LES
ROUTIERS

# BRITAIN

## AND THE NORTH OF IRELAND

### QUALITY AND VALUE
### FOOD AND ACCOMMODATION

1994

IN ASSOCIATION WITH

BRITANNIA
RESCUE

# Introduction and Welcome

*A personal introduction from Duncan Bradbury, Managing Director of Les Routiers*

Welcome to the Les Routiers *Guide to Britain and the North of Ireland 1994*.

If you are looking for interesting places at which to dine or stay at good value, you will enjoy looking through this guide. This is the 15th edition of the Les Routiers guide and it is easily the best we have ever produced, listing over 1,500 establishments throughout the UK and the north of Ireland. There's more choice and the best-ever range of welcoming establishments which we feel you will want to visit time after time.

The entries featured range from quiet country hotels and beamed coaching inns to fashionable town and city restaurants, from bracing seaside guest houses to grandiose Victorian rectories. Meet a resident ghost . . . retrace the steps of Bonnie Prince Charlie at Scotland's oldest hotel . . . raise a glass in the smallest inn in London or sample a tasty treat from Desperate Dan's 3 ft frying pan – the choice is endless and you will be sure to find exactly what you are looking for.

**No truly contemporary guide can ignore the influence of the various kinds of ethnic cuisine currently available**. In this guide you will find not only some of the best British cuisine, but many outstanding examples of Greek, Indian, Chinese, Italian and even Mongolian. Exciting flavours and greatly enhanced variety have now made such an impact on traditional British and French cooking that we have to constantly reassess the basis on which our inspectors can judge food.

Good food and accommodation, value for money and a warm and friendly welcome towards guests have always been the criteria for selecting establishments for membership of Les Routiers, and this year is no exception. Interestingly enough, we are aware that only in recent years have some people rediscovered such values. We have an extensive nationwide team of over 100 inspectors who visit each establishment anonymously before it is accepted into the guide – and despite rising standards generally, our inspectors find that many still do not meet these simple, but well-tested standards.

Whether you are visiting family or friends, planning a holiday, a business trip or simply getting away for a lazy weekend, the *Les Routiers Guide to Britain and the North of Ireland 1994* has something for everyone. I sincerely hope that you find this guide easy to use, very accurate and thoroughly enjoyable.

Sincerely,

Duncan Bradbury

First published in the United Kingdom in 1994
Alan Sutton Publishing Ltd
Phoenix Mill · Far Thrupp · Stroud
Gloucestershire GL5 2BU

First published in the
United States of America in 1994
Alan Sutton Publishing Inc.
83 Washington Street
Dover · NH 03820

ISBN 0-7509-0546-8

Les Routiers inspectors visit each establishment anonymously and settle their bill before revealing their identity. Complimentary meals and/or accommodation are not accepted.

**Prices for FOOD in this guide are based on a 3-course evening meal, excluding wine and service.**
**Prices for ACCOMMODATION in this guide are per person based on two people sharing a room.**

Les Routiers, 25 Vanston Place, London SW6 1AZ

For reservations and further information – Les Routiers Booking Line: 071 610 1856
Club Bon Viveur: 071 610 1857.
Partnership Protection Insurance: 071 610 3266.

*Editor:* Malcolm Morris
*Maps:* Martin Latham
*Cover illustration:* Gary Brazier

Typeset by Alan Sutton Publishing Limited.
Printed in Great Britain by
The Bath Press, Bath, Avon.

# Your Personal Assurance

For over twenty-two years, Les Routiers have been inspecting and recommending hotels and restaurants, guest houses and inns throughout the UK which provide good quality food and accommodation, value for money and a warm and friendly welcome – the 1994 *Guide to Britain and the North of Ireland* offers a superb choice of establishments – just look out for the distinctive red and blue Les Routiers symbol!

**For reservations and further information, phone the Les Routiers**
**BOOKING & INFORMATION LINE on 071 610 1856 (Fax 071 385 7136)**

# Contents

# Guide Entries

# 60 Years of Tradition

Having been established in France for 60 years, we feel we have come to understand the importance attached to the meaning of 'good food', the concept of combining 'quality' and 'value for money' and the genuine sense of hospitality that accompanies a 'warm welcome'.

Indeed, in a country as discerning as France, no symbol could have possibly become such a household name without representing the sort of standards that have stood the test of time. After 60 years we feel Les Routiers can confidently be said to have proved that it is an inspiration to those of you who share a high regard for food, value for money and hospitality.

Today, the red and blue Les Routiers sign is as familiar a sight in Britain as it is in France, but it is far more than just another sign – it is your personal assurance! We hope that in using this guide you will come to enjoy the confidence that goes with every Les Routiers recommendation.

## A Recognized Standard

The Les Routiers sign represents a recognized and reliable standard of achievement of quality in all types of cuisine and comfortable accommodation at hotels, restaurants, guest houses and inns, from Land's End to the Shetland Isles and Clwyd to Cambridgeshire.

## Anonymous Inspections

Before any establishment can achieve the Les Routiers recommendation, it must first pass a rigorous inspection to ensure that it meets the exacting standards which have been set. Each inspection is undertaken anonymously and covers everything from food and service to comfort and hygiene.

## Maintaining Standards

Once accepted by Les Routiers, an establishment is then regularly re-inspected to ensure that the proper standards are maintained. Only on this basis may the famous Les Routiers sign be displayed by our members.

## Recommended or Not?

So how can you be sure that an establishment is actually Les Routiers recommended? The first and most obvious clue is to look out for the red and blue sign. Any establishment displaying this sign is committed to providing quality and value for their customers. Secondly, it must be displaying a current certificate showing the proprietor's or manager's name. Sometimes, however, there are establishments who continue to display the sign when they are no longer Les Routiers recommended. If you know of such an establishment please let us know immediately. Your cooperation is invaluable in helping us to maintain the high standards on which Les Routiers have established their proud reputation. You will find an Opinion Page on page 421 which you are invited to fill in and return to us.

**Look out for the sign – it's your personal assurance!**

# See Why Our Members Prefer Us

**BRITANNIA RESCUE**

# We Offer You the Choice

## Road Rescue – What price peace of mind?
## Answer –
## Less than you'd think!

For ten years Britannia Rescue has been providing a fast, efficient breakdown and recovery service, originally exclusively for members of the CSMA. But now, this excellent service is offered to buyers of the Les Routiers Guides to Britain and France. Britain's leading consumer testing magazine in their April 1992 issue, voted Britannia Rescue as their 'Best Buy' with an average callout time of 34 minutes, well ahead of the AA, RAC and National Breakdown.

## What services can you have?

### Superstart – a home start-up service from £26.50 per year

An economically priced service, ideal for drivers who use their cars infrequently or for shorter journeys. If your car will not start at home, or if you break down within half a mile of home, our agent will come to your assistance. If the car cannot be started you can be taken to a single destination of your choice (within 10 miles) while your car is transported to a local garage.

### Rescue Plus – roadside assistance and local recovery service from £40.00 per year

Designed to offer protection against minor breakdowns away from your home. If your problem can't be solved at the roadside we will transport you, your vehicle and up to five passengers to a nearby garage. We will also reimburse you up to £12 towards the cost of a taxi or other alternative transport.

## Standard Cover – roadside assistance and recovery to nearby garage or home or to an onward destination from £54.50 per year or £5.50 per month*

Cover offers protection from every breakdown situation while away from the vicinity of your home, both for your car and for you. We will endeavour to fix any minor problems on the spot as quickly as possible. If, however, this is not possible, our agent will transport you, your vehicle and up to five passengers home or to the destination of your choice.

## Comprehensive Cover – roadside assistance, recovery, attendance at home from £72.00 per year or £7.25 per month*

This cover gives you complete peace of mind. We cater for annoying non-start problems such as flat batteries and damp engines to roadside breakdowns and accident recovery. We also include Housecall, covering you at home or within half a mile radius of home. It should be noted that Housecall is not intended as a home maintenance service and we would not expect to attend to recurring faults.

## Deluxe Cover – roadside assistance, recovery, attendance at home, free car hire or hotel accommodation from £88.00 per year or £8.75 per month*

As the name suggests, this is the highest level of cover. You and your vehicle are not only catered for both at home and on the road, but if your car cannot be repaired the same day you can choose between a free replacement car (for up to 48 hours), or assistance with overnight hotel accommodation. Please note that car hire is subject to the terms and conditions of Britannia Rescue's car companies, minimum age of drivers must be 23 years.

## Personal Cover – £18.00 per year or £1.80 per month*

Whichever Britannia Rescue cover you choose, for just £18 we will extend the cover to include any car you or your spouse may drive.

## * Monthly Premiums

Monthly premiums are available on the top three levels of service – Standard, Comprehensive and Deluxe – when paying by Direct Debit.

# All Part of Our Service

## Legal advice and defence

We offer every member a 24 hour legal advice service. We can also provide representation in magistrates' courts.

## Assistance after theft and vandalism

In the case of vehicle immobilization, we will provide roadside repair or transport to a local garage or on to your destination.

## Relief driver

Britannia Rescue will arrange a relief driver to assist you in case of illness, injury or severe mental distress.

## Tyres and windscreens

We assist on less serious, but often annoying occasions, such as punctures, shattered windscreens, lack of fuel or even locking your keys in the car.

## Caravans and trailers

These are covered free of charge (excluding Housecall).

**BRITANNIA RESCUE**

# Why choose Britannia Rescue?

- Dedicated to providing every member with a fast, caring road rescue service

- 34 minutes average callout time

- Over 3,000 trained personnel on call 24 hours a day 365 days a year

- A BSI registered firm committed to consistent service quality

- Value for money prices with easy payment methods

- Recommended by Britain's leading consumer watchdog as 'Best Buy'

# How to apply for Britannia Rescue membership

Turn to pages 417 and 419 for an application form and direct debit mandate. Or if you wish to join immediately by telephone, simply ring FREE on 0800 591563 and quote your credit card number!

MasterCard    VISA

# Travelling abroad

Available to anyone, whether covered by Britannia Rescue in the UK or not, Britannia Continental is a superb emergency breakdown service, competitively priced, and designed to cover any mishap while travelling abroad. There are two types of cover, one for travel with a vehicle in Europe, and the other for travel anywhere in the world. Personal Insurance includes medical repatriation by air ambulance. For further details and a brochure, ring 0484 514848.

# What's in This Guide

This guide is designed to help you easily locate a Les Routiers to suit any occasion, be it an annual holiday, a weekend break or dinner with friends.

## Regions of the UK

Our establishments stretch the length and breadth of the United Kingdom, and for your convenience the guide has been divided into regional sections: London, South East England and East Anglia, South West England, the Channel Islands, Central England, Northern England and the Isle of Man, Wales, Scotland, and the North of Ireland.

Within each regional section, individual entries are listed alphabetically by town. There are also colour maps at the front and indexes at the back of the guide to help you. The red and blue symbols on the maps will show you instantly which establishments offer food, accommodation, or both.

*We hope you will have no trouble in finding the Les Routiers of your choice, but if in doubt, just phone our Booking & Information line on 071 610 1856.*

# Introductory Vouchers

*As an introduction to the world of Les Routiers – that's if you haven't already discovered it – you will find something rather special on page 377 of your guidebook . . .*

### *Up to £500 worth of Introductory Vouchers!*

These vouchers are for use exclusively at nearly 200 Les Routiers recommended establishments, where savings can be made on food, wine and accommodation.

Each voucher carries the name and address of the establishment with details of its offer. Some vouchers may have one, two or *all* offers, although you may only select one. Terms and conditions are printed on the reverse of each voucher, and are subject to the individual establishment's regulations which apply at all times.

There are three different offers which you can take advantage of:

(a) 10% off a food bill
(b) 10% off standard accommodation
(c) a free bottle of house wine

Look out for entries bearing the 'Special Welcome' symbol indicating the Les Routiers establishment where the Introductory Vouchers may be used!

# Quality and Value for Money

The Les Routiers recommendation is given to those who offer a much sought after combination of quality and value for money, and where your host has a ready welcome. All establishments listed in this guide have achieved our recommendation by offering precisely that. Their prices and services form the basis of consistent and accurate research by ourselves to bring you, the guide reader, the very best in hospitality. In addition, those establishments which – in our opinion – have consistently offered outstanding quality of service and above average cuisine are awarded the Les Routiers **Casserole Award** (see page 55).

*Every establishment in this guide includes a carefully researched estimate of cost so that you will know what to expect.*

**FOOD**
**Prices given are based on a 3-course meal excluding wine and service.**

up to £15 per person
between £15 and £20 per person
between £21 and £25 per person
between £26 and £30 per person

**ACCOMMODATION**
**Prices given are based per person on two people sharing a double room.**

up to £20 per person
between £21 and £30 per person
between £31 and £40 per person
between £40 and £50 per person
over £50 per person

*Please note:* **The price bands are intended to give an indication of the range of meals and accommodation available, reflecting regional price variations. All prices are based on information supplied to us by the establishment, and although the prices quoted are correct at the time of going to press, they cannot be guaranteed.**

**Prices quoted for food refer to evening restaurant meals, taken from the table d'hôte menu. Prices quoted for accommodation refer to double rooms, many of which have *en suite* facilities.**

# Symbols Used in This Guide

As you browse through your Les Routiers guide, you will see that many of the establishments featured have the following symbols. These symbols are in recognition of a special achievement by the establishment, signifying that it has received one or more of our prestigious annual awards for outstanding and consistent presentation of food or wine or cheeseboards.

### CASSEROLE AWARD

Awarded to establishments which have consistently offered outstanding service and an impressive ability to present above average cuisine. Refer to pages 55–8 for a complete list of Casserole Award holders.

### CHEESEBOARD

Indicates a Les Routiers establishment where you have the opportunity to sample a superb selection of well-chosen and prepared cheeses, including less common local varieties. Refer to pages 66–7 for a complete list of Cheeseboard Award holders.

### WINE
**The Les Routiers 'Corps D'Elite'**

This symbol is awarded to Les Routiers establishments who offer an interesting, carefully selected and easily understood variety of wines. Refer to pages 69–70 for a complete list of Wine Award holders.

In addition to awards, we also make special mention of two valuable offers available to you from our members.

### CLUB BON VIVEUR
**'The Ultimate Dining Scheme'**

Establishment entries bearing this sign offer, on less busy nights of the week, exceptional discounts to Club Bon Viveur members. To find out how you can rediscover the *Joie de Vivre*, refer to pages 415–16 for full details of how to join.

### INTRODUCTORY OFFERS
**'A Valuable Introduction to Les Routiers'**

All entries bearing this symbol offer a 'Special Welcome' by way of an introductory reduction on food or accommodation charges, or in some cases a free bottle of house wine.

# List of Maps

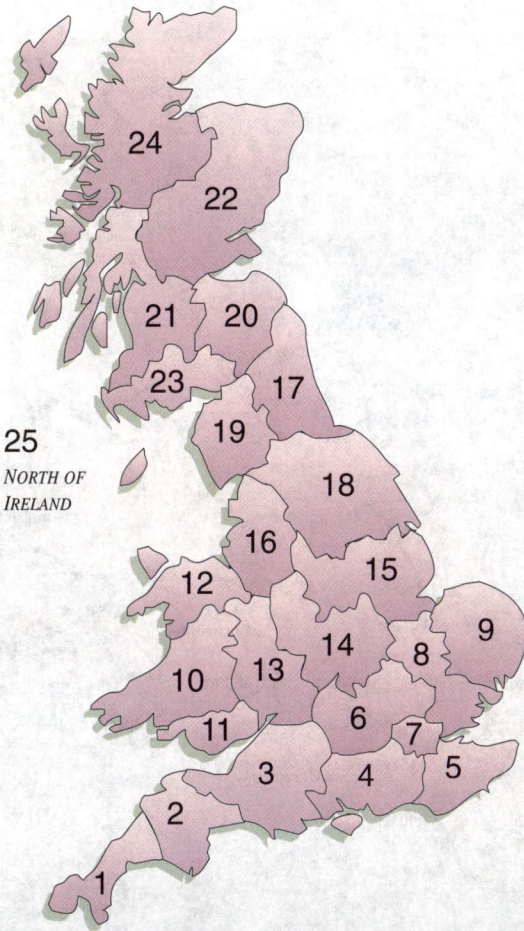

1 Cornwall
2 Devon
3 Somerset, Avon, Dorset, Wiltshire
4 Hampshire, Surrey, West Sussex, Isle of Wight
5 Kent, East Sussex, Channel Islands
6 Berkshire, Oxfordshire, Buckinghamshire, Bedfordshire, Hertfordshire
7 Greater London
8 Cambridgeshire, Essex
9 Norfolk, Suffolk
10 Dyfed, Powys
11 West Glamorgan, Mid Glamorgan, South Glamorgan, Gwent
12 Gwynedd, Clwyd
13 Shropshire, Hereford and Worcester, Gloucestershire
14 Leicestershire, Northamptonshire, Warwickshire, Staffordshire, West Midlands
15 Derbyshire, Lincolnshire, Nottinghamshire
16 Lancashire, Merseyside, Greater Manchester, Cheshire
17 Northumberland, Durham, Cleveland, Tyne and Wear
18 North Yorkshire, West Yorkshire, South Yorkshire, Humberside
19 Isle of Man, Cumbria
20 Lothian, Borders
21 Strathclyde, Isle of Arran, Isle of Iona, Isle of Mull
22 Grampian, Tayside, Central, Fife
23 Dumfries and Galloway
24 Highlands, Western Isles, Orkney Islands, Shetland Islands
25 North of Ireland

## KEY TO MAP SYMBOLS

CITY

MOTORWAY

COUNTY BOUNDARY

MAIN TOWN

MAIN ROAD

FOOD and ACCOMMODATION available

FOOD ONLY available

ACCOMMODATION ONLY available

MAP 2

Bude

Boscastle
Tintagel

Port Isaac

Constantine Bay
Rock

Padstow

Wadebridge

**BODMIN
MOOR**

Gunnislake

Bodmin

Newquay

Cubert

Lostwithiel

Perranporth

St Austell
Carlyon Bay
Fowey

Looe

St Agnes

Grampound
Tregony

Polperro

Truro

Mevagissey

St Ives

Phlleigh

**CORNWALL**

Mylor Bridge

St Just

Falmouth
Portscatho

Penzance

Sennen
St Just in Penwith

Land's End

Coverack

The Lizard

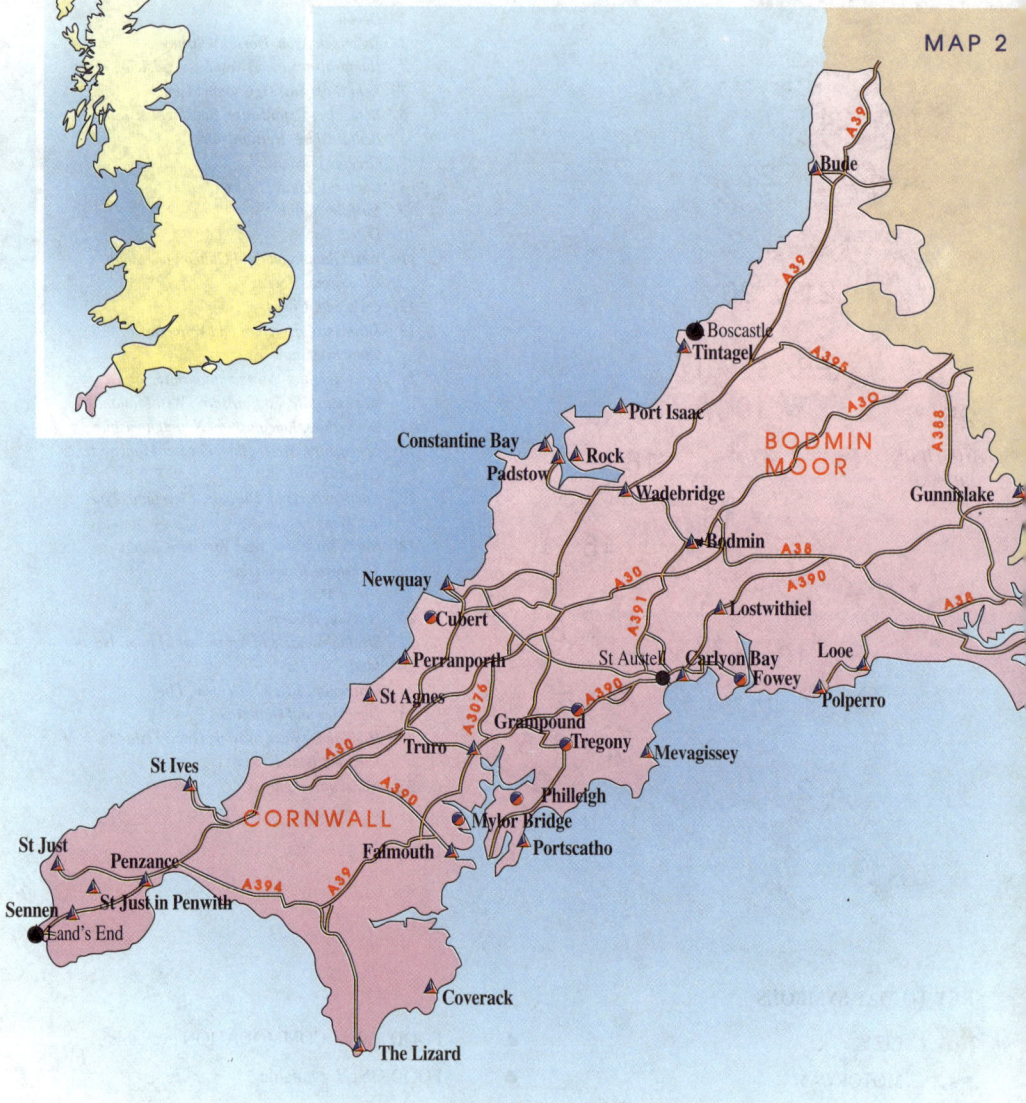

SCALE: 13 MILES TO 1 INCH

| | | | | | |
|---|---|---|---|---|---|
| Bodmin | ⚠ | Lostwithiel | ⚠ | Rock | ⚠ |
| Bude | ⚠ | Mevagissey | ⚠ | Sennen | ⚠ |
| Carlyon Bay | ⚠ | Mylor Bridge | ◐ | St Agnes | ⚠ |
| Constantine Bay | ⚠ | Newquay | ⚠ | St Ives | ⚠ |
| Coverack | ⚠ | Padstow | ⚠ | St Just | ⚠ |
| Cubert | ◐ | Penzance | ⚠ | St Just in Penwith | ⚠ |
| Falmouth | ⚠ | Perranporth | ⚠ | The Lizard | ⚠ |
| Fowey | ◐ | Phlleigh | ◐ | Tintagel | ⚠ |
| Grampound | ◐ | Polperro | ⚠ | Tregony | ◐ |
| Gunnislake | ⚠ | Port Isaac | ⚠ | Truro | ⚠ |
| Looe | ⚠ | Portscatho | ⚠ | Wadebridge | ⚠ |

MAP 3

Lynton
Lynmouth
Ilfracombe
Combe Martin
Mortehoe
EXMOOR
Braunton

A361
A361

Bideford
South Molton
Bampton

A39

A386
A377

Thelbridge
Tiverton

Wembworthy
Bickleigh

Honiton
A35
Axminster

DEVON
A377
Whimple

Clawton
A30
Throwleigh
Chagford
Moretonhampstead
Exeter
Sidford
Sidmouth
Beer
Axmouth

Lydford
Lifton

DARTMOOR
Haytor
Bovey Tracey
Exmouth
Dawlish

MAP 1
A386
Tavistock
Dartmoor
Bickington
Newton Abbot
Shaldon

Yelverton
Totnes
Torquay
Paignton

A38
Ivybridge
Halwell
Brixham

Plymouth
Dartmouth

Kingsbridge
Chillington

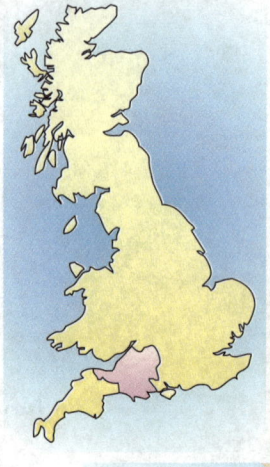

MAP 11

Clevedon

Weston-Super-Mare

Brent Knoll

Burnham-on-Sea

Panborough

Minehead

Exford

Dunster

Watchet

Glastonbury

Exmoor

Bridgwater

SOMERSE

Dulverton

Exebridge

Taunton

MAP 2

Crewkerne

Chard

Misterto

ALDERNEY

Holywell

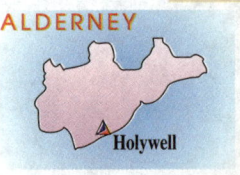

SCALE: 4 MILES TO 1 INCH

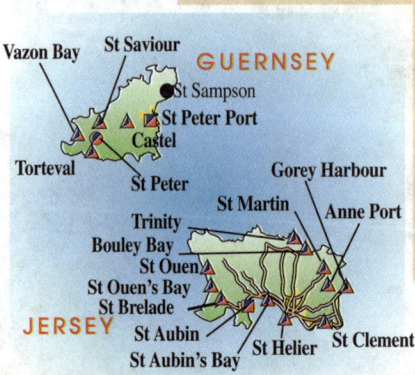

Charmouth

Lyme Regis

Chideock

Bridpor

Vazon Bay

St Saviour

GUERNSEY

St Sampson

St Peter Port

Castel

Torteval

St Peter

Gorey Harbour

St Martin

Anne Port

Trinity

Bouley Bay

St Ouen

St Ouen's Bay

St Brelade

JERSEY

St Aubin

St Helier

St Clement

St Aubin's Bay

SCALE: 13 MILES TO 1 INCH

MAP 13

MAP 6

MAP 4

Rangeworthy
Old Sodbury
Sherston
Swindon
Ford
Chippenham
Ogbourne St George
Bristol
AVON
Freshford
Corsham
Bath
Melksham
Chelwood
Devizes
Pewsey
Bradford-on-Avon
Trowbridge
WILTSHIRE
Woolverton
Westbury
Frome
Warminster
Litton
lls
Mere
Amesbury
Bruton
Tisbury
Burcombe
Salisbury
Wincanton
Holton
Shaftesbury
Trent
Sturminster Newton
ute
DORSET
Blandford Forum
A354
Zelston
Longham
Dorchester
Poole
Bournemouth
Wareham
Christchurch
Studland
Weymouth
West Lulworth
Swanage
Portland
Lulworth Cove

SCALE: 13 MILES TO 1 INCH

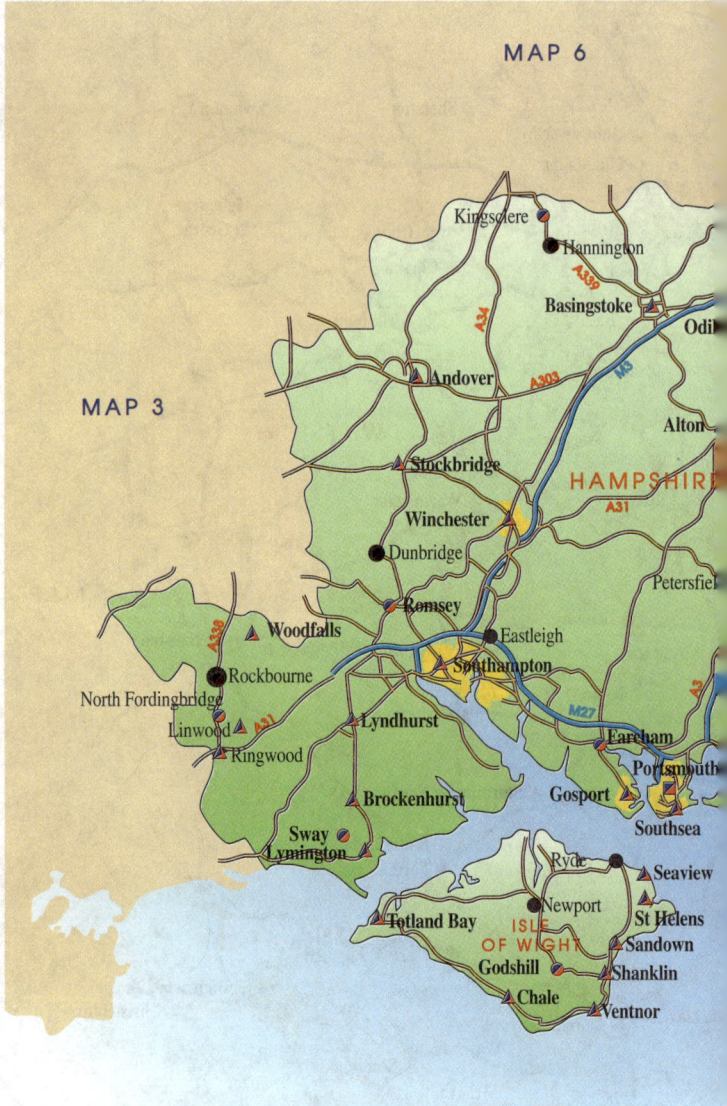

MAP 6

MAP 3

Kingsclere

Hannington

A339

Basingstoke

Odi

A34

Andover

A303

M3

HAMPSHIRE

Alton

Stockbridge

A31

Winchester

Dunbridge

Petersfiel

Woodfalls

Romsey

Eastleigh

A33

Rockbourne

Southampton

North Fordingbridge

A338

M27

Fareham

Linwood

A31

Lyndhurst

Ringwood

Portsmouth

Brockenhurst

Gosport

Sway

Southsea

Lymington

Ryde

Seaview

Newport

Totland Bay

St Helens

ISLE

OF WIGHT

Sandown

Godshill

Shanklin

Chale

Ventnor

SCALE: 13 MILES TO 1 INCH

MAP 7

Egham
Staines
Walton on Thames
Knaphill
Esher
Sutton
Croydon
Ripley
Epsom
South Croydon
Woking
Kenley
Leatherhead
Tadworth
M25
Farnborough
Limpsfield
Aldershot
Guildford
Reigate
Bletchingly
Dorking
Redhill
Farnham
SURREY
Godalming
Newdigate
Copthorne
Bordon
Cranleigh
Gatwick
Crawley
East Grinstead
Haslemere
Baynards
Horsham
Fernhurst
Lindfield
Trotton
Haywards Heath
Midhurst
st Marden
Henfield
Hurstpierpoint
sworth
WEST SUSSEX
Steyning
MAP 5
Lavant
Arundel
Chichester
Lancing
West Wittering
Worthing
ling
Bognor Regis
nd

MAP 7

Dartford

Gravesend

Bromley

Rochester
Chatham

M25

M26

Westerham

Sevenoaks

Maidstone

A21

MAP 4

Edenbridge

Tonbridge

Penshurst

Tunbridge Wells

A21

Crowborough

A26

Wadhurst

Salehurst

A272

Uckfield

EAST SUSSEX

Wivelsfield Green

A22

Battle

Lewes

Bexhill-on-Sea

A27

Brighton

Brighton & Hove

A27

A259

Newhaven

Alfriston

Eastbourne

Seaford

SCALE: 13 MILES TO 1 INCH

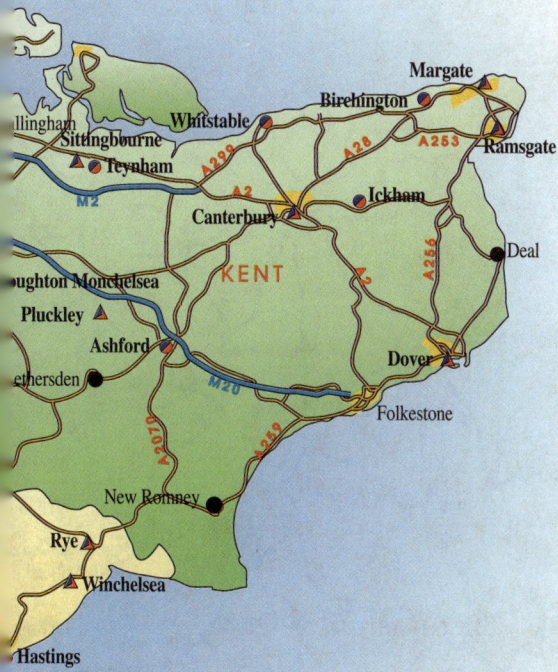

Margate
Birchington
Whitstable
Ramsgate
Ickham
Canterbury
Deal
KENT
oughton Monchelsea
Pluckley
Ashford
ethersden
Dover
Folkestone
New Romney
Rye
Winchelsea
Hastings
Sittingbourne
Teynham
llingham

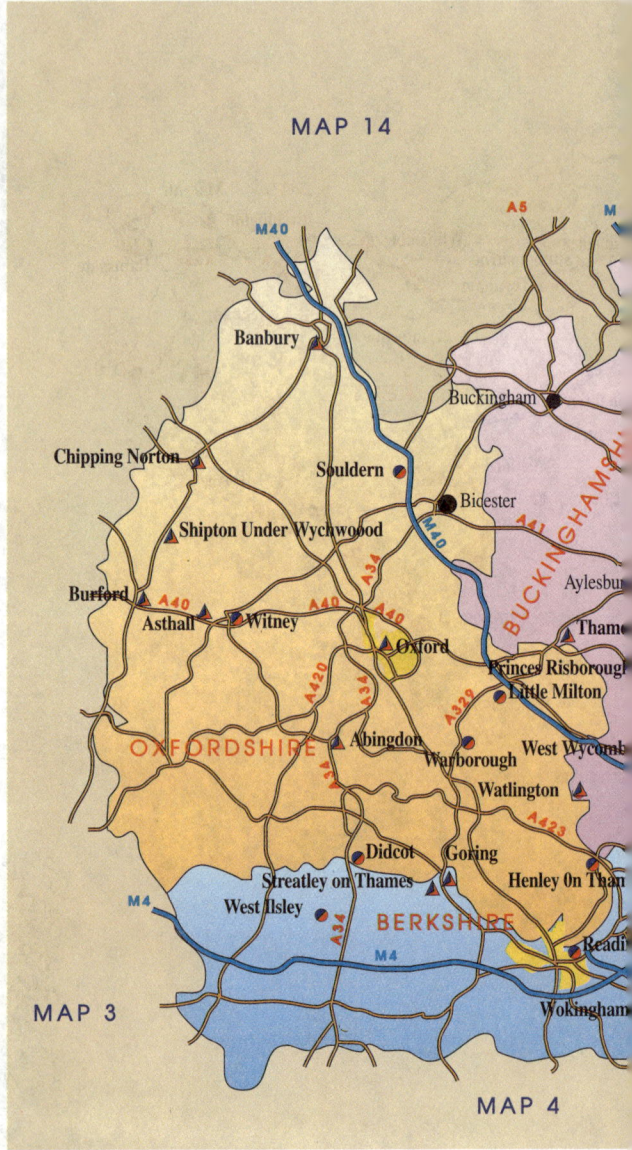

MAP 14

MAP 3

MAP 4

SCALE: 13 MILES TO 1 INCH

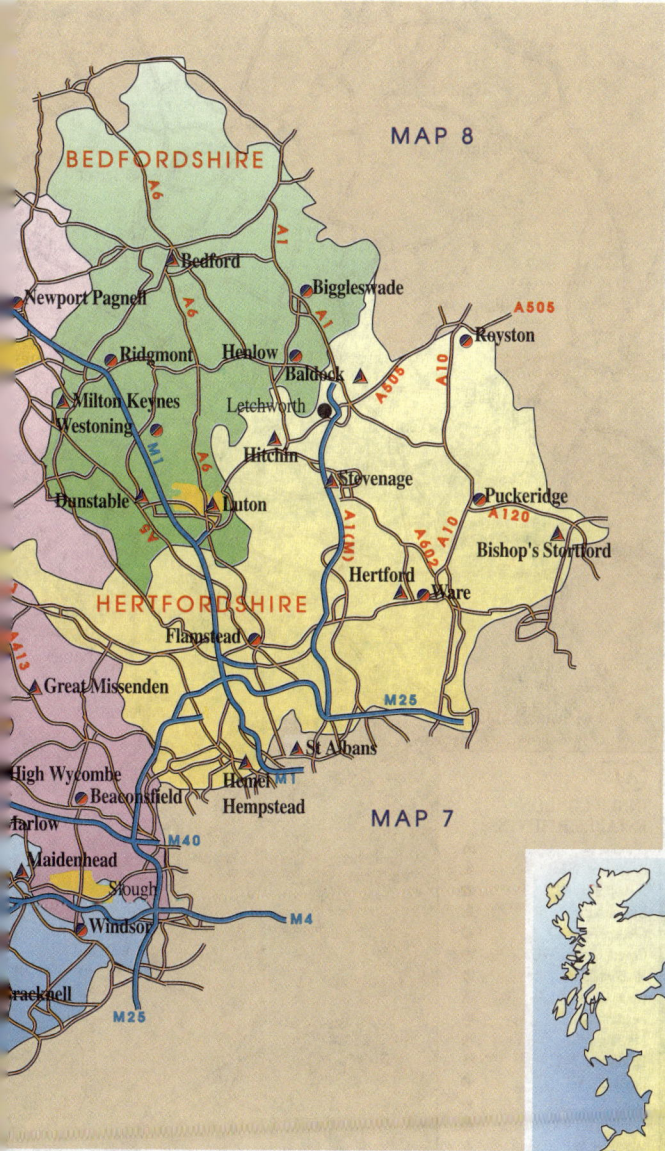

MAP 8

BEDFORDSHIRE

A6

A1

Bedford

Newport Pagnell

Biggleswade

A505

Royston

Ridgmont

A6

Henlow

A505

A10

Baldock

Milton Keynes

Letchworth

Westoning

M1

A6

Hitchin

Dunstable

A5

Luton

Stevenage

Puckeridge

A120

A1(M)

A602

A10

Bishop's Stortford

HERTFORDSHIRE

Hertford

Flamstead

Ware

Great Missenden

M25

A413

St Albans

High Wycombe

Hemel

M1

MAP 7

Beaconsfield

Hempstead

Harlow

M40

Maidenhead

Slough

M4

Windsor

Bracknell

M25

MAP 6

GREAT

Watford

Rickmansworth

Barnet

Muswell Hill

Harrow

Ruislip

Wembley

Hamps

West Hampstead

Uxbridge

Greenford

Ealing

Notting Hill

Kens

Ealing Common

Shepherds Bush

Chiswick

Hammersmith

Kew

Earls Court

Barnes

Chelsea

Mortlake

Fulham

Bat

Parsons Green

Staines

Putney

Teddington

Wimbledon

Kingston upon Thames

Esher

Sutton

Epsom

MAP 4

**Ⓐ**

**INNER LONDON
ESTABLISHMENTS:**

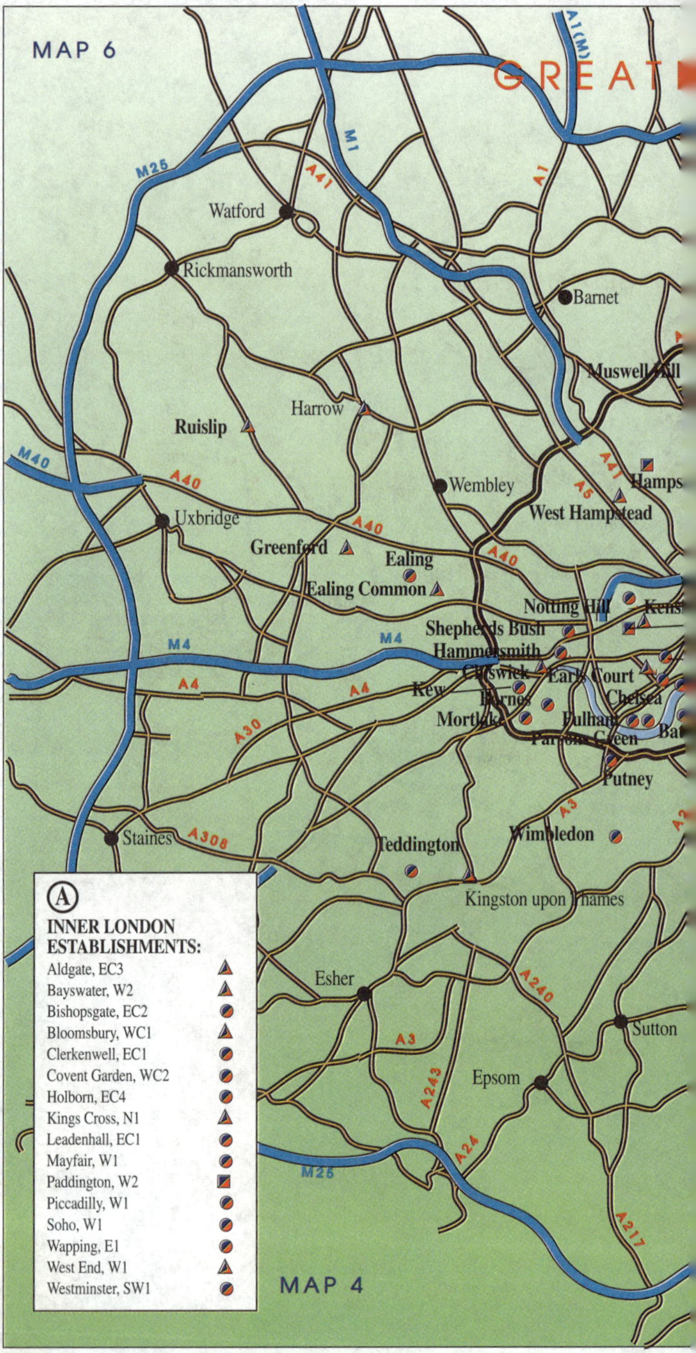

SCALE: 5 MILES TO 1 INCH APPROX

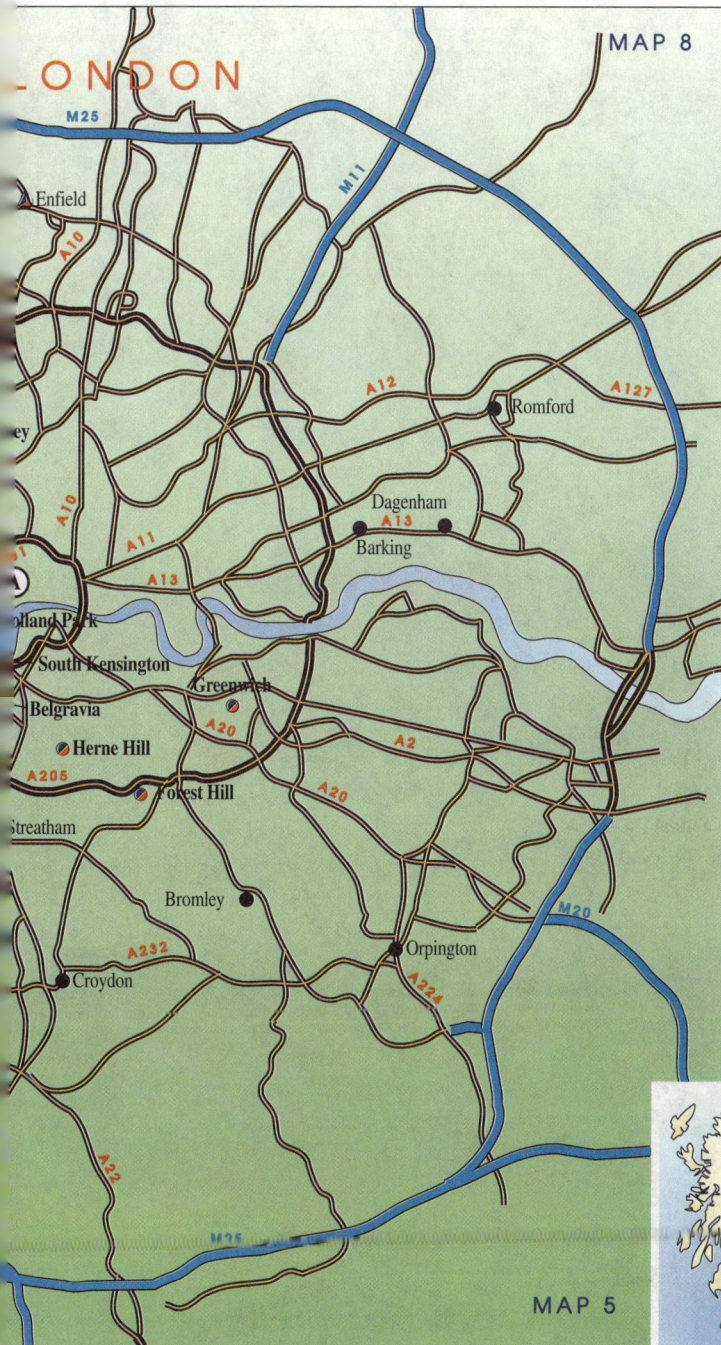

MAP 8

LONDON

M25

M11

Enfield

A10

A12

A127

Romford

A10

A11

Dagenham

A13

Barking

A13

Holland Park

South Kensington

Greenwich

Belgravia

A20

A2

Herne Hill

A205

Forest Hill

A20

Streatham

Bromley

Orpington

M20

A232

Croydon

A224

A22

M25

MAP 5

MAP 8

Stamford

A15

A47

Peterborough

A47

A605

Whittlesey

A1

A141

Chatteris

A142

A10

Ely

A141

A142

CAMBRIDGESHIRE

A14

Huntingdon

St Ives

A10

A142

A11

A604

A45

MAP 9

A1

M11

A45

A10

Cambridge

Newmarket

A1

A10

A11

Linton

A604

MAP 6

Duxford

A505

Saffron Walden

M11

A131

Halstead

A12

A131

Colchester

A120

A120

A120

A12

MAP 7

A120

Witham

Clacton-on-Sea

ESSEX

A414

Chelmsford

A12

A130

M25

A12

A129

Billericay

Brentwood

SCALE 13 MILES TO 1 INCH

M11

Romford

M25

Basildon

Southend

Shoeburyness

Rainham

Westcliff-on Sea

Stansted

SCALE: 13 MILES TO 1 INCH

| Billericay | ⊘ | Duxford | △ | Rainham | ⊘ | Stansted | △ |
| Brentwood | ⊘ | Ely | △ | Romford | △ | St Ives | △ |
| Cambridge | △ | Harwich | △ | Saffron Walden | △ | Westcliff-on-Sea | ⊘ |
| Chelmsford | △ | Linton | ⊘ | Shoesburyness | ⊘ | Whittlesey | △ |
| Colchester | △ | Peterborough | △ | Southend | △ | | |

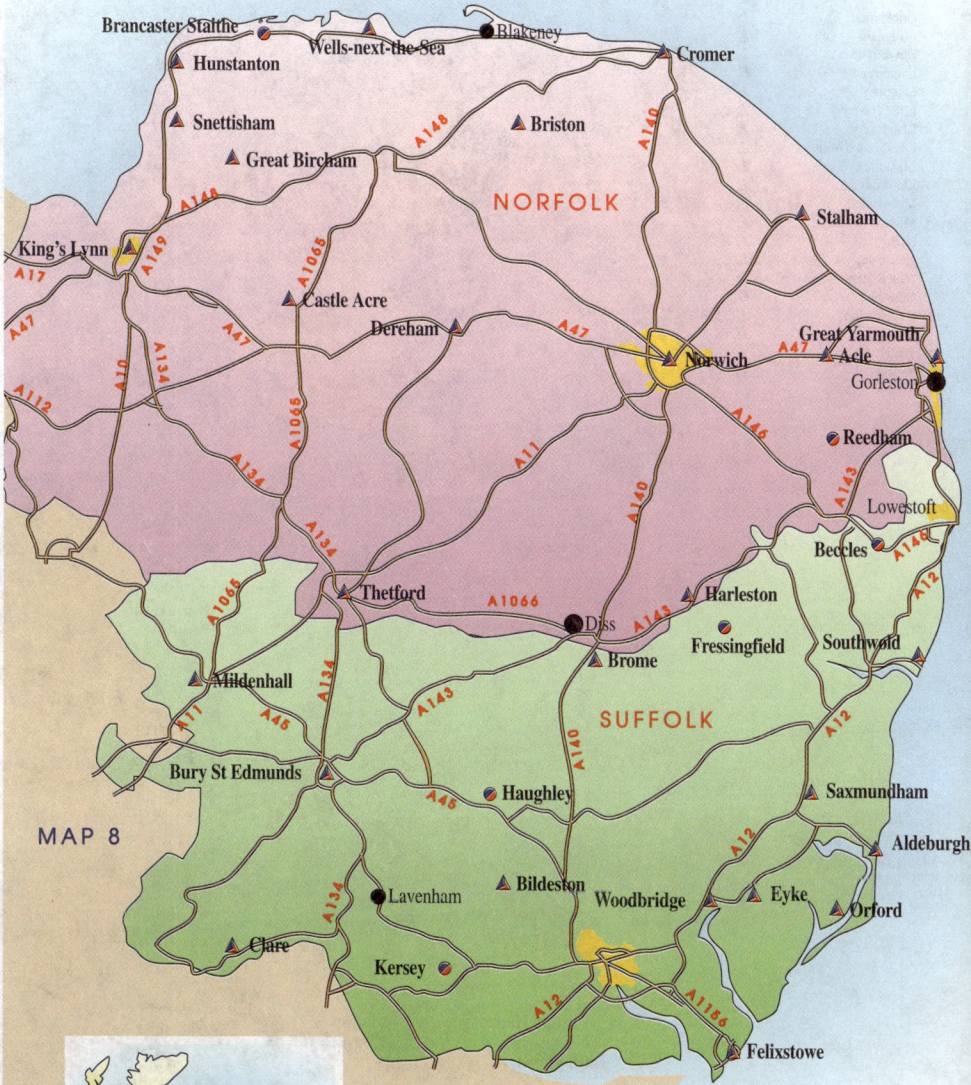

## MAP 9

Brancaster Staithe
Wells-next-the-Sea
Blakeney
Cromer
Hunstanton
Snettisham
Briston
Great Bircham

**NORFOLK**

Stalham

King's Lynn

A17
A149
A148
A1065

Castle Acre
Dereham
A47
Norwich
Great Yarmouth
Acle
Gorleston

A47
A1112
A134
A1065
A134
A11
A146
Reedham
Lowestoft

A1065
A134
Thetford
A1066
Diss
Harleston
Beccles
A143
A12

Mildenhall
Brome
Fressingfield
Southwold
A11
A48
A143
A134

**SUFFOLK**

Bury St Edmunds
A46
Haughley
A140
Saxmundham
A12
A12
Aldeburgh

**MAP 8**

Lavenham
Bildeston
Woodbridge
Eyke
Orford
A134
Clare
Kersey
A12
A1156
Felixstowe

| | | | |
|---|---|---|---|
| Acle | △ | Harleston | △ |
| Aldeburgh | △ | Haughley | ◐ |
| Beccles | ◐ | Hunstanton | △ |
| Bildeston | △ | Kersey | ◐ |
| Brancaster Staithe | ◐ | Kings Lynn | △△△ |
| Briston | △ | Lavenham | ◐△ |
| Brome | △ | Mildenhall | △△ |
| Bury St Edmunds | △ | Norwich | △△ |
| Castle Acre | △ | Orford | △△△ |
| Clare | △ | Reedham | ◐ |
| Cromer | △ | Saxmundham | △ |
| Dereham | △ | Snettisham | △ |
| Eyke | △ | Southwold | △△ |
| Felixstowe | △ | Stalham | △ |
| Fressingfield | ◐ | Thetford | △ |
| Great Bircham | △ | Wells Next The Sea | △ |
| Great Yarmouth | △ | Woodbridge | △△△ |

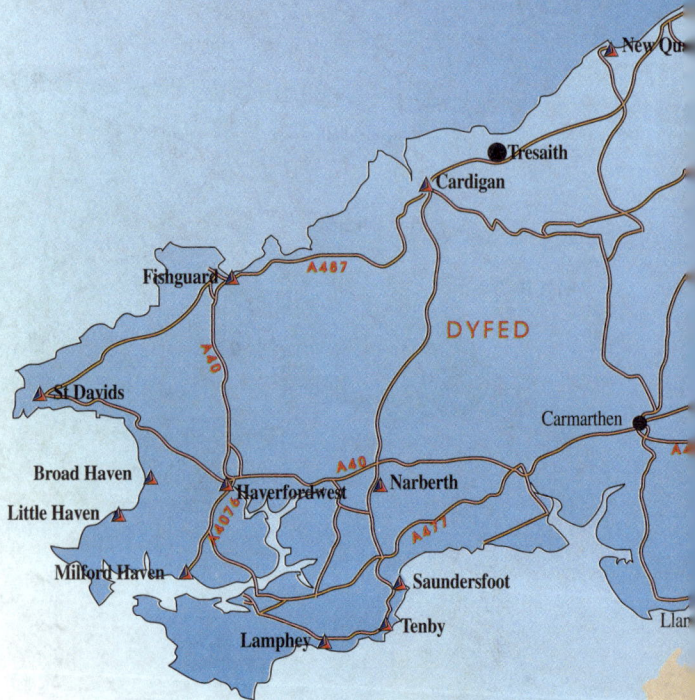

New Qu

Tresaith

Cardigan

Fishguard

A487

DYFED

St Davids

A40

Carmarthen

Broad Haven

Haverfordwest

A40

Narberth

Little Haven

Milford Haven

A477

Saundersfoot

Tenby

Lamphey

Llan

MAP 12

▲ Llanwddyn

A458

Welshpool

POWYS

A470

A470

A489

Machynlleth

A483

A492

Newtown

A470

A489

MAP 13

A44

Aberystwyth

Llanidloes

A483

A44

Llandrindod Wells ▲ New Radnor

A44

A470

Lampeter

▲ Builth Wells

A483

Llandovery

A438

echfa

A40

A436

A470

A479

Brecon

Llandeilo

A470

Crickhowell ▲

Llandybie

MAP 11

SCALE: 13 MILES TO 1 INCH

**11**

MAP 10

MA

West Glamorgan
Mid Glamorgan
South Glamorgan
Gwent

M4
A465
A470
A40
A465
A4042
A40
A449
A48
A473
A48

Merthyr Tydfil
Ebbw Vale
Abergavenny
Aberdare
Pontypool
Llantrissent
Tre
Neath
Cwmbran
Shirenewton
Swansea
Port Talbot
Pontypridd
Caerphilly
Newport
Gower
Oxwich
Bridgend
Cardiff
South Glamorgan
Barry

MAP

Abergavenny
Bridgend
Cardiff
Chepstow
Cwmbran
Gower
Llantrissent
Monmouth
Newport
Pontypridd
Shirenewton
Swansea
Tintern
Trellech

SCALE: 13 MILES TO 1 INCH

Angl
Holyhead
Trearddur

Nefyn
Pwllheli
Llanbedrog
Abersoch

SCALE: 13 MILES TO 1 INCH

Abergele
Abersoch
Anglesey
Bala
Barmouth
Beddgelert
Betws y Coed
Caernarfon
Capel Curig
Colwyn Bay
Conwy
Criccieth
Denbigh
Dolgellau
Harlech
Holyhead
Llanbedr
Llanberis
Llandudno
Llanfairpwll
Llangollen
Maentwrog
Mold
Nefyn
Porthmadog
Prestatyn
Pwllheli
Ruthin
St Asaph
Tal-y-Bont
Trearddur Bay
Wrexham

MAP 16

Llandudno
Conwy
Menai Bridge
fair
Bangor
Tal y bont
Caernarfon
Llanberis
Capel Curig
Betws-y-coed
GWYNEDD
Beddgelert
Blaenau Ffestiniog
Porthmadog
Maentwrog
Harlech
Llanbedr
Dolgellau
Barmouth

Prestatyn
Abergele
Colwyn Bay
St Asaph
A55
A470
Chester
A55
Denbigh
Mold
A494
Ruthin
CLWYD
Wrexham
A494
A5
A483
Llangollen

A5
A487
A470
A458
MAP 10

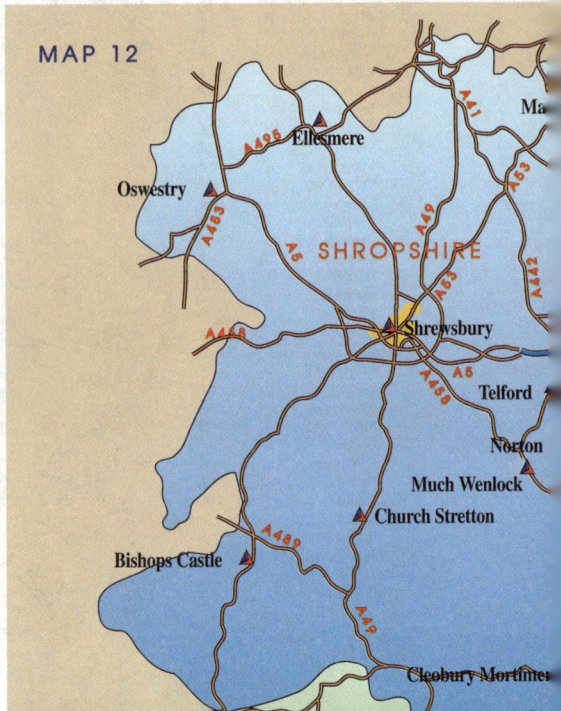

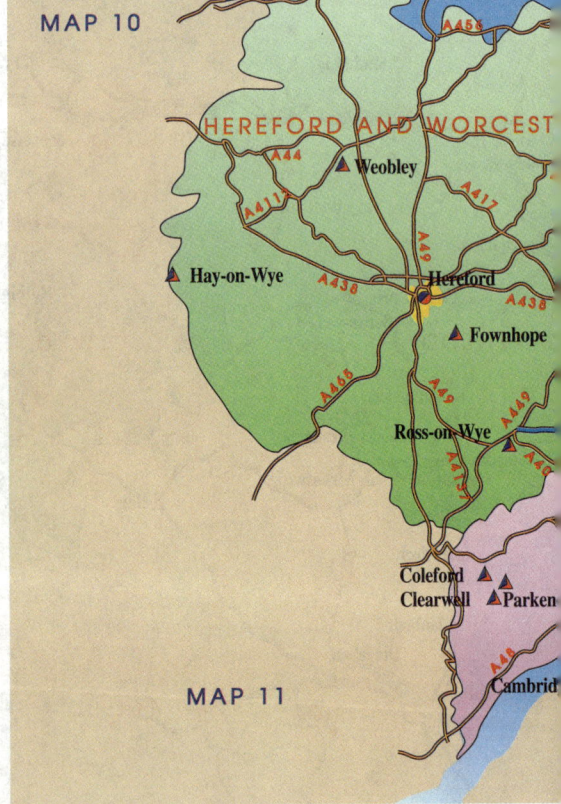

MAP 12

Ellesmere

Oswestry

SHROPSHIRE

Shrewsbury

Telford

Norton

Much Wenlock

Church Stretton

Bishops Castle

Cleobury Mortimer

MAP 10

HEREFORD AND WORCEST

Weobley

Hay-on-Wye

Hereford

Fownhope

Ross-on-Wye

Coleford
Clearwell Parken

MAP 11

Cambrid

Ma

SCALE: 13 MILES TO 1 INCH

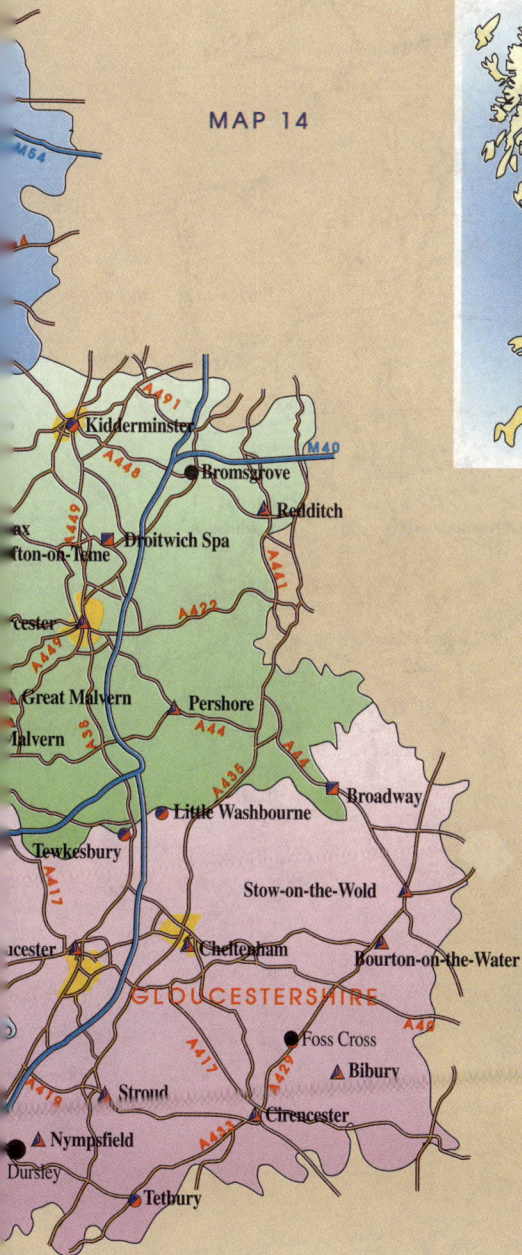

MAP 14

Kidderminster

Bromsgrove

Redditch

Droitwich Spa

ax
ton-on-Teme

cester

Great Malvern

Malvern

Pershore

Little Washbourne

Broadway

Tewkesbury

Stow-on-the-Wold

cester

Cheltenham

Bourton-on-the-Water

GLOUCESTERSHIRE

Foss Cross

Bibury

Stroud

Cirencester

Nympsfield

Dursley

Tetbury

MAP 16

MAP 13

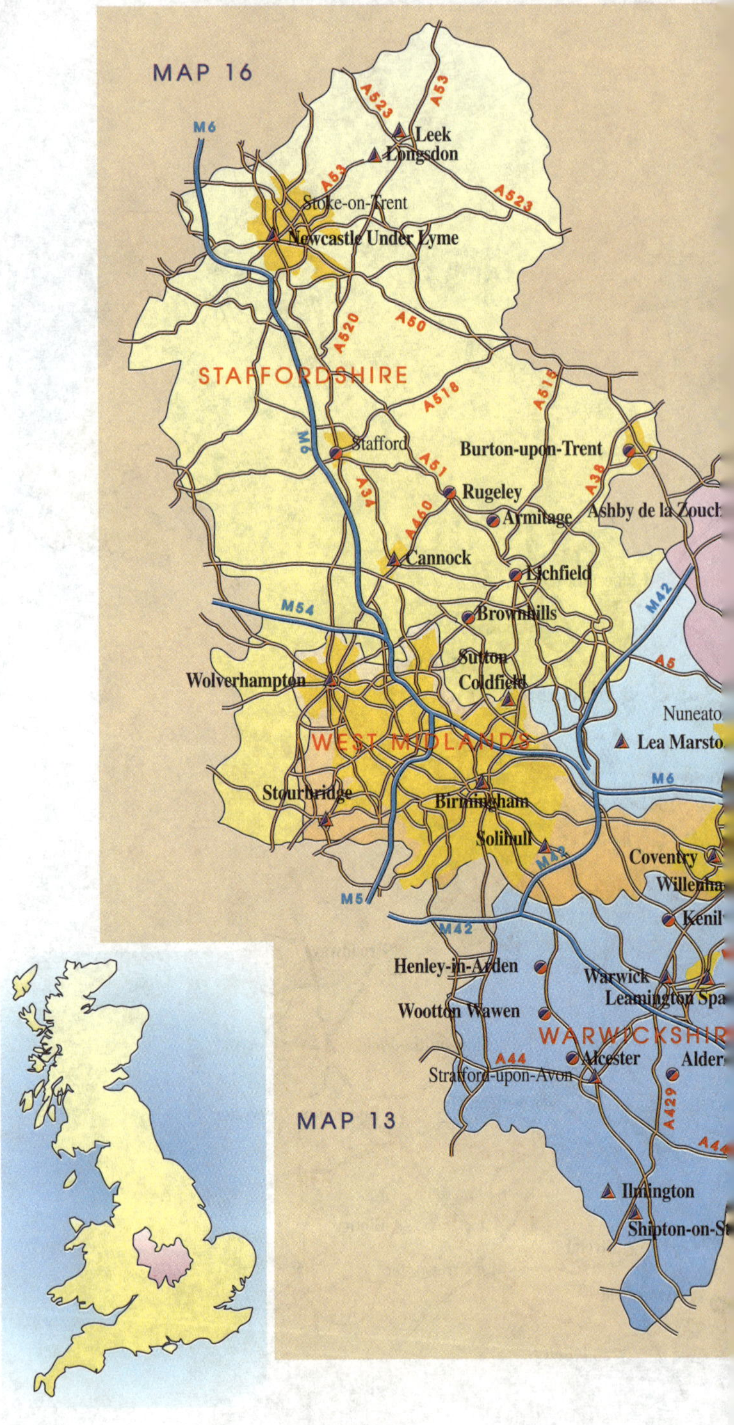

MAP 15

M1

Castle Donnington

Hoton Old Dalby
Burton-on-the-Wolds
Loughborough Melton Mowbray
A607
Rothley A6 A607 A606 Rutland
Sileby Oakham
A50
LEICESTERSHIRE
own Linford
Leicester A6003

A47 Uppingham
Lyddington

A6

Hinckley
Upper Benefield A427 Oundle
A5 A427
A605
Market Harborough
utterworth A43
Welford
Kettering
NORTHAMPTONSHIRE A14
Rugby Crick A6
M45 Wellingborough
A43 A508
Daventry A46
Weedon A45 Northampton

A5

A508

M1

A43

MAP 6

M40

SCALE: 13 MILES TO 1 INCH

MAP 18

MAP 14

A628

DERBYSHIRE

A623

Buxton

A6

A515

Bakewell

Chesterfield

A619

A619

A617

Matlock

A61

Wirksworth

Alfreton

Ashbourne

A52

Belper

Kimberley

Ikeston

Derby

A52

Shardlow

A6

Long Eaton

A50

A514

M1

Worksop

A57

A614

Edwinstowe

A615

Mansfield

A617

A60

Southwell

NOTTINGHAMSH

A612

Gunthorpe

Nottingham

Colston Bass

A648

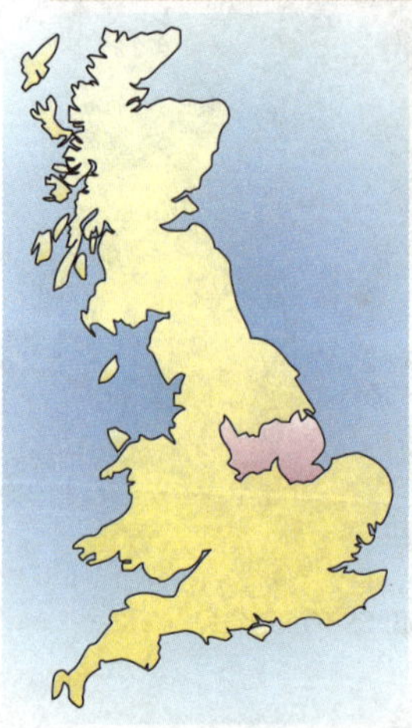

Gainsborough

Market Rasen

Louth

Mablethorpe

Donington-on-Bain

A46

A18

A16

A15

A1103

A46

A57

A46

A158

Lincoln

A158

A16

A1028

LINCOLNSHIRE

Spilsby

A158

Skegness

A16

Newark

A417

Leadenham

Sleaford

A1121

Boston

A17

A52

Grantham

A17

Gedney Dyke

Spalding

A1

A15

A16

Stamford

MAP 9

MAP 8

SCALE. 13 MILES TO 1 INCH

MAP 19

MAP 18

M6

Carnforth
Hornby
Bolton le Sands
Morecambe
Lancaster

A683

LANCASHIRE

Fleetwood

A6

Clitheroe

A59

A6068

Blackpool

Longridge

A59

M55

Burnley

Preston
A646

Lytham St Annes

Blackburn

A666

M65

M61

Southport

Chorley

Ramsbottom

Rochdale

M62

Eccleston
Mawdesley

A565

A5209

Bolton

Bury

M66

A58

Ormskirk

Standish

GREATER MANCHESTER

A580

Bootle

Salford
Manchester
Hyde

MERSEYSIDE

Newton-le-Willows

A57
A628

Wallasey

A5

Altrincham

Stockport

Birkenhead

Liverpool

Widnes

Warrington

MAP 15

A41

Thornton Hough

Parkgate

Knutsford

Frodsham

Macclesfield

Northwich

A34
A536

A556

Chester

Middlewich

A54

A51

A55

Congleton

MAP 12

CHESHIRE

A530

Alsager

Crewe

MAP 14

A41
A49

A51

M6

SCALE: 13 MILES TO 1 INCH

| | | | | | |
|---|---|---|---|---|---|
| Alsager | ⛺ | Crewe | ⛺ | Morecambe | ⛺ |
| Altrincham | ⛺ | Eccleston | ⛺ | Newton le Willows | ⛺ |
| Birkenhead | ⛺ | Frodsham | ⛺ | Northwich | ⛺ |
| Blackburn | ⛺ | Hyde | ⛺ | Preston | ⦿ |
| Blackpool | ⛺ | Knutsford | ⛺ | Ormskirk | ⦿ |
| Bolton | ⛺ | Lancaster | ⛺ | Parkgate | ⦿ |
| Bolton Le Sands | ⦿ | Liverpool | ⦿ | Preston | ⛺ |
| Bury | ⛺ | Longridge | ⦿ | Ramsbottom | ⛺ |
| Carnforth | ⛺ | Lytham St Annes | ⛺ | Salford | ⛺ |
| Chester | ⛺ | Macclesfield | ⛺ | Southport | ⛺ |
| Chorley | ⛺ | Manchester | ⛺ | Standish | ⛺ |
| Clitheroe | ⛺ | Mawdesley | ⦿ | Thornton Hough | ⛺ |
| Congleton | ⛺ | Middlewich | ⛺ | Wallasey | ⛺ |

SCALE: 13 MILES TO 1 INCH

| Alnmouth | ⚑ | Consett | ⚑ | Hexham | ⚑ | Sunderland | ⚑ |
| Alnwick | ⚑ | Corbridge | ⚑ | Longframlington | ⚑ | Thornaby | ⚑ |
| Bamburgh | ⚑ | Cornhill on Tweed | ⚑ | Newcastle Upon Tyne | ⚑ | Warkworth | ⊘ |
| Belford | ⚑ | Durham | ⚑ | Newton Aycliffe | ⚑ | Whitley Bay | ⚑ |
| Bellingham | ⚑ | Gateshead | ⚑ | Otterburn | ⚑ | Yarm | ⊘ |
| Berwick-Upon-Tweed | ⚑ | Greenhead | ⊘ | Rothbury | ⚑ | | |
| Billingham | ⚑ | Hartlepool | ⚑ | Seahouses | ⚑ | | |
| Bishop Auckland | ⊘ | Haydon Bridge | ⚑ | South Shields | ⚑ | | |

MAP 17

Darlington
A66 A1(M) A66(M)
Middleton Tyas
Stoke
A1
A19
Richmond
Reeth
Osmotherley
Northaller
Askrigg
Wensleydale
Leeming Bar
Bainbridge
Thirsk

NORTH YORKSHIRE

A65
Ripon
Austwick
Settle
Grassington
Long Preston
Wigglesworth
A59
Harrogate
A1
A58

MAP 16
Skipton
A65
Ilkley
Otley
A660
Keighley
Bingley
A61
A58
Haworth
Shipley
A629
Bradford
Leeds
Fairburn
A650
WEST YORKSHIRE
Castleford
A646
Halifax
Wakefield
Elland
A642
A638
Huddersfield
A629
A63
A628
M62
Holmfirth
SOUTH YORKSHIRE
Rotherham
Sheffield

Ellerby
Whitby
Castleton
Goathland
Rosedale Abbey
Kirkbymoorside
Appleton-le-Moors
Helmsley
East Ayton
Scarborough
Filey
Hovingham
Malton
Bridlington
Little Driffield
Driffield
York
HUMBERSIDE
Beverley
Cottingham
Ellerker
Hull
Blacktoft
Snaith
Scunthorpe
Grimsby
Cleethorpes
Brigg
caster

A171
A64
A1079
A163
A1079
A1035
A6
A63
M62
A164
A63
A15
A18
A180
A16
A18
A168
A166
A165
A19

MAP 15

SCALE: 13 MILES TO 1 INCH

**19**

MAP 23

MAP 17

MAP 18

Longtown

Brampton

M6

A74

A7

A69

Silloth on Solway

Carlisle

A596

A595

Melmerby

A66

Penrith

Bassenthwaite

Bassenthwaite Lake

Workington

Emerdale Bridge

Keswick

Thirlmere

Whitehaven

Buttermere

Borrowdale

Appleby in Westmorland

St. Bees

CUMBRIA

Brough Sowerby

A595

A591

Grasmere

A6

A685

Ambleside

Eskdale Green

Far Sawrey

Grizedale

A591

Coniston

Windermere

Hawkshead

Bowness on Windermere

Kendal

Sedbergh

Broughton in Furness

A5092

Newby Bridge

A590

A5900

A595

Witherslack

A65

Ulverston

Grange-over-Sands

Kirkby Lonsdale

Barrow-in-Furness

Sulby

Ramsey

Glen Helen

ISLE OF MAN

Douglas

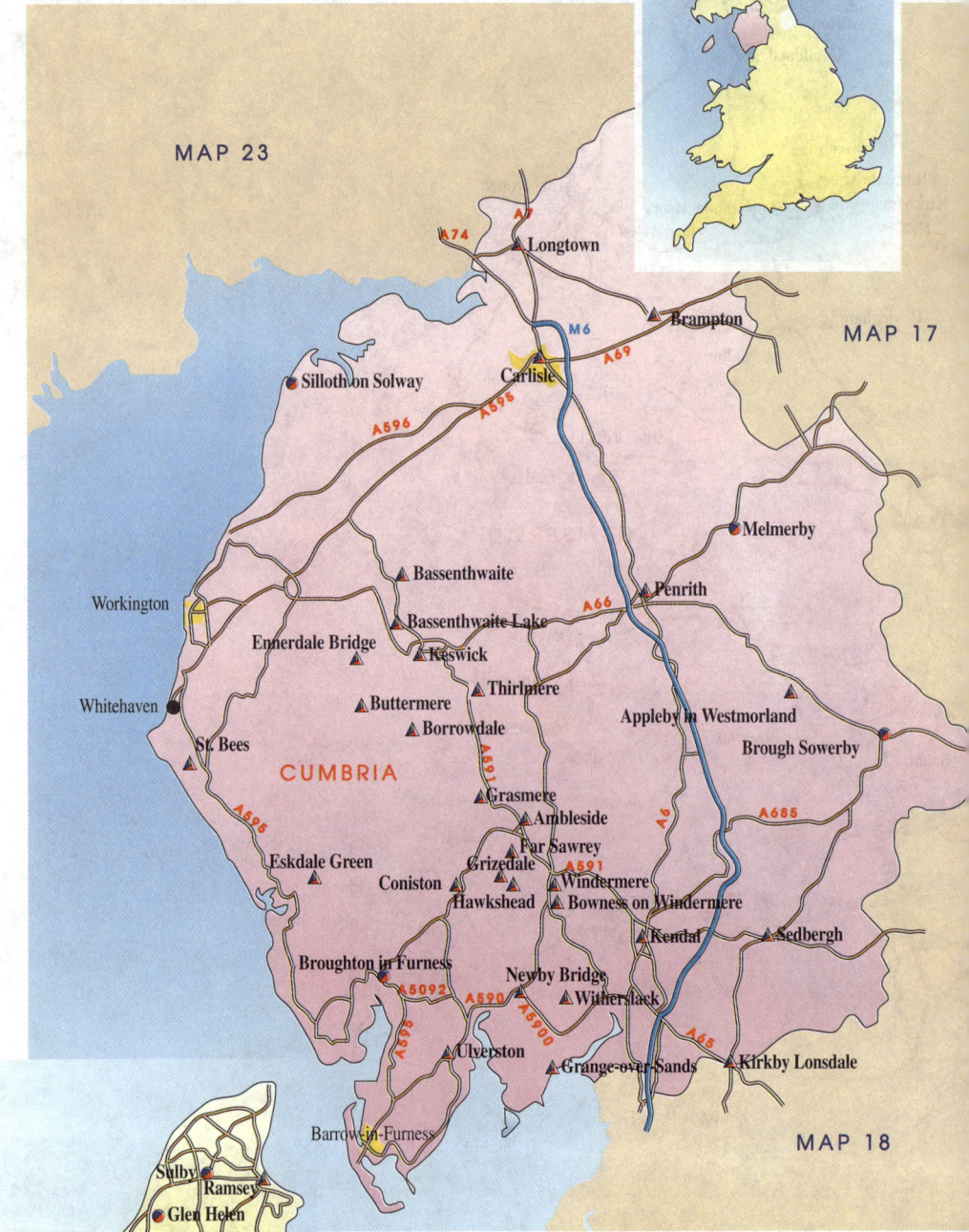

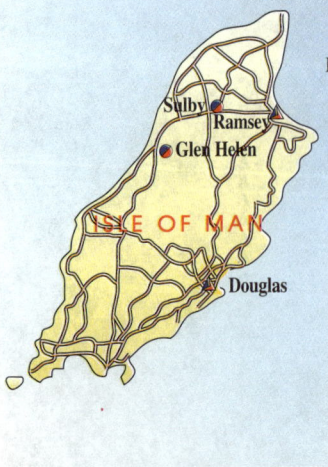

SCALE: 13 MILES TO 1 INC

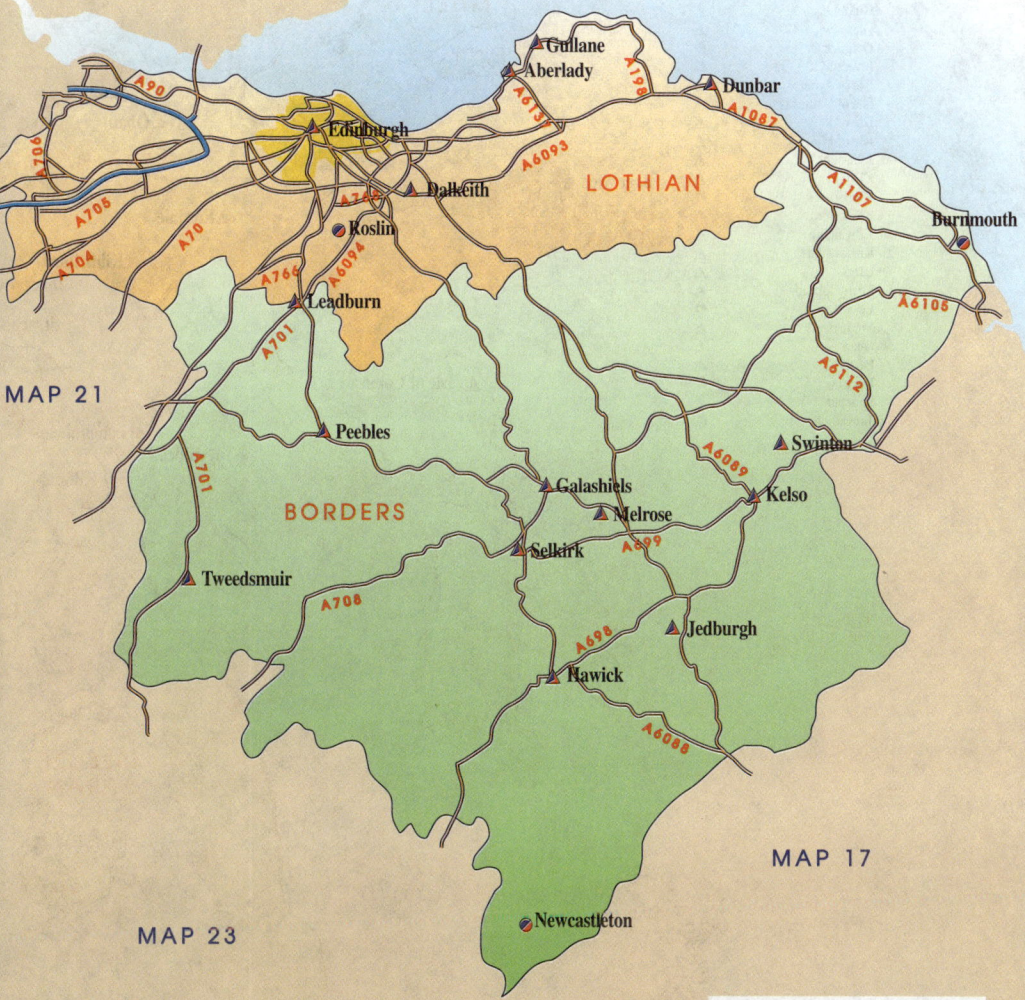

**20**

MAP 22

Gullane
Aberlady
Dunbar

Edinburgh
LOTHIAN
Dalkeith
Burnmouth
Roslin

Leadburn

MAP 21

Peebles
Swinton
Galashiels
Kelso
BORDERS
Melrose
Selkirk
Tweedsmuir
Jedburgh
Hawick

MAP 17

MAP 23

Newcastleton

SCALE: 13 MILES TO 1 INCH

| Aberlady | | Gullane | | Newcastleton | |
| Burnmouth | | Hawick | | Peebles | |
| Dalkeith | | Jedburgh | | Roslin | |
| Dunbar | | Kelso | | Selkirk | |
| Edinburgh | | Leadburn | | Swinton | |
| Galashiels | | Melrose | | Tweedsmuir | |

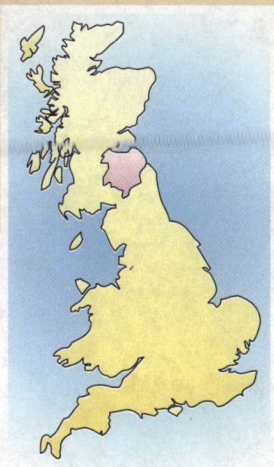

Road numbers: A90, A702, A901, A198, A6137, A1087, A705, A703, A70, A705, A704, A766, A6094, A6093, A1107, A6105, A701, A6112, A701, A6089, A899, A708, A698, A6088

**ISLE OF MULL**

Salen

**ISLE OF IONA**

Baile Mór

Bunessan

Pennyghael

Oban

**STRATHCLYDE**

A828

A85

Easdale

Kilmelford

Inveraray

Strachur

A815

Isle of Colonsay

A886

Lochgilphead

Tayvallich

Kilfinan

A8003

A83

Catacol

**ISLE OF ARRAN**

Whiting Bay

A841

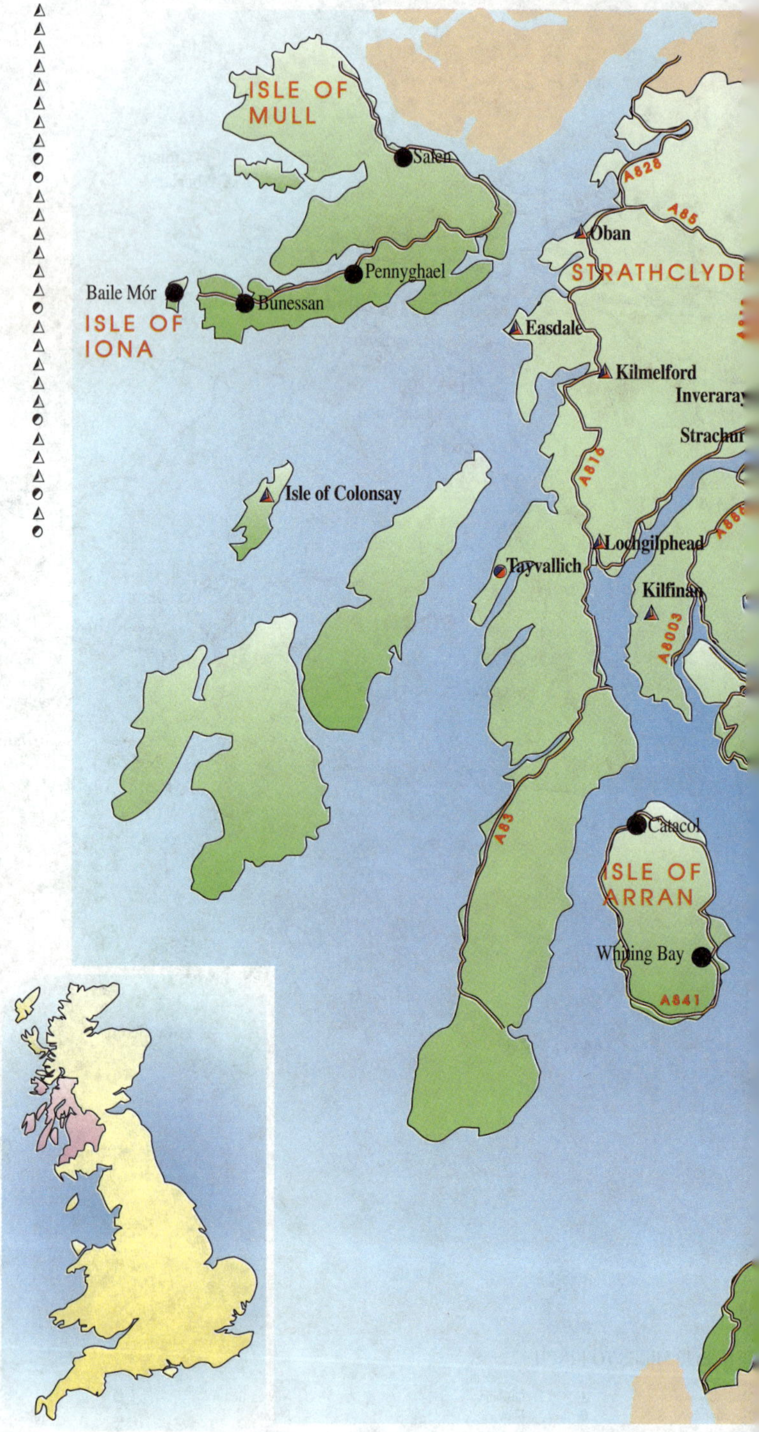

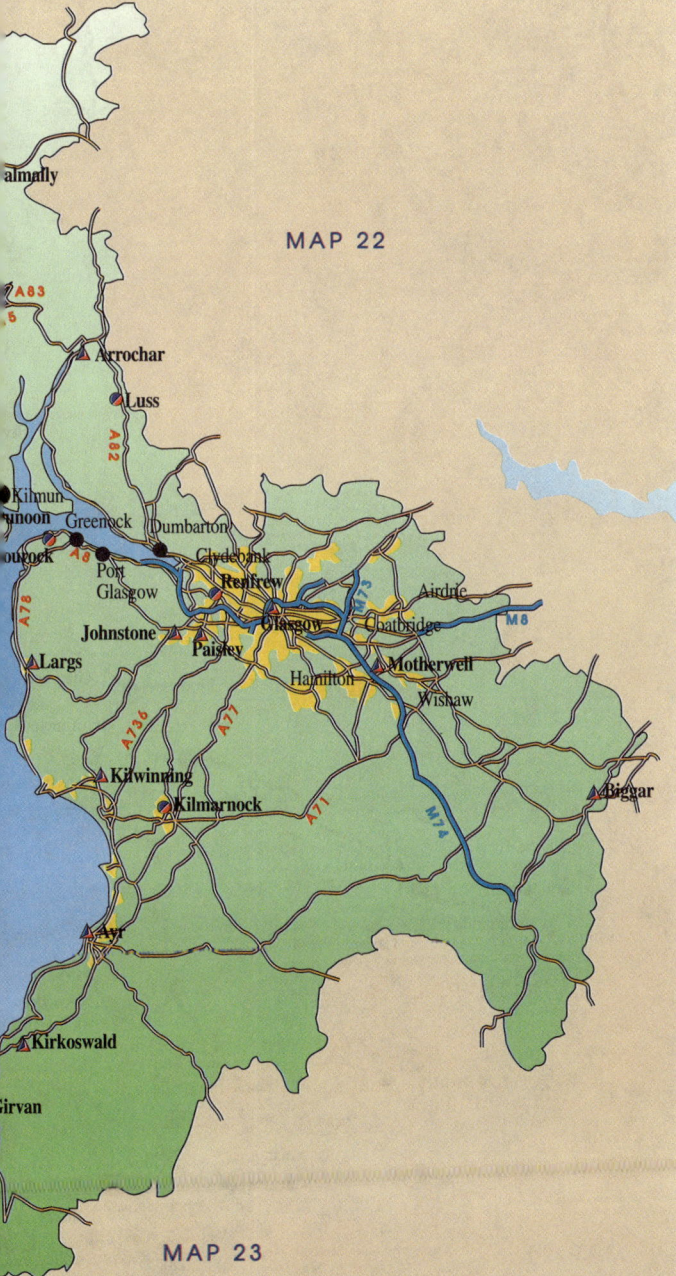

MAP 24

MAP 22

A83

5

Arrochar

A82

Luss

Kilmun

unoon

Kilmun

Greenock

Dumbarton

ourock

A8

Port
Glasgow

Clydebank

Renfrew

A78

Johnstone

Paisley

Glasgow

Airdrie

Coatbridge

M8

M73

Largs

A736

Hamilton

Motherwell

Wishaw

A77

Kilwinning

Kilmarnock

A71

M74

Biggar

Ayr

Kirkoswald

Girvan

MAP 23

SCALE: 17 MILES TO 1 INCH

MAP 24

Br

A96

A9

TAYSIDE

Pitlochry

Glen Isla

Kirkmichael

Aberfeldy

Kenmore

A9

Killin

A85

St Fillans

Crieff

Perth

A82

Tyndrum

Crianlarich

Lochearnhead

A85

A85

M90

A82

CENTRAL

A84

A9

Auchterarder

Aucht

Callander

Milnathort

Kinross

Port of Menteith

Dunblane

A811

M9

A91

A977

Stirling

Kincardine-on-Forth

Dunfermline

Stenhousemuir

A985

Bo'ness

M80

Falkirk

Grangemouth

Rosyt

M9

MAP 21

Fraserburgh

Buckie  Cullen  Banff

A98  A98  A92  A952

gin

A96

A411

Aberlour

A92

Peterhead

A96

A952

olivet

Insch

GRAMPIAN

Inverourie

A92

Alford

A96

Balmedie

Glenshee by Blairgowrie  Aberdeen

A93

rathie

A93

Aboyne  Banchory

A92

Ballater

Deeside  Stonehaven

A94

A92

Edzell

Montrose

Brechin

A94

Forfar

Blairgowrie

A929  A92

Arbroath

A85

Dundee  Carnoustie

Newport on Tay

A914

Letham  St Andrews

A914  Cupar  A91

Freuchie  FIFE  Crail

Glenrothes  Lundin Links

West Wemyss

Kirkcaldy

Burntisland

SCALE: 17 MILES TO 1 INCH

MAP 21

DUMFRIES
AND
GALLOWAY

New Gallowa

Newton Stewart

Gatehouse-of-F

Stranraer

Portpatrick

Isle of Whithor

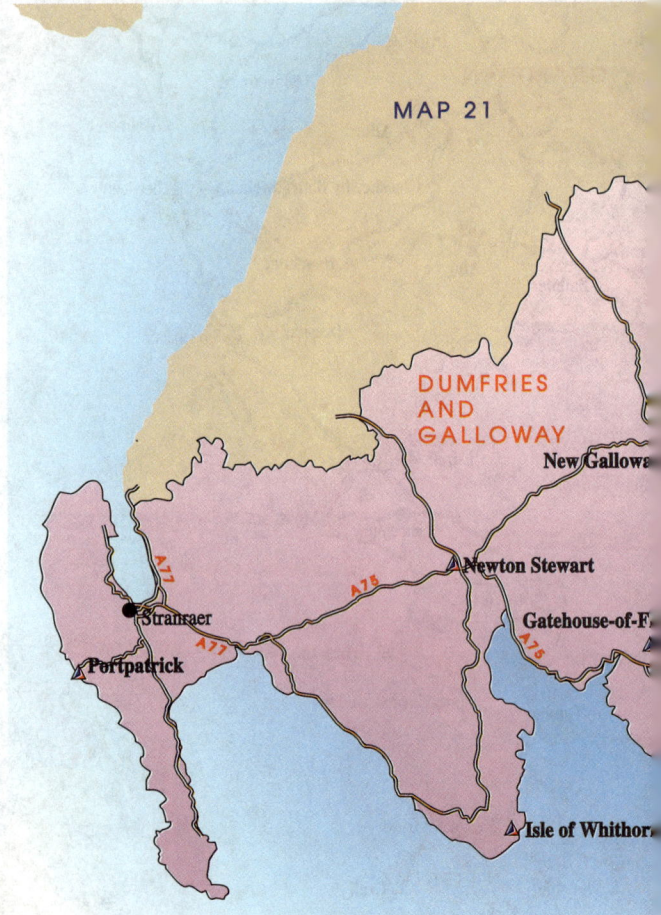

SCALE: 13 MILES TO 1 INCH

MAP 20

A76

A74 ▲Moffat

▲Thornhill

A701

A74

▲Lockerbie

A75

A76

A75
Dumfries

A75
Annan▲  ● Gretna

A7

kcudbright

MAP 19

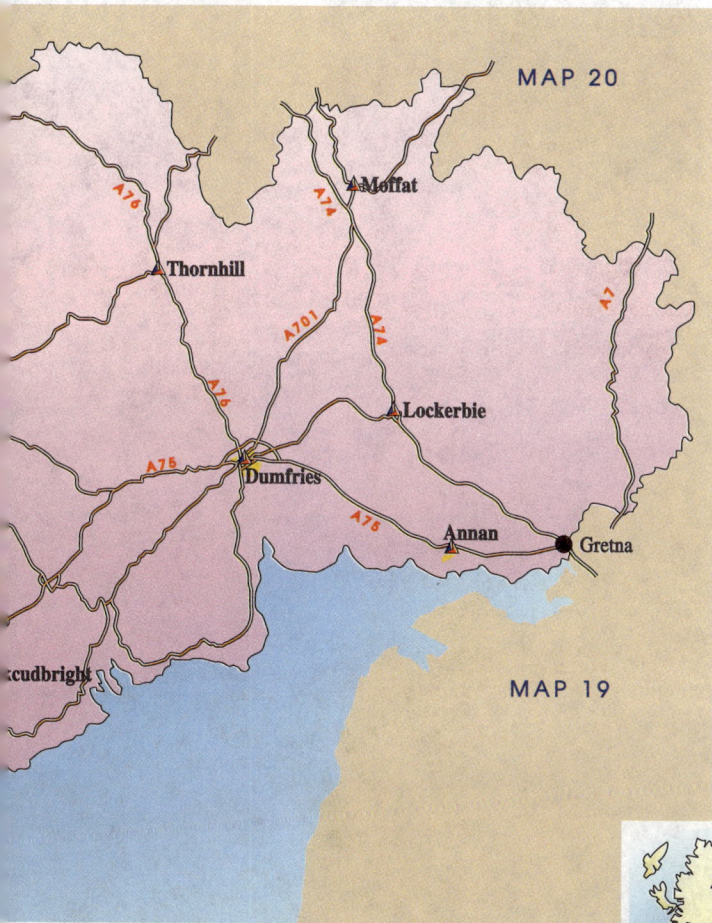

| Annan | ⚑ |
| Dumfries | ⚑ |
| Gatehouse of Fleet | ⚑ |
| Isle of Whithorn | ⚑ |
| Kirkcudbright | ⚑ |
| Lockerbie | ⚑ |
| Moffat | ⚑ |
| New Galloway | ⚑ |
| Newton Stewart | ⚑ |
| Portpatrick | ⚑ |
| Thornhill | ⚑ |

## WESTERN ISLES

SCALE: 26 MILES TO 1 INCH

ISLE OF LEWIS

Stornoway

Tarbert

ISLE OF NORTH UIST

ISLE OF HARRIS

Lochmaddy

ISLE OF BENBECULA

Liniclett

ISLE OF SOUTH UIST

Daliburgh

ISLE OF BARRA

Castlebay

Scouri

Lochniver

Laide

**Gairloch**
**Poolewe**

Kinloch

Shieldaig

HIG

Staffin

Uig

**Dunvegan**

Skeabost

Portree

Lochcarron

Kyleakin

ISLE OF SKYE

Isleornsay

A87

Glenmo

**Mallaig**

**Arisaig**

Glenfinnan

Fort William

Acharacle

**Glenborrodale**

Strontian

Kinlochlever

G

SCALE: 17 MILES TO 1 INCH

24

Durness
Tongue
Thurso
Halkirk
John o' Groats
A882
Wick
Altnaharra
A895
Dunbeath
A9
Helmsdale
Rosehall
Lairg
Dornoch
Tain
Invergordon
Cromarty
Dingwall
Contin by Strathpeffer
Nairn
A96
Beauly
Inverness
nnich
Drumnadrochit
Grantown-on-Spey
A82
Invermoriston
87
Nethybridge
A95
Fort Augustus
A9
Aviemore
Kincraig
Invergarry
Kingussie
Newtonmore
A86
ean Bridge
Dalwhinnie

MAP 22

SHETLAND
ISLANDS
Hillswick

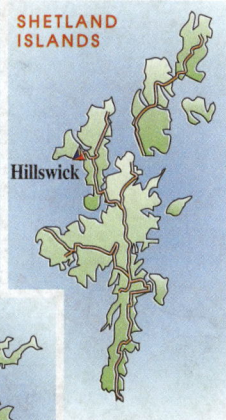

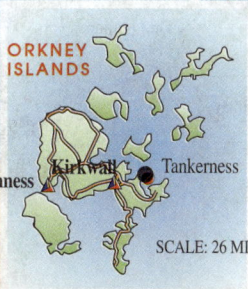

ORKNEY
ISLANDS
Stromness
Kirkwall
Tankerness
SCALE: 26 MILES TO 1 INCH

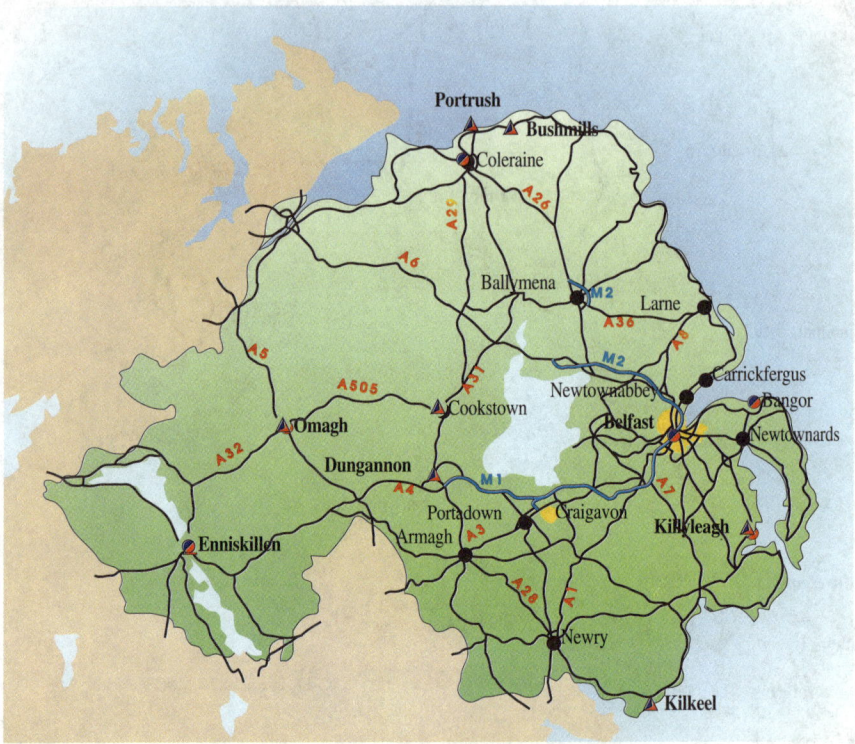

SCALE: 28 MILES TO 1 INCH

| | |
|---|---|
| Bangor | ⊙ |
| Belfast | ⊙ |
| Bushmills | △ |
| Coleraine | ⊙ |
| Cookstown | △ |
| Dungannon | △ |
| Enniskillen | ⊙ |
| Kilkeel | △ |
| Killyleagh | △ |
| Omagh | △ |
| Portrush | △ |

# The 1994 Casserole Awards

The 'Casserole' represents the finest of Les Routiers culinary traditions and is awarded annually to our members who offer that little something extra.

Whenever you visit a Casserole award-winning establishment, whatever dish you order, it will have that extra thoughtful finishing touch. You will experience an exciting new world of wonderful sensations through the clever use of herbs and aromatic spices, combinations of carefully matched colours and varying textures, all immaculately prepared and professionally presented.

To qualify for the Casserole Award an establishment must demonstrate that they have maintained the required standards for a minimum period of one year. Winners are allowed to display a prestigious certificate and receive a Casserole symbol against their entry in the guide.

| | | |
|---|---|---|
| Aberlour | Grampian | Archiestown Hotel |
| Abersoch | Gwynedd | The White House Hotel |
| Ambleside | Cumbria | The Riverside Hotel |
| Arisaig | Highlands | The Old Library Lodge & Restaurant |
| Ayr | Strathclyde | Fouters Bistro |
| Bampton | Devon | The Swan Hotel |
| Banchory | Grampian | Banchory Lodge Hotel |
| Bangor | Co. Down | Gillespies' Place / Gryphon Restaurant |
| Bassenthwaite Lake | Cumbria | The Pheasant Inn |
| Battersea | London | Buchan's |
| Battersea | London | Jack's Place |
| Battle | East Sussex | Powdermills Hotel |
| Beaconsfield | Buckinghamshire | The Royal Standard of England |
| Bedford | Bedfordshire | The Knife & Cleaver |
| Bedford | Bedfordshire | Three Cranes |
| Betws y Coed | Gwynedd | Ty Gwyn Hotel |
| Biggleswade | Bedfordshire | La Cachette |
| Bildeston | Suffolk | The Crown Hotel |
| Birchington | Kent | Smugglers Restaurant |
| Bloomsbury | London | Academy Hotel |
| Boughton Monchelsea | Kent | Tanyard |
| Bovey Tracey | Devon | The Edgemoor Hotel |
| Bowness on Windermere | Cumbria | Blenheim Lodge |
| Bradford on Avon | Wiltshire | Widbrook Grange |
| Brighton | East Sussex | Le Grandousier Restaurant |
| Burntisland | Fife | Kingswood Hotel |
| Bury | Greater Manchester | Rosco's Eating House |
| Bury St Edmunds | Suffolk | The Six Bells Inn |
| Bushmills | Antrim | Hillcrest Country House & Restaurant |
| Cardigan | Dyfed | Skippers |
| Castle Donington | Leicestershire | Le Chevalier |
| Chelwood | Avon | Chelwood House Hotel |
| Chester | Cheshire | Francs Restaurant |
| Chester | Cheshire | Redland Hotel |
| Chichester | West Sussex | Platters Restaurant |

| | | |
|---|---|---|
| Chippenham | Wiltshire | The Three Crowns |
| Cirencester | Gloucestershire | Wild Duck Inn |
| Clearwell | Gloucestershire | Wyndham Arms |
| Colwyn Bay | Clwyd | Edelweiss Hotel |
| Corsham | Wiltshire | Rudloe Park Hotel & Restaurant |
| Criccieth | Gwynedd | Bron Eifion Country House Hotel |
| Criccieth | Gwynedd | The Moelwyn Restaurant |
| Cullen | Grampian | Bayview Hotel |
| Cwmbran | Gwent | The Parkway Hotel & Conference Centre |
| Dolgellau | Gwynedd | Clifton House Hotel |
| Durness | Highland | Far North Hotel |
| Duxford | Cambridgeshire | Duxford Lodge Hotel |
| Edenbridge | Kent | Castle Inn |
| Edinburgh | Lothian | The Tattler |
| Edinburgh | Lothian | Verandah Tandoori Restaurant |
| Elland | West Yorkshire | Berties Bistro |
| Exebridge | Somerset | Anchor Inn Hotel |
| Exeter | Devon | The Old Thatch Inn |
| Glasgow | Strathclyde | Ewington Hotel |
| Glasgow | Strathclyde | La Fiorentina |
| Grange Over Sands | Cumbria | Netherwood Hotel |
| Grizedale | Cumbria | Grizedale Lodge Hotel & Restaurant |
| Guildford | Surrey | The Spread Eagle |
| Halifax | West Yorkshire | Collyers Hotel |
| Halifax | West Yorkshire | Imperial Crown Hotel |
| Harrogate | North Yorkshire | Grundy's Restaurant |
| Harrow | Middlesex | Cumberland Hotel |
| Harrow | Middlesex | Fiddler's Restaurant |
| Hay on Wye | Hereford & Worcester | The Old Black Lion |
| Helmsley | North Yorkshire | The Feversham Arms Hotel |
| Inverness | Highlands | Whinpark Hotel & Restaurant |
| Isle of Skye | Highlands | Flodigarry Country House Hotel |
| Isle of Skye | Highlands | Kinloch Lodge |
| Kilwinning | Strathclyde | Montgreenan Mansion House Hotel |
| Kirkcudbright | Dumfries & Galloway | Selkirk Arms Hotel |
| Lancaster | Lancashire | Springfield House Hotel & Restaurant |
| Leamington Spa | Warwickshire | Eathorpe Park Hotel |
| Leeds | West Yorkshire | Olive Tree Greek Restaurant |
| Little Driffield | Humberside | Downe Arms |
| Llanbedr | Gwynedd | Llew Glas |
| Llanberis | Gwynedd | Lake View Hotel |
| Llandudno | Gwynedd | Dunoon Hotel |
| Longridge | Lancashire | Corporation Arms |
| Longsdon | Staffordshire | Bank End Farm Motel |
| Longtown | Cumbria | The Sportsman's Restaurant |
| Lyme Regis | Dorset | Bensons Restaurant |
| Lynmouth | Devon | Rising Sun Hotel |
| Lynton | Devon | Millslade Country House Hotel |
| Malton | North Yorkshire | Cornucopia |
| Manchester | Greater Manchester | The Mock Turtle Restaurant & Carroll's |

| | | |
|---|---|---|
| Melmerby | Cumbria | Shepherds Inn |
| Midhurst | West Sussex | The Spread Eagle Hotel |
| Monmouth | Gwent | The Crown at Whitebrook |
| Nairn | Highlands | Ramleh Hotel & Fingal's Restaurant |
| Norton | Shropshire | The Hundred House Hotel Restaurant |
| Odiham | Hampshire | La Foret |
| Old Dalby | Leicestershire | The Crown Inn |
| Omagh | County Tyrone | The Woodlander |
| Oswestry | Shropshire | Restaurant Sebastian |
| Oundle | Northamptonshire | Fitzgeralds Restaurant |
| Oxford | Oxfordshire | Belfry Hotel |
| Peebles | Borders | Cringletie House Hotel |
| Peebles | Borders | Peebles Hotel Hydro |
| Pinner | Middlesex | La Giralda |
| Pitlochry | Tayside | Green Park Hotel |
| Plymouth | Devon | Trattoria Pescatore |
| Plymouth | Devon | The Weary Friar Inn |
| Polperro | Cornwall | The Kitchen |
| Poole | Dorset | Allans Seafood Restaurant |
| Preston | Lancashire | The Bushells Arms |
| Preston | Lancashire | Ferraris Restaurant |
| Putney | London | Gavin's Restaurant |
| Pwllheli | Gwynedd | Twnti Seafood Restaurant |
| Ramsey | Isle of Man | Harbour Bistro |
| Ramsgate | Kent | Morton's Fork |
| Renfrew | Strathclyde | Piccolo Mondo & La Toscanella |
| Rotherham | South Yorkshire | The Elton Hotel |
| Rutland | Leicestershire | The Shires Hotel |
| Seaview | Isle of Wight | Seaview Hotel & Restaurant |
| Selkirk | Borders | Philipburn House Hotel & Restaurant |
| Snettisham | Norfolk | The Rose & Crown Freehouse |
| Souldern | Oxfordshire | Fox Inn |
| St Brelade | Jersey | La Place Hotel |
| St Davids | Dyfed | Harbour House Hotel & Restaurant |
| St Ives | Cornwall | Pedn-Olva Hotel & Restaurant |
| St Ouen's Bay | Jersey | The Lobster Pot Hotel & Restaurant |
| Stafford | Staffordshire | The Moat House Restaurant |
| Stamford | Lincolnshire | Candlesticks Hotel & Restaurant |
| Stokesley | North Yorkshire | Millers Restaurant |
| Stow on the Wold | Gloucestershire | Grapevine Hotel |
| Strachur | Strathclyde | The Creggans Inn |
| Teddington | Middlesex | The Italian Place Brasserie |
| Telford | Shropshire | Raphaels Restaurant |
| Thirsk | North Yorkshire | Nags Head Hotel & Restaurant |
| Thirsk | North Yorkshire | Sheppard's Hotel, Restaurant & Bistro |
| Tongue | Highland | Ben Loyal Hotel |
| Torquay | Devon | Jingle's Restaurant |
| Truro | Cornwall | Alverton Manor |
| Vazon Bay | Guernsey | La Grande Mare |
| Wadhurst | East Sussex | The Old Vine |

| | | |
|---|---|---|
| Watlington | Oxfordshire | The Well House Restaurant & Hotel |
| West End | London | Don Pepe Restaurant |
| Westerham | Kent | The Kings Arms Hotel |
| Weymouth | Dorset | Sea Cow Restaurant |
| Whitby | North Yorkshire | The Magpie Cafe |
| Whitstable | Kent | Giovannis Restaurant |
| Wirksworth | Derbyshire | Le Bistro |
| Witherslack | Cumbria | The Old Vicarage Country House Hotel |
| Woodbridge | Suffolk | Captain's Table |
| York | North Yorkshire | Mount Royale |

# Les Routiers Awards 1994

All establishments listed in this guide have attained the prestigious Les Routiers 'recommendation' only by meeting our exacting standards, providing *quality, value for money and a warm welcome*. There are some, however, whose efforts have far exceeded the required standards, and our expectations, by making a concerted effort towards achieving *total customer satisfaction*, offering that something extra. In recognition of their achievements, each year we present a number of awards.

*Restaurant of the Year* – a restaurant or bistro which offers a full and varied menu with imaginative, mouthwatering dishes served by knowledgeable, efficient and friendly staff.

*Pub of the Year* – an establishment which echoes the true traditions of the English inn. Essential factors are a cheerful friendly greeting, relaxed informality, a place for families and a place where one can enjoy traditional wholesome food and carefully selected fine ales.

*Accommodation of the Year* – a hotel or guest house where you start to relax the instant you arrive. Rooms should be inviting, clean and comfortable, with special touches like fresh flower arrangements, a hairdryer for women, a trouser press for men and visitor information. Little extras such as these clearly demonstrate further consideration towards the guest. Good food and welcoming hospitality are two other important ingredients in an award-winning hotel.

*Newcomer of the Year* – any hotel, guest house, restaurant or inn which is being featured in the Les Routiers guide for the very first time and is clearly already offering an outstanding level of service. Nominations for this award are usually instantly recognizable from the glowing report which follows their inspection.

*Cheeseboard of the Year* – awarded for the most exceptional cheeseboard at a Les Routiers establishment. Cheese is a serious business at this establishment and in almost every case the proprietor and staff will be able to provide customers with expert knowledge of the varieties of cheeses which they are being offered.

*Prix D'Elite* (**Wine of the Year**) – the award for most exceptional wine list at a Les Routiers establishment. Like the cheeseboard winner, wine plays a very important role in the daily programme. Although the establishment may specialize in certain varieties and vintages, the customer is assured that the list is easily readable and that they will be able to receive sound advice on the perfect selection.

*Symbol of Excellence* – not an annual award, but given to an establishment which has been recommended by Les Routiers for at least a decade. Over this period of time, it will have consistently provided its customers with an outstanding level of service. This award has been presented on only three occasions since its creation.

*Your Recommendations Please . . .*
We welcome your help and opinions which are invaluable in helping us to make our selection of award winners. On page 421 of this guide, you will find an Opinion Form which gives you the opportunity to nominate your favourite Les Routiers establishment, or perhaps somewhere new that you have recently discovered. If you prefer not to remove this page, you may write to us at: **Les Routiers, 25 Vanston Place, London SW6 1AZ**, with details of your recommendation, outlining why you feel this particular establishment should be considered for an award.

# Restaurant of the Year

## RAMLEH HOTEL & FINGAL'S RESTAURANT

### Nairn, Highlands

After earning itself an enviable reputation for its excellent quality food, Fingal's Restaurant – also known as the best place to eat in Nairn – is a deserved winner of this award.

Theme Nights are a regular and highly popular feature at the Ramleh. To name just a few: Malaysian Magic, Out of Africa, Way Out West, A Taste of 19th-Century Scotland, Turkish Delight, A Taste of Thailand, Viva Espana, A Feast of Caribbean Creations – the list goes on and on. These 'fixed menu' theme nights allow diners to sample some of the most exciting culinary sensations of worldwide ethnic cuisine, without having to search too far, although it is true to say that many do come from miles away to participate in these colourful gourmet feasts. Meals can be enjoyed in either the splendid new conservatory, or in the elegant and intimate surroundings of the newly refurbished restaurant – the hotel also has forty-nine comfortable bedrooms, most of which have excellent *en suite* facilities.

Where finer a place to enjoy a delicious meal than in Nairn, nestling on the south shore of the Moray Firth looking northwards to the Black Isle and the mountains of Ross and Sutherland. The Ramleh Hotel offers a fine selection of tasty British and continental cuisine, for which the chef delights in using local and regional fresh Scottish produce. Diners can choose from a mouthwatering selection of Scottish seafood dishes, including tipsy trout – an oven-baked rainbow trout with a sherry and walnut stuffing, and wild salmon steak – gently grilled with maitre d'hôte butter. Dishes selected from the game and poultry menu may include duckling exotique, a duckling breast in a deliciously different sauce made with ginger, mango and spring onion, or perhaps auld alliance – Scottish venison cooked to an old French recipe, marinaded in red wine and herbs for four days to produce a rich and satisfying sauce. Fresh local produce has also been used to full effect in the Ramleh's meat dishes menu, where one can select a succulent range of steaks, such as Gaelic steak – a sirloin or fillet of fresh Aberdeen Angus studded with garlic, steeped in whisky and combined with cream for a braw sauce; or for those with a really healthy appetite, there is a 14 oz T-bone. Veal Romana uses a delicate blend of mushrooms, baby onions, wine and cream, while Fingal's pork fillet uses medallions of pork, seasoned and cooked with red and green peppers in marsala wine. To ensure that every taste is catered for, there is a good vegetarian menu available offering some real treats with all dishes accompanied by fresh salad or vegetables and a choice of creamed, parsley, baked, chipped or sautéd potatoes.

# Restaurant of the Year

## HILLCREST COUNTRY HOUSE AND RESTAURANT

### Bushmills, County Antrim

An increasing number of overseas visitors to the land of blue mountains, forest parks, mazy lakes and windswept moors, has enabled us to offer you an even wider choice of fine hotels and restaurants in the north of Ireland for 1994.

They all have their own very special qualities, but after much deliberation we are delighted to name the Hillcrest Country House and Restaurant in County Antrim as our 'Restaurant of the Year' in Ireland for 1994.

Situated in a lovely position, with spectacular views over the Atlantic and the lush green hills of Donegal on the road to the mysterious Giant's Causeway, the Hillcrest is a top quality guest house and restaurant, renowned for its good food and fine wines. The Hillcrest has received many previous accolades, including two Galtee Irish Breakfast awards and membership of 'A Taste of Ulster'. By setting and maintaining meticulously high standards, proprietor Michael McKeever has created here what must surely be one of the finest restaurants in the north of Ireland which is widely renowned for its excellent cuisine and friendly efficient service. The extensive à la carte menu offers such delicacies as grilled venison Bushmills – rosettes of venison, lightly grilled, served on a crouton with game mousseline and finished with a sauce prepared from redcurrant jelly, laced with the famous whisky, Black Bush, or roast leg of lamb with minted peach or minted cream. Fish dishes include salmon Portbradden – a fillet of wild salmon baked in the oven and accompanied by a cucumber, sliced mushroom and fennel sauce, or supreme of sole Inishowen – fillets of sole poached in white wine, garnished with prawns and shallots and smothered in a creamy fish velouté, and who could fail to resist baked trout almondine – a whole rainbow trout, baked in the oven, off the bone and garnished with toasted almonds and nut brown butter. Round off your meal with one of the sumptuous desserts of which butterscotch meringues and banoffi pie are just two superb examples.

The Hillcrest is an ideal place for businessmen, families and couples, also offering four comfortably furnished *en suite* rooms equipped with a range of modern facilities to make any stay here truly memorable.

# Pub of the Year

## WILD DUCK INN

### Drakes Island, Ewen, nr Cirencester, Gloucestershire

If any establishment has adequately fulfilled our criteria for this award – it is the Wild Duck Inn.

Dating back to 1563 and uniquely situated in a country setting in the quiet Cotswold village of Ewen, the Wild Duck Inn has a timeless quality about it. The warm and welcoming Post Horn Bar, with its gleaming copper and brass, stately grandfather clock, leather fireside chairs and bar stools, serves a varied choice of piping-hot food in plentiful proportions and an excellent range of traditional fine ales and wines. It is an extremely popular gathering place with both local businessmen, families and holiday makers touring the Cotswolds. The patter is often of an equestrian nature, due to the many major local events, such as polo at Cirencester Park, Gatcombe Horse Trials, Badminton Horse Trials and Cheltenham Races. Outside, there is a delightful garden where in fine weather families or couples can relax and enjoy 'al fresco' dining in pleasant surroundings. The Wild Duck is also popular with visitors from overseas who come to sample the outstanding selection of exotic and colourful fish dishes, from oceans from all around the world.

For those not in a hurry, the Wild Duck provides a welcome resting place to weary travellers by offering traditionally furnished *en suite* rooms of a very high standard, all equipped with colour television and tea and coffee-making facilities. Interestingly, two of these rooms are located in the oldest part of the building and have garden views and marvellous four-poster beds with furnishings to match. The country-style restaurant has a warm, welcoming ambience, with a delicious ever-changing menu specializing in fresh seasonal fare. The Grouse Room allows diners and residents to unwind beside the Elizabethan inglenook fireplace with its antique furnishings. A cool room in the summer months, but on a winter's day guests can curl up with a favourite book in front of the roaring log fire.

The Wild Duck is ideally situated being just minutes away from the M4 and M5 motorways, thirty minutes from Swindon, Cheltenham and Gloucester and less than an hour's drive from 'Roman' Bath. Open every day of the week throughout the year, this family-run establishment ensures a friendly, comfortable atmosphere with good food and pleasing wines and ales. Nearby is the Cotswold Water Park, which covers many acres and has eighty lakes, where you can enjoy excellent birdwatching, sailing, windsurfing, swimming and more, or simply take the Gloucestershire air. Oaksey Park, just 2 miles away, offers golf, tennis and clay-pigeon shooting among its many interesting features.

# Accommodation of the Year

## THE ROYAL OAK INN

### Winsford, Exmoor National Park, Somerset

The Royal Oak Inn is set in the picturesque village of Winsford, on the edge of the Exmoor National Park, and are deserved winners of this award. The style of accommodation offered is everything one would expect of a traditional English Country Inn of this nature, and befits its character and timeless charm with absolute precision.

Each bright and airy bedroom has been furnished with enormous care to retain the cosy atmosphere of this quaint 12th-century inn. Fresh, clean and inviting, The Royal Oak has carefully selected traditional country-style furnishings, such as liberal displays of fresh dried flowers, floral-patterned cushions with deep, comfy armchairs, matching drapes and heavy mullioned windows. Within the courtyard of this old inn is The Annexe, which has been restored and redecorated to provide a further six attractive bedrooms, including a delightful family cottage. Each room has its own private bathroom and many other cleverly integrated modern facilities, including colour television and tea-making facilities.

The inn retains many of its original features, including a charming thatched roof, open inglenook fireplaces and heavy oak beams. Furnished to a high standard of elegance are the relaxing lounges, where you can read a book or enjoy a coffee. The restaurant prides itself on its freshly cooked cuisine and a small but select wine cellar. Menus are changed daily to give guests the widest possible selection of traditional English dishes. And if your appetite does not require a meal, then the ideal alternative is to have a light meal in one of the quaint bars.

Winsford itself was described by W.H. Hudson in 1909 as 'fragrant, cool, grey green – immemorial peace – second to no English village in beauty, running waters, stone thatched cottages, hoary church tower'. Today little has changed and the area is ideal for walking, fishing, riding and shooting. Within 2 miles is the Caratacus Stone on Winsford Hill, thought to have been inscribed in the Dark Ages. On the same hill are the Wambarrows – three buried mounds probably of the Beaker period or Bronze Age and between 2,500 and 4,000 years old. Minehead and Porlock are within easy distance as are a wealth of charming, unspoilt villages. Your stay at this inn will not only give you an opportunity to enjoy wonderful accommodation, but to explore a beautiful, unspoilt part of This England.

Anyone considering a stay at The Royal Oak Inn is recommended to phone or write first for full details of their special Getaway Breaks programme.

# Newcomer of the Year

## RIVERDALE HALL HOTEL

### Bellingham, Hexham, Northumberland

The Riverdale Hall Hotel – undoubtedly one of Northumbria's most outstanding country house hotels – was chosen to receive this award from hundreds of new entries to the guide this year.

Tastefully converted from a Victorian mansion by its present owners, Mr and Mrs John Cocker, this elegant building on the edge of the Northumberland National Park, is superbly situated in its own large grounds alongside the North Tyne River and reflects the character and charm of bygone days in its appearance, ambience and atmosphere.

The hotel has special appeal to sports and leisure enthusiasts. In the grounds is a large heated indoor swimming pool and sauna, providing fun and relaxation whatever the weather. The pool opens onto a lawned, sheltered sunbathing terrace, a charming spot in which to laze on sunny days. Also in the grounds is a beautiful cricket field, which is skirted by the picturesque and idyllic river, noted for its freshwater fishing. Opposite the hotel is Bellingham Golf Course, with its well-kept greens and fairways.

The elegantly furnished restaurant – where numerous showbusiness and sporting personalities mingle with regular diners – provides a warm, relaxing setting for enjoying a meal and offers a high standard of cuisine, complemented by well-chosen wines and friendly, efficient service. Regional specialities include Northumbrian lamb, Kielder venison and Angus steaks, with salmon and trout caught from their own stretch of river. The attractive bar-lounge with its cosy, inviting log fire, is a popular rendezvous where guests and locals soon become acquainted over a drink and convivial conversation. For guests who prefer a more secluded environment, there is a residents' lounge and a diners' bar. Fully centrally heated, the Riverdale Hall is comfortable, intimate and friendly. All bedrooms are very well appointed and offer a wide range of facilities to cater for every need. Some of the bedrooms have four-poster beds and others have the spaciousness to accommodate additional beds for families who wish to be together. The ground-floor bedrooms in the Museum Wing are popular with the infirm and disabled. The hotel is a perfect venue for weekday and weekend small business meetings or conferences. Privacy and security is assured and the management welcome the opportunity to discuss individual requirements.

Riverdale Hall is an ideal base from which to tour, as it is within easy reach of the many scenic attractions the region has to offer. Nearby are Kielder Water and Forest, Hadrian's Wall, Cragside House and Gardens, and the market town of Hexham with its abbey and lovely riverside walks. The surrounding countryside provides excellent walking opportunities and the renowned Pennine Way flanks the hotel.

**Mr and Mrs Cocker extend a warm welcome and their hospitality guarantees the visitor a most enjoyable, rewarding and memorable experience at any time of the year.**

# Symbol of Excellence

## CASTLE INN

### Chiddingstone, Edenbridge, Kent

The number 'thirteen' may be unlucky for some, but not for the Castle Inn who, having enjoyed the Les Routiers 'recommendation' for the same number of years, have received our highest accolade – the Symbol of Excellence.

A delightful oak-beamed inn, nestling in the centre of one of Kent's most unspoilt villages on the edge of the castle grounds. The public bar has enormous character, with its open fireplace, low ceilings, decorative beaded windows and dark wooden furniture. Here you can enjoy traditional English bar food of the highest quality at exceptional prices from the comfort of the Saloon Bar, or in the pretty courtyard cottage garden during summertime. Since 1981, through their hard work, proprietor Nigel Lucas and his team have created a proud reputation for providing a unique blend of good old-fashioned hospitality, efficiency and warmth, which attracts visitors from far afield. It is a truly remarkable achievement and we applaud their efforts by presenting them with this award.

A particularly nice idea are the specially tailored seasonal menus, which include such delicacies as poached salmon with fennel mayonnaise and venison in a red wine sauce, followed by homemade blackcurrant cheesecake, chocolate torte, strawberries and cream. And who could resist the breast of duck in a cherry sauce and lobster thermidor, with a compote of summer fruits, profiteroles with chocolate sauce and lemon syllabub. A separate restaurant with formal waiter service and an ever changing menu, offers English and continental dishes with European overtones. Dishes include roast rib of beef, roast rack of lamb, and local game, fresh fish and vegetables, complemented by an extensive wine list of over 150 wines and three exceptional hand-pumped draught ales. All this washed down with a speciality liqueur coffee provides the perfect end to an exquisite, enjoyable, tasty meal.

# Les Routiers Cheeseboard Awards 1994

'I applaud Les Routiers' initiatives to encourage its members to provide more imaginative cheese selections. Several cheeseboard prizes are awarded each year guaranteeing that wherever you may travel in Britain and the north of Ireland, a delicious meal with a fine cheeseboard is not far away.'

Jenny Muir
Editor, *Good Cheese*

The variety of cheeses now generally available in the UK is wider and more unusual than ever before.

However, it is not just the selection or variety which makes a good cheeseboard. There are many important factors which constitute a good cheeseboard. We put ourselves in the customer's shoes and looked for TASTE through expert selection. We looked for VARIETY with an imaginative use of traditional, new and local cheeses. PRESENTATION requires not only good use of colour, texture and shape to create a mouthwatering display, but careful handling and storage to bring out the best in cheese. And finally, we looked for KNOWLEDGE of the cheeses offered. We hope you will discover that cheese is fun, and that in this guide there are a vast range of establishments offering an infinite and mouthwatering choice of cheeses. English, Scottish and Welsh cheeses to European varieties and many interesting regional specialities, complemented by well-matched vintage wines.

After careful consideration, the following establishments have all been judged worthy of inclusion in the Les Routiers Cheeseboard Honours List. From this list, one establishment has been selected as the overall winner and receives the prestigious Les Routiers Cheeseboard of the Year Award 1994.

| | | |
|---|---|---|
| Alnmouth | Northumberland | Saddle Hotel & Saddle Grill Restaurant |
| Alnwick | Northumberland | The Cottage Inn Hotel |
| Ayr | Strathclyde | Fouters Bistro |
| Ballater | Grampian | Alexandra Hotel |
| Biggar | Strathclyde | Tinto Hotel |
| Bolton Le Sands | Lancashire | Deerstalker Restaurant |
| Broughton in Furness | Cumbria | Beswicks Restaurant |
| Cambridge | Cambridgeshire | The Three Hills |
| Chester | Cheshire | The Blue Bell Restaurant |
| Chester | Cheshire | Francs Restaurant |
| Clitheroe | Lancashire | The Inn At Whitewell |
| Covent Garden | London | Le Cafe Des Amis Du Vin |
| Ely | Cambridgeshire | The Anchor Inn |
| Falmouth | Cornwall | Green Lawns Hotel |
| Gateshead | Tyne & Wear | Beamish Park Hotel |
| Glenshee By Blairgowrie | Tayside | The Blackwater Inn |
| Grange Over Sands | Cumbria | Abbot Hall |
| Hammersmith | London | 103 |

| Haughley | Suffolk | The Old Counting House Restaurant |
| Helmsley | North Yorkshire | The Feversham Arms Hotel |
| Huddersfield | West Yorkshire | The Lodge Hotel |
| Leadenham | Lincolnshire | George Hotel |
| Leeds | West Yorkshire | Pinewood Private Hotel |
| Leeming Bar | North Yorkshire | Motel Leeming |
| Llanymynech | Shropshire | Bradford Arms & Restaurant |
| Looe | Cornwall | Allhays Country House |
| Maidenhead | Berkshire | Chauntry House Hotel |
| Moretonhamstead | Devon | Cookshayes Guest House |
| Nairn | Highlands | Ramleh Hotel & Fingal's Restaurant |
| Newark | Nottinghamshire | New Ferry Restaurant |
| Newby Bridge | Cumbria | Swan Hotel |
| Newdigate | Surrey | Gammage's Restaurant |
| North Uist | Western Isles | Lochmaddy Hotel |
| Ormskirk | Lancashire | Beaufort Hotel |
| Shrewsbury | Shropshire | Sydney House Hotel |
| Torquay | Devon | Livermead Cliff Hotel |
| Vazon Bay | Guernsey | La Grande Mare |
| Wells | Somerset | Fountain Inn & Boxers Restaurant |
| West Ilsley | Berkshire | The Harrow |

# Cheeseboard of the Year

## THE FEVERSHAM ARMS HOTEL

### Helmsley, North Yorkshire

'Those restaurateurs who take up the challenge to offer an interesting cheeseboard are rewarded not only with loyal customers who look forward to tasting a little bit of this, a little piece of that, and just a smidgeon of that funny looking one over there, but also provide a valuable service to both tourists and the cheese trade. Trying local specialities is just one of the great pleasures of travelling, and the memories of good flavour stay with you long after you have eaten. From the winner of the Les Routiers "Cheeseboard of the Year", you are particularly sure of a superb offering.'

Jenny Muir
Editor, *Good Cheese*

Who says that hard work doesn't pay? For their consistency in presenting an outstanding cheeseboard for a number of years, The Feversham Arms have been rewarded with the coveted title of *Cheeseboard of the Year* for 1994.

This attractive, historic coaching inn, nestling in the beautiful North Yorkshire Moors National Park, is certainly no stranger to awards, having won the Les Routiers 'Cheese', 'Wine' and 'Casserole' awards on several previous occasions. Their list – although not extensive – encourages experimentation by offering customers an interesting selection of both British and foreign cheeses. British cheeses, to name just a few, include Blue Stilton, Blue Wensleydale, Cotswold, Cheddar, Double Gloucester, Emmerdale Gloucester, Lancashire, Goats Swaledale, Smoked Applewood, Stilton and Apricot, Smoked Cheddar and Leicester. Unusual foreign cheeses mingle delightfully among more common varieties: Mauchego, Cambazada, Dolcelatte, Emmental, Jarlsburg, Mycella, Port Salut, Old Amsterdam, Vignote, Austrian Smoked, Brie, Danish Blue, Edam, Gouda, and Gruyère. All cheeses are attractively displayed with an imaginative range of accompaniments, such as asparagus, palm hearts, artichokes, pickled walnuts, radishes, strawberries and biscuits. The cheeseboard is replaced daily, in fact when we asked them for their opinion of what makes a good cheeseboard they confidently replied 'Freshness, freshness, freshness!'

In addition to an excellent cheeseboard, visitors to The Feversham Arms Hotel can enjoy fine English and continental cuisine in the Goya Restaurant, which specializes in serving shellfish and game (in season). An extensive wine list includes a good selection of French Grand Cru Classes and Spanish Gran Reservas. Set in an acre of beautiful walled gardens, the hotel offers a superb all-weather hard tennis court and an outdoor heated swimming pool, with golf and riding nearby.

# Les Routiers Corps D'Elite (Wine Awards) 1994

As the consumption of wine and demand for variety continue to grow in the UK, Les Routiers are playing a vital role by meeting customers' requests for more adventurous selections.

Wine should be as important to an establishment as the food it serves, in much the same way as a good port complements a fine cheese. A well-balanced wine list should offer an interesting selection of different wines with varying tastes to suit all palates and at good value for money. Equally important is an easy-to-read wine list which is free of jargon, the provision of half-bottles throughout the range, and the enthusiasm displayed by the proprietor in giving advice on selection. When visiting Les Routiers establishments you will be able to choose from a comprehensive range of imaginative wines from both the UK and Europe, as well as from other countries all around the world, including Australia, New Zealand, Chile, Germany, Russia or Lebanon to name a few.

The following list of establishments are all those who have been judged as combining all of the essential qualities that constitute a good wine list. From this list, one establishment has been selected for the most outstanding wine list of all, and receives the coveted Les Routiers Prix D'Elite Award for 1994.

| | | |
|---|---|---|
| Aberlady | Lothian | Green Craigs |
| Ayr | Strathclyde | Fouters Bistro |
| Banbury | Oxfordshire | The White Horse Inn |
| Bangor | Co. Down | Gillespies' Place / Gryphon Restaurant |
| Bedford | Bedfordshire | The Knife & Cleaver |
| Bellingham | Northumberland | Riverdale Hall Hotel |
| Biggleswade | Bedfordshire | La Cachette |
| Billericay | Essex | Duke of York |
| Brancaster Staithe | Norfolk | The Jolly Sailors |
| Brough Sowerby | Cumbria | The Black Bull Inn |
| Broughton in Furness | Cumbria | Beswicks Restaurant |
| Bury St Edmunds | Suffolk | The Six Bells Inn |
| Buttermere | Cumbria | Bridge Hotel |
| Cambridge | Cambridgeshire | The Ancient Shepherds |
| Chale | Isle of Wight | Clarendon Hotel & Wight Mouse Inn |
| Chichester | West Sussex | Platters Restaurant |
| Clawton-Holesworthy | Devon | Court Barn Country House Hotel |
| Dorchester | Dorset | The Manor Hotel |
| Duxford | Cambridgeshire | Duxford Lodge Hotel |
| Ely | Cambridgeshire | The Anchor Inn |
| Falmouth | Cornwall | Green Lawns Hotel |
| Glasgow | Strathclyde | Cathay Cuisine |
| Glasgow | Strathclyde | Ewington Hotel |
| Harlech | Gwynedd | Castle Cottage Hotel & Restaurant |
| Helmsley | North Yorkshire | The Feversham Arms Hotel |
| Holborn | London | Bleeding Heart Wine Bar |
| Isle of Skye | Highlands | Hotel Eilean Iarmain |

| | | |
|---|---|---|
| Leeming Bar | North Yorkshire | Motel Leeming |
| Lincoln | Lincolnshire | The Grand Hotel & Restaurant |
| Llangollen | Clwyd | Gales |
| Llanymynech | Shropshire | Bradford Arms & Restaurant |
| Monmouth | Gwent | The Crown at Whitebrook |
| Nairn | Highlands | Ramleh Hotel & Fingal's Restaurant |
| Newark | Nottinghamshire | New Ferry Restaurant |
| Newby Bridge | Cumbria | Swan Hotel |
| Newdigate | Surrey | Gammage's Restaurant |
| Newquay | Cornwall | The Headland Hotel |
| Omagh | Co. Tyrone | The Mellon Country Inn |
| Pewsey | Wiltshire | Woodbridge Inn |
| Port Isaac | Cornwall | The Cornish Arms |
| Rotherham | South Yorkshire | The Elton Hotel |
| Settle | North Yorkshire | New Inn Hotel |
| Shipton under Wychwood | Oxfordshire | The Shaven Crown Hotel |
| Shrewsbury | Shropshire | Sydney House Hotel |
| St Davids | Dyfed | Ramsey House |
| St Helier | Jersey | Millbrook House |
| Strachur | Strathclyde | The Creggans Inn |
| Teynham | Kent | The Ship Inn & Smugglers Restaurant |
| Tunbridge Wells | East Sussex | Winston Manor Hotel |
| Watlington | Oxfordshire | The Well House Restaurant & Hotel |
| Weobley | Hereford & Worcester | Ye Olde Salutation Inn |
| West Wittering | West Sussex | The Lamb Inn West Wittering |

# Prix D'Elite
# 'WINE' OF THE YEAR
## THE CROWN AT WHITEBROOK

### Monmouth, Gwent

Chosen from a short-list of almost 300, 'The Crown at Whitebrook' has been declared the overall winner of this award, for what is a truly exceptional wine list.

Personally run by Roger and Sandra Bates, this small, intimate restaurant and hotel – our Newcomer of the Year in 1991 – is remotely situated among breathtaking and beautiful scenery close to the English border. The wine list? Well, in the first instance it has everything one would expect of a first-class wine list, and furthermore, it is so refreshing to discover that the only thing which is absent are the baffling descriptions of the wines available, which can only be deciphered by wine experts. Each wine on the list is accompanied by an understandable and accurate description enabling easy selection.

Unlike some wine lists, you are most certainly not limited by choice. Selected specifically for their variety of flavours and value for money, there is an excellent range of both red and white wines, such as a 1987 Margaux Private Reserve Schroder et Schyler at £16.95, Macon Villages 1992 Domaine de Terraux – a good quality fresh dry white with a touch of honey, Pouilly Fuisse 1991/2 Verry Pere et Fils – an attractive, light and elegant wine, Cabernet d'Anjou Rose 1991 P Godinat, which conjures up hot summers on the banks of the Loire, and Cornas Chante Perdriv 1986 Domaine Delas Freres, that will make a pheasant or even a partridge sing. An outstanding selection of world wines are also available: from Germany there are wines as refreshing as the bite of an apple; from Italy – rich, dark wines with fruity aromas; from sun-drenched Spain – full-flavoured lemon fresh whites; from Australia and New Zealand – fruity wines with overtones of honey and peaches; dry, full-bodied wines from California; spicy full-flavoured cask-aged reds and whites from South Africa; from Lebanon – dried raisons on the palate . . . and even their own from their native Wales would you believe – chosen from an exceptional site near the River Wye!

There is a interesting choice of dessert wines to accompany the sweets and puddings offered, served by the bottle or by the glass, including Muscat de Beaumes de Venise – golden sweet rich and grapey, and Morris of Rutherglen Liqueur Muscat – sticky toffee pudding in a glass. Also, Single Quinta Ports and Vintage Ports to classic Wood Aged Tawnies, aged in the wood for many years to ensure their exquisite flavour. Well-chosen, sensibly priced, there is literally something to suit every palate and pocket. Anyone visiting The Crown may also care to take advantage of the comfortably furnished accommodation, after sampling the culinary delights of Sandra Bates who specialises in creating original dishes from fresh local ingredients.

# Official UK Tourist Boards

**ENGLISH TOURIST BOARD**
Thames Tower
Black's Road
Hammersmith
London W6 9EL
Tel: 081 846 9000

**CUMBRIA TOURIST BOARD**
Ashleigh
Holly Road
Windermere LA23 2AQ
Tel: (05394) 44444

**EAST ANGLIA TOURIST BOARD**
Toppesfield Hall
Hadleigh
Suffolk IP7 7DN
Tel: (0473) 822922

**EAST MIDLANDS TOURIST BOARD**
Exchequergate
Lincoln LN2 1PZ
Tel: (0522) 531521

**HEART OF ENGLAND TOURIST BOARD**
Larkhill Road
Worcester WR5 2EF
Tel: (0905) 763436

**LONDON TOURIST BOARD**
26 Grosvenor Gardens
London SW1W 0DU
Tel: 071 730 3488

**NORTHUMBRIA TOURIST BOARD**
Aykley Heads
Durham DH1 5UX
Tel: (091) 384 6905

**SOUTHERN TOURIST BOARD**
40 Chamberlayne Road
Eastleigh
Hants SO5 5JH
Tel: (0703) 620006

**SOUTH EAST ENGLAND TOURIST BOARD**
The Old Brew House
Warwick Park
Tunbridge Wells
Kent TN2 5TU
Tel: (0892) 540766

**WEST COUNTRY TOURIST BOARD**
60 St David's Hill
Exeter EX4 4SY
Tel: (0392) 211171

**YORKSHIRE & HUMBERSIDE TOURIST BOARD**
312 Tadcaster Road
York YO2 2HF
Tel: (0904) 707961

**NORTHERN IRELAND TOURIST**
St Anne's Court
59 North Street
Belfast BT1 1NB
Tel: (0232) 231221/246609

**NORTHERN IRELAND TOURIST BOARD (LONDON)**
11 Berkeley Street
London W1X 5AD
Tel: 071 493 0601

**SCOTTISH TOURIST BOARD**
23 Ravelston Terrace
Edinburgh EH4 3EU
Tel: 031 332 2433

**SCOTTISH TOURIST BOARD**
19 Cockspur Street
London SW1Y 5BL
Tel: 071 930 8661

**WALES TOURIST BOARD**
Brunel House
2 Fitzalan Road
Cardiff CF2 1UY
Tel: (0222) 499909

**WALES TOURIST BOARD (LONDON)**
12 Lower Regent Street
London SW1A 4PQ
Tel: 071 409 0969

**JERSEY TOURISM**
Liberation Square
St Helier
Jersey JE1 1BB
Channel Islands
Tel: (0534) 78000

**STATE OF GUERNSEY TOURIST
BOARD**
PO Box 23
White Rock
St Peter Port
Guernsey
Channel Islands
Tel: (0481) 723552

**ISLE OF MAN DEPARTMENT OF
TOURISM LEISURE & TRANSPORT**
C Terminal Building
Douglas
Isle of Man
Tel: (0624) 686801

# Useful Telephone Numbers

**EMERGENCY NUMBERS**
Ambulance
Cave Rescue
Coastguards      999
Fire
Mountain Rescue
Police

| | |
|---|---|
| **TOURIST INFORMATION CENTRES** | 071 846 9000 |
| **BRITISH TRAVEL CENTRE** | 071 730 3400 |
| **LONDON TOURIST BOARD** | |
| (Central London Telephone Information Service) | 071 730 3488 |
| Riverboat Information | 071 730 4812 |
| London Special Events | 0836 401295 |

**ROADWATCH**

| | |
|---|---|
| National Motorways | 0836 401280 |
| West Country | 0836 401281 |
| Wales | 0836 401282 |
| Midlands | 0836 481283 |
| East Anglia | 0836 401274 |
| NW England | 0836 401285 |
| NE England | 0836 401286 |
| Scotland | 0836 401287 |
| N. Ireland | 0836 401288 |
| Central London | 0836 401289 |
| Motorways & Roads between M4 & M1 | 0836 401290 |
| Motorways & Roads between M1 & M23 | 0836 401292 |
| Motorways & Roads between M23 & M4 | 0836 401293 |
| M25 London Orbital Only | 0836 401294 |
| Continental Roadwatch – Ferry News – Weather | 0836 401296 |

**AIRPORTS**

| | |
|---|---|
| London – Gatwick | 0293 535353 |
| London – Heathrow | 081 759 4321 |
| London – Stansted | 0279 680500 |
| Luton | 0582 405100 |
| Manchester | 061 489 3000 |
| Aberdeen | 0224 722331 |
| Glasgow | 041 887 1111 |
| Edinburgh | 031 333 1000 |

# LONDON

As one of the most exciting and colourful cities in the world, London offers the traveller, the tourist or the casual visitor a world of adventure!

The city is saturated with historical landmarks which are as popular with visitors as the famous red London buses which weave their course around them. Taking a guided bus tour is, of course, the ideal way to see London and there are many different tours available throughout the year, all of which pass the principal sights such as the Tower of London, the Houses of Parliament, Trafalgar Square, St Paul's Cathedral and many more.

There is a wealth of fine museums and galleries to visit, the most popular including the Natural History Museum, the Science Museum, the British Museum and the Victoria & Albert Museum. One which has gained increasing popularity is the Museum of the Moving Image, which resurrects the history of film and television through technical wizardry. The Theatre Museum in Covent Garden traces the history of the stage from Shakespeare to the present day and at the London Dungeon (not for the faint-hearted) you can witness the macabre sights and sounds from the Dark Ages to the late seventeenth century. The Imperial War Museum offers a vivid portrayal of military history, while Madame Tussaud's Waxworks, with its images of famous personalities, is a long-time favourite. At the Trocadero Centre in Piccadilly you can visit the Guinness World of Records, with the Rock Circus nearby.

For the shopper, London caters for every taste and pocket, from bustling Oxford Street,with its huge department stores and glitzy boutiques, to the grandeur of Regent Street and Hamley's – the world's largest toy shop. Other popular locations include Bond Street, Burlington Arcade, Brompton Arcade, Kensington High Street and last but not least, the list simply wouldn't be complete without a mention of Harrods! Whether you come to browse or buy, the street markets at Portobello Road, Petticoat Lane and Camden Lock are well worth a visit simply to soak up the sights and sounds of true Cockney London.

If it's entertainment you are seeking, then London has it all – from dazzling West End shows to world-class opera and ballet; from characteristic pubs to chic nightclubs where you may find yourself mingling with the rich and famous. No less than five of the world's finest orchestras are based in London, with three central concert halls, the Royal Festival Hall, the Barbican, and the Royal Albert Hall. Rock and pop venues include the Hammersmith Apollo (formerly the Odeon), Wembley Arena, and the London Arena in Docklands.

Naturally, London would be incomplete without a mention of its pomp and ceremony – major events include Trooping the Colour on Horse Guard's Parade to celebrate the Queen's Birthday each June, the Lord Mayor's Show and the famous Changing of the Guard at Buckingham Palace!

For details of where to visit and what to see in London, contact the London Tourist Board, 26 Grosvenor Gardens, London SW1W 0DU. Tel: 071 730 3488, or the English Tourist Board on 081 846 9000.

---

## ALDGATE, London Map 7

### THE GREAT EASTERN HOTEL, Liverpool Street

*Set in the famous Square Mile, amongst the country's leading banks and insurance companies, The Great Eastern has 163 rooms equipped with the most modern facilities. A Hair & Beauty Salon is open Monday to Friday and there are two excellent restaurants to choose from. There are twelve rooms available for hire to suit interviews, or conferences catering for 100. Close to the Barbican Arts Centre.*

ACCOMMODATION £41–£50
FOOD £21–£25
**Hours:** breakfast 7am – 10am; bar snacks 11am – 10:30pm; lunch 12noon – 3pm; dinner 6:30pm – 10pm.
**Cuisine:** English:- Traditional carvery. **Rooms:** 159 bedrooms 20 singles, 21 singles ensuite, 7 twins, 57 twins ensuite, 6 doubles, 21 doubles ensuite, 2 triples, 14 triples ensuite, 4 quads ensuite, 7 family rooms ensuite. **Credit cards:** Visa, Access, Diners, AmEx. **Other**

points: open bank holidays, no-smoking area, afternoon teas, disabled access, residents' lounge, vegetarian meals, children catered for – please check for age limits, residents' bar. **Directions:** Liverpool Street, right by Liverpool Street station.
Tel (071) 283 4363, fax (071) 283 4897.

## BATTERSEA, London Map 7

### BUCHAN'S, 62–4 Battersea Bridge Road
*An attractive shop fronted restaurant/wine bar which serves outstanding French cuisine in a bustling, friendly atmosphere. The service is welcoming and efficient. Although the cuisine is French, Buchan's also offers Scottish specialities such as Arbroath smokie mousse, Scotch fillet steak flambed in whisky and a Scottish based cheeseboard.*
*FOOD up to £15* 🍷 CLUB
**Hours:** lunch 12noon – 2:45pm; dinner 6pm – 10:45pm; closed bank holidays. **Cuisine:** French:- Specialities include some Scottish dishes. Menu changes weekly. Master chef: Alain Jeannon. **Credit cards:** Visa, Access, Diners, AmEx. **Other points:** licensed, Sunday lunch, children catered for – please check for age limits, pets allowed. **Directions:** 200yds from Battersea Bridge, on the south side of River Thames.
JEREMY & DENISE BOLAM, tel (071) 228 0888, fax (071) 924 1718.

### JACK'S PLACE, 12 York Road
*This restaurant has a friendly, relaxed and informal atmosphere. The walls are covered in memorabilia which keeps the customers interested between courses. With excellent food and substantial portions, Jack's Place is very highly recommended.*
*FOOD £15–£20* 🍷
**Hours:** lunch 12noon – 3pm; dinner 6:30pm – 11pm; closed Monday. **Cuisine:** English:- Steaks and fresh fish are specialities. Sunday lunch is available from September until Easter. **Credit cards:** Visa, Access. **Other points:** Sunday lunch, children catered for – please check for age limits. **Directions:** close to Clapham Junction station.
MR JACK KING, tel (071) 228 8519, (071) 228 1442.

## BAYSWATER, London Map 7

### GARDEN COURT HOTEL, 30/31
### Kensington Garden Square
*Situated in a calm leafy Victorian garden square in central London, the Garden Court built in 1870 is a family run hotel within walking distance of many of the city's finest tourist attractions, including Kensington Palace and Portobello Antique market. Its location allows easy access to buses and the underground.*
*ACCOMMODATION £21–£30*
**Hours:** breakfast 7:30am – 9:30am. **Cuisine:** breakfast:- Full English breakfast, a selection of fruits and yoghurts. **Rooms:** 35 bedrooms all with tea making facilities, radio, TV: 12 singles, 1 single ensuite, 4 doubles, 3 doubles ensuite, 2 twins, 6 twins ensuite, 3 triples, 2 triples ensuite, 1 family room, 1 triple ensuite. **Credit cards:** Visa, Access. **Other points:** baby-listening device, cots, children catered for – please check for age limits, open bank holidays. **Directions:** 4 minute walk from Bayswater tube, 6 minutes from Queensway tube.
CONNOLLY PARTNERSHIP, tel (071) 229 2553, fax (071) 727 2749.

### MITRE HOUSE HOTEL, 178–184 Sussex Gardens
*The Mitre Hotel has been run by the same family for over 25 years, and this is reflected in it's comfortable atmosphere and ambiance. Ideally located on the north side of Hyde Park, central London is easily accessible, and should you require a hired car or a sightseeing tour, the helpful staff will be happy to assist.*
*ACCOMMODATION £31–£40*
**Hours:** breakfast 7:30am – 9am. **Rooms:** 60 bedrooms all with tea making facilities, telephone, radio, TV: 6 singles ensuite, 18 doubles ensuite, 26 twins ensuite, 7 family rooms ensuite, 3 suites. **Credit cards:** Visa, Access, Diners, AmEx. **Other points:** children catered for – please check for age limits. **Directions:** south of Paddington tube, parallel to Praed St.
SANGARIDES & CO LTD, tel (071) 723 8040, fax (071) 402 0990.

## BELGRAVIA, London Map 7

### NAG'S HEAD, 53 Kinnerton Street
*Built in 1780 this has been called the smallest pub in London and is thought to be a former gaol. In 1921 it was sold for 11 7s 6d – almost the price of a couple of rounds of drinks today. The Nag's Head, the village pub in Belgravia is now a free house in the real sense. Since December 1992 the pub has become an independent, one of the very few in the heart of London.*
*FOOD up to £15*
**Hours:** meals all day – everyday 12noon – 10pm. **Cuisine:** English:- Traditional home cooked pub food with daily specials and daily roasts – Irish stew, various curries, chilli con carne, home-made pies. **Other points:** licensed, open-air dining, Sunday lunch, no-smoking area, children catered for – please check for age limits. **Directions:** near to Hyde Park Corner tube, Kinnerton St is off Wilton Road.
KEVIN MORAN, tel (071) 235 1135.

## BISHOPSGATE, London Map 7

### CITY LIMITS RESTAURANT & WINE BAR, 16-18 Brushfield Street
*A buzzing, ground floor wine bar with restaurant downstairs, which doubles as an evening private function room. Situated between the market and offices with good car parking facilities very close by.*
*FOOD £15–£20*
**Hours:** bar meals 11:30am – 2:30pm; lunch 12noon – 3pm; bar meals 5pm – 8pm; closed Saturday; closed

Sunday. **Cuisine:** international:- Varied international foods; speciality starters, fresh fish, excellent gateaux. Imaginative wine list, international and unusual beers (non-draught). **Credit cards:** Visa, Access, AmEx. **Other points:** children catered for – please check for age limits, parking. **Directions:** situated in Spitalfields, near the Bishopsgate Institution.
DAVID HUGHES, tel (071) 377 9877.

## BLOOMSBURY, London Map 7

### ACADEMY HOTEL, 17–21 Gower Street
*The Academy Hotel is a beautifully appointed hotel set in a listed building, providing comfort and personal service for tourists and business travellers. Ideally situated for theatreland and many historical places of interest, including the British Museum, Jewish Museum and Covent Garden. Conference facilities are available for 6 to 40 people.*
*ACCOMMODATION £41–£50*
*FOOD up to £15* 🍴
**Hours:** breakfast 7am – 10:30am; lunch 12noon – 2:30pm; dinner 6:30pm – 12midnight. **Cuisine:** English:- Own club/restaurant, GHQ, with Les Routiers Golden Casserole award winning cuisine, predominantly European/English dishes. Good reasonably priced wine list. **Rooms:** 9 single, 7 twin, 17 double, and 2 studio suites, 26 en suite with TV, tea/coffee making facilities and room-service. beautifully decorated. **Credit cards:** Visa, Access, Diners, AmEx. **Other points:** licensed, Sunday lunch, children catered for – please check for age limits, afternoon tea, garden, conferences, library. **Directions:** Nearest tube: Goodge St, Tottenham Court Rd or Russell Square.
ALAN RIVERS, tel (071) 631 4115, fax (071) 636 3442.

### THE BONNINGTON IN BLOOMSBURY, Southampton Row
*Owned and run by the Frame family since its construction in 1911, the Bonnington with its Edwardian facade offers up-to-the-minute standards of comfort at value for money prices. With 200 comfortable bedrooms, imposing lounges and a splendid dining room, an eighty-year tradition of friendly service and hospitality awaits. The hotel offers eight flexibly-designed function rooms and provides the ideal venue for anything from a small committee meeting to a major conference or luncheon. Its central location makes it ideal for visitors to London.*
*ACCOMMODATION £41–£50*
*FOOD £15–£20*
**Hours:** breakfast 7am – 10am; lunch 12noon – 2.30pm; bar snacks 12noon – 2:30pm; bar snacks 5pm – 9:30pm; dinner 5:30pm – 10:30pm; restaurant closed Saturday & Sunday lunch. **Cuisine:** international:- A la carte and table d'hote menus. **Rooms:** 215 bedrooms all with tea making facilities, telephone, radio, TV: 108 singles ensuite, 43 doubles ensuite, 44 twins ensuite, 20 family rooms ensuite. **Credit cards:** Visa, Access, Diners, AmEx. **Other points:** children catered for – please check for age limits, open bank holidays, no-smoking

rooms, afternoon tea, disabled access, pets allowed, residents' lounge, vegetarian meals, conferences, functions, foreign exchange, 24 hr reception, residents' bar, baby sitting, baby-listening device, cots. **Directions:** in the heart of London, just minutes from Holborn underground station.
BONNINGTON HOTELS LIMITED, tel (071) 242 2828, fax (071) 831 9170.

### EURO & GEORGE HOTELS, 51–53 Cartwright Gardens
*The Euro and George Hotels are situated in a quiet crescent of historically listed buildings. Both provide a high standard of service and comfort at good value prices. Its central position offers easy access to the West End and local attractions such as the British Museum.*
*ACCOMMODATION £21–£30*
**Hours:** breakfast 7:30am – 9am. **Cuisine:** breakfast. **Rooms:** 84 bedrooms all with tea making facilities, telephone, radio, TV: 4 singles ensuite, 24 singles, 4 twins ensuite, 17 twins, 3 doubles ensuite, 3 doubles, 3 triples ensuite, 15 triples, 1 quad ensuite, 10 quads. **Credit cards:** Visa, Access, AmEx. **Other points:** children catered for – please check for age limits, residents' lounge, garden, in-house films, tennis, residents' lounge, garden, cots. **Directions:** close to Kings Cross, Euston and Russell Square tube stations.
PETER EVANS, tel (071) 387 8777, (071) 387 6789, fax (071) 383 5044.

### THE HERMITAGE, 19 Leigh Street
*Situated in a 'city village' area, this delightful restaurant offers typically French cuisine with speciality dishes. Very popular with locals and tourist's, it is furnished in a French theme and has lots of character. Near to the British Museum and various theatres.*
*FOOD: up to £15*
**Hours:** closed Saturday morning; closed Sunday evening; Sunday 10:30am – 2:30pm; lunch 11:30am – 2:30pm; dinner 6pm – 10pm. **Cuisine:** French. **Credit cards:** Visa, Access, AmEx. **Directions:** 300 yds from Kings Cross and Euston.
AMR LTD, tel (071) 387 8034.

### ST GILES HOTEL, Bedford Avenue
*A luxury, modern international hotel, where guests receive a warm welcome by friendly and courteous staff in the elegant entrance lobby. All 600 bedrooms have been decorated and furnished to a high standard. Guests can relax in the comfort of the hotel lounge or the warm atmosphere of the panelled Clock Bar. The La Bagatelle Bistro offers French cuisine and wines, and Osbournes Coffee Shop serves a sumptuous breakfast buffet. There is a convention room for over 200 delegates and access to the private sports club beneath the hotel.*
*ACCOMMODATION £41–£50*
*FOOD up to £15*
**Hours:** breakfast 7am – 11am; meals all day 11am – 11pm. **Cuisine:** English / international. **Credit cards:** Visa, Access, Diners, AmEx. **Other points:** children

catered for – please check for age limits, creche available, open bank holidays, afternoon tea, residents' lounge, vegetarian meals. **Directions:** situated on the corner of Tottenham Court Road and Oxford Street. MR TAYLOR, tel (071) 636 8616, fax (071) 631 1031.

## CAMDEN, London Map 7

### NONTAS, 14 Camden High Street

*Nontas is the perfect answer for those who prefer the personal atmosphere and warm hospitality of a family-run establishment. Specialising in Greek cuisine, The Ouzerie provides a relaxing place for socialising, with its attractive Cocktail Bar and open fireplace. All rooms are spacious and elegant with most modern facilities. Ideal location for visiting London's famous Theatreland.*

ACCOMMODATION £21–£30

FOOD up to £15

**Hours:** closed Sunday & bank hols 11am; breakfast 8am – 10am; bar snacks 10am – 12:30am; lunch 12noon –3:15pm; dinner 6pm – 12:30am. **Cuisine:** Greek. **Credit cards:** Visa, Access, Diners, AmEx. **Other points:** garden dining, residents' lounge. **Directions:** situated between Camden underground and Mornington Crescent underground. MR N VASSILAKAS, tel (071) 388 4611, fax (071) 383 0335.

## CHELSEA, London Map 7

### CAFE ROUGE, 390 Kings Road

**Hours:** meals all day 10am – 11pm; meals all day –Sunday 10am – 10:30pm. **Cuisine:** French:- Traditional French food. Full a la carte. Light meals available. Good wine list. **Credit cards:** Visa, Access. **Other points:** bank holidays, children catered for – please check for age limits, licensed. **Directions:** nearest underground is Sloane Square. GILLES GAUBERT (MGR), tel (071) 352 2226, fax (071) 352 8006.

### GLAISTERS CAFE BAR AND RESTAURANT, 4 Hollywood Road

*One of the many inviting features at Glaister's is the beautiful garlanded garden where one can dine alfresco enjoying excellent home-cooked cosmopolitan dishes prepared with great care at very reasonable prices. And if it rains, there's an automatic roof which rolls back to keep you dry! On Sundays, parents can enjoy their lunch in peace and quiet by leaving the children next door at a registered creche. The garden is also an ideal location for cocktail parties, wedding receptions and birthday parties for up to 40 guests. Balloons or flowers can be supplied and every effort is taken to ensure your party is a success.*

FOOD up to £15

**Hours:** lunch 12noon – 3pm; lunch – Sunday 12noon – 4pm; dinner 7:30pm – 11:30pm. **Cuisine:** English / cosmopolitan. **Credit cards:** Visa, Access, Diners, AmEx. **Other points:** Sunday lunch, vegetarian meals, open-air dining, licensed. **Directions:** off Fulham Road, opposite the new Chelsea and Westminster Hospital. STEPHEN GLAISTER, tel (071) 352 0352.

## CHISWICK, London Map 7

### CHISWICK HOTEL, 73 Chiswick High Road

*A well appointed luxuriously furnished Victorian hotel offering an ideal base for families visiting London. Under the same ownership for 19 years, it has a warm and welcoming atmosphere and has been steadily improved to an extremely high standard with many modern facilities. Special weekend rates are available on request.*

ACCOMMODATION £31–£40

FOOD up to £15

**Hours:** breakfast 7am –9am; dinner 6.30pm –9pm. **Cuisine:** English. Rooms: 33 bedrooms all with telephone, tea making facilities, TV. **Credit cards:** Visa, Access, AmEx, Diners, Switch. **Other points:** parking, children catered for – check for age limits, open bank holidays, pets allowed, residents' lounge, vegetarian meals, garden. **Directions:** turn north from A4 between M4 and Hammersmith roundabout. The hotel is at junction with Chiswick High Post Office. Nearest underground: Turnham Green (District line). 30 minutes to Heathrow. BRYN DREW, tel (081) 994 1712, fax (081) 742 2585.

## CLAPHAM, London Map 7

### WINDMILL ON THE COMMON, Southside, Clapham Common

*First mentioned in local records in 1729, The Windmill retains much of its Victorian character and charm. Prize-winning traditional beers are complemented by modern hotel accommodation offering peace and tranquility. An ideal venue for meetings, luncheons, wedding receptions and cocktail parties. Clapham Common is nearby.*

ACCOMMODATION £31–£40

FOOD up to £15

**Hours:** breakfast 7am – 10am; bar snacks 12noon – 2:30pm; dinner 7pm – 10pm; bar snacks 7pm – 10pm. **Cuisine:** British. **Credit cards:** Visa, Access, Diners, AmEx. **Other points:** parking, children catered for – please check for age limits, no-smoking area, disabled access, pets, garden, vegetarian meals, open-air dining. **Directions:** follow south circular to where it crosses A24, turn towards central London on A24 – quarter of a mile on common side. Tel (081) 673 4578, fax (081) 675 1486.

## CLERKENWELL, London Map 7

### CAFE ST PIERRE, 29 Clerkenwell Green, Nr Farringdon Road

*A converted pub with a typical French atmosphere close to Farringdon tube. Situated alongside the Clerks Well in the historic village of Clerkenwell. Close to the Barbican and St Pauls.*

FOOD up to £15

**Hours:** lunch 12noon – 3pm; dinner 5:30pm – 10pm; closed Saturday; closed Sunday. **Cuisine:** French:- Daily fresh fish dishes. Regional French cuisine in the Brasserie and Traditional French cuisine in the Restaurant. **Credit cards:** Visa, Access, Diners, AmEx. **Other points:** licensed, open-air dining, children catered for – please check for age limits. **Directions:** near Farringdon tube on metropolitan and circle lines. JIMMY LAHOUD, tel (071) 251 6606.

### THE HELLENIK RESTAURANT, 86 St John Street

*A family run, fully licensed Greek/Cypriot restaurant where good food at reasonable prices matters. Situated near Smithfield and the Barbican it is ideal for pre or post theatre meals.*
*FOOD up to £15*
**Hours:** lunch 11:45am – 3pm; dinner 6pm – 11pm; closed August 3 weeks; closed bank holidays; closed Sundays. **Cuisine:** Greek / Cypriot:- Kleftico, moussaka, meze, souvlaki. Special lunch menu 11 dips & 4 dishes for 8.50 per person. **Credit cards:** Visa, Access, AmEx. **Other points:** children catered for – please check for age limits, street parking. **Directions:** 500yds from Smithfield market. (Farringdon & Barbican stations). MR & MRS P & A KRASE, tel (071) 253 0754.

## COVENT GARDEN, London Map 7

### FOOD FOR THOUGHT, 31 Neal Street

*Ideal for the hungry traveller, this busy vegetarian restaurant provides a warm welcome and quick, friendly service. Menu changed twice a day. Take-away meals and snacks also available.*
*FOOD up to £15* ★
**Hours:** meals – except Sunday 10:30am – 8pm; meals – Sunday 10:30am – 4:30pm; closed Christmas; closed New Year. **Cuisine:** vegetarian:- Wide range of vegetarian dishes all prepared on premises from fresh produce – daily specials. **Other points:** no-smoking area, children catered for – please check for age limits, parking. **Directions:** close to Covent Garden tube. JERZY PAJDAK & VANESSA GARRETT, tel (071) 836 0239, (071) 836 9072, fax (071) 379 1249.

### FUNG-SHING, 15 Lisle Street

*Fung-Shing is situated in a converted Victorian warehouse. Customers can enjoy a wide variety of competently served Cantonese dishes.*
*FOOD up to £15*
**Hours:** meals all day 12noon – 11:30pm. **Cuisine:** Cantonese:- Cantonese: Crispy duck, Sizzling prawns. **Credit cards:** Visa, Access, Diners, AmEx. **Other points:** licensed, Sunday lunch, private dining. **Directions:** in Chinatown. JIMMY CHIM, tel (071) 437 1539.

### HENRY'S CAFE BAR (COVENT GARDEN), 27–29 Endell Street

*Set amongst a terrace of small shops, Henry's is modelled on an American-style cafe bar. It has a quiet, relaxing atmosphere, dark wooden furniture and art deco lamps.*

*Diners can choose from an extensive range of international fast-food, complemented by some interesting wines. Royal Opera House, Covent Garden market, Transport Museum and many more attractions nearby.*
*FOOD up to £15*
**Hours:** 12noon. **Cuisine:** international. **Credit cards:** Visa, Access. **Other points:** children catered for – please check for age limits, open bank holidays, no-smoking area, afternoon teas, disabled access, vegetarian meals. MR B PETERSON, tel (071) 379 8500.

### LE CAFE DES AMIS DU VIN, 12 Hanover Place (off Long Acre)

*This restaurant offers good value for money in that the food is well prepared, cooked and served, the service is friendly and you can enjoy your meal amidst pleasant surroundings. Popular basement wine bar for theatre goers. Adjacent to the Royal Opera House. Routiers Cheeseboard of the Year Award 1991/2/3.*
*FOOD £15–£20* ⏰ CLUB
**Hours:** meals all day 11:30am – 11:30pm. **Cuisine:** French:- Charcuterie, plats du jour. French cheese and wines. **Credit cards:** Visa, Access, Diners, AmEx. **Other points:** open-air dining, children catered for – please check for age limits. **Directions:** nearest tube – Covent Garden on the Piccadilly line. MR P NOTTAGE/CAFE DES AMIS LIMITED, tel (071) 379 3444, fax (071) 379 9124.

### SMITH'S RESTAURANT & WINE BAR, 25 Neal Street

*Situated beneath Smith's Art Galleries. Large, spacious restaurant with contemporary paintings. The restaurant, galleries and cafe Casbar are all available for private hire. Robust European cooking.*
*FOOD £21–£25*
**Hours:** last orders 11:30am – 11:30pm; meals – weekdays 12noon – 12midnight; dinner – weekend 6pm – 12midnight; closed Sunday. **Cuisine:** modern English:- New English style cuisine from Head Chef, Ralph Nuttal. **Credit cards:** Visa, Access, Diners, AmEx. **Other points:** licensed, children catered for – please check for age limits, disabled access. **Directions:** 2 minutes from Covent Garden tube, off Neal St opposite tube station. Tel (071) 379 0310, fax (071) 836 4769.

## EALING, London Map 7

### ANNE-MARIE AT THE 'TASTE OF THE TAJ', 4 Norbreck Parade

*The warmth and efficiency of the staff here, make this a pleasant and enjoyable place to spend an evening, sampling cuisine of a high-quality. The Proprietor, Anne-Marie is pleased to guide you through the many different dishes, which are offered at varying levels of hotness. The service is friendly and efficient and the atmosphere calm and welcoming.*
*FOOD up to £15*

**Hours:** lunch 12noon – 2:30pm; dinner 6pm – 11:30pm; closed Christmas 25/12; closed Saturday lunch; closed Sunday lunch. **Cuisine:** Indian:- Comprehensive choice of fine Indian style cuisine. **Credit cards:** Visa, Access, Diners, AmEx. **Other points:** licensed, children catered for – please check for age limits, disabled access, vegetarian meals, bank holidays, street parking. **Directions:** Hanger Lane Gyratory System. Please telephone us for "directions", which are essential. ANNE-MARIE DUBREIL, tel (081) 991 5366, (081) 991 5209.

## CHARLOTTE'S PLACE, 16 St Matthews Road, Ealing Common

*A small, cosy restaurant providing imaginative French cuisine. Candlelit tables add to the overall ambiance, which attracts a young, friendly crowd, including business clientele.*

FOOD £15–£20

**Hours:** lunch 12:30pm – 2pm; dinner 7:30pm – 10pm; closed Saturday lunch; closed Sunday. **Cuisine:** French:- French cuisine, complemented by a fine Wine List. **Credit cards:** Visa, Access, Diners, AmEx. **Other points:** licensed, children catered for – please check for age limits, vegetarian meals. **Directions:** just off Uxbridge Road, overlooking Ealing Common. JOHN & CHARLOTTE KEARNS, tel (081) 567 7541.

# EALING COMMON, London Map 7

## CARNARVON HOTEL

*A modern well appointed hotel overlooking Ealing Common, offering both the business visitor and tourist a convenient and comfortable base just fifteen minutes from central London. Spacious and comfortable lounges with a well stocked residents bar. The Gunnersby Suite is ideal for meetings and training seminars. Ideally located for quick and easy access to motorways, airport and tube stations.*

ACCOMMODATION over £50

FOOD £15–£20

**Hours:** breakfast 7am – 9:30am; bar snacks 12noon – 2:30pm; lunch 12:30pm – 2:30pm; dinner 6:30pm – 9:30pm. **Cuisine:** English:- A la carte and snack menus available. **Rooms:** 146 bedrooms all with telephone, radio, TV: 100 twins ensuite, 46 doubles ensuite. **Credit cards:** Visa, Access, Diners, AmEx. **Other points:** conferences, functions, parking, children catered for – please check for age limits, Sunday lunch, open bank holidays, no-smoking area, residents' lounge, vegetarian meals. **Directions:** located at the junction of the A406 North Circular and Uxbridge Road A4020, overlooking Ealing Common. CARNAVON HOTELS LTD, tel (081) 992 5399, fax (081) 992 7082.

# EARLS COURT, London Map 7

## AMSTERDAM HOTEL, 7 Trebovir Road

*Situated close to Earls Court Exhibition Centre, catering for the tourist and businessman alike. Recently modernised and refurbished, the Amsterdam offers a refreshingly clean and bright environment with a pleasing atmosphere. Ideal for visiting South Kensington's Museums.*

ACCOMMODATION £21–£30

**Hours:** open all year 6:30pm. **Cuisine:** breakfast:- continental. **Rooms:** 19 bedrooms 2 singles ensuite, 8 doubles ensuite, 3 twins ensuite, 2 triples ensuite, 4 quads ensuite. **Credit cards:** Visa, Access, AmEx. **Other points:** open bank holidays. **Directions:** the hotel is close to Earls Court tube station and readily visible from junction with Earls Court Road. MR JAJBHAY, tel (071) 3705084, fax (071) 2447608.

## KENSINGTON COURT HOTEL, 33 Nevern Place

*A typical 1970's development which has currently undergone refurbishment. Catering for businessmen and tourists, it is an ideal location for short-stay guests. Nearby for south Kensington Museums.*

**Hours:** breakfast 7am – 9:30am. **Cuisine:** breakfast. **Other points:** parking, children catered for – please check for age limits. **Directions:** off Earls Court Road, just a few minutes walk from Earls Court Underground. MR S KADIR, tel (071) 370 5151, fax (071) 370 3499.

# FINCHLEY, London Map 7

## RANI VEGETARIAN RESTAURANT, 7 Long Lane, Finchley Central

*A high-class and well known speciality restaurant, offering an extensive choice of Indian vegetarian dishes. All produce is freshly prepared by family chefs. Bright and welcoming with a warm and friendly atmosphere.*

FOOD up to £15

**Hours:** closed Christmas day 7am; lunch 12:15pm – 4pm; dinner 6pm – 12midnight; closed lunchtime Monday & Saturday. **Cuisine:** Indian vegetarian. **Credit cards:** Visa, Access, AmEx. **Other points:** children catered for – please check for age limits, Sunday lunch, open bank holidays, no-smoking area, disabled access. **Directions:** 5 minute walk from Finchley Central underground. JYOTINDRA PATTNI, tel (081) 349 4386, fax (081) 349 4386.

# FOREST HILL, London Map 7

## BABUR BRASSERIE, 119 Brockley Rise

*A stylish, up-market restaurant providing comfortable dining in smart surroundings. The Moghul-style menu spoils you for choice, ranging from the tasty appetizers through the Tandoori selection, Fish, Prawn and vegetable dishes. Babur specialities: Shugati Masala (chicken in spices and a masala sauce enriched with coconut and poppy seeds), and Babur-e-Bhojan (a selection of Murgh Tikka, Boti Kebab, Sali Jardaloo and Makhani with Nan and Basmati rice). Although not listed seperately, the chef will prepare any traditional dishes, such as Rogan Josh, Dupeaza or Dhansak at your request.*

FOOD up to £15

# PHEASANT INN

## BASSENTHWAITE LAKE, NR COCKERMOUTH, CUMBRIA CA13 9YE
### Telephone: (07687) 76234

### OUR "SYMBOL OF EXCELLENCE" WINNERS– 1993

Barrie and Mary Wilson (centre right), of the Pheasant Inn at Bassenthwaite Lake in Cumbria, receiving our highest accolade, the "Symbol of Excellence" Award for 1993, from Les Routiers Membership Manager Gordon Wilson and Britannia Rescue Marketing Director, Gail Fee

For full details see Bassenthwaite Lake, Northern England

# KENSINGTON
## INTERNATIONAL HOTEL

### NO. 4
### TEMPLETON PLACE
### LONDON, W. 1.
### TEL: (071) 370 4333

For full details see London, Kensington

# PATSHULL PARK HOTEL
## GOLF & COUNTRY CLUB

PATTINGHAM, WOLVERHAMPTON WV6 7HR
*Telephone: (0902) 700100*

For full details see Central England, Wolverhampton

# CHASE LODGE
## HOTEL

10 PARK ROAD, HAMPTON WICK, KINGSTON-UPON-THAMES, SURREY.
TEL. (081) 943 1862

For full details see South East, Kingston-upon-Thames

# THE CAIRNDALE

## HOTEL AND LEISURE CLUB

ENGLISH STREET, DUMFRIES. TEL (0387) 54111

For full details see Scotland, Dumfries

# MILLBROOK HOUSE

*Rue De Trachy, St Helier, Jersey, C. I. Tel. (0534) 33036*

For full details see Channel Islands, St Helier

# The Falls of Lora Hotel

## Connel Ferry, by Oban, Argyll PA37 IPB

Proprietor: Mrs C.M. Webster
Telephone: (0631) 71 483

For full details see Scotland, Oban

# HOTEL
# EILEAN
# IARMAIN

Eilean Iarmain, Sleibhte, An T-Eilean Sgitheanach IV43 8QR
Telephone: (04713) 332

For full details see Scotland, Isle of Skye

**Hours:** lunch 12noon – 2:30pm; dinner 6pm – 11:30pm; closed Christmas 25/12 – 26/12. **Cuisine:** Moghul. **Credit cards:** Visa, Access, Diners, AmEx. **Other points:** licensed, Sunday buffet lunch, children catered for – please check for age limits, air-conditioned. **Directions:** Brockley Rise is off the south circular – Stansted Road.
BABUR LTD, tel (081) 291 2400, (081) 291 4881.

## FULHAM, London Map 7

### CAFE ROUGE, 855 Fulham Road

*A cafe/restaurant with a genuine French feel and character, serving excellent traditional bistro food. Cappuccino and light meals are served all day and the restaurant offers full a la carte. The atmosphere is cosmopolitan and the French staff are very friendly yet professional. Popular with all ages.*
*FOOD £15–£20*
**Hours:** breakfast 10am – 12noon; lunch 1pm – 3pm; bar meals 3pm – 7pm; dinner 7pm – 11pm. **Cuisine:** French:- Traditional French cuisine. Menu changes every 3 months, but generally includes Marmite Dieppoise, Entrecote Bearnaise. Lighter meals also served. **Credit cards:** Visa, Access. **Other points:** licensed, Sunday lunch, children catered for – please check for age limits, bank holidays, afternoon tea. **Directions:** on corner of Munster Road.
CAFE ROUGE LTD, tel (071) 371 7600.

### CIAO CAFE WINE BAR, 222 Munster Road

*'Ciao', situated on Munster Road and seating 80 people, provides good food at excellent value for money in attractive surroundings and friendly, very efficient service. Offering a wide selection of tasty, well presented dishes including many fresh pasta specialities, you will find the relaxing candlelit atmosphere an excellent backdrop for business or pleasure.*
*FOOD up to £15*
**Hours:** lunch 12noon – 3:30pm; dinner 6pm – 10pm; closed Christmas 3 days over Christmas. **Cuisine:** continental:- Brasserie cuisine, fresh pasta dishes and daily specialities. **Credit cards:** Visa, Access, AmEx. **Other points:** open-air dining, Sunday lunch, children catered for – please check for age limits, bank holidays. **Directions:** between Fulham Road and Lillie Road, north of Parsons Green.
MARK MILTON, tel (071) 381 6137.

## GREENWICH, London Map 7

### SPREAD EAGLE RESTAURANT, 1&2 Stockwell Street

*A tavern since before the 1650's and later a thriving coaching inn and hostelry. Strong 19th century music hall connections. The Spread Eagle is a truly fascinating place steeped in history, much of it still visible. Providing business lunches, bar snacks and pre-theatre suppers. 3 dining areas. Private party facilities. A visit is highly recommended.*
*FOOD £15–£20*

**Hours:** lunch 12noon – 3pm; dinner 6:30pm – 10:30pm. **Cuisine:** French. **Other points:** children catered for – please check for age limits, disabled access, vegetarian meals. **Directions:** situated just off the A2 and A206 opposite the Greenwich Theatre.
MR R MOY, tel (081) 853 2333, fax (081) 305 1666.

## HAMMERSMITH, London Map 7

### 103, Black Lion Lane

*Sample the delights of a typical French bistro – in England! Flickering candles, red and white tablecloths, low ceilings, French posters adorning the walls, music and first-class service. The intimacy and ambiance of this restaurant will have you imagining that you are, just for a moment, in wartime Paris!*
*FOOD £15–£20* ⊕
**Hours:** lunch 12noon – 2:30pm; dinner 7pm – 10:30pm; closed Saturday lunch; closed evenings Sunday & Monday. **Cuisine:** French:- French brasserie/bistro style cuisine, offering a range of imaginative traditional French dishes. Blackboard menu, changes regularly. **Credit cards:** Visa, Access, Diners, AmEx. **Other points:** vegetarian meals, licensed. **Directions:** off King Street. Underground stop – Stamford Brook.
ANDREW HUNTER & JEAN LOUIS COMMEUREUC, tel (081) 748 9070.

### DALMACIA HOUSE, 71 Shepherds Bush Road

*This recently refurbished Victorian terraced house offers comfortable accommodation and value for money. The family who run the hotel speak French and Serbo-Croat. Situated midway between Central London and Heathrow. Olympia and Kensington nearby.*
**Hours:** breakfast 7am – 9:30am; dinner 6pm – 8:30pm. **Cuisine:** breakfast. **Rooms:** 16 bedrooms all with telephone, TV: 3 singles ensuite, 6 twins ensuite, 3 doubles ensuite, 4 triples ensuite. **Credit cards:** Visa, Access, Diners, AmEx. **Other points:** children catered for – please check for age limits, cots, left luggage. **Directions:** on A219, north of Hammersmith tube. Identified in 'Airbus' leaflet.
GEORGE KRIVOSIC, tel (071) 603 2887, fax (071) 602 9226.

### LA PLUME DE MA TANTE, 381 King Street

*This delightful French bistro-style restaurant is a little piece of France on the borders of Hammersmith and Chiswick. The chef, originally from Burgundy, prepares imaginative, high quality food using fresh ingredients. Refreshingly unpretentious and with friendly staff, La Plume de Ma Tante consistently serves up excellent cuisine at a reasonable price.*
*FOOD £15–£20*
**Hours:** lunch 12noon – 2:30pm; dinner 7pm – 11pm; closed bank holidays; closed Saturday lunch; closed Sunday. **Cuisine:** French:- Dishes may include Roast Duck Fillet served pink in apricot sauce, Veal Casserole

in cream sauce, Rack of Lamb with rosemary. **Credit cards:** Visa, Access, AmEx, Switch. **Other points:** licensed, children catered for – please check for age limits, guide dogs, disabled access, vegetarian meals. **Directions:** on the left-hand side, approaching from Hammersmith Broadway.
MICHEL PIQUET, tel (081) 748 8270.

## ST PETERS HOTEL, 407–411 Goldhawk Road

*A small personally run hotel offering clean and comfortable accommodation to suit both business and tourist clientele. On the bus route for Kew Gardens, the River Thames and the West End.*
*ACCOMMODATION £21–£30*
**Hours:** breakfast 7am – 9:30am. **Cuisine:** English. **Rooms:** 18 bedrooms 1 single, 1 double, 2 twins, 4 singles ensuite, 4 doubles ensuite, 6 twins ensuite. **Credit cards:** Visa, Access, AmEx. **Other points:** children catered for – please check for age limits, open bank holidays, afternoon tea, residents' lounge, residents' bar. **Directions:** opposite Stamford Brook underground station. Close to M4, Junction: Goldhawk Rd/Chiswick High Rd.
MR M COSIC, tel (081) 741 4239, fax (081) 748 3845.

## HAMPSTEAD, London Map 7

### CAFE ROUGE, 19 High Street

*A French cafe/restaurant, serving traditional bistro food in an informal, but professional atmosphere. Serves cappuccino and light meals all day in the cafe area and the restaurant offers full a la carte.*
*FOOD £15–£20*
**Hours:** meals all day 10am – 11pm. **Cuisine:** French:- Traditional French cuisine. Menu changes every 3 months, but generally offers Marmite Dieppoise, Cochonaille and plats du jour. **Credit cards:** Visa, Access. **Other points:** licensed, Sunday lunch, no-smoking area, children catered for – please check for age limits, bank holidays.
**Directions:** nearest tube is Hampstead.
CAFE ROUGE LTD, tel (071) 433 3404.

## HIGHGATE, London Map 7

### CAFE ROUGE, 6-7 South Grove

**Hours:** meals all day 10am – 11pm; meals all day – Sunday 10am – 10:30pm. **Cuisine:** French:- Traditional French cuisine including Marmite Dieppoise, Saucisses Fumees, and sandwiches. Good wine list. **Credit cards:** Visa, Access. **Other points:** bank holidays, licensed. **Directions:** near Highgate tube.
JOE BOTINDARI (MGR), tel (081) 342 9797, fax (081) 342 9503.

## HOLBORN, London Map 7

### BLEEDING HEART WINE BAR, Bleeding Heart Yard, Greville Street

*The Bleeding Heart is well-hidden beneath historic Bleeding Heart Yard off Greville Street, near Farringdon tube. Not only does the Yard feature in Dickens' novel Little Dorrit – hence the Dickensian atmosphere and first editions – but it is said to be haunted by the ghost of Lady Hatton. Terrace for outdoor eating in summer.*
*FOOD £15–£20* ☉
**Hours:** lunch 12noon – 3pm; dinner 5:30pm – 10:30pm; closed Saturday; closed Sunday. **Cuisine:** French:- Charcoal grilled meats, French regional dishes (especially Provencal). Over 200 wines, many by the glass. **Credit cards:** Visa, Access, Diners, AmEx. **Other points:** licensed, open-air dining, coach/prior arr. **Directions:** nearest tube – Farringdon.
MR R WILSON, tel (071) 242 8238, (071) 242 2056.

### HODGSON'S, 115 Chancery Lane

*This attractive restaurant, once the legal book depositary for Sothebys, serves beautifully presented food in generous portions. The a la carte menu is changed every 6 weeks and there is a daily table d'hote lunch menu offering a choice of three starters, main courses and desserts representing excellent value for money.*
*FOOD £15–£20*
**Hours:** bar meals 11am – 11pm; lunch 12noon – 2:30pm; dinner 5pm – 11pm; closed Saturday – Sunday. **Cuisine:** continental:- Nouvelle Cuisine style a la carte and table d'hote menus. Includes Roast Monkfish Teriyaki, Magret of Duck, Roast rack of lamb. **Credit cards:** Visa, Access, Diners, AmEx. **Other points:** children catered for – please check for age limits. **Directions:** off Fleet Street.
DENISE SOLLIS (MANAGER), tel (071) 242 2836.

## THE MAGPIE AND STUMP, 20 Old Bailey Road

*Over 300 years ago, the Magpie & Stump faced the notorious Newgate gaol, where the hangings provided occasions for gruesome festivity. Today, this bustling city pub has three floors, where you can sample fine hand-drawn ales and good food combined with quality of service. Downstairs you will find a more intimate atmosphere, offering specialist wines and select hot dishes.*
*FOOD up to £15*
**Hours:** lunch 12noon – 2:30pm; closed Saturday – Sunday. **Cuisine:** English:- Daily menu of grills and traditional English food, freshly made sandwiches and baguettes. Sausages from different countries. Draught beers and fine wines. **Credit cards:** Visa, Access, Diners, AmEx. **Other points:** licensed, no-smoking area, children catered for – please check for age limits, vegetarian meals, real ales. **Directions:** opposite the Old Bailey Law Courts.
BASS TAVERNS, tel (071) 248 5085.

## HOLLAND PARK, London Map 7

### THE HOLLAND PARK HOTEL, 6 Ladbroke Terrace

*Situated in a quiet tree-lined area close to Kensington Palace, this Victorian Town House has been extensively*

renovated and restored to provide fine accommodation in relaxed and comfortable surroundings. There is an elegant sitting room an a beautiful garden. Close to shops and restaurants, with major train, bus and underground services just minutes away.
ACCOMMODATION £31–£40
**Cuisine:** continental:- continental breakfast. **Rooms:** 27 bedrooms all with tea making facilities, telephone, radio, TV: 4 singles ensuite, 4 singles ensuite, 5 singles, 4 twins ensuite, 1 twins, 4 doubles ensuite, 3 doubles, 1 triple ensuite, 1 triple. **Credit cards:** Visa, Access, Diners, AmEx. **Other points:** licensed, children catered for – please check for age limits, residents' lounge, garden, bank holidays, cots, 24hr reception. **Directions:** on the boundary of Holland Park and Notting Hill Gate.
YAZIM NANJI, tel (071) 792 0216, fax (071) 727 8166.

## HORNSEY, London Map 7

### L'AMICO ITALIAN RESTAURANT, 12 Crouch End Hill
A bright and cheerful Italian restaurant, appropriately furnished with paintings and artefacts, serving a wide range of fresh, well prepared dishes.
FOOD up to £15
**Hours:** lunch 12noon – 2:30pm; dinner 5:30pm – 11:30pm; closed Christmas 25/12. **Cuisine:** Italian / continental:- Modern European and Italian menu, offering an extensive choice of dishes, supplemented by an excellent wine list. Vegetarian menu also available. **Credit cards:** Visa, Access, AmEx. **Other points:** licensed, Sunday lunch, no-smoking area, children catered for – please check for age limits. **Directions:** at the bottom of Crouch End Hill, in the centre of Crouch End.
MRS ATANANCIA NICOLAOU, tel (081) 340 5143.

## KENSINGTON, London Map 7

### ABCONE HOTEL, 10 Ashburn Gardens
Located in a quiet street in the heart of Kensington, the Abcone is ideal for business or pleasure. All rooms are equipped with many modern facilities, including in-house video and satellite movies. Full secretarial services are available to all business clients. Just a short walk away from Hyde Park, Natural History and Victoria & Albert Museums, and the world famous Harrods.
ACCOMMODATION £31–£40
**Hours:** breakfast 7:30am – 9:30am. **Cuisine:** breakfast. **Rooms:** 69 bedrooms: 5 singles, 11 singles ensuite, 3 twins ensuite, 4 doubles, 11 doubles ensuite, 5 singles, 12 singles ensuite, 3 twins ensuite, 4 doubles, 11 doubles ensuite. **Credit cards:** Visa, Access, Diners, AmEx. **Other points:** children catered for – please check for age limits, residents' lounge. **Directions:** off Cromwell Road, turn on to Ashburn Gardens.
MR A A SADRUDDIN, tel (071) 370 3383, fax (071) 373 3082.

### AL BASHA RESTAURANT, 222 High Street
This traditional Lebanese restaurant offers a wide range of dishes and a house-speciality of charcoal grilled food. The friendly staff are very willing to give advice about ordering for those who may not be familiar with the menu. Live music is featured nightly from 8.00pm.
FOOD £15–£20
**Hours:** open all year 7:30am; open bank holidays 7:30am; meals all day 12noon – 12midnight. **Cuisine:** Lebanese:- Traditional Lebanese cooking including meze. **Credit cards:** Visa, Access, Diners, AmEx. **Other points:** licensed, open-air dining, Sunday lunch, children catered for – please check for age limits, disabled access. **Directions:** situated next to Holland Park and Commonwealth Institute.
MR KUDSI, tel (071) 938 1794, fax (071) 937 0340.

### AMBER HOTEL, 101 Lexham Gardens
Located in London's "green heart", near Kensington Gardens, Hyde Park and Holland Park, The Amber Hotel offers smart, friendly accommodation with personal attention. All rooms have elegant interiors and are equipped with many modern facilities. Ideal for the business traveller with personal computer, photocopier and fax machine available. Earls Court Exhibition Centre and Olympia are both nearby.
ACCOMMODATION £31–£40
FOOD up to £15
**Hours:** breakfast 7am – 10am. **Rooms:** 40 ensuite bedrooms. **Credit cards:** Access, Diners, AmEx. **Other points:** residents' bar, satellite TV, pets allowed. **Directions:** from Earls Court Underground turn left, walk 300m, cross junction. The hotel is on the right.
MR JONATHAN TOMKINSON, tel (071) 373 8666, fax (071) 835 1194.

### BEAVER HOTEL, 57–59 Philbeach Gardens
Situated in a quiet, tree-lined crescent of late Victorian houses, Beaver Hotel is ideally placed for Earls Court, Olympia and central London. Car Park for hotel guests.
ACCOMMODATION £21–£30
**Hours:** breakfast 7:30am – 9:30am. **Cuisine:** breakfast. **Rooms:** 38 bedrooms all with telephone, radio, TV: 4 singles ensuite, 14 singles, 8 twins ensuite, 2 twins, 6 doubles ensuite, 4 triples ensuite. **Credit cards:** Visa, Access, AmEx. **Other points:** children catered for – please check for age limits, pets allowed, baby sitting, cots, left luggage, residents' lounge, residents' bar. **Directions:** just off the A4 Cromwell Road.
JAN LIS, tel (071) 373 4553, fax (071) 373 4555.

### CAFE ROUGE, 2 Lancer Square, (off Kensington Church Street)
**Hours:** meals all day 10am – 11pm; meals all day – Sunday 10am – 10:30pm. **Cuisine:** French:- Traditional French food. Full a la carte with a good wine list. Light meals available all day. **Credit cards:** Visa, Access.

**Other points:** children catered for – please check for age limits, bank holidays, licensed. **Directions:** few minutes walk from High Street Kensington underground. GIAMPIERO MARTIGNONI (MGR), tel (071) 938 4200.

## CAPS, 64 Pembridge Road, Notting Hill Gate

*Close to the famous Portobello Road antique market, and within easy access of the West End, Caps is an attractive restuarant with a relaxed atmosphere. The menu offers a mix of French and English dishes with daily extras. The walls are covered with school caps and 'Williams Room', named after Prince William, is available for private parties.*
*ACCOMMODATION over £50*
*FOOD up to £15* CLUB ★

**Hours:** dinner 6pm – 1am; last orders 11:15pm; closed Sunday. **Cuisine:** English / French:- Specialities include avocado salad, roast rack of lamb with rosemary and honey, fillet of beef with madeira and truffles. **Rooms:** 21 bedrooms 4 singles ensuite, 8 twins ensuite, 9 doubles ensuite. **Credit cards:** Visa, Access, Diners, AmEx. **Other points:** licensed, no-smoking area, children catered for – please check for age limits. **Directions:** close to Notting Hill Gate tube. Top end of Portobello Road.
PAUL CAPRA, tel (071) 229 5177, fax (07) 727 4982.

## DINO'S (KENSINGTON), 7 Kensington High Street

*A typical Italian-style taverna, traditionally furnished with tiled floors and fresh flowers on the tables. Excellent service from helpful friendly staff. Mixed upmarket clientele.*
*FOOD up to £15*

**Hours:** lunch 12noon – 2:45pm; dinner 5:30pm – 11:30pm. **Cuisine:** Italian. **Credit cards:** Visa, Access, Diners, AmEx. **Other points:** children catered for – please check for age limits, disabled access, vegetarian meals. **Directions:** situated in Kensington High Street, minutes from tube.
Tel (071) 938 1944, fax (071) 370 1316.

## IL PORTICO, 227 Kensington High Street

*A popular high-street restaurant, offering a good selection of Italian style cuisine. The atmosphere is warm and friendly, attracting a regular clientele, mostly local. Ideally situated for visiting the famous Albert Hall, Hyde Park, and many other London tourist attractions.*
*FOOD £21–£25*

**Hours:** lunch 12noon – 3pm; dinner 6pm – 11:30pm. **Cuisine:** Italian:- A la carte menu, offering a wide range of Italian style cuisine. Vegetarian dishes available. **Credit cards:** Visa, Access, AmEx. **Other points:** no-smoking area, children catered for – please check for age limits, vegetarian meals. **Directions:** easy to locate. Situated almost opposite the Commonwealth Institute.
ANNA & PINO CHIAVARINI, tel (071) 602 6262.

## KENSINGTON INTERNATIONAL HOTEL, 4 Templeton Place

*A delightful Victorian hotel, recently renovated to a high standard. An inventive decorating scheme means every floor follows a different theme (e.g. Art Deco, Chinese, Tudor). Imaginative lunch and dinner scheme involving local restaurants. Extremely friendly, helpful staff. Altogether, outstanding value for money. (See colour advertisement in centre section.)*
*ACCOMMODATION £31–£40*
*FOOD up to £15*

**Hours:** breakfast 8am – 10am; bar meals 6pm – 11pm. **Cuisine:** English / continental:- Substantial continental or English breakfast. Lunch and dinner provided by local Chinese, Italian or Indian restaurant using hotel voucher. **Rooms:** 56 bedrooms all with tea making facilities, telephone, TV: 15 singles ensuite, 24 twins ensuite, 15 doubles ensuite, 2 triples ensuite. **Credit cards:** Visa, Access, Diners, AmEx. **Other points:** room-service, conservatory, bank holidays, residents' bar, children catered for – please check for age limits, residents' lounge, garden, baby sitting, cots, 24hr reception, left luggage, vegetarian meals, parking. **Directions:** close Earls Court tube, between Warwick Road and Earls Court Road.
MR PATEL, tel (071) 370 4333, fax (071) 244 7873.

## MICHEL'S BRASSERIE, 6 Holland Street

*Tucked away on a lovely street just off Kensington High Street this "petite" brasserie has been recently completely refurbished. Like all the Michels it has a relaxed and welcoming atmosphere. There are a la carte and set menus, including the "rapido" for those in a hurry, and everything is prepared fresh in the restaurant in that typical Michel's style.*
*FOOD up to £15*

**Hours:** closed 01/01; lunch 12noon – 2:30pm; dinner 6pm – 10:30pm; closed Christmas 25/12 – 26/12; closed some bank holidays. **Cuisine:** French:- French Brasserie/Bistro style cuisine, complemented by a fine Wine List. 3 Course Lunch menu. Vegetarian dishes available. **Credit cards:** Visa, AmEx, Diners. **Other points:** licensed, Sunday lunch, children catered for – please check for age limits. **Directions:** High Street Kensington tube.
MICHEL SADONES (MANAGING DIRECTOR), tel (071) 937 3367.

# KINGS CROSS, London Map 7

## GREAT NORTHERN HOTEL

*Opened in 1854, The Great Northern Hotel is situated between Kings Cross and St Pancras main line stations. The atmosphere is of a warm and friendly modern establishment. Squires Carving Restaurant is an ideal venue for lunch and dinner, before retiring to the Potters Bar. The hotel also has a choice of 13 Meeting Rooms and private catering arrangements with seating for up to 100.*
*ACCOMMODATION £41–£50*
*FOOD £15–£20*

**Hours:** breakfast 7am – 10am; breakfast – Sunday 8am – 10:30am; lunch 12noon – 3pm; lunch – weekends 12noon – 2pm; dinner 5:30pm – 10pm; dinner – weekends 5:30pm – 9pm; closed Christmas eve – Boxing day. **Cuisine:** English. **Rooms:** 89 bedrooms all with tea making facilities, telephone, TV: 13 singles ensuite, 60 doubles ensuite, 16 family rooms ensuite. **Credit cards:** Visa, Access, Diners, AmEx. **Other points:** parking, children catered for – please check for age limits, afternoon teas, vegetarian meals, residents' lounge, residents' bar. **Directions:** access from Pancras Road.
Tel (071) 837 5454, fax (071) 278 5270.

### THE PLACE CAFE, *17 Dukes Road*

*London's only restaurant which is shared by dancers and the public alike. The food is English home cooking and the atmosphere is leisurely and relaxed, with flickering candles and music in the evenings. Ideal for visiting the sights or as a lunchtime break.*
*FOOD up to £15*
**Hours:** meals all day 10am – 4pm; lunch 12noon – 2:30pm; dinner – performance evngs 5:30pm – 8pm. **Cuisine:** English:- Cafe style snack menu, offering hot & cold buffets, sandwiches, pastries and pasta, all dishes are vegetarian. Menu changes daily. **Other points:** licensed, no-smoking area, children catered for – please check for age limits, afternoon tea. **Directions:** 100yds from Euston station on the east side of St Pancras church.
VICAR OF ST MARTIN IN THE FIELDS, tel (071) 383 5469.

## LEADENHALL, London Map 7

### BEAUCHAMPS RESTAURANT, *23-25 Leadenhall Market*

*A turn-of-the-century city restaurant, tastefully furnished in darkwood and brass, situated within the confines of Leadenhall Market. A range of quality fish, speciality dishes are available. The restaurant being unique in London by owning its own fishmonger 'Ashdown,' with live holding tanks for shellfish. Attractions nearby, include Lloyds, Stock Exchange & Bank of England.*
*FOOD £21–£25*
**Hours:** morning coffee 9:30am – 11:30am; meals all day 11:30am – 6:30pm; closed some bank holidays. **Cuisine:** seafood:- Excellent selection of fish speciality dishes, including Lobster with ginger and spring onion, Halibut steak with thyme, parsley and cream. Often 2 or 3 daily specials. **Credit cards:** Visa, Access, Diners, AmEx. **Other points:** licensed, children catered for – please check for age limits, vegetarian meals, hard to park. **Directions** take either the Bank or Monument tube. Just off Leadenhall Street.
JOHN BEAUCHAMP BLACKETT, tel (071) 621 1331, fax (071) 626 5889.

### THE LEADENHALL CANTINA, *22 Leadenhall Market*

*A fashionable wine bar and bistro, situated within the confines of the old Victorian Leadenhall Market. Nearby attractions include the Tower of London, Tower Bridge and the Lloyd's building.*
*FOOD up to £15*
**Hours:** bar 11:30am – 10pm; meals all day 11:30am – 3pm. **Cuisine:** continental:- Delicious tapas buffet. House specialities include Gambas Pil-pil, Pincho Moruno and Paella Deluxe. **Credit cards:** Visa, Access, Diners, AmEx. **Other points:** functions, licensed. **Directions:** situated in Leadenhall market.
THE PELICAN GROUP PLC, tel (071) 623 1818.

## MAYFAIR, London Map 7

### DINO'S (MAYFAIR), *33 North Audley Street*

*Forming part of an attractive Edwardian terrace, Dino's is divided into three sections and decorated accordingly: Coffee Bar, Trattoria and Restaurant. It offers a typical Italian menu and the atmosphere is lively with an upmarket clientele.*
*FOOD up to £15*
**Hours:** meals all day 8am – 11:30pm. **Cuisine:** Italian. **Credit cards:** Visa, Access, Diners, AmEx. **Other points:** children catered for – please check for age limits, afternoon teas, disabled access, vegetarian meals. **Directions:** situated just off Oxford Street, close to Selfridges and minutes from the tube.
Tel (071) 629 7070, fax (071) 370 1316.

## MORTLAKE, London Map 7

### THE DEPOT CAFE WINE BAR, *Tideway Yard, Mortlake High Street*

*Built from original Victorian stables, the Depot is an attractive 80 seat cafe offering excellent value for money. Pine tables and pitch pine flooring with the friendly bustle of customers give the restaurant an authentic atmosphere. Stunning views of the River Thames from the terrace.*
*FOOD £15–£20*
**Hours:** lunch 12noon – 3pm; dinner 6pm – 11pm; closed 3 days over Christmas. **Cuisine:** English / continental:- Brasserie/wine bar style: fresh pasta, lemon sole, fricassee of chicken. **Credit cards:** Visa, Access, AmEx. **Other points:** licensed, Sunday lunch, children catered for – please check for age limits, afternoon tea. **Directions:** near Barnes railway bridge, just off Mortlake High Street.
MARK MILTON, tel (081) 878 9462.

## NOTTING HILL, London Map 7

### CAFE ROUGE, *31 Kensington Park Road*

*A traditional French bistro/bar open for meals and snacks throughout the day. Whether you dine a la carte or choose a lighter snack, all dishes are very well cooked using fresh ingredients. A welcoming and relaxed atmosphere prevails and the professional but young and friendly staff will go out of their way to ensure that you enjoy your visit.*
*FOOD £15–£20*

**Hours:** meals all day 10am – 11pm; closed Christmas 25/12; closed August bank holiday. **Cuisine:** French:- Traditional French cuisine such as Marmite Dieppoise, Entrecote Bearnaise and Plats du Jour. Also French snacks and sandwiches. **Credit cards:** Visa, Access. **Other points:** licensed, Sunday lunch, children catered for – please check for age limits, functions. **Directions:** close to Portobello market.
CAFE ROUGE LTD, tel (071) 221 4449, fax (071) 738 5301.

## PADDINGTON, London Map 7

### ASHLEY HOTEL, *15 Norfolk Square*
*The Ashley Hotel is flanked by its sister hotels, The Tregaron and The Oasis, and all three adjoin one another and are interconnected. Very centrally situated in a pretty garden square, a few minutes bus ride from Oxford St and close to Paddington Station. The Norfolk Gardens were re-designed in 1990 to recreate the Victorian era. A lovely and quiet place to sit and take your ease.*
*ACCOMMODATION £21–£30*
**Hours:** closed Christmas, August bank holiday; breakfast 7:30am – 9am. **Cuisine:** breakfast:- Full English Breakfast. **Rooms:** 52 bedrooms all with tea making facilities, radio, TV: 6 singles ensuite, 12 singles, 9 twins ensuite, 5 twins, 12 doubles ensuite, 2 doubles, 1 triple ensuite, 3 quads ensuite, 2 quads.

**Credit cards:** Visa, Access. **Other points:** central heating, children catered for – please check for age limits, no evening meal, residents' lounge, TV all rooms, left luggage. **Directions:** situated between Praed Street & Sussex Gardens. 3 minutes from Paddington.
MESSRS W J & D E GEORGE, tel (071) 723 3375, fax (071) 723 0173.

## PARSONS GREEN, London Map 7

### THE WHITE HORSE ON PARSONS GREEN, *1–3 Parsons Green*
*A large, comfortable Victorian pub with plenty of character and a reputation for good beer, wine and food. It has won many awards and in 1990 was the London Evening Standard's Pub of the Year. The rooms overlook Parsons Green and are suitable for a variety of uses, including lectures, exhibitions, press launches, and much more. A very popular pub with a lively clientele.*
*FOOD up to £15*
**Hours:** lunch 11:30am – 3pm; dinner 5pm – 10pm; closed Christmas 25/12. **Cuisine:** English:- Traditional pub-style cuisine, with set prices. 'Mega breakfast' from 11am at weekends. Outstanding reasonably priced wine list. **Credit cards:** Visa, Access, AmEx. **Other points:** licensed, open-air dining, Sunday lunch, no-smoking area, functions. **Directions:** situated at the northern end of Parsons Green.
BASS TAVERNS, tel (071) 736 2115.

## PICCADILLY, London Map 7

### HENRY'S CAFE BAR (PICCADILLY), 80 Piccadilly

*An attractive cafe-bar with art-deco interior serving an extensive range of international fast-food dishes, speciality cocktails and American beers. Very popular with businessmen and tourists and busy at lunchtimes. Near for many major tourist attractions, including Buckingham Palace and The Royal Academy.*
*FOOD up to £15*
**Hours:** meals all day 8am – 11pm. **Cuisine:** international. **Credit cards:** Visa, Access. **Other points:** children catered for – please check for age limits, open bank holidays, afternoon teas, no-smoking area, disabled access, vegetarian meals.
Tel (071) 491 2522.

## PUTNEY, London Map 7

### BANGLADESH CURRY MAHAL, 294 Upper Richmond Road

*A Bangladeshi restaurant serving a high standard of food in a typical Indian decor. Friendly staff will advise on your choice of dishes and the service is efficient yet relaxed. With the good food, faultless service and a friendly, warm atmosphere, it is easy to understand the popularity of this restaurant. Frequented by all ages, including families.*
*FOOD £15–£20*
**Hours:** closed Christmas 8am; lunch 12noon – 3pm; dinner 6pm – 12midnight. **Cuisine:** Bangladeshi / Indian:- Bangladeshi/Indian dishes using chicken, meat, shell fish and vegetables. Tandoori specialities. Fried scampi for the less adventurous. **Credit cards:** Visa, Access, Diners, AmEx. **Other points:** licensed, Sunday lunch, children catered for – please check for age limits, bank holidays. **Directions:** opposite Putney police station, just west of Putney High Street.
NURUL ISLAM, tel (081) 789 9763.

### CAFE ROUGE, 200–204 Putney Bridge Road

*A French cafe/restaurant, serving traditional bistro food in an informal but professional atmosphere. Cappuccino and light meals are served all day in the cafe area and the restaurant offers full a la carte. Attractively decorated in reds and dark wood, the atmosphere is busy yet relaxing. Popular with all ages.*
*FOOD £15–£20*
**Hours:** meals all day 10am – 11pm; closed Christmas 25/12. **Cuisine:** French:- French dishes such as Normandy Fish Stew, Entrecote Bearnaise. Snacks include Baguette du Cafe Rouge (hot steak sandwich), Croque Monsieur. **Credit cards:** Visa, Access. **Other points:** licensed, open-air dining, Sunday lunch, children catered for – please check for age limits, pets allowed, street parking. **Directions:** left off Putney High St at the Cannon cinema. Very close Putney bridge.
MR I WILDE, tel (081) 788 4257, fax (081) 789 8562.

### GAVIN'S RESTAURANT, 5 Lacy Road

*This lively Putney restaurant has an interesting menu with imaginative brasserie style dishes and an excellent choice of fresh pasta with a wide selection of sauces, all complemented by a well selected wine list. It has a great atmosphere and a well established local reputation.*
*FOOD up to £15* 🍽
**Hours:** lunch 12noon – 3:30pm; dinner 6pm – 11pm. **Cuisine:** eclectic continental:- A la carte menu specialising in brasserie and fresh pasta dishes. **Credit cards:** Visa, Access, AmEx, Diners, Switch. **Other points:** Sunday lunch, children catered for – please check for age limits. **Directions:** Lacy Road runs off Putney High Street, opposite Marks & Spencers.
MARK MILTON & GAVIN BARLOW, tel (081) 785 9151, fax (081) 788 1703.

### MYRA RESTAURANT, 240 Upper Richmond Road

*This cosy Victorian-fronted restaurant is situated close to the junction with Putney High Street and welcomes family groups to complement its strong local patronage. Theme nights are a popular 'speciality' – so book ahead to avoid disappointment! An International menu, all home cooked by Myra, and a warm welcome guarantee satisfaction.*
*FOOD £15–£20* CLUB ★
**Hours:** lunch – except Sunday 12noon – 2:30pm; lunch – Sunday 12:30pm – 4pm; dinner 6:30pm – 11pm. **Cuisine:** International:- A la carte, fixed price 3 course menu. **Credit cards:** Visa, Access, Diners, AmEx. **Other points:** licensed, open-air dining, Sunday lunch, children catered for – please check for age limits, garden. **Directions:** south circular, near Putney bridge.
MISS MOLONY, tel (081) 788 9450.

### TRAPPERS, 148 Upper Richmond Road

*Decorated in the style of a Canadian log cabin close to Putney High Street. Very popular with all ages with its interesting selection of dishes, cocktail list and special children's menu.*
*FOOD up to £15*
**Hours:** dinner – weekend 12noon – 11pm; dinner – weekdays 6pm – 11:30pm; closed Christmas 25/12 – 26/12; closed Easter Sunday. **Cuisine:** international:- Dishes include char-grilled steaks, burgers and chicken. Pasta, pizza, curry and vegetarian dishes. Plus a selection of daily specials. **Credit cards:** Visa, Access, Diners, AmEx. **Other points:** open-air dining, Sunday lunch, children catered for – please check for age limits. **Directions:** on the south circular road, 3 minutes walk from east Putney tube.
MR J CORY, tel (081) 788 6324, fax (081) 780 1728.

## SHEPHERDS BUSH, London Map 7

### BALZAC BISTRO, 4 Wood Lane

*A typical bistro style restaurant offering typically French cuisine of high quality. A pleasant, warm and friendly atmosphere abounds. Metred parking during the day.*
*FOOD £15–£20*

Hours: closed bank holidays Easter Sunday; closed sat lunch & Sunday; lunch 12noon – 2:30pm; dinner 7pm – 11pm. **Cuisine:** French. **Credit cards:** Visa, Access, Diners, AmEx. **Other points:** children catered for – please check for age limits, vegetarian meals. **Directions:** corner of Sheperds Bush Green and Wood Lane.
MR P TARELLI, tel (081) 743 6787.

## SOHO, London Map 7

### MING, 35 Greek Street
*Ming offers an extensive a la carte menu of traditional and imaginative Chinese dishes and an additional 4 set menus. The food is beautifully cooked and the large choice ensures plenty of scope for exploration of new dishes for even the most regular customers. The simple decor is in keeping with the calm, relaxed atmosphere of the restaurant.*
*FOOD up to £15*
**Hours:** meals all day 12noon – 11:45pm; closed Christmas 25/12 – 26/12; closed Sunday – except Chinese New Year. **Cuisine:** Chinese:- northern Chinese. Special menu with more unusual, innovative dishes. Ming Bowl menu featuring one dish meal and pre-theatre menu. **Credit cards:** Visa, Access, Diners, AmEx. **Other points:** licensed, no-smoking area, children catered for – please check for age limits, private dining. **Directions:** corner of Greek St & Romilly St Nearest tube: Leicester Square.
CHRISTINE YAU, tel (071) 734 2721, fax (071) 435 0812.

## SOUTH KENSINGTON, London Map 7

### BANGKOK RESTAURANT, Bute Street
*This lively popular restaurant is handy for the Natural History and Victoria and Albert Museums. The traditional dishes are well presented in generous portions and the service is swift and courteous.*
*FOOD up to £15*
**Hours:** lunch 12:15pm – 2:15pm; dinner 7pm – 11:15pm; closed bank holidays; closed Sunday. **Cuisine:** Thai:- Traditional Thai cuisine mainly stir fried chicken and beef dishes. **Credit cards:** Visa, Access. **Other points:** licensed, children catered for – please check for age limits, pets allowed, bank holidays. **Directions:** close South Kensington tube station.
T BUNNAG, tel (071) 584 8529, fax (071) 823 7883.

## TOWER HILL, London Map 7

### CAFE ROUGE, Hays Galleria, Tooley Street
*Lively French cafe with warm, vibrant decor. Continental atmosphere conducive to lingering after a meal. Friendly, efficient service and frothy cappuccino.*
*FOOD up to £15*
**Hours:** meals all day – weekdays 10am – 10pm; meals all day – weekends 10am – 6pm. **Cuisine:** French:- Lively French cuisine. Light meals available. French

pizzeria open at lunch time. **Credit cards:** Visa, Access, Diners, AmEx. **Other points:** bank holidays, children catered for – please check for age limits. **Directions:** few minutes walk from London Bridge underground Station.
JASON DANCIGER (MGR), tel (071) 378 0097, fax (071) 378 6317.

## WAPPING, London Map 7

### HENRY'S CAFE BAR (WAPPING), Tobacco Dock
*A glass-fronted, wooden beamed building which was opened as part of the Tobacco Dock Development Project. Serving an extensive range of international fast-food, it has a bustling atmosphere with warm, courteous waitress service. The Tower of London and St Katherine's Dock are within easy reach.*
*FOOD up to £15*
**Hours:** meals all day 11am – 11pm. **Cuisine:** international. **Credit cards:** Visa, Access. **Other points:** parking, children catered for – please check for age limits, open bank holidays, no-smoking area, afternoon teas, disabled access, vegetarian meals.
Tel (071) 481 0004.

## WEST END, London Map 7

### ARRAN HOUSE HOTEL (ARRAN HOTEL), 77-79 Gower Street
*A small English family-run hotel offering warmth and hospitality which has brought back the same dedicated clientele for many years. A 200 year-old Georgian building in the centre of 'Literary Bloomsbury', it offers guests a wide range of modern facilities to ensure a comfortable stay. Within walking distance of the British Museum, Piccadilly Circus, Oxford Street and London's theaterland.*
*ACCOMMODATION £21–£30*
**Hours:** breakfast 7:30am – 9am; breakfast / Sunday 8am – 9:30am. **Cuisine:** English. **Other points:** parking, residents' lounge, vegetarian meals, garden. **Directions:** situated in Gower Street, between Chenies Street and Torrington Place.
MR J RICHARDS, tel (071) 637 1140, (071) 636 2186, fax (071) 436 5328.

### BIAGIO CHEZ VICTOR, 45 Wardour Street
*In the heart of London's West End, this cosy, continental restaurant is ideally situated for both theatres and cinema. Friendly staff serve well-prepared food in an intimate atmosphere, making for an excellent night out.*
*FOOD £21–£25*
**Hours:** meals all day 12noon – 11:30pm. **Cuisine:** Italian / French:- Italian and French cooking – prepared to high standards. **Credit cards:** Visa, Access, Diners, AmEx. **Other points:** licensed, Sunday lunch, children catered for – please check for age limits. **Directions:** corner of Shaftesbury Ave and Wardour St.
BIAGIO CAROLEO, tel (071) 437 6523, fax (071) 734 3123.

## CAFE IN THE CRYPT, St Martin In The Fields

*A unique cafe, situated immediately underneath the famous Church of St Martin in the Fields, Trafalgar Square. Generous portions of wholesome food are offered at outstanding value for money. Meals can be enjoyed beneath the vaulted ceilings in what must be one of the most unusual eating places in London. Centrally situated and very close to the National Gallery.*
FOOD up to £15
**Hours:** meals all day 10am – 9pm; meals all day – Sunday 12noon – 6pm. **Cuisine:** English:- English home cooking. Self-service. Menu changes daily. **Credit cards:** Visa, Access. **Other points:** licensed, Sunday lunch, children catered for – please check for age limits, afternoon tea. **Directions:** nearest tubes: Leicester Sq & Charing Cross. Entrance – Duncannon Street.
THE VICAR OF ST MARTIN IN THE FIELDS, tel (071) 839 4342.

## CAFE PELICAN, 48 St Martin's Lane

*French cafe and brasserie restaurant, situated in a popular part of London, offering an extensive range of imaginative French dishes and fine wines. Good access for disabled persons.*
FOOD up to £15
**Hours:** meals all day 12noon – 12midnight. **Cuisine:** French:- French bistro style cuisine, complemented by a fine wine list. **Credit cards:** Visa, Access, Diners, AmEx. **Other points:** children catered for – please check for age limits, bank holidays. **Directions:** St Martin's Lane.
THE PELICAN GROUP PLC, tel (071) 379 0309, fax (071) 379 9782.

## CAFE ROUGE, 46–48 James Street

*A warm and friendly French cafe with lively decor and atmosphere. Good location in London's busy West End with good access to shops, cinema and theatres. Efficient, friendly staff make you feel welcome. Continental ambiance will make you want to linger*
FOOD up to £15
**Hours:** meals all day – Sunday 9am – 4pm; meals all day 10am – 11pm. **Cuisine:** French:- Traditional French cuisine. Full a la carte. Light meals available. Good selection of wines. **Credit cards:** Visa, Access. **Other points:** children catered for – please check for age limits, bank holidays. **Directions:** closest underground station is Bond Street.
CLAUDE LALANDE (MGR), tel (071) 407 4847, fax (071) 935 2631.

## DON PEPE RESTAURANT, 99 Frampton Street

*Founded by the present owner 20 years ago, this was one of London's first Tapas Bars. Today, it is undoubtedly one of the capital's premier Spanish restaurants, offering a wide range of excellent Spanish cuisine. This popular restaurant offers live music and alfresco dining in summertime. Ideal for Lord's cricket ground and Little Venice canal.*
FOOD up to £15 ⏱
**Hours:** closed Sunday evening 10am; closed Christmas day 10am; lunch 12noon – 3pm; dinner 7pm – 1am. **Cuisine:** Spanish. **Other points:** children catered for – please check for age limits, vegetarian meals, open bank holidays. **Directions:** just off Edgeware Road, between Lisson Grove and Edgeware Road itself.
Tel (071) 262 3834, (071) 723 9749, fax (071) 724 8305.

## EDWARD LEAR HOTEL, 28/30 Seymour Street

*Formerly the home of the famous Victorian painter and poet, Edward Lear. The Hotel offers cheerful rooms with all the usual facilities and is in the perfect location: just minutes away from Hyde Park, Speakers Corner and Oxford Street.*
ACCOMMODATION £21–£30
**Hours:** breakfast 7:30am – 9:15am. **Cuisine:** breakfast. **Rooms:** 22 bedrooms all with tea making facilities, telephone, radio, TV: 12 singles, 5 twins, 1 double ensuite, 1 double, 2 triples ensuite, 1 triple. **Credit cards:** Visa, Access. **Other points:** children catered for – please check for age limits, in-house films, residents' lounge, baby-listening device, cots, vegetarian meals, parking, disabled access. **Directions:** close to Marble Arch tube and a minutes walk from Oxford Street.
PETER EVANS, tel (071) 402 5401, fax (071) 706 3766.

## MARCHE RESTAURANT – THE SWISS CENTRE, 1 Swiss Court

*Continental cafe meets outdoor market. Choose the ingredients for your meal from diverse stations, then watch it being cooked before your eyes. An unusual set-up, but the cheerful, cafe-type decor and helpful service makes for an interesting, enjoyable meal.*
FOOD up to £15
**Hours:** breakfast 7am – 11am; meals all day 11am – 12midnight; closed Christmas 25/12. **Cuisine:** Swiss / German:- Swiss with Germanic influence. Fresh ingredients, varied menu at reasonable prices. **Credit cards:** Visa, Access, Diners, AmEx. **Other points:** licensed, Sunday lunch, no-smoking area, children catered for – please check for age limits, bank holidays. **Directions:** London underground: Piccadilly and Leicester Square.
MICHAEL BURKE – MANAGER, tel (071) 494 0498, fax (071) 494 0502.

## PARKWOOD HOTEL, 4 Stanhope Place

*An attractive town house situated in a quiet, residential street, but just a short walk away from Oxford Street, Marble Arch and Hyde Park. The Parkwood is under excellent management, offering spotlessly clean and airy bedrooms serviced by friendly and efficient staff.*
ACCOMMODATION £21–£30
**Hours:** breakfast 7:30am – 9:15am. **Cuisine:** breakfast. **Rooms:** 18 bedrooms all with tea making facilities, telephone, radio, TV: 3 singles, 4 twins ensuite, 4 twins, 4 doubles ensuite, 2 triples ensuite, 1 triple. **Credit**

cards: Visa, Access. **Other points:** children catered for
– please check for age limits, in-house films, left
luggage, launderette, baby-listening device, cots, left
luggage, hair dryers, satellite TV. **Directions:** a minutes
walk from Marble Arch tube station.
PETER EVANS, tel (071) 402 2241, fax (071) 402 1574.

## PICCADILLY RESTAURANT, 31 Great Windmill Street

*Centrally situated in the heart of theatreland and on the
fringes of Soho. The restaurant is on two levels and both
have a cosy informal atmosphere. Excellent for eating
either before or after the theatre.*
*FOOD £15–£20*
**Hours:** lunch 12noon – 2:30pm; dinner 5:30pm –
11:15pm; closed bank holidays; closed Sunday. **Cuisine:**
Italian:- Italian cuisine. **Credit cards:** Visa, Access,
AmEx. **Other points:** children catered for – please
check for age limits, guide dogs. **Directions:** nearest
tube, Piccadilly.
CLAUDIO MUSSI, tel (071) 734 4956.

---

For reservations & further information,
phone:

# LES ROUTIERS

Ø

Booking & Information Line

Tel: 071-610-1856
Fax: 071-385-7136

---

## LES ROUTIERS GUIDE TO FRANCE 1994

Over 1,700 recommended establishments
in France.

Available at all good bookshops, or direct
from the publishers.

**£8.99**

---

## WEST HAMPSTEAD, London

### CHARLOTTE RESTAURANT & GUEST HOUSE, 221 West End Land

*An old established restaurant and guest house, 2 minutes
from West Hampstead tube (Jubilee line) and direct
British Rail link to Gatwick and Luton Airports. A free
London Travel Card is issued to guests staying one week
or more. The restaurant is tastefully decorated and the
ample portions are served by cheerful staff. The
accommodation is unbeatable value and comfortable.*
*ACCOMMODATION under £20*
*FOOD up to £15*

**Hours:** breakfast 7:30am – 11:30am; lunch 12noon –
4pm; dinner 6pm – 11pm; closed Sunday. **Cuisine:**
English / continental:- English and continental cooking
from liver Bavaria and deubreziner sausages to stir-fried
vegetables with rice and prawn and poussin a la diable.
**Rooms:** 36 bedrooms all with TV: 6 singles, 6 singles
ensuite, 6 doubles, 18 doubles ensuite. **Other points:**
children catered for – please check for age limits.
**Directions:** 2 minutes from West Hampstead tube
(Jubilee Line).
MR L KOCH, tel (071) 794 6476, fax (071) 431 3584.

### NO 77 WINE BAR, 77 Mill Lane

*A popular wine bar decorated in pine with old film bills
on the walls. International theme evenings such as Burns
Night, July 4th, Greek Evening. The in-house club sails,
plays cricket, rugby and golf tournaments.*
*FOOD £15–£20*
**Hours:** closed Christmas Sunday; lunch 12noon – 3pm;
dinner 6pm – 11pm; closed bank holidays; closed good
Friday. **Cuisine:** English:- Homemade soups, lamb
Shrewsbury. **Credit cards:** Visa, Access. **Other points:**
children catered for – please check for age limits, street
parking. **Directions:** Mill Lane is off the Edgware Rd
between Kilburn and Cricklewood.
DAVID BLAKEMORE, tel (071) 435 7787.

---

## WESTMINSTER, London Map 7

### BUMBLES RESTAURANT, 16 Buckingham Palace Road

*Friendly English restaurant with cartoons and old prints
lining the walls, padded bench-style seating set in
alcoves and a spacious basement which is also air-
conditioned. Places of interest nearby include
Buckingham Palace, Westminster Abbey and local
theatres.*
*FOOD £15–£20* CLUB
**Hours:** lunch 12noon – 2:15pm; dinner 6pm – 10:45pm;
closed bank holidays; closed Saturday lunch; closed
Sunday. **Cuisine:** English / international:-
English/International cuisine: fresh fish, savoury
pancakes, lamb, duck, home-made pies. Super puddings.
Extensive wine list. Choice of set menus. **Credit cards:**
Visa, Access, Diners, AmEx. **Other points:** children
catered for – please check for age limits, functions.
**Directions:** 200yds from Victoria station going towards
Buckingham Palace.
PHILIP BARNETT, tel (071) 828 2903.

---

## WIMBLEDON, London Map 7

### CAFE ROUGE, 26 High Street

*A lively, Parisian-style cafe with genuine French feel
and character, serving excellent traditional bistro food.
Light meals and cappuccino served all day. Full a la
carte. Continental atmosphere conducive to lingering.*
*FOOD up to £15*
**Hours:** meals all day 10am – 11pm; meals all day –
Sunday 10am – 10:30pm. **Cuisine:** French:- Traditional

French cuisine. House speciality Marmite Dieppoise. Good selection of wines. Light meals available. **Credit cards:** Visa, Access. **Other points:** bank holidays, children catered for – please check for age limits. **Directions:** nearest underground is Wimbledon. GEORGE MULLER (MGR), tel (081) 944 5131, fax (081) 947 6610.

## GOURMET RESTAURANT, 2a Kings Road

*A modern style restaurant situated just off Wimbledon Broadway and close to the theatre, offering an excellent mix of French cuisine with continental influence. The spacious and comfortable interior is attractively decorated around a large central chimney feature, amidst subtle lighting and gentle background music providing a perfect setting for diners. The staff are friendly and efficient, and in summer alfresco dining on pavement tables is an additional attraction.*
*FOOD up to £15*
**Hours:** lunch 10am – 3pm; dinner 5:30pm – 11:30pm. **Cuisine:** French. **Credit cards:** Visa, Access, Diners, AmEx. **Other points:** children catered for – please check for age limits, Sunday lunch, open bank holidays, vegetarian meals. **Directions:** just off Wimbledon Broadway.
ABDDOLLAH SHIRAZI, tel (081) 540 5710, (081) 543 6416.

## ENFIELD, Middlesex Map 7

### OAK LODGE HOTEL, 80 Village Road, Bush Hill Park

*An exclusive country-style hotel set in secluded gardens, offering a personal atmosphere and service. English Tourist Board 3 Crown Highly Commended, it has a reputation as the 'Directors Choice.' Favoured at weekends by visiting family wedding guests or newlyweds who are attracted by the romantic atmosphere. Luxurious and well-appointed with a unique personal charm.*
*ACCOMMODATION £41–£50*
*FOOD up to £15*
**Hours:** breakfast 7am – 10am; dinner 7pm – 10pm. **Cuisine:** English / continental:- Connoisseur A la carte and Table d'hote menu's available. A la carte menu also available for celebratory dinner parties, for up to 14 covers. **Rooms:** 6 bedrooms, all en suite, furnished to an extremely high standard of comfort, with many extras provided. **Credit cards:** Visa, Access, Diners, AmEx. **Other points:** licensed, open-air dining, Sunday lunch, children catered for – please check for age limits, pets/prior arr, parking, residents' lounge, garden, honeymoon suite, functions. **Directions:** 1 mile from A10. Turn right at 7th set of lights from exit 25 of M25. JOHN BROWN, tel (081) 360 7082.

## GREENFORD, Middlesex Map 7

### THE BRIDGE HOTEL, Western Avenue

*A tasteful combination of the 'old' and the 'new', The Bridge Hotel has always enjoyed an excellent reputation for its quality beers and delightful atmosphere. Ideally situated on the A40, it is easily accessible from all routes. The private bedrooms have every modern facility, including satellite TV, and the lounge and saloon bars proudly boast their beautiful original wood panelling. The new superbly appointed restaurant offers a wide range of appetising alternatives to the most discerning of palates.*
*ACCOMMODATION £41–£50*
*FOOD up to £15*
**Hours:** 7pm. **Cuisine:** French. **Other points:** parking, disabled access, residents' lounge, vegetarian meals. **Directions:** A4127 off A40. Greenford underground (Central line) is a few minutes walk from the hotel. Tel (081) 566 6246, fax (081) 566 6140.

## HARROW, Middlesex Map 7

### CRESCENT LODGE HOTEL, 58–62 Welldon Crescent

*This is a family owned and run hotel situated in Harrow, providing guests with personal service and a comfortable, carefree stay. Happy to cater for conferences. A genuine warm welcome is extended to all visitors and the accommodation is of a very high standard.*
*ACCOMMODATION £21–£30*
*FOOD up to £15* ★
**Hours:** breakfast 7:30am – 9am. **Cuisine:** English:- Varied menu, including Kosher and Vegetarian. Dishes may include, Venison in Red Wine, Provencale Nut Wellington, Chicken Satay with Noodles, Steaks. **Rooms:** 21 bedrooms all with tea making facilities, telephone, radio, TV: 4 singles ensuite, 5 singles, 4 twins ensuite, 3 twins, 3 doubles ensuite, 1 triple ensuite, 1 quad ensuite. **Credit cards:** Visa, Access, AmEx. **Other points:** children catered for – please check for age limits, bank holidays, conferences, secretary available, baby-listening device, cots, 24hr reception, foreign exchange, left luggage, vegetarian meals, residents' bar, residents' lounge. **Directions:** off Headstone Road, onto Hindes Road then Welldon Crescent. ZENNIE & SHIRAZ JIVRAJ, tel (081) 863 5491, fax (081) 427 5965.

### CUMBERLAND HOTEL, St John's Road

*Relax in the unrushed peaceful atmosphere of this long established hotel. The Restaurant offers generous portions of freshly prepared food to suit all tastes. Every care is taken by the attentive staff to make all visitors feel relaxed and welcome. Highly recommended.*
*ACCOMMODATION £31–£40*
*FOOD up to £15* ☕
**Hours:** breakfast 7am – 9:30am; lunch 12noon – 2pm; dinner 7pm – 9:30pm. **Cuisine:** French / continental:- Dishes are mainly French on the a la carte menu, with various specialities on the fixed price choice menu, eg. Baked Swordfish, Cajun Chicken. **Rooms:** 81 bedrooms all with tea making facilities, telephone, radio, TV: 40 singles ensuite, 13 twins ensuite, 23 doubles ensuite, 3 triples ensuite, 2 quads ensuite. **Credit cards:** Visa,

Access, Diners, AmEx. **Other points:** open-air dining, Sunday lunch, no-smoking area, conferences, gym facilities, children catered for – please check for age limits, baby-listening device, cots, 24hr reception, parking, vegetarian meals, disabled access. **Directions:** leave M4, Exit 3. Follow the A312 to Harrow. MR I KAY – MANAGER, tel (081) 863 4111.

## FIDDLER'S RESTAURANT, 221–225 High Road, Harrow Weald

*Part of a 1930's row of shops, 'Fiddlers' has a black and white mock Tudor frontage. Inside, Tudor decor, bric a brac and mirrors create warm, attractive surroundings in which to enjoy the excellent food. All dishes are well cooked and well presented. Everything is done to ensure that customers enjoy their meal and the service and atmosphere is warm and welcoming.*
FOOD up to £15 🍲 CLUB

**Hours:** last orders 7pm – 11:30pm; last orders – fri/sat 7pm – 12midnight; lunch 12noon – 2:30pm; dinner – except fri/sat 7pm – 1am; dinner – Friday/Saturday 7pm – 2am. **Cuisine:** Italian / French:- Wide selection of Italian & French cuisine such as Duck with orange sauce; Beef al Pepe -with a crushed pepper, brandy & cream sauce; Calamari Fritti. **Credit cards:** Visa, Access, AmEx, Switch. **Other points:** licensed, Sunday lunch, no-smoking area, children catered for – please check for age limits, entertainment, conferences, functions, air-conditioned. **Directions:** A409, between Harrow Wealdstone station and Uxbridge Road roundabout.
ANTONIO BRANCA, tel (081) 863 6066, (081) 427 1931, fax (081) 861 2807.

## OLD ETONIAN RESTAURANT, 38 High Street, Harrow On The Hill

*An 18th century French bistro-style restaurant, situated in the town centre near the famous Harrow Public School, combining the qualities of excellent food and service with comfortable and relaxed surroundings.*
FOOD up to £15

**Hours:** lunch 12noon – 2:30pm; dinner 7pm – 11pm; closed bank holidays; closed Saturday lunch; closed Sunday. **Cuisine:** French:- French cuisine, featuring seafood pancake, Steak Dijon, roast duck in orange sauce, with guava, chocolate mousse, creme brulee. **Credit cards:** Visa, Access, Diners, AmEx. **Other points:** licensed, children catered for – please check for age limits, parking. **Directions:** off Uxbridge road, in the town centre near the school.
MR PELAEZ, tel (081) 422 8482.

# PINNER, Middlesex Map 7

## LA GIRALDA, 66 Pinner Green

*Situated just north of Pinner village amongst a parade of shops, this tastefully furnished restaurant has 4 rooms of different Spanish styles and serves authentic Spanishcuisine. Fixed price menu using finest fresh produce. Believed to own one of the finest lists of Spanish wine in Britain.*
FOOD £15–£20 🍲

**Hours:** lunch 12noon – 2:30pm; dinner 6:30pm – 10:30pm; closed Monday; closed Sunday evening. **Cuisine:** Spanish:- Paella, fish – fixed price menus. **Credit cards:** Visa, Access, AmEx. **Other points:** licensed, children catered for – please check for age limits, street parking. **Directions:** situated north of Pinner village.
MR D BROWN, tel (081) 868 3429, (081) 868 3193, fax 081 868 1218.

# RUISLIP, Middlesex Map 7

## BARN HOTEL & CONFERENCE CENTRE, West End Road

*Set in 2 acres of landscaped lawns and gardens, The Barn Hotel combines Olde Worlde charm with all the comforts you would expect from a first class hotel. This traditional English style retreat is grouped around a Grade II listed barn. All bedrooms are individually furnished to an exceptionally high standard. For breakfast, lunch or dinner, enjoy the finest food in the Leaning Bar Restaurant with its low oak beamed ceiling and views over the lawns. Ideal for conferences, seminars and wedding hire.*
ACCOMMODATION £41–£50
FOOD up to £15

**Hours:** breakfast 7am – 9:30am; lunch 12noon – 2pm; bar snacks 12noon – 2pm; dinner 7pm – 9:30pm; bar snacks 7pm – 9:30pm. **Cuisine:** English/French. **Rooms:** 61 bedrooms 27 singles ensuite, 22 doubles ensuite, 12 twins ensuite. **Credit cards:** Visa, Access, Diners, AmEx. **Other points:** parking, children catered for – please check for age limits, Sunday lunch, open bank holidays, Sunday dinner, disabled access, pets allowed, vegetarian meals, open-air dining, garden, conferences, weddings. **Directions:** next to Ruislip underground station on the A4180. Easy access from M4, M1 and M25.
MR F SMITH, tel (0895) 636057, fax (0895) 638379.

## RUISLIP TANDOORI, 115 High Street

*A 60-seater tandoori restaurant serving Nepalese cuisine. The atmosphere is set by subdued lighting and soft background music. Well patronised by the locals. Established since 1980.*
FOOD up to £15

**Hours:** lunch 12noon – 2:30pm; dinner 6pm – 11:30pm; closed Christmas 25/12 – 26/12. **Cuisine:** Nepalese:- Chicken Zhal Frazi, Chicken Gurkhali, Butter Chicken, Chicken Nepal, Chicken Chilly Massala. Karai dishes and Kathmandu dishes. Set Nepalese Thali and set dinner. Special Sunday lunch buffet, 12 dishes to choose from £6.95 per adult and £3.50 for children. **Credit cards:** Visa, Access, Diners, AmEx. **Other points:** Sunday lunch, children catered for – please check for age limits, no service charge. **Directions:** situated centrally on Ruislip High Street.
K B RAICHHETRI, tel (0895) 632859, (0895) 674890.

## TEDDINGTON, Middlesex Map 7

### THE ITALIAN PLACE BRASSERIE,
### 38 High Street

*An excellent Italian restaurant in the centre of
Teddington. The menu offers an extensive choice of
authentic and creative Italian dishes at very reasonable
prices, with all meals freshly cooked and well presented.
Highly recommended for the excellent food and
welcoming service in a lively yet relaxed atmosphere.
Special Sunday Brunch from £3.75 and half price large
pizzas Saturday lunch from £2.30.*

*FOOD up to £15* ☕

**Hours:** open bank holidays 25/12; Sunday brunch
11am – 1pm; lunch 12noon – 2:30pm; lunch –
Sunday 12noon – 3pm; dinner 6:30pm – 11pm; dinner –
Sunday 7pm – 10:30pm. **Cuisine:** Italian:- Italian
cuisine, dishes may include – Polenta con Funghi,
Fettuccine al Salmon, Manzo alla Mostarda, Insalata
Marinara. Specials change daily. **Credit cards:** Visa,
Access, Diners, AmEx. **Other points:** licensed,
Sunday lunch, no-smoking area, children catered for –
please check for age limits. **Directions:** on Teddington
High Street.

FEDERICO SECOLA, tel (081) 943 2433.

# SOUTH EAST ENGLAND & EAST ANGLIA

However long your stay, you will not exhaust the pleasures and warm welcome offered by the beautiful regions of the South East and East Anglia – from the rolling North and South Downs to the wide open skies of East Anglia, from the charming chocolate-box villages of the Thames and Chilterns to the Lincolnshire fens, all are steeped in history and heritage from Roman and Norman times.

East Anglia, although bordering London, has retained its true character and integrity. A place of wild natural beauty with its ancient forests, reed-fringed waterways and windswept sand dunes. Essex, with its bustling market towns, is full of white weatherboarded villages and winding river estuaries. Colchester is England's oldest recorded town, with its magnificent Norman castle built on the foundations of a Roman temple. The countryside along the Essex/Suffolk border with its willow trees, cattle-grazed water meadows and gently flowing river, is virtually untouched since John Constable and Gainsborough both painted here.

The Suffolk wool town of Lavenham is England's best preserved medieval town boasting a wealth of magnificent timbered buildings. Along East Anglia's 200 mile coastline, the seaside towns of Aldeburgh and Southwold are particularly charming with their pretty pebble beaches and fleet of tiny fishing boats. Wide salt flats and wild yellow gorse-covered heathlands attract an enormous variety of wildlife in their natural habitats.

Norwich has an abundance of tiny narrow medieval streets, hidden courtyards and leafy lanes running down to the Rivers Yare and Wensum, which wind slowly through the heart of the city. On the famous 'Broads' are vast sluggish rivers and acres of whispering sedge.

A day in Cambridge simply isn't long enough. King's College Chapel is a wedding cake made of stone, while the Backs, the cool green river, and an extraordinary variety of bookshops make this university town a delight to visit. Not far away, Ely's mellow stone buildings cluster around the skirts of the cathedral whose Lantern Tower is a masterpiece of medieval engineering, balancing mighty oak trees 60 feet high above an awe-inspiring lofty nave.

Discover the 'American connection' in Lincolnshire – home of the Pilgrim Fathers. Shop for antiques in Lincoln's ancient cobbled streets or visit the International Antique and Collectors Fair, held several times a year at the Winthorpe Showground.

The counties of the Thames and Chilterns encompass some of the most charming and unspoilt countryside in England and has something for everyone.

The Thames and Chilterns may be 'landlocked', but are far from being high and dry. Brightly painted canal boats, punts and pleasure cruisers ply the waterways across the region. In July, Henley's famed Royal Regatta draws competitors and spectators from around the globe. Stately homes saturate the landscape reflecting centuries of colourful history. Bedfordshire is home to Woburn Abbey and Luton Hoo, while Berkshire has Highcliffe Castle, Cliveden and Windsor Castle – home of English monarchs since William the Conqueror. Buckinghamshire is renowned for its constellation of Rothschild residences and it was at Hatfield House in Hertfordshire, the childhood home of Elizabeth I, where she learned of her accession to the throne. Oxford – city of dreaming spires, magnificent golden limestone architecture and a world famous university. Blenheim Palace, birthplace of Winston Churchill and ancestral home of the Dukes of Marlborough, is the jewel in Oxfordshire's crown.

The famous holiday coastline of the South East, includes the popular resorts of Worthing, Brighton, Eastbourne, Hastings, Ramsgate, Margate, Folkestone and Dover. Attractions are many and include wildlife parks, steam railway museums and vineyards. For a real taste of the countryside, visit Hampshire's Test Valley with its tranquil waterways, reminiscent of Kenneth Grahame's writings of Ratty, Toad and Mole in his famous novel *Wind in the Willows*. Explore the network of footpaths and bridleways through the New Forest where ponies and deer still wander freely. An area rich in quality restaurants and quaint inns where a warm and hospitable welcome awaits.

For details of where to visit and what to see in South East England and East Anglia, contact the East Anglia Tourist Board, Toppesfield Hall, Hadleigh, Suffolk IP7 7DN. Tel: (0473) 822922.

## ACLE, Norfolk Map 9

### MANNINGS HOTEL & RESTAURANT, South Walsham Road

*A small family-run hotel, set in peaceful landscaped gardens. All rooms are elegantly furnished and comfortable. The licensed restaurant is open to non-residents, offering cuisine which is believed to be the best in the area. Centrally situated for touring the Norfolk Broads and for exploring the beautiful Norfolk countryside.*
*ACCOMMODATION £21–£30*
*FOOD up to £15*
**Hours:** breakfast 7:30am – 9am; lunch 12noon – 2pm; bar meals 12noon – 2pm; dinner 7pm – 9:30pm.
**Cuisine:** English:- Full a la carte and table d'hote menus offering a very high standard of catering, using only the freshest of produce. **Rooms:** 10 bedrooms all with tea making facilities, telephone, radio, TV: 3 singles ensuite, 3 twins ensuite, 4 doubles ensuite. **Credit cards:** Visa, Access, AmEx. **Other points:** licensed, open-air dining, Sunday lunch, children catered for – please check for age limits, pets allowed, parking, garden, vegetarian meals. **Directions:** midway between Great Yarmouth (9 miles), and Norwich (11 miles).
ROBERT MANNING, tel (0493) 750377, fax (0493) 751220.

## ALDEBURGH, Suffolk Map 9

### AUSTINS HOTEL & RESTAURANT, 243 The High Street

*Situated at the end of the High-Street, a short walk from the beach, the Yacht Club and the marshes, Austins is distinguished by its warm and intimate atmosphere. Furnished with antiques and paintings, there is a very attractive and welcoming restaurant, drawing room and Bar. Internationally renowned as the home of the Music Festival, Aldeburgh has much to offer.*
*ACCOMMODATION £41–£50*
*FOOD £15–£20*
**Hours:** breakfast 7am – 9:30am; lunch 12:30pm; dinner 7:30pm. **Cuisine:** English / seafood:- A la carte and Table d'hote, with the accent on local fresh fish dishes. **Rooms:** 7 bedrooms, all en suite and centrally heated, with bathroom or luxurious shower, colour TV, direct-dial telephone and tea/coffee making facilities. **Credit cards:** Visa, Access. **Other points:** licensed, Sunday lunch, residents' lounge, street parking.
**Directions:** situated in the town centre at the end of the High Street.
ROBERT SELBIE & JULIAN ALEXANDER-WORSTER, tel (0728) 453932, fax (0728) 453 6680.

## ALFRISTON, East Sussex Map 5

### DRUSILLAS PARK

*The attractive Toucan's thatched restaurant forms part of a leisure park which includes a zoo – known as the best small zoo in the south. Set in large well kept grounds, it was established in 1924 and is still a family run business. Toucans was Egon Ronay's Family Restaurant of the Year 1991. Toy boxes & Sunday lunchtime entertainment.*
*FOOD up to £15*
**Hours:** lunch 12noon – 6pm; closed evenings. **Cuisine:** international:- Family menu in 'Toucans' Restaurant. Pub food in 'Inn at the Zoo'. **Credit cards:** Visa, Access.
**Other points:** licensed, Sunday lunch, children catered for – please check for age limits, zoo, playland. **Directions:** off the A27 between Lewes and Polegate.
MR M ANN, tel (0323) 870656, fax (0323) 870846.

### LITLINGTON GARDENS, Litlington

*Set in a charming, unspoilt corner of Sussex, the Victorian Gardens and traditional cream teas were established over 150 years ago. Relax and enjoy good food surrounded by a colourful array of plants and flowers. At the weekend the Gourmet Lunches prepared by Chef Christophe Buey and his team are quite outstanding (Reservations Only). A welcoming establishment.*
*FOOD up to £15*
**Hours:** meals all day 11am – 5:30pm; closed November – March. **Cuisine:** English / French:- Morning coffee. Licensed, Garden lunches, snacks, light & gourmet lunches. Traditional English Cream Teas with home-made cakes, and light refreshments. **Other points:** licensed, open-air dining, Sunday lunch, no-smoking area, children catered for – please check for age limits, bank holidays, afternoon tea, pets allowed. **Directions:** between Alfriston & Seaford. 5 minutes drive from Alfriston.
CHRISTOPHE BUEY, tel (0323) 870222.

## ASHFORD, Kent Map 5

### THE ROYAL STANDARD, Ashford Road, Bethersden

*A popular freehouse with a warm and friendly atmosphere offering a very good selection of meals at reasonable prices. Dine in the restaurant or the bar, beside the warmth of log fires in winter or in the large garden during summer, a visit at anytime of the year is memorable.*
*FOOD up to £15*

Hours: open bank holidays November; lunch 12noon –
2pm; dinner 7pm – 9:30pm. **Cuisine:** English:-
Traditional featuring home-made pies. **Credit cards:**
Visa. **Other points:** licensed, open-air dining, Sunday
lunch, playland, garden. **Directions:** on A28 between
Ashford and Tenterden.
ROGER HAMBERG, tel (0233) 820280.

## BALDOCK, Hertfordshire Map 6

### THE JESTER HOTEL, 116 Station Road, Odsey
*Set in pleasant gardens, the Jester Hotel offers*
*comfortable accommodation and well presented meals at*
*value for money prices. Popular with locals, the hotel*
*enjoys a relaxed atmosphere.*
ACCOMMODATION £21–£30
FOOD up to £15
Hours: breakfast 7am – 10am; bar meals 11:30am –
2:30pm; lunch 12noon – 3pm; bar meals 6:30pm –
10pm; dinner 7pm – 10pm. **Cuisine:** English:- Serving
bar snacks, table d'hote and full a la carte menu. Dishes
may include Shelley salad, poached lemon sole with
lobster sauce & choice of sweets. **Rooms:** 14 bedrooms
5 singles ensuite, 1 twin ensuite, 8 doubles ensuite.
**Credit cards:** Visa, Access, AmEx. **Other points:**
licensed, open-air dining, Sunday lunch, no-smoking
area, children catered for – please check for age limits.
**Directions:** between Royston & Baldock. Turn off
Steeple Morden Ashwell St.
MR MILDENHALL-CLARKE, tel (046274) 2011.

## BATTLE, East Sussex Map 5

### BURNT WOOD HOUSE HOTEL, Powdermill Lane
*An Edwardian country house set in 18 acres of lawns,*
*gardens and woodland. Ideal location for exploring this*
*historic area. Excellent French & English Cuisine, with*
*good selection of wines. Warm and relaxing atmosphere,*
*in heart of tranquil Sussex countryside.*
ACCOMMODATION £31–£40
FOOD £15–£20
Hours: breakfast 7:30am – 9:30am; lunch 12noon –
2pm (last orders); dinner 7pm – 9:30pm (last orders);
restaurant closed Sunday evening. **Cuisine:** English /
French:- A la carte, table d'hote and bar meals. **Rooms:**
10 bedrooms 2 singles ensuite, 1 twin ensuite, 7 doubles
ensuite. **Credit cards:** Visa, Access, Diners, AmEx.
**Other points:** parking, children catered for – please
check for age limits, swimming pool, tennis, croquet,
pets, residents' lounge, vegetarian meals, garden dining.
**Directions:** turn right onto B2095 Catsfield Road – 1.5
miles on left. Between Battle and Catsfield.
MR M HOGGARTH, tel (0424) 775151.

### POWDERMILLS HOTEL, Powdermill Lane
*Set in 150 acres of park-like grounds and with fishing*
*lakes and woodlands, this hotel is ideal for those*
*wanting to return to nature. The Orangery Restaurant*

*serves imaginative and exciting meals and the Hotel*
*offers accommodation of a very high standard. Highly*
*recommended.*
ACCOMMODATION £31–£40
FOOD £21–£25 🍽 ★
Hours: breakfast 7:30am – 9:30am; lunch 12noon –
2pm; dinner 7pm – 9pm. **Cuisine:** English:- Full a la
carte menu, table d'hote and bar snacks. Vegetarian
menu. **Rooms:** 17 bedrooms all with telephone, TV: 6
twins ensuite, 11 doubles ensuite. **Credit cards:** Visa,
Access, AmEx. **Other points:** licensed, open-air dining,
Sunday lunch, children catered for – please check for
age limits, morning & afternoon tea, swimming pool,
golf nearby, riding, dogs allowed, disabled access,
vegetarian meals, residents' lounge, residents' bar.
**Directions:** through Battle toward Hastings, first right
turn. Opposite railway station.
D & J COWPLAND CHEF – PAUL WEBBE, tel (0424)
775511, fax (0424) 774540.

### THE SQUIRREL INN, North Trade Rd
*A freehouse with its own restaurant serving traditional*
*fayre, including bar snacks. Close for Battle Abbey, Bodiam*
*Castle, Driscilla's Zoo and many other attractions.*
FOOD up to £15
Hours: lunch 12noon – 2:30pm; dinner – Mon-Sat 6pm
– 9:30pm; dinner – Sunday 7pm – 9:30pm; closed
Sunday night winter. **Cuisine:** English. **Credit cards:**
Visa, Access, AmEx. **Other points:** parking, children
catered for – please check for age limits, Sunday lunch,
open bank holidays, no-smoking area, disabled access,
pets allowed, vegetarian meals, open-air dining,
licensed. **Directions:** located on A271, just before
approaching A2100 and Battle.
BOB & KATH BRITT, tel (0424) 772717.

## BAYNARDS, West Sussex Map 4

### THURLOW ARMS, Nr Rudgwick
*This building stands alongside the newly opened Downs*
*Link Bridlepath. The Thurlow Arms serves a wide range*
*of traditional beers and home cooked food.*
ACCOMMODATION under £20
FOOD up to £15
Hours: lunch 12noon – 2:20pm; dinner 6pm – 10:30pm.
**Cuisine:** English:- Seafood, grills , steaks and a large
variety of bar snacks and home cooked sauces. **Rooms:**
2 bedrooms 2 twins ensuite. **Credit cards:** Visa, Access.
**Other points:** open-air dining, Sunday lunch, children
catered for – please check for age limits, garden.
**Directions:** situated off A281 between Guildford and
Horsham, at Baynards disused railway station.
RICHARD & MAXINE CHISHOLM, tel (0403) 822459.

## BEACONSFIELD, Buckinghamshire Map 6

### THE ROYAL STANDARD OF ENGLAND, Forty Green
*Famous old English pub boasting a beautiful country*
*atmosphere, in character with its surroundings. Reputed*

to be one of the oldest public houses in England. English
and continental draught beers.

**FOOD** up to £15 ☞

**Hours:** lunch 11am – 3pm; dinner 5:30pm – 11pm.
**Other points:** licensed, open-air dining, Sunday lunch,
children catered for – please check for age limits, pets
allowed. **Directions:** between Beaconsfield and Forty
Green.

MR P W ELDRIDGE, tel (0494) 673382.

---

## BECCLES, Suffolk Map 9

### QUIGGINS RESTAURANT, 2 High Street, Wrentham

*An elegant, yet comfortable and relaxing, beamed
restaurant, decorated with plants, family pictures and
knick-knacks to create a homely atmosphere. The food is
well-cooked and presented. A choice of main course may
include Filet au Fromage, Huntsman's (Game) Pie, and
Salmon Royale, amongst others. Warm and courteous
service. Wide range of wines with emphasis on New
World varieties. Quiggins adhere to the BTA's recently
introduced "Restaurant Customers Charter".*

**FOOD** £15–£20 CLUB ★

**Hours:** lunch 11:30am – 2pm; dinner 7pm – 10pm;
closed Sunday evening – Monday. **Cuisine:** English /
international:- English and international cuisine, all
made from fresh ingredients, including English
puddings. Established reputation for quality seafood.
**Credit cards:** Visa, Access. **Other points:** licensed,
open-air dining, Sunday lunch, no-smoking area,
children catered for – please check for age limits, close
to beach. **Directions:** situated on crossroads in centre of
Wrentham. On the A12.

DUDLEY & JILL MCNALLY, tel (050275) 397.

---

## BEDFORD, Bedfordshire Map 6

### EDWARDIAN HOUSE HOTEL, Shakespeare Road

*On a beautiful tree lined road in the Poets area of
Bedford, just a few minutes from the town centre, this
charming, family run hotel offers modern facilities,
excellent service and a friendly atmosphere. The hotel is
very tastefully decorated and the accommodation is of a
high standard. Enjoy good, freshly prepared food in the
restaurant and relax in the hotel's bar and lounge.*

**ACCOMMODATION** £21–£30

**FOOD** up to £15

**Hours:** breakfast 7:30am – 9am; bar meals 6:30pm –
8:45pm. **Cuisine:** English. **Rooms:** 19 bedrooms all with
tea making facilities, telephone, TV: 11 singles ensuite,
2 twins ensuite, 5 doubles ensuite, 1 family room
ensuite. **Credit cards:** Visa, Access, AmEx. **Other
points:** children catered for – please check for age
limits, conferences, vegetarian meals. **Directions:**
centrally located in Bedford, a few minutes from railway
station.

JOHN & ROSSLYN ALLEN, GRAHAM & LYNDSEY
WOOD, tel (0234) 211156.

---

### THE KNIFE & CLEAVER, The Grove, Houghton Conquest

*In a prominent position opposite the medieval church in
Houghton Conquest. The restaurant is an airy Victorian-
style conservatory and the innovative menu which
changes monthly incorporates seasonal specialities
made from the finest fresh produce. Fresh shellfish,
lobster and vegetarian dishes. List of 100 well chosen
wines. Flowery terrace. Easy reach of Woburn Abbey
and Luton Airport.*

**ACCOMMODATION** £21–£30

**FOOD** £15–£20 ♟ ☞ ★

**Hours:** breakfast – weekdays 7:30am; breakfast –
weekends 8:30am; lunch 12noon – 2:30pm; bar meals
12noon – 2:30pm; dinner 7pm – 10pm; bar meals 7pm –
10pm. **Cuisine:** English / French:- Modern English and
French cuisine. A speciality is the 'Knife & Cleaver
Hors d'Oeuvre', almost a meal in itself. **Rooms:** 9
bedrooms all with tea making facilities, radio, TV: 4
doubles ensuite, 5 twins ensuite. **Credit cards:** Visa,
Access, Diners, AmEx. **Other points:** licensed, Sunday
lunch, children catered for – please check for age limits,
pets allowed, bank holidays, functions. **Directions:**
between A6 and B530, 5m south of Bedford and 2m
north of Ampthill.

DAVID & PAULINE LOOM, tel (0234) 740387, fax
(0234) 740900.

---

### THE LAWS HOTEL, High Street, Turvey

*Situated in the pleasant village of Turvey, this hotel
offers attractive and comfortable accommodation. The
restaurant serves well presented meals and provides
excellent service in a light and relaxed atmosphere.
Close to Woburn Abbey and Whipsnade Park Zoo.*

**ACCOMMODATION** £21–£30

**FOOD** £15–£20

**Hours:** breakfast 7am – 8:30am; lunch 12noon – 2pm;
dinner 7pm – 9:45pm. **Cuisine:** English / seafood:- A
wide selection of dishes on the a la carte menu plus a
table D'Hote menu featuring specials; Fillet Steak &
Lobster Tail, Queen Scallops, Dover Sole. **Rooms:** 19
bedrooms all with tea making facilities, telephone, radio,
TV: 2 singles ensuite, 17 doubles ensuite. **Credit cards:**
Visa, Access, AmEx. **Other points:** licensed, open-air
dining, Sunday lunch, children catered for – please
check for age limits, afternoon tea, pets allowed,
residents' lounge, residents' bar. **Directions:** follow A6,
take exit for A428 to Bedford. Continue to Turvey.

JEROME & FRANCESCA MACK, tel (0234) 881213,
fax (0234) 888864.

---

### THREE CRANES, High Street, Turvey

*Set in the centre of the attractive village of Turvey next
to the ancient Turvey church, the Three Cranes offers
very good food, a welcoming atmosphere and excellent
service. All meals are well cooked and presented, served
by friendly and efficient staff. The Three Cranes is a very
popular pub and well worth a visit.*

**ACCOMMODATION** under £20

**FOOD** up to £15 ☞

**Hours:** breakfast 7:30am – 9:30am; bar meals 12noon – 2pm; bar meals – Sun-Wed 6:30pm – 9:30pm; bar meals – Thur-Sat 6:30pm – 10pm. **Cuisine:** English:- Wide choice of dishes such as Crane's Mixed Grill, salads, steaks. Blackboard specials including fresh fish dishes, especially at the weekend. **Rooms:** 5 bedrooms 2 singles ensuite, 3 doubles ensuite. **Credit cards:** Visa, Access. **Other points:** licensed, open-air dining, Sunday lunch, beer garden, parking. **Directions:** on A428 midway between Bedford and Northampton.
DAVID & SANDRA ALEXANDER, tel (0234) 881305.

---

## BEXHILL-ON-SEA, East Sussex Map 5

### THE NORTHERN HOTEL, 72–78 Sea Road
*Adjacent to the seafront, the hotel is just one minute's walk from the sea. Comfortable accommodation which has been decorated and furnished to a high standard. The Georgian style restaurant serves well prepared and well presented food at very good value for money. Quiet and relaxing atmosphere, as is the tradition of a family run hotel.*
*ACCOMMODATION £31–£40*
*FOOD up to £15*
**Hours:** breakfast 8am – 9:30am; lunch 12noon – 2pm; dinner 6pm – 8pm. **Cuisine:** English:- varied high quality selection on Table D'Hote, A La Carte and Bar Snack Menu. Vegetarians catered for. **Rooms:** 21 bedrooms 6 singles ensuite, 7 twins ensuite, 7 doubles ensuite, 1 family room ensuite. **Credit cards:** Visa, Access, AmEx. **Other points:** licensed, children catered for – please check for age limits, afternoon tea, pets allowed. **Directions:** off the A259.
THE SIMS FAMILY, tel (0424) 212836, fax (0424) 213036.

---

## BIGGLESWADE, Bedfordshire Map 6

### LA CACHETTE, 61 Hitchin Street
*A welcoming restaurant offering an imaginative menu and excellently cooked, fresh food. A separate menu caters for vegetarian guests and provides an equally good choice and high standard of cuisine. With a warm atmosphere and excellent service, La Cachette is definitely worth a visit.*
*FOOD £15–£20* ♀ ⌒ ★
**Hours:** dinner 7pm – 10pm; closed Sunday – Monday. **Cuisine:** French / continental:- Imaginative cuisine which also features speciality dishes from around the world. Dishes may include Tiger Prawn Mille Feuille with Brandy Sauce, Pork Fillet stuffed with apricots, Kleftico. Extensive vegetarian choice. **Credit cards:** Visa, Access, AmEx. **Other points:** licensed, children catered for – please check for age limits, street parking. **Directions:** A1M follow signs to town centre. 2 minutes walk from Market Square.
RICHARD & MARGARET POOL, tel (0767) 313508.

---

## BILDESTON, Suffolk Map 9

### THE CROWN HOTEL, 104 High Street
*A 15th Century coaching inn in the heart of the Suffolk countryside. Along with excellent food and*
*accommodation, The Crown Hotel offers guests the chance to spot one of its several ghosts!*
*ACCOMMODATION £21–£30*
*FOOD up to £15* ⌒
**Hours:** breakfast 7:30am – 10am; lunch – except Sunday 12noon – 2pm; lunch – Sunday 12:30pm – 2:30pm; dinner 7pm – 9:30pm. **Cuisine:** English:- Traditional English. Victorian Diable mixed meats in a spicy sauce is a speciality. **Rooms:** 15 bedrooms all with TV: 1 single ensuite, 2 twins, 3 twins ensuite, 8 doubles ensuite, 1 triple. **Credit cards:** Visa, Access. **Other points:** licensed, open-air dining, Sunday lunch, children catered for – please check for age limits, garden, afternoon tea, residents' bar, baby-listening device, baby sitting. **Directions:** in the village on the B1115.
MR HENDERSON, tel (0449) 740510, fax (0449) 740224.

---

## BILLERICAY, Essex Map 8

### DUKE OF YORK, Southend Road, South Green
*A pub and restaurant offering good value meals and efficient, friendly service. The Duke of York was a beer house in 1868 and the restaurant has since been sympathetically added to complement the original building. Customers will find a warm, cosy atmosphere in which to enjoy their meal and the pub comes complete with its own ghost in residence, 'Swanee'.*
*FOOD £21–£25* ♀
**Hours:** lunch 12noon – 2pm; dinner 7pm – 10pm. **Cuisine:** French / English:- Choice of menus. Large choice of bar snacks. Hot & cold bar snacks Sunday lunchtime. Traditional Sunday roast £4.25. **Credit cards:** Visa, Access, Diners, AmEx. **Other points:** licensed, children catered for – please check for age limits. **Directions:** A129 Billericay – Wickford road. 1 mile from Billericay High Street.
MRS EDNA WHITE, tel (0277) 651403.

---

## BIRCHINGTON, Kent Map 5

### SMUGGLERS RESTAURANT, 212 Canterbury Road
*A comfortable, welcoming restaurant which offers a very extensive choice of well-cooked food. The cuisine is predominantly French with dishes ranging from Salmon with a prawn and dill sauce to Fillet steak cooked in Brandy and French mustard. All dishes are made from fresh ingredients and attractively presented. The quality of the food is complemented by excellent service.*
*FOOD £15–£20* ⌒
**Hours:** lunch 12noon – 2pm; dinner 7pm – 10pm; closed Monday lunch. **Cuisine:** French / English:- Table d'hote menus and extensive a la carte menu. Duckling aux Cerises, Chateaubriand, fish dishes. **Credit cards:** Visa, Access, Diners, AmEx. **Other points:** licensed, open-air dining, Sunday lunch, children catered for –

please check for age limits, functions. **Directions:** on road to Margate from Thanet Way, just past Birchington roundabout.
BOB & SUE SHERMAN, tel (0843) 41185.

# BISHOPS STORTFORD, Hertfordshire
Map 6

## PEARSE HOUSE, Parsonage Lane
*Pearse House is an established Management Training and Conference Centre, offering residential conference facilities of the highest standard. It is easily accessible by road rail and air, and just 1 hour from London. All rooms are equipped with the most modern business facilities. The attractive modern bedrooms offer comfortable accommodation and leisure facilities are also available on-site and close by.*
ACCOMMODATION £21–£30
FOOD up to £15
**Hours:** breakfast 7am – 9am; lunch 12noon – 2pm; dinner 7pm – 9pm; bar snacks 7pm – 10:30pm. **Cuisine:** British. **Credit cards:** Visa, Access, AmEx. **Other points:** parking, children catered for – please check for age limits, disabled access, residents' lounge, vegetarian meals, conferences. **Directions:** situated in Parsonage Lane off Dunmow Road (B1250) which leads from town centre to M11. From motorway (M11) 2 minutes drive following signs to Bishop's Stortford; or follow signs from by-pass or Stansted Road (B1184). 10 minutes from Stansted Airport.
VALERIE MCGREGOR, tel (0279) 757400, fax (0279) 506591.

# BLETCHINGLEY, Surrey Map 4

## WILLIAM IV, Little Common Lane
*A traditional unspoilt British village pub with compact bars and an old English garden. The pub offers an extensive a la carte and bar meals menu with dishes ranging from salmon en croute to home-made steak and kidney pie. Friendly, efficient service complements the warm, bustling atmosphere of the pub. Ideally situated for walks over the North Downs and Tillgates Gardens.*
FOOD up to £15
**Hours:** bar 11am – 3pm; lunch 12noon – 2pm; bar 6pm – 11pm; dinner 7pm – 9:15pm. **Cuisine:** English / international:- Extensive menu including grills, home-made pies, curries, pizzas, fish dishes. Daily specials and bar meals. Dining room. **Credit cards:** Visa, Access. **Other points:** licensed, open-air dining, children catered for – please check for age limits, beer garden, pets allowed. **Directions:** Little Common Lane is located at top of Bletchingley High St (A25). Signposted to Merstham.
BRIAN & SANDRA STRANGE, tel (0883) 743278.

# BOGNOR REGIS, West Sussex Map 4

## THE ROYAL HOTEL, The Esplanade
*A Victorian Hotel situated only yards from the sea with unimpeded views from the restaurant, bars and coffee shop.*
ACCOMMODATION £21–£30
FOOD £15–£20 CLUB
**Hours:** breakfast 7:30am – 9:30am; bar meals 11:30am – 10:30am; lunch 12noon – 2:30pm; dinner 6pm – 10:30pm. **Cuisine:** English:- Prawns, pasta, lobster & continental. **Rooms:** 40 bedrooms, all en suite. **Credit cards:** Visa, Access, Diners, AmEx. **Other points:** licensed, Sunday lunch, children catered for – please check for age limits, coach/prior arr. **Directions:** Bognor Regis seafront, 50yds west of the pier.
DAVID M COOMBS, tel (0243) 864665, (0243) 864666.

# BOUGHTON MONCHELSEA, Kent
Map 5

## TANYARD, Wierton Hill, Nr Maidstone
*Tanyard is a small medieval country house hotel situated in the heart of rural Kent, with the welcoming feel of a private Country Home, rather than a hotel. Full of character, the accommodation and reception rooms are of a very high standard. The 4 course menu is imaginative and well cooked using fresh local ingredients. Les Routiers Newcomer of the Year 1991.*
ACCOMMODATION £41–£50
FOOD £21–£25 ☜
**Hours:** breakfast – weekdays 7:30am – 9:30am; breakfast – weekends 8:15am – 9:30am; closed Christmas day – New Years day. **Cuisine:** English:- English and French cuisine, the daily menu may include breast of duck in a bigerard sauce, rack of lamb with a tomato and ginger coulis or supreme of chicken with sesame seeds in a lime cream and mango sauce. Enquire for meal times. **Rooms:** 6 bedrooms all with tea making facilities, telephone, radio, TV: 1 suite, 1 single ensuite, 2 twins ensuite, 2 doubles ensuite. **Credit cards:** Visa, Access, Diners, AmEx. **Other points:** children catered for – please check for age limits, vegetarian meals. **Directions:** off B2163 between Langley & Linton.
JAN DAVIES, tel (0622) 744705, fax (0622) 741998.

# BRANCASTER STAITHE, Norfolk Map 9

## THE JOLLY SAILORS, Brancaster Staithe
*Records of The Jolly Sailors date back to 1789 – a popular haunt with locals where beer is still drawn by hand pumps. It is ideally situated for good beaches, sailing, bird reserves and many places of interest, including Sandringham House and Halkham Hall. Award winning wine list.*
FOOD up to £15 ♟ ★
**Hours:** closed Christmas day; dinner 7pm – 9pm; lunch 12noon – 2pm; meals all day July – August. **Cuisine:** English:- Staithe mussels, lasagne, game casserole. All food prepared and cooked on the premises. Bar food and restaurant available. **Rooms:** bed and breakfast can be arranged in local houses. **Credit cards:** Visa, Access. **Other points:** licensed, open-air dining, Sunday lunch, pets allowed, children catered for – please check for age

limits, log fire, no music, playland, tennis. **Directions:** on A149 coast road, halfway between Hunstanton & Wells-Next-The-Sea.
ALISTER BORTHWICK, tel (0485) 210314, fax (0485) 210158.

## BRENTWOOD, Essex Map 8

### THE BLACK HORSE, Ongar Road, Pilgrims Hatch

*Dating back to the 14th century, this delightful converted farmhouse retains its rustic charm and atmosphere. Warm and friendly staff make guests welcome. Substantial, well prepared meals are complemented by a good range of beers.*
FOOD up to £15
**Hours:** meals all day 11am – 11pm; last orders 10pm.
**Cuisine:** English:- Traditional English, eg. steak & kidney pie, mixed grills, fresh fish, steaks. **Credit cards:** Visa, Access. **Other points:** children catered for – please check for age limits, licensed, garden, parking, disabled access. **Directions:** in village of Pilgrims Hatch on A128, 4 miles from Brentwood.
DAVID AND JAYNE TAYLOR, tel (0277) 372337.

## BRIGHTON, East Sussex Map 5

### DONATELLO RESTAURANT, 3 Brighton Place, The Lanes

*A popular and well run Italian restaurant specialising in pasta dishes, pizzas and Italian ice cream. The menu offers an extensive choice of dishes at good value for money. A lively restaurant with friendly service and a warm, relaxed atmosphere.*
FOOD up to £15
**Hours:** meals all day 11:30am – 11:30pm. **Cuisine:** Italian:- Extensive menu of Italian dishes including pasta, pizzas, fish and meat dishes. Italian ice cream. **Credit cards:** Visa, Access, AmEx, Diners, Switch. **Other points:** licensed, Sunday lunch, children catered for – please check for age limits. **Directions:** in centre of Brighton's Lanes.
MR PIETRO ADDIS, tel (0273) 775477, fax (0273) 677659.

### ENGLISH'S OYSTER BAR & SEAFOOD RESTAURANT, 29/31 East Street

*The restaurant is housed in three fishermen's cottages on the edge of Brighton's historic Lanes. For more than 200 years, English's Oyster Bar has been a family business, selling oysters and fish without a break in tradition. Enjoy the pleasures of dining 'al fresco' on our outside terrace.*
FOOD up to £15
**Hours:** meals all day 12noon – 10:15pm; meals all day – Sunday 12:30pm – 9:30pm; closed Boxing day; closed Christmas eve; closed Christmas day; closed New Years day. **Cuisine:** seafood:- Seafood, including oysters, Dover sole, plaice, monkfish, mussels, fresh crab and lobsters. Special two-course menu for £5.95. Daily

specialities. **Credit cards:** Visa, Access, Diners, AmEx. **Other points:** Sunday lunch, no-smoking area, children catered for – please check for age limits, bank holidays. **Directions:** in the heart of Brighton Lanes, 2 minutes' walk from Royal Pavilion.
MRS P M LEIGH-JONES, tel (0273) 327980, (0273) 325661.

### KEMPTON HOUSE HOTEL, 33/34 Marine Parade

*A friendly, family run hotel situated opposite the beach and famous Palace Pier and within minutes of all amenities. Mr & Mrs Swaine assure a warm welcome and real 'home from home' atmosphere. With a high standard of accommodation, a patio overlooking the seafront, residential bar and comfortable surroundings, an enjoyable stay is guaranteed.*
ACCOMMODATION £21–£30 ★
**Hours:** breakfast 8:30am – 9am; dinner 6pm. **Cuisine:** English. **Rooms:** 12 bedrooms all with tea making facilities, telephone, radio, TV: 3 family rooms ensuite, 2 twins ensuite, 7 doubles ensuite. **Credit cards:** Visa, Access, Diners, AmEx. **Other points:** children catered for – please check for age limits, pets allowed, residents' lounge, garden, vegetarian meals, street parking, residents' bar. **Directions:** A23 London Road until Palace Pier roundabout. Left onto A259. 200yds on left.
PHILIP & VALERIE SWAINE, tel (0273) 570248, fax (0273) 570248.

### THE LATIN IN THE LANE, 10/11 Kings Road

*A popular Italian restaurant, decorated in cool 1930's Italian designs with tiled floor, marble tables and peach and white colours. A varied menu is complemented by a good selection of wines. Situated just off the seafront close to the Palace Pier.*
FOOD £15–£20
**Hours:** lunch 12noon – 2:15pm; dinner 6pm – 11pm. **Cuisine:** Italian:- Very extensive menu offering an excellent choice of starters, pasta, meat and fish dishes. **Credit cards:** Visa, Access, Diners, AmEx. **Other points:** licensed, Sunday lunch, children catered for – please check for age limits, disabled access. **Directions:** just off the seafront, behind the Queen's Hotel.
MR CAPPAI, tel (0273) 328672, fax (0273) 321690.

### LE GRANDOUSIER RESTAURANT, 15 Western Street

*A small restaurant serving authentic French cuisine in the best French tradition. The 6-course set menu is beautifully presented by friendly staff. Les Routiers Symbol of Excellence Award winner 1992 for consistently providing outstanding quality and value.*
FOOD £15–£20 ☜
**Hours:** lunch 12:30pm – 2:30pm; dinner 7:30pm – 10:15pm; closed Sunday. **Cuisine:** French:- Panier de crudites, panier de saucissons, terrine de foie de volaille poivre vert. **Credit cards:** Visa, Access, AmEx. **Other**

points: children catered for – please check for age limits. **Directions:** in Brighton, at the bottom of Norfolk Square.
MR LEWIS HARRIS, tel (0273) 772005.

## MELFORD HALL HOTEL, 41 Marine Parade

*A seafront hotel on a corner position of a garden square and close to all main amenities. Melford Hall also overlooks the beach. The accommodation is en suite and ground floor rooms and four poster bedrooms are available. Under the personal supervision of the resident proprietors.*

ACCOMMODATION £21–£30 ★
**Hours:** breakfast 8am – 9am. **Cuisine:** breakfast.
**Rooms:** 25 bedrooms all with tea making facilities, radio, TV: 2 singles ensuite, 8 twins ensuite, 11 doubles ensuite, 3 triples ensuite, 1 quad ensuite. **Credit cards:** Visa, Access, Diners, AmEx. **Other points:** children catered for – please check for age limits, residents' lounge. **Directions:** A259 Newhaven to Brighton. A259 Marine Parade, close to Palace Pier.
IAN DIXON, tel (0273) 681435, fax (0273) 624186.

## NEW STEINE HOTEL, 12a New Steine

*A Grade II listed building in a Regency square, within easy walking distance of the town centre, conference centre and the famous Royal Pavilion. Pleasantly decorated and comfortably furnished, an enjoyable stay is assured.*

ACCOMMODATION under £20
**Hours:** breakfast 8am – 9am. **Cuisine:** breakfast.
**Rooms:** 11 bedrooms all with tea making facilities, TV: 3 singles, 5 doubles ensuite, 1 twin, 2 family rooms ensuite. **Other points:** children catered for – please check for age limits, pets allowed, central heating, residents' lounge, street parking. **Directions:** in a Regency square just off the main promenade.
MESSRS SHAW & MILLS, tel (0273) 681546.

## PASKINS HOTEL, 19 Charlotte Street

*Paskins Hotel is part of an elegant Georgian terrace in one of Brighton's conservation areas. Centrally located, the hotel is just 2 minutes from the beach and 5 minutes from the town and conference centres. Friendly and efficient staff ensure a warm welcome and a pleasant stay and the accommodation is of a very high standard. Meals include organic produce. Highly recommended.*

ACCOMMODATION £21–£30
FOOD up to £15 ★
**Hours:** breakfast 8am – 9am; dinner 6pm – 8:30pm.
**Cuisine:** English. **Rooms:** 19 bedrooms all with tea making facilities, telephone, TV: 1 single, 4 singles ensuite, 1 twin, 2 twins ensuite, 1 double, 9 doubles ensuite, 1 family room ensuite. **Credit cards:** Visa, Access. **Other points:** pets allowed, vegetarian meals. **Directions:** follow the A23 to Brighton Centre. Turn left at sea-front.
SUE PASKINS, tel (0273) 601203, fax (0273) 621973.

## PINOCCHIO, 22 New Road

*A traditional Italian meal at a reasonable price in pleasant, unpretentious and relaxed surroundings. This is a very popular restaurant with travellers and locals alike.*

FOOD up to £15
**Hours:** lunch – weekdays 12noon – 2:30pm; meals all day – weekends 12noon – 11:30pm; dinner – weekdays 5pm – 11:30pm. **Cuisine:** Italian / continental:- Pizza and pasta. Selection of chicken, veal, and fish dishes. **Credit cards:** Visa, Access, Diners, AmEx. **Other points:** Sunday lunch, children catered for – please check for age limits. **Directions:** easily located opposite the Pavilion Theatre.
MR PIETRO ADDIS, tel (0273) 677676, fax (0273) 677659.

## REGENCY RESTAURANT, 131 Kings Road

*A friendly, relaxed restaurant with welcoming staff where good food can be enjoyed throughout the day. The restaurant specialises in locally caught fresh fish with a wide choice of other dishes including roasts, grills and steaks. All food is well-cooked and offers good value for money. In fine weather tables are available outside on the seafront.*

FOOD up to £15 CLUB
**Hours:** meals all day 10am – 11pm; closed Christmas 23/12 – 10/01. **Cuisine:** seafood / English:- A wide range of meals with locally caught fresh fish a speciality. **Credit cards:** Visa, Access, Diners. **Other points:** licensed, Sunday lunch, children catered for – please check for age limits, morning tea, afternoon tea, parking. **Directions:** A259. Opposite West Pier, Brighton seafront.
ROVERTOS & EMILIO SAVVIDES, tel (0273) 325014.

## TROUVILLE HOTEL, 11 New Steine

*A Regency grade II listed Townhouse tastefully restored and furnished, enhanced with window boxes, conveniently situated in a seafront square. The town centre, marina, Pavilion, lanes and conference centre are all within easy walking distance.*

ACCOMMODATION under £20 ★
**Hours:** breakfast – weekdays 8:15am – 9am; breakfast – weekends 8:45am – 9:15am. **Cuisine:** breakfast.
**Rooms:** 9 bedrooms all with tea making facilities, TV: 2 singles, 1 double, 3 doubles ensuite, 1 twin, 1 twin ensuite, 1 family room ensuite. **Credit cards:** Visa, Access, AmEx. **Other points:** central heating, children catered for – please check for age limits, residents' lounge. **Directions:** just off the seafront, 300 yd east of Palace Pier off A259.
MR & MRS J P HANSELL, tel (0273) 697384.

# BRIGHTON & HOVE, East Sussex Map 5

## COSMOPOLITAN HOTEL, 31 New Steine, Marine Parade

*Overlooking the beach and Palace Pier, the Cosmopolitan Hotel is a friendly, comfortable place to stay and popular with holiday-makers and business*

*visitors alike. There is a cosy residential licensed bar
and the hotel is very central for shopping,
entertainments and conference centres.*
ACCOMMODATION £21–£30 ★
**Hours:** breakfast 8am – 9am. **Cuisine:** breakfast.
**Rooms:** 24 bedrooms all with tea making facilities,
telephone, radio, TV: 4 singles, 6 singles ensuite, 3
twins, 1 twin ensuite, 1 double, 9 family rooms ensuite.
**Credit cards:** Visa, Access, Diners, AmEx. **Other
points:** children catered for – please check for age
limits, TV lounge, residents' bar. **Directions:** A23 to
Brighton seafront, turn left onto A259 Marine Parade –
quarter mile.
C PAPANICHOLA, tel (0273) 682461.

### KIMBERLEY HOTEL, *17 Atlingworth Street*

*A friendly, family hotel with clean, comfortable rooms, a
resident's lounge and bar facilities. Centrally situated,
being only 2 minutes from the seafront, with the Royal
Pavilion, Palace Pier and Marina nearby.*
ACCOMMODATION under £20
**Hours:** breakfast – weekdays 8am – 9am; breakfast –
weekends 8:30am – 9:30am. **Cuisine:** breakfast.
**Rooms:** 16 bedrooms all with tea making facilities, TV:
3 singles, 2 doubles ensuite, 2 doubles, 3 twins ensuite, 3
twins, 3 family rooms ensuite. **Credit cards:** Visa,
Access, Diners, AmEx. **Other points:** children catered
for – please check for age limits, bank holidays,
residents' lounge. **Directions:** situated between Brighton
Marina and Palace Pier off the A259.
MRS R LISS & MRS M ROLAND, tel (0273) 603504,
fax (0273) 685373.

### ST CATHERINES LODGE HOTEL, *Seafront, Kingsway*

*A 150 year old Victorian gabled hotel, centrally situated
on the seafront, with full accommodation facilities. Good
food at value for money prices is served by well trained
attentive staff in attractive surroundings. Located nearby
is the King Alfred Leisure Centre with swimming pools,
waterslides and ten-pin bowling.*
ACCOMMODATION £31–£40
FOOD up to £15 CLUB ★
**Hours:** breakfast 7:45am – 9:30am; lunch 12:30pm –
2pm; dinner 7pm – 9pm. **Cuisine:** English:- Extensive a
la carte. Dishes include roast carved at table. **Rooms:**
49 bedrooms all with telephone, TV: 8 singles ensuite, 2
singles, 1 twin, 6 doubles, 4 family rooms ensuite,
11 twins ensuite, 15 doubles ensuite, 2 suites.
**Credit cards:** Visa, Access, Diners, AmEx.
**Other points:** Sunday lunch, children catered for –
please check for age limits, garden, games room,
residents' lounge, afternoon tea, conferences,
functions, residents' bar, vegetarian meals, parking,
foreign exchange. **Directions:** hotel is on A259 coast
road, on the seafront in the centre of Hove. Near King
Alfred Sports centre.
JOHN HOULTON, tel (0273) 778181, fax (0273)
774949.

## BRISTON, Norfolk Map 9

### THE JOHN H STRACEY, *West End, Nr Melton Constable*

*Professional and friendly staff take special care to make
guests feel at home. Mr Fox is at present offering Bargain
Breaks. With the good food and relaxing surroundings, this
promises to be a popular bargain indeed.*
ACCOMMODATION under £20
FOOD up to £15
**Hours:** lunch 12noon – 2:15pm; bar meals 12noon –
2:15pm; dinner 7pm – 9:30pm; bar meals 7pm – 10pm.
**Cuisine:** international:- Comprehensive menu including
Salmon a la Stracey (fresh salmon steaks, poached in
white wine, with prawns and parsley). **Rooms:** 3
bedrooms all with TV: 1 double, 1 twin, 1 double
ensuite. **Credit cards:** Access, AmEx. **Other points:**
licensed, Sunday lunch, children catered for – please
check for age limits, vegetarian meals, afternoon tea.
**Directions:** on B1354 close to Melton Constable and en
route to Aylsham and Fakenham.
MR & MRS R E FOX, tel (0263) 860891.

## BROME, Suffolk Map 9

### BROME GRANGE HOTEL

*Massive oak timbers and huge open fires in the reception,
bar and restaurant reflect this hotel's medieval origins.
Every visitor to Brome Grange receives caring, personal
service – and if you are fond of a friendly bar with plenty of
atmosphere, that serves real ales and freshly prepared food
– you will not be disappointed. For functions, Brome
Grange offers a beautiful Tithe Barn.*
ACCOMMODATION £41–£50
FOOD up to £15
**Hours:** open all year 7pm; breakfast 7:30am – 9:30am;
lunch 12noon – 2pm; dinner 7pm – 10pm. **Cuisine:**
English:- Excellent choice of English dishes, using the
best locally-grown produce, with fresh fish from nearby
ports, and game when in season. **Rooms:** 22 bedrooms,
all en suite, chalet style with central heating, private
bathroom, colour TV, radio, telephone, trouser-press and
hot drinks facilities. **Credit cards:** Visa, Access, Diners,
AmEx. **Other points:** licensed, open-air dining, Sunday
lunch, children catered for – please check for age limits,
pets allowed, afternoon tea, parking, residents' lounge,
garden, disabled access. **Directions:** on the A140
Ipswich to Norwich road, approximately halfway.
WAVENEY INNS, tel (0379) 870456, fax (0379)
870929.

## BROMLEY, Kent Map 5

### HENRY'S CAFE BAR (BROMLEY), *2–4 Ringers Road*

*Situated just off Bromley High Street, this popular cafe-
bar serves an extensive range of international fast-food
and American and non-alcoholic beers and speciality
cocktails. Busy at lunchtimes.*
FOOD up to £15

**Hours:** closed Sunday 7pm; meals all day 10:30am – 6:30pm. **Cuisine:** international. **Credit cards:** Visa, Access. **Other points:** children catered for – please check for age limits, open bank holidays, no-smoking area, afternoon teas, disabled access, vegetarian meals. **Directions:** off High Street Bromely south.
GRAEME COLLINS, tel (081) 313 0980.

## BURY ST EDMUNDS, Suffolk Map 9

### THE GRANGE HOTEL, Thurston

*Attractive mock Tudor country house hotel with a large garden for alfresco dining. Very helpful and welcoming staff who are eager to please. Kilverstone Wildlife Park, Cambridge, Ickworth Hall and Anglo-Saxon village all nearby.*
*ACCOMMODATION £21–£30*
*FOOD £15–£20*
**Hours:** breakfast 7am – 9:30am; lunch 12noon – 2:30pm; bar meals 12noon – 2:30pm; dinner 7pm – 10pm; bar meals 7pm – 10pm. **Cuisine:** English / French:- English and French cuisine, specialities including lemon sole stuffed with prawns in a prawn and basil sauce. **Rooms:** 14 bedrooms all with tea making facilities, TV: 2 twins, 1 single ensuite, 8 doubles ensuite, 2 twins ensuite, 1 family room ensuite. **Credit cards:** Visa, Access. **Other points:** licensed, Sunday lunch, children catered for – please check for age limits, pets allowed, bank holidays. **Directions:** A45 to Bury St Edmunds, exit at Sugar Beet factory and follow A143.
MR & MRS E G WAGSTAFF, tel (0359) 31260, fax (0359) 31260.

### THE SIX BELLS INN, The Green, Bardwell

*A traditional 16th Century coaching inn, situated just off the village green near the duck pond in the peaceful Suffolk village of Bardwell. Offering all the delights of a country free house – good food and drink in a friendly hospitable and informal atmosphere, the Six Bells with its lovely accommodation in converted barn stables, makes a delightful stop.*
*ACCOMMODATION £21–£30*
*FOOD up to £15* ♀ ☜
**Hours:** breakfast – weekdays 7:30am – 9:15am; breakfast – weekends 8:30am – 9:45am; lunch 12noon – 2:30pm; dinner – except Sunday 7pm – 11pm; dinner – Sunday 7pm – 10:30pm; last orders lunch – 1:30pm – dinner – 9:30pm. **Cuisine:** innovative English:- Scrumptious specialities – Tipsy Lamb, Stilton Steak, Peppered Chicken, Salmon and Sole Strudel, Game Pie, plus Traditional Puds. **Rooms:** 8 bedrooms all with tea making facilities, telephone, TV: 3 twins ensuite, 3 doubles ensuite, 2 family rooms ensuite. **Credit cards:** Visa, Access. **Other points:** Sunday lunch, children catered for – please check for age limits, garden, special breaks available, parking, vegetarian meals, residents' bar. **Directions:** off A143, 8 miles from Bury St Edmunds, follow signs for Bardwell.
RICHARD & CAROL SALMON, tel (0359) 50820.

## CAMBRIDGE, Cambridgeshire Map 8

### THE ANCIENT SHEPHERDS, High Street, Fen Ditton

*A very friendly country inn, circa 1540, serving well-cooked and presented food. Very pleasant atmosphere, with a good cross-section of business people, students and locals.*
*FOOD up to £15* ♀
**Hours:** closed Christmas 1 week; lunch 12noon – 2:15pm; bar meals 12noon – 2:15pm; bar meals 6:30pm – 9:30pm; dinner 7pm – 9:30pm; closed Sunday night only. **Cuisine:** English / continental:- Varied a la carte menu, including moules marinieres, and fresh fish. Bar meals include Chicken Ancient Shepherds – chicken with apricots, brandy & cream. **Credit cards:** Visa, Access. **Other points:** children catered for – please check for age limits, pets allowed, garden, bank holidays. **Directions:** B1047 from A45 travelling east. Turn right into Fen Ditton High St.
HILTON ROSE, tel (0223) 293280.

### ARUNDEL HOUSE HOTEL, 53 Chesterton Road

*Overlooking the River Cam and Jesus Green, the Arundel House Hotel is one of the few privately owned hotels in Cambridge. Within easy walking distance of the city centre and university colleges. An elegant conversion of fine Victorian terraced houses with a reputation for some of the best food in the area.*
*ACCOMMODATION £31–£40*
*FOOD up to £15*
**Hours:** lunch 12:15pm – 1:45pm; dinner 6:30pm – 9:30pm. **Cuisine:** French / English:- (Children's and vegetarian meals and extensive range of bar meals also available.). **Rooms:** 105 bedrooms all with tea making facilities, telephone, radio, TV: 23 twins ensuite, 33 doubles ensuite, 37 singles ensuite, 6 family rooms ensuite, 1 twin, 5 singles. **Credit cards:** Visa, Access, Diners, AmEx. **Other points:** licensed, Sunday lunch, children catered for – please check for age limits, limited disabled access. **Directions:** on the A1303. Exit Junction 13 on M11.
Tel (0223) 67701, fax (0223) 67721.

### BENSON HOUSE, 24 Huntingdon Road

*A well established guest house offering comfortable accommodation, only 10 minutes walk from the city centre and university. The breakfasts are hearty and a choice is offered.*
**Hours:** breakfast 8am – 9am. **Rooms:** 9 bedrooms all with TV, tea making facilities, some with ensuite: 2 single, 3 double, 2 twin, 2 family rooms. **Other points:** central heating, children catered for – check for age limits, pets allowed, residents' lounge. **Directions:** in north Cambridge on A1307, opposite Newhall College.
*ACCOMMODATION £21–£30*
MRS DOWLING & MR D MANSFIELD, tel (0223) 311594.

## HENRY'S CAFE BAR (CAMBRIDGE),
### Quayside

A popular cafe-bar in the centre of this beautiful University town, close to Magdalen College. Serving an extensive range of international fast-food, it is extremely popular with businessmen, students and tourists.
**FOOD** up to £15
**Hours:** meals all day 11am – 11pm. **Cuisine:** international. **Credit cards:** Visa, Access. **Other points:** children catered for – please check for age limits, open bank holidays, no-smoking area, afternoon teas, disabled access, vegetarian meals.
JON SHAW, tel (0223) 324649.

## MICHEL'S BRASSERIE,
### 21–24 Northampton Street

This beautiful brasserie combines the modern and the traditional in the manner characteristic of all the Michel's. There are a la carte and set menus, including the "rapido" for people in a hurry; everything is prepared by our own chefs with the flair and imagination that typifies Michel. There is a wine bar on the first floor and a room available for private parties.
**FOOD** up to £15
**Hours:** closed 01/01; lunch 12noon – 2:30pm; dinner 6pm – 11pm; closed Christmas 25/12 – 26/12. **Cuisine:** French:- French Brasserie/Bistro style cuisine, complemented by a fine Wine List. **Credit cards:** Visa, Access, Diners, AmEx. **Other points:** licensed, Sunday lunch, children catered for – please check for age limits, vegetarian meals, bank holidays. **Directions:** on the A1303, just outside Cambridge Town centre.
MICHEL SADONES (MANAGING DIRECTOR), tel (0223) 353110.

## THE SUFFOLK HOUSE, 69 Milton Road

A large 1930's gable fronted detached house, set in a large secluded garden. A high standard of comfort and cleanliness is maintained by Mary and Michael who extend a warm welcome to their guests. Less than 20 minutes walk from the city centre.
**ACCOMMODATION** £21–£30
**Hours:** breakfast – weekdays 8am – 8:45am; breakfast – weekends 8:30am – 9:15am. **Cuisine:** breakfast.
**Rooms:** 10 bedrooms all with TV: 4 doubles ensuite, 2 twins ensuite, 4 family rooms ensuite. **Credit cards:** Visa, Access. **Other points:** central heating, children catered for – please check for age limits, residents' lounge, garden. **Directions:** situated on the A1309, leave the A45 at A10 Ely and A1309 junction.
MR & MRS CUTHBERT, tel (0223) 352016.

## THE THREE HILLS, Bartlow

A 16th century village inn set in glorious countryside off the beaten track, but well worth checking out. The bar and restaurant are a wealth of old beams, with inglenook fire in winter. For the summer, there is a walled garden and covered patio. A popular pub with a growing reputation.
**FOOD** up to £15 ⊗

**Hours:** lunch 12noon – 1:45pm; dinner 7pm – 9:30pm.
**Cuisine:** English:- Homemade specials every day plus fine steaks, grills and fresh fish. Only fresh local produce used, when possible. **Credit cards:** Visa, Access. **Other points:** licensed, open-air dining, vegetarian meals, parking. **Directions:** 1 mile off the A604 Cambridge to Haverhill Road (Linton by-pass).
SUE & STEVE DIXON, tel (0223) 891259.

# CANTERBURY, Kent Map 5

## THE GREEN MAN, Shatterling,
### Nr Wingham

Old English country inn with garden, set in an area known for its hop growing and vine culture. 2 'bat & trap pitches'. Easy access to Dover and Ramsgate ports.
**ACCOMMODATION** under £20
**FOOD** up to £15
**Hours:** breakfast 7:45am – 9am; lunch 12noon – 2pm; dinner 7pm – 8:45pm; closed Sunday evening to non-res. **Cuisine:** English:- Genuine English home cooking.
**Rooms:** 3 bedrooms all with tea making facilities, TV: 2 twins, 1 family room ensuite. **Credit cards:** Visa, Access. **Other points:** open-air dining, Sunday lunch, children catered for – please check for age limits, coach/prior arr. **Directions:** on the A257 between Wingham and Ash.
MESSRS FERNE & GREENWOOD, tel (0304) 812525.

## POINTERS HOTEL, 1 London Road

A Grade II listed Georgian hotel situated near the City centre offering comfortable accommodation in a warm and friendly atmosphere. Enjoy good food at reasonable prices and easy access to shopping, entertainment and historical sites.
**ACCOMMODATION** £21–£30
**FOOD** up to £15
**Hours:** breakfast 7:30am – 9am; dinner 7:30pm – 9pm.
**Cuisine:** English:- Traditional. **Rooms:** 14 bedrooms all with tea making facilities, telephone, radio, TV: 2 family rooms ensuite, 1 twin ensuite, 1 twin – shower only, 4 doubles ensuite, 1 double – shower only, 1 single ensuite, 1 single, 3 doubles. **Credit cards:** Visa, Access, Diners, AmEx. **Other points:** residents' lounge, children catered for – please check for age limits, pets allowed. **Directions:** northside of Canterbury. On London Road opposite parish church.
MR & MRS O'BRIEN, tel (0227) 456846, (0227) 831131.

# CASTLE ACRE, Norfolk Map 9

## THE OSTRICH INN, Stocks Green,
### Nr Kings Lynn

Large 16th century coaching inn with two big open fires in the lounge bar. On the A1065 in a typical, small Norfolk village which has the Peddars Way running through it. Many National Trust attractions nearby.
**ACCOMMODATION** under £20
**FOOD** up to £15

**Hours:** bar meals 12noon – 2pm; bar meals 7:30pm – 10:30pm; closed Christmas 25/12 – 26/12. **Cuisine:** international:- Bar meals ranging from sausages to caviar, cockles to T-bone steaks. Daily specials from all over the world, cooked by the chef/proprietor. **Rooms:** 2 bedrooms 2 twins. **Other points:** licensed, Sunday lunch, children catered for – please check for age limits, coach/prior arr. **Directions:** on the A1065 between Swaffham and Fakenham on the village green. RAYMOND H WAKELEN, tel (0760) 755398.

## CHELMSFORD, Essex Map 8

### MIAMI HOTEL, Princes Road

*The Miami Hotel is a family run business for the past 30 years with 3 generations working in the hotel. 55 bedrooms, all twin /double size but let as single if required. All rooms have colour TV, Sky TV, trouser-press and tea making facilities. Easy access from all main routes, M25, A12 and A1016. Close to all major Airports for the international traveller. The Miami Hotel offers value, comfort and hospitality.*
*ACCOMMODATION £21–£30*
**Hours:** breakfast 7:30am – 9am; lunch 12noon – 2:30pm; dinner 6:30pm – 9:30pm. **Cuisine:** continental:- Filet Mignon, Steak au Poivre, Beef Stroganoff. **Rooms:** 55 bedrooms all with tea making facilities, TV: 16 doubles ensuite, 39 twins ensuite. **Credit cards:** Visa, Access, AmEx, Diners, Switch. **Other points:** Sunday lunch, children catered for – please check for age limits. **Directions:** by the A1016 Billericay roundabout. MR C NEWCOMBE, tel (0245) 269603, (0245) 264848, fax (0245) 259860.

### THE PLOUGH INN, Springfield Road

*This is a lively 19th century pub with a busy, family atmosphere. It has a pleasing, rustic decor with comfortable chairs. The staff are helpful and friendly.*
*FOOD up to £15*
**Hours:** meals all day 11am – 10pm. **Cuisine:** English:- Traditional English pub food. Generous portions. Daily blackboard specials. **Credit cards:** Visa, Access. **Other points:** children catered for – please check for age limits, bank holidays, licensed. **Directions:** from A12, take the A138 Chelmsford then A113. Pub half mile on left. TONY AND MARGARET HURDING, tel (0245) 353375.

### SOLE MIO ITALIAN RESTAURANT, 11–13 Baddow Road

*Authentic Italian dishes are served in this restaurant close to the town centre. Enjoy a choice of two set menus Monday to Friday, and there is a private room catering for parties or conferences. Multi storey car park is adjacent.*
*ACCOMMODATION £21–£30*
*FOOD up to £15* CLUB ★
**Hours:** lunch 12noon – 2pm; dinner 7pm – 11pm; closed bank holidays; closed Sundays. **Cuisine:** Italian:- Grilled fresh sardines, Lombatine Mariapia. Vegetarian

menu. **Credit cards:** Visa, Access, Diners, AmEx. **Other points:** licensed, children catered for – please check for age limits. **Directions:** old Baddow Road is in the town centre, on the one-way system. A A SOLDANI, tel (0245) 250759, fax (0245) 496450.

### SOUTH LODGE HOTEL, 196 New London Road

*A busy commercial hotel close to the town centre and County Cricket Ground. South Lodge is a converted Victorian residence standing in its own mature gardens. Full conference, function and leisure facilities available.*
*ACCOMMODATION £31–£40*
*FOOD up to £15*
**Hours:** breakfast 7:30am – 9:30am; lunch 12:30pm – 2:30pm; dinner 7pm – 10pm. **Cuisine:** English / inter-national:- international and New English cuisine. **Rooms:** 41 bedrooms all with tea making facilities, telephone, TV: 20 singles ensuite, 10 twins ensuite, 9 doubles ensuite, 2 triples ensuite. **Credit cards:** Visa, Access, Diners, AmEx. **Other points:** licensed, Sunday lunch, no-smoking area, children catered for – please check for age limits, cots. **Directions:** off the A12 close to the town centre. MR A A SOLDANI, tel (0245) 264564, fax (0245) 492827.

## CHERTSEY, Surrey Map 4

### THE CROWN HOTEL, 7 Lonor Street

*This comfortable hotel is popular with tourists and locals alike, whether relaxing in the bar or soaking up the atmosphere and sampling the fine food in the restaurant. The private bedrooms have every possible modern facility to make you feel at home. The special conference suite, accommodating up to 100 people, can also be used for private celebrations and dinner dances. Ideally located for London, Heathrow and Gatwick, not to mention the tourist areas of Hampton Court, Windsor and Windsor Safari Park.*
*FOOD up to £15*
*ACCOMMODATION £41–£50*
**Hours:** breakfast 7am –10am, lunch 12 noon – 2pm, dinner 7pm – 10pm, bar snacks 6.30pm – 9pm, closed Saturday lunch. **Cuisine:** British. **Rooms:** 30 ensuite bedrooms all with TV, telephone, tea making facilities. **Credit cards:** Visa, Access, AmEx, Diners. **Other points:** parking, children catered for – check for age limits, no smoking area, disabled access, pets allowed, residents' lounge, garden, vegetarian meals, open air dining. **Directions:** off M25 (Junction 11), follow signs for Chertsey town centre. We are situated behind Sainsbury Centre. MR W PEITERS, tel (0932) 564657, fax (0932) 570839.

## CHICHESTER, West Sussex Map 4

### ANGLESEY ARMS, Halnaker

*A small, friendly traditional pub serving real ales. The single bar and attractive garden are both very popular. Only 2 miles from Goodwood Racecourse and 4 miles from Chichester harbour. There is a separate restaurant area.*

FOOD up to £15

**Hours:** closed Christmas day 7pm; closed New Years day 7pm; last orders 7pm – 10pm; lunch 12noon – 2pm; dinner 7:30pm – 12midnight. **Cuisine:** English:- Peppered fillet steak, fresh Selsey lobster and crab, locally smoked salmon and ham, traditional roast Sunday lunch. **Credit cards:** Visa, Access, Diners, AmEx. **Other points:** licensed, children catered for – please check for age limits. **Directions:** close to the A27. Take the A285 to Halnaker. Pub is 1 mile up on right, just after Halnaker cross roads.
CHRISTOPHER & TESSA HOUSEMAN, tel (0243) 773474, fax (0243) 530034.

### EARL OF MARCH, Mid Lavant
*Excellent service by well-trained staff will make this a good stop for those travelling in the area. Comfortable surroundings and good food can be found here.*
FOOD up to £15
**Hours:** last orders 7:30pm – 10pm; lunch 12:30pm – 2pm; dinner – except Sunday 6pm – 11pm; dinner – Sunday 7pm – 9:30pm. **Cuisine:** English:- Varied selection of traditional cuisine. Special vegetarian dishes. Bar food. **Credit cards:** Visa, Access.
**Other points:** licensed, open-air dining, Sunday lunch, children catered for – please check for age limits, pets allowed. **Directions:** 2 miles from Chichester on the A286.
MR A L LAURIN, tel (0243) 774751.

### EASTON HOUSE, Chidham Lane, Chidham
*A former 16th century farmhouse situated on the Chidham peninsula. Within easy reach of Goodwood, Chichester, Portsmouth and the New Forest. Uncrowded and peaceful waterside walks within 5 minutes of the house. The bedrooms overlook either farmland, the harbour or the garden.*
ACCOMMODATION £21–£30
**Hours:** breakfast 8am – 9am. **Cuisine:** breakfast. **Rooms:** 1 double with en suite and 1 twin bedroom. tea/coffee making facilities. 1 bathroom. 1 shower. **Other points:** central heating, no evening meal, children catered for – please check for age limits, residents' lounge, garden. **Directions:** 1 mile south of the A259.
MRS C M HARTLEY, tel (0243) 572514.

### MICAWBER'S RESTAURANT, 13 South Street
*Situated just south of the Cross, this popular restaurant has a provincial French character. The fruits de mer are cooked by the chef directly after he gets them from the local fishermen.*
FOOD up to £15 : CLUB
**Hours:** lunch 11:30am – 2:30pm; dinner 6pm – 10:30pm; closed Sunday. **Cuisine:** French / English:- Wide selection of fish dishes, and shellfish, fresh meat and vegetables all from local markets. **Credit cards:**

Visa, Access, Diners, AmEx. **Other points:** children catered for – please check for age limits, French spoken. **Directions:** situated just south of the Cross at Chichester.
PHILIP COTTERILL & THIERRY BOISHU, tel (0243) 786989.

### PLATTERS RESTAURANT, 15 Southgate
*A sumptuous meal in this Mediterranean-style restaurant is assured with very personal attention from the friendly staff. House specialities change from day to day and you may even be treated to an explanation of the more interesting ingredients, such as local wild mushrooms. Chefs, enjoying a break from other restaurants, are known to eat meals here – high praise indeed.*
FOOD £15–£20 ♟ ↽ CLUB ★
**Hours:** lunch 12noon – 2pm; dinner 7pm; closed Sunday; closed Tuesday. **Cuisine:** Mediterranean:- A la carte and Table d'hote offering a range of imaginative dishes with daily changes. Vegetarian dishes always available daily. **Credit cards:** Visa, Access, AmEx. **Other points:** licensed, open-air dining, children catered for – please check for age limits, street parking. **Directions:** 100yds north of railway and bus station, opposite magistrates court.
NICHOLAS WESTACOTT, tel (0243) 530430.

## CHITTERING, Cambridgeshire Map 8

### TRAVELLERS REST, Ely Road
*A 300 year old beamed public house with its own restaurant decorated throughout with a cottage theme, providing a perfect atmosphere for families and caravanners. Carvery offering 3 course meals. Ideal location for visiting Anglesey Abbey and Wicken Fen, or for touring Cambridge, Bury St Edmunds and Newmarket.*
FOOD up to £15
**Hours:** lunch 12noon – 2:30pm; dinner – Mon-Sat 6pm – 9:30pm; dinner – Sunday 7pm – 9pm. **Cuisine:** English / continental:- Quality a la carte. **Credit cards:** Visa, Access, AmEx. **Other points:** parking, children catered for – please check for age limits, no-smoking area, disabled access, vegetarian meals, open-air dining. **Directions:** on A10, exactly halfway between Ely and Cambridge (8 miles each way).
KEITH AND ALEXANDRA RICHARDSON, tel (0223) 860751.

## CLACTON ON SEA, Essex Map 8

### THE ROBIN HOOD, 221 London Road
*Originally a farmhouse, this delightful pub has retained its rustic charm. Hot, home-style meals at affordable prices and friendly staff will make you feel at home. There is a family atmosphere as children are particularly welcome.*
FOOD up to £15
**Hours:** meals all day 11am – 11pm. **Cuisine:** English:- Good selection of pub style food. Blackboard specials

daily. Children's menu. Enormous portions at extremely reasonable prices. **Credit cards:** Visa, Access. **Other points:** children catered for – please check for age limits, bank holidays, licensed. **Directions:** on A133, follow signs to Clacton centre. On right.
JOHN AND BARBARA TAYLOR, tel (0255) 421519.

## CLARE, Suffolk Map 9

### THE CLARE HOTEL, Nethergate Street
*Recently renovated 17th century inn, in a picturesque market town, close to the market place, park and castle ruins. Large bar and restaurant, decorated in antiques, serving excellent cuisine accompanied by superb wine list. Beautiful landscaped garden with garden restaurant for summer evenings.*
*ACCOMMODATION £21–£30*
*FOOD up to £15*
**Cuisine:** English / French:- English & French cafe/restaurant style. **Rooms:** 5 bedrooms 2 doubles ensuite, 1 twin ensuite, 1 twin, 1 single. **Credit cards:** Visa, Access, AmEx. **Other points:** licensed, Sunday lunch, children catered for – please check for age limits, pets allowed. **Directions:** easy to locate in the town centre.
MR & MRS ROSS, tel (0787) 277449, fax (0787) 278270.

## COLCHESTER, Essex Map 8

### JACKLINS RESTAURANT, 147 High Street
*A first floor restaurant, situated in the town centre on the site of the pottery shops of Roman Colchester. Delightful oak panelled rooms where breakfasts, lunches and afternoon teas are served. Also specialist shop downstairs for tobacco products, teas and confectionery.*
*FOOD up to £15*
**Hours:** meals all day 9:15am – 5pm; closed bank holidays; closed Sunday. **Cuisine:** English:- Breakfasts, lunches, light meals and afternoon teas. **Credit cards:** Visa, Access, AmEx. **Other points:** children catered for – please check for age limits, parking. **Directions:** 100 yds west of the Town Hall in the High Street.
MR S H JACKLIN, tel (0206) 572157.

### ROSE & CROWN HOTEL, East Gate
*The original style of this Tudor building has been retained and is the oldest Inn in Britain's oldest recorded town. The restaurant has a cosy cocktail bar and offers fresh home-made food every day of the year. A delightful place for lovers of history.*
*ACCOMMODATION over £50*
*FOOD up to £15* ★
**Hours:** breakfast 7am – 9:30am; lunch 12noon – 2pm; dinner 7pm – 10pm. **Cuisine:** French / English:- A la carte, fixed price menu, French/English cuisine. **Rooms:** 31 bedrooms all with tea making facilities, telephone, TV: 13 singles ensuite, 3 twins ensuite, 11 doubles ensuite, 4 family rooms ensuite. **Credit cards:** Visa, Access, Diners, AmEx. **Other points:** licensed, children

catered for – please check for age limits, conferences, residents' lounge, residents' bar. **Directions:** in town centre off A12. East Gate area.
MR BAGHERZADEH, tel (0206) 866677, fax (0206) 866616.

### THE SHEPHERD & DOG, Moor Road, Langham
*Set in a small village near Colchester, this pub offers tasty meals presented with care. As this is a free house there is a good selection of beers. Booking recommended as restaurant can be busy.*
*FOOD up to £15*
**Hours:** last orders 7pm – 10pm; lunch 11am – 3pm; bar meals 11am – 2:30pm; dinner 4pm – 12midnight; bar meals 6pm – 11pm. **Cuisine:** English / continental:- Bar and restaurant meals. Predominantly English and continental cuisine. **Credit cards:** Visa, Access, AmEx. **Other points:** licensed, open-air dining, Sunday lunch, children catered for – please check for age limits, bank holidays, pets allowed.
**Directions:** first exit off A12 north of Colchester (signed Langham).
MR PAUL BARNES & MISS JANE GRAHAM, tel (0206) 272711.

## COPTHORNE (NR GATWICK), West Sussex Map 4

### LINCHENS, New Domewood
*Linchens is situated in 3 and a half acre woodland garden on a private estate a quarter of an hour from Gatwick Airport and airport parking. Each room has adequate facilities, including colour television. Late arrivals or early departures are welcome.*
**Hours:** breakfast 5am – 9am. **Cuisine:** English. **Other points:** parking, children catered for – please check for age limits, open bank holidays, no-smoking, pets allowed, vegetarian meals, garden. **Directions:** M23, Junction 10, take A264 towards East Grinstead, after 3 miles (garage on right "Airport Parking") turn left into New Domewood. Signed private, take first right road then bend sharply to left. "Linchens" is the first house on the right.
JOHN AND SALLY SMYTH, tel (0342) 713085.

## CRANLEIGH, Surrey Map 4

### BRICKS RESTAURANT, Smithbrook Kilns
*Situated in a multi-workshop craft centre in an old brickworks. Self-service from kitchen counter with table service for drinks, desserts and coffee. Waitress service in evenings.*
*FOOD up to £15*
**Hours:** closed 01/01; lunch 12noon – 2pm; dinner 7:30pm – 9:45pm; closed Christmas 25/12 – 27/12; closed bank holidays. **Cuisine:** international:- Menus change daily offering a selection of casseroles with hot potatoes, salads, French bread and butter. All desserts are made on the premises. **Credit cards:** Visa, Access.

**Other points:** open-air dining, Sunday lunch, children catered for – please check for age limits, coach/prior arr. **Directions:** on A281 just north of crossroads with B2127.
MRS H RUSSELL-DAVIS, tel (0483) 276780.

### LA SCALA RESTAURANT, High Street
A well established and popular restaurant under the current ownership for over 20 years. Situated on the first floor above a jeweller's shop on the High Street. The menu offers an interesting selection of Italian favourites and regional cuisine.
FOOD up to £15
**Hours:** lunch 12noon – 2pm; dinner 6:30pm – 11pm; last orders 10.45pm; closed Monday; closed Sunday. **Cuisine:** Italian:- Veal escalopa a la crema, sole Isoladoro, fettucini crema, mussels. **Credit cards:** Visa, Access. **Other points:** open-air dining, children catered for – please check for age limits. **Directions:** on the A281 Guildford to Horsham road.
ROSARIO MAZZOTTA, tel (0483) 274900.

---

## CRAWLEY, West Sussex Map 4

### GOFFS PARK HOTEL, Goffs Park Road
Goff's Park Hotel is a modern country house situated in a peaceful residential area, close to Crawley town centre and within easy reach of the M23 and Gatwick Airport. The newly refurbished restaurant offers imaginative table d'hote and a la carte menus, complemented by an interesting wine list. All rooms are furnished to a very high standard with many modern facilities.
ACCOMMODATION £21–£30
FOOD up to £15
**Hours:** closed Saturday lunch; breakfast 7am – 9:30am; breakfast – Sunday 8am – 10am; lunch 12:30pm – 2pm; dinner 7pm – 9:30pm. **Cuisine:** English / Italian. **Credit cards:** Visa, Access, Diners, AmEx. **Directions:** Brighton Road off A23, then onto Goff's Park Road.
COMPASS GROUP, tel (0293) 535447, fax (0293) 542050.

---

## CROWBOROUGH, East Sussex Map 5

### BOARS HEAD INN, Eridge Road, Boarshead
A real old country inn with flagstone floors and oak beams, virtually untouched by the passing of 600 years. Open fires, a warm friendly ambiance and well cooked and presented food have drawn people to the Boars Head from miles around.
FOOD £15–£20
**Hours:** lunch 12noon – 2pm. **Cuisine:** English:- Fresh trout in season, steak, poultry. Table d'hote menu by reservation. Bar snacks. **Credit cards:** Visa, Access. **Other points:** licensed, open-air dining, Sunday lunch. **Directions:** on the A26 in Boarshead, between Crowborough and Eridge.
JILLIENNE & GORDON MCKENZIE, tel (0892) 652412.

---

## CROYDON, Surrey Map 4

### BRIARLEY HOTEL, 8 Outram Road
A Victorian exterior but inside everything you expect from a hotel in the 90's including colour TV, tea facilities and direct-dial telephone. Quietly situated but excellent for public transport. Private car park. Launderette.
ACCOMMODATION £41–£50
FOOD up to £15
**Hours:** lunch – Sunday 12noon – 1:30pm; dinner – except Sunday 6:30pm – 10pm. **Cuisine:** English:- Traditional home-made food with soups, steaks, Briarleyburger and fresh vegetables, and all the usual favourites associated with the a la carte menu. **Rooms:** 38 bedrooms all with tea making facilities, telephone, radio, TV: 18 singles ensuite, 8 twins ensuite, 7 doubles ensuite, 5 family rooms ensuite. **Credit cards:** Visa, Access, Diners, AmEx. **Other points:** licensed, Sunday lunch, children catered for – please check for age limits, baby-listening device, cots, bar, lounge, central heating. **Directions:** Outram Rd runs between the A232 and A222, near East Croydon station.
MRS S P MILLS, tel (081) 654 1000, fax (081) 656 6084.

### MARKINGTON HOTEL, 9 Haling Park Road
This comfortable, friendly hotel is situated in a quiet area, yet is very close to the commercial centre of Croydon. After a days shopping in the under-cover shopping centre, you can relax in the bar lounge or have a game of pool!
ACCOMMODATION £21–£30
FOOD up to £15 ★
**Hours:** breakfast 7am – 9am; dinner 6:30pm – 8:30pm. **Cuisine:** English. **Rooms:** 22 bedrooms all with tea making facilities, telephone, radio, TV: 9 singles ensuite, 9 doubles ensuite, 3 twins ensuite, 1 family room ensuite. **Credit cards:** Visa, Access, AmEx. **Other points:** children catered for – please check for age limits, garden, billiards, vegetarian meals, parking, residents' lounge, residents' bar. **Directions:** just off A235 Brighton, opposite Croydon bus garage.
MR & MRS MICKELBURGH, tel (081) 681 6494, fax (081) 688 6530.

---

## DISS, Norfolk Map 9

### SCOLE INN, Scole
Built in 1655 by a wealthy Norwich wool merchant, this magnificent listed inn can be found in the picturesque village of Scole near Diss. Elegantly finished in authentic decor, including oak beams, heavy oak doors and a gleaming oak staircase, the Scole Inn also boasts warming inglenook fireplaces and even an occasional ghost or two.
ACCOMMODATION £31 –£40
FOOD up to £15
**Hours:** breakfast 7:30am – 9:30am; lunch 12noon – 2pm; bar snacks 12noon – 2:30pm; bar snacks 6pm – 10pm; dinner 7pm – 9:30pm. **Cuisine:** English:-

Traditional East Anglian cooking. House specials include Steak and Kidney Pie, Roast Norfolk Duckling and local game. Bar snacks. Good range of real ales. **Credit cards:** Visa, Access, Diners, AmEx. **Other points:** afternoon tea, pets allowed, residents' lounge, garden, children catered for – please check for age limits. **Directions:** situated on the A140, 2 miles east of Diss.
ROGER HALES, tel (0379) 740481, fax (0379) 740762.

## DUNSTABLE, Bedfordshire Map 6

### BELLOWS MILL, Bellows Mill, Eaton Bray

*For a truly memorable break, this delightful mill, set in its own grounds and dating back to the Domesday Book, is idyllic. The accent is on highly personal attention to your needs and facilities include an all-weather tennis court, snooker table, even fishing by arrangement. Bellows Mill is also ideal for private receptions and small conferences.*
*ACCOMMODATION £21–£30*
*FOOD up to £15*
**Hours:** open all year 7pm; breakfast 7am – 10:30am; dinner 7pm – 9pm. **Cuisine:** English / international:- Fixed price menu. Dishes may include, Pheasant Normande, Chicken in Lemon & Coriander (Indian style), and Lamb Noisettes. Vegetarian – by arrangement. **Rooms:** 6 bedrooms all with tea making facilities, telephone, TV: 3 twins ensuite, 2 doubles ensuite, 1 family room ensuite. **Credit cards:** Visa, Access. **Other points:** licensed, open-air dining, residents' lounge, garden, disabled access, parking, children catered for – please check for age limits, pets/prior arr, bank holidays. **Directions:** follow signs for Zoo at 'Plough Pub.' Take road to east Bray.
RACHAEL HODGE, tel (0525) 220548, (0525) 220536.

## DUXFORD, Cambridgeshire Map 8

### DUXFORD LODGE HOTEL, Ickleton Road

*Duxford Lodge has been carefully converted and refurbished to form a luxurious country house hotel. The accommodation is outstanding with all bedrooms individual in design. The restaurant serves a high standard of traditional cuisine, cooked by the proprietor, at excellent value for money and within attractive, elegant surroundings. Duxford Lodge is an ideal choice for a meal or overnight stay.*
*ACCOMMODATION £21–£30*
*FOOD up to £15* ♈ ☕
**Hours:** breakfast 7:15am – 9:30am; lunch 12noon – 2pm; dinner 7pm – 9:30pm. **Cuisine:** English:- Table d'hote and a la carte menus. Dishes may include Dover Sole, Chicken Duxford, Rack of Lamb, Steak au Poivre. **Rooms:** 15 bedrooms, all en suite. **Credit cards:** Visa, Access, Diners, AmEx. **Other points:** licensed, Sunday lunch, conferences, functions. **Directions:** the first or second right turn after exiting from the M11 onto the A505 eastbound will bring you directly to the hotel.
RONALD & SUZANNE CRADDOCK, tel (0223) 836444, fax (0223) 832271.

## EASTBOURNE, East Sussex Map 5

### ADRIAN HOUSE HOTEL, 24 Selwyn Road

*A small, family-run hotel set in a quiet location in one of Britain's most popular holiday resorts. Fully centrally-heated, there is a comfortable T.V. lounge, and guests all have their own keys. Offering good home cooking, special diets are also catered for.*
*ACCOMMODATION under £20*
*FOOD up to £15*
**Hours:** breakfast – Saturday 8:30am; breakfast 9am; dinner 6pm. **Cuisine:** English. **Other points:** parking, children catered for – please check for age limits, no-smoking area, pets, residents' lounge, garden, vegetarian meals. **Directions:** half mile north of station, on right after pedestrian crossing.
MR AND MRS B MILES, tel (0323) 720372.

### THE CHATSWORTH HOTEL, Grand Parade

*The Chatsworth Hotel is a traditional English Hotel. The atmosphere is both pleasant and relaxing. It is ideally situated on the Grand Parade only a minute away form the beach and promenade. With the staff always ready to help in any way, the Chatsworth is a very comfortable, family hotel.*
*FOOD £15–£20*
**Hours:** breakfast 8am – 9:45am; lunch – except Sunday 12noon – 1:45pm; lunch – Sunday 12:30pm – 2pm; dinner 7pm – 8:30pm. **Cuisine:** English:- A wide range of food including dishes such as avocado and prawns, soup, rosset of lamb, escalope of turkey, strawberry gateaux and crepes Normand. **Rooms:** 92 bedrooms all with telephone, radio, TV: 12 singles ensuite, 24 twins ensuite, 8 doubles ensuite, 1 triple ensuite, 2 quads ensuite. **Credit cards:** Visa, Access. **Other points:** licensed, Sunday lunch, children catered for – please check for age limits, pets allowed, conferences, cots, left luggage. **Directions:** corner of the Grand Parade and Hartington Place. Very near bandstand.
MRS G H BENZMANN, tel (0323) 411016, fax (0323) 643270.

### WEST ROCKS HOTEL, Grand Parade

*A friendly, family owned and managed hotel, occupying one of Eastbourne's finest seafront locations. Three elegant and spacious lounges afford magnificent views over the Parades and the Channel. The 54 comfortable bedrooms – the majority with sea views – have many modern facilities, and there is also a passenger lift. As one of the sunniest resorts in Great Britain, Eastbourne is the ideal place for your summer holiday.*
*ACCOMMODATION £21–£30*
*FOOD up to £15*
**Hours:** breakfast 8am – 9:30am; bar snacks 12noon – 2pm; dinner 6:45pm – 8pm; closed mid November – mid March. **Cuisine:** English / continental. **Rooms:** 54 bedrooms all with tea making facilities, telephone, TV: 10 singles, 1 twin, 1 double, 6 singles ensuite, 16 twins ensuite, 17 doubles ensuite, 3 family rooms ensuite.

**Credit cards:** Visa, Access, Diners, AmEx. **Other points:** children catered for – please check for age limits, no-smoking area, residents' lounge, vegetarian meals, residents' bar. **Directions:** western end past the bandstand. MR K B SAYERS, tel (0323) 725217, fax (0323) 720421.

## WISH TOWER HOTEL, *King Edward's Parade*

*Ideally situated on the seafront, the Wish Tower Hotel provides splendid views across to the Esplanade and beach beyond. There is a friendly, relaxing atmosphere in which to enjoy the well cooked food, with locally caught fish and seafood always available. With efficient, courteous service, and comfortable furnishings, the Wish Tower is a popular rendezvous.*

ACCOMMODATION £31–£40

FOOD up to £15

**Hours:** breakfast 7am – 9:30am; lunch – except Sunday 12noon – 2pm; lunch – Sunday 12:30pm – 2pm; dinner 7pm – 8:45pm. **Cuisine:** English:- Table d'hote menu. Fish is the speciality but dishes include Roast Sirloin of Scotch Beef with Burgundy Wine Sauce. Lunchtime hot and cold Buffet. **Rooms:** 65 bedrooms 11 doubles ensuite, 29 twins ensuite, 25 singles ensuite. **Credit cards:** Visa, Access, Diners, AmEx. **Other points:** licensed, Sunday lunch, no-smoking area, children catered for – please check for age limits, afternoon tea, pets allowed, conferences, parking. **Directions:** on the promenade overlooking 'The Wish Tower', museum and sea. JOHN RAFFERTY, tel (0323) 722676, fax (0323) 721474.

## EDENBRIDGE, Kent Map 5

### Symbol of Excellence
### CASTLE INN, *Chiddingstone*

*The Castle Inn is a delightful oak beamed pub in the centre of one of Kent's most unspoilt villages. Enjoy traditional English bar food from the comfort of the Saloon Bar or in the pretty cottage garden during summertime. There is a separate restaurant with formal waiter service and an ever changing menu. Extensive list of over 150 wines and three hand-pumped draught beers.*

FOOD £15–£20

**Hours:** lunch 12noon – 2pm; dinner 7:30pm – 9:30pm. **Cuisine:** English / continental:- Mainly British with European overtones. Roast rib of beef, roast rack of lamb, local game, fresh fish, fresh vegetables. **Credit cards:** Visa, Access, Diners, AmEx. **Other points:** licensed, Sunday lunch, children catered for – please check for age limits. **Directions:** 1.5 miles south of the B2027 Edenbridge to Tonbridge Road. NIGEL D LUCAS, tel (0892) 870247.

## ELY, Cambridgeshire Map 8

### THE ANCHOR INN, *Sutton Gault*

*A traditional old Fen riverside pub, approximately 350 years old, lit by gas lamps and with old beams, scrubbed wooden tables and chairs. Frequented by locals and tourists alike, the atmosphere is homely and welcoming with efficient service. Recognised in all the guides. Ideal base for visiting Ely Cathedral, the Ouse Washes, Welney Wildfowl Reserve, and for exploring the real Fen country.*

FOOD up to £15 ♀ ♨

**Hours:** last orders 7:30pm – 9:30pm; closed Sunday evening 01/10 – Easter; lunch 12noon – 2:30pm; dinner 6:30pm – 11pm. **Cuisine:** English:- A la carte menu, offering an extensive range of imaginative dishes, changes daily. **Credit cards:** Visa, Access. **Other points:** licensed, open-air dining, Sunday lunch, no-smoking area, children catered for – please check for age limits, bank holidays. **Directions:** signposted Sutton Gault, just south of Sutton village (B1381). 7 miles west of Ely. HEATHER & ROBIN MOORE, tel (0353) 778537, fax (0353) 776180.

## EPSOM, Surrey Map 4

### EPSOM DOWNS HOTEL, *9 Longdown Road*

*A friendly hotel with a cosy, inviting atmosphere and excellent, individual service. Comfortably furnished and attractively decorated, the hotel offers well-appointed accommodation and very good food. All dishes are tasty and served in generous portions. You are guaranteed the warmest of welcomes by the manager, Jenny Clark, and her staff.*

ACCOMMODATION £31–£40

FOOD £15–£20

**Hours:** breakfast – weekdays 7:30am – 9:30am; breakfast – weekends 8:30am – 10:30am; closed Christmas 1 week; lunch 12:30pm – 2pm; dinner 7:30pm – 9:30pm. **Cuisine:** English / continental:- Traditional English and continental cuisine such as Lemon Sole, Rack of Lamb roasted with honey and served with a herb and garlic sauce. **Rooms:** 14 bedrooms all with tea making facilities, telephone, TV: 7 singles ensuite, 2 singles, 2 twins ensuite, 3 doubles ensuite. **Credit cards:** Visa, Access, Diners, AmEx. **Other points:** licensed, children catered for – please check for age limits, residents' lounge, garden, cots, 24hr reception. **Directions:** quiet, residential area on the eastern (Banstead) side of Epsom. JENNY CLARK – MANAGER, tel (0372) 740643, fax (0372) 723259.

## ESHER, Surrey Map 4

### ALBERT ARMS, *82 High Street*

*Situated close to Hampton Court and to Sandown Park and Kempton race courses, The Albert Arms is a traditional pub with a restaurant extension.*

FOOD up to £15

**Hours:** breakfast 10:30am – 12noon; bar meals 11am – 3pm; lunch 12noon – 3pm; dinner 7:30pm – 10pm; bar meals 7:30pm – 10pm. **Cuisine:** English / Italian:- Wide

range of dishes including grills, salads, steaks, pies, casseroles and Italian specialities. **Credit cards:** Visa, Access, Diners, AmEx. **Other points:** licensed, Sunday lunch, children catered for – please check for age limits. **Directions:** off the A3 London – Guildford on the A304 in Esher.
JEAN & BRUCE MONTGOMERY, tel (0372) 465290, fax (0372) 469217.

## EYKE, Suffolk Map 9

### THE OLD HOUSE, Nr Woodbridge
*This friendly guest house is a listed building dating back to 1600, with oak beams and open fires. Situated in the small village of Eyke on the A1152, the heritage coast, Sutton Hoo, Aldeburgh and Snape Maltings are all nearby. All food is prepared on the premises using home and local produce, all diets are catered for.*
*ACCOMMODATION under £20*
**Hours:** breakfast 6am – 10am; dinner 6pm – 8:30pm.
**Cuisine:** English. **Rooms:** 3 double bedrooms (can be let as twin, single or family rooms), all ensuite colour TV, tea/coffee making facilities, radio/alarm in all rooms. **Other points:** central heating, children catered for – please check for age limits, residents' lounge, garden. **Directions:** situated on the A1152 in the village of Eyke.
JAN & TONY WARNOCK, tel (0394) 460213.

## FARNHAM, Surrey Map 4

### SEVENS WINE BAR & BISTRO, 7 The Borough
*An 18th century beamed black and white restaurant situated in the centre of Farnham serving tasty, well prepared food. In summer you can dine in the garden but whatever the month and setting, the food is always good and the service excellent. The friendly, welcoming staff and relaxing, informal atmosphere makes this bistro a pleasure to visit. Fully air-conditioned.*
*FOOD up to £15*
**Hours:** morning coffee 9:30am – 12noon; lunch 12noon – 2:30pm; afternoon tea 2:30pm – 6:30pm; dinner 6:30pm – 11pm; closed Sunday. **Cuisine:** French:- French style bistro, including home-made dishes, home-made sweets. Menu's change monthly & Blackboard Specials daily. **Credit cards:** Visa, Access. **Other points:** licensed, children catered for – please check for age limits, garden, afternoon tea, barbecues. **Directions:** in the centre of Farnham, very close to Castle Street and market.
MR A C GREEN, tel (0252) 715345.

## FELIXSTOWE, Suffolk Map 9

### MARLBOROUGH HOTEL, Sea Front
*An Edwardian building facing the sea, offering panoramic views from many of the rooms. The staff are very friendly and promote a high standard of service, all the rooms being very clean and the food well-cooked and*

prepared. *Conveniently situated, close to Felixstowe leisure centre and the Spa Pavilion.*
*ACCOMMODATION £21–£30*
*FOOD up to £15*
**Hours:** breakfast 7am – 9:30pm; lunch 12noon – 2:30pm; bar meals 12noon – 2:30pm; dinner Mon–Thurs 6:30pm – 9pm; bar meals – except Sunday 6:30pm – 9:30pm; breakfast 7pm – 9:30pm; dinner Fri–Sat 7pm – 9:45pm; Sun 6.30pm – 8:45pm; bar meals – Sunday 7pm – 9pm. **Cuisine:** English / French:- English and French traditional cuisine, including carvery. Good wine list. **Rooms:** 94 bedrooms all with tea making facilities, telephone, radio, TV: 5 singles ensuite, 22 twins ensuite, 20 doubles ensuite. **Credit cards:** Visa, Access, AmEx. **Other points:** licensed, Sunday lunch, no-smoking area, children catered for – please check for age limits, pets allowed, afternoon tea, bank holidays, baby-listening device, cots, foreign exchange. **Directions:** second turn off roundabout at end of A45, to port. At port, take first turning. Proceed over traffic lights, taking first left. Hotel is 250yds on the left.
OHI (UK) LTD, tel (0394) 285621.

### THE WAVERLEY HOTEL, Wolsey Gardens
*The Waverley is a beautiful, recently refurbished Victorian Hotel standing high on the cliff, offering spectacular views of the sea and promenade. The Wolsey Restaurant provides an excellent a la carte menu as well as specially priced changing daily menus. There is always a selection of fresh fish and seafood available. Lighter meals available in Gladstones Bar and Brasserie. Real ales.*
*ACCOMMODATION £21–£30*
*FOOD up to £15* ★
**Hours:** lunch 12noon – 2pm; dinner 6:30pm – 10pm. **Cuisine:** English / continental:- Varied a la carte menu in the restaurant. Bar meals include grills, fresh fish, chilli, lasagne, salads and home made pies. Daily changing specials. **Rooms:** 20 bedrooms all with tea making facilities, telephone, TV: 4 singles ensuite, 7 twins ensuite, 8 doubles ensuite, 1 family room ensuite. **Credit cards:** Visa, Access, Diners, AmEx. **Other points:** Sunday lunch, children catered for – please check for age limits, weekend breaks. **Directions:** On upper sea-cliff road, 1 minute from main street.
MR AVERY, tel (0394) 282811, fax (0394) 670185.

## FERNHURST, West Sussex Map 4

### THE RED LION, The Green
*One of the oldest buildings in the village, The Red Lion is an attractive stone built inn overlooking the village green. With exposed beams and open log fires to add to the cosy atmosphere, you will find the good food and Mrs Heath's hospitality hard to pass by.*
*FOOD up to £15*
**Hours:** lunch 12noon – 2:30pm; dinner 7pm – 10:30pm.
**Cuisine:** English / continental:- English/Continental,

including Breast of pigeon in a blackberry sauce, Peppered chicken in a cream and Dijon sauce. **Credit cards:** Visa, Access. **Other points:** licensed, Sunday lunch, no-smoking area, children catered for – please check for age limits, garden. **Directions:** off the A286, situated in Fernhurst, 3 miles from Haslemere.
MRS BRENDA HEATH, tel (0428) 643112, (0428) 653304.

## FRESSINGFIELD, Suffolk Map 9

### THE FOX AND GOOSE INN, Nr Diss

*Nestling next to the church in the centre of the beautiful Suffolk village of Fressingfield, this 480 year old inn with its beams and timbers is a delight to visit. A welcoming atmosphere prevails and although a 'local restaurant' it is still widely renowned for its diversity of a la carte dishes, from English and French through to Italian or Japanese, all home-cooked using fresh produce. It is ideally situated for exploring rural Suffolk and for visiting such attractions as Framlingham Castle, Blooms Garden Centre & Steam Museum, and many more.*
*FOOD £15–£20*
**Hours:** lunch 12noon – 2pm; bar snacks 12noon – 2pm; dinner 7pm – 9:30pm; bar snacks 7pm – 9:30pm. **Cuisine:** international:- Ranging from Japanese deep-fried fish and vegetable tempure to seized local cod with garlicky saffron potato puree or home-made sausages, mash, onion and gravy. **Other points:** parking, children catered for – please check for age limits, Sunday lunch, vegetarian meals, open-air dining, licensed. **Directions:** on A140 south of Scole, take B1118 to Stradbroke, turn left to Fressingfield after approx 5 miles.
RUTH WATSON, tel (0379) 86247, fax (0379) 868107.

## GATWICK, Surrey Map 4

### RUSS HILL HOTEL, Russ Hill, Charlwood

*Built in the late 1800's as a fine country manor house, this hotel is rich in Victorian charm and elegance, enjoying panoramic views of Surrey's hills. All 150 air-conditioned bedrooms feature the most modern facilities, with furnishings of the highest standard. Superb health and leisure centre, conference and banqueting facilities are also available. Ideal for Gatwick Airport and many nearby places of interest. A courtesy coach to Gatwick Airport is available to guests.*
*ACCOMMODATION £21–£30*
*FOOD up to £15*
**Hours:** breakfast 6:30am – 10am; bar snacks 12noon – 12midnight; dinner 7pm – 10pm. **Cuisine:** international – **Rooms:** 150 bedrooms 19 singles ensuite, 10 twins ensuite, 109 doubles ensuite, 12 family rooms ensuite. **Other points:** parking, children catered for – please check for age limits, open bank holidays, Sunday dinner, disabled access, pets allowed, residents' lounge, vegetarian meals, conferences, garden, leisure club. **Directions:** from A23 follow signs to Charlwood. At the

end of the village turn left into Rectory Lane, hotel is at the top of the hill.
MR R IBBOTT (DEPUTY GENERAL MANAGER), tel (0293) 862171, fax (0293) 862390.

## GODALMING, Surrey Map 4

### THE MONGOLIAN, 10–14 Wolf Street

*Discover the spirit of creation with a style of eating which exemplifies an age old tradition from the homelands of Mongolia, where the great Khans barbecued slivers of meat on their upturned shields. Fill your bowl with a selection of meats and vegetables, add herbs and then watch your creation being barbecued on the Mongolian hotplate. Young, enthusiastic friendly crowd.*
*FOOD up to £15*
**Hours:** closed 01/01; lunch 12noon – 5pm; dinner 6:30pm – 12midnight; closed Christmas 25/12. **Cuisine:** Mongolian:- Barbecue style cuisine, enhanced with aromatic spices and seasonings. **Credit cards:** Visa, Access, AmEx. **Other points:** licensed, Sunday lunch, children catered for – please check for age limits, bank holidays. **Directions:** on junction of B3001 and B2130, opposite the police station.
GLENN MATTHEWS & ANTHONY WILSON, tel (0483) 414155.

## GREAT BIRCHAM, Norfolk Map 9

### THE KINGS HEAD HOTEL, Great Bircham, Kings Lynn

*A country hotel near Sandringham, Kings Lynn and the coast. With open country on three sides, the outlook is decidedly rural and quiet. There is a pleasant grassed area for summer dining. An extremely popular eating place with tourists and locals, in the bar and restaurant. French, Italian and Spanish are spoken.*
*ACCOMMODATION £21–£30*
*FOOD up to £15* ★
**Hours:** breakfast 8am – 9:30am; lunch 12noon – 2pm; dinner 7pm – 10pm. **Cuisine:** English / continental:- Stuffed sardines in herbs, brodetto, duckling a l'orange, halibut, Grenobloise, fresh Norfolk seafood and produce. **Rooms:** 5 bedrooms all with tea making facilities, TV: 3 twins ensuite, 2 doubles ensuite. **Credit cards:** Visa, Access. **Other points:** open-air dining, children catered for – please check for age limits, ample parking. **Directions:** on the edge of Royal Sandringham Estate beside the B1153.
IRIS & ISIDORO VERRANDO, tel (048523) 265.

## GREAT MISSENDEN, Buckinghamshire Map 6

### THE GEORGE, 94 High Street

*Many levelled, old beamed and tastefully furnished pub which offers excellent food, competent service, a very pleasant atmosphere at very good value.*
*ACCOMMODATION £21–£30*
*FOOD up to £15* ★

**Hours:** last orders 7pm – 9:45pm; bar snacks all day 7pm; lunch 12noon – 2pm; dinner 7pm – 11:30pm. **Cuisine:** English / continental:- Steaks, pasta and vegetarian selections. **Rooms:** 6 bedrooms 4 doubles ensuite, 2 family rooms ensuite. **Credit cards:** Access, Visa, Switch. **Other points:** licensed, open-air dining, Sunday lunch, children catered for – please check for age limits. **Directions:** ¼ mile from A413 between Amersham & Wendover. In town's main st. GUY & SALLY SMITH, tel (0494) 862084, fax (0494) 865622.

## GREAT YARMOUTH, Norfolk Map 9

### CARLTON HOTEL, Marine Parade
*This original 1840's hotel has been tastefully modernised to the most luxurious current day standards, creating one of East Anglia's leading hotels and is an ideal base for the business executive or for that special break. The Carlton also has its own Hairdressing Salon. The highly trained staff will ensure every need is catered for. Conference and Function Suites.*
*ACCOMMODATION £31–£40*
*FOOD up to £15*
**Hours:** breakfast 7am – 9:30am; bar meals 11am – 3pm; lunch 12noon – 3pm; bar meals 5pm – 10:30pm; dinner 7pm – 9:30pm. **Cuisine:** English:- A la carte & Table d'hote, offering good English food & fine wines. Penny's Cafe Bar provides meals and snacks all day. Vegetarian meals available. **Rooms:** 88 bedrooms all with tea making facilities, telephone, radio, TV: 35 singles ensuite, 11 twins ensuite, 33 doubles ensuite, 5 triples ensuite, 4 quads ensuite. **Credit cards:** Visa, Access, Diners, AmEx. **Other points:** licensed, Sunday lunch, pets allowed, afternoon tea, vegetarian meals, parking, bank holidays, children catered for – please check for age limits, baby sitting, baby-listening device, cots, 24hr reception, foreign exchange, residents' bar, residents' lounge. **Directions:** located on Great Yarmouth seafront. Corner of Marine Parade & Albert Square.
WAVENEY INNS, tel (0493) 855234, fax (0493) 852220.

### THE CLIFF HOTEL, Cliff Hill, Gorleston-on-Sea
*A welcoming business and holiday hotel overlooking the harbour on the quieter side of Great Yarmouth. The chefs and their staff provide a large selection of English dishes, offering the opportunity to sample the best from the produce of Norfolk farms and market gardens.*
*ACCOMMODATION £21–£30*
*FOOD £15 £20*
**Hours:** open all year 7pm; breakfast 7:30am – 9:45am; lunch 12:30pm – 2pm; dinner 7pm – 9:30pm. **Cuisine:** English:- Traditional roasts. **Rooms:** 39 bedrooms, all en suite. **Credit cards:** Visa, Access, Diners, AmEx. **Other points:** Sunday lunch, children catered for – please check for age limits. **Directions:** overlooking the harbour at Great Yarmouth on A47.
MR R W SCOTT, tel (0493) 662179.

### THE GALLON POT, Market Place
*A traditional town centre public house which has built up a fine reputation for good quality bar food at very reasonable prices. Popular with locals of all ages the pub also appeals to seasonal holiday-makers. A relaxed and comfortable atmosphere.*
*FOOD up to £15*
**Hours:** bar – except Sunday 10am – 11pm; lunch – except Sunday 11:30am – 2:30pm; lunch – Sunday 12noon – 2:30pm; dinner – except Sunday 7pm – 10pm; dinner – Sunday 7pm – 9:30pm. **Cuisine:** English:- Traditional pub food. Special weekend and lunchtime menus. **Other points:** licensed, open-air dining, children catered for – please check for age limits, parking. **Directions:** in town centre, in open market square. Next to large public car park.
MICHAEL & MARIA SPALDING, tel (0493) 842230.

### IMPERIAL HOTEL, North Drive
*For many years The Imperial has enjoyed an outstanding reputation for its quality of food and wine. The Rambouillet with its quiet intimacy offers a wide range of dishes to appeal to both the gourmet and traditional diner. The excellently appointed rooms are equipped with all modern facilities, and many have glorious sea views. A perfect base for touring East Anglia.*
*ACCOMMODATION £31–£40*
*FOOD £15–£20*
**Hours:** open all year 7pm; breakfast 7:30am – 9:30am; lunch 12:30pm – 2:30pm; dinner 7pm – 10pm. **Cuisine:** English / French:- Regional English and French cuisine of the highest quality, complemented by a superb wine list. Special gastronomique weekends are held each year. **Rooms:** 39 bedrooms all with tea making facilities, telephone, radio, TV: 4 singles ensuite, 12 twins ensuite, 23 doubles ensuite. **Credit cards:** Visa, Access, Diners, AmEx. **Other points:** licensed, Sunday lunch, children catered for – please check for age limits, afternoon tea, residents' lounge, pets allowed, conferences. **Directions:** situated on seafront opposite the Waterways.
ROGER MOBBS, tel (0493) 851113, fax (0493) 852229.

### REGENCY HOTEL, 5 North Drive
*A modern seaside hotel offering comfortable accommodation in a good seafront location. Guests can choose from table d'hote or a la carte menus at dinner and there is a good choice at breakfast. The Regency Hotel is popular with holiday-makers and business people alike.*
*ACCOMMODATION £21–£30*
*FOOD up to £15*
**Hours:** breakfast 8am – 9:30am; dinner – Sunday 5pm – 8pm; dinner 6pm – 8:30pm. **Cuisine:** English. **Rooms:** 13 bedrooms 3 singles ensuite, 9 doubles ensuite, 1 family room ensuite. **Credit cards:** Visa, Access, Diners, AmEx. **Directions:** on the seafront in Great Yarmouth.
J BARNETT, tel (0493) 843759.

## GUILDFORD, Surrey Map 4

### KINGS SHADE COFFEE HOUSE,
*20 Tunsgate*
*Well situated between the famous Guildhall clock and the superb Castle gardens. Kings Shade Coffee House is open all day and is a very popular venue in which to enjoy a meal or snack. The menu is extensive, the atmosphere bustling and the service friendly and efficient. The home-made sweets are particularly recommended.*
**FOOD up to £15** CLUB
**Hours:** meals all day 8:30am – 6pm; closed Sunday.
**Cuisine:** English:- House specialities include Steak & Kidney Pie, Chicken & Spinach Gratin, Lasagne, Salads, toasted savouries, stuffed baked potatoes, sandwiches. Morning coffee, lunch, light meals and afternoon tea are also available. **Other points:** licensed, afternoon tea.
**Directions:** off the High Street, opposite the Guild Hall.
DAVID GOLDSBY, tel (0483) 576718.

### THE SPREAD EAGLE, 46 Chertsey Street
*A split-level older style pub, with exposed walls, specialising in real ale. The stables have been converted to a family room and children's dining area. Close to the town's shops and offices.*
**FOOD up to £15** 🍽
**Hours:** lunch 12noon – 2pm. **Cuisine:** English:- Bar meals – lamb provencale, moussaka, lasagne, beef and mushroom pie, asparagus quiche. **Other points:** licensed, open-air dining, children catered for – please check for age limits.
**Directions:** off the main street in Guildford.
MR & MRS OLIVER, tel (0483) 35018.

## HARWICH, Essex Map 8

### CLIFF HOTEL, Marine Parade, Dovercourt
*Overlooking the seafront, this large Victorian hotel is decorated and furnished in keeping with the character of the building. Attractively presented meals are served by friendly, competent staff and the accommodation is very comfortable. Ideally located on the seafront for holiday-makers.*
**ACCOMMODATION £21–£30**
**FOOD up to £15** ★
**Hours:** breakfast 7:30am – 9:30am; bar meals 12noon – 2pm; lunch 12:30pm – 2pm; bar meals 6pm – 9pm; dinner 6:30pm – 9pm. **Cuisine:** English:- Wide choice of dishes including fresh fish. **Rooms:** 27 bedrooms 2 singles, 1 single ensuite, 11 doubles ensuite, 8 twins ensuite, 5 family rooms ensuite. **Credit cards:** Visa, Access, Diners, AmEx. **Other points:** licensed, Sunday lunch, children catered for – please check for age limits, bank holidays, afternoon tea.
**Directions:** on seafront at Dovercourt.
D A HUTCHINS, tel (0255) 503345, fax (0255) 240358.

### NEW FARM HOUSE, Spinnel's Lane, Wix, Manningtree
*A large modern farmhouse, set in its own well-tended gardens situated on the outskirts of the quiet village of Wix. Comfortable, clean bedrooms complemented by a relaxing and friendly atmosphere.*

**ACCOMMODATION under £20**
**FOOD up to £15**
**Hours:** breakfast 8am – 10am; dinner 6:30pm – 7pm.
**Cuisine:** English. **Rooms:** 11 bedrooms all with tea making facilities, TV: 2 singles, 1 single ensuite, 2 twins ensuite, 1 double ensuite, 2 family rooms, 3 family rooms ensuite. **Credit cards:** Visa, Access. **Other points:** children catered for – please check for age limits, playland, pets allowed, vegetarian meals.
**Directions:** follow A120 from Colchester to Harwich. Turn into Wix village.
THE MITCHELL FAMILY, tel (0255) 870365, fax (0255) 870837.

### TOWER HOTEL, Main Road, Dovercourt
*Built in 1885 the main feature of the building is a tower in the north-east corner. Inside, it retains many original architectural features with friezes, cornices and architraves. The Pattrick Suite is a magnificent function room which is available for private hire.*
**ACCOMMODATION £21–£30**
**FOOD up to £15**
**Hours:** breakfast 8am – 9:30am; lunch 12noon – 2pm; dinner 6:30pm – 9:30pm. **Cuisine:** English / seafood:- Fresh local lobster and Dover sole. **Rooms:** 15 bedrooms 3 singles ensuite, 8 doubles ensuite, 2 twins ensuite, 2 family rooms ensuite. **Credit cards:** Visa, Access, Diners, AmEx. **Other points:** licensed, Sunday lunch, children catered for – please check for age limits.
**Directions:** on the left side of A136 (Harwich bound) near Dovercourt Station.
DOUGLAS HUTCHINS, tel (0255) 504952.

## HASTINGS, East Sussex Map 5

### RESTAURANT TWENTY SEVEN,
*27 George Street, Hastings Old Town*
*Attractive French restaurant set in the old part of town near the seafront. All food is freshly prepared for each customer and, with its impressionist paintings and soft gallic style music, the atmosphere is both intimate and relaxing.*
**FOOD £15–£20**
**Hours:** dinner 7pm – 10:30pm; closed Monday.
**Cuisine:** French:- French dishes including Salad Maconnaise, Cassoulet de Lotte, Boeuf en Croute, Maigret di Canard, Steak au Poivre. Traditional Sunday lunch. **Credit cards:** Visa, Access. **Other points:** licensed, Sunday lunch. **Directions:** east end of the seafront, pedestrianised area of the old town.
P ATTRILL & E GIBBS CHEF – C ATTRILL, tel (0424) 420060.

## HAUGHLEY, Suffolk Map 9

### THE OLD COUNTING HOUSE RESTAURANT, Nr Stowmarket
*Typical Suffolk timber-framed house dating back to the 1500's when it was a bank. Now you may dine at tables set with damask linen, fine glassware and classic cutlery.*
**FOOD £15–£20** 🐕

**Hours:** lunch 12noon – 2pm; dinner 7:30pm – 9:30pm; closed Sunday July – August. **Cuisine:** English / French:- Lunch – 2 or 3 course table d'hote plus a la carte. Dinner – 4 course table d'hote, 6 choices for each course, changed every 3 weeks. Also a la carte dinner menu. Sunday lunch is available September to June. **Credit cards:** Visa, Access, AmEx. **Other points:** licensed, children catered for – please check for age limits. **Directions:** 3 miles west of Stowmarket, 1.5 miles A45. Haughley centre.
MR & MRS P WOODS, tel (0449) 673617.

## HAYWARDS HEATH, West Sussex Map 4

### INN THE PRIORY, Syresham Gardens
*Lovely restaurant set in the surroundings of a Victorian priory chapel, with stained glass windows, ornate wood carvings and a turret clock; offering a freshly prepared carvery menu of high quality and good value. Conference facilities available. National Trust gardens and Bluebell steam railway located nearby.*
*FOOD up to £15* CLUB
**Hours:** lunch – Sunday 11:45am – 4pm; lunch – except Sunday 12noon – 3pm; dinner 7pm – 11:30pm. **Cuisine:** English:- Traditional English carvery. Fish and vegetarian menus available. **Credit cards:** Visa, Access, Diners, AmEx. **Other points:** licensed, Sunday lunch, children catered for – please check for age limits.
**Directions:** take Caxton Way off Sussex Square roundabout on South Road.
DAVID & MARTINA WHITE, tel (0444) 459533, fax (0444) 459340.

### THE SLOOP INN , Freshfield Lock
*This attractive public house offers good quality bar meals in comfortable surroundings. The service is warm and courteous and the pub enjoys a friendly, welcoming atmosphere.*
*FOOD up to £15*
**Hours:** lunch 12 noon – 2pm; dinner Sunday till Thursday 7pm – 9.30pm, Friday & Saturday 7pm –10pm. **Cuisine:** English, extensive menu displayed on blackboards changes daily. **Credit cards:** Visa, Access, Diners. **Other points:** children catered for – please check for age limits, dogs allowed (in public bar), garden, games room, disabled access, parking, vegetarian meals. **Directions:** off the A272 at Scaynes Hill near Haywoods Heath.
DAVID MICHAEL & MARILYN MILLS, tel (0444) 831219.

## HEMEL HEMPSTEAD, Hertfordshire Map 6

### THE BOBSLEIGH INN, Hempstead Road, Bovingdon
*The Bobsleigh Inn has an established reputation for good food and customer care, with visitors from around the world. Enjoy a candle-lit dinner in the elegant restaurant overlooking the garden, or relax with a cocktail, liqueur or late night coffee in the conservatory. Conference facilities for up to 40 persons. Banqueting for up to 90, and Wedding Receptions are a speciality.*
*ACCOMMODATION £21–£30*
*FOOD £15–£20*
**Hours:** no lunch or dinner Sunday; no lunch Monday; breakfast 7am – 9:30am; lunch 12noon – 2pm; dinner 7pm – 9:30pm; closed 26 December – 6 January. **Cuisine:** English / international. **Rooms:** 39 bedrooms 5 singles ensuite, 4 twins ensuite, 28 doubles ensuite, 2 family rooms ensuite. **Credit cards:** Visa, Access, AmEx, Diners, Switch. **Other points:** parking, children catered for – please check for age limits, disabled access, pets, residents' lounge, garden, vegetarian meals, open-air dining. **Directions:** M1 Junction 8 / M25 Junction 20, take A41 to Aylesbury after Hemel Hempstead train station, turn left at Swan Public House and follow B4505. The Inn is 2 miles on the left-hand side.
MR A RICKETT & MRS C DERBYSHIRE, tel (0442) 833276, fax (0442) 832471.

## HENFIELD, West Sussex Map 4

### TOTTINGTON MANOR HOTEL & RESTAURANT, Edburton
*This typical Sussex Country Manor House, set in 4 acres of well kept grounds, dates back to the 16th Century, and commands magnificent views over the South Downs and Weald. The Chef/Proprietor was formerly head chef at the Ritz in London. Guests will find the accommodation to as high a standard as the fine cuisine.*
*ACCOMMODATION £21–£30*
*FOOD £15–£20*
**Hours:** breakfast 7:30am – 9:30am; lunch 12noon – 9:15pm; dinner 7pm – 9:15pm. **Cuisine:** English / continental:- A la carte, Table d'hote and Bar menu. Traditional English, classical and international cuisine. **Rooms:** 6 bedrooms, all en suite. TV, telephones, tea & coffee making facilities. **Credit cards:** Visa, Access, Diners, AmEx. **Other points:** licensed, Sunday lunch, no-smoking area, conferences. **Directions:** off the A2037.
DAVID & KATE MILLER, tel (0903) 815757, fax (0903) 879331.

## HERTFORD, Hertfordshire Map 6

### SALISBURY ARMS HOTEL, Fore Street
*Hertford's oldest hostelry, offering guests the opportunity to enjoy excellent food, traditional ales and a warm welcome in surroundings that retain all the character and charm of a bygone age. The oak-beamed and wood panelled restaurant offers exceptional cuisine, and the well appointed bedrooms are furnished in a blend of subtle pastel shades, complementing the cottage atmosphere.*
*ACCOMMODATION £31–£40*
*FOOD up to £15*
**Hours:** breakfast 7am – 9am; lunch 12noon – 2pm; dinner 7pm – 10pm. **Cuisine:** international. **Credit**

cards: Visa, Access, Diners, AmEx. **Other points:**
parking, children catered for – please check for age
limits, residents' lounge, vegetarian meals. **Directions:**
A414 to Hertford from A10.
JOEY & TINA O'REGAN, tel (0992) 583091, fax
(0992) 552510.

## HIGH WYCOMBE, Buckinghamshire Map 6

### DRAKE COURT HOTEL, 141 London Road
*A small, friendly hotel situated close to the centre of
historic High Wycombe. The staff are welcoming and
efficient. Convenient for the M40 London – Oxford
motorway and for touring the Thames Valley, Oxford and
the Cotswolds.*
*ACCOMMODATION under £20*
*FOOD up to £15*
**Hours:** breakfast 7:30am – 8:30am; dinner 7pm –
9:30pm. **Cuisine:** English / continental:- Traditional
English and continental cuisine. **Rooms:** 20 bedrooms, 8
en suite. **Credit cards:** Visa, Access, Diners, AmEx.
**Other points:** licensed, children catered for – please
check for age limits, bank holidays, residents' lounge,
swimming pool. **Directions:** A40 London Road, close to
High Wycombe. Approx 1 mile M40 motorway.
IAN CLARK, tel (0494) 523639, fax (0494) 472696.

## HITCHIN, Hertfordshire Map 6

### REDCOATS FARMHOUSE HOTEL,
Redcoats Green
*A 15th century farmhouse set in beautiful grounds
amidst the rolling Hertfordshire countryside near Little
Wymondley village, yet only minutes from the A1. Full of
English charm, with its beamed and comfortable
interior, bar and lounge, the intimate quiet of the dining
rooms and individual character of the bedrooms,
Redcoats exudes an air of peace and tranquillity.
Excellent food and efficient service. Ideally situated for
visiting Knebworth and Woburn Parks.*
*ACCOMMODATION £31–£40*
*FOOD £21–£25*
**Hours:** breakfast 7am – 9am; lunch 12noon – 1:30pm; club
lunch 12noon – 2pm; dinner 7pm – 9:30pm; club supper
from 7pm. **Cuisine:** English/French. **Rooms:** 14 bedrooms
1 single, 10 doubles, 3 twins. **Credit cards:** Visa, Access,
Diners, AmEx. **Other points:** parking, children catered for
– please check for age limits, no-smoking area, residents'
lounge, vegetarian meals, open-air dining. **Directions:**
Junction 8 on A1M south of Little Wymondley. Follow
signs for Todds Green. Then Redcoats Green.
PETER BUTTERFIELD AND JACKIE GAINSFORD,
tel (0438) 729500, fax (0438) 723322.

## HORSHAM, West Sussex Map 4

### COUNTRYMAN INN, Shipley
*A traditional old country pub with a very friendly
atmosphere, set in 3000 acres of Sussex farmland.
Customers can enjoy delicious home-cooked meals,*
*especially the deep dish pies which are made with fresh
meat from the local farm. A very popular pub with the
local community and country walkers. Places of interest
nearby include Knepp Castle and Shipley Mill.*
*FOOD up to £15*
**Hours:** lunch 12noon – 2pm; bar meals 12noon – 2pm;
dinner 7pm – 9:30pm; bar meals 7pm – 9pm. **Cuisine:**
English:- Rural English cuisine, including speciality
'deep dish' pies and fresh fish. Good wine list. **Credit
cards:** Visa, Access. **Other points:** open-air dining,
Sunday lunch, children catered for – please check for
age limits, bank holidays, functions. **Directions:** follow
A24 to Worthing; A272 signs to Billingshurst. Second
turn left, then 1 mile to bottom of lane.
ALAN VAUGHAN, tel (0403) 741383.

## HOVE, East Sussex Map 5

### SACKVILLE HOTEL, 189 Kingsway
*The hotel has a commanding sea-front position, looking
out over the bowling greens and the beaches. Oak
panelling, luxurious furnishings and ornamental high
ceilings create the feeling of space and comfort. The
restaurant menu places a strong accent on local fresh
produce such as seafood. The hotel was completely
refurbished at the beginning of 1993 and many of the 45
ensuite bedrooms have seaviews and balconies.*
*ACCOMMODATION £21–£30*
*FOOD up to £15* `CLUB`
**Hours:** breakfast 7:30am – 9:30am; bar lunches
11:30am – 2pm; lunch 12:30pm – 2pm; dinner 7:30pm –
9:30pm. **Cuisine::-** English, French, Chinese. Including
a special hors d'oeuvres selection and carving trolley.
**Rooms:** 45 bedrooms 13 singles ensuite, 7 twins ensuite,
22 doubles ensuite, 3 suites. **Credit cards:** Visa, Access,
Diners, AmEx. **Other points:** children catered for –
please check for age limits, no-smoking area, pets
allowed, residents' lounge, vegetarian meals, parking.
**Directions:** A259, sea-front road – west out of Brighton.
ANDREW BORLAND (GENERAL MANAGER),
tel (0273) 736292, fax (0273) 205759.

## HUNSTANTON, Norfolk Map 9

### CALEY HALL MOTEL AND
RESTAURANT, Old Hunstanton
*The resident proprietors of Caley Hall have skilfully
converted the outbuildings of their 17th century Manor
House to provide a comfortable bar and restaurant
facilities. Chalets have been sympathetically added and
are closely in keeping with the overall architectural
style. The restaurant serves a wide range of good food
which is well presented and offers good value for money.*
*ACCOMMODATION £21–£30*
*FOOD up to £15*
**Hours:** breakfast 8am – 9:30am; lunch 12noon – 2pm;
dinner 7pm – 9pm. **Cuisine:** French / British:- Table
d'hote and a la carte menus. French and British cuisine
specialising in steaks and fish. Childrens portions
available. **Rooms:** 29 bedrooms 4 singles ensuite, 9

twins ensuite, 3 chalets, 13 doubles ensuite. **Credit cards:** Visa, Access. **Other points:** licensed, Sunday lunch, children catered for – please check for age limits, pets allowed, residents' lounge. **Directions:** A149. Just off the coast road between Brancaster and Hunstanton. CLIVE KING, tel (0485) 533486.

### GATE LODGE GUEST HOUSE, 2 Westgate
*Gate Lodge is a family run Guest House offering comfortable accommodation and meals of a high standard. The beach, leisure complex, shopping centre and bus station are all within easy reach. Gate Lodge provides an ideal base for touring the unspoilt north Norfolk Heritage coast and countryside. Sandringham is within easy reach. Birdwatching. Windsurfing. Bowling. Tennis. Croquet.*
*ACCOMMODATION under £20*
*FOOD up to £15*
**Hours:** closed 01/12 – 31/12; breakfast 8:45am; dinner 6:45pm. **Cuisine:** English:- Menu's are chosen daily, prepared with fresh seasonal produce to a very high standard. **Rooms:** 7 bedrooms all with tea making facilities, TV: 1 single ensuite, 3 doubles ensuite, 3 twins ensuite. **Other points:** security parking, pets allowed, residents' lounge, vegetarian meals, special diets, disabled access. **Directions:** A149 from Kings Lynn. Left at Hunstanton roundabout. Down hill and turn right. GUY & ROISIN WELLARD, tel (0485) 533549.

### NORTHGATE HOUSE, 46 Northgate
*Northgate House is a family run Guest House with comfortable, spacious accommodation, close to Hunstanton's Blue Flag beach, shops and theatre. Nearby are bird reserves, golf courses, several Stately Homes, Peddars Way, and the Norfolk Coast Path.*
*ACCOMMODATION under £20*
*FOOD up to £15*
**Hours:** breakfast 8:30am – 9am; dinner 6:30pm. **Cuisine:** breakfast. **Rooms:** 1 single, 2 double & 1 family bedroom, 1 en suite & all with shaver points. 1 bathroom/shower. Tea/coffee making facilities in all bedrooms. TV in all rooms. **Other points:** central heating, vegetarian meals, children catered for – please check for age limits, residents' lounge. **Directions:** off the A149, turn right into Austin St which leads to Northgate. MR & MRS M R SNARE, tel (0485) 533269.

## ICKHAM, Kent Map 5

### THE DUKE WILLIAM, The Street
*A 16th century freehouse in a picturesque village surrounded by farmlands. There is a lovely garden to the rear with ponds, a fountain and flowers, as well as swings for the children. Situated only 10 minutes from Canterbury, Ickham is central for Kent's many tourist attractions.*
*FOOD £21–£25*
**Hours:** open bank holidays 6:30pm; lunch 12noon – 2pm; bar meals 12noon – 2pm; dinner 7pm – 10pm; bar meals 7pm – 10pm; closed Monday. **Cuisine:** English / international:- Extensive seafood menu, beef, lamb, poultry, veal. In the bar: omelettes, fish, home-made

soup, chilli, home baked bread. Exciting bar meals. **Credit cards:** Visa, Access, Diners, AmEx. **Other points:** licensed, open-air dining, Sunday lunch, children catered for – please check for age limits, pets allowed, conservatory, garden. **Directions:** in the centre of Ickham which is signposted from the A257. MR A ROBIN & MRS C A MCNEILL, tel (0227) 721308.

## KERSEY, Suffolk Map 9

### BELL INN, The Street
*A 14th century timber-framed inn situated in a village that has become known as the 'prettiest village in the world'. An extensive selection of well presented tasty cuisine at excellent value for money. The friendly informal atmosphere and delightful surroundings make this a lovely place to dine.*
*FOOD £15–£20*
**Hours:** dinner – except Sunday 10am – 10pm; lunch 11:30am – 2pm; dinner 7pm – 9:30pm; closed Christmas evening; closed Boxing Day.**Cuisine:** English:- Extensive menu including boneless fillet of poached Scotch Salmon, steaks, salads, grills, home cooking and puddings. Good choice of vegetarian dishes. **Credit cards:** Visa, Access, Diners, AmEx. **Other points:** children catered for – please check for age limits, garden, afternoon tea. **Directions:** signposted off A1141, north of Hadleigh, Suffolk. ALEC & LYNNE COOTE, tel (0473) 823229.

## KEW, Surrey Map 7

### PISSARRO'S WINE BAR, 1 Kew Green, Richmond
*A roaring open fire, oak beams, a host of antique curios, some 50 wines and a delicious selection of home-made foods are all there to welcome and tempt you. Pissarro once painted the buildings where this enchanting wine bar now stands.*
*FOOD up to £15*
**Hours:** bar – except Sunday 11:30am – 11pm; bar – Sunday 12noon – 3pm; bar – Sunday 7pm – 10:30pm; closed Christmas 25/12 – 26/12; closed Easter Sunday. **Cuisine:** English:- Homemade country pies, delicious soups, fresh vegetables, a hearty selection of cheeses plus our daily cold buffet with special slimmer's salads, mouthwatering desserts and a traditional Sunday lunch. **Credit cards:** Visa, Access. **Other points:** licensed, open-air dining, Sunday lunch, disabled access, no children. **Directions:** on the A205 (south circular), south of Kew Bridge just off Kew Green. PAUL & PENNY CARVOSSO, tel (081) 940 3987.

## KINGS LYNN, Norfolk Map 9

### GUANOCK HOTEL, Southgates
*Close to the historic Southgates and adjacent to Jubilee Gardens. Just a few minutes from the town centre in a pleasant area of town.*

ACCOMMODATION under £20

FOOD up to £15

**Hours:** breakfast 7am – 8:30am; dinner 6pm – 7pm.
**Cuisine:** breakfast:- Full English or your choice from a
large selection. **Rooms:** 17 bedrooms all with tea
making facilities, radio, TV: 5 singles, 4 doubles, 3
twins ensuite, 5 family rooms. **Credit cards:** Visa,
Access, AmEx. **Other points:** central heating, children
catered for – please check for age limits, residents'
lounge, roof patio garden, billiards. **Directions:** on the
London road, enter Kings Lynn via Southgates.
TERRY PARCHMENT, tel (0553) 772959, fax (0553)
772959.

## KINGSTON UPON THAMES, Surrey
Map 4

### CHASE LODGE HOTEL, 10 Park Road,
Hampton Wick

Set on a quiet residential street in Hampton Wick, this
tranquil hotel is a real gem. Tastefully furnished with a
conservatory and a well tended garden, it strives to
provide personal service and attention to detail, and
offers a welcome retreat in a busy world. (See colour
advertisement in centre section.)

ACCOMMODATION £21–£30

FOOD up to £15 ★

**Hours:** breakfast 7am – 9am; dinner 7pm – 9:30pm.
**Cuisine:** English:- Traditional English cuisine with
imaginative sauces. Prepared to a high standard. Good
selection of wines. **Rooms:** 9 bedrooms 2 twins, 1 single
ensuite, 5 doubles ensuite, 1 twin ensuite. **Credit cards:**
Visa, Access, AmEx. **Other points:** no-smoking area,
parking, residents' lounge, garden. **Directions:** from
south take A93 Blairgowrie to Braemar road. 9 miles
north of Blairgowrie on left-hand side of the road,
Kingston-upon-Thames, near Hampton Court.
MR & MRS STAFFORD HAWORTH, tel (081) 943
1862, fax (081) 943 9363.

## KNAPHILL, Surrey Map 4

### FROGGIES WINE BAR & RESTAURANT,
42/44 High Street

'Froggies' offers three seating areas for an enjoyable
meeting and eating place, making it popular with locals
and travellers alike. Established since 1980.

FOOD £15–£20

**Hours:** lunch – weekdays 12noon – 2:30pm; dinner –
weekdays 7pm – 11pm; dinner – Saturday 7pm – 11pm;
closed Sunday. **Cuisine:** international:- Fresh
ingredients used on a daily produced menu
encompassing European and Far Eastern selected dishes.
Well-known for its soup, fresh fish and puddings.
**Credit cards:** Visa, Access, Diners, AmEx. **Other
points:** open-air dining, children catered for – please
check for age limits, private dining, parking.
**Directions:** a short drive from the main M3 in the centre
of Knaphill.
MR ROBIN DE WINTON, tel (0483) 480835.

## LANCING, West Sussex Map 4

### MINSTRELS GALLERY, Old Salts Farm Road

This 500 year old farmhouse has been beautifully upheld
and the restaurant offers an extensive French/English
menu. The atmosphere is warm and service excellent,
finished off with live piano music during the week.

FOOD £21–£25

**Hours:** lunch 12noon – 1:45pm; dinner 7pm – 8:45pm;
closed Monday; closed Saturday lunchtime; closed
Sunday evening. **Cuisine:** English / French:- Fixed price
menu, English-French cuisine. **Credit cards:** Visa,
Access, AmEx. **Other points:** Sunday lunch.
**Directions:** on A259, main coast road.
MR & MRS DAVIS, tel (0903) 766777, fax (0903)
764404.

### THE SUSSEX PAD HOTEL

The ambiance, service and cuisine at The Sussex Pad
combine to make dining here a special experience.
Renowned for its seafood – particularly lobsters, which
are kept alive in basement tanks until required for the
table. A boardroom style conference room is available
for up to 20 persons.

ACCOMMODATION £31–£40

FOOD up to £15

**Hours:** breakfast 7:30am – 10am; meals all day 11am –
10pm; lunch 12noon – 2pm; dinner 7pm – 10pm.
**Cuisine:** English:- Speciality: a seasonally-changing fish
menu featuring fresh lobster. **Rooms:** 19 bedrooms 9
doubles ensuite, 10 twins ensuite. **Credit cards:** Visa,
Access, Diners, AmEx. **Other points:** licensed, open-air
dining, children catered for – please check for age limits,
afternoon tea, pets allowed, conservatory. **Directions:** on
the A27 by Lancing College.
MR PACK, tel (0273) 454647, fax (0273) 453010.

## LAVENHAM, Suffolk Map 9

### THE TIMBERS RESTAURANT, High Street

15th century building which, as the name suggests, has
many exposed beams. Low ceilings and oak tables
complete the cosy and friendly atmosphere. Full a la
carte and table d'hote menus available in the evenings,
plus blackboard specials.

FOOD £15–£20

**Hours:** lunch 12noon – 2pm; dinner 7pm – 9:30pm; closed
Monday in summer; closed Sunday in summer. **Cuisine:**
English:- Daily specials on the blackboard at lunch.Evening:
A la carte. **Credit cards:** Visa, Access. **Directions:** on the
A1141 Sudbury to Bury St Edmunds road.
MISS B A PREECE & A M TRODD, tel (0787) 247218.

## LEATHERHEAD, Surrey Map 4

### THE STAR, Kingston Road

In a convenient position close to Chessington World of
Adventures and the M25, The Star serves good-quality
bar meals. A very popular, busy pub.

FOOD up to £15

**Hours:** lunch 12noon – 2pm; dinner 5:30pm – 10pm. **Cuisine:** English:- House speciality – fresh Scottish beef steaks cooked over charcoal. **Credit cards:** Visa, Access, Diners, AmEx. **Other points:** licensed, open-air dining, Sunday lunch, coach/prior arr. **Directions:** on the A243 1 mile from Leatherhead. Close to Chessington and M25.
COLIN & IRENE SUCKLING, tel (037 284) 2416.

## LEWES, East Sussex Map 5

### LA CUCINA RESTAURANT, 13 Station Street
*Outstanding food and excellent service can be found at this Italian restaurant in the centre of Lewes. The menu offers an extensive choice of authentic Italian dishes, superbly cooked and served in generous portions. Highly recommended for the high standard of cuisine and service within an atmosphere of peace and calm.*
FOOD £15–£20
**Hours:** lunch – Thur-Sat 12noon – 2pm; dinner – Mon-Sat 6:30pm – 10:30pm; closed Sunday/bank holidays. **Cuisine:** Italian:- Seasonal specialities may include, Fresh Mussels Marinara, Pesce Misto Marinara, Pollo alla Cacciatora, Sussex Lamb, Strawberries & Cream or Maraschino. **Credit cards:** Visa, Access, AmEx. **Other points:** licensed, children catered for – please check for age limits, parking. **Directions:** 200 metres from station towards the High Street.
JOSE VILAS MAYO, tel (0273) 476707.

### WHITE HART HOTEL, High Street
*An historic 16th century coaching house with a modern extension, tastefully blended to the original architecture. Well placed for exploring the Sussex coast, the hotel offers comfort, good food and warm hospitality.*
ACCOMMODATION £41–£50
FOOD up to £15
**Hours:** breakfast 8am – 9:30am; lunch 12:30pm – 2pm; dinner 7pm – 10:15pm. **Cuisine:** English / French:- A la carte, English and French. Carvery, set price with fish or vegetarian option. **Rooms:** 48 bedrooms, 44 en suite. **Credit cards:** Visa, Access, Diners, AmEx. **Other points:** licensed, Sunday lunch, children catered for – please check for age limits, pets allowed, conferences, afternoon tea. **Directions:** 7 miles from Brighton on A26.
MR AYRIS, tel (0273) 476694.

## LINDFIELD, West Sussex Map 4

### BENT ARMS, 98 High Street
*The Bent Arms is part of a 16th century coaching inn, that sits in a typical English village with half timbered houses, a lake and swans. It is popular with locals and has a friendly and relaxed atmosphere.*
ACCOMMODATION £21–£30
FOOD up to £15 CLUB ★
**Hours:** breakfast 7:30am; lunch 12noon – 2:15pm; dinner 6:15pm – 10:15pm. **Cuisine:** English:- A la carte,

bar meals/snacks. The speciality is Spit Roast Beef in bar – sliced to order, hot. **Rooms:** 9 bedrooms all with tea making facilities, TV: 1 single ensuite, 4 twins ensuite, 4 doubles ensuite. **Credit cards:** Visa, Access, Diners, AmEx. **Other points:** licensed, open-air dining, Sunday lunch, children catered for – please check for age limits, garden, pets allowed. **Directions:** 2 miles outside Haywards Heath station.
MR HOYLE, tel (0444) 483146.

## LINTON, Cambridgeshire Map 8

### THE CROWN INN, High Street
*A lime-washed Georgian pub, situated in the centre of the pleasant village of Linton, offering a choice of tasty bar meals or an interesting a la carte menu in their restaurant. Excellent service and a very warm welcome typical of a charming village pub, makes a visit here well worthwhile.*
ACCOMMODATION under £20
FOOD up to £15
**Hours:** lunch 12noon – 2pm; bar 12noon – 3pm; dinner 6:30pm – 10pm; bar 6:30pm – 11pm. **Cuisine:** English:- Home cooked food using fresh ingredients. **Rooms:** four self-contained rooms, all en suite and with TV, tea/coffee making facilities. **Credit cards:** Visa, Access. **Other points:** licensed, open-air dining, Sunday lunch, no-smoking area, children catered for – please check for age limits, garden. **Directions:** off A604, near the Water tower.
JOEL PALMER, tel (0223) 891759.

## LOWESTOFT, Suffolk Map 9

### WHERRY HOTEL, Bridge Road, Oulton Broad
*Easy access and a first class setting allow guests to relax in the hotel or take in the sights along the delightful inland waterways, renowned as the famous Norfolk Broad. The Wherry Hotel has been completely refurbished and offers a variety of amenities for the guests convenience and comfort. Large conference facilities, catering for up to 140, are available for conferences and functions.*
**Hours:** breakfast 7:30am – 9am; lunch 12noon – 2pm; bar meals 12noon – 2pm; dinner 7pm – 10pm; bar meals 7pm – 9pm. **Credit cards:** Visa, Access, Diners, AmEx. **Other points:** children catered for – please check for age limits, parking, vegetarian meals, pets. **Directions:** A117. From London A12 towards Lowestoft, follow signs to Oulton Broad.
MR A LOCK, tel (0502) 573521, fax (0502) 501350.

## LUTON, Bedfordshire Map 6

### LEASIDE HOTEL, 72 New Bedford Road
*A Victorian hotel, set in its own well tended gardens with large patio. Pleasantly decorated with comfortable furnishings and serving well cooked food, attractively presented from a comprehensive menu, the light*

pleasant atmosphere attracts tourists and business persons alike.
ACCOMMODATION £31–£40
FOOD £15–£20
**Hours:** breakfast 7am – 9am; lunch 12noon – 2pm; dinner 7pm – 9:30pm; closed Christmas 25/12 – 26/12. **Cuisine:** English:- A la carte menu, fixed price 3 course menu, bar meals/snacks and vegetarian meals available. **Rooms:** 14 bedrooms 10 singles ensuite, 1 twin ensuite, 2 doubles ensuite, 1 family room ensuite. **Credit cards:** Visa, Access, Diners, AmEx. **Other points:** licensed, Sunday lunch, children catered for – please check for age limits, garden. **Directions:** on A6 near Moor Park. MRS C A GILLIES, tel (0582) 417643, fax (0582) 34961.

## MAIDSTONE, Kent Map 5

### THE LIMETREE RESTAURANT AND HOTEL, The Limes, The Square, Lenham
Situated in the picturesque old Kentish village of Lenham, this family run establishment is steeped in history boasting timber frames dating back to the 14th century. Sympathetically renovated and refurbished, the hotel still retains many traditional features of a 600 year old building. The seven en suite bedrooms are all comfortably furnished and the restaurant specialises in classic French and continental cuisine. The atmosphere is relaxed and informal and small weddings and parties can be catered for. Ideally located for motorway and Channel ports, with the beautiful Leeds Castle just five miles away.
ACCOMMODATION £21–£30
**Hours:** breakfast 7am – 9am; lunch 12noon – 2:30pm; bar snacks 12noon – 2:30pm; dinner 7pm – 10:30pm; bar snacks 7pm – 10:30pm. **Cuisine:** English / French:- An extensive a la carte menu and set menu Monday to Sunday. **Rooms:** 7 bedrooms all with tea making facilities, telephone, TV: 1 4-poster ensuite, 3 twins ensuite, 2 doubles ensuite, 1 family room ensuite. **Other points:** parking, children catered for – please check for age limits, Sunday lunch, open bank holidays, no-smoking area, afternoon tea, vegetarian meals, open-air dining, garden, licensed. **Directions:** situated in the square just off the A20.
MUSA KIVRAK, tel (0622) 859509, fax (0622) 850096.

## MARGATE, Kent Map 5

### THE FOUR LANTERNS, 6 Market Place
The Four Lanterns is an attractive restaurant offering a wide variety of Greek and English food. Greek music and ornaments add to the friendly atmosphere in the restaurant. During the summer, meals are served in the Market Place which is just one of Margate's tourist attractions.
FOOD up to £15
**Hours:** lunch – Tue-Fri 12noon – 2pm; dinner 6pm – 11pm; closed lunchtime Sat-Mon. **Cuisine:** Greek / continental:- Specialising in fish dishes. Fresh lobster, sea bass and red snapper. Superb fish or meat meze. **Credit cards:** Visa, Access, AmEx. **Other points:**

children catered for – please check for age limits, entertainment, open-air dining. **Directions:** in the Market Place off the pier.
GEORGE PTOHOPOULOS, tel (0843) 293034.

### IVYSIDE HOTEL, 25 Sea Road, Westgate-on-Sea
The Ivyside overlooks the sea standing in its own grounds. Tourists, conferences and families blend well to make an excellent atmosphere. Good value, open 24 hours, with super sports complex.
ACCOMMODATION £31–£40
**Hours:** breakfast 7:30am – 9am; bar meals 12noon – 2pm; lunch 12:30pm – 2pm; bar meals 6pm – 10pm; dinner 6:30pm – 8:45pm. **Cuisine:** traditional English:- Traditional English, a la carte and vegetarian. **Rooms:** 70 bedrooms – TV, phone, satellite TV. **Credit cards:** Visa, Access, AmEx. **Other points:** indoor swimming, steamroom, Sunday lunch, no-smoking area, children catered for – please check for age limits, swimming pool, Jacuzzi, sauna, squash, launderette, entertainment. **Directions:** A28 from Canterbury. Close to Herne Bay and Ramsgate.
MICHAEL WISEMAN, tel (0843) 831082, fax (0843) 831082.

### KINGSDOWN HOTEL, 59–61 Harold Road, Cliftonville
A Victorian hotel, situated near the main shopping area and seafront, offering pleasantly decorated and spotlessly clean accommodation. The warm and courteous service and welcoming atmosphere attracts business people and tourists alike.
ACCOMMODATION under £20 ★
**Hours:** breakfast 9am – 9:30am; bar snacks 12:30pm – 2pm; dinner 6pm. **Cuisine:** English. **Rooms:** 12 bedrooms 6 singles, 4 twins ensuite, 1 double, 1 double ensuite. **Credit cards:** Visa, Access, AmEx. **Other points:** children catered for – please check for age limits, afternoon tea, parking. **Directions:** follow A28 to Margate or follow the Isle of Thanet signs.
MR JAMES WILLIAMS, tel (0843) 221672.

## MARLOW, Buckinghamshire Map 6

### YE OLDE DOG & BADGER, Henley Road, Medmenham
Lovely olde worlde pub, with delightful atmosphere and good food. Oak beams, gleaming brass, friendly staff to be found along a windy country road. Overflowing flower baskets make an attractive finish.
FOOD up to £15
**Hours:** lunch 12noon – 12:30pm; bar meals 12noon – 2:30pm; bar meals 5:30pm – 9:30pm; dinner 7pm – 9:30pm. **Cuisine:** English:- Traditional English pub food. Delicious, well-cooked, satisfying. **Credit cards:** Visa, Access, Diners, AmEx. **Other points:** licensed, Sunday lunch, children catered for – please check for age limits, bank holidays. **Directions:** on A4155 midway between Henley and Marlow.
MR & MRS FARRELL, tel (0491) 571362.

## MIDHURST, West Sussex Map 4

### THE SPREAD EAGLE HOTEL, South Street

*This attractive hotel started its days as a tavern in 1430 and expanded as a famous coaching inn. Excellent restaurant and bar facilities with a 17th century Jacobean Hall used for banqueting and conferences. Dine by candlelight in the beautiful restaurant, complete with huge coppered inglenook fireplace and dark oak beams. The ideal choice for that special occasion.*
*FOOD £26–£30* ⏝

**Hours:** open 24 hours; breakfast 8am – 10am; lunch 12:30pm – 2:15pm; dinner 7:30pm – 9:30pm. **Cuisine:** English:- Modern British cooking. The Fixed price menu changes every 2 weeks. **Rooms:** 41 bedrooms, all en suite. **Credit cards:** Visa, Access, Diners, AmEx. **Other points:** Sunday lunch, children catered for – please check for age limits. **Directions:** south-east outskirts of Midhurst. Off the High Street.
THE GOODMAN FAMILY & GEORGE MUDFORD, tel (0730) 816911.

## MILDENHALL, Suffolk Map 9

### THE SMOKE HOUSE, Beck Row

*Tony and Inez Warin extend a warm welcome to this atmospheric 16th century establishment, set in the heart of the East Anglian countryside. It has an established reputation for its friendly staff and caring attitude, good food and accommodation. Ideal for the country lover and sportsman, offering fishing, shooting, riding, and horseracing at nearby Newmarket. Ten golf courses nearby.*
*ACCOMMODATION £41–£50*
*FOOD £15–£20* ★

**Hours:** open all year 7:30pm; breakfast 7am – 9:30am; bar meals 11am – 2:30pm; lunch 12noon – 2pm; dinner 5pm – 10pm; bar meals 5pm – 11pm. **Cuisine:** English:- A la carte and Table d'hote, offering a wide range of traditional English dishes. **Rooms:** 104 bedrooms all with tea making facilities, telephone, radio, TV: 86 twins ensuite, 18 doubles ensuite. **Credit cards:** Visa, Access, Diners, AmEx. **Other points:** licensed, Sunday lunch, no-smoking area, children catered for – please check for age limits, afternoon tea, residents' lounge, garden, parking, baby-listening device, 24hr reception, foreign exchange. **Directions:** 4 miles from A11 Barton Mills roundabout on A1101, near Mildenhall.
TONY & INEZ WARIN, tel (0638) 713223, fax (0638) 712202.

## MILTON KEYNES, Buckinghamshire Map 6

### THE CARRINGTON ARMS, Cranfield Road, Nr Newport Pagnell

*Set in 1.5 acres of gardens, this hotel has recently been refurbished and decorated. Light background music and friendly staff help create the relaxed atmosphere in which you can enjoy generous meals presented with care and flair. Comfortable accommodation.*
*ACCOMMODATION £21–£30*
*FOOD up to £15*

**Hours:** last orders 5pm – 9:30pm; breakfast 7:30am – 9:30am; lunch 12noon – 3pm; bar meals 12noon – 3pm; dinner 6pm – 11pm; bar meals 6pm – 9:30pm. **Cuisine:** modern English:- Dishes may include supreme of chicken, mushrooms and nut fettucini, rainbow trout. Daily specials. **Rooms:** 8 bedrooms all with tea making facilities, telephone, radio, TV: 5 twins ensuite, 3 doubles ensuite. **Credit cards:** Visa, Access. **Other points:** licensed, open-air dining, Sunday lunch, children catered for – please check for age limits, bank holidays. **Directions:** Junction 14, M1, towards Newport Pagnell, approx 50yds right to Moulsoe.
STEVE CHESTERMAN, tel (0908) 615721, fax (0908) 615721.

## NEWDIGATE, Surrey Map 4

### GAMMAGE'S RESTAURANT, The Forge, Parkgate Road

*In keeping with French tradition, Gammage's is independently run by a husband and wife team. Situated in rural Newdigate, a warm welcome and outstanding Anglo-French cuisine await you. The food is superbly cooked and presented, complemented by a relaxing atmosphere and pleasing surroundings.*
*ACCOMMODATION under £20*
*FOOD up to £15* ♟ ⟨⟩ ⟦CLUB⟧ ★

**Hours:** dinner – Tue-Sun 7pm – 9:30pm; closed 2 weeks end of August; closed Easter. **Cuisine:** English / French:- Anglo-French cuisine using the best fresh ingredients. Dishes may include creamy soups, Foie gras, turbot with champagne & passionfruit, roast grouse. **Rooms:** 2 bedrooms 1 single, 1 double. **Credit cards:** Visa, Access, Diners, AmEx. **Other points:** licensed, no-smoking area, children catered for – please check for age limits, parking. **Directions:** 15 minutes from Gatwick airport. Opposite Surrey Oaks pub.
GARY & DEBBIE GAMMAGE, tel (0306) 631664.

## NEWPORT PAGNELL, Buckinghamshire Map 6

### MYSORE INDIAN CUISINE, 97–101 High Street

*The Mysore restaurant offers a wide range of high quality traditional Indian and Persian cuisine with takeaway menu also available. For special occasions a Mysore table of Murgh Masala or Kurzi Lamb can be ordered for four or more people at 48 hours notice. On Sundays a special hot buffet lunch is available for a very reasonable set price.*
*FOOD up to £15*

**Hours:** closed Christmas; open bank holidays, Easter; lunch 12noon – 2:30pm; dinner 6pm – 11:30pm. **Cuisine:** Indian:- Indian cuisine with tandoori specialities. **Credit cards:** Visa, Access, AmEx. **Other points:** licensed, Sunday lunch, no-smoking area,

children catered for – please check for age limits.
**Directions:** M1: Junction 14. Situated in centre of Newport Pagnell.
MR ODUD, tel (0908) 216426.

## NORWICH, Norfolk Map 9

### GRANGE HOTEL, 230 Thorpe Road
*Formerly an old Manor House and now tastefully restored, The Grange Hotel provides comfortable accommodation to the casual visitor and businessman alike. The comfortable bar is an ideal spot in which to spend a relaxing evening or enjoy a pre-dinner drink. Sauna and Solarium available. Available for special and private function hire. Ideal for touring Norfolk.*
*ACCOMMODATION £31–£40*
*FOOD £15–£20* ★
**Hours:** breakfast 7:30am – 9am; dinner 6:30pm – 9:30pm; closed Christmas 25/12 – 31/12. **Cuisine:** English:- A la Carte and Table d'Hote. Dishes may include, Roast Aylesbury Duckling, Lamb Cutlets Marchale, Supreme of Chicken, Darne of Salmon Rouge. Vegetarian. **Rooms:** 35 bedrooms all with tea making facilities, telephone, TV: 16 singles ensuite, 6 twins ensuite, 12 doubles ensuite, 1 quad ensuite. **Credit cards:** Visa, Access, Diners, AmEx. **Other points:** licensed, no-smoking area, children catered for – please check for age limits, parking, residents' lounge, disabled access, cots, functions, vegetarian meals, residents' bar. **Directions:** 1 mile from Norwich station, travelling towards Great Yarmouth.
ROBERT HARGREAVES, tel (0603) 34734, fax (0603) 34734.

### THE LARDER AND "UPSTAIRS" AT THE LARDER, 19 Bedford Street
*Good food and a warm welcome can be found at this establishment which is personally run by the proprietors and divided into 3 sections: A sandwich bar, a waitress service tea room and snack restaurant; while "Upstairs" is a small and intimate restaurant providing quality English and continental food with a daily special menu at reasonable prices in attractive surroundings.*
*FOOD up to £15*
**Hours:** breakfast 9am – 10:30am; meals all day 10:30am – 4:45pm. **Cuisine:** English / continental:- Three sections: sandwich bar – fresh baps & sandwiches to order, waitress service tea room & luncheon restaurant and a intimate a la carte restaurant, offering both English and continental food. **Other points:** licensed, no-smoking area, children catered for – please check for age limits, afternoon tea, guide dogs.
**Directions:** near the market place.
LAURENCE DYER AND MARTYN ROBERTS, tel (0603) 622641.

### OAKLANDS HOTEL, 89 Yarmouth Road, Thorpe St Andrews
**Hours:** breakfast 7am – 9:30am; lunch 12noon – 3pm; dinner 6pm – 9:30pm. **Cuisine:** English:- Traditional

English food prepared on the premises. Fresh local produce and good quality ingredients.
**Rooms:** 38 bedrooms all with tea making facilities, telephone, radio, TV: 6 singles ensuite, 12 twins ensuite, 16 doubles ensuite, 3 triples ensuite, 1 quad ensuite. **Credit cards:** Visa, Access, Diners, AmEx. **Other points:** children catered for – please check for age limits, bank holidays, residents' lounge, garden, baby-listening device, cots, 24hr reception, residents' bar. **Directions:** A47 Norwich to Great Yarmouth ring road, east of Norwich centre.
PETER CRONIN, tel (0603) 34471, fax (0603) 700318.

## ORFORD, Suffolk Map 9

### CROWN & CASTLE HOTEL, Nr Woodbridge
*Set in the Market Square next to Orford Castle, on the beautiful Suffolk coast, the Crown & Castle is tastefully and comfortably furnished and provides good, traditional fare. Popular with all ages, the hotel enjoys a pleasant, relaxed atmosphere. Ten ensuite rooms have private access to a garden overlooking the castle.*
*ACCOMMODATION £21–£30*
*FOOD up to £15*
**Hours:** breakfast 8am – 9:30am; lunch 12noon – 2pm; dinner 7pm – 9pm. **Cuisine:** English:- Predominantly English cuisine. **Rooms:** 20 bedrooms all with tea making facilities, telephone, TV: 1 single, 2 twins, 10 twins ensuite, 1 double, 5 doubles ensuite, 1 single ensuite. **Credit cards:** Visa, Access, Diners, AmEx. **Other points:** licensed, open-air dining, Sunday lunch, children catered for – please check for age limits, bank holidays, afternoon tea, pets allowed. **Directions:** turn off the A12 at Woodbridge.
SARAH MANN, tel (0394) 450205, fax (0394) 450176.

## PENSHURST, Kent Map 5

### THE BOTTLE HOUSE INN & RESTAURANT, Smarts Hill
*A very popular country pub set high on a hill. T he interior has an olde worlde feel with exposed beams, oak tables and chairs. The cuisine is mainly British and European with all dishes very well cooked and attractively presented. With friendly service, a relaxed atmosphere, excellent food and a garden for summer, the Bottle House is a good choice for an enjoyable meal.*
*FOOD up to £15*
**Hours:** bar meals 11am – 2:30pm; dinner 6pm – 11pm; closed Sunday evening. **Cuisine:** British / continental:- Dishes in the restaurant may include Fresh Fish, Mediterranean King Prawns, Fillet Steak Voronof. Bar meals menu and specials board. **Credit cards:** Visa, Access. **Other points:** licensed, open-air dining, Sunday lunch, pets allowed, disabled access. **Directions:** take the B2176 then the B2110.
GORDON & VALERIE MEER, tel (0892) 870306, fax (0892) 871094.

## THE SPOTTED DOG, *Smarts Hill*

*Originally established in 1520, having started life as a row of cottages. The pub sign was to represent the coat of arms of the Sydney family who resided at Penshurst Place. A short-sighted painter mistook the leopard on the family crest for a spotted hunting dog, since when the pub has been known as the Spotted Dog. A typical Kentish pub with good food and a warm, hearty welcome. A large garden and terraced area complements the warm atmosphere inside.*

FOOD up to £15

**Hours:** bar meals 12noon – 2:15pm; bar meals 7pm – 9:45pm; dinner 7:15pm – 10pm. **Cuisine:** English / French:- Traditional English and French, complemented by a fine Wine List. Dishes may include, Roast Half Rack of Lamb, and Monkfish Goujons. **Credit cards:** Visa, Access, Diners, Switch. **Other points:** licensed, open-air dining, Sunday lunch, children catered for – please check for age limits, parking, vegetarian meals. **Directions:** B2176 & B2110. Through Penshurst village – third turning on the right.

ANDY & NIKKI TUCKER, tel (0892) 870253.

## PETERBOROUGH, Cambridgeshire Map 8

### BELL INN HOTEL, *Great North Road*

*This hotel has been built around the courtyard of an historic inn. It offers old world charm, relaxing comfort and modern facilities. The Inn has a history dating back to 1500 and is a dream for history lovers.*

ACCOMMODATION £21–£30

**Hours:** breakfast 7am – 9am; lunch 12noon – 2pm; dinner 7pm – 9:30pm. **Cuisine:** English:- A la carte. Dishes include Byron Fillet of Beef, Wild Salmon Dumpling, Vegetable Filo Parcels. **Rooms:** 18 bedrooms 13 doubles ensuite, 1 family room ensuite, 2 singles ensuite, 2 twins ensuite. **Credit cards:** Visa, Access, AmEx. **Other points:** open-air dining, Sunday lunch, no-smoking area, garden, conferences. **Directions:** ½ mile off A1 northbound. 5 miles south of Peterborough.

MR & MRS MCGIVERN, tel (0733) 241066.

### HAWTHORN HOUSE HOTEL, *89 Thorpe Road*

*A small family run hotel centrally situated in this beautiful Cathedral city and within walking distance of main shops. All bedrooms are fully equipped with modern facilities and there is a wide selection of good home-made fast food to choose from. An ideal position for visiting the East of England Showground.*

ACCOMMODATION £21–£30

FOOD up to £15

**Credit cards:** Visa, Access. **Other points:** parking, no-smoking area, garden. **Directions:** A1179. Follow signs to centre and district hospital.

MR & MRS FEW, tel (0733) 340608.

## PLUCKLEY, Kent Map 5

### THE DERING ARMS, *Station Road, Nr Ashford*

*Originally built as a hunting lodge for the Dering family, the inn has some unusual features such as the curved Dutch gables and the windows. Visitors to the Dering Arms are assured of a varied choice of real ales and fine wines. Good home-made food is served 7 days a week and comfortable accommodation is available throughout the year. Friendly and welcoming.*

ACCOMMODATION under £20

FOOD up to £15

**Hours:** lunch – except Sunday 12noon – 3pm; last orders 2pm; lunch – Sunday 12noon – 2pm; dinner 6:30pm – 11pm; last orders 10pm. **Cuisine:** English:- Continually changing menu – Seafood specials and Daily specials. Restaurant and bar menus. **Rooms:** 3 bedrooms 1 twin, 2 doubles. **Credit cards:** Visa, Access. **Other points:** licensed, Sunday lunch, garden. **Directions:** on Bethersden Road, 100yds from Pluckley railway station.

MR JAMES BUSS, tel (0233) 840371, fax (0233) 840498.

## PRINCES RISBOROUGH, Buckinghamshire Map 6

### KING WILLIAM IV FREEHOUSE & RESTAURANT, *Hampden Road, Speen*

*A Grade II listed building, originally an old farmhouse dating from 1668, offering a combination of good food and unobtrusive expert service. The fresh flowers on every table are an additional bonus. Ideally situated for visiting Hughenden Manor, and the Home of Rest for Horses.*

FOOD £15–£20

**Hours:** last orders 6:30pm – 9:30pm; lunch 12noon – 3pm; dinner 7pm – 11pm; closed Monday evening; closed Sunday evening. **Cuisine:** English:- A la carte and Table d'hote menu's, offering a changing menu of freshly prepared English cuisine. The "Farmhouse Menu" is available at lunch or dinner, this is regularly changed but some examples are Roast Topside of Beef, Seafood Crepe, locally made sausages. **Credit cards:** Visa, Access. **Other points:** licensed, open-air dining, Sunday lunch, no-smoking area, children catered for – please check for age limits, parking, bank holidays. **Directions:** from High Wycombe – take Hughenden Valley road (A4128).

GEOFFREY & SANDRA CARTER, tel (0494) 488329, fax (0494) 488301.

## RAINHAM, Essex Map 8

### PORKY'S, *Unit 1, Manor Way Business Centre, Fairview Industrial Estate*

*Quite unlike any other eating establishment in the UK, Porky's may be described as having a hint of original Les Routiers French truck stop cafe whilst serving*

*exceptional traditional British food. Situated on a large modern industrial estate, it is extremely popular with intercontinental truckers, it even operates a timed phone-in delivery service to businesses on the estate. The attractive decor complements dark timber furniture, circular tables, saloon style chairs, a full bar and seating for 80.*
*FOOD up to £15*
**Hours:** closed Sunday evening; meals all day 7am – 11pm; meals all day – Saturday 7am – 12noon. **Cuisine:** English. **Other points:** parking, children catered for – please check for age limits, no-smoking area, afternoon tea, disabled access, vegetarian meals. **Directions:** Manor Way, off A13, alongside Rainham Steel.
JENNY FIGGANS, tel (0708) 630552, (0708) 630553.

## RAMSGATE, Kent Map 5

### MORTON'S FORK, 42 Station Rd, Minster, Nr Ramsgate
*A charming 17th century restaurant and wine bar, situated in a quiet, historical village, only 5 miles from Ramsgate. The atmosphere is relaxed and friendly and the menu offers imaginative dishes. The guest rooms have been attractively refurbished, retaining character yet providing modern conveniences.*
*ACCOMMODATION £21–£30*
*FOOD up to £15* 🛏 ★
**Hours:** lunch 11:30am – 2pm; dinner 6:30pm – 10pm. **Cuisine:** British / continental:- British and continental cuisine, including salmon parcel and chicken stuffed with crab. Good vegetarian dishes available. **Rooms:** 3 bedrooms all with tea making facilities, telephone, TV: 3 doubles ensuite. **Credit cards:** Visa, Access, Diners, AmEx. **Other points:** Sunday lunch, children catered for – please check for age limits, parking, vegetarian meals, residents' bar, disabled access. **Directions:** follow the A28, exit onto A253. Turn left for Minster village.
MR DAVID J SWORDER, tel (0843) 823000.

## REEDHAM, Norfolk Map 9

### REEDHAM FERRY & INN,
*Situated on the River Yare, adjacent to the Ferry crossing, this popular old inn provides a pleasant stop for locals and tourists alike. Well presented, well served good value meals and welcoming family atmosphere. Riverside tables and chairs with garden. Adjoining the Inn is the Reedham Ferry Camping & Caravan Park, four acres of landscaped grounds and modern facilities next to the River Yare.*
*FOOD up to £15*
**Hours:** lunch 12noon – 2:15pm; dinner 7pm – 10pm. **Cuisine:** English:- A changing season menu using only fresh produce, with prime meat from local butchers and hand-picked fish from Lowestoft Market. Chef's own daily specials, vegetarian and diet conscious dishes. A selection of salads, fresh filled rolls and sandwiches. **Credit cards:** Visa, Access. **Other points:** open-air dining, Sunday lunch, children catered for – please check for age limits, pets allowed. **Directions:** just off the B1140 in Reedham on the north side of the ferry.
MR D N ARCHER, tel (0493) 700429.

## REIGATE, Surrey Map 4

### BRIDGE HOUSE HOTEL & RESTAURANT, Reigate Hill
*Situated high on Reigate Hill, The Bridge House Hotel, open all year round, provides an elegant and sophisticated setting to complement the high quality cuisine. The extensive wine list offers a range of excellent house wines to rare vintages. Dinner dances with a resident band are regularly featured. Private parties and individual celebrations catered for.*
*ACCOMMODATION £21–£30*
*FOOD £15–£20*
**Hours:** breakfast 7:30am – 9:30am; lunch 12:30pm – 2:15pm; dinner 7:30pm – 10pm. **Cuisine:** English / continental:- English and continental cuisine of a high standard. Dishes may include, Timbale of Salmon with Monkfish, Scampi Funghetto, Magret of Duck Noisse-Be. **Rooms:** 37 bedrooms all with tea making facilities, telephone, radio, TV: 8 singles ensuite, 20 twins ensuite, 6 doubles ensuite, 3 quads ensuite. **Credit cards:** Visa, Access, Diners, AmEx. **Other points:** licensed, Sunday lunch, children catered for – please check for age limits, parking, disabled access, vegetarian meals, conferences, functions, baby-listening device, cots, 24hr reception, residents' bar. **Directions:** from Junction 8 of M25, take A217 to Reigate. Hotel is 2 mins on left under bridge.
BRIDGE HOUSE HOTEL (REIGATE) LIMITED, tel (0737) 246801, fax (0737) 223756.

### CRANLEIGH HOTEL, 41 West Street
*The Cranleigh Hotel is set in one of the last unspoilt towns fringing the magnificent forested North Downs, famous for its Pilgrims, Romans and spring-waters. Owned and managed by the Bussandri family for over 20 years, who have in this time achieved an unsurpassable reputation for friendliness, care and quality hospitality. The house has been carefully restored to include luxurious bedrooms, fine public rooms and a grand conservatory leading on to their pride of a garden and orchard, overlooking a swimming pool and tennis courts.*
*ACCOMMODATION £21–£30*
*FOOD up to £15*
**Hours:** breakfast 7:30am – 9:30am; dinner 7pm – 9pm; closed for Christmas 24 December – 26 December (incl). **Cuisine:** international. **Other points:** parking, children catered for – please check for age limits, residents' lounge, garden, vegetarian meals, open-air dining. **Directions:** on A25, end of Reigate High Street going west.
MR G BUSSANDRI, tel (0737) 223417, fax (0737) 223734.

### THE MARKET HOTEL, High Street
*Situated in the centre of Reigate, this lively pub does much to justify its continuing popularity. A good*

*selection of real ales, bottled and continental lagers make the perfect complement to well-cooked food – all at reasonable prices.*
*FOOD up to £15*
**Hours:** open all year; open bank holidays; meals all day 12noon – 9:30pm. **Cuisine:** English:- Traditional English pub food, prepared to a high standard. Generous portions complemented by a fine selection of wines, ales and lagers. **Credit cards:** Visa, Access. **Other points:** licensed, open-air dining, Sunday lunch, no-smoking area, children catered for – please check for age limits, morning tea, afternoon tea, garden. **Directions:** centre of town, by clocktower.
MARKET TAVERNS LIMITED, tel (0737) 240492, fax (0737) 226221.

---

## RICHMOND, Surrey Map 4

### CAFE ROUGE, 7a Petersham Road
*A lively bar and restaurant, with rear conservatory, polished wood floors, chandeliers, oil paintings and posters. The food is fresh, of excellent quality and served in ample proportions. River Thames, Kew gardens, Richmond Park and Hampton Court nearby.*
*FOOD up to £15*
**Hours:** meals all day 10am – 11pm. **Cuisine:** French:- Traditional French cuisine. Menu changes every 3 months, but generally offers Toulouse Sausages, Marmite Dieppoise and Plats du Jour. **Credit cards:** Visa, Access. **Other points:** Sunday lunch, no-smoking area, children catered for – please check for age limits, afternoon tea, bank holidays, licensed. **Directions:** through Richmond from A3, follow one-way to Petersham, past Odeon.
CAFE ROUGE LTD, tel (081) 332 2423, fax (081) 332 2534.

### CAFFE MAMMA, 24 Hill Street
*Decorated in the style of a Neapolitan cafe with typical Italian ambiance. Situated in the main shopping area of Richmond, not far from the river. Caffe Mamma enjoys a good reputation in the area and is popular with all ages.*
*FOOD up to £15*
**Hours:** meals all day 12noon – 12midnight; closed Christmas 25/12 – 26/12; closed 31/12. **Cuisine:** Italian:- Italian, specialising in pasta dishes. **Credit cards:** Visa, Access, AmEx. **Other points:** Sunday lunch, children catered for – please check for age limits. **Directions:** in the centre of Richmond, near Odeon cinema.
TIM DIXON-NUTTALL, tel (081) 940 1625, fax (081) 948 7330.

### HENRY'S CAFE BAR (RICHMOND), Riverside Development, Riverside
*A popular split-level cafe-bar serving an extensive range of international fast-food, American and non-alcoholic beers and speciality cocktails. Comfortable, friendly interior with live music at weekends. Ideal location for those wanting to take a riverboat excursion along the Thames.*
*FOOD up to £15*

**Hours:** meals all day 11am – 10pm. **Cuisine:** international. **Credit cards:** Visa, Access. **Other points:** children catered for – please check for age limits, open bank holidays, no-smoking area, afternoon teas, disabled access, vegetarian meals. **Directions:** situated behind the Town Hall.
ANN CLANCY, tel (081) 332 2492.

### JASPER'S BUN IN THE OVEN, 11 Kew Green
*French – international cuisine served in this charming Georgian house overlooking Kew Green. Jasper's offers winter dining in front of log fires and summer dining in the courtyard. Great value set price menu and extensive a la carte menu. Special Sunday menu. Open for lunch and dinner except Sunday evening. Extensive wine list.*
*FOOD £15–£20*
**Hours:** lunch 12:30pm – 3pm; dinner 7pm – 11pm; closed Christmas 24/12 – 26/12; closed Good Friday; closed Sunday evening. **Cuisine:** French:- French style cuisine, complemented by an extensive Wine List. **Credit cards:** Visa, Access, Diners, AmEx. **Other points:** licensed, garden, children catered for – please check for age limits, vegetarian meals. **Directions:** situated on Kew Green.
MR CARVOSSO, tel (081) 940 3987, fax (081) 940 6387.

### THE ORANGE TREE PUBLIC HOUSE & MASQUERADES WINE BAR, 45 Kew Road
*The Orange Tree is a unique 18th century pub, and home of the Orange Tree theatre – the first ever licensed theatre pub of its kind. It has its own Wine Bar 'Masquerades' – a popular haunt of actors and actresses performing nearby, and is appropriately furnished with authentic theatrical memorabilia. Masquerades is cosy and intimate, whilst the Orange Tree is lively and bustling.*
*FOOD up to £15*
**Hours:** bar meals 11am – 10pm; lunch 12noon – 2:30pm; dinner 5:30pm – 10pm. **Cuisine:** international:- A la carte menu offering a wide range of dishes from oriental to steaks and fish. Vegetarian meals also available. Over 20 wines available by the glass. **Credit cards:** Visa, Access, Diners, AmEx. **Other points:** licensed, open-air dining, Sunday lunch, no-smoking area, children catered for – please check for age limits, functions. **Directions:** situated at the junction of the A316, close to British rail station.
CARL & JUDITH MARTIN, tel (081) 940 0944, fax (081) 332 6414.

### THE RIVER TERRACE, The Tower, Bridge Street
*A Regency style building, recently renovated, with a balcony which overlooks the River Thames. The chef prides himself on his imaginative dishes, one of which is a scooped-out pineapple filled with seafood, herbs and spices, vegetables and rice in a coconut sauce, served*

with a tropical salad. Service is very efficient, and staff are pleased to offer advice on various dishes.
FOOD up to £15
**Hours:** meals all day 11am – 11pm. **Cuisine:** international:- Breast of Duckling with Blueberries, Char-grilled Swordfish Steak with Yoghurt & Coriander. Fillet of Beef with Oyster sauce & noodles. **Credit cards:** Visa, Access, Diners, AmEx. **Other points:** licensed, open-air dining, Sunday lunch, children catered for – please check for age limits. **Directions:** situated on the Richmond side of Richmond Bridge, overlooking river.
RIVER TERRACE LTD, tel (081) 332 2524, fax (081) 332 6136.

## RIDGMONT, Bedfordshire Map 6

### THE ROSE & CROWN, 89 High Street
A 300 year old country pub with a prize-winning large garden. Patio for barbecues. Games room and conference and private party facilities. Recommended for its traditional ales and also offers an extensive wine list. 20 years in the Good Beer Guide.
FOOD up to £15
**Hours:** lunch 12noon – 2pm; dinner 6:30pm – 10:30pm.
**Cuisine:** English:- Bar: a comprehensive menu including specials of the day eg tarragon lamb, lemon chicken, beef olives, etc. **Credit cards:** Visa, Access, Diners, AmEx. **Other points:** open-air dining, Sunday lunch. **Directions:** on the main street in Ridgmont, (A507) 2 miles from Junction 13 of M1.
NEIL & ELIZABETH MCGREGOR, tel (0525280) 245.

## ROMFORD, Essex Map 8

### THE SCHOOLHOUSE, Church Road, Noak Hill
As the name suggests, the building is a converted schoolhouse which has been tastefully redecorated. Drinks served on a pretty patio. Flowers presented at table by prior order. Celebration sponge cakes made to order. Selection of paintings by local artists always available.
FOOD up to £15
**Hours:** last orders 6:30pm – 9pm; lunch 12noon – 2:30pm; dinner 7pm – 11pm; closed bank holidays; closed Sunday evenings. **Cuisine:** English / vegetarian:- Wide choice of dishes including home-made Steak & Kidney Pie, Trout, vegetarian dishes. Traditional Sunday lunches. **Credit cards:** Visa, Access, Diners. **Other points:** licensed, Sunday lunch, children catered for – please check for age limits. **Directions:** from A12 at Gallow's Corner, take Straight Rd to end and turn right.
FIONA RICHARDS & TONY MERRY, tel (0708) 349900.

## ROYSTON, Hertfordshire Map 6

### BRITISH RAJ INDIAN RESTAURANT, 55 High Street
Reputed to be one of East Anglia's best Indian restaurants and one of the top 100 curry houses. A varied menu, dishes may include such specialities as Shooting Bird Bhuna, Fixed Bayonet Poussin and Crab Rezalla. Bronze Award Winner in Best Menu Category, Top 30 in Best Britain Category, listed in Pataks Real Curry Restaurant Guide and Good Curry Guide amongst others. Highly recommended.
FOOD up to £15 CLUB
**Hours:** lunch 12noon – 3pm; dinner 6pm – 12midnight.
**Cuisine:** Indian:- Lamb masala – a whole leg of lamb cooked for four. Tandoori, royal, karai dishes. English menu also available. Thalia dishes including wedding feast.
**Credit cards:** Visa, Access, Diners, AmEx. **Other points:** Sunday lunch, children catered for – please check for age limits. **Directions:** situated in Royston, on the A10.
NAZIR UDDIN CHOUDHURY, tel (0763) 241471.

## RUSTINGTON, West Sussex Map 4

### MAYDAY HOTEL, Broadmark Lane
Situated just 400 yd from the beach and shops, the Mayday is a small hotel which offers a friendly atmosphere, good food and comfortable surroundings. Magnificent award-winning garden "Arun in Bloom" 1988 & 1990, overflowing with colourful blooms throughout Summer. Personal attention by husband and wife team, Pat and Terry Shorrock towards guests makes a visit highly desirable.
ACCOMMODATION £21 – £30
FOOD up to £15
**Hours:** breakfast 8.15am – 9am, dinner from 6.30pm, closed October. **Cuisine:** English/International. **Rooms:** 10 bedrooms all with tea making facilities, TV, radio, alarm. **Other points:** children catered for – check for age limits, parking, no smoking area, residents' lounge, vegetarian meals, open air dining. **Directions:** 400 yds from the seafront.
TERENCE SHORROCK, tel (0903) 771198.

## RYE, East Sussex Map 5

### THE OLD FORGE RESTAURANT, 24 Wish Street
Originally a forge, the building was bought and converted by the present owner. Highly recommended for its good food within a reasonable price limit, friendly service and informal atmosphere. A large open fire adds to the character and atmosphere of the restaurant during winter.
FOOD up to £15
**Hours:** lunch 12:30pm – 2pm; dinner 6:30pm – 10pm; closed Monday; closed Sunday; closed Tuesday lunch; closed Wednesday lunch. **Cuisine:** English:- Specialities include fresh local fish, shellfish and chargrilled steaks.
**Credit cards:** Visa, Access. **Other points:** licensed, children catered for – please check for age limits, street parking. **Directions:** on western side of Rye where Wish St joins the main A259.
DEREK BAYNTUN, tel (0797) 223227.

### THE SHIP INN, Strand Quay
An attractive 16th century Inn, set amongst the historic Strand Quay warehouses, where confiscated contraband

was once stored by revenue men as records show. All
bedrooms are equipped with modern facilities for
maximum comfort and the Inn provides guests with
details of where to visit and what to see in the area.
Special Breaks are available throughout the year.
ACCOMMODATION £21–£30

FOOD up to £15

**Hours:** breakfast 8am – 9:45am; bar snacks 12noon –
3pm; lunch 12:30pm – 2:30pm; bar snacks 7pm –
9:30pm; dinner 7:30pm – 9:15pm. **Cuisine:** English.
**Credit cards:** Visa, Access. **Other points:** parking,
children catered for – please check for age limits,
residents' lounge, vegetarian meals. **Directions:**
amongst Warehouses (18th Century) on Strand Quay,
foot of Mermaid Street.
MR M GREGORY, tel (0797) 222233, fax (0797)
223892.

## SAFFRON WALDEN, Essex Map 8

### SAFFRON HOTEL, 10–18 High street
This listed building with 16th century origins, in
'Lovejoy country', has recently been refurbished. The
award winning restaurant enjoys an excellent reputation
for a high standard of imaginatively prepared cuisine.
You can enjoy table d'hote and a la carte meals in the
elegant conservatory restaurant, or bar meals in the
popular bar, with real ales. The accommodation is
comfortable and well equipped and includes three rooms
with four poster beds.
ACCOMMODATION £31 –£40

FOOD £16 to £20

**Hours:** breakfast 7.30am – 9.15am, lunch and bar meals 12
noon – 2.15pm, dinner and bar meals 6.45pm – 9.30pm
(last orders 9pm), open Christmas day. **Cuisine:** dishes
include steak and kidney pie and bread and butter pudding.
**Rooms:** 24 bedrooms, 21 ensuite. **Credit cards:** Access,
Visa, AmEx, Diners. **Other points:** children catered for –
check for age limits, residents' lounge, garden, weddings,
special romantic weekends and functions, conference
facilities, parking, disabled access, vegetarian meals.
**Directions:** take the M11 junction 9. Hotel is on the A30 in
the centre of Saffron Walden.
DAVID BALL, tel (0799) 522676, fax (0799) 513979.

## SEAFORD, East Sussex Map 5

### THE OLD PLOUGH, 20 Church Street
A delightful 17th century coaching inn, situated on the
beautiful East Sussex Downs, bordering Newhaven. The
inn is extremely popular with tourists who are attracted
to the area, which is steeped in history as a result of the
Norman Conquests. The nearby Heritage Centre is well
worth a visit.
FOOD up to £15

**Hours:** open all year 7pm; lunch 12noon – 2:30pm;
dinner 7pm – 10pm. **Cuisine:** English:- Traditional
homestyle cooking, offering an extensive selection of
dishes, including speciality home-made pies and
steamed puddings. Steaks cut to order and fresh fish.
**Credit cards:** Visa, Access, Diners. **Other points:**
licensed, open-air dining, Sunday lunch, no-smoking
area, children catered for – please check for age limits,
parking. **Directions:** situated off A259 in Seaford
adjoining the parish church.
JOHN BOOTS, tel (0323) 892379.

## SEVENOAKS, Kent Map 5

### MOORINGS HOTEL, 97 Hitchen Hatch Lane
A small, friendly family hotel offering a high standard of
accommodation for tourists and business travellers. One
especially pleasant feature is the range of garden patio
bedrooms which are arranged like a small motel around a
secluded lawn. Sevenoaks is a pleasant Kentish market town
within easy reach of many places of historical interest. The
newly refurbished restaurant opened in January 1994.
ACCOMMODATION £21–£30

FOOD up to £15

**Hours:** breakfast – weekdays 7:30am – 9am; breakfast –
weekends 8am – 9am; dinner 7pm – 9pm. **Cuisine:**
international. **Credit cards:** Visa, Access, AmEx. **Other
points:** children catered for – please check for age
limits, no-smoking area, vegetarian meals, garden,
residents' bar, residents' lounge, satellite TV, parking.
**Directions:** situated on the A224, 2 minutes from the
M25. 200yds from Sevenoaks BR station.
FIONA & TIM RYAN, tel (0732) 452589, fax (0732)
456462.

### SEVENOAKS PARK HOTEL, Seal Hollow Road
The Sevenoaks Park Hotel is a charming building
standing in 3 acres of Elizabethan gardens overlooking
superb views of Knole Park. Offering well cooked and

presented cuisine and attractive comfortable accommodation, the hotel provides guests with a pleasant and welcoming atmosphere. An ideal base for touring areas of interest such as Royal Tunbridge Wells and Leeds Castle.
*ACCOMMODATION under £20*
*FOOD up to £15*
**Hours:** breakfast 7am – 9:30am; dinner 7pm – 9:30pm. **Cuisine:** modern English:- A la carte, table d'hote, dishes include Poached salmon served in lemon & mustard sauce, Breast of duck fried and served with strawberry & blackcurrant. **Rooms:** 33 bedrooms all with telephone, radio, TV: 2 singles, 10 twins, 10 twins ensuite, 4 doubles, 6 doubles ensuite, 1 family room ensuite. **Credit cards:** Visa, Access, Diners, AmEx. **Other points:** licensed, open-air dining, Sunday lunch, children catered for – please check for age limits, afternoon tea, swimming pool. **Directions:** off A225. MR NOBLE & MR HUNTLEY, tel (0732) 454245, fax (0732) 457468.

## SHOESBURYNESS, Essex Map 8

### THE POLASH RESTAURANT, 84/86 West Road

Authentic Bangladeshi and Indian music unobtrusively relaxes diners and gives an aura of tranquillity. One of the top thirty out of 10,500 Indian Restaurants in the United Kingdom, nominated by Pataks for food, quality and service.
*FOOD up to £15* ★
**Hours:** lunch 12noon – 3pm; dinner 6pm – 12midnight. **Cuisine:** Bangladeshi:- Bangladeshi food, eg. Kim's dish, Kipling's favourites, Passage to India, Sunset in Ganges. Authentic tandoori and bhoona dishes. **Credit cards:** Visa, Access, Diners, AmEx. **Other points:** Sunday lunch, children catered for – please check for age limits, air-conditioned. **Directions:** Southend-on-Sea road A127 – A13.
MR A KHALIQUE, tel (0702) 293989, (0702) 294721.

## SITTINGBOURNE, Kent Map 5

### CONISTON HOTEL, 70 London Road

The hotel is very well placed for visiting Kent's many sights and attractions. The ballroom can seat 160 people and is available for private hire.
*ACCOMMODATION £21–£30*
*FOOD up to £15*
**Hours:** open 7 days 6pm; breakfast 7:30am – 9:30am; lunch 12noon – 2:30pm; dinner 7pm – 10pm. **Cuisine:** English / seafood:- Speciality: Dover sole. **Rooms:** 51 bedrooms all with tea making facilities, telephone, TV: 16 singles ensuite, 14 doubles ensuite, 16 twins ensuite, 5 family rooms ensuite. **Credit cards:** Visa, Access, Diners, AmEx. **Other points:** Sunday lunch, children catered for – please check for age limits, coach/prior arr, pets/charge. **Directions:** on the A2 half a mile from town centre.
MR S KLECZKOWSKI, tel (0795) 472131, (0795) 472907, fax (0795) 428056.

## SNETTISHAM, Norfolk Map 9

### THE ROSE & CROWN FREEHOUSE, Old Church Road

Situated just off the A149, this 14th century pub offers good food, real ales and a friendly welcoming atmosphere. A large collection of old farming implements is on display. Children have their own menu and a large, separate room, personally supervised by the proprietor.
*ACCOMMODATION under £20*
*FOOD up to £15* ☺ ★
**Hours:** lunch 12noon – 2pm; dinner 6:30pm – 10:30pm. **Cuisine:** English:- Rare roast beef, quality steaks, good selection of vegetarian dishes, dish of the day – good home cooking. **Rooms:** 3 bedrooms 1 double ensuite, 1 double, 1 twin. **Credit cards:** Visa, Access. **Other points:** open-air dining, Sunday lunch, children catered for – please check for age limits, coach/prior arr, garden. **Directions:** from Kings Lynn – A149 north, 10 miles, signs for Snettisham.
MARGARET GODDARD, tel (0485) 541382.

## SOUTHEND-ON-SEA, Essex Map 8

### ROSLIN HOTEL, Thorpe Esplanade, Thorpe Bay

Situated on the seafront, the Roslin Hotel boasts one of the finest views of the Thames Estuary in residential Thorpe Bay. Facilities for golfing, sailing, tennis, bowling, horse riding, ten-pin bowling. Weekend bargain breaks. Temporary membership of local leisure centre for residents.
*ACCOMMODATION £31–£40*
*FOOD up to £15*
**Hours:** lunch 12:30pm – 2pm; dinner 6:30pm – 9:30pm. **Cuisine:** English:- Noisette of lamb Gascoigne, Veal Millanaise, local trout with chestnut and cucumber. Sunday lunches. Vegetarian menu. A la carte and table d'hote menus. **Rooms:** 40 bedrooms all with tea making facilities, telephone, radio, TV: 10 singles ensuite, 10 twins ensuite, 7 doubles ensuite, 3 triples ensuite. **Credit cards:** Visa, Access, Diners, AmEx. **Other points:** Sunday lunch, children catered for – please check for age limits, residents' lounge, residents' bar, disabled access. **Directions:** close to the seafront.
MR K G OLIVER, tel (0702) 586375.

### LA POUBELLE, 50a Hamlet Court Road, Westcliff

A small, friendly family-run restaurant with an emphasis on good, honest, fresh food in comfortable surroundings. An informal atmosphere provides the ideal ambiance for pleasant dining. Very popular locally so booking advised.
*FOOD up to £15*
**Hours:** last orders 6:30pm – 10:30pm; lunch 12:30pm – 2:15pm; dinner 7pm; closed lunch except Sunday; closed Monday; closed Sunday evening. **Cuisine:**

international:- Paella, chicken breast in stilton sauce, local fish, home smoked produce. A varied and interesting menu – all dishes home prepared and cooked. **Credit cards:** Visa, Access. **Other points:** licensed, Sunday lunch-winter, children catered for – please check for age limits, low price menu. **Directions:** on shopping street near Westcliff railway station, 5 mins from seafront and Cliffs Pavilion.
MR & MRS R C BERNER, tel (0702) 351894.

### THE MAYFLOWER HOTEL, 6 Royal Terrace
*Built in 1792, this grade II listed house still retains many original Georgian features. A mass of flowers in hanging baskets are draped over the balcony and on the terrace. The hotel overlooks the Thames estuary and the Pier.*
*ACCOMMODATION under £20*
**Hours:** closed Christmas Sunday evening; breakfast 6:45am – 9am. **Cuisine:** breakfast. **Rooms:** 24 bedrooms all with TV: 7 singles, 5 doubles, 4 doubles ensuite, 5 twins, 3 family rooms ensuite. **Other points:** central heating, no evening meal, children catered for – please check for age limits, residents' lounge. **Directions:** A127 to southend on Sea, Hotel overlooks the Thames estuary.
CHRISTOPHER POWELL, tel (0702) 340489.

### TOWER HOTEL AND RESTAURANT, 146 Alexandra Road
*Built in 1901 as a unique gentleman's residence "Taranaki", it first became a hotel in 1923. Fully renovated and restored in the elegant ambiance of the era, it combines every modern convenience and luxury. Many of the splendid "Tower" rooms afford views of the Thames Estuary and the Kent coastline. To complement a comfortable stay in luxurious accomodation, a superb English Breakfast is served daily. Just a few minutes walk from the town's finest amenities.*
*ACCOMMODATION £21–£30*
*FOOD up to £15*
**Hours:** closed Sunday evening; breakfast weekdays 7am – 9am; breakfast weekends 8am – 10am; dinner 6:30pm – 9:30pm; bar snacks 6:30pm – 11pm. **Cuisine:** English. **Rooms:** 33 bedrooms 3 family rooms ensuite, 5 twins ensuite, 12 doubles ensuite, 13 singles ensuite. **Credit cards:** Visa, Access, Diners, AmEx. **Other points:** children catered for – please check for age limits, Sunday lunch, disabled access, pets allowed, residents' lounge, vegetarian meals. **Directions:** Alexandra Road is off High Street Southend.
MR M TAYLOR, tel (0702) 348635, fax (0702) 433044.

## SOUTHWOLD, Suffolk Map 9

### SUTHERLAND HOUSE RESTAURANT, 56 High Street
*Built in the 16th century, Sutherland House was once the headquarters of an Admiral who became King of England, James II. Today it carefully preserves its historic past and specialises in good food and refreshment of high quality. You can be assured of welcoming service, well presented, fresh home cooked food, and good value for money prices.*
*ACCOMMODATION under £20*
*FOOD up to £15*
**Hours:** closed Wednesday 6:30pm; breakfast 9am – 10am; lunch - Sat & Sun 12noon – 2pm; dinner 7pm – 9pm; dinner – 7 days Easter – October; dinner – Thur-Sat October – Easter. **Cuisine:** English:- A daily menu featuring all fresh, home cooked local produce. Fresh, local fish dishes are a speciality. Informal Brasserie-style cuisine. **Rooms:** 3 bedrooms all with tea making facilities, TV: 3 doubles ensuite. **Credit cards:** Visa, Access. **Other points:** licensed, Sunday lunch, no-smoking in bedroom. **Directions:** 4 miles from A12. On High Street in the centre of Southwold.
PAUL & MARGARET SAMAIN, tel (0502) 722260.

## ST ALBANS, Hertfordshire Map 6

### NEWPARK HOUSE HOTEL, North Orbital Road, Nr London Colney Roundabout
*A family run, welcoming guest house offering comfortable accommodation and full English breakfast at very reasonable prices. Only 18 minutes by train from London, and close to the centre of the historic city of St Albans. There is an excellent garden for guests use and the hotel enjoys a warm and friendly atmosphere. A good base for holiday-makers, tourists and business people alike.*
*ACCOMMODATION under £20*
*FOOD up to £15* ★
**Hours:** breakfast 6:45am – 8:45am; dinner 6pm – 8pm. **Cuisine:** English. **Rooms:** 14 bedrooms all with tea making facilities, TV: 9 singles, 5 twins. **Credit cards:** Visa, Access. **Other points:** children catered for – please check for age limits, garden, picnic lunches, pets allowed, conferences. **Directions:** A414 dual carriageway, 400yds from London Colney roundabout.
DENNIS & VIOLET BYGRAVE, tel (0727) 824839, fax (0727) 826700.

## ST IVES, Cambridgeshire Map 8

### THE DOLPHIN HOTEL, Bridge Foot, London Road
*The Dolphin is a small friendly hotel situated in the old town of St Ives, on the banks of the Great Ouse. Diners have a pleasant view over the river which makes for a particularly relaxed atmosphere in which to enjoy the good food. Children are welcome and charged at a reduced price.*
*ACCOMMODATION £31–£40*
*FOOD up to £15*
**Hours:** breakfast 7:30am – 9:30am; lunch 12noon – 2pm; dinner 7pm – 9:30pm. **Cuisine:** English / French:- English and French cuisine, with a comprehensive wine list. Sunday lunch also served. **Rooms:** 47 bedrooms all with tea making facilities, telephone, radio, TV: 2 singles ensuite, 13 doubles ensuite, 32 twins ensuite. **Credit cards:** Visa, Access, Diners, AmEx. **Other**

points: licensed, Sunday lunch. **Directions:** from A604 to St Ives, first roundabout take first exit then immediately right.
H R WADSWORTH, tel (0480) 466966, (0480) 497497, fax (0480) 495597.

## STALHAM, Norfolk Map 9

### SUTTON STAITHE HOTEL, Sutton Staithe, Sutton

*Situated by the waterside at the head of Sutton Broad, the inn is popular with boat people. The food is plentiful, well cooked and well presented.*
ACCOMMODATION £31–£40
FOOD up to £15
**Hours:** lunch 12noon – 2pm; dinner 7pm – 9:30pm. **Cuisine:** English / seafood:- Local game and fish in season. **Rooms:** 10 bedrooms, 6 en suite. **Credit cards:** Visa, Access, Diners, AmEx. **Other points:** licensed, open-air dining, Sunday lunch, children catered for – please check for age limits, fishing. **Directions:** just off the A149 Yarmouth to North Walsham road.
M K & D P TAYLOR, tel (0692) 580244.

## STANSTED, Essex Map 8

### CRICKETERS ARMS, Rickling Green

*This large village pub and restaurant faces the oldest cricket grounds in Essex, where cricket is played on summer weekends. It is lively and popular, with an imaginative menu. The pub is within easy travelling distance of London and 10 minutes drive from Stansted Airport. Accommodation, off-airport parking and a courtesy car to airport if requested.*
ACCOMMODATION £31–£40
FOOD £15–£20
**Hours:** bar meals 12noon – 2pm; lunch – except Sunday 12noon – 2pm; lunch – Sunday 12noon – 3:30pm; bar meals 7pm – 10pm; dinner – except Sunday 7pm – 9:45pm; dinner – Sunday 7pm – 9pm. **Cuisine:** English:- Bar: a range of grills and casseroles, steak and kidney pie, mussels a speciality. Restaurant: The table d'hote menu in the restaurant offers English and French cooking. **Rooms:** 18 bedrooms all with tea making facilities, telephone, radio, TV: 7 singles ensuite, 6 twins ensuite, 1 double ensuite, 2 triples ensuite, 2 quads ensuite. **Credit cards:** Visa, Access, Diners, AmEx. **Other points:** licensed, open-air dining, Sunday lunch, children catered for – please check for age limits, garden, baby-listening device, baby sitting, cots. **Directions:** off the A11 in Rickling Green opposite the village green.
TIM & JO PROCTOR, tel (0799) 543210, fax (0799) 543512.

## STEYNING, West Sussex Map 4

### OLD TOLLGATE RESTAURANT & HOTEL, The Street, Bramber

*Travellers passing through Bramber were, at one time, obliged to interrupt their journey to pay a few pence at a Tollgate for the right to continue on their way. Today, many still stop there but only to enjoy the good food and hospitality offered by this establishment, which stands on the original site. Ideal for touring, or for visiting the ruins of nearby Bramber Castle.*
ACCOMMODATION over £50
FOOD £15–£20
**Hours:** open all year 7pm; breakfast 7:30am – 9:30am; lunch 12noon – 2pm; bar meals 12noon – 2pm; dinner 7pm – 9:30pm. **Cuisine:** English:- Traditional Olde English cuisine, including shellfish, meats and salads, roasts, casseroles, poultry and savoury pies. Special Christmas menu. **Rooms:** 29 bedrooms all with tea making facilities, telephone, TV: 2 suites, 17 doubles ensuite, 10 twins ensuite. **Credit cards:** Visa, Access, Diners, AmEx. **Other points:** licensed, Sunday lunch, children catered for – please check for age limits, residents' lounge, garden, parking, functions, conferences, residents' bar, disabled access, vegetarian meals. **Directions:** on A283. Situated in Bramber village, 4 miles from Shoreham-by-Sea.
PETER SARGENT, tel (0903) 879494, fax (0903) 813399.

### SPRINGWELLS HOTEL, 9 High Street

*A delightful 17th century Georgian hotel, with ivy wall covering and large Georgian windows, situated on the High Street of the charming, unspoilt town of Steyning. Under the personal supervision of the owners, this hotel has been arranged and fitted to ensure maximum comfort for guests by providing attractive bedrooms and a large sunny dining room for hearty English breakfasts.*
ACCOMMODATION £21–£30
**Hours:** breakfast 7:15am – 10am. **Cuisine:** breakfast. **Rooms:** 2 single, 2 twin, 6 double, 1 family bedroom: 9 en suite. all rooms have TV, and telephone. coffee/tea making facilities on request. Four posters. **Credit cards:** Visa, Access, Diners, AmEx. **Other points:** children catered for – please check for age limits, swimming pool, residents' lounge, garden, vegetarian meals. **Directions:** off A283.
MRS J HESELGRAVE, tel (0903) 812446, (0903) 812043.

## SUTTON, Surrey Map 4

### ASHLING TARA HOTEL, 44–50 Rosehill

*A family run hotel with a friendly and welcoming atmosphere situated within easy walking distance of Sutton town centre and directly opposite the Rose Hill Tennis Centre and Sports complex. With the comfort of her guests in mind, Mrs Harold has succeeded in offering a combination of tasty home cooked meals to complement comfortable attractive accommodation. A pleasure to visit.*
ACCOMMODATION £21–£30
FOOD up to £15  ★
**Hours:** breakfast 7:30am – 8:45am; dinner 7pm – 9pm. **Cuisine:** English. **Rooms:** 16 bedrooms all with tea making facilities, telephone, radio, mini bar, TV: 2 family rooms ensuite, 4 twins ensuite, 3 singles ensuite, 5 doubles ensuite,

1 single, 1 twin. **Credit cards:** Visa, Access, Diners, AmEx.
**Other points:** children catered for – please check for age
limits, bank holidays, residents' lounge, garden, launderette,
fax. **Directions:** near Angel Hill.
CATHERINE HAROLD, tel (081) 641 6142, fax (081)
644 7872.

## THATCHED HOUSE HOTEL, 135 Cheam Road
*Situated a short walk from Sutton centre and Cheam
village, this lovely thatched cottage has been completely
modernised and offers good food, comfortable
accommodation and a friendly welcome. Close proximity
to Epsom Downs, Wimbledon Tennis, Hampton Court,
Windsor Castle and RHS Gardens at Wisley. Golf can be
arranged at Banstead Downs only a mile from the Hotel.*
*ACCOMMODATION £31–£40*
*FOOD up to £15*
**Hours:** breakfast 7:30am – 9am; dinner 7pm – 9pm.
**Cuisine:** English:- English fare. Chefs specials daily.
**Rooms:** 23 bedrooms all with tea making facilities,
telephone, TV: 8 twins ensuite, 10 doubles ensuite, 3
singles ensuite, 2 singles. **Credit cards:** Visa, Access.
**Other points:** licensed, children catered for – please
check for age limits, afternoon tea, functions,
conferences, garden. **Directions:** on the A232, opposite
Sutton Cricket and Squash Club.
MR & MR P SELLS, tel (081) 642 3131.

## TEYNHAM, Kent Map 5

## THE SHIP INN & SMUGGLERS RESTAURANT, Conyer Quay, Nr Sittingbourne
*Hidden away in the picturesque village of Conyer which
nestles amongst the orchards and hopfields of the marsh
farms but well worth searching for. An attractive pub
and restaurant offering good food and a warm and
friendly atmosphere. The interior is full of character.
Mercier Corps d'Elite 1991/1992 for their excellent wine
list, over 60 bottled beers and 250 different whiskies.*
*FOOD £21–£25* ♟
**Hours:** lunch 12noon – 2:30pm; dinner 7pm – 10:30pm.
**Cuisine:** English / continental:- Moules Marinieres,
King Neptunes banquet, steak au poivre. Huge choice of
whiskies, rums, brandies, liqueurs, wine, real ales,
draught and bottled beers. **Credit cards:** Visa, Access,
AmEx. **Other points:** licensed, open-air dining, Sunday
lunch, children catered for – please check for age limits,
pets allowed. **Directions:** 2 miles off the A2 in village of
Conyer. On waters edge.
ALEC HEARD, tel (0795) 521404.

## THETFORD, Norfolk Map 9

## WEREHAM HOUSE HOTEL, 24 White Hart Street
*A small, well-run, family hotel set in pleasant
surroundings. In a relaxed, friendly atmosphere you can
enjoy the tasty meals which are on offer. Comfortable
accommodation.*
*ACCOMMODATION £21–£30*
*FOOD up to £15*
**Hours:** breakfast 7am – 9am; bar meals 12noon – 2pm;
dinner 7pm – 9:30pm. **Cuisine:** English / continental:-
Dishes may include Rainbow Trout, Salmon Steak with
Hollandaise sauce, Roasted Duck. **Rooms:** 9 bedrooms 2
singles ensuite, 3 twins ensuite, 4 doubles ensuite.
**Credit cards:** Visa, Access. **Other points:** licensed,
Sunday lunch, children catered for – please check for
age limits, bank holidays, AA – 1 star, ETB – 2 crown.
**Directions:** A134 Thetford – Bury Rd, into Bridge St,
leads to White Hart St.
COLIN ROGERS, tel (0842) 761956.

## TONBRIDGE, Kent Map 5

## THE CHASER INN, Stumble Hill, Shipbourne
*Built in the 1880's, The Chaser Inn is an attractive
colonial style building. An extensive and imaginative
range of food is offered in the bars and a creative set
menu can be enjoyed in the restaurant which features a
beamed vaulted ceiling and panelled walls. Only minutes
from the M25, M20 and M26 motorway networks, The
Chaser Inn is well placed to greet travellers.*
*ACCOMMODATION £21–£30*
*FOOD £21–£25* ★
**Hours:** breakfast 7:30am – 9:30am; bar meals 12noon –
2pm; lunch 12:30pm – 2pm; bar meals 7pm – 9:30pm;
dinner 7:30pm – 9:30pm. **Cuisine:** English / French:-
Table d'hote menu in restaurant. Dishes may include
Lamb fillet on a raspberry & mint sauce, Lemon sole.
Also bar snacks. **Rooms:** 15 bedrooms all with tea
making facilities, telephone, TV: 5 singles ensuite, 4
twins ensuite, 6 doubles ensuite. **Credit cards:** Visa,
Access, AmEx. **Other points:** licensed, open-air dining,
Sunday lunch, children catered for – please check for
age limits, functions, baby-listening device, cots, 24hr
reception, residents' bar, vegetarian meals, parking,
residents' lounge, disabled access. **Directions:** A227,
north of Tonbridge. Next to Shipbourne Church &
opposite green.
MICHAEL AND VIVIEN NIX, tel (0732) 810360, fax
(0732) 810941.

## THE OFFICE WINE BAR, 163 High Street
*A 16th century half-brick timbered building in Tonbridge
High Street, offering a very warm and friendly bistro-
style atmosphere. The menu and wine list is extensive,
the service polite and efficient. An ideal stop-off for
tourists who wish to visit Tonbridge Castle, Penshurst
Place, Tunbridge Wells, and the beautiful Kent
countryside.*
*FOOD up to £15*
**Hours:** bar 10:30am – 2:30pm; lunch 12noon – 2pm; bar
6pm – 11pm; dinner 7pm – 9:30pm; closed bank
holidays; closed Sunday. **Cuisine:** English / French:-
English bistro style menu, with an added touch of

French. Wide choice of dishes, nicely presented. Vegetarian menu also available. **Credit cards:** Visa, Access, Diners, AmEx. **Other points:** licensed, children catered for – please check for age limits. **Directions:** situated at north end of High Street, near Tonbridge School.
JERRY HALFHIDE, tel (0732) 353660.

## TUNBRIDGE WELLS, Kent Map 5

### PORTOVINO'S RESTAURANT, Church Road
*An attractive Edwardian style house, with a delightfully furnished green and white interior and fresh flowers. Comfortable, clean and very efficiently run, offering fine food and wine in a restful and pleasing atmosphere.*
FOOD £15–£20
**Hours:** closed 01/01 – 07/01; lunch 12noon – 2:30pm; dinner 7pm – 10pm; closed Sunday evening – Monday. **Cuisine:** English:- A la carte and Table d'hote menus, offering an extensive selection of dishes, complemented by a fine wine list. Vegetarian meals also available. **Credit cards:** Visa, Access, AmEx. **Other points:** licensed, Sunday lunch, children catered for – please check for age limits, parking. **Directions:** off Southborough Common on A26 between Tunbridge and Tunbridge Wells.
ANDREW BOND, tel (0892) 513161, fax (0892) 513161.

### RUSSELL HOTEL, 80 London Road
*The Russell Hotel is a large Victorian House furnished to a high standard. It is situated facing the Common and is only a few minutes walk from the town centre. This hotel offers generous portions of appetising meals, cooked from local fresh produce. The staff are welcoming and helpful making a stay here very comfortable.*
ACCOMMODATION £41–£50
FOOD up to £15
**Hours:** breakfast – except Sunday 7am – 9:30am; breakfast – Sunday 8am – 10am; dinner – except Sunday 7pm – 9:30pm; dinner – Sunday 7pm – 9pm. **Cuisine:** modern English:- A la carte menu, fixed 3 course menu, bar snacks. Dishes include stuffed mushrooms, veal cooked in marsala & cream, grilled steak in mustard sauce. **Rooms:** 26 bedrooms all with tea making facilities, telephone, TV: 2 singles ensuite, 13 twins ensuite, 11 doubles ensuite. **Credit cards:** Visa, Access, Diners, AmEx. **Other points:** children catered for – please check for age limits, foreign exchange, residents' lounge, residents' bar, vegetarian meals, parking. **Directions:** take M25; exit 5. Follow A21 south, join A26. On A26 near A264 junction.
MR & MRS K A WILKINSON, tel (0892) 544833, fax (0892) 515846.

### WINSTON MANOR HOTEL, Beacon Road, Crowborough
*This large, late Victorian Hotel is set in the heart of the Ashdown Forest within easy reach of Gatwick and the*
*south coast, offering excellent facilities including a leisure club. The atmosphere is quiet and relaxed and the food and service outstanding.*
ACCOMMODATION £31–£40
FOOD £15–£20 ⚏ ★
**Hours:** breakfast 7:30am – 9:30am; meals all day 7:30am – 10pm; dinner 7:30pm – 9:30pm. **Cuisine:** French / English:- A la carte, Table d'hote and Coffee Shop menus. Childrens menu available. Imaginative dishes for vegetarians. **Rooms:** 54 bedrooms all with tea making facilities, telephone, TV: 1 single ensuite, 17 twins ensuite, 35 doubles ensuite, 1 triple ensuite. **Credit cards:** Visa, Access, AmEx, Diners, Switch. **Other points:** licensed, Sunday lunch, no-smoking area, children catered for – please check for age limits, garden, pets allowed, afternoon tea, conferences, functions, baby-listening device, baby sitting, cots, 24hr reception, residents' lounge, residents' bar, swimming pool, vegetarian meals, parking. **Directions:** hotel is on the A26 between Tunbridge Wells and Uckfield.
MR FRAZIER, tel (0892) 652772.

## UCKFIELD, East Sussex Map 5

### HALLAND FORGE HOTEL & RESTAURANT, Halland
*All dishes are cooked to order for the restaurant, whilst the coffee shop is self-service. A family-run hotel in its own grounds which include lawns, flower beds and woodlands. Its location is ideal for the South Downs, Ashdown Forest and the coast at Eastbourne and Brighton.*
ACCOMMODATION £21–£30
FOOD up to £15
**Hours:** breakfast 8am – 12noon; lunch 12noon – 2pm; dinner 7pm – 9:30pm. **Cuisine:** English / French / Italian:- Only fresh ingredients. **Rooms:** 20 bedrooms all with tea making facilities, telephone, radio, TV: 7 twins ensuite, 11 doubles ensuite, 2 triples ensuite. **Credit cards:** Visa, Access, Diners, AmEx. **Other points:** Sunday lunch, children catered for – please check for age limits, residents' lounge, residents' bar. **Directions:** at the junction of the A22 and B2192 4 miles south of Uckfield.
MR & MRS J M HOWELL, tel (0825) 840456, fax (0825) 840773.

## WADHURST, East Sussex Map 5

### THE GREYHOUND, St James Square
*An historical coaching inn with heavily beamed and half-panelled bar, inglenook fireplace and photographs of past eras. Variety of draught lagers and real ales, plus a fine selection of wines.*
FOOD up to £15
**Hours:** lunch 12noon – 2pm; dinner 7pm – 9:30pm. **Cuisine:** English:- House menu contains a large range of fish, poultry, veal & beef dishes – all of a very high standard. Separate Sunday Roast luncheon menu. **Credit cards:** Visa, Access. **Other points:** Sunday lunch,

children catered for – please check for age limits.
**Directions:** situated in the centre of Wadhurst.
ROBIN & TANNIA HEALE, tel (0892) 783224, (0892)
784090.

### THE OLD VINE, *Cousley Wood*
*The Old Vine provides an extensive choice of excellently
cooked food in the bar and restaurant. All meals are
freshly prepared and attractively presented whilst
offering excellent value for money. The service is
friendly and efficient, in keeping with the busy, friendly
atmosphere. Very highly recommended by the Les
Routiers inspector.*
*FOOD £15–£20* ☕
**Hours:** last orders 7pm – 9:30pm; Sunday lunch 12noon
– 2pm; bar meals 12noon – 2pm; bar meals 6pm –
9:30pm; dinner 7pm – 11:30pm. **Cuisine:** continental:-
Modern European cuisine with a good vegetarian
selection. Dishes may include Peppered Sirloin, Chicken
Caprice. **Credit cards:** Visa, Access, Diners. **Other
points:** licensed, Sunday lunch, children catered for –
please check for age limits, pets allowed, reservations,
entertainment. **Directions:** off the A21 at Lamberhurst
onto B2100 direction Wadhurst.
ANTHONY PEEL, tel (0892) 782271.

## WALTON ON THAMES, Surrey Map 4

### SIXTIES WINE BAR, *New Zealand Avenue*
*The small bar area of the 36-seater wine bar leaves
plenty of room for the restaurant. The cosy atmosphere,
varied wine list and good food make this a popular spot
with the locals.*
*FOOD £15–£20*
**Hours:** lunch 12noon – 2:15pm; dinner 6pm – 10:15pm;
closed Monday evening; closed Sunday. **Cuisine:**
English:- Fresh, local produce. Each dish cooked to
order. No frozen foods. **Credit cards:** Visa, Access,
Diners, AmEx. **Directions:** Walton on Thames is
situated 1 mile from the A3.
MR & MRS NEIL BARKBY, tel (0932) 221685.

## WELLS NEXT THE SEA, Norfolk Map 9

### CROWN HOTEL & RESTAURANT, *The Buttlands*
*The hotel is ideally situated for visiting historic
churches, priories and stately homes including Holkham
Hall and Sandringham. Both table d'hote and a la carte
menus are available in the restaurant.*
*ACCOMMODATION £31–£40*
*FOOD up to £15*
**Hours:** lunch 12noon – 2pm; dinner 7pm – 9:30pm.
**Cuisine:** English:- Sea and shellfish, steak and kidney
pie, home-made soups, pate and French specialities.
Local produce used where possible. **Rooms:** 15
bedrooms 2 doubles, 1 family room, 1 twin, 1 single
ensuite, 5 twins ensuite, 5 doubles ensuite. **Credit
cards:** Visa, Access, Diners, AmEx. **Other points:**
licensed, Sunday lunch, children catered for – please

check for age limits. **Directions:** The Buttlands is a tree-
lined square in the centre of town.
MR & MRS W FOYERS, tel (0328) 710209.

## WEST MARDEN, West Sussex Map 4

### VICTORIA INN, *Nr Chichester*
*A deservedly popular pub in the heart of the Sussex
countryside. The Inn is family-run and enjoys a friendly
atmosphere. Well cooked and presented meals are served in
the bar and in the small restaurant and the emphasis is on
home cooked dishes. Vegetarian dishes on request. The Inn
has a well appointed garden and terrace. Draught beers,
including Gibbs Mews, Bishops Tipple and Bass.*
*FOOD up to £15*
**Hours:** lunch 12noon – 2pm; dinner 7pm – 9:30pm;
dinner – Sunday 7pm – 9pm. **Cuisine:** English:- All
dishes home cooked. Daily blackboard menu served in
both bar and restaurant. **Credit cards:** Visa, Access,
AmEx. **Other points:** licensed, Sunday lunch, beer
garden, bank holidays. **Directions:** on B2146 between
coast and Petersfield, 9 miles west of Chichester.
JAMES NEVILLE, tel (0705) 631330, fax (0705)
631722.

## WEST WITTERING, West Sussex Map 4

### THE LAMB INN WEST WITTERING, *Chichester Road*
*This traditional Sussex country freehouse specialises in real
ales and home cooking; the pies and toasted sandwiches
are particularly recommended. The evening menu also
features a range of local fresh fish, and during summer
months (weather permitting) there is a salad bar and
weekend evening barbecue in the pretty pub garden. With
its good value and warm welcome, the Lamb Inn is popular
with locals, visiting sailors and windsurfers.*
*FOOD up to £15* ☗
**Hours:** bar – except Sunday 11am – 2:30pm; bar –
Sunday 12noon – 3pm; lunch 12noon – 2pm; bar –
except Sunday 6pm – 11pm; bar – Sunday 7pm –
10:30pm; dinner 7pm – 9pm. **Cuisine:** English:-
Homemade food including pies and fresh fish
(evenings). **Credit cards:** Visa, Access. **Other points:**
licensed, open-air dining, limited Sunday lunch menu,
no-smoking area, open bank holidays, dogs allowed (on
lead), barbecues, parking, disabled access, vegetarian
meals. **Directions:** on B2179 500yds beyond Itchenor
turn. Sign opposite pub.
MR NIGEL CARTER, tel (0243) 511105.

## WEST WYCOMBE, Buckinghamshire Map 6

### GEORGE & DRAGON, *High Street*
*This charming country inn is situated in a National Trust
village with several tourist attractions within walking
distance. Renowned for traditional English home
cooking, The George & Dragon offers superior
accommodation for that special stay. Private room
available for functions.*

ACCOMMODATION £21–£30

FOOD up to £15

**Hours:** lunch 12noon – 2pm; dinner 6pm – 9:30pm.
**Cuisine:** English:- Home cooking, local game in season.
**Rooms:** 8 bedrooms, all en suite, 2 with four-posters and
1 family room. **Credit cards:** Visa, Access, Diners,
AmEx. **Other points:** licensed, open-air dining, Sunday
lunch. **Directions:** on the A40 in West Wycombe village,
3 miles west of High Wycombe.
PHILIP TODD, tel (0494) 464414, fax (0494) 462432.

## WESTERHAM, Kent Map 5

### THE KINGS ARMS HOTEL, Market Square

A privately owned, elegant Georgian Coaching Inn
offering a relaxed, peaceful atmosphere, comfortable
accommodation and professional, welcoming staff. The
restaurant provides traditional but imaginative dishes,
freshly prepared and cooked to order. The good food is
complemented by a comprehensive wine list. Ideal
location for business and pleasure.

ACCOMMODATION £41–£50

FOOD £15–£20 ♈ ☋

**Hours:** breakfast – weekdays 7:30am – 9:30am;
breakfast – weekends 8am – 10am; lunch 12noon – 2pm;
bar meals 12noon – 2pm; dinner 7pm – 10pm; bar meals
7pm – 10pm. **Cuisine:** English:- Table d'hote and a la
carte menus using fresh ingredients. Dishes may include,
pot-roasted Guinea Fowl, Supreme of Chicken,
Rossettes of Lamb. **Rooms:** 16 bedrooms 1 single
ensuite, 9 doubles ensuite, 4 twins ensuite, 1 triple
ensuite, 1 family room ensuite. **Credit cards:** Visa,
Access, Diners, AmEx. **Other points:** licensed, open-air
dining, Sunday lunch, children catered for – please
check for age limits, residents' lounge, garden,
conferences, terrace bar. **Directions:** Junction 6, M25.
Follow A25 into Westerham.
KEN EATON, tel (0959) 562990, fax (0959) 564240.

## WESTONING, Bedfordshire Map 6

### THE CHEQUERS, Park Road

A 17th Century thatched inn, retaining all of its original
character. The stables have been tastefully re-decorated
to form an outstanding restaurant offering good value
for money. Very highly recommended.

FOOD up to £15

**Hours:** bar meals – except Sunday 11am – 11pm; lunch
12noon – 2pm; bar meals – Sunday 12noon – 3pm;
dinner 7pm – 11pm; bar meals – Sunday 7pm –
10:30pm. **Cuisine:** English / international:- Fixed price
menu. English cuisine. Dishes include Char grilled
steaks, lamb steaks, Cajun chicken. Extensive bar food
menu. Daily specials on blackboards. **Credit cards:**
Visa, Access, Diners, AmEx. **Other points:** children
catered for – please check for age limits, courtyard,
Sunday lunch. **Directions:** on A5120, in centre of
village.
PAUL WALLMAN, tel (0525) 713125, fax (0525)
716702.

## WHITSTABLE, Kent Map 5

### GIOVANNIS RESTAURANT, 49–55 Canterbury Road

This fully air-conditioned cocktail bar and restaurant is
very popular and booking is recommended. Established
in 1968, Giovanni's is owner-managed with an
enthusiastic continental staff.

FOOD £15–£20 ☋

**Hours:** lunch 12noon – 2:30pm; dinner 6pm – 10:30pm;
closed Sunday evening. **Cuisine:** Italian / French.
**Credit cards:** Visa, Access, Diners, AmEx. **Other
points:** licensed, Sunday lunch, children catered for –
please check for age limits. **Directions:** on the A290
near the railway bridge.
GIOVANNI FERRARI, tel (0227) 273034.

## WHITTLESEY, Cambridgeshire Map 8

### THE FALCON HOTEL, Paradise Lane, Whittlesey, Nr Peterborough

Extensively refurbished, the Falcon Hotel provides
excellent quality food in a warm and friendly
atmosphere. Renowned for their imaginative bar meals
and gourmet dishes which attract a regular clientele.

ACCOMMODATION £21–£30

FOOD £15–£20

**Hours:** open all year; open bank holidays; breakfast
7:30am – 10am; lunch 12noon – 2pm; dinner 6:30pm –
11pm. **Cuisine:** modern English:- Gourmet dishes and
Speciality Bar Meals, including Roast Duckling with a
Rum and Honey Sauce, and Escalopes of Veal with
strawberry syrup. **Rooms:** 8 bedrooms, 2 en suite
with colour TV, radio, trouser-press, telephone, and
tea/coffee making facilities. Room-service provided.
**Credit cards:** Visa, Access, Diners, AmEx. **Other
points:** licensed, Sunday lunch, children catered for –
please check for age limits, parking, vegetarian meals.
**Directions:** situated off the B005, Church Street
Whittlesey.
D THOMPSON, tel (0733) 350318.

## WOODBRIDGE, Suffolk Map 9

### BULL HOTEL, Market Hill

A 16th century coaching inn on the A12 in the centre of
town. Facilities for conferences, private hire and
receptions.

ACCOMMODATION £21–£30

FOOD up to £15

**Hours:** breakfast 7:30am – 9:30am; lunch 12noon –
2pm; dinner 7pm – 10pm. **Cuisine:** English:-
Homemade soup, steaks, bar snacks. **Rooms:** 25
bedrooms all with tea making facilities, telephone, TV: 1
single, 9 doubles ensuite, 1 double, 1 twin, 7 twins
ensuite, 3 singles ensuite, 1 family room ensuite, 1
triple, 1 triple ensuite. **Credit cards:** Visa, Access,
Diners, AmEx. **Other points:** Sunday lunch, no-
smoking area, children catered for – please check for age

limits, residents' lounge, residents' bar. **Directions:** on
A12 in town centre.
NEVILLE & ANNE ALLEN, tel (0394) 382089, fax
(0394) 384902.

## CAPTAIN'S TABLE, 3 Quay Street

*This fish and seafood restaurant has a timbered interior
with a distinct nautical flavour to the decor. Very close
to the river and the town centre.*
*FOOD £15–£20* 🍲
**Hours:** lunch 12noon – 2pm; dinner 6:30pm – 9:30pm;
closed Monday. **Cuisine:** seafood:- Local seafood.
**Credit cards:** Visa, Access, Diners, AmEx. **Other
points:** open-air dining, no-smoking area, children
catered for – please check for age limits. **Directions:**
near the railway station and the quayside.
MR A J PRENTICE, tel (0394) 383145.

# WORTHING, West Sussex Map 4

## THE COURT HOUSE, Sea Lane,
## Goring By Sea

*Goring is just west of Worthing town. The Court House
is an historic listed building within walking distance of
the sea. There are train and bus services to the town
centre, Sussex and London. Local attractions include
yachting and windsurfing, the National Bowls Centre
and other sports facilities.*
*ACCOMMODATION under £20*
**Hours:** breakfast 8:15am – 9am. **Cuisine:** breakfast.
**Rooms:** 1 single, 2 twin and 3 family bedrooms, 3 with
en suite facilities. 1 bathroom and 1 shower. Colour TV
and tea/coffee making facilities in all rooms. **Credit
cards:** Access. **Other points:** children catered for –
please check for age limits, pets allowed, residents'
lounge, garden, German spoken, French spoken, Dutch
spoken. **Directions:** A259 from Worthing, 2 miles.
MRS I GOMME, tel (0903) 248473.

## KINGSWAY HOTEL, Marine Parade

*This four storey hotel, ideally situated for the
promenade, town centre shopping and entertainments,
has been under the personal supervision of the Howlett
family for over twenty years. Offering good cuisine, with
a choice of a la carte, carvery or bar meals, the
Kingsway Hotel has very comfortable accommodation,
complemented by friendly and attentive service.*
*ACCOMMODATION £41–£50*
*FOOD up to £15* ★
**Hours:** breakfast 7:45am – 9:30am; lunch 12noon –
2pm; dinner – except Sunday 7pm – 9pm; dinner –
Sunday 7pm – 8:30pm. **Rooms:** 29 bedrooms all with
tea making facilities, telephone, radio, mini bar, TV: 14
singles ensuite, 7 doubles ensuite, 8 twins ensuite.
**Credit cards:** Visa, Access, Diners, AmEx. **Other
points:** licensed, Sunday lunch, children catered for –
please check for age limits, afternoon tea, pets allowed,
lift, residents' lounge, patio, functions, residents' bar.
**Directions:** on Marine Parade, near the Pier. To the
west.
BRIAN & ANN HOWLETT, tel (0903) 237542, (0903)
237543, fax (0903) 204173.

## WINDSOR HOUSE HOTEL,
## 14–20 Windsor Road

*This family owned and run hotel is situated close to the
sea and a short walk from the town centre. Well
maintained and attractively decorated, it offers a
friendly atmosphere and good service to both business
people and holiday-makers. The hotel enjoys an
attractive bar and gardens and three comfortable
lounges. It also has a private car park.*
*ACCOMMODATION £21–£30*
*FOOD up to £15* ★
**Hours:** breakfast 7:30am – 9:15am; lunch 12:30pm –
2:30pm; dinner 6pm – 9:30pm. **Cuisine:** English:- A la
carte menu, fixed price 3 course menu, bar meals/snacks
and vegetarian meals. **Rooms:** 30 bedrooms all with tea
making facilities, telephone, radio, TV: 1 single ensuite,
12 twins ensuite, 8 doubles ensuite, 3 triples ensuite, 6
quads ensuite. **Credit cards:** Visa, Access. **Other
points:** licensed, Sunday lunch, children catered for –
please check for age limits, garden, afternoon tea, baby-
listening device, cots. **Directions:** take A24 to A259.
MR & MRS ARMSTRONG, tel (0903) 239655, fax
(0903) 210763.

# SOUTH WEST ENGLAND

The counties of South West England make up England's most popular holiday areas.

The West Country is a region rich in ingredients for the traveller or tourist, where the scenery seems to almost change with every bend in the road. You can explore the miles of cliff paths, visit castles, ancient monuments, shop in peaceful little towns, fish for shark, sail, surf, or simply find your own secluded cove and bask in the sun. Much of Cornwall's Celtic coastline is best explored on foot or by horseback. The narrow country lanes and quaint fishing villages are truly fascinating. Washed by Atlantic breakers and a favourite with surfers, Cornwall has some magnificent beaches with vast stretches of golden sand. From the clifftop castle at Tintagel, with its legends of King Arthur, to the rugged open uplands of Bodmin Moor – it offers immense variety for visitors of all ages.

Few other counties can rival the sheer beauty of Devon – a region of chocolate-box cottages and gardens full of old fashioned sweet-scented flowers. Thatched villages, cream teas, craft centres, historic houses and gardens abound. Dorset, too, has some of the loveliest scenery in England with dramatic changes in landscape and some 88 miles of coastline. Bournemouth is Dorset's largest resort, with Poole nearby. There are many tiny villages to visit, like Milton Abbas and Tolpuddle where, in 1883, farm labourers rebelled against a fall in farm wages and formed a union to stand against the landowners. Christchurch is a charming heritage town dominated by its magnificent Priory Church and is an ideal centre for touring Dorset and the New Forest. An area of 235 square miles, nothing can compare with the rolling hills of North Dorset once ruled by famous kings. Often called 'a photographer's paradise', where many will have snapped the famous Gold Hill at Shaftesbury featured in the Hovis advertisement.

Everybody knows that Somerset is cider country – but there is far more to discover. The magnificent heather-covered scenery of the Exmoor National Park with its quaint villages of Dunster and Porlock; tiny Culbone church; the clapper bridge at Tarr Steps with walks up to the top of Dunkery Beacon. Charming country towns like Crewkerne, Chard, Ilchester, Ilminster and Yeovil, all provide a warm and hearty welcome for the visitor. Visit Cadbury Castle, claimed to be the site of Arthur's Camelot, the National Trust's Montacute House, or the wildlife park at Cricket St Thomas. The Somerset coast and its vast expanse of golden sand offers superb opportunities for fishing, boating and a whole range of water sports and other activities. Travel from Bridgwater Bay across the broad sands to the Quantock Hills and on to the popular resort of Minehead.

Stonehenge, Avebury and Old Sarum are names that immediately spring to mind when one mentions Wiltshire. In the south lies Salisbury Plain stretching from Pewsey Vale with its chalk downlands, ancient tracks, paths and avenues of grand trees which make up Savernake Forest. Historic houses include Longleat, famous for its lions, Wilton, Lacock Abbey and many more, all open to the public.

Historic Salisbury boasts the highest spire in England at 404 ft, and to the north are many fascinating towns including Malmesbury and Bradford-on-Avon with its curious lock-up. Visit the Great Western Railway Museum in Swindon, which also has a modern shopping centre, or travel to Castle Combe, nestling in the heart of the Cotswold Valley.

Centred on Bath and Bristol is the county of Avon. Stretching westwards towards Weston-Super-Mare are the Mendip Hills and in the south is the man-made lakeland of the Chew Valley and Blagdon, both of which offer superb scope for birdwatching, fishing, sailing and picnics. Bristol, the largest city in the West Country, is steeped in history with its cobbled King Street, famous for the Theatre Royal and almshouses at Llandoger Trow. A busy setting with a thriving arts centre, shops, restaurants, pubs and the centre for numerous festivals throughout the year. At Clifton is Brunel's famous Suspension Bridge which spans the Avon

Gorge, and a visit to Bristol Zoo is highly recommended. Up river is Bath, Britain's oldest spa town and once a popular resort with the Romans.

For details of where to visit and what to see in Southern England, contact the following tourist boards: South East England Tourist Board, 40 Chamberlayne Road, Eastleigh, Hants SO5 5JH. Tel: (0703) 620006. West Country Tourist Board, 60 St David's Hill, Exeter EX4 4SY. Tel: (0392) 211171.

## AXMINSTER, Devon Map 2

### THE NEW COMMERCIAL INN, Trinity Square

*This restaurant is found in a natural stone Victorian building in the centre of Axminster and offers excellent service and menu variety, including a special children's menu. The value for money is outstanding.*
FOOD up to £15
**Hours:** breakfast 7:30am – 12noon; lunch 12noon – 2pm; afternoon tea 2pm – 5:30pm; dinner 6pm – 10:30pm. **Cuisine:** English / international:- Separate Breakfast, Lunch, Afternoon Tea and Children's menu. Meal menu includes dishes such as fish, steak, chilli con carne and pizza. **Credit cards:** Visa, Access, Diners, AmEx. **Other points:** licensed, children catered for – please check for age limits, afternoon tea, street parking, bread shop. **Directions:** in the main square in Axminster. THE WALDEN FAMILY, tel (0297) 33225.

## AXMOUTH, Devon Map 2

### THE SHIP INN, Nr Seaton

*A small, popular pub on the road from Seaton serving an extensive range of lunchtime and evening meals in both bars and the garden. Real ales.*
FOOD up to £15
**Hours:** lunch 12noon – 2pm; dinner 7:30pm – 9pm. **Cuisine:** English:- Deep sea surprise, baked plaice with seafood stuffing, accent on local game and seafood in season. Homegrown fruit, vegetables and herbs. **Other points:** children catered for – please check for age limits, garden, games room. **Directions:** 1 mile south of the A3052 Lyme Regis – Exeter road towards Seaton. MR & MRS C CHAPMAN, tel (0297) 21838.

## BAMPTON, Devon Map 2

### THE SWAN HOTEL, Station Road

*A 15th century building which retains its old charm and character. Originally, The Swan housed the stone masons who built the nearby church. Close to Exmoor, Bickley Mill and Wimbleball Lake.*
ACCOMMODATION £21–£30
FOOD up to £15 ○ ★
**Hours:** breakfast 8am – 9:30am; lunch 12noon – 2pm; bar meals 12noon – 2pm; bar meals 6pm – 10pm; dinner 7pm – 10pm. **Cuisine:** English:- Home style traditional cooking, using fresh produce such as local trout and fresh vegetables. **Rooms:** 6 rooms, 2 en suite. **Credit cards:** Visa, Access, Diners. **Other points:** licensed,

Sunday lunch, bank holidays, children catered for – please check for age limits, pets allowed, afternoon tea. **Directions:** on main Barnstable – Taunton Rd on B3227. Close to public car park. BRIAN & PAM DUNESBY, tel (0398) 331257.

## BASINGSTOKE, Hampshire Map 4

### FERNBANK HOTEL, 4 Fairfields Road

*A newly refurbished hotel situated in a quiet, residential road by the cricket ground, a few minutes walk from restaurants, the shopping centre and sports facilities. Mr & Mrs White extend a warm welcome and friendly personal service to all guests. Ideal for exploring the beautiful Hampshire countryside. Spanish is also spoken.*
ACCOMMODATION £21–£30
**Hours:** breakfast 7:15am – 9am; bar snacks varies. **Cuisine:** English. **Rooms:** 17 bedrooms 5 singles, 4 singles ensuite, 1 twin, 2 twins ensuite, 5 doubles ensuite. **Other points:** parking, children catered for – please check for age limits, open bank holidays, no-smoking area, afternoon tea, residents' lounge, vegetarian meals, satelite TV. **Directions:** from Junction 6 (M3) turn left at first roundabout, right at next roundabout, then left at Lambs Pub. MR & MRS WHITE, tel (0256) 21191, fax (0256) 21191.

## BATH, Avon Map 3

### BAILBROOK LODGE, 35/37 London Road West

*A splendid listed Georgian mansion designed by John Everlaigh and situated on the outskirts of Bath. The building retains many features from the period; furniture, oil paintings, crystal chandeliers, and a quiet, friendly atmosphere prevails throughout. A small bar is available on a self-service basis. The emphasis at the Bailbrook is on a high standard of service and hospitality towards guests.*
ACCOMMODATION £21–£30
**Hours:** breakfast 8am – 9:30am. **Cuisine:** breakfast. **Rooms:** 12 bedrooms all with tea making facilities, TV: 4 twins ensuite, 4 doubles ensuite. **Credit cards:** Visa, Access, Diners, AmEx. **Other points:** parking, children catered for – please check for age limits, afternoon teas, residents' lounge, vegetarian meals, garden. **Directions:** Junction 18 off M4, take A46 to Bath, at T junction turn left onto A4 towards Chippenham. Bailbrook Lodge is 300yds on the left. MARGARET ADDISON, tel (0225) 859090.

## BROMPTON HOUSE, St Johns Road

*A former Georgian Rectory of 1777, now converted and extended it is set amidst a prize-winning garden. All rooms have been tastefully furnished to an extremely high standard with guests comfort in mind, and although remodernised, the building still retains the Georgian era with oil paintings, furniture and fittings of the period. A very friendly and courteous welcome is assured from both the management and helpful staff in the relaxing, informal atmosphere.*

ACCOMMODATION £31–£40

**Hours:** breakfast 8:15am – 9:30am; closed 23 December – 2 January. **Cuisine:** breakfast. **Rooms:** 18 bedrooms all with tea making facilities, telephone, radio, TV: 2 singles ensuite, 11 doubles ensuite, 4 twins ensuite, 1 family room ensuite. **Credit cards:** Visa, Access. **Other points:** parking, children catered for – please check for age limits, open bank holidays, no-smoking area, residents' lounge, vegetarian meals, garden. **Directions:** exit 17 or 18 off M4 to A4, Bath Road. At traffic lights take A35, Warminster Road, crossing Cleveland Bridge first right. Brompton House is on left next to church.
SELBY, DAVID AND SUSAN, tel 0225 420972.

## THE CANARY CAFE, 3 Queen Street

*The Canary Cafe has become one of Bath's most popular and well-established restaurants. The chefs produce an array of international dishes to suit all tastes and times of day. Teatime is a speciality and The Canary was the winner of the Tea Council's Top Tea Place Award of the Year in 1989. Over 40 different teas are served with an impressive selection of patisserie.*

FOOD up to £15

**Hours:** closed 01/01; meals all day 9am – 8pm; meals all day – Sunday 11am – 6pm; closed Christmas 25/12 – 26/12. **Cuisine:** international:- Varied and interesting range of international cuisine, with Award Winning Speciality Teas. **Credit cards:** Visa, Access. **Other points:** children catered for – please check for age limits, parking. **Directions:** on A4. 9 miles off M4 on A46.
MR DAVIES, tel (0225) 424846.

## COMPASS ABBEY HOTEL, North Parade

*Originally built as a wealthy merchants house in the 1740's, the Compass Abbey Hotel re-opened in May 1990 after a complete refurbishment. Just a minute's walk from the Abbey, Roman Baths and Pump Room, it offers comfortable accommodation with many luxuries, including Sky TV. Wedgwood's Restaurant, Coffee House and bar are ideal meeting places whilst exploring the European Heritage City of Bath. The Fernley and Orchard Rooms are available for meeting and conference hire.*

ACCOMMODATION £31–£40

FOOD £15–£20

**Hours:** breakfast 7:15am – 9:30am; bar snacks 10am – 6pm; lunch 12noon – 2pm; dinner 7:15pm – 9:15pm. **Cuisine:** English. **Rooms:** 54 bedrooms 12 singles ensuite, 16 twins ensuite, 26 doubles ensuite. **Credit**

cards: Visa, Access, AmEx, Diners, Switch. **Other points:** children catered for – please check for age limits, no-smoking, afternoon teas, disabled access, pets, residents' lounge, vegetarian. **Directions:** right in the city centre.
DAVID PRIOR, tel (0225) 461603, fax (0225) 447758.

## THE COURT HOTEL, Emborough, Chilcompton

*An attractive Victorian stone manor house, this recently refurbished hotel is set in the beautiful countryside of Avon. Tastefully decorated, the rooms are light and airy with good views. Superb food is served in the tranquil dining room. Conference facilities.*

ACCOMMODATION £31–£40

FOOD up to £15

**Hours:** breakfast 6:45am – 9:30am; lunch 12:15pm – 2:15pm; dinner 7:30pm – 9:30pm. **Cuisine:** English:- Mainly traditional English and French cuisine. Imaginative cooking. Good selection of wines. **Rooms:** 12 bedrooms all with tea making facilities, TV: 3 singles ensuite, 5 doubles ensuite, 3 twins ensuite, 1 family room ensuite. **Credit cards:** Visa, Access, AmEx. **Other points:** licensed, open-air dining, Sunday lunch, children catered for – please check for age limits, bank holidays, afternoon teas, residents' lounge, garden. **Directions:** take A367 from Bath to Radstock, then Wells Road.
MISS COLLINS, tel (0761) 232237, fax (0761) 233730.

## CROSS KEYS INN, Midford Road, Combe Down

*An attractive olde worlde pub with a friendly, welcoming atmosphere. The food is well cooked and offers variety and good value for money. The B3110 is a scenic alternative to the main A36 and is worth taking even if only to visit the Cross Keys for its good food, warm welcome and friendly service. In the garden there is an interesting well stocked aviary.*

FOOD up to £15

**Hours:** lunch 12noon – 2pm; dinner 7pm – 10pm. **Cuisine:** English:- Bar meals including a large selection of home-made foods. **Other points:** licensed, Sunday lunch, children catered for – please check for age limits, garden, pets allowed, public aviary. **Directions:** B3110 overlooking Bath. Near St Martin's Hospital.
MARK & CAROLINE PALMER, tel (0225) 832002.

## DORIAN HOUSE, 1 Upper Oldfield Park

*A gracious Victorian home with parking. Situated on the southern slopes overlooking Bath, yet only ten minutes stroll to the city centre. There are seven charming bedrooms, all en suite. The lounge and small licensed bar provide a pleasant atmosphere for friends to meet. There is a full English breakfast menu and a warm welcome for all guests.*

ACCOMMODATION £21–£30

**Hours:** breakfast 8am – 9am. **Cuisine:** breakfast. **Rooms:** 7 bedrooms all with tea making facilities, telephone, radio, TV: 1 single ensuite, 4 doubles ensuite, 2 family rooms ensuite. **Credit cards:** Visa, Access,

Diners, AmEx. **Other points:** children catered for – please check for age limits, residents' lounge, garden, vegetarian meals. **Directions:** up A367 Wells Rd for 250m to left-hand bend. First right/3rd house on left. IAN & DOREEN BENNETTS, tel (0225) 426336, fax (0225) 444699.

## GEORGES HOTEL, 2/3 South Parade

*Situated in the very heart of historic Bath, the hotel is part of an elegant terrace built in the 1740's. Guests can enjoy well appointed accommodation and a well stocked Georgian bar. For a touch of Greece, the Acropolis Restaurant below the hotel offers a wide range of traditional Greek and English dishes. Private Parties and Weddings are a speciality.*

*ACCOMMODATION £21–£30*

*FOOD up to £15*

**Hours:** breakfast 7:30am – 9:30am; restaurant 11am – 11pm. **Cuisine:** Greek / English. **Rooms:** 19 bedrooms all with telephone, TV: 4 family rooms ensuite, 7 doubles ensuite, 8 twins ensuite. **Credit cards:** Visa, Access, AmEx, Diners, Switch. **Other points:** children catered for – please check for age limits, open Sunday lunch, open bank holidays, no-smoking area, afternoon tea, open Sunday dinner, residents' lounge, disabled access, pets allowed, weddings, vegetarian meals, conferences. **Directions:** proceed Junction 18 M4, signed Bath. Located on north Parade Bridge in centre of Bath.

MR G M PAPANICOLAOU, tel (0225) 464923, fax (0225) 425471.

## LEIGHTON HOUSE, 139 Wells Road

*A well appointed Victorian residence that has been tastefully furnished by Kathy and Dave Slape, who have successfully created a warm and friendly haven for their guests. With the emphasis on comfort, warm hospitality and attention to detail, guests can be assured of an enjoyable stay. Situated just 10 minutes from the City centre, Leighton House comes highly recommended.*

*ACCOMMODATION £21 £30* ★

**Hours:** breakfast 8am – 9am. **Cuisine:** English:- Traditional. Vegetarian dishes. **Rooms:** 8 bedrooms all with tea making facilities, telephone, radio, TV: 3 twins ensuite, 3 doubles ensuite, 1 triple ensuite, 1 quad ensuite. **Credit cards:** Visa, Access. **Other points:** children catered for – please check for age limits, residents' lounge, garden, special breaks, baby-listening device, cots. **Directions:** situated on the southern side of Bath on the A367 Exeter road.

DAVE & KATHY SLAPE, tel (0225) 314769.

## THE NORTHEY ARMS HOTEL, Bath Road, Box

*The Northey Arms dates back to the 1840's when it served the needs of the Box Quarrymen. Extended in 1934 by Maisie Gay, a star of stage and screen, Noel Coward once served behind the bar. Situated within easy reach of the historic city of Bath with its Georgian houses, it is ideal for midweek business or a weekend break. Nearby, there are many places of interest to visit.*

*ACCOMMODATION £41–£50*

*FOOD up to £15*

**Hours:** open all year 7:30pm; breakfast 8am – 9:30am; bar meals 12noon – 2pm; dinner 7pm – 10pm. **Cuisine:** English:- Good old fashioned homecooked pub-style food. Good vegetarian menu. **Rooms:** 4 bedrooms, all en suite, with colour TV, telephone, trouser-press, hair dryer and tea/coffee making facilities. A cot is available on request. **Credit cards:** Visa, Access. **Other points:** licensed, open-air dining, Sunday lunch, children catered for – please check for age limits, parking. **Directions:** Junction 17 or 18 of M4 motorway. On the A4 Bath road.

PAUL DICKENSON (WADWORTH & CO LTD), tel (0225) 742333.

## THE OLD MALT HOUSE HOTEL, Radford, Timsbury, Nr Bath

*Only 6 miles from Bath the hotel is an excellent base to explore the West Country and guests are welcome at the farm run by the same family with its famous Shire Horses. The comfortable relaxed restaurant is renowned for its excellent English food. Full English breakfast is included in all B&B rates.*

*ACCOMMODATION £31–£40*

*FOOD up to £15* ★

**Hours:** breakfast 7:45am – 9am; lunch 12noon – 2pm; dinner 7pm – 8:30pm; closed 25 December – 1 January. **Cuisine:** English:- Traditional English, including pheasant, duck, venison, steak, rabbit and vegetarian dishes. Locally grown vegetables and additive free meat are used. **Rooms:** 10 bedrooms all with tea making facilities, telephone, TV: 1 single ensuite, 3 twins ensuite, 4 doubles ensuite, 2 triples ensuite. **Credit cards:** Visa, Access, Diners, AmEx. **Other points:** licensed, open-air dining, parking, children catered for – please check for age limits, afternoon tea, residents' lounge, garden, disabled access, vegetarian meals, residents' bar. **Directions:** off A367. Follow Radford Farm signs.

MICHAEL & MARGUERITE HORLER, tel (0761) 470106, fax (0761) 472616.

## THE OLD SCHOOL HOUSE, Church Street, Bathford

*Built in 1837 on the site of the Old Manor Court Barn. After 140 years it closed as the village school and now provides comfortable accommodation and the ambiance of a peaceful country home with the added charm of log fires in winter. Situated within a conservation area with beautiful views over the Avon Valley.*

*FOOD £16 – £20*

*ACCOMMODATION £31–£40*

**Hours:** breakfast 8am – 9am, dinner – to be ordered in advance 7pm – 8pm. **Food:** English. **Rooms:** 4 double bedrooms with TV, telephone, tea making facilities. **Credit cards:** Visa, Access. **Other points:** Fully no smoking, parking, residents' lounge, vegetarian meals. **Directions:** leave A4 at junction with A363, turn under

Brunel railway bridge, left at the Crown public house, proceed then take first turning on the right, Church Street. Hotel is at the far end.
MR R STONE, tel (0225) 859593, fax (0225) 859950.

## ORCHARD LODGE, *Warminster Road, Bathampton*
*A modern hotel situated in the picturesque village of Bathampton, just one and a half miles from Bath city centre. The Lodge has a good reputation for its fine food, comfortable accommodation and friendly service. All food is freshly prepared and special diets can be catered for. Guests can take advantage of a superb health area, including both sauna and solarium. Enjoys magnificent views of the Avon Valley and hills beyond.*
*ACCOMMODATION £21–£30*
*FOOD £21–£25*
**Hours:** restaurant closed Sundays and 25 December; breakfast 7:30am – 9am; breakfast – weekends 8am – 9:30am; dinner 6:30pm – 9pm. **Cuisine:** English. **Credit cards:** Visa, Access, Diners, AmEx. **Other points:** parking, children catered for – please check for age limits, no-smoking area, disabled access, pets, residents' lounge, vegetarian meals. **Directions:** proceed from Bath on A36, signposted Warminster. Orchard Lodge is situated approx 2 miles from centre on left.
MR M CURTIS, tel (0225) 466115, fax (0225) 446050.

## RAJPOOT, *4 Argyle Street*
*The restaurant is in the cellar of a Georgian building. Its layout comprises 3 large spacious halls with typically Indian decor including painted wooden images of Hindu gods. The menu offers a wide choice of well cooked Indian dishes. The Rajpoot is an internationally renowned establishment and appears in many national and international good food guides.*
*FOOD up to £15*
**Hours:** lunch 12noon – 2:30pm; dinner 6pm – 11pm; closed Christmas 25/12 – 26/12. **Cuisine:** Indian:- northern Indian Cuisine. **Credit cards:** Visa, Access, Diners, AmEx. **Other points:** Sunday lunch, children catered for – please check for age limits, disabled access. **Directions:** by the Pulteney Bridge next to Great Pulteney Street.
A & M CHOWDHURY, tel (0225) 466833, (0225) 464758, fax (0225) 442462.

## RASCALS BISTRO, *Pierrepont Place*
*Rascals is situated in a listed building in converted cellars and is entered via a main staircase. Its original stone walls give it a warm, intimate atmosphere, where you can sample imaginative international cuisine and an excellent wine list. The staff are polite and courteous and the service friendly and efficient. Ideal base for touring the beautiful historic Roman city of Bath.*
*FOOD up to £15*
**Hours:** lunch 11:30am – 2:30pm; bar snacks 11:30am – 2:30pm; dinner – weekends 5:30pm – 11pm; dinner – weekdays 6pm – 10:30pm. **Cuisine:** international:- All meals are prepared on the premises and all ingredients

are bought fresh each day. **Credit cards:** Access, Visa, Switch. **Other points:** children catered for – please check for age limits, open bank holidays, no-smoking area, pets allowed, vegetarian meals, open-air dining. **Directions:** near Pulteney Bridge off Pierrepont Street, through stone pillars behind Compass Hotel.
NICK ANDERSON & NIGEL MANNING-MORTON, tel (0225) 330201.

## THE ROOKERY, *Wells Road, Radstock*
*Set amidst a pleasant garden with flowers and shrubs, this 200 year old country house is now a homely guest-house offering every comfort, good food, personal attention, a happy and friendly atmosphere and olde world charm. Separate guest lounge is available for small conferences. Ideal location for touring the West Country.*
*ACCOMMODATION £21–£30*
*FOOD up to £15*
**Hours:** closed Xmas day (non res) 6pm; breakfast 7:30am – 9:30am; lunch 12noon – 2pm; bar snacks 12noon – 2pm; dinner 7pm – 9:30pm; bar snacks 7pm – 9:30pm. **Cuisine:** English. **Rooms:** 9 bedrooms all with tea making facilities, telephone, TV: 4 twins ensuite, 2 doubles ensuite, 3 family rooms ensuite. **Credit cards:** Visa, Access, Diners. **Other points:** parking, children catered for – please check for age limits, open bank holidays, no-smoking area, afternoon tea, disabled access, pets allowed, residents' lounge, vegetarian meals, garden, licensed. **Directions:** take A367 from Bath to Radstock, approx. 8 miles to The Rookery.
ANN & ROGER SIMS, tel (0761) 432626.

## THE WIFE OF BATH RESTAURANT, *12 Pierrepont Street*
*This well established bistro style restaurant is close to Bath Abbey and the famous Pump Rooms. A series of Georgian cellars of great character open onto a walled garden. The atmosphere is informal and staff are welcoming and friendly. The good food is complemented by an interesting wine list. Attractive decor, with quarry-tiled floors, stone walls and provencal printed fabrics.*
*FOOD up to £15*
**Hours:** lunch 12:15pm – 2:15pm; dinner 5:30pm – 11pm; closed Sunday lunch. **Cuisine:** English:- Casseroles, stuffed peppers, steaks, fresh fish, daily specials, toasted sandwiches at lunchtime. **Credit cards:** Visa, Access, AmEx. **Other points:** licensed, open-air dining, no-smoking area, children catered for – please check for age limits, vegetarian meals, no-smoking, garden. **Directions:** situated close to Bath Abbey.
DICK & AINSLIE ENSOM, tel (0225) 461745.

# BEER, Devon Map 2

## GARLANDS, *Stovar Long Lane*
*An Edwardian character house set in an acre of ground on the main coast road between Seaton and Beer. There are superb views from the house both of the sea and the Devon countryside, and the beach is within easy walking*

*distance. Fishing trips can be arranged – and your catch cooked for supper.*

ACCOMMODATION *under £20*

FOOD *up to £15* ★

**Hours:** last orders Sunday lunch – 12noon; breakfast 8:30am – 9:30am; dinner 6:30pm – 9:30pm. **Rooms:** 7 bedrooms all with tea making facilities: 1 single, 1 double, 1 double ensuite, 1 twin ensuite, 3 family rooms ensuite. **Credit cards:** Visa, Access. **Other points:** central heating, children catered for – please check for age limits, residents' lounge. **Directions:** turn south off A3052 at Hangmans Stone onto B3174. Signposted. ANN & NIGEL HARDING, tel (0297) 20958.

## BICKINGTON, Devon Map 2

### THE DARTMOOR HALFWAY, Nr Newton Abbot

*A charming pub, aptly named, halfway between Ashburton and Newton Abbot. The Dartmoor Halfway offers first class food and service.*

FOOD *up to £15*

**Hours:** bar meals 11am – 10:30pm; closed Christmas 25/12. **Cuisine:** English:- English home cooking. **Credit cards:** Visa, Access, Diners, AmEx. **Other points:** licensed, Sunday lunch, children catered for – please check for age limits, caravan facilities. **Directions:** on the A383, halfway between Ashburton and Newton Abbot. MESSRS B R & M D HUGGINS, tel (0626) 821270.

## BIDEFORD, Devon Map 2

### RIVERSFORD HOTEL, Limers Lane

*A country house hotel in 3 acres of gardens, affording magnificent views of the River Torridge. Ideal touring centre for beaches and countryside or discovering the hidden charms of Devon and Exmoor.*

ACCOMMODATION *£31–£40*

FOOD *up to £15* ★

**Hours:** open all year. **Cuisine:** English:- Homemade country fare, eg. home-made sweets, Devonshire cream teas and interesting wines. Traditional Sunday lunch. Extensive snack meals. **Rooms:** 16 bedrooms, 14 en suite. **Credit cards:** Visa, Access, Diners, AmEx. **Other points:** licensed, open-air dining, Sunday lunch, children catered for – please check for age limits. **Directions:** Limers Lane is on the right, 1 mile north of Bideford on the A386. MAURICE & MERRILYN JARRAD, tel (0237) 474239, (0237) 470381, fax (0237) 421661.

### YEOLDON COUNTRY HOUSE HOTEL & RESTAURANT, Durrant Lane, Northam

*Set beside the River Torridge, with lawns sloping down toward the river, you will find a warm welcome at Yeoldon Country House. Excellent cuisine, using local fresh produce wherever possible, and luxury accommodation are complemented by friendly efficient service, making this hotel a pleasure to visit.*

ACCOMMODATION *£21–£30*

FOOD *£15–£20*

**Hours:** breakfast 8am – 9:30am; breakfast – Sunday 8:30am – 9:45am; lunch – Sunday 12noon – 2:30pm; lunch – except Sunday 12:30pm – 2pm; dinner 7pm – 9:15pm. **Cuisine:** English / continental:- English and continental dishes, using local fresh produce wherever possible. Chef's home-made sweet table. **Rooms:** 10 luxury bedrooms, all en suite. Honeymoon suite available. **Credit cards:** Visa, Access. **Other points:** Sunday lunch, garden, afternoon tea, residents' lounge, room-service, parking, residents' bar, children catered for – please check for age limits. **Directions:** leave M5, exit 27. Take A361 (Bideford) then A386 to Northam. SONIA, RIC AND GARY CHEESEWRIGHT, tel (0237) 474400, fax (0237) 476618.

## BLANDFORD FORUM, Dorset Map 3

### ANVIL HOTEL AND RESTAURANT, Salisbury Road, Pimperne, Blandford

*Situated in the pretty Dorset village of Pimperne, this beautifully maintained 16th century hotel, just two minutes from Blandford is steeped in history. The well appointed restaurant offers quality dishes prepared by a Savoy-trained chef and personally supervised by Carolann Palmer. Ideally situated for touring Dorset and the surrounding counties of Wiltshire, Hampshire, Somerset and Devon. Enquire about clay pigeon tuition and flying tuition.*

ACCOMMODATION *£31–£40*

FOOD *up to £15*

**Hours:** breakfast 7:30am – 9:30am; lunch 12noon – 2:30pm; dinner 7pm – 9:45pm; bar snacks 7pm – 9:45pm. **Cuisine:** English / continental:- Varied menu, freshly prepared. **Rooms:** 9 bedrooms all with tea making facilities, telephone, TV: 1 single ensuite, 2 twins ensuite, 5 doubles ensuite, 1 family room ensuite. **Credit cards:** Visa, Access, Diners, AmEx. **Other points:** parking, children catered for – please check for age limits, open bank holidays, disabled access, pets allowed, residents' lounge, vegetarian meals, garden, open-air dining, entertainment, residents' bar, cots. **Directions:** 2 miles out of Blandford on A354 road to Salisbury. CAROLANN PALMER, tel (0258) 453431, (0258) 480182.

## BODMIN, Cornwall Map 1

### ASTERISK RESTAURANT WITH ROOMS, A30 Mount Pleasant, Roche

*Situated west of Bodmin, this is an ideal spot from which to visit Lands End and many other fascinating places of interest. Offering good home cooking, dishes may include Fillet in Stout Beef fillet, Duck Chartreuse, and Pork Fillet Oriental. Tasty desserts.*

ACCOMMODATION *under £20*

FOOD *up to £15*

**Hours:** dinner 7pm – 10pm; breakfast as required. **Cuisine:** English. **Credit cards:** Visa, Access, AmEx. **Other points:** parking, children catered for – please

check for age limits, open bank holidays, Sunday dinner, pets allowed, residents' lounge, vegetarian meals, garden. **Directions:** A30 two miles due west of Bodmin roundabout.
MR F ZOLA, tel (0726) 890863.

## BORDON, Hampshire Map 4

### THE CROWN INN, Arford, Headley

Situated in the picturesque village of Arford, the Crown Inn is a cosy, village pub with a friendly atmosphere and good food. There is a large garden leading down to a stream and there are plenty of tables for customers' use during the summer months. Two large log fires welcome you during the winter months.
FOOD up to £15
**Hours:** lunch 12noon – 2:15pm; dinner 6:30pm – 10pm; dinner – Sunday 7pm – 9:30pm. **Cuisine:** English:- Stuffies – large, hot baps – variety of fillings, chilli with avocado dip, salmon steaks, homemade steak & kidney pie, trout, meringues. Vegetarian and childrens menus. **Credit cards:** Visa, Access. **Other points:** open-air dining, Sunday lunch, beer garden, pets allowed, children catered for – please check for age limits. **Directions:** off the A325, onto the B3002. South of Farnham.
COLIN AND JANE GREENHALGH, tel (0428) 712150.

## BOURNEMOUTH, Dorset Map 3

### BAY VIEW COURT HOTEL, 35 East Overcliffe Drive, East Cliff

A recently completely refurbished 64 bedroom hotel situated in its own delightful garden with breathtaking views across the bay. This hotel offers the highest standards for business customers, conference delegates and holiday-makers, all who can enjoy the indoor pool, snooker room, games room and bars. The hotel is family run and we guarantee a warm welcome with excellent food and service.
ACCOMMODATION £31–£40
FOOD £15–£20
**Hours:** breakfast 8am – 9:30am; bar snacks 12noon – 2pm; dinner 6:30pm – 8:30pm; bar snacks 6:30pm – 8:30pm. **Cuisine:** English / continental:- Very high quality. **Rooms:** 65 bedrooms 9 singles ensuite, 20 twins ensuite, 27 doubles ensuite, 9 family rooms ensuite. **Other points:** parking, children catered for – please check for age limits, Sunday lunch, open bank holidays, no-smoking area, vegetarian meals, functions, indoor swimming pool. **Directions:** from A338 Bournemouth Ring Road (Wessex Way) and A35 Christchurch Road. At St Pauls roundabout near Central Station turn left to Manor Road and continue to East Overcliff Drive overlooking the sea.
MR L COX, tel (0202) 294449, fax (0202) 292883.

### BELVEDERE HOTEL – CECIL RESTAURANT, Bath Road

Positioned atop Bath Hill, the Belvedere has impressive sea views from most south facing rooms and is just a short stroll from shops, beach and other amenities. The Cecil Restaurant has a long established local reputation for fine food and welcoming service. Recently refurbished, a good meal can be enjoyed in elegant, comfortable surroundings.
ACCOMMODATION £31–£40
FOOD up to £15
**Hours:** breakfast 7:30am – 9:30am; bar meals 12noon – 2:30pm; lunch 12:30pm – 2pm; bar meals 6pm – 9pm; dinner 6:30pm – 9pm. **Cuisine:** English:- Predominantly English cuisine including Carvery. **Rooms:** 62 bedrooms all with tea making facilities, telephone, radio, TV: 12 singles ensuite, 8 family rooms ensuite, 22 twins ensuite, 20 doubles ensuite. **Credit cards:** Visa, Access, Diners, AmEx. **Other points:** licensed, Sunday lunch, 24hr reception, residents' lounge, entertainment, conferences, children catered for – please check for age limits, baby sitting, baby-listening device, cots, central heating, residents' bar. **Directions:** centre of Bournemouth on approach road to pier.
MAUREEN PELLATT, tel (0202) 297556, fax (0202) 294699.

### BURLEY COURT HOTEL, Bath Road

A well-known hotel, which has been in the same family over 40 years, and where the continuing aims are good quality food, courteous service and a high standard of cleanliness. The hotel is large enough to offer every luxury, yet not too large to be personally supervised throughout. A welcoming, comfortable hotel.
ACCOMMODATION £31–£40
FOOD up to £15 ★
**Hours:** breakfast 8am – 9:30am; bar meals 12noon – 2:30pm; dinner 6:30pm – 8:30pm. **Cuisine:** English:- Traditional English dishes. Snack lunches available in Lounge bar, or by the pool. Vegetarian by arrangement. **Rooms:** 38 bedrooms 6 singles ensuite, 11 doubles ensuite, 12 twins ensuite, 9 family rooms ensuite. **Credit cards:** Visa, Access. **Other points:** licensed, open-air dining, Sunday lunch, children catered for – please check for age limits, afternoon tea, pets allowed, residents' lounge, lift, games room, swimming pool, solarium. **Directions:** East Cliff near Bournemouth Railway Station.
MASLYN & JAN HASKER, tel (0202) 552824, fax (0202) 298514.

### CHINE HOTEL, 25 Boscombe Spa Road

Constructed during 1874 on Sir Henry Drummond-Wolff's estate, The Chine overlooks Poole Bay and the beautifully landscaped Boscombe Chine Gardens. Excellent service and old world charm combine to create a warm, friendly atmosphere. The Bay Restaurant enjoys sea views and offers a high standard of freshly prepared meals for guests and non-residents.
ACCOMMODATION £41–£50
**Hours:** breakfast 8am – 9:30am; lunch 12:30pm – 2pm; dinner 7pm – 8:30pm. **Cuisine:** English:- Dishes include Fillet steak topped with mushroom and stilton, Paupiette of Plaice with Asparagus. Lunchtime cold buffet and

carvery. **Rooms:** 97 bedrooms 9 singles ensuite, 39 twins ensuite, 30 doubles ensuite, 19 family rooms ensuite. **Credit cards:** Visa, Access, Diners, AmEx. **Other points:** licensed, Sunday lunch, children catered for – please check for age limits, garden, afternoon tea. **Directions:** overlooking Poole Bay to the south. MR J G J BUTTERWORTH, tel (0202) 396234.

## CHINEHURST HOTEL, Studland Road, Alumchine, Westbourne

*A family run hotel overlooking the beautiful Alum Chine. Tastefully decorated throughout, this is a medium sized establishment with all the facilities of a large hotel. Close to the sea and shops on the West Cliff. Entertainment weekly. Separate special Italian restaurant – "Mr Macaws".*

*ACCOMMODATION £21–£30*

*FOOD up to £15*

**Hours:** breakfast 7:30am – 9:30am; lunch 12noon – 2:30pm; bar meals 12noon – 1:45pm; dinner 6:30pm – 10:30pm. **Cuisine:** English:- Wide selection. Table d'hote menu changes daily – roasts, sole in white wine, steaks. A la carte menu also available. **Rooms:** 29 bedrooms all with tea making facilities, telephone, radio, TV: 2 singles ensuite, 15 doubles ensuite, 6 twins ensuite, 6 family rooms ensuite. **Credit cards:** Visa, Access, Diners, AmEx. **Other points:** licensed, Sunday lunch, no-smoking area, children catered for – please check for age limits, pets/prior arr, afternoon tea, garden, barbecues, residents' lounge, residents' bar. **Directions:** west of the pier overlooking Alum Chine close to the seafront. MR C K GRIFFIN, tel (0202) 764583, fax (0202) 765854.

## THE CLIFFSIDE HOTEL, East Overcliff Drive

*The Cliffside Hotel, overlooking the sea, is suitable for all ages. Well cooked food and friendly, efficient service are complemented by the comfortable furnishings throughout. In an excellent position, close to shops, theatres, the BIC, and with plenty of activities: golf, windsurfing, tennis and pony trekking to name a few. Complimentary membership to Queensbury Leisure Club.*

*ACCOMMODATION £31–£40*

*FOOD up to £15*

**Hours:** breakfast 8am – 9:30am; lunch – Sunday 12:30pm – 2pm; lunch – except Sunday 12:45pm – 2pm; dinner 6:45pm – 8:30pm. **Cuisine:** English:- Dishes include grilled lamb cutlet garni and grilled whole Dover sole maitre d'hotel. Cold buffet. **Rooms:** 62 rooms. 5 single, 25 twin and 24 double with 8 family rooms. all rooms with colour TV, telephone, radio, and tea/coffee facilities. **Credit cards:** Visa, Access. **Other points:** licensed, Sunday lunch, no-smoking area, children catered for – please check for age limits, pets/prior arr, afternoon tea, swimming pool, games room, conferences. **Directions:** A31 to Bournemouth. Close to shops, overlooking the sea. MR A D YOUNG, tel (0202) 555724.

## CORIANDER RESTAURANT, 14 Richmond Hill

*A long established town-centre restaurant catering for many tastes, including vegetarian. Open all day, travellers and visitors are able to obtain almost anything, from a light snack and Mexican beer to full three-course meal.*

*FOOD up to £15*

**Hours:** open all day – Mon-Sat 11am – 10pm. **Cuisine:** Mexican / international:- Wide selection of authentic Mexican dishes, plus 'Gringo' steaks, chicken and fish. Special vegetarian dishes. Daily blackboard specials. Homemade sweets. **Credit cards:** Visa, Access. **Other points:** children catered for – please check for age limits, no-smoking area, coach/prior arr. **Directions:** in the heart of Bournemouth. CHRISTINE MILLS, tel (0202) 552202.

## CUMBERLAND HOTEL, East Overcliff Drive

*A purpose-built hotel providing luxurious accommodation and facilities. Situated on the famous East Cliff there are superb sea views from the Purbeck Hills to the Isle of Wight. The elegant oak-panelled restaurant offers a varied menu, carefully selected wine list and efficient, courteous service. A family run hotel which provides excellent standards.*

*ACCOMMODATION £31–£40*

*FOOD £15–£20*

**Hours:** breakfast – except Sunday 8am – 9:30am; lunch 12:30pm – 1:45pm; bar meals 12:30pm – 2pm; dinner 7pm – 8:30pm; bar meals 7pm – 8:30pm. **Cuisine:** modern English:- 4 course Table d'Hote menu. Dishes may include Poached fillet of sole, Medallions of Pork Tenderloin with a Calvados Cream Sauce. Bar snacks. **Rooms:** 100 bedrooms all with tea making facilities, telephone, radio, TV: 12 singles ensuite, 44 twins ensuite, 32 doubles ensuite, 8 triples ensuite, 4 quads ensuite. **Credit cards:** Visa, Access, AmEx. **Other points:** licensed, Sunday lunch, no-smoking area, children catered for – please check for age limits, residents' lounge, swimming pool, garden, conferences, parking, vegetarian meals, disabled access, residents' bar. **Directions:** M3 – M27 – Wessex Way – East Cliff. ARTHUR YOUNG HOTELS LTD, tel (0202) 290722, fax (0202) 311394.

## DORSET RIVERS, 17 Drummond Road

*A quiet, well maintained, personally run guest house situated near Boscombe Gardens and the sea, offering comfortable accommodation. Ideally located for exploring the New Forest and the Dorset and Hampshire countryside. Within easy reach of Poole Harbour, Corfe Castle and the ancient towns of Wimborne Minster and Blandford Forum, as are Dorchester and Salisbury. Just a short distance to the beach, Bournemouth town centre and Boscombe shopping centre.*

*ACCOMMODATION under £20*

*FOOD up to £15*

**Hours:** breakfast 9am; dinner 6pm. **Cuisine:** English.

**Rooms:** 7 bedrooms all with tea making facilities, TV: 1 single ensuite, 1 double, 2 doubles ensuite, 1 twin ensuite, 1 family room ensuite, 1 family room. **Credit cards:** Visa, Access, Diners, AmEx. **Other points:** parking, children catered for – please check for age limits, open bank holidays, no-smoking area, residents' lounge, vegetarian meals, picnic lunches. **Directions:** A338, left at first roundabout, left at Christchurch Road, second roundabout, then left at the top of the hill. FRANK JOYCE, tel (0202) 396550.

## DURLSTON COURT HOTEL, 47 Gervis Road, East Cliff

*Situated on Bournemouth's East Cliff in a quiet tree-lined road close to the cliff top, town centre and Pavilion. Here, you can enjoy excellent food in comfortable surroundings from a sandwich to a candlelit dinner. The hotel is equipped with saunas, solarium, Jacuzzi and mini gymnasium, and there are several bars to choose from offering a wide range of drinks.*
ACCOMMODATION £21–£30
FOOD up to £15
**Hours:** breakfast 8am – 9.30am; bar snacks 12.30pm – 1.45pm; dinner 7pm –7.30pm. **Cuisine:** English/Continental. **Rooms:** 60 ensuite bedrooms all with tea making facilities, telephone, TV, radio. **Credit cards:** Visa, Access, AmEx, Diners. **Other points:** parking, children catered for – please check for age limits, no smoking area, disabled access, pets allowed, residents' lounge, vegetarian meals, garden. **Directions:** approximately half a mile from Bournemouth Travel Interchange.
MS Z INVERNE, tel (0202) 291488, fax (0202) 290335.

## EMBASSY HOTEL, Meyrick Road, East Cliff

*Set in a prime position on Bournemouth's beautiful East Cliff, close to the sea and within walking distance of the town centre shops, the Embassy offers high standards, comfortable accommodation and a friendly atmosphere. It is set in attractive gardens with its own large heated swimming pool, presenting an ideal location for holiday or business visitors.*
ACCOMMODATION £21–£30
FOOD £15–£20
**Hours:** breakfast 8am – 9am; bar snacks 11:30am – 2pm; dinner 6:30pm – 8pm. **Cuisine:** English / French. **Rooms:** 72 bedrooms 8 singles ensuite, 22 doubles ensuite, 30 twins ensuite, 12 family rooms ensuite. **Other points:** parking, children catered for – please check for age limits, open bank holidays, afternoon tea, pets allowed, residents' lounge, vegetarian meals. **Directions:** leave A338 to East Cliff and head for Lansdown roundabout. Meyrick Road can be found second left off roundabout.
ANTHONY EDEN, tel (0202) 290751, fax (0202) 557459.

## GRANGE HOTEL, Southbourne Overcliffe Drive, Southbourne

*Situated in a premier position by the sea and overlooking beautiful Bournemouth Bay with scenic views from the Isle of Wight in the east to the Isle of Purbeck in the west. Offering quality accommodation and service, many rooms have balconies with excellent sea views. A passenger lift – wheelchair friendly – serves all floors. The sun terrace and barbecue area is open during the summer season.*
ACCOMMODATION £21–£30
FOOD up to £15
**Hours:** breakfast 8am – 9:30am; Sunday lunch 12noon – 2:30pm; bar snacks 6pm – 11pm; dinner 6:30pm – 8:30pm. **Cuisine:** English / continental. **Rooms:** 31 bedrooms 6 singles ensuite, 16 doubles ensuite, 6 twins ensuite, 3 family rooms ensuite. **Credit cards:** Access, Visa, Switch. **Other points:** children catered for – please check for age limits, parking, no-smoking area, afternoon teas, disabled access, pets, residents' lounge, vegetarian meals. **Directions:** seafront between Christchurch and Boscombe (Fishermans Walk).
BLAKEY, GORDON & KAY, tel (0202) 433093/4, fax (0202) 424228.

## HOTEL MON BIJOU, 47 Manor Road, East Cliff

*Once a Victorian Coach House, the building, set in a lovely tree-lined avenue has been skilfully converted to provide a luxurious and elegantly furnished small private hotel. Poole Harbour and sandbanks are a short distance to the west with ferries to Swanage and Studland Bay. The historic towns of Wimborne Minster and Ringwood for the New Forest are within easy reach and Christchurch Priory is just a few minutes drive away. Also ideal for Beaulieu Motor Museum, Compton Acres, Bournemouth beach and shopping centre.*
**Hours:** breakfast 8am – 9am; lunch 12:30pm – 2pm; bar snacks 12:30pm – 2pm; dinner 6:30pm – 7:30pm; bar snacks 6:30pm – 7:30pm. **Cuisine:** English. **Other points:** parking, children catered for – please check for age limits, no-smoking in bedrooms, afternoon teas, disabled access, pets allowed, residents' lounge, vegetarian meals, open-air dining, garden. **Directions:** from Bournemouth Town Centre, take the town bypass along Wessex Way on the A338. The hotel is on the Manor Road, adjacent to East Cliff.
MR & MRS SHEARS, tel (0202) 551389.

## MAE-MAR HOTEL, 91–93 Westhill Road, Westcliff

*An attractive hotel situated in the heart of the Westcliff area. Within walking distance of both beach and town, the Mae-Mar provides a friendly family retreat at the end of the day.*
ACCOMMODATION under £20
**Hours:** open all year; last orders for dinner 4:30pm; breakfast 8am – 9:15am; dinner 6pm – 6:30pm. **Cuisine:** English. **Rooms:** 39 bedrooms all with tea making facilities, TV: 4 singles ensuite, 5 singles, 8 doubles ensuite, 4 doubles, 11 twins ensuite, 1 twin, 6 family rooms ensuite. **Credit cards:** Visa, Access. **Other points:** central heating, children catered for – please

check for age limits, pets/prior arr, residents' lounge, lift. **Directions:** A31 to Bournemouth, situated in Westcliff area.
MRS JANET CLEAVER, tel (0202) 553167, fax (0202) 313911.

## OAK HALL HOTEL, 9 Wilfred Road, Boscombe Manor
*A comfortable, family-run hotel with a homely atmosphere, which has been thoroughly refurbished and modernised whilst retaining many of its old world features. Resident proprietors Margaret and Joe McDonnell and their staff extend a warm, hearty welcome to all. Oak Hall is adjacent to Shelley Park with its bowls and tennis courts, and is just a short walk away from the seafront.*
*ACCOMMODATION £21–£30*
*FOOD up to £15*
**Hours:** closed New Year 6pm; breakfast 9am – 10am; dinner 6pm – 7pm. **Cuisine:** English. **Rooms:** 13 bedrooms 2 singles ensuite, 5 doubles ensuite, 6 family rooms ensuite. **Credit cards:** Visa, Access, AmEx. **Other points:** parking, children catered for – please check for age limits, pets, residents' lounge, vegetarian meals, garden. **Directions:** A35 Christchurch Road into Bournemouth or Bournemouth Ring Road (Wessex Way), observe sign post for Boscombe and Boscombe Pier.
J AND M MCDONNELL, tel (0202) 395062.

## PARKLANDS HOTEL, 4 Rushton Crescent
*A charming family run hotel, situated within the area of Meyrick Park, where excellent facilities exist for golf, tennis, bowls and squash. Bournemouth, with its miles of golden sands, award winning gardens and wonderful shops, is just one mile from the hotel. Most bedrooms are ensuite with tea and coffee making facilities and personal attention by the owners ensure cuisine of the highest standard. The hotel has a cosy residential bar and residents lounge.*
*ACCOMMODATION under £20*
*FOOD up to £15*
**Hours:** breakfast 8:30am – 9am; dinner 6pm. **Cuisine:** English:- Well cooked meals with plenty of variety. **Rooms:** 10 rooms, 7 ensuite. **Credit cards:** Visa, Access, AmEx. **Other points:** parking, open bank holidays, no-smoking area, residents' lounge, special breaks, golf, tennis, bowls, squash. **Directions:** follow Wimborne Road, A347, follow Winton signs. The hotel is on the edge of Meyrick Park.
ALAN & SYLVIA CLARK, tel (0202) 552529, fax (0202) 552529.

## THE QUEENS HOTEL, Meyrick Road, East Cliff
*A comfortable family-run hotel which caters for every taste, offering full a la carte, table d'hote and bar menus. Situated on the East Cliff, a minute's walk from the town centre and a host of local amenities. Other attractions like Lulworth Cove and Brownsea Island are also within easy reach. New leisure club for 1993, inc. indoor pool, sauna, Jacuzzi and steam room.*
*ACCOMMODATION £31–£40*
*FOOD £15–£20* ★
**Hours:** breakfast 7:30am – 9:45am; bar meals 12noon – 3pm; lunch 12:45pm – 1:45pm; bar meals 6pm – 10pm; dinner 7pm – 9pm. **Cuisine:** English / French. **Rooms:** 111 bedrooms all with tea making facilities, telephone, radio, TV: 14 singles ensuite, 43 twins ensuite, 36 doubles ensuite, 12 family rooms ensuite, 6 suites. **Credit cards:** Visa, Access. **Other points:** licensed, Sunday lunch, children catered for – please check for age limits, pets allowed, bank holidays, conferences. **Directions:** A338 Wessex Way into Bournemouth, then signs to East Cliff.
MR A D YOUNG, tel (0202) 554415, fax (0202) 294810.

## TROUVILLE HOTEL, Priory Road, West Cliff
*Centrally situated within walking distance of all the main amenities in Bournemouth, the Trouville provides high standards of food and accommodation. The restaurant overlooks the town and offers first-class table d'hote cuisine, excellently presented and served in pleasant and relaxed surroundings. The leisure facilities include a sauna, trymnasium, Jacuzzi and solarium.*
*ACCOMMODATION £21–£30*
*FOOD up to £15*
**Hours:** breakfast 8am – 9:30am; lunch 12:15pm – 1:45pm; dinner 7pm – 8:30pm. **Cuisine:** English:- Dishes may include Cubes of Salmon, Monkfish and Scampi in a Tarragon Cream and a Flaky Pastry Case, Braised Scotch Steak, Roast Loin of Pork. **Rooms:** 78 bedrooms all with tea making facilities, telephone, TV: 11 singles ensuite, 24 twins ensuite, 20 doubles ensuite, 20 triples ensuite, 3 quads ensuite. **Credit cards:** Visa, Access, AmEx. **Other points:** licensed, Sunday lunch, no-smoking area, children catered for – please check for age limits, afternoon tea, residents' lounge, pets allowed, leisure centre, conferences, 24hr reception, baby-listening device, baby sitting, cots, residents' bar. **Directions:** Adjacent to Bournemouth International Centre. Very central.
DAVID ARTHUR YOUNG, tel (0202) 552262, fax (0202) 293324.

## WENMAUR HOUSE HOTEL, 14 Carysfort Road, Boscombe
*Ideally located for the Beaulieu Car Museum, beautiful Poole Harbour and the New Forest, this is a hotel for those seeking a more leisurely pace of life. All bedrooms are neatly furnished and there is a licensed bar overlooking an enclosed garden. Guests comfort and enjoyment is the main concern and every need is catered for.*
*ACCOMMODATION under £20*
*FOOD up to £15*
**Hours:** breakfast 8am – 9am; dinner 6pm – 8pm; bar meals 6pm – 8pm. **Cuisine:** English. **Rooms:** 11 bedrooms 2 singles, 2 family rooms ensuite, 4 doubles ensuite, 3 doubles. **Credit cards:** Visa, Access. **Other**

points: parking, children catered for – please check for age limits, open bank holidays, no-smoking area, pets allowed, residents' lounge, vegetarian meals, garden, licensed. **Directions:** Carysfort Road is off Hamilton Road between Boscombe centre and Boscombe Gardens. MR D FARMER, tel (0202) 395081.

# BOVEY TRACEY, Devon Map 2

## THE EDGEMOOR HOTEL, *Lowerdown Cross, Haytor Road*

*A 19th century country house, surrounded by extensive well tended lawns and gardens, lovingly decorated and comfortably furnished in keeping with the era. Offering good quality food, excellently cooked and presented, complemented by a distinguished wine list and attentive well trained staff. A delightful establishment not to be missed. Highly recommended.*

*ACCOMMODATION £41–£50*

*FOOD £15–£20* ☕

**Hours:** breakfast 8am – 9:30am; lunch 12noon – 2pm; dinner 7:30pm – 9pm. **Cuisine:** French / English:- Dishes include: curried cream prawns in a filo pastry croustade, roast duck glazed with orange and Cointreau, roast sirloin of beef with red wine and mushrooms. **Rooms:** 12 bedrooms 3 singles ensuite, 2 twins ensuite, 6 doubles ensuite, 1 family room ensuite. **Credit cards:** Visa, Access, Diners, AmEx. **Other points:** licensed, Sunday lunch, children catered for – please check for age limits, garden, afternoon tea, pets allowed. **Directions:** 7 minutes from A38, 1 mile from Bovey Tracey.
ROD & PATRICIA DAY, tel (0626) 832466, fax (0626) 834760.

# BRACKNELL, Berkshire Map 6

## OSCARS, *South Hill Park Arts Centre*

*Situated in a large, elegant mansion now used as an art centre. The food is excellently prepared – an ideal accompaniment to an evening at the theatre or cinema on the same site.*

*FOOD £15–£20*

**Hours:** closed Christmas 7:30pm; bar meals 12noon – 2pm; bar meals 6:15pm – 7:30pm; dinner 6:30pm – 9:30pm; closed Monday; closed Sunday. **Cuisine:** international:- Ethnic, vegetarian, seafood, steaks, game and special Supper Parties and Wines. All main dishes freshly cooked to order. **Credit cards:** Visa. **Other points:** licensed, children catered for – please check for age limits, coach/prior arr, disabled access, parking. **Directions:** from the A3095 or the A322 follow signs to South Hill Park.
MARK BRIDGES, tel (0344) 59031, fax (0344) 411427.

# BRADFORD ON AVON, Wiltshire Map 3

## RIVERSIDE INN HOTEL & RESTAURANT, *49 St Margarets Street*

*Overlooking the Avon River, this charming 17th century inn has a long tradition of hospitality and good service. Well-located to serve as a base from which to explore the many nearby attractions, the Riverside offers comfortable accommodation and excellent home cooking. Their succulent steak and kidney pies are renowned.*

*ACCOMMODATION under £20*

*FOOD up to £15*

**Hours:** breakfast 7:30am – 9am; bar meals 12noon – 2:30pm; dinner 6pm – 10pm; bar meals 6pm – 10pm. **Cuisine:** English:- Traditional home-made English cuisine. A la carte or Table d'hote menus available. Bar meals also available. **Rooms:** 14 bedrooms 4 doubles ensuite, 8 twins ensuite, 2 family rooms ensuite. **Credit cards:** Access, Visa, Switch. **Other points:** open-air dining, Sunday lunch, children catered for – please check for age limits, bank holidays.
NOAH STEFANICKJ, tel (0225) 863526, fax (0225) 868082.

## WIDBROOK GRANGE, *Trowbridge Road*

*An impressive building set in 11 acres, expertly converted to provide luxurious accommodation whilst retaining the atmosphere of a traditional English farmhouse. Inside, the decor and furnishings are elegant and provide the best in comfort. Widbrook Grange enjoys a welcoming, gracious atmosphere and is highly recommended as a delightful place to stay or as an elegant conference venue.*

*ACCOMMODATION £31–£40*

*FOOD £15–£20* ☕ ★

**Hours:** breakfast 7:30am – 9:45am; dinner 6:30pm – 8pm. **Cuisine:** international:- An evening meal is available Monday to Thursday. Fresh, local produce is used in preparing the daily changing menu. Orders for dinner are requested by 6.00pm. **Rooms:** 18 bedrooms all with tea making facilities, telephone, TV: 1 single, 1 suite, 1 family room ensuite, 5 twins ensuite, 10 doubles ensuite. **Credit cards:** Visa, Access, AmEx. **Other points:** children catered for – please check for age limits, residents' lounge, garden, conferences, indoor swimming pool. **Directions:** 1 mile from town centre, 200m past canal towards Trowbridge.
JOHN & PAULINE PRICE, tel (0225) 864750, (0225) 863173, fax (0225) 862890.

# BRAUNTON, Devon Map 2

## PRESTON HOUSE HOTEL

*A grand Victorian Country House overlooking the 10 mile sweep of Barnstaple's sandy bay. Built in 1895, the stained glass windows, moulded ceilings, period furnishings, paintings and ornaments all recreate the glory of the period. Golf, riding, fishing and water sports are all available nearby and the hotel has its own heated outdoor swimming pool.*

*ACCOMMODATION £21–£30*

*FOOD up to £15*

**Hours:** breakfast 8:30am – 9:30am; lunch 12noon – 2pm; dinner 7pm – 8:30pm. **Cuisine:** English:- Table d'hote menu – changes daily. All dishes prepared and cooked on the premises. **Rooms:** 14 bedrooms all with tea making facilities, telephone, radio, TV: 2 singles ensuite, 7 twins

ensuite, 5 doubles ensuite. **Credit cards:** Visa, Access. **Other points:** licensed, Sunday lunch, solarium, sauna, spa-bath, residents' lounge, garden, conservatory, residents' bar, swimming pool. **Directions:** take the A361 to Braunton. Follow signposts to Saunton.
ANN COOK, tel (0271) 890472, fax (0271) 890555.

## BRENT KNOLL, Somerset Map 3

### BATTLEBOROUGH GRANGE COUNTRY HOTEL, Bristol Road

*This hotel and restaurant nestles in its own grounds at the foot of the historic Iron Age fort known as Brent Knoll. Both the restaurant and bar offer imaginative, well presented home made food. The proprietors and their staff ensure that each guest enjoys their visit.*
ACCOMMODATION £21–£30
FOOD £15–£20
**Hours:** breakfast 7:30am – 9:30am; lunch 12noon – 2pm; bar meals 12noon – 2pm; dinner 7pm – 9pm. **Cuisine:** modern English:- Peking prawns, Scampi Pernod, Grange fillet steak. **Rooms:** 18 bedrooms, 14 en suite. **Credit cards:** Visa, Access, Diners, AmEx. **Other points:** licensed, open-air dining, Sunday lunch, afternoon tea. **Directions:** 1 mile from M5 junction 22 on A38.
TONY & CAROL WILKINS, tel (0278) 760208.

## BRIDGWATER, Somerset Map 3

### WALNUT TREE INN, North Petherton

*Set in the heart of Somerset, this fully modernised 18th Century Coaching Inn makes an ideal touring centre for many attractions. Two popular restaurants, friendly bar, spacious decorated luxury bedrooms, including a 4-Poster and Suites. Quietly located, The Walnut Tree offers everything for a touring holiday base or restful short break. Ample parking.*
ACCOMMODATION £21–£30
FOOD up to £15 ★
**Hours:** lunch 12noon – 2pm; dinner 7pm – 10pm. **Cuisine:** English:- Local produce, fresh meat, duck, local dishes. **Rooms:** 28 bedrooms all with tea making facilities, telephone, radio, TV: 2 singles ensuite, 6 twins ensuite, 20 doubles ensuite. **Credit cards:** Visa, Access, Diners, AmEx. **Other points:** Sunday lunch, children catered for – please check for age limits, baby-listening device, baby sitting, cots, disabled access, 24hr reception, foreign exchange, residents' bar, residents' lounge, central heating, vegetarian meals, parking. **Directions:** exit 24 of M5 to Taunton (¼ mile). Signs to North Petherton. On A38.
RICHARD & HILARY GOULDEN, tel (0278) 662255, fax (0278) 663946.

## BRIDPORT, Dorset Map 3

### GEORGE INN, Chideock

*A 16th century thatched inn offering an extensive menu with daily extras and prices to suit all pockets. Restaurant, beer garden, family room with pool, darts*
*and skittles. A true local welcome is assured in this Dorset Evening Echo 1985 Pub of the Year.*
FOOD up to £15
**Hours:** open all year 7pm; last orders 7pm – 9:30pm; lunch 12noon – 2pm; dinner 6:45pm – 10:30pm. **Cuisine:** English:- Specialities – omelettes with various fillings. Steaks including massive mixed grill. Salads, fish, gammon. Daily specials, eg. venison, lamb, trout. **Other points:** licensed, open-air dining, Sunday lunch, children catered for – please check for age limits. **Directions:** On the A35, 2 miles west of Bridport in the east of Chideock.
MIKE & MARILYN TUCK, tel (0297) 89419.

### HADDON HOUSE HOTEL, West Bay

*Regency style 3 star country house hotel with a reputation for fine cuisine. Situated approximately 300 yd from the picturesque harbour and coast of west Bay, overlooking Dorset's beautiful countryside. Amenities available to visitors, include deep sea fishing, riding, tennis and 18 hole golf course opposite hotel. Ideally situated for touring Dorset, Devon and Somerset.*
ACCOMMODATION £21–£30
FOOD up to £15
**Hours:** breakfast 7:45am – 9:15am; lunch 12noon – 1:30pm; dinner 7pm – 9pm. **Cuisine:** English:- Fresh local fish, grills, own label wines. **Rooms:** 13 bedrooms all with tea making facilities, telephone, radio, TV: 4 twins ensuite, 1 family room ensuite, 6 doubles ensuite, 2 singles ensuite. **Credit cards:** Visa, Access, Diners, AmEx. **Other points:** Sunday lunch, children catered for – please check for age limits, coach/prior arr, residents' bar. **Directions:** ½ mile south of main A35 at Bridport. Follow signpost to West Bay.
MR & MRS P W LOUD, tel (0308) 423626, (0308) 425323.

## BRISTOL, Avon Map 3

### 51 PARK STREET, 51 Park Street

*Prominently positioned in Bristol's shopping area, 51 Park Street is well decorated and offers a wide variety of dishes at value for money prices. Frequented by holiday-makers and locals alike, and of appeal to all age groups.*
FOOD £15–£20 CLUB
**Hours:** open bank holidays 7pm; meals all day 12noon – 11pm; meals all day – Sunday 12noon – 10pm; closed Christmas 25/12 – 26/12; closed Monday; closed New Years day. **Cuisine:** international:- Mainly English with French and Asiatic influences. Specialities include modern American dishes and European brasserie food. **Credit cards:** Visa, Access, Diners, AmEx. **Other points:** licensed, open-air dining, Sunday lunch, no-smoking area, children catered for – please check for age limits, afternoon tea. **Directions:** from City centre follow route to Bristol University.
MRS H.L. TIMMONS, tel (0272) 268016.

### ARCHES HOTEL, 132 Cotham Brow, Cotham

*A small and attractive Victorian house hotel, set in quiet, comfortable surroundings. English Tourist Board 'One*

Crown' approved. Convenient for Bristol city centre and within easy reach of Broadmead shopping centre, theatres and exhibition centres. Clifton suspension bridge and waterfront are nearby. Main bus station half a mile.
**ACCOMMODATION £21–£30** ★
**Hours:** breakfast – weekdays 7:15am – 8:30am; breakfast – Saturday 8am – 9am; breakfast – Sunday 8:30am – 9:30am; closed Christmas – New Year.
**Cuisine:** continental. **Rooms:** 10 bedrooms all with tea making facilities, TV: 3 singles, 3 doubles, 1 double ensuite, 2 twins, 1 twin ensuite. **Credit cards:** Visa, Access. **Other points:** no-smoking area, children catered for – please check for age limits, pets allowed, bank holidays, vegetarian meals, parking. **Directions:** half-mile from Bus Station, north on A38, turn left at first mini roundabout.
MR & MRS D LAMBERT, tel (0272) 247398.

## CHINA PALACE RESTAURANT, 18a Baldwin Street

The China Palace, the largest Cantonese restaurant in the west of England, is air-conditioned, has 2 attractive bars and facilities for dancing. Extensive menu, with all food beautifully cooked and presented.
**FOOD £15–£20**
**Hours:** lunch – Mon-Sat 12noon – 2:30pm; meals all day – Sunday 12noon – 11:30pm; dinner 6pm – 11:30pm. **Cuisine:** Chinese:- Chinese cuisine, with Cantonese, Szechuan and Pekinese specialities. **Credit cards:** Visa, Access, AmEx. **Other points:** Sunday lunch, no-smoking area. **Directions:** in the centre of Bristol, near theatre and cathedral on Baldwin St.
KAM WONG, tel (0272) 262719, fax (0272) 256168.

## THE GANGES, 368 Gloucester Road, Horfield

A friendly restaurant, tastefully decorated in Indian style, with intimate alcoves for romantic dining. The service is courteous and efficient and the menu includes some lesser known Indian dishes.
**FOOD £15–£20**
**Hours:** lunch 12noon – 2:30pm; dinner 6pm – 11:30pm; closed Christmas 25/12 – 26/12. **Cuisine:** Indian:- north Indian. **Credit cards:** Visa, Access, Diners, AmEx.
**Other points:** licensed, Sunday lunch, children catered for – please check for age limits. **Directions:** on the A38, Gloucester Road.
MR CHOWDHURY, tel (0272) 428505, (0272) 245234.

## GRASMERE COURT HOTEL, 22–24 Bath Road, Keynsham

Situated approximately halfway between Bath and Bristol city centre, this hotel has recently been renovated and modernised to provide a compact 'Country Style' hotel with a friendly atmosphere. The residents lounge offers a haven of peace in which to relax in comfort after a strenuous day exploring the nearby Mendip Hills, shopping or sightseeing.
**ACCOMMODATION £21–£30**
**FOOD up to £15**

**Hours:** breakfast 7:30am – 9:30am; bar snacks 12noon – 2pm; dinner 6pm – 7:30pm; bar snacks 6pm – 9:30pm.
**Cuisine:** English / cosmopolitan:- Attractively presented, home style meals. **Rooms:** 16 bedrooms 10 doubles ensuite, 4 twins ensuite, 2 singles ensuite.
**Credit cards:** Visa, Access, AmEx. **Other points:** parking, children catered for – please check for age limits, open bank holidays, no-smoking rooms, afternoon tea, residents' lounge, vegetarian meals, garden. **Directions:** on main road between Bristol and Bath.
JOHN BARRINGTON LLEWELLIN & M LLEWELLIN, tel (0272) 862662, fax (0272) 862762.

## HENRY AFRICA'S HOTHOUSE, 65 Whiteladies Road, Clifton

This lively restaurant with its extensive cocktail list, busy happy hour and Cajun & Tex-Mex specialities is extremely popular, whether for snacks and drinks at the bar or for a full meal in the attractive upstairs restaurant.
**FOOD up to £15**
**Hours:** Sunday breakfast 10am – 5:30pm; meals all day 12noon – 11pm. **Cuisine:** Tex-Mex:- Grills, Barbecue, Cajun and Tex-Mex specialities. Magnificent selection of Cocktails, Wines and Beers, including non-alcoholic.
**Credit cards:** Visa, Access. **Other points:** licensed, Sunday lunch, no-smoking area, children catered for – please check for age limits, afternoon tea, bank holidays.
**Directions:** just north of the BBC on Whiteladies Road, Clifton, Bristol.
ANDREW MURDEN, tel (0272) 238300, fax (0272) 467893.

## JUBILEE INN, Flax Bourton

An olde worlde stone-built inn, partly covered by creepers and hanging baskets. Fresh produce is used to provide well-cooked meals and all dishes offer good value for money. Traditional English dishes are cooked with an imaginative touch. For warmer days there is an attractive garden for customers use.
**FOOD up to £15**
**Hours:** breakfast 8:15am – 9:15am; lunch 12noon – 2pm; dinner 7:30pm – 10pm. **Cuisine:** English:- Traditional English home-made dishes. Specialities include the Special Seafood Pie (fresh salmon, white fish and prawns, topped with potato). **Rooms:** 4 bedrooms.
**Other points:** licensed, Sunday lunch, garden, pets allowed. **Directions:** between Bristol and Weston Super Mare.
BRIAN HAYDOCK, tel (0275) 462741.

## LA CANTINA MEXICAN RESTAURANT, 1 Chandos Road, Redland

An authentic Mexican restaurant, appropriately furnished, offering a good selection of authentic Mexican dishes. Places to visit nearby include Clifton Suspension Bridge, and Bristol Zoo. Convenient for shopping in Bristol city centre.
**FOOD up to £15**

**Hours:** lunch 12noon – 2pm; dinner 7pm – 12midnight; closed Christmas 25/12 – 26/12. **Cuisine:** Tex-Mex:- Wide and varied range of authentic Mexican dishes, including Tex-Mex – the Americanised version of Mexican food. Vegetarian dishes available & specials board. Large selection of Mexican beers and tequilas. **Credit cards:** Visa, Access, AmEx. **Other points:** licensed, Sunday lunch, children catered for – please check for age limits, disabled access. **Directions:** from Bristol city centre, up St Michael's Hill – ½ mile turn right.
PAUL GERRARD, tel (0272) 744801.

### NATRAJ TANDOORI (NEPALESE & INDIAN CUISINE), 185 Gloucester Road, Bishopston

*Natraj offers an excellent mix of traditional Tandoori with more unusual Nepalese dishes. Try Momocha (spiced minced lamb in pastry served with Nepalese pickle) as one of the many Nepalese specialities on offer, or one of the set menus. Friendly, helpful staff will help you choose from the extensive menu. Generous helping of food in comfortable, oriental surroundings.*
FOOD up to £15
**Hours:** lunch – Fri-Sat 12noon – 2pm; dinner – Mon-Thur 6pm – 12midnight; dinner – Fri-Sat 6pm – 12:30am; dinner – Sunday 6pm – 12midnight. **Cuisine:** Nepalese / Indian:- Nepalese and Indian dishes. Specialities include Gurkha chicken, Momocha, Murgi Mussalam, Thuckpa. continental dishes and a la carte or special buffet. **Credit cards:** Visa, Access, Diners, AmEx. **Other points:** licensed, no-smoking area, children catered for – please check for age limits, functions. **Directions:** A38, north of city centre. Opposite Bristol North Swimming Baths.
MR D KARKI, tel (0272) 248145.

### THE OAKDENE HOTEL, 45 Oakfield Road, Clifton

*A large Georgian House hotel set in a quiet tree lined avenue, close to the university, zoo, hospitals, restaurants, shops, cinemas, theatres and Clifton Suspension Bridge.*
ACCOMMODATION £31–£40
**Hours:** breakfast 7am – 9am. **Cuisine:** breakfast.
**Rooms:** 4 single, 6 double, 4 twin bedrooms, 7 en suite. colour TV, tea/coffee facilities, shaver points in all rooms. **Other points:** children catered for – please check for age limits, garden. **Directions:** off the A4018. BRIAN & PAUL INE JOHNSON JONES, tel (0272) 735900.

### RAINBOW CAFE, 9–10 Waterloo Street, Clifton

*The combination of home-made meat and vegetarian dishes on offer has made this small restaurant very popular. Quality secondhand books on sale and monthly exhibitions of work by local artists.*
FOOD up to £15
**Hours:** snacks 10am – 5:30pm; lunch 12noon – 2:30pm; closed Christmas 25/12 – 01/01; closed bank holidays;

closed Sunday. **Cuisine:** English / vegetarian:- Fish and meat dishes. The lunch menu varies daily and all food is fresh each day. **Other points:** licensed, no-smoking area, children catered for – please check for age limits. **Directions:** from Bristol City centre follow Clifton signs. Off Princess Street.
ALISON MOORE & TIM ANSELL, tel (0272) 738937.

### RING OF BELLS, Henfield Road, Coalpit Heath

*A 400 year old Grade II listed building steeped in history, which was used as a Coroner's Court for judging pit deaths and accidents from the 18th century. Boasting a wealth of oak beams and a characteristic inglenook fireplace, the inn has been tastefully refurbished to retain its olde worlde image. Frequented by local folk, the atmosphere inside is warm and welcoming and staff most helpful. Ideal for Bristol Zoo, Cheddar Caves and much more.*
FOOD up to £15
**Hours:** lunch 12noon – 2pm; dinner 7pm – 10pm.
**Cuisine:** English / continental. **Other points:** open bank holidays, children catered for – please check for age limits, parking, disabled access, vegetarian meals, parking, open-air dining. **Directions:** from Bristol A432 to Chipping Sodbury, right at traffic lights at Coalpit. H T SMITH, tel (0454) 772818.

## BRIXHAM, Devon Map 2

### POOPDECK RESTAURANT, 15 The Quay

*Situated overlooking the harbour opposite the replica of the Golden Hind. The building started life in 1830 as a fish shop.*
FOOD £15–£20
**Hours:** dinner 6:30pm – 10pm; closed February; closed January. **Cuisine:** Italian / English:- Locally caught fish and seafood and Anglo/Italian meat and fish dishes. **Credit cards:** Visa, Access, Diners, AmEx. **Other points:** Sunday lunch, children catered for – please check for age limits. **Directions:** on the quayside, overlooking the harbour.
EDWARD C ALLEN, tel (0802) 857415.

### RADDICOMBE LODGE, 120 Kingswear Road

*The latticed windows and pitched ceilings give this country house a cottage atmosphere. Most rooms have a fine sea or country view. A good base for touring the Devon coast and Dartmoor.*
ACCOMMODATION under £20
**Hours:** breakfast 8am – 9am. **Cuisine:** breakfast.
**Rooms:** 8 bedrooms all with tea making facilities, TV: 2 doubles ensuite, 3 doubles, 1 twin, 1 family room ensuite, 1 family room. **Credit cards:** Visa, Access, Diners. **Other points:** central heating, children catered for – please check for age limits, residents' lounge, garden, vegetarian meals. **Directions:** on the B3205 between Brixham and Dartmouth.
MR & MRS GLASS, tel (0803) 882125.

# BROCKENHURST, Hampshire Map 4

## THE WATERSPLASH HOTEL, The Rise

*A family-run Victorian country house hotel set in 2 acres of secluded gardens. The hotel is noted for good food, friendly service and comfortable accommodation. The menu offers imaginative and well cooked food. Situated in the centre of the New Forest.*

ACCOMMODATION £41–£50

FOOD £15–£20

**Hours:** bar meals 12noon – 2pm; lunch 1pm – 2pm; dinner 7:30pm – 8:30pm. **Cuisine:** English:- Specialities include pot roast haunch of New Forest venison. **Rooms:** 23 bedrooms, all en suite. Colour TV, tea/coffee making facilities and direct-dial telephones in all rooms. **Credit cards:** Visa, Access. **Other points:** licensed, open-air dining, Sunday lunch, no-smoking area, children catered for – please check for age limits, garden, pets allowed, afternoon tea. **Directions:** off A337 south of Lyndhurst. Turning to The Rise opposite Shell Garage.

ROBIN & JUDY FOSTER, tel (0590) 22344.

# BRUTON, Somerset Map 3

## THE OLD RED LION, North Brewham

*The Old Red Lion is an old bar and light cottage type restaurant with lovely views across the valley. This is a rural public house, popular with locals and travellers alike.*

FOOD up to £15

**Hours:** lunch 12noon – 2pm; dinner 7pm – 10pm. **Cuisine:** English:- Sandwiches, snacks, salads, traditional bar meals, a full a la carte menu is also available. **Credit cards:** Visa, Access. **Other points:** licensed, open-air dining, Sunday lunch, free house. **Directions:** off B3092. On Maiden Bradley/Bruton Road. Signs for North Brewham.

MR & MRS T O'TOOLE, tel (0749) 850287.

# BUDE, Cornwall Map 1

## THE FALCON HOTEL, Breakwater Road

*Character hotel in unique position overlooking the historic Bude Canal and yet only a short stroll from the sandy beaches and shops. Renowned for the quality of the food, whether for the high class menu in the Candlelit Restaurant, or from the extensive bar snack menu in the Coachmans Bar.*

ACCOMMODATION £31–£40

FOOD £15–£20

**Hours:** breakfast 8am – 9:30am; lunch 12noon – 2pm; dinner 7pm – 9pm; closed Christmas 25/12. **Cuisine:** English / French:- A la carte and Table d'hote menus of an English and French style are served in the Restaurant. An international menu of great variety is available in the Bar. **Rooms:** 18 bedrooms all with tea making facilities, TV: 5 singles ensuite, 9 doubles ensuite, 1 twin ensuite, 3 triples ensuite. **Credit cards:** Visa, Access, AmEx, Diners, Switch. **Other points:** licensed, children catered

for – please check for age limits, pets allowed, garden, car park. **Directions:** on western side of Bude, easily seen from the main road.

TIM & DOROTHY BROWNING, tel (0288) 352005, fax (0288) 356359.

## MAER LODGE HOTEL, Crooklets Beach

*Maer Lodge Hotel serves excellent and extremely varied home cooked food. The quality of the ingredients and the care in preparation and presentation are paramount. A friendly, family hotel with first class personal service.*

ACCOMMODATION £21–£30

FOOD up to £15  CLUB  ★

**Hours:** breakfast 8:30am – 9:15am; lunch 12noon – 1:45pm; dinner 7pm – 8pm. **Cuisine:** English / continental. **Rooms:** 19 rooms all with tea making facilities, telephone, radio, TV: 2 singles ensuite, 2 singles, 3 twins ensuite, 1 twin, 7 doubles ensuite, 1 double, 2 triples ensuite, 1 quad ensuite. **Credit cards:** Visa, Access, Diners, AmEx. **Other points:** pets allowed, children catered for – please check for age limits, baby sitting, baby-listening device, cots, 24hr reception, foreign exchange, left luggage, residents' lounge, residents' bar. **Directions:** overlooking Golf Course and close to the beach.

MR & MRS STANLEY, tel (0288) 353306, fax (0288) 353306.

## MORNISH HOTEL, 20 Summerleaze Crescent

*The Mornish Hotel offers magnificent views from a prime location in Bude overlooking the beach. Centrally situated, with shops, golf course and beach nearby.*

ACCOMMODATION under £20

FOOD up to £15

**Hours:** order by 5:30pm; breakfast 8:30am – 9am; dinner 6:30pm – 7pm; closed November – February. **Cuisine:** English:- B&B includes a full English breakfast. Dinner – Home-cooking to a very high standard. £8.50 for 5 courses – if you can manage them. **Rooms:** 10 bedrooms all with tea making facilities, TV: 5 doubles ensuite, 2 twins ensuite, 3 family rooms ensuite. **Credit cards:** Visa, Access, Diners, AmEx. **Other points:** central heating, children catered for – please check for age limits, residents' lounge, vegetarian meals, residents' bar. **Directions:** from town centre, turn left at Post Office corner, towards sea.

JOHN & JULIA HILDER, tel (0288) 352972.

## STAMFORD HILL HOTEL, Stratton

*A Georgian Manor set in five acres of wooded grounds on the famous Stamford Hill battle site. Retaining many of its original features including a magnificent stained glass window, the hotel is ideally situated for touring both Cornwall and Devon. A games room provides table tennis, poll and darts, or for the ultimate relaxation, an outdoor heated swimming pool and sauna. Specialised golfing holidays and breaks enable the golfer to choose from a wide and varied range of courses. There is also a putting green and childrens play area.*

ACCOMMODATION £21–£30
FOOD up to £15
**Hours:** early b/fast available November; breakfast
8:30am – 9:30am. **Rooms:** 15 bedrooms 6 doubles
ensuite, 6 twins ensuite, 2 family rooms ensuite, 1 suite.
**Credit cards:** Visa, Access. **Other points:** children
catered for – please check for age limits, residents'
lounge, garden, pets allowed, special breaks.
IAN & JOY MCFEAT, tel (0288) 352709, fax (0288)
352709.

## BURCOMBE, Wiltshire Map 3

### SHIP INN, Nr Wilton
A delightful country inn which is well signposted from
the A30. In the cold winter months, real log fires help to
ease the chill, while in summer, the large garden running
down to the river is popular.
FOOD up to £15
**Hours:** lunch 12noon – 2pm; dinner 6:30pm – 11pm.
**Cuisine:** English:- Grills, bar snacks. **Credit cards:**
Visa, Access. **Other points:** open-air dining, Sunday
lunch, children catered for – please check for age limits,
coach/prior arr. **Directions:** off the A30.
MR T BAXTER, tel (0722) 743182.

## BURNHAM ON SEA, Somerset Map 3

### ROYAL CLARENCE HOTEL, 31 Esplanade
Old coaching inn situated on the Esplanade. Convenient
for town centre and the adjacent countryside. Self-
contained banquet/ballroom for private functions of up
to 200 people.
ACCOMMODATION £21–£30
FOOD up to £15
**Hours:** breakfast 8am – 9:30am; bar meals 11:30am –
2:30pm; lunch 12noon – 2:15pm; bar meals 6pm –
9:30pm; dinner 7pm – 8:30pm. **Cuisine:** English:-
Traditional British cooking. **Rooms:** 19 bedrooms all
with tea making facilities, telephone, radio, TV: 1 single,
4 twins ensuite, 4 family rooms ensuite, 9 doubles
ensuite, 1 single ensuite. **Credit cards:** Visa, Access,
Diners, AmEx. **Other points:** Sunday lunch, children
catered for – please check for age limits, coach/prior arr.
**Directions:** 3 miles off M5 on B3140. Situated on the
Esplanade.
D Q & P Q DAVEY, tel (0278) 783138, (0278) 783139,
fax (0278) 792965.

## CALNE, Wiltshire Map 3

### LANSDOWNE STRAND HOTEL,
The Strand
Situated in the picturesque market town of Calne on the
edge of the Marlbourgh Downs, this original 16th
century Coaching Inn with its courtyard and medieval
brew-house is of particular historic interest. Today, after
thoughtful refurbishment, it offers many modern
amenities, with well appointed bedrooms, three friendly
bars and an excellent restaurant serving imaginative

fare. The area is steeped in history and this is an ideal
touring base.
ACCOMMODATION £21–£30
FOOD up to £15
**Hours:** breakfast 7am – 9:30am; lunch 12noon –
2:30pm; dinner 7pm – 9:30pm. **Cuisine:** English. **Credit
cards:** Visa, Access, Diners, AmEx. **Other points:** bar,
children catered for – please check for age limits,
parking, disabled access, pets allowed, vegetarian meals.
**Directions:** right in the centre of Calne.
MR N RUSSELL, tel (0249) 812488, fax (0249) 815323.

## CARLYON BAY, Cornwall Map 1

### PORTH AVALLEN HOTEL, Sea Road
Situated in several acres of gardens with panoramic
views over Carlyon Bay and its rugged coastline, this
well-appointed hotel offers perfect peace and quiet. The
oak panelled residents' lounge opens onto the terrace,
and is a cosy retreat during the winter months. The 40
seater restaurant maintains a very high standard, as
does the accommodation. Ideal base for touring.
ACCOMMODATION £41–£50
FOOD £15–£20
**Hours:** breakfast 7:30am – 9:30am; lunch 12noon –
2pm; dinner 7pm – 9pm; closed Christmas 25/12 –
02/01. **Cuisine:** British:- British cuisine, with a touch of
French. Dishes may include: Magret Duck, Roast Rack
of Lamb, Scottish Fillet Steak, and Dover Sole.
Vegetarian dishes. **Rooms:** 24 bedrooms all with tea
making facilities, radio, TV: 1 twin, 3 singles ensuite, 4
twins ensuite, 10 doubles ensuite, 5 family rooms
ensuite, 1 self-catering room. **Credit cards:** Visa,
Access, AmEx. **Other points:** licensed, Sunday lunch,
children catered for – please check for age limits,
afternoon tea, residents' lounge, garden, parking,
functions, conferences. **Directions:** from Plymouth –
take A390 – 45 minutes. On outskirts of St Austell.
N & M PERRETT & G & K SIM, tel (0726) 812802,
(0726) 812183, fax (0726) 817097.

## CHAGFORD, Devon Map 2

### THE THREE CROWNS HOTEL
Situated in the pretty village of Chagford, within the
Dartmoor National Park, this 13th century inn retains its
olde worlde charm with its open fires and four poster beds.
ACCOMMODATION £21–£30
FOOD up to £15
**Hours:** breakfast 8.30am – 9:30am; lunch 12noon –
2pm; dinner 7pm – 9:30pm. **Cuisine:** English:- Bar
menu, eg. home-made steak and kidney pie,
ploughman's, seafood, special vegetarian meals and
table d'hote menus available. **Rooms:** 17 bedrooms, 13
en suite. **Credit cards:** Visa, Access, AmEx. **Other
points:** Sunday lunch, children catered for – please
check for age limits. **Directions:** 3 miles off
A382(B3206). Situated within the village.
MR & MRS J GILES, tel (0647) 433444, fax (0647)
433117.

## CHALE, Isle Of Wight Map 4

### CLARENDON HOTEL AND WIGHT MOUSE INN

*A charming 17th century Inn overlooking Chale Bay in the south of the Island, a few minutes from Blackgang Chine. The hotel enjoys a fine reputation for good food, wine, comfort and hospitality. With over 365 whiskies, real ales and open fires, a warm, friendly atmosphere is assured! Children are most welcome.*

ACCOMMODATION £21–£30

FOOD £15–£20 ♀ ★

**Hours:** open all year 7pm; bar – except Sunday 11am – 12midnight; bar – Sunday 12noon – 3pm; restaurant 12noon – 10pm; bar – Sunday 7pm – 10:30pm. **Cuisine:** international:- Wight Mouse Inn: Island Steaks, local fish, crab, home made pizzas, curries, lasagne, chilli, etc, all home-made. Clarendon Hotel: fresh vegetables, fresh local fish, meat and game. **Rooms:** 13 bedrooms all with tea making facilities, radio, TV: 1 double ensuite, 3 doubles, 7 quads ensuite, 2 suites. **Credit cards:** Visa, Access. **Other points:** open-air dining, Sunday lunch, no-smoking area, children catered for – please check for age limits, entertainment, baby sitting, baby-listening device, cots, vegetarian meals, parking, residents' bar, residents' lounge. **Directions:** on B3399, 50yds from the Military road, B3055, in Chale.

MR & MRS J BRADSHAW, tel (0983) 730431, fax (0983) 730431.

## CHARMOUTH, Dorset Map 3

### HENSLEIGH HOTEL, Lower Sea Lane

*A comfortable, well-equipped family run hotel in a quiet position. A friendly, homely atmosphere is complemented by good home cooking using local produce. The rolling hills of Dorset and stunning cliff walks are on the doorstep.*

ACCOMMODATION £21–£30

FOOD up to £15

**Hours:** breakfast 8am – 9am; lunch 12noon – 2pm; dinner 6:45pm – 7:30pm; closed November – February. **Cuisine:** English. **Rooms:** 10 bedrooms all with tea making facilities, radio, mini bar, TV: 2 singles ensuite, 3 doubles ensuite, 3 twins ensuite, 2 family rooms ensuite. **Other points:** central heating, children catered for – please check for age limits, pets allowed, residents' lounge, garden. **Directions:** Midway between the village and beach off the A35.

MALCOLM & MARY MACNAIR, tel (0297) 60830.

### NEWLANDS HOUSE, Stonebarrow Lane

*A former 16th century farmhouse, family run and situated in approximately 2 acres of garden and old orchard at the foot of Stonebarrow Hill, which is part of the National Trust Golden Cap Estate. Newlands House makes an ideal centre for walking and touring and is just minutes away from the famous fossil cliffs and beaches of Lyme Bay. 6 miles east of Axminster.*

ACCOMMODATION £21–£30

FOOD up to £15

**Hours:** breakfast 8:30am – 9:15am; dinner 7pm – 7:30pm; open March – October. **Cuisine:** English / continental:- Cordon bleu cuisine. Home-produced dishes. **Rooms:** 12 bedrooms all with tea making facilities, TV: 1 single, 2 singles ensuite, 3 twins ensuite, 4 doubles ensuite, 2 family rooms ensuite. **Other points:** licensed, no-smoking area, children catered for – please check for age limits, pets/prior arr, residents' lounge, garden. **Directions:** A35, 7 miles west of Bridport at foot of Stonebarrow Lane.

ANNE & VERNON VEAR, tel (0297) 60212.

## CHELWOOD, Avon Map 3

### CHELWOOD HOUSE HOTEL, Nr Bristol

*A listed historic house of charm and character, built in 1681 with panelled lounges and glorious rural views in every direction. There is a delightful new 'Restaurant in a Garden' – a conservatory-type dining room with the ambiance of a garden – tastefully decorated public rooms, and individually furnished bedrooms. A family concern with a welcoming atmosphere.*

ACCOMMODATION £31–£40

FOOD up to £15 🍽

**Hours:** last orders 9pm; breakfast 7:30am – 9:30am; dinner 7:30pm – 11:30pm; closed Christmas 2 weeks; closed Sunday evening to non residents. **Cuisine:** English / German:- Traditional English and German cuisine. **Rooms:** 11 bedrooms all with tea making facilities, telephone, TV: 2 singles ensuite, 2 twins ensuite, 7 doubles ensuite. **Credit cards:** Visa, Access, Diners, AmEx. **Other points:** licensed, children catered for – please check for age limits. **Directions:** just south of Chelwood Bridge on the A37 between Pensford & Clutton.

JILL & RUDI BIRK, tel (0761) 490730, fax (0761) 490730.

## CHIPPENHAM, Wiltshire Map 3

### CROWN INN, Giddeahall, Bristol Road

*Formerly four cottages and a farm building with a small pub at the front, dating back to the 15th century. The interior has maintained its original style and has open log fires and beams, with brasses and farming implements. Offering farm house cooking and dishes from the Far East, it is very popular with locals and tourists alike.*

**Hours:** breakfast 7am – 9:30am; lunch 12noon – 2:30pm; bar snacks 12noon – 2:30pm; dinner 7pm – 9:30pm; bar snacks 7pm – 9:30pm. **Cuisine:** English. **Credit cards:** Visa, Access. **Other points:** parking, children catered for – please check for age limits, no-smoking area, residents' lounge, vegetarian meals, outdoor dining. **Directions:** from Chippenham proceed along the A420 for approx. 3 miles. The hotel is situated on the left before the Ford.

MR E OLDLAND, tel (0249) 782229.

### THE OLD HOUSE AT HOME, Burton

*Originally a 17th century coaching inn built in soft Cotswold stone with oak beams and leaded windows*

*throughout. Offering good home cooked English and continental cuisine for which it has a renowned reputation, this is a truly upmarket public house with a loyal clientele.*
*FOOD up to £15*
**Hours:** closed Tuesday lunchtime; lunch 12noon – 2pm; dinner 7pm – 8pm; Sunday dinner 7pm – 9:30pm; closed Christmas day – Boxing day. **Cuisine:** English / continental:- Good choice of meals cooked fresh daily, vegetarian options are available. **Credit cards:** Visa, Access. **Other points:** parking, open bank holidays, no-smoking area, disabled access, vegetarian meals, garden, open-air dining. **Directions:** off A46 from Bath, from Bristol Junction 18 M4 to Acton Turville. Situated on the B4039.
DAVE AND SALLY WARBURTON, tel (0454) 218227.

### THE THREE CROWNS, Brinkworth
*A stone built, 18th century pub situated on the village green. There is an extensive menu with an emphasis on fresh produce. All dishes are cooked to order and served with a minimum of 6 fresh vegetables. The Three Crowns is justifiably proud of its award-winning cuisine. Good service and a relaxed, friendly atmosphere will add to the enjoyment of your meal.*
*FOOD up to £15* 🍽
**Hours:** lunch – except Sunday 10am – 2:30pm; lunch – Sunday 12noon – 3pm; dinner – except Sunday 6pm – 11pm; dinner – Sunday 7pm – 10:30pm. **Cuisine:** English:- Blackboard menu – changes daily according to the availability of fresh produce. Eg. locally smoked Chicken, Rack of lamb, steaks, fresh fish. **Credit cards:** Visa, Access, AmEx. **Other points:** licensed, Sunday lunch, children catered for – please check for age limits, garden, pets allowed. **Directions:** on the B4042, next to the village church in Brinkworth.
MR A WINDLE, tel (0666) 510366.

## CHRISTCHURCH, Dorset Map 3

### BEVERLY GLEN GUEST HOUSE, 1 Stuart Road, Highcliffe
*A very attractive family-run guest house situated in the popular seaside village of Highcliffe, with its sea-front, gently sloping grass and shrub covered cliffs leading down to a sand and shingle beach. Fishing is available on the Stour and Avon rivers, and just 4 miles away is Christchurch with its famous priory and museums. En suite bedrooms with many modern facilities, good food and comfort ensures a comfortable stay.*
*ACCOMMODATION under £20*
*FOOD up to £15*
**Hours:** breakfast 8am – 8:45am; dinner 6pm. **Cuisine:** English:- A varied menu with fresh produce used whenever possible. **Rooms:** 7 bedrooms all with tea making facilities, radio, TV: 2 doubles, 2 singles ensuite, 2 doubles ensuite, 1 family room ensuite. **Other points:** parking, children catered for – please check for age limits, no-smoking in bedrooms, residents' lounge, licensed. **Directions:** situated on A337, eastern end of the village, first turning right after the traffic lights if travelling towards Lymington.
MR P BOURN, tel (0425) 273811.

### THE COPPER SKILLET, 17 Church Street
*A licensed steak house and family restaurant situated in the old part of Christchurch close to the town quay, priory and castle ruins.*
*FOOD up to £15* CLUB ★
**Hours:** meals all day 9am – 9pm; closed Christmas 25/12 – 26/12. **Cuisine:** English:- Steaks and grills, and weekly fresh fish and vegetarian specialities. **Rooms:** self catering accommodation. **Credit cards:** Visa, Access. **Other points:** Sunday lunch, children catered for – please check for age limits, coach/prior arr. **Directions:** Off main A35 into Christchurch High St, take Church St toward Priory.
MICHAEL DEVALL, tel (0202) 485485, fax (0202) 475866.

### THE FISHERMAN'S HAUNT HOTEL, Salisbury Road, Winkton
*Superior 2 star/4 crowns country house hotel on the banks of the River Avon. The restaurant overlooks the river and there is an attractive beer garden with children's play area. Situated on the edge of the New Forest. A freehouse serving real ales.*
*ACCOMMODATION £31–£40*
*FOOD up to £15*
**Hours:** breakfast 7:30am – 9:30am; breakfast – Sunday 8am – 9:30am; bar 10am – 2:30pm; bar – Sunday 12noon – 3pm; lunch 12noon – 2pm; bar 6pm – 11pm; bar – Sunday 7pm – 10:30pm; dinner 7pm – 10pm; closed Christmas 25/12. **Cuisine:** English:- Fresh Christchurch salmon, Avon trout, steak and kidney pie. **Rooms:** 20 bedrooms, most en suite. Limited accommodation over Christmas week. **Credit cards:** Visa, Access, Diners, AmEx. **Other points:** licensed, open-air dining, Sunday lunch, children catered for – please check for age limits. **Directions:** On the B3347 between Christchurch and Ringwood.
MR J BOCHAN, tel (0202) 477283.

### LE PETIT ST TROPEZ, 3 Bridge Street
*The ambiance, cuisine and service at Le Petit St Tropez combine to make dining here a special experience. This genuine French family run restaurant has a choice of fixed price or a la carte menu, including their own seasonal specialities.*
*FOOD up to £15*
**Hours:** lunch 12noon; dinner 7pm. **Cuisine:** French:- Traditional French from Provence. Seasonal specialities. **Credit cards:** Visa, Access. **Other points:** open-air dining, children catered for – please check for age limits, bank holidays, functions. **Directions:** Between the two bridges, 100 metres from the Civic Offices.
MARCEL & DEBORAH DUVAL, tel (0202) 482522, fax (0202) 470048.

## CLAWTON-HOLESWORTHY, Devon Map 2

### COURT BARN COUNTRY HOUSE HOTEL
*A country house of great character and charm, with antiques, pictures and flowers throughout, Court Barn is*

the perfect touring hotel for Dartmoor, Bodmin and Exmoor. Les Routiers/Mercier Wine List of the Year 1989, Corps d'Elite 1990, 1991 and 1992. Tea Council 'Best Teas in Britain' 1987 and 1989. National Awards for cuisine. A Devon's 'Hotel of Distinction.'
ACCOMMODATION £31–£40
FOOD £15–£20 ♀ ★
**Hours:** closed 01/01 – 07/01; morning coffee 10am – 12noon; lunch 12noon – 2pm; afternoon tea 3pm – 5pm; dinner 7:30pm – 9pm. **Cuisine:** English / French:- Cordon Bleu cuisine. 5 course candlelit dinners. Fresh local produce. Vegetarian dishes. Menu changes daily. Award winning cream teas and restaurant awards. **Rooms:** 7 bedrooms all with tea making facilities, telephone, TV: 3 doubles ensuite, 3 twins ensuite, 1 single ensuite. **Credit cards:** Visa, Access, Diners, AmEx. **Other points:** licensed, Sunday lunch, children catered for – please check for age limits, pets allowed, garden, tennis, croquet, residents' lounge, library, games room, residents' bar, swimming pool. **Directions:** 3 miles south of Holesworthy, off A388. Next to 12th century church.
ROBERT & SUSAN WOOD, tel (040927) 219.

## CLEVEDON, Avon Map 3

### CASA TOMAS RISTORANTE, Millcross, Southern Way
For a true taste of Italy, one need go no further than this lively restaurant in the heart of Clevedon. Warm, friendly service and a vibrant atmosphere complement the first class Italian food.
FOOD £15–£20
**Hours:** dinner 7:30pm – 10:30pm; closed Sunday. **Cuisine:** Italian:- Distinctive Italian cuisine, with vegetarian meals also provided. **Credit cards:** Visa, Access. **Other points:** children catered for – please check for age limits. **Directions:** ½ mile off Junction 20 of M5.
TOMAS MEDINA, tel (0275) 343578.

## COMBE MARTIN, Devon Map 2

### RONE HOUSE HOTEL, King Street
A small, privately-run hotel where the emphasis is on comfort, relaxation and superb food and service. Nearby are fine sandy beaches, Exmoor, beautiful hills and valleys, such as Valley of the Rocks, Watersmeet and Doone and the famous Dartington Glass Factory.
ACCOMMODATION £21–£30
FOOD £15–£20 CLUB
**Hours:** breakfast 8:30am – 9:15am; lunch 12:30pm – 2pm; dinner 6:30pm – 9pm. **Cuisine:** modern English. **Rooms:** 4 doubles, 4 family rooms, all en suite. 2 twins and 1 single. **Credit cards:** Visa, Access. **Other points:** garden, children catered for – please check for age limits, special breaks, pets allowed, swimming pool. **Directions:** Junction 27 on M5. Then follow A369 link road to sign for Combe Martin.
GRAHAM & ELSPETH COTTAGE, tel (0271) 883428.

### SANDY COVE HOTEL, Berrynarbor
The hotel stands in 20 acres of gardens featuring woods, cliffs and coves. Other facilities include indoor swimming pool, sauna and whirlpool.
ACCOMMODATION £31–£40
FOOD up to £15 ★
**Hours:** breakfast 8:30am – 9:30am; bar 11am – 11pm; lunch 12:30pm – 2:30pm; afternoon tea 3pm – 5pm; dinner 7pm – 9:30pm. **Cuisine:** international:- Fondue, kebabs, 5 variations of lobster. Large a la carte menu. **Rooms:** 33 bedrooms all with tea making facilities, telephone, TV: 15 doubles ensuite, 2 singles ensuite, 5 twins ensuite, 11 family rooms ensuite. **Other points:** licensed, Sunday lunch, children catered for – please check for age limits, coach/prior arr, vegetarian meals, disabled access, swimming pool, residents' bar. **Directions:** on the A399 (coast road), 1 mile from Combe Martin.
MRS DARLINGTON, tel (0271) 882243, (0271) 882888, fax (0271) 883830.

## CORSHAM, Wiltshire Map 3

### RUDLOE PARK HOTEL & RESTAURANT, Leafy Lane
A peaceful 19th century country house hotel set in 4 acres of beautiful gardens with extensive views to and beyond the Georgian city of Bath. The restaurant has received many awards for their wine and cheeseboard. Les Routiers "Cheeseboard of the Year 1993", and Casserole Award holder.
ACCOMMODATION £31–£40
FOOD £15–£20 ♀ ⌂ ★
**Hours:** breakfast 7:30am – 9:30am; lunch 12noon – 2pm; dinner 7pm – 10pm. **Cuisine:** English:- Large fixed price menus with freshly cooked food. Vegetarian and dietary meals available. Lounge food. Extensive selection of excellent cheeses and wines. **Rooms:** 11 bedrooms all with tea making facilities, telephone, radio, TV: 3 twins ensuite, 8 doubles ensuite. **Credit cards:** Visa, Access, Diners, AmEx. **Other points:** licensed, Sunday lunch, no-smoking area, children catered for – please check for age limits, pets allowed. **Directions:** on the A4 between Bath and Chippenham at the top of Box Hill.
IAN & MARION OVEREND – RESIDENT DIRECTOR, tel (0225) 810555, fax (0225) 811412.

## COVERACK, Cornwall Map 1

### THE BAY HOTEL
Set in the unspoilt Cornish countryside of the beautiful Lizard Peninsula, providing the perfect location for that 'away from it all' feeling. Furnished to an extremely high standard, most rooms have wonderful sea views. Cornish proprietors Lorraine and David Goldsworthy have succeeded in providing a comfortable and friendly atmosphere.
ACCOMMODATION £21–£30
FOOD up to £15
**Hours:** open Christmas 7pm; open New Year 7pm; breakfast 8:30am – 9:30am; bar snacks 12noon – 2pm;

dinner 6:30pm – 8:30pm; closed November – February. **Cuisine:** English:- All meals are cooked to order with fresh local produce. **Rooms:** 14 bedrooms all with tea making facilities, TV: 1 single ensuite, 3 twins ensuite, 10 doubles ensuite. **Credit cards:** Visa, Access. **Other points:** parking, Sunday lunch, open bank holidays, disabled access, pets allowed, residents' lounge, vegetarian meals, garden, licensed, central heating. **Directions:** from Helston take B3292 to St Keverne, Coverack is signed.
LORRIANE & DAVID GOLDSWORTHY, tel (0326) 280464.

## CREWKERNE, Somerset Map 3

### THE GEORGE HOTEL AND RESTAURANT, Market Square
*An interesting building with a fascinating history dating back to the 17th century. With an excellent restaurant and accommodation of the highest standard, it provides an ideal base for touring the counties of Somerset, Dorset and the borders.*
*ACCOMMODATION £21–£30*
*FOOD up to £15*
**Hours:** breakfast 7:30am – 9:30am; lunch 12noon – 2pm; dinner 6:30pm – 9:30pm. **Cuisine:** English / continental. **Credit cards:** Visa, Access, Diners, AmEx. **Other points:** children catered for – please check for age limits, Sunday lunch, residents' lounge, vegetarian meals. **Directions:** halfway between Yeovil and Chard.
GARY ROBERT GILMORE, tel (0460) 73650, fax (0460) 72974.

## DARTMOUTH, Devon Map 2

### ROYAL CASTLE HOTEL, The Quay
*Standing on the quayside of the River Dart, this hotel was a coaching inn and has a fascinating history. The ceiling of the bar is reputed to have been constructed with timber from the wreckage of the Armada. The hotel's elegant atmosphere is reflected in the traditional English cooking and service.*
*ACCOMMODATION £31–£40*
*FOOD up to £15* ★
**Hours:** breakfast 8am – 9:30am; bar meals 12noon – 9:45pm; lunch 12:30pm – 2:15pm; dinner 7pm – 9:45pm. **Cuisine:** English:- Seafood, traditional roasts. **Rooms:** 25 bedrooms all with tea making facilities, telephone, radio, TV: 4 twins ensuite, 21 doubles ensuite. **Credit cards:** Visa, Access. **Other points:** Sunday lunch, children catered for – please check for age limits, afternoon tea, pets allowed, weekend breaks, Jacuzzi, parking. **Directions:** from A38 take A384 to Totnes, A381 to Halwell, then B3207.
MR NIGEL WAY, tel (0803) 833033, fax (0803) 835445.

### SLOPING DECK RESTAURANT, The Butterwalk
*The Sloping Deck consists of a bakery on the ground floor and a restaurant on the first floor, both offering quality food at very good value. Situated in one of Dartmouth's most famous historic buildings.*
*FOOD up to £15*
**Hours:** meals all day 9am – 5:30pm. **Cuisine:** English:- English home-cooking, including fresh fish and steak and kidney pie. **Credit cards:** Visa, Access. **Other points:** licensed, Sunday lunch, no-smoking area, children catered for – please check for age limits, pets allowed, afternoon tea. **Directions:** in Butterwalk, centre of town. Historic building.
MR & MRS BARNES, tel (0803) 832758.

### STOKE LODGE HOTEL, Stoke Fleming
*Situated on the scenic coastal road between historic Dartmouth and Kingsbridge, this charming hotel is very popular locally and offers first class service and comfort with fresh local food, 3 acres of grounds and every facility for a truly relaxing holiday.*
*ACCOMMODATION £31–£40*
*FOOD up to £15*
**Hours:** breakfast 8:30am – 9:45am; lunch 12:30pm – 2pm; dinner 7pm – 9pm. **Cuisine:** English / French:- A large variety of English/French cuisine using only the best local fresh ingredients, eg. Poached salmon with Hollandaise sauce. **Rooms:** 29 bedrooms all with tea making facilities, telephone, radio, TV: 3 singles ensuite, 8 twins ensuite, 9 doubles ensuite, 7 triples ensuite, 2 quads ensuite. **Credit cards:** Visa, Access. **Other points:** licensed, outdoor swimming pool, indoor swimming pool, Jacuzzi, tennis, sauna, fishing, river trips, bird-watching, garden, children catered for – please check for age limits, pets allowed, baby-listening device, baby sitting, cots. **Directions:** A379. 2 miles south of Dartmouth.
STEVEN MAYER, tel (0803) 770523, fax (0803) 770851.

## DAWLISH, Devon Map 2

### LANGSTONE CLIFF HOTEL, Mount Pleasant Road, Dawlish Warren
*Set in 19 acres of wooded grounds and only 500 yd from the beach, this hotel offers the warmest of welcomes and the best in friendly service with special consideration for families and children. Superbly decorated, the hotel provides a high standard of food and accommodation and there is a host of activities for all ages to enjoy. Set in an area of outstanding beauty.*
*ACCOMMODATION £31–£40*
*FOOD up to £15*
**Hours:** breakfast 7:30am – 10am; lunch 12:30pm – 2pm; dinner 7pm – 9pm. **Cuisine:** English:- Traditional English cuisine. Table d'hote dinner menu and carvery. Coffee shop offering light refreshments. **Rooms:** 68 bedrooms all with tea making facilities, telephone, radio, TV: 6 singles ensuite, 21 doubles ensuite, 25 triples ensuite, 16 quads ensuite. **Credit cards:** Visa, Access, Diners, AmEx. **Other points:** licensed, Sunday lunch, children catered for – please check for age limits, games room, tennis, swimming pool, dinner dances,

conferences, baby sitting, baby-listening device, cots, 24hr reception, residents' lounge, residents' bar. **Directions:** 1 mile off the A379. 1 mile north of Dawlish.
GEOFFREY ROGERS, tel (0626) 865155, fax (0626) 867166.

## DEVIZES, Wiltshire Map 3

### THE BEAR HOTEL, Market Place
*A 16th century coaching inn where you will find friendly, helpful service and many historic associations. Within easy reach of Bath, Swindon, Salisbury and a host of stately homes and gardens. Weekend breaks.*
*FOOD £15–£20*
**Hours:** open all day 7am; lunch 12noon – 2pm; dinner 7pm – 9:30pm. **Cuisine:** English:- Devizes pie, roast joints carved at your table daily, charcoal grills in the Lawrence room. **Rooms:** 25 bedrooms, all en suite.
**Credit cards:** Visa, Access, AmEx. **Other points:** open-air dining, Sunday lunch, children catered for – please check for age limits. **Directions:** 15 miles off M4, A350 to Melksham, the A365 to Devizes.
MR W K DICKENSON, tel (0380) 722444, fax (0380) 2450.

## DORCHESTER, Dorset Map 3

### THE ACORN INN HOTEL, 28 Fore Street, Evershot
*Dating from the 16th century, The Acorn Inn Hotel nestles in an unspoilt and peaceful village, set in the heart of Thomas Hardy's Dorset. A warm welcome awaits you from the resident owners and their friendly staff in this totally refurbished establishment. An imaginative a la carte menu is available from plain and simple cooking to the diverse using local produce when in season.*
*ACCOMMODATION £31–£40*
*FOOD up to £15*
**Hours:** open all year 7pm; breakfast 8am – 9:30am; lunch 12noon – 2pm; dinner 6:30pm – 9:45pm. **Cuisine:** English:- Dishes may include Game Bordeaux, Pork Wellington, and Duck with Orange & Grand Marnier. Speciality Main Course changes daily. Excellent wine selection. **Rooms:** 8 bedrooms, all with en suite facilities, including four poster beds. **Credit cards:** Visa, Access. **Other points:** licensed, open-air dining, Sunday lunch, no-smoking area, children catered for – please check for age limits, afternoon tea, residents' lounge, garden, pets allowed. **Directions:** Off A37 towards Evershot, in main street before church.
DENISE MORLEY, tel (0935) 83228.

### CHURCHVIEW GUEST HOUSE, Winterbourne Abbas
*A delightful family run guest house with comfortable accommodation and with a very high standard of wholesome English cooking and varied menu, served in the charming period dining room. Each bedroom has its own character and warmth. The Churchview is superbly situated to visit many places of interest throughout the beautiful Dorset countryside and close to the coast.*
*ACCOMMODATION under £20*
*FOOD up to £15*
**Hours:** breakfast 8:15am – 8:45am; dinner 7pm. **Cuisine:** English. **Credit cards:** Visa, Access. **Other points:** children catered for – please check for age limits, pets, disabled access, parking, residents' lounge. **Directions:** on A35 5 miles west of Dorchester.
MR M DELLER, tel (0305) 889296.

### JUDGE JEFFREYS RESTAURANT, 6 High West Street
*In 1685 the notorious Judge Jeffreys lodged at this famous Dorchester House during the time of 'The Bloody Assize'. Today the original beamed building houses a restaurant which provides very good food and polite, friendly service. Highly recommended for its warm welcome, good food and value for money prices.*
*FOOD up to £15*
**Hours:** morning coffee 9:30am – 12noon; lunch 12noon – 2:30pm; dinner 7pm – 9:30pm. **Cuisine:** English:- Wide range of lunchtime specials which change daily. Evening a la carte menu. Morning coffee and afternoon teas. **Credit cards:** Visa, Access. **Other points:** licensed, no-smoking area, children catered for – please check for age limits, pets allowed, afternoon tea, parking. **Directions:** In centre of town on main road. Public car parks nearby.
IAN AND PAT MCLELLAN, tel (0305) 264369.

### THE MANOR HOTEL, Beach Road, West Bexington
*17th century manor house 500 yd from Chesil Beach. Panoramic views from most bedrooms of unspoilt Dorset coastline. Three real ales served in character cellar bar. Log fires. Private dining room for up to 40. Facilities for conferences, buffets, receptions.*
*ACCOMMODATION £31–£40*
*FOOD £21–£25* ☿ ★
**Hours:** breakfast 8:30am – 9:30am; lunch 12noon – 2pm; dinner 7pm – 10pm. **Cuisine:** English / seafood:- Local seafood and imaginative dishes. **Rooms:** 13 bedrooms all with tea making facilities, telephone, radio, TV: 9 doubles ensuite, 1 single ensuite, 3 twins ensuite. **Credit cards:** Visa, Access, Diners, AmEx. **Other points:** licensed, Sunday lunch, children catered for – please check for age limits, parking. **Directions:** on the B3157 Bridport to Weymouth coast road.
RICHARD & JAYNE A CHILDS, tel (0308) 897616, fax (0308) 897035.

### NEW INN, West Knighton
*Attractive old pub with hanging baskets and jasmine creeper. Cheerful, relaxed atmosphere. Efficient service provided by friendly staff.*
*FOOD up to £15*
**Hours:** open all year 7pm; lunch 12noon – 2pm; dinner 7pm – 9pm. **Cuisine:** English:- Well-cooked traditional

pub food. Wide selection. Sunday lunches and sizzling dishes a speciality. Extensive specials board. Vegetarian menu. **Credit cards:** Visa, Access. **Other points:** licensed, open-air dining, Sunday lunch, children catered for – please check for age limits, pets allowed. **Directions:** Situated off the A352 at West Knighton. RODGER & JULIA GILBEY, tel (0305) 852349.

### WESSEX ROYALE HOTEL, 32 High Street
*Dating back to the 1600's, the hotel was originally built as a town house for the Earl of Ilchester. Generously proportioned rooms with feature fireplaces, the hotel has been substantially refurbished to provide a friendly, relaxing atmosphere. Bedrooms are attractively furnished with many modern facilities, and the restaurant offers a high standard of continental and English cuisine. A conservatory is available for banquets and weddings for up to 100 people. Ideal location for the leisure traveller exploring Dorset.*
*ACCOMMODATION under £20*
*FOOD up to £15*
**Hours:** breakfast 7:30am – 10am; dinner 6pm – 10:30pm. **Cuisine:** English / continental. **Credit cards:** Visa, Access, Diners, AmEx. **Other points:** children catered for – please check for age limits, no-smoking area, residents' lounge, garden, pets, vegetarian meals, open bank holidays. **Directions:** on main road in centre of Dorchester.
MR M BOWLEY, tel (0305) 262660, fax (0305) 251941.

## DULVERTON, Somerset Map 3

### CARNARVON ARMS HOTEL
*An imposing Victorian hotel set in 50 acres of grounds which stands guard at one of the entrances to the Exmoor National Park near the banks of the River Barle. Billed as a 'fine English country sporting hotel', fishing, shooting and swimming are available, and first class English cooking guaranteed.*
*ACCOMMODATION £31–£40*
*FOOD £21–£25*
**Hours:** open all year 6pm; breakfast 8am – 9:30am; bar meals 12noon – 2pm; lunch 12:30pm – 1:30pm; bar meals 7pm – 9pm; dinner 7:30pm – 9pm. **Cuisine:** English:- Good wholesome English cooking – all home prepared using fresh local produce. **Rooms:** 22 bedrooms all with telephone, TV: 1 suite, 3 singles ensuite, 7 twins ensuite, 11 doubles ensuite. **Credit cards:** Visa, Access. **Other points:** Sunday lunch, no-smoking area, children catered for – please check for age limits, pets allowed, afternoon tea. **Directions:** 1 mile south of Dulverton on B3222 on the edge of Brushford Village.
MRS TONI JONES, tel (0398) 23302, fax (0398) 24022.

### THE LION HOTEL, Bank Square
*Set in the heart of the Exmoor National Park, the Lion is an ideal base for exploring this beautiful, unspoilt corner of England. It offers a warm welcome, comfortable accommodation and good food at excellent value for money. The wide range of holiday breaks cater*

for every interest, including those who fancy a trip in a hot air balloon.
*ACCOMMODATION £21–£30*
*FOOD £15–£20*
**Hours:** breakfast 8:30am – 9:30am; lunch 12noon – 2pm; dinner – except Sunday 6:30pm – 9pm; dinner – Sunday 7pm – 9pm. **Cuisine:** English:- Fresh Exmoor produce including salmon, trout, game birds and venison, traditionally cooked and available in the restaurants and bars. **Rooms:** 13 bedrooms all with tea making facilities, telephone, TV: 4 singles ensuite, 4 twins ensuite, 4 doubles ensuite, 1 family room ensuite. **Credit cards:** Visa, Access. **Other points:** Sunday lunch, children catered for – please check for age limits, pets/charge, special breaks, shooting, hunting, fishing. **Directions:** Junction 27, off M5. Then off A396, between Tiverton and Minehead.
DUNCAN & JACKIE MACKINNON – MANAGERS, tel (0398) 23444.

## DUNSTER, Somerset Map 3

### THE TEA SHOPPE, 3 High Street
*15th century tea rooms in lovely medieval village close to National Trust castle. Norman and Pam can boast 32 years experience and specialise in home cooking. A well presented tea room offering all sorts of unusual teas, jams, coffees, etc.*
*FOOD up to £15*
**Hours:** meals all day 10am – 5:30pm; closed January – February(incl); open March – October(incl); closed weekdays November – December(incl). **Cuisine:** English:- Homemade soups and traditional recipes. Delicious puddings and home-made cakes. **Credit cards:** Visa, Access. **Other points:** Sunday lunch, no-smoking area, children catered for – please check for age limits, pets allowed, licensed. **Directions:** situated on the town's main road at the end nearest the castle.
NORMAN & PAM GOLDSACK, tel (0643) 821304.

### YARN MARKET HOTEL, 25/27 High Street
*A small family run hotel with a warm and friendly atmosphere and situated in Dunster High Street opposite the famous Yarn Market, offering splendid views of the castle with the hills beyond. Accommodation is available throughout the year and Dunster village has many attractions, including the water mill and priory church together with local shops full of historic artefacts. Dunster is also the gateway to the walkers paradise of Exmoor National Park which offers a whole range of fascinating outdoor pursuits.*
*ACCOMMODATION £21–£30*
*FOOD up to £15* ★
**Hours:** breakfast – Mon-Sat 8am – 9am; breakfast – Sunday 8:30am – 9:30am; dinner 7pm – 8pm. **Cuisine:** English:- A good mixture of modern and traditional meals, likely features on the menu include traditional roast, pork chop with apricot, vegetarian lasagne. International:- Italian, French, American, Mexican, Oriental. **Rooms:** 4 bedrooms all with tea making facilities, TV: 1 single ensuite, 2 doubles ensuite, 1

family room ensuite. **Credit cards:** Visa, Access,
AmEx. **Other points:** parking, children catered for –
please check for age limits, open bank holidays,
pets/prior arr, picnic lunches, drying facilities, Sunday
lunch, no-smoking area, afternoon teas, residents'
lounge, vegetarian meals, conferences. **Directions:** from
Junction 23 (M5) take A39, or from Junction 25 (M5)
take A358 to Minehead and follow directions to Dunster.
The hotel is in the centre of Dunster village beside the
Historic Yarn Market. 2 minutes from A1(M) off A167,
signposted Brafferton.
SARAH ASHMAN (MANAGERESS), tel (0643)
821425.

## EMSWORTH, Hampshire Map 4

### JINGLES, 77 Horndean Road
*A homely Victorian building flanked by open
countryside. All bedrooms are individually decorated
and provide comfortable accommodation. Under the
personal supervision of Kit & Angela Chapman, the
atmosphere and service are welcoming and friendly.*
*ACCOMMODATION £21–£30*
*FOOD up to £15*
**Hours:** breakfast 7:15am – 9am; lunch – Sunday 12noon
– 2pm; dinner 7pm – 9pm. **Cuisine:** English /
international. **Rooms:** 14 bedrooms all with tea making
facilities, TV: 5 singles, 1 twin, 2 twins ensuite, 5
doubles ensuite, 1 family room. **Credit cards:** Visa,
Access. **Other points:** children catered for – please
check for age limits, central heating, residents' lounge,
pets allowed, garden, afternoon tea, vegetarian meals,
disabled access, parking, residents' bar. **Directions:**
follow the A259 to Emsworth. Proceed north from
village onto B2148.
KIT & ANGELA CHAPMAN, tel (0243) 373755.

## EXEBRIDGE, Somerset Map 3

### ANCHOR INN HOTEL, Nr Dulverton
*A 300 year old residential inn on the banks of the River
Exe, with fishing from the hotel grounds. Standing in an
acre of grounds, the Anchor Inn provides a high standard
of comfort and tranquillity. The restaurant is set in a
converted stable block overlooking the lawned garden and
river. Excellent a la carte menu includes trout from the
River Exe. Ideal base for exploring Exmoor.*
*ACCOMMODATION £31–£40*
*FOOD £15–£20* 🍽
**Hours:** open all year 7pm; breakfast 8:30am – 9:30am;
lunch 12noon – 2pm; dinner 7pm – 9pm. **Cuisine:**
modern English:- Good home cooking with local
produce used where possible, including Chef who bakes
own bread and makes home-made desserts. **Rooms:** 6
bedrooms 3 doubles ensuite, 3 twins ensuite. **Credit
cards:** Visa, Access. **Other points:** open-air dining, beer
garden, reservations, children catered for – please check
for age limits, playland. **Directions:** on the B3222, just
off the A396, north east of Bampton.
JOHN & JUDY PHRIPP, tel (0398) 23433.

## EXETER, Devon Map 2

### THE ANGLERS REST, Fingle Bridge, Drewsteignton
*A family-run restaurant and lounge bar with riverside
terraces. Adjoining Fingle Bridge on the banks of the
River Teign deep in Fingle Gorge, The Anglers Rest
provides a starting point for miles of walks, fishing and
bird-watching.*
*FOOD up to £15*
**Hours:** lunch – summer 11am – 5:30pm; lunch – winter
11am – 2:30pm; dinner – summer 7pm – 9pm; dinner –
winter 7pm – 11pm. **Cuisine:** English / international:-
Steak & Kidney pie, Devon steaks, salmon, trout. Bar
meals. Devonshire cream teas. Vegetarian dishes.
Homemade speciality curries and pasta dishes. **Credit
cards:** Visa, Access. **Other points:** open-air dining,
Sunday lunch, children catered for – please check for
age limits, functions. **Directions:** next to Fingle Bridge
in Drewsteignton.
THE PRICE FAMILY, tel (064 721) 287.

### LAMB'S, Under The Iron Bridge, 15 Lower North Street
*A Grade II listed building approximately 200 years old,
providing modern English food in a delightful, friendly
setting. The restaurant has a courtyard at the rear
alongside the original Roman city wall. Ideal location
for exploring Exeter and for visiting Devon's many
attractions.*
*FOOD £15–£20*
**Hours:** lunch 12noon – 2:30pm; dinner 6pm –
12midnight. **Cuisine:** English. **Credit cards:** Visa,
Access, AmEx, Switch. **Other points:** Sunday lunch,
vegetarian meals. **Directions:** 100yds from Harlequin
Car Park under the Iron Bridge.
ALDRIDGE, IAN & ALISON, tel (0392) 54269, fax
(0392) 431145.

### THE OLD THATCH INN, Cheriton Bishop
*Traditional 16th century thatched free house, originally
built as a coaching house. Just 10 miles from Exeter and
inside the Eastern border of Dartmoor National Park.
"Les Routiers of the Year 1985".*
*ACCOMMODATION £21–£30*
*FOOD up to £15* 🍽
**Hours:** lunch 12noon – 2:15pm; dinner – except Sunday
6:30pm – 9:30pm; dinner – Sunday 7pm – 9pm.
**Cuisine:** English:- Homemade food using traditional
recipes. Dishes may include steak & kidney pudding,
Thatch mixed grill, baked stuffed aubergine, sole
fourees. **Rooms:** 3 bedrooms all with tea making
facilities, radio, TV: 3 doubles ensuite. **Credit cards:**
Visa, Access. **Other points:** licensed, Sunday lunch,
children catered for – please check for age limits.
**Directions:** from the A30, 10 miles west of Exeter, take
Cheriton Bishop road.
BRIAN & HAZEL BRYON-EDMOND, tel (0647)
24204.

## PARK VIEW HOTEL, *8 Howell Road*

*A popular hotel in the centre of Exeter, which offers comfortable accommodation and excellent full breakfasts. Attractively decorated, Park View Hotel provides a comfortable, welcoming base from which to visit Exeter, whether on business or for pleasure. Very close to the University and station.*

ACCOMMODATION under £20

**Hours:** breakfast 7:30am – 9am; breakfast – Sunday 8:30am – 9:30am; closed Christmas 25/12. **Cuisine:** breakfast. **Rooms:** 15 bedrooms all with tea making facilities, telephone, TV: 4 singles, 1 twin, 1 double, 2 twins ensuite, 5 doubles ensuite, 2 family rooms ensuite. **Credit cards:** Visa, Access. **Other points:** children catered for – please check for age limits, residents' lounge. **Directions:** B3183 to clock tower roundabout – third exit. At end turn Left.
MR & MRS BATHO, tel (0392) 71772.

---

## EXFORD, Somerset Map 3

## THE EXMOOR WHITE HORSE INN

*Your dream of an olde worlde inn with log fires comes true before your eyes. Standing on the green by the side of a trickling stream in one of Exmoors' most beautiful villages. Horses all around, the blacksmith busy over the road and rolling moors await you at the edge of the village.*

ACCOMMODATION £41–£50
FOOD up to £15

**Hours:** breakfast 8:30am – 9:30am; lunch 12noon – 2:30pm; dinner 7pm – 9:30pm. **Cuisine:** English:- Steaks, seafood, venison, and extensive bar snacks. **Rooms:** 18 bedrooms all with tea making facilities, radio, TV: 3 twins ensuite, 3 family rooms ensuite, 12 doubles ensuite. **Other points:** licensed, Sunday lunch, children catered for – please check for age limits, garden, vegetarian meals, residents' lounge, residents' bar, parking, disabled access. **Directions:** from Taunton take the A358, then the B224 to Exford.
MRS DARLINGTON, tel (064383) 229.

---

## EXMOOR, Somerset Map 3

## KARSLAKE HOUSE HOTEL, *Winsford, Exmoor National Park*

*Situated on the edge of the wild yet beautiful Exmoor National Park, this 15th century establishment provides good quality food and service in a pleasant and comfortable atmosphere. Ideal for exploring the moors, or visiting nearby tourist attractions, including Tarr Steps, Dunkery Beacon, and Dunster Castle.*

ACCOMMODATION £21–£30
FOOD up to £15

**Hours:** closed 01/07 – 14/07; breakfast 8:30am – 9:30am; dinner 7:30pm – 8pm; closed November – March. **Cuisine:** English:- Table d'hote menu, predominantly English cuisine. Dishes may include, Loin of Lamb, Guinea Fowl in Red Wine, and Halibut Steak. Vegetarians catered for. **Rooms:** 7 bedrooms all

with tea making facilities, TV: 2 doubles ensuite, 2 twins ensuite, 2 doubles, 1 twin. **Other points:** children catered for – please check for age limits, pets allowed, parking, residents' lounge, garden, bank holidays. **Directions:** Junction 27 link road to A396 towards Bridgetown. Left to Winsford.
FRED ALDERTON & JANE YOUNG, tel (064) 385242.

---

## THE ROYAL OAK INN, *Withypool*

*Set in the beautiful village of Withypool in the middle of Exmoor, this is an ideal base from which to ride, hunt, shoot, fish or simply take a leisurely walk. All bedrooms are individually furnished with their own characters and the two bars with their beamed ceilings are everything you would expect of an old country inn. R.D. Blackmore stayed here whilst writing his famous novel* Lorna Doone.

ACCOMMODATION £31–£40
FOOD £15–£20

**Hours:** breakfast 8:30am – 9:30am; bar snacks 12noon – 2pm; bar snacks 6:30pm – 9:30pm; dinner 7pm – 9pm. **Cuisine:** English / continental. **Rooms:** 8 bedrooms 6 doubles ensuite, 1 twin ensuite, 1 family room ensuite. **Credit cards:** Visa, Access, Diners, AmEx. **Other points:** parking, children catered for – please check for age limits, pets allowed, residents' lounge, vegetarian meals, open-air dining. **Directions:** leave the M5 at Tiverton and take the A361. Turn left for North Molton and Withypool. The establishment is in the centre of Withypool.
MR M BRADLEY, tel (064383) 506, (064383) 507, fax (064383) 659.

---

## Accommodation of the Year
### ROYAL OAK INN, *Winsford*

*Nestling in the picturesque village of Winsford on the edge of the Exmoor National Park, the inn dates from the 12th century. Its charming thatched roof, open fireplaces and oak beams have been subtly combined with many modern facilities to ensure guests comfort. The restaurant prides itself on its freshly cooked cuisine and the lounges are furnished to a high standard of elegance, as are the bedrooms which maintain cosiness and charm. This is a superb location for exploring Exmoor and its ancient history. A winner of many outstanding awards.*

ACCOMMODATION £41–£50
FOOD £21–£25

**Hours:** open all year; bar 11:30am – 2:30pm, 6pm – 11pm. **Cuisine:** English. **Rooms:** 15 bedrooms 2 twins ensuite, 11 doubles ensuite, 1 family room ensuite, 1 suite. **Other points:** parking, children catered for – please check for age limits, bank holidays, afternoon teas, pets, residents' lounge, garden dining, vegetarian meals. **Directions:** M5 south, off at junction 27, on to A396.
CHARLES STEVEN, tel (064385) 455, fax (064385) 388.

# EXMOUTH, Devon Map 2

## BALCOMBE HOUSE HOTEL, Stevenstone Road

*The Balcombe House Hotel is an oasis of peace and tranquillity within half an acre of garden. A short walk away from the seafront with its two miles of golden sands and wealth of leisure activities. The town centre is also close at hand. Very comfortably furnished to a high standard with a well stocked licensed bar in a sunny lounge overlooking the gardens and a second no-smoking lounge. There may be impromptu musical entertainment from the proprietoress; a professional musician of high standing. The extended hours of service allow guests to dine early or late, choosing from the many and varied dishes on offer. Open all year with special Christmas, New Year and Easter programmes.*
ACCOMMODATION £21–£30

FOOD up to £15

**Hours:** breakfast 8am – 9:30am; lunch 12noon – 2pm; dinner 6:30pm – 9pm. **Cuisine:** English. **Rooms:** 12 bedrooms all with tea making facilities, radio, TV: 2 singles ensuite, 4 doubles ensuite, 4 twins ensuite, 2 family rooms ensuite. **Credit cards:** Visa, Access, Eurocard. **Other points:** parking, children catered for – please check for age limits, no-smoking area, afternoon teas, disabled access, residents' lounge, garden, vegetarian meals, functions. **Directions:** follow road to Sandy Bay, bear right at Littleham Cross, third turn on left.
MR O SMALDON, tel (0395) 266349.

# FALMOUTH, Cornwall Map 1

## GREEN LAWNS HOTEL, Western Terrace

*An elegant chateau-style hotel situated midway between town and beaches. Renowned a la carte restaurant and full banqueting/conference facilities available. The hotel's 'Garras Leisure Complex' consists of indoor heated swimming pool, Jacuzzi, sauna, solarium and gymnasium. Honeymoon and Executives suites available.*
ACCOMMODATION £31–£40

FOOD £15–£20 ⛾ ⊕ ★

**Hours:** breakfast 7am – 9:30am; lunch 12noon – 2pm; dinner 6:45pm – 10pm. **Cuisine:** modern English:- Fresh local seafood and speciality steaks. **Rooms:** 40 bedrooms all with tea making facilities, telephone, radio, TV: 6 singles ensuite, 15 twins ensuite, 11 doubles ensuite, 8 triples ensuite. **Credit cards:** Visa, Access, Diners, AmEx. **Other points:** licensed, Sunday lunch, children catered for – please check for age limits, coach/prior arr, honeymoon suite, baby sitting, baby-listening device, cots, 24hr reception. **Directions:** on the main road into Falmouth heading towards the main beaches.
WENDY SYMONS, tel (0326) 312734, fax (0326) 211427.

## THE GROVE HOTEL, Grove Place

*Overlooking the harbour, close to shops, quays, railway station and ideally situated for exploring the Cornish coastline, the Grove Hotel was established in 1946. Although the building itself has been changed, you will still find the same relaxed and friendly atmosphere under the second generation of the Corks.*
FOOD up to £15 ★

**Hours:** breakfast 8am – 9am; dinner 7pm – 9pm. **Cuisine:** English / vegetarian:- English, international, Vegetarian. **Rooms:** 15 bedrooms all with tea making facilities, TV: 2 singles, 5 doubles ensuite, 4 twins ensuite, 4 family rooms ensuite. **Credit cards:** Visa, Access. **Other points:** central heating, children catered for – please check for age limits, residents' lounge, street parking, vegetarian meals. **Directions:** off the A39. Take harbour road to Grove Place near the Dinghy park.
PETER & JANET CORK, tel (0326) 319577, fax (0326) 319577.

## GYLLYNGVASE HOUSE HOTEL, Gyllyngvase Road

*Personally supervised by the owners, this is a small hotel which extends the warmest of welcomes to all its guests. The fine cuisine includes seafood specialities, and even special diets and picnic lunches can be arranged. There is an attractive lounge bar and garden terrace, and comfortably furnished rooms in colour co-ordinated schemes. Gyllyngvase is Falmouth's main beach – a wide sweep of golden sands making it an ideal location for a family holiday.*
ACCOMMODATION under £20

FOOD up to £15

**Hours:** breakfast 8:30am – 9am; dinner 6:30pm – 7pm; closed mid December – mid January. **Cuisine:** English. **Other points:** children catered for – please check for age limits, no-smoking area, vegetarian meals, afternoon teas, pets, residents' lounge, garden, parking.
**Directions:** from Truro take A3078 to traffic lights, go straight on to Melville Road. Hotel on right.
MR C LE MAITRE, tel (0326) 312956.

# FORD, Wiltshire Map 3

## THE WHITE HART, Nr Chippenham

*Reputedly built in 1533 and listed as being of architectural and historical interest, this attractive West Country inn was featured in the film Dr Doolittle. In spring and summer, the terrace overlooking the Bybrook River is an ideal spot to eat, drink and contemplate the abundance of nature. The interior is pleasantly decorated and there is an abundance of oak beams. The atmosphere and ambiance lends itself well to the olde worlde image and the inn has a proud reputation for good food and ale at value for money prices.*
ACCOMMODATION £21–£30

FOOD up to £15

**Cuisine:** English / French. **Rooms:** 11 bedrooms 1 twin ensuite, 10 doubles ensuite. **Credit cards:** Visa, Access, Diners, AmEx. **Other points:** parking, children catered for – please check for age limits, open bank holidays, pets allowed, vegetarian meals, open-air dining.

**Directions:** situated on A420, exit Junction 17 or 18 from Chippenham.
CHRIS AND JENNY PHILLIPS, tel (0249) 782213, fax (0249) 783075.

## FOWEY, Cornwall Map 1

### STANTON'S RESTAURANT, 11 The Esplanade

*Family owned and run restaurant with superb views over moorings on the River Fowey estuary and harbour. The emphasis is on quality, freshness and real home cooking. Established and renowned since 1980, Stanton's is 35 yd along the Esplanade on the left-hand side (almost invisible until you reach us).*
FOOD £15–£20
**Hours:** dinner 7pm – 10:30pm; closed Monday. **Cuisine:** international:- Local seafood and fish, char-grilled steaks. **Credit cards:** Visa, Access, Diners, AmEx. **Other points:** open-air dining, Sunday lunch, children catered for – please check for age limits, disabled access, vegetarian meals, parking nearby. **Directions:** descend hill into Fowey. Turn Rt into Esplanade. 35 yd on left.
PETER & ANN WILKES, tel (0726) 832631, fax (0726) 832631.

## FRESHFORD, Avon Map 3

### THE INN AT FRESHFORD, Freshford, Nr Bath

*An attractive stone-built inn with hanging baskets adding to its charm, situated in beautiful countryside. The pleasant interior is enhanced by fresh flowers and a friendly, relaxed atmosphere. There is an extensive choice of meals which are well-cooked and served by cheerful, efficient staff. A good choice for an enjoyable meal in attractive, welcoming surroundings.*
FOOD up to £15
**Hours:** bar meals 11am – 2pm; lunch 12noon – 2pm; dinner 6pm – 10pm; bar meals 6pm – 10pm. **Cuisine:** English:- Extensive choice of predominantly traditional English cuisine, and a large daily specials board. **Credit cards:** Visa, Access. **Other points:** licensed, open-air dining, Sunday lunch, children catered for – please check for age limits, pets allowed, beer garden, functions. **Directions:** off A36, 5 miles south of Bath. Between Limpley Stoke & Bradford on Avon.
JOHN THWAITES, tel (0225) 722250.

## FROME, Somerset Map 3

### THE GEORGE HOTEL, Market Place

*An old coaching inn, now completely modernised but retaining its original character. There is a choice of bars and a dining room where you can enjoy good food at very reasonable prices. The menu changes frequently to use the best of seasonal produce. The bedrooms are comfortable and attractively furnished with local wooden furniture. A cheerful, friendly hotel.*

ACCOMMODATION £31–£40
FOOD up to £15
**Hours:** breakfast 7:30am – 9:30am; lunch 12noon – 2pm; bar meals 12noon – 2pm; bar meals 6:30pm – 9:30pm; dinner 7pm – 9:30pm. **Cuisine:** English:- A la carte, table d'hote and bar meals. English cuisine with char grills a speciality. **Rooms:** 20 bedrooms, all en suite. **Credit cards:** Visa, Access, Diners, AmEx. **Other points:** licensed, Sunday lunch, children catered for – please check for age limits, afternoon tea, residents' lounge, pets allowed, disabled access, residents' bar, vegetarian meals, parking. **Directions:** from the A36/361 west from Bath, travel to Frome. In town centre.
MR N J BICKHAM, tel (0373) 462584.

## GLASTONBURY, Somerset Map 3

### THE RED LION HOTEL, Glastonbury Road, West Pennard

*Built around 1678, the Red Lion has been sympathetically restored to retain the original flag stone floors, log fires and beam and stone interior. The atmosphere is relaxed and friendly, enhanced by welcoming staff, and provides an ideal setting in which to enjoy the excellent food. All dishes are individually prepared, beautifully presented and in generous portions.*
ACCOMMODATION £31–£40
FOOD up to £15
**Hours:** breakfast 8am – 9:30am; lunch 12noon – 2:30pm; dinner 7pm – 9pm. **Cuisine:** English / continental:- Restaurant menu and bar snacks. Dishes may include Breast of Duck with Cherry Sauce, Veal Portuguese. All dishes individually prepared. **Rooms:** 7 bedrooms, all en suite. **Credit cards:** Visa, Access, AmEx. **Other points:** licensed, Sunday lunch, children catered for – please check for age limits. **Directions:** A361 between Shepton Mallet and Glastonbury in West Pennard.
BOB BUSKIN, LORRAINE JESSEMEY & PARTNERS, tel (0458) 832941.

## GODSHILL, Isle Of Wight Map 4

### ESSEX COTTAGE, High Street

*One of the oldest buildings in Godshill and listed in the Domesday Book, Essex Cottage now houses an excellent restaurant. The menus offer a good choice of well-cooked, imaginative dishes featuring predominantly fresh, local produce. An interesting restaurant with a good reputation for the high quality food, good value for money, and warm welcome. Booking recommended.*
FOOD £15–£20
**Hours:** bar meals 10am – 9:30pm; lunch 12noon – 2:30pm; dinner 7pm – 9:30pm. **Cuisine:** English / French:- Anglo/French cuisine including old English style dishes such as Pheasant in sherry with cream, apples & raisins, Lamb with Lavender. Vegetarian & vegan. **Credit cards:** Visa, Access. **Other points:** licensed, open-air dining, Sunday lunch, no-smoking

area, children catered for – please check for age limits, afternoon tea. **Directions:** A3020, on the main Newport to Shanklin road in Godshill.
ROY & CHRISTINE DALBY, tel (0983) 840232.

## GOSPORT, Hampshire Map 4

### ALVERBANK HOUSE HOTEL, Stokesbay Road, Alverstoke
Victorian country house comfortably furnished and decorated with excellent views of the bay. Popular with both holiday-makers and locals, this establishment enjoys a lively atmosphere. Offering generous portions of good food, first class service, and accommodation of a high quality.
ACCOMMODATION £21–£30
FOOD up to £15  ★
**Hours:** breakfast 7am – 9am; lunch 12noon – 2:30pm; bar meals 12noon – 2:30pm; dinner 7pm – 9:30pm; bar meals 7pm – 9:30pm. **Cuisine:**- A la carte and fixed price menus, using local fresh produce where possible. **Rooms:** 8 bedrooms all with tea making facilities, telephone, TV: 1 single, 1 twin, 1 twin ensuite, 2 doubles, 3 doubles ensuite. **Credit cards:** Visa, Access, Diners, AmEx. **Other points:** fully licensed, open-air dining, Sunday lunch, children catered for – please check for age limits, afternoon tea, parking, vegetarian meals, disabled access. **Directions:** exit M27 to Fareham, follow A32 for 3 miles, signposted Stokes Bay.
MR PATRICK DOYLE, tel (0705) 510005, fax (0705) 520864.

### BELLE VUE HOTEL, 39 Marine Parade East, Lee-on-the-Solent
Situated on the seafront, overlooking the Solent this modern yet traditional hotel offers comfortable accommodation for a wide range of visitors. The food in the restaurant can be enjoyed in relaxed surroundings.
ACCOMMODATION £21–£30
FOOD up to £15
**Hours:** open bank holidays 7pm; breakfast 7:15am – 9:15am; lunch 12noon – 2pm; bar meals 12noon – 2pm; dinner 7pm – 9:45pm. **Cuisine:** English:- Menu includes a good selection of fish, meat, grills and vegetarian dishes and may feature potted prawns and avocado fans. Grilled whole lemon sole, rack of English lamb set on a delicious sauce. **Rooms:** 27 bedrooms 4 singles ensuite, 19 doubles ensuite, 4 twins ensuite. **Credit cards:** Visa, Access, AmEx. **Other points:** licensed, open-air dining, Sunday lunch, no-smoking area, children catered for – please check for age limits, patio, entertainment. **Directions:** M27 Junction 8 or 11, to Fareham – to Lee on Solent, approx 8 mins.
MR T BELLASIS, tel (0705) 550258, fax (0705) 552624.

## GRAMPOUND, Cornwall Map 1

### EASTERN PROMISE CHINESE RESTAURANT, 1 Moorview
Attractive and roomy, beautifully decorated with matching furnishings, flowers on the tables, and comfortable chairs. Excellent cuisine, efficient and personal service, and a quiet, friendly atmosphere all adds to overall ambiance of this professional restaurant.
FOOD £15–£20
**Hours:** dinner 6pm – 11pm; closed Wednesday.
**Cuisine:** Chinese:- A la carte and Table d'hote menus, offering dishes of the highest quality of China's most famous regional cuisine, such as Cantonese, Peking and Szechuan, complemented by an extensive Wine list. Vegetarian meals available. **Credit cards:** Visa, Access, Diners, AmEx. **Other points:** licensed, children catered for – please check for age limits, vegetarian meals, parking, bank holidays, air-conditioned. **Directions:** between Truro and St Austell.
PHILIP & LISA TSE, tel (0726) 883033.

## GUNNISLAKE, Cornwall Map 1

### HINGSTON HOUSE COUNTRY HOTEL, St Ann's Chapel
A charming Georgian country house, set in spacious gardens and with breathtaking views of the Tamar Valley, offering good food and accommodation in attractive, relaxed surroundings. Mr & Mrs Shelvey have created a relaxed and delightful hotel where their hospitality and warm welcome extends to each and every guest. An ideal central base for touring Devon and Cornwall.
ACCOMMODATION £21–£30
FOOD up to £15  ★
**Hours:** breakfast 7am – 9am; dinner 7:30pm – 8pm.
**Cuisine:** English:- Varied selection of home cooked meals – 4 course with coffee and mints. We also offer an alternative menu, including fish, scampi, chicken, steak, etc, served with vegetables, salad, etc. **Rooms:** 10 bedrooms all with tea making facilities, TV: 1 single ensuite, 1 double, 1 twin, 1 family room ensuite, 1 twin ensuite, 5 doubles ensuite. **Credit cards:** Visa, Access. **Other points:** licensed, open-air dining, no-smoking area, children catered for – please check for age limits, pets allowed, bank holidays, residents' lounge, residents' bar, vegetarian meals, parking. **Directions:** on A390, between Tavistock & Callington. Near St Mellion Golf Course.
MR W A SHELVEY, tel (0822) 832468.

## HAYTOR, Devon Map 2

### THE MOORLAND HOTEL, Nr Newton Abbot, Dartmoor
Nestling at the southern foot of Haytor rocks, the Moorland Hotel is set in a delightful aspect of the moors commanding spectacular views across the rolling Devonshire countryside. All bedrooms are equipped with many modern facilities and two rooms have traditional four-poster beds. The elegant and comfortable Agatha Christie Lounge with its stylish cocktail bar is named after the famous author who completed her first novel whilst staying here. A function room provides a perfect venue for wedding receptions. There is a patio

restaurant which is ideal for bar meals, mid-morning coffee and traditional cream teas.
*ACCOMMODATION £31–£40*
*FOOD up to £15*
**Hours:** breakfast 8am – 9:30am; lunch 12noon – 2pm; bar snacks 12noon – 2pm; bar snacks 6:30pm – 9:45pm; dinner 7pm – 9:30pm. **Cuisine:** English. **Credit cards:** Visa, Access. **Other points:** children catered for – please check for age limits, parking, afternoon teas, disabled access, pets, garden, open-air dining, vegetarian meals, functions. **Directions:** from Bovey Tracey pick up Haytor/Widecombe signs.
MONICA ANN SIMPSON, tel (0364) 661407, fax (0364) 661573.

## HOLTON, Somerset Map 3

### THE OLD INN, Nr Wincanton
*The Old Inn is a 350 year old coaching inn with a small, intimate restaurant. The bar has an original flagstone floor and inglenook fireplace. The Inn is situated halfway between London and the West Country.*
*FOOD up to £15*
**Hours:** last orders 7pm – 10pm; bar – weekdays 11:30am – 3pm; bar – Saturday 11:30am – 11pm; lunch 12noon – 2pm; bar – Sunday 12noon – 3pm; dinner 7pm – 12midnight; bar – Sunday 7pm – 10:30pm. **Cuisine:** English:- A la carte menu, extensive wine list. 4 course Sunday lunch if booked by previous Saturday. Wide range of bar meals from sandwiches to steaks. **Credit cards:** Visa, Access. **Other points:** licensed, open-air dining, Sunday lunch, beer garden, pets allowed, coach/prior arr. **Directions:** just off A303 in centre of Holton, 1 mile from Wincanton.
MARTIN & LINDA LUPTON, tel (0963) 32002.

## HONITON, Devon Map 2

### MONKTON COURT INN, Monkton, Nr Honiton
*An imposing building approximately 300 years old, offering a warm and friendly welcome, good food and drink in a convivial and rambling country-style atmosphere. Recommended!*
*ACCOMMODATION £21–£30*
*FOOD up to £15*
**Hours:** breakfast 8am – 9am; bar meals 11:30am – 2pm; bar meals 6:30pm – 9:30pm; dinner 6:30pm – 9:30pm. **Cuisine:** English:- English homestyle country cooking at its best, offering local fresh fish, West Country salads, garnishes & tasty sauces. Bar Meals & Restaurant A la carte and Table D'Hote. **Rooms:** 8 bedrooms all with tea making facilities, telephone, radio, TV: 1 single, 1 twin, 4 doubles ensuite, 1 twin ensuite, 1 family room ensuite. **Credit cards:** Visa, Access. **Other points:** licensed, open-air dining, Sunday lunch, children catered for – please check for age limits, garden, parking, residents' bar, residents' lounge. **Directions:** on south side of A30/303, 2 miles east of Honiton, in village of Monkton, opposite Church.
JOHN & MARGERY TAYLOR, tel (0404) 42309.

## ILFRACOMBE, Devon Map 2

### DEDES HOTEL AND WHEEL INN, PUB AND RESTAURANT, 1–3 The Promenade
*Situated on the Victorian promenade overlooking the sea, incorporating the wheel room. A delightful character restaurant and bar featuring exposed stonework, beams and old coaching wheels.*
*ACCOMMODATION under £20*
*FOOD up to £15*
**Hours:** breakfast 8am – 10am; lunch 12noon – 2pm; dinner 6pm – 10pm. **Cuisine:** modern English:- Quality steaks and fresh, local seafood in season including fresh lobster. **Rooms:** 17 bedrooms all with tea making facilities, TV: 5 singles, 3 twins ensuite, 3 doubles ensuite, 4 triples ensuite, 2 quads ensuite. **Credit cards:** Visa, Access, Diners, AmEx. **Other points:** Sunday lunch, disabled access, children catered for – please check for age limits, cots. **Directions:** A361 to Ilfracombe, situated on the promenade.
MR & MRS C I CAWTHORNE, tel (0721) 862545.

### HEADLANDS HOTEL, 7 Capstone Crescent
*A 100 year-old terraced hotel set in its own cliff garden in a popular holiday resort. Offering good wholesome food, nothing is too much trouble for the proprietors whose aim is to please. Older, retired clientele. Near to harbour.*
*ACCOMMODATION up to £20*
*FOOD up to £15*
**Hours:** breakfast 8.30am, dinner 6.15pm. **Cuisine:** English. **Rooms:** 19 bedrooms, some ensuite. **Other points:** parking nearby, pets allowed, residents' lounge, garden. **Directions:** in the harbour area, near Royal Britannia Public Hospital.
J, V, D & B ANGOLD, tel (0271) 862887.

### THE ILFRACOMBE CARLTON, Runnacleave Road
*Situated in a central location adjacent to the beach, this hotel offers fresh, well cooked food in pleasant surroundings. Comfortable accommodation and friendly attentive service. Ilfracombe offers its visitors a choice of recreational and sporting activities, a spectacular coastline and secluded bays.*
*ACCOMMODATION under £20*
*FOOD up to £15* ★
**Hours:** breakfast 8:30am – 9:30am; lunch 12noon – 2pm; dinner 7pm – 8:30pm. **Cuisine:** English:- Traditional English food. **Rooms:** 48 bedrooms all with tea making facilities, telephone, radio, TV: 8 singles ensuite, 18 twins ensuite, 15 doubles ensuite, 6 triples ensuite, 1 quad ensuite. **Credit cards:** Visa, Access, Diners, AmEx. **Other points:** Sunday lunch, children catered for – please check for age limits, afternoon tea, baby-listening device, cots, 24hr reception, residents' lounge, residents' bar. **Directions:** off the A361, close to the beach front.
DAWN MARSHALL, tel (0271) 862446, fax (0271) 865379.

### SHELLEYS COTTAGE HOTEL,
Watersmeet Road, Lynton
*A quiet, peaceful hotel and restaurant set in its own shrub gardens in a beautiful Devon village. The proprietors personally supervise the day-to-day running of the hotel, ensuring that every guests need is catered for. Ideal base from which to explore the Valley of Rocks, Glen Lyn Gorge and the Devon countryside.*
ACCOMMODATION up to £20
FOOD up to £15
**Hours:** breakfast 8.30am – 9.30am, lunch 12 noon – 2.30pm, dinner 7pm – 9pm, closed December and January except New Years Day. **Cuisine:** English. **Rooms:** 10 bedrooms all with TV, radio, tea making facilities. **Credit cards:** Visa, Access, AmEx. **Other points:** children catered for – check for age limits, no smoking area, pets allowed, residents' lounge, vegetarian meals, garden. **Directions:** A39, end of Watersmeet Road, bottom of Lynmouth Hill.
MRS & MRS PRIDEAUX, tel (0598) 53219.

### ST BRANNOCKS HOUSE HOTEL,
St Brannocks Road
*A detached Victorian hotel set in its own grounds and close to the beautiful Bicclescombe Park, Cairn Nature Reserve, town centre and seafront. The cosy well stocked bar is an ideal place to relax and socialise, the dining room offers generous portions of good home cooked food and a selection of table wines. An ideal base for a perfect family holiday or special break.*
ACCOMMODATION up to £20
FOOD up to £15
**Hours:** breakfast 8.30am – 9am; dinner at 6.30pm; bar snacks 12 noon – 2pm and 8pm – 9.30pm. **Cuisine:** English. **Rooms:** 16 bedrooms all with tea making facilities, TV, radio. **Credit cards:** Visa, Access, AmEx. **Other points:** children catered for – please check for age limits, parking, pets allowed, residents' lounge. **Directions:** approach from Barnstaple on A361. Hotel is on left side heading into town.
MRS B CLARKE, tel (0271) 863873.

### TORRS HOTEL, Torrs Park
*This hotel is in a commanding position at the end of the Torrs Walk which follows the cliff along the coast. The hotel has lovely views of the surrounding countryside.*
ACCOMMODATION £21–£30
FOOD up to £15
**Hours:** breakfast 8:30am – 9:30am; dinner 6:30pm – 7:30pm; closed November – February. **Cuisine:** English:- Roasts, grills, home cooked dishes. **Rooms:** 14 bedrooms all en suite and with colour TV, clock radio and tea/coffee facilities. **Credit cards:** Visa, Access, Diners, AmEx. **Other points:** licensed, open-air dining, Sunday lunch, special diets, children catered for – please check for age limits. **Directions:** off the A399 or A361 at the end of the Torrs Walk.
MR R I COOK, tel (0271) 862334.

### TRAFALGAR HOTEL, Larkstone Terrace,
Hillsborough Road
*A 250 year old Grade II listed hotel, retaining many of its original features and furnished to a high standard. Offering excellent sea and woodland views from comfortable rooms, a pleasant, relaxing stay is assured. Live music is provided at weekends.*
ACCOMMODATION £21–£30
FOOD up to £15
**Hours:** breakfast 8:30am – 9:30am; lunch 12noon – 2pm; bar snacks 6pm – 9pm; dinner 6:30pm – 8pm. **Cuisine:** English. **Credit cards:** Visa, Access, Diners, AmEx. **Other points:** parking, children catered for – please check for age limits, afternoon teas, pets, residents' lounge, vegetarian meals. **Directions:** continuation of High Street from A361 direction.
TONY AND JUNE WHITE, tel (0271) 862145, (0271) 863745.

### UPSTAIRS RESTAURANT, Mullacott Cross
*High above Ilfracombe with unrestricted views to Lundy Isles, the Welsh coast and Exmoor.*
FOOD up to £15
**Hours:** dinner 6pm – 10pm; closed October – Easter. **Cuisine:** modern English:- Carvery with best quality steaks. Children's menu. **Credit cards:** Visa, Access, Diners, AmEx. **Other points:** open-air dining, Sunday lunch, children catered for – please check for age limits. **Directions:** found on the A361 Mullacott roundabout.
MRS C J NAPPER, tel (0271) 863780, (0271) 865500.

## IVYBRIDGE, Devon Map 2

### THE CROOKED SPIRE INN, Ermington
*A quiet, comfortable inn, in the middle of Ermington village square – best kept village in 1985 and 1986, where the welcome is warm and friendly. Booking advisable.*
ACCOMMODATION £21–£30
FOOD up to £15
**Hours:** breakfast 7am – 10am; lunch 11:30am – 2:30pm; dinner 7pm – 11pm; closed Christmas 25/12. **Cuisine:** English:- At least 2 dozen varied main courses always available. All prepared on the premises. **Rooms:** 3 bedrooms all with colour TV. **Credit cards:** Visa, Access. **Other points:** open-air dining, Sunday lunch, children catered for – please check for age limits, vegetarian meals, parking. **Directions:** 2 miles south of A38 at Ivybridge Junction.
JIM SHIELD & GERALDINE TAYLOR, tel (0548) 830202.

### IMPERIAL INN, 28 Western Road
*A charming Olde Worlde village pub adorned with window boxes with a large welcoming open fire and a warm welcome to match. There is a large beer garden and a separate children's play area with playground equipment.*
FOOD up to £15
**Hours:** lunch 12noon – 2pm; dinner 6pm – 10pm. **Cuisine:** modern English:- Many daily specials – home cooked meals to hot beef curry, variety of local fresh fish

including our fresh Avon mussels in wine and cream sauce. From sauted lambs kidneys to chicken marengo and much more. **Other points:** open-air dining, Sunday lunch, children catered for – please check for age limits, coach/prior arr. **Directions:** follow A38 from Plymouth (7 miles). PHILIP GRIMES, tel (0752) 892269.

## KINGSBRIDGE, Devon Map 2

### THE ASHBURTON ARMS, West Charleton
*A very friendly pub, serving excellent home-made food at good value for money. The steaks are particularly good, served on hot stones so they continue to cook at the table, and there is a good wine list. The pub is set on a main tourist route, in an area of outstanding natural beauty. Well worth visiting.*
ACCOMMODATION under £20
FOOD up to £15
**Hours:** lunch 12noon – 1:45pm; dinner 7pm – 9pm. **Cuisine:** English:- Dishes include speciality 'steak on the rocks', served on hot stones. Vegetarian dish of the day. Desserts such as pavlova & treacle tart. All home-made. Fresh fish always on the menu. **Rooms:** 4 bedrooms all with tea making facilities, radio, TV: 1 double, 1 twin, 2 singles. **Credit cards:** Visa, Access. **Other points:** Sunday lunch, no-smoking area, children catered for – please check for age limits. **Directions:** on A379, 1.5 miles east of Kingsbridge on Tor crossroads. BRIAN & ELIZABETH SAUNDERS, tel (0548) 531242.

### ASHLEIGH HOUSE, Ashleigh Road
*An elegant white painted Victorian house with bright, airy rooms, tastefully decorated and furnished and situated only a short walk from the town centre. An ideal place to relax. The Towners pride themselves on their personal service and relaxed atmosphere.*
ACCOMMODATION under £20
FOOD up to £15
**Hours:** open all year 7pm; breakfast 8:30am – 9:15am; dinner 6:45pm. **Cuisine:** English. **Rooms:** 4 double, 3 twin and 1 family bedroom. 2 showers. All first floor rooms have private facilities at £2.50 extra. Tea/coffee making facilities in all rooms. **Credit cards:** Visa, Access. **Other points:** children catered for – please check for age limits, pets allowed, residents' lounge, TV lounge, garden, ETB – 2 crowns. **Directions:** Ashleigh Rd is off the A381 towards Salcombe on the edge of town. MRS C TOWNER, tel (0548) 852893, fax (0548) 852893

### WHITE HOUSE HOTEL, Chillington
*The White House Hotel is a lovely Georgian house set in an acre of lawned and terraced gardens and is just two miles from the coast. It offers excellent food and friendly service in peaceful and relaxed surroundings.*
ACCOMMODATION £31–£40
FOOD up to £15
**Hours:** breakfast 8:30am – 9:30am; dinner 7pm – 10pm. **Cuisine:** English:- All dishes are home made with constant change of fixed menu eg. Roast rack of lamb,

fresh lemon sole. **Rooms:** 7 bedrooms, all ensuite. TV and direct-dial telephone in all rooms. **Credit cards:** Visa, Access. **Other points:** licensed, children catered for – please check for age limits, pets/prior arr, residents' lounge, TV all rooms. **Directions:** on A379 between Kingsbridge and Dartmouth. MICHAEL ROBERTS & DAVID ALFORD, tel (0548) 580580, fax (0548) 581124.

## KINGSCLERE, Hampshire Map 4

### THE VINE INN, Hannington
*An exceptional country inn in a prime location off the A339 in this charming village. The Vine incorporates a large freehouse pub, new 42 seater Conservatory, and an a la carte restaurant, offering varied menus seven days a week. The Matthews have gained a considerable reputation locally for their food.*
FOOD up to £15
**Hours:** lunch 12noon – 2pm; dinner 6:30pm – 9:30pm. **Cuisine:** English:- Famous pies, reputable steaks, choice of vegetarian meals in bar and conservatory and a seasonally changing a la carte menu. **Credit cards:** Visa, Access, Diners, AmEx. **Other points:** open-air dining, children catered for – please check for age limits. **Directions:** off the A339. MR & MRS MATTHEWS, tel (0635) 298525.

## LIFTON, Devon Map 2

### LIFTON COTTAGE HOTEL
*A Gothic-style building, most of which is 400 years old, situated in Lifton, one of the earliest Saxon villages in Devon. Ideal for touring both Devon and Cornwall, the village being halfway between the outstanding wild country of the great moors – Dartmoor and Bodmin Moor. Fishing, shooting, riding, golf and water sports available in the immediate area.*
ACCOMMODATION £21–£30
FOOD up to £15
**Hours:** breakfast 8am – 9am; lunch 12noon – 2pm; bar meals 12noon – 2pm; dinner 7pm – 9pm; bar meals 7pm – 10pm. **Cuisine:** English:- English and international cuisine with an interesting wine list. **Rooms:** 12 bedrooms all with tea making facilities, telephone, TV: 1 single ensuite, 3 singles, 2 twins ensuite, 3 doubles ensuite, 2 triples ensuite, 1 quad ensuite. **Credit cards:** Visa, Access, Diners, AmEx. **Other points:** licensed, Sunday lunch, children catered for – please check for age limits, pets allowed, bank holidays, cots, log fires. **Directions:** A30, halfway through village on main road. MR & MRS DODDS, tel (0566) 784863, fax 0566 784770.

## LINWOOD, Hampshire Map 4

### HIGH CORNER INN, Nr Ringwood
*A 17th century inn tucked well away in the heart of the New Forest. Situated some 6 miles north of Ringwood with indoor and outdoor facilities for children.*

*ACCOMMODATION £31–£40*
*FOOD up to £15*
**Hours:** lunch – except Sunday 12noon – 2pm; lunch –
Sunday 12noon – 2:15pm; dinner – except Sunday
6:30pm – 10pm; dinner – Sunday 7pm – 10pm. **Cuisine:**
English:- Venison in season, homecooked food including
steak & kidney pie and daily specials. **Rooms:** 7
bedrooms all en suite, ETB 3 crowns commended.
**Credit cards:** Visa, Access, Diners, AmEx. **Other
points:** Sunday lunch, children catered for – please
check for age limits, squash, forest walks, playland, d.i.y
stables. **Directions:** between the A31 and the A338, 6
miles north of Ringwood.
MR & MRS R KERNAN, tel (0425) 473973, fax (0425)
480015.

---

## LONGHAM, Dorset Map 3

### ANGEL INN, Wimborne
*Situated on the busy road between Poole and
Southampton. The menu is varied and quite extensive
with the emphasis on well cooked, generous portions of
food.*
*FOOD up to £15*
**Hours:** lunch 12noon – 2pm; dinner 6pm – 9:30pm.
**Cuisine:** English:- Dorset pate, steak and kidney pie,
steaks, daily specials. **Credit cards:** Visa, Access.
**Other points:** Sunday lunch, children catered for –
please check for age limits, garden, playland.
**Directions:** On the Poole to Southampton Road.
MR B SIMS, tel (0202) 873778.

---

## LOOE, Cornwall Map 1

### ALLHAYS COUNTRY HOUSE, Talland Bay
*A period country house standing in 'an English country
garden' with spectacular views over to Talland Bay. A
Victorian style conservatory extends the dining room
into the garden for dining alfresco whatever the weather.
Allhays has an enviable reputation for its food.*
*ACCOMMODATION £31–£40*
*FOOD up to £15* ⓒ ★
**Hours:** breakfast 8:30am – 9am; dinner 7pm. **Cuisine:**
modern English:- New English cuisine using the finest
local and homegrown produce, freshly prepared and
cooked in the Aga by chef Patronne Lynda Spring.
British cheeses. **Rooms:** 7 bedrooms all with tea making
facilities, telephone, radio, TV: 2 twins ensuite, 1 twin, 3
doubles ensuite, 1 double. **Credit cards:** Visa, Access,
AmEx. **Other points:** pets allowed, children catered for
– please check for age limits, vegetarian meals, parking,
residents' bar, residents' lounge, disabled access.
**Directions:** turn left 2.5 miles from Looe on A387.
Follow Hotel signposts.
BRIAN & LYNDA SPRING, tel (0503) 72434, fax
(0503) 72929.

### COOMBE FARM, Widegates
*Delightful country house in ten acres of grounds with
superb views to the sea, and with glorious walks and*
*beaches nearby. Coombe Farm has a croquet lawn,
heated outdoor pool and snooker and table tennis
facilities, and there are many birds and animals in the
grounds, including horses and peacocks. The food is
superb and can be enjoyed in candlelit surroundings
with real log fires.*
*ACCOMMODATION £21–£30*
*FOOD up to £15*
**Hours:** breakfast 8:30am – 9am; dinner 7pm – 7:30pm;
closed November – February. **Cuisine:** breakfast.
**Rooms:** 10 bedrooms all with tea making facilities,
telephone, radio, TV: 3 doubles ensuite, 3 twins ensuite,
4 family rooms ensuite. **Other points:** central heating,
children catered for – please check for age limits,
residents' lounge, garden, swimming pool. **Directions:**
just south of Widegates on the B3253, between Looe and
Hessonford.
ALEXANDER & SALLY LOW, tel (05034) 223.

### PANORAMA HOTEL, Hannafore Road,
West Looe
*Superbly situated with outstanding views over the
harbour, cliffs and beaches, The Panorama is a well-
appointed, family run hotel. Friendly, welcoming service
is just one illustration of the care shown to ensure that
guests have an enjoyable stay. Good, wholesome food
awaits you in the Tudor dining room and there is a
lounge bar in which to relax.*
*ACCOMMODATION £31–£40*
*FOOD up to £15*
**Hours:** breakfast 8:30am – 9am; dinner 6:30pm – 7pm.
**Cuisine:** English:- Good homecooking using fresh
produce and locally caught fish whenever available.
Non-residents welcome for dinner. **Rooms:** 10 bedrooms
all with tea making facilities, TV: 2 singles ensuite, 1
twin ensuite, 4 doubles ensuite, 3 family rooms ensuite.
**Credit cards:** Visa, Access. **Other points:** licensed,
children catered for – please check for age limits, special
diets, special breaks, garden, parking, residents' bar.
**Directions:** take the A387 to West Looe (10 miles west
of Plymouth).
JACKIE & ALAN RUSSELL, tel (0503) 262123.

### PELYNT DAGGER RESTAURANT,
14 Barton Meadow, Pelynt By Looe
*A warm welcome awaits you at this popular family-run
restaurant, serving quality meals at value for money
prices. Comfortable lounge area to sit and make your
choice from our comprehensive menu, in a relaxing and
friendly atmosphere.*
*FOOD up to £15* CLUB
**Hours:** last orders 6:30pm – 8:45pm; dinner 6pm –
11:30pm; closed end October – December. **Cuisine:**
English / continental:- Local beef, steak Portuguese,
Awarding winning duckling, Roast Sunday Lunch.
**Credit cards:** Visa, Access, AmEx. **Other points:**
licensed, open-air dining, Sunday lunch, children catered
for – please check for age limits, parking. **Directions:** 4
miles from Looe on B3359 in Pelynt village.
JOHN & JOAN BLAKE, tel (0503) 220386.

**PUNCHBOWL INN,** *Lanreath, Nr Looe*
*This oak-beamed inn is over 400 years old and has served as the Court House, a Coaching Inn and Smugglers' Distribution House in its time! It now offers visitors a chance to enjoy traditional hospitality within its historic walls.*
ACCOMMODATION £21–£30
FOOD up to £15
**Hours:** breakfast 8:30am – 9:30am; lunch 12noon – 2pm; dinner 7pm – 9pm. **Cuisine:** English:- Table d'Hote and a la carte. Traditional English, seasonal fish menu and ice cream specialities. Bar snack menu. **Rooms:** 14 bedrooms, 12 en suite. **Credit cards:** Visa, Access. **Other points:** licensed, Sunday lunch, no-smoking area, children catered for – please check for age limits, pets allowed, beer garden, vegetarian meals, residents' bar, residents' lounge, parking. **Directions:** off the B3359 in the centre of Lanreath village. HARVEY & SYLVIA FRITH, tel (0503) 220218.

---

# LULWORTH COVE, Dorset Map 3

## MILL HOUSE HOTEL & BISHOP'S COTTAGE, West Lulworth, Wareham
*Once the Bishop of Salisbury's home, the house stands in its own grounds on the edge of the Cove and is sheltered by Bindon Hill. The grounds have direct access to coastal heritage cliffs and the Cove.*
ACCOMMODATION £21–£30
FOOD up to £15
**Hours:** open all year 7pm; breakfast 8am – 9:30am; lunch 12noon – 2:30pm; bar meals 12noon – 2:30pm; dinner 6pm – 10pm; bar meals 6pm – 10pm. **Cuisine:** seafood:- Seafood, local fish, vegetarian dishes. **Rooms:** 26 bedrooms all with tea making facilities, telephone, radio, TV: 3 singles, 5 doubles, 16 doubles ensuite, 2 family rooms ensuite. **Credit cards:** Visa, Access. **Other points:** licensed, Sunday lunch, children catered for – please check for age limits, swimming pool, pets allowed. **Directions:** Overlooking Lulworth Cove. MRS ELIZABETH RUDD, tel (092941) 261, (092941) 404.

---

# LYDFORD, Devon Map 2

## THE CASTLE INN HOTEL, Okehampton
*A delightful 16th Century Free House, overlooked by Lydford Castle, and set in one of the loveliest parts of Devon. Featured in the film* The Hound of the Baskervilles, *The Castle Inn is a traditional West Country Inn, offering good food, fine ales, comfortable accommodation and a very warm welcome. Nearby visitor attractions, include Lydford Gorge and the beautiful wild moors.*
ACCOMMODATION £21–£30
FOOD up to £15
**Hours:** breakfast 8am – 9am; bar meals 12noon – 2:30pm; bar meals 6:30pm – 9:30pm; dinner 7pm – 9:30pm. **Cuisine:** English:- A la carte and table d'hote menus, using freshly cooked food and local produce.

Dishes may include, Guinea Fowl, Whiskied Steak, and Salmon Cutlets. **Rooms:** 8 bedrooms all with tea making facilities, radio, TV: 2 twins ensuite, 3 doubles ensuite, 2 doubles, 1 triple ensuite. **Credit cards:** Visa, Access, Diners, AmEx. **Other points:** licensed, open-air dining, Sunday lunch, no-smoking area, children catered for – please check for age limits, pets allowed, parking, garden, disabled access, residents' lounge, vegetarian meals, cots, 24hr reception, left luggage. **Directions:** take the Lydford turning off A386 between Okehampton & Tavistock. CLIVE & MO WALKER, tel (082282) 242, fax (0822882) 454.

---

# LYME REGIS, Dorset Map 3

## BELL CLIFF RESTAURANT, 5/6 Broad Street
*A small, homely restaurant, slightly Dickensian in appearance, with excellent service, quality and ambiance. The building dates from the 16th century and was used in the film* The French Lieutenants Woman *as the 'Old Fossil Depot'. Well placed in the centre of town and popular with both locals and holiday-makers.*
FOOD up to £15
**Hours:** meals all day – summer 8:30am – 6pm; meals all day – winter 9am – 5pm. **Cuisine:** English:- English home cooking. Specialities include home-made sweets and cakes. **Other points:** licensed, Sunday lunch, children catered for – please check for age limits, disabled access, pets allowed, afternoon tea, parking. **Directions:** Off A35 on A3052 or A3070. At sea end of main thoroughfare (A3052). RICHARD & AUDREY EVANS, tel (0297) 442459.

## BENSONS RESTAURANT, 65 Broad Street
*A small, elegantly furnished restaurant offering outstanding food at reasonable prices. The a la carte menu provides a good choice of imaginative, excellently cooked and presented dishes. Welcoming and efficient service and a good wine list complement the quality of the food. A varying fixed price menu is available on weekdays.*
FOOD up to £15
**Hours:** dinner 6:30pm – 9pm; closed Sundays except August – and bank holidays; closed – Sunday & Monday mid-October – Easter. **Cuisine:** French:- Predominantly French-style cuisine. House specialities include Salmon Fillet with Asparagus, Benson's Tournedos, Scampi Portugaise, Pork Normandy, Sole Veronique, Sole Fine Herbes. **Credit cards:** Visa, Access, AmEx. **Other points:** licensed, children catered for – please check for age limits. **Directions:** At bottom of hill on main street, next to car park, opposite sea. WILLIAM ROBERT BENSON, tel (0297) 442049.

## KERSBROOK HOTEL & RESTAURANT, Pound Road
*A thatched 18th century listed house, set in its own gardens overlooking Lyme Bay. Carefully modernised to retain the original character of the building and to offer*

a high standard of comfort and convenience. The food is of a high standard and the restaurant boasts an extensive wine list for every occasion.
ACCOMMODATION £31–£40
FOOD £15–£20 CLUB
**Hours:** breakfast 8:30am – 9:30am; lunch 12:15pm – 2:15pm. **Cuisine:** English / continental:- Full a la carte menu and table d'hote. **Rooms:** 10 double, 2 twin all en suite. **Credit cards:** Visa, Access, Diners, AmEx. **Other points:** licensed, residents' lounge, garden. **Directions:** From main Lyme Regis – Exeter road, turn right opp. main car park.
ERIC HALL STEPHENSON, tel (0297) 442596.

### ROYAL LION HOTEL, Broad Street
A 17th Century Coaching Inn in the centre of this attractive little town, equipped with a large games room, with snooker and table tennis tables. Apart from being the home town of many writers, artists and artisans, Lyme Regis is famous for being the location of United Artists' French Lieutenants' Woman.
FOOD up to £15
**Hours:** breakfast 8:30am – 9:30am; lunch 12noon – 2pm; dinner 6:30pm – 9:30pm. **Cuisine:** English:- Fresh sirloin steak. **Rooms:** 30 bedrooms all en suite. **Credit cards:** Visa, Access, Diners, AmEx. **Other points:** Sunday lunch, children catered for – please check for age limits, coach/prior arr, leisure centre, swimming pool. **Directions:** In the centre of Lyme Regis.
MR & MRS B A SIENESI, tel (02974) 445622, (02974) 442014.

## LYMINGTON, Hampshire Map 4

### PEELERS BISTRO, Gosport Street
Built in 1700 as a Police Station, Peelers no longer dishes out law and order but rather serves a wide range of delicious food with a well deserved reputation for its fish. An extremely popular restaurant especially in the evenings. Close to the Isle of Wight ferry in a mainly cobbled road. Acclaimed as "Restaurant of the Year" in 1992, where to eat in Hants/Wilts.
ACCOMMODATION under £20
FOOD up to £15
**Hours:** breakfast 8:30am – 9am; lunch 12noon – 1:45pm; dinner (July–Sept.) 6:30pm – 10:30pm; dinner 7pm – 10:15pm. **Cuisine:** modern English:- Fresh fish and pasta. **Rooms:** 2 bedrooms all with TV: 2 doubles ensuite. **Credit cards:** Visa, Access. **Other points:** licensed, open-air dining, Sunday lunch, children catered for – please check for age limits. **Directions:** bottom of Lymington High Street, turn left into Gosport St, Peelers is 100 yd along on the left-hand side.
MR & MRS W J SMITH, tel (0590) 676165.

## LYNDHURST, Hampshire Map 4

### BELL INN HOTEL, Brook
17th century building set in the New Forest, but only 1 mile from Jct 1, on the M27. The food is of an excellent standard, and beautifully presented, and the rooms are very comfortable, many with forest views. A lovely friendly atmosphere prevails. The Inn has its own three 18 hole golf courses.
ACCOMMODATION over £50
FOOD £21–£25
**Hours:** breakfast 7:30am – 9:30am; lunch 12noon – 2pm; dinner 7:30pm – 9:30pm. **Cuisine:** English:- Dishes include Magret of Duckling, Scollops of Scottish Beef, Ragout of seafood, saddle of hare. Bar meals available, fresh local fish and game a speciality. **Rooms:** 20 bedrooms all with tea making facilities, telephone: 3 singles ensuite, 10 twins ensuite, 7 doubles ensuite. **Credit cards:** Visa, Access. **Other points:** children catered for – please check for age limits, pets allowed, garden. **Directions:** junction 1, M27 – B3078.
GAVIN SCOTT (MANAGER), tel (0703) 812214, fax (0703) 813958.

### THE NEW FOREST INN, Emery Down
In a delightful setting, in the heart of the New Forest, the inn dates back to the early 1700's when a caravan stood on this site claiming squatter's rights. Today, the caravan now forms part of the porchway.
FOOD up to £15
**Hours:** breakfast 8am – 9am; lunch 11:30am – 2pm; dinner 6pm – 9:30pm. **Cuisine:** English:- Game in season, eg. pheasant, venison. Old English recipes. **Rooms:** 4 bedrooms, all en suite. **Credit cards:** Visa, Access. **Other points:** open-air dining, Sunday lunch, children catered for – please check for age limits, coach/prior arr. **Directions:** located between A31/M27 and A35.
SUE & NICK EMBERLEY, tel (0703) 282329.

## LYNMOUTH, Devon Map 2

### THE BATH HOTEL, Lynmouth Street
Centrally located by picturesque Lynmouth Harbour, the hotel has a relaxed, friendly atmosphere in an ideal position for exploring Exmoor and many local attractions. The sun lounge serving traditional afternoon teas is open to non-residents. Two bars and garden serving bar lunches, and in the restaurant a set 5 course dinner menu is available, offering excellent value and a wide choice of different dishes.
ACCOMMODATION £21–£30
FOOD up to £15
**Hours:** breakfast 8:30am – 9:30am; bar meals 12noon – 2:15pm; lunch 12:30pm – 2pm; dinner 7pm – 8:30pm; closed November – March. **Cuisine:** English:- Bar snacks, lunches, teas and set dinner menu featuring specials and a vegetarian dish. Speciality of Wild Lyn Salmon, caught in our own trap, and Lynmouth Lobster dishes. **Rooms:** 24 bedrooms 1 single ensuite, 8 twins ensuite, 11 doubles ensuite, 4 family rooms ensuite. **Credit cards:** Visa, Access, Diners, AmEx. **Other points:** licensed, open-air dining, Sunday lunch, no-smoking area, children catered for – please check for age limits, afternoon tea, garden, pets allowed. **Directions:** situated on the A39 at Lynmouth.
MRS DALGARNO, tel (0598) 52238.

## CORNER HOUSE, *Riverside Road*

*A pleasant and comfortable establishment with large restaurant, spacious, airy rooms and garden with attractive shrubs and flowers overlooking the river and Lyn Valley. Ideal for visiting Exmoor, the Valley of Rocks and Waters Meet. Outside paved area for alfresco dining at umbrella tables.*

*ACCOMMODATION under £20*

*FOOD up to £15*

**Hours:** breakfast 8:30am – 11am; bar snacks 11:30am – 5pm; dinner 6pm – late; last orders 9pm; closed November – February; restaurant closed Saturday; restaurant closed Tuesday evening. **Cuisine:** English. **Rooms:** 3 bedrooms all with tea making facilities, TV: 3 doubles ensuite. **Credit cards:** Visa, Access. **Other points:** residents' parking, children catered for – please check for age limits, Sunday lunch, open bank holidays, afternoon tea, vegetarian meals, open-air dining, licensed. **Directions:** A39, on entry into Lynmouth you will see the black and white umbrellas along the river.
WHITWELL, ROBERT & PENELOPE, tel (0598) 53300.

## RISING SUN HOTEL, *Harbourside*

*A lovely 14th century thatched smugglers inn overlooking a small picturesque harbour and Lynmouth Bay. The hotel offers free salmon fishing for residents. The buildings were once smugglers' cottages with a wealth of intriguing staircases and narrow passages.*

*ACCOMMODATION £31–£40*

*FOOD £15–£20*

**Hours:** open all year Tuesday evening; breakfast 8:30am – 9:30am; lunch 12:30pm – 2pm; dinner 7pm – 9pm. **Cuisine:** English:- Seafood, game in season. **Rooms:** 16 bedrooms all with tea making facilities, telephone, radio, TV: 1 single ensuite, 3 twins ensuite, 11 doubles ensuite, 1 suite. **Credit cards:** Visa, Access, AmEx. **Other points:** licensed, open-air dining, Sunday lunch, coach/prior arr, baby-listening device, cots, residents' bar, residents' lounge, vegetarian meals, parking, children catered for – please check for age limits. **Directions:** exit 23 on the M5, then A39 to Lynmouth. Opposite sea harbour.
MR F ST H JEUNE, tel (0598) 53223, fax (0598) 53480.

## ROCK HOUSE HOTEL

*Perched on the waters edge overlooking Lynmouth's picturesque harbour, the Rock House Hotel has a backdrop of wooded trees. Tastefully decorated, the rooms are spacious and airy. Serving quality food at good value prices, the hotel is very popular with locals and holiday-makers alike, with its cheerful atmosphere.*

*ACCOMMODATION £21–£30*

*FOOD up to £15*

**Hours:** breakfast 8:45am – 9:45am; lunch 12noon – 2pm; dinner 7pm – 9pm. **Cuisine:** international:- Large and varied menu. Dishes include Crab soup, Escargots Bourguignonne, Guinea fowl, Hawaiian Duck, Peppered Steak, Steak Exmoor and a variety of sweets. **Rooms:** 6 rooms. 2 twin and 4 double bedrooms. 4 en suite. **Credit**

cards: Visa, Access, Diners, AmEx. **Other points:** licensed, open-air dining, Sunday lunch, garden, afternoon tea, pets/prior arr, picnic lunches. **Directions:** A39 to Lynton, then follow the short road down to Lynmouth.
MR MILLETT, tel (0598) 53508.

# LYNTON, Devon Map 2

## THE EXMOOR SANDPIPER INN, *Countisbury*

*A long, white, 13th century building of considerable charm and character at the top of Countisbury Hill with stunning views over Exmoor. The area is distinctly rural with sheep roaming the grounds, but the food and accommodation are sophisticated yet homely. An excellent base for walkers.*

*ACCOMMODATION £31–£40*

*FOOD £15–£20*

**Hours:** breakfast 8:30am – 9:30am; bar 11am – 11pm; lunch 12noon – 2:30pm; dinner 7pm – 10pm. **Cuisine:** English:- Large selection, table d'hote evening meal including garlic prawns, local venison in red wine, steaks, lobster, cold seafood platter, home-made soups. **Rooms:** 16 bedrooms all with tea making facilities, radio, TV: 2 twins ensuite, 2 family rooms ensuite, 12 doubles ensuite. **Other points:** licensed, open-air dining, Sunday lunch, children catered for – please check for age limits, pets/prior arr, parking, residents' lounge, residents' bar. **Directions:** on the A39 at the top of Countisbury Hill, outside of Lynton.
PERSONALLY RUN HOTELS LTD, tel (05987) 263, fax (05987) 358.

## MILLSLADE COUNTRY HOUSE HOTEL, *Brendon*

*An 18th century country house set in 9 acres of grounds in a quiet spot on the edge of Brendon village, surrounded by the forest and River Lynn. The hotel has fishing rights (salmon and trout) for their guests to enjoy and there are plenty of local attractions including Doone valley, Barnstaple and Minehead.*

*ACCOMMODATION £31–£40*

*FOOD £15–£20*

**Hours:** breakfast 8:30am – 9:30am; lunch 12noon – 2:30pm; dinner 7pm – 9:30pm. **Rooms:** 4 double, 2 twin and 1 family room, 5 en suite. Also 3 four-poster suites available. All rooms have colour TV and tea making facilities. **Credit cards:** Visa, AmEx, Diners. **Other points:** licensed, Sunday lunch, children catered for – please check for age limits, pets allowed, afternoon tea, bank holidays, residents' lounge, garden. **Directions:** 2 miles from Lynton, just off the A39.
E M FREWER, tel (05987) 322.

# MAIDENHEAD, Berkshire Map 6

## ANTONIA'S BAR BISTRO, *11 Bridge Street*

*Originally an old pub, and now tastefully redecorated in bistro style, offering a cosy, warm welcome in pleasant*

surroundings. The River Thames and Boulters Lock are just two of the many nearby places of interest to visit and explore.
FOOD up to £15

**Hours:** lunch 12noon – 2:30pm; meals all day – Sunday 12noon – 11pm; dinner 6pm – 11pm. **Cuisine:** Italian:- Country Italian style cuisine, offering a different house speciality every day. Vegetarian dishes also available. Good wine list. **Credit cards:** AmEx. **Other points:** licensed, open-air dining, no-smoking area, children catered for – please check for age limits, bank holidays, parking. **Directions:** situated off the A4.
ANTONIA TARTAGLIONE, tel (0628) 23670.

## CHAUNTRY HOUSE HOTEL, Bray On Thames

*An outstanding 18th century country house hotel situated in a delightful village close to Windsor and Heathrow Airport. No visitor can fail to be impressed by the friendly and relaxed atmosphere in this intimate restaurant.*
ACCOMMODATION £41–£50
FOOD £15–£20 ⓐ

**Hours:** breakfast 7:30am – 9:30am; lunch 12noon – 2pm; dinner 7:30pm – 9:30pm. **Cuisine:** English:- Imaginative English cuisine. Menu changes seasonally. House speciality – a selection of wild mushrooms tossed in butter with a julienne of bacon and a hint of garlic, served on a bed of winter leaves. **Rooms:** 13 bedrooms all with tea making facilities, telephone, mini bar, TV: 2 singles ensuite, 5 twins ensuite, 6 doubles ensuite. **Credit cards:** Visa, Access, Diners, AmEx. **Other points:** licensed, open-air dining, conferences, functions. **Directions:** M4 J8/9. A308 to Windsor, B3028 to Bray. Last building on right.
ANN YOUNG, tel (0628) 73991, fax (0628) 773089.

# MERE, Wiltshire Map 3

## THE BUTT OF SHERRY, Castle Street

*A 17th century pub with atmospheric low ceilings and uneven floors offering a fine selection of traditional home-made cuisine. Popular with locals and tourists alike. The staff are friendly and efficient, whilst the proprietor speaks fluent French and is popular with holiday-makers from France. An ideal stop-off point for touring the Wiltshire countryside.*
FOOD up to £15

**Hours:** open all year 7am; lunch 12noon – 2:30pm; dinner 6:30pm – 9:30pm. **Credit cards:** Visa, Access. **Other points:** licensed, open-air dining, Sunday lunch, children catered for – please check for age limits, pets allowed, parking, disabled access, playland. **Directions:** on the B3092, situated just off A303 on the edge of the village.
JOHN QUIRK, tel (0747) 860352.

# MEVAGISSEY, Cornwall Map 1

## HARBOUR LIGHTS, Polkirt Hill, Nr St Austell

*A family-run fully licensed freehouse with letting accommodation in one of the finest locations in*

Cornwall. Situated on the cliff-top with panoramic views over Mevagissey and St Austell Bay from all public rooms and most of the bedrooms. Comfort and atmosphere are guaranteed.
ACCOMMODATION under £20
FOOD up to £15

**Hours:** breakfast 8:30am – 9am; lunch 12noon – 2pm; dinner 6:30pm – 9pm. **Cuisine:** English / continental:- Extensive bar menu served in public bar or dining room, where smoking is not permitted. **Rooms:** 7 bedrooms all with tea making facilities, telephone, radio, TV: 2 twins ensuite, 3 doubles ensuite, 2 singles. **Credit cards:** Visa, Access. **Other points:** licensed, Sunday lunch, children catered for – please check for age limits, no dogs, parking, special breaks. **Directions:** B3273 to Mevagissey from A390. Follow Gorren Haven sign post.
MR & MRS SHENTON AND MR & MRS QUINN, tel (0726) 843249.

## MR BISTRO, East Quay

*This restaurant is situated facing the harbour in a town with a long established fishing history. The menu, needless to say, specialises in fish dishes. The 'Dish of the Day' depends on the fishermen's catch of the day!*
FOOD £15–£20

**Hours:** lunch 12noon – 2pm; dinner 7pm – 10pm; closed November – January. **Cuisine:** English / seafood:- Fresh fish and shellfish, sweet trolley. **Credit cards:** Visa, Access, Diners, AmEx. **Other points:** Sunday lunch, children catered for – please check for age limits. **Directions:** on the harbour front.
CHRIS & ROMER ROBINS, tel (0726) 842432.

## SHARKSFIN HOTEL & RESTAURANT, The Quay, Nr St Austell

*Occupying a commanding and unrivalled position on Mevagissey Quay overlooking the quaint Cornish harbour, the Sharksfin provides a cheerful and lively atmosphere for its guests. The restaurant, with its fishing theme decor, offers a wide and varied menu and has a well stocked bar. Most of the eleven bedrooms have views over the harbour and the sea and all are equipped with modern facilities for extra comfort. Its location makes the hotel an ideal base from which to tour the nearby historic towns and villages, such as the cathedral city of Truro, also Newquay, Looe and Bodmin Moor.*
ACCOMMODATION £21–£30
FOOD up to £15

**Hours:** breakfast from 7.30am, lunch 12 noon – 2.30pm, dinner 7pm – 9.50pm; closed January and February. **Cuisine:** English:- local fish and shellfish, lobster a speciality. Extensive a la carte menu. **Rooms:** 11 bedrooms all with tea making facilities, telephone, radio, mini bar, TV; 2 singles, 4 doubles, 1 family, 4 doubles ensuite. **Credit cards:** Visa, Access, AmEx, Diners. **Other points:** children catered for – please check for age limits, afternoon teas, vegetarian meals, residents' lounge. **Directions:** Sharksfin Hotel is an old historic building situated right on the quay in the

picturesque fishing village of Mevagissey, accessed by the B3273.
MR & MRS GOODHEW, tel (0726) 843241, fax (0726) 842552.

## MINEHEAD, Somerset Map 3

### BEACONWOOD HOTEL, Church Road, North Hill

*A 16 bedroom Edwardian Country House Hotel which stands in over two acres of terraced gardens, with panoramic views over Exmoor and sea. A warm welcome awaits you and the quiet, friendly atmosphere guarantees a peaceful and relaxing stay. There is a bar decorated like an old country inn, a spacious dining room serving good food and the accommodation is of a very high standard.*
ACCOMMODATION £21–£30
**Hours:** breakfast 8:30am – 9:15am; lunch 12noon – 1pm; dinner 6:30pm – 8pm. **Cuisine:** English. **Rooms:** 16 bedrooms all with tea making facilities, telephone, radio, TV: 1 single ensuite, 2 twins, 5 twins ensuite, 6 doubles ensuite, 2 family rooms ensuite. **Credit cards:** Visa, Access. **Other points:** children catered for – please check for age limits, garden, pets allowed, special breaks, tennis, swimming pool. **Directions:** close to St Michaels Church, off St Michaels Road.
MR T ROBERTS, tel (0643) 702032.

### THE REST & BE THANKFUL INN, Wheddon Cross

*Blazing log fires and a warm courteous welcome await you at this charming, olde style inn with a patio and views over the moors. Good food in a friendly atmosphere and comfortable accommodation ensure a restful stay and an entirely enjoyable visit. Children are especially welcome, with the Buttery Bar dedicated to parents with children and a games room with skittles and videos.*
ACCOMMODATION £21–£30
FOOD up to £15
**Hours:** breakfast 8am – 9:30am; lunch 12noon – 2pm; dinner 7pm – 10pm. **Cuisine:** English:- Traditional English bar meals. Full menu with recommended house specials. **Rooms:** three ensuite rooms, furnished to a high standard. **Credit cards:** Visa, Access, Diners, AmEx. **Other points:** licensed, open-air dining, Sunday lunch, no-smoking area, children catered for – please check for age limits, residents' lounge, bank holidays. **Directions:** Nine miles south of Minehead on A396 to Tiverton.
MR M WEAVER, tel (0643) 841222.

## MONTACUTE, Somerset Map 3

### KINGS ARMS INN

*A 16th century Inn constructed of local stone and set in one of Somerset's most picturesque villages. It provides an ideal touring base for those wishing to explore the West Country, offering a relaxing stay in comfortable,*

*attractively furnished accommodation. The elegant Abbey Room restaurant offers a wide selection of classical and unusual dishes, complemented by a good wine list.*
ACCOMMODATION £31–£40
FOOD £15–£20
**Hours:** breakfast 8am – 9am; lunch 12noon – 2pm; bar snacks 12noon – 2pm; bar snacks 7pm – 10pm; dinner 7:30pm – 9pm; closed Christmas day – Boxing day (incl). **Cuisine:** English / continental. **Rooms:** 11 bedrooms 3 twins ensuite, 8 doubles ensuite. **Credit cards:** Visa, Access, Diners, AmEx. **Other points:** Sunday lunch, parking, children catered for – please check for age limits, no-smoking area, disabled access, afternoon teas, vegetarian meals, residents' lounge, garden. **Directions:** on A3088, 3 miles west of Yeovil just off the main A303.
MICHAEL & VICKI HARRISON, tel (0935) 822513, fax (0935) 826549.

## MORETONHAMPSTEAD, Devon Map 2

### COOKSHAYES GUEST HOUSE, 33 Court Street

*A 19th century granite villa standing in 1 acre of well-tended, south-facing garden in the heart of Dartmoor National Park. The house is tastefully furnished with antiques, china and glass. Delicious home-cooking using fresh, local produce. An ideal location for touring the Devon area.*
ACCOMMODATION under £20
FOOD up to £15 ☺
**Hours:** last orders for dinner – 5pm; breakfast 8:30am – 9am; dinner 7pm; closed November – mid-March. **Cuisine:** English:- All food is prepared daily, and may include dishes like baked lemon sole with a crab and seafood sauce, Chicken Chasseur, roast Devon topside of beef. **Rooms:** 8 bedrooms all with tea making facilities, TV: 1 single, 1 double, 3 doubles ensuite, 3 twins ensuite. **Credit cards:** Visa, Access, AmEx. **Other points:** central heating, children catered for – please check for age limits, residents' lounge, garden, four poster bed, licensed. **Directions:** on B3212 on the west edge of the village.
MRS VERONICA HARDING, tel (0647) 40374.

## MORTEHOE, Devon Map 2

### LUNDY HOUSE HOTEL, Chapel Hill, Woolcombe

*Spectacularly situated on the cliff-side opposite secluded beach, with magnificent sea views over Morte Bay to Lundy Island. Terraced gardens, comfortable licensed bar lounge, separate colour TV, video and satellite TV lounges. Traditional home from home cooking. Vegetarian and special diets catered for.*
ACCOMMODATION under £20
FOOD up to £15
**Hours:** breakfast 8:30am – 9:30am; dinner 7:30pm; closed November – January. **Cuisine:** English. **Rooms:**

2 single, 3 double, 5 family bedrooms, 6 en suite. 1 bathroom, 1 WC. **Other points:** pets allowed, special breaks. **Directions:** situated between Woolacombe and Mortehoe off the A361 on the B3343.
ROGER & DENA SELLS, tel (0271) 870372.

# MYLOR BRIDGE, Cornwall Map 1

### THE PANDORA INN, *Restronguet Creek, Nr Falmouth*

*A picture book 13th century thatched inn reputedly owned by Capt. Edwards of Bounty mutiny fame. Flagstone floors, low beamed ceilings & gleaming brasswork complete the picture book setting. Come by car or by boat – yachts may be moored on the 140ft pontoon at the front, and enjoy the famous, fine cuisine.*
FOOD up to £15
**Hours:** last orders 7:30pm – 10pm; bar meals 12noon – 2:15pm; bar meals 6:30pm – 10pm; dinner 7pm – 12midnight. **Cuisine:** English:- Local fresh fish and fresh produce. Cornish specialities. Afternoon teas. **Credit cards:** Visa, Access. **Other points:** licensed, open-air dining, Sunday lunch, disabled access, pets allowed, afternoon tea, vegetarian meals. **Directions:** from A39 in Falmouth take Mylor turn then down hill to Pandora.
MR AND MRS R HOUGH, tel (0326) 372678.

# NEWQUAY, Cornwall Map 1

### BON AMI HOTEL, *3 Trenance Lane*

*A well established family-run hotel, ideally situated in a peaceful area of Newquay, overlooking the boating lakes and within easy reach of lovely beaches and the town centre. There is a terrace with lake views where refreshments can be obtained. The hotels policy is one of courteous, efficient service with an informal but friendly atmosphere. Close by are the beautiful Trenance Gardens which lead to Waterworld Leisure Park, Indoor Swimming Pool and Zoo and much more.*
ACCOMMODATION under £20
FOOD up to £15
**Hours:** breakfast 8:30am – 9:15am; bar snacks 1pm – 2pm; dinner 6:30pm – 7:15pm; bar snacks 9pm – 11pm; closed October – Easter. **Cuisine:** English:- Home-cooked meals using only the freshest produce. **Rooms:** 9 bedrooms all with tea making facilities: 1 single ensuite, 1 twin ensuite, 6 doubles ensuite, 1 triple ensuite. **Credit cards:** Visa, Access. **Other points:** parking, afternoon tea, residents' lounge, vegetarian meals, bar, central heating. **Directions:** A30 to junction A392, follow signs for Newquay. At roundabout opposite boating lake keep left on A392. First turning on right is Trenance Lane. Hotel is 500yds on the left.
MR M LEVY, tel (0637) 874009.

### CORISANDE MANOR HOTEL, *Riverside Avenue, Pentire*

*Built in 1900 of Austrian design, standing in 3 acres of grounds with private foreshore. The Painters have owned and run the hotel since 1968 and they offer many facilities, such as rowing boats, a putting green, crocquet and giant outdoor chess. Advance booking is strongly recommended.*
ACCOMMODATION £21–£30
FOOD up to £15
**Hours:** breakfast 8:30am – 9:30am; closed 09/10 – 14/05; bar meals 12:30pm – 1:30pm; dinner 7pm – 7:30pm. **Cuisine:** breakfast. **Rooms:** 19 bedrooms all with tea making facilities, radio, TV: 3 singles ensuite, 2 singles, 2 twins ensuite, 1 twin, 8 doubles ensuite, 1 triple ensuite, 2 quads ensuite. **Credit cards:** Visa, Access. **Other points:** central heating, children catered for – please check for age limits, residents' lounge, garden. **Directions:** off B3282 on the Gannel Estuary.
DAVID PAINTER, FHCIMA, tel (0637) 872042.

### THE GREAT WESTERN HOTEL, *Cliff Road*

*An imposing cream building perched on the cliff above Great Western Beach offering magnificent seaviews. The hotel comprises a lawned garden, indoor swimming pool and Jacuzzi and serves traditional English food with traditional hospitality.*
ACCOMMODATION £21–£30
FOOD up to £15 ★
**Hours:** breakfast 8am – 9:30am; lunch 12noon – 2pm; bar meals 12noon – 2pm; bar meals 6pm – 9:30pm; dinner 7pm – 8:45pm. **Cuisine:** English:- Homemade dishes. **Rooms:** 72 bedrooms all with tea making facilities, telephone, radio, TV: 12 singles ensuite, 18 twins ensuite, 21 doubles ensuite, 18 triples ensuite, 3 quads ensuite. **Credit cards:** Visa, Access, Diners, AmEx. **Other points:** licensed, Sunday lunch, children catered for – please check for age limits, coach/prior arr, baby-listening device, cots, foreign exchange, residents' lounge, residents' bar, swimming pool. **Directions:** on the cliff road near the railway station.
MR FITTER, tel (0637) 872010, fax (0637) 874435.

### THE HEADLAND HOTEL

*Standing on its own headland with the sea on three sides, the hotel enjoys magnificent sea views. A wide choice of meals and an extensive selection of wines and vintage port are on offer in the restaurant. Probably unique in having its own hot-air balloon but due to its superb position there are many other sports facilities available, making The Headland a sportman's paradise.*
ACCOMMODATION £31–£40
FOOD up to £15 ☖
**Hours:** open New Year 7pm; lunch 12:30pm – 2pm; dinner 7:30pm – 9pm; closed mid-November – mid March. **Cuisine:** English:- English and continental dishes including local crab and lobster. Table d'hote & a la carte. Snacks, home-made cakes and scones served in coffee shop. **Rooms:** 104 bedrooms all with tea making facilities, telephone, radio, TV: 11 singles ensuite, 15 twins ensuite, 22 doubles ensuite, 40 family rooms ensuite, 16 suites. **Credit cards:** Visa, Access, AmEx. **Other points:** licensed, Sunday lunch, children catered

for – please check for age limits, afternoon tea, pets allowed, residents' lounge, garden, swimming pool, tennis, billiards, putting green, residents' bar. **Directions:** follow directions to Fistral beach.
MR & MRS ARMSTRONG, tel (0637) 872211.

## TREGURRIAN HOTEL, Watergate Bay
*A modern hotel overlooking the surf beach of Watergate Bay. Offering comfortable accommodation, there are excellent facilities for family holidays, with heated swimming pool, games room, laundry room etc. A wide range of bar meals are available and with childrens early light teas. Only 100 yd from the beach, it is suitable for all ages and offers excellent surfing conditions. Central location.*
*ACCOMMODATION £21–£30*
**Hours:** breakfast 8:30am – 9:15am; lunch 12:30pm – 1:30pm; dinner 6:45pm – 7:30pm. **Cuisine:** English.
**Rooms:** 28 bedrooms 2 singles, 2 singles ensuite, 2 twins ensuite, 1 twin, 11 doubles ensuite, 2 doubles, 7 family rooms ensuite. **Credit cards:** Visa, Access.
**Other points:** children catered for – please check for age limits, garden, afternoon tea, pets allowed.
**Directions:** 3 miles form Newquay, on the B3276.
MR & MRS MOLLOY, tel (0637) 860280.

## TRENANCE LODGE, 83 Trenance Road
*Situated in its own grounds overlooking the Lake and Gannel Valley, this fine restaurant has an established reputation for its seafood and game. The Daily Blackboard menu offers locally caught fish and shellfish, together with vegetarian dishes. Small weddings, private and business parties are catered for.*
*ACCOMMODATION £21–£30*
*FOOD £15–£20*
**Hours:** breakfast 7am – 10am; dinner 7pm – 11pm.
**Cuisine:** modern English:- An established reputation for excellent seafood, game and steaks. Extensive wine list. Vegetarians catered for. Daily Blackboard Specials.
**Rooms:** 5 bedrooms all with tea making facilities, telephone, radio, TV; 1 twin ensuite, 4 doubles ensuite.
**Credit cards:** Visa, Access. **Other points:** licensed, open all year, parking, residents' lounge, garden, bank holidays, swimming pool. **Directions:** overlooking the Gannel Valley.
MICHAEL MACKENZIE, tel (0637) 876702.

## TYGWYN, 107 Pentire Avenue
*A luxury split-level chalet bungalow set high on the cliff-top overlooking the beach, with sea views from every room. On the food side, the emphasis is on fresh produce with a choice of menu. The Tygwyn may be small but the welcome is warm and served with true Cornish hospitality. Tygwyn offers it's guests the convenience of on-site parking.*
*ACCOMMODATION under £20*
*FOOD up to £15*
**Hours:** breakfast 8:30am – 8:45am; dinner 6pm – 8pm; closed November – February. **Cuisine:** English. **Rooms:** 6 bedrooms all with tea making facilities, TV: 1 single, 3 doubles ensuite, 1 twin ensuite, 1 family room ensuite.

**Other points:** central heating, children catered for – please check for age limits, residents' lounge, garden, special diets. **Directions:** from the centre of Newquay, take the road to Pentire headland.
MEL, CLIVE & MARK GRIFFIN, tel (0637) 874480.

## WHIPSIDERRY HOTEL, Porth
*The Whipsiderry commands a superb position overlooking Porth beach and bay, with breathtaking views of both sea and country. Whether exploring the rugged Cornish coastland or venturing inland, the hotel provides a friendly retreat. On fine summer evenings enjoy a barbecue on the terrace, and at night, watch the badgers feed and play only a few feet away.*
*ACCOMMODATION £21–£30*
*FOOD up to £15*
**Hours:** open Christmas; breakfast 8:30am – 9am; lunch 12noon – 2pm; dinner 6:30pm – 8pm; closed November – March. **Cuisine:** English:- Varied table d'hote menu changes daily. **Rooms:** 23 bedrooms all with tea making facilities, radio, TV: 4 family rooms ensuite, 14 doubles ensuite, 3 twins ensuite, 2 childrens rooms. **Other points:** licensed, open-air dining, Sunday lunch, central heating, children catered for – please check for age limits, pets allowed, swimming pool, sauna, billiards, launderette. **Directions:** Trevelgue Road leads off Watergate Road (the seafront).
RICHARD & ANN DRACKFORD, tel (0637) 874777.

## WHITE LODGE HOTEL, Mawgan Porth
*Family owned and run, the hotel is beautifully situated in an elevated position, just 100 yd from the golden sands of Mawgan Porth. Excellent views of the sea and cliffs from the dining room, bar and most of the bedrooms. Comments from recent visitors highly praise the White Lodge and commend the comfortable accommodation, good food and welcoming, friendly service.*
*ACCOMMODATION under £20*
*FOOD up to £15* ★
**Hours:** breakfast 8am – 9am; bar snacks 12noon – 2pm; dinner 6pm – 8pm; closed November – February.
**Cuisine:** English. **Rooms:** 13 bedrooms all with tea making facilities, TV: 1 chalet, 6 family rooms ensuite, 1 single ensuite, 1 single, 4 doubles. **Credit cards:** Visa, Access, AmEx. **Other points:** children catered for – please check for age limits, afternoon tea, pets allowed, residents' lounge, picnic lunches, vegetarian meals, games room, garden. **Directions:** B3276 coast road between Newquay & Padstow 5 miles from Newquay.
JOHN & DIANE PARRY, tel (0637) 860512.

# NEWTON ABBOT, Devon Map 2

## QUEEN HOTEL, Queen Street
*Situated in the bustling market town of Newton Abbot, the Queen's Hotel provides a perfect place to stay for West Country race goers and tourists alike. Visit the nearby coastal towns of Torbay, Paignton and Babbacombe, or take a peaceful stroll in Dartmoor's*

National Park. For racing enthusiasts, the Newton Abbot racecourse and also the Devon & Exeter course are nearby.

ACCOMMODATION £31–£40

FOOD up to £15

**Hours:** breakfast 7:30am – 9am; lunch 11:45am – 2pm; bar meals 11:45am – 1:45pm; dinner 6:45pm – 9pm; bar meals 6:45pm – 8:45pm. **Cuisine:** English:- A la Carte & Table d'Hote menus, offering traditional Devonian cooking. Extensive Wine List. Daily bar lunches in Queen's Bar. Vegetarians catered for. **Rooms:** 25 bedrooms all with tea making facilities, telephone, radio, TV: 5 singles ensuite, 4 singles, 6 twins ensuite, 8 doubles ensuite, 1 double, 1 quad ensuite. **Credit cards:** Visa, Access, AmEx. **Other points:** licensed, children catered for – please check for age limits, pets allowed, parking, bank holidays, afternoon tea, baby-listening device, cots, vegetarian meals, residents' bar. **Directions:** adjacent to Courtenay Park, opposite British Rail station. TONY & FAY JELLEY, tel (0626) 63133, fax (0626) 64922.

# NORTH FORDINGBRIDGE,

Hampshire Map 4

## ROSE & THISTLE, Rockbourne, Nr Fordingbridge

A beautiful 16th century thatched roof inn, situated in a picture postcard village in the New Forest. A popular haunt of tourists and walkers who are drawn by the warm, homely atmosphere and olde worlde interior, offering log fires, oak beams and low ceilings. Fine quality, imaginative fresh food, with excellent wines and real ales available daily.

FOOD up to £15

**Hours:** open all year 6:45pm; lunch 12noon – 2:30pm; dinner 7pm – 10pm; closed Sunday evening. **Cuisine:** British:- Fresh fish and shellfish available daily, including Lobster Thermidor and a huge Dover Sole. Also, traditional Scottish grouse, pheasant and beef. **Credit cards:** Visa, Access. **Other points:** licensed, open-air dining, Sunday lunch, children catered for – please check for age limits, afternoon tea, disabled access, pets allowed. **Directions:** from Fordingbridge A3078 Sandleheath sign for the Roman Villa. TIM NORFOLK, tel (07253) 236.

# ODIHAM, Hampshire Map 4

## LA FORET, High Street

This intimate French restaurant, situated on the main street of the delightful country town of Odiham, provides excellently cooked French cuisine in attractive comfortable surroundings. Using an imaginative menu which has obviously been devised by a creative and caring chef, you will find excellent service and candlelit surroundings complement your gastronomic delights.

FOOD £21–£25 ☺

**Hours:** lunch 12:30pm – 2pm; dinner 7pm – 9:45pm. **Cuisine:** French:- Classic French cuisine, including

extensive selection of fish specialities. **Credit cards:** Visa, Access, Diners, AmEx. **Other points:** licensed, Sunday lunch, children catered for – please check for age limits. **Directions:** on the main street in Odiham. MR & MRS HOULKER, tel (0256) 702697.

# OLD SODBURY, Avon Map 3

## SODBURY HOUSE HOTEL, Badminton Road

Set in large attractive grounds with ample off road parking, this former 1830's farmhouse has been tastefully converted into a hotel retaining the character but providing the facilities that todays guest expects. All 14 rooms are ensuite and have direct-dial telephone, colour TV, hair dryer, trouser-press and welcome tray. Most rooms have mini bars. A self contained conference facility is situated in the Coach House. The hotel caters for small weddings, and private dinner parties. Bed & Breakfast is provided at an all inclusive rate. Ideally situated for visiting Bath, Bristol and the Cotswolds. An ideal stop over en route to the West Country, Wales and Ireland.

ACCOMMODATION £21–£30

**Hours:** breakfast – weekdays 7:30am – 8:30am; breakfast – w'ends/b.hols 8:30am – 9:30am; closed 24 December – 4 January. **Cuisine:** breakfast. **Rooms:** 7 bedrooms all with tea making facilities, telephone, mini bar, TV: 4 doubles ensuite, 2 twins ensuite, 1 family room ensuite. **Credit cards:** Visa, Access. **Other points:** parking, children catered for – please check for age limits, open bank holidays, afternoon tea, pets/prior arr, vegetarian meals, garden, open-air dining, residents' lounge. **Directions:** from Junction 18 – M4, take A46 for 3 miles, left at traffic lights, A432. 12 miles from Junction 14 on M5. WARREN, DAVID & MARGARET, tel (0454) 312847, fax (0454) 273105.

# PADSTOW, Cornwall Map 1

## THE OLD MILL COUNTRY HOUSE, Little Petherick

This 16th Century converted corn mill complete with waterwheel is situated in the pretty village of Little Petherick and is a grade 11 listed building set within its own gardens next to a stream that dawdles into the Carmel Estuary. It retains much of its original character and charm whilst providing guests with modern amenities amidst a welcoming and friendly atmosphere. A unique feature of the Old Mill is the kitchen which is available for residents inspection of the cuisine of which the proprietors Michael & Pat Walker are justifiably proud.

ACCOMMODATION £21–£30

FOOD up to £15

**Hours:** breakfast 9am; dinner 7pm; closed November – February. **Cuisine:** traditional:- Freshly prepared and traditionally cooked. **Rooms:** 6 bedrooms all with tea making facilities: 3 doubles ensuite, 3 twins ensuite.

Other points: parking, no-smoking area, residents' lounge, vegetarian meals, Sunday dinner, garden, residents' bar. Directions: A39 then A389.
WALKER, MICHAEL AND PAT, tel (0841) 540388.

## PAIGNTON, Devon Map 2

### BARTON PINES INN, Blagdon Road, Higher Blagdon
*Elizabethan style manor in extensive grounds with superb views, offering self catering apartments, touring caravans, tennis court, heated pool, and solarium. Quality home cooking. Personally run by the proprietors.*
ACCOMMODATION £31–£40
FOOD up to £15
Hours: lunch 12noon – 2:30pm; dinner 7pm – 10:30pm.
Cuisine: English:- Home cooking, eg. steak and kidney pie, curry, and lasagne. Extensive menu and daily specials board. Sunday lunch off season. Rooms: 8 bedrooms all with tea making facilities, radio, TV: 8 self-catering rooms. Credit cards: Visa. Other points: licensed, children catered for – please check for age limits, disabled access, 24hr reception, foreign exchange, self catering, baby-listening device, cots.
Directions: from A380, Torbay Ring Road, take unclassified road to Marldon & Berry Pomeroy.
MR & MRS P B DEVONSHIRE, tel (0803) 553350.

### THE INN ON THE GREEN, Seafront
*A holiday complex set in 2 acres right on the seafront, yet within a 2 minute walk from shops, theatre and other attractions. The menu is very extensive, offering a wide range of dishes, well-cooked and presented, and the apartments are very comfortable. An ideal place for family holidays, as children are well catered for with sandpits, Wendy House and own discos.*
ACCOMMODATION under £20
FOOD up to £15
Hours: lunch 12noon – 3pm; dinner – except Sunday 6:30pm – 12midnight; dinner – Sunday 7pm – 10:30pm.
Cuisine: international:- Very extensive menu, including traditional English, Indian, and Italian dishes. Children's own menu. Desserts include Olde English puddings.
Rooms: 82 self-catering apartments. Maid service.
Other points: Sunday lunch, children catered for – please check for age limits, pets allowed, garden, playland, swimming pool, launderette, games room.
Directions: end of M5 to Torbay. Directly on seafront opposite the pier.
BRIAN SHONE, tel (0803) 557811, fax (0803) 550044.

### REDCLIFFE HOTEL, Marine Drive
*Situated in one of Britain's most popular seaside resorts. This is an ideal location from which to visit Paignton Zoo and explore the Devon countryside.*
FOOD up to £15
Hours: breakfast 8am – 9:30am; bar snacks 12noon – 2pm; Sunday lunch 12:45pm – 2pm; dinner 7pm – 8:30pm. Cuisine: English/French. Credit cards: Visa, Access. Other points: parking, children catered for –

please check for age limits, afternoon teas, residents' lounge, vegetarian meals, garden, leisure centre, indoor pool. Directions: take the A385 or A380 and head for Paignton sea-front. The hotel is at the Torquay end of Paignton Green.
MR S TWIGGER, tel (0803) 526397, fax (0803) 528030.

### SOUTH SANDS HOTEL, 12 Alta Vista Road
*South Sands Hotel, situated close to Goodrington Sands, enjoys outstanding views of the bay. Under the personal supervision of the proprietors, visitors are assured of a warm welcome, comfortable, well-equipped bedrooms, and superb freshly prepared food. Very good value for money. Ideally located for the beach, town centre and water adventure park. Free car park.*
ACCOMMODATION under £20
FOOD up to £15
Hours: breakfast 8am – 9am; dinner 6pm – 7pm.
Cuisine: English / continental. Rooms: 62 bedrooms all with tea making facilities, telephone, radio, TV: 2 singles ensuite, 44 twins ensuite, 3 doubles ensuite, 5 triples ensuite, 8 quads ensuite. Credit cards: Visa.
Other points: children catered for – please check for age limits, vegetarian meals, afternoon tea, pets allowed, garden, residents' lounge, baby sitting, baby-listening device, cots, left luggage. Directions: keep Paignton harbour on left, go over top of hill. First hotel on right.
TONY & CECILE CAHILL, tel (0803) 557231, (0803) 529947.

## PANBOROUGH, Somerset Map 3

### THE PANBOROUGH INN
*A late 17th century inn situated in the hamlet of Panborough, and offering a quiet, relaxing atmosphere. The well-maintained frontage with hanging baskets and manicured gardens are a joy in Summer. Good traditional food in delightful surroundings!*
FOOD up to £15
Hours: open all year 6pm; lunch 11:30am – 2:30pm; dinner 6:30pm – 10pm. Cuisine: English:- A la carte and Table d'hote menu's offering a wide range of traditional style dishes. Good choice of steaks. Vegetarian dishes also available. Credit cards: Visa, Access. Other points: licensed, open-air dining, Sunday lunch, children catered for – please check for age limits, pets allowed, bank holidays, disabled access.
Directions: situated on the B3139 Burnham-on-Sea – Wedmore – Wells Road.
JOHN HALLIWELL & KENNETH HARGREAVES, tel (0934) 712554.

## PENZANCE, Cornwall Map 1

### BLUE SEAS HOTEL, Regent Terrace, Promenade
*Set in a quiet, south facing terrace overlooking the promenade, this family owned and run hotel offers a high standard of comfort and friendly service.*

*Specialising in home cooking using local fresh produce. Bus and rail stations within easy walking distance, also the Ilses of Scilly boat 2 minutes walk. Ideal for Land's End and Lizard Point.*
ACCOMMODATION *under £20*
FOOD *up to £15*
**Hours:** breakfast 7:30am – 9:30am; dinner 6:30pm. **Cuisine:** English:- Varied daily menus using fresh local produce. **Rooms:** 8 bedrooms all with tea making facilities, TV: 1 single, 5 doubles ensuite, 2 twins ensuite. **Other points:** parking, open bank holidays, no-smoking area, afternoon tea, residents' lounge, vegetarian meals, garden. **Directions:** A30 to Penzance, follow seafront to start of Promenade. The hotel is set back in the terrace.
DAVENPORT, DEREK AND PAT, tel (0736) 64744, fax (0736) 330701.

## CARNSON HOUSE HOTEL, *East Terrace*
*This small, comfortable, private hotel enjoys one of Penzance's most central positions. Close to harbour and beaches, it is an ideal base for touring the Lands End Peninsula with its dramatic scenery of coves and cliffs. Tourist information and excursion booking service available. French and German spoken.*
ACCOMMODATION *under £20*
**Hours:** breakfast 8am – 8:30am; dinner 6:15pm; last orders 4pm. **Cuisine:** English. **Rooms:** 8 bedrooms all with tea making facilities, TV: 3 singles, 3 doubles, 2 doubles ensuite. **Credit cards:** Visa, Access, Diners, AmEx. **Other points:** central heating, residents' lounge, garden. **Directions:** on the right side of main road entering Penzance from the A30 east.
RICHARD & TRISHA HILDER, tel (0736) 65589.

## HIGHER FAUGAN COUNTRY HOUSE HOTEL, *Newlyn*
*A gracious Country House, built at the turn-of-the-century, surrounded by 10 acres of lawns and woodlands. The rooms are tastefully furnished and the standard of accommodation is excellent. The dinner menu is changed daily and uses fresh, local produce. With personal service and a warm, welcoming atmosphere, this hotel is highly recommended.*
ACCOMMODATION *£41–£50*
FOOD *up to £15*
**Hours:** open all year 6:15pm; last orders 6:15pm – 7pm; breakfast 7:30am – 10am; bar snacks 12noon – 2pm; dinner 7:30pm – 8:30pm. **Cuisine:** English. **Rooms:** 12 bedrooms all with tea making facilities, telephone, TV: 2 family rooms ensuite, 5 twins ensuite, 4 doubles ensuite, 1 single ensuite. **Credit cards:** Visa, Access, AmEx. **Other points:** children catered for – please check for age limits, pets allowed, residents' lounge, garden, billiards, swimming pool, tennis, putting green. **Directions:** off B3315. 2 miles west of Penzance in Newlyn fishing village.
MICHAEL & CHRISTINE CHURCHMAN, tel (0736) 62076, fax (0736) 51648.

## LYNWOOD GUEST HOUSE, *41 Morrab Road*
*A comfortable, well-appointed family guest house built in Victorian times. Situated between the promenade and the town centre, Lynwood is convenient for all amenities and close to the sub-tropical gardens. An ideal base for visiting Lands' End and the Lizard Peninsula, St Michael's Mount and the Isles of Scilly.*
ACCOMMODATION *under £20*
**Hours:** breakfast 8am – 8:45am. **Cuisine:** breakfast. **Rooms:** 7 bedrooms all with tea making facilities, radio, TV: 1 single, 1 double, 2 twins, 3 family rooms. **Credit cards:** Visa, Access, Diners, AmEx. **Other points:** central heating, children catered for – please check for age limits, no evening meal, residents' lounge. **Directions:** Morrab Road is a turning off the Seafront.
MRS JOAN WOOD, tel (0736) 65871.

## MOUNT HAVEN HOTEL & RESTAURANT, *Turnpike Road, Marazion*
*Situated in its own grounds on the outskirts of the ancient market town of Marazion, Mount Haven is just a few minutes walk from the sea. There are superb views over St Michael's Mount from the garden and sun terrace. With both a la carte and table d'hote menus guests have a good choice of meals in the restaurant and the service is friendly and efficient.*
ACCOMMODATION *£21–£30*
FOOD *up to £15*
**Hours:** breakfast 8am – 9:15am; lunch 12noon – 2pm; dinner 7pm – 9pm. **Cuisine:** English:- A la carte and table d'hote menus. Specialities include local crab and fish, brought fresh to the restaurant from Newlyn fishing port. **Rooms:** 17 bedrooms all with tea making facilities, telephone, radio, TV: 3 singles ensuite, 2 twins ensuite, 7 doubles ensuite, 3 triples ensuite, 2 quads ensuite. **Credit cards:** Visa, Access, AmEx. **Other points:** licensed, Sunday lunch, no-smoking area, children catered for – please check for age limits, garden, afternoon tea, pets allowed, vegetarian meals, parking, residents' lounge, residents' bar. **Directions:** Marazion exit from A30, through village. Hotel on right-hand side.
JOHN & DELYTH JAMES, tel (0736) 710249, fax (0736) 711658.

## UNION HOTEL, *Chapel Street*
*Steeped in history, the hotel dates back to the 17th Century. It was here that news of Nelson's death and victory at the Battle of Trafalgar was first announced. Today, well-cooked and presented meals are served in a cosy atmosphere and the accommodation is comfortable. Log fires in winter add to the warm welcome extended to all guests.*
ACCOMMODATION *£31–£40*
FOOD *up to £15*
**Hours:** breakfast 8am – 9:30am; bar meals 12noon – 2pm; dinner 6pm – 9:30pm; bar meals 6pm – 9pm. **Cuisine:** English:- Full a la carte menu, table d'hote and bar snacks. **Rooms:** 28 bedrooms, 24 en suite. **Credit cards:** Visa, Access, Diners, AmEx. **Other points:**

licensed, Sunday lunch, children catered for – please check for age limits. **Directions:** take the A30 or A394 to Penzance. Follow town centre one way system. MR KENNEDY, tel (0736) 62319.

## WOODSTOCK GUEST HOUSE, 29 Morrab Road

*A large Victorian terrace house, converted into a very comfortable and friendly guest house, complemented by the delightful Morrab Gardens nearby. Highly recommended and excellent value for money.*
*ACCOMMODATION under £20*
**Hours:** breakfast 8am – 8:30am. **Cuisine:** breakfast.
**Rooms:** 5 bedrooms all with tea making facilities, radio, TV: 1 single, 1 double, 1 double ensuite, 1 twin, 1 family room. **Credit cards:** Visa, Access, Diners, AmEx.
**Other points:** children catered for – please check for age limits, street parking. **Directions:** off the promenade, close to Morrab Gardens.
CHERRY HOPKINS, tel (0736) 69049.

## PERRANPORTH, Cornwall Map 1

### BEACH DUNES HOTEL, Ramoth Way, Reen Sands

*Roomy, comfortably furnished hotel, with colour co-ordinated decor and pleasant, cheerful atmosphere. The Hotel is situated in the sand dunes above the beach, and adjoins the golf course.*
*ACCOMMODATION £21–£30*
*FOOD up to £15* ★
**Hours:** closed November – December; breakfast 8:15am – 9:30am; bar meals 12noon – 2pm; dinner 6pm – 11pm.
**Cuisine:** English:- Traditional English homecooked food. Fixed menu which changes daily. **Rooms:** 8 bedrooms all with tea making facilities, telephone, radio, TV: 4 doubles ensuite, 2 triples ensuite, 2 quads ensuite. **Credit cards:** Visa, Access, AmEx. **Other points:** no-smoking area, children catered for – please check for age limits, afternoon tea, parking, residents' lounge, garden, indoor swimming pool, squash. **Directions:** B3285. Situated along a private road – 400 metres from main road.
KEITH WOOLDRIDGE, tel (0872) 572263, fax (0872) 573824.

## PEWSEY, Wiltshire Map 3

### WOODBRIDGE INN, North Newnton

*This popular 17th century country riverside inn, located in the tranquil Vale of Pewsey, is unique in offering the best of both worlds. The inn is busy and lively with a friendly atmosphere yet not rowdy. The award-winning food and drink is imaginatively different and excellent. The rooms are comfortable and well-appointed, you can really relax. Yet if you want to see the sights make this location your ideal base; Stonehenge – 15mins, Bath – 55mins, Avebury – 10mins, Marlborough – 10mins, Salisbury – 25mins, the south coast – 1 hour.*
*ACCOMMODATION under £20*
*FOOD up to £15* ♀ ★

**Hours:** meals all day 11am – 11pm; lunch – Sunday 12noon – 3pm; dinner – Sunday 7pm – 10:30pm. **Cuisine:** international:- A wide range of international dishes featuring Cajun, Indonesian, Classical French and English and Mexican specialities, such as sizzling fajita, vegetable chimichanga, chicken burrito. Traditional Sunday roasts. Reservations essential to avoid disappointment. **Rooms:** 3 bedrooms all with tea making facilities, telephone, radio, TV: 1 twin, 1 double ensuite, 1 double. **Credit cards:** Visa, Access, Diners, AmEx. **Other points:** licensed, open-air dining, Sunday lunch, children catered for – please check for age limits, beer garden, petanque pistes, caravan facilities, conferences, cots. **Directions:** 3 miles south of Pewsey on the A345, on the roundabout.
LOU & TERRY VERTESSY, tel (0980) 630266, fax (0980) 630266.

## PHILLEIGH, Cornwall Map 1

### SMUGGLERS COTTAGE OF TOLVERNE

*This 500 year-old thatched cottage has been run by the Newman family for over 60 years. Situated on the banks of the River Fal, near the King Harry car ferry on the Roseland Peninsula, with own landing stage and moorings. Smugglers Cottage offers a selection of over 70 different malt whiskies.*
*FOOD up to £15*
**Hours:** morning coffee 10:30am; lunch 12noon – 2pm; cream teas 3pm – 5:30pm; dinner 7:30pm – 9pm.
**Cuisine:** English:- Daily changing menu of home cooked dishes using fresh local produce, particularly fish and seafood. **Credit cards:** Visa, Access. **Other points:** open-air dining, Sunday lunch, children catered for – please check for age limits. **Directions:** near King Harry car ferry on Roseland Peninsula.
ELIZABETH & PETER NEWMAN, tel (0872) 580309, fax (0872) 580216.

## PLYMOUTH, Devon Map 2

### CRANBOURNE HOTEL, 282 Citadel Road, The Hoe

*A clean, family run town house hotel close to the city centre with all its attractions. Cranbourne Hotel is a convenient two minute walk from the Ferry Port and has its own hairdressing salon.*
*ACCOMMODATION under £20*
**Hours:** breakfast 7am – 9am. **Cuisine:** breakfast.
**Rooms:** 14 bedrooms all with tea making facilities, TV: 2 singles, 2 doubles, 1 twin, 6 twins ensuite, 3 family rooms – shower only. **Credit cards:** Visa, Access, AmEx. **Other points:** children catered for – please check for age limits, pets allowed, parking. **Directions:** close to city centre, 200 yds from Hoe Promenade.
PETER & VALERIE WILLIAMS, tel (0752) 661400, fax (0752) 263858.

### OLIVERS HOTEL & RESTAURANT, 33 Sutherland Road

*A family-run luxury hotel in the north east corner of the city centre off the B3241. The Pursers have tastefully, and*

carefully, modernised the building to ensure that modern comforts can be enjoyed in Victorian splendour and ambiance.
ACCOMMODATION £21–£30
FOOD £15–£20
**Hours:** breakfast 7:45am – 9am; dinner – Monday 6pm – 8pm; dinner – Tuesday 6pm – 8pm; dinner – Wednesday 6pm – 8pm; dinner – Thursday 6pm – 8pm; dinner – Friday 7pm – 9pm; dinner – Saturday 7pm – 9pm. **Cuisine:** English / continental:- Traditional 5 course breakfast, daily plats du jour, eg. coq au vin, beef Wellington, and seafood provencal. **Rooms:** 6 bedrooms, 4 en suite. **Credit cards:** Visa, Access, Diners, AmEx. **Other points:** licensed, Sunday lunch, no-smoking area, children catered for – please check for age limits. **Directions:** less than a mile from the Hoe, to the east of the railway station.
JOY & MIKE PURSER, tel (0752) 663923.

## SMEATONS TOWER HOTEL, 40–44 Grand Parade, The Hoe
A small, friendly family run hotel situated close to the seafront and 12–15 minutes walk from the city centre. A popular holiday and commercial hotel.
ACCOMMODATION under £20
FOOD up to £15
**Hours:** breakfast 7am – 9am; lunch 12noon – 2pm; bar meals 12noon – 3pm; dinner 6pm – 8:30pm; bar meals 6pm – 11pm. **Cuisine:** English / continental:- Table d'hote and full a la carte menus. **Rooms:** 18 bedrooms all with tea making facilities, telephone, TV: 4 family rooms ensuite, 4 twins ensuite, 10 doubles ensuite. **Credit cards:** Visa, Access. **Other points:** licensed, Sunday lunch, no-smoking area, children catered for – please check for age limits, afternoon tea. **Directions:** adjacent to Plymouth Hoe.
BRIAN & May MASON, tel (0752) 221007, fax (0752) 221664.

## TRATTORIA PESCATORE, 36 Admiralty Street, Stonehouse
A small Italian restaurant situated in an old Victorian building. Hand painted murals on the walls add to the truely Italian atmosphere of the restaurant. All food is freshly cooked to order and seafood is the house speciality. Delicious food and friendly, efficient service. Highly recommended.
FOOD £15–£20
**Hours:** lunch 12noon – 2pm; dinner 7pm – 11pm; closed Saturday lunch; closed Sunday. **Cuisine:** Italian:- The traditional Italian cuisine selection includes Stuffed sole with crab, special vegetarian pastas. **Credit cards:** Visa, Access. **Other points:** licensed, open-air dining, children catered for – please check for age limits. **Directions:** approx 1 mile from city centre, near Plymouth to Roscoff ferry port.
GIAN PIERO CALIGARI & RITA ATKINSON, tel (0752) 600201.

## THE WEARY FRIAR INN, Pillaton, Nr Saltash
A famous old 12th century inn, situated next to the Church of St Odolphus, where you will find true character and

atmosphere. Today the Weary Friar welcomes you to imaginative food of a high standard, suberb surroundings and comfortable accommodation. Highly recommended for its high quality food and the excellent combination of modern comforts with 12th century character.
ACCOMMODATION £21–£30
FOOD up to £15
**Hours:** breakfast 7:30am – 10am; lunch 12noon – 2pm; dinner 7pm – 10pm. **Cuisine:** modern English:- Dishes may include Fillets of Sole Champagne, Honey Roast Saddle of Lamb, Smokey Carpetbag Steak (with oysters), Vegetable & Nut Salousie. **Rooms:** 14 bedrooms, all en suite. **Credit cards:** Visa. **Other points:** licensed, open-air dining, Sunday lunch, children catered for – please check for age limits, afternoon tea, residents' lounge. **Directions:** between Saltash & Callington, 2 miles west of A388. Near St Mellion.
SUE & ROGER SHARMAN, tel (0579) 50238.

# POLPERRO, Cornwall Map 1

## THE KITCHEN, The Coombes
A small, informal, licensed restaurant specialising in high quality dishes prepared by the owners who have a well deserved reputation for imaginative food.
FOOD £15–£20
**Hours:** dinner 6:30pm – 9:30pm; closed Sunday to Thursday – November to March. **Cuisine:** modern English:- Fish, lobster, crab, duck, steak, lamb, and vegetarian menu. **Credit cards:** Visa, Access. **Other points:** parking, disabled access. **Directions:** on the walk down to the harbour.
IAN & VANESSA BATESON, tel (0503) 72780.

## NELSON'S RESTAURANT, Big Green
A large, olde worlde restaurant with a distinct nautical flavour, reflecting the proprietor's long connection with the sea. The table d'hote menu changes with the availability of fresh produce. An intimate restaurant with a friendly atmosphere.
FOOD £15–£20
**Hours:** lunch 11:45am – 2pm; dinner 7pm – 10pm; closed mid-January – mid-February; closed Monday; closed Saturday lunch. **Cuisine:** English / French /seafood:- Fresh seafood, roasts, grills. **Credit cards:** Visa, Access, Diners, AmEx. **Other points:** licensed, Sunday lunch, children catered for – please check for age limits, pets/prior arr. **Directions:** on the Saxon bridge in Polperro.
PETER NELSON, tel (0503) 72366.

## PENRYN HOUSE HOTEL, The Coombes
Located on the main village road in a tranquil setting, the hotel offers imaginative food using mostly local fresh produce. Enjoy individual attention and quality of service, whilst relaxing in the comfortable surroundings. An exciting range of Special Interest Holidays are also offered, including Watercolour Painting Weekends, Walking Weekend, and Murder Mystery.
ACCOMMODATION £21–£30
FOOD £15–£20

**Hours:** open all year Saturday lunch; breakfast 8:30am – 9:30am; dinner 7pm – 9pm. **Cuisine:** English / continental:- English and continental cuisine, with a varied selection of vegetarian dishes also available. **Rooms:** 13 bedrooms, 10 en suite, with central heating, colour TV, and tea/coffee making facilities. A family suite is available. Provision of a cot for a baby. **Credit cards:** Visa, Access, Diners. **Other points:** licensed, open-air dining, no-smoking area, children catered for – please check for age limits, pets allowed, parking, residents' lounge, afternoon tea, bank holidays. **Directions:** A387 to Polperro from A38.
MS C KAY, tel (0503) 72157.

## POOLE, Dorset Map 3

### ALLANS SEAFOOD RESTAURANT, 8 Bournemouth Road
*A small seafood restaurant offering extremely fresh, perfectly prepared seafood of all types. The exterior of the restaurant is unpretentious and the interior has the feel of a French rural restaurant which is in keeping with the very helpful, friendly service. Considering the high cost of seafood, this restaurant offers excellent value for money. Highly recommended.*
FOOD £21–£25 CLUB
**Hours:** lunch 12noon – 2pm; dinner 6:30pm – late; closed Sunday lunch. **Cuisine:** seafood:- Fresh local fish, fresh lobster, crab – all year. Alternative dishes include – steaks, veal, duck and chicken. Special lunch menu. **Credit cards:** Visa, Access. **Other points:** licensed, street parking. **Directions:** main road from Bournemouth to Poole.
A D TOMLINSON, tel (0202) 741489.

### CORKERS CAFE BAR & RESTAURANT, 1 High Street, The Quay
*Adjacent to Poole Quay with views overlooking the harbour, the ground floor is a cafe bar, the first floor a licensed restaurant and the second floor bed and breakfast accommodation.*
ACCOMMODATION under £20
FOOD £15–£20
**Hours:** cafe bar – except Sunday 10am – 12midnight; cafe bar – Sunday 10am – 10:30pm; lunch 12noon – 2pm; dinner 7pm – 11pm. **Cuisine:** English / seafood:- Seafood a speciality. **Rooms:** 4 bedrooms 1 double, 3 twins. **Credit cards:** Visa, Access, Diners, AmEx. **Other points:** disabled access, children catered for – please check for age limits. **Directions:** adjacent to the quayside.
NICHOLAS CONSTANDINOS, tel (0202) 601393.

### HAVEN HOTEL, Banks Road, Sandbanks
*An attractive building standing on the seafront with magnificent views across to the Purbeck Hills and Poole Harbour. Like its sister hotels, the Sandbanks and Chine, an informal atmosphere reigns despite its size and sophistication. The Haven Hotel has a purpose built Sports and Leisure Centre, and a newly built Business Centre Complex.*

ACCOMMODATION over £50
FOOD £15–£20 ★
**Hours:** breakfast 8am – 10am; lunch 12:30pm – 2pm; dinner 7pm – 9:30pm. **Cuisine:** English / international:- Traditional and international cuisine. **Rooms:** 94 bedrooms all with tea making facilities, telephone, TV: 18 singles ensuite, 29 twins ensuite, 39 doubles ensuite, 2 suites, 1 triple ensuite, 3 quads ensuite, 2 family rooms ensuite. **Credit cards:** Visa, Access, Diners, AmEx. **Other points:** licensed, Sunday lunch, vegetarian meals, swimming pool, residents' lounge, residents' bar. **Directions:** adjacent to the ferry in the Sandbanks area of Poole.
BROWNSEA HAVEN PROPERTIES, tel (0202) 707333, fax (0202) 708796.

### SANDBANKS HOTEL, 15 Banks Road, Sandbanks
*Sandbanks occupies a superb position right on the beach with lovely views of the sea and Poole harbour. The beach has the coverted E.E.C. Blue Flag Award for clean beaches. A large, fully equipped hotel with the atmosphere and charm of a smaller establishment.*
ACCOMMODATION £41–£50
FOOD £15–£20
**Hours:** breakfast 8am – 9:45am; lunch 12:30pm – 2pm; dinner 7pm – 9pm. **Cuisine:** English:- Table d'hote menu changes daily – steaks, game, fish dishes. A la Carte restaurant also available. **Rooms:** 105 bedrooms, all en suite. **Credit cards:** Visa, Access, Diners, AmEx. **Other points:** licensed, Sunday lunch, children catered for – please check for age limits, garden. **Directions:** from Bournemouth follow signs to Sandbanks Ferry. On the seafront.
SANDBANKS HOTEL LIMITED, tel (0202) 707377, fax (0202) 708885.

### SEA-WITCH HOTEL, 47 Haven Road, Canfords Cliffs
*Sea-Witch Licenced Hotel, with its friendly atmosphere, is set amidst pine trees near Canford Cliffs village. Within easy reach of Bournemouth, Poole Quay, Sandbanks, golf courses, sailing and windsurfing. Only a short stroll through pine-wooded chines to some of the finest sandy beaches in England. All rooms fully en-suite, with tea/coffee making facilities, colour TV, radio, telephone, etc. Ample parking in hotel grounds. Convenient to ferry for France and Channel Islands. Open all year round. For full tariff and brochure, please phone or write to Jo & Tony Sweeting.*
ACCOMMODATION £21–£30
FOOD up to £15
**Hours:** breakfast 7:30am – 9am; lunch – Sunday only 12noon – 2pm; dinner 6:30pm. **Cuisine:** English. **Rooms:** 10 bedrooms 4 doubles ensuite, 4 twins ensuite, 2 family rooms ensuite. **Credit cards:** Visa, Access. **Other points:** parking, no-smoking area, pets allowed, vegetarian meals. **Directions:** from Westbourne take the avenue to Canford Cliffs village, or from Poole, take Sandbanks Road, turn left at Compton Acres sign post.
JO AND TONY SWEETING, tel (0202) 707697.

## PORT ISAAC, Cornwall Map 1

### THE CORNISH ARMS, Pendoggett

*This typical Cornish 16th Century Coaching Inn, located on the perimeter of the small village of Pendoggett, is indeed charming. The excellent cuisine is served in a relaxed and friendly atmosphere, and the choice of fresh seafood, from the local fishing villages, makes it well worth a visit!*
*ACCOMMODATION £21–£30*
*FOOD up to £15* 🍷
**Hours:** last orders 6:30pm – 9:30pm; breakfast 8:30am – 9:30am; lunch 12:30pm – 2:30pm; dinner 7:15pm – 12midnight. **Cuisine:** English / seafood:- A la carte and Bar menu. Fresh local lobster, crab, lemon soles and fillet steak filled with sauted mushrooms and smoked oysters, specialities. **Rooms:** 7 bedrooms all with tea making facilities, telephone, TV: 1 twin, 2 twins ensuite, 1 double, 3 doubles ensuite. **Credit cards:** Visa, Access, Diners, AmEx. **Other points:** licensed, open-air dining, Sunday lunch, no-smoking area, pets allowed, children catered for – please check for age limits, disabled access, residents' lounge, residents' bar, vegetarian meals. **Directions:** off A30, follow A395 until A39 T junction. Left – first right onto B3314.
JOHN ROBINSON & MERVYN GILMOUR, tel (0208) 880263, fax (0208) 880335.

### OLD SCHOOL HOTEL, Fore Street

*The Old School dates from 1875 and stands sentinel on the cliff-top overlooking the harbour and out to sea. The accommodation is excellent, tastefully furnished to provide a high standard of comfort yet retaining the original character of the building. The restaurant specialises in local fish and seafood. Deep-sea fishing, riding, golf and sailing are all available nearby.*
*ACCOMMODATION £21–£30*
*FOOD up to £15*
**Hours:** open all year 7:15pm; breakfast 8am – 11am; lunch 11am – 3pm; bar snacks 11am – 9:30pm; dinner 7pm – 9:30pm. **Cuisine:** seafood:- Restaurant specialises in fish and seafood dishes such as Whole Grilled Lemon Sole, Lobster Thermidor, Mariner's Fish Pie. Bar meals. **Rooms:** 13 bedrooms all with TV: 3 family rooms ensuite, 3 suites, 6 doubles ensuite, 1 twin ensuite. **Credit cards:** Visa, Access. **Other points:** licensed, open-air dining, Sunday lunch, children catered for – please check for age limits, afternoon tea, residents' lounge, pets allowed, garden, barbecues, medieval banquets. **Directions:** 9 miles N of Wadebridge on B3314 until left turn on B3267.
MICHAEL WARNER, tel (0208) 880721.

### BAY HOTEL & RESTAURANT, 1 The Terrace

*Small, friendly, family run hotel at the top of this Cornish fishing village with views out to sea and cliffs. Ideal for a quiet holiday. 3 and 4 night mini-breaks available out of main season.*
*ACCOMMODATION under £20*
*FOOD up to £15*
**Hours:** breakfast 8:30am – 9:30am; bar snacks 11am – 10pm; dinner 7pm – 8pm; closed November – Easter. **Cuisine:** English / continental:- Fresh local crab and seafood, including lobster, home baked pies and pastries. Vegetarians catered for. **Rooms:** 10 bedrooms all with tea making facilities: 2 family rooms ensuite, 2 doubles ensuite, 1 double, 1 twin, 2 singles, 2 family rooms. **Other points:** licensed, Sunday lunch, children catered for – please check for age limits, parking, pets allowed. **Directions:** on the B3267 at the top of the cliff opposite main public car park.
JIM & MARY ANDREWS, tel (0208) 880380.

## PORTLAND, Dorset Map 3

### ALESSANDRIA HOTEL AND ITALIAN RESTAURANT, 71 Wakeham, Easton, Nr Weymouth

*An excellent family run hotel and Italian restaurant, ideally situated to explore Portland's historical interests, and yet close to the beach and shopping centre of Weymouth and the beautiful Dorset coast.*
*Accommodation is of a very high standard and the a la carte menu offers a wide range of traditional Italian, English & French dishes.*
*ACCOMMODATION £21–£30*
*FOOD £15–£20*
**Hours:** breakfast 7:30am – 9:30am; dinner 7pm – 9pm. **Cuisine:** continental / English:- All fresh produce, cooked to order by Giovanni, Chef Proprietor 30 years, 5 star experience. Most salads and vegetables from our own garden. **Rooms:** 17 bedrooms all with tea making facilities, TV: 3 singles, 1 single ensuite, 2 doubles, 5 doubles ensuite, 3 twins ensuite, 3 family rooms ensuite. **Credit cards:** Visa, Access, Diners, AmEx. **Other points:** parking, children catered for – please check for age limits, open bank holidays, disabled access, residents' lounge, vegetarian meals, residents' bar. **Directions:** from Weymouth take main road for Portland, A354.
GIOVANNI BISOGNO, tel (0305) 822270, (0305) 820108.

## PORTSCATHO, Cornwall Map 1

### PENDOWER BEACH HOUSE HOTEL, Gerrans Bay, Ruan High Lanes

*The hotel occupies a prime position on the beautiful Roseland Peninsula. It boasts extensive grounds where peacocks and ducks roam freely. The choice of cuisine is excellent specialising in local fresh fish served in a relaxing atmosphere.*
*ACCOMMODATION over £50*
*FOOD £15–£20*
**Hours:** breakfast 8:45am – 9:15am; lunch 12noon – 2pm; dinner 7:30pm – 9pm. **Cuisine:** English:- A la carte, fixed 5 course menu or bar snacks available. **Rooms:** 13 bedrooms 2 family rooms ensuite, 3 twins ensuite, 2 singles, 6 doubles ensuite. **Credit cards:** Visa, Access. **Other points:** licensed, open-air dining, no-smoking area,

children catered for – please check for age limits, afternoon tea, garden, pets allowed. **Directions:** A3078, turning 6 miles N of St Mawes. End of lane to 'Pink Hotel'.
PETER & CAROL BEETHAM, tel (0872) 501241.

---

## PORTSMOUTH, Hampshire Map 4

### SEAFARER STEAK HOUSE AND FISH RESTAURANT, 177–185 Elm Grove, Southsea

*A steak-house style restaurant, situated 5 minutes by car from the continental ferry port near the central shopping centre, offering good grills, interesting fish dishes and a daily market produce board. Friendly and efficient service and a welcoming pre-dinner bar.*
FOOD up to £15
**Hours:** dinner – Saturday 6pm – 11pm; dinner – Friday 6:30pm – 10:30pm; dinner – Monday 7pm – 10pm; dinner – Tuesday 7pm – 10pm; dinner – Wednesday 7pm – 10pm; dinner – Thursday 7pm – 10pm; closed Sunday. **Cuisine:** English:- English with strong European influence, using fresh daily market produce. **Credit cards:** Visa, Access. **Other points:** children catered for – please check for age limits. **Directions:** M275 to Portsmouth; first exit at roundabout, over 3 roundabouts; restaurant on right.
TIM HUNT, tel (0705) 827188.

### UPLANDS, 34 Granada Road, Southsea

*2 minutes from seafront, 10 minutes from continental car ferries. Reduced rates for children sharing parent's room. Special rates for OAPs in September. Stay seven nights – pay for six nights! Or 20% discount for 2 persons sharing, 2 nights minimum.*
ACCOMMODATION under £20
**Hours:** breakfast 6am – 9am; dinner 6pm. **Cuisine:** breakfast. **Rooms:** 11 bedrooms 1 single, 2 singles ensuite, 2 doubles ensuite, 1 twin ensuite, 2 family rooms, 3 family rooms ensuite. **Credit cards:** Visa, Access. **Other points:** children catered for – please check for age limits, TV lounge, satellite TV. **Directions:** off M27 to Portsea, follow the Southsea sign to South Parade Pier.
MRS H ZANELLOTTI, tel (0705) 821508, fax (0705) 870126.

---

## RANGEWORTHY, Avon Map 3

### RANGEWORTHY COURT HOTEL, Church Lane, Wotton Road, Nr Bristol

*An attractive, historic country house set in its own grounds with the church. Inside, the lounges have log fires and candles in winter, flowers all year and a relaxing atmosphere. Food is considered an important feature of the hotel and the restaurant has a strong local following. Enjoy welcoming service, well cooked food and the peace and quiet of this country house.*
ACCOMMODATION £31–£40
FOOD up to £15 CLUB
**Hours:** breakfast 7:15am – 9:30am; lunch – except

Sunday 12noon – 2pm; lunch – Sunday 12noon – 1:45pm; dinner – except Sunday 7pm – 9pm; dinner – Sunday 7pm – 8:30pm. **Cuisine:** English:- Dishes may include Devilled crab, Lamb steak in Madeira & rosemary sauce, Fresh salmon, Turbot. Vegetarian and Vegan dishes. **Rooms:** 16 bedrooms all with tea making facilities, telephone, radio, TV: 5 singles ensuite, 1 twin ensuite, 8 doubles ensuite, 2 triples ensuite. **Credit cards:** Visa, Access, Diners, AmEx. **Other points:** licensed, Sunday lunch, children catered for – please check for age limits, garden, pets allowed, functions, conferences, baby-listening device, cots, residents' bar, residents' lounge, vegetarian meals, parking, swimming pool. **Directions:** from Bristol, M32 Exit 1, then B4058 to Rangeworthy.
MERVYN & LUCIA GILLETT, tel (0454) 228347, fax (0454) 228945.

---

## READING, Berkshire Map 6

### HONG HONG RESTAURANT, 14 West Street

*A friendly, traditional Chinese restaurant serving an interesting selection of regional Chinese specialities, wines and liqueurs.*
FOOD £15–£20
**Hours:** meals all day – Monday 12noon – 11:30pm; meals all day – Tuesday 12noon – 11:30pm; meals all day – Wednesday 12noon – 11:30pm; meals all day – Thursday 12noon – 11:30pm; meals all day – Friday 12noon – 12midnight; meals all day – Saturday 12noon – 12midnight; meals all day – Sunday 1pm – 11:30pm. **Cuisine:** Cantonese / Pekinese:- Peking, Cantonese and Szechuan food – crispy aromatic duck, Peking style imperial hors d'oeuvres, Cantonese style spicy Szechuan prawn. **Credit cards:** Visa, Access, Diners, AmEx. **Other points:** licensed, Sunday lunch, children catered for – please check for age limits, functions. **Directions:** in the town centre opposite the Co-op, next to Prontaprint.
NGHU CHAN & GENEVIEVE ONG, tel (0734) 585372, (0734) 507472.

### MICHEL'S BRASSERIE, 62 Christchurch Road

*Recently refurbished in the typical Michel's style there is a modern brasserie on the ground floor and more traditional dining rooms on the first floor. As in all the Michel's restaurants there is a variety of a la carte dishes and set menus with a special "rapide" menu for those in a hurry. Everything is prepared on the premises using fresh ingredients. There are no-smoking areas and rooms available for private hire.*
FOOD up to £15
**Hours:** closed Christmas 1pm; closed 01/01; lunch 12noon – 2:30pm; dinner 6pm – 10:30pm; closed bank holidays. **Cuisine:** French:- Turbot Brasserie/Bistro style cuisine, complemented by a fine Wine List. 3 Course lunch menu. Vegetarian dishes available. **Credit cards:** Visa, Access, Diners, AmEx. **Other points:**

licensed, Sunday lunch, children catered for – please check for age limits, disabled access. **Directions:** close to Reading University and main traffic lights, in shopping parade.
MICHEL SADONES (MANAGING DIRECTOR), tel (0734) 872823.

## RINGWOOD, Hampshire Map 4

### THE OLD COTTAGE RESTAURANT,
14 West Street
*A unique and beautiful 14th century thatched restaurant, reported to be the oldest building in the area. Retaining many historical features, it offers excellent English and continental cuisine in an atmosphere of Olde Worlde charm. The proprietors personally supervise the day-to-day running of this extremely popular restaurant in a beautiful part of England.*
FOOD £15–£20
**Hours:** closed Boxing day and bank holidays; lunch 12noon – 2:30pm; dinner 7pm – 10:30pm. **Cuisine:** English / continental. **Credit cards:** Visa, Access, AmEx. **Other points:** parking, children catered for – please check for age limits, Sunday lunch, open bank holidays, no-smoking area, disabled access, vegetarian meals, open-air dining. **Directions:** A31 across New Forest towards Bournemouth, turn off at A31 Ringwood roundabout and proceed to High Street. West Street is a continuation of High Street.
TRICIA AND PAUL HARPER, tel (0425) 474283.

### TOAD HALL HOTEL AND
RESTAURANT, The Cross, Burley
*Nestling in the heart of the New Forest, Toad Hall is a perfect retreat whatever time of year. A beautiful Victorian country house, privately owned and operated, it offers a relaxed and friendly atmosphere. The bedrooms are furnished to a high standard and the restaurant offers elegant dining in the traditional English manner.*
ACCOMMODATION £21–£30
FOOD £15–£20
**Hours:** breakfast 8am – 9:30am; dinner 7pm – 9:30pm; closed Christmas day – Boxing day (inclusive). **Cuisine:** modern English. **Credit cards:** Visa, Access, Diners, AmEx. **Other points:** parking, vegetarian meals, pets, residents' lounge, garden. **Directions:** on A31 before Ringwood, Burley is signposted at Picket Post.
CHRIS SPRAGUE, tel (0425) 403448, fax (0425) 402505.

## ROCK, Cornwall Map 1

### ROSKARNON HOUSE HOTEL, Rock,
Nr Wadebridge
*By the golden sands of Rock and the open sea of the Camel Estuary, the Roskarnon House Hotel is an ideal place in which to enjoy the delights of a holiday in Cornwall. This small, unpretentious hotel offers all the essentials and amenities to make your stay a happy one. Simple, home cooked food.*
ACCOMMODATION under £20
FOOD up to £15
**Hours:** breakfast 8:30am – 9:30am; lunch 12noon – 1:30pm; dinner 7pm – 8pm. **Cuisine:** English:- Dishes include Vegetarian Lasagne, Roast Chicken and poached Salmon with butter sauce. **Rooms:** 12 bedrooms, 7 en suite. **Credit cards:** AmEx. **Other points:** children catered for – please check for age limits, garden, afternoon tea. **Directions:** overlooking Camel Estuary. Off A39 and B3314.
IAN VEALL, tel (0208) 862329.

## ROMSEY, Hampshire Map 4

### COBWEB TEA ROOMS, 49 The Hundred
*Situated in the town centre of Romsey, this friendly tea room has a restful atmosphere with a soft green colour scheme inside and an attractive Tea Garden. Broadlands and Romsey Abbey are nearby places of interest to visit.*
FOOD up to £15
**Hours:** open bank holidays 7pm; morning coffee 10am – 12noon; lunch 12noon – 2pm; afternoon tea 2pm – 5:30pm; closed Monday; closed Sunday. **Cuisine:** English:- Homemade cakes and sweets. Toasted sandwiches. Light lunches. **Other points:** open-air dining, children catered for – please check for age limits, disabled access, parking, no-smoking area. **Directions:** in the main street in Romsey on the A27, 100yds from Broadlands Estate.
MISS ANGELA WEBLEY, tel (0794) 516434.

### SOUTH GARDEN CANTONESE &
PEKINESE CUISINE, 9 Bell Street
*An elegant restaurant in the centre of Romsey offering excellent food in comfortable surroundings. All dishes are cooked from fresh ingredients and beautifully presented. Cantonese cuisine is based on freshness and stir-fried cooking whilst Pekinese cuisine is more spicy and aromatic. The wine list includes Chinese wines. Excellent, welcoming service.*
FOOD up to £15
**Hours:** lunch – Thur-Sun 12:15pm – 2:15pm; dinner 6pm – 11:30pm. **Cuisine:** Cantonese / Pekinese:- Cantonese & Pekinese cusine including Sizzling dishes and a wide choice of seafood dishes. Extensive menu. Set dinners and English dishes also available. **Credit cards:** Visa, Access, AmEx. **Other points:** licensed, Sunday lunch, no-smoking area, children catered for – please check for age limits, parking. **Directions:** centre of Romsey, approx 200yds from Romsey Abbey. Behind Town Hall.
JASON MAN, tel (0794) 514428.

## SALISBURY, Wiltshire Map 3

### ANTROBUS ARMS HOTEL, 15 Church
Street, Amesbury
*Situated on a quiet thoroughfare the Antrobus Arms Hotel is a traditional hotel offering a warm welcome,*

good food in both our bar and renowned restaurant, comfortable accommodation with large public rooms and open fires in winter. There is a large walled garden with a two-tier fountain in the centre. There is also excellent fishing nearby on the river Avon. Stonehenge is only two miles from the hotel, and the Cathedral City of Salisbury six miles.

*ACCOMMODATION £21–£30*

*FOOD up to £15*

**Hours:** breakfast 7:30am – 9:30am; lunch 12noon – 2:30pm; bar meals 12noon – 2:30pm; dinner 7pm – 10pm; bar meals 7pm – 10pm. **Cuisine:** English:- Serving bar snacks, full a la carte menu and table d'hote. Vegetarian meals available. **Rooms:** 20 bedrooms 4 singles, 4 singles ensuite, 1 twin, 5 twins ensuite, 1 double, 4 doubles ensuite, 1 family room ensuite. **Credit cards:** Visa, Access, Diners, AmEx. **Other points:** licensed, open-air dining, Sunday lunch, children catered for – please check for age limits, afternoon tea, pets allowed. **Directions:** 6 miles north of Salisbury A345, ½ mile off the A303, 11 miles west of Andover. JOHN HALLIDAY, tel (0980) 623163, fax (0980) 622112.

## FINDERS KEEPERS, *Southampton Road, Landford*

*This cottage-style building is surrounded by well kept grounds which are lit up at night. It is decorated in a light attractive colour scheme and comfortably furnished. Serving well presented and cooked meals, the atmosphere is relaxed and is complemented by the soft tones of music in the background. Excellent value.*

*FOOD up to £15*

**Hours:** lunch – except Sunday 10:30am – 5:30pm; lunch – Sunday 12noon – 5:30pm; dinner 6:30pm – 9:30pm. **Cuisine:** English:- A wide variety of traditional fare and local dishes with the emphasis on fresh produce and all home-made sweets. **Credit cards:** Visa, Access, AmEx. **Other points:** licensed, Sunday lunch, children catered for – please check for age limits, garden, afternoon tea. **Directions:** on A36, on the left travelling west from Southampton. KIM & SUZANNE SPROAT, tel (0794) 390331.

## GEORGE & DRAGON, *85 Castle Street*

*A small family pub dating back to the early 16th century within 5 minutes walk of the city centre. Real ales, keg bitters, bottled beers and an extensive wine list are offered to complement the variety of meals available. Enjoy the riverside garden – or barbecue your own meal in summer.*

*FOOD up to £15*

**Hours:** lunch 12noon – 2:30pm; dinner – except Sunday 6pm – 9pm; dinner – Sunday 7pm – 9pm; closed Christmas 25/12. **Cuisine:** English:- Grills, roasts, salads and daily specials. All meals prepared with fresh vegetables and produce wherever possible. **Credit cards:** Visa, Access, Diners, AmEx. **Other points:** open-air dining, Sunday lunch, pets allowed, barbecues. **Directions:** by the river in Salisbury. JOHN & WENDY WADDINGTON, tel (0722) 333942.

## HOGS HEAD, *Wilton Road*

*Offers a wide range of food at excellent value. Very friendly pub atmosphere.*

*FOOD up to £15*

**Hours:** lunch 12noon – 2:15pm; dinner 6pm – 10pm. **Cuisine:** English / international:- Wide range of pub food from chilli/curry to steak and kidney pies and battered squid rings. Desserts include sherry trifle and pancake rolls. **Other points:** Sunday lunch, no children. **Directions:** A36 to Wilton/Bath, just past Salisbury station. T C BROOK, tel (0722) 327064.

## THE KINGS ARMS HOTEL, *7a–11 St Johns Street*

*Standing in the heart of Salisbury and surrounded by picture-book English countryside, this hotel is full of lovely old oak beams, slanting staircases and sloping floors. Evenings can be spent dining by candlelight in the informal atmosphere of the restaurant. The 'Snug Bar' offers real timeless character whilst the bedrooms are individually decorated to a very high standard. Stonehenge and Salisbury Cathedral are nearby.*

*ACCOMMODATION £31–£40*

*FOOD up to £15*

**Hours:** breakfast 7:30am – 9am; bar snacks 11:30am – 3pm; lunch 12noon – 2:30pm; dinner 6pm – 10pm; bar snacks 6pm – 10pm. **Cuisine:** English / continental. **Rooms:** 13 bedrooms 1 single, 3 doubles ensuite, 8 twins ensuite, 1 family room ensuite. **Credit cards:** Visa, Access, Diners, AmEx. **Other points:** parking, children catered for – please check for age limits, Sunday lunch, no-smoking area, pets, residents' lounge, vegetarian meals. **Directions:** opposite St Anne Gate to Cathedral in St Johns Street. MR & MRS R STOKES, tel (0722) 327629, fax (0722) 414246.

## PEMBROKE ARMS HOTEL, *Minster Street*

*A Georgian-style hotel and restaurant, set in an attractive garden complete with a small stream. The accommodation is outstanding and the restaurant offers very good food at very reasonable prices. With welcoming service and a friendly atmosphere, the Pembroke Arms is well worth a visit.*

*ACCOMMODATION £31–£40*

*FOOD up to £15*

**Hours:** breakfast 7am – 9:30am; lunch 12noon – 2pm. **Cuisine:** continental:- Dishes may include Beef Wellington, Duck a l'orange, Scampi Provencale, Mushroom Stroganoff. **Rooms:** 8 bedrooms all with tea making facilities, telephone, radio, TV. 1 single ensuite, 2 twins ensuite, 5 doubles ensuite. **Credit cards:** Visa, Access, Diners, AmEx. **Other points:** licensed, open-air dining, Sunday lunch, afternoon tea, residents' lounge, garden, 24hr reception, children catered for – please check for age limits, baby-listening device, cots, vegetarian meals, residents' bar, disabled access. **Directions:** A36, opposite Wilton House Stately Home. Approx. 2 miles from the city centre. GENERAL MANAGER, tel (0722) 743328, fax (0722) 744886.

## SANDOWN, Isle Of Wight Map 4

### CULVER LODGE HOTEL & RESTAURANT, 17 Albert Road

*A family run hotel with glass frontage which looks out on shrubs and flower beds. Just a few minutes from beaches and entertainment for all ages, summer theatre and shops.*
ACCOMMODATION *under £20*
FOOD *up to £15* ★

**Hours:** breakfast 8:30am – 9am; lunch 12noon – 2pm; dinner 6pm – 7pm. **Cuisine:** modern English:- Table d'hote menu. **Rooms:** 20 bedrooms all with tea making facilities, radio, TV: 3 singles ensuite, 6 twins ensuite, 9 doubles ensuite, 1 triple ensuite, 1 quad ensuite. **Credit cards:** Visa, Access. **Other points:** licensed, special diets, children catered for – please check for age limits, cots, residents' lounge, residents' bar. **Directions:** Albert Road runs off the main shopping street, parallel to High Street, half mile to train station.
MRS LE LIEVRE, tel (0983) 403819.

### OAKLANDS HOTEL, Yarbridge

*A friendly, family run, licensed hotel at the foot of the Brading Downs, offering cheerful efficient service. Local activities include fishing, swimming, golf and sailing. Ideal for walking holidays. The pool is heated to at least 82 degrees Farenheit, June to September.*
ACCOMMODATION *£31–£40* ★

**Hours:** breakfast 8:30am – 9am; dinner (low season) 6:30pm – 7pm; bar snacks (high season) 9pm – 10:30pm. **Cuisine:** breakfast. **Rooms:** 1 single, 3 double, 2 twin, 3 family bedrooms, 1 family suite, 9 en suite including 2 four posters. Colour TV with in-house video, hair dryer, clock radio and tea/coffee makers in all rooms. Trouser-press/ironing facilities. Central heating. **Credit cards:** Visa, Access. **Other points:** children catered for – please check for age limits, garden, pets allowed, swimming pool, floodlit boules, aerospa, vegetarian meals. **Directions:** on Ryde – Sandown road, 1 mile from Sandown in direction of Brading.
JOAN RAWLINGS & FAMILY, tel (0983) 406197.

## SEAVIEW, Isle Of Wight Map 4

### SEAVIEW HOTEL & RESTAURANT, High Street

*This Edwardian hotel is situated in the heart of the pretty village of Seaview. It is possible to while away many hours looking at the unique collection of prints of old ships and liners that once passed the hotel. Frequented by local characters and the visiting yachtsmen. Routiers Restaurant of the Year 1989.*
ACCOMMODATION *£31–£40*
FOOD *£15–£20* 👄

**Hours:** breakfast 8am – 9:30am; lunch 12noon – 2pm; dinner 7:30pm – 9:45pm. **Cuisine:** English / seafood:- Local fish and shellfish. **Rooms:** 16 bedrooms, all en suite. **Credit cards:** Visa, Access, Diners, AmEx. **Other points:** open-air dining, Sunday lunch, children catered for – please check for age limits, residents' lounge, residents' bar, vegetarian meals, parking. **Directions:** take B3330 to Seaview. At Nettlestone Green turn left into village.
MR & MRS NICHOLAS HAYWARD, tel (0983) 612711, fax (0983) 613729.

## SENNEN, Cornwall Map 1

### THE LAND'S END STATE HOUSE, Land's End

*Situated right on the cliff-top at Land's End, the State House is a superb hotel with awe-inspiring views across the sea to the Scilly Isles. The all-glass observatory restaurant provides special surroundings in which to enjoy the high-quality food and welcoming service. Comfortable accommodation and an outstanding situation.*
ACCOMMODATION *£31–£40*
FOOD *£15–£20*

**Hours:** breakfast 8am – 9:30am; lunch 12noon – 2pm; dinner 7pm – 9:30pm. **Cuisine:** English / seafood:- Table d'hote and gourmet menus based on high quality local produce. Fresh fish and seafood a speciality. Bar snacks also available. **Rooms:** 34 bedrooms 1 single ensuite, 15 doubles ensuite, 18 twins ensuite. **Credit cards:** Visa, Access, AmEx. **Other points:** licensed, open-air dining, Sunday lunch, no-smoking area, children catered for – please check for age limits, afternoon tea, conferences, functions.
BILL JOHNSON, tel (0736) 871844, fax (0736) 871599.

## SHAFTESBURY, Dorset Map 3

### THE BENETT ARMS, Semley

*Built in the 17th century, 'The Benett Arms' overlooks the village green. A choice of freshly cooked, interesting meals and knowledgeable advice on wine make this traditional pub extremely popular with both locals and many foreign travellers. In summer, you can enjoy a barbecue on the common itself. Special events such as steam rallies, jazz bands, etc. are sometimes organised.*
ACCOMMODATION *£31–£40*
FOOD *up to £15* ★

**Hours:** breakfast 8:30am – 9:30am; lunch 12noon – 2pm; dinner 7pm – 10pm. **Cuisine:** English / continental:- Dishes in the restaurant may include steaks, Chicken Trois Frere, Traditional bar meals in the bar. **Rooms:** 5 bedrooms, all en suite. **Credit cards:** Visa, Access, Diners, AmEx. **Other points:** licensed, Sunday lunch, children catered for – please check for age limits, garden, pets allowed, vegetarian meals, parking, residents' bar, disabled access, residents' lounge. **Directions:** 2 miles off the A350, north of Shaftesbury. Turn right to Semley (1 mile).
J C M DUTHIE, tel (0747) 830221, fax (0747) 830152.

## SHALDON, Devon Map 2

### THE NESS HOUSE HOTEL, Marine Parade, Teignmouth

*Formerly a private country house, the hotel sits in beautiful gardens and enjoys wonderful views of the coast and the Teign Estuary. A friendly hotel serving good food.*

ACCOMMODATION £31–£40

FOOD £15–£20 CLUB ★

**Hours:** breakfast 8am – 10am; lunch 12noon – 2pm; bar meals 12noon – 2pm; bar meals 6:30pm – 10pm; dinner 7pm – 10pm. **Cuisine:** French:- A large choice of traditional French dishes. Coquille St Jacques aux safran, mignon de veau aux fraises. **Rooms:** 12 bedrooms all with tea making facilities, telephone, TV: 2 family rooms ensuite, 10 doubles ensuite. **Credit cards:** Visa, Access, AmEx. **Other points:** licensed, open-air dining, Sunday lunch, children catered for – please check for age limits, afternoon tea, garden, residents' bar, residents' lounge. **Directions:** on A379 (Teignmouth – Torquay road) in Shaldon. Parkland.

PETER & JANE REYNOLDS, tel (0626) 873480, fax (0626) 873486.

---

# SHANKLIN, Isle Of Wight Map 4

## BRAEMAR HOTEL, 1 Grange Road

*The Braemar is tucked away in Shanklin's Old Village. Probably the Island's most attractive corner, it is ideally placed for the beach, chine, shops and countryside. All bedrooms are tastefully decorated providing a cosy, relaxing retreat. A large sunbathing balcony is available to all guests, and at mealtimes, individual tables with waitress service makes dining here a real pleasure. Entertainment is provided in the comfortable surroundings of the Olde Worlde Thatched bar, which also has its own dance floor. A happy, friendly atmosphere prevails.*

ACCOMMODATION under £20

FOOD up to £15

**Hours:** breakfast 8:45am; dinner 6pm. **Cuisine:** English:- English with a touch of continental style. **Credit cards:** Visa, Access, AmEx. **Other points:** parking, children catered for – please check for age limits, no-smoking area, pets, vegetarian meals. **Directions:** Grange Road is directly off Shanklin High Street.

MRS P WILSON, tel (0983) 863172.

## BURLINGTON HOTEL, 6 Chine Avenue

*An attractive stone building, constructed in the reign of Queen Victoria as a gentleman's residence. Standing in its own grounds overlooking the sea, it is a comfortable family hotel for those seeking the traditional seaside holiday. Traditional home cooking with a pleasant lounge bar and residents lounge with sea view.*

ACCOMMODATION £21–£30

**Rooms:** 20 bedrooms all with tea making facilities, TV: 6 singles, 3 twins, 1 double, 4 doubles ensuite, 3 family rooms, 3 family rooms ensuite. **Other points:** parking, children catered for – please check for age limits, residents' lounge, vegetarian meals, garden, residents' bar, cots. **Directions:** B3328 to Chine Avenue, turn right.

MR J W ELLYAT, tel (0983) 862090.

## THE HAMBLEDON HOTEL, 11 Queens Road

*A detached family run hotel surrounded by well kept gardens. Tastefully decorated in a traditional style to a high standard, the accommodation is very comfortable. This is an ideal place to stay if you have young children as there are special provisions for very young children including baby sitting – Mrs Birch is a trained nursery nurse.*

ACCOMMODATION under £20

**Hours:** breakfast 8:30am – 9am; dinner 6:30pm. **Cuisine:** breakfast. **Rooms:** 11 bedrooms all with telephone, radio, TV: 1 single ensuite, 1 twin ensuite, 6 doubles ensuite, 3 family rooms ensuite. **Credit cards:** Visa, Access. **Other points:** children catered for – please check for age limits, garden, nursery, special diets. **Directions:** from Fishbourne Ferry; take A3055 to Shanklin. Near Cliff Top lift.

NORMAN & BERYL BIRCH, tel (0983) 862403.

## QUEENSMEAD HOTEL, Queens Road

*Positioned close to the famous Keats' Green area of Shanklin, just minutes from the sea, town and Old Village. An elegant Victorian villa with modern additions, the hotel has a large heated outdoor swimming pool and a sheltered rose arbor in the garden. The dining room is also open to non-residents, space allowing. Guaranteed personal all day service.*

ACCOMMODATION £31–£40

**Hours:** open Christmas 6:30pm; breakfast 7:30am – 9am; lunch 12noon – 2:30pm; dinner 6:30pm; closed December – February. **Cuisine:** English. **Rooms:** 31 bedrooms all with tea making facilities, TV: 2 singles ensuite, 10 twins ensuite, 13 doubles ensuite, 6 family rooms ensuite. **Credit cards:** Visa, Access. **Other points:** children catered for – please check for age limits, vegetarian meals, garden, residents' lounge. **Directions:** opposite the Church of St Saviour (very tall spire) on the cliff.

KEN, JEAN & JULIAN CHAPMAN, tel (0983) 862342.

## WEST COOMBE HOTEL, West Hill Road

*Situated in a delightful tree lined drive, West Coombe Hotel stands in a secluded garden setting enjoying a southerly position on the edge of the picturesque Old Village of Shanklin. It's informal country setting makes it ideal for newlyweds, but is also just minutes away from theatre, cinema and main shopping centre. The hotel has an enviable reputation for its good food and fine wines.*

FOOD up to £15

**Hours:** breakfast 8:30am – 9am; dinner 6:15pm – 7pm; closed November – March. **Cuisine:** English. **Credit cards:** Visa, Access, AmEx. **Other points:** parking, children catered for – please check for age limits, no-smoking area, residents' lounge, vegetarian meals, garden. **Directions:** turn off A3020 third mile from junction A3055.

MRS B STARKEY, tel (0983) 866323.

## SHERSTON, Wiltshire Map 3

### RATTLEBONE INN, Church Street

*An old Cotswold pub in the time-honoured setting opposite the church. The lounge bar is full of nooks and crannies, while the roof of the dining room is festooned with tankards, water jugs and bottles. The Games Bar walls are covered with boozy cartoons. The attractive walled garden has a boules pitch.*

*FOOD up to £15*

**Hours:** lunch 12noon – 2pm; dinner 7pm – 9:45pm. **Cuisine:** English:- A wide range of meat, fish and vegetarian dishes, together with constantly changing Blackboard Specials, with fresh vegetables. **Credit cards:** Visa, Access, AmEx, Diners, Switch. **Other points:** licensed, Sunday lunch, children catered for – please check for age limits, disabled access. **Directions:** 5 miles from Malmesbury on B4040 towards Bristol.
ANNE & DAVE REES, tel (0666) 840871, fax By Prior Arrangement.

## SIDFORD, Devon Map 2

### THE BLUE BALL INN, Nr Sidmouth

*Dating back to 1385, 'The Blue Ball Inn' is thatched and made of cob and flint. Fresh flowers add to the tasteful decor of the building and outside customers can enjoy barbecues in the garden during summer. Run by the same family since 1912, the pub provides well cooked food in a busy but relaxed atmosphere. Excellent, friendly service.*

*ACCOMMODATION under £20*

*FOOD up to £15*

**Hours:** breakfast 8:30am – 10am; lunch 10:30am – 2pm; dinner 6:30pm – 10pm. **Cuisine:** English:- Home made specialities include steak and kidney pie, chicken mornay, chilli con carne and local fish. **Rooms:** 3 bedrooms 3 twins. **Credit cards:** Visa, Access. **Other points:** licensed, open-air dining, Sunday lunch, children catered for – please check for age limits, garden, barbecues, pets allowed, functions. **Directions:** on the A3052, just outside Sidmouth.
MR ROGER NEWTON, tel (0395) 514062.

## SIDMOUTH, Devon Map 2

### BYES LINKS HOTEL, Sid Road

*The Byes Links nestles close to the heart of Sidmouth adjacent to the Byes, an extensive sylvan glade which lies alongside the River Sid. This family-owned hotel aims to provide an atmosphere of friendliness and attention to guests comforts. A gracious lounge with bar facilities overlooks the heated swimming pool and gardens. Ideally located for touring and exploring.*

*ACCOMMODATION £21–£30*

*FOOD up to £15*  ★

**Hours:** open all year 6:30pm; open bank holidays 6:30pm; breakfast 8am – 9:45am; lunch 12noon – 2:30pm; dinner 6:45pm – 10pm. **Cuisine:** modern English:- Fixed price menu, offering the highest standards of cuisine, in conjunction with a Master of Wine who has personally selected the cellar. **Rooms:** 18 bedrooms all with tea making facilities, radio, TV: 3 family rooms ensuite, 9 doubles ensuite, 6 twins ensuite. **Other points:** licensed, open-air dining, Sunday lunch, no-smoking area, children catered for – please check for age limits, pets allowed, garden, afternoon tea, honeymoon suite. **Directions:** take the Sidmouth turning off the Exeter to Lyme Regis road.
CLIFFORD HARROP, tel (0395) 513129.

### FORTFIELD HOTEL

*Overlooking Sidmouth cricket field and the sea, this elegant hotel is comfortably furnished and serves good food in generous portions. With a beauty treatment and indoor swimming pool, this hotel is ideal for those wishing to keep in trim or take advantage of the coastal views.*

*ACCOMMODATION under £20*

*FOOD up to £15*  ★

**Hours:** breakfast 8:30am – 9:30am; lunch 12noon – 2pm; dinner 7pm – 8:30pm. **Cuisine:** English:- Prawn and apple cocktail, deep-fried mushroom rossini, pork fillet cider and apple sauce, escalope of veal Italian, traditional steak and kidney pudding. **Rooms:** 50 bedrooms all with tea making facilities, telephone, radio, TV: 11 doubles ensuite, 5 singles ensuite, 5 family rooms ensuite, 29 twins ensuite. **Credit cards:** Visa, Access, Diners, AmEx. **Other points:** licensed, open-air dining, Sunday lunch, no-smoking area, children catered for – please check for age limits, beauty therapy, gym facilities, afternoon tea, pets allowed. **Directions:** from Exeter take A3052. Turn right at Bowd Inn. Hotel on right just before seafront.
ANDREW TORJUSSEN, tel (0395) 512403, fax (0395) 512403.

### KINGSWOOD HOTEL, Esplanade

*An excellent family run establishment on the sea-front with an award winning and colourful terraced garden. Fully modernised, the interior is spacious and many of the rooms look out over the Devon coast. Personally supervised by the proprietors, the food and service are excellent. The Kingswood is now licensed with a good selection of reasonably priced wines.*

*ACCOMMODATION £21–£30*

*FOOD up to £15*

**Hours:** breakfast 8:15am – 9:15am; lunch 12:30pm – 12:45pm; dinner 6:30pm – 7pm. **Cuisine:** English. **Rooms:** 26 bedrooms all with tea making facilities, telephone, TV: 8 singles ensuite, 6 doubles ensuite, 7 twins ensuite, 5 family rooms ensuite. **Other points:** central heating, children catered for – please check for age limits, pets allowed, residents' lounge, baby-listening device, picnic lunches. **Directions:** on the seafront.
JOY, COLIN, MARK & JOANNA SEWARD, tel (0395) 516367, (0395) 513185, fax (0395) 513185.

### WESTCLIFF HOTEL, Manor Road

*Delightful family run hotel, set in 2 acres of beautiful gardens. In a prime position for access to the town centre, Connaught Gardens, beach and golf club.*

Fabulous coastal views and excellent dining at affordable prices make this hotel a definite stop for tourists.

ACCOMMODATION £41–£50

FOOD £21–£25 ★

**Hours:** breakfast 8:30am – 9:30am; bar meals 12:30pm – 1:45pm; lunch 1pm – 2pm; dinner 7:15pm – 9:30pm; closed November – February. **Cuisine:** international:- Sunday lunch and bar lunches. **Rooms:** 40 bedrooms all with tea making facilities, telephone, radio, TV: 13 family rooms ensuite, 15 twins ensuite, 5 doubles ensuite, 7 singles ensuite. **Credit cards:** Visa, Access. **Other points:** licensed, Sunday lunch, no-smoking area, children catered for – please check for age limits, afternoon tea, residents' lounge, residents' bar, swimming pool. **Directions:** off the A3052. Situated along the sea-front.

MRS P HARDING/MR & MRS MALLOCH BROWN, tel (0395) 513252, fax (0395) 578203.

# SOUTH MOLTON, Devon Map 2

## THE GEORGE HOTEL, Broad Street

Dating from the 1600's, this is an old Posting House situated in the centre of a delightful village. Steeped in history, it has a magnificent old staircase, which has a preservation order. A warm, friendly atmosphere prevails. "Asterisk Restaurant" with rooms.

ACCOMMODATION under £20

FOOD up to £15

**Hours:** breakfast 8am – 9am; breakfast – Sunday 9am – 10am; lunch 12noon – 2pm; dinner 7pm – 9pm. **Cuisine:** English:- Traditional English cuisine, with a good range of bar snacks. **Credit cards:** Visa, Access. **Other points:** licenced, children catered for – please check for age limits, parking, Sunday lunch.

MR D & MRS J MACK, tel (0769) 572514.

## MARSH HALL COUNTRY HOUSE HOTEL, North Molton Road

Marsh Hall is a small friendly, independent country house hotel steeped in the peace and quiet of the rolling north Devonshire countryside. Dating from the 17th century with a Victorian frontage, it is reputed to have been built by the local squire for his mistress. Marsh Hall is proud of its reputation for top quality cuisine using fresh local produce. The bedrooms are equipped with many modern facilities and there is a magnificently proportioned Squire's Room with large four-poster and elegant curved bathroom.

FOOD £15–£20

**Hours:** breakfast 8am – 9.15am, dinner 7pm – 8:30pm. **Cuisine:** English:- Extremely good food, using top quality local produce and home-grown herbs, vegetables and fruit. **Rooms:** 7 bedrooms 2 twins ensuite, 4 doubles ensuite, 1 single ensuite. **Other points:** parking, open bank holidays, no-smoking area, residents' lounge, vegetarian lounge, garden, residents' bar. **Directions:** take North Molton Road off A361, take first right and right again.

TONY AND JUDY GRIFFITHS, tel (0769) 572666, fax (0769) 574230.

## PARTRIDGE ARMS FARM, Yeo Mill, West Anstey

Formerly a country inn, Partridge Arms Farm is set in over 200 acres of land. Ideally suited for touring or walking in the Exmoor National Park and the many local coastal beauty spots. Trout fishing and pony trekking also available.

ACCOMMODATION under £20

FOOD up to £15

**Hours:** open all year 7pm; last orders 7pm – 5pm; breakfast 8:30am – 9am; dinner 6:45pm. **Cuisine:** English. **Rooms:** 9 bedrooms 1 single, 1 single ensuite, 1 double, 5 doubles ensuite, 1 family room ensuite. **Other points:** central heating, children catered for – please check for age limits, residents' lounge. **Directions:** off A361, 8 miles W of Bampton. Follow directions for West Anstey.

MRS H J MILTON, tel (03984) 217.

## STUMBLES HOTEL & RESTAURANT, 131–134 East Street

Stumbles is situated on the edge of Exmoor in a bustling market town with its many fine antique shops and historical buildings. The attractive and spacious 30 seater restaurant with its secluded tables and soft lighting, offers fresh food daily. Stumbles have their own hotel offering very comfortable accommodation all ensuite. The bar and courtyard are open for morning coffees and lunches with barbecues in summmer.

ACCOMMODATION £21–£30

FOOD up to £15

**Hours:** restaurant closed Sunday 6:45pm; breakfast 8am – 9am; lunch 12:30pm – 2pm; dinner 7pm – 9:30pm. **Cuisine:** English/French:- Fresh produce used for the daily changing menu. **Rooms:** 11 bedrooms all with tea making facilities, telephone, TV: 5 doubles ensuite, 3 twins ensuite, 3 singles ensuite. **Credit cards:** Visa, Access. **Other points:** parking, children catered for – please check for age limits, no-smoking area, disabled access, pets, residents' lounge, garden, vegetarian meals, open-air dining. **Directions:** town centre, just off the Square.

MR & MRS M POTTER, tel (0769) 574145, fax (0769) 572558.

# SOUTHAMPTON, Hampshire Map 4

## AVENUE HOTEL, Lodge Road

Privately owned, the Avenue Hotel is situated in the tree-lined avenue. A friendly, welcome awaits you at this modern comfortably furnished hotel. The restaurant offers fine food and wine served in a convivial ambiance, so providing an excellent venue to entertain and to be entertained. Conveniently located, with direct access from motorways to the city centre.

ACCOMMODATION £21–£30

FOOD up to £15

**Hours:** breakfast 7am – 9:30am; lunch – except Sunday 12noon – 2:30pm; lunch – Sunday 12noon – 3pm; dinner – except Sunday 6:30pm – 10pm; dinner – Sunday 6:30pm – 9:30pm. **Cuisine:** English:- A la carte and

table d'hote menus. All dishes are home-made. **Rooms:** 48 bedrooms, all en suite. **Credit cards:** Visa, Access, AmEx. **Other points:** licensed, Sunday lunch, no-smoking area, children catered for – please check for age limits, afternoon tea, pets allowed, conferences, functions. **Directions:** off the A33.
A WYLIE, tel (0703) 229023.

## GOLDEN PALACE RESTAURANT,
### 17a Above Bar
*This restaurant is popular with the student population of Southampton offering a 10% discount to those holding a National Student Card. The food is well-presented, plentiful and very good value for money.*
*FOOD up to £15*
**Hours:** meals all day 11:45am – 12midnight. **Cuisine:** Cantonese:- Dim Sum, Cantonese dishes and seafood. **Credit cards:** Visa, Access, Diners, AmEx. **Other points:** Sunday lunch, children catered for – please check for age limits. **Directions:** M3 or M27 to Southampton.
MR DAVID LAI, tel (0703) 226636.

## LA MARGHERITA RESTAURANT,
### 6 Commercial Road
*A busy, friendly bistro type restaurant near the Mayflower Theatre. Popular with theatre goers and TV stars. Repartee and good humour flow as fast as the Italian red wine.*
*FOOD up to £15* CLUB
**Hours:** open bank holidays 11:45am; lunch 12noon – 2:30pm; dinner 6:30pm – 11:30pm. **Cuisine:** continental:- Langostinos, steak Diane, freshly made pizzas, and home-made lasagne. Desserts include creme caramel. **Credit cards:** Visa, Access, Diners, AmEx. **Other points:** disabled access, children catered for – please check for age limits. **Directions:** from main BR station, turn right at traffic lights into Commercial Rd.
FRANCESCO FANTINI, tel (0703) 333390.

## LANGLEY'S BISTRO, 10/11 Bedford Place
*Situated in a busy area, this is a popular city centre bistro offering fine English and continental dishes to a sophisticated business clientele. Spacious with an attractive bar and furnishings, a comfortable atmosphere prevails.*
*FOOD up to £15*
**Hours:** lunch 12noon – 2pm; dinner 6:30pm – 10:30pm. **Cuisine:** English / continental. **Credit cards:** Visa, Access, Eurocard. **Other points:** children catered for – please check for age limits, open bank holidays, disabled access, vegetarian meals. **Directions:** via Winchester, from M3 Motorway take A33 to Southampton.
MR TUCKER, tel (0703) 224551.

## SOUTHSEA, Hampshire Map 4

## BEAUFORT HOTEL, 71 Festing Road
*The Beaufort Hotel has achieved an outstanding reputation for comfort and excellence. You can relax in a*

*warm and friendly atmosphere where the emphasis is on service and quality, confident that your stay will be an enjoyable and memorable one. The hotel is situated in a beautiful part of Southsea, overlooking the Canoe Lake and the colourful Rose Garden, with the seafront and promenade just a short stroll away.*
*ACCOMMODATION £31 – £40*
*FOOD up to £15*
**Hours:** dinner 6.30pm – 8pm. **Cuisine:** English/European; a la carte and table d'hote. **Rooms:** 18 ensuite bedrooms. **Other points:** children catered for – please check for age limits, parking, licensed, residents' lounge. **Directions:** Festing Road is a quiet road 250yds from the seafront.
MR A FREEMANTLE, tel (0705) 823707, fax (0705) 870270.

## ST ANDREWS LODGE, 65 St Andrews Road
*A pleasant, newly renovated guest house situated minutes from the seafront and continental ferry port, and close to the motorway. All rooms have been thoughtfully furnished and are bright and clean throughout.*
**Hours:** closed Christmas 6:30pm; breakfast 6am – 9am. **Cuisine:** breakfast. **Rooms:** 1 single, 2 doubles, 3 twins and 3 family bedrooms. 1 bathroom, 1 shower. colour TV and tea/coffee facilities in all bedrooms. **Other points:** central heating, children catered for – please check for age limits, residents' lounge, garden, street parking, vegetarian meals. **Directions:** just off the B2151.
MRS D ROWLING & MRS B WATSON, tel (0705) 827079.

## ST AGNES, Cornwall Map 1

## PENKERRIS, Penwinnick Road
*Enchanting Edwardian residence with garden and large lawn in an unspoilt Cornish village. Dramatic cliff walks, beaches, swimming, surfing all nearby. Superb home cooking – traditional roasts, home made fruit tarts with local fresh produce. Touches of the exotic with excellent curries, pastas and vegetable dishes.*
*ACCOMMODATION under £20*
*FOOD up to £15*
**Hours:** breakfast 8:30am; dinner 6:30pm. **Cuisine:** English / international. **Rooms:** 1 single, 2 double, 1 twin and 1 family bedroom, 1 en suite, all with TV and kettles. 2 bathrooms, 1 shower. **Credit cards:** Visa, Access. **Other points:** central heating, children catered for – please check for age limits, residents' lounge, garden, piano, log fire, video. **Directions:** take B3277 off A30 at Chiverton Roundabout. 3 miles into village.
DOROTHY GILL-CAREY, tel (0872) 552262.

## ST HELENS, Isle Of Wight Map 4

## ST HELENS RESTAURANT, Lower Green Road
*This cosy English restaurant with a big log fire in winter, has a cheerful, relaxed atmosphere and overlooks the*

*largest green in England. The home cooking is excellent value and tastes delicious!*
ACCOMMODATION £21–£30
FOOD up to £15
**Hours:** last orders January – 10pm; lunch 12noon – 2pm; dinner 6:30pm – 12:30am; closed Monday. **Cuisine:** English:- A la carte menu, fixed 3 course menu. Mainly traditional English with vegetarian choice. **Credit cards:** Visa, Access. **Other points:** licensed, Sunday lunch, children catered for – please check for age limits. **Directions:** B3330 to St Helens, right onto Lower Green.
FRANK & ROSEMARY BALDRY, tel (0983) 872303.

## ST IVES, Cornwall Map 1

### BOSKERRIS HOTEL, *Carbis Bay*
*A family run hotel, set in private gardens with a heated swimming pool, noted for its fine wines and good food. Overlooks Carbis Bay, with magnificent views across to St Ives Harbour on one side and Godrevy Head on the other.*
**Hours:** breakfast 8:30am – 9:30am; bar meals 12:30pm – 1:30pm; dinner 7pm – 8:30pm. **Cuisine:** English. **Rooms:** 2 single, 10 double (3 of which convert to family rooms), 6 twin and 1 suite. 17 rooms are en suite. All have colour TV, radio, alarm, telephones and tea/coffee facilities. Baby-listening devices also available. **Credit cards:** Visa, Access, Diners. **Other points:** children catered for – please check for age limits, pets allowed, afternoon tea, bank holidays, special breaks. **Directions:** along A30 to St Ives. Third turning on right as you enter Carbis Bay.
MR & MRS MONK, tel (0736) 795295, fax (0736) 798632.

### CHY-AN-DOUR HOTEL, *Trelyon Avenue*
*This 19th century, former sea captain's home has been extended to form a most attractive hotel with superb panoramic views over St Ives Bay and harbour. All bedrooms are en suite, most with breathtaking views.*
ACCOMMODATION £21–£30
FOOD £15–£20 ★
**Hours:** breakfast 8:30am – 9:30am; bar meals 12noon – 2pm; dinner 7pm – 8pm. **Cuisine:** English:- 6 course table d'hote dinner menu. Main course dishes include a choice of meat, fish, salad and vegetarian. **Rooms:** 23 bedrooms all with tea making facilities, telephone, radio, TV: 10 doubles ensuite, 10 twins ensuite, 3 family rooms ensuite. **Credit cards:** Visa, Access. **Other points:** licensed, no-smoking area, children catered for – please check for age limits, residents' lounge, garden, residents' bar, baby sitting, baby-listening device, cots. **Directions:** A3074, on main road into St Ives.
DAVID & RENEE WATSON, tel (0736) 796436, fax (0736) 795772.

### PEDN-OLVA HOTEL & RESTAURANT, *Porthminster Beach*
*'Pedn-Olva' means look-out on the headland and this hotel, built with its series of towers, is situated on a*

*rocky promontory overlooking the ancient town, the harbour and bay. Beautifully presented and served, the quality of food and wine offered here only just surpasses the restaurants seascape view. Attractive balcony bedrooms provide guests with a relaxing holiday setting.*
ACCOMMODATION £41–£50
FOOD £15–£20 ☜
**Hours:** breakfast 8am – 9:15am; lunch 12noon – 2pm; dinner 6:30pm – 9:30pm. **Cuisine:** English:- Wide selection of table d'hote or a la carte menu, using fresh quality produce, including seafood specialities. **Rooms:** 35 bedrooms, 33 en suite. **Credit cards:** Visa, Access. **Other points:** licensed, Sunday lunch, children catered for – please check for age limits, afternoon tea, swimming pool, residents' lounge, pets allowed. **Directions:** A3074, hotel overlooks the town, harbour and bay.
KENNETH GEORGE EVANS, tel (0736) 796222.

### PORTHMINSTER HOTEL, *The Terrace*
*The hotel stands above the bay enjoying superb views of the harbour and beaches. The leisure complex complements the existing hotel facilities. St Ives has always been a prosperous town and home to many artists and craftsmen, as well as the new Tait Gallery of St Ives.*
ACCOMMODATION £41–£50
FOOD £15–£20
**Hours:** breakfast 8am – 9:30am; lunch 12:15pm – 2pm; bar meals 12:15pm – 2pm; dinner 7:15pm – 8:30pm. **Cuisine:** English:- Buffet lunch every day with a daily 'special' and roasts on Sundays. Vegetarian by prior arrangement. **Rooms:** 48 bedrooms 5 singles ensuite, 15 doubles ensuite, 18 twins ensuite, 10 family rooms ensuite. **Credit cards:** Visa, Access, Diners, AmEx. **Other points:** licensed, Sunday lunch, children catered for – please check for age limits, coach/prior arr, leisure centre, swimming pool, spa-bath, sauna, solarium, trimnasium. **Directions:** on the A3074, the main road in St Ives.
TREVOR & ROSALIND RICHARDS, tel (0736) 795221.

### SKIDDEN HOUSE HOTEL & RESTAURANT, *Skidden Hill*
*Welcoming and comfortable, the Skidden House Hotel is set in the centre of St Ives and dates back through almost 500 years of history. Today, under the ownership of Michael and Dennis, the hotel enjoys a fine reputation for its cuisine and comfortable accommodation. With a peaceful, olde world atmosphere, it is an ideal place to relax and enjoy the delights of Cornwall.*
ACCOMMODATION £31–£40
FOOD £15–£20
**Hours:** breakfast 8:30am – 9:30am; lunch 12noon – 1:30pm; dinner 7:30pm – 8:30pm. **Cuisine:** English:- A la Carte and table d'hote menus. Dishes may include Wild Salmon, poached in wine with King Scallops, served in Scallop & cream sauce, Tornedos Rossini. **Rooms:** 8 bedrooms all with tea making facilities, telephone, TV: 7 doubles ensuite, 1 twin ensuite. **Credit

**cards:** Visa, Access, Diners, AmEx. **Other points:** licensed, no-smoking area, children catered for – please check for age limits, afternoon tea, pets allowed, vegetarian meals, residents' bar, residents' lounge. **Directions:** take A30 then A3074 to St Ives. Turn right after bus/ train station.
MR HOOK & MR STOAKES, tel (0736) 796899, fax (0736) 798619.

## THE ST UNY HOTEL, *Carbis Bay*
*Suberb position overlooking the bay with excellent views from most rooms. Originally a private mansion, now a thoroughly refurbished hotel with an atmosphere of calm and relaxation. Standing in 2 acres of sheltered gardens with semi-tropical trees and shrubs.*
FOOD £15–£20
**Hours:** breakfast 8:45am – 9:30am; bar snacks 12noon – 2pm; dinner 7pm – 8pm. **Cuisine:** English. **Rooms:** 30 bedrooms, 19 en suite. **Credit cards:** Visa, Access. **Other points:** Sunday lunch, children catered for – please check for age limits, parking, afternoon tea. **Directions:** from A30 take the A3074, the hotel is close to Carbis Bay Station.
T & B C CARROLL, tel (0736) 795011.

## ST JUST, Cornwall Map 1

### BOSCEAN COUNTRY HOTEL, *Bosweddon Road*
*This peaceful Edwardian hotel is an ideal place to 'get away from it all'. Surrounded by fields and moorlands, this stately building overlooks the sea and, with its spacious oak-panelled interior, is a delightful holiday spot. Friendly staff and loyal clientele give it a welcoming atmosphere.*
ACCOMMODATION under £20
FOOD up to £15
**Hours:** breakfast 8:30am – 9:15am; dinner 7pm. **Cuisine:** English:- Traditional home cooked English cuisine. Fresh produce. Fixed daily menu with ample choice of appetizers and sweets. **Rooms:** 12 bedrooms all with tea making facilities: 4 family rooms ensuite, 4 doubles ensuite, 4 twins ensuite. **Credit cards:** Visa, Access, Eurocard. **Other points:** children catered for – please check for age limits, pets allowed, garden, parking. **Directions:** A3071 to St Just Sq. Turn left by Barclays Bank into Boswedden Rd.
ROY & JOYCE LEE, tel (0736) 788748.

## ST JUST IN PENWITH, Cornwall Map 1

### WELLINGTON HOTEL, *Market Square*
*In the centre of St Just-in-Penwith, the Wellington Hotel is well located to explore Cornwall. Extensively modernised in recent years this comfortable, family-run hotel is noted for its excellent food. All room bookings include a full English breakfast and a menu with daily specials is available for non-residents at lunch and dinner times. Ideal centre for walking, climbing, water sports and relaxing holidays, golf and beaches.*
ACCOMMODATION under £20
FOOD up to £15 ★
**Hours:** open all year 7pm; breakfast 8am – 8:30am; lunch 12noon – 2pm; dinner 6pm – 8:30pm. **Cuisine:** English:- Cuisine for all the family – pub style, including traditional Sunday lunch and children's menu. Vegetarians also catered for. Fresh local fish and crab, steaks, etc. **Rooms:** 13 bedrooms, 6 en suite with toilet, bath, shower, colour TV, hair dryer, trouser-press, direct-dial telephone and tea/coffee making facilities. **Credit cards:** Visa, Access. **Other points:** licensed, open-air dining, Sunday lunch, children catered for – please check for age limits, bank holidays, pets allowed, residents' lounge. **Directions:** take A3071 from Penzance to St Just (6 miles).
RODERICK & JENNIFER GRAY, tel (0736) 787319, (0736) 787906.

## STOCKBRIDGE, Hampshire Map 4

### THE GREYHOUND HOTEL
*This small hotel situated in a delightful small Hampshire town has log fires and oak beams and the restaurant offers a wide selection of seafood dishes, including Lobster, Crepe Fruits de Mer and Smoked Trout. The hotel has its own stretch of the famous River Test – day tickets available. Golf day fees can also be arranged, along with Clay Pigeon Shooting.*
ACCOMMODATION £31–£40
FOOD up to £15
**Hours:** breakfast 7:30am – 9:30am; lunch 12noon – 2pm; dinner 6pm – 9:30pm. **Cuisine:** English / seafood:- A la carte including a range of seafood, crepes, and Ploughman's. **Rooms:** 10 rooms, 5 en suite. **Credit cards:** Visa, Access, AmEx. **Other points:** licensed, open-air dining, Sunday lunch, children catered for – please check for age limits, afternoon tea, garden, pets allowed. **Directions:** Stockbridge is located at the intersection of the A30 and A3057.
MR GUMBRELL, tel (0264) 810833.

## STOGUMBER, Somerset Map 3

### CURDON MILL, *Lower Vellow, Near Taunton*
*Curdon Mill nestles in a beautiful, tranquil setting at the foot of the Quantock Hills and is ideal for the country-lover wishing to explore this picturesque part of Somerset. The bedrooms are prettily decorated and in the comfortable lounge there are chintz chairs and fresh flowers. A cosy atmosphere prevails welcoming guests from far and wide. Idyllic setting for weddings and private parties with the hills providing a perfect backdrop. Has its own heated outdoor swimming pool.*
**Hours:** breakfast 8am – 9am; lunch 12noon – 2pm; bar snacks 6:30pm – 8:30pm. **Cuisine:** English. **Other points:** parking, afternoon teas, no-smoking area, pets, garden, residents' lounge, open-air dining, vegetarian meals. **Directions:** off A358 for Vellow – 1 mile down the road.
MR R CRIDDIE, tel (0984) 56522, fax (0984) 56197.

## STUDLAND, Dorset Map 3

### THE MANOR HOUSE, Beach Road, Studland Bay

An 18th century Gothic manor in 16 acres of secluded, mature grounds with 2 tennis courts, overlooking the sea and 3 miles of sandy beach. The house has been in the Rose family since 1950 and has been fully modernised whilst retaining the original features and character. Wonderful coastal walks.

ACCOMMODATION over £50

FOOD £15–£20 ★

**Hours:** breakfast 8:30am – 9:30am; lunch 12noon – 2pm; closed 17/12 – 29/01; dinner 7pm – 8:30pm. **Cuisine:** English:- Local venison, duckling and fresh local seafood. **Rooms:** 20 bedrooms all with tea making facilities, telephone, radio, TV: 6 twins ensuite, 6 doubles ensuite, 2 triples ensuite, 6 quads ensuite. **Credit cards:** Visa, Access. **Other points:** open-air dining, Sunday lunch, children catered for – please check for age limits, golf nearby, tennis, residents' lounge, residents' bar. **Directions:** 3 miles from Swanage, 3 miles from Sandbanks Ferry.
MR RICHARD ROSE, tel (092944) 288.

## STURMINSTER NEWTON, Dorset Map 3

### STOURCASTLE LODGE, Goughs Close

Stourcastle Lodge was originally a farmhouse known as The Cottage. Centrally located in the medieval market town of Sturminster Newton, it offers relaxing all year round hospitality, from blazing log fires in winter to a pretty cottage garden in summer. An exhausting day exploring the Dorset countryside will prepare you for a delectable four course dinner in the evening.
**Hours:** open all year 7pm; breakfast 7:30am – 9:30am; dinner 7:30pm – 9:30pm. **Cuisine:** English / continental:- Delicious and imaginative English and continental cuisine. Fixed menus. **Rooms:** 5 bedrooms, 4 en suite, all with radio, alarm, telephone, tea/coffee making facilities, some with whirlpool bath and TV. Antique brass bedsteads! **Credit cards:** Visa, Access. **Other points:** children catered for – please check for age limits, residents' lounge, garden, parking, vegetarian meals. **Directions:** B3092. Off Town Square.
KEN & JILL HOOKHAM-BASSETT, tel (0258) 472320, fax (0258) 473381.

## SWANAGE, Dorset Map 3

### HAVENHURST HOTEL, Cranborne Road

A comfortable hotel standing in its own grounds, just a short stroll from the shops, the safe sandy beach and all other amenities. With good home cooked food, a comfortable lounge bar and a spacious colour TV lounge, Havenhurst also offers a high standard of accommodation. The proprietors extend a warm and friendly welcome to all guests.

ACCOMMODATION under £20

FOOD up to £15

**Hours:** breakfast 8:30am – 9:15am; bar meals 12noon – 2pm; dinner 7pm. **Cuisine:** English. **Rooms:** 17 bedrooms all with tea making facilities: 3 singles ensuite, 4 twins ensuite, 8 doubles ensuite, 2 family rooms ensuite. **Other points:** children catered for – please check for age limits, garden, afternoon tea, TV lounge, hair dryers, launderette. **Directions:** close to the beach. Off Rempstone Road.
MRS CHERRETT & MRS ROBSON, tel (0929) 424224.

### MOWLEM RESTAURANT, Shore Road

Situated on the beach road with views over the beach and bay. Very popular with families as it has a special children's menu and everyone can enjoy watching their meals being prepared in front of them.

FOOD £15–£20

**Hours:** lunch 12noon – 2pm; dinner 7pm – 10pm; closed Christmas 25/12. **Cuisine:** English:- Seafood, steaks, salads, children's menu. **Credit cards:** Visa, Access. **Other points:** Sunday lunch, children catered for – please check for age limits, coach/prior arr. **Directions:** on the beach road.
MR SM HOUSLEY, tel (0929) 422496.

## SWINDON, Wiltshire Map 3

### BLUNSDON HOUSE HOTEL, Blunsdon

Close to junction 15 on the M4, this hotel caters for every type of traveller. It is family owned and managed with a pleasant, friendly, relaxed atmosphere. The restaurant has developed a strong local following.

ACCOMMODATION £41–£50

FOOD up to £15

**Hours:** open 24 hours 25/12; breakfast 7am – 9:30am; lunch 12noon – 2:15pm; dinner 7pm – 10:30pm. **Cuisine:** English:- Fillet steak Blunsdon-style. **Rooms:** 88 bedrooms all with tea making facilities, telephone, radio, TV: 9 singles ensuite, 51 doubles ensuite, 18 twins ensuite, 10 family rooms ensuite. **Credit cards:** Visa, Access, Diners, AmEx. **Other points:** licensed, Sunday lunch, children catered for – please check for age limits, leisure centre, swimming pool, sauna, creche available, beauty therapy, 9 hole golf course. **Directions:** 2 miles north of Swindon just off A419 at "Broad Blunsdon".
MR P CLIFFORD, tel (0793) 721701, fax (0793) 721056.

## TAUNTON, Somerset Map 3

### THE CAREW ARMS, Crowcombe

Nestling in the Somerset countryside yet conveniently situated for access to the south west, the Carew Arms is the ideal place to stay when exploring the West Country.

ACCOMMODATION under £20

FOOD up to £15

**Hours:** breakfast 8am – 9am; dinner 8pm – 9pm. **Cuisine:** English. **Rooms:** 4 bedrooms 4 doubles.

Credit cards: Visa, Access. Other points: children catered for – please check for age limits. Directions: off A358 Taunton – Minehead road. 10 miles Taunton. 4 miles Williton.
MRS C BREMNER, tel (09848) 631.

### THE CORNER HOUSE, Park Street
*A Victorian hotel of character, situated close to the centre of Taunton. Lunch and dinner is served in the Parkfield Restaurant, offering food and wine of fine quality and the staff are efficient and friendly. Close to Exmoor, Dartmoor, Quantocks, and Yeovilton Air Museum.*
*ACCOMMODATION £21–£30*
*FOOD up to £15*
Hours: breakfast 7am – 9:30am; lunch 12noon – 1:30pm; dinner 7pm – 10pm. Cuisine: English / French:- English and French cuisine, including trout served with almonds and chateaubriand. Good wine list. Rooms: 29 bedrooms all with tea making facilities, telephone, radio, TV: 2 singles, 6 singles ensuite, 13 twins ensuite, 4 doubles ensuite, 4 family rooms ensuite. Credit cards: Visa, Access. Other points: licensed, no-smoking area, children catered for – please check for age limits, bank holidays, vegetarian meals, parking, residents' lounge, residents' bar, disabled access. Directions: A38, on south side of Taunton town centre. MR R IRISH, tel (0823) 284683.

### THE ROSE & CROWN EAST LYNG, East Lyng
*A 400 year old Coaching Inn, situated in beautiful countryside with panoramic views over the Somerset levels. Chintz furnishings against old oak beams and a welcoming log fire in winter. Residents' have use of the Sitting Room which is tastefully furnished with antiques. Nearby attractions, include the Taunton & Bridgwater Canal, Glastonbury Tor, Wells Cathedral and many more.*
*ACCOMMODATION under £20*
*FOOD up to £15*
Hours: lunch 11am – 2:30pm; bar meals 12noon – 2pm; dinner 6:30pm – 11pm; bar meals 7pm – 10pm. Cuisine: English / international:- Dishes may include, Rainbow Trout with Almonds, Chicken with Garlic & Herb butter. Steaks. Roast Lunches on Sundays. Rooms: 2 bedrooms all with tea making facilities, radio, TV: 2 doubles ensuite. Credit cards: Visa. Other points: licensed, open-air dining, Sunday lunch, children catered for – please check for age limits, vegetarian meals, parking, residents' lounge, garden, skittle alley. Directions: 6 miles out of Taunton on the A361 Taunton/Glastonbury road.
PETER JOHN THYER & DEREK MASON, tel (0823) 698235.

## TAVISTOCK, Devon Map 2

### THE OLD PLOUGH INN, Bere Ferrers, Nr Yelverton
*A 16th century Inn, situated beside the River Tavy in the scenic village of Bere Ferrers, in an unspoilt area of* outstanding beauty. A wide range of home-made food and ales are offered in the bar, restaurant or beer garden. Open log fires in winter.
*FOOD up to £15*
Hours: lunch 12noon – 3pm; dinner 7:30pm – 10:30pm; closed Christmas evening only. Cuisine: English:- Menus change daily, including, when available, fresh fish and 'Maggies Monster' home-made pies. Locally grown vegetables. All dishes home-made. Credit cards: Visa, Access, AmEx. Other points: licensed, open-air dining, Sunday lunch. Directions: from Plymouth – A386, follow signs for Bere Alston and Bere Ferrers.
ADRIAN & MARGARET HOOPER, tel (0822) 840358.

## THE LIZARD, Cornwall Map 1

### THE CAERTHILLIAN, Helston
*A Victorian building, in the centre of the village, retaining much of its character with some of the original furnishings and fireplaces, yet recently refurbished to provide modern standards of comfort. Set in the beautiful surroundings of the Lizard Peninsula. Restaurant serves a selection of sensibly priced home-cooked food, offering quality and real value.*
*ACCOMMODATION under £20*
*FOOD up to £15*
Hours: breakfast 8:30am – 9:30am; lunch 12noon – 2pm; dinner 6pm – 9pm; restaurant closed Sunday evening & Monday; restaurant closed (winter) Tuesday. Cuisine: international:- international cuisine, with Italian bias. Dishes may include, Guinea Fowl and Mushrooms in Red Wine, Grilled Whole Lemon Sole, Homemade Pasta Dishes. Rooms: 4 bedrooms all with tea making facilities, radio, TV: 1 double, 1 double ensuite, 1 twin ensuite, 1 family room ensuite. Credit cards: Visa, Access, AmEx. Other points: licensed, Sunday lunch, children catered for – please check for age limits, pets – prior arrangement, parking, vegetarian meals. Directions: in The Lizard village, opposite the post office.
JACK & PENNY GAYTON, tel (0326) 290019.

### HOUSEL BAY HOTEL, Housel Bay
*An elegant Victorian hotel in a spectacular clifftop position, with a secluded sandy cove and extensive grounds. Offers well equipped, comfortable rooms and value for money food. Kynance Cove, The Lizard and Goonhilly Downs all nearby.*
*ACCOMMODATION £31–£40*
*FOOD £15–£20*
Hours: closed 01/01 – 08/02; breakfast 8:30am – 10am; bar meals 11:30am – 1:45pm; dinner 7:30pm – 9:30pm; bar meals 7:30pm – 9:30pm. Cuisine: English:- Traditional English cuisine, including fresh fish and seafood. Rooms: 23 bedrooms all with tea making facilities, telephone, radio, TV: 4 singles ensuite, 8 twins ensuite, 11 doubles ensuite. Credit cards: Visa, Access. Other points: Sunday lunch, no-smoking area, children catered for – please check for age limits, pets allowed, afternoon tea, bank holidays, disabled access, residents'

lounge, residents' bar. **Directions:** at The Lizard town signpost, take the left fork following hotel signs. FREDA & DEREK OSWALD, tel (0326) 290417, fax (0326) 290359.

## THROWLEIGH, Devon Map 2

### WELL FARM, Okehampton
*Relax in beautiful and peaceful surroundings at Well Farm – a Grade II listed medieval Dartmoor longhouse. It is a working family run dairy and outdoor pig farm with peacocks, ornamental pheasants, free-range poultry. Fresh produce is served in a relaxed, family atmosphere.*
ACCOMMODATION *under £20*
FOOD *up to £15*  ★
**Hours:** closed Christmas 7:30pm; breakfast 9am; dinner 8pm – 9pm. **Cuisine:** English. **Rooms:** 3 bedrooms all with tea making facilities: 1 twin ensuite, 2 family rooms ensuite. **Other points:** children catered for – please check for age limits, residents' lounge, vegetarian meals, working farm. **Directions:** 1.5 miles from the A30 in the Dartmoor National Park.
MRS SHEELAGH KNOX, tel (064723) 294.

## TINTAGEL, Cornwall Map 1

### BOSSINEY HOUSE HOTEL & RESTAURANT
*A large country house standing in its own grounds. Tastefully decorated using light colours and comfortably furnished. The restaurant offers traditional English fare. All rooms are very well decorated in a variety of styles. This hotel overlooking the north Cornish coast is an ideal base for those wanting to explore 'King Arthur's Country'.*
ACCOMMODATION *£21–£30*
FOOD *up to £15*  ★
**Hours:** breakfast 8:45am – 9:15am; lunch 12noon – 3pm; dinner 7pm – 10pm. **Cuisine:** English:- Menu changes daily. Dishes include home made vegetable soup, roast leg of pork served with apple sauce, strawberry cheesecake. Table d'hote & a la carte. **Rooms:** 18 bedrooms 7 twins ensuite, 10 doubles ensuite, 1 family room ensuite. **Credit cards:** Visa, Access, Diners, AmEx. **Other points:** licensed, children catered for – please check for age limits, garden, afternoon tea, pets allowed, putting green, swimming pool, sauna, solarium, vegetarian meals, residents' bar, residents' lounge, disabled access. **Directions:** M5 Junction 31. On the A30 then A395. Follow signs to Tintagel
MR & MRS R L SAVAGE & MR & MRS C J SAVAGE, tel (0840) 770240, fax (0840) 770501.

### THE PORT WILLIAM, Trebarwith Strand
*Beautifully situated on top of the cliffs at Trebarwith overlooking the bay, this cheerful 19th century pub provides good food and a vibrant atmosphere in which to enjoy it. An excellent selection of home-cooked food and seafood at reasonable prices. Live music in the evenings.*
FOOD *up to £15*

**Hours:** lunch 12noon – 2:30pm; dinner 6pm – 9:30pm; closed Christmas 25/12. **Cuisine:** English:- A la carte menu offering traditional homestyle cooking. Speciality dishes include shellfish and seafood, with daily changing blackboard specials. **Credit cards:** Visa, Access. **Other points:** licensed, open-air dining, Sunday lunch, children catered for – please check for age limits, pets allowed, parking, afternoon tea, bank holidays, disabled access. **Directions:** follow the B3263 – off the Tintagel/Camelford road – 3 miles.
PETER & GILLIAN HALE, tel (0840) 770230.

## TIVERTON, Devon Map 2

### BRIDGE GUEST HOUSE, 23 Angel Hill
*Situated on the main road bridge over the River Exe in the centre of the town, all rooms overlook the river. There is a pleasant riverside tea garden. Fishing rights.*
ACCOMMODATION *under £20*
FOOD *£15–£20*
**Hours:** open all year; breakfast 7:30am – 9am; dinner 6:30pm – 7:30pm. **Cuisine:** English. **Rooms:** 10 bedrooms all with tea making facilities, TV: 4 singles, 1 single ensuite, 1 twin, 2 doubles ensuite, 2 family rooms ensuite. **Other points:** central heating, children catered for – please check for age limits, residents' lounge, bar. **Directions:** off M5 exit Junction 27, link road to town centre, beside River Exe.
BOB & SUE COXALL, tel (0884) 252804.

### THE HARTNOLL COUNTRY HOUSE HOTEL, Bolham Road, Bolham
*This lovely Georgian hotel has a cosy and intimate atmosphere which is very welcome after an active day prowling through the surrounding Devon countryside. A mill-stream runs through the hotel grounds, giving you a delightful feeling of 'getting away from it all'. Friendly and courteous staff help make your stay memorable.*
ACCOMMODATION *£21–£30*
FOOD *up to £15*
**Hours:** breakfast 7:30am – 10am; lunch 12noon – 2pm; dinner 7pm – 9pm. **Cuisine:** English / French:- Mixture of traditional English and French cuisine. Regular a la carte plus Table d'hote which changes daily. **Rooms:** 16 rooms all en suite. remote control TV, direct-dial telephone, tea/coffee making facilities in every room. **Credit cards:** Visa, Access. **Other points:** licensed, open-air dining, Sunday lunch, children catered for – please check for age limits, pets allowed, bank holidays, residents' lounge, residents' bar, vegetarian meals, parking. **Directions:** after Junction 27 on M5, take first roundabout (6 miles). A396 third exit right.
SALLY PRICE AND MAGDI SOLIMAN, tel (0884) 252777.

### THE MERRIEMEADE HOTEL, 1 Lower Town, Sampford Peverell
*Formerly a Georgian style Gentlemans Residence, The Merriemeade Hotel overlooks the Blackdown Hills. This hotel caters for all ages with a childrens play area in the*

rear garden. Its food is both varied and excellently cooked. The rooms are also of high standard. Great value for money.
ACCOMMODATION under £20
FOOD up to £15
**Hours:** breakfast 7:30am – 9am; lunch – except Sunday 11:30am – 2pm; lunch – Sunday 12noon – 2:30pm; dinner – except Sunday 6:45pm – 10:30pm; dinner – Sunday 7pm – 9:30pm. **Cuisine:** English / French:- A la carte menu, bar meals and snacks. **Rooms:** 5 bedrooms 1 single ensuite, 1 twin ensuite, 1 double ensuite, 2 family rooms ensuite. **Credit cards:** Visa, Access. **Other points:** licensed, open-air dining, Sunday lunch, children catered for – please check for age limits, pets allowed. **Directions:** 1 mile from Junction 27 of the M5 and north Devon link road. On A373.
MR L J AFFLECK & MR P J P COURT, tel (0884) 820270, fax (0884) 821614.

## TORQUAY, Devon Map 2

### THE DEVONSHIRE HOTEL, Parkhill Rd
A large, luxurious and quiet 100 year old hotel where guests are warmly welcomed with Porter Service. A distinct feature are the original doors and high corniced ceilings leading to the beautiful dining rooms and bar lounges which are decorated in restful colours. Nearby for theatre visits and boat excursions.
ACCOMMODATION £31–£40
FOOD up to £15
**Hours:** bar snacks 12noon – 2:30pm; bar snacks 6:30pm – 8:45pm; dinner 7pm – 8:45pm. **Cuisine:** English:- Traditional cuisine and grill options. **Rooms:** 71 bedrooms all with tea making facilities, telephone, TV: 8 singles ensuite, 14 doubles ensuite, 40 twins ensuite, 9 family rooms ensuite. **Credit cards:** Visa, Access, Diners. **Other points:** parking, children catered for – please check for age limits, open bank holidays, afternoon teas, disabled access, pets allowed, residents' lounge, vegetarian meals, garden, residents' bar, swimming pool. **Directions:** at the harbour clock turn right along harbour side and proceed up the hill toward Meadfoot Beach. The hotel is at the crest of the hill.
THE DEVONSHIRE HOTEL (TORQUAY) LTD, tel (0803) 291123, fax (0803) 291710.

### HOTEL SYDORE, Meadfoot Road
A Georgian villa set in 2 acres of wooded gardened grounds, only a short walk to Blue Flag Meadfoot Beach and town centre. The restaurant offers good food at value for money and the accommodation is of a high standard. Personally owned and operated by the professional but jocular Jane and John Rowe. Those with special diets are well catered for.
ACCOMMODATION £21–£30
FOOD up to £15 CLUB ★
**Hours:** breakfast 8:30am – 9:30am; bar meals 11am – 10pm; lunch 12:30pm – 2pm; dinner 6:30pm – 8:30pm. **Cuisine:** English / continental:- Dishes may include

poached Fillet of Salmon steak with Hollandaise sauce, Roast leg of Lamb. Vegetarian menu. **Rooms:** 13 bedrooms, all en suite and with colour TV, tea maker, hair dryer, trouser-press and radio. **Credit cards:** Visa, Access. **Other points:** licensed, open-air dining, Sunday lunch, no-smoking area, children catered for – please check for age limits, afternoon tea, pets allowed, residents' lounge, garden, games room, patio. **Directions:** Strand, Inner harbour, left into Torwood Street, first right.
JANE & JOHN ROWE, tel (0803) 294758.

### INGOLDSBY HOTEL, Chelston Road
A truly delightful hotel where you can relax in the attractive garden or take a short stroll to the seafront or into Cockington Village. The spacious dining room overlooks the garden and there are comfortable bedrooms and a quiet television room. An ideal base for a family hotel or seasonal break.
**Hours:** bar snacks all day 6:30pm; breakfast 8:45am – 9:30am; dinner 6pm – 7pm. **Cuisine:** English. **Other points:** parking, children catered for – please check for age limits, open bank holidays, disabled access, residents' lounge, vegetarian meals, garden. **Directions:** from seafront, turn right by Grand Hotel, first left then right at crossroads.
MR R WELLS, tel (0803) 607497.

### JINGLE'S RESTAURANT, 34 Torwood Street
An American themed restaurant offering a good variety of very well cooked dishes to suit all tastes. Choice of dishes includes char-grilled steaks, hamburgers and vegetarian meals. House specialities are Mexican dishes such as Sizzling Fajita, a traditional Mexican style of cooking. The good food is complemented by generous portions and welcoming service. International beers.
FOOD up to £15 ☕
**Hours:** lunch – summer only 12noon – 3pm; dinner 6pm – 11pm; closed Sunday lunch. **Cuisine:** American / Mexican:- Wide choice of dishes including chargrilled steaks, Cajun dishes, Mexican dishes, vegetarian meals, hamburgers and deep pan pizzas. **Credit cards:** Visa, Access, AmEx. **Other points:** licensed, children catered for – please check for age limits, street parking, parking nearby. **Directions:** 100 yd from Clock Tower on harbourside.
JOHN & PAT GOLDER, tel (0803) 293340.

### LANSDOWNE HOTEL, Babbacombe Road
A relaxed but lively south-facing holiday hotel, spacious and comfortable with a suntrap patio, swimming pool and full centrally heated for those cooler evenings. Nightly entertainment is provided, with Cabaret, live music and a family disco in the spacious ballroom, with special entertainment for children. Good traditional cuisine with a wide choice of drinks and cocktails. Many nearby attractions.
ACCOMMODATION £21–£30
FOOD up to £15
**Hours:** breakfast 8:30am – 10am; lunch 12noon –

1:30pm; dinner 7pm – 8:30pm. **Cuisine:** English. **Credit cards:** Visa, Access. **Other points:** parking, children catered for – please check for age limits, no-smoking area, pets, residents' lounge, vegetarian meals, garden. **Directions:** to Torquay Harbour, turn left at clock tower. The hotel is quarter of a mile on the left.
MR & MRS RIDLER, tel (0803) 299599.

## LIVERMEAD CLIFF HOTEL, *Sea Front*

*A comfortable family hotel situated on the seafront at waters' edge yet only a few minutes' level walk from the centre of town and English Riviera Centre. The hotel is tastefully decorated and offers a high standard of comfort, which is complemented by the friendly and efficient service. All meals are cooked on the premises using fresh ingredients.*
*ACCOMMODATION £31–£40*
*FOOD £15–£20* 🐕

**Hours:** open all year 7pm; bar meals 12noon – 2pm; lunch 1pm – 2pm; bar meals 6:30pm – 8:30pm; dinner 7pm – 8:30pm. **Cuisine:** English / continental:- Locally caught fish, Devon meats and poultry. **Rooms:** 64 bedrooms all with tea making facilities, telephone, radio, TV: 12 singles ensuite, 16 twins ensuite, 15 doubles ensuite, 16 triples ensuite, 5 quads ensuite. **Credit cards:** Visa, Access, Diners, AmEx. **Other points:** licensed, Sunday lunch, children catered for – please check for age limits, afternoon tea, swimming pool, solarium, garden, conferences, baby-listening device, cots, baby sitting, vegetarian meals, parking, residents' bar, residents' lounge, disabled access. **Directions:** from M5, exit onto A380 to Torquay, right at seafront, 600 yards.
MR JOHN PERRY, tel (0803) 299666, fax (0803) 294496.

# TOTLAND BAY, Isle Of Wight Map 4

## SENTRY MEAD HOTEL, *Madeira Road*

*An imposing Victorian country house on the west coast heudland, yet just a two minute walk from the beach, providing good quality, comfortable accommodation in attractive pleasant surroundings. You can be assured of a warm welcome from resident proprietors, Mike and Julie Hodgson. Ideal base for countryside and coastal walking.*
*ACCOMMODATION £21–£30*
*FOOD up to £15*

**Hours:** breakfast 8:30am – 9:15am; lunch 12noon – 2pm; dinner 7pm – 8pm. **Cuisine:** English:- Fixed price menu. Imaginative homestyle cooking. Dishes may include, Turkey Breast in a cream & brandy sauce, Lemon Sole, and Lamb Maroc. **Rooms:** 14 bedrooms all with tea making facilities, radio, TV: 2 singles ensuite, 5 doubles ensuite, 3 twins ensuite, 3 triples ensuite, 1 family room ensuite. **Credit cards:** Visa, Access, AmEx. **Other points:** children catered for – please check for age limits, garden, pets allowed. **Directions:** on the Headland, opposite Turf Walk.
MIKE & JULIE HODGSON, tel (0983) 753212.

# TOTNES, Devon Map 2

## THE OLD CHURCH HOUSE INN,
*Torbryan, Ipplepen*

*Many kings of England have dined at this Inn which is steeped in history and is also recognised as one of the most haunted inns in the West Country. Owned by the Pimm family since 1984, the Church House Inn is renowned for its warm hospitality and its unique atmosphere. The old Inglenook fireplace provides a magic atmosphere to enhance that romantic evening. The Locals Bar is well known for the quality of its beer and allows guests to mingle informally with local folk. These bars have been used extensively over the years for TV and radio for programmes such as* Ripping Yarns *and* The Most haunted Inn.
*ACCOMMODATION £21–£30*
*FOOD up to £15*

**Hours:** breakfast 8:30am – 10am; bar snacks 12noon – 3pm; dinner 7pm – 10:30pm. **Cuisine:** English:- Traditional English, freshly cooked and prepared daily from local produce. **Rooms:** 9 bedrooms all with tea making facilities, TV: 7 doubles ensuite, 2 singles ensuite. **Credit cards:** Visa, Access. **Other points:** parking, children catered for – please check for age limits, Sunday lunch, bank holidays, no-smoking area, disabled access, residents' lounge, vegetarian meals, open-air dining, garden, licensed, open to non residents'. **Directions:** leave A381 at Ipplepen sign, through village, past Church to Torbryan, on left. Turn off the A382 Newton Abbot to Totnes road to Ipplepen. Go through the village to Orley Common then follow signs to the inn.
PIMM, CHRISTINE AND ERIC, tel (0803) 812372.

# TREGONY, Cornwall Map 1

## KEA HOUSE RESTAURANT, *69 Fore Street*

*A 2 storey stone building facing the main street, tastefully decorated with a warm welcoming atmosphere. Excellent cuisine with seafood and fish specialities (in season) and special selection of malt whiskies.*
*FOOD £21–£25*

**Hours:** closed 01/11 – 30/11; lunch – summer 10:30am – 4:30pm; dinner 7pm; closed Sunday. **Cuisine:** English:- Chicken with fresh herbs and spices fried in filo pastry served in plum sauce, also fish and cheeseboard. **Credit cards:** Visa, Access, AmEx. **Other points:** licensed, disabled access. **Directions:** on the B3287, west of Truro.
MR & MRS A NIXON, tel (087253) 642.

# TRENT, Dorset Map 3

## THE ROSE AND CROWN, *Nr Sherborne*

*A 16th century part thatched freehouse, which could have been plucked from a picture postcard. There are 3 open fires and stone floors – a traditional atmosphere in which to sample traditional ales and cider and tasty home-cooked food, without the intrusion of juke boxes or fruit machines. Won national awards for cuisine in 1989 and 1990.*
*FOOD up to £15*

**Hours:** last orders Sunday – 9:30pm; lunch 12noon – 2:30pm; bar meals 12noon – 1:45pm; dinner 7pm – 11pm; bar meals 7pm – 9:30pm; closed Christmas 25/12. **Cuisine:** international:- Fish and game – using local ingredients. Menu changes weekly. Specialities – Cajun and Creole Cuisine from Louisiana. **Credit cards:** Visa, Access. **Other points:** licensed, open-air dining, Sunday lunch, children catered for – please check for age limits, pets allowed, open-air dining. **Directions:** A30 between Sherborne – Yeovil, take Trent turn, approx 1–2 miles. MR C F MARION-CRAWFORD, tel (0935) 850776.

# TRURO, Cornwall Map 1

### ALVERTON MANOR, Tregolls Road
Situated in the heart of Truro, this building was in the Tweedy family for over 150 years. The interior is tastefully decorated and furnished to a high standard. In a pleasant atmosphere and delightful, elegant surroundings, you can enjoy 'superbly cooked and presented' meals. Highly recommended.
ACCOMMODATION £31–£40
FOOD £15–£20 ☺
**Hours:** breakfast 7:30am – 9:45am; lunch 12noon – 1:45pm; dinner 7:15pm – 9:45pm. **Cuisine:** modern English:- Dishes may include Pepper Mousse with Salad, Baked Loin of Pork with an Apple and Plum Tartlet, Fresh Peaches in Champagne. **Rooms:** 25 bedrooms, all en suite. **Credit cards:** Visa, Access, Diners, AmEx. **Other points:** licensed, open-air dining, Sunday lunch, no-smoking area, children catered for – please check for age limits, bank holidays, afternoon tea, pets allowed. **Directions:** on A390 approach road to Truro from St Austell.
MR EDWARD BENCE, tel (0872) 76633, fax (0872) 222989.

### THE WITHIES, Penmount Farm, Newquay Road
An interesting old farmhouse which has been upgraded to a fine restaurant offering fine traditional cuisine using fresh garden produce. A friendly old world atmosphere prevails. Morning coffee and tea are served, and customers can purchase willow baskets, herbs, preserves and dried flowers.
FOOD up to £15
**Hours:** lunch 10.30am – 5pm, dinner 7pm – 11pm; closed Mondays and Saturdays October until June 1st. **Cuisine:** English; home cooked traditional meals. **Other points:** parking, children catered for – please check for age limits, Sunday lunch, no smoking area, disabled access, vegetarian meals, open air dining. **Directions:** 2 miles from Truro on A3076.
MR C J ELLIS, tel (0872) 70007.

# VENTNOR, Isle Of Wight Map 4

### OLD PARK HOTEL, St Lawrence
Games room, under fives supper between 4.30pm and 5.30pm, sauna, solarium, swimming pool, and no danger from traffic – all this plus comfortable accommodation, good food and a friendly atmosphere, adds up to a fantastic family holiday. Mr Thornton has created a fun safe haven for children, whilst providing all the qualities of a good hotel.
ACCOMMODATION £21–£30
FOOD up to £15
**Hours:** breakfast 8:30am – 9:30am; bar meals 12noon – 2pm; dinner 7:30pm – 8:30pm. **Cuisine:** English:- Extensive fixed price 5 course menu (pies, pasties/traditional English). **Rooms:** 34 bedrooms all with tea making facilities, TV: 1 single ensuite, 6 doubles ensuite, 4 twins ensuite, 3 family rooms ensuite, 20 suites. **Credit cards:** Visa, Access. **Other points:** licensed, children catered for – please check for age limits, garden, afternoon tea, pets allowed, sauna, solarium, swimming pool, special breaks, residents' lounge, residents' bar, foreign exchange. **Directions:** A3055 to St Lawrence.
MR R W THORNTON, tel (0983) 852583, fax (0983) 854920.

### ST MAUR HOTEL, Castle Road
St Maur is beautifully situated on town level, only minutes from Ventnor beach and Steephill Cove. All bedrooms have views over the hotel gardens and some have sea views.
ACCOMMODATION under £20
FOOD up to £15
**Hours:** breakfast 8:30am – 9am; dinner 6:30pm – 7pm; closed December – February. **Cuisine:** English. **Rooms:** 3 single, 4 double, 4 twin and 4 family rooms, 13 of them en suite. All rooms have tea/coffee making facilities. Colour TVs in rooms can be arranged. **Credit cards:** Visa, Access. **Other points:** children catered for – please check for age limits. **Directions:** west of Ventnor, St Maur is 100yds up Castle Road at end of Park Ave – A3055.
D J GROOCOCK, tel (0983) 852570, fax (0983) 852306.

# WADEBRIDGE, Cornwall Map 1

### THE MOLESWORTH ARMS HOTEL, Molesworth Street
True Cornish hospitality can be found at this 16th century Coaching Inn. The traditional furnishings and old beamed ceilings retain the character and olde-worlde elegance of the Inn whilst providing comfortable surroundings in which to enjoy the best in fresh local produce and the friendly, caring atmosphere.
ACCOMMODATION £21–£30
FOOD up to £15
**Hours:** breakfast 8am – 10am; bar meals 12noon – 2:30pm; bar meals 6:30pm – 9:30pm; dinner 7pm – 9:30pm. **Cuisine:** English:- Traditional English cuisine using local produce. Cornish produce includes local shell fish, salmon and speciality steaks. **Rooms:** 9 bedrooms all with tea making facilities, TV: 1 single, 1 single ensuite, 1 twin, 4 twins ensuite, 2 family rooms

ensuite. **Credit cards:** Visa, Access, AmEx. **Other points:** licensed, open-air dining, Sunday lunch, children catered for – please check for age limits, afternoon tea, pets allowed, residents' lounge, conferences. **Directions:** A30 to Bodmin, A389 to Wadebridge. Left over bridge. Parking at rear.
NIGEL CASSIDY, tel (0208) 812055, fax (0208) 814254.

## WAREHAM, Dorset Map 3

### WOODS EDGE COUNTRY RESTAURANT, Wareham Road, Sandford

*Woods Edge Country Restaurant offers excellent home cooking by the proprietor. Ideally located for visiting Lulworth Cove, Corfe Castle, Bovingdon Army Tank Museum, or exploring the beautiful surrounding countryside and beaches of the Purbecks.*
FOOD up to £15
**Hours:** lunch 12noon – 2:30pm; dinner 6:30pm – 10pm; morning coffee from 10:30am. **Cuisine:** English / French. **Credit cards:** Visa, Access. **Other points:** parking, open bank holidays, no-smoking area. **Directions:** from A35 Poole/Dorchester Road, 1 mile on left before Wareham town. Restaurant situated on Island.
MR BERRYMAN, tel (0929) 556959.

## WARMINSTER, Wiltshire Map 3

### THE FARMERS HOTEL, 1 Silver Street

*Centrally located in the town centre, this family run hotel, whose buildings date back to the 17th century, is comfortably furnished and decorated. The hotel offers good quality food and accommodation in pleasant surroundings, ideal for exploring West Country attractions, including Longleat and Stonehenge.*
ACCOMMODATION £21–£30
FOOD up to £15
**Hours:** breakfast 7am – 9:30am; lunch 12noon – 2pm; dinner 6:15pm – 12midnight; last orders 10.45pm. **Cuisine:** English / continental:- English, French & Italian cooking, extensive a la carte and set menus and bar meals. Dishes include fettucine alla carbonara, veal marsala and steak and kidney pie. **Rooms:** 18 bedrooms, 11 en suite. **Credit cards:** Visa, Access, Diners, AmEx. **Other points:** coach/prior arr, disabled access, children catered for – please check for age limits, functions, coaches, parking, vegetarian meals. **Directions:** on the A36.
MR G BRANDANI, tel (0985) 213815, (0985) 212068.

### OLD BELL HOTEL, 42 Market Place

*Part of the Old Bell dates from 1483 and much of the character and old English charm has been retained whilst adding modern comforts. Enjoy the high standard of English cuisine in the candlelit restaurant or good bistro and bar meals. On warm days relax in the attractive courtyard or by the open log fires in winter. Luxury accommodation and excellent, welcoming service.*
ACCOMMODATION £21–£30
FOOD up to £15 CLUB

**Hours:** breakfast 7:30am – 9:30am; lunch 12noon – 2:30pm; bar meals 12noon – 2:30pm; dinner 7pm – 10:30pm; bar meals 7pm – 9pm; closed Christmas 24/12 – 26/12. **Cuisine:** English / international:- A la carte and bistro menus and bar meals. Mexican, Italian and American. **Rooms:** 20 bedrooms all with tea making facilities, telephone, TV: 1 single ensuite, 8 doubles ensuite, 3 twins ensuite, 2 family rooms ensuite, 2 singles, 3 doubles, 1 twin. **Credit cards:** Visa, Access, AmEx. **Other points:** licensed, Sunday lunch, children catered for – please check for age limits, pets allowed, residents' lounge, functions, residents' bar. **Directions:** in the centre of Warminster.
MERVYN PARRISH, tel (0985) 216611, fax (0985) 217111.

## WATCHET, Somerset Map 3

### WEST SOMERSET HOTEL, Swain Street

*A 2 Crown town pub situated in the ancient port of Watchet. The hotel can arrange sea, fresh water fishing, clay pigeon shooting, golf and horseriding. For fossil hunters, the local cliffs are of interest. Also, an ideal base for cycling and walking holidays in Somerset and Devon.*
ACCOMMODATION under £20
FOOD up to £15
**Hours:** breakfast 8:30am – 10am; lunch 12noon – 2pm; dinner 7pm – 10pm. **Cuisine:** English:- Imaginative cuisine using local produce plus standard back-up menu and daily specials. Wine list includes interesting & excellent locally grown wines. **Rooms:** 12 bedrooms, most with en suite facilities. **Credit cards:** Visa, Access. **Other points:** open-air dining, Sunday lunch, children catered for – please check for age limits, pets allowed. **Directions:** on the A358 in Watchet.
MR & MRS CLIFFORD & VICTORIA BARBER, tel (0984) 34434.

## WELLS, Somerset Map 3

### THE BULL TERRIER, Croscombe

*An old stone-built country pub with stone flagged floors, open inglenook fireplace and an attractive garden. Reputed for its good food and value for money, The Bull Terrier has an atmosphere which is warm and inviting, to locals and holiday-makers alike.*
ACCOMMODATION £21–£30
FOOD up to £15 ★
**Hours:** breakfast 8:15am – 9am; closed all day Monday 1 October – 31 March; lunch – except Sunday 12noon – 2pm; lunch – Sunday 12noon – 1:45pm; dinner – except Sunday 7pm – 9:30pm; dinner – Sunday 7pm – 9pm. **Cuisine:** English / continental:- Dishes include Tuna and Egg Mayonnaise, Scampi, Turkey Cordon Bleu, Spiced Brazil Nut Roast, hot Butterscotch & Walnut Fudge Cake. **Rooms:** 3 bedrooms 1 single, 1 twin ensuite, 1 double ensuite. **Credit cards:** Visa, Access. **Other points:** licensed, Sunday lunch, garden, children catered for – please check for age limits, real ales. **Directions:** on A371, in the village of Croscombe, near Wells.
MR & MRS LEA, tel (0749) 343658.

### CROSSWAYS INN, North Wootton

*Located in the heart of the country, off the A361 and midway between Wells, Glastonbury, Shepton Mallet. Overlooking the historic Valley of Avon and Glastonbury Tor. Advance booking recommended.*

ACCOMMODATION under £20

FOOD £15–£20

**Hours:** lunch 12noon – 2:30pm; dinner 7pm – 10pm. **Cuisine:** English:- Full a la carte menu plus daily specials in the buffet bar, hot and cold bar meals. **Rooms:** 17 bedrooms, all en suite. **Credit cards:** Visa, Access. **Other points:** Sunday lunch, children catered for – please check for age limits, coach/prior arr. **Directions:** on the A361 midway between Wells, Glastonbury, Shepton Mallet.
JOHN KIRKHAM, tel (0749) 890237, (0749) 890476.

### FOUNTAIN INN & BOXERS RESTAURANT, 1 St Thomas Street

*Georgian style building, 50 yd from Wells Cathedral, enjoying a local reputation for fine food, using the freshest ingredients. Good selection of Spanish wines. Restaurant decorated with pine, local prints and Laura Ashley fabrics.*

FOOD up to £15 ♇ ☺

**Hours:** lunch 11:30am – 2pm; dinner 6pm – 10pm; closed Christmas 25/12 – 26/12. **Cuisine:** modern English:- Local produce mainly used; Lamb & redcurrant & rosemary sauce. Fresh fish daily. Interesting selection of West Country cheeses. **Credit cards:** Visa, Access, AmEx. **Other points:** licensed, Sunday lunch, children catered for – please check for age limits, real ales. **Directions:** in the centre of town behind the cathedral.
ADRIAN LAWRENCE, tel (0749) 672317.

## WEMBWORTHY, Devon Map 2

### LYMINGTON ARMS, Lama Cross

*Late Georgian country Coaching Inn midway between Exmoor and Dartmoor surrounded by panoramic views and extensive forest walks. Almost equidistant from Torrington (15 miles), S.Molton (15 miles), Crediton (15 miles) and Okehampton (13 miles). High quality, freshly cooked food at good value prices.*

ACCOMMODATION under £20

FOOD up to £15

**Hours:** lunch 12noon – 2pm; dinner 6pm – 11pm; closed Christmas 25/12. **Cuisine:** English / continental:- Homemade soups, pate, casseroles. Interesting variety of home-made puddings, sweets etc. **Rooms:** 1 double room with childs bed and en suite facilities. **Credit cards:** Visa, Access. **Other points:** licensed, open-air dining, Sunday lunch, beer garden, children catered for – please check for age limits, pets allowed, vegetarian meals. **Directions:** 2 miles west of Eggesford Station (A377), 2 miles east of Winkleigh B3220.
PAMELA & ALEC ROUD, tel (0837) 83572.

## WEST ILSLEY, Berkshire Map 6

### THE HARROW, West Ilsley

*A village pub standing on the edge of the cricket green opposite the duck pond. The village is situated on the edge of the Berkshire Downs. Beer garden and children's play area. The interior structure has been refurbished giving increased space. Visitors enjoy a high standard of home cooking using fresh ingredients with the emphasis on traditional British dishes.*

FOOD up to £15 ☺

**Hours:** lunch 12noon – 2:15pm; dinner 6pm – 9:15pm. **Cuisine:** English:- Rabbit pie with lemon, herbs and bacon. Traditional English puddings. English farmhouse cheese. **Credit cards:** Visa, Access. **Other points:** open-air dining, Sunday lunch, children catered for – please check for age limits, coach/prior arr. **Directions:** 1 mile off the A34 – follow the signs to West Ilsley.
MRS HEATHER HUMPHREYS, tel (0635) 281260.

## WEST LULWORTH, Dorset Map 3

### THE CASTLE INN, Main Street

*A charming thatched building dating back to the 1600's and close to the famous Lulworth Cove. The large garden is very popular – barbecues are held in summer.*

ACCOMMODATION £21–£30

FOOD up to £15

**Hours:** breakfast 7am – 9:30am; bar meals 11am – 2:30pm; lunch 12noon – 2:30pm; bar meals 7pm – 11pm; dinner 7:30pm – 11pm. **Cuisine:** English:- Homemade raised pies, fillet Stilton, spicy lamb, pork in whisky. **Rooms:** 15 bedrooms 2 singles, 2 twins, 8 doubles ensuite, 2 twins ensuite, 1 family room ensuite. **Credit cards:** Visa, Access, Diners, AmEx. **Other points:** licensed, open-air dining, Sunday lunch, children catered for – please check for age limits, coach/prior arr. **Directions:** on the B3070 road from Wareham in the centre of West Lulworth.
GRAHAM & PATRICIA HALLIDAY, tel (092941) 311.

## WESTBURY, Wiltshire Map 3

### CEDAR HOTEL AND RESTAURANT, Warminster Road

*Built towards the end of the 18th century, this personally-run hotel has a relaxed and informal atmosphere. Retaining much of its olde worlde character, the friendly staff will ensure that your stay is both comfortable and relaxing. The Regency Restaurant offers superb English and continental cuisine using fresh local produce. An ideal base for exploring the beautiful counties of Wiltshire, Somerset, Dorset and Devon.*

ACCOMMODATION £21–£30

FOOD up to £15

**Hours:** breakfast – daily 7:30am – 9:30am; breakfast – weekends 8am – 10am; lunch 12noon – 2pm; bar snacks 12noon – 2pm; dinner 7pm – 10pm; bar snacks 7pm – 9:30pm. **Cuisine:** English. **Rooms:** 16 bedrooms 1 single ensuite, 12 doubles ensuite, 3 twins ensuite.

**Other points:** parking, children catered for – please check for age limits, Sunday lunch, open bank holidays, Sunday dinner, disabled access, pets allowed, residents' lounge, vegetarian meals, open-air dining, garden. **Directions:** on A350 from Trowbridge / Warminster, situated on right side.
MRS L & MR T FROST, tel (0373) 822753, fax (0373) 858423.

## WESTBURY HOTEL, Market Place
*A Grade II listed building dating back to 1545 standing on the site of an old coaching halt known as the St George & Dragon. After major refurbishment, the hotel now boasts luxurious accommodation with many modern facilities, whilst retaining many of its original features, including oak beams and an open stone fireplace. A warm and courteous service is extended to all guests from both the proprietors and staff. The wine list is a connoisseurs delight. Ideally located for visiting major attractions such as Longleat and Stonehenge. Some rooms have four poster beds and spa-baths.*
ACCOMMODATION £21–£30
**Hours:** breakfast 7am – 9am; lunch 12noon – 2pm; bar meals 12noon – 2pm; dinner 7pm – 9:30pm; bar meals 7pm – 9:30pm. **Cuisine:** English:- A la carte, table d'hote and extremely cheap, good, bar meals. **Rooms:** 11 bedrooms 3 twins ensuite, 8 doubles ensuite. **Other points:** parking, Sunday lunch, open bank holidays, afternoon tea, residents' lounge, vegetarian meals, garden. **Directions:** A350 Warminster Rd from Melksham. Westbury Hotel is situated in the market place at Westbury which is in the centre of town.
MS R BAKER, tel (0373) 822500, fax (0373) 824144.

# WESTON SUPER MARE, Avon Map 3

## CARRINGTON HOTEL, 28 Knightstone Road
*A Victorian terraced house overlooking the beach and the pier, with a patio to the front laid with tables and umbrellas for ulfresco dining in summer. Situated near to the Winter Gardens, and with all the facilities of a British seaside town on the doorstep.*
ACCOMMODATION £21–£30
FOOD up to £15
**Hours:** breakfast 8:30am – 9:30am; bar meals 11am – 9:30pm; lunch 11:30am – 3pm; dinner 6pm – 9:30pm. **Cuisine:** English:- In the restaurant: steaks, grills, salads, omelettes, fish. In the bar: homemade steak and kidney pie, cottage pie, home-made sweets. **Rooms:** 16 bedrooms, 6 en suite. **Credit cards:** Access. **Other points:** licensed, open-air dining, Sunday lunch, no-smoking area, children catered for – please check for age limits. **Directions:** on the seafront between the Grand Pier and Marine Lake.
MR & MRS ARNAOUTI, tel (0934) 626621.

## THE COMMODORE HOTEL, Beach Road, Sand Bay, Kewstoke
*On the seafront at Sand Bay with extensive views across the Bristol Channel and the local countryside. Good access to*
*West Country attractions and several National Trust walks. Golfing discounts and riding can be arranged.*
ACCOMMODATION £41–£50
FOOD £15–£20
**Hours:** breakfast – weekdays 7:30am – 9:30am; breakfast – weekends 8am – 10am; lunch 12noon – 2pm; dinner 6:30pm – 9:30pm. **Cuisine:** modern English:- Lounge Buffet-Carvery and a la carte restaurant with international and modern English cuisine. **Rooms:** 20 bedrooms, 16 en suite all with tea/coffee facilities and TVs. **Credit cards:** Visa, Access, Diners, AmEx. **Other points:** licensed, Sunday lunch, disabled access, children catered for – please check for age limits, functions, conferences. **Directions:** overlooking beach in Sand Bay, 1.5 miles north of Weston on Toll Rd.
JOHN STOAKES, MHCIMA, MBIM, tel (0934) 415778, fax (0934) 636483.

## PEARL DE MARE CHINESE CUISINE, 15–18 Alexandra Parade
*An opportunity to sample excellent cuisine in delightful surroundings. The restaurant is tastefully furnished and comfortable, with pleasant, restful background music. Service is highly efficient and courteous. Executive business lunches available. Situated within easy reach of many major tourist attractions, from the seafront to the beautiful surrounding countryside.*
FOOD up to £15 [CLUB]
**Hours:** lunch 12noon – 2pm; dinner 6pm – 11:30pm; closed Sunday lunch. **Cuisine:** Chinese:- Chinese Cantonese and Peking cuisine of an extremely high standard and beautifully presented. Fixed price Executive lunches available. **Credit cards:** Visa, Access, Diners, AmEx. **Other points:** licensed, children catered for – please check for age limits, disabled access, vegetarian meals, street parking. **Directions:** situated in the town centre, opposite the Odeon cinemas.
MR CHIM ('JIM'), tel (0934) 621307, (0934) 626104.

# WEYMOUTH, Dorset Map 3

## BEECHCROFT HOTEL, 128–129 The Esplanade
*The Beechcroft Hotel is situated in a prime seafront position, only 5 minutes level walk to the city centre and the stations.*
ACCOMMODATION under £20
FOOD up to £15
**Hours:** last orders Sunday lunch – 4:30pm; breakfast 8:30am – 9am; dinner 6pm; closed October – March. **Cuisine:** English. **Rooms:** 30 bedrooms all with TV, 6 singles, 2 singles ensuite, 2 twins, 2 twins ensuite, 3 doubles, 3 doubles ensuite, 4 family rooms, 8 family rooms ensuite. **Credit cards:** Visa, Access. **Other points:** children catered for – please check for age limits, pets/prior arr, residents' lounge. **Directions:** A354 or A353 to Weymouth, hotel is on the Esplanade between pier bandstand and Jubilee Clock.
MESSRS THOMPSON, CLAYDEN & EVANS-JONES, tel (0305) 786608.

## THE CHATSWORTH, 14 The Esplanade

*An attractive Georgian building with excellent views over Weymouth Bay and the Sands to the front and the picturesque Harbour to the rear. The Chatsworth offers a friendly and comfortable base for short breaks and family holidays. All the amenities of an English seaside town are nearby and it is an ideal centre from which to tour Hardy's Dorset.*

ACCOMMODATION under £20

**Hours:** closed Christmas; breakfast 8am – 9am; dinner 6pm – 7pm. **Cuisine:** English. **Rooms:** all rooms fully en suite – 2 single, 4 double , 4 twin or trebles and 1 family bedroom. Colour TV, tea/coffee making facilities, radio, direct-dial telephones and central heating in all rooms. **Credit cards:** Visa, Access, AmEx. **Other points:** central heating, children catered for – please check for age limits, pets allowed, residents' lounge, garden. **Directions:** Situated on the Esplanade, opposite Alexandra Gardens. MR S ROBERTS, tel (0305) 785012, fax (0305) 766342.

## MOONFLEET MANOR, Moonfleet

*A complete resort hotel set in 5 acres of countryside by the sea. Many sports facilities including indoor pool, gymnasium, 4 rink indoor Bowls Hall, 9-pin automatic skittles, 2 tennis courts, 2 squash, 2 snooker tables, childrens indoor and outdoor play areas.*

ACCOMMODATION £31–£40

FOOD up to £15

**Hours:** lunch – except Saturday 12:30pm – 2pm; dinner 7pm – 9pm. **Cuisine:** English:- Trenchards – Carvery, buffet, Sunday Roasts, Table d'hote. **Rooms:** 6 single, 16 double, 6 twin and 9 family rooms – 37 en suite. **Credit cards:** Visa, Access, Diners, AmEx. **Other points:** licensed, Sunday lunch, no-smoking area, children catered for – please check for age limits, vegetarian meals, parking, residents' bar, residents' lounge, disabled access. **Directions:** take the B3157 to Weymouth, turn towards sea at Chickerell. JAN HEMINGWAY, tel (0305) 786948.

## THE PEBBLES GUEST HOUSE, 18 Kirtleton Avenue

*Situated in a quiet and peaceful residential area of Weymouth, with the beach and town shopping centre just minutes away. A warm and courteous welcome is assured and the accommodation, like the traditional English cooking, is of a high standard. An ideal base for guests wishing to explore beautiful Dorset.*

ACCOMMODATION under £20

FOOD up to £15

**Hours:** breakfast 8am – 9am; dinner 5:30pm – 6:30pm. **Cuisine:** English. **Rooms:** 8 bedrooms 2 singles, 3 doubles, 2 family rooms, 1 family room ensuite. **Other points:** children catered for – please check for age limits, no-smoking area, residents' lounge, vegetarian meals, garden, parking. **Directions:** A354 Dorchester to Weymouth Road, just before entering the centre of Weymouth turn into Carlton Road North. Kirtleton Avenue is first on left. Hotel is on the left. SHEILA AND BARRY SINGLE, tel (0305) 784331.

## SEA COW RESTAURANT, 7 Custom House Quay

*With a prominent quayside position this restaurant specialises in fresh fish and also offers a wide variety of meat, poultry and game. Very popular with visitors to this picturesque town.*

FOOD £15–£20 🍲

**Hours:** coffee shop – summer only 10am – 4:30pm; lunch 12noon – 2pm; dinner 7pm – 10pm. **Cuisine:** English:- Fresh mussels and scallops in season, fresh local lobster, skate, lemon sole. Game in season, Dorset Blue Steak. Chocolate mousse. **Credit cards:** Visa, Access, Eurocard. **Other points:** children catered for – please check for age limits, street parking, vegetarian meals, Sunday lunch. **Directions:** on the quayside. MR & MRS T M WOOLCOCK, tel (0305) 783524.

## THE SHIP INN RESTAURANT, Custom House Quay

*Overlooking the harbour, this traditional quayside pub has an upstairs restaurant offering food at excellent value for money. There is also a full range of children's facilities and a wide range of home-cooked bar snacks.*

FOOD up to £15

**Hours:** lunch – except Sunday 10:30am – 2:30pm; lunch – Sunday 12noon – 2:30pm; dinner 7pm – 10:30pm. **Cuisine:** English / seafood:- Fresh, local seafood. **Credit cards:** Visa, Access, Diners. **Other points:** Sunday lunch, children catered for – please check for age limits. **Directions:** On the quayside. R S CROW, tel (0305) 773879, fax (0305) 761206.

## SOU'WEST LODGE HOTEL, Rodwell Road

*An extremely pleasant, well kept hotel with first class furnishings throughout. A warm friendly atmosphere has been created by Michael & June Moxham, who will endeavour to make your stay enjoyable. There is a cosy intimate bar to relax in at the end of the day.*

ACCOMMODATION £21–£30

FOOD up to £15

**Hours:** closed Christmas 7pm; last orders 7pm – 3pm; breakfast 7:30am – 8:30am; dinner 6pm. **Cuisine:** English. **Rooms:** 8 bedrooms all with tea making facilities, TV: 1 twin ensuite, 2 family rooms ensuite, 5 doubles ensuite. **Other points:** children catered for – please check for age limits, pets allowed, residents' lounge, patio. **Directions:** situated off harbour road to Portland, over Boot Hill. MICHAEL & June MOXHAM, tel (0305) 783749.

## SUNNINGDALE HOTEL, Preston Road, Preston

*Set in one and a half acres of grounds, all bedrooms enjoy fine views over the gardens or fields. Although only 600 yds from the sea, the heated outdoor swimming pool is always popular, especially with small children.*

ACCOMMODATION under £20

FOOD up to £15

**Hours:** breakfast 8:15am – 9:15am; dinner 6:15pm – 7:15pm; closed mid-October – March. **Cuisine:** English. **Rooms:** 21 bedrooms all with tea making facilities, radio: 1 single, 6 doubles ensuite, 2 doubles, 3 twins ensuite, 3 twins, 6 family rooms ensuite. **Credit cards:** Visa, Access, Diners. **Other points:** children catered for – please check for age limits, residents' lounge, garden, swimming pool, putting green, games room, pets allowed. **Directions:** off the A353, through Preston village towards the sea.
MR & MRS TONY FLUX, tel (0305) 832179.

## WHIMPLE, Devon Map 2

### THE PADDOCK INN, London Road
*A large, country pub offering a daily changing menu in comfortable, relaxed surroundings. The service is welcoming and efficient. Places of interest nearby include Ottery St Mary (Coleridge's birthplace), Escot Aquarium, Killerton House and the attractions of Exeter. The proprietor also speaks French & German.*
*FOOD up to £15* CLUB
**Hours:** bar meals 11am – 2:30pm; lunch 12noon – 2pm; bar meals 6pm – 10pm; dinner 6:30pm – 9:30pm; closed Saturday a/noon – winter. **Cuisine:** English:- Daily changing menu using predominantly fresh produce. Children's menu. **Credit cards:** Visa, Access, Diners, AmEx. **Other points:** licensed, open-air dining, Sunday lunch, children catered for – please check for age limits, beer garden. **Directions:** halfway between Honiton & Exeter on A30. Approx. 9 miles each way.
ROBERT PUSEY, tel (0404) 822356.

## WHITCHURCH, Hampshire Map 4

### THE WHITE HART HOTEL, The Square
*Set in the picturesque town of Whitchurch, at the foot of the beautiful Hampshire downs, this family-run hotel has been welcoming travellers since 1461. Steeped in period history and atmosphere, this traditional Coaching Inn offers endless hospitality in warm and friendly surroundings and is widely renowned for its excellent cuisine.*

*ACCOMMODATION £21–£30*
*FOOD up to £15*
**Hours:** breakfast 7am – 9am, lunch 12 noon – 2pm, dinner 7pm – 9pm; closed Christmas day after lunch only. **Cuisine:** English/Continental. **Rooms:** 18 bedrooms all with TV, telephone, tea making facilities. **Credit cards:** Visa, Access, Diners, AmEx. **Other points:** parking, children catered for – please check for age limits, no smoking area, disabled access, pets allowed, vegetarian meals. **Directions:** A34, the hotel is situated in the centre of Whitchurch.
MESSRS KAVANAGH AND THORPE, tel (0256) 892900, fax (0256) 896628.

## WINCANTON, Somerset Map 3

### HOLBROOK HOUSE HOTEL, Holbrook
*A genuine country house hotel, set in 15 acres of its own grounds in unspoilt countryside. Behind the walled garden & dovecote lie the squash and tennis court. The old orchard provides a delightful setting for the outdoor heated pool. A splendid wine list complements the interesting variety of well cooked food. A lovely hotel providing a relaxing and pleasant atmosphere.*
*ACCOMMODATION £31–£40*
*FOOD up to £15*
**Hours:** breakfast 8:15am – 9:15am; lunch 1pm – 2pm; dinner 7:30pm – 8:30pm. **Cuisine:** English:- A la carte, table d'hote, using freshest ingredients available. **Rooms:** 20 bedrooms all with tea making facilities, telephone, radio: 5 singles ensuite, 2 singles, 4 twins ensuite, 1 twin, 4 doubles ensuite, 2 triples ensuite, 2 quads ensuite. **Credit cards:** Visa, Access, AmEx. **Other points:** licensed, open-air dining, Sunday lunch, children catered for – please check for age limits, pets allowed, tennis, squash, swimming pool, games room, golf, riding, fishing, croquet, residents' lounge, baby-listening device, cots, residents' bar. **Directions:** 1.5 miles off A303 on the A371 towards Castle Cary and Shepton Mallet.
MR & MRS G E TAYLOR, tel (0963) 32377.

# HOLBROOK HOUSE
## HOTEL

Holbrook, Nr. Wincanton, Somerset BA9 8BS
*Telephone: (0963) 32377*

## WINCHESTER, Hampshire Map 4

### THE ABBEY BAR & COURTYARD CAFE,
**The Guildhall, The Broadway**
*Situated within the delightful Victorian building of Winchester Guildhall this is an ideal place to stop, meet and visit. Winchester Guildhall is an ideal venue for banqueting, promotions and conferences. Good food is provided in comfortable friendly surroundings.*
**FOOD up to £15**  ★
**Hours:** open bank holidays 7:30pm; morning coffee 10am – 12noon; lunch 12noon – 2pm. **Cuisine:** English:- Serving morning coffee, bar meals, salad bar and carvery. **Other points:** Sunday lunch, no-smoking area, afternoon tea, parking. **Directions:** approx 75yds from King Alfred Statue in city centre and 200yds from Winchester Cathedral.
MRS SHIRLEY MORRISSEY, tel (0962) 848368, fax (0962) 878458.

### HARESTOCK LODGE HOTEL & RESTAURANT, Harestock Road
*The hotel is situated on the edge of historic Winchester, which was once the capital of England. Owned and run by the Bishop family, the hotel has characterised rooms and large secluded gardens as befits a country house which originates from 1885. Facilities include open-air swimming pool and indoor spa pool. The superb restaurant offers fine food from A La Carte and Table D'Hote menus. Everything for a relaxing stay.*
**ACCOMMODATION £21–£30**
**FOOD up to £15**
**Hours:** breakfast 7:30am – 9am; lunch 12noon – 2:30pm; dinner 6:30pm – 10pm. **Cuisine:** English. **Credit cards:** Visa, Access, AmEx. **Other points:** parking, children catered for – please check for age limits, afternoon teas, disabled access, pets, residents' lounge, garden, vegetarian meals, open-air dining. **Directions:** 1 mile north of Winchester, A34 (dual carriageway).
BISHOP, PETER & NICK, tel (0962) 881870, fax (0962) 880038.

### THE ROYAL HOTEL, St Peter Street
*Formally a Bishop's residence, the Royal Hotel was built in the 16th century and has been a hotel for about 150 years. The restaurant offers well cooked, imaginative dishes using predominantly fresh, local produce. The hotel is furnished and decorated to a very high standard, providing attractive surroundings and comfortable accommodation. 2 minutes from main Shopping Street.*
**ACCOMMODATION £31–£40**
**FOOD up to £16–£20**  ★
**Hours:** breakfast – weekdays 7am – 9:30am; breakfast – weekends 8am – 10am; bar meals 12noon – 2:30pm; dinner – Sunday 7pm – 9:30pm. **Cuisine:** modern English:- A la carte and table d'hote menus. Dishes may include Baked local Pink Trout, Navarin of Spring lamb, Medallions of Beef in a green peppercorn sauce. **Rooms:** 75 bedrooms, all en suite. **Credit cards:** Visa,

Access, Diners, AmEx. **Other points:** licensed, open-air dining, Sunday lunch, afternoon tea, residents' lounge, special breaks, children catered for – please check for age limits, residents' bar, vegetarian meals, parking, disabled access. **Directions:** M3: exit 9. Follow one way system to St Georges Street then turn right.
TONY & PAMELA SMITH, tel (0962) 840840, fax (0962) 841582.

## WINDSOR, Berkshire Map 6

### CHRISTOPHER HOTEL, 110 High Street, Eton
*A former coaching inn situated in Eton High Street, close to the famous school and within walking distance of Windsor Castle. The restaurant serves an excellent selection of home cooked meals.*
**FOOD £15–£20** CLUB
**Hours:** breakfast 7:15am – 9:30am; lunch 12noon – 2pm; dinner 7pm – 10pm. **Cuisine:** English:- Traditional English cuisine. **Rooms:** 33 bedrooms all with tea making facilities, telephone, TV: 1 single ensuite, 1 twin ensuite, 23 doubles ensuite, 5 triples ensuite, 3 quads ensuite. **Credit cards:** Visa, Access, Diners, AmEx. **Other points:** open-air dining, children catered for – please check for age limits, pets allowed, baby-listening device, cots, foreign exchange, left luggage. **Directions:** 2 miles off the M4.
MRS MARTIN, tel (0753) 852359, (0753) 857091.

## WOKINGHAM, Berkshire Map 6

### CANTLEY HOUSE HOTEL, MARYLINE'S BRASSERIE, Milton Road
*A converted Victorian country house set in pleasant parklands with easy access to the M4. The Penguin & Vulture Pub and Maryline's Brasserie are situated in a converted 17th century barn in a secluded courtyard. A charming, character restaurant with old oak beams and sunken lounge around a warming log fire.*
**ACCOMMODATION £31–£40**
**FOOD £15–£20**
**Hours:** breakfast 7:30am – 10am; lunch 12noon – 2pm. **Cuisine:** modern English:- Fine modern English cuisine. **Rooms:** 29 bedrooms 15 singles ensuite, 2 twins ensuite, 12 doubles ensuite. **Credit cards:** Visa, Access, AmEx, Diners, Switch. **Other points:** Sunday lunch, pets allowed, children catered for – please check for age limits. **Directions:** from M4, Junction 10 follow signs to Wokingham. Off A321 towards Henley.
MR MAURICE MONK, tel (0734) 789912, fax (0734) 774294.

### EDWARD COURT HOTEL, Wellington Road
*Situated in the heart of Berkshire and easily accessible by rail and road, this hotel provides comfortable accommodation and well cooked and presented meals. Local produce is used wherever possible.*
**ACCOMMODATION £31–£40**
**FOOD up to £15**
**Hours:** breakfast 7:30am – 9am; lunch 12noon – 2pm;

dinner 7:30pm – 9:30pm; closed Christmas 24/12 – 02/01. **Cuisine:** French:- Dishes May include – smoked mackerel salad with grated apple and horseradish sauce, saute of veal strips in creamy sauce with apple. **Rooms:** 25 bedrooms 8 singles ensuite, 17 doubles ensuite. **Credit cards:** Visa, Access, Diners, AmEx. **Other points:** licensed, conferences, functions. **Directions:** leave M4 Junction 10, onto A329M. Follow signs for Wokingham, 100 yd from BR Station.
JUDITH SIMPSON, tel (0734) 775886, fax (0734) 772018.

### THE HANSOM CABIN, *Lower Wokingham Road, Crowthorne*
*The Hansom Cabinn is an attractive cabin-like restaurant surrounded by roses. Inside, you will find pine panelling and pictoral reference to Hansomcabs. Fresh ingredients are used imaginatively to produce well cooked meals, simply and thoughtfully presented. Good, welcoming service and a happy and relaxed atmosphere prevails.*
*FOOD up to £15*
**Hours:** last orders 24/12 – 9:30pm; lunch 12noon – 2pm; dinner – except Sunday 7pm – 12:30am; dinner – Sunday 7pm – 9:30pm; closed Saturday lunch; closed Sunday lunch. **Cuisine:** English:- Starters range from sliced smoked trout, fresh soup or prawns. House specialites are duck or salmon en croute. Desserts includes home-made ice creams. **Credit cards:** Visa, Access. **Directions:** alongside A321.
MR JOHN HANSOM, tel (0344) 772450.

## WOKINGHAM, Hampshire Map 4

### LE TOAD AND STUMPS BISTRO, *The Green, Eversley Cross*
*A popular bar/bistro offering fine English and continental cuisine. Attractively furnished throughout, it has a distinct cosmopolitan atmosphere. A guitarist often plays in the bistro.*
**Hours:** lunch 12noon – 2:30pm; bar snacks 12noon – 10pm; dinner 7pm – 10:30pm. **Cuisine:** English / continental. **Other points:** parking, children catered for – please check for age limits, disabled access, vegetarian meals, open-air dining. **Directions:** leave the M3 at junction 4 and travel through Blackwater and Yateley. The establishment is situated on the B3272 at Eversley Cross, just before Eversley.
MR T PAINE, tel (0734) 731126, fax (0734) 731126.

## WOODFALLS, Hampshire Map 4

### THE WOODFALLS INN, *The Ridge*
*Located in the village of Woodfalls, nestling on the north edge of the New Forest, Woodfalls has provided hospitality to travellers seeking rest and refreshment since 1870. On arrival, guests will find that the hospitality and welcome remains as warm as ever. A well stocked bar includes a fine choice of properly stored cask conditioned ales. Ideal for touring the New Forest.*
*ACCOMMODATION under £20*
*FOOD up to £15*

**Hours:** breakfast 7:30am – 11:45am; bar meals 11:30am – 3pm; lunch 12noon – 3pm; dinner 6:30pm – 9:30pm; bar meals 6:30pm – 10pm. **Cuisine:** English:- Traditional and wholesome English cooking. Frequently changing menus to suit every palate, using a wide variety of fresh locally grown produce. **Rooms:** 8 bedrooms 4 doubles ensuite, 4 twins ensuite. **Credit cards:** Visa, Access. **Other points:** licensed, open-air dining, Sunday lunch, no-smoking area, children catered for – please check for age limits, pets allowed, afternoon tea, parking, residents' lounge, residents' bar, disabled access, vegetarian meals.
**Directions:** exit M27 Junction 1. Take B3078 to Telegraph Corner – B3080 to Woodfalls.
MICHAEL ELVIS, tel (0725) 513222, fax (0725) 513220.

## WOOLACOMBE, Devon Map 2

### BAYCLIFFE HOTEL, *Chapel Hill, Mortehoe*
*Small, family run hotel offering good service, comfortable rooms and superb views of the bay. Beaches are just a few minutes away and places of interest include an 11th century church. Also, being adjacent to National Trust land, walkers will find this an ideal spot.*
**Hours:** breakfast 9am – 10am; dinner 7pm – 8pm. **Cuisine:** English. **Rooms:** 2 single, 7 double and 1 family room all en suite. Colour TV, telephone, tea/coffee making facilities in bedrooms. Four poster suites available. **Credit cards:** Visa, Access. **Directions:** B3343 to Mortehoe village.
MR & MRS MCFARLANE, tel (0271) 870393.

## WOOLVERTON, Somerset Map 3

### WOOLVERTON HOUSE HOTEL
*Woolverton House was built in the early 19th century as a rectory, and has been sympathetically converted to a splendid hotel. Set in its own 2 and a half acre grounds with scenic views, it offers all the facilities you would expect from an elegant country house. Surrounded by beautiful countryside, this is an ideal location for a leisurely break.*
*ACCOMMODATION £21–£30*
*FOOD up to £15*
**Hours:** breakfast 7:30am – 9am; lunch 12noon – 2pm; dinner 7pm – 9pm; closed 24/12 – 03/01. **Cuisine:** English. **Rooms:** 16 bedrooms 3 singles ensuite, 13 doubles ensuite. **Credit cards:** Visa, Access, AmEx. **Other points:** parking, children catered for – please check for age limits, open bank holidays, no-smoking area, disabled access, pets allowed, residents' lounge, vegetarian meals, open-air dining, residents' garden.
**Directions:** 9 miles south of Bath on A36.
GEORGE & VERA WILKES, tel (0373) 830415, fax (0373) 830415.

## ZELSTON, Dorset Map 3

### THE BOTANY BAY INNE, *Winterbourne*
*A friendly country pub with a delightful restaurant offering a wide variety of home cooked fresh food,*

*served in immaculate and comfortable surroundings.
Ideal as a refreshment stop for lunch or excellent bar
snacks whilst visiting some of the places of interest
within the idyllic countryside. A comfortable and
sophisticated atmosphere.*

*FOOD up to £15*

**Hours:** closed Christmas day; lunch 11am – 2:30pm;
dinner 6pm – 10pm. **Cuisine:** English / continental.
**Credit cards:** Visa, Access, Diners. **Other points:**
children catered for – please check for age limits,
parking, vegetarian meals, pets, open-air dining.
**Directions:** A31, between Winborne and Dorchester.
CHRIS & BEVERLEY MASSEY, tel (0929) 45227.

# THE CHANNEL ISLANDS

For those who are really seeking solitude, the Channel Islands of Jersey, Guernsey, Alderney and Sark, are the perfect location. The island of Guernsey is very different to that of Jersey, having retained its Norman-French character. A visit to the capital at St Peter Port is a delightful experience with its quaint town built on a hill above the main harbour. One of the main attractions here is Shell Beach.

Jersey's most spectacular asset is its dramatic coastline. Inland, tiny narrow lanes meander gently through villages untouched by modern progress and woods, pastures and rich farmland melt into gorse-covered cliffs. The churches and manor houses built by the Normans still remain, notably the magnificent Mont Orgueil Castle which was built to defend the island. Another superb castle which appears to be floating on the water is found at St Aubin's Bay. It was named Fort Isabella by Sir Walter Rayleigh, who became governor of Jersey in 1600.

Known as the 'Gem of the Channel Isles' is tiny Sark, unspoiled by aircraft or cars. The traditional and leisurely way to travel the island is by horse-drawn carriage, and for the more energetic, bicycles can be hired for exploring the many superb cliff walks. An ideal visitors' retreat throughout the year.

For details of where to visit and what to see in the Channel Islands, contact the following tourist boards: Jersey Tourism, Liberation Square, St Helier, Jersey JE1 1BB. Tel: (0534) 78000. State of Guernsey Tourist Board, PO Box 23, White Rock, St Peter Port, Guernsey. Tel: (0481) 723552.

## ANNE PORT, Jersey Map 3

### ANNE PORT BAY HOTEL, St Martins
*Situated in the picturesque and unspoilt bay of Anne Port, this small country inn, taking 26 guests, is owned and run by a Jersey family. Over several years, they have built a fine reputation for excellent food and a high level of personal service and comfort. The beach is quiet, sandy and safe for bathing. There are many exciting places of interest to visit nearby.*
*ACCOMMODATION £21–£30*
*FOOD up to £15*
**Hours:** breakfast 8:30am – 9:15am; bar meals 12noon – 1:45pm; dinner 6:30pm – 7:15pm; closed November – March. **Cuisine:** English:- A la carte and Table d'hote menus, offering homestyle cuisine. Vegetarians catered for. **Rooms:** 14 bedrooms all with tea making facilities, radio, TV: 2 singles ensuite, 4 twins ensuite, 8 doubles ensuite. **Credit cards:** Visa, Access. **Other points:** licensed, children catered for – please check for age limits, parking, residents' lounge, baby-listening device, cots, left luggage. Directions: first bay north of Gorey on east of Jersey.
MRS RUTH CAVEY, tel (0534) 852058, fax (0534) 857887.

## BOULEY BAY, Jersey Map 3

### WATERS EDGE HOTEL, Les Charrieres Du Boulay
*Set in its own terraced gardens in a commanding position of outstanding natural beauty. Panoramic windows in nearly all public areas take advantage of the vista afforded by Bouley Bay, boats and the coast of France. There is outdoor dining in the beautiful terraced gardens and a swimming pool, heated from April to October.*
*ACCOMMODATION £41–£50*
*FOOD £21–£25*
**Hours:** breakfast 8am – 9:30am; bar snacks 12noon – 1:45pm; lunch 12:30pm – 1:45pm; dinner 7pm – 9:45pm. **Cuisine:** French:- French a la carte and table d'hote lunch and dinner menus. Wide choice of dishes and local fresh fish specialities. The Hotel offers an extensive wine list and a selection of banqueting menus for up to 140 people. **Rooms:** 51 bedrooms all with tea making facilities, telephone, radio, mini bar, TV: 13 doubles ensuite, 3 family rooms ensuite, 3 suites, 1 penthouse suite, 7 singles ensuite, 24 twins ensuite. **Credit cards:** Visa, Access, Diners, AmEx. **Other points:** children catered for – please check for age limits, pets allowed, afternoon tea, residents' lounge, garden, parking, licensed. **Directions:** take A8/B31 from St Helier, 300m from Trinity church turn left.
SHELDRAKE INVEST CO LTD, tel (0534) 862777, fax (0534) 863615.

## CASTEL, Guernsey Map 3

### COBO BAY HOTEL, Cobo Bay
*Cobo Bay Hotel is situated in one of the finest locations in the Channel Islands, overlooking the golden sands of Cobo Bay with its glorious sunsets. The hotel has a reputation for excellent cuisine. There are two luxury self-catering apartments, a sun terrace and a complimentary health suite for guests.*

*ACCOMMODATION £21–£30*
*FOOD up to £15*
**Hours:** breakfast 7:30am – 9:30am; lunch 12noon – 2pm; dinner 6:45pm – 9:45pm; open all year except February. **Cuisine:** English / continental:- international cuisine with a large variety of fresh Guernsey seafood. **Rooms:** 38 bedrooms all with tea making facilities, telephone, radio, TV: 3 singles ensuite, 20 twins ensuite, 11 doubles ensuite, 1 triple ensuite, 1 family room ensuite, 2 self-catering rooms. **Credit cards:** Visa, Access. **Other points:** licensed, Sunday lunch, children catered for – please check for age limits, bank holidays, parking, sauna, Jacuzzi, baby-listening device, cots, left luggage. **Directions:** located on West Coast Road in the centre of Cobo Bay.
DAVID & JULIE NUSSBAUMER, tel (0481) 57102, fax (0481) 54542.

## ST ANNES, Alderney Map 3

### INCHALLA HOTEL
*A modern hotel with first class facilities, including sauna, Jacuzzi and solarium. A pleasant and relaxing atmosphere in a hotel situated in lovely grounds overlooking the sea.*
*ACCOMMODATION £21–£30*
*FOOD up to £15*
**Hours:** breakfast 8:30am – 9:30am; lunch – Sunday 1pm – 2pm; dinner 7pm – 8:30pm. **Cuisine:** English / French. **Rooms:** 10 bedrooms all with tea making facilities, telephone, radio, mini bar, TV: 4 doubles ensuite, 4 twins ensuite, 2 family rooms ensuite. **Credit cards:** Visa, Access, AmEx. **Other points:** central heating, children catered for – please check for age limits, residents' lounge, garden. **Directions:** at the edge of St Annes overlooking the sea.
MRS VALERIE WILLS, tel (048182) 3220.

### ROSE & CROWN, Le Huret
*Constructed of Alderney granite around 1770, this hotel is situated in one of the most attractive yet peaceful parts of St Anne. It offers a friendly, homely atmosphere and is tastefully furnished to a very high standard with added comfort. Picnic lunches are available to those who wish to spend the day walking, exploring or relaxing on the beach. Attractive garden.*
*ACCOMMODATION under £20*
*FOOD up to £15*
**Hours:** breakfast 9am – 9:30am; bar meals 12noon – 2pm; bar meals 6:30pm – 9pm. **Cuisine:** English / international:- Traditional English pub cuisine, and a wide choice of international specialities. Daily Blackboard Specials. Vegetarians catered for. **Rooms:** 6 bedrooms, 4 en suite, centrally heated, with colour TV and sky channel, direct-dial telephones, and tea/coffee making facilities. Tastefully furnished. **Credit cards:** Visa, Access. **Other points:** licensed, open-air dining, picnic lunches, children catered for – please check for age limits, garden, bank holidays. **Directions:** situated in the centre of St Anne in a quiet area.
BASIL BLUMBERG (MANAGING DIRECTOR), tel (0481) 823414, fax (0481) 823615.

## ST AUBIN'S BAY, Jersey Map 3

### BRYN-Y-MOR, Route De La Haule, Beaumont
*A large Georgian house, set in well tended gardens, with a magnificent view of the beautiful bay of St Aubin. The combination of friendly attentive service, blended with comfortable surroundings and a fine location. Situated just two hundred yards from three miles of golden beach makes the 'Bryn-Y-Mor' a must for all visitors – be it business or leisure. Open throughout the year.*
*ACCOMMODATION £21–£30*
*FOOD up to £15* ★
**Hours:** breakfast 8:30am – 9:30am; dinner 6:30pm – 7:30pm. **Cuisine:** English / continental. **Rooms:** 4 family, 1 single and 9 double/twin bedrooms, 11 en suite. Reductions for children sharing parents room. Intercom, direct-dial telephone, tea & coffee making facilities in all rooms. Baby sitting by arr. permanent residents' welcome. **Credit cards:** Visa, Access, Diners, AmEx. **Other points:** children catered for – please check for age limits, TV lounge, picnic lunches, pets allowed. **Directions:** on the A1, situated on the main south coast road.
MISS M F TEMPLETON, tel (0534) 20295, fax (0534) 24262.

## ST BRELADE, Jersey Map 3

### LA PLACE HOTEL, Route Du Coin, La Haule
*Dating from 1640 and farmhouse in style, this delightful hotel has two very attractive courtyards, one with swimming pool, where meals can be enjoyed alfresco. Inside, the hotel has large fireplaces and wood beams, combining charm with top comfort. Fresh, local produce and high culinary standards are found in the award-winning restaurant. Excellent service.*
*ACCOMMODATION £41–£50*
*FOOD £15–£20* ☕
**Hours:** breakfast 8am – 9:30am; bar meals 11am – 5pm; lunch 12:30pm – 2pm; dinner 7pm – 9:30pm; bar meals 7pm – 9:30pm. **Cuisine:** French:- Classical French cuisine with seafood specialities. Table d'hote, a la carte, Pool-side and Courtyard menus. **Rooms:** 40 bedrooms, all en suite, including 2 family rooms and 1 honeymoon suite. **Credit cards:** Visa, Access, Diners, AmEx. **Other points:** licensed, open-air dining, Sunday lunch, children catered for – please check for age limits, residents' lounge, swimming pool, dinner dress code. **Directions:** 4 miles from St Helier. At the top of La Haule Hill, St Brelade.
DELRICH HOTELS LTD, tel (0534) 44261.

## ST CLEMENT, Jersey Map 3

### BELLE PLAGE HOTEL, Green Island
*A small family run hotel where personal attention is paid to guests by a friendly management and staff. A genuine seaside location. Cosy bar and lounge available for guests to relax in at the end of the day. Varied menus and a selected wine list are available in the restaurant.*
*ACCOMMODATION £21–£30*

**Hours:** breakfast 8:30am – 9:30am; dinner 7pm – 8pm; closed October – March. **Cuisine:** English. **Rooms:** 20 bedrooms, all en suite. rooms with private balconies and sea views available. TV rental if required. **Credit cards:** Visa, Access, AmEx. **Other points:** children catered for – please check for age limits, vegetarian meals, swimming pool. **Directions:** seaside location at St Clement.
F B HOUSE & W B YATES, tel (0534) 853750, fax (0534) 853894.

## ST HELIER, Jersey Map 3

### THE BERKSHIRE HOTEL & LILLIE LANGTRY BAR, La Motte Street
*Situated in the business district and near the Yacht Harbour, the main Shopping Precinct, Park and Leisure complex, this is an ideal base for touring St Helier. Offering good meals with an emphasis on fresh seafood, and comfortable accommodation. Frequented by mixed ages the hotel enjoys a convivial atmosphere.*
ACCOMMODATION £21–£30
FOOD up to £15
**Hours:** lunch 12noon – 3pm; dinner 7pm – 10pm.
**Cuisine:** continental:- Predominantly continental cuisine such as Moules Lillie Langtry, Fruits De Mer, Chicken Camembert, Lobster, Daily specials. **Rooms:** 64 bedrooms all with tea making facilities, radio, TV: 8 singles ensuite, 8 family rooms ensuite, 24 doubles ensuite, 24 twins ensuite. **Credit cards:** Visa, Access, Diners, AmEx. **Other points:** licensed, open-air dining, parking. **Directions:** at top of main shopping precinct.
MICHAEL BARNES, tel (0534) 23241, fax (0534) 32986.

### GLENTHORNE, Elizabeth Place
*A welcoming guest house situated close to the town and beach. Glenthorne is family run and offers a friendly, homely atmosphere, good home cooking and good value for money. The proprietors are always at hand to assist guests and to ensure that your stay in Jersey is enjoyable.*
ACCOMMODATION under £20
FOOD up to £15 ★
**Hours:** breakfast 8:30am – 9am; bar 5:45pm – 1am; dinner 6:30pm – 7pm. **Cuisine:** English. **Rooms:** 18 bedrooms all with tea making facilities, telephone, radio, TV: 6 doubles ensuite, 3 twins ensuite, 5 family rooms ensuite, 3 doubles, 1 twin. **Credit cards:** Visa, Access, Diners, AmEx. **Other points:** children catered for – please check for age limits, pets allowed, afternoon tea, residents' lounge, garden, picnic lunches, safe facilities, fax. **Directions:** close to St Helier and beach.
MR WAYNE RHODES, tel (0534) 22817, fax (0534) 58002.

### GREENWOOD LODGE, Roseville Street
*Situated in a quieter part of St Helier, this family run hotel is decorated to a high standard. The accommodation is bright and airy and more than comfortable. Serving quality food prepared under the personal supervision of the proprietors. Staff are helpful*

*and friendly adding to the hotels popularity with the holiday-makers.*
ACCOMMODATION under £20
FOOD up to £15
**Hours:** breakfast 8:30am – 9:30am; dinner 6:30pm – 7:30pm; closed mid November – end February. **Cuisine:** seafood:- A good selection of traditional English cuisine specialising in seafood. **Rooms:** 33 bedrooms all with tea making facilities, telephone, radio, TV: 2 singles, 13 doubles ensuite, 10 doubles, 4 twins ensuite, 4 family rooms ensuite. **Credit cards:** Visa, Access, AmEx, Switch. **Other points:** children catered for – please check for age limits, pets allowed, vegetarian meals, residents' lounge, bank holidays. **Directions:** from Weighbridge, through the tunnel and take second right. The Lodge is the first building on the left.
HOWARD & SUE SNOW, tel (0534) 67073, fax (0534) 67876.

### MILLBROOK HOUSE, Rue De Trachy
*Built around 1790, the combination of Georgian and Colonial architectural features sympathetically modernised, and spacious 10 acre gardens and grassland gives an atmosphere of great ease and tranquillity. Situated 500 yd from the beach with stupendous views overlooking St Aubin's Bay, Millbrook House is an ideal setting for an away from it all restful holiday. Comprehensive menu, extensive wine list, comfortable accommodation. (See colour advertisement in centre section.)*
ACCOMMODATION £21–£30
FOOD up to £15 ♈
**Hours:** breakfast 7:30am – 9:30am; dinner 6:30pm – 8:30pm. **Cuisine:** English. **Rooms:** 21 bedrooms all with tea making facilities, telephone, TV: 2 family rooms ensuite, 19 doubles ensuite. **Credit cards:** AmEx. **Other points:** children catered for – please check for age limits, lift, special diets, vegetarian meals. **Directions:** off the A1, 1.5 miles west of St Helier.
MR G. PIROUET – G.T.P. (JERSEY) LTD, tel (0534) 33036, fax (0534) 24317.

### MONT MILLAIS HOTEL, Mont Millais
*Set in own attractive terraced gardens, only 5 mins away from town centre. Decorated in light shades of welcoming colours and offering accommodation of a high standard. The restaurant enjoys a friendly atmosphere, in which you can indulge in a really good meal made even more enjoyable by the excellent service. Highly recommended.*
ACCOMMODATION £21–£30
FOOD up to £15
**Hours:** breakfast 8:15am – 9:30am; bar meals 12noon – 2pm; dinner 7pm – 9pm; closed January – April. **Cuisine:** English / continental:- Homemade Soups and Sweets. Fresh local Fish. **Rooms:** 44 bedrooms, all en suite. **Credit cards:** Visa, Access. **Other points:** licensed, Sunday lunch, children catered for – please check for age limits, afternoon tea, coach/prior arr, dry cleaning, picnic lunches. **Directions:** from Howard Davis Park approx 400m toward Five Oaks.
COLIN KIRKHAM, tel (0534) 30281, fax (0534) 66849.

## UPLANDS HOTEL, St Johns Road

*A spacious and well decorated hotel with a welcoming atmosphere and a high standard of accommodation. The attractive sun-lounge opens on to a patio overlooking the swimming pool and provides an ideal place to relax. English and continental cuisine is served in the restaurant and some nights entertainment can be enjoyed in the bar in the main season. A comfortable, friendly hotel.*
ACCOMMODATION £31–£40
FOOD up to £15
**Hours:** breakfast 8:30am – 9:30am; bar snacks 12noon – 1:30pm; dinner 6:30pm – 7:30pm. **Cuisine:** English. **Rooms:** 43 bedrooms all with tea making facilities, telephone, radio, TV: 17 twins ensuite, 19 doubles ensuite, 3 triples ensuite, 4 singles ensuite. **Credit cards:** Visa, Access. **Other points:** children catered for – please check for age limits, afternoon tea, garden, sun lounge, patio, swimming pool. **Directions:** top of Queens Rd, first Left turn 100yds, hotel on the right.
MORVAN FAMILY HOTELS, tel (0534) 73006, fax (0534) 68804.

## ST OUEN'S BAY, Jersey Map 3

### L'ETACQUEREL, L'Etacq

*Small country hotel with glorious sea views and a German bunker in the grounds. Every comfort is provided including teamakers, hair dryers, clock/radios and ironing facilities. 20 minutes' drive from St Helier overlooking a long, sweeping sandy beach.*
ACCOMMODATION under £20
**Hours:** breakfast 8am – 9am; dinner 6:30pm – 7pm; closed October – March. **Cuisine:** English. **Rooms:** 3 single, 7 double, 2 twin and 1 family bedroom, 4 en suite. 1 bathroom, 2 showers, 2 WC. **Other points:** central heating, residents' lounge, TV lounge, children catered for – please check for age limits. **Directions:** follow signs to L'Etacquerel, hotel opposite Lobster Pot Restaurant.
MAUREEN ASHWORTH, MRS, tel (0534) 482492.

### THE LOBSTER POT HOTEL & RESTAURANT, L'Etacq

*A 17th century French style granite farmhouse enjoying sweeping panoramic views of the Atlantic Ocean. The restaurant is internationally famous for its cuisine and offers a mouth watering selection of seafood. The seafaring name of the restaurant is reflected in the decor and the walls are festooned with Lobster Pots. Excellent food in a friendly and comfortable atmosphere.*
ACCOMMODATION £31–£40
FOOD up to £15 🍽
**Hours:** breakfast 8am – 9:15am; bar meals 10:30am – 6pm; lunch 12:30pm – 2:15pm; dinner 7:30pm – 12:30am; last orders – 10:15pm. **Cuisine:** seafood / international:- Lobster, shellfish, fish, steaks and veal dishes. **Rooms:** 13 bedrooms all with tea making facilities, telephone, TV: 3 twins ensuite, 9 doubles ensuite, 1 family room ensuite. **Credit cards:** Visa,

Access, Diners, AmEx. **Other points:** licensed, open-air dining, Sunday lunch, children catered for – please check for age limits, afternoon tea. **Directions:** set on the seafront at St Ouen's Bay.
GERALD HOWE, tel (0534) 482888, fax (0534) 481574.

## ST PETER, Jersey Map 3

### THE STAR & TIPSY TOAD BREWERY, St Peters Village

*Originally a small Victorian pub and now recently refurbished and extended, this is the first pub in Jersey to house its own brewery. Very popular with locals and families alike, and customers can view the brewery by prior arrangement. Nearby tourist attractions, include a German Underground Hospital, Car Museum and an excellent beach for surfing.*
FOOD up to £15
**Hours:** lunch 12noon – 2:15pm; dinner 6pm – 8:15pm. **Cuisine:** English:- Extensive menu offering Steak, Prawn, Chicken, Fish, Salad & Pork dishes. Children's menu. Chef's Specials. Vegetarian dishes available. Good Wine List. **Other points:** licensed, open-air dining, children catered for – please check for age limits, pets allowed, parking, garden, patio, disabled access, playland. **Directions:** on the A12 in St Peter's village, near airport.
STEVE & SARAH SKINNER, tel (0534) 485556, fax (0534) 485559.

## ST PETER PORT, Guernsey Map 3

### LE NAUTIQUE RESTAURANT, Quay Steps

*Black oak beams and whitewashed walls, adorned with various fishing items all add up to create a nautical ambiance. Meals of the highest quality are served by friendly, efficient staff. Frequented by business people and locals alike, Le Nautique has its fair share of regulars – a tribute to the consistently good food and service. Established for 30 yrs, 15 under Mr Graziani.*
FOOD £21–£25
**Hours:** open bank holidays 6pm; closed 01/01 – 14/01; lunch 12noon; dinner 7pm; closed Sunday. **Cuisine:** seafood:- Fish dishes a speciality. Dishes may include – Huitres de Sur Epinars au Currie, Turbot Grille Au Poche-Sauce Hollandaise. **Credit cards:** Visa, Access, Diners, AmEx. **Other points:** private dining. **Directions:** town centre. On seafront overlooking St Peter Port Yacht Marina.
CARLO GRAZIANI, tel (0481) 721714.

### MARINE HOTEL, Well Road

*A comfortable town hotel enjoying a delightful view of the harbour and islands. Guests can relax on the attractive sun patio overlooking the sea. There are many good restaurants offering reasonably priced meals within walking distance of the hotel and the picturesque shopping centre is close by.*
ACCOMMODATION under £20

**Hours:** breakfast 8am – 8:45am. **Cuisine:** breakfast:- Packed lunches also, if ordered the day before. **Rooms:** 11 bedrooms all with tea making facilities, TV: 3 family rooms ensuite, 3 twins ensuite, 4 doubles ensuite, 1 single ensuite. **Credit cards:** Visa, Access, Eurocard. **Other points:** children catered for – please check for age limits, vegetarian meals, picnic lunches, lounge. **Directions:** 30 yd from sea-front and new marina. Off Glategny Esplanade.
MR & MRS CLEGG, tel (0481) 724978.

## ST SAVIOUR, Guernsey Map 3

### LA HOUGUE FOUQUE FARM HOTEL, Les Bas Courtils
*Originally an old Guernsey farmhouse, now extensively adapted and refurbished to provide one of the finest hotels on the island, combining comfort and atmosphere. For the ultimate in luxury, the La Hougue suite can be reserved. A meeting place for locals, the attractive well-stocked bar is ideal for evening relaxation, where a resident pianist entertains frequently.*
*ACCOMMODATION £21–£30*
*FOOD up to £15*
**Hours:** open all year 8am; breakfast 7:30am – 9:30am; lunch 12noon – 1:45pm; dinner 6:30pm – 9:30pm. **Cuisine:** English / continental:- Using fresh produce, prime meats and local fish. Shellfish and lobster is available to special order. **Rooms:** 15 bedrooms all with tea making facilities, radio, TV: 4 doubles ensuite, 3 suites, 1 twin ensuite, 6 triples ensuite, 1 family room ensuite. **Credit cards:** Visa, Access, Diners, AmEx. **Other points:** licensed, open-air dining, Sunday lunch, no-smoking area, children catered for – please check for age limits, afternoon tea, parking, swimming pool. **Directions:** near Les Vaubelets Little Chapel, 1 mile from the airport.
ANTON NUSSBAUMER, tel (0481) 64181, fax (0481) 66272.

## TORTEVAL, Guernsey Map 3

### IMPERIAL HOTEL, BARS & RESTAURANT, Pleinmont
*The Imperial has proved a popular rendezvous with tourists and locals alike for over 100 years, with its unequalled views of the west coast and safe, sandy beaches. The cuisine too is excellent with seafood specialities and shellfish fresh from the bay. The main restaurant offers superb cuisine for that special candlelit dinner with fine wines and friendly service. In the bars meals are served all year round, in the summer you can enjoy your lunch or supper in the garden or on the terrace.*
*ACCOMMODATION £21–£30*
*FOOD up to £15*
**Hours:** breakfast 8:15am – 9:15am; lunch 12noon – 1:30pm; bar meals 12noon – 2pm; dinner 6:30pm – 9pm; bar meals 7pm – 9pm; closed (hotel only) November – March. **Cuisine:** French:- Traditional French haute cuisine with seafood specialities. A la carte, table d'hote and bar menus. **Rooms:** 17 bedrooms all with tea

making facilities, telephone, TV: 4 twins ensuite, 9 doubles ensuite, 3 family rooms ensuite, 1 single ensuite. **Credit cards:** Visa, Access. **Other points:** licensed, Sunday lunch, children catered for – please check for age limits, disabled access. **Directions:** south western tip of the island, overlooking Rocquaine Bay.
PATRICK & DIANA LINDLEY, tel (0481) 64044, fax (0481) 66139.

## TRINITY, Jersey Map 3

### COTE DU NORD HOTEL, Cote Du Nord
*Standing in its own grounds on the north east coast, the Cote Du Nord has a spectacular view of the sea and surrounding country, and is within walking distance of the harbour and village of Rozel. The restaurant is known locally for the high standard of cuisine and service it offers.*
*ACCOMMODATION £21–£30*
*FOOD £15–£20*
**Hours:** closed Christmas November; breakfast 8am – 9:30am; lunch 12noon – 2pm; dinner 7pm – 10pm. **Cuisine:** French:- A la carte, Table d'hote and Bar menus. French cuisine – seafood speciality. **Rooms:** 12 bedrooms all with tea making facilities, radio, TV: 2 singles ensuite, 4 doubles ensuite, 2 twins ensuite, 2 triples ensuite, 2 family rooms ensuite. **Credit cards:** Visa, Access, Diners, AmEx. **Other points:** licensed, open-air dining, Sunday lunch, children catered for – please check for age limits, afternoon tea. **Directions:** off the C93, on left towards Rozel.
MR HODSON, tel (0534) 861171, (0534) 861122, fax (0534) 865119.

## VAZON BAY, Guernsey Map 3

### LA GRANDE MARE, Castel
*La Grande Mare, situated in its own grounds of over 100 acres, enjoys delightful views. Friendly, caring and efficient service complements the high quality food on offer at this hotel, golf and country club. The restaurant specialises in seafood, shellfish and top class a la carte cuisine, and an extended wine list. Casserole award winner 1990, 1991, 1992 and 1993, also Corps D'Elite.*
*ACCOMMODATION over £50*
*FOOD £21–£25*
**Hours:** lunch 12noon – 2pm; dinner 7pm – 9.45pm. **Cuisine:** continental:- Fresh seafood, shellfish, flambe and the modern interpretation of classical dishes using the best of home-grown and local produce. Extensive wine list. Restaurant of the Year 1993. **Rooms:** 36 bedrooms, all en suite, furnished to an extremely high standard. **Credit cards:** Visa, Access, Diners, AmEx. **Other points:** licensed, Sunday lunch, no-smoking area, children catered for – please check for age limits, swimming pool, spa-bath, golf, fishing. **Directions:** fronts directly on to the Vazon Bay. Only 15 minutes from St Peter Port and 10 minutes from the airport.
MR P M VERMEULEN, tel (0481) 56576, fax (0481) 56532.

# CENTRAL ENGLAND

No other part of England offers a greater variety of countryside, town and village than can be found in the Heart of England.

Stratford-upon-Avon, world famous as the home of Shakespeare, is an ideal centre for touring other historic towns in the area. The Cotswolds are considered to be one of the most beautiful areas in England, with its soft natural limestone and wealth of historic buildings – the result of the wool trade which once prospered here. Surrounding the hills are many fine cathedral cities and Cheltenham with its magnificent Regency architecture.

Staffordshire, the land of peaks and potteries in the north of the region, offers many fascinating contrasts. Discover the history of the potteries with a visit to a museum, or a leisurely wander through the rugged moorland landscape. Nearby is the old city of Lichfield and home of England's leading leisure theme park, Alton Towers. To the west, you can escape to 'The Marches' where England meets Wales and enjoy the dramatic panoramic views.

Hereford and Worcester are for true lovers of the countryside. A combination of sweet-smelling hop fields surrounded by high flowering hedges and vast orchards of apple, pear and cherry; a patchwork of cornfields, grazing pastures and water meadows, interspersed by old broad-leaved woodland with rolling hills and ridges. To the north lies ancient Leominster with its pretty black and white villages, while to the south lies the dramatic Wye Valley and Forest of Dean. Hereford and Worcester each have their own cathedral, river bridge and quaint paved streets, separated only by the romantic Malvern Hills boasting the finest ridge walk in England. Birmingham, the capital, is all you would expect from a lively welcoming city with its concert halls, shops, and mixture of old and new architecture. Not far away is the Black Country, famed for its black puddings and the centre of traditional glass making. A visit to this area provides the tourist with a fascinating insight into England's industrial past.

Follow the story of the English Civil War from Nottinghamshire to Northamptonshire; in Leicestershire, walk the Battlefield Trail at Bosworth and enjoy the spectacle of Belvoir Castle's world famous medieval jousting tournaments. Derbyshire's Calke Abbey is well worth a visit as 'the house that time forgot'.

For the adventurous the region offers extensive scope, with climbing, caving, cycling, sailing, horse-riding or hill-walking and more. For the less energetic, there are trips available by steam train or tram, the leisurely pace of a canal boat or breathtaking panoramic views to be enjoyed over the Derbyshire dales from cable cars at the Height of Abraham. Stop for a drink at the Talbot Inn where the ghost of Mary, Queen of Scots – executed at nearby Fotheringham – is still said to walk, or visit Ye Old Trip to Jerusalem, reputedly the oldest inn in England, hewn out of rock on which Nottingham Castle stands. Enjoy the taste of Bakewell's famous pudding, Ashbourne's gingerbread, or pork pies and Stilton from Melton Mowbray.

Any visitor to this lovely part of England can certainly be assured of one thing – fine cooking and a range of accommodation to suit every taste and pocket, with the accent on quality and service.

For details of where to visit and what to see in Central England, contact the East Midlands Tourist Board, Exchequergate, Lincoln LN2 1PZ. Tel: (0522) 531521, or the Heart of England Tourist Board, Larkhill Road, Worcester WR5 2EF. Tel: (0905) 763436.

# ABINGDON, Oxfordshire Map 6

## ABINGDON LODGE HOTEL, Marcham Road

*A distinctive, octagon shaped modern hotel opened in 1986. At the heart of the hotel overlooking the pergola patio is the Octagon restaurant and attractively designed bar in conservatory fashion with trestle ceilings and hanging ivy. Close to Oxford and the Cotswolds.*
ACCOMMODATION over £50
FOOD up to £15
**Hours:** breakfast 7am – 9:30am; lunch 12noon – 2pm; bar meals 12noon – 2pm; bar meals 6pm – 10pm; dinner 7pm – 10pm. **Cuisine:** English:- All meals prepared with fresh produce. Carvery every lunchtime and Friday & Saturday evenings. Full a la carte menu every evening. **Rooms:** 53 bedrooms all with tea making facilities, telephone, radio, mini bar: 32 twins ensuite, 21 doubles – shower only. **Credit cards:** Visa, Access, Diners, AmEx. **Other points:** licensed, Sunday lunch, children catered for – please check for age limits, afternoon tea, baby-listening device, cots, 24hr reception, residents' lounge, residents' bar, parking, vegetarian meals, disabled access, foreign exchange. **Directions:** off the A34/A415 intersection. Situated on west entry into town.
JOHN OLDMAN, tel (0235) 553456, fax (0235) 554117.

# ALCESTER, Warwickshire Map 14

## ROSSINI RESTAURANT, 50 Birmingham Road

*A well-maintained traditional Italian restaurant, offering good food and wine in comfortable, friendly surroundings. The 100 year old Victorian building is pleasantly furnished throughout, and the service highly efficient. Nearby places of interest include Ragley Hall, Coughton Court, and Stratford-upon-Avon.*
FOOD £15–£20
**Hours:** lunch 12noon – 2pm; dinner 6:30pm – 10:30pm. **Cuisine:** Italian:- A la carte and Table d'hote menus. Traditional Italian style cuisine, including a wide choice of Pasta dishes, complemented by a good Wine List. **Credit cards:** Visa, Access, Diners, AmEx. **Other points:** licensed, Sunday lunch, children catered for – please check for age limits, disabled access, parking. **Directions:** situated on the main Evesham to Birmingham A435 road.
CARMINE SACCO, tel (0789) 762764.

# ALDERMINSTER, Warwickshire Map 14

## BELL BISTRO

*Standing on the A3400, the Bell is an old Coaching Inn with flagstones, beams and fireplaces. All food is freshly prepared and cooked on the premises and because of the use of fresh produce the menu changes daily. Traditional, predominantly English cuisine is imaginatively cooked. A friendly atmosphere prevails.*
FOOD £15–£20
**Hours:** lunch 12noon – 2:30pm; dinner 7pm – 11pm. **Cuisine:** English:- Menu written on blackboards –

changes daily. Fresh fish a speciality. Slimmers & Vegetarian dishes always available. All freshly prepared. **Credit cards:** Visa, Access. **Other points:** licensed, Sunday lunch, no-smoking area, children catered for – please check for age limits, conferences. **Directions:** on the A3400, 4 miles south of Stratford-upon-Avon.
KEITH & VANESSA BREWER, tel (0789) 450414, fax (0789) 450998.

# ALSAGER, Cheshire Map 16

## MANOR HOUSE HOTEL, Audley Road

*A friendly country hotel set in its own grounds, approximately two and a half miles from junction 16 of the M6. It retains the original oak beams from the farm around which it was built. Morning coffee and teas are served in the lounge. For sports enthusiasts there is an indoor swimming pool, snooker and pool room and a golf club opposite. Excellent conference facilities are available in a purpose-built 1,895 square foot air-conditioned centre.*
ACCOMMODATION £21–£30
FOOD £15–£20
**Hours:** 7:15am – 9:15am; 12:30pm – 2:30pm; dinner 7pm – 9:45pm. **Cuisine:** English. **Rooms:** 52 bedrooms all with tea making facilities, telephone, TV: 3 singles ensuite, 9 twins ensuite, 29 doubles ensuite, 5 family rooms ensuite, 6 singles – shower only. **Credit cards:** Visa, Access, Diners, AmEx. **Other points:** parking, children catered for – please check for age limits, no-smoking area, disabled access, pets, garden, vegetarian meals, swimming pool, residents' bar, residents' lounge. **Directions:** 2–3 miles from Junction 16 (A500) off M6.
MR M MITCHELL, tel (0270) 884000, fax (0270) 882483.

# ALTON, Staffordshire Map 14

## WILD DUCK INN, New Road

*A country house built by Earl John. Elegant bar and family restaurant with comfortable and reasonably priced letting bedrooms. Set in Churnet Valley overlooking Alton Towers Leisure Park.*
ACCOMMODATION under £20
FOOD up to £15
**Hours:** breakfast 8:30am – 9:30am; dinner 7pm – 8:30pm. **Cuisine:** English:- Traditional pub food in the bar. English style food and snacks served in the restaurant. **Rooms:** 6 bedrooms 1 family room ensuite, 5 family rooms. **Credit cards:** Visa, Access. **Other points:** licensed, Sunday lunch, children catered for – please check for age limits, coach/prior arr. **Directions:** off the B5032. Follow directions for Alton Towers.
MR & MRS KEITH MURDOCH, tel (0538) 702218.

# ASHBOURNE, Derbyshire Map 15

## THE BENTLEY BROOK INN, Fenny Bentley

*This traditional timbered inn, set in 2 acres of well tended gardens, provides wonderfully cooked food using only the freshest produce – no frozen food here. With a daily changing menu, you will find their tasty main*

dishes with crisp fresh vegetables and home-made sweets a delight, especially when teamed with their comprehensive list of wines. Good accommodation & welcome.
ACCOMMODATION £21–£30
FOOD up to £15 CLUB
**Hours:** breakfast 7am – 10am; meals all day 11am – 9:30pm. **Cuisine:** English:- Dishes include savoury Derbyshire oatcake, Prime Steaks, selection of home-made sweets. **Rooms:** 9 bedrooms all with tea making facilities, telephone, radio, TV: 1 single ensuite, 1 twin ensuite, 2 twins, 4 doubles ensuite, 1 double. **Credit cards:** Visa, Access, Diners, AmEx. **Other points:** licensed, Sunday lunch, children catered for – please check for age limits, garden, pets allowed. **Directions:** on junction of the A515 to Buxton and B5056 to Bakewell.
MR & MRS ALLINGHAM, tel (033529) 278, fax (033529) 422.

### STANSHOPE HALL, Stanshope
A 17th century country house with beautiful south-facing views, standing on the brow of a hill above Dovedale in the Peak National Park. The rooms are large and comfortable featuring unusual decorations such as hand-painted walls. Atmosphere of a country house and family home combined with the standards and features of a hotel. Ideal for walkers. 30 mins Alton Towers.
ACCOMMODATION £21–£30
FOOD £15–£20 ★
**Hours:** breakfast 8:30am – 9:30am; dinner 7pm. **Cuisine:** English:- 3 course dinner. Home cooking and vegetables from the garden. Home made chocolates served with the coffee. Vegetarians welcome. **Rooms:** 3 bedrooms all with tea making facilities, telephone, TV: 1 twin ensuite, 2 doubles ensuite. **Other points:** licensed, children catered for – please check for age limits, pets allowed, garden, residents' lounge. **Directions:** off A515 Ashbourne to Buxton in the hamlet of Stanshope.
NAOMI CHAMBERS & NICK LOURIE, tel (0335) 27278, fax (0335) 27470.

## ASHBY DE LA ZOUCH, Leicestershire Map 14

### LA ZOUCH RESTAURANT, 2 Kilwardby Street
A renovated Georgian building, tastefully decorated and furnished and with a walled garden, cottage style with pebble water feature. There is a small intimate bar with a larger lounge bar upstairs and private functions and dinner parties can be arranged. The restaurant offers a large selection of English and continental dishes.
FOOD £15–£20 CLUB
**Hours:** closed 01/01 – 15/01; closed 01/07 – 14/07; lunch 12noon – 2pm; dinner 7pm – 10pm; closed Monday; closed Sunday evening. **Cuisine:** English / continental:- Grilled Salmon & Cucumber sauce, Rump steak and mustard sauce. Homemade sweets. Speciality; Colston Bassett Stilton. **Credit cards:** Visa, Access,

Diners, AmEx. **Other points:** licensed, open-air dining, Sunday lunch, children catered for – please check for age limits, parking, vegetarian meals. **Directions:** at the crossroads of the A50 and B5006 in town centre.
GEOFFREY & LYNNE UTTING, tel (0530) 412536.

### THE MEWS WINE BAR & RESTAURANT, 8 Mill Lane
Situated in a pedestrian mews in this historic market town, this popular Queen Anne listed building in a conservation area has a reputation for excellent home cooked food in its Garden Room restaurant. Under same ownership for 12 years.
FOOD up to £15
**Hours:** lunch 12noon – 2:30pm; dinner 6pm – 10:30pm; closed Monday; closed Sunday. **Cuisine:** English:- Traditonal English cooking with a different menu using only fresh supplies. **Credit cards:** Visa, Access, AmEx. **Other points:** no-smoking area, children catered for – please check for age limits. **Directions:** 30 yd from the junction of the A50/A453.
IAN G BRIDGE, tel (0530) 416683, fax (0530) 415111.

## ASTHALL, Oxfordshire Map 6

### THE MAYTIME INN, Nr Burford
Situated in a tiny hamlet, 2.5 miles from Burford, the Maytime Inn has retained much of its centuries-old Cotswold charm. In addition to a spacious bar, there is a dining room seating 80 where one can wine and dine in style and comfort.
ACCOMMODATION £21–£30
FOOD up to £15
**Hours:** open bank holidays, Sunday; breakfast 8am – 11am; lunch 11am – 2:30pm; dinner 7pm – 10pm. **Cuisine:** English / international:- Daily specials, eg Steak and Kidney pie, fish pie, medallions of fillet steak Chinese style, fresh local salmon. **Rooms:** 6 bedrooms 4 twins ensuite, 2 doubles ensuite. **Credit cards:** Visa, Access, AmEx. **Other points:** licensed, open-air dining, Sunday lunch, children catered for – please check for age limits. **Directions:** down a narrow country lane from the A40 between Witney & Burford.
T M & M MORGAN, tel (099382) 2068.

## BAKEWELL, Derbyshire Map 15

### ASHFORD HOTEL & RESTAURANT, Church Street, Ashford-in-the-Water
An 18th century Grade II listed building with traditional oak beams and open fires. A family run hotel with a warm welcome and personal service. Good food is beautifully presented in the restaurant and a wide range of bar meals are also available. Behind the hotel and extending down to the River Wye is a large beer garden, a perfect place to enjoy a snack in summer.
ACCOMMODATION £31–£40
FOOD up to £15
**Hours:** breakfast 8am – 9:30am; lunch – Sunday 12noon – 2pm; bar meals 12noon – 2pm; dinner 7pm – 9:30pm. **Cuisine:** French:- French cuisine specialising in fish

dishes including salmon, Dover sole and trout. A la carte and table d'hote menus. **Rooms:** 7 bedrooms 5 doubles ensuite, 1 twin ensuite, 1 single ensuite. **Credit cards:** Visa, Access. **Other points:** licensed, open-air dining, Sunday lunch, children catered for – please check for age limits, beer garden, afternoon tea, pets allowed, residents' lounge. **Directions:** 2.5 miles outside Bakewell, off the A6 towards Buxton.
JOHN & SUE DAWSON, tel (0629) 812725.

## BANBURY, Oxfordshire Map 6

### THE MOON & SIXPENCE, Hanwell
*Snuggling in the old Anglo-Saxon village of Hanwell, deep in the Oxfordshire countryside, the Moon & Sixpence offers luxurious accommodation. The attractive split-level restaurant seats up to 100 in comfort to enjoy the excellent freshly prepared cuisine and fine wines. The Oak Room is available for private hire, as are many other rooms – details on request.*
*ACCOMMODATION £21–£30*
*FOOD £21–£25*
**Hours:** closed part of August 7pm; lunch 12noon – 3:30pm; dinner 7pm – 10pm. **Cuisine:** international:- Finest Scottish beef dishes. Poached Scotch Salmon, Grilled Dover Sole feature among the fresh fish selection. Involtini Della Mamma. **Rooms:** 3 bedrooms 2 doubles ensuite, 1 twin ensuite. **Credit cards:** Visa, Access. **Other points:** licensed, patio, children catered for – please check for age limits, residents' lounge, parking, disabled access. **Directions:** close to Junction 11 of M40 between A423 & B4100, north from Banbury.
LEONARDO & GILLIAN DE FELICE, tel (0295) 730544, fax (0295) 730147.

### ROEBUCK INN, Drayton
*The 16th century stone built village pub offers excellent value bar meals and a good a la carte menu with fish, steak and vegetarian specialities, served in a friendly atmosphere.*
*ACCOMMODATION under £20*
*FOOD up to £15*
**Hours:** breakfast 8am – 9am; lunch 11:30am – 2pm; dinner 7pm – 9:30pm. **Cuisine:** English:- A la carte. **Rooms:** 2 bedrooms 1 double, 1 twin. **Credit cards:** Visa, Access. **Other points:** licensed, Sunday lunch, children catered for – please check for age limits. **Directions:** A422, just outside Banbury.
MICHAEL & LIZ BROWN, tel (0295) 730542.

### THE WHITE HORSE INN, Duns Tew
*A Grade 1 listed XVIIth century Inn, constructed of Cotswold stone. The interior is heavily beamed and the walls adorned with saddlery and horse-brasses which add to the quaintness. As the only pub in the village, it is a firm favourite with locals who visit regularly. Nearby places of interest are Blenheim Palace, Oxford (15 miles) and Stratford (18 miles). The Hotel now has its own 18 hole golf course, Par 72, 6100 yds.*
*ACCOMMODATION £21–£30*
*FOOD up to £15* ♀
**Hours:** breakfast 8:30am – 9:30am; lunch 12:30pm – 2pm;

dinner 7:30pm – 9:30pm. **Cuisine:** English:- A la carte and Table d'hote menus offering traditional English fare. **Rooms:** 13 bedrooms all with tea making facilities, TV: 7 twins ensuite, 6 doubles ensuite. **Credit cards:** Visa, Access. **Other points:** licensed, open-air dining, Sunday lunch, children catered for – please check for age limits, residents' lounge, parking, disabled access, vegetarian meals, air-conditioned. **Directions:** 5 miles from Junction 10 on M40. 2 miles south of Deddington.
E SINCLAIR, tel (0869) 40272, fax (0869) 47732.

## BELPER, Derbyshire Map 15

### THE HANGING GATE, Ashbourne Road, Shottle Gate
*This attractive, popular pub has an extensive menu of well presented traditional pub food with a special children's menu. Within reach of the Peak District and Alton Towers. The Hanging Gate occasionally features live piano music and traditional 'sing alongs'. There is a wine list with a choice of about a dozen reasonably priced wines to accompany meals.*
*FOOD up to £15*
**Hours:** meals all day 11am – 11pm; Sunday 12noon – 10:30pm. **Cuisine:** English:- Traditional English pub meals and snacks with a wide range of home made desserts. **Credit cards:** Visa, Access. **Other points:** licensed, open-air dining, Sunday lunch, no-smoking area, children catered for – please check for age limits, afternoon tea. **Directions:** Situated on the A517 Ashbourne Road 2 miles from Belper.
JEREMY & LINDA BRADSHAW, tel (0773) 550363.

## BIBURY, Gloucestershire Map 13

### JANKOWSKIS BRASSERIE, The Swan Hotel
*Located in the centre of Bibury near the bridge, this 300 year old building offers excellent British cuisine with French overtones. The atmosphere is relaxed and friendly with a mixed clientele. Live Jazz is provided on Wednesday evenings. Accommodation is available at the adjoining Swan Hotel.*
*ACCOMMODATION over £50*
*FOOD £15–£20*
**Hours:** meals all day 10am – 10pm. **Cuisine:** British / French. **Credit cards:** Visa, Access, AmEx. **Other points:** parking, children catered for – please check for age limits, disabled access, vegetarian meals, open-air dining. **Directions:** located in the centre of Bibury, adjacent to the bridge. In the heart of the Cotswolds, 7 miles from Cirencester.
MRS E A HAYLES & MR J A FURTEK, tel (0285) 740695, fax (0285) 740473.

## BIRMINGHAM, West Midlands Map 14

### FOUNTAIN COURT HOTEL, 339–343 Hagley Road, Edgbaston
*A friendly, family run hotel located on a main road about 3 miles from the city centre. Good location for*

access to M5 and the international Conference Centre. The hotel is well-maintained and has been recently refurbished. Especially popular with business travellers and weekenders.

ACCOMMODATION £21–£30

FOOD up to £15

**Hours:** breakfast 6:45am – 9am; dinner 6:30pm – 8:30pm. **Cuisine:** English:- Table d'hote menu. Dishes may include roast pork, Chilli con Carne, grilled gammon. **Rooms:** 25 bedrooms all with tea making facilities, telephone, TV: 13 singles ensuite, 6 twins ensuite, 6 doubles ensuite. **Credit cards:** Visa, Access, AmEx. **Other points:** licensed, Sunday lunch, children catered for – please check for age limits, garden, afternoon tea, pets allowed. **Directions:** A456. Corner of Hagley Road and Fountain Road. 2 miles from Junction 3, M5.

GLADYS, STELLA & RICHARD SMITH, tel (021) 429 1754, fax (021) 429 1209.

## GREAT BARR HOTEL, Peartree Drive, Great Barr

Conveniently situated on the outskirts of Birmingham, this beautifully decorated and furnished 3 Star hotel is an ideal venue for family stop-overs, week-end/Short Breaks or for the Business person looking for a comfortable and friendly hotel. The Partridge Restaurant has a reputation for an interesting selection of food and fine wines.

ACCOMMODATION £21–£30

FOOD £15–£20

**Hours:** breakfast 7am – 9:30am; lunch 12:30pm – 2pm; dinner 7pm – 9:45pm. **Cuisine:** English / continental:- A la Carte and Table d'hote menus, offering an imaginative selection of English and continental cuisine. **Rooms:** 110 bedrooms all with tea making facilities, telephone, radio, TV: 77 singles ensuite, 4 twins ensuite, 29 doubles ensuite. **Credit cards:** Visa, Access, Diners, AmEx. **Other points:** licensed, open-air dining, Sunday lunch, children catered for – please check for age limits, afternoon tea, residents' lounge, garden, parking, functions, baby-listening device, baby sitting, cots, 24hr reception, foreign exchange, residents' bar, vegetarian meals. **Directions:** M6-exit 7, A34 to B'ham. Take first right at lights onto Newton Road, the hotel is 1 mile on the right.

MORGAN SINCLAIR, tel (021) 357 1141, fax (021) 357 7557.

## HAGLEY COURT HOTEL, 229 Hagley Road, Edgbaston

A Georgian mansion, set back from the main road leading into the city. The Conference Centre is only one mile from the hotel, making it an ideal place for delegates to stay. The hotel is renowned for its comfortable and homely accommodation.

ACCOMMODATION £21–£30

FOOD up to £15 ★

**Hours:** breakfast 7am – 9am; dinner 6pm – 9:30pm. **Cuisine:** French / English:- A la carte, Table d'hote and Bar menus. French/English – steaks, chicken, fish. **Rooms:** 27 bedrooms all with tea making facilities,

telephone, radio, TV: 8 singles ensuite, 3 twins ensuite, 16 doubles ensuite. **Credit cards:** Visa, Access, AmEx, Diners, Switch. **Other points:** licensed, children catered for – please check for age limits, cots, residents' bar, residents' lounge, parking. **Directions:** on A456.

CHRISTOPHER PHILIPPIDES, tel (021) 454 6514, fax (021) 456 2722.

## HEATH LODGE HOTEL, 117 Coleshill Road, Marston Green

Family-run hotel, with cosy lounge and coal-effect fire, quietly situated just a short distance away from NEC and Birmingham international Airport. Courtesy car available for airport travellers and long-term car parking.

ACCOMMODATION under £20

FOOD up to £15

**Hours:** dinner 6:30pm – 9pm. **Cuisine:** international:- Farmhouse grill, fillet steak, Chicken Kiev, salmon, halibut. **Rooms:** 18 bedrooms all with tea making facilities, telephone, TV: 1 single, 7 singles ensuite, 4 twins, 2 twins ensuite, 4 doubles ensuite. **Credit cards:** Visa, Access, Diners, AmEx. **Other points:** licensed, children catered for – please check for age limits, pets allowed, bank holidays, residents' bar, residents' meals, vegetarian meals, parking. **Directions:** hotel located 1 mile from entrance to Birmingham airport.

SIMEON COLLINS, tel (021) 779 2218, fax (021) 779 5673.

## HENRY'S CAFE BAR (BIRMINGHAM), 1 Victoria Square

A popular cafe-bar situated in the city centre, close to shops and serving an extensive range of international fast-food, American beers and speciality cocktails. Lively and very popular, lunchtimes are busy.

FOOD up to £15

**Hours:** closed Sunday 6:30pm; meals all day 10:30am – 9:30pm. **Cuisine:** international. **Credit cards:** Visa, Access. **Other points:** children catered for – please check for age limits, open bank holidays, no-smoking area, afternoon teas, disabled access, vegetarian meals. **Directions:** 5 minute walk from European Conference Centre.

MR D SAMPSON, tel (021) 631 3827, (021) 631 3834.

## LYNDHURST HOTEL, 135 Kingsbury Road, Erdington

Family owned and run. Recently refurbished to a high standard but maintaining a relaxed family atmosphere. On the route of the 114 and 116 buses which go to the city centre.

ACCOMMODATION £21–£30

FOOD up to £15 ★

**Hours:** closed Christmas 10:30am; breakfast 7:30am – 8:30am; dinner 6:30pm – 8:30pm. **Cuisine:** English. **Rooms:** 14 bedrooms all with tea making facilities, TV: 2 singles, 6 singles ensuite, 4 twins ensuite, 2 family rooms ensuite. **Credit cards:** Visa, Access, Diners, AmEx. **Other points:** central heating, children catered

for – please check for age limits, residents' lounge, garden, vegetarian meals. **Directions:** on the A38, half mile from M6 turn-off Junction 6.
MR & MRS R WILLIAMS, tel (021) 373 5695, fax (021) 373 5695.

### PINOCCHIOS RESTAURANT, Chad Square, Hawthorne Road
*A traditional Italian decor sets the scene in which to enjoy quality Italian meals generously served. With its warm, friendly and relaxed atmosphere, it is the perfect place for a quiet or romantic dinner. Fresh fish and vegetables are bought daily. Situated just minutes from the City on the Harborne/Edgbaston border, Pinocchios is a real taste of Italy in Birmingham.*
*FOOD £21–£25*
**Hours:** lunch 12noon – 2:30pm; dinner 7pm – 11pm; closed bank holidays; closed Sunday. **Cuisine:** Italian:- Extensive menu – dishes may include Filetto Farfalla, Calamari alla Livornese, Sogliola di Dover Grigliata, Pollo alla Pinocchio. **Credit cards:** Visa, Access, Diners, AmEx. **Other points:** licensed, children catered for – please check for age limits. **Directions:** opposite White Swan pub, just off Harborne Road. Near Botanical Gardens.
MR SILVIO NOVELLI, tel (021) 454 8672.

### WESTBOURNE LODGE HOTEL, 27/29 Fountain Road, Edgbaston
*Family-run hotel ideally situated for I.C.C, N.E.C, National Indoor Arena and Edgbaston Cricket ground. Located 1¹/₂ miles from city in a quiet suburb, 200 yd off the A456 Hagley Road. A warm welcome, good food, free parking, and all rooms en suite.*
*ACCOMMODATION £21–£30*
*FOOD up to £15*
**Hours:** closed Christmas Sunday; breakfast 7am – 9am; lunch 12:30pm – 2pm; dinner 6pm – 9pm. **Cuisine:** English. **Rooms:** 11 single, 2 double, 3 twin and 2 family bedrooms – 18 of them en suite. Telephones, TV, radio and tea/coffee making facilities in rooms. **Credit cards:** Visa, Access, AmEx. **Other points:** central heating, children catered for – please check for age limits, patio, garden, residents' lounge, vegetarian meals. **Directions:** off the A456, 200yds from the corner of Hagley and Fountain Road.
MR & MRS J H HANSON, tel (021) 429 1003, fax (021) 429 7436.

## BISHOPS CASTLE, Shropshire Map 13

### THE BOARS HEAD, Church Street
*A 16th century Inn and restaurant in a historic Shropshire market town. The Inn has a comfortable dining area with an extensive menu ranging from bar snacks to full a la carte meals. The stable block behind the Boars Head has been converted to provide 4 comfortable bedrooms. All food is well-cooked and provides good value for money. A relaxed, friendly atmosphere prevails.*
*ACCOMMODATION £21–£30*
*FOOD up to £15* ★

**Hours:** breakfast 8am – 9am; bar meals 12noon – 2pm; dinner 7pm – 9:30pm; bar meals 7pm – 10pm. **Cuisine:** English:- Bar snacks and a la carte meals. Predominantly English cuisine. **Rooms:** 8 bedrooms all with tea making facilities, telephone, TV: 2 twins ensuite, 1 double ensuite, 1 family room ensuite, 3 twins ensuite, 1 double ensuite. **Credit cards:** Visa, Access. **Other points:** licensed, children catered for – please check for age limits, pets allowed, cots, parking. **Directions:** from A488, signs to livestock market & car park before crossroads.
GRANT PERRY, tel (0588) 638521.

## BOURTON-ON-THE-WATER, Gloucestershire Map 13

### BO-PEEP TEA ROOMS, Riverside
*'Olde worlde' riverside tea rooms and licensed restaurant. The spacious interior has fitted carpets, panelling and exposed Cotswold stone walls. A homely, comfortable atmosphere prevails and the service is efficient and welcoming. All dishes are freshly cooked, well served and presented. The menu offers a good choice including vegetarian dishes. A beautiful setting. Chosen by the Tea Council as one of the top ten places in Britain for both 1992 and 1993.*
*FOOD up to £15*
**Hours:** winter (closed some w'days) 10am – 5:30pm; summer 10am – 9pm. **Cuisine:** English:- Homemade. Large Cornish clotted cream teas. **Credit cards:** Visa, Access, Diners, AmEx. **Other points:** licensed, Sunday lunch, no-smoking area, children catered for – please check for age limits, afternoon tea, pets allowed, bank holidays. **Directions:** off A429 Fosse Way. Opposite side of river to village green.
JUDY & BOB HISCOKE, tel (0451) 822005.

### OLD NEW INN
*A traditional country inn built in 1709, situated in the heart of the Cotswolds on the banks of the River Windrush and set in attractive gardens. Antique furnishings, warming log fires and traditional home cooking set the atmosphere. Run by the Morris family for over 60 years.*
*ACCOMMODATION £21–£30*
**Hours:** breakfast 8:15am – 9:15am; lunch 12:30pm – 1:30pm; dinner 7:30pm – 8:30pm; closed Christmas Day. **Cuisine:** English:- Traditional home cooking. **Rooms:** 20 bedrooms all with tea making facilities, TV: 4 singles, 1 single ensuite, 2 twins, 5 twins ensuite, 2 doubles, 6 doubles ensuite. **Credit cards:** Visa, Access. **Other points:** open-air dining, Sunday lunch, children catered for – please check for age limits, pets allowed. **Directions:** off the A429. Turn off Fosseway down to the High Street.
PETER MORRIS, tel (0451) 820467, fax (0451) 810236.

### THE OLD MANSE HOTEL, Victoria Street
*Built in 1748 as the home of the Reverend Benjamin Beddome, the village's Baptist pastor, this traditional Cotswold stone building stands on the south bank of the leisurely River Windrush which flows gently by. Fully centrally heated, there is a spacious 60 seater restaurant*

which is elegantly decorated and furnished offering excellent cuisine, using fresh local produce wherever possible, complemented by an extensive wine list. Special dishes can be prepared on request. Places of interest nearby include Birdland, Perfumery, Motor Museum, Model Village and Model Railway Exhibition.
ACCOMMODATION £21–£30
FOOD up to £15
**Hours:** breakfast 8am – 9:30am; bar snacks 11am – 11pm; Sunday lunch 12noon – 2:30pm; bar snacks – Sunday 12noon – 3pm; dinner – Mon-Sat 6pm – 9pm; dinner – Sunday 7pm – 9pm; bar snacks – Sunday 7pm – 10:30pm. **Cuisine:** English / French. **Credit cards:** Visa, Access, Diners, AmEx. **Other points:** children catered for – please check for age limits, parking, disabled access, pets, residents' lounge, garden, vegetarian meals, open-air dining. **Directions:** on the banks of the river Windrush overlooking the village green and the High Street.
MR & MRS DOCKERY, tel (0451) 820082, fax (0451) 810381.

## BROADWAY, Hereford & Worcestershire Map 13

### BELL INN, Main Street, Willersey
A large public house built in traditional Cotswold stone, the Bell Inn serves excellent food within comfortable, relaxed surroundings. The food is made from fresh local produce and is superbly cooked and presented. Highly recommended for its welcoming service and excellent food at very good value for money.
FOOD up to £15
**Hours:** lunch 12noon – 2pm; dinner – except Sunday 6pm – 9:30pm; dinner – Sunday 7pm – 9pm. **Cuisine:** English:- Daily changing menu. Dishes may include Lemon Sole, Salmon en Croute, traditional Game Pie, Steak au Poivre, as well as a standard menu. **Credit cards:** Visa, Access, AmEx. **Other points:** licensed, open-air dining, Sunday lunch, children catered for – please check for age limits, beer garden. **Directions:** B4632 Broadway (1.5 miles) to Stratford-upon-Avon. By the Duck Pond.
WILLIAM MOORE, tel (0386) 858405.

## BROUGHTON, Cheshire Map 16

### THE SPINNING WHEEL TAVERN, The Old Warren, Nr Chester
Old roadside pub, attractively furnished and decorated with copper antiques and brass horse artifacts. Freshly prepared traditional meals are served in a convivial, welcoming atmosphere. Friendly staff and efficient service make the meal complete. Good value for money.
FOOD up to £15
**Hours:** lunch 11:30am – 2:30pm; dinner 6pm – 10:30pm. **Cuisine:** English / international:- Specialities may include Sole Spinning Wheel (with white wine, mushrooms, prawns & cream), Tournedos Rossini. Blackboard specials change daily. **Credit cards:** Visa, Access, Diners, AmEx. **Other points:** licensed, Sunday lunch, children catered for – please check for age limits,

bank holidays, functions. **Directions:** on Old Main Rd from Broughton to Buckley, 6 miles from Chester.
MIKE & MAGGIE VERNON, tel (0244) 531068, (0244) 533637.

## BROWNHILLS, West Midlands Map 14

### TERRACE RESTAURANT, 9 Watling Street, Newtown
A modern 150 seater restaurant which has deservedly won awards for its delightful floral gardens. The interior of the restaurant is modern and comfortable with fresh flowers in abundance. Well-cooked, attractively presented food is served in generous portions.
FOOD up to £15 ★
**Hours:** lunch 12noon – 2:30pm; dinner 7pm – 10pm; closed Sunday evening. **Cuisine:** English:- Traditional English cuisine. Specialities include Beef Wellington and fresh fish. **Credit cards:** Visa, Access, Diners, AmEx. **Other points:** licensed, Sunday lunch, children catered for – please check for age limits, functions, conferences, weddings. **Directions:** main A5 trunk road. 7 miles east of M6. 5 miles north east of Walsall.
MR ADSHEAD, tel (0543) 378291, (0543) 360456.

## BURFORD, Oxfordshire Map 6

### COTSWOLD GATEWAY, Cheltenham Road Roundabout
Situated in the enchanting town of Burford with its 1,000 inhabitants, the Cotswold Gateway has for more than two hundred years provided a welcome stop-over for travellers. Today, guests can expect personal and caring attention in a friendly and intimate atmosphere from the highly trained staff. Burford, set on the valley side of the River Windrush and surrounded by old hay meadow and cornfields has changed little since the early 17th century and is also an important centre for reputable antique dealers.
ACCOMMODATION £31–£40
FOOD £15–£20
**Hours:** breakfast 7:30am – 9:30am; lunch 12noon – 2pm; bar snacks 12noon – 2pm; dinner 7pm – 9:30pm; bar snacks 7pm – 9:30pm. **Cuisine:** modern English:- Great attention paid to quality and presentation. **Rooms:** 16 bedrooms 1 single ensuite, 9 doubles ensuite, 2 twins ensuite, 4 family rooms ensuite. **Credit cards:** Visa, Access, Diners, AmEx. **Other points:** parking, children catered for – please check for age limits, Sunday lunch, open bank holidays, afternoon tea, disabled access, pets allowed, residents' lounge, vegetarian meals, licensed. **Directions:** on the A40 main road, right by roundabout at the top of Burford Hill.
RAY & JOYCE FORD, tel (0993) 822695, fax (0993) 823600.

## BURTON-ON-THE-WOLDS, Leicestershire Map 14

### GREYHOUND INN, 25 Melton Road
A traditional coaching inn renovated in 1991. All the food is home cooked and supported by a comprehensive

*wine list. British Institute of Innkeeping (East Midlands Section) Pub of the Year 1988 and 1989.*
**FOOD** up to £15
**Hours:** lunch 12noon – 2pm; dinner 7pm – 10pm.
**Cuisine:** English:- Home cooked specials. "Big Steak Night" every Thursday. **Credit cards:** Visa, Access, AmEx, Diners, Switch. **Other points:** open-air dining, Sunday lunch, children catered for – please check for age limits, coach/prior arr. **Directions:** B676 Loughborough to Melton Mowbray road.
PHILIP & ANN ASHLEY, tel (0509) 880860, fax (0509) 881709.

## BUXTON, Derbyshire Map 15

### OLD HALL HOTEL, *The Square*
*This historic hotel dating back to the 16th century has entertained thousands of visitors including Mary Queen of Scots. Overlooking the Pavilion Gardens and Opera House, it is an ideal base for those wishing to visit the theatre. Good food and comfortable accommodation.*
*ACCOMMODATION £31–£40*
*FOOD up to £15*
**Hours:** breakfast 7:30am – 9:30am; lunch 12noon – 2:30pm; dinner 6pm – 11pm; bar meals 6pm – 11pm.
**Cuisine:** English:- Serving bar snacks, full a la carte menu and table d'hote. **Rooms:** 38 bedrooms, 32 en suite.
**Credit cards:** Visa, Access, AmEx, Diners, Switch. **Other points:** licensed, open-air dining, Sunday lunch, children catered for – please check for age limits, afternoon tea, functions, conferences, foreign exchange, residents' lounge, residents' bar. **Directions:** Centre of Buxton, past the crescent.
GEORGE & LOUISE POTTER, tel (0298) 22841, fax (0298) 72437.

## CAMBRIDGE, Gloucestershire Map 13

### THE GEORGE INN, *Bristol Road*
*Nestling on the banks of the River Cam, The George Inn is the ideal stepping stone to many of Gloucestershire's premier tourist attractions. The oak-beamed dining areas have a unique style with tables made from original Singer sewing machine treadles. Meals also available in the garden or on the patio.*
*FOOD up to £15*
**Hours:** last orders 10pm; lunch 12noon – 2pm; dinner 7pm – 11pm. **Cuisine:** English / Italian:- Traditional Gloucestershire fayre to international cuisine. **Credit cards:** Visa, Access, Diners, AmEx. **Other points:** licensed, open air dining, Sunday lunch, children catered for – please check for age limits, garden, coach/prior arr. **Directions:** on the A38, three miles south of Junction 13, M5.
ALISTAIR & JANE DEAS, tel (0453) 890270.

## CANNOCK, Staffordshire Map 14

### SALEEM BAGH, *Queens Square*
*A popular air-conditioned restaurant offering an extensive menu of traditional Indian cuisine with*

*speciality dishes, all freshly prepared. A 4-course Businessman's Lunch is also available.*
*FOOD up to £15*
**Hours:** closed Sunday 7pm; open Christmas day 7pm; lunch 12noon – 2:30pm; dinner 5pm – 11pm. **Cuisine:** Indian. **Credit cards:** Visa, Access, Diners, AmEx.
**Other points:** children catered for – please check for age limits, open bank holidays, no-smoking area, disabled access, vegetarian meals. **Directions:** close to town centre on the ringway.
MR M NANU, tel (0543) 505089.

## CASTLE DONINGTON, Leicestershire Map 14

### DONINGTON MANOR HOTEL, *High Street*
*An 18th century Regency Coaching Inn, popular with race-goers. Donington Manor provides the epitome of traditional British hospitality.*
*ACCOMMODATION £31–£40*
*FOOD up to £15*
**Hours:** meals 7am – 12midnight; last orders 9:30pm; closed 27/12 – 30/12. **Cuisine:** English:- Melton fillet, fresh duckling, game dishes and fresh fish in season.
**Rooms:** 27 bedrooms 17 singles ensuite, 5 twins ensuite, 4 doubles ensuite, 1 family room ensuite. **Credit cards:** Visa, Access, Diners, AmEx. **Other points:** Sunday lunch, conferences. **Directions:** off M1 at Junction 24, 2 miles along A6 to Derby, turn left at B6540.
MR N GRIST, tel (0332) 810253.

### LE CHEVALIER, *2 Borough St*
*A small, intimate personally run restaurant with a well-established reputation for its good food and friendly atmosphere. It now has a number of lovely rooms around the rear courtyard and makes an ideal base for exploring the surrounding area, with Donington Park Racetrack, Nottingham, Derby and Alton Towers nearby.*
*ACCOMMODATION under £20*
*FOOD up to £15* CLUB
**Hours:** breakfast 7:30am – 8:30am; lunch 12noon – 2pm; dinner 6:30pm – 11pm. **Cuisine:** French / continental:- French and continental cuisine, specialities including Boudin a l'Anglaise and Filet de Boeuf Chevalier. **Rooms:** 4 bedrooms all with tea making facilities, telephone, radio, TV: 2 doubles ensuite, 1 family room ensuite, 1 twin ensuite. **Credit cards:** Visa, Access, Diners, AmEx.
**Other points:** licensed, children catered for – please check for age limits, bank holidays, garden. **Directions:** just off B6540 – Jct 24 of M1. On main street of Castle Donington.
MR JAD OTAKI & LYNN OTAKI, tel (0332) 812106, (0332) 812005.

## CHELTENHAM, Gloucestershire Map 13

### BELOW STAIRS RESTAURANT, *103 Promenade*
*Situated in the town centre with front entrance from the promenade and rear access with evening and weekend*

parking in Montpellier Street. Cooking is personally supervised by the Chef/Proprietor.

FOOD up to £15 CLUB ★

**Hours:** lunch – except Sunday 12noon; dinner – except Sunday 6pm; closed bank holidays; closed Sunday. **Cuisine:** English / seafood:- Fresh seafood a speciality. Traditional cooking and fresh vegetables. Vegetarian and vegan dishes available. **Credit cards:** Visa, Access, Diners, AmEx. **Other points:** open-air dining, no-smoking area, children catered for – please check for age limits, disabled access. **Directions:** in the town centre. MR J B LINTON, tel (0242) 234599.

## COTSWOLD GRANGE HOTEL, Pittville Circus Road

Built as the fine country house of a London solicitor, this attractive, mellow, Cotswold stone building is set in a tree-lined avenue in a pleasant location close to the centre of Cheltenham. The hotel is a friendly, family run establishment and offers quality food at excellent prices.

ACCOMMODATION £21–£30

FOOD up to £15

**Hours:** breakfast 7:15am – 9am; lunch 12noon – 2pm; bar meals 12noon – 2pm; dinner 6pm – 7:30pm; closed Christmas – New Year; closed Sunday. **Cuisine:** English. **Rooms:** 32 bedrooms all with tea making facilities, telephone, radio, TV: 12 singles ensuite, 7 twins ensuite, 9 doubles ensuite, 4 triples ensuite. **Credit cards:** Visa, Access, AmEx. **Other points:** licensed, no-smoking area, children catered for – please check for age limits, pets allowed, bank holidays, baby sitting, baby-listening device, cots, residents' lounge, residents' bar. **Directions:** at roundabout on Prestbury road, take right for Pittville Circus. MR PAUL WEAVER, tel (0242) 515119, fax (0242) 241537.

## THE HARE & HOUNDS, Foss Cross, Nr Chedworth

Located in open countryside, the pub dates back to the 17th century with many original features. They now offer a separate function area. All food is home made. Registered caravan site for up to 5 vehicles adjacent.

FOOD up to £15

**Hours:** closed Christmas day Sunday; bar – weekdays 11am – 3pm; bar – weekends 12noon – 3pm; bar – weekdays 6pm – 11pm; bar – weekends 7pm – 10:30pm; bar meals from 7pm. **Cuisine:** English:- Steak & kidney with dumplings cooked in ale, grills, and a selection of various home-made dishes, including vegetarian. **Credit cards:** Visa, Access, Diners, AmEx. **Other points:** licensed, open-air dining, Sunday lunch, children catered for – please check for age limits, coach/prior arr, functions. **Directions:** halfway between Cirencester and Northleach on A429. THE TURNER FAMILY, tel (0285) 720288.

## THE RETREAT, 10/11 Suffolk Parade

Lively, friendly bar with fresh food cooked daily on the premises. Its central location and distinctive atmosphere makes The Retreat a popular rendezvous.

FOOD up to £15

**Hours:** lunch 12noon – 2:15pm; closed Sunday. **Cuisine:** international:- Prepared in our own kitchen using fresh produce. Wide range of cold meats, salads and fish from servery. Home made puddings, cheesecakes, tarts. Extensive hot menu with a wide range of vegetarian food. **Credit cards:** Visa, Access, Diners, AmEx. **Other points:** open-air dining, children catered for – please check for age limits. **Directions:** in the centre of Cheltenham's Antique area of town. MIKE DEY, tel (0242) 235436.

## CHESTER, Cheshire Map 16

## THE BLUE BELL RESTAURANT, 65 Northgate Street

The Blue Bell is Chester's oldest surviving domestic structure and the city's only example of a medieval inn. Dating back to the 15th century, the Blue Bell has been beautifully restored as a restaurant and displays a wealth of antique furniture, and a resident ghost. Serving fine English food combining tradition with imagination and noted for its extensive wine list, the Blue Bell offers discreet and efficient service and is the perfect venue for a relaxing lunch or evening meal. Excellent value for money.

FOOD up to £15 ♈ ☺

**Hours:** lunch 12noon – 2:30pm; dinner 7pm – 10pm. **Cuisine:** English / French. **Credit cards:** Visa, Access. **Other points:** licensed, Sunday lunch & evening, no-smoking area, children catered for – please check for age limits, garden. **Directions:** 9 miles south of M53 and M56 intersection. MRS GLENYS EVANS, tel (0244) 317758.

## CHEYNEY LODGE HOTEL, 77–79 Cheyney Road

Half a mile from the City's Roman Wall, Cheyney Lodge was originally three houses. Recently completely refurbished, the hotel is now attractively decorated and provides good quality accommodation, a cosy bar, small dining room and separate lounge. A small, well-furnished hotel with a welcoming atmosphere and good, homecooked meals, offering good value for money.

ACCOMMODATION under £20

FOOD up to £15

**Hours:** breakfast 8am – 9am; lunch 12noon – 2pm; dinner 6:30pm – 9pm. **Cuisine:** English. **Rooms:** 8 bedrooms all with tea making facilities, radio, TV: 5 doubles ensuite, 1 family room ensuite, 2 twins ensuite. **Credit cards:** Visa, Access. **Other points:** children catered for – please check for age limits, residents' lounge, ETB – 3 crowns. **Directions:** from the city centre take A540 – Hoylake, left into Cheyney Rd. KEVIN DIXON – MANAGER, tel (0244) 381925.

## FRANCS RESTAURANT, 14 Cuppin Street

A 17th century oak-beamed building within the City walls serving top quality, exclusively French cuisine. Wide choice of dishes whether you are looking for 'un petit morceau' or a whole feast. The wine list has been

produced to complement their menus and there is a wide range of French aperitifs and liqueurs. A friendly, relaxing and informal atmosphere.
FOOD up to £15 ⌣ ⌣ ★
**Hours:** open 7 days 6:30pm; plats du jour 12noon – 6pm; a la carte menu 12noon – 11pm. **Cuisine:** Provincial French cuisine. House specialities include traditional French Savoury Crepes, Boudins and vegetarian dishes. **Credit cards:** Visa, Access, AmEx. **Other points:** licensed, children catered for – please check for age limits, parking, air-conditioned, disabled access, parties catered for. **Directions:** off Grosvenor Rd, near main north Wales roundabout and Police Station.
D JOHNSTON-CREE, tel (0244) 317952, fax (0244) 342767.

### MAMMA MIA, St Werburgh Street
A friendly Italian pizzeria with a lively atmosphere. Diners can watch chefs preparing and cooking pizzas in the traditional way in the open plan kitchen. Popular with locals and tourists alike.
FOOD up to £15
**Hours:** lunch 12noon – 2:30pm; dinner 6pm – 11pm; dinner – Sunday 6pm – 8pm; closed Sunday lunch. **Cuisine:** Italian:- Authentic Italian dishes – pizzas, pasta, calamari, sirloin. **Credit cards:** Visa, Access, Diners, AmEx. **Other points:** licensed, children catered for – please check for age limits. **Directions:** next to the Cathedral.
GIUSEPPE & ANNA LABELLA, tel (0244) 314663.

### REDLAND HOTEL, 64 Hough Green
An exquisite hotel with a unique Victorian ambiance recreated with genuine antiques, tasteful period furnishings and original wood panelling. Each of the rooms has been individually decorated and comprises all the facilities of a large hotel but with great character, charm and friendliness. The Redland turns a night away from home into a special experience.
ACCOMMODATION £31–£40
FOOD £26–£30 ⌣
**Hours:** breakfast 7:30am – 9:30am. **Cuisine:** breakfast. **Rooms:** 2 single, 6 double and 3 twin bedrooms, all en suite. TV and tea/coffee making facilities in all rooms. Routiers accommodation of the year 1988. **Other points:** children catered for – please check for age limits, pets/prior arr, residents' lounge, honeymoon suite, garden. **Directions:** on the A5104, 1 mile from the city centre.
MRS THERESA WHITE, tel (0244) 671024.

### ROWTON HALL HOTEL, Rowton Lane, Whitchurch Road
A Georgian manor house converted to an hotel in 1955, 3 miles from Chester city. Set in 8 acres of gardens, the hall stands on Rowton Moor, site of one of the major battles in the English Civil War. The Health and Leisure Club, Hamiltons, provides excellent facilities.
FOOD £15–£20
**Hours:** lunch 12noon – 2pm; dinner 7pm – 9:30pm. **Cuisine:** French / English:- Game (in season), local

salmon and trout. **Rooms:** 42 bedrooms en suite. **Credit cards:** Visa, Access, Diners, AmEx. **Other points:** licensed, Sunday lunch, children catered for – please check for age limits, leisure centre. **Directions:** just off the A41 Chester to Whitchurch road. Jct 13, M53.
S D BEGBIE, tel (0244) 335262.

## CHURCH STRETTON, Shropshire Map 13

### LONGMYND HOTEL, Cunnery Road
Longmynd Hotel stands in 10 acres of woodland commanding panoramic views of the south Shropshire hills. Amenities include a swimming pool, pitch and putt, trim gym, sauna, solarium and pavement chess. 1 bedroom cottages in the grounds and 2 bedroom apartments nearby (both self-catering).
ACCOMMODATION £41–£50
FOOD £15–£20
**Hours:** breakfast 8am – 9:30am; bar meals 12noon – 2pm; lunch 12:30pm – 2pm; bar meals 6:30pm – 9:30pm; dinner 7pm – 9:30pm. **Cuisine:** English:- Grilled fish, roasts, flambe dishes, salads. **Rooms:** 50 bedrooms, all en suite. Colour TV in all rooms, with satellite TV and video. **Credit cards:** Visa, Access, Diners, AmEx. **Other points:** Sunday lunch, children catered for – please check for age limits, coach/prior arr. **Directions:** on the A49 between Ludlow and Shrewsbury.
MISS SMITH – DIRECTOR, tel (0694) 722244.

## CIRENCESTER, Gloucestershire Map 13

### THE CROWN OF CRUCIS HOTEL & RESTAURANT, Ampney Crucis
A well patronised, pleasant hotel and restaurant with good home cooking. On fine days the tables beside the stream are very popular with families. Facilities for private parties of up to 100 people.
ACCOMMODATION £21–£30
FOOD up to £15 ★
**Hours:** open all year 7pm; lunch 12noon – 2:30pm; dinner 7pm – 10pm. **Cuisine:** English:- Daily specials, home-made desserts, traditional English cooking including award winning steak and kidney pies. **Rooms:** 27 bedrooms all with tea making facilities, telephone, radio, TV: 17 twins ensuite, 8 doubles ensuite, 2 quads ensuite. **Credit cards:** Visa, Access, Diners, AmEx. **Other points:** licensed, open-air dining, Sunday lunch, children catered for – please check for age limits, parking, garden, baby sitting, baby-listening device, cots, left luggage. **Directions:** on the A417 between Cirencester and Fairford.
MR R K MILLS, tel (0285) 851806, fax (0285) 851735.

### HARRY HARE'S RESTAURANT & BRASSERIE, 3 Gosditch Street
The wide ranging menu at this restaurant and brasserie caters for all tastes, from those wanting an a la carte lunch or dinner to those seeking a traditional breakfast

or just coffee and a cake. The menu changes monthly and includes steaks, pasta, salads, sauteed king prawns in garlic butter on a julienne of vegetables. All are very fresh; local suppliers deliver twice daily.
FOOD up to £15
**Hours:** meals all day 11am – 11pm; open for lunch Christmas day. **Cuisine:** English / continental:- Very varied brasserie style food including breakfast, brunch and tea. **Credit cards:** Visa, Access, AmEx. **Other points:** licensed, open-air dining, Sunday lunch, children catered for – please check for age limits, bank holidays, afternoon tea. **Directions:** just off west Market Place, 200 yd from parish church.
MARK R STEPHENS, tel (0285) 652375, fax (0285) 640197.

## KINGS HEAD HOTEL, Market Place
Retaining its olde worlde charm, this delightful hotel has an innkeeping tradition dating back 300 years. Paintings, panelling and high ceilings add atmosphere whilst the accommodation has been furnished with attention to comfort.
ACCOMMODATION £31–£40
FOOD up to £15 ★
**Hours:** breakfast 7:30am – 9:15am; lunch 12:15pm – 2pm; dinner 7pm – 9pm; closed 27/12 – 30/12.
**Cuisine:** English:- Appetising traditional English fare – creative omelettes a house specialty. **Rooms:** 66 bedrooms all with tea making facilities, telephone, radio, TV: 15 singles ensuite, 26 twins ensuite, 20 doubles ensuite, 5 family rooms ensuite. **Credit cards:** Visa, Access, Diners, AmEx. **Other points:** licensed, Sunday lunch, children catered for – please check for age limits, pets allowed, residents' lounge, bank holidays, baby-listening device, cots, residents' bar. **Directions:** situated in the town centre opposite parish church tower.
MR & MRS BANNERMAN, tel (0285) 653322, fax (0285) 655103.

## THE VILLAGE PUB, Barnsley
A traditional Cotswold stone country pub in the centre of Barnsley village. The food is well cooked and presented and served in generous portions. The country style accommodation boasts low beams. Welcoming service and a friendly atmosphere.
ACCOMMODATION £21–£30
FOOD up to £15
**Hours:** breakfast 7:30am – 9am; lunch 12noon – 2pm; dinner 7pm – 9:30pm; closed Christmas 25/12. **Cuisine:** English:- Bar meals and A la Carte menu. Dishes include local Bibury Trout, Deep Fried Halibut, Gammon Steak, Bean and Vegetable Casserole. **Rooms:** 5 bedrooms 4 doubles ensuite, 1 twin ensuite. **Credit cards:** Visa, Access, AmEx. **Other points:** licensed, Sunday lunch, children catered for – please check for age limits, garden, pets allowed, afternoon tea. **Directions:** B4425 in the centre of Barnsley.
MRS S WARDROP, tel (0285) 740421.

## CLEARWELL, Gloucestershire Map 13

## TUDOR FARMHOUSE HOTEL, Nr Coleford
Delightful 13th century stone farmhouse in a peaceful village setting. The hotel features an abundance of oak beams, original wall-panelling and 15th century spiral staircase. Ideal for the Forest of Dean and Wye Valley.
ACCOMMODATION £21–£30
FOOD up to £15
**Hours:** breakfast 7:30am – 9:30am; dinner 7:30pm – 9pm. **Cuisine:** English / international:- A la carte and Table d'hote, with menu changes daily. Dishes may include, Cajun Whitefish, Roast Rack of Lamb, Guinea Fowl. Vegetarian dishes. **Rooms:** 9 bedrooms all with tea making facilities, telephone, TV: 6 doubles ensuite, 3 family rooms ensuite. **Credit cards:** Visa, Access, AmEx. **Other points:** licensed, open-air dining, children catered for – please check for age limits, pets allowed, disabled access, 24 hr reception, residents' bar, residents' lounge, cots, baby-listening device. **Directions:** Clearwell is north of the A48 and east of A466.
DEBORAH & RICHARD FLETCHER, tel (0594) 833046, fax (0594) 837093.

## WYNDHAM ARMS, Nr Coleford
Situated within easy reach of Chepstow and Lydney, yet peaceful and secluded, off the main route. The Wyndham Arms has beautifully decorated rooms and offers food of excellent quality. It deservedly won the Routiers Accommodation of the Year Award in 1990.
ACCOMMODATION £21–£30
FOOD up to £15 🍽
**Hours:** lunch 12noon – 2pm; dinner 7pm – 9:30pm; bar open all day. **Cuisine:** English:- Fresh food using home-grown fruit and vegetables where possible. Homemade puddings. **Rooms:** 17 bedrooms all with tea making

facilities, telephone, radio, TV: 2 singles ensuite, 8 twins ensuite, 5 doubles ensuite, 2 triples ensuite. **Credit cards:** Visa, Access, Diners, AmEx. **Other points:** licensed, Sunday lunch, children catered for – please check for age limits, pets allowed, baby-listening device, cots, 24hr reception. **Directions:** in the centre of Clearwell village, 2 miles from Coleford.
MR J STANFORD, tel (0594) 833666, fax (0594) 836450.

## CLEOBURY MORTIMER, Shropshire

Map 13

### THE REDFERN HOTEL, Nr Kidderminster
*The hotel lies between Kidderminster and Ludlow within easy reach of junctions 3 and 6 on the M5. The Redfern provides the best in food and accommodation and there are many places of local interest for the visitor to see including the Ironbridge Museum and the Severn Valley Railway.*
ACCOMMODATION £31–£40
FOOD up to £15  ★
**Hours:** breakfast – weekdays 8am – 9:30am; breakfast – weekends 8:30am – 9:30am; bar 10:30am – 2:30pm; lunch 12noon – 2pm; bar 6pm – 10:30pm; dinner 7:30pm – 9:30pm. **Cuisine:** English:- Shropshire chicken, stuffed loin of lamb, steak and kidney pie. **Rooms:** 11 bedrooms all with radio, TV: 5 twins ensuite, 5 doubles ensuite, 1 family room ensuite. **Credit cards:** Visa, Access, Diners, AmEx. **Other points:** licensed, Sunday lunch, children catered for – please check for age limits, pets allowed, parking, vegetarian meals, residents' bar, residents' lounge. **Directions:** Cleobury Mortimer is on the A4117, 11 miles west of Kidderminister.
MR & MRS J REDFERN, tel (0299) 270395, fax (0299) 271011.

## COLEFORD, Gloucestershire Map 13

### OREPOOL INN AND MOTEL, St Briavels Road, Sling, Nr Coleford
*Charming motel and inn dating from the mid 17th century. Friendly staff ensure a warm welcome. Busy family atmosphere. Conference facilities. Coach parties welcome by prior appointment. C.L. site (five caravans at any one time).*
ACCOMMODATION under £20
FOOD up to £15
**Hours:** breakfast 7am – 9:30am; bar snacks 11am – 10:30pm. **Cuisine:** English:- Substantial English or continental breakfast. Extensive bar menu and Specials Board which changes on a daily basis. **Rooms:** 10 bedrooms all with tea making facilities, telephone, TV: 2 singles ensuite, 2 twins ensuite, 4 doubles ensuite, 2 family rooms ensuite. **Credit cards:** Visa, Access, AmEx. **Other points:** licensed, open-air dining, Sunday lunch, afternoon tea, children catered for – please check for age limits, disabled access. **Directions:** B4228 Coleford to Chepstow Road.
JIM AND JOAN WILSON, tel (0594) 833277.

## COLSTON BASSETT, Nottinghamshire

Map 15

### THE MARTINS ARMS INN, School Lane
*Housed in an attractive period building, the Martins Arms offers excellent food and and a warm welcome. Only fresh produce is used and the menu offers a good choice of very well-cooked and presented dishes. During summer, drinks and meals can be enjoyed in the garden. Under the same ownership as The Crown Inn, Old Dalby – winner of the Les Routiers Pub of the Year Award 1991.*
FOOD £15–£20
**Hours:** lunch 12noon – 2pm; dinner 6pm – 9:30pm. **Cuisine:** English / continental:- Dishes may include Roast Rack of English Lamb served with a fresh Tarragon & Cream sauce, Freshly made Tagliatelle with spicy Chicken pieces. **Other points:** licensed, open-air dining, Sunday lunch, beer garden. **Directions:** A46 Bingham roundabout, left on A52, 1 mile first right for Langar & C.B.
LYNNE BRYAN & SALVATORE INGUANTA, tel (0949) 81361.

## CONGLETON, Cheshire Map 16

### SANDHOLE FARM, Hulme Walfield
*Sandhole Farm's high class quality farm accommodation is popular with both business people and holiday-makers alike. A converted stable-block offers rooms with the most modern facilities. The lounge is a special feature with French Windows opening out onto a small garden and undulating fields. A new dining room/conservatory seats up to 30 guests and has breathtaking views of the peaceful rural setting.*
ACCOMMODATION under £20
**Hours:** breakfast 7am – 9am. **Cuisine:** breakfast. **Credit cards:** Visa, Access. **Other points:** children catered for – please check for age limits, parking, disabled access, pets, residents' lounge, vegetarian meals, garden.
**Directions:** 2 miles north of Congleton on A34 opposite Waggon & Horses Public House.
VERONICA WORTH, tel (0260) 224419, fax (0260) 224766.

## COVENTRY, West Midlands Map 14

### LADY GODIVA HOTEL, 80/90 Holyhead Road
*Situated on the main Coventry/Birmingham road only 11 miles from Birmingham Airport. Good facilities for conferences and private functions of up to 300. Central for the Cotswolds and Shakespeare Country.*
ACCOMMODATION £31–£40
FOOD £15–£20
**Hours:** breakfast 7am – 9:30am; lunch 12:30pm – 2:30pm; dinner 7:30pm – 10pm. **Cuisine:** modern English:- Nouvelle cuisine, eg. salmon with maltaise sauce, mille feuilles of scampi tomato, garlic, herbs. **Rooms:** 105 bedrooms 60 singles ensuite, 33 twins ensuite, 9 doubles ensuite, 3 triples ensuite. **Credit**

**cards:** Visa, Access, Diners, AmEx. **Other points:** Sunday lunch, children catered for – please check for age limits, coach/prior arr, parking, disabled access, lift. **Directions:** 10 minutes walk from city centre, 9 miles from NEC. MR GAUNT – CHIEF EXECUTIVE, tel (0203) 258585, fax (0203) 225547.

## CREWE, Cheshire Map 16

### SLEEPERS HOTEL, The Wharf, Thomas Street

*This restaurant specialises in hearty home-cooked casseroles and stews. Brian and Joan have owned and run this restaurant for many years and the hotel is a natural addition. Attractively converted railway stables with private cobbled car park near the town centre.*

*ACCOMMODATION under £20*

*FOOD up to £15*

**Hours:** lunch – Mon-Fri 12noon – 2pm; dinner – Mon-Fri from 7pm; bar open to residents Saturday; closed Sunday. **Cuisine:** English:- Casseroles, black pepper steak. **Rooms:** 13 bedrooms 3 doubles ensuite, 8 twins ensuite, 2 family rooms ensuite. **Credit cards:** Visa, Access, Diners, AmEx. **Other points:** children catered for – please check for age limits, sun terrace, barbecues. **Directions:** on A532, runs between A530 and A534. BRIAN & JOAN SHANNON, tel (0270) 585479, (0270) 585555, fax (0270) 585479.

## CRICK, Northamptonshire Map 14

### EDWARDS OF CRICK, The Wharf

*Situated on the canal side, an ideal location for those seeking the more leisurely pace of life. Enjoy a romantic candelit dinner in the spacious upstairs restaurant, or a pot of fresh-ground coffee in the informal ground floor coffee house. While waiting for your meal, you can play bagatelle or solitaire, read the magazines, feed the ducks, or simply watch the boats go by.*

*FOOD £15–£20*

**Hours:** meals all day from 10:30am; closed Sunday evening – Monday. **Cuisine:** English:- A la carte menu, offering an interesting selection of freshly home-made dishes, in both restaurant and coffee house. **Credit cards:** Visa, Access, Diners, AmEx. **Other points:** licensed, open-air dining, Sunday lunch, children catered for – please check for age limits, afternoon tea, disabled access, vegetarian meals, parking. **Directions:** situated at the Eastern end of Crick off the A428. RICHARD COLEMAN, tel (0788) 822517.

## DERBY, Derbyshire Map 15

### CAVENDISH ARMS, London Road, Shardlow

*An attractive building, enhanced by displays of fresh flowers both inside and out. Some imaginative dishes are served in the comfortable dining room, where the emphasis is on good food in relaxed, informal surroundings.*

*FOOD up to £15*

**Hours:** lunch 12noon – 2:30pm; dinner 7pm – 10pm. **Cuisine:** English:- Soups, rainbow trout, scampi, chicken chasseur, steaks etc. **Credit cards:** Visa, Access. **Other points:** licensed, Sunday lunch, children catered for – please check for age limits, garden. **Directions:** on the main A6 near to Cavendish Bridge at Shardlow. PETER DALTON-PRIOR, tel (0332) 792216.

### HOTEL RISTORANTE LA GONDOLA, 220 Osmaston Road

*The Hotel Ristorante La Gondola is situated 5 minutes from Derby city centre, 15 minutes from the scenic Peak District. The hotel is elegantly decorated and very comfortable. Meals are cooked from fresh produce and served in generous portions which are enjoyed by locals and holiday-makers alike. Staff are friendly and pleasant, adding to the relaxed atmosphere of the hotel.*

*ACCOMMODATION £41–£50*

*FOOD £15–£20*

**Hours:** breakfast 7am – 9am; lunch 12:15pm – 2pm; dinner 7pm – 10pm. **Cuisine:** Traditional English and continental. Dishes include Pork Cutlet Pizzaiola, Rainbow Trout, Roast duckling. **Rooms:** 20 bedrooms all with tea making facilities, telephone, radio, mini bar, TV: 2 twins ensuite, 11 doubles ensuite, 6 triples ensuite, 1 quad ensuite. **Credit cards:** Visa, Access, AmEx. **Other points:** licensed, children catered for – please check for age limits, afternoon tea, conferences, baby-listening device, cots, 24hr reception, residents' lounge, residents' bar, parking, vegetarian meals, disabled access. **Directions:** Hotel is located off the A514 dual carriageway into Derby. MR R GIOVANNELLI, tel (0332) 32895, fax (0332) 384512.

## DIDCOT, Oxfordshire Map 6

### THE RED LION, Nottingham Fee, Blewbury

*A very old, traditional country pub, tucked away in the pretty village of Blewbury. The interior has an olde worlde appearance and an informal, relaxed atmosphere in which to enjoy the good bar meals.*

*FOOD up to £15*

**Hours:** lunch 12noon – 2pm; dinner 6pm – 9:30pm; Sunday evening 7pm – 7:30pm. **Cuisine:** English:- Bar meals including daily specials, especially fresh fish. **Credit cards:** Visa, Access, Diners, AmEx. **Other points:** licensed, Sunday lunch, children catered for – please check for age limits, garden, disabled access. **Directions:** off the A417. ROGER SMITH, tel (0235) 850403.

## DONINGTON ON BAIN, Lincolnshire Map 15

### THE BLACK HORSE, Louth

*Nestling in the heart of the Wolds on the Viking Way, this truly delightful 200 year old inn has been extensively and sympathetically refurbished. An intimate snug bar seating 10 people is ideal for family celebrations. Join*

*the locals in a game of darts, pool or dominoes. Close to Cadwell motor racing circuit, Mabelthorpe and Woodhall Spa.*
ACCOMMODATION *under £20*
FOOD *up to £15*
**Hours:** breakfast 7am – 9:30am; lunch 12noon – 3pm; bar meals 12noon – 3pm; dinner 7pm – 10:30pm; bar meals 7pm – 11:30pm. **Cuisine:** English:- A la carte menu offering traditional English fair, cooked to order using local produce and served in olde worlde surroundings. Good selection of sweets. **Rooms:** 8 bedrooms all with tea making facilities, TV: 6 twins ensuite, 2 family rooms ensuite. **Other points:** licensed, open-air dining, Sunday lunch, children catered for – please check for age limits, disabled access, garden, vegetarian meals, parking. **Directions:** off the A153 Horncastle/Louth and adjoining roads. Well signposted.
TONY & JANINE PACEY, tel (0507) 343640.

---

# DROITWICH SPA, Hereford & Worcestershire Map 13

## HADLEY BOWLING GREEN INN, Hadley Heath
*The Hadley Bowling Green Inn is ideally situated for both businessmen and holiday-makers alike. Just 10 minutes drive from Worcester and Droitwich, it offers a friendly, relaxed atmosphere to welcome you during your stay. Two delightful furnished bars with open log fires in winter offer real draught ales, cider and Irish Stout. An extensive a la carte menu is available in the intimate 30 seater dining room. Accommodation is of the highest standard with some rooms boasting four poster beds. Weddings can also be adequately catered for. The area is steeped in history and is well worth a visit.*
ACCOMMODATION *£21–£30*
**Hours:** breakfast 7:30am – 9am; lunch 12noon – 2pm; dinner 6pm – 9:30pm. **Cuisine:** English. **Other points:** children catered for – please check for age limits, parking, afternoon teas, open-air dining, vegetarian meals, residents' lounge, garden. **Directions:** take A4133 to Ombersley out of Droitwich and follow the sign to Ladywood, at next junction turn left and the inn is on the left.
MRS P RICHARDS, tel (0905) 620294.

---

# ELLESMERE, Shropshire Map 13

## STANWARDINE HOUSE, Cockshutt
*A 17th century Grade II listed building which has been newly furnished throughout in country house style. One room boasts a four poster, delightfully swathed in green and burgundy roseprint, with wallpaper to match. Ideal for visiting Chirk Castle, Hodnet Hall and Gardens, the Roman town of Wroxeter and North Wales.*
ACCOMMODATION *£21–£30*
FOOD *£15–£20*
**Hours:** breakfast – as required; dinner 7:30pm – 8pm. **Cuisine:** good home cooking based on local organic produce. **Rooms:** 2 bedrooms all with tea making facilities, TV: 2 doubles ensuite. **Other points:** parking,

children catered for – please check for age limits, open bank holidays, no-smoking, residents' lounge, garden, vegetarian meals on request. **Directions:** 5 miles south of Ellesmere, 12 miles north of Shrewsbury.
NEVILLE AND PAT GLEAVE, tel (0939) 270534.

---

# FOWNHOPE, Hereford & Worcestershire Map 13

## THE GREEN MAN INN
*A 15th century country inn set in the heart of the beautiful Wye Valley, popular for businessmen, families, wedding parties or small functions. Ideal centre for fishing with some of England's best salmon reaches nearby.*
ACCOMMODATION *£21–£30*
FOOD *up to £15*
**Hours:** breakfast 8:15am – 9am; lunch 12noon – 2pm; bar meals 12noon – 2pm; bar meals 6pm – 10pm; dinner 7pm – 9pm. **Cuisine:** English:- A la carte and bar food menus. Dishes include beef, mushroom and ale pie. **Rooms:** 20 bedrooms 7 twins ensuite, 13 doubles ensuite. **Credit cards:** Visa, Access, AmEx. **Other points:** open-air dining, Sunday lunch, children catered for – please check for age limits. **Directions:** on B4224, midway between Ross on Wye and Hereford.
ARTHUR & MARGARET WILLIAMS, tel (0432) 860243, fax (0432) 860207.

---

# FRODSHAM, Cheshire Map 16

## OLD HALL HOTEL, Main Street
*This 15th century house has been beautifully renovated and modernised and is set amongst other old buildings in the centre of Frodsham. The restaurant serves an imaginative variety of dishes, all of which are beautifully presented and served by friendly attentive staff.*
ACCOMMODATION *£41–£50*
FOOD *£15–£20*
**Hours:** breakfast 6am – 10am; lunch 12noon – 2pm; dinner 7pm – 10pm. **Cuisine:** English:- A la carte menu. Dishes include sea bass champagne, roast duckling cerises. **Rooms:** 23 rooms. 7 single, 2 twin, 13 double and 1 family bedroom, all en suite. **Credit cards:** Visa, Access, Diners, AmEx. **Other points:** licensed, open-air dining, Sunday lunch, children catered for – please check for age limits, garden, afternoon tea, pets allowed, parking, residents' lounge, residents' bar. **Directions:** M5 junction 12.
MR & MRS WINDFIELD, tel (0928) 732052.

---

# GEDNEY DYKE, Lincolnshire Map 15

## THE CHEQUERS, Nr Spalding
*A small, homely country freehouse with restaurant. The bar and dining room have low ceilings with exposed beams and have been attractively furnished. Good food and a friendly, welcoming atmosphere have made this restaurant and freehouse deservingly popular.*
FOOD *up to £15*
**Hours:** lunch 12noon – 1:45pm; dinner 7pm – 9:30pm; dinner – Mon-Wed 7pm – 9pm; no meals Boxing day; no

meals Christmas day; no meals Sunday evenings
November – March. **Cuisine:** English:- Cooked on the
premises, with local fresh fish and vegetables and light
meals in the bar. Full a la carte menu in the comfortably
furnished restaurant. **Credit cards:** Visa, Access,
Diners, AmEx. **Other points:** licensed, open-air dining,
Sunday lunch, children catered for – please check for
age limits, garden. **Directions:** take B1359 north of the
A17 and turn left at the Post Office.
JUDITH & ROB MARSHALL, tel (0406) 362666.

# GLOUCESTER, Gloucestershire Map 13

## MORAN'S EATING HOUSE, 23 Worcester Street

*Centrally situated, Moran's is made up of two*
*restaurants seating 120 people. One in brick and pine*
*with a large skylight, the other with old and antique*
*mirrors, plus a private room for 60. Blackboard menu*
*changes daily. A variety of drinks and cocktails.*
*FOOD £15–£20*
**Hours:** lunch 11:30am – 2pm; dinner 6:30pm –
10:45pm; closed Monday lunch; closed Sunday lunch.
**Cuisine:** modern English:- Curried parsnip soup, fillet
of pork with cranberry and orange sauce. **Other points:**
Sunday lunch, children catered for – please check for
age limits. **Directions:** in the centre of Gloucester.
BRIAN MORAN, tel (0452) 422024.

# GORING ON THAMES, Oxfordshire
Map 6

## THE MILLER OF MANSFIELD HOTEL, High Street

*A beautiful 18th century building decorated in line with the*
*period and with many antiques. The hotel is situated close*
*to the river in the village centre. The Goring Gap is an area*
*of outstanding natural beauty. 9 miles from Reading, 15*
*miles from Oxford, and with easy access from the M4.*
*ACCOMMODATION £21–£30*
*FOOD up to £15* ★
**Hours:** breakfast 7:30am – 9am; lunch 12noon – 2pm;
dinner 7pm – 10pm. **Cuisine:** English:- Varied a la carte
menu including grills, plus extensive bar food menus.
**Rooms:** 10 bedrooms all with tea making facilities,
radio, TV: 1 single, 2 twins ensuite, 1 twin, 4 doubles
ensuite, 2 doubles. **Credit cards:** Visa, Access. **Other**
**points:** licensed, Sunday lunch, children catered for –
please check for age limits, baby-listening device, cots,
residents' bar. **Directions:** from A329, take the B4009 at
Streatley, cross river, 200yds on left.
MARTIN WILLIAMSON, tel (0491) 872829, fax (0491)
874200.

# GRANTHAM, Lincolnshire Map 15

## THE ROYAL OAK, Swayfield

*This traditional stone built country inn has been*
*excellently maintained and is set amidst the attractive*
*Lincolnshire countryside. Offering well cooked and*

*presented food, with 'Special dishes' each day, served by*
*helpful and friendly staff. Outside dining in well tended*
*beer garden during the summer months. Listed in the*
*Good Beer Guide. Enquire about new accommodation*
*available in spring 1994.*
*FOOD up to £15*
**Hours:** lunch – except Sunday 11am – 2:30pm; lunch –
Sunday 12noon – 3pm; dinner – except Sunday 6pm –
10:30pm; dinner – Sunday 7pm – 10:30pm. **Cuisine:**
English:- A la carte with special Sunday lunch menu and
special Sunday supper menu. Mon-Fri lunch 3 course
Table d'hote and a la carte. **Credit cards:** Visa, Access.
**Other points:** licensed, Sunday lunch, children catered
for – please check for age limits, garden, pets allowed.
**Directions:** A1 south from Grantham. Left at
Colsterworth roundabout. 2 miles, follow signs for
Swayfield.
DAVID COOKE, tel (0476) 550247.

# GREAT MALVERN, Hereford &
Worcestershire Map 13

## MOUNT PLEASANT HOTEL, Belle Vue Terrace

*An attractive early Georgian building and orangery set*
*in 1.5 acres of mature terraced gardens with lovely*
*views across the town. Close to the theatre and shops yet*
*only seconds from the Malvern Hills rising behind the*
*hotel. An informal hotel with all the facilities of a larger*
*establishment.*
*ACCOMMODATION £31–£40*
*FOOD up to £15*
**Hours:** breakfast 7:45am – 9:30am; coffee shop 10am –
6pm; lunch 12noon – 2pm; bar meals 12noon – 2pm;
dinner 7pm – 9:30pm; bar meals 7pm – 9pm; closed
Christmas 25/12 – 26/12. **Cuisine:** international:- In the
restaurant: Salmon in plum sauce, paellas, gazpacho,
guacamole, turkey quajalote and vegetarian menu.
Excellent home cooked bar meals, and table d'hote
menu. **Rooms:** 15 bedrooms all with tea making
facilities, telephone, radio, TV: 2 singles ensuite, 6 twins
ensuite, 7 doubles ensuite. **Credit cards:** Visa, Access,
Diners, AmEx. **Other points:** licensed, Sunday lunch,
children catered for – please check for age limits,
conferences, functions, cots, left luggage, vegetarian
meals, residents' bar, residents' lounge. **Directions:** take
M5; exit 7. Follow A449 to Malvern. Near church in
town centre.
SOL AND GEOFF PAYNE, tel (0684) 561837, fax
(0684) 569968.

## SIDNEY HOUSE, 40 Worcester Road

*An attractive, white Georgian listed building standing in*
*an elevated position in Great Malvern, with stunning*
*views over the Severn Valley, towards the Vale of*
*Evesham and the Cotswolds. The town centre, Winter*
*gardens, Malvern Festival theatre, Priory Park and the*
*Hills are only a few minutes walk away.*
*ACCOMMODATION £21–£30*
*FOOD up to £15*

**Hours:** breakfast 8am – 9am; dinner 7pm. **Cuisine:** breakfast. **Rooms:** 8 bedrooms all with tea making facilities, TV: 1 single, 1 double, 4 doubles ensuite, 1 twin, 1 twin ensuite. **Credit cards:** Visa, Access, Diners, AmEx. **Other points:** central heating, children catered for – please check for age limits, pets/prior arr, residents' lounge. **Directions:** on the A449, 150yds on right from junction with Church Street.
TOM J S & MARGARET E HAGGETT, tel (0684) 574994.

## GREAT RISSINGTON, Gloucestershire
Map 13

### THE LAMB INN
*Situated in the heart of the Cotswolds, Great Rissington is popular with tourists. Locally there is the Cotswold Wildlife Park and slightly further afield, Oxford and Stratford-upon-Avon.*
*ACCOMMODATION £21–£30*
*FOOD up to £15*
**Hours:** breakfast 8:30am – 9am; lunch 12noon – 1:45pm; dinner – weekdays 7pm – 9pm; dinner – weekends 7pm – 9pm. **Cuisine:** English:- Steaks, Cotswold trout, pates, soups, casseroles. **Rooms:** 8 rooms most ensuite. **Credit cards:** Visa, Access. **Other points:** children catered for – please check for age limits.
MR & MRS CLEVERLY, tel (0451) 820388.

## GUNTHORPE, Nottinghamshire Map 15

### THE TOLL HOUSE RESTAURANT,
*Riverside*
*First class service is upheld in this small, friendly restaurant. The building itself used to be the Toll House to the first Gunthorpe bridge built in 1875.*
*FOOD £15–£20*
**Hours:** dinner 7pm – 10pm; closed Sunday evenings. **Cuisine:** English / French:- moules Mariniere, Salmon & Smoked Salmon Mousse, fish, meat and fresh pasta dishes with a selection of desserts and cheeses. **Credit cards:** Visa, Access. **Other points:** licensed, Sunday lunch, no-smoking area, Sunday lunch. **Directions:** from Nottingham, turn left immediately before Gunthorpe bridge.
MR CLIVE HARRIS, tel (0602) 663409.

## HAY-ON-WYE, Hereford & Worcestershire
Map 13

### THE OLD BLACK LION, Lion Street
*Oliver Cromwell is reputed to have stayed at the Old Black Lion whilst the Roundheads besieged Hay Castle which was a Loyalist stronghold. Whether you be loyalist or roundhead, this old coaching inn extends a warm welcome to all who visit today by serving delicious country cooking. Hay is the world centre for second hand books with over 2 million books in 27 bookshops.*
*ACCOMMODATION under £20*
*FOOD up to £15* 🍵

**Hours:** breakfast 8:30am – 9:15am; lunch 12noon – 2:30pm; dinner 7pm – 9pm. **Cuisine:** international:- Home country cooking with international flair, house specials being steaks, seafood, game and vegetarian. 38 Wines from around the world. **Rooms:** 10 bedrooms all with tea making facilities, telephone, radio, TV: 4 twins ensuite, 4 doubles ensuite, 1 family room ensuite, 1 single. **Credit cards:** Visa, Access. **Other points:** licensed, Sunday lunch, children catered for – please check for age limits, pets allowed, fishing. **Directions:** 50yds off the B4352 Hereford to Hay road.
JOHN & JOAN COLLINS, tel (0497) 820841.

## HENLEY-IN-ARDEN, Warwickshire
Map 14

### ARDEN TANDOORI RESTAURANT,
*137 High Street*
*Situated right in the centre of the historic town of Henley-in-Arden. The interior has been tastefully decorated with an air of subdued elegance. The Arden offers a warm welcome and excellent food.*
*FOOD £15–£20* CLUB
**Hours:** lunch 12noon – 2:30pm; dinner 5:30pm – 11:30pm; closed Christmas 25/12. **Cuisine:** Indian:- Kurzi lamb, lamb pasanda Nawabi, Makhon chicken and Balti dishes. **Credit cards:** Visa, Access, Diners, AmEx. **Other points:** open-air dining, Sunday lunch, coach/prior arr, children catered for – please check for age limits. **Directions:** on the A34 between Solihull and Stratford-upon-Avon.
NANU MIAH, tel (0564) 792503.

## HEREFORD, Hereford & Worcestershire Map 13

### THE TASTE OF RAJ, 67 St Owen Street
*A comfortably furnished Indian restaurant providing freshly prepared and individually cooked dishes. Extensive menu with all dishes carefully explained and English meals available for the less adventurous. Good wine list with the additional choice of Indian wine, beer and liquors to complement the food.*
*FOOD £15–£20*
**Hours:** lunch 12noon – 2:30pm; dinner 6pm – 11:30pm. **Cuisine:** Regional Indian dishes. Specialities include Tandoori trout, mughlai mosollah, lamb pasanda. Set meals for 2 and 4 persons. **Credit cards:** Visa, Access, Diners, AmEx. **Other points:** licensed, Sunday lunch, children catered for – please check for age limits. **Directions:** on same street as Hereford Town Hall. In centre near Cathedral.
MR S RAHMAN, tel (0432) 351075, (0432) 351076.

## HINCKLEY, Leicestershire Map 14

### WOODSIDE FARM GUEST HOUSE,
*Ashby Road, Stapleton*
*A working farm in a rural and tranquil setting, where Julia Furniss and her husband provide a warm welcome for all guests. Comfortable lounge and dining room with*

traditional farmhouse furniture. Ideally situated for
visiting nearby Bosworth Battle Centre, Kirkby Mallory
Race Track and Twycross Zoo.
ACCOMMODATION under £20
FOOD up to £15
**Hours:** open all year 6pm; breakfast 7am– 9am; dinner
6:30pm – 9:30pm. **Cuisine:** English:- Good homely
cooking using the freshest of local produce, cooked and
served by the owners. **Rooms:** 10 bedrooms all with tea
making facilities, radio, TV: 4 singles ensuite, 2 twins
ensuite, 3 doubles ensuite, 1 triple ensuite.
**Credit cards:** Visa, Access. **Other points:** licensed,
open-air dining, Sunday lunch, children catered for –
please check for age limits, vegetarian meals, residents'
lounge, garden, parking, cots. **Directions:** 3 miles
north of Hinckley on left-hand side, past Woodlands
Nursery.
JULIA FURNISS, tel (0455) 291929, fax (0455)
291929.

## HYDE, Cheshire Map 16

### NEEDHAMS FARM, Uplands Road, Werneth Low, Gee Cross
A small working farm, dating to the 16th century, which
offers very comfortable accommodation and food of an
excellent standard. The inspector declared it 'a
wonderful place to stay', and noted it was ideal for
children as there are many friendly animals on the farm.
Perfect base for walking, riding, and golf, with many
local places of interest nearby. Highly recommended.
ACCOMMODATION £31–£40 ★
**Hours:** breakfast 6:30am – 11am; dinner 7pm – 9:30pm.
**Cuisine:** English. **Rooms:** 6 bedrooms all with tea
making facilities, telephone, radio, TV: 1 single ensuite,
1 twin, 1 double, 1 triple ensuite, 2 doubles ensuite.
**Credit cards:** Visa, Access. **Other points:** children
catered for – please check for age limits, special breaks,
residents' lounge, cots. **Directions:** junction 15, M66 –
off A560. Between Werneth Low Country Park and
Etherow Valley.
MRS WALSH, tel (061) 368 4610, fax (061) 367 9106.

### SHIRE COTTAGE FARMHOUSE, Benches Lane, Chisworth
A typical country farmhouse commanding breathtaking
views over the wooded hills across the Cheshire Plains.
Furnished in traditional farmhouse style with restful
colours, it offers a perfect retreat from the pressures of
modern day living. Ideal location for touring the Peak
District and for visiting the many nearby places of
interest, including Lyme Park and a number of Country
Houses.
ACCOMMODATION under £20
FOOD £15–£20
**Hours:** breakfast 7am – 9am. **Cuisine:** breakfast.
**Rooms:** 4 bedrooms all with tea making facilities, TV: 2
doubles ensuite, 2 twins. **Other points:** children catered
for – please check for age limits, bank holidays,
residents' lounge, vegetarian meals. **Directions:** A626

from Marple, Glossop Road. Turn into Benches Lane
opposite Woodheys Restaurant at Chisworth, 4th on
right up Benches Lane.
MONICA SIDEBOTTOM, tel (0457) 866536.

## ILMINGTON, Warwickshire Map 14

### THE HOWARD ARMS, Lower Green
This tranquil 16th century inn provides a delightful
setting in which to sample some delectable English
cuisine. Fresh ingredients and an imaginative,
constantly changing menu can tempt even the most
particular palate.
ACCOMMODATION £21–£30
FOOD up to £15
**Hours:** breakfast 8am – 9:30am; lunch 12noon – 2pm;
dinner – Sun-Thur 7pm – 9pm; dinner – Fri-Sat 7pm –
9:30pm; no accommodation 24/12 – 27/12. **Cuisine:**
Classic English cuisine with a regularly changing menu,
served in bar, restaurant or garden. **Rooms:** 2 bedrooms
with tea making facilities, TV: 1 twin ensuite, 1 double
ensuite. **Credit cards:** Visa, Access, AmEx. **Other
points:** licensed, open-air dining, Sunday lunch, children
catered for – please check for age limits, garden.
**Directions:** from Stratford-upon-Avon, turn off A3400
Shipston on Stour Rd. Turn right and follow for 4 miles.
MESSRS SMART & THOMPSON, tel (0608) 682226,
fax (0608) 682226.

## KEGWORTH, Leicestershire Map 14

### THE CAP AND STOCKING, 20 Borough Street
A 100 year old building which is well known for its
excellent jug ales. Serving good wholesome home-made
food, there is also a sheltered garden with tables.
FOOD up to £15
**Hours:** lunch 11.30am – 3pm; dinner 6pm – 11pm;
closed Christmas night. **Cuisine:** International:- varied
to suit all tastes. **Other points:** children catered for –
please check for age limits, open bank holidays, pets
allowed, vegetarian meals, open air dining. **Directions:**
off A6 Kegworth village.
PIERS RUPERT BEAUMONT-BAILEY, tel (0509)
674814.

## KENILWORTH, Warwickshire Map 14

### CLARENDON ARMS, 44 Castle Hill
An olde worlde inn in an historic, picture-postcard
location opposite the entrance to Kenilworth castle.
Dine in the small intimate bar, or in the larger dining
area on the first floor – either way the cheerful
ambiance and good home-cooked fare is sure to please.
FOOD up to £15
**Hours:** lunch 12noon – 3pm; dinner – except Sunday
5:30pm – 11pm; dinner – Sunday 7pm – 10:30pm.
**Cuisine:** English / international:- Giant chargrilled
steaks, chicken terriyaki, traditional pub meals. **Credit
cards:** Visa, Access, Diners, AmEx. **Other points:**

licensed, open-air dining, Sunday lunch, children catered for – please check for age limits. **Directions:** opposite the entrance to Kenilworth castle.
PATRICK MCCOSKER & MAURICE KUTNER, tel (0926) 52017, fax (0926) 50229.

## KIDDERMINSTER, Hereford & Worcestershire Map 13

### THE COLLIERS ARMS, Clows Top

*This two-storey rendered country pub is set in its own gardens with delightful pergola and surrounded by pleasant open countryside. Providing excellent service and value for money. Daily Chef's Specials.*
FOOD up to £15
**Hours:** lunch 12noon – 2pm; dinner 7pm – 10pm; closed Sunday evening – winter. **Cuisine:** English.
**Credit cards:** Visa, Access. **Other points:** licensed, Sunday lunch, children catered for – please check for age limits, garden, pets allowed. **Directions:** A456 at Clows Top. Highest point locally.
THE SANKEY FAMILY, tel (0299) 832242.

## KIMBERLEY, Nottinghamshire Map 15

### THE NELSON & RAILWAY INN, Station Road

*The Nelson & Railway Inn is a traditional village pub with original beamed lounges. Good basic home cooked food and a warm welcome are guaranteed. Good beers and a Happy Hour between 5pm and 7pm. Daily specials on blackboard.*
ACCOMMODATION under £20
FOOD up to £15
**Hours:** lunch 12noon – 2:30pm; dinner 5pm – 9pm. **Cuisine:** English:- Traditional home-made pub meals. **Rooms:** 2 bedrooms 2 twins. **Other points:** licensed, open-air dining, Sunday lunch, children catered for – please check for age limits, pets allowed, beer garden. **Directions:** 1 mile north Junction 26 on M1. On B600.
HARRY BURTON, tel (0602) 382177.

## KNUTSFORD, Cheshire Map 16

### LONGVIEW HOTEL AND RESTAURANT, Manchester Road

*A period hotel, recently refurbished to enhance its Victorian splendour. With many antiques, this hotel offers a relaxed and comfortable atmosphere from its open log fires to the quality of its award winning restaurant and welcome. Just minutes away from Junction 19, M6. Set overlooking the town common in this attractive Cheshire market town.*
ACCOMMODATION £21–£30
FOOD up to £15
**Cuisine:** British / continental:- An ever changing menu which draws on the best of continental foods as well as the rich heritage of British cooking. **Rooms:** 23 bedrooms all with tea making facilities, telephone, radio, TV: 5 singles ensuite, 11 doubles ensuite, 7 twins ensuite. **Credit cards:**

Visa, Access, Diners, AmEx. **Other points:** children catered for – please check for age limits, pets allowed, bank holidays. **Directions:** junction 19 M6, A556 towards Chester. Left at lights. Left at roundabout.
PAULINE & STEPHEN WEST, tel (0565) 632119, fax (0565) 652402.

## LEADENHAM, Lincolnshire Map 15

### GEORGE HOTEL, High Street

*A family-run old coaching inn on the A17. The George is renowned for its well-stocked bar – a whisky drinker's delight with over 500 varieties of whisky and drinks from around the world.*
ACCOMMODATION under £20
FOOD up to £15 ⊕
**Hours:** last orders 10pm; lunch 10:30am – 2:30pm; dinner 6pm – 11pm. **Cuisine:** English:- Steaks, Lincolnshire duckling a l'orange, Georgian trout. **Rooms:** 7 bedrooms all with tea making facilities, TV: 2 singles, 2 twins, 1 twin ensuite, 1 double, 1 double ensuite. **Credit cards:** Visa, Access, Diners, AmEx. **Other points:** open-air dining, Sunday lunch, children catered for – please check for age limits. **Directions:** at the junction of the A17 and the A607, 8 miles from the A1.
MR G M WILLGOOSE, tel (0400) 72251.

## LEAMINGTON SPA, Warwickshire Map 14

### EATHORPE PARK HOTEL, Fosse Way, Eathorpe

*An 1860 Victorian house situated within 11 acres of parklands, surrounded by panoramic views. The hotel is near to the M1, M40, M6 and M42 motorways and within easy access of the historic neighbouring towns, Stratford-upon-Avon, Warwick, Rugby, Leamington Spa and Coventry. Whether you choose an overnight stay or a leisurely few days a warm friendly welcome awaits.*
ACCOMMODATION £21–£30
FOOD up to £15 ⊕
**Hours:** breakfast 7:30am – 9:30am; lunch 12noon – 2pm; dinner 7pm – 10pm. **Cuisine:** English / continental:- Full a la carte menu, table d'hote and bar snacks. Speciality menus from around the world throughout the year. **Rooms:** 18 bedrooms 3 family rooms ensuite, 4 singles ensuite, 11 doubles ensuite. **Credit cards:** Visa, Access, Diners, AmEx. **Other points:** nightclub, Sunday lunch, children catered for – please check for age limits, bank holidays, afternoon tea, garden, vegetarian meals, residents' bar, residents' lounge. **Directions:** take M40, exit 11 for Banbury, A423 – A425 – B429 for Leamington Spa.
MR & MRS GRINNELL, tel (0926) 632632, fax (0926) 632481.

### EATON COURT HOTEL, 1–7 St Marks Road

*Located in a calm backwater close to the centre of Leamington Spa, the Eaton family are directly involved in running this comfortable hotel. The spacious and comfortable bedrooms are furnished to a high standard* and provide a convenient base from which to explore the Warwickshire countryside. The superb cuisine uses a wide range of freshly prepared produce, and special diets can be arranged. Ideal for the business traveller, conferences and weddings can also be catered for. Some rooms are no-smoking.

ACCOMMODATION £31–£40

FOOD up to £15

**Hours:** lunch by arrangement; breakfast 7am – 9:30am; dinner 7pm – 12midnight. **Cuisine:** English / French. **Credit cards:** Visa, Access. **Other points:** parking, children catered for – please check for age limits, no-smoking area, pets, residents' lounge, garden, vegetarian meals, open-air dining. **Directions:** off A452 Leamington – Warwick Road on northern side of Leamington town. VINCE & BARBARA EATON, tel (0926) 885848, fax (0926) 885848.

### REGENCY FARE, 86 Regent Street

Situated near the main shopping centre, the Regency Fare offers well cooked 'Home Cooking', with delightful desserts at very good value.

FOOD up to £15

**Hours:** breakfast 9am – 11:45am; lunch 12noon – 5:30pm; closed bank holidays; closed Sunday. **Cuisine:** English:- 'Home cooking'. House specialities: Steak and kidney pie and meringues with toasted almonds. **Credit cards:** Visa, Access, AmEx. **Other points:** children catered for – please check for age limits, afternoon tea. **Directions:** on Regent Street, off main shopping street. MRS S J HELM, tel (0926) 425570.

## LEEK, Staffordshire Map 14

### HOTEL RUDYARD, Lake Road, Rudyard

An impressive Victorian building overlooking Rudyard Lake in an attractive rural setting. The hotel enjoys a relaxed, family atmosphere and the accommodation is of a high standard. With friendly and efficient service, well-cooked food and generous portions, the Carvery restaurant provides an enjoyable meal at excellent value for money.

ACCOMMODATION £21–£30

FOOD up to £15

**Hours:** 11am – 3pm, 6pm – 11pm. **Cuisine:** English:- Carvery and bar meals. **Rooms:** 18 bedrooms, all en suite. **Credit cards:** Visa, Access. **Other points:** licensed, open-air dining, Sunday lunch, children catered for – please check for age limits, disabled access, residents' lounge. **Directions:** Leek to Macclesfield A523, 1 mile turn left for Rudyard. RONALD WILLIAM & JEAN LLOYD, tel (053833) 208, fax (053833) 249.

### THE THREE HORSESHOES INN & RESTAURANT, Buxton Road, Blackshaw Moor

Situated in a lovely country setting with beautiful views towards the moors and Pennines. First class accommodation in cottage-style bedrooms. Dinner/dance at weekends.

ACCOMMODATION £21–£30

FOOD up to £15  ★

**Hours:** breakfast 7:30am – 9:30am; lunch 12noon – 2pm; dinner 7pm – 9:30pm. **Cuisine:** English:- Bar Carvery at lunch and in the evening plus restaurant a la carte and table d'hote menus in the evening. **Rooms:** 6 bedrooms all with tea making facilities, telephone, radio, TV: 4 doubles ensuite, 2 twins ensuite. **Credit cards:** Visa, Access. **Other points:** Sunday lunch, children catered for – please check for age limits, garden. **Directions:** located on A53 Leek–Buxton Road. WILLIAM KIRK, tel (0538) 300296, fax (0538) 300320.

## LEICESTER, Leicestershire Map 14

### THE COTTAGE IN THE WOOD, Maplewell Road, Woodhouse Eaves

Situated in the heart of Charnwood forest, the cottage restaurant has a warm, local atmosphere. The menu features seasonal monthly specials and also includes a wide choice for vegetarians. Places to explore include Bradgate deer park, Beacon Hill, Broombrigs working farm and the Great Central Railway. A function room is available with a dance floor for dinners and receptions.

FOOD up to £15

**Hours:** lunch – Sunday 12noon – 2:30pm; dinner – Wednesday 7:30pm – 9:30pm; dinner – Thursday 7:30pm – 9:30pm; dinner – Friday 7:30pm – 9:30pm; dinner – Saturday 7:30pm – 9:30pm. **Cuisine:** English / continental:- Steak, lamb, lasagne and Javanese chicken with a choice of home-made sweets. A la carte menu featuring traditional favourites, and imaginative dishes all prepared from fresh local produce. Carvery menu, roast Scottish sirloin of Beef with Yorkshire pudding. Home made steak and kidney pie. **Credit cards:** Visa, Access. **Other points:** licensed, Sunday lunch, children catered for – please check for age limits, afternoon teas, no-smoking area, parking, vegetarian meals. **Directions:** off A6 by the B591 road to Woodhouse Eaves. ANDREW & GILL HARRIS, tel (0509) 890318, fax (0509) 890718.

### OLD TUDOR RECTORY, Main Street, Glenfield

A Tudor hotel with Jacobean and Queen Anne additions, set in its own acre of well tended gardens, offering attractive and comfortable accommodation. The tasteful well selected interior adds to the friendly relaxed atmosphere and outstanding hospitality of Mrs Weston.

ACCOMMODATION £21–£30

FOOD up to £15

**Hours:** breakfast 7:30am – 9am; breakfast – Sun/bank hols 8:30am – 9:45am; dinner 7pm – 9:30pm. **Cuisine:** English / continental. **Rooms:** 16 bedrooms all with tea making facilities, telephone, TV: 3 singles ensuite, 3 twins ensuite, 8 doubles ensuite, 2 family rooms ensuite. **Credit cards:** Visa, Access, Diners, AmEx. **Other points:** children catered for – please check for age limits, garden, pets allowed, beauty therapy, gym facilities, solarium, parking, vegetarian meals, residents' lounge, residents' bar. **Directions:** leave M1; exit 22. Take the A50 to Leicester. Opposite Forge Berni Inn. MRS B A WESTON, tel (0533) 320220, fax (0533) 876002.

## OLDE LANCASTER INN, Station Road, Desford

*On the outskirts of Leicester, this original coaching house dating back to the 1860s retains much of its old world charm, with 3 lounge bars and a cosy, intimate restaurant offering a variety of popular home-made dishes.*
*FOOD up to £15*
**Hours:** lunch 12noon – 2pm; dinner 7:30pm – 10pm. **Cuisine:** continental:- Steak Cafe Ootmarsum – rump or fillet steak with special Dutch recipe sauce. **Credit cards:** Visa, Access. **Other points:** open-air dining, Sunday lunch, children catered for – please check for age limits, pets allowed. **Directions:** on B5380 adjacent to the railway.
MR PHILIP LIDDELL, tel (0455) 822589.

## LICHFIELD, Staffordshire Map 14

## THE BULLS HEAD, Birmingham Road, Shenstone

*Having undergone extensive refurbishment throughout, The Bulls Head now offers a relaxed and friendly atmosphere in pleasant surroundings. Very popular with locals and tourists alike, who come to sample the good wholesome English cuisine. Close to the famous Belfry Golf Club.*
*FOOD up to £15*
**Hours:** meals all day 11am – 10pm. **Cuisine:** English:- Traditional style menu, offering mixed grill specialities, and imaginative desserts. Children's menu. Daily specials. Traditional beers. **Credit cards:** Visa, Access. **Other points:** licensed, open-air dining, Sunday lunch, no-smoking area, children catered for – please check for age limits, disabled access, parking. **Directions:** take A5127 off A5 or A38 to Sutton Coldfield. Half a mile on right.
WARREN ASHCROFT, tel (0543) 480214.

## LINCOLN, Lincolnshire Map 15

## THE GRAND HOTEL AND RESTAURANT, St Marys Street

*A family hotel of distinctive character, which has been run by the Hubbard family for over 50 years. The Grand Hotel has a strong local following for its traditional fare and good value and, situated in the heart of Lincoln, is an ideal base whether your interest is shopping, leisure or history.*
*ACCOMMODATION £21–£30*
*FOOD up to £15* ♀
**Hours:** breakfast 7am – 9:30am; meals all day 10am – 10pm; meals all day – Sunday 11am – 9pm; lunch 12noon – 2pm; dinner 7pm – 9pm. **Cuisine:** English / French:- A la carte and table d'hote. English and French. **Rooms:** 48 bedrooms all with tea making facilities,

telephone, radio, TV: 19 singles ensuite, 11 doubles ensuite, 13 twins ensuite, 1 triple ensuite, 4 suites. **Credit cards:** Visa, Access, Diners, AmEx. **Other points:** licensed, Sunday lunch, children catered for – please check for age limits, pets allowed, special breaks, conferences, residents' lounge, residents' bar. **Directions:** in the heart of Lincoln city centre.
MRS HUBBARD & MRS WOOTTON, tel (0522) 524211, fax (0522) 537661.

## HILLCREST HOTEL, 15 Lindum Terrace

*A former Victorian rectory situated in a quiet avenue yet only 5 minutes walk to Cathedral, museums and shops. The Hillcrest offers a chance to relax and enjoy a drink or meal in our wonderful conservatory, with views over garden and parkland. Non-smoking restaurant and some non-smoking bedrooms.*
*ACCOMMODATION £21–£30*
*FOOD up to £15* ★
**Hours:** breakfast 7:15am – 9am; lunch 12noon – 2pm; dinner 7pm – 8:45pm; bar meals – not Sun. Dinner 7:30pm – 9:30pm. **Cuisine:** modern English:- Dishes may include Lamb noisettes, Gammon in peaches and honey, Steaks, Vegetarian dishes, Pork with honey and apple. **Rooms:** 17 bedrooms all with tea making facilities, telephone, radio, TV: 6 singles ensuite, 2 twins ensuite, 5 doubles ensuite, 4 triples ensuite. **Credit cards:** Visa, Access, AmEx, Switch. **Other points:** licensed, no-smoking area, children catered for – please check for age limits, pets allowed, afternoon tea, baby-listening device, cots, left luggage, vegetarian meals, parking, residents' bar, residents' lounge. **Directions:** off the A115 Wragby road, close to Cathedral.
JENNIFER BENNETT, tel (0522) 510182, fax (0522) 510182.

## KINGS HEAD, 31 High Street, Navenby

*Situated in the attractive village of Navenby, this is a friendly and welcoming Inn, frequented by the locals. Proprietors Cliff and Beryl Freeman both wait and serve at the bar to ensure personal service at all times. The ancient Viking Way passes close by.*
*ACCOMMODATION under £20*
*FOOD up to £15*
**Hours:** lunchtime 11am – 2:30pm; Saturday 11am – 11pm; evening 5pm – 11pm. **Cuisine:** English:- Constantly changing black-board menu and fixed menu. Seafood specialities. **Rooms:** 2 bedrooms 2 doubles ensuite. **Credit cards:** Visa, Access. **Other points:** parking, children catered for – please check for age limits, open bank holidays, no-smoking area, disabled access, vegetarian meals, open-air dining. **Directions:** on the A607 between Lincoln and Grantham.
CLIFF & BERYL FREEMAN, tel (0522) 810367.

## MINSTER LODGE HOTEL, 3 Church Lane

*Minster Lodge Hotel is a delightful, small hotel refurbished to the highest standards with a good reputation for its warm welcome. Full English breakfasts are provided in the superbly appointed dining room and all rooms offer the discerning guest many modern*

*facilities. It is situated close to Newport Arch – the only remaining Roman arch still in use today. A good base for visiting all the major attractions in Lincoln and its colourful, characteristic shops.*
ACCOMMODATION £21–£30
**Hours:** breakfast 8am – 9am. **Rooms:** 6 ensuite bedrooms all with tea making facilities, telephone, TV, radio, alarm. **Credit cards:** Visa, Access. **Other points:** parking, children catered for – please check for age limits, pets allowed, residents' lounge, vegetarian meals. **Directions:** A15 north Lincoln, quarter of a mile past the cathedral.
MR R H BROWN, tel (0522) 513220, fax (0522) 513220.

### THE PENNY FARTHING INN, Station Road, Timberland
*An attractive 18th century inn set in a pretty village, with a warm and welcoming atmosphere and offering clean and comfortable accommodation. Good spot for visiting Tattershall Castle, Woodhall Spa, Lincoln and for discovering the famous fens.*
ACCOMMODATION under £20
FOOD up to £15
**Hours:** closed Monday lunch; breakfast 7am – 10am; bar snacks 12noon – 2pm; bar snacks 7pm – 10pm; dinner 7:30pm – 9:30pm. **Cuisine:** English:- A la carte and bar menus. **Rooms:** 6 bedrooms all with tea making facilities, telephone, TV: 4 twins, 2 doubles. **Credit cards:** Visa, Access, Diners, AmEx. **Other points:** parking, children catered for – please check for age limits, open bank holidays, pets allowed, residents' lounge, vegetarian meals, golf nearby. **Directions:** situated on the B1189.
ANTHONY DANIEL, MICHAEL DOBSON, tel (0526) 378359, (0526) 378492, fax (0526) 378359.

### PORTLAND HOTEL, 49–55 Portland Street
*Situated 5 minutes from the city centre and close to the railway and coach stations, this guest house is ideally situated for the passing traveller or for visitors to the city. The reception is friendly and cheerful.*
ACCOMMODATION under £20 ★
**Hours:** open all year 7:30pm; breakfast 7:30am – 9am. **Cuisine:** breakfast. **Rooms:** 14 bedrooms all with TV: 7 singles, 3 twins, 3 doubles, 1 family room. **Credit cards:** AmEx, Diners. **Other points:** central heating, no evening meal, children catered for – please check for age limits, residents' lounge, games room, garden, bar. **Directions:** off the High Street, opposite the 'Ritz Theatre'.
DAVID HALLGATH, tel (0522) 521098.

### WASHINGBOROUGH HALL COUNTRY HOUSE HOTEL, Church Hill, Washingborough
*Set in 3 acres of lawns and woodland, on the edge of Washingborough village. The bar serves real ales and the Wedgwood dining room serves an interesting and comprehensive menu as well as an excellent wine list. Outdoor heated swimming pool.*
ACCOMMODATION £31–£40
FOOD up to £15

**Hours:** breakfast 7:30am – 9am; dinner 7pm – 9pm. **Cuisine:** English:- Traditional cuisine. **Rooms:** 14 bedrooms 5 twins ensuite, 7 doubles ensuite, 2 singles ensuite. **Credit cards:** Visa, Access, Diners, AmEx. **Other points:** licensed, Sunday lunch, no-smoking area, children catered for – please check for age limits, pets allowed, afternoon tea, swimming pool, residents' lounge, residents' bar, vegetarian meals, parking. **Directions:** from Lincoln town centre, take B1190 for Bardney. Turn right after 2 miles.
MARY & BRIAN SHILLAKER, tel (0522) 790340, fax (0522) 792936.

## LITTLE MILTON, Oxfordshire Map 6

### THE LAMB INN, High Street
*A stone-built 17th century thatched inn where good food is served at reasonable prices. Popular with locals, there is a friendly atmosphere. The surrounding farmland and countryside is now a conservation area.*
FOOD up to £15
**Hours:** lunch 12noon – 2pm; dinner 7pm – 10pm. **Cuisine:** English:- Steaks, salads, grilled swordfish and prawns, smoked quail, venison in red wine. **Credit cards:** AmEx, Diners. **Other points:** open-air dining, Sunday lunch, children catered for – please check for age limits, garden. **Directions:** on the A329, 2 miles south of the M40, Junction 7.
DAVID J G BOWELL, tel (0844) 279527.

## LITTLE WASHBORNE, Gloucestershire Map 13

### THE HOBNAILS INN, Nr Tewkesbury
*Dating back to 1474, the inn has been run by the same family since 1743. A delightful location in a valley sweeping down to the River Severn at the foot of the Cotswolds.*
FOOD £15–£20
**Hours:** bar meals 12noon – 2pm; bar meals 7pm – 10pm; dinner – Friday 7pm – 9:30pm; dinner – Saturday 7pm – 9:30pm; closed Christmas 25/12 – 26/12. **Cuisine:** English:- Hobnails Baps – soft round rolls with 52 different fillings from sausage to steak and mushrooms. Homemade gateaux and flans. **Credit cards:** Visa, Access. **Other points:** open-air dining, Sunday lunch, children catered for – please check for age limits, pets allowed. **Directions:** situated on the B4077 Tewkesbury to Stow road.
MR & MRS S FARBROTHER, tel (0242) 620237.

## LLANYMYNECH, Shropshire Map 13

### BRADFORD ARMS AND RESTAURANT, Nr Oswestry
*Old coaching inn on A483 which was 'victorianised' in 1902. Comfortably and traditionally furnished with soft lighting, Victorian marble fireplace and mahogany bar. Sheltered patio area to the side. Large car park to the rear and on road parking.*
FOOD up to £15 ♈ ⊕

**Hours:** open bank holidays; lunch – except Sunday 12noon – 2pm; lunch – Sunday 12noon – 1:45pm; dinner – except Sunday 7pm – 10pm; dinner – Sunday 7pm – 9:45pm; closed 3 weeks mid October – November; closed Boxing day; closed Christmas day; closed Monday. **Cuisine:** modern English:- Bar – all home-made. Soups, bread, filled brioches, mushrooms in port, hot baked avocado & prawns, devilled crab, steak kebabs, salmon & mushroom au gratin, chicken in stilton chive sauce, beef provencale. Restaurant – Loin of lamb in garlic sauce, veal with apple & calvados, fillet steak dyonnais, vegetarian dishes. Always fresh vegetables and home-made desserts. Large selection of farmhouse cheeses. Dinner can be enjoyed in the restaurant, and bar food is available at lunchtime and in the evenings. **Other points:** licensed, open-air dining, Sunday lunch, children catered for – please check for age limits. **Directions:** off the A483, situated on the main road in Llanymynech.
ANNE & MICHAEL MURPHY, tel (0691) 830582.

## LONGSDON, Staffordshire Map 14

### BANK END FARM MOTEL, *Leek Old Road*
*A 14th century stone barn converted to provide single-storey accommodation. Very convenient for the Potteries, the Peak District and Alton Towers. The motel's swimming pool and views over Endon Brook Valley make it popular with tourists and businessmen. Les Routiers Casserole Award winner.*
ACCOMMODATION £21–£30
FOOD up to £15
**Hours:** breakfast 7:30am – 9:30am; dinner 7pm – 8:30pm. **Cuisine:** English / French. **Rooms:** 10 bedrooms 1 single, 1 single ensuite, 1 double, 2 doubles ensuite, 3 twins ensuite, 2 family rooms ensuite. **Other points:** central heating, children catered for – please check for age limits, residents' lounge, garden. **Directions:** situated 2 miles south-west of Leek on A53.
MRS BARBARA ROBINSON, tel (0538) 383638.

## LOUGHBOROUGH, Leicestershire Map 14

### THE GEORGE HOTEL, *17 Market Place, Belton*
*This old coaching inn dating back to 1753 is set in the rural village of Belton near the church. It offers a warm welcome and good wholesome food to travellers and locals alike. Near Castle Donington, race track and east Midland Airport.*
ACCOMMODATION £21–£30
FOOD up to £15
**Hours:** breakfast 7:30am – 9:30am; lunch 12noon – 2:30pm; bar meals 12noon – 2:30pm; dinner 7pm – 11pm; bar meals 7pm – 11pm. **Cuisine:** English:- Homemade bar meals and very good a la carte menu available. **Rooms:** 20 bedrooms, 16 en suite. **Credit cards:** Visa, Access, Diners, AmEx. **Other points:** licensed, Sunday lunch, vegetarian meals, children

catered for – please check for age limits, pets allowed, afternoon tea, disabled access, parking. **Directions:** 5 minutes from M1, junction 23 or 24.
MR HOUSTON, tel (0530) 222426.

### THE PACKE ARMS, *Rempstone Arms, Hoton*
*The pub has undergone a £500,000 refurbishment. There are facilities for all the family with a beer garden, play area, barbecue and petanque available. Private parties and receptions catered for.*
FOOD up to £15
**Hours:** lunch 12noon – 2pm; lunch – Sunday 12noon – 2:30pm; dinner – Fri-Sat 6pm – 10pm; dinner – Mon-Thur 6:30pm – 9pm; dinner – Sunday 7pm – 9pm. **Cuisine::-** Extensive menu plus specials of the day. Most dishes are home-made. Vegetarian dishes always available. **Rooms:** 3 bedrooms. **Credit cards:** Visa, Access, AmEx. **Other points:** open-air dining, Sunday lunch, children catered for – please check for age limits, playland, coach/prior arr, beer garden, disabled access. **Directions:** on A60 Loughborough to Nottingham road.
PETER & SANDRA NEWMAN, tel (0509) 880662.

## LOUTH, Lincolnshire Map 15

### BRACKENBOROUGH ARMS HOTEL, *Cordeaux Corner*
*Set in the heart of the Lincolnshire Wolds, the hotel is situated in pleasant surroundings noted for its natural beauty and within easy reach of all major routes. The bedrooms feature the best in home comforts with many modern facilities. A beautifully furnished lounge boasts traditional low beams and log fire, and there is a superb Dining Room offering the finest in fresh cuisine. Nearby are the coastal towns of Mabelthorpe and Skegness, Market Rasen Racecourse and Cadwell Park, with historic Lincoln just an hour away.*
ACCOMMODATION £21–£30
FOOD £15–£20
**Hours:** breakfast 7am – 10:30am; lunch 12noon – 3pm; bar snacks 12noon – 3pm; bar snacks 6:30pm – 11pm; dinner 7pm – 11pm; closed Christmas day – Boxing day (inclusive). **Cuisine:** English. **Credit cards:** Visa, Access, Diners, AmEx. **Other points:** children catered for – please check for age limits, open-air dining, vegetarian meals, garden, parking, disabled access. **Directions:** A16 Louth to Grimsby, 1 mile outside Louth.
J, D AND A LIDGARD, tel (0507) 609169, fax (0507) 609413.

### MR CHIPS FISH RESTAURANT, *17–21 Aswell Street*
*A bright and roomy restaurant which provides excellent value in both quantity and quality. Seating for 300. Self-service.*
FOOD up to £15
**Hours:** open bank holidays; meals all day 9am – 11pm; closed Boxing day; closed Christmas; closed New Year's day; closed Sunday. **Cuisine:** English:- Fresh North Sea haddock, cod, plaice, scampi with chips & mushy peas.

Lincolnshire sausages, Norfolk chicken, Vegetarian. Selection of sweets. **Other points:** licensed, no-smoking area, children catered for – please check for age limits, parking, air-conditioned, coach/prior arr, baby changing room. **Directions:** from Market Place, turn into Queen St, then first right into Aswell St.
THE HAGAN FAMILY, tel (0507) 603756, fax (0507) 601255.

## LYDDINGTON, Leicestershire Map 14

### MARQUESS OF EXETER HOTEL, Main Street, Nr Uppington

*Ideally situated for visiting nearby Rockingham Castle and Rutland Water.*
*ACCOMMODATION £31–£40*
*FOOD up to £15*
**Hours:** open all year; breakfast 7:30am – 9:30am; bar meals 12:15pm – 2pm; bar meals 7:15pm – 10pm; dinner 7:30pm – 9:30pm. **Cuisine:** modern English:- Chicken Andree, Noisettes of Lamb with Peppers and Tomato, Fillet of Beef. **Rooms:** 17 bedrooms, all en suite. **Credit cards:** Visa, Access, Diners, AmEx. **Other points:** licensed, open-air dining, Sunday lunch, children catered for – please check for age limits, pets allowed, residents' lounge, garden, parking, afternoon tea, disabled access. **Directions:** 2 miles south of Uppingham, off the A6003 Oakham – Kettering road.
MR L S EVITT, tel (0572) 822477, fax (0572) 821343.

### OLD WHITE HART COUNTRY INN & RESTAURANT, 51 Main Street

*Situated in an unspoilt village, this stone building with its walled garden is opposite the village green. Decorated to a high standard it is furnished with good, solid yet comfortable furniture. In the restaurant you can enjoy quality food, appealingly presented and served in generous portions. The staff are skilled and helpful while the atmosphere is friendly and relaxed.*
*FOOD up to £15*
**Hours:** lunch 12noon – 2pm; dinner 6:30pm – 10am. **Cuisine:** English:- Full restaurant and bar menus, most popular dishes are mushrooms Lyddington, chicken in filo pastry with asparagus sauce and Sussex pond pudding. **Credit cards:** Visa, Access. **Other points:** licensed, Sunday lunch, garden, pets allowed. **Directions:** 1 mile south of Uppingham, follow 'Bede House' signs.
DIANE & BARRY BRIGHT, tel (0572) 821703, fax (0572) 821965.

## MACCLESFIELD, Cheshire Map 16

### SUTTON HALL, Bullocks Lane, Sutton

*Once the baronial residence of the Sutton family and more recently a convent, Sutton Hall has been sympathetically restored to create a unique 'Inn' of distinction, affording the weary traveller superb food, good ales and truly sumptuous accommodation. The fully licensed lounge bar, open to non-residents, boasts a wealth of 16th century oak beams, and 3 open log fires.*
*ACCOMMODATION £41–£50*
*FOOD £15–£20*
**Hours:** open all year 6:30pm; breakfast 7:30am – 10am; lunch 12noon – 2:30pm; dinner 7pm – 10pm. **Cuisine:** international:- a changing range of fresh seasonal dishes traditionally prepared from the finest fresh ingredients. Fine ales and wines. **Rooms:** 10 bedrooms all with tea making facilities, telephone, TV: 10 doubles ensuite. **Credit cards:** Visa, Access. **Other points:** licensed, open-air dining, Sunday lunch, garden, pets allowed. **Directions:** south of Macclesfield A523, left Byrons Lane, right Bullocks Lane.
ROBERT BRADSHAW, tel (0260) 253211, fax (0260) 252538.

## MANSFIELD, Nottinghamshire Map 15

### MAID MARIAN RESTAURANT, 8 Church Street, Edwinstowe

*Legend has it that Maid Marian and Robin Hood were married in the church opposite this restaurant. Still celebrating the occasion, the a la carte menu offers dishes such as Will Scarlet's Feast and Robin's Reward.*
*FOOD up to £15*
**Hours:** meals all day 9am – 10pm. **Cuisine:** English:- Extensive grill, snack, table d'hote and a la carte menus. Excellent choice and good value for money. **Credit cards:** Visa, Access, Diners, AmEx. **Other points:** Sunday lunch, children catered for – please check for age limits, coach/prior arr. **Directions:** situated on the B6034 in the heart of Sherwood forest.
MR & MRS C A BENNETT, tel (0623) 822266.

## MARKET DRAYTON, Shropshire Map 13

### BOWMANS, High Street

*Built in 1774 as an old Coaching Inn, this is now Ellesmere's premier hotel having undergone extensive refurbishment and modernisation. There are tastefully furnished rooms for overnight stays and a lovely function suite for weddings and parties. Located in the town centre, it offers a wide variety of good food and drink in hospitable surroundings.*
*FOOD up to £15*
**Hours:** meals all day 9am – 1am. **Cuisine:** British. **Credit cards:** Visa, Access, Diners. **Other points:** children catered for – please check for age limits, vegetarian meals, garden, disabled access, parking. **Directions:** on the town square – opposite The Corset Arms Hotel.
MR PAUL ALCOCK, tel (0630) 658728.

## MARKET RASEN, Lincolnshire Map 15

### JOSSALS, 48–50 Queen Street

*An attractive terrace-style restaurant with adjoining coffee shop, situated on the main street of Market Rasen, offering very good food at very reasonable prices. The combination of well cooked and prepared food and the genuinely friendly welcome makes this restaurant a must for those in the area interested in the local horse racing or touring the beautiful Lincolnshire Wolds. Outside catering specialists.*

*FOOD up to £15*

**Hours:** coffee shop 9am – 4:30pm; Sunday lunch 12noon – 1:30pm; dinner Thurs-Sat from 7pm; private parties accepted Sunday – Wednesday. **Cuisine:** English:- Extensive a la carte menu, featuring home cooking using fresh local produce. Coffee shop: home-made hot & cold snacks, home baking. **Credit cards:** Visa, Access. **Other points:** licensed, Sunday lunch, no-smoking area, children catered for – please check for age limits, afternoon tea. **Directions:** on the A631, main high street of Market Rasen. Below railway bridge. JO PARSONS & SALLY GRAHAM, tel (0673) 843948.

## MATLOCK, Derbyshire Map 15

### BOWLING GREEN INN, *East Bank, Winster*
*Situated in a popular and picturesque Derbyshire village, the Bowling Green Inn with its characteristic fireplace is thought to be of 15th century origin. Along with the resident ghost, Dave and Jayne Bentley extend a warm and friendly welcome to all. The inn is ideally located for touring nearby attractions, such as Chatsworth House, Haddon Hall, Tissington and Dove Dale.*

*FOOD up to £15*

**Hours:** lunch 12noon – 2pm; bar meals 2pm – 9pm; no food Sunday evening. **Cuisine:** English:- Good selection with fresh daily specials, including vegetarian speciality dishes. Traditional Sunday Roast of Beef, Lamb or Pork. Good selection of home-made sweets. **Credit cards:** Visa, Access. **Other points:** open-air dining, Sunday lunch, children catered for – please check for age limits, disabled access, parking, bank holidays, vegetarian meals, garden. **Directions:** Matlock – A6 north 1½ miles. Turn left onto B5057 for 2½ miles. DAVID & JAYNE BENTLEY, tel (0629) 650219.

### THE ELIZABETHAN RESTAURANT, *4 Crown Square*
*This attractive restaurant is located right in the centre of the picturesque town of Matlock on the A6. It offers a warm, friendly welcome and excellent food in idyllic surroundings.*

*FOOD up to £15*

**Hours:** open every day Sunday evening; morning coffee 10am – 12noon; lunch 12noon – 3pm; afternoon tea 3pm – 5pm; dinner 7:30pm – 10pm. **Cuisine:** English / continental:- Steak and kidney pie, savoury filled pancakes. Homemade, continental dishes. Roasts daily. **Credit cards:** Visa, Access. **Other points:** Sunday lunch, children catered for – please check for age limits, coach/prior art. **Directions:** On the A6 in the centre of town. MR G E FAULKNER, tel (0629) 583533.

## MELTON MOWBRAY, Leicestershire Map 14

### HUNTERS ARMS HOTEL, *Edmondthorpe Road, Wymondham*
*Old stone built country house offering beautifully cooked cuisine in the restaurant and a good snack for the*

traveller passing through. The hotel has a large garden at the rear, real ales and warm and friendly service.
*ACCOMMODATION under £20*

*FOOD up to £15*

**Hours:** bar meals 12noon – 2pm; dinner 7pm – 9:30pm; bar meals 7pm – 9:30pm; closed Monday. **Cuisine:** English:- Medallion of fillet steak flamed with brandy, mushroom and cream. Specials of the day, eg. Lamb's liver Provencale, fillet of lemon sole, prawn and cream sauce, beef Wellington, Bouillabaisse. **Rooms:** 2 bedrooms all with tea making facilities, TV: 2 twins. **Credit cards:** Visa, Access, Diners, AmEx. **Other points:** licensed, Sunday lunch, vegetarian meals, pets allowed, children catered for – please check for age limits. **Directions:** from the A607 onto the B676, past Wymondham. MR & MRS M MASCARO, tel (057284) 633.

### SYSONBY KNOLL HOTEL AND RESTAURANT, *Asfordby Road*
*A family-run hotel, set in 2 acres of grounds with river frontage, the Sysonby Knoll has beautifully decorated rooms with quality furnishings. The restaurant offers an imaginative menu which our inspector comments 'gives excellent value for money'.*

*ACCOMMODATION £21–£30*

*FOOD up to £15*

**Hours:** breakfast 7:30am – 9:30am; lunch 12noon – 2pm; dinner 7pm – 10pm. **Cuisine:** English:- Extensive a la carte menu which includes a vegetarian selection. **Rooms:** 24 bedrooms all with tea making facilities, telephone, radio, TV: 6 singles ensuite, 6 twins ensuite, 10 doubles ensuite, 2 triples ensuite. **Credit cards:** Visa, Access. **Other points:** Sunday lunch, children catered for – please check for age limits, pets allowed, garden, baby-listening device, cots, vegetarian meals, parking, residents' lounge, residents' bar, disabled access. **Directions:** take A606/607 to Melton Mowbray. Follow A6006, half mile from town centre. MRS S BOOTH, tel (0664) 63563.

## MIDDLEWICH, Cheshire Map 16

### THE KINDERTON HOUSE HOTEL, *Kinderton Street*
*An attractive mock tudor hotel and restaurant offering traditional English cuisine in pleasant, informal surroundings. Weddings and private functions are a speciality.*

*ACCOMMODATION £21–£30*

*FOOD up to £15*

**Hours:** breakfast 7am – 9am; lunch 12noon – 2pm; bar snacks 12noon – 9pm; dinner 7pm – 9pm. **Cuisine:** English. **Credit cards:** Visa, Access, Diners. **Other points:** children catered for – please check for age limits, vegetarian meals, no-smoking area, disabled access, residents' lounge, garden, parking. **Directions:** A54, 2 minutes from junction 18 on the M6. CHRISTOPHER DEVANEY, tel (0606) 834325.

## MUCH WENLOCK, Shropshire Map 13

### THE WENLOCK EDGE INN, Hilltop, Wenlock Edge

*Stone built in the 17th century, this traditional country Inn is family-run and provides a delightful rural retreat. The Inn is comfortable and the home-cooking is of a high standard. Welcoming service and a relaxed atmosphere ensure an enjoyable meal or stay. Highly recommended.*

ACCOMMODATION £21–£30

FOOD up to £15

**Hours:** breakfast 8:30am – 9:30am; lunch 12noon – 2pm; dinner 7pm – 9pm. **Cuisine:** Traditional English cuisine. Pies and puddings – house specialities. **Rooms:** 5 bedrooms, all en suite. **Credit cards:** Visa, Access. **Other points:** Sunday lunch, no-smoking area, children catered for – please check for age limits, bank holidays, pets allowed. **Directions:** from Much Wenlock take B4371. Approx 4 miles along on left side. THE WARING FAMILY, tel (074 636) 403.

## NEWARK, Nottinghamshire Map 15

### NEW FERRY RESTAURANT, Riverside, Farndon

*Standing attractively by the River Trent, the New Ferry Restaurant serves generous portions of well-cooked food in a relaxed and friendly atmosphere. The menus offer a wide choice of dishes and the specialities change 3 times a week to make use of the best in fresh produce. The high standard of the food is complemented by a good, varied wine list.*

FOOD up to £15 ♀ 🐕 CLUB

**Hours:** open bank holidays 7pm; lunch 12noon – 2pm; dinner 7pm – 10pm; closed Monday. **Cuisine:** Mediterranean influenced cuisine. Dishes may include fresh salmon with a fennel & cream sauce, rack of lamb with a redcurrant & port sauce. Fresh Lobster, Shellfish, etc always available. **Credit cards:** Visa, Access, Diners, AmEx. **Other points:** licensed, open-air dining, Sunday lunch, children catered for – please check for age limits. **Directions:** off A46, Nottingham to Newark road. 5 minutes from Newark by River Trent. JOSE & PAM GOMES, tel (0636) 76578.

### THE WILLOW TREE INN, Front Street, Barnby-in-the-Willows

*This delightful 17th century inn was a former stop for drivers on the heavy horse route from Newark to the coast. Retaining its welcoming aspect and atmosphere, this heavily beamed, typical country inn is nestled in the conservation village of Barnby-in-the-Willows and makes a charming resting place for anyone who appreciates good food and good beer.*

ACCOMMODATION under £20

FOOD up to £15 ★

**Hours:** last orders Monday – 10:30pm; breakfast 7:45am – 9am; lunch 12noon – 2:30pm; dinner 7pm – 12midnight; bar meals 7pm – 10:30pm; closed

Christmas day. **Cuisine:** Traditional English cuisine with regular daily specials. Occasional menu features traditional main courses such as rabbit pie, game pie. Good desserts. **Rooms:** 5 bedrooms all with tea making facilities, radio, TV: 1 single, 1 double ensuite, 1 double, 1 triple ensuite, 1 triple. **Credit cards:** Visa, Access, AmEx. **Other points:** licensed, Sunday lunch, children catered for – please check for age limits, parking, vegetarian meals, bank holidays, cots. **Directions:** near Newark golf course. Turn off A17 (signposted Barnby). DONALD & MARY-ANNE GRANT, tel (0636) 626613, fax (0636) 626613.

## NEWCASTLE-UNDER-LYME, Staffordshire Map 14

### GABLES HOTEL, 570–572 Etruria Road

*The Gables is a fine Edwardian townhouse set in extensive gardens. Situated next to the new Victoria Theatre and ideal for visitors to Stoke on Trent's pottery factories (e.g. Wedgwood, Spode and Royal Doulton) and to Alton Towers.*

ACCOMMODATION under £20

**Hours:** breakfast 7:15am – 8:45am; dinner 6pm – 8:30pm. **Cuisine:** English. **Rooms:** 6 double, 1 twin and 6 family bedrooms all en suite. 2 bathrooms and 1 shower. **Other points:** central heating, children catered for – please check for age limits, pets allowed, residents' lounge, garden. **Directions:** on the A53 half mile from town centre next to New Victoria Theatre. ROSEMARY BRASSINGTON, tel (0782) 619748.

### BRUNSWICKS RESTAURANT, 10 Brunswick Street

*A Victorian type building brightly and tastefully decorated, only 2 minutes walk from the town centre. This restaurant serves a range of European dishes in a bright and busy atmosphere.*

FOOD £15–£20

**Hours:** lunch – Tue-Fri 12noon – 2pm; dinner 6:30pm; closed Monday; closed Sunday. **Cuisine:** continental:- European cuisine. House specialities are steaks served with a variety of sauces, and evening blackboard specials feature many fresh fish dishes. **Credit cards:** Visa, Access, AmEx. **Other points:** licensed, children catered for – please check for age limits. **Directions:** on Brunswick St between Fatty Arbuckles Nightclub and Baths. Opposite Berkley Court. MRS M ARCHER, tel (0782) 635999.

## NEWTOWN LINFORD, Leicestershire Map 14

### THE JOHNSCLIFFE HOTEL & RESTAURANT, 73 Main Street

*The Johnscliffe provides a varied and exciting menu served by friendly and efficient staff. Set in its own wooded grounds, this elegant building has sunlit rooms and a quiet, relaxing atmosphere. Places to visit include*

*Bradgate park, the home of Lady Jane Grey, Castle Donington race track.*
ACCOMMODATION £41–£50
FOOD £15–£20
**Hours:** lunch 12noon – 2pm; dinner 7pm – 9:30pm.
**Cuisine:** English / continental:- Crab, chicken, pheasant, fish and steak in interesting sauces.
**Rooms:** 15 bedrooms, all en suite. **Credit cards:** Visa, Access, AmEx. **Other points:** licensed, Sunday lunch, children catered for – please check for age limits, pets allowed. **Directions:** 5 minutes from Junction 22 off the M1.
MR & MRS DEVONPORT, tel (0533) 242228.

## NORTHAMPTON, Northamptonshire Map 14

### COACH HOUSE HOTEL, 8–10 East Park Parade, Kettering Road
*Popular among business people, this charming Victorian hotel offers comfortable accommodation, good food and friendly service at reasonable prices. Close to the centre of town.*
ACCOMMODATION £31–£40
FOOD up to £15
**Hours:** breakfast 7:30am – 10am; dinner 7pm – 9:30pm.
**Cuisine:** English:- Traditional English cooking. Generous portions at reasonable prices. Real ales.
**Rooms:** 29 bedrooms, 21 en suite. **Credit cards:** Visa, Access, Diners, AmEx. **Other points:** licensed, children catered for – please check for age limits, afternoon tea, pets allowed, residents' lounge, residents' bar, satellite TV, vegetarian meals, parking. **Directions:** half mile from town centre on A43 Northampton to Kettering road.
MRS LONG, tel (0604) 250981.

### RED LION HOTEL, Main Street, East Haddon
*Its welcoming old world atmosphere, comfortable decor and good food has given this establishment a well deserved reputation as the ideal location for a peaceful weekend break. It is within easy reach of Althorp House, Guilsbrough Wild Life Park and facilities for golf, trout fishing, sailing and horse riding.*
ACCOMMODATION under £20
FOOD £15–£20
**Hours:** open all year 7pm; open bank holidays 7pm; breakfast 7:30am – 9:30am; lunch 12:30pm – 2pm; dinner 7pm – 9:30pm. **Cuisine:** English:- Traditional English cooking with some more adventurous menu items. Examples of what you may find on the menu include fresh crab claws, Rabbit & Hare pie, supreme of chicken Roquefort. **Rooms:** 5 bedrooms all with tea making facilities: 1 single, 2 doubles, 2 twins. **Credit cards:** Visa, Access, Diners, AmEx. **Other points:** licensed, open-air dining, Sunday lunch, children catered for – please check for age limits, residents' lounge, garden. **Directions:** off A428 between Northampton and Rugby, 7 miles from Junction 18 (M1).
IAN KENNEDY, tel (0604) 770223, fax (0604) 645866.

### WESTONE MOAT HOUSE, Ashley Way, Weston Favell
*This old country house was originally owned by the Sears family who founded Truform shoes. Now it provides a haven for visitors, overlooking peaceful lawns, set in a quiet residential area and offering facilities for croquet, mini-gym, sauna and solarium.*
ACCOMMODATION £31–£40
FOOD up to £15
**Hours:** breakfast 7:30am – 9:30am; lunch 12:30pm – 1:45pm; dinner 7pm – 9:45pm. **Cuisine:** English / French:- Avocado Thermidor, Scampi Marsala and Chicken Duxelle en croute. **Rooms:** 66 bedrooms all with tea making facilities, telephone, TV: 27 singles ensuite, 21 twins ensuite, 12 doubles ensuite, 3 triples ensuite, 1 quad ensuite, 2 suites. **Credit cards:** Visa, Access, Diners, AmEx. **Other points:** licensed, Sunday lunch, children catered for – please check for age limits, pets allowed, Sunday lunch, bank holidays. **Directions:** the hotel is signed off the A4500 in Weston Favell.
MR G FEHLER – MANAGER, tel (0604) 406262, fax (0604) 415023.

## NORTON, Shropshire Map 13

### HUNDRED HOUSE HOTEL, RESTAURANT & INN, Bridgnorth Road
*An award-winning, family run, country inn with character, charm and a warm atmosphere. It has patchwork themed bedrooms with antique furnishings and all facilities, and offers superb European and English food. Only 45 mins from Birmingham international Airport, Conference and Exhibition Centres and an ideal location to explore Ironbridge Gorge museums and the Severn Valley.*
ACCOMMODATION £31–£40
FOOD up to £15 ⌣ ★
**Hours:** breakfast 7:30am – 9:30am; lunch 11:30am – 2:30pm; dinner 6pm – 10pm. **Cuisine:** English / continental:- Varied menu which changes frequently: local game, char-grilled meats, traditional roasts, home-made steak and kidney pies, lasagne and moussaka. **Rooms:** 10 luxury bedrooms, all en suite, with some honeymoon suites and family rooms. **Credit cards:** Visa, Access. **Other points:** licensed, open-air dining, Sunday lunch, children catered for – please check for age limits, garden. **Directions:** situated on the A442 Bridgenorth – Telford road, in Norton village.
HENRY & SYLVIA & DAVID PHILLIPS, tel (095271) 353, fax (095271) 355.

## NOTTINGHAM, Nottinghamshire Map 15

### BELL INN, Old Market Square
*A 15th century traditional inn, situated in the historic heart of Nottingham, offering well presented appetising English fare complemented by warm and courteous service. Owned and operated by the same family for over 95 years, the Bell Inn, with its original oak beams and*

ancient flagstones, makes a pleasant lunchtime stop for locals and tourists alike.

**FOOD** up to £15

**Hours:** lunch 11:30am – 2:15pm; closed evenings; restaurant closed Sunday. **Cuisine:** English:- Good English fare at reasonable prices. **Credit cards:** Visa, Access, Diners, AmEx. **Other points:** children catered for – please check for age limits, pets allowed, street parking. **Directions:** situated in Old Market Square in the centre of Nottingham.

DAVID R JACKSON, tel (0602) 475241, fax (0602) 475502.

## THE HAVEN, *Grantham Road, Whatton*

*The Haven is a pleasant, homely hotel, situated in 5 acres of grassland in the beautiful Vale of Belvoir. Offers food of fine quality, in generous proportions, at very good value for money.*

ACCOMMODATION £31–£40

FOOD up to £15

**Hours:** breakfast 7am – 9:30am; lunch 12noon – 2pm; dinner 6pm – 10pm. **Cuisine:** English, including Belvoir Steak and speciality flambe. **Rooms:** 2 single, 17 double, 10 twin, and 4 family rooms, all en suite. All rooms have colour TV, telephone and tea/coffee facilities. Four posters available. **Credit cards:** Visa, Access, AmEx. **Other points:** licensed, open-air dining, Sunday lunch, no-smoking area, children catered for – please check for age limits, pets allowed, bank holidays, afternoon tea. **Directions:** between Notts and Grantham. Corner of A52 and road to Belvoir Castle.

LESLIE & BETTY HYDES, tel (0949) 50800.

## JALLANS, *9 Byard Lane*

*A victorian flagged floor building situated up a small alley in the heart of the city of Nottingham, providing an ideal meeting place for lunch in a friendly and lively atmosphere. The decor is bright and welcoming with dried flower arrangements, patterned tablecloths and wooden chairs and the food well presented with good use of garnishes. Ideal location for visitors to the city, with Tales of Robin Hood, the Theatre Royal, Concert hall and shops all within walking distance.*

FOOD up to £15

**Hours:** meals all day 11am – 7pm; closed Christmas day; closed New Year's day. **Cuisine:** international. **Credit cards:** Visa, Access, Diners, AmEx. **Other points:** children catered for – please check for age limits, open bank holidays, afternoon tea, disabled access, vegetarian meals, licensed. **Directions:** situated in the city centre, off Bridlesmith Gate – opposite Paul Smith.

MR ROMER, MR VIGGERS, MR BRADFIELD, tel (0602) 506684.

## THE TOWN HOUSE, *8–10 Low Pavement*

*The Town House restaurant and coffee house are two grade II listed buildings in Victorian Gothic and Edwardian style, set in a pedestrianized area in the heart of the city of Nottingham. Popular with the local business community, it has an informal atmosphere*

where you can enjoy good food in generous portions. Ideal for shopping or for visiting Nottingham Castle, opposite.

FOOD up to £15

**Hours:** meals all day, Mon, Tue, Sat, 8.30am – 6pm, Wed, Thur, Fri, 8.30am – 9pm; closed Sunday. **Cuisine:** modern British:- Pizza, pasta. **Credit cards:** Visa, Switch. **Other points:** children catered for – please check for age limits, vegetarian meals, no smoking area, open air dining, baby changing room. **Directions:** situated in the heart of the city by Marks and Spencer.

CHRIS & LINDSAY DEERING, tel (0602) 470074.

## WALTON'S HOTEL, *North Lodge, The Park*

*Originally the hunting lodge to the Castle Deer Park, Walton's Hotel is a Regency house furnished with antiques and offering food and accommodation of a very high standard. The atmosphere is pleasant and welcoming and guests can relax and enjoy the good food and wine in the comfort of the elegant dining room. Within walking distance of the city centre, theatres and Castle.*

ACCOMMODATION £31–£40

FOOD up to £15

**Hours:** breakfast 7:30am – 10am; lunch 12:30pm – 2pm; dinner 7:30pm – 9:30pm. **Cuisine:** French:- Dishes include scallops in ginger sauce, chicken in hazelnut sauce, and a large selection of steaks but fish is their speciality. **Rooms:** 17 bedrooms 2 singles ensuite, 2 twins ensuite, 13 doubles ensuite. **Credit cards:** Visa, Access, AmEx. **Other points:** licensed, open-air dining, Sunday lunch, children catered for – please check for age limits, garden, afternoon tea, pets allowed, residents' lounge. **Directions:** A6200. From A52 follow city centre signs. 200yds from police station.

G L FLANDERS & T W K WALTON, tel (0602) 475215, fax (0602) 475053.

# NYMPSFIELD, Gloucestershire Map 13

## ROSE & CROWN INN, *Stonehouse*

*A 300 year-old coaching inn in an extremely quiet Cotswold village. Close to the Cotswold Way and Nympsfield Gliding Club. A friendly, local inn which is an ideal base for touring, and within easy access of the M4 and M5.*

ACCOMMODATION under £20

FOOD up to £15

**Hours:** breakfast 8am – 9am; lunch 12noon – 2pm; bar meals 6:30pm – 9:30pm. **Cuisine:** English / international:- Good bar food with sandwiches, salads, steaks, fish meals, spicy dishes. Packed lunch available. Choice of over 40 main meals. **Rooms:** 4 bedrooms 4 family rooms. **Credit cards:** Visa, Access, AmEx. **Other points:** licensed, Sunday lunch, children catered for – please check for age limits, coach/prior arr. **Directions:** off the B4066 Dursley–Stroud road. Situated in village centre.

BOB AND LINDA WOODMAN, NEIL SMITH, tel (0453) 860240, fax (0453) 860240.

## OLD DALBY, Leicestershire Map 14

### THE CROWN INN, Debdale Hill, Nr Melton Mowbray

Tucked away in a corner of the village and approached through the large car park, the Crown Inn offers the facilities of a croquet lawn, large garden and a petanque pitch. The beer is drawn straight from the wood and the bar menu is interesting and extensive. Routiers Pub of the Year 1991.

FOOD £15–£20 ☺

**Hours:** lunch 12noon – 2pm; dinner 6pm – 9:30pm.
**Cuisine:** modern English:- Fresh, seasonal dishes.
**Other points:** licensed, open-air dining, Sunday lunch, children catered for – please check for age limits.
**Directions:** off the A46 and the A606 in Old Dalby.
LYNNE BRYAN & SALVATORE INGUANTA, tel (0664) 823134.

## OSWESTRY, Shropshire Map 13

### RESTAURANT SEBASTIAN, 45 Willow Street

Pleasantly decorated with oak beams and panelling, Restaurant Sebastian enjoys a relaxed atmosphere. The French provincial cuisine is of the highest standard and elegantly presented. A popular restaurant and highly recommended for its outstanding food, welcoming service and attractive surroundings.

FOOD £21–£25 ☺

**Hours:** dinner 6:30pm – 10:30pm; closed Sunday – Monday. **Cuisine:** French:- Table d'hote and a la carte menus featuring predominantly French cuisine. The restaurant also offers a 3 course Routiers menu @ £9.95 and a Tourist menu @ £13.95. **Credit cards:** Visa, Access, AmEx. **Other points:** licensed. **Directions:** close to the town centre.
MICHELLE & MARK SEBASTIAN FISHER, tel (0691) 655444, fax (0691) 655444.

### STARLINGS CASTLE, Bron y Garth

An 18th century sandstone farmhouse, previously a shooting lodge, surrounded by the deep foliage of rhododendrons and conifers and standing within sight of Offas Dyke, the plain of Shropshire and the hidden valleys and mountains of Berwyn. Ideally situated within reach of many interesting activities; salmon and trout fishing, walking, horse and pony trekking, canoeing, canal cruising and golf. Chirk Castle, Erddig Hall and the medieval flower town of Shrewsbury are all just a short distance away.

ACCOMMODATION under £20
FOOD £15–£20

**Hours:** breakfast 8am – 9:30am; Sunday lunch 12:30pm – 2:30pm; dinner 7:30pm – 9:30pm. **Cuisine:** eclectic.
**Rooms:** 8 bedrooms 2 singles, 2 twins, 4 doubles.
**Credit cards:** Visa, Access, Diners, AmEx. **Other points:** parking, children catered for – please check for age limits, disabled access, pets, residents' lounge, vegetarian meals, garden, open-air dining. **Directions:** situated off B4579.
MR A & MRS J PITT, tel (0691) 718464, fax (0691) 718464.

## OUNDLE, Northamptonshire Map 14

### FITZGERALDS RESTAURANT, 26 West Street

A 17th century, Grade II listed building in the heart of Oundle, which has been converted to a 32 seat restaurant with walled courtyard. All dishes are home-made using fresh, seasonal produce. The Routiers inspector was impressed by the very well cooked food and welcoming service. Exposed oak beams and solid pine furniture add to the cosy, homely atmosphere. Good value.

FOOD up to £15 ☺

**Hours:** morning coffee 10:30am – 12noon; dinner 7pm – 10pm; closed Sunday. **Cuisine:** English / French:- An English country bistro offering regional French cuisine and traditional English fayre. **Credit cards:** Visa, Access. **Other points:** licensed, open-air dining, children catered for – please check for age limits, patio, no-smoking area. **Directions:** A605. 300m beyond Oundle War Memorial, towards Corby.
NIALL FITZGERALD, tel (0832) 273242.

### MILL AT OUNDLE, Barnwell Road

A friendly pub/restaurant, set in an 11th century restored watermill, offering a choice of eating and drinking venues on the banks of the River Nene. Mill race can be seen from the bars and it is situated close to Barnwell Country Park and Oundle Marina.

FOOD up to £15 ★

**Hours:** lunch 12noon – 3pm; dinner 7pm – 11pm.
**Cuisine:** English:- 'Granary' Restaurant serving English fayre, and 'La Trattoria' serving continental dishes with pizzas, steaks, fajitas, kebabs and seafood. **Credit cards:** Visa, Access, AmEx. **Other points:** open-air dining, Sunday lunch, no-smoking area, children catered for – please check for age limits, bank holidays.
**Directions:** off A605 to Oundle. Signs to Barnwell Country Park.
MR N TULLEY & MRS L TULLEY, tel (0832) 272621, fax (0832) 272166.

## OXFORD, Oxfordshire Map 6

### BELFRY HOTEL, Brimpton Grange, Milton Common

Set in the Oxfordshire countryside approximately 10 minutes from Oxford. Decorated and furnished to a high standard and enjoying a friendly atmosphere. Good food and comfortable accommodation. Highly recommended.

ACCOMMODATION £11–£50
FOOD £21–£25 ☺

**Hours:** breakfast – weekdays 7:30am – 9:30am; breakfast – weekends 8:30am – 9:30am; lunch 12:30pm – 2pm; bar meals 12:30pm – 2pm; dinner 7:30pm – 9:30pm; closed Christmas 24/12 – 31/12. **Cuisine:** English:- Serving bar snacks, full a la carte menu and table d'hote. **Rooms:** 81 bedrooms all with tea making facilities, telephone, radio, TV: 11 singles ensuite, 30 twins ensuite, 36 doubles ensuite, 4 twins ensuite.
**Credit cards:** Visa, Access, Diners, AmEx. **Other**

points: licensed, Sunday lunch, children catered for – please check for age limits, leisure centre, conferences, baby sitting, cots, 24hr reception. **Directions:** situated on A40 between Junctions 7 and 8.
MR BARBER, tel (0844) 279381, fax (0844) 279624.

## CAFE FRANCAIS, 146 London Road, Headington

*Located on the main road just outside central Oxford in Headington this is a convenient place for either lunch or dinner. The relaxed, traditional style of this restaurant/bar has its own character, and its interesting menu offers something a little different and is sure to please everyone. The dishes on the a la carte and special menus are prepared fresh in the restaurant with the flair for which Michel is known.*

*FOOD up to £15*

**Hours:** lunch 12noon – 2:15pm; dinner 7pm – 10:30pm; closed Christmas 25/12; closed bank holidays. **Cuisine:** French:- French Brasserie/Bistro style cuisine. Vegetarian menu. **Credit cards:** Visa, Access, Diners, AmEx. **Other points:** licensed, Sunday lunch, children catered for – please check for age limits. **Directions:** town centre, over Magdalen bridge, left at roundabout, up hill on right.
MICHEL SADONES (MANAGING DIRECTOR), tel (0865) 62587.

## GABLES GUEST HOUSE, 6 Cumnor Hill

*Gables is a very attractive detached house in a select residential area of the city. Easy access to ring road and 5 minutes drive into centre. Guests are always assured of a very warm welcome and personal service.*

*ACCOMMODATION under £20*

**Hours:** breakfast 7am – 9am; closed Christmas 25/12 – 26/12. **Cuisine:** breakfast. **Rooms:** 6 bedrooms all with tea making facilities, TV: 2 singles ensuite, 2 doubles ensuite, 1 twin ensuite, 1 family room ensuite. **Credit cards:** Visa, Access. **Other points:** central heating, children catered for – please check for age limits, residents' lounge, payphone avail. **Directions:** 1.5 miles west of the city centre.
MR & MRS TOMPKINS, tel (0865) 862153.

## HOPCROFTS HOLT HOTEL, Steeple Aston

*A large 15th century coaching inn, which has been extensively refurbished to offer well appointed bedrooms, good food and a relaxed informal atmosphere. Situated very close to the delightful village of Steeple Aston, the hotel is an ideal base for touring north Oxfordshire and the northern Cotswolds.*

*ACCOMMODATION £21–£30*

*FOOD £15–£20* CLUB

**Hours:** breakfast 7:30am – 9:30am; lunch 12noon – 2pm; dinner – except Sunday 7pm – 9:45pm; dinner – Sunday 7pm – 8:30pm. **Cuisine:** modern English:- Escalope of salmon and crunchy vegetables with lemon butter, fillet beef with a celery and stilton jus, poached supreme of chicken and fresh salad. **Rooms:** 19 single, 26 twin, 42 double and 1 family bedroom, all en suite. **Credit cards:** Visa, Access, Diners, AmEx. **Other**

points: licensed, Sunday lunch, children catered for – please check for age limits, garden, afternoon tea, pets allowed, parking, vegetarian meals, residents' lounge, residents' bar, disabled access. **Directions:** midway between Oxford and Banbury on A4260.
MR S MYLCHREEST – GENERAL MANAGER, tel (0869) 40259, fax (0869) 40865.

## MICHEL'S BRASSERIE, 10 Little Clarendon Street

*Located in the centre of town this pleasant brasserie is a popular place to meet a friend or to have a break during a busy day. All the dishes on the a la carte and set menus are prepared on the premises using fresh ingredients in the typical Michel's style. It is a perfect spot for tourists visiting Oxford and other nearby attractions such as Blenheim Palace.*

*FOOD up to £15*

**Hours:** closed 01/01; lunch 12noon – 2:30pm; dinner 6pm – 11pm; closed Christmas 25/12 – 26/12. **Cuisine:** French:- French Brasserie/Bistro style cuisine, complemented by a fine Wine List. **Credit cards:** Visa, Access, Diners, AmEx. **Other points:** licensed, Sunday lunch, children catered for – please check for age limits, bank holidays, vegetarian meals. **Directions:** in Oxford town centre.
MICHEL SADONES (MANAGING DIRECTOR), tel (0865) 52142.

## PICKWICKS, 17 London Road, Headington

*A comfortable, quiet and efficiently managed hotel with first class decor and facilities. Large, clean, well appointed dining room and comfortable residents' lounge. A welcoming and helpful attitude will be found here.*

*ACCOMMODATION under £20*

*FOOD up to £15*

**Hours:** breakfast – except Sunday 7am – 8:30am; breakfast – Sunday 8am – 9am. **Cuisine:** breakfast. **Rooms:** 3 single, 5 double, 3 twin and 3 family bedrooms: 10 en suite. Direct-dial phones, colour TV and tea/coffee making facilities in all rooms. **Credit cards:** Visa, Access. **Other points:** children catered for – please check for age limits, garden. **Directions:** 0.25 mile from Oxford centre on London Road (A420).
G J & P MORRIS, tel (0865) 750487, (0865) 69413, fax (0865) 742208.

# PARKEND, Gloucestershire Map 13

## PARKEND HOUSE HOTEL, Nr Lydney

*A small country house hotel set in three acres of parkland. Over 200 years old, the house has been tastefully converted to retain its country house atmosphere. The restaurant offers a varied menu of well-cooked dishes at good value for money, served in pleasing surroundings. A welcoming hotel where guests can relax within the peaceful surroundings of the Royal Forest of Dean.*

*ACCOMMODATION under £20*

*FOOD up to £15* ★

**Hours:** breakfast 8:30am – 9:30am; bar meals 12noon – 2pm; dinner 7pm – 8pm. **Cuisine:** English / continental:- Table d'hote menu with a of choice of English and

continental dishes. **Rooms:** 8 bedrooms all with TV: 3 twins ensuite, 5 doubles ensuite. **Credit cards:** Visa, Access. **Other points:** licensed, children catered for – please check for age limits, afternoon tea, pets allowed, residents' lounge, garden, croquet. **Directions:** A48 Chepstow/Gloucester to Lydney. In Lydney take B4234 to Parkend.
MRS ROBERTA POOLE, tel (0594) 563666.

## PARKGATE, Cheshire Map 16

### THE BOATHOUSE, 1 The Parade
*This is an establishment which certainly has a history. First recorded on this site was The Beer House in 1664. Today, the Boathouse has been recently refurbished and pleasantly decorated. Good portions of value for money meals are served in a quiet and friendly atmosphere.*
*FOOD up to £15*
**Hours:** open bank holidays 7pm; bar meals 11:30am – 11pm; lunch 12noon – 2pm; dinner 6:30pm – 9:30pm. **Cuisine:** Welsh:- Classical home cooking, which has won many awards, dishes may include Welsh trimmed lamb with elderberry sauce, saddle of hare or barbary duck. **Credit cards:** Visa, Access, AmEx. **Other points:** licensed, open-air dining, Sunday lunch, children catered for – please check for age limits. **Directions:** 1 mile off A50, 15 miles to Manchester.
KEITH PARR, tel (051) 336 4187.

## PERSHORE, Hereford & Worcestershire Map 13

### CHEQUERS INN, Chequers Lane, Fladbury
*Situated at the end of a quiet lane in Fladbury, this old English village inn, parts of which date from the 14th century, offers exceptional accommodation and is renowned for its hospitality and excellent food. Warm and comfortable, there is a tradtional country lounge bar with magnificent open fire, cosy restaurant and endless beams. Ideal location for both tourists and business people.*
*ACCOMMODATION £21–£30*
*FOOD up to £15*
**Hours:** breakfast 7:15am – 9:30am; lunch 12noon – 2pm; bar snacks 12noon – 2pm; bar snacks 6pm – 10pm; dinner 7:30pm – 10pm. **Cuisine:** English. **Rooms:** 8 bedrooms 4 doubles ensuite, 4 twins ensuite. **Credit cards:** Visa, Access. **Other points:** parking, children catered for – please check for age limits, Sunday lunch, open bank holidays, vegetarian meals, garden. **Directions:** between Evesham and Pershore. Off A44 or off B4084.
MR A & MRS D CORFIELD, tel (0386) 860276, fax (0386) 860527.

## REDDITCH, Hereford & Worcestershire Map 13

### HOTEL MONTVILLE & GRANNY'S RESTAURANT, 101 Mount Pleasant, Southcrest
*A fine 16 bedroomed hotel, offering exceptional quality. The latest addition is 'Granny's Restaurant,' where the majority of guests dine, and also popular with the locals.*

*The residents' lounge is comfortably furnished and has a writing desk. The hotel can arrange for guests to play squash, snooker, golf and use the gymnasium.*
*ACCOMMODATION £31–£40*
*FOOD up to £15*
**Hours:** breakfast 7:30am – 9:30am; lunch 12noon – 2pm; dinner 6:30pm – 9:30pm. **Cuisine:** English:- English Home Cooking, using freshly cooked vegetables and salads, with traditional home-made puddings. Vegetarians are also well catered for. **Rooms:** 16 bedrooms, 12 en suite, tastefully furnished, with central heating, showers or baths, colour TV, telephone, and tea/coffee making facilities. **Credit cards:** Visa, Access, Diners, AmEx. **Other points:** Sunday lunch, no-smoking area, children catered for – please check for age limits, pets allowed, residents' lounge, parking. **Directions:** Redditch ring road. Left, for Southcrest. Turn right into Tunnel Drive.
MARY WARNER, tel (0527) 544411.

## ROSS-ON-WYE, Hereford & Worcestershire Map 13

### ARCHES COUNTRY HOUSE HOTEL, Walford Road
*A small, family run hotel set in half an acre of lawned gardens only 10 minutes walk from the town centre. Easy access to many places of interest in the beautiful Wye Valley. All bedrooms are decorated and furnished to a high standard and overlook the gardens. Renowned for good food and a warm and friendly atmosphere with personal service.*
*ACCOMMODATION under £20*
**Hours:** closed Christmas 6:30pm; breakfast 8am; dinner 7pm. **Cuisine:** English:- Dinner is available on request. An excellent and varied menu, offers home cooked dishes using local homegrown produce whenever possible. **Rooms:** 7 bedrooms all with tea making facilities, TV: 1 twin ensuite, 1 twin, 2 doubles ensuite, 2 family rooms ensuite, 1 single. **Other points:** central heating, children catered for – please check for age limits, residents' lounge, garden, pets/prior arr. **Directions:** A40 then on to B4234.
JEAN JONES, tel (0989) 63348.

### LOUGHPOOL INN, Sellack
*A 16th century pub with oak beams, a large open fireplace and original flagstone flooring. Outside, the inn is set in a large garden, facing a pool surrounded by willows. On the main Hoarwithy road – a popular tourist route.*
*FOOD up to £15*
**Hours:** open all year 7pm; lunch 12noon – 2:30pm; dinner 7pm – 9:30pm. **Cuisine:** English / international. **Credit cards:** Visa, Access. **Other points:** open-air dining, Sunday lunch, garden. **Directions:** turn off the A49, to the Sellack to Hoarwithy road. The Loughpool Inn is midway between Hoarwithy and Ross.
PHILIP & JANET MORAN, tel (0989) 87236.

## THE OLD COURT HOTEL & RESTAURANT, Symonds Yat West

*This old 16th century manor house is situated in a most beautiful part of the Wye Valley. The carefully selected menus in the Tudor restaurant offer a wide variety of dishes and the charming Cotswold bar serves a wide choice of hot and cold bar food and a comprehensive selection of ales, lagers and wines. Excellent accommodation and service.*

ACCOMMODATION £21–£30

FOOD £15–£20 ★

**Hours:** bar meals 12noon – 2pm; bar meals 6pm – 10pm; dinner 7pm – 9:30pm. **Cuisine:** English:- Fixed 3 course menu and bar menu. **Rooms:** 20 bedrooms 6 doubles, 11 doubles ensuite, 3 family rooms ensuite. **Credit cards:** Visa, Access, Diners, AmEx. **Other points:** licensed, open-air dining, Sunday lunch, no-smoking area, children catered for – please check for age limits, afternoon tea, pets allowed, swimming pool, conservatory. **Directions:** within the Wye Valley on A40, 1 mile from end of M50.

JOHN & ELIZABETH SLADE, tel (0600) 890367.

## ROTHLEY, Leicestershire Map 14

### THE RED LION INN

*An old farmhouse converted to a coaching inn, and trading since about 1725. Bar platters and snacks are served every day. Extensive table d'hote.*

FOOD £15–£20

**Hours:** open all year 7pm; lunch 12noon – 2pm; bar meals 12noon – 2pm; bar meals 6pm – 10pm; dinner 7pm – 10pm; closed Saturday lunch; closed Sunday dinner. **Cuisine:** modern English:- Regional French and English dishes complemented by an extensive wine list. Traditional Sunday lunch. Extensive Bar Snacks. Vegetarian menu. Summer barbecue. **Credit cards:** Visa, Access, Diners, AmEx. **Other points:** licensed, Sunday lunch, children catered for – please check for age limits, playland, disabled access. **Directions:** between Leicester & Loughborough at Rothley crossroads. B5328 & Loughborough Road.

MRS IRENE DIMBLEBEE, tel (0533) 302488.

## RUGELEY, Staffordshire Map 14

### CEDAR TREE HOTEL, Main Road

*Listed William and Mary building with furnishings in the restaurant to reflect the era. Located close to Cannock Chase, an outstanding beauty spot, the hotel is easy to spot by the vast cedar tree growing outside.*

FOOD £15–£20 CLUB

**Hours:** breakfast 7am – 9am; lunch 12noon – 2pm; dinner 7pm – 10pm. **Cuisine:** continental:- Flambe dishes. **Rooms:** 30 bedrooms, 21 en suite. **Credit cards:** Visa, Access, Diners, AmEx. **Other points:** Sunday lunch, children catered for – please check for age limits. **Directions:** 5 miles from Lichfield.

S E ROWE, tel (0889) 584241, (0889) 584242.

## RUTLAND, Leicestershire Map 14

### THE SHIRES HOTEL, Great North Road, Stretton

*A blend of old worldly charm and home-from-home comforts await you at this 200 year old Georgian FreeHouse. The Rutlander Bar offers a good choice of bar meals and the candlelit restaurant features genuine English and classical French cuisine. The food is excellently cooked and presented and the portions are more than adequate. A warm welcome and friendly, courteous service are assured.*

ACCOMMODATION under £20

FOOD up to £15 ☞

**Hours:** breakfast 7:30am – 9:30am; lunch 12noon – 3pm; dinner 7pm – 11pm. **Cuisine:** French / English:- A la carte – Classical French and English cuisine. Carvery. **Rooms:** 4 bedrooms all with tea making facilities, radio, TV: 4 doubles. **Credit cards:** Visa, Access. **Other points:** licensed, Sunday lunch, children catered for – please check for age limits, garden, afternoon tea, pets allowed, games room, functions, conferences. **Directions:** A1 Stretton Junction, signposted for R.A.F Cottesmore.

MRS A M BOWEN, tel (0780) 410332.

## SHEFFIELD, Derbyshire Map 15

### LONGLAND'S EATING HOUSE, Main Road, Hathersage

*Large country style cafe/restaurant with exposed beams and wood floor, offering well presented, generous portions of good food at excellent value for money. Situated in the main street of an attractive Peak District Village.*

FOOD up to £15

**Hours:** breakfast – weekends 9am – 11:30am; meals all day 11:30am – 5pm; dinner 6:45pm – 9:30pm; closed evenings Sunday – Thursday. **Cuisine:** international:- The menu is half vegetarian: stilton and walnut tagliatelli, spicy chick peas, old English beef in ale. **Credit cards:** Visa, Access. **Other points:** children catered for – please check for age limits, afternoon tea, pets allowed. **Directions:** off the A625, situated on the main road in Hathersage.

MR PJN LONGLAND, tel (0433) 651978.

## SHIPSTON-ON-STOUR, Warwickshire Map 14

### THE HORSESHOE INN, Church Street

*This popular inn, situated in the centre of Shipton-on-Stour, is a favourite with travellers and locals alike. The menu is varied and the service is efficient and friendly. The bedrooms are comfortable and clean, the perfect place to rest your weary head after a day's sightseeing in nearby Stratford-upon-Avon, Warwick and Stow on the Wold.*

ACCOMMODATION under £20

FOOD up to £15

**Hours:** breakfast 8am – 10:30am; lunch 12noon – 3pm; dinner 7pm – 10pm. **Cuisine:** English. **Credit cards:** Visa, Access, Diners, AmEx. **Other points:** children catered for – please check for age limits, parking, disabled access, pets allowed, vegetarian meals, open-air dining. **Directions:** located in the centre of Shipston-on-Stour.
MRS S A WILLIAMS, tel (0608) 661225, fax (0608) 663762.

# SHIPTON UNDER WYCHWOOD,
Oxfordshire Map 6

## THE SHAVEN CROWN HOTEL, Chipping Norton
Built c.1380 as a hospice to Bruern Abbey, The Shaven Crown is now one of the ten oldest inns in England. An attractive building of honey coloured stone around a medieval courtyard with a fountain, in the heart of the Cotswolds. In fine weather, dine alfresco in the courtyard.
ACCOMMODATION £31–£40
FOOD up to £15 ⏣
**Hours:** breakfast 8:30am – 9:30am; bar meals 12noon – 2pm; dinner – except Sunday 7:30pm – 9:30pm; dinner – Sunday 7:30pm – 9pm; bar meals 7:30pm – 9:30pm. **Cuisine:** English:- An excellent selection of a la carte and bar meal dishes. **Rooms:** 9 bedrooms, all en suite. **Credit cards:** Visa, Access. **Other points:** licensed, open-air dining, Sunday lunch, children catered for – please check for age limits, afternoon tea. **Directions:** 4 miles north of Burford on the A361, opposite the church and green.
TREVOR & MARY BROOKES, tel (0993) 830330.

# SHREWSBURY, Shropshire Map 13

## LION & PHEASANT HOTEL, 49 Wyle Cop
Dating from the 17th century, the Lion & Pheasant provides an atmosphere of warmth and friendliness within its characterful surroundings. There is an excellent choice of meals and snacks in the bar areas and full meals can be enjoyed in the intimate restaurant. The bedrooms have been individually furnished and retain the character of the building. A very welcoming hotel.
ACCOMMODATION £41–£50
FOOD up to £15
**Hours:** last orders 9:45pm; breakfast 7:30am – 9:30am; lunch 12noon – 2pm; bar meals 12noon – 2pm; dinner 7pm 11pm; bar meals 7pm – 10:30pm. **Cuisine:** English / continental:- Extensive selection of bar meals. Regularly changing restaurant menu. **Rooms:** 20 bedrooms, 17 en suite. **Credit cards:** Visa, Access, Diners, AmEx. **Other points:** licensed, Sunday lunch, children catered for – please check for age limits, afternoon tea, residents' lounge, conferences. **Directions:** A5112 in town centre. Town side of English Bridge.
ERNEST & DOROTHY CHIDLOW, tel (0743) 236288, fax (0743) 343740.

## ROWTON CASTLE HOTEL, Halfway House
A magnificent location for history lovers! Mentioned in the Domesday Book and standing on the site of a Roman fort, Rowton Castle has been splendidly restored and converted. Here you can enjoy the peace and tranquillity of the country, yet just 10 minutes drive from the historic market town of Shrewsbury. The timbered panelled restaurant comfortably seats 40 guests, and offers dishes to tempt the most discerning palate. Each bedroom has a unique charm and character and many modern facilities expected in a hotel of quality. The Cardeston Suite offers conferencing facilities for 150 and The Oak Room can seat up to 20 at a table for private meetings and meals.
ACCOMMODATION £41–£50
FOOD up to £15
**Hours:** 24 hour room-service; breakfast 7am – 10am; lunch 12:30pm – 2pm; dinner 7pm – 9pm. **Cuisine:** English:- Traditional English with continental flavour. **Rooms:** 19 bedrooms all with tea making facilities, telephone, radio, TV: 3 singles ensuite, 6 twins ensuite, 10 doubles ensuite. **Credit cards:** Visa, Access, AmEx. **Other points:** parking, children catered for – please check for age limits, no-smoking area, afternoon teas, pets, residents' lounge, vegetarian meals, garden, open-air dining, residents' bar. **Directions:** follow M54 on to A5, take A458 to Welshpool. The hotel is 3 miles on right.
HUGH PHELAN, tel (0743) 884 044, fax (0743) 884 949.

## SHELTON HALL HOTEL, Shelton
A manor house set in 3 and a half acres of beautiful landscaped gardens. Extensive facilities for weddings, parties, meetings and conferences. The bedrooms are comfortably furnished with TV, radio, direct-dial telephone and tea/coffee facilities.
ACCOMMODATION £31–£40
FOOD £15–£20
**Hours:** breakfast 7:30am – 9:30am; lunch 12:30pm – 2pm; dinner 7:30pm – 9:30pm; closed Boxing day. **Cuisine:** English:- Fixed price menus with variety of dishes, eg. rainbow trout Cleopatra, roast duck Olde Englande, steak chasseur. Popular for Sunday lunch. **Rooms:** 9 bedrooms all with tea making facilities, telephone, radio, TV: 2 family rooms ensuite, 2 twins ensuite, 4 doubles ensuite, 1 single. **Other points:** Sunday lunch, children catered for – please check for age limits. **Directions:** 1.5 miles north west of the town on the old A5.
MR GEOFFREY LARKIN, tel (0743) 343982, fax (0743) 241515.

## SYDNEY HOUSE HOTEL, Coton Crescent, Coton Hill
This Edwardian Hotel is within ten minutes walk of Shrewsbury's historic town centre. The restaurant boasts an extensive wine list and some excellent ports. You are assured of a warm welcome at the restaurant as the staff aim to make all guests feel at home.
ACCOMMODATION £21–£30
FOOD up to £15 ⏣ ⌾ ★

**Hours:** breakfast 7:30am – 9:15am; closed 1 week over Christmas; dinner 7:30pm – 9pm. **Cuisine:** English:- Fixed price menu. **Rooms:** 7 bedrooms all with tea making facilities, telephone, radio, TV: 1 single, 1 single ensuite, 1 twin, 1 twin ensuite, 2 doubles ensuite, 1 family room. **Credit cards:** Visa, Access, AmEx. **Other points:** licensed, no-smoking area, children catered for – please check for age limits. **Directions:** off the A528 and B5067, just outside the town centre.
TERENCE & PAULINE HYDE, tel (0743) 354681.

---

## SILEBY, Leicestershire Map 14

### THE WHITE SWAN, Swan Street

*1930s style pub with garden at rear. Large collection of ornamental frogs and bottled beers! Close to Bradgate Park and Charnwood Forest.*
FOOD up to £15
**Hours:** lunch – Tue-Sun 12noon – 2pm; dinner – Tue-Sat 7:30pm – 10pm. **Cuisine:** English:- A la carte menu in the evening and lunchtime. Fish, steaks, home-made dishes and puddings. Bar snacks. Tuesday night is speciality night. **Credit cards:** Visa, Access. **Other points:** licensed, children catered for – please check for age limits, skittle alley, coach/prior arr. **Directions:** on the B674 between the A6 and the A46.
MRS THERESA MILLER, tel (050981) 4832.

---

## SKEGNESS, Lincolnshire Map 15

### THE CRAWFORD HOTEL, 104 South Parade

*A very attractive and well-organised hotel, offering a high standard of service, with comfortable rooms and good food. Mr & Mrs Willis ensure their guests have every satisfaction: a full English breakfast is provided, but vegetarian, continental and any other dietary requirement will be catered for on request.*
ACCOMMODATION £21–£30
FOOD up to £15
**Hours:** breakfast 8:30am – 9:15am; lunch 12:30pm – 1:30pm; dinner 7pm. **Cuisine:** breakfast. **Rooms:** 20 bedrooms all with tea making facilities, radio, TV: 3 singles ensuite, 9 doubles ensuite, 8 family rooms ensuite. **Credit cards:** Visa, Access. **Other points:** children catered for – please check for age limits, afternoon tea, residents' lounge, swimming pool, sauna, solarium. **Directions:** A52. Clock tower – right end of parade.
MR & MRS WILLIS, tel (0754) 764215, fax (0775) 710074.

### CROWN HOTEL, Drummond Road

*Completely refurbished, the Crown Hotel provides first-class service with an ambiance of quiet unobtrusiveness and efficiency in full traditional English style. Enjoy a swim in the hotel pool or a game of golf on one of the many nearby well known professional courses. Ideally situated for touring the area's many attractions, such as the famous Gibralter Point nature reserve.*

ACCOMMODATION £31–£40
FOOD up to £15
**Hours:** breakfast 7:30am – 10am; lunch 12noon – 2pm; bar meals 12noon – 2pm; dinner 7pm – 9:30pm. **Cuisine:** English:- A la carte and table d'hote menus. Dishes may include Pork Escallope with Cider Cream and Apples, Poached Salmon Steak. Vegetarian and children's dishes. **Rooms:** 26 bedrooms all with tea making facilities, telephone, TV: 1 single ensuite, 13 twins ensuite, 4 doubles ensuite, 7 family rooms ensuite, 1 suites. **Credit cards:** Visa, Access, Diners, AmEx. **Other points:** licensed, open-air dining, Sunday lunch, parking, children catered for – please check for age limits, residents' lounge, garden, functions, conferences. **Directions:** A52 to Skegness. Lumley Rd. Take last turning right before seafront.
PETER MCGONAGLE, tel (0754) 610760, fax (0754) 610847.

---

## SLEAFORD, Lincolnshire Map 15

### MILLERS WINE BAR, Mill Court, Carre Street

*A delightful 150 year old red brick barn set in the market town of Sleaford, and which has been carefully renovated to provide a wine bar of character, with large oak beams and attractive patterned furnishings. Set in a secluded situation, it offers garden dining during the summer months and is extremely popular with people of all ages. Good location for visiting the RAF Museum at Cranwell and Heckington mill.*
FOOD up to £15
**Hours:** closed Christmas day 7pm; Sunday – bookings only 7pm; lunch 12noon – 2pm; bar snacks 12noon – 2pm; dinner 7pm – 12midnight; bar snacks 7pm – 10:30pm. **Cuisine:** English:- Healthy, wholesome and delicious. **Credit cards:** Visa, Access, AmEx, Switch. **Other points:** parking, children catered for – please check for age limits, open bank holidays, disabled access, pets allowed, vegetarian meals, open-air dining. **Directions:** A153 to Skegness in centre of Sleaford, turn right opposite church and right into the carpark.
ROWENA MARY DROWLEY, tel (0529) 413383.

---

## SOLIHULL, West Midlands Map 14

### FLEMINGS HOTEL, 141 Warwick Road, Olton

*A patron run hotel situated only 5.5 miles from the centre of Birmingham. A high standard of comfort and service are provided at reasonable prices and the restaurant offers both a la carte and table d'hote menus. Has the homely friendliness of a small hotel.*
ACCOMMODATION £21–£30
FOOD £15–£20
**Hours:** closed Christmas 7pm; lunch 12noon – 2pm; lunch 12noon – 2pm; dinner 6:30pm – 9:30pm; dinner 6:30pm – 9:30pm; Christmas day lunch only. **Cuisine:** English:- Seafood special, steaks, beef stroganoff. **Rooms:** 78 bedrooms all with tea making facilities,

radio, TV: 16 doubles ensuite, 7 twins ensuite, 4 family rooms ensuite, 51 singles ensuite. **Credit cards:** Visa, Access, Diners, AmEx. **Other points:** licensed, Sunday buffet lunch, open-air dining, children catered for – please check for age limits, pets allowed. **Directions:** on A41, 250yds from Olton station.
W FLEMING, tel (021) 706 0371, fax (021) 706 4494.

## SOULDERN, Oxfordshire Map 6

### FOX INN, Fox Lane

*A traditional 19th century stone-built inn, situated 7 miles north of Bicester off the B4100 in a beautiful Cotswold stone village. Ideal for Oxford, Stratford, the Cotswolds, Warwick and Silverstone motor racing circuit.*
*FOOD £15–£20* 🍲
**Hours:** no food Sunday evening, lunch only; last orders 9:30pm; breakfast 8am – 9:30am; lunch 12noon – 2pm; bar meals 12noon – 2pm; dinner 7pm – 12midnight; bar meals 7pm – 9:30pm. **Cuisine:** European:- Roast Sunday lunch, table d'hote and a la carte menu, daily specials in both Bar and Restaurant. **Rooms:** 4 bedrooms all with tea making facilities, TV: 1 twin, 1 double, 2 doubles ensuite. **Credit cards:** Visa, Access, AmEx. **Other points:** open-air dining, Sunday lunch, children catered for – please check for age limits, fishing nearby, golf nearby. **Directions:** follow Souldern signs off the B4100, situated on left in village, 200yds past pond. 3 miles from Junction 10 of M40.
IAN MACKAY, tel (0869) 345284, fax (0869) 40074.

## SPALDING, Lincolnshire Map 15

### THE RED LION HOTEL, Market Place

*Sympathetically refurbished 18th century town centre Hotel offering en suite accommodation, real ales, real food, a warm welcome and value for money. Local facilities include beautiful gardens and nurseries, fishing, clay pigeon shooting and golf.*
*ACCOMMODATION £21–£30*
*FOOD up to £15* ★
**Hours:** breakfast 7:30am – 9:30am; lunch 12noon – 2pm; dinner 7pm 9:30pm. **Cuisine:** English. **Rooms:** 15 bedrooms all with tea making facilities, telephone, TV: 7 twins ensuite, 7 doubles ensuite, 1 single ensuite. **Credit cards:** Visa, Access, Diners, AmEx. **Other points:** Sunday lunch, children catered for – please check for age limits, disabled access. **Directions:** centre of Spalding.
MRS J M WILKINS & MR N J WILKINS, tel (0775) 722869.

## SPILSBY, Lincolnshire Map 15

### RED LION INN/LE BARON RESTAURANT, Raithby-by-Spilsby

*A pleasant Tudor style country pub (a listed building), attractively furnished with brick tiled floor, original beams and comfortable seating. The atmosphere is warm and friendly, as locals and tourists mix together to enjoy good food. Nearby places of interest include Wesley Chapel, Old Bolingbroke Castle, and the famous Lincolnshire Wolds.*
*ACCOMMODATION under £20*
*FOOD up to £15*
**Hours:** breakfast 7:30am – 10am; bar meals 12noon – 3pm; lunch – by arrangement 12noon – 2:30pm; bar meals 7pm – 10:30pm; dinner 7:15pm – 10:30pm. **Cuisine:** English / French:- fish and game speciality dishes. Vegetarian meals available. **Rooms:** 3 bedrooms all with tea making facilities: 2 doubles ensuite, 1 double. **Credit cards:** Visa, Access. **Other points:** licensed, open-air dining, Sunday lunch, pets allowed, disabled access, residents' lounge, parking, bank holidays. **Directions:** Lincoln road out of Spilsby – turn right after Hundleby for Raithby.
ROGER & MAGGIE SMITH, tel (0790) 53727.

## STAFFORD, Staffordshire Map 14

### THE MOAT HOUSE RESTAURANT, Lower Penkridge Road, Acton Trussell

*A 13th century moated manor house set in 6 acres of landscaped grounds and overlooking the canal, yet only 1 mile from the M6. The delightful restaurant provides excellent food with all dishes home-made, including the bread and petit fours. The food is of the highest quality, beautifully served in generous portions. An outstanding restaurant in all aspects.*
*FOOD £21–£25* 🍲 ★
**Hours:** lunch 12noon – 2pm; bar meals 12noon – 2pm; dinner 7pm – 9:30pm; closed Sunday evening. **Cuisine:** Traditional English cuisine. A la carte menu in evenings and table d'hote luncheon and dinner during the week. Traditional Sunday lunch. **Credit cards:** Visa, Access, AmEx. **Other points:** licensed, open-air dining, Sunday lunch, no-smoking area, children catered for – please check for age limits, patio, disabled access, functions, conservatory. **Directions:** Junction 13, M6. A449 toward Stafford, first right to village. Near church.
JOHN & MARY LEWIS, tel (0785) 712217, fax (0785) 715364.

## STAMFORD, Lincolnshire Map 15

### CANDLESTICKS HOTEL & RESTAURANT, 1 Church Street

*Occupying the corner unit of a stone Victorian building, the Candlesticks has been established for over 16 years. During that time the restaurant has gained a fine reputation for the very high standard of food and good value prices. After an enjoyable meal it is worth taking a walk around the historic stone built town of Stamford. Highly recommended.*
*ACCOMMODATION £21–£30*
*FOOD up to £15* 🍲
**Hours:** lunch 12noon – 2pm; dinner – except Sunday 7pm – 9:30pm; dinner – Sunday 7pm – 8:45pm; closed Monday. **Cuisine:** French / continental:- Specialities include Portuguese fish dishes. Menu changes monthly. **Rooms:** 8 bedrooms all with tea making facilities,

telephone, TV: 3 doubles ensuite, 3 twins ensuite, 2 singles ensuite. **Credit cards:** Visa, Access. **Other points:** licensed, Sunday lunch, children catered for – please check for age limits. **Directions:** opposite St Martin's Church. MANUEL PINTO, tel (0780) 64033.

## STOURBRIDGE, West Midlands Map 14

### KINFAYRE HOTEL & RESTAURANT, 41 High Street, Kinver

*Built in 1690, the Kinfayre was originally The Crown public house and still retains its distinctive olde-worlde charm. Hanging flower baskets and wooden beams add to a pleasant atmosphere where you can enjoy well-cooked food and friendly service.*

ACCOMMODATION £21–£30

FOOD up to £15

**Hours:** open all year Monday; open bank holidays Monday; breakfast 7am – 9am; lunch 12noon – 2:30pm; dinner 7pm – 10pm. **Cuisine:** English. **Rooms:** 11 bedrooms all en suite. **Credit cards:** Visa, Access. **Other points:** licensed, Sunday lunch, no-smoking area, children catered for – please check for age limits, afternoon tea, residents' lounge, garden. **Directions:** situated off the A449, 7 miles south of Wolverhampton. MR & MRS WILLIAMS, tel (0384) 872565, fax (0384) 877724.

### THE RETREAT, 157 Hagley Road, Old Swinford

*A stylish and popular bar and bistro, situated in the village of Old Swinford, serving fine quality food and drink, six days per week. The brasserie-style menu offers light snacks and full meals, served in an informal atmosphere in pleasant surroundings. Places of interest nearby include Hagley Hall, Harvington Hall, and an interesting glassworks.*

FOOD up to £15

**Hours:** lunch 12noon – 2:30pm; dinner – Thurs-Sat 6:30pm – 11pm; dinner – Mon-Wed 7pm – 11pm; closed Christmas 25/12 – 26/12. **Cuisine:** English:- Full a la carte menu, offering a wide selection of imaginative dishes. Vegetarian meals available. Business Lunches & Small Parties catered for. **Credit cards:** Visa, Access. **Other points:** licensed, disabled access, vegetarian meals, bank holidays. **Directions:** 1 mile outside the town centre on the left of the A491. PAT & PETER GULLY, tel (0384) 396290.

## STOW-ON-THE-WOLD, Gloucestershire Map 13

### GRAPEVINE HOTEL, Sheep Street

*Be pampered at this welcoming, award winning hotel with its romantic vine clad conservatory restaurant, imaginative cuisine, high quality soft furnishings and caring staff, for whom nothing is too much trouble.*

ACCOMMODATION £41–£50

FOOD £21–£25 ⌣ ★

**Hours:** breakfast 8:30am – 9:45am; bar meals 12noon – 2pm; dinner 7pm – 9:30pm; bar meals 7pm – 9:30pm;

closed Christmas 24/12 – 11/01. **Cuisine:** French / English. Bar: Delicious selection of unusual dishes. Restaurant: English & French haute cuisine. Changing menu with fresh ingredients. Typically local and national traditional dishes. **Rooms:** 23 bedrooms all with tea making facilities, telephone, radio, TV: 1 single ensuite, 11 twins ensuite, 9 doubles ensuite, 2 quads ensuite. **Credit cards:** Visa, Access, AmEx, Diners, Switch. **Other points:** licensed, open-air dining, Sunday lunch, children catered for – please check for age limits, afternoon tea, garden, baby-listening device, cots, left luggage, tennis. **Directions:** from A429, take A436 towards Chipping Norton, 150yds on right. MRS SANDRA ELLIOTT, tel (0451) 830344, fax (0451) 832278.

### THE WHITE HART HOTEL, Market Square

*A 17th century coaching inn which still retains much of its old character and ambiance. It provides an ideal base for touring the Cotswolds and the food and service are of a high standard.*

ACCOMMODATION under £20

FOOD up to £15

**Hours:** breakfast 8:15am – 9:15am; lunch 11:45am – 2:15pm; dinner – except Sunday 6pm – 10pm; dinner – Sunday 7pm – 9pm. **Cuisine:** English:- Homemade traditional pies, local grilled trout. **Rooms:** 7 bedrooms all with tea making facilities, TV: 3 family rooms ensuite, 3 doubles, 1 family room. **Credit cards:** Visa, Access, Diners, AmEx. **Other points:** Sunday lunch, children catered for – please check for age limits. **Directions:** off A429. Turn off at town centre sign, left side of main square. COLIN & ALISON HEWETT & CLARE PEASTON, tel (0451) 830674, fax (0451) 830090.

### THE LIMES, Evesham Road

*A Victorian style building quietly situated in a large garden offering clean and comfortable accommodation in neatly decorated rooms, one of which has a genuine Victorian four poster bed. Many places of interest to visit and explore nearby. Four minutes from town centre.*

ACCOMMODATION under £20

**Hours:** breakfast 8am – 8:45am; closed 23 December – 1 January inclusive. **Cuisine:** breakfast:- All varieties of English breakfast, vegetarians also catered for. **Rooms:** 3 bedrooms all with tea making facilities, TV: 1 twin, 1 double ensuite, 1 family room ensuite. **Other points:** parking, children catered for – please check for age limits, pets, residents' lounge, vegetarian meals, garden. **Directions:** from town centre join A429 at lights, cross the road, left at lights, right of "V", second on left. MRS V KEYTE, tel (0451) 830034.

### THE OLD STOCKS HOTEL, The Square

*A 17th Century Grade II listed Hotel, one of the original buildings in the square, and facing the quiet village green on which the original penal stocks still stand. Refurbished to combine modern comforts with original charm and character. Friendly and caring staff make this an ideal base for exploring the beautiful Cotswolds.*

ACCOMMODATION £31–£40

FOOD £15–£20

**Hours:** breakfast 8:15am – 9:15am; lunch 12noon – 2pm; dinner 7pm – 9pm. **Cuisine:** English / vegetarian:- Extensive Table d'hote and very popular Special Value Menu specialising in traditional home cooked dishes and also catering for the vegetarian. **Rooms:** 19 bedrooms all with tea making facilities, TV: 1 single ensuite, 1 family room ensuite, 2 twins ensuite, 15 doubles ensuite. **Credit cards:** Visa, Access. **Other points:** licensed, Sunday lunch, children catered for – please check for age limits, garden, patio, pets allowed, disabled access. **Directions:** take A429 to Stow-on-the-Wold. Hotel in town centre next to the green.

ALAN & CAROLINE ROSE, tel (0451) 830666.

# STRATFORD-UPON-AVON,
Warwickshire Map 14

## *AMBLESIDE GUEST HOUSE, 41 Grove Road*
Small, homely guest house run by the Barnacles since 1961. Centrally located opposite Verdant Park, only a few minutes walk from the town centre. Special off season mini breaks.

ACCOMMODATION £21–£30

**Hours:** closed Christmas 7pm; breakfast 7:45am – 8:45am. **Cuisine:** breakfast. **Rooms:** 2 single, 1 double, 1 twin and 3 family bedrooms, 2 en suite. 1 bathroom. colour TV and tea/coffee making facilities in all rooms. **Credit cards:** Visa, Access. **Other points:** central heating, children catered for – please check for age limits. **Directions:** centrally located in Stratford-upon-Avon opposite Verdant Park.

RON & PAM BARNACLE, tel (0789) 297239, (0789) 295670.

## *BROOK LODGE, 192 Alcester Road*
This well appointed guest house with its tasteful decorations and furnishings provides a comfortable and enjoyable place to stay. Located within 5 minutes walk of Anne Hathaway's cottage, Brook Lodge is in an ideal position for visiting Stratford-Upon-Avon, Warwick, the Cotswolds and the many other nearby places of interest.

ACCOMMODATION £21–£30

**Hours:** closed Christmas 7:45am; breakfast 8:30am – 9:15am. **Cuisine:** breakfast. **Rooms:** 7 bedrooms 3 doubles ensuite, 1 twin ensuite, 3 family rooms ensuite. **Credit cards:** Visa, Access, AmEx. **Other points:** central heating, children catered for – please check for age limits, parking, residents' lounge. **Directions:** leave M40 from Warwick; take A46. Exit left onto A422 towards Stratford-Upon-Avon.

YVONNE & ROB CHARLETT, tel (0789) 295988.

## *CRAIG CLEEVE HOUSE, 67–69 Shipston Road*
A licensed Private Hotel retaining a family atmosphere where the sole aim is to make guests feel comfortable and welcome. Good friendly service, comfortable rooms

of a high standard, and a breakfast where no one is left feeling hungry! Quality, value for money and a warm welcome are guaranteed. Only 5 minutes walk from the town centre and within easy reach of the Cotswolds.

ACCOMMODATION under £20

**Hours:** breakfast 7:30am – 9am. **Cuisine:** breakfast. **Rooms:** 15 bedrooms all with tea making facilities, TV: 2 singles, 2 doubles, 5 doubles ensuite, 2 twins, 2 twins ensuite, 2 family rooms ensuite. **Credit cards:** Visa, Access, Diners, AmEx. **Other points:** children catered for – please check for age limits, afternoon tea, pets allowed, residents' lounge, parking, coach/prior arr. **Directions:** A3400 Stratford to Oxford Road. 5 minutes walk to town centre.

TERRY & MARGARITA PALMER, tel (0789) 296573, fax (0789) 299452.

## *HARDWICK GUEST HOUSE, 1 Avenue Road*
A large Victorian House, in a quiet tree lined avenue, only a few minutes walk from the centre of town with all it's attractions. The Coulson family will welcome you into their comfortable home, which is ideally situated near the Warwick Road for visitors to Warwick Castle.

ACCOMMODATION £21–£30  ★

**Hours:** breakfast 8am – 9:15am. **Cuisine:** breakfast:- Snacks are also available during the day. **Rooms:** 14 bedrooms all with tea making facilities, TV: 2 singles, 3 doubles, 3 doubles ensuite, 2 twins, 1 twin ensuite, 3 family rooms ensuite. **Credit cards:** Visa, Access, AmEx. **Other points:** children catered for – please check for age limits. **Directions:** off Warwick Road, corner of St Gregorys Road and Avenue Road.

JILL & ERNIE COULSON, tel (0789) 204307, fax (0789) 296760.

## *HUSSAINS INDIAN CUISINE, 6a Chapel Street*
A superior northern Indian restaurant where freshly blended spices and fragrances distinguish the cuisine. The meal is complemented by a good wine list, elegant surroundings and is popular with people of all ages.

FOOD up to £15

**Hours:** lunch 12noon – 2pm; dinner 5pm – 11:45pm. **Cuisine:** Indian:- Dishes with emphasis on milder northern Indian fragrances and spices. **Credit cards:** Visa, Access, Diners, AmEx. **Other points:** no dogs. **Directions:** off the A34.

N I HUSSAIN, tel (0789) 267506.

## *MARLOWE'S RESTAURANT, 18 High Street*
Marlowe's, originally an Elizabethan town house, is now a first class restaurant with an enviable clientele, including actors Anthony Quayle, Vanessa Redgrave, Sir John Gielgud, Sir Alec Guinness and many more. It has enjoyed a long association with the Royal Shakespeare Theatre and was once the home of Denny Gilkes, the famous opera singer and actress. Enjoy excellent cuisine from the Charcoal Grill, to fish, meat and poultry dishes,

*including vegetarian specials. The restaurant will also cook any speciality or Gourmet/party meal with prior notice.*
FOOD £15–£20
**Hours:** lunch 12noon – 2:30pm; dinner 5:45pm – 10:30pm. **Cuisine:** English. **Credit cards:** Visa, Access, Diners, AmEx. **Other points:** Sunday lunch, open bank holidays, vegetarian. **Directions:** centre of Stratford-upon-Avon.
MR GEORGE KRUSZYNSKYI, tel (0789) 204999, fax (0789) 204171.

## MOONRAKER HOUSE, 40 Alcester Road
*Moonraker House comprises three attractive white houses situated in a pleasant area in the north-west of the town. Very tastefully decorated and comfortably furnished throughout, the atmosphere is friendly and relaxed. An ideal location for touring Shakespeare country, the Cotswolds, and the many castles and places of interest nearby.*
ACCOMMODATION £21–£30
**Hours:** breakfast 8am – 9:30am. **Cuisine:** breakfast. **Rooms:** 11 double, 4 twin and 4 family rooms all ensuite. TV, hair dryer and clock radio in rooms. For special occasions there are 4 luxury four poster suites with own garden terrace and lounge. Champagne/flowers on request. **Credit cards:** Visa, Access. **Other points:** central heating, children catered for – please check for age limits, pets/prior arr, residents' lounge, garden, patio. **Directions:** on the A422 in the centre of town, close to railway station.
MR & MRS M S SPENCER, tel (0789) 267115, (0789) 299346, fax (0789) 295504.

## THE OPPOSITION RESTAURANT,
*13 Sheep Street*
*A 500 year old, half-timbered grade II listed 16th century building, converted to a popular bistro with candle lit dining. Home-made Italian, American and continental dishes. Dine before or after the theatre – which is only 5 minutes away.*
FOOD up to £15
**Hours:** morning coffee 11am – 12noon; lunch 12noon – 2pm; dinner 5:30pm – 11pm. **Cuisine:** American / continental:- Eclectic Bistro. **Credit cards:** Visa, Access. **Other points:** licensed, Sunday lunch, children catered for – please check for age limits, garden, street parking. **Directions:** 3 minutes from Royal Shakespeare Theatre.
MR NIGEL LAMBERT, tel (0789) 269980.

## SEQUOIA HOUSE PRIVATE HOTEL,
*51 Shipston Road*
*Beautifully appointed, quietly run, private licensed hotel, superbly situated across the River Avon opposite the Royal Shakespeare Theatre. Large private car park. Delightful garden walk to the Theatre, Riverside Gardens and town centre. Fully air-conditioned dining room and conference facility.*
ACCOMMODATION under £20
**Hours:** breakfast 7:30am – 9am. **Cuisine:** breakfast. **Rooms:** 2 single, 7 double, 6 twin and 6 family bedrooms,

21 bedrooms en suite. 5 bathrooms. 2 showers. Colour TV in all bedrooms and direct-dial telephones. **Credit cards:** Visa, Access, Diners, AmEx. **Other points:** central heating, children catered for – please check for age limits, residents' lounge, air conditioned, conferences, vegetarian meals. **Directions:** located on A34 approach road from the south, near Clopton Bridge.
MR P L EVANS, tel (0789) 268852.

## SWAN HOUSE HOTEL, The Green, Wilmcote
*An attractive listed building overlooking Mary Arden's House. Swan House occupies a rural setting, yet is close enough to Birmingham to be a good centre for business conferences etc.*
ACCOMMODATION £21–£30
FOOD up to £15
**Hours:** closed 03/01 – 06/01; breakfast 7:30am – 9:30am; lunch 12noon – 2pm; dinner 7:30pm – 9:30pm. **Cuisine:** English:- Extensive range of home-made bar meals – steak and mushroom pie, lasagne. A la carte – duckling, salmon, peppered sirloin. **Rooms:** 8 bedrooms all with tea making facilities, radio, TV: 1 family room ensuite, 1 single ensuite, 3 doubles ensuite, 3 twins ensuite. **Credit cards:** Visa, Access, AmEx. **Other points:** Sunday lunch, children catered for – please check for age limits, disabled access. **Directions:** from the A3400, 3 miles north west of Stratford take the Wilmcote turn off.
IAN & DIANA SYKES, tel (0789) 267030, fax (0789) 204875.

## THE VINTNER CAFE, WINE BAR,
*5 Sheep Street*
*The Vintner's name derives from 1601 when John Smith lived at this address working as a vintner, and the Elizabethan decor reflects this association. An extensive, international wine, beer and spirits list and prompt service makes this cafe wine bar popular with theatregoers and locals alike. Open for coffees to three-course meals. Family run.*
FOOD up to £15
**Hours:** meals all day 10:30am – 11:30pm; closed Christmas 25/12 – 26/12. **Cuisine:** modern English:- Wide selection of homecooked soups, vegetarian dishes, steaks and salads. Superb sweets. Full menu is accompanied by many daily changing chef specials. **Credit cards:** Visa, Access, AmEx. **Other points:** licensed, Sunday lunch, children catered for – please check for age limits, pets/prior arr, coach/prior arr. **Directions:** off A34, 1st right as approaching Theatre on waterside near Town Hall.
MR N MILLS, tel (0789) 297259.

# STROUD, Gloucestershire Map 13

## LONDON HOTEL, 30–31 London Road
*A very friendly, welcoming hotel situated in the small industrial town of Stroud, where 5 valleys meet in the beautiful Cotswolds. The food in the candlelit restaurant*

is of excellent quality, and the accommodation is very comfortable. Places of interest nearby include Gatcombe Park, Gloucester Cathedral, and Slimbridge Wild Fowl Trust.

ACCOMMODATION £21–£30
FOOD up to £15

**Hours:** breakfast 7:30am – 9:30am; lunch 12noon – 2pm; dinner 7pm – 9:30pm. **Cuisine:** continental:- dishes including sirloin steak Francaise, Hawaian duck, and Romany chicken. A la carte, table d'hote and bar meals. Good wine list. **Rooms:** 12 bedrooms all with tea making facilities, telephone, radio, TV: 1 single ensuite, 3 singles, 3 twins ensuite, 4 doubles ensuite, 1 double. **Credit cards:** Visa, Access, Diners, AmEx. **Other points:** licensed, no-smoking area, children catered for – please check for age limits, bank holidays, residents' lounge, afternoon tea, baby-listening device, cots. **Directions:** from Stroud town centre, take A419 towards Cirencester.
MR & MRS PORTAL, tel (0453) 759992, fax (0453) 753363.

## THE RAGGED COT INN, Hyde, Chalford

Located in a supremely ideal position, deep in the heart of the Cotswolds and surrounded by a wealth of picturesque villages, this Inn is personally supervised by the owners. The cosy, intimate restaurant offers imaginative award-winning food, and all bedrooms are equipped with the most modern facilities to provide a comfortable, relaxing stay. The Bar is warm and friendly, with lots of character and open log fires. Ideal base for visiting the many important equestrian events which are held annually in this area.

ACCOMMODATION £21–£30
FOOD up to £15

**Hours:** closed Christmas day 7pm; breakfast 8am – 9:30am; lunch 12noon – 2:30pm; dinner 7pm – 9:30pm. **Cuisine:** English. **Credit cards:** Visa, Access, AmEx. **Other points:** children catered for – please check for age limits, disabled access, vegetarian meals, open-air dining, garden, no-smoking area, parking. **Directions:** Junction 15 off M4, A419 to Cirencester or Junction 13 off M5 to Stroud. Follow signs to Hyde out of Chalford and turn left at junction.
MARGARET ANN AND MICHAEL CASE, tel (0453) 884643, (0453) 731333, fax (0453) 731166.

## SUTTON COLDFIELD, West Midlands Map 14

### SUTTON COURT HOTEL, 66 Lichfield Road

A hotel which has succeeded in retaining its Victorian elegance yet combines to give the best of modern facilities and old fashioned hospitality. The restaurant enjoys a good reputation for dishes prepared from fresh ingredients. This popular restaurant offers efficient, friendly service.

ACCOMMODATION £31–£40
FOOD up to £15

**Hours:** last orders 10pm; breakfast 7:30am – 9:30am; lunch 12noon – 2pm; bar meals 12noon – 2pm; dinner 7pm – 12midnight; bar meals 7pm – 10:30pm. **Cuisine:** French:- Traditional French dishes, Vegetarian meals. **Rooms:** 64 bedrooms all with tea making facilities, telephone, radio, mini bar, TV: 17 singles ensuite, 24 doubles ensuite, 23 twins ensuite. **Credit cards:** Visa, Access, Diners, AmEx. **Other points:** children catered for – please check for age limits, airport nearby, baby sitting, baby-listening device, cots, 24hr reception, foreign exchange. **Directions:** off A38 on corner of A5127 and A453.
PETER JOHN BENNETT, tel (021) 355 6071.

## TELFORD, Shropshire Map 13

### THE OAKS HOTEL & RESTAURANT, Redhill, Nr St Georges

A family-run hotel, in a secluded countryside setting on the A5, 2.5 miles from Telford, offering a varied menu cooked to a high standard by our chef Paul Marshall. The combination of good food, comfortable accommodation and a friendly, welcoming atmosphere provides guests with an enjoyable visit. Ideally situated to see all that Shropshire has to offer. Conference facilities.

ACCOMMODATION £21–£30
FOOD up to £15

**Hours:** breakfast 7:30am – 9am; lunch 12noon – 2pm; dinner 7pm – 9:30pm. **Cuisine:** English / continental:- Venison steak marinated in red wine served with stilton sauce, half roast duckling with blackcurrant sauce. **Rooms:** 12 bedrooms 5 singles ensuite, 2 doubles ensuite, 3 twins ensuite, 2 family rooms ensuite. **Credit cards:** Visa, Access, Diners, AmEx. **Other points:** licensed, open-air dining, Sunday lunch, children catered for – please check for age limits, bank holidays, conferences. **Directions:** on the A5, 2 and a half miles from Telford, 4 miles from Weston Park.
ROBERT & JILL MOORE, tel (0952) 620126, fax (0952) 620257.

### RAPHAELS RESTAURANT, 4 Church Street, Shifnal

Highly recommended by the Routiers inspector, Raphaels Restaurant offers an imaginative menu of excellently cooked dishes to suit both vegetarians and non-vegetarians alike. The quality of the food and service is outstanding. An ideal choice for excellent food in attractive and comfortable surroundings.

FOOD £15–£20 ✪ ★

**Hours:** last orders 9:30pm; lunch – Sunday 12noon – 2:30pm; dinner 7:30pm – 12midnight; closed Monday; closed Sunday evening. **Cuisine:** French, British and Vegetarian Gourmet Food. A la carte and Table d'hote menus. Dishes may include, Salmon in Champagne, Venison with a Game Sauce. **Credit cards:** Visa, Access. **Other points:** licensed, no-smoking area, children catered for – please check for age limits. **Directions:** 2 miles Junction 4, M54. Off A464 in centre of Shifnal, one-way street.
ROGER & MARY WILD, tel (0952) 461136.

## THE VALLEY HOTEL, Ironbridge

*Originally an 18th century Country House, this beautifully refurbished Georgian listed building is set in its own secluded and spacious grounds. The industrious owner, Mr Arthur Maw conducted his tile manufacturing business in the nearby Gorge which is now the Jackfield Tile Museum. The 'Chez Maw Restaurant' offers an extensive range of fine accommodation and there are exceptional conference and business facilities available. All bedrooms are equipped with the most up-to-date facilities. A superb location for exploration in a stunning setting.*

ACCOMMODATION £31–£40

FOOD up to £15

**Hours:** breakfast 7:30am – 9:30am; lunch 12noon – 3pm; bar snacks 12noon – 3pm; dinner 7pm – 12midnight. **Cuisine:** international:- innovative. **Rooms:** 34 ensuite bedrooms. **Credit cards:** Visa, Access, AmEx. **Other points:** parking, children catered for – please check for age limits, open bank holidays, disabled access, no-smoking area, afternoon teas, Sunday dinner, residents' lounge, vegetarian meals, garden, open-air dining, conferences. **Directions:** on B4380. M54 to Junction 6 onto A5223 to Ironbridge.

MR P CASSON, tel (0952) 432247, fax (0952) 432308.

## TEWKESBURY, Gloucestershire Map 13

### GUPSHILL MANOR, Gloucester Road

*A timbered 15th century manor house and site of the 1491 Battle of Tewkesbury. Margaret of Anjou is rumoured to have watched the battle from the precarious safety of one of the bedrooms. The battles are over now, and Gupshill has been tastefully restored, offering a peaceful setting to enjoy good food.*

FOOD £15–£20

**Hours:** bar meals 12noon – 2:15pm; dinner 7pm – 9:30pm; bar meals 7pm – 9:30pm. **Cuisine:** English:- All home cooked and menu in carvery changes daily. **Credit cards:** Visa, Access, Diners, AmEx. **Other points:** licensed, open-air dining, Sunday lunch, children catered for – please check for age limits. **Directions:** on the A38 on the edge of Tewkesbury, 5 minutes from the M5.

MARK & KAY RATCLIFFE, tel (0684) 292278.

## THAME, Oxfordshire Map 6

### ABINGDON ARMS, 21 Cornmarket

*A large Victorian public house which adequately caters for families and tourists to the area. There is a large beer garden with children's climbing frame, swing and sandpit. Barbecues are frequently held in the garden or barn, which is available for private hire and live bands and discos can be provided.*

FOOD up to £15

**Hours:** breakfast 8am – 10:30am; lunch 12noon – 2:30pm; dinner 6pm – 9pm. **Cuisine:** English / continental. **Credit cards:** Visa, Access. **Other points:** children catered for – please check for age limits, parking, disabled access, vegetarian meals, open-air dining. **Directions:** enter Thame from Oxford direction, in main High Street at first zebra crossing and lights – on right.

WAYNE BONNER, tel (0844) 260332, fax (0844) 260338.

## UPPINGHAM, Leicestershire Map 14

### FALCON HOTEL, High Street East

*This renowned coaching inn of great charm and character, in the former county of Rutland, offers warmth and comfort in a convivial atmosphere where you will be welcomed by the efficient and friendly staff. The hotel has long served as a popular meeting place on Uppingham's market square with its traditional architecture and Dickensian style shop fronts which reflect a timeless quality. Situated a short distance from the A1 and M1 motorways, there are many nearby attractions including Rutland Water which is famous for its water sports and fishing, Burghley House and Rockingham Castle.*

ACCOMMODATION £21–£30

FOOD up to £15  ★

**Hours:** breakfast 7:30am – 9:30am; breakfast – weekends 8am – 10am; lunch 12noon – 2pm; dinner 7pm – 9:30pm. **Cuisine:** English / international. **Rooms:** 25 bedrooms all with tea making facilities, telephone, TV: 5 singles ensuite, 12 doubles ensuite, 6 twins ensuite, 2 suites. **Credit cards:** Visa, Access, Diners, AmEx. **Other points:** licensed, parking, children catered for – please check for age limits, Sunday lunch, open bank holidays, afternoon tea, disabled access, pets allowed, residents' lounge, vegetarian meals, open-air dining. **Directions:** near to Corby/Kettering on A6003 to Oakham.

RICHARD & JOANNE BATTERSBY, tel (0572) 823535, fax (0572) 821620.

## WARBOROUGH, Oxfordshire Map 6

### THE SIX BELLS, The Green South

*A delightful 15th century thatched inn housing its own restaurant, offering outstanding British cuisine with Nouvelle Cuisine influences. It has undergone considerable refurbishment to provide a comfortable atmosphere with attractive furnishings. The River Thames, Dorchester Abbey, Henley on Thames and the City of Oxford are within easy reach.*

FOOD up to £15

**Hours:** bar snacks 12noon – 2:30pm; dinner 7pm – 10pm. **Cuisine:** British. **Credit cards:** Visa, Access. **Other points:** parking, Sunday lunch, open bank holidays, no-smoking areas, disabled access, vegetarian meals, open-air dining. **Directions:** A329, 2 miles from Wallingford off Henley to Oxford road.

MR C DAVEY, tel (086732) 8265, fax (086732) 8556.

## WARWICK, Warwickshire Map 14

### TUDOR HOUSE INN, West Street

*A privately owned inn of great charm and character. Dating from 1472 it retains a wealth of timbers many of which were used in old warships. It is also one of the few buildings to survive the great fire of Warwick in 1694. The Inn offers*

*good, plentiful food at reasonable prices in a very friendly and welcoming atmosphere, along with good value wines.*
*ACCOMMODATION £21–£30*
*FOOD up to £15*
**Hours:** breakfast 7am – 9:30am; lunch 12noon – 3pm; dinner 6pm – 11pm. **Cuisine:** English:- Traditional English cuisine. **Rooms:** 11 bedrooms all with tea making facilities, telephone, TV: 2 doubles – shower only, 4 doubles ensuite, 1 twin ensuite, 1 twin – shower only, 3 singles. **Credit cards:** Visa, Access, Diners, AmEx. **Other points:** licensed, open-air dining, Sunday lunch, children catered for – please check for age limits, afternoon tea, garden, residents' bar. **Directions:** on the A429, almost opposite the entrance to Warwick Castle. MR P MCCOSKER & MR M KUTNER, tel (0926) 495447.

## WATLINGTON, Oxfordshire Map 6

### THE WELL HOUSE RESTAURANT & HOTEL, *34–40 High Street*
*An elegant 15th century house in a small picturesque town at the foot of the Chilterns, some 40 miles from London and 30 minutes from Heathrow Airport. The Well House restaurant comprises an attractive cocktail bar and dining room with inglenook fireplace. Close to National Trust woodlands.*
*ACCOMMODATION £21–£30*
*FOOD £15–£20* ♀ ⊕
**Hours:** lunch 12noon – 2pm; dinner 7:30pm – 9:30pm. **Cuisine:** English / international:- Seasonal specials, eg boned quail with hazelnut stuffing, salmon en croute with ginger and herb sauce. Chocolate velvet cake and creme brulee. **Rooms:** 10 bedrooms all with telephone, TV: 1 single ensuite, 4 twins ensuite, 5 doubles ensuite. **Credit cards:** Visa, Access, Diners, AmEx. **Other points:** Sunday lunch, children catered for – please check for age limits. **Directions:** on the main street in Watlington, 2 miles from M40 at Junction 6. ALAN & PAT CRAWFORD, tel (0491) 613333, fax (0491) 612025.

## WEEDON, Northamptonshire Map 14

### HEART OF ENGLAND, *Daventry Road*
*Recently refurbished, this hotel offers a welcome retreat for individual tourists and families, with a large garden and children's play area. It is ideally situated for sporting enthusiasts who wish to visit nearby Silverstone Race Track, and Towcester Racecourse. Warwick Castle is another nearby popular tourist attraction.*
*ACCOMMODATION £31–£40*
*FOOD up to £15*
**Hours:** open all year 7:30pm; breakfast 7:30am – 9am; lunch 12noon – 2:30pm; dinner 6pm – 9:30pm. **Cuisine:** English:- Traditional pub style cuisine, with daily changing blackboard specials and vegetarian dishes. **Rooms:** 9 bedrooms, all en suite, with colour TV, trouser-press, telephone, and tea/coffee making facilities. 1 four-poster suite available. **Credit cards:** Visa, Access, Diners, AmEx.

**Other points:** licensed, Sunday lunch, no-smoking area, children catered for – please check for age limits, parking, afternoon tea, garden, playland. **Directions:** 200yds from crossroads with A5 at Weedon. DERICK LLOYD, tel (0327) 40335, fax (0327) 40531.

## WELFORD, Northamptonshire Map 14

### THE SHOULDER OF MUTTON INN, *12 High Street*
*Charming 17th century low beamed village inn on the A50. There is a large beer garden, and the play area will keep the liveliest children amused. Good home cooked food served with a ready smile.*
*FOOD up to £15*
**Hours:** lunch 12noon – 2pm; dinner 7pm – 9:30pm. **Cuisine:** international:- Varied menu to suit all tastes, in addition to daily home-made specials, ie. Indian curries, beef stroganoff and chicken dishes. **Credit cards:** Visa, Access, AmEx. **Other points:** licensed, open-air dining, Sunday lunch, children catered for – please check for age limits, free house. **Directions:** on the A50, midway between Leicester and Northampton. ARTHUR & JUDY CORLETT, tel (0858) 575375.

## WEOBLEY, Hereford & Worcestershire Map 13

### YE OLDE SALUTATION INN, *Market Pitch*
*Dating back over 500 years, this former Ale & Cider house, offers a traditional setting and friendly atmosphere in which to spend a pleasant lunchtime or evening out. A main feature of the comfortable lounge is a large inglenook fireplace, leading into the 40-seater Oak Room Restaurant. The local area offers many activities, including fishing, horseriding, hiking and golf.*
*ACCOMMODATION £21–£30*
*FOOD £15–£20* ♀ ★
**Hours:** enquire for early b'fast 7pm; breakfast 9am – 9:30am; lunch 12noon – 2pm; dinner 7pm – 9pm. **Cuisine:** English:- Traditional English fare of excellent quality, using fresh local produce. All dishes are cooked to order. Vegetarian dishes also available. **Rooms:** 4 bedrooms all with tea making facilities, radio, TV: 1 twin ensuite, 3 doubles ensuite. **Credit cards:** Visa, Access, Diners, AmEx. **Other points:** licensed, open-air dining, Sunday lunch, no-smoking area, pets allowed, lounge, bar, baby-listening device. **Directions:** situated 8 miles from Leominster on the A4112 Brecon road. CHRISTOPHER ANTHONY, tel (0544) 318443, fax (0544) 318216.

## WILLENHALL, West Midlands Map 14

### YE OLDE TOLL HOUSE RESTAURANT, *40 Walsall Street*
*An 18th century toll house which has been renovated to a high standard incorporating original features, eg. oak beams. Table d'hote menu includes starter, main course, cheese and biscuits, wine and liqueur coffee.*
*FOOD £15–£20*

**Hours:** lunch 12noon – 3pm; dinner 7pm – 9:30pm. **Cuisine:** English:- Large, varied selection of fresh fish. Fresh vegetables, home-made desserts. **Credit cards:** Visa, Access. **Other points:** children catered for – please check for age limits. **Directions:** situated on A454 in the centre of Willenhall.
MR BRIAN FRENCH, tel (0902) 605575, fax (0902) 605575.

# WIRKSWORTH, Derbyshire Map 15

## LE BISTRO, 13 St John Street
*Built in 1760, this is a candlelit cellar restaurant approached by a spiral staircase from the reception bar. Situated in the centre of this quaint market town, the freshly prepared, rural French style cuisine is very popular. The friendly efficent service complements a wonderful meal. International evenings monthly. Highly recommended.*
*FOOD up to £15* 🍽
**Hours:** dinner 6:30pm – 9:30pm; closed Sunday. **Cuisine:** French:- Sauce dishes – Marget de Canard in Grand Marnier and fresh orange sauce, Steaks, seafood and an extensive vegetarian menu. Game in season. **Credit cards:** Visa, Access, Diners, AmEx. **Other points:** licensed, children catered for – please check for age limits, disabled access, parking. **Directions:** in the centre of Wirksworth opposite Lloyds Bank.
MARK FOX, tel (0629) 823344.

# WITNEY, Oxfordshire Map 6

## THE COUNTRY PIE, 63 Corn Street
*A 16th century building of Cotswold stone, a short walk from Buttercross. Recent extensive modernisation has not detracted from the old world charm. Here, good food is served in congenial surroundings with an air of calm efficiency.*
*FOOD £15–£20*
**Hours:** lunch – Tue-Sun 12noon – 2pm; dinner – Tue-Sat 7pm – 9:45pm; closed Monday; closed Sunday evening. **Cuisine:** English / continental:- Traditional English and continental cuisine. Table d'hote and a la carte menus available. **Credit cards:** Visa, Access, Diners, AmEx. **Other points:** licensed, open-air dining, Sunday lunch, coach/prior arr, children catered for – please check for age limits, street parking. **Directions:** from the A40, follow signs to town centre.
JANET & ALAN DIXEY, tel (0993) 703590.

# WOLVERHAMPTON, Shropshire Map 13

## PATSHULL PARK HOTEL GOLF & COUNTRY CLUB, Pattingham
*Set in 280 acres of parkland alongside 80 acres of trout & coarse fishing. The 18 hole championship golf course was designed by John Jacobs. Inside, the hotel is comfortable and spacious and the restaurant provides a pleasing variety of well presented dishes. A quiet, relaxed atmosphere prevails. In the Shropshire*
*countryside yet only 10 minutes from the M54 and M6. (See colour advertisement in centre section.)*
*ACCOMMODATION £31–£40*
*FOOD £15–£20*
**Hours:** breakfast 7:30am – 9:30am; lunch 12noon – 2pm; dinner 7:30pm – 9:30pm. **Cuisine:** English / continental:- A la carte and table d'hote menus. Coffee shop open all day. **Rooms:** 48 bedrooms all with tea making facilities, radio, TV: 38 twins ensuite, 5 doubles ensuite, 1 suites, 4 triples ensuite. **Credit cards:** Visa, Access, AmEx. **Other points:** licensed, open-air dining, Sunday lunch, children catered for – please check for age limits, afternoon tea, pets/prior arr, conferences, golf, special breaks, fishing, leisure centre, tennis, swimming pool, parking, vegetarian meals, residents' lounge, residents' bar. **Directions:** 5 miles from Junction 3, M54. 8 miles from Wolverhampton. Near Pattingham.
PATSHULL PARK LTD, tel (0902) 700100, fax (0902) 700874.

## PURBANI TANDOORI, 41/43 Birch Street
*An immaculately furnished Indian Restaurant, popular with all ages and providing traditional and English cuisine of an exceptional standard. Fresh flowers on the tables, the staff wait in dinner jackets and the service is polite and efficient. One nice touch is the complimentary liqueur which is presented with the bill. Highly recommended.*
*FOOD £15–£20*
**Hours:** dinner 6pm – 12midnight. **Cuisine:** Indian. **Credit cards:** Visa, Access, Diners, AmEx. **Other points:** children catered for – please check for age limits, open bank holidays, disabled access, vegetarian meals. **Directions:** approach via Waterloo Road and Clarence Street.
MR L HUSSAIN, tel (0902) 24030.

# WOOTTON WAWEN, Warwickshire Map 14

## NAVIGATION INN, Stratford Road
*A friendly, family pub, serving good quality food in generous portions. An excellent place to take children as it has a large garden and adventure playground and, being situated on the canal side, there are walks along the tow-path with plenty of narrow boats to look at.*
*FOOD up to £15*
**Hours:** lunch 11:30am – 3pm; bar meals 11:30am – 3pm; dinner 6pm – 10pm; bar meals 6pm – 10pm. **Cuisine:** English / international:- Home-made dishes, with grills, seafood casserole, lasagne and crispy chicken. Home-made sweets include apple pie and cheesecake. **Credit cards:** Visa, Access, Diners, AmEx. **Other points:** licensed, Sunday lunch, children catered for – please check for age limits, pets allowed, bank holidays. **Directions:** on main A34 Birmingham – Stratford road, 6 miles north of Stratford.
MARK SMITH, tel (0564) 792676, fax (0564) 792228.

## WORCESTER, Hereford & Worcestershire
Map 13

### LENCHFORD HOTEL, Shrawley

*Stephen and Karen Horn offer you a warm welcome and personal attention in the relaxed atmosphere of this splendid late Georgian house which still retains many of its original features. Log fires in Winter and riverside lawns in Summer. The large restaurant offers superb views across the river Severn which flows gently by. 100-seater Banqueting Suite available for hire.*
*ACCOMMODATION £21–£30*
*FOOD £15–£20*

**Hours:** breakfast 7:30am – 9am; bar meals 12noon – 2pm; dinner 7pm – 9:30pm; closed Christmas 24/12 – 30/12. **Cuisine:** English / continental:- Extensive a la carte lunch and dinner menus Monday – Saturday. Carvery – Sunday lunchtimes. Bar meals available. **Rooms:** 16 bedrooms all with tea making facilities, telephone, radio, TV: 3 singles ensuite, 1 single, 4 twins ensuite, 7 doubles ensuite, 1 triple ensuite. **Credit cards:** Visa, Access, Diners, AmEx. **Other points:** licensed, open-air dining, Sunday lunch, children catered for – please check for age limits, parking, residents' lounge, garden, vegetarian meals, baby-listening device, cots, residents' bar. **Directions:** on the A443 – B1496 6 miles north of Worcester. 7 miles from M5 Junctions 5 & 6. STEPHEN & KAREN HORN, tel (0905) 620229.

## WORKSOP, Nottinghamshire Map 15

### LION HOTEL, 112 Bridge Street

*A 16th century Coaching Inn situated in the centre of Worksop, offering a warm welcome and comfortable accommodation. The restaurant provides well-cooked and presented meals with a good choice of traditional and more imaginative dishes. Bar meals are served in the popular, lively bar, adjoining the restaurant. Close to Sherwood Forest, Clumber Park and Creswell Crags.*
*ACCOMMODATION £31–£40*
*FOOD £21–£25*

**Hours:** breakfast 7am – 9:30am; bar meals 11:30am – 2:30pm; lunch 12noon – 2pm; dinner 7pm – 9:45pm; bar meals 7pm – 9:30pm. **Cuisine:** English / continental:- Carte de jour and table d'hote menus featuring traditional English and more imaginative dishes. Good vegetarian menu. Traditional Sunday lunch. **Rooms:** 30 bedrooms, 2 luxury suites, all en suite with direct-dial telephones and free sky t.v. **Credit cards:** Visa, Access, AmEx. **Other points:** licensed, Sunday lunch, children catered for – please check for age limits, pets allowed, residents' lounge, gym facilities, sauna, solarium, functions. **Directions:** Market Square, turn right at Eyres Furniture Store, then sharp right.
COOPLANDS (DONCASTER) LTD, tel (0909) 477925, fax (0909) 479038.

# NORTHERN ENGLAND AND THE ISLE OF MAN

Located in the centre of Great Britain, Yorkshire and Humberside is a region of great cultural and scenic diversity.

York, the region's capital, is dominated by its huge medieval Minster cathedral. Ringed by ancient walls it is a treasure trove of history dating back to the Roman occupation nearly 2,000 years ago. Many other cultures have also left their mark on the city, notably the Vikings who sailed up the river and made York their capital. This slice of history is recaptured at the Jorvik Viking Centre, where visitors can travel back in 'time cars' experiencing the sights, sounds and smells of Viking York. Aside from being a shoppers' paradise, York also boasts the finest preserved medieval street in the whole of Europe – The Shambles. Savour authentic Yorkshire with a visit to the bustling and colourful market towns of Otley and Pateley Bridge, each with its own special character.

For the English nobility and gentry, Yorkshire and Humberside's lush pastureland and rolling hills and dales presented ideal locations for their stately homes. Among the most famous is Castle Howard, setting for the epic television drama *Brideshead Revisited*. The countryside has inspired many world famous artists and writers – for example, the wild moors around Haworth in West Yorkshire have become famous through the books of the Brontë sisters. Famed painter J.M.W. Turner also found inspiration in the Yorkshire landscape. Here, too, are cliffs, coves and sandy beaches overlooking quiet fishing villages like Robin Hood's Bay, tiny Staithes, once the haunt of smugglers, the clifftop abbey at Whitby and Bridlington with its 900-year-old harbour.

Northumberland echoes with history too. A fine and rugged country with many miles of still unspoilt coastline upward from the Tyne, past Holy Lindisfarne to the Tweed and bygone centuries of border warfare. The North Pennines is Britain's largest official area of outstanding natural beauty where walkers and naturalists abound. Wander up the Cheviot Hills through which winds the most northerly stretch of the Pennine Way, long distance walk or simply relax and capture the freshness of the hills and moors. Many natural advantages ensure that Northumbria is ideal for recreational activities – with centres for trekking, trail riding, white-water canoeing, sailing and windsurfing.

Often called the most beautiful corner of England, Cumbria is a region of uncomparable richness and variety in its landscape, climate, culture and history. At the heart of the region lies the Lake District with its core of dramatic mountains and rugged fells from which pastoral and forested valleys radiate, studded with gleaming lakes and natural watercourses. Visit the home and birthplace of famous poet William Wordsworth who lived at Dove Cottage and later at Rydal Mount. Take time to unwind and enjoy a day out at a nostalgic steam railway or a trip aboard one of the lake steamers. Evidence of Cumbria's rich heritage can be found in the historic houses, castles, museums and galleries scattered throughout the county. Cumbria's traditional sports, rural shows and celebrations are an ideal way of meeting the local folk to enjoy their warm hospitality.

Despite its industrial history of cotton production, Lancashire is a surprisingly beautiful county. Country lovers can enjoy the sweeping hills of Bowland, the lovely Ribble Valley and the open moors of Rossendale. The moors, which descend to the very edges of the textile towns of Nelson, Colne, Burnley, Accrington and Blackburn, are wild and beautiful and many have prehistoric tumuli and earthworks. Lancaster is an ancient city boasting the largest castle in England, dating back to Norman times. Lancashire's coastal resorts are legendary with Blackpool, undoubtedly, being queen of them all with her miles of illuminations.

For details of where to visit and what to see in Northern England and the Isle of Man, contact the following tourist boards: Northumbria Tourist Board, Aykeley Heads, Durham DH1 5UX. Tel: (091) 384 6905. Cumbria Tourist Board, Ashleigh, Holly Road, Windermere LA23 2AQ. Tel: (05394) 44444. Yorkshire & Humberside Tourist Board, 312 Tadcaster Road, York YO2 2HF. Tel: (0904) 707961. Isle of Man Department of Tourism, Leisure & Transport, C Terminal Building, Douglas, Isle of Man. Tel: (0624) 686801.

## ALNMOUTH, Northumberland Map 17

### FAMOUS SCHOONER HOTEL,
*Northumberland Street*
*Listed Georgian Coaching Inn, situated only 100 yds from the beach, river and golf course. The Schooner is of 4 Crown standard (ETB), and is renowned for its superb food and its extensive selection of Real Ales.*
ACCOMMODATION £31–£40
FOOD up to £15 CLUB
**Hours:** breakfast 7:30am – 9:30am; lunch 12noon – 3pm; dinner 7pm – 11pm. **Cuisine:** English / French:- Superb English/French cuisine, and also a 'Bistro' Restaurant and conservatory. **Rooms:** 25 rooms. 3 single, 19 double/twin and 3 family rooms, all en suite. **Credit cards:** Visa, Access, Diners, AmEx. **Other points:** licensed, Sunday lunch, children catered for – please check for age limits, garden, afternoon tea, pets allowed, squash, solarium, conservatory, conferences, free house. **Directions:** next to the 9 hole village golf course. 5 miles A1, Alnwick exit.
MR ORDE, tel (0665) 830216, fax (0665) 830216.

### SADDLE HOTEL & SADDLE GRILL
### RESTAURANT, 24 Northumberland Street
*Alnmouth is a picturesque village perched above the mouth of the Aln. An attractive old building, recently refurbished and redecorated.*
ACCOMMODATION £21–£30
FOOD up to £15 ⊕
**Hours:** lunch 12noon – 2pm; dinner 6pm – 9pm. **Cuisine:** English:- Locally caught salmon, plaice, trout, cod, sole, crab, haddock. Beef Elizabeth, Northumberland sausage and chicken pancake. **Rooms:** 9 bedrooms all with telephone, TV: 4 doubles ensuite, 4 twins ensuite, 1 family room ensuite. **Credit cards:** Access, Visa, Switch. **Other points:** licensed, Sunday lunch, children catered for – please check for age limits, conferences, functions. **Directions:** on the B1338, on the main street in Alnmouth.
STAN & MARY TAIT, tel (0665) 830476.

## ALNWICK, Northumberland Map 17

### THE COTTAGE INN HOTEL, Dunstan
*Village, Craster*
*Recently modernised, the Cottage Inn is situated in the heart of the beautiful Northumbrian countryside, and just a few minutes from the sea. Craster is the ideal base for touring the wealth of nearby historic buildings which include Alnwick Castle and Wallington House. Hosts Lawrence and Shirley Jobling offer you good food, service, and an olde-world atmosphere.*
ACCOMMODATION £21–£30
FOOD up to £15 ⊕
**Hours:** breakfast 8:30am – 9:30am; lunch 12noon – 2:30pm; bar meals 12noon – 2:30pm; bar meals 6pm – 9:30pm; dinner 7pm – 9:30pm. **Cuisine:** English:- A la carte, table d'hote and extensive Bar Menu. Dishes may include, Pigeon, Escalopes of Venison and Monkfish in

filo pastry. Vegetarian dishes. **Rooms:** 10 bedrooms all with tea making facilities, telephone, TV: 8 twins ensuite, 2 doubles ensuite. **Credit cards:** Visa, Access. **Other points:** licensed, open-air dining, Sunday lunch, no-smoking area, parking, children catered for – please check for age limits, garden, bank holidays, residents' bar, disabled access, listening device, cots. **Directions:** 6 miles east of Alnwick and half a mile from Craster harbour.
LAWRENCE & SHIRLEY JOBLING, tel (0665) 576658.

### HOTSPUR HOTEL, Bondgate Without
*A former coaching house converted into a comfortable, family-run hotel. There is a choice of dining in the restaurant or in the wine and food bar. Friendly and polite service.*
ACCOMMODATION £31–£40
FOOD £15–£20
**Hours:** closed 01/01; lunch 12noon – 2pm; dinner 7pm – 9pm; closed Christmas 25/12 – 26/12. **Cuisine:** English:- Steaks, wild salmon. **Rooms:** 26 bedrooms, 23 en suite. **Credit cards:** Visa, Access, Diners, AmEx. **Other points:** licensed, Sunday lunch, children catered for – please check for age limits, pets allowed, parking, vegetarian meals. **Directions:** on B6346 just outside city wall approaching from A1.
MR D COZENS, tel (0665) 510101.

## ALTRINCHAM, Greater Manchester Map 16

### CRESTA COURT HOTEL, Church Street
*A unique combination of amenities and location make the Cresta Court a perfect base, whether travelling on business, taking a holiday break or looking for a venue for a private function. The hotel has been well furnished to offer comfort and a warm atmosphere prevails. There is a bar, 2 restaurants and a cocktail lounge bar where you can relax over a drink before you dine.*
ACCOMMODATION £21–£30
FOOD up to £15
**Hours:** breakfast 7:15am – 9:45am; bar meals 10am – 6:30pm; lunch 12noon – 2pm; dinner 6:30pm – 10:30pm. **Cuisine:** English:- 2 Restaurants: Lodge Restaurant and the Trellis Restaurant (a la carte). Bar meals in Townfields Bar. **Rooms:** 139 bedrooms all with tea making facilities, telephone, radio, TV: 114 singles ensuite, 7 twins ensuite, 11 doubles ensuite, 3 family rooms ensuite, 2 luxury twins, 2 luxury doubles. **Credit cards:** Visa, Access, Diners, AmEx. **Other points:** licensed, Sunday lunch, children catered for – please check for age limits, afternoon tea, pets allowed, conferences, functions. **Directions:** on A56 at junction of Woodlands Road. 600yds from Altrincham station.
ANTHONY BRITTON, tel (061) 927 7272, fax (061) 926 9194.

### FRANCS RESTAURANT, 2 Goose Green
*Francs Restaurant, overlooking Goose Green conservation area, offers first-class French cuisine in an informal and relaxed atmosphere which truly captures the essence of France. Furnished in typically French style, the service is friendly and efficient, making it a*

very popular choice with both tourists and local businessmen. Very highly recommended.

FOOD up to £15

**Hours:** lunch 12noon – 3pm; dinner 6pm – 10:30pm; dinner – Fri-Sat 6pm – 11pm. **Cuisine:** French. **Credit cards:** Visa, Access, Diners, AmEx. **Other points:** parking, children catered for – please check for age limits, Sunday lunch, vegetarian meals, open-air dining. **Directions:** off New Stanford Road, turn left after Barclays Bank. MR N J BANKS, tel (061) 941 3954.

---

## AMBLESIDE, Cumbria Map 19

### COMPSTON HOUSE HOTEL, Compston Road

A family run hotel, beautifully situated opposite park and fells. Ann and Graham Smith offer excellent food and friendly service in cosy surroundings. Most rooms have views of the park where you may play tennis, croquet and bowls or test your skills on the putting green. Guided fell walking, rock climbing, pony trekking and riding can be arranged. Excellent water sports nearby. Recomended by major guides.

ACCOMMODATION £21–£30

FOOD up to £15

**Hours:**  breakfast 8:30am – 9am; dinner 7pm, order by 5pm. **Cuisine:** English. **Rooms:** 8 bedrooms all with tea making facilities, TV: 6 doubles ensuite, 1 twin ensuite, 1 family room ensuite. **Other points:** central heating, children catered for – please check for age limits, lounge, patio, parking, vegetarian meals, special diets. **Directions:** leave M6, Junction 36. Follow A59O/591 bypassing Kendal and Windermere – leading straight on to the centre of Ambleside village. The hotel is situated on the corner, overlooking the park. ANN & GRAHAM SMITH, tel (05394) 32305.

### LYNDHURST HOTEL, Wansfell Road

A small, friendly family run hotel of traditional Lakeland slate, just two minutes walk from the delightful Victorian market town of Ambleside and close to the shores of Lake Windermere. Set in its own garden, it offers comfortable accommodation and imaginative, excellent home cooking, freshly prepared and cooked, and a well stocked bar. Ambleside is the centre of the Lake District and a place to visit in all seasons.

ACCOMMODATION under £20

FOOD up to £15

**Hours:** breakfast 8:45am – 9:30am; dinner 6:30pm – 7:30pm. **Cuisine:** English:- Imaginative home cooking, freshly prepared. **Rooms:** 8 bedrooms 6 doubles ensuite, 2 twins ensuite. **Other points:** parking, children catered for – please check for age limits, open bank holidays, residents' lounge, vegetarian meals. **Directions:** off M6 junction 36, northbound A591 to Ambleside. CHRIS & HELEN GREEN, tel (05394) 32421.

### THE RIVERSIDE HOTEL, Near Rothay Bridge, Upper Loughrigg

A small, family-run hotel in a peaceful riverside setting in a typical English country lane. The Haineys are Scots with a welcome to match in their classic hotel. Excellent food – booking highly recommended. A few minutes from the centre of Ambleside.

ACCOMMODATION £31–£40

FOOD £15–£20 🍵

**Hours:** breakfast 8:30am – 9:30am; dinner 7pm – 8pm. **Cuisine:** English:- A la carte and table d'hote menu – changes daily. **Rooms:** 10 bedrooms all with tea making facilities, telephone, radio, TV: 2 twins ensuite, 8 doubles ensuite. **Credit cards:** Visa, Access. **Other points:** licensed. **Directions:** from A591 take A593 to Coniston, left over Rothay Bridge then right. JIM & JEAN HAINEY, tel (05394) 32395.

---

## APPLEBY IN WESTMORELAND, Cumbria Map 19

### NEW INN, Brampton

The New Inn is in fact a very old inn built around 1730 and charmingly restored with hanging baskets which enhance its appearance. Inside, low beams, open log fires and flag stone floors take you back to a bygone era. A delightfully setting in the Vale of Eden, and an ideal stop for the tourist.

ACCOMMODATION under £20

FOOD up to £15

**Hours:** breakfast 7:30am – 9:30am; lunch 12noon – 2pm; dinner 7:30pm – 9:30pm. **Cuisine:** English:- Steaks, grills, curried nut roast, pork chops in cider, westmorland sweetbake, chocolate fudge cake. **Rooms:** 3 bedrooms all with tea making facilities, TV: 1 twin, 2 doubles. **Other points:** licensed, open-air dining, Sunday lunch, children catered for – please check for age limits, beer garden. **Directions:** from Appleby, follow signs to Brampton, 1.5 miles away. ROGER & ANNE CRANSWICK, tel (07683) 51231, fax (07683) 53130.

---

## APPLETON LE MOORS, North Yorkshire Map 18

### APPLETON HALL COUNTRY HOUSE HOTEL

A delightful country house set in attractive gardens with lovely views over the Yorkshire moors. In fine weather, afternoon teas can be enjoyed on the terrace, the quality of which earned Appleton Hall the place of 'Tea Council Finalist' in 1989. For a more substantial meal, the dining room provides a pleasant ambiance in which to enjoy the excellent cuisine.

ACCOMMODATION £21–£30

FOOD £15–£20

**Hours:** breakfast 8:30am – 9:30am; dinner 7pm – 8:30pm. **Cuisine:** English:- English cuisine, with home-made soups and puddings. **Rooms:** 10 bedrooms all with tea making facilities, telephone, radio, TV: 3 suites, 1 twin ensuite, 3 doubles ensuite, 3 singles ensuite. **Credit cards:** Visa, Access, AmEx. **Other points:** licensed, Sunday lunch, afternoon tea, pets allowed, children

catered for – please check for age limits, lift, vegetarian meals, parking, residents' lounge, residents' bar.
**Directions:** 1.75 miles from the A170. Follow signs for 'Appleton-le-Moors'.
GRAHAM & NORMA DAVIES, tel (0751) 417227, fax (0751) 417540.

## ASKRIGG, North Yorkshire Map 18

### KING'S ARMS HOTEL AND RESTAURANT, *Askrigg in Wensleydale*

*A Grade II listed coaching inn, with atmosphere and character which began life as the famous 18th century racing stable of John Pratt. The bars, once the tack and harness rooms, are familiar to many as the 'Drovers Arms' of Darrowby in the BBC TV series of James Herriot's 'All Creatures Great and Small'. Famous for good food, wine and real ales.*
*ACCOMMODATION £31–£40*
*FOOD up to £15*
**Hours:** breakfast 8:30am – 9:30am; bar meals 12noon – 2pm; bar meals 6:30pm – 9pm; dinner 7:30pm – 9pm.
**Cuisine:** English / French:- Meat, game, fresh fish and vegetarian dishes cooked to order in restaurant, grill room and bar. **Rooms:** 9 bedrooms, all en suite, 1 suite, 1 family room, colour TV, telephone, radio, tea/coffee making facilities. Four poster and half tester beds available. **Credit cards:** Visa, Access. **Other points:** licensed, open-air dining, Sunday lunch, no-smoking area, disabled access, children catered for – please check for age limits. **Directions:** 1 mile off the A684 at Bainbridge, in the market square in Askrigg.
LIZ & RAY HOPWOOD, tel (0969) 650258, fax (0969) 650635.

## AUSTWICK, North Yorkshire Map 18

### THE TRADDOCK, *Via Lancaster*

*Situated among the breathtaking scenery of the Yorkshire Dales National Park, an area of outstanding natural beauty, the Traddock offers you the perfect base for a walking or touring holiday or break. Comfortable accommodation and a high standard of home cooking are complemented by a warm welcome. Highly recommended by the Routiers inspector and well worth a visit.*
*ACCOMMODATION £21–£30*
*FOOD up to £15*
**Hours:** open all year 7:30pm; breakfast 8:30am – 9:30am; lunch 12noon – 2pm; dinner 7:30pm – 8:30pm. **Cuisine:** international.- All dishes home made and may include Chicken in Calvados Cream, Halibut with Tomato & Orange sauce, Vegetable Paella. Reasonably priced wine list. **Rooms:** 11 bedrooms all with tea making facilities, telephone, TV: 3 family rooms ensuite, 4 doubles ensuite, 3 twins ensuite, 1 single ensuite. **Credit cards:** Visa, Access. **Other points:** licensed, Sunday lunch, no-smoking area, children catered for – please check for age limits, garden, afternoon tea. **Directions:** A65. Half a mile off the main road in a very quiet situation.
FRANCES & RICHARD MICHAELIS, tel (05242) 51224.

## BAINBRIDGE, North Yorkshire Map 18

### RIVERDALE COUNTRY HOUSE HOTEL, *Bainbridge, Leyburn*

*Situated in the centre of a country village in Upper Wensleydale amongst hills and moors, Riverdale Country House is an ideal base for touring and walking. Used in the filming of James Herriot's novels.*
*ACCOMMODATION £21–£30*
*FOOD up to £15*
**Hours:** breakfast 8:30am – 9am; dinner 7:30pm; closed December – February. **Cuisine:** English. **Rooms:** 14 bedrooms 1 double, 1 twin, 5 doubles ensuite, 5 twins ensuite, 2 family rooms ensuite. **Other points:** central heating, children catered for – please check for age limits, residents' lounge. **Directions:** follow A684 to Bainbridge, hotel overlooks the green.
MRS A HARRISON, tel (0969) 50311.

## BASSENTHWAITE, Cumbria Map 19

### LAKESIDE, *Bassenthwaite Lake, Cockermouth*

*Lakeside is a small guest-house set in peaceful surroundings near the shore of Bassenthwaite Lake. The residents' lounge overlooks the Lake and has colour T.V. All bedrooms have hot and cold water and tea or coffee making facilities. A warm and friendly welcome awaits you from Eric and Joan Murray.*
*ACCOMMODATION under £20*
*FOOD up to £15*
**Hours:** breakfast 8:30am – 9am; dinner 7pm. **Cuisine:** English. **Rooms:** 8 bedrooms 3 doubles, 4 doubles ensuite, 1 single. **Other points:** parking, children catered for – please check for age limits, open bank holidays, no-smoking area, residents' lounge, vegetarian meals, garden. **Directions:** M6 to junction 40, A66 Keswick to Cockermouth, 6 miles from Keswick. Turn right at sign to Dubwath B5291, 100yds right again, 50yds on left, Lakeside.
MR E & MRS J MURRAY, tel (07687) 76358.

## BASSENTHWAITE LAKE, Cumbria Map 19

### THE PHEASANT INN, *Nr Cockermouth*

*The hotel is an excellent base from which to tour the Lake District as well as the Roman Wall and Border country, the Eden Valley and Cumbrian coast. It has all the charm and character of a typical old inn and is well known for its excellent English cooking, service and friendliness. (See colour advertisement in centre section.)*
*ACCOMMODATION £41–£50*
*FOOD £15–£20*
**Hours:** breakfast 8:30am – 9:45am; lunch 12noon – 2pm; dinner 7pm – 10:30pm; closed Christmas 25/12 – 26/12. **Cuisine:** English:- Roast meats – pheasant, venison (in season), roast duckling with orange sauce,

Silloth shrimps. **Rooms:** 20 bedrooms 1 twin ensuite, 5 singles ensuite, 14 doubles ensuite. **Credit cards:** Visa, Access. **Other points:** licensed, Sunday lunch, no-smoking area, children catered for – please check for age limits, parking. **Directions:** just off the A66, 7 miles west of Keswick.
MR W E BARRINGTON WILSON, tel (07687) 76234, fax (07687) 76002.

## BELFORD, Northumberland Map 17

### *BLUE BELL, Market Square*

*A 17th century coaching inn set in the heart of a peaceful Northumbrian village. An ideal stop-over for north/South travellers or those exploring Northumbria's wonderful beaches and historic castles.*
*ACCOMMODATION £31–£40*
*FOOD up to £15*
**Hours:** breakfast 8am – 9:30am; lunch 12noon – 2pm; dinner 7pm – 9pm. **Cuisine:** English:- Fresh local produce, eg fish. lamb and game. **Rooms:** 17 bedrooms 4 twins – shower only, 4 twins ensuite, 8 doubles ensuite, 1 single ensuite. **Credit cards:** Visa, Access, AmEx. **Other points:** open-air dining, Sunday lunch, children catered for – please check for age limits, pets allowed, coach/prior arr. **Directions:** situated on the B6349 just off the A1.
MRS J SHIRLEY, tel (0668) 213543, fax (0668) 213787.

## BELLINGHAM, Northumberland Map 17

### Newcomer of the Year
### *RIVERDALE HALL HOTEL*

*Undoubtedly one of Northumbria's most outstanding country house hotels, having been tastefully converted from a Victorian mansion. It stands in its own large grounds on the edge of the small town of Bellingham close to the beautiful Northumberland National Park. The elegantly furnished restaurant provides a warm, relaxed setting in which to enjoy a high standard of cuisine including regional specialities, complemented by well chosen wines. It is a magnet for sports and leisure enthusiasts and an ideal base from which to tour the countryside and coastline, and explore the many nearby attractions.*
*ACCOMMODATION £31–£40*
*FOOD £15–£20* 🍸
**Hours:** open all year 7pm; breakfast 7:45am – 10am; lunch 12noon – 2pm; dinner 6:45pm – 9:30pm; bar snacks 6:45pm – 9:30pm. **Cuisine:** English:- English cuisine with French influences, chicken au poivre, monkfish thermidore, poached asparagus glazed with cheese. **Rooms:** 20 bedrooms 3 singles ensuite, 12 doubles ensuite, 5 family rooms ensuite. **Credit cards:** Visa, Access, AmEx, Diners, Switch. **Other points:** parking, children catered for – please check for age limits, Sunday lunch, no-smoking area, afternoon tea, Sunday dinner, residents' lounge, residents' garden, vegetarian meals, open-air dining, pets allowed. **Directions:** situated in Bellingham on the B6320, 17 miles north of Hexham, between Hadrian's Wall and Kielder Water and Forest.
MR J COCKER, tel (0434) 220254, fax (0434) 220457.

## BERWICK-UPON-TWEED, Northumberland Map 17

### *BLACK BULL INN, Main Street, Lowick*

*A 300 year old Northumbrian pub with good local trade and excellent visitor trade in summer. Due to this pub's popularity, the proprietors, Anne & Tom Grundy, have expanded the food side of the business and can now offer larger dining room facilities where real ales are also served. Booking is advised for evenings and weekends. A cottage attached to the pub, but with independent access, provides accommodation for up to 6 people.*
*ACCOMMODATION under £20*
*FOOD up to £15*
**Hours:** lunch 12noon – 2pm; dinner 6:30pm – 9:30pm; closed Monday October – Easter. **Cuisine:** English:- Well known for home-made pies and local fish. **Rooms:** 1 bedroom with TV, self-catering rooms. **Credit cards:** Visa. **Other points:** licensed, open-air dining, Sunday lunch, children catered for – please check for age limits, coach/prior arr, disabled access. **Directions:** on B6353 between Coldstream and Holy Island.
ANNE & TOM GRUNDY, tel (0289) 88228.

### *THE CAT INN, Cheswick*

*The Cat Inn is situated on the A1, four miles south of Berwick-on-Tweed, a Border town of great architectural diversity. Offering superb en suite accommodation and beautifully cooked meals, it is surrounded by open fields and just 1 and a half miles from the sea. Close to excellent golfing and fishing facilities.*
*ACCOMMODATION under £20*
*FOOD up to £15*
**Hours:** restaurant open all day October; breakfast 9am – 11am; closed Sunday afternoon 3pm – 7pm. **Cuisine:** English. **Other points:** parking, children catered for – please check for age limits, Sunday lunch, open bank holidays, afternoon teas, Sunday dinner, disabled access, pets allowed, vegetarian meals, open-air dining. **Directions:** on the A1. 4 Miles south of Berwick-upon-Tweed.
MR W L KEITH, tel (0289) 87251, fax (0289) 87251.

## BEVERLEY, Humberside Map 18

### *THE LAIRGATE HOTEL, Lairgate*

*A delightful Georgian house in the centre of this busy market town, famous for its Minster, racecourse and Saturday market. This hotel has a relaxed, happy atmosphere with friendly, conscientious staff.*
*ACCOMMODATION under £20*
*FOOD £15–£20*
**Hours:** meals all day 7:30am – 9:30pm. **Cuisine:** English / continental:- All dishes are home-made. Fisherman's pie, steak and kidney pie, moussaka and

steaks. Flambee and fondue served in the piano bar atmosphere. **Rooms:** 24 bedrooms, 18 en suite. **Credit cards:** Visa, Access. **Other points:** Sunday lunch, no-smoking area, children catered for – please check for age limits, coach/prior arr. **Directions:** in the centre of Beverley – Lairgate runs parallel to Market Square. PETER WALSHAW, tel (0482) 882141, (0482) 861901.

## RUDSTONE WALK FARM, *South Cave, Brough*

*A beautiful 400 year old farmhouse mentioned in the Domesday Book, nestling into the foot of the Yorkshire Wolds in an area steeped in history and charm. The farm offers unrivalled views across the countryside towards nearby York, Beverley and the East Riding. Luxurious, serviced, self-contained cottages in the grounds are available for hire all year round. Convenient for the M62.*
ACCOMMODATION £21–£30
FOOD up to £15
**Hours:** breakfast 7am – 8:30am; dinner 7pm – 8:20pm. **Cuisine:** English:- Traditional home cooking. **Rooms:** 14 bedrooms all with tea making facilities, TV: 7 doubles ensuite, 7 twins ensuite. **Credit cards:** Visa, Access. **Other points:** central heating, children catered for – please check for age limits, TV lounge, garden, vegetarian meals. **Directions:** situated on the B1230, off M62. MRS PAULINE GREENWOOD, tel (0430) 422230, fax (0430) 424552.

# BILLINGHAM, Cleveland Map 17

## BILLINGHAM ARMS HOTEL, *The Causeway*

*A conveniently located, modern hotel, 5 minutes from Billingham railway station and 10 miles from Teesside Airport. Berties Restaurant is renowned for its good food and friendly service. An ideal hotel for tourists and business-people alike.*
ACCOMMODATION £31–£40
FOOD up to £15
**Hours:** breakfast 7am – 10am; lunch 12noon – 2pm; dinner 6pm – 11pm. **Cuisine:** English / continental:- eg. Croissant filled with diced chicken & bacon in a cream cheese & mushroom sauce; Strips of beef cooked at your table in a sherry & oyster sauce. **Rooms:** 69 bedrooms all with tea making facilities, telephone, TV: 17 singles ensuite, 41 doubles ensuite, 10 twins ensuite, 1 suites. **Credit cards:** Visa, Access, Diners, AmEx. **Other points:** licensed, Sunday lunch, no-smoking area, pets allowed, coach/prior arr, children catered for – please check for age limits, disabled access, residents' lounge, residents' bar, vegetarian meals. **Directions:** from A19, in town square next to Forum Sports Centre and theatre. MESSRS SNAITH & HUGHES, tel (0642) 553661, (0642) 360880, fax (0642) 552104.

# BINGLEY, West Yorkshire Map 18

## OAKWOOD HALL HOTEL, *Lady Lane*

*A family-run hotel set in a quiet woodland. The decor of the hotel is of a very high standard with furnishings of*

great taste. A relaxed place to visit, serving superb food with unusual starters and sweets.
ACCOMMODATION £31–£40
FOOD up to £15 CLUB ★
**Hours:** breakfast 7:30am – 9:30am; lunch – except Sunday 12noon – 2pm; lunch – Sunday 12:30pm – 2pm; dinner 7:30pm – 9:30pm. **Cuisine:** English:- A la carte menu, fixed 3 course menu, bar meals and bar snacks. **Rooms:** 16 rooms, some with 4 poster and half tester beds, all en suite. **Credit cards:** Visa, Access, Diners, AmEx. **Other points:** Sunday lunch, children catered for – please check for age limits, garden, pets allowed, conferences, functions. **Directions:** off A650. MRS K BRASSINGTON, tel (0274) 564123, fax (0274) 561477.

# BIRKENHEAD, Merseyside Map 16

## THE YEW TREE HOTEL, *56–58 Rock Lane West, Rock Ferry*

*Set in a quiet backwater of the River Mersey, the Yew Tree provides an atmosphere of warmth and charm. All food is freshly prepared and homecooked using vegetables from the hotel's own kitchen garden. The low black-beamed Dining Room has arches with hand cut bricks fired with 140 year old coal. Situated within easy reach of Albert Dock, Mersey Ferries and Birkenhead centre. The newly opened "Mariner's Cavern Restaurant and Bar" with sun patio adds the final touches to this popular hotel.*
ACCOMMODATION under £20
FOOD up to £15 ★
**Hours:** open all year 7:30pm; breakfast 7am – 9am; dinner 5pm – 9:30pm. **Cuisine:** modern British:- Table d'Hote and a la carte. Also vegetarians catered for. **Rooms:** 23 bedrooms all with tea making facilities, radio, TV: 6 singles, 7 singles ensuite, 3 doubles ensuite, 6 twins ensuite, 1 triple. **Credit cards:** Visa, Access, AmEx. **Other points:** children catered for – please check for age limits, parking, residents' lounge, no-smoking area. **Directions:** off New Chester Road (old A41). From Liverpool, towards Rock Ferry. RAYMOND ARNOLD & DILLY ARNOLD, tel (051) 645 4112, fax (051) 645 4112.

# BISHOP AUCKLAND, County Durham Map 17

## BISHOPS BISTRO, *17 Cockton Hill Road*

*Old converted cottages with plenty of character situated in the main street from the town centre. Personally run by the chef/proprietor, there is a restaurant and a separate bar area where diners may enjoy pre-dinner drinks. Efficient service and well cooked cuisine in an informal atmosphere.*
FOOD £15–£20
**Hours:** lunch 12noon – 1:30pm; dinner 7pm – 9pm; last orders 7pm – 9:30pm; closed Sunday – Monday. **Cuisine:** English / continental:- Dishes may include; Honey roast breast of duckling, Braised Guinea fowl,

Escalope of veal. Daily specials displayed on blackboard. Choice of vegetarian dishes. **Credit cards:** Visa, Access, Diners, AmEx. **Other points:** licensed, children catered for – please check for age limits. **Directions:** 2 minutes from the new railway station opposite the hospital.
CHARLES & KATE DAVIDSON, tel (0388) 602462.

## BLACKBURN, Lancashire Map 16

### MILLSTONE HOTEL, Church Lane, Mellor

Set in a small Lancashire village, the Millstone combines the cosy atmosphere of a traditional country inn with all the conveniences of a modern hotel. Bedrooms are very well appointed and boast fine furnishings and delightful decor. The restaurant specialises in local market produce, selected according to the season and freshly prepared for the table. Within easy reach of the remote Trough of Bowland, with Blackpool just 45 minutes away.
ACCOMMODATION £41–£50
FOOD £15–£20
**Hours:** breakfast 7am – 9:30am; lunch 12noon – 2pm; dinner 7pm – 9:45pm. **Cuisine:** English / continental. **Rooms:** 21 bedrooms all with tea making facilities, telephone, radio, TV: 6 singles ensuite, 1 twin ensuite, 12 doubles ensuite, 1 family room ensuite, 1 suite. **Credit cards:** Visa, Access, AmEx, Diners, Switch. **Other points:** children catered for – please check for age limits, parking, no-smoking area, pets, residents' lounge, vegetarian meals, residents' bar, disabled access. **Directions:** A59/A667. 10 minutes drive from Junction 31 of M6.
Tel (0254) 813333, fax (0254) 812628.

## BLACKPOOL, Lancashire Map 16

### HILL'S TUDOR ROSE HOTEL, 435–437 South Promenade

A comfortable, medium sized family hotel overlooking the sea and only a few minutes away from the Sandcastle. Friendly, personal service will ensure that your stay is as enjoyable as possible. The Lounge Bar makes a good rendezvous for a drink before dinner.
ACCOMMODATION £21–£30
**Hours:** breakfast 8:30am – 9:30am; dinner 5:30pm. **Cuisine:** English. **Rooms:** 5 single, 5 twin, 23 double and 6 family bedrooms, 17 en suite. **Credit cards:** Visa, Access, Diners, AmEx. **Other points:** children catered for – please check for age limits, snack lunches. **Directions:** on the Promenade near the south Pier.
STAN HILL, tel (0253) 42656.

### NEWLYN PRIVATE HOTEL, 31/33 Northumberland Avenue, North Shore

Friendly private hotel personally run by owners. Adjacent to Promenade and Boating Pool. Many guests return yearly to sample the good home cooking and hospitality. Comfortable accommodation with standard and ensuite rooms available.
ACCOMMODATION under £20
FOOD up to £15

**Hours:** breakfast 8:30am; dinner 5pm. **Cuisine:** English. **Rooms:** 15 bedrooms all with tea making facilities, TV: 3 singles, 7 doubles, 2 twins, 3 family rooms. **Credit cards:** Visa, Access. **Other points:** children catered for – please check for age limits, licensed, residents' lounge. **Directions:** off Queens Promenade.
MRS S HARGREAVES, tel (0253) 353230.

### NEWLYN REX HOTEL, 56–58 Central Drive

A 'typical seaside resort hotel', traditionally furnished and situated opposite Blackpool's municipal car park. There is a separate lounge and bar room with two good size dining rooms in the basement. Ideal for conference delegates being only 100 yd from main conference halls. Bookings welcomed from illumination parties. The famous Tower and Town Centre are close by.
ACCOMMODATION under £20
FOOD up to £15
**Hours:** breakfast 9am – 9:30am; bar snacks 11am – 4pm; dinner 5pm – 5:30pm. **Cuisine:** English. **Rooms:** 34 bedrooms all with tea making facilities, telephone, TV: 13 doubles ensuite, 4 family rooms ensuite, 6 singles, 2 family rooms, 7 doubles, 2 twins. **Credit cards:** Visa, Access, Diners. **Other points:** children catered for – please check for age limits, afternoon tea, pets allowed, vegetarian meals, TV lounge, special breaks. **Directions:** situated at the far end of municipal car park, corner of Hornby road.
TERENCE DOHERTY, tel (0253) 25444.

### SUNRAY, 42 Knowle Avenue, off Queens Promenade

A cheerful and comfortable guest house that has been family run for the past 21 years under the capable hands of Mrs Jean Dodgson. With all your needs catered for by this friendly and welcoming establishment, you will find The Sunray an ideal place to stay whilst in the area. It provides the facilities you would only expect from a large hotel; direct-dial telephone, TV, hair dryer and more.
ACCOMMODATION £21–£30
FOOD up to £15 ★
**Hours:** breakfast 8:30am – 9:15am; dinner 5:30pm – shows. **Cuisine:** breakfast. **Rooms:** 9 bedrooms 3 singles ensuite, 2 twins ensuite, 2 doubles ensuite, 2 family rooms ensuite. **Credit cards:** Visa, Access. **Other points:** children catered for – please check for age limits, garden, pets allowed, vegetarian meals. **Directions:** 2 miles north of Blackpool Tower, along promenade. Turn right at Uncle Toms Cabin.
JEAN & JOHN DODGSON, tel (0253) 351937.

### THE TOWN AND COUNTRY RESTAURANT, 4 Queens Square

A popular restaurant, well known in Blackpool, with a reputation for its excellent cuisine, fine wines and efficient service. All staff are dressed in black and white, the waiters wearing bow ties. The tastefully furnished interior offers a comfortable and relaxed atmosphere, having undergone extensive refurbishment. Ideal for visiting the Tower, Piers and Winter gardens.

FOOD £15–£20

**Hours:** closed Sunday. **Cuisine:** international:-
A la carte and table d'hote cuisine. Dishes may include, Scallop & Monkfish Pottage, Royal Grouse, and Crispy Roast Duckling. Excellent Wine List. Good Dessert selection. **Credit cards:** Visa, Access, Diners, AmEx. **Other points:** licensed, children catered for – please check for age limits, silver service. **Directions:** proceed past Blackpool north Pier – first turning on the right.
STEVEN LAWRENCE & CATHERINE COOKE, tel (0253) 293277.

## WHITE TOWER RESTAURANT, Balmoral Road

The White Tower Restaurant serves excellent food and wine in very pleasant, elegant surroundings. From its penthouse position, high in the exciting 'Wonderful World Building', the restaurant has splendid views overlooking the Promenade and the famous Illuminations.

FOOD up to £15

**Hours:** closed 01/01 – 31/01; meals all day 7am – 10:45pm; lunch – Sunday 12noon – 4pm. **Cuisine:** continental:- Extensive a la carte menu. Dishes may include Chateaubriand, Dover Sole. continental dishes. Excellent wine list. **Credit cards:** Visa, Access, Diners, AmEx. **Other points:** Sunday lunch, children catered for – please check for age limits, guide dogs, conferences, functions. **Directions:** M55. Yeadon Way, near Pleasure Beach/Sandcastle Centre.
BLACKPOOL PLEASURE BEACH LTD, tel (0253) 346710, (0253) 341036, fax (0253) 401098.

## BLACKTOFT, Humberside Map 18

## THE COURTYARD TEAROOMS AND RESTAURANT, South Farm Craft Gallery, Staddlethorpe Lane

A mellow brick building situated close to the Humber Estuary, where the restaurant is part of a renovated farm. Good English cuisine with a continental influence ensures that guests return time after time. Ideal location for visiting The Pottery or for exploring the peaceful scenic countryside.

FOOD up to £15

**Hours:** closed Monday & Tuesday 12noon; meals all day – Wed-Sat 10am – 10pm; meals all day Sun & hols 11am – 5pm. **Cuisine:** English:- Home-made with continental influences. **Credit cards:** Visa, Access. **Other points:** parking, children catered for – please check for age limits, Sunday lunch, open bank holidays, no-smoking, afternoon tea, disabled access, vegetarian meals, open-air dining, licensed. **Directions:** from B1230 in Gilberdyke, follow brown signs to South Farm Craft Gallery.
BREALEY, SALLY-ANN & CHRIS, tel (0430) 441889.

## BOLTON, Lancashire Map 16

## GEORGIAN HOUSE HOTEL, Manchester Road, Blackrod

This large Georgian building is decorated to a high standard and provides a very comfortable stay. Attractive meals are presented in the relaxed atmosphere of the restaurant. With its five conference suites and banqueting facilities it is ideal for either weddings or conferences. Dinner dances on Fridays and Saturdays in the Regency Restaurant.

ACCOMMODATION £31–£40

FOOD up to £15

**Hours:** breakfast 7am – 10am; bar snacks 11am – 3pm; lunch 12noon – 2pm; dinner 7pm – 10pm. **Cuisine:** English / continental:- Dishes may include Georgian House Pate, Egg and Prawn Marie Rose, Supreme of Chicken, Quenelles of Seafood. Flambe specialities on the a la carte menu. **Rooms:** 101 bedrooms all with tea making facilities, telephone, radio, TV: 26 twins ensuite, 15 singles ensuite, 49 doubles ensuite, 8 suites, 3 family rooms ensuite. **Credit cards:** Visa, Access, Diners, AmEx. **Other points:** licensed, Sunday lunch, children catered for – please check for age limits, afternoon tea, pets allowed, leisure centre. **Directions:** on the A6, 1.5 from the M61 Junction 6.
MRS DIANE NORBURY – DIRECTOR, tel (0942) 814598.

## BOLTON LE SANDS, Lancashire Map 16

## DEERSTALKER RESTAURANT, 4 Main Road

A 3 storey stone-built restaurant, decorated in olde worlde style, with many interesting pieces of railway memorabilia. The food is freshly prepared and beautifully presented – complemented by a good wine list. The service is excellent, very efficient but warm and friendly.

FOOD £15–£20 ⓒⓣ

**Hours:** lunch 12noon – 2:30pm; dinner 6:30pm – 9:30pm; closed Monday. **Cuisine:** English and continental cuisine, with dishes such as Filet mignon, Boeuf bourguignon, Tournedos Deerstalker, and Sole meuniere. **Credit cards:** Visa. **Other points:** licensed, Sunday lunch, children catered for – please check for age limits. **Directions:** exit 35 off M6, then take A6. Near garage.
MR & MRS WOODS, tel (0524) 732841.

## BOWNESS ON WINDERMERE, Cumbria Map 19

## KNOLL HOTEL, Lake Road

A large Victorian country house set in an acre of gardens and woodland, offering superb views over Lake Windermere, yet within easy reach of the shops and the bay.

ACCOMMODATION £21–£30

FOOD up to £15

**Hours:** breakfast 8:45am – 9:15am; dinner 7pm – 7:30pm. **Cuisine:** English. **Rooms:** 12 bedrooms all with

tea making facilities, telephone, TV: 3 singles, 1 single ensuite, 4 doubles ensuite, 2 twins ensuite, 2 family rooms ensuite. **Credit cards:** Visa, Access. **Other points:** children catered for – please check for age limits, garden, leisure centre. **Directions:** between Windermere Station and the pier.
MRS BERRY, tel (05394) 43756.

## BLENHEIM LODGE, Brantfell Road
*A beautiful lake land hotel overlooking Lake Windermere, Blenheim Lodge offers peace and quiet yet is close to the Lake and shops. Jacqueline Sanderson is an expert in traditional English cuisine and guests' admiration for the food has resulted in the Sandersons' own award-winning cookbook. Repeat visits vouch for the warm welcome and quality that are to be found here. Winner of Les Routiers "Accommodation of the Year" and "Casserole Award" in 1992.*
*ACCOMMODATION £31–£40*
*FOOD up to £15* 🍽
**Hours:** breakfast 8:30am – 9am; dinner 7pm. **Cuisine:** English:- English – Traditional and Victorian dishes. All home-made. Fresh home-grown produce. Extensive Vegetarian fare. **Rooms:** 11 bedrooms, all en suite.
**Credit cards:** Visa, Access, Diners, AmEx. **Other points:** licensed, no-smoking area, children catered for – please check for age limits, residents' lounge.
**Directions:** from M6 turn left off A591 to Windermere. Opposite St Martins Church.
FRANK SANDERSON, tel (05394) 43440.

## QUINN'S RESTAURANT, Royal Square
*A corner site restaurant in Royal Square, on two floors. Tastefully and simply decorated with cane furniture and pretty lakeland pictures. A friendly atmosphere is created with unobtrusive background music in which to enjoy well-cooked and well-presented cuisine.*
*FOOD £15–£20*
**Hours:** lunch 12noon – 2:30pm; dinner 6pm – 10pm; closed mid-January – mid-February. **Cuisine:** British:- Full a la carte and table d'hote menus. Sunday roasts. **Credit cards:** Visa, Access, AmEx. **Other points:** licensed, children catered for – please check for age limits. **Directions:** in Royal Square in Bowness.
MR & MRS QUINN, tel (05394) 45510.

## RASTELLI RESTAURANT & PIZZERIA, Lake Road
*A bright, airy and modern restaurant situated in the centre of Bowness. Home baked pizzas and excellent Italian cuisine make this a firm favourite with locals, tourists – and Italians alike.*
*FOOD up to £15*
**Hours:** closed 01/10 – 31/01; dinner 6pm – 10:45pm; closed Wednesday. **Cuisine:** English / continental:- Pizzas, pasta and meat dishes. **Credit cards:** Visa, Access. **Other points:** open-air dining, Sunday lunch.
**Directions:** in the shopping centre in Bowness.
MR RASTELLI, tel (05394) 44227.

## DAMSON DENE HOTEL, Crosthwaite, Lyth Valley
*Lying in the heart of the Lyth Valley in the beautiful Lake District National Park, the Damson Dene is luxury throughout. Log fires in winter, patios and three acres of landscaped gardens to enjoy in summer. Both the restaurant and bar enjoy stunning views across the fields to the fells beyond. Excellent leisure facilities including a swimming pool and squash court, and an entertainment suite with dance floor for special functions. An ideal base for touring the lakes.*
*ACCOMMODATION £41–£50*
*FOOD £15–£20*
**Hours:** breakfast 8am – 9:30am; Sunday lunch 12noon – 2pm; bar meals 12noon – 2pm; dinner 7pm – 9pm. **Cuisine:** English. **Credit cards:** Visa, Access. **Other points:** children catered for – please check for age limits, Sunday lunch, parking, no-smoking area, afternoon teas, disabled access, residents' lounge, garden, vegetarian meals, garden dining. **Directions:** exit 36 of M6 – A590, then A5074.
MR PHILIP COULSON, tel (05395) 68676, fax (05395) 68227.

# BRAMPTON, Cumbria Map 19

## ABBEY BRIDGE INN, Lanercost
*This inn is in a superb setting on the banks of the River Irthing amid the Borders and gently rolling fells. Proprietor, Philip Sayers is an authority on "real ale" and an alternative real ale is offered every week. The rooms in the hotel are attractively furnished in shades of bright pastel. The excellent cuisine attracts local and foreign tourists visiting Hadrian's Wall and the many other nearby attractions.*
*ACCOMMODATION under £20*
*FOOD £15–£20*
**Hours:** closed Christmas day; breakfast 8am – 9am; lunch 12noon – 2:30pm; dinner 7pm – 9:30pm. **Cuisine:** English:- Mainly modern English, but also includes some international flavour. **Rooms:** 7 bedrooms 1 single, 1 double, 3 doubles ensuite, 1 twin, 1 twin ensuite. **Credit cards:** Visa, Access. **Other points:** parking, children catered for – please check for age limits, no-smoking area, disabled access, pets, residents' lounge, vegetarian meals, open-air dining, garden. **Directions:** 1 mile off A69 north of Brampton.
MR P SAYERS, tel (06977) 2224.

# BRIDLINGTON, Humberside Map 18

## SEACOURT HOTEL, 76 South Marine Drive
*The Seacourt Hotel stands quietly in a prime position overlooking the beautiful south Bay, with panoramic views of the Old Harbour, town and Flamborough Head. A refurbishment project has transformed this former large Edwardian house into a delightful small hotel of distinction. Bridlington and the surrounding area offers a virtually endless combination of attractions.*

*ACCOMMODATION £21–£30*
*FOOD up to £15*
**Hours:** open all year; lunch 12noon – 2pm; dinner 6:30pm – 10pm. **Cuisine:** English:- Table d'hote and a la carte menus, with fish dishes, both sea and freshwater, a house speciality. Vegetarian meals are available. Children's menu. **Rooms:** 12 bedrooms all with tea making facilities, telephone, TV: 3 singles, 2 doubles, 3 doubles ensuite, 3 twins ensuite, 1 family room ensuite. **Credit cards:** Visa, Access. **Other points:** licensed, Sunday lunch, no-smoking area, children catered for – please check for age limits, meals all day, residents' lounge, functions. **Directions:** on South Marine Drive overlooking the bay.
ANNE & GEOFFREY HOLMES, tel (0262) 400872.

## BRIGG, Humberside Map 18

### ARTIES MILL, Wressle Road, Castlethorpe
*This charming old Windmill dates back to 1790 and the adjoining grain sheds have been converted into bars and restaurants with a pleasant and friendly atmosphere whilst still retaining the fascinating mill features. Good food, comfortable accommodation and the warm friendly welcome from the proprietors, Mr & Mrs Briggs, combines to make this hotel 'highly recommended'.*
*ACCOMMODATION £21–£30*
*FOOD up to £15*
**Hours:** breakfast 7am – 9am; bar meals 11am – 10pm; dinner 7pm – 10pm. **Cuisine:** English:- A la carte, table d'Hote, bar meals. **Rooms:** 49 bedrooms all with tea making facilities, telephone, radio, mini bar, TV: 14 twins ensuite, 2 twins, 7 doubles ensuite, 1 triple ensuite, 1 family room, 2 twins, 7 doubles ensuite, 1 family room ensuite, 14 twins ensuite. **Credit cards:** Visa, Access, Diners, AmEx. **Other points:** licensed, open-air dining, Sunday lunch, children catered for – please check for age limits, garden, functions, private dining, cots, 24hr reception, left luggage. **Directions:** 1 mile from Brigg on the A18 and 5 miles from Scunthorpe.
IAN & DOREEN BRIGGS, tel (0652) 652094, fax (0652) 657107.

### EXCHANGE COACH HOUSE INN, Bigby Street
*Dating back to the 1760s, The Exchange is a Grade II listed building, set in the centre of the bustling market town of Brigg and has been fully restored back to its former glory. Attractively furnished rooms all have their own bath and shower, and an a la carte restaurant and carvery specialises in traditional English Fare. The Gaslamp Lounge offers live traditional jazz music at weekends and there is a Cocktail Bar, Conference and Function Rooms. Conveniently located for Humberside Airport, with Hull and Lincoln just half an hour away.*
*ACCOMMODATION £21–£30*
*FOOD up to £15*
**Hours:** breakfast 7am – 9am; lunch 11am – 2pm; dinner 6pm – 11pm. **Cuisine:** English. **Credit cards:** Visa, Access, AmEx. **Other points:** children catered for –

please check for age limits, no-smoking area, disabled access, residents' lounge, garden, vegetarian meals, open-air dining, parking. **Directions:** Junction 5 off M180 and carry along on the A18.
MR J MULLEN, tel (0652) 657633, fax (0652) 657636.

## BROUGH SOWERBY, Cumbria Map 19

### THE BLACK BULL INN, Nr Kirkby Stephen
*A Country Inn where the staff are keen to make guests feel at home, the food is professionally prepared, and the steaks are served in particularly generous portions. Situated within easy reach of the Yorkshire Dales and the Lake District National Park.*
*FOOD up to £15* ♀
**Hours:** bar meals 11:30am – 2pm; bar meals 6pm – 9pm; basket meals 9pm – late. **Cuisine:** international:- Barbequed spare ribs, chicken kiev, lasagne and bar snacks. **Other points:** licensed, Sunday lunch, no-smoking area, beer garden, afternoon tea, children catered for – please check for age limits, pets allowed. **Directions:** on A685 between Brough and Kirkby Stephen in the Upper Eden valley.
MR G DUTTON, tel (07683) 41413.

## BROUGHTON IN FURNESS, Cumbria Map 19

### BESWICKS RESTAURANT, Langholme House, The Square
*A traditional Lakeland house facing the square in the village of Broughton, well-decorated and comfortably furnished. The 5 course set menu offers a good choice of English/French dishes. The tranquil and unhurried atmosphere, unobtrusive classical music and excellent service, ideally complement the high standard of cuisine with all dishes freshly cooked to order.*
*FOOD £21–£25* ♀ 🏧 CLUB ★
**Hours:** last orders 9pm – 9:30pm; dinner 7:30pm – 12midnight; generally closed Sunday – Tuesday. **Cuisine:** English / French:- 5 course table d'hote menu with regular changes. Main courses may include Rack of Lamb with Cumberland sauce, Roast Quail, and Poached Salmon Steak. **Credit cards:** Visa, Access. **Other points:** licensed, no-smoking area, children catered for – please check for age limits. **Directions:** Junction of A595 & A593, in the centre of Broughton in Furness.
CHRISTINE ROE, tel (0229) 716285.

## BURY, Greater Manchester Map 16

### THE BOLHOLT, Walshaw Road
*A large extended country house set in 50 acres of parkland and lakes. The warm and courteous hospitality, open fires and elegant surroundings make this hotel a joy to visit.*
*ACCOMMODATION £21–£30*
*FOOD up to £15*
**Hours:** breakfast 7am – 8:45am; lunch 12noon – 2pm; dinner 7pm – 9:30pm. **Cuisine:** English:- A la carte. Traditional English – Fillet Steak Wellington. **Rooms:** 48

bedrooms 1 suite, 2 singles, 28 doubles ensuite, 7 twins ensuite, 10 singles ensuite. **Credit cards:** Visa, Access, Diners, AmEx. **Other points:** licensed, Sunday lunch, children catered for – please check for age limits, garden, pets allowed. **Directions:** A58 from Bury towards Bolton, follow signs for Hington, fork left at Dusty Miller Pub. STEFAN SIKORSKI, tel (061) 764 3888, fax (061) 763 1789.

### ROSCO'S EATING HOUSE, 173 Radcliffe Road

*Owned and run by 2 chefs, the atmosphere is definitely 'foody'. The unassuming frontage hides a simple and welcoming restaurant which specialises in original dishes served in a distinctive style. The charcoal grill is placed so that everyone can see their steaks cooking. Booking advisable at weekends as Rosco's is very popular with locals & other caterers – hence the late opening.*
*FOOD up to £15* ☞

**Hours:** dinner Saturday 4:30pm – 4am; dinner Friday 6:30pm – 4am; dinner Sunday 7:30pm – 12midnight; dinner Wednesday 7:30pm – 12midnight; dinner Thursday 7:30pm – 12midnight; closed Monday; closed Tuesday. **Cuisine:** English / international:- From simple meals costing a few pounds to original dishes with imaginative sauces freshly made to order. Large selection of fresh vegetables. **Credit cards:** Visa, Access. **Other points:** Sunday lunch, limited disabled access, children catered for – please check for age limits, coach/prior arr. **Directions:** Whitfield Road from centre, right at traffic lights near Pack Horse Pub. STUART AND JACQUELINE RUSCOE, tel (061) 797 5404.

# BUTTERMERE, Cumbria Map 19

### BRIDGE HOTEL

*In a beautiful and unspoiled lakeland valley with easy access to both Buttermere Lake and Crummock Water, this hotel is set in superb unrestricted walking country with wonderful mountain scenery. The home-made food is freshly prepared daily. The comfortable, inviting lounges provide an ideal place in which to relax.*
*ACCOMMODATION £41–£50*
*FOOD £15–£20* ♀

**Hours:** open all year Tuesday; bar meals 12noon – 9:30pm. **Cuisine:** French / Cumbrian:- Traditional Cumbrian dishes and French Cuisine eg. Cumberland hot pot with black pudding, Cumbrian sausages. **Rooms:** 22 bedrooms all with private bathroom. **Other points:** Sunday lunch, children catered for – please check for age limits, pets allowed. **Directions:** on the B5289 Keswick to Buttermere Road. PETER MCGUIRE, tel (07687) 70252, (07687) 70266.

# CARLISLE, Cumbria Map 19

### ANGUS HOTEL, 14 Scotland Road

*At the Angus hotel you will find a warm welcome and an emphasis on making guests feel at home. Good home cooked food is available from our licensed restaurant, open 6 evenings per week. Fresh soup and home baked bread complement a menu which offers very good value for money. The spotlessly clean and comfortable accommodation offers tea/coffee and colour TV's in all rooms. En-suite rooms have radio alarms and hair dryers too. A friendly place to stay at very reasonable prices.*
*ACCOMMODATION under £20*
*FOOD up to £15*

**Hours:** open all year 12noon; breakfast 7:30am – 8:45am; dinner 6:30pm – 9pm. **Cuisine:** British. **Rooms:** 12 bedrooms 1 single, 1 single ensuite, 2 twins, 2 twins ensuite, 1 double, 1 double ensuite, 1 family room, 3 family rooms ensuite. **Credit cards:** Visa, Access, AmEx. **Other points:** children catered for – please check for age limits, pets allowed, vegetarian meals, residents' lounge. **Directions:** leave M6/A74 at Jct. 44. Hotel at 5th set of traffic lights. A7. ELAINE & GEOFF WEBSTER, tel (0228) 23546.

### CRAIGBURN FARMHOUSE, Catlowdy, Penton, Nr Longtown

*An 18th century working farm in a quiet rural area. Only a few miles from M6 and A7 – a perfect stopping place for north/South travellers. However, for those staying longer there is plenty to do both on the farm and locally. Finalist in national cookery competition.*
*ACCOMMODATION under £20*
*FOOD up to £15*

**Hours:** closed 01/12 – 31/12; breakfast 8am – 8:30am; lunch – Sunday 1pm; dinner 7pm, order by 5pm. **Cuisine:** English:- Traditional cooking, vegetarian. **Rooms:** 6 bedrooms all with tea making facilities: 2 twins ensuite, 2 doubles ensuite, 2 family rooms ensuite. **Other points:** central heating, children catered for – please check for age limits, residents' lounge, garden, licensed. **Directions:** situated on B6318 3 miles from the Scottish border. MRS JANE LAWSON, tel (0228) 577214.

### THE ROYAL OAK, Scotby

*A very popular public house in the attractive north Cumbrian village of Scotby. The Royal Oak has a good reputation locally for its well cooked bar meals. Welcoming staff and a friendly atmosphere. Only 3 miles from the historic city of Carlisle.*
*FOOD up to £15*

**Hours:** bar meals 12noon – 2pm; dinner – except Sunday 6pm – 8:30pm; dinner – Sunday 7pm – 8:30pm. **Cuisine:** English:- Bar meals including Goujons of Plaice, Farmhouse Grill, Cumberland Sausage, Lasagne, Mediterranean Bake, 'T'bone steak, salads and rolls. **Other points:** licensed, open-air dining, Sunday lunch, children catered for – please check for age limits, pets allowed, beer garden, bank holidays. **Directions:** 2 miles east of Carlisle on A69. Cross M6, first right to Scotby. GEOFF & LINDA MITCHELL, tel (0228) 513463.

## CARNFORTH, Lancashire Map 16

### NEW CAPERNWRAY FARM, Capernwray, Nr Lancaster

*A 17th century former farmhouse with exposed beams and stone walls. Peace and quiet, good food and elegant comfort all contribute to make this a very popular little establishment and a national prize-winner.*

ACCOMMODATION £21–£30

FOOD £15–£20

**Hours:** breakfast 8:30am; dinner 7:30pm. **Cuisine:** English. **Rooms:** 1 double & 1 twin with en suite and 1 twin with private facilities. Colour TV in all bedrooms. **Credit cards:** Visa, Access. **Other points:** central heating, children catered for – please check for age limits, residents' lounge, garden, pets allowed, vegetarian meals. **Directions:** exit 35, M6. Take B6254 to Over Kellet. Left at village green, 2m. MRS SALLY TOWNEND, tel (0524) 734284, fax (0524) 734284.

## CASTLETON, North Yorkshire Map 18

### MOORLANDS HOTEL, 55 High Street

*A 100 year old stone building with modern furnishings and walls decorated with pictures by a local artist. Good traditional cuisine and a la carte menu. Close to North Yorkshire Moors.*

ACCOMMODATION £21–£30

FOOD £15–£20

**Hours:** breakfast 8:30am – 9:30am; bar snacks 10am – 10pm; dinner 7pm – 10pm. **Cuisine:** English / international. **Credit cards:** Visa, Access. **Other points:** children catered for – please check for age limits, parking, pets, garden, vegetarian meals, open-air dining, residents' lounge, residents' bar. **Directions:** 4 miles south of A171 Whitby to Middlesboro Road. 15 miles west of Whitby, 40 miles north of York. A AND A ABRAHAMS, tel (0287) 660206.

## CHORLEY, Lancashire Map 16

### HARTWOOD HALL HOTEL, Preston Road

*Situated 1 mile from the centre of Chorley and convenient for the M6 and M61. There are facilities for conferences, private buffets, dinners, dances or wedding receptions for up to 120 people.*

ACCOMMODATION £21–£30

FOOD up to £15

**Hours:** breakfast 7:30am – 9am; lunch 12noon – 2pm; dinner 7pm – 9pm. **Cuisine:** English. Steak Diane, Trout Cleopatra, Beef Strogonoff. **Rooms:** 22 bedrooms, most en suite. **Credit cards:** Visa, Access, Diners, AmEx. **Other points:** licensed, Sunday lunch, children catered for – please check for age limits. **Directions:** 1 mile north of Chorley on the A6 Preston road. J E PILKINGTON, tel (0257) 269966, fax (0257) 241678.

### SHAW HILL HOTEL, GOLF & COUNTRY CLUB, Preston Road, Whittle le Woods

*Set in beautiful countryside midway between Chorley and Preston, Shaw Hill is a perfect venue for golf, business seminars, weddings and private functions. Vardons Restaurant is, without doubt, one of the finest a la carte dining facilities in the north west. The luxuriously furnished suites offer quiet and comfort, with magnificent views over the golf course and greens.*

ACCOMMODATION £31–£40

FOOD £15–£20

**Hours:** breakfast – weekdays 7am – 9:30am; bar meals 11am – 7pm; lunch 12noon – 2pm; dinner 7pm – 9:45pm. **Cuisine:** international:- Fillet with Woodpigeon, Venison with Blackcurrants, Pork with Savoury Scones, Veal with Truffle, Duck with Candied Vegetables. **Rooms:** 22 luxury colour co-ordinated suites, with satellite TV, direct-dial telephones, radio, trouser-press, power showers, and a well chilled mini-bar. **Credit cards:** Visa, Access, AmEx. **Other points:** licensed, Sunday lunch, children catered for – please check for age limits, pets allowed, afternoon tea, parking, residents' lounge, garden, special breaks. **Directions:** Junction 28 of M6 and follow signs for Whittle-le-Woods. Junction of A6. JS STORES & CO LTD, tel (0257) 269221, fax (0257) 261223.

## CLEETHORPES, Humberside Map 18

### AGRAH INDIAN RESTAURANT, 7–9 Seaview Street

*The Agrah Indian Restaurant is decorated with brightly coloured pictures, illustrating a story, and with Muslim style wall panels. A broad clientele, including many thespians from the seasonal summer shows.*

FOOD up to £15

**Hours:** lunch 12noon – 2:30pm; dinner 6pm – 12midnight. **Cuisine:** Indian:- Tandoori dishes. **Credit cards:** Visa, Access. **Other points:** licensed, open-air dining, Sunday lunch, children catered for – please check for age limits. **Directions:** Cleethorpes is 4 miles south of Grimsby on A46 and A16. BASHIR MIAH, tel (0472) 698669.

### STEELS CORNER HOUSE RESTAURANT, 11–13 Market Street

*A popular and friendly restaurant which continues to provide excellent value for money.*

FOOD up to £15

**Hours:** breakfast 9am – 11am; meals all day 9am – 10pm; meals all day – Saturday 9am – 11pm. **Cuisine:** English:- Fish and Chips. Grills. Business lunches. **Credit cards:** Visa, Access, Diners, AmEx. **Other points:** Sunday lunch, children catered for – please check for age limits. **Directions:** in the market place behind the Dolphin Hotel. MESSRS P & K OLIVER, tel (0472) 692644.

## CLITHEROE, Lancashire Map 16

### BAYLEY ARMS, Hurst Green, nr Whalley

*Situated in the delightful village of Hurst Green, the Bayley Arms offers warm hospitality all year round.*

Comfortable chairs, gleaming brass and welcoming log fires contribute to a relaxing, unhurried atmosphere.
ACCOMMODATION £21–£30
FOOD up to £15 ★
Hours: breakfast 8.30am – 10am; lunch 12 noon – 2pm; dinner 7pm – 9pm. Cuisine: English:- Satisfying English fare. Generous portions at affordable prices. Rooms: 8 bedrooms all with tea making facilities, TV: 2 singles ensuite, 1 twin, 3 doubles ensuite, 2 triples ensuite. Credit cards: Visa, Access. Other points: licensed, Sunday lunch, children catered for – please check for age limits, bank holidays, cots. Directions: in village of Hurst Green close to Stonyhurst College.
MR TAYLOR, tel (0254) 826478, fax (0254) 826797.

### CALF'S HEAD HOTEL, Worston
Nestling in the historic village of Worston, the hotel offers a variety of dining locations, including a beautiful walled garden with stream and rustic bridge for warm summer days. In winter, roaring fires in the a la carte dining room or intimate Tudor Room and Bar Lounge area will melt away the chill.
ACCOMMODATION £21–£30
FOOD up to £15
Hours: breakfast 7:30am – 10am; lunch 12noon – 2pm; dinner 7pm – 9:30pm. Cuisine: English:- Full a la carte menu, bar meals, Sunday 'Hot Calfery' (12 noon – 6pm). Barbeques on request. All food home-made using fresh, local produce. Rooms: 6 bedrooms all with tea making facilities, telephone, TV: 4 doubles ensuite, 1 twin ensuite, 1 single ensuite. Credit cards: Visa, Access, Diners, AmEx. Other points: open-air dining, Sunday lunch, pets allowed, children catered for – please check for age limits, weekend breaks. Directions: situated just off A59.
MR & MRS DAVIS, tel (0200) 441218, fax (0200) 441510.

### THE INN AT WHITEWELL, Forest of Bowland
A lovely riverside setting with 6 miles of salmon, sea trout and trout fishing for residents. Log fires and antique furniture create a homely atmosphere. The inn has magnificent views across the trough of Bowland and provides an ideal location for exploring the surrounding countryside on foot.
ACCOMMODATION £21–£30
FOOD up to £15 ⏎
Hours: bar open 11am – 3pm; bar open 6pm – 11pm; dinner 7:30pm – 9:15pm. Cuisine: English:- Homemade soups. Steak, kidney and mushroom pie. Local lamb. Homemade ice cream. Rooms: 9 bedrooms, all en suite. Credit cards: Visa, Access, Diners, AmEx. Other points: licensed, children catered for – please check for age limits. Directions: follow signs to Whitewell from roundabout in Longridge centre.
RICHARD & PAM BOWMAN, tel (0200) 448222.

### SPREAD EAGLE HOTEL, Sawley
Owing to its popularity it is advisable to book for Sunday lunch, Friday and Saturday dinner. Situated on a bend of the River Ribble with lovely views across the river to the surrounding countryside. An excellent base from which to tour the Dales and the Lake District.
ACCOMMODATION £41–£50
FOOD £15–£20 ★
Hours: open all year 7:30pm; lunch 12:30pm – 2pm; dinner 7pm – 9pm. Cuisine: English / continental:- All steaks – beef from Aberdeen Angus stock. Regional specialities. Rooms: 10 bedrooms all with tea making facilities, telephone, radio, TV: 2 singles ensuite, 3 doubles ensuite, 5 twins ensuite. Credit cards: Visa, Access, Diners, AmEx. Other points: licensed, Sunday lunch, children catered for – please check for age limits. Directions: off the A59, half mile down the road to Sawley Village.
THE TRUEMAN FAMILY, tel (0200) 441202, (0200) 441406, fax (0200) 441973.

## CONISTON, Cumbria Map 19

### CONISTON LODGE HOTEL, Sunny Brow
A family run hotel offering very high standards of comfort yet retaining a homely feel with country cottage-style furnishing. The dining room serves excellent home-made cuisine, presented with originality and flair. Comfortable accommodation with beautiful views. The warm welcome and good service is vouched for by the large number of repeat bookings every year.
ACCOMMODATION £31–£40
FOOD £15–£20
Hours: closed Christmas 7pm; breakfast 8:30am – 9:30am; dinner 7pm – 7:30pm. Cuisine: English:- Traditional English and local dishes such as freshly caught Coniston Char. Full Lakeland-style breakfast. Rooms: 6 bedrooms all with tea making facilities, radio, TV: 3 twins ensuite, 3 doubles ensuite. Credit cards: Visa, Access, AmEx. Other points: licensed, no-smoking area, residents' lounge, vegetarian meals. Directions: turn up hill at crossroads by filling station on A593.
ANTHONY & ELIZABETH ROBINSON, tel (05394) 41201.

## CONSETT, Northumberland Map 17

### ROYAL DERWENT HOTEL, Hole Row, Allensford
The Royal Derwent has the ambiance and style of a medieval mansion. Timber beamed bedrooms are furnished with either queen or king size beds and equipped with many modern facilities. Enjoy fine cuisine in the Cutlers Restaurant, with its crackling winter log fire, or morning and afternoon teas in the lounge. This hotel is an ideal venue for visiting Hadrian's Wall, Durham Cathedral, the north Pennines and Lake District.
ACCOMMODATION £21–£30
FOOD up to £15
Hours: breakfast 7am – 10am; lunch 12noon – 2:30pm; bar meals 12noon – 2:45pm; dinner 6:30pm – 9:45pm; bar meals 7pm – 9:45pm. Cuisine: English. Rooms: 45 bedrooms all with tea making facilities, telephone, TV: 31 twins ensuite, 11 doubles ensuite, 3 suites. Credit

cards: Visa, Access, Diners, AmEx. **Other points:** parking, children catered for – please check for age limits, no-smoking area, afternoon teas, disabled access, pets, residents' lounge, vegetarian meals, residents' bar. **Directions:** 1 mile north of Castleside.
COMPASS GROUP, tel (0207) 592000, fax (0207) 502472.

# CORNHILL ON TWEED,
Northumberland Map 17

## TILLMOUTH PARK HOTEL
*A country-house hotel set in extensive grounds, with very comfortable surroundings and food and accommodation of a high standard.*
ACCOMMODATION £41–£50
FOOD up to £15
**Hours:** breakfast 8am – 9:45am; lunch 12:30pm – 2pm; dinner 7:30pm – 9:30pm. **Cuisine:** English:- Tweed salmon, local pheasant, Cheviot lamb. **Rooms:** 14 bedrooms all with tea making facilities, telephone, radio, TV: 1 single ensuite, 6 twins ensuite, 6 doubles ensuite, 1 family room ensuite. **Credit cards:** Visa, Access, Diners, AmEx. **Other points:** Sunday lunch, children catered for – please check for age limits, pets allowed. **Directions:** on A698 Cornhill to Berwick-on-Tweed road. 3 miles from main A697.
R M DOLLERY, tel (0890) 882255, fax (0890) 882540.

# COTTINGHAM, Humberside Map 18

## MANDARIN RESTAURANT, 119 Hallgate
*A typically furnished Chinese style restaurant, offering excellent cuisine in a friendly, warm atmosphere. Conveniently located. Helpful staff assist you in making a selection so that you will be sure to enjoy your meal.*
FOOD up to £15
**Hours:** lunch 12noon – 2pm; dinner 5pm – 12midnight. **Cuisine:** oriental / vegetarian:- Peking, Cantonese and Vegetarian cuisine. Coffee Specialities. **Credit cards:** Visa, Access, Diners, AmEx. **Other points:** licensed, Sunday lunch, children catered for – please check for age limits, parking. **Directions:** situated in Cottingham village centre.
WAI LUN CHUNG, tel (0482) 843475, fax (0482) 875795.

# DARLINGTON, County Durham Map 17

## THE FOX AND HOUNDS, Neasham
*This village pub is situated on the banks of the river Tees in Neasham, 2 miles south of Darlington. With a large beer garden, family room and children's play area, this is a must for the family on the move.*
FOOD up to £15
**Hours:** bar meals 12noon – 2pm; family meals 5pm – 7pm; bar meals 7:30pm – 9:30pm; indoor bbq – weekend 7:30pm – 9:30pm. **Cuisine:** English:- Extensive bar meal menu. Daily specials. **Credit cards:** Access. **Other points:** licensed, open-air dining, Sunday lunch, no-smoking area, beer garden, children catered for – please check for age limits, conservatory. **Directions:** from the A67 or the A167 follow signs to Neasham.
MIKE ANDERSON, tel (0325) 720350.

## GEORGE HOTEL, Piercebridge
*This 17th Century Coaching Inn is set on the grassy banks of the River Tees. The restaurant offers excellent value for money dishes, complemented by a varied selection of good wines. Comfortable accommodation and friendly efficient service.*
ACCOMMODATION £21–£30
**Hours:** breakfast 7:30am – 11am; lunch 11:30am – 3pm; dinner 6:30pm – 10pm. **Cuisine:** English:- A la carte menu and bar meals. **Rooms:** 24 rooms. all en suite. **Credit cards:** Visa, Access, Diners, AmEx. **Other points:** licensed, open-air dining, Sunday lunch, children catered for – please check for age limits, garden, afternoon tea, coach/prior arr, disabled access, vegetarian meals, residents' lounge, residents' bar. **Directions:** follow A1; exit to B6275 to Piercebridge. Hotel located in village.
MR & MRS WAIN, tel (0325) 374576, fax (0325) 374577.

## HALL GARTH GOLF AND COUNTRY CLUB HOUSE, Coatham Mundeville
*This hotel offers a unique blend of style and the best of English tradition. Although dating back to 1540, the hotel has undergone a thoughtful and interesting renovation to retain the elegance of the time. It has an enviable reputation for its imaginative cuisine, luxury and service which complement the exquisite surroundings.*
ACCOMMODATION £41–£50
FOOD £15–£20
**Rooms:** 39 bedrooms 17 doubles ensuite, 4 twins ensuite, 18 singles ensuite. **Credit cards:** Visa, AmEx, Diners. **Other points:** indoor pool, leisure club, golf, gymn facilities, tennis, sauna, solarium.
MRS I FREEMAN, tel (0325) 300400, fax (0325) 310083.

## THE OLD FARMHOUSE, Mortons Plams, Middleton St George
*This delightful converted farmhouse retains its rustic charm. With comfortable furnishings and a lively atmosphere, it is a lovely setting for an enjoyable meal. Courteous, efficient service and friendly staff put the seal on a good meal out.*
**Hours:** meals all day 11am – 10pm. **Cuisine:** English:- Traditional English pub food, prepared to a high standard. Fresh. **Credit cards:** Visa, Access. **Other points:** bank holidays, children catered for – please check for age limits. **Directions:** off the main Middlesborough to Darlington road near Teeside airport.
KEN AND SUE POTTS, tel (0325) 333372.

# DONCASTER, South Yorkshire Map 18

## THE REGENT HOTEL, PARADE BAR & RESTAURANT, Regent Square
*Established under same family ownership for 50 years, this well preserved, town centre Victorian building has*

the unique advantage of being situated in a small Regency Park on the A638. Close to Doncaster racecourse and an ideal stopping place when travelling north or south.
ACCOMMODATION £31–£40
FOOD £15–£20
**Hours:** breakfast 7:30am – 9am; lunch 12noon – 2pm; dinner 6pm – 10pm. **Cuisine:** international:- Wide chioce of menus and dishes includes table d'Hote, a la carte, steak house menu, Sunday lunch, Tapas and vegetarian dishes. Giant menu. **Rooms:** 50 bedrooms, all en suite. **Credit cards:** Visa, Access, Diners, AmEx. **Other points:** licensed, Sunday lunch, children catered for – please check for age limits, coach/prior arr. **Directions:** on the main A638 road through Doncaster.
MICHAEL LONGWORTH, tel (0302) 364180.

## DOUGLAS, Isle of Man Map 19

### LA BRASSERIE, The Empress Hotel, Central Promenade
An excellent restaurant situated below the Empress Hotel, serving an extensive choice of meals throughout the day. All dishes are prepared from fresh produce, well cooked and attractively presented in generous proportions. The high quality food is complemented by a good wine list and excellent service. Enjoy your meal in comfortable surroundings with a pleasant, relaxed atmosphere.
ACCOMMODATION £31–£40
FOOD up to £15
**Hours:** open all year 6pm; meals all day 10am – 10:45pm; childrens menu available until 7:30pm. **Cuisine::**- Extensive menu featuring eg. Fresh Scallops wrapped in bacon with garlic butter, Kidney & Guiness pie, Salmon Hollandaise. Complemented by a good wine list. **Rooms:** 102 bedrooms all with tea making facilities, telephone, radio, TV: 28 singles ensuite, 17 twins ensuite, 53 doubles ensuite, 4 suites. **Credit cards:** Visa, Access, AmEx, Diners, Switch. **Other points:** children catered for – please check for age limits, open all day, no-smoking area, afternoon tea, street parking, vegetarian meals, disabled access. **Directions:** directly beneath the Empress Hotel, Douglas Promenade. Seafront.
MR JOHN TURNER, tel (0624) 661155, fax (0624) 673554.

### SEFTON HOTEL, Harris Promenade
Adjacent to the Gaiety Theatre, this hotel offers special 'Island Theatre Weekends'. Whether you wish to enjoy a play or two, or simply relax, the Sefton Hotel is ideal. Good food is served in a pleasantly relaxed atmosphere. With a health club, indoor heated swimming pool, and comfortable accommodation, this is just the place to return to after discovering the island. There are 2 bedrooms suitable for the disabled.
ACCOMMODATION £31–£40
FOOD up to £15
**Hours:** open bank holidays; breakfast 7:30am – 9:45am; bar snacks 9:45am – 11pm; lunch 12:30pm – 2pm; dinner 7:15pm – 9:30pm. **Cuisine:** modern English:- Dishes may include – mushroom crepes with sauce

mornay, grilled salmon with cucumber sauce, Manx ice cream. **Rooms:** 80 bedrooms 13 singles ensuite, 31 twins ensuite, 31 doubles ensuite, 4 family rooms ensuite, 1 suites. **Credit cards:** Visa, Access, AmEx, Diners, Switch. **Other points:** licensed, pool side bar, no-smoking area, children catered for – please check for age limits, afternoon tea, solarium, gym facilities, swimming pool, beauty therapy, sauna, coffee shop, conferences, disabled access, steam room. **Directions:** centre of Douglas Promenade. Next to the Gaiety Theatre.
CHRIS ROBERTSHAW – MANAGING DIRECTOR, tel (0624) 626011, fax (0624) 676004.

## DURHAM, County Durham Map 17

### HALLGARTH MANOR HOTEL, Pittington
Located in the small village of Pittington, this hotel is brightly yet tastefully decorated. Frequented by all ages the hotel enjoys a relaxed atmosphere. First class food and accommodation of a high standard.
ACCOMMODATION £31–£40
FOOD £21–£25 CLUB
**Hours:** breakfast 7:30am – 9:30am; lunch 12noon – 2pm; bar snacks 12noon – 2pm; bar snacks 5:30pm – 9:30pm; dinner 7pm – 9:15pm. **Cuisine:** English:- A la carte menu, table d'hote and bar snacks. **Rooms:** 23 bedrooms, all en suite. **Credit cards:** Visa, Access, Diners, AmEx. **Other points:** licensed, open-air dining, Sunday lunch, children catered for – please check for age limits, afternoon tea, pets allowed. **Directions:** 3.5 miles from Durham city centre.
ALAN DUMIGHAM & TERENCE ROBSON, tel (091) 372 1188, fax (091) 372 1249.

### KENSINGTON HALL HOTEL, Kensington Terrace, Willington, Crook
A delightful old village hall which has been tastefully converted to a hotel of a very high standard. It is widely renowned for its excellent cuisine. The Regency Function Suite is available for private hire. Good base for exploring Durham Cathedral and Beamish Museum.
ACCOMMODATION £21–£30
FOOD up to £15
**Hours:** lunch 11.30am – 2pm; dinner 7pm – 9.30pm. **Cuisine:** English. **Rooms:** 10 ensuite rooms with tea making facilities, TV, radio, alarm. **Credit cards:** Visa, Access, AmEx, Diners. **Other points:** parking, children catered for – please check for age limits, Sunday lunch, open bank holidays, Sunday dinner, disabled access, vegetarian meals. **Directions:** on A690 8 miles from Durham, 2 miles from Crook.
MR R SMEATON, tel (0388) 745071, fax (0388) 745800.

### NEVILLE'S CROSS HOTEL, Darlington Road, Neville's Cross
A small family run hotel on the outskirts of Durham with open fires which create a warm convivial atmosphere. English Tourist Board classification – 2 Crowns.
ACCOMMODATION under £20
FOOD up to £15

**Hours:** breakfast – except Sunday 8am – 9am; lunch 12noon – 2pm; bar meals 12noon – 2pm; bar meals 6:30pm – 9:30pm; dinner 7pm – 9pm. **Cuisine:** English:- Homemade steak and kidney pie, steaks grilled in red wine, veal flambe. **Rooms:** 5 bedrooms. **Credit cards:** Visa, Access, AmEx. **Other points:** Sunday lunch, children catered for – please check for age limits, pets allowed, coach/prior arr. **Directions:** on the crossroads of the A167 and A690.
MR & MRS J B HOLLAND, tel (091) 384 3872.

## RAMSIDE HALL HOTEL, *Carrville*

*A Country House type hotel set into 280 acres of farm and parkland. Choice of three eating areas and musical entertainment seven nights a week. The Ramside Hall Hotel provides an ideal venue for conferences, functions and weddings.*
*ACCOMMODATION £41–£50*
*FOOD up to £15*
**Hours:** breakfast 7:30am – 10:30am; lunch 12noon – 2pm; dinner 7pm – 9:30pm. **Cuisine:** English:- 3 eating areas – A La Carte Restaurant (fixed price), Carvery, Grill Room. **Rooms:** 82 bedrooms all with tea making facilities, telephone, radio, TV: 5 singles ensuite, 30 twins ensuite, 45 doubles ensuite, 2 suites. **Credit cards:** Visa, Access, Diners, AmEx. **Other points:** Sunday lunch, no-smoking area, children catered for – please check for age limits, coach/prior arr. **Directions:** on A690, just off the A1 motorway.
MR R J SMITH, tel (091) 386 5282, fax (091) 386 0399.

## SEVEN STARS INN, *Shincliffe Village*

*1725 coaching inn in charming village, in a conservation area one mile from Durham City. The atmosphere is very relaxed and friendly, the food is well prepared and served in generous proportions, and the accommodation is very comfortable with all major facilities, plus thoughtful extra touches. Close to Durham Cathedral, castle and museums.*
*ACCOMMODATION £21–£30*
*FOOD up to £15*
**Hours:** breakfast 8am – 9am; lunch 12noon – 2pm; bar meals 12noon – 2pm; dinner 7pm – 9pm; bar meals 7pm – 9:30pm. **Cuisine:** English:- English cuisine, with traditional roasts, home-made lasagne, pies, and steaks. **Rooms:** 8 bedrooms all with tea making facilities, telephone, radio, TV: 1 single ensuite, 6 doubles ensuite, 1 twin ensuite. **Credit cards:** Visa, AmEx, Diners. **Other points:** Sunday lunch, no-smoking area, children catered for – please check for age limits, bank holidays, residents' lounge, Hungarian spoken. **Directions:** from A1 take A177 to Bowburn, then main road into Shincliffe village.
ANDREW WINTERHALTER, tel (091) 384 8454.

## EAST AYTON, North Yorkshire Map 18

## CHURCH FARMHOUSE HOTEL AND COTTAGES, *3 Main Street*

*Listed 18th century farmhouse with many original features. Very handy for the coast, historic houses,* *Abbeys, York, Whitby, Beverley and other attractions. Mrs Chamberlain creates a homely and relaxing atmosphere. Full disabled access. 'Tourism for All' Award 1991. Y.H.T.B.*
*ACCOMMODATION £21–£30*
**Hours:** dinner from 7.30pm; breakfast 8:30am – 10am. **Cuisine:** English. **Rooms:** 1 single, 1 double, 1 twin and 2 family bedrooms, most en suite. Colour TV, tea/coffee making, hair dryer etc. ETB 3 crowns commended. Holiday cottages, ETB 5 keys commended. Twin bedrooms, central heating, all facilities very comfortable. **Other points:** central heating, children catered for – please check for age limits, residents' lounge, garden, games room, vegetarian meals. **Directions:** situated on the A170 in the north Yorks. National Park.
MRS SALLY CHAMBERLAIN, tel (0723) 862102, (0723) 865028.

## ECCLESTON, Lancashire Map 16

## THE ORIGINAL FARMERS ARMS, *Towngate*

*A country style pub with a warm, family atmosphere. Friendly staff combined with a wide choice of good food served in generous portions illustrate why the Farmers Arms enjoys such popularity. For those wishing to stay in the area, or for travellers on the M6, there are 4 comfortable bedrooms.*
*ACCOMMODATION under £20*
*FOOD up to £15* ★
**Hours:** breakfast 7am – 9am; meals all day 12noon – 10pm; dinner 5:30pm – 10pm. **Cuisine:** English / international:- Wide choice of dishes such as home made steak & kidney pie, rack of lamb and mixed grill. Plus a vast selection of home made specials which are written on blackboard. **Rooms:** 4 bedrooms all with tea making facilities, radio, TV: 2 doubles, 1 twin, 1 twin ensuite. **Credit cards:** Visa, Access. **Other points:** licensed, open-air dining, Sunday lunch, children catered for – please check for age limits, beer garden, afternoon tea. **Directions:** B5250 west of M6 near Chorley. 2 miles Charnock Richard service area M6.
BARRY S NEWTON, tel (0257) 451594, fax (0257) 453329.

## ELLAND, West Yorkshire Map 18

## BERTIES BISTRO, *7–10 Town Hall*

*All menus and wine lists are on blackboards on the walls, which change every week. Fresh produce is always used and the result is an excellent standard of well cooked and presented food.*
*FOOD up to £15* 🍽
**Hours:** dinner – Sunday 5pm – 9pm; dinner – Saturday 6:30pm – 11pm; dinner – Tues-Fri 7pm – 10:30pm; closed Monday. **Cuisine:** English / continental:- Salad of smoked turkey and quail eggs; tartlette of mushrooms, scallops and dill; griddled lamb steak with fresh basil; and Berties bombe. **Other points:** licensed, children

catered for – please check for age limits, parking.
**Directions:** Elland is 1 mile from exit 24 on the M62,
next to the Town Hall.
MR G BRETT WOODWARD, tel (0422) 371724, fax
(0422) 372830.

## ELLERBY, North Yorkshire Map 18

### THE ELLERBY HOTEL, *Hinderwell,*
### *Saltburn by the Sea*
*An attractive residential country inn situated in the*
*north Yorkshire Moors National Park in the small hamlet*
*of Ellerby. Just 1 mile from the picturesque fishing*
*village of Runswick Bay.*
ACCOMMODATION £21–£30
FOOD up to £15
**Hours:** lunch 12noon – 2pm; dinner 7pm – 10pm.
**Cuisine:** international:- An extensive range of meals
including a specials board. 9 course Chinese banquets on
specified dates. **Rooms:** 9 bedrooms, all en suite and
with colour TV, tea/coffee making facilities and
telephone. **Credit cards:** Access, Visa, Switch. **Other
points:** Sunday lunch, children catered for – please
check for age limits, coach/prior arr. **Directions:** off the
A174, 8 miles north of Whitby – take Ellerby turn off.
D R ALDERSON, tel (0947) 840342, fax (0947) 841221.

## ELLERKER, Humberside Map 18

### KINGSTONS BLACK HORSE INN, *Church*
### *Lane*
*Set in the pretty little village of Ellerker, 14 miles outside*
*Hull, the Black Horse offers excellent value for money.*
*The low lighting and an interesting use of mirrors*
*combine to give a continental feel, even if the food is*
*predominantly English. You can be sure of a warm*
*welcome in this popular and atmospheric pub.*
FOOD up to £15
**Hours:** open all year 7pm; last orders 10pm; lunch
12noon – 3pm; dinner 6:30pm – 12midnight; closed
Monday lunch; closed Tuesday lunch. **Cuisine:**
continental, with a variety of steaks, fish, chicken and
venison on offer. Dishes include Dover Sole Veronique,
Chicken a la Pernod, Fillet Steak Princess. **Other
points:** licensed, open-air dining, Sunday lunch, children
catered for – please check for age limits. **Directions:**
situated 1 mile off the A63 in Ellerker village.
BARBARA & MICHAEL KINGSTON, tel (0430)
423270.

## ENNERDALE BRIDGE, Cumbria Map 19

### THE SHEPHERD'S ARMS HOTEL
*Village centre hotel with central heating and log fires.*
*Personal service and informal atmosphere. Walking and*
*climbing. Children sharing with parents have free*
*accommodation.*
ACCOMMODATION £21–£30
FOOD up to £15
**Hours:** closed 01/01 – 08/01; dinner from 7pm, last

orders 8.30pm. **Cuisine:** English:- All home cooked
food – home smoked salmon, local game and fish.
Sunday lunch is available, but must be booked in
advance. **Rooms:** 6 bedrooms all with tea making
facilities: 2 doubles ensuite, 1 twin ensuite, 1 twin, 1
double, 1 single. **Credit cards:** Visa, Access, Diners,
AmEx. **Other points:** open-air dining, Sunday lunch,
disabled access, children catered for – please check for
age limits. **Directions:** on A66 at Cockermouth take
B5086 south. Signposted Ennerdale Bridge.
DAVID WHITFIELD BOTT, tel (0946) 861249.

## ESKDALE GREEN, Cumbria Map 19

### BOWER HOUSE INN
*An historic inn, with the ambiance of a fine old*
*Cumbrian hostelry, set in its own gardens. Good food*
*and olde worlde charm can be found here.*
ACCOMMODATION £31–£40
FOOD £15–£20
**Hours:** breakfast 7:30am – 9:30am; lunch 12noon –
2pm; bar meals 6:30pm – 9:30pm; dinner 7pm – 9pm.
**Cuisine:** French:- Freshly cooked predominantly French
cuisine including game. All dishes home prepared and
cooked. **Rooms:** 22 bedrooms, all en suite and with
direct-dial telephone, tea/coffee making facilities.
**Credit cards:** Visa, Access. **Other points:** licensed,
Sunday lunch, children catered for – please check for
age limits, pets allowed. **Directions:** turn inland at
Holmrook, from the coast road A595 for Eskdale Green.
MR & MRS CONNOR, tel (09467) 23244, fax (09467)
23308.

## FAIRBURN, North Yorkshire Map 18

### THE BAY HORSE, *Silver Street*
*The Bay Horse is near the turn-off between Ferrybridge*
*and Selby Fork, and is easily accessible from both*
*carriageways of the A1.*
FOOD up to £15
**Hours:** lunch 12noon – 2pm; dinner 7pm – 10pm.
**Cuisine:** English / continental:- Dishes may include
Noisettes of lamb, Caserole of beef and Guinness, Salmon
en croute. **Credit cards:** Visa, Access, Diners. **Other
points:** open-air dining, Sunday lunch, children catered for
– please check for age limits, functions. **Directions:** on the
A1 northbound at the Fairburn turn-off.
J M & P S PALFREYMAN, tel (0977) 607265, fax
(0977) 670553.

## FAR SAWREY, Cumbria Map 19

### THE SAWREY HOTEL, *Nr Ambleside*
*This family run country hotel provides a welcoming and*
*friendly service and excellent home cooking. Close to*
*Windermere car ferry and Hawkshead, ideally situated*
*for touring the Lake District.*
ACCOMMODATION £21–£30
FOOD £15–£20
**Hours:** lunch – except Sunday 11am – 2:30pm; lunch –
Sunday 12noon – 2:30pm; dinner 7pm – 8:45pm; closed

mid December – end December. **Cuisine:** English:-
Windermere char (in season), fresh and smoked
Esthwaite trout, home-made soups and gateaux. **Rooms:**
17 bedrooms all with tea making facilities, telephone,
TV: 1 twin, 3 singles, 7 doubles ensuite, 3 twins ensuite,
3 family rooms ensuite. **Other points:** licensed, Sunday
lunch, children catered for – please check for age limits,
vegetarian meals. **Directions:** on the B5285 road to
Hawkshead, 1 mile from Windermere car ferry.
DAVID D BRAYSHAW, tel (05394) 43425.

## FILEY, North Yorkshire Map 18

### SEAFIELD HOTEL, 9–11 Rutland Street
*A pleasant, family run guest house, conveniently situated
for the beautiful Crescent Gardens in the traditional
seaside resort of Filey. Close to the railway and bus
stations. Offering good food, comfortable
accommodation and a friendly, 'home from home'
atmosphere.*
*ACCOMMODATION under £20*
*FOOD up to £15*
**Hours:** breakfast 8:45am – 9am; dinner 6pm. **Cuisine:**
English. **Rooms:** 13 bedrooms all with tea making
facilities, TV: 1 single, 3 doubles ensuite, 1 double, 3
triples ensuite, 4 quads ensuite, 1 quad. **Credit cards:**
Visa, Access. **Other points:** children catered for –
please check for age limits, residents' lounge, special
breaks, baby-listening device, cots, left luggage.
**Directions:** Rutland Street runs off The Crescent.
JILL & DON DRISCOLL, tel (0723) 513715.

## GATESHEAD, Tyne & Wear Map 17

### BEAMISH PARK HOTEL, Beamish Burn Road, Marley Hill
*Surrounded by some of the finest north Eastern
Heritage, the Beamish Park Hotel offers a perfect blend
of food and accommodation in relaxing and comfortable
surroundings. Convenient for visiting Beamish, the
North of England Open Air Museum, The Metro Centre,
Metroland and Newcastle city centre. Perfect for an
overnight stay or family break.*
*ACCOMMODATION under £20*
*FOOD up to £15* ☕
**Hours:** breakfast 7:30am – 9:30am; lunch 12noon –
2:30pm; dinner 7pm – 10:15pm. **Cuisine:** English:-
A la carte & table d'hote. Extensive choice of blackboard
specials. Dishes include, Poached Fillet of Salmon,
Grilled Duck Breast, Roast English Lamb. Rooms: 47
bedrooms all with tea making facilities, telephone, radio,
TV: 9 singles ensuite, 14 twins ensuite, 24 doubles
ensuite. **Credit cards:** Visa, Access, Diners, AmEx. **Other
points:** licensed, Sunday lunch, children catered for –
please check for age limits, bank holidays, parking, baby
sitting, cots, 24hr reception, foreign exchange. **Directions:**
A1 to Chester le Street, then Stanley, taking A6076 to
Gateshead.
WILLIAM WALKER, tel (0207) 230666, fax (0207)
281260.

## GOATHLAND, North Yorkshire Map 18

### INN ON THE MOOR
*Rooms are comfortably furnished and service in the
restaurant is friendly, yet prompt. The Inn overlooks the
Yorkshire moors, offering the ideal opportunity to
explore the countryside. Places of interest include the
waterfalls and the Roman Road.*
*ACCOMMODATION £21–£30*
*FOOD up to £15*
**Hours:** breakfast 8:45am – 9:30am; lunch 12noon –
2pm; dinner 7pm – 8:30pm. **Cuisine:** English. **Rooms:**
24 en suite rooms, 6 four poster, 1 family suite. **Credit
cards:** Visa, Access, AmEx. **Other points:** licensed,
Sunday lunch, children catered for – please check for
age limits, pets allowed, parking. **Directions:** 9 miles
from Whitby, 14 miles from Pickering.
MALCOLM SIMPSON, tel (0947) 86296, fax (0947)
86484.

## GRANGE-OVER-SANDS, Cumbria Map 19

### ABBOT HALL, Kents Bank
*Situated in the wooded area of Kents Bank, the Abbot
Hall is run by the Methodist Guild. You can enjoy a
peaceful atmosphere, perhaps stemming from the
morning and evening devotions you may be invited to
join. Good food, comfortable accommodation and
friendly staff will help you to enjoy your stay. Mothers
can make the most of the hair salon while children enjoy
the play area.*
*ACCOMMODATION £21–£30*
*FOOD up to £15* ☕ ☕
**Hours:** breakfast 9am; lunch 12noon – 2pm; dinner
6:45pm. **Cuisine:** British:- Dishes may include – Fennel
& Almond Soup, Stilton Pate, Wild Salmon Steak,
lakeland Pork en croute, home-made puddings, north
Yorkshire Cheeses. **Rooms:** 56 bedrooms, 24 en suite.
hotel is ETB recommended. **Other points:** Sunday
lunch, no-smoking area, children catered for – please
check for age limits, afternoon tea, table-tennis, tennis,
games room, lawn bowls, putting green, croquet, tennis.
**Directions:** B5277 through Grange-Over-Sands towards
Allithwaite. Left for K.Bank.
METHODIST GUILD HOLIDAYS, tel (05395) 32896,
fax (05395) 35200.

### NETHERWOOD HOTEL, Lindale Road
*An imposing hotel enjoying a prime position overlooking
Morecambe Bay on the fringe of the Lake District.
Inside, the oak panelling and log fires provide an
atmosphere of old world luxury and comfort. In the
restaurant, dishes include Roast Rack of Venison
Caroline: Local venison roasted pink, served on a bed of
tagliatelle with wild mushrooms, and a sauce Robert.*
*ACCOMMODATION £41–£50*
*FOOD £15–£20* ☕
**Hours:** open all year 6:45pm; breakfast 8am – 10am;
lunch 12:30pm – 2pm; dinner 7:30pm – 9:30pm.

**Cuisine:** modern English:- Imaginative home-cooked dishes using local produce eg. Breast of chicken filled with Cumberland sausagemeat, apples and cranberries, wrapped in puff pastry. **Rooms:** 29 bedrooms 3 singles ensuite, 8 twins ensuite, 9 doubles ensuite, 8 family rooms ensuite, 1 suite. **Credit cards:** Visa, Access. **Other points:** Sunday lunch, children catered for – please check for age limits, swimming pool, spa-bath, sauna, beauty salon, solarium. **Directions:** 600 yd from Grange-over-Sands Railway Station.
MESSRS J D & M P FALLOWFIELD, tel (05395) 32552, fax (05395) 34121.

## GRASSINGTON, North Yorkshire Map 18

### GRASSINGTON HOUSE HOTEL, Skipton

*Built in the early 18th century and situated in the renowned cobbled square, the hotel enjoys an atmosphere of warmth and friendliness. The food is outstanding, imaginatively cooked from fresh ingredients and beautifully presented. The traditional decor of the dining room is delightful and forms an ideal setting for your meal. Well situated in the heart of the Yorkshire Dales.*
*ACCOMMODATION £31–£40*
*FOOD £15–£20*
**Hours:** breakfast 8am – 9am; bar meals 12noon – 2pm; dinner 7pm – 9:30pm; bar meals 7pm – 9:30pm. **Cuisine:** English:- Monthly changing table d'hote dinner menu eg. Guinea Fowl, Venison. **Rooms:** 10 bedrooms all with tea making facilities, TV: 2 twins ensuite, 2 singles ensuite, 6 doubles ensuite. **Credit cards:** Visa. **Other points:** licensed, children catered for – please check for age limits, pets allowed, residents' lounge. **Directions:** B6265 from Skipton or Ripon. In Grassington Square.
GORDON & LINDA ELSWORTH, tel (0756) 752406, fax (0756) 752135.

## GRIZEDALE, Cumbria Map 19

### GRIZEDALE LODGE HOTEL & RESTAURANT, Hawkshead

*Situated 2 miles south of Hawkshead on the Satterthwaite road in the heart of Grizedale Forest, midway between Coniston Water and Lake Windermere. The hotel is approached down a small country road and provides an elegant and relaxing retreat in a superb, peaceful setting. Routiers Newcomer of the Year 1986.*
*ACCOMMODATION £31–£40*
*FOOD £15–£20*
**Hours:** breakfast 8:30am – 9:15am; lunch 12:15pm – 1:45pm; dinner 7pm – 8pm; closed January – mid-February. **Cuisine:** English / French:- Cumbrian specialities such as Derwentwater duck, Grizedale venison and Lake Esthwaite trout. **Rooms:** 9 bedrooms all with telephone, TV: 2 twins ensuite, 6 doubles ensuite, 1 triple ensuite. **Credit cards:** Visa, Access. **Other points:** licensed, Sunday lunch, no-smoking area, residents' lounge, residents' bar. **Directions:** on the road to Grizedale Visitor Centre from Hawkshead.
JACK & MARGARET LAMB, tel (05394) 36532, fax (05394) 36572.

## HALIFAX, West Yorkshire Map 18

### COLLYERS HOTEL, Burnley Road, Luddendenfoot

*A former Victorian stone-built mill owners house, beautifully refurbished and overlooking the Calder Valley. Both accommodation and food are of a superb standard, the inspector remarking that it would be 'a pleasure to return'. Everything is beautifully clean, with pot pourri, plants and paintings adding to the charm of the furnishings. Friendly atmosphere.*
*ACCOMMODATION £21–£30*
*FOOD up to £15* 🍽 CLUB
**Hours:** last orders January – 9pm; breakfast – weekdays 7:30am – 9am; breakfast – weekends 8:30am – 9:30am; morning coffee 10:30am – 12noon; lunch 12noon – 2pm; bar meals 12noon – 2pm; afternoon tea 3:30pm – 5pm; dinner 7pm – 12midnight. **Cuisine:** modern English:- A la carte menu includes dishes such as pork fillet in wine and coriander, roast guinea fowl and entrecote steak. Vegetarian selection. Good wine list. **Rooms:** 10 bedrooms all with tea making facilities, telephone, radio, TV: 4 singles ensuite, 2 singles, 2 twins ensuite, 2 doubles – shower only. **Credit cards:** Visa, Access, Diners, AmEx. **Other points:** Sunday lunch, children catered for – please check for age limits, pets allowed, afternoon tea, baby sitting, baby-listening device, cots, 24hr reception, left luggage, residents' bar, residents' lounge, parking, disabled access, vegetarian meals. **Directions:** leave M62, exit 22 or 24, then to Sowerby Bridge, follow signs Burnley A646 to Luddendenfoot. Hotel on A646 in centre of village.
D F NORTHEY & N A SKELTON, tel (0422) 882624, fax (0422) 883897.

### DUKE OF YORK INN, Brighouse & Denholmegate Road, Stone Chair

*A former 17th Century coaching inn, this establishment lavishly displays pots and pans from the ceiling. Tasty meals at value for money prices and a wide range of ales, spirits and malt whiskies are offered. Friendly, efficient staff help create the relaxed atmosphere which is enjoyed by all ages.*
*ACCOMMODATION £21–£30*
*FOOD up to £15*
**Hours:** breakfast 7am – 9am; lunch 12noon – 2pm; dinner 5pm – 9pm. **Cuisine:** English:- Home cooked food, wide and varied menu. Daily specials. **Rooms:** 12 bedrooms all with tea making facilities, TV: 7 doubles ensuite, 2 twins ensuite, 1 single ensuite, 2 family rooms ensuite. **Credit cards:** Visa, Access, AmEx, Diners, Switch. **Other points:** licensed, open-air dining, Sunday lunch, children catered for – please check for age limits.

**Directions:** between Bradford and Halifax, 2 miles from M62 on main Howarth Road.
STEPHEN WHITAKER, tel (0422) 202056, fax (0422) 206618.

## IMPERIAL CROWN HOTEL,
### 42–46 Horton Street
*The Hotel is under the personal supervision of the proprietors who, together with the local staff, take every care to look after their guests' comforts and needs. Within the atmosphere of informality and friendliness, the hotel provides an excellent standard of both food and accommodation. Well situated in the heart of historic Halifax. Extensive facilities for functions.*
*ACCOMMODATION £41–£50*
*FOOD £15–£20* 🍽
**Hours:** breakfast 7am – 9am; bar snacks 5pm – 10pm; dinner 7pm – 10pm. **Cuisine:** French:- Excellent French cuisine. A la carte and table d'hote menus. **Rooms:** 40 bedrooms, all en suite. **Credit cards:** Visa, Access, Diners, AmEx. **Other points:** licensed, Sunday lunch, children catered for – please check for age limits, residents' lounge, functions, conferences. **Directions:** Junction 24, M62. Directly opposite main railway station in Halifax.
C & C H TURCZAK, tel (0422) 342342, fax (0422) 349866.

## ROCK INN HOTEL & CHURCHILL'S RESTAURANT, *Holywell Green*
*A 17th century inn set in rural surroundings, recently refurbished to include large Conservatory and Patio areas. Open all day, every day. Close to Elland and Bradley Hall Golf courses, with 'Last Of The Summer Wine' country just a few miles away. Ideal facilities for conferences and receptions, accommodating 160 people in comfort, choice of suites for smaller parties.*
*ACCOMMODATION £31–£40*
*FOOD up to £15*
**Hours:** breakfast 7am – 9am; meals all day 12noon – 10pm. **Cuisine:** English:- Steak a la Churchills and traditional Sunday lunch. **Rooms:** 18 bedrooms all with tea making facilities, telephone, radio, mini bar, TV: 14 doubles ensuite, 2 twins ensuite, 1 triple ensuite, 1 family room ensuite. **Credit cards:** Visa, Access, Diners, AmEx. **Other points:** Sunday lunch, children catered for – please check for age limits, pets allowed, vegetarian meals, residents' bar, residents' lounge, disabled access. **Directions:** situated 1.5 miles Junction 24 on the M62.
ROBERT VINSEN, tel (0422) 379121, fax (0422) 379110.

---

# HARROGATE, North Yorkshire Map 18

---

## ARDEN HOUSE HOTEL, *69–71 Franklin Road*
*A comfortable family-run hotel offering a warm and personal welcome. Situated within easy walking distance of the town centre, Valley Gardens and Royal Hall. It is tastefully decorated and noted for its high standards of traditional English cooking. A popular meeting place is the Victorian Bar where guests can relax.*
*ACCOMMODATION £21–£30*
*FOOD up to £15*
**Hours:** closed Christmas day 12noon; closed New Year's day 12noon; breakfast 8:45am – 9am; dinner 7pm. **Cuisine:** English. **Rooms:** 14 bedrooms all with tea making facilities, telephone, radio, TV: 4 singles ensuite, 4 twins ensuite, 5 doubles ensuite, 1 triple ensuite. **Credit cards:** Visa, Access. **Other points:** parking, children catered for – please check for age limits, no-smoking area, afternoon teas, pets, residents' lounge, vegetarian meals, garden, residents' bar, cots.
**Directions:** A61 Harrogate, Kings Road, Strawberry Dale avenue then turn left to Franklin Road.
MR & MRS K LYNCH, tel (0423) 509224.

## BRITANNIA LODGE HOTEL, *16 Swan Road*
*A family run hotel in a very good position for all the attractions of Harrogate. Refurbished to a high standard, the hotel provides comfortable facilities for its guests and prides itself on personal service. Weekend/Midweek breaks available at most times.*
*ACCOMMODATION £21–£30*
*FOOD up to £15*  ★
**Hours:** breakfast 7:30am – 9am; dinner 6:30pm – 8pm. **Cuisine:** English:- Full English breakfast. Evening menu consists of traditional Yorkshire home cooking. **Rooms:** 12 bedrooms all with tea making facilities, telephone, radio, TV: 4 singles ensuite, 3 twins ensuite, 4 doubles ensuite, 1 family room ensuite. **Credit cards:** Visa, Access, AmEx. **Other points:** children catered for – please check for age limits. **Directions:** close to Royal Hall, Valley Gardens and Exhibition complex.
P & E M J CULLING, tel (0423) 508482, fax (0423) 508482.

## GRUNDY'S RESTAURANT, *21 Cheltenham Crescent*
*An excellent restaurant serving first class meals in comfortable surroundings. The cuisine is predominantly Modern English and all dishes are freshly cooked to order. The outstanding food is complemented by a good wine list, excellent service and a friendly, warm atmosphere. The fixed price menu offers particularly good value for money.*
*FOOD up to £15* 🍽
**Hours:** dinner 6:30pm – 10pm; closed 2 weeks Jul/Aug; closed bank holidays; closed January 2 weeks; closed Sunday. **Cuisine:** modern English:- Menu may feature – Baked fresh salmon with white wine, cream and chive sauce, English lamb with a rosemary & Port wine sauce. Table d'hote and a la carte. **Credit cards:** Visa, Access, AmEx. **Directions:** in town centre, approx 2 mins walk from Royal Hall/Conference Centre.
VAL & CHRIS GRUNDY, tel (0423) 502610.

## THE LANGHAM HOTEL, *21–27 Valley Drive*
*Run by 3 members of the Ward family, this beautiful old hotel is in the heart of Harrogate, overlooking the*

renowned Valley Gardens. The Langham is a friendly comfortable establishment, offering good food, with the table d'hote menu of particularly good value. National parks, stately homes and golf courses nearby.
ACCOMMODATION £41–£50
FOOD £15–£20
**Hours:** dinner 7:30pm – 9:30pm. **Cuisine:** Traditional English and French cuisine. **Rooms:** 50 bedrooms, all en suite. **Credit cards:** Visa, Access, Diners, AmEx. **Other points:** licensed, Sunday lunch, children catered for – please check for age limits, bank holidays, vegetarian meals, residents' bar, residents' lounge. **Directions:** take A1; exit onto the A59 for Harrogate. Opposite Valley Gardens. THE WARD FAMILY, tel (0423) 502179.

## SHANNON COURT HOTEL, 65 Dragon Avenue
A beautiful Victorian house with character and charm, bordering on the 'Stray' in High Harrogate. This family run hotel offers its guests a warm and friendly atmosphere in pleasant surroundings and your stay would be a happy one with Tricia and Mike on hand to welcome you. Within easy driving distance of the Yorkshire Dales and North Yorkshire Moors National Park.
ACCOMMODATION £21–£30
FOOD up to £15
**Hours:** breakfast 8am – 9am; dinner 7pm. **Cuisine:** English:- Traditional. **Rooms:** 8 bedrooms all with tea making facilities, TV: 2 singles ensuite, 3 doubles ensuite, 1 twin ensuite, 2 family rooms ensuite. **Credit cards:** Visa, Access. **Other points:** children catered for – please check for age limits, residents' lounge, vegetarian meals, no-smoking. **Directions:** off the A59 Skipton road.
TRICIA & MIKE YOUNG, tel (0423) 509858, fax (0423) 530606.

## STUDLEY HOTEL, Swan Road
Attractively situated adjacent to the beautiful Valley Gardens but within easy walking distance of Harrogate town centre, the Studley Hotel has all amenities. All bedrooms have private facilities. Le Breton French Restaurant has a genuine charcoal grill and, in addition, there is a meeting room/private party room available, for up to 15 people.
ACCOMMODATION £31–£40
FOOD up to £15
**Hours:** breakfast 7:30am – 10am; lunch 12:30pm – 2pm; dinner 7pm – 10pm. **Cuisine:** international:- Extensive a la carte menu, inc. charcoal grilled steaks, fish, chicken, seafood, kebabs. Luncheon – steak and kidney pie. Bar snacks available. **Rooms:** 36 bedrooms all with tea making facilities, telephone, radio, TV: 15 singles ensuite, 11 twins ensuite, 10 doubles ensuite. **Credit cards:** Visa, Access, Diners, AmEx. **Other points:** licensed, Sunday lunch, pets/prior arr, vegetarian meals, children catered for – please check for age limits. **Directions:** adjacent to Valley Gardens.
MR G G DILASSER, tel (0423) 560425, fax (0423) 530967.

# HARTLEPOOL, Cleveland Map 17

## GRAND HOTEL, Swainson Street
A Grade II listed Victorian hotel situated in the town centre. Victoria's Lounge Bar serves popular bar food Monday to Saturday lunchtime, whilst Piper's Restaurant provides a Carvery and a la carte menus. The food is well cooked and served in generous portions. Excellent, welcoming service adds to the relaxed, friendly atmosphere of the Grand Hotel.
ACCOMMODATION £31–£40
FOOD up to £15
**Hours:** breakfast 7:30am – 9:30am; lunch 12noon – 2pm; dinner 7:30pm – 10pm; dinner – Sunday 7:30pm – 9pm. **Cuisine:** English / continental:- Carvery and a la carte menu. The specialities are steaks – Steak Diane, Surf and Hoof etc. **Rooms:** 47 bedrooms all with tea making facilities, telephone, radio, TV: 18 doubles ensuite, 14 twins ensuite, 15 singles ensuite. **Credit cards:** Visa, Access, Diners, AmEx. **Other points:** licensed, Sunday lunch, children catered for – please check for age limits, afternoon tea, pets allowed, conferences, functions, 24 hr reception, foreign exchange, residents' bar, residents' lounge, baby-listening device, cots, disabled access. **Directions:** town centre by Civic Centre and Cenotaph.
WEST HARTLEPOOL HOTELS LTD, tel (0429) 266345, fax (0429) 265217.

## KRIMO'S, 8 The Front, Seaton Carew
An outstanding restaurant with Mediterranean style decor, popular with both locals and visitors and offering a relaxed, welcoming atmosphere. The food is well cooked, well presented, and is highly recommended.
FOOD £15–£20
**Hours:** lunch 12noon – 1:30pm; dinner 7:30pm – 9:30pm; closed Monday; closed Saturday lunch; closed Sunday. **Cuisine:** Mediterranean food – steaks, fish. **Credit cards:** Visa, Access. **Other points:** licensed, children catered for – please check for age limits, street parking. **Directions:** on sea-front, off A689.
KRIMO BOUABDA, tel (0429) 266120.

# HAWKSHEAD, Cumbria Map 19

## KINGS ARMS HOTEL, The Square
Situated in the picturesque village of Hawkshead, close to Beatrix Potter's house, this 16th century pub is ideally positioned for fishing and walking. Fishing holidays arranged at no extra charge.
ACCOMMODATION £21–£30
FOOD up to £15
**Hours:** bar open 11am – 11pm; bar open – Sunday 12noon – 3pm; lunch 12noon – 2:30pm; lunch – Sunday 12noon – 2:30pm; dinner 6pm – 9:30pm; dinner – Sunday 7pm – 9:30pm. **Cuisine:** English:- Home-cooking eg. steak and kidney pie, Kings Arms chicken supreme. **Rooms:** 12 bedrooms 5 doubles, 4 doubles ensuite, 2 family rooms, 1 self-catering room. **Credit cards:** Visa, Access. **Other points:** Sunday lunch,

children catered for – please check for age limits, pets allowed. **Directions:** situated within the village of Hawkshead on B5285.
MRS R JOHNSON, tel (05394) 36372.

## HELMSLEY, North Yorkshire Map 18

### Cheeseboard of the Year
### THE FEVERSHAM ARMS HOTEL, 1 High Street

*Attractive historic coaching Inn, modernised retaining its old charm, set in the North Yorkshire Moors National Park. Accommodation includes 5 four-poster bedrooms, one suite, 6 ground floor bedrooms. Tennis court, heated outdoor swimming pool (May to October) and gardens for guests use. Golf and riding nearby.*
*ACCOMMODATION £31–£40*
*FOOD £15–£20* ☿ ☂ ☺

**Hours:** breakfast 7:30am – 10am; lunch 12noon – 3pm; last orders – lunch 2pm; dinner 6pm – 11pm; last orders – dinner 9:30pm. **Cuisine:** English / continental:- Fresh shellfish, game (in season), Spanish paella (if booked in advance). Wide range of continental dishes complemented by impressive Spanish wine list. **Rooms:** 18 bedrooms all with tea making facilities, telephone, radio, TV: 8 twins ensuite, 9 doubles ensuite, 1 suite. **Credit cards:** Visa, Access, Diners, AmEx. **Other points:** licensed, Sunday lunch, children catered for – please check for age limits, special breaks, parking, vegetarian meals, residents' bar, residents' lounge, disabled access. **Directions:** at the junction of the A170 and B1257 in Helmsley.
THE FEVERSHAM ARMS HOTEL LTD, tel (0439) 70766, fax (0439) 70346.

### PHEASANT HOTEL, Harome

*Near the North Yorkshire Moors National Park in the charming village of Harome. The hotel was originally 2 blacksmiths' cottages and a shop which have been carefully converted with spacious rooms and much character. Many of the rooms overlook the village pond.*
*ACCOMMODATION £21–£30*
*FOOD up to £15*

**Hours:** closed 01/01 – 28/02; breakfast 8:30am – 9:30am; lunch 12noon – 2pm; dinner 7:30pm – 8pm. **Cuisine:** English:- Steak & Kidney pie, fresh local meat fish and poultry. **Rooms:** 12 bedrooms 2 singles ensuite, 5 doubles ensuite, 5 twins ensuite. **Other points:** licensed, open air dining Sunday lunch, no-smoking area, indoor swimming pool. **Directions:** 3 miles from Helmsley off the A170.
MR & MRS KEN & CHRISTOPHER BINKS, tel (0439) 771241.

## HEXHAM, Northumberland Map 17

### BEAUMONT HOTEL, Beaumont Street

*A busy, family run hotel incorporating a wine bar and cocktail bar, The Park Restaurant and conference facilities. Close to the centre of this historic market town*
*in the heart of Northumbria, The Beaumont is a popular hotel with tourists and businessmen.*
*ACCOMMODATION £31–£40*
*FOOD £15–£20*

**Hours:** closed 01/01; breakfast 7:30am – 9:45am; lunch 12noon – 2pm; bar meals 12noon – 2pm; dinner 7pm – 9:45pm; closed 26/12. **Cuisine:** French:- Steaks, Pheasant, Guinea Fowl, Lamb. **Rooms:** 23 bedrooms all with tea making facilities, telephone, radio, TV: 6 singles ensuite, 5 twins ensuite, 11 doubles ensuite, 1 quad ensuite. **Credit cards:** Visa, Access, Diners, AmEx. **Other points:** licensed, Sunday lunch, children catered for – please check for age limits, lift, baby-listening device, baby sitting, cots, 24hr reception, parking, vegetarian meals, residents' bar, residents' lounge. **Directions:** on the A69 overlooking the Abbey and the park in the town centre.
MARTIN & LINDA OWEN, tel (0434) 602331, fax (0434) 602331.

### COUNTY HOTEL, Priestpopple

*A homely, privately run by real Northumbrians who understand the meaning of real hospitality. Its old fashioned atmosphere provides a warm, relaxing and comfortable retreat. Conveniently situated between train and bus stations.*
*ACCOMMODATION £21–£30*
*FOOD up to £15*

**Hours:** meals all day 7:30am – 10pm; lunch 12:05pm – 2:15pm; dinner 7pm – 9:30pm. **Cuisine:** English:- Fresh, traditional British dishes. **Rooms:** 9 bedrooms all with tea making facilities, telephone, radio, TV: 2 singles ensuite, 3 twins ensuite, 4 doubles ensuite. **Credit cards:** Visa, Access, AmEx. **Other points:** licensed, Sunday lunch, children catered for – please check for age limits, coach/prior arr, baby-listening device, baby sitting, cots, 24hr reception. **Directions:** from A69, follow signs to Hexham. Hotel is on the main street.
MR KEN WATTS, tel (0434) 602030.

### LANGLEY CASTLE HOTEL, Langley on Tyne

*Set in 10 acres of lush mowed lawns surrounded by woodland, this fascinating 14th century castle combines contemporary conveniences with the authentic reminiscent of yesteryear. The food is cooked to an extremely high standard and beautifully presented, with attention to detail. The spacious surroundings and sense of history make this a glorious setting for any visit.*
*ACCOMMODATION £41–£50*
*FOOD £15–£20* ★

**Hours:** breakfast 8am – 9:30am; lunch 12noon – 2pm; bar meals 12noon – 2pm; dinner 7pm – 9pm. **Cuisine:** French:- Imaginative menu, including daily specialities. **Rooms:** 8 bedrooms all with tea making facilities, telephone, radio, TV: 2 twins ensuite, 6 doubles ensuite. **Credit cards:** Visa, Access, Diners, AmEx. **Other points:** licensed, Sunday lunch, children catered for – please check for age limits, afternoon tea, pets allowed, residents' lounge, baby-listening device, cots.

**Directions:** follow the A69 to Haydon Bridge, then A686 1.5 miles to Langley.
MR ANTON PHILLIPS – GENERAL MANAGER, tel (0434) 688888, fax (0434) 684019.

# HOLMFIRTH, West Yorkshire Map 18

## LA GRENOUILLE, Stable Coast, Huddersfield Road

*Formerly a coaching inn, this charming French restaurant is located in the heart of the 'Summer Wine country.' Set in a comfortable, rustic and spacious setting, the restaurant has a lively and vibrant atmosphere. The cuisine is outstanding and is matched with pleasant service.*
*FOOD £15–£20*
**Hours:** lunch 12noon – 1:30pm; dinner 6:45pm – 9:30pm; closed Sunday – Monday. **Cuisine:** French country cooking, specialising in fresh fish and game, and. **Other points:** licensed, children catered for – please check for age limits, air-conditioned. **Directions:** off A6024. Just off main Hudds Road into Holmfirth. Near fire station.
CLIVE JONES, tel (0484) 687955.

# HOVINGHAM, North Yorkshire Map 18

## THE WORSLEY ARMS HOTEL, Main Street

*This attractive stone-built Georgian coaching inn is set in the historic and unspoilt village of Hovingham, near York. Having exhausted yourself exploring the numerous local landmarks, you can spend a restful evening in this spacious and peaceful hotel. The rooms are tastefully decorated and meet all the modern needs of the discerning traveller.*
*ACCOMMODATION £41–£50*
*FOOD £15–£20*
**Hours:** open all year; breakfast 7:30am – 10am; lunch 12noon – 2pm; dinner 7pm – 9:30pm. **Cuisine:** English:- Table d'hote menu offering a strong style of English cuisine. Game from the estate is a particular speciality. Wine List offers quality and variety. **Rooms:** 22 bedrooms all with radio, TV: 3 singles ensuite, 11 doubles ensuite, 8 twins ensuite. **Credit cards:** Visa, Access. **Other points:** licensed, open-air dining, Sunday lunch, no-smoking area, children catered for – please check for age limits, pets allowed, parking, residents' lounge, garden, afternoon tea. **Directions:** take A64 to Malton – then the B1257 to Hovingham.
ARNOLD SCHNEGG (MANAGER), tel (0653) 628234, fax (0653) 628130.

# HUDDERSFIELD, West Yorkshire Map 18

## ELM CREST GUEST HOUSE, 2 Queens Road

*A pleasant 1860s house with car park and attractive conservatory. The owners, Derek & Hilary Gee, prepare and cook all meals using only fresh local produce. Ideally located near town centre and other amenities.*

*ACCOMMODATION £21–£30*
*FOOD up to £15* ★
**Hours:** breakfast 7:30am – 8:30am; lunch 12noon – 2pm; dinner 7pm – 9:30pm. **Cuisine:** English:- Table d'hote menu offering a good selection of interesting dishes. Good selection of cheeses and wines. **Rooms:** 8 bedrooms all with tea making facilities, telephone, radio, TV: 2 singles ensuite, 1 single, 1 twin ensuite, 2 twins, 1 double ensuite, 1 triple ensuite. **Credit cards:** Visa, Access, AmEx, Switch. **Other points:** garden, afternoon tea, parking, left luggage. **Directions:** follow A629 ring road. Over traffic lights. Centre lane for right turn.
DEREK & HILARY GEE, tel (0484) 530990, fax (0484) 516227.

## HUDDERSFIELD HOTEL/ROSEMARY LANE BISTRO, 33–47 Kirkgate

*The hotel is made up of a bistro, formal hotel, pub, wine bar, all-day brasserie and night club all under the same roof. The Brasserie is air-conditioned and serves food from 10am, closing at 11pm, seven days a week.*
*ACCOMMODATION £21–£30*
*FOOD up to £15*
**Hours:** breakfast 7:30am – 10am; brasserie 10am – 11pm; lunch 12noon – 2pm; dinner 7pm – 11pm. **Cuisine:** English:- Grills, fish and British cooking. **Rooms:** 56 bedrooms all with tea making facilities, telephone, radio, TV: 16 singles ensuite, 20 doubles ensuite, 17 twins ensuite, 1 suites, 2 family rooms ensuite. **Credit cards:** Visa, Access, Diners, AmEx. **Other points:** licensed, children catered for – please check for age limits, coach/prior arr. **Directions:** off A62, on main ring road in town centre, opposite sports centre.
JOE MARSDEN, tel (0484) 512111, fax (0484) 435262.

## THE LODGE HOTEL, 48 Birkby Lodge Road, Birkby

*A fine Victorian gentleman's residence sympathetically restored as Huddersfield's first country house hotel and set in 2 acres of mature gardens. The 50-seater restaurant offers excellent and innovative cuisine using fresh seasonal foods, supplemented by an excellent wine list. An ideal venue for business luncheons, conferences, private functions and family Sunday lunch.*
*ACCOMMODATION £21–£30*
*FOOD £15–£20* 🍷
**Hours:** breakfast 7:30am – 9:45am; lunch 12noon – 2pm; dinner 7:30pm – 9:45pm; closed 26/12 – 28/12. **Cuisine:** modern English:- Fixed price speciality menus. Dishes to choose from include Pan Fried Venison, Sauted Pork Fillet, Ballantine of Duck. Vegetarian menu available. **Rooms:** 11 bedrooms all with tea making facilities, telephone, radio, TV: 4 singles ensuite, 3 twins ensuite, 4 doubles ensuite. **Credit cards:** Visa, Access, AmEx. **Other points:** licensed, open-air dining, Sunday lunch, no-smoking area, children catered for – please check for age limits, afternoon tea, residents' lounge, garden, parking, AA – 2 star, baby-listening device, cots,

24hr reception. **Directions:** 1 mile from Huddersfield town centre. 2 miles from M62 motorway. GARRY & KEVIN BIRLEY, tel (0484) 431001, fax (0484) 421590.

### THE WHITE HOUSE, Slaithwaite

*A 200 year old pub situated on the Lancashire-Yorkshire packhorse route, with commanding views of the local countryside. The interior has been carefully restored with original flag stone floors, wooden beams and open fires.*
*ACCOMMODATION under £20*
*FOOD up to £15*
**Hours:** breakfast 7:30am – 9am; lunch 12noon – 1:45pm; Sunday lunch 12:15pm – 1:45pm; dinner 6pm – 9:30pm. **Cuisine:** English:- Extensive menu served in the bar/restaurant with additional specialities and daily blackboard changes. **Rooms:** 8 bedrooms 4 doubles ensuite, 1 twin ensuite, 1 single ensuite, 2 doubles. **Credit cards:** Visa, Access, Diners, AmEx. **Other points:** Sunday lunch, children catered for – please check for age limits, pets/prior arr. **Directions:** off B6107. Turn off A62 in Slaithwaite village. MRS GILLIAN SWIFT, tel (0484) 842245.

## HULL, Humberside Map 18

### KINGSTOWN HOTEL, Hull Road, Hedon

*A family-run hotel with very high standards and a friendly atmosphere. Good food excellently served in the restaurant and bar. Ideally situated for the continental Ferry, the coastal resorts of Holdferness, the historic towns of Hedon and Beverley, and the important city of Hull.*
*ACCOMMODATION £31–£40*
*FOOD £15–£20* ★
**Hours:** breakfast 7am – 9:30am; lunch 12noon – 2:30pm; dinner 7pm – 10pm. **Cuisine:** English:- A la carte and table d'hote menus served in the restaurant and lounge bar. **Rooms:** 34 bedrooms all with tea making facilities, telephone, radio, TV: 10 singles ensuite, 4 twins ensuite, 20 doubles ensuite. **Credit cards:** Visa, Access, AmEx. **Other points:** licensed, Sunday lunch, no-smoking area, children catered for – please check for age limits, guide dogs, residents' lounge, conferences, baby sitting, cots, 24hr reception, left luggage. **Directions:** on Eastern outskirts of Hull, opposite continental Ferry Terminal. PETER READ, tel (0482) 890461, fax (0482) 890713.

### PEARSON PARK HOTEL, Pearson Park

*Situated within a public ornamental park, one mile north of the city centre. Very popular with families and businessmen. The establishment has been under the same ownership for the last 27 years.*
*ACCOMMODATION £31–£40*
*FOOD up to £15*
**Hours:** breakfast 7:30am – 9:15am; lunch 12:30pm – 2pm; dinner 6:30pm – 9pm. **Cuisine:** French / English:- Daily specials, fresh local produce. **Rooms:** 59

bedrooms all with tea making facilities, telephone, radio, TV: 10 singles ensuite, 17 doubles ensuite, 9 singles ensuite, 16 doubles ensuite, 6 twins ensuite, 1 family room ensuite. **Credit cards:** Visa, Access, Diners, AmEx. **Other points:** Sunday lunch, children catered for – please check for age limits, cots, 24hr reception, parking, residents' bar, residents' lounge, disabled access. **Directions:** take A1079 Bevereley Road from city centre. Pearson avenue on left. MR & MRS D A ATKINSON, tel (0482) 43043.

## ILKLEY, West Yorkshire Map 18

### COW & CALF HOTEL, Ilkley Moor

*A country house on Ilkley Moor adjacent to the Cow and Calf rocks, from which it takes its name. All bedrooms are fully en suite and offer a high standard of comfort, and the well cooked food is served lunchtime and evening. The restaurant has unrivalled views of Wharfedale and the moors, immortalised by the song 'On Ilkley Moor Bahtat', are a mere 20 yd walk away.*
*ACCOMMODATION £31–£40*
*FOOD up to £15* ★
**Hours:** breakfast 7:30am – 9:30am; lunch 12noon – 2pm; dinner 7:15pm – 9:30pm; closed Christmas 25/12. **Cuisine:** modern English:- A la carte menu in Panorama restaurant, eg. Panorama pate, chicken Panorama (chicken in chef's orange and tarragon sauce). Fish available also. **Rooms:** 17 bedrooms all en suite, including 1 family room, 5 executive rooms, 1 4-poster. **Credit cards:** Visa, Access, Diners, AmEx. **Other points:** Sunday lunch, children catered for – please check for age limits, parking, residents' bar, residents' lounge. **Directions:** located one mile off A65. Follow signs for Cow & Calf Rocks. THE NORFOLK FAMILY, tel (0943) 607335, fax (0943) 816022.

## KEIGHLEY, West Yorkshire Map 18

### OLD WHITE LION HOTEL, West Lane, Haworth

*An old inn at the centre of this famous village on the A629 and close to the M62 motorway. A convenient location for visitors to the Bronte Museum, parsonage and Worth Valley Steam Railway.*
*ACCOMMODATION £21–£30*
*FOOD up to £15*
**Hours:** breakfast 7am – 9am; lunch 11:30am – 2:30pm; dinner 6:30pm – 9:30pm. **Cuisine:** English & international:- Dover sole, boeuf à l Americaine, seafood pie and game in season. **Rooms:** 14 bedrooms all with tea making facilities, telephone, radio, TV: 2 singles ensuite, 1 twin ensuite, 9 doubles ensuite, 2 family rooms ensuite. **Credit cards:** Visa, Access, Diners, AmEx. **Other points:** Sunday lunch, children catered for – please check for age limits, coach/prior arr. **Directions:** off M62 take A629 through Halifax and turn off before Keighley. MR KEITH BRADFORD, tel (0535) 642313, fax (0535) 646222.

## KENDAL, Cumbria Map 19

### FINKLES RESTAURANT, Yard 34, Finkle Street
*A 300 year old building occupying one of Kendal's famous labyrinthine 'yards' behind the main street. A variety of dishes are served by friendly, efficient staff. Seating now available for up to 130 people.*
FOOD up to £15
**Hours:** meals all day 9:30am – 9:30pm; closed Sunday. **Cuisine:** continental:- Crepes, pizzas, Gateaux. **Other points:** pets allowed, coach/prior arr, children catered for – please check for age limits, afternoon tea. **Directions:** behind the main street in Kendal.
MR & MRS STANWORTH, tel (0539) 727325.

### THE KENDAL ARMS HOTEL, 72 Milnthorpe Road
*A listed building of around 150 years old, serving wholesome good pub food in pleasant surroundings. It is a typical town style pub, very popular with locals and business people working nearby. Ideal location from which to tour and explore all other Lakeland amenities.*
ACCOMMODATION under £20
FOOD up to £15
**Hours:** breakfast 7am – 10:30am; meals all day 11am – 9:30pm. **Cuisine:** English:- Good pub food, including quality Steaks, with good wine list. **Rooms:** 8 bedrooms, all en suite, with colour TV, radio, and tea/coffee making facilities. large function/meeting room available. **Credit cards:** Visa, Access. **Other points:** licensed, open-air dining, Sunday lunch, children catered for – please

check for age limits, pets allowed, residents' lounge, garden, parking, afternoon tea. **Directions:** close to the town centre, on the main road into Kendal.
GEORGE WARDMAN, tel (0539) 720956, fax (0772) 722470.

## KESWICK, Cumbria Map 19

### ALLERDALE HOUSE, 1 Eskin Street
*Quiet location only 5 minutes walk from the town centre off AmblesideRoad, and only 15 minutes stroll from the lake side. David & Ellen Stephenson have built up a reputation for their good food and hospitality with people returning time after time. Advanced booking recommended. Off street parking for 6 cars.*
**Hours:** open all year 11am; breakfast 8:30am – 9am; dinner 6:30pm. **Cuisine:** breakfast. **Rooms:** 3 double and 3 family bedrooms, all en suite. 1 separate WC. TV, radio, hair dryer and telephone in all rooms. **Credit cards:** Visa, Access. **Other points:** central heating, children catered for – please check for age limits, residents' lounge, garden. **Directions:** A66 or A591 to Keswick, 5 minutes walk from town centre.
DAVID & ELLEN STEPHENSON, tel (07687) 73891.

### CHAUCER HOUSE HOTEL, Ambleside Road
*Quietly situated in Keswick on the old Ambleside Road by the parish church and away from the bustle of everyday traffic. This family-owned and managed hotel near Lake Derwentwater is based on attentive and friendly service without undue formality. Relax in the bright, comfortable lounge bars, furnished with*

*craftsman-built local stone fireplaces and lakeland scenes by local artists. All bedrooms have full en suite facilities for maximum comfort. A beautiful place in a beautiful setting for people of all ages.*
**Hours:** breakfast 8:15am – 9am; dinner 6:30pm – 9pm; bar snacks all day, to order. **Cuisine:** English. **Other points:** parking, children catered for – please check for age limits, open bank holidays, no-smoking area, Sunday dinner, disabled access, residents' lounge, pets allowed. **Directions:** Ambleside Road, opposite St John's church. MR K AND MRS J PECHARTSCHECK, tel (07687) 72318, (07687) 73223.

## HIGHFIELD HOTEL, *The Heads*
*Friendly, family-run hotel with superb views of Derwentwater and the mountains. The hotel is opposite the miniature golf course, on a quiet road only minutes from the lake and Market Square. Bread baked on the premises and fresh produce used in all dishes.*
*ACCOMMODATION £21–£30*
*FOOD up to £15*
**Hours:** breakfast 8:30am – 9:15am; dinner 6:30pm – 7:30pm, order by 6pm; closed November – March. **Cuisine:** British. **Rooms:** 19 bedrooms 4 singles, 1 single ensuite, 7 doubles ensuite, 4 twins ensuite, 3 family rooms ensuite. **Other points:** central heating, children catered for – please check for age limits, residents' lounge, garden. **Directions:** A66 to Keswick, second entry to Keswick via roundabout, left at T junction, next right signed "Borrowdale", second right after petrol station. MR & MRS R M JORDAN, tel (07687) 72508.

## IVY HOUSE HOTEL, *Braithwaite*
*Once a 17th century yeoman farmer's house, this beautiful oak-beamed building is tucked away in the corner of a typical Cumbrian village. The restaurant offers an interesting and imaginative menu and both the proprietors and staff pride themselves in offering a warm welcome and personal service.*
*ACCOMMODATION £41–£50*
*FOOD up to £15*
**Hours:** closed 01/01 – 31/01; breakfast 8:30am – 9am; dinner 7pm – 7:30pm. **Cuisine:** modern English:- Chicken stuffed with mango served with a creamy saffron sauce, Salmon with ginger & sultanas, Haunch of venison with port wine and redcurrant sauce. **Rooms:** 12 bedrooms, all en suite. **Credit cards:** Visa, Access, Diners, AmEx. **Other points:** licensed, no-smoking area, pets/prior arr. **Directions:** NW from Keswick on A66. Braithwaite signposted after 2 miles. NICK & WENDY SHILL, tel (07687) 78338.

## KITCHINS BISTRO, *18–20 Lake Road*
*This friendly, family run bistro and cellar bar is as equally popular with the locals as it is with travellers and tourists. The first class cuisine is predominantly traditional English with distinct French overtones, and is complemented by a superb wine list. Nearby visitor attractions include the beautiful Lake District and Keswick Motor Museum.*
*FOOD up to £15* CLUB
**Hours:** closed Christmas day; lunch 11:30am – 2pm;

dinner 4pm – 9:30pm. **Cuisine:** modern English & English / French:- Dishes include Cumberland sausage with apple sauce, Chicken Kiev, Steaks, Thai style vegetables, Nut roast salad with Cumberland sauce. **Credit cards:** Visa, Access. **Other points:** children catered for – please check for age limits, parking, Sunday lunch, Sunday dinner, disabled access, vegetarian meals, open-air dining. **Directions:** from the A66 take the A591 to Keswick. Located in the town centre. GEOFREY KITCHIN, tel (07687) 72990.

## QUEENS HOTEL, *Main Street*
*An old coaching inn, originally the posting house. The town is on the busy A66 to the north of the Lakes. The hay loft and stables have been converted to provide a cosy bar known as Ye Olde Queens Head.*
*ACCOMMODATION £21–£30*
*FOOD up to £15*
**Hours:** breakfast 8am – 9:30am; lunch 10am – 5pm; bar meals 12noon – 9pm; dinner 6:30pm – 9pm. **Cuisine:** English:- Traditional British dishes. **Rooms:** 36 bedrooms 9 singles ensuite, 5 twins ensuite, 13 doubles ensuite, 9 family rooms ensuite. **Credit cards:** Visa, Access, Diners, AmEx. **Other points:** licensed, Sunday lunch, children catered for – please check for age limits, coach/prior arr. **Directions:** in the market square in Keswick. Off the A66. PETER JAMES WILLIAMS, tel (07687) 73333, fax (07687) 71144.

## SPRINGS FARM, *Springs Road*
*Large 19th century house with views of Walla Crag and Lake Derwentwater. Meals are prepared and cooked on the premises and the menus feature traditional British dishes. This is a working dairy farm with a small flock of sheep. For the children there is also a garden with swings and banana slide.*
*ACCOMMODATION under £20*
*FOOD up to £15*
**Hours:** closed November – March. **Cuisine:** British. **Rooms:** 5 bedrooms 2 singles, 2 doubles, 1 family room. **Other points:** children catered for – please check for age limits, residents' lounge, garden. **Directions:** A66 or A591 to Keswick. MRS ANNIE HUTTON, tel (07687) 72144.

# KIRBY LONSDALE, Cumbria Map 19
## THE COPPER KETTLE, *3–5 Market Street*
*A 16th century building on the main street of this busy market town. Mr Chubb is a member of the Societe Gastronomique Francaise, evident in the excellent meals produced. Kirkby Lonsdale is a charming market town, and a good base for touring the Lakes and the Yorkshire Dales.*
*ACCOMMODATION under £20*
*FOOD up to £15*
**Hours:** meals all day 12noon – 9pm. **Cuisine:** English:- Roasts, steaks and dishes cooked in wine. **Rooms:** 4 bedrooms all with TV and tea/coffee making facilities. **Credit cards:** Visa, Access, Diners, AmEx. **Other**

points: licensed, Sunday lunch, children catered for – please check for age limits. **Directions:** From M6 junction 36, follow signs to Kirkby Lonsdale, Market St on left.
MR & MRS GAMBLE, tel (05242) 71714.

### THE SUN HOTEL, *Market Street*

*A 17th century Coaching House in the delightful market town of Kirkby Lonsdale. The atmosphere is that of a small, friendly country pub yet The Sun Hotel combines 'olde wordle' charm with modern comforts. Comfortable accommodation, friendly service, good home-made food and value for money prices will be found here.*
*ACCOMMODATION under £20*
*FOOD up to £15*
**Hours:** open all year 12noon; lunch 11am – 2pm; dinner 6pm – 10pm. **Cuisine:** English:- Dishes include home-made soups, steak & Kidney pie, pizza. There are 3 or 4 daily specials in addition. **Rooms:** 9 bedrooms, 5 en suite. **Credit cards:** Visa, Access, Diners. **Other points:** licensed, Sunday lunch, children catered for – please check for age limits, residents' lounge. **Directions:** Situated in the centre of Kirkby Lonsdale.
ANDREW WILKINSON, tel (05242) 71965, fax (05242) 72489.

# KIRKBYMOORSIDE, North Yorkshire

Map 18

### THE GEORGE & DRAGON, *17 Market Place*

*Situated in the ancient cobbled market square of Kirkbymoorside, the George & Dragon has provided travellers with hospitality perfected over centuries. Full of olde worlde charm and antiquity, this delightful hotel dating from the 13th century combines comfort, service and excellent cuisine with true Yorkshire tradition. An ideal centre for holiday and business guests. Private functions and weddings can also be catered for.*
*ACCOMMODATION £21–£30*
*FOOD up to £15*
**Hours:** breakfast 7:30am – 9:30am; lunch 12noon – 2pm; bar snacks 12noon – 2pm; bar snacks 6:30pm – 9:30pm; dinner 7pm – 9:15pm. **Cuisine:** English. **Credit cards:** Visa, Access. **Other points:** parking, children catered for – please check for age limits, no-smoking area, pets allowed, residents' lounge, vegetarian meals, open-air dining, garden. **Directions:** situated in the Town Centre, just off the A170 between Thirsk and Scarborough.
STEPHEN COLLING, tel (0751) 31637, fax (0751) 33334.

# LANCASTER, Lancashire Map 16

### SPRINGFIELD HOUSE HOTEL & RESTAURANT, *Wheel Lane, Pilling*

*A Georgian country house hotel set in extensive, attractive grounds with walled gardens and pools. The two dining rooms, The Corless Room and Miss Ciceleys,*

*are sympathetically decorated in keeping with the 1840s style of building. Very well-cooked and presented meals offering outstanding value for money are served in a relaxed atmosphere by polite, efficient staff.*
*ACCOMMODATION £21–£30*
*FOOD £15–£20* 🍽
**Hours:** lunch 12noon – 2pm; dinner 7pm – 9pm. **Cuisine:** international:- Monthly changing table d'hote menu may include Trout Dundee (in a whisky & orange sauce), duckling, steak, chicken Maryland and medallions Carribean. **Rooms:** 7 bedrooms, all en suite and with full facilities. Some four poster beds. Midweek break speciality. **Credit cards:** Visa, Access. **Other points;** licensed, Sunday lunch, children catered for – please check for age limits, pets allowed, afternoon tea, residents' lounge, garden, functions. **Directions:** off A588 Blackpool – Lancaster road, to the west of Pilling village.
GORDON & ELIZABETH COOKSON, tel (0253) 790301, fax (0253) 790907.

# LEEDS, West Yorkshire Map 18

### AVALON GUEST HOUSE, *132 Woodsley Road*

*A Victorian family house situated close to the University. Comfortable and well maintained, the Avalon Guest House has a homely atmosphere. Popular with business travellers and visitors to the University.*
*ACCOMMODATION £21–£30*
**Hours:** breakfast 7:30am – 8:45am. **Cuisine:** breakfast. **Rooms:** 10 bedrooms all with tea making facilities, TV: 2 singles, 2 singles ensuite, 2 twins, 1 twin ensuite, 1 double, 1 double ensuite, 1 family room ensuite. **Credit cards:** Visa, Diners. **Other points:** garden, pets allowed, cots, baby sitting, disabled access, central heating. **Directions:** half a mile from the city centre in the University area.
ELIZABETH DEARDEN, tel (0532) 432848, (0532) 432545, fax (0532) 420649.

### THE BUTLERS HOTEL, *Cardigan Road, Headingley*

*Overlooking Headingley Cricket Ground and only 2 minutes from the City centre, this hotel offers excellent, luxurious accommodation and a friendly, welcoming atmosphere. The superbly appointed licensed restaurant provides a wide choice of well-cooked dishes such as Entrecote au Paivie and Chicken Chasseur. An elegant, comfortable and welcoming place to stay.*
*ACCOMMODATION £31–£40*
*FOOD up to £15* ★
**Hours:** breakfast 7:30am – 9am; lunch 12noon – 2pm; bar meals 12noon – 12midnight; dinner 7pm – 9pm. **Cuisine:** English / French. **Rooms:** 8 bedrooms all with tea making facilities, telephone, radio, TV: 3 singles ensuite, 3 twins ensuite, 1 double ensuite, 1 quad ensuite. **Credit cards:** Visa, Access, Diners, AmEx. **Other points:** children catered for – please check for age limits, pets allowed, residents' lounge, afternoon tea,

special breaks, vegetarian meals, baby-listening device, cots, 24hr reception, conferences, weekend breaks, residents' lounge, parking. **Directions:** link road between A65 Skipton & A660 Otley Road. Next to Headingley cricket ground.
DAVID HARRY BUTLER, tel (0532) 744755, fax (0532) 744755.

## OLIVE TREE GREEK RESTAURANT,
### Oaklands, Rodley Lane, Rodley
*The regional food from Corfu, Cyprus, Salonica and Athens is finely judged; the tastes are intense, balanced and true. The technical expertise and skills have elevated Greek cooking, not highly regarded by everyone, to dizzy heights. The explosion of these flavours, textures, colours and tastes have come to prominence and fruition. King Constantine of the Hellenes has tasted the Olive Tree's cuisine. George and his wife Vasoulla have appeared on numerous T.V. programmes most notably the BBC 2's 'Food and Drink'.*
*FOOD £15–£20*
**Hours:** lunch 12noon – 2:30pm; dinner 6:30pm – 11:30pm; closed Saturday lunch. **Cuisine:** Greek:- Choice of special meze including vegetarian and seafood, blackboard specials, home-made Greek pastries. **Credit cards:** Visa, Access, AmEx. **Other points:** licensed, Sunday lunch, children catered for – please check for age limits. **Directions:** by Rodley roundabout on the Leeds ring road.
GEORGE & VASOULLA PSARIAS, tel (0532) 569283.

## PINEWOOD PRIVATE HOTEL,
### 8 Potternewton Lane
*Set in a quiet residential area, the Pinewood offers a very good standard of cooking and accommodation. All food is cooked and prepared by the proprietors themselves using fresh ingredients. Traditional standards of comfort and cleanliness are maintained at all times.*
*ACCOMMODATION £41–£50*
*FOOD up to £15* ★
**Hours:** breakfast 7:30am – 8:30am; meals – prior arrangement 2pm – 7pm; dinner – Friday 7pm – 10:30pm; dinner – Saturday 7pm – 10:30pm; dinner – weekdays 8pm – 10:30pm. **Cuisine:** modern English:- Chimes Restaurant, offering a la carte and table d'hote menus. Calves liver in Madeira, rack of lamb with mustard & nut crust, wild mushrooms in basil sauce on a herb crouton. **Rooms:** 10 bedrooms all with tea making facilities, radio, TV: 4 singles ensuite, 2 twins ensuite, 2 doubles ensuite, 1 family room ensuite, 1 triple ensuite. **Credit cards:** Visa, Access. **Other points:** licensed, weekend breaks, children catered for – please check for age limits, residents' lounge, garden, vegetarian meals, street parking, cots, left luggage. **Directions:** leave Leeds on A61 to Harrogate, approx 2 miles from centre on dual carriageway. Turn right at first roundabout, 600yds on left.
CHARLES MICHAEL & WENDY STUBLEY, tel (0532) 622561, fax (0532) 622561.

## LEEMING BAR, North Yorkshire Map 18

## MOTEL LEEMING, Great North Road, Bedale
*Motel Leeming has easy access to both carriageways of the A1 and is open and serving meals 24 hours a day.*
*ACCOMMODATION £21–£30*
*FOOD up to £15* ★
**Hours:** open 24 hours. **Cuisine:** English:- Farmhouse platter, cheese fritters, traditional Sunday lunch, fresh fish dishes. Award-winning cheeseboard. Only fresh produce from local suppliers is used. **Rooms:** 40 bedrooms 18 doubles ensuite, 8 twins ensuite, 10 singles ensuite, 4 family rooms ensuite. **Credit cards:** Visa, Access, Diners, AmEx. **Other points:** Sunday lunch, children catered for – please check for age limits. **Directions:** take A1; exit at the A684. Bedale sits on the A1/A684 junction.
CARL LES, tel (0677) 422122, (0677) 423611, fax (0677) 424507.

## LITTLE DRIFFIELD, Humberside Map 18

## DOWNE ARMS
*A delightful 16th century public house and restaurant opposite the village green in Little Driffield. Separate lunch and dinner menus offer an extensive choice of excellently cooked dishes. The high standard of food is complemented by the comfortable, attractive decor, first class service and a warm and friendly atmosphere. Highly recommended whether for lunch for dinner.*
*FOOD up to £15*
**Hours:** lunch 12noon – 2pm; dinner 7pm – 9:30pm; Sunday dinner bookings only. **Cuisine:** English:- A la carte menu, table d'hote and bar meals. Dishes include Beef Wellington, Rack of Lamb, Tangy Chicken, Scampi a la creme, Duck a l'orange. Traditional Sunday lunch. **Credit cards:** Visa, Access. **Other points:** licensed, open-air dining, Sunday lunch, children catered for – please check for age limits. **Directions:** turning on right, 1 mile before Driffield on A166 from York.
STUART WOOD, tel (0377) 252243.

## LIVERPOOL, Merseyside Map 16

## MAYFLOWER RESTAURANT, 48 Duke Street
*A large, modern Chinese restaurant with a warm and relaxed atmosphere. The restaurant serves Pekingese, Cantonese and Schezuan dishes including crispy fragrant duck served with pancakes. As the restaurant is open until 4am, it is ideal for anyone looking for a peaceful restaurant in which to enjoy good food, but outside the more usual opening hours.*
*FOOD up to £15*
**Hours:** meals all day 12noon – 4am. **Cuisine:** pekingese / Cantonese:- Peking and Cantonese cuisine, with vegetarian and seafood specialities. **Credit cards:** Visa, Access, AmEx, Diners, Switch. **Other points:** licensed, children catered for – please check for age limits, air-

conditioned, parking, disabled access. **Directions:** 2 minutes from main shopping area. Near Pier Head and Albert Dock.
MR SIM, tel (051) 709 6339.

## LONG PRESTON, North Yorkshire Map 18

### MAYPOLE INN, Nr Skipton

*17th century village inn situated on the Maypole Green in the Yorkshire Dales National Park. Interesting selection of real ales in cosy bars with open fires, and a restaurant with a good local following, serving generous portions of home cooked food. Close to Malham, the Settle/Carlisle railway and the starting point for many beautiful walks. Easy drive to the Lake District and Forest of Bowland.*
*ACCOMMODATION under £20*
*FOOD up to £15*
**Hours:** lunch – weekdays 12noon – 2pm; dinner – Sunday 5pm – 9pm; dinner – Saturday 5:30pm – 9:30pm; dinner – weekdays 6:30pm – 9pm; closed Christmas. **Cuisine:** English:- Traditional home cooking. Beef in ale pie, braised shoulder of lamb, trout, Yorkshire ham and eggs, 20oz rump or vegetarian selection. **Rooms:** 6 bedrooms: 3 doubles ensuite, 1 single ensuite, 2 family rooms ensuite. **Credit cards:** Visa, Access, Diners, AmEx. **Other points:** licensed, Sunday lunch, children catered for – please check for age limits, coach/prior arr, residents' lounge.
**Directions:** on the A65 between Settle and Skipton.
ROBERT & ELSPETH PALMER, tel (0729) 840219.

## LONGRIDGE, Lancashire Map 16

### CORPORATION ARMS, Lower Road, Nr Preston

*Situated in the wilds of Lancashire on the borders of the Fell country, this pub provides a warm and friendly welcome to its customers. The food and service are excellent, making it highly recommended.*
*FOOD up to £15*
**Hours:** lunch 12:15pm – 2pm; dinner 7pm – 9:30pm; closed Christmas 25/12. **Cuisine:** English:- Eg. Pan Fried Chicken, Beef Strogonoff, home-made Steak, Kidney & Mushroom Pie, Stuffed Mushrooms, Hot Chocolate Fudge Cake, Hot Sticky Toffee Pudding. **Credit cards:** Visa, Access, Diners, AmEx. **Other points:** Sunday lunch & evening. **Directions:** on the B6245 Longridge–Blackburn road, half mile from Longridge Centre.
MR A GORNALL, tel (0772) 782644.

## LONGTOWN, Cumbria Map 19

### THE SPORTSMAN'S RESTAURANT, MARCH BANK, Scotsdyke

*The 'Last Hotel in England' is an old country house with beautiful views over the River Esk. Personally run by the Moore family, you are assured a warm welcome and excellent service in both the hotel and restaurant. The food is of a very high standard yet offers excellent value for money. Highly recommended. Private Fishing for residents. A Routiers Casserole award winner for 3 years running.*
*ACCOMMODATION £21–£30*
*FOOD up to £15*
**Hours:** breakfast 8am – 9am; lunch 12noon – 2pm; dinner 6pm – 9pm. **Cuisine:** British:- Specialities include Locally Smoked Salmon, Whole Roast Leg of Lamb (for 4 persons at 24 hours notice), Scotch steaks, Game. **Rooms:** 4 bedrooms all with tea making facilities, TV: 3 doubles ensuite, 1 single. **Credit cards:** Visa, Access, Diners, AmEx. **Other points:** licensed, Sunday lunch, no-smoking area, children catered for – please check for age limits, fishing. **Directions:** 3 miles north of Longtown on the A7. 9 miles M6, Junction 44.
THE MOORE FAMILY, tel (0228) 791325.

## LYTHAM ST ANNES, Lancashire Map 16

### BEDFORD HOTEL, 307–311 Clifton Drive South

*Exclusive family-run hotel, with a reputation for comfort and cuisine. Situated 200 yd from shops, beach and swimming pool with 4 golf courses nearby. Other places of nearby interest include Blackpool, Liverpool Docks, Wigan Pier and the Lake District which are all easily accessible, as the motorway is 10 mins away.*
*ACCOMMODATION £31–£40*
*FOOD up to £15*
**Hours:** breakfast 7:30am – 9:30am; lunch 12noon – 5pm; dinner 6:30pm – 8:30pm. **Cuisine:** English / continental. **Rooms:** 36 bedrooms, all en suite. **Credit cards:** Visa, Access. **Other points:** licensed, Sunday lunch, no-smoking area, children catered for – please check for age limits, pets allowed, leisure centre.
**Directions:** off M6 to M55. Turn off at Junction 4, then left, following signs.
J P & T BAKER, tel (0253) 724636, fax (0253) 729244.

### CHADWICK HOTEL & LEISURE COMPLEX, South Promenade

*A modern, family-run hotel commanding lovely sea views. Spacious lounges overlook the seafront and indoor Leisure Pool. Other facilities include a spa-bath, Turkish room, sauna and solarium. The Clipper Restaurant serves generous portions of very good food and the bedrooms are comfortable and well-furnished.*
*ACCOMMODATION £21–£30*
*FOOD up to £15*
**Hours:** open all year 6:30pm; breakfast 7:30am – 10am; bar meals 12noon – 2pm; lunch 1pm – 2pm; dinner 7pm – 8:30pm. **Cuisine:** English:- Traditional English cooking, local seafood specialities. 24 hour menu. **Rooms:** 72 bedrooms all with tea making facilities, telephone, radio, TV: 11 singles ensuite, 31 twins ensuite, 10 doubles ensuite, 12 triples ensuite, 8 quads ensuite. **Credit cards:** Visa, Access, Diners, AmEx. **Other points:** Sunday lunch, children catered for – please check for age limits, baby-listening device, baby

sitting, cots, 24hr reception, foreign exchange, 24hr room-service, parking, vegetarian meals, residents' lounge, residents' bar, disabled access. **Directions:** off the M6 to M55, take Junction 4. Turn left following signposts.
MR CORBETT, tel (0253) 720061, fax (0253) 714455.

## THE LINDUM HOTEL, 65/76 South Promenade

*Open all year round, the Lindum Hotel has 80 bedrooms, all with private bath, and modern facilities. Lounge entertainment and children's parties are held regularly throughout the season. The food is all home-cooked and offers good value for money.*
ACCOMMODATION £21–£30
FOOD up to £15  ★
**Hours:** breakfast 8:30am – 9:15am; bar meals 12noon – 2pm; lunch – Sunday 12:45pm – 1:45pm; dinner 6pm – 7pm. **Cuisine:** English:- Dishes include Sardines with Saffron Rice, Roast beef and Yorkshire Pudding, Poached Salmon with Cucumber Sauce, Sticky Toffee Pudding. **Rooms:** 80 bedrooms, all en suite. **Credit cards:** Visa, Access, AmEx. **Other points:** licensed, Sunday lunch, children catered for – please check for age limits, pets allowed, sauna, solarium, Jacuzzi, night porter. **Directions:** near St Annes Pier, on the seafront.
LINDUM HOTEL LTD, tel (0253) 721534.

## FERNLEA HOTEL & LEISURE COMPLEX, 15 South Promenade

*Situated on St Annes' south Promenade, the Fernlea is a large comfortable family run hotel, with lots of fun things to do. They serve well prepared, generous portions of food and the accommodation is of a high standard.*
ACCOMMODATION £41–£50
FOOD £15–£20
**Hours:** breakfast 8am – 9:30am; lunch 12:30pm – 1:30pm; dinner 7pm – 8:30pm. **Cuisine:** English:- Fixed price 4 course menu and bar snacks at lunchtime.
**Rooms:** 110 bedrooms all with tea making facilities, telephone, TV: 19 singles ensuite, 2 suites, 30 twins ensuite, 15 doubles ensuite, 44 family rooms ensuite.
**Credit cards:** Visa, Access, Diners, AmEx. **Other points:** licensed, Sunday lunch, children catered for – please check for age limits, pets allowed, swimming pool, gym facilities, solarium, squash, aerobics, sauna.
**Directions:** 5 miles from Blackpool. Close to the Pier.
TONY P CROSTON, tel (0253) 726726.

## MALTON, North Yorkshire Map 18

## CORNUCOPIA, 87 Commercial Street, Norton

*Set in the heart of the horseracing capital of the north, the restaurant is appropriately adorned with horseracing memorabilia. The menu is extensive and innovative with a wine list to suite most palates. An award winning pub and a finalist in the Steak and Kidney Pie competition.*
FOOD up to £15  ☜

**Hours:** lunch 12noon – 2pm; dinner 6:30pm – 10pm.
**Cuisine:** English:- Halibut, salmon & prawn mornay, boned duckling, traditional Sunday lunch. Braised beef simmered in ale & herb dumplings, pork casserole & apple fritters. **Credit cards:** Visa, Access. **Other points:** licensed, open-air dining, Sunday lunch, children catered for – please check for age limits, beer garden.
**Directions:** off the A64 in the centre of Norton.
HAROLD ST QUINTON, tel (0653) 693456.

## KINGS HEAD HOTEL, 5 Market Place

*A delightful welcome awaits you when you visit this establishment. Serving good food at value for money prices, in a down to earth, homely and relaxing atmosphere.*
FOOD up to £15  CLUB  ★
**Hours:** bar snacks 11am – 2:30pm; lunch 12noon – 2pm; dinner 7pm – 9:30pm; bar snacks 7pm – 9:30pm; last orders 9pm. **Cuisine::-** Menu feature Wensleydale mushrooms, Yorkshire Puddings in onion gravy, a large range of traditional home made dishes together with steaks and grills. **Credit cards:** Visa, Access, Diners, AmEx. **Other points:** Sunday lunch, children catered for – please check for age limits, parking. **Directions:** located at top of market place.
CHRISTOPHER BARLOW, tel (0653) 692289.

## THE MOUNT HOTEL, Yorkersgate

*An attractive hotel with a fascinating interior in the form of over 700 jugs and a collection of racing memorabilia, Malton being a racehorse breeding centre. Very popular with local racing folk who gather in the old fashioned mahogany bar to enjoy the excellent home cooking. Ideal location for touring the North Yorkshire Moors and visiting Castle Howard and Eden Camp.*
ACCOMMODATION £21–£30
FOOD up to £15
**Hours:** lunch 12noon – 2pm; dinner 7pm – 9pm.
**Cuisine::-** Home cooked country fare at value for money prices. **Rooms:** 12 bedrooms: 4 singles, 2 twins, 1 double, 2 doubles ensuite, 3 family rooms ensuite.
**Credit cards:** Visa, Access. **Other points:** street parking, children catered for – please check for age limits, no-smoking area, afternoon tea, open all day, disabled access, vegetarian meals, air-conditioned, residents' garden. **Directions:** off the A64 York to Scarborough Road. First hotel on left in Malton.
MR GIBSON, tel (0653) 692608, fax (0653) 692608.

## MANCHESTER, Greater Manchester Map 16

## CRESCENT GATE HOTEL, Park Crescent, Victoria Park

*The Crescent Gate is situated in Victoria Park, one of the pleasant park estates to be found near to the city centre. Set in a quiet tree-lined avenue, the hotel is an ideal place to wind down after a long journey or a hard day's work.*
ACCOMMODATION £21–£30
FOOD up to £15
**Hours:** breakfast 7:30am – 9am; bar meals 12noon – 2pm; bar meals 6:30pm – 10:30pm; dinner 7pm – 8pm.

**Cuisine:** English. **Rooms:** 26 bedrooms all with tea making facilities, telephone, radio, TV: 13 singles ensuite, 8 singles, 2 twins ensuite, 2 doubles ensuite, 1 triple ensuite. **Credit cards:** Visa, Access, Diners, AmEx. **Other points:** licensed, no-smoking area, children catered for – please check for age limits, pets allowed, bank holidays, afternoon tea, baby-listening device, cots, foreign exchange, parking, vegetarian meals, residents' bar, residents' lounge. **Directions:** B5166, to city for 4 miles. Park Crescent third right after Platt Fields Park.
TERRY HUGHES, tel (061) 224 0672, fax (061) 257 2822.

## ELM GRANGE HOTEL, 561 Wilmslow Road, Withington

*A family run commercial hotel situated approximately 20 minutes drive from the City centre, Exhibition centre and the Airport. In a main road position with a good bus service to the main shopping area it is easily located by following the signposts to Christie Hospital which is opposite the hotel. Good food from an extensive menu.*
ACCOMMODATION under £20
FOOD up to £15
**Hours:** breakfast 7:15am – 9:45am. **Cuisine:** English. **Rooms:** 32 bedrooms all with tea making facilities, telephone, radio, TV: 9 singles, 8 singles ensuite, 5 twins, 6 twins ensuite, 2 doubles, 2 doubles ensuite. **Credit cards:** Visa, Access, AmEx. **Other points:** children catered for – please check for age limits, central heating, residents' lounge. **Directions:** from A34 at west Didsbury, take B5117 to Didsbury, hotel 1 mile on right.
GORDON W DELF, tel (061) 445 3336, fax (061) 445 3336.

## GALLERY BISTRO, Whitworth Art Gallery, University of Manchester

*A charming bistro situated within the Whitworth Art Gallery (admission free). Good food is served at very reasonable prices and in fine weather meals can be enjoyed alfresco. Partly self-service but the staff are friendly and efficient. Varied and well-presented meals – all fresh and home-made.*
FOOD up to £15
**Hours:** morning coffee from 10.30am; closed Sunday; lunch 12noon – 2:15pm. **Cuisine:** English:- Home made soups and pates. Home made fresh salmon fishcakes, savoury pithivier, carrot cake, French almond tart. **Other points:** open-air dining, children catered for – please check for age limits, no-smoking area, no pets, parking, disabled access, vegetarian meals. **Directions:** on Oxford Road, opposite the Royal Infirmary and adjoining Whitworth Park.
MRS ROSEMARY WATTS, tel (061) 273 1249, fax (061) 274 4543.

## GARDENS HOTEL, 55 Piccadilly

*Located in the heart of the city, "Gardens Hotel" is only minutes away from Piccadilly station and within easy access of Manchester International Airport and the famous G-Mex centre. Overlooking the Piccadilly Gardens, it provides stylish comfort and is an ideal base for both businessmen and tourists alike. Ed's Bar is available for private functions and there are also three conference suites accommodating up to 70 people.*
ACCOMMODATION £21–£30
FOOD up to £15
**Hours:** breakfast 7am – 9:30am; lunch 12noon – 2pm; bar snacks 12noon – 10pm; dinner 6:30pm – 10pm. **Cuisine:** English. **Credit cards:** Visa, Access, Diners, AmEx. **Other points:** children catered for – please check for age limits, pets, entertainment. **Directions:** on Piccadilly, in the heart of the city.
MR B COWLEY, tel (061) 236 5155, fax (061) 228 7287.

## GAYLORD INDIA RESTAURANT, Amethyst House, Spring Gardens

*A well-known restaurant, part of an international chain. You can watch your dishes being prepared through the tandoor's window. Being situated in the heart of the city, this is a very popular lunch time rendezvous.*
FOOD up to £15
**Hours:** lunch 12noon – 3pm; dinner 6pm – 11:30pm; closed Christmas 25/12. **Cuisine:** Indian:- north Indian Tandoori dishes, eg. kebab, tikka, pakora. Vegetarian dishes such as Saag paneer, Onion kulcha. **Credit cards:** Visa, Access, Diners, AmEx. **Other points:** Sunday lunch, no-smoking area, children catered for – please check for age limits, street parking. **Directions:** centre of Manchester.
PARDEEP CHADHA, tel (061) 832 6037, (061) 832 4866.

## HENRY'S CAFE BAR (MANCHESTER), Parsonage Gardens

*A lively, popular cafe-bar serving an extensive range of international fast-food, American and non alcoholic beers and speciality cocktails. Very busy at lunchtimes.*
FOOD up to £15
**Hours:** closed Sunday 25/12; meals all day 10.30am – 11pm. **Cuisine:** international. **Credit cards:** Visa, Access. **Other points:** children catered for – please check for age limits, open bank holidays, no-smoking area, afternoon teas, disabled access, vegetarian meals. **Directions:** behind Kendals – off Deansgate.
PHILLIP YATES, tel (061) 832 7935.

## THE MOCK TURTLE RESTAURANT & CARROLL'S, 256 Wilmslow Road, Fallowfield

*An intimate, candlelit, French-style restaurant in a delightful old church building. The menu offers imaginative dishes, excellently cooked and presented, and served by friendly and efficient staff. The restaurant is attached to a 24-bedroom hotel complete with heated indoor swimming pool, and to the Queen of Hearts Pub.*
ACCOMMODATION £31–£40
FOOD up to £15 ♨
**Hours:** breakfast 7am – 9am; dinner 6pm – 10:30pm. **Cuisine:** French:- Predominantly French cuisine

specialising in fish, game and vegetarian dishes. Only the finest fresh ingredients used. **Rooms:** 8 single, 8 double and 8 twin bedrooms, all en suite. **Credit cards:** Visa, Access, Diners, AmEx. **Other points:** licensed, children catered for – please check for age limits, functions. **Directions:** Oxford Rd from City centre for 3 miles. Opposite student residences.
MR D SANDWITH, tel (061) 224 2340, fax (061) 257 2046.

## THAT CAFE, 1031–1033 Stockport Road, Levenshulme
*Situated 3 miles from Manchester city centre, That Cafe offers a good variety of both meat and vegetarian dishes. The atmosphere and decor are unique with open fires, bric a brac and 30s and 40s music.*
*FOOD up to £15*
**Hours:** lunch – Sunday 12:30pm – 2:30pm; dinner 7pm – 11pm; closed Sunday evenings. **Cuisine:** English / continental:- Special £12.95 Table d'hote menu, exclusive of coffee/tea, Monday, Tuesday, Wednesday and Thursday evenings. Weekly menu change. Fresh fish. 3 course Sunday Lunch £10.95, main courses £5.95. A la carte menu changes monthly. **Credit cards:** Visa, Access, AmEx, Switch. **Other points:** Sunday lunch, children catered for – please check for age limits, functions. **Directions:** on the A6 between Manchester and Stockport.
JOSEPH QUINN & STEPHEN KING, tel (061) 432 4672.

## MAWDESLEY, Lancashire Map 16

### ROBIN HOOD INN, Bluestone Lane
*A small family pub set in a rural area and humming with local life. Prompt friendly service and special Robin Hood dishes such as the Friar Tuck grill.*
*FOOD up to £15*
**Hours:** lunch 12noon – 2pm; dinner 6:30pm – 9:30pm. **Cuisine:** English:- Traditional, varied menu available in bar. Restaurant menu: steaks, fish, chicken. **Credit cards:** Visa, Access. **Other points:** licensed, Sunday lunch, children catered for – please check for age limits, afternoon tea – Sunday, bank holidays. **Directions:** take B5246 to Mawdesley. Through village, turn left.
DAVID CROPPER, tel (0704) 822275.

## MELMERBY, Cumbria Map 19

### SHEPHERDS INN, Nr Penrith
*An 18th century pub, built of traditional Cumberland stone, nestling at the foot of Hartside Pass in the northern Pennines. Serves fine traditional beers and extensive, original, home prepared meals. Winner of the 1990 Dairy Crest Cheese Symbol of Excellence for their outstanding cheese selection. Casserole Award winner 1991, 1992 and 1993. 1993 Publican Catering Pub of the Year. Holiday cottages available in village; brochure on request.*
*FOOD up to £15* 🍽
**Hours:** lunch – except Sunday 11am – 2:30pm; lunch – Sunday 12noon – 2pm; dinner – except Sunday 6pm – 10pm; dinner – Sunday 7pm – 10pm; closed Christmas

25/12. **Cuisine:** English:- Many home made dishes such as Spare ribs, Chicken Leoni, Rogan Gosht. Choice of 26 different cheeses for Ploughmans and a range of exotic Pickles. **Credit cards:** Visa, Access, Diners, AmEx. **Other points:** open-air dining, Sunday lunch, children catered for – please check for age limits. **Directions:** On the A686 in Melmerby.
MARTIN & CHRISTINE BAUCUTT, tel (0768881) 217.

## MIDDLETON TYAS, North Yorkshire
Map 18

### SHOULDER OF MUTTON INN, Richmond
*Built 300 years ago as a farmhouse, the Shoulder of Mutton has been tastefully restored retaining all the charm and character of a bygone era. The Shoulder of Mutton makes an ideal stop-over on the route to Scotland.*
*FOOD £15–£20*
**Hours:** lunch 12noon – 2pm; bar meals 12noon – 2pm; dinner 7pm – 10pm; bar meals 7pm – 10pm. **Cuisine:** English:- Steaks, fish, poultry. Menu changes weekly. **Credit cards:** Visa, Access, AmEx. **Other points:** licensed, Sunday lunch, children catered for – please check for age limits. **Directions:** half mile from the Scotch Corner roundabout on the A1.
MR & MRS TWEEDY, tel (0325) 377271.

## MORECAMBE, Lancashire Map 16

### CRAIGWELL HOTEL & TEDDY'S RESTAURANT, 372 Marine Road East
*A terraced bay-fronted property on the sea-front with splendid views to the Lakeland Hills. The hotel has been extensively refurnished to provide guests with a high level of comfort and convenience. Teddy's Restaurant provides well cooked and attractively presented food, served by warm and courteous staff.*
*ACCOMMODATION under £20*
*FOOD up to £15*
**Hours:** breakfast 8am – 9:30am; lunch – Sunday only 12:30pm – 3:30pm; dinner 6pm – 9:30pm. **Cuisine:** English:- Table d'hote menu and a la carte menu. **Rooms:** 13 bedrooms 5 singles ensuite, 5 doubles ensuite, 1 twin ensuite, 2 family rooms ensuite. **Credit cards:** Visa, Access, AmEx. **Other points:** parking, children catered for – please check for age limits, Sunday lunch, open bank holidays, residents' lounge, vegetarian meals, licensed, specials breaks, central heating. **Directions:** between the Town Hall and The Broadway.
MR N PETERS, tel (0524) 410095.

## NEWBY BRIDGE, Cumbria Map 19

### SWAN HOTEL, Nr Ulverston
*A 16th century coaching inn in a superb location at the southern end of Lake Windermere. The Mailcoach Wine Bar serves informal meals in a relaxed atmosphere, whilst The Tithe Barn Restaurant overlooking Newby Bridge and the River Leven offers a more extensive menu in a traditional setting.*

*ACCOMMODATION £41–£50*

*FOOD £15–£20* 🍷 ⊕

**Hours:** breakfast – weekdays 7:30am – 9:30am; breakfast – weekend 8am – 10am; bar meals 11:45am – 2:45pm; bar meals 6:30pm – 9:45pm; dinner 7pm – 9pm; dinner – Saturday 7pm – 9:30pm. **Cuisine:** English / French:- English – featuring, when available, Char, Venison, Cumberland Farmhouse cheese and ocasional continental dishes. **Rooms:** 36 bedrooms all with tea making facilities, telephone, radio, mini bar, TV: 7 singles ensuite, 10 twins ensuite, 18 doubles ensuite, 1 suite. **Credit cards:** Visa, Access, Diners, AmEx. **Other points:** licensed, Sunday lunch, children catered for – please check for age limits, baby-listening device, cots, residents' lounge, residents' bar. **Directions:** Junction 36 of M6, A590 towards Barrow; overlooking Newby Bridge.

JAMES A BERTLIN, MANAGER, tel (05395) 31681, fax (05395) 31917.

# NEWCASTLE UPON TYNE,

Tyne & Wear Map 17

## COURTNEY'S RESTAURANT, *5–7 The Side, Quayside*

*A small restaurant, well decorated in a simple style to provide a restful setting in which to enjoy the good food. Only the freshest and best ingredients are used and all dishes are well cooked and presented. The service is welcoming and efficient and complements the warm, relaxed atmosphere in the restaurant.*

*FOOD £15–£20*

**Hours:** closed Christmas 1 week; lunch 12noon – 2pm; dinner 7pm – 10:30pm; closed bank holidays; closed May (2 weeks); closed Saturday lunch; closed Sunday. **Cuisine:** international:- Modern international cuisine. Emphasis on fresh and quality ingredients. Daily specials and a good vegetarian choice. **Credit cards:** Visa, Access, AmEx. **Other points:** licensed, guide dogs. **Directions:** bottom of Dean St. Right hand side before roundabout at Quayside.

MICHAEL & KERENSA CARR, tel (091) 232 5537.

## THE BLACK BULL, *Matfen*

*Situated in a picture postcard village, this delightful inn has low beamed ceilings, a log-burning stone fireplace, and offers a very warm welcome. Good quality traditional fare in an pleasant and intimate atmosphere. Tourist attractions nearby include Hadrian's Wall, Kielder Reservoir and the Metro Centre.*

*ACCOMMODATION £21–£30*

*FOOD up to £15*

**Hours:** breakfast 7:30am – 9am; lunch 12noon – 2pm; bar meals 12noon – 2pm; bar meals 6:30pm – 9pm; dinner 7pm – 9:30pm. **Cuisine:** English:- A la carte menu. Steamed Salmon Fillet, Assorted Game, King Prawns. Excellent Wine List. Vegetarian dishes available. **Rooms:** 3 bedrooms all with tea making facilities, radio, TV: 3 doubles ensuite. **Credit cards:** Visa, Access. **Other points:** licensed, open-air dining,

Sunday lunch, children catered for – please check for age limits, disabled access, parking, garden, bank holidays. **Directions:** leave A69 at Corbridge to join B6318. 2 miles north of this road.

COLIN & MICHELLE SCOTT, tel (0661) 886330.

## THE FERNCOURT HOTEL, *34 Osborne Road, Jesmond*

*An attractive, spacious hotel, with easy access to Hadrian's Wall and other local tourist attractions. Pleasant surroundings, comfortably furnished to appeal to business executives and holiday-makers alike. Well-prepared Tex-Mex food, attractively presented in a lively atmosphere. English Tourist Board 3 Crown Commended.*

*ACCOMMODATION £21–£30*

*FOOD up to £15*

**Hours:** open all year; open bank holidays; breakfast – weekdays 7am – 9am; breakfast – weekends 8am – 9:30am; dinner – weekdays 6:30pm – 10:30pm; dinner – weekends 7pm – 10pm. **Cuisine:** Tex-Mex:- Large and varied menu, featuring authentic Texan and Mexican food. **Rooms:** 16 bedrooms all with tea making facilities, TV: 4 singles, 1 single ensuite, 3 doubles, 3 doubles ensuite, 1 twin, 1 family room, 3 family rooms ensuite. **Credit cards:** Visa, Access, Diners, AmEx. **Other points:** licensed, children catered for – please check for age limits, vegetarian meals, pets allowed, parking. **Directions:** off the A1058, left at roundabout on to Osborne Road.

MR CLARK, tel (091) 281 5418, (091) 281 5377, fax (091) 212 0783.

## SACHINS, *Forth Banks*

*An authentic Punjabi restaurant in a grade II listed building situated at the head of the Forth Banks close to the River Tyne. The menu offers a range of speciality Punjabi dishes, flavoured with the freshest of produce with the delicate aromas of herbs and spices, prepared by one of the top Punjabi chefs in Britain. The atmosphere is relaxed and comfortable.*

*FOOD £15–£20*

**Hours:** closed Sunday 7pm; lunch 12noon – 2:15pm; dinner 6pm – 11:15pm. **Cuisine:** Punjabi:- The fine menu offers a splendid array of the most exotic and enticing dishes. **Credit cards:** Visa, Access, Diners, AmEx. **Other points:** parking, children catered for – please check for age limits, vegetarian meals, licensed. **Directions:** easy to find behind the Central Station.

RAWLEY, DINESH, tel (091) 261 9035, (091) 232 4660.

## SURTEES HOTEL/WINGS RESTAURANT, *12–16 Dean Street*

*A 100 year old building which has been lovingly restored to its former glory, providing visitors to the city of Newcastle with a high degree of comfort, elegance and charm. Each of the 27 beautifully decorated bedrooms has been individually and tastefully decorated to give a homely touch. Below the hotel is "Wings" Restaurant, which has been transformed into Newcastle's*

most interesting theme eating-house, with an abundance of aeroplanes from ceiling to carpet, and open 7 days a week. There are rooms which can be hired for meetings, full fax facilities and supervised car parking, everything you would expect from a first class hotel.
ACCOMMODATION £21–£30
FOOD up to £15
**Hours:** meals all day 7am – 11pm; meals all day – Sunday 8am – 11pm. **Rooms:** 27 bedrooms 12 singles ensuite, 6 twins ensuite, 9 doubles ensuite. **Credit cards:** Visa, Access, Diners, AmEx.
BRIAN MACKAY & JOHN MONK, tel (091) 261 7771, fax (091) 230 1322.

## NEWTON AYCLIFFE, County Durham Map 17

### THE GRETNA HOTEL AND RESTAURANT, Great North Road
Situated just a short drive away from Darlington Intercity Railway, the Gretna is an ideal place to stay when touring the north east with its many interesting attractions. Formerly the Wedding Inn, it has recently undergone extensive refurbishment to provide a high level of comfort. A function room is available for private hire for up to 100 guests.
ACCOMMODATION £21–£30
FOOD up to £15
**Hours:** breakfast 7am – 9.30am; lunch 11.30am – 2pm; dinner 6.30pm – 10pm. **Cuisine:** English/International. **Rooms:** 9 ensuite bedrooms all with TV, telephone, tea making facilities. **Credit cards:** Visa, Access. **Other points:** parking, children catered for – please check for age limits, disabled access, pets allowed, vegetarian meals, open air dining, garden.
MR G HAMILTON, tel (0325) 300100, fax (0325) 300949.

## NORTHALLERTON, North Yorkshire Map 18

### DUKE OF WELLINGTON INN, Welbury
A family-run, rural village Inn with a warm, welcoming atmosphere enhanced by real log fires in winter. All food is fresh, well-cooked and attractively presented, the service warm and courteous. For a friendly, relaxed atmosphere, good food and service, the Duke of Wellington is well worth a visit.
FOOD up to £15
**Hours:** bar meals 12noon – 2pm; bar meals 7pm – 10pm; closed Monday lunch; closed Tuesday lunch. **Cuisine:** English:- Traditional home-made cuisine. Dishes may include Duck a l'orange, Steak Diane, Steak & Kidney pie. Vegetarian dishes. **Rooms:** adjoining cottage available for holiday let. **Credit cards:** Visa, Access. **Other points:** licensed, children catered for – please check for age limits, beer garden, playland. **Directions:** between A19 & A167. 7 miles north of Northallerton, 3 miles west of A19.
MR & MRS THOMPSON, tel (0609) 882464.

## ORMSKIRK, Lancashire Map 16

### BEAUFORT HOTEL, High Lane, Burscough
A welcoming hotel offering excellent food and comfortable accommodation. These high standards are matched by friendly and efficient service and the prices, especially in the restaurant, are very reasonable. Close to M6 and M58, the hotel is within easy travelling distance of Liverpool and Southport.
ACCOMMODATION £31–£40
FOOD £15–£20 ⓒ⑰
**Hours:** breakfast 7am – 9:30am; lunch 12noon – 2pm; dinner 7pm – 10pm. **Cuisine:** English / continental:- French table d'hote and a la carte menus. **Rooms:** 21 bedrooms: 2 singles ensuite, 11 twins ensuite, 7 doubles ensuite, 1 suite. **Credit cards:** Visa, Access, Diners, AmEx. **Other points:** licensed, Sunday lunch, children catered for – please check for age limits, pets allowed. **Directions:** 2 miles north of Ormskirk on A59, corner of Pippin St & High Lane.
DUNCAN REICH, tel (0704) 892655, fax (0704) 895135.

## OSMOTHERLEY, North Yorkshire Map 18

### THREE TUNS INN, South End, Nr Northallerton
Situated on the edge of the beautiful north Yorkshire moors in an old village, the Three Tuns is an early 18th century inn, with a walled garden. Ideal place for a relaxing meal, at good value, especially after tackling one of the nearby walks: Lyke Wake, Hambleton Hobble and Cleveland Way.
ACCOMMODATION £41–£50
FOOD up to £15
**Hours:** lunch 12noon – 2:30pm; dinner 7pm – 9:30pm. **Cuisine:** English / French:- home-cooked using fresh produce, the speciality being seafood. **Rooms:** 3 en suite twin bedded rooms. **Credit cards:** Visa, Access. **Other points:** licensed, Sunday lunch, children catered for – please check for age limits, pets allowed. **Directions:** from north & south, A19 turn left signposted Northallerton/Osmotherley.
H & J DYSON, tel (0609) 883301.

## OTLEY, West Yorkshire Map 18

### CHEVIN LODGE COUNTRY PARK HOTEL, Yorkgate
Delightful Scandinavian Lodge Style building, with pine furniture and a unique layout. Large windows give a good view to the abundant wildlife which can be watched from the warm and friendly atmosphere of this country hotel. Enjoy an intimate, special ambiance and excellent food at reasonable prices served by competent staff.
ACCOMMODATION £41–£50
FOOD £21–£25
**Hours:** breakfast 7am – 9:30am; lunch 12:30pm – 2:30pm; dinner 7pm – 9:30pm. **Cuisine:** English:-

Predominantly English cuisine using fresh, local produce. **Rooms:** 52 bedrooms, all en suite. **Credit cards:** Visa, Access, AmEx. **Other points:** open-air dining, Sunday lunch, children catered for – please check for age limits, bank holidays, afternoon tea, pets allowed, tennis, games room, sauna. **Directions:** A659, 10 miles north west of Leeds.
MR PETER CAULFIELD, tel (0943) 467818, fax (0943) 850335.

## THE WHITE HART, *Main Street, Pool in Wharfedale*

*This delightful converted farmhouse has a pleasant, unpretentious atmosphere in keeping with its rustic origins. Good, well-cooked food and friendly staff make for an enjoyable visit. Children particularly welcome.*
*FOOD up to £15*
**Hours:** bar – except Sunday 11am – 11pm; bar – Sunday 12noon – 10:30pm. **Cuisine:** English:- Traditional English pub food. Generous proportions at reasonable prices. Daily specials. Fresh fish daily. Vegetarian specialities. Imaginative children's menu. Food available every day. **Credit cards:** Visa, Access. **Other points:** children catered for – please check for age limits, open bank holidays, open-air dining, parking. **Directions:** on main street of Pool on A6589 Bradford to Harrogate Road.
DAVID & EMMA MCHATTIE, tel (0532) 843011.

# OTTERBURN, Northumberland Map 17

## OTTERBURN TOWER HOTEL

*A spacious, adapted castellated country house in extensive grounds. 3-course menu and bar meals are offered in the traditionally furnished and wood-panelled dining room and lounges. Steeped in history, the hotel is reputedly haunted! Private fishing on 3.5 miles of the River Rede.*
*ACCOMMODATION £31–£40*
*FOOD up to £15*
**Hours:** open all day 7am – 11:30pm. **Cuisine:** English. **Rooms:** 12 bedrooms, 8 en suite. **Credit cards:** Visa, Access, Diners, AmEx. **Other points:** Sunday lunch, children catered for – please check for age limits, garden. **Directions:** the entrance to the hotel is at the junction of the A696 and B6320.
PETER HARDING, tel (0830) 20620.

# PENRITH, Cumbria Map 19

## KNOTT'S MILL COUNTRY LODGE, *Watermillock, Ullswater*

*Originally a sawmill, Knott's Mill has recently been refurbished to provide comfortable accommodation in the beautiful Ullswater countryside. The house is set in a secluded position, and all rooms have views of the fells. Sailing boats and windsurfing boards may be hired in Glenridding, and a steamer trip offers a scenic trip of the lake. Many nearby picturesque valleys and villages.*
*ACCOMMODATION £21–£30*
*FOOD up to £15*

**Hours:** open all year; breakfast 8:15am – 9:15am; dinner 6:30pm – 8:30pm. **Cuisine:** British:- A la carte menu, offering a range of traditional homestyle cuisine. **Rooms:** 9 bedrooms all with tea making facilities, TV: 1 twin ensuite, 2 family rooms ensuite, 6 doubles ensuite. **Credit cards:** Visa, Access. **Other points:** licensed, children catered for – please check for age limits, morning tea, afternoon tea, garden, parking. **Directions:** From Jct. 40 on M6, follow A66 to Keswick – then A592 for 6 miles.
JANE JONES, tel (07684) 86472, fax (07684) 86699.

## TEBAY MOUNTAIN LODGE HOTEL, *Orton*

*The Tebay Mountain Lodge is a beautiful new concept in hotel accommodation. Each Studio is custom-built, offering every modern day comfort, and enjoying magnificent views of the Cumbrian hills. Not only does it provide a stop-over for business travellers and families, but is also an excellent base for holidaying and exploring the unspoilt valleys and historical attractions.*
*ACCOMMODATION £31–£40*
*FOOD up to £15*
**Hours:** open all year 6:30pm; breakfast 7:30am – 9am; dinner 7pm – 9pm. **Cuisine:** English / continental:- A la carte menu, offering a combination of English and continental dishes. **Rooms:** 30 large studio bedrooms, all with en suite facilities, private bathroom, colour TV, telephone and radio, and tea/coffee making facilities. **Credit cards:** Visa, Access, Diners, AmEx. **Other points:** licensed, no-smoking area, children catered for – please check for age limits, pets allowed, residents' lounge, parking. **Directions:** 1 mile north of Jct 36 of M6 motorway. Turn into Tebay Service area.
MR BULT, tel (05396) 24511, fax (05874) 354.

## WREAY FARM COUNTRY GUESTHOUSE, *Lake Ullswater, Watermillock*

*Built in 1787, Wreay Farm has been completely modernised to provide a high standard of comfort. Situated on the brow of a hill near Bennet Head in a quiet, peaceful area, it affords spectacular views of Lake Ullswater. Offering exceptional cuisine using only the freshest of local produce, it is an ideal choice for a family hotel. A list of 'Places to Visit' is provided for all guests.*
*ACCOMMODATION £21–£30*
*FOOD up to £15*
**Hours:** breakfast 8:30am; dinner 7:30pm; closed December – January (inclusive). **Cuisine:** English. **Other points:** parking, children catered for – please check for age limits, dogs allowed, residents' lounge, vegetarian meals. **Directions:** come to Lake Ullswater, turn right, go up lake for 2 miles until you reach the Brackenrigg Hotel, turn right, go up hill and the guest house is at the top on the right.
D H N WINDLE, tel (07684) 86296.

## PRESTON, Lancashire Map 16

### THE BUSHELLS ARMS, Church Lane, Goosnargh

A friendly village hostelry, which offers a superb variety of dishes. There is both a standard menu and a 'specials' board. The ever changing but comprehensive wine list is selected to complement the style of food. All meals are home-made and the puddings are sumptuous. Visitors can enjoy all this at very reasonable prices and relax in the friendly surroundings.

FOOD up to £15 ♀ ⌣

Hours: lunch 12noon – 2:30pm; dinner 7pm – 10pm; closed Christmas 25/12; closed occasional Mondays. Cuisine: international:- Dublin Coddle, Kefta Tagine, Jambalaya. Comprehensive choice of 'specials'. Changing wine list. Vegetarian. Other points: licensed, open-air dining, Sunday lunch, no-smoking area, children catered for – please check for age limits, beer garden. Directions: M6 Junction 32 north on A6 towards Garstang, turn right at lights. DAVID & GLYNIS BEST, tel (0772) 865235, fax (0772) 861837.

### CARAVELA RESTAURANT, Preston New Road, Freckleton

A Portuguese restaurant, attractively decorated with pine wood furniture, fishing nets and old schooner paintings to create a Portuguese feel. The a la carte menu offers a wide choice of Portuguese dishes whilst the table d'hote provides a more British alternative. Excellently cooked and presented food and friendly, efficient service. Good selection of Portuguese wines.

FOOD £15–£20

Hours: lunch 12noon – 2pm; dinner 6:30pm – 10:30pm; closed Monday; closed Saturday lunch. Cuisine: Portuguese:- 3 course weekday lunch menu, Sunday lunch menu and A La Carte. Wide choice of Portuguese specialities. Credit cards: Visa, Access. Other points: licensed, Sunday lunch, vegetarian meals, children catered for – please check for age limits. Directions: A584 Preston – Lytham road. A FIGUEIRA & M DE NOBREGA, tel (0772) 632308.

### FERRARIS RESTAURANT, West End, Great Eccleston

An excellent English and continental restaurant in the village of Great Eccleston. The interior is very Italian in style, with an accent on Ferrari cars and provides attractive, comfortable surroundings in which to enjoy the first-class cuisine. The meals are beautifully cooked and presented, complemented by welcoming and efficient service. Excellent food and atmosphere.

FOOD £15–£20 ⌣

Hours: dinner 6:30pm – 10:30pm. Cuisine: English / continental:- Table d'hote, and extensive a la carte menu. English and continental dishes. Credit cards: Visa, Access. Other points: licensed, children catered for – please check for age limits. Directions: from M55 at Kirkham, take A585 to Larbreck, then right on A586. SUSAN & VIRGINIO FERRARI, tel (0995) 70243.

### RUNSHAW COLLEGE SCHOOL OF CATERING, Langdale Road, Leyland

The Fox Holes Restaurant is part of a tertiary college allowing students an opportunity to practise skills in food service and kitchen work.

FOOD up to £15

Hours: closed – Sat/Sun/Tuesday lunch; lunch 11:45am – 2pm; last orders – lunch 12:45pm; dinner 6:30pm – 10pm; last orders – dinner 7:45pm; closed July – August. Cuisine: English / French & continental:- A varied menu. Dishes include Steak Pie, Tagliatelle carbonara, Champignon stroganoff, Tournedo de saumon avec beurre citron. Other points: parking, children catered for – please check for age limits, no-smoking area, disabled access, vegetarian meals. Directions: From M6 junction 28, follow signs for Leyland, take second road on left – Bent Lane. Follow to end, turn right and first left for Langdale Road. MR LITTLEWOOD, tel (0772) 432511, fax (0772) 622295.

### YE HORN'S INN, Horns Lane, Gooshargh

This delightful oak-beamed inn offers good home cooked English country fare, using local farm produce. Private parties catered for. Small private rooms available. Set in rural countryside, the Inn provides an ideal base from which to visit nearby beauty spots such as Beacon Fell, The Trough of Bowland and the Hodder Valley.

ACCOMMODATION £41–£50

FOOD £15–£20

Hours: lunch 12noon – 2pm; dinner 7pm – 9:15pm; closed Monday lunch. Cuisine: English:- Home cooking, eg. roast duckling. Rooms: 6 bedrooms, all en suite. Credit cards: Visa, Access, Diners, AmEx. Other points: Sunday lunch, no-smoking area, children catered for – please check for age limits, disabled access, residents' bar, vegetarian meals. Directions: M6: exit 36. Off the B5269 near Whittingham Hospital. MRS E WOODS, tel (0772) 865230.

## RAMSBOTTOM, Lancashire Map 16

### OLD MILL HOTEL & RESTAURANT, Springwood

Originally an old mill, this hotel has been completely refurbished achieving an attractive yet comfortable atmosphere. With a combination of a good choice of food and wine and attentive service both restaurants are well worth a visit.

ACCOMMODATION £31–£40

FOOD up to £15

Hours: breakfast 7:30am – 9:30am; lunch 12noon – 2:30pm; dinner 6:30pm – 10:30pm. Cuisine: French / Italian:- 2 Restaurants. French cuisine – fish, steak, shellfish, casseroles. Comprehensive wine list. Italian cuisine – pastas, pizzas. Rooms: 36 bedrooms all with tea making facilities, telephone, TV: 12 singles ensuite, 12 twins ensuite, 12 doubles ensuite. Credit cards: Visa, Access, Diners, AmEx. Other points: licensed, open-air dining, Sunday lunch, swimming pool, sauna,

solarium, leisure centre, children catered for – please check for age limits, residents' lounge, garden. **Directions:** off Junction M66 with A56, situated on A676 north of Manchester.
KAREN SACCO, tel (070682) 2991.

## RAMSEY, Isle of Man Map 19

### HARBOUR BISTRO, 5 East Street
*Comfortably furnished and enjoying a relaxed atmosphere, the Harbour Bistro offers an extensive menu with an emphasis on seafood. All dishes are well cooked, attractively presented and served by helpful, friendly staff. Good wine list. Popular with locals and holiday-makers alike, the atmosphere is welcoming and relaxed.*
*FOOD up to £15* 🍷 ☕
**Hours:** lunch 12noon – 2:15pm; dinner 6:30pm – 10:30pm; closed Good Friday; closed for 2 weeks October. **Cuisine:** continental:- Dishes may include – Traditional Roast Duck with Walnut stuffing, Baked Chicken Breast and Asparagus. Seafood specialities and fresh lobster and Dover sole when available. **Credit cards:** Visa, Access. **Other points:** licensed, Sunday lunch, children catered for – please check for age limits, special diets, street parking. **Directions:** between Harbour and Parliament Street.
KEN DEVANEY & KAREN WONG, tel (0624) 814182.

## REETH, North Yorkshire Map 18

### KINGS ARMS HOTEL, High Row
*18th century listed building situated in the heart of Swaledale. Original beams and open log fires add to the cosy and friendly atmosphere of this village 'local'.*
*ACCOMMODATION £21–£30*
*FOOD up to £15*
**Hours:** bar meals 12noon – 2pm; bar meals 6:30pm – 9pm. **Cuisine:** English. **Rooms:** 4 bedrooms all with tea making facilities, TV: 1 family room ensuite, 1 twin ensuite, 2 doubles ensuite. **Other points:** licensed, open-air dining, children catered for – please check for age limits, coach/prior arr. **Directions:** leave the A6108 at Richmond and take B6270 to Reeth.
ASHLEY MARKHAM & ARTHUR COOK, tel (0748) 84259.

## RICHMOND, North Yorkshire Map 18

### A66 MOTEL, Smallways
*The A66 Motel was originally a 17th century farm. Situated close to the Dales and areas of historic interest, the motel is conveniently placed for visiting this beautiful part of England.*
*ACCOMMODATION £21–£30*
*FOOD £15–£20*
**Hours:** breakfast 7am – 10am; lunch 12noon – 2pm; bar meals 12noon – 2:30pm; dinner 7pm – 10:30pm; bar meals 7pm – 10:30pm. **Cuisine:** modern English:- Fresh salmon salad, Aylesbury duckling, steaks with sauce Espagnole. **Rooms:** 6 bedrooms. **Credit cards:** Visa, Access, Diners, AmEx. **Other points:** licensed, Sunday

lunch, children catered for – please check for age limits, pets allowed, garden. **Directions:** on the A66 near Scotch Corner.
SONIA HALL, tel (0833) 27334, fax (0833) 627334.

### PEAT GATE HEAD, Low Row in Swaledale
*A 300 year old Dales house standing in 2 acres of grounds with magnificent and memorable view up dale to the Pennines and down to Richmond. An ideal stop for travellers to explore the bewitching countryside. All food is home-made using fresh, seasonal produce. Special diets, likes and dislikes are catered for. A friendly, welcoming place to stay.*
*ACCOMMODATION under £20*
*FOOD £15–£20*
**Hours:** breakfast 8:30am; dinner 7pm. **Cuisine:** English. **Rooms:** 1 single, 2 double and 3 twin bedrooms, 3 en suite. 1 bathroom, 1 shower. 1 ground floor bedroom especially designed for the disabled. **Other points:** central heating, children catered for – please check for age limits, residents' lounge, garden, vegetarian meals. **Directions:** situated off B6270 on Langthwaite road.
ALAN EARL, tel (0748) 86388.

## RIPON, North Yorkshire Map 18

### STAVELEY ARMS (SPIT ROAST), North Stainley
*Charming country pub oozing with atmosphere. Flagged floors, log fires and candlelight. Bygone farming paintings and country tools adorn the walls. Delightful rural setting, 3 miles from Fountains Abbey, 1 mile from Lightwater Valley Theme Park on the main A6108 road to the beautiful Yorkshire Dales.*
*ACCOMMODATION under £20*
*FOOD up to £15*
**Hours:** lunch 12noon – 2pm; dinner 7pm – 9:30pm; bar meals 7pm – 9:30pm. **Cuisine:** English:- Famous Spit turns Thursday – Sunday. Excellent bar meals every evening. Choose from blackboard, vegetarian dishes available. **Rooms:** 5 bedrooms all with tea making facilities, TV: 2 twins ensuite, 3 doubles ensuite. **Credit cards:** Visa, Access. **Other points:** licensed, open-air dining, Sunday lunch, children catered for – please check for age limits, parking. **Directions:** A6108 north out of Ripon, 4 miles towards north Stainley.
R M STAVELEY, tel (0765) 635439, fax (0765) 635359.

## ROSEDALE ABBEY, North Yorkshire Map 18

### BLACKSMITH'S ARMS HOTEL, Hartoft End, Nr Pickering
*A family-run hotel at the foot of Rosedale in the north Yorkshire Moors National Park, an area renowned for its scenic beauty. The original farmhouse dates back to the 16th century and commands extensive views of the surrounding moors and dales. Ideal centre for touring and riding.*
*FOOD £15–£20*
**Hours:** lunch 12noon – 2pm. **Cuisine:** French /

English:- Hot or cold meals available in bar eg. supreme of chicken filled with garlic butter. Table d'hote e.g. fresh local lobster. **Rooms:** 14 bedrooms. **Credit cards:** Visa, Access. **Other points:** children catered for – please check for age limits. **Directions:** set within the North Yorkshire Moors National Park.
ANTHONY & MARGARET FOOT, tel (07515) 331.

## THE MILBURN ARMS HOTEL,
### Nr Pickering
*Set in the heart of the North Yorkshire Moors National Park, this hotel is an ideal centre for walking and touring as many places of scenic and historical interest are within easy reach. The atmosphere is most convivial, with low beams, log fires and real ales. Award winning cuisine.*
*ACCOMMODATION £31–£40*
*FOOD up to £15* ★
**Hours:** breakfast 8am – 9:30am; lunch 12noon – 2pm; dinner 7pm – 8:30pm. **Cuisine:** English:- Extensive range of bar food including grilled Farndale goats cheese, Lastingham lamb hot-pot, pan-fried supreme of salmon, home-made steamed treacle and ginger pudding. **Rooms:** 11 bedrooms all with tea making facilities, telephone, TV: 9 doubles ensuite, 2 twins ensuite. **Credit cards:** Visa, Access, Diners. **Other points:** licensed, open-air dining, Sunday lunch, children catered for – please check for age limits, parking, vegetarian meals, no dogs. **Directions:** from the A170 at Wrelton follow the sign to Rosedale Abbey.
TERRY & JOAN BENTLEY, tel (07515) 312, fax (07515) 312.

# ROTHBURY, Northumberland Map 17

## COQUET VALE HOTEL, Station Road
*A Victorian type building constructed for the railways, it was previously called the Station Hotel. Situated on the B6341 this hotel is very well placed for north/South travellers and for those wanting to discover the delights of the area and the Borders.*
*ACCOMMODATION £21–£30*
*FOOD £15–£20*
**Hours:** breakfast 7:30am – 9:30am; lunch 12noon – 2pm; dinner 7pm – 9pm. **Cuisine:** English:- English and French cuisine: real Yorkshire pudding with onion gravy, and baked halibut and salmon parcels. Pan fried collops of venison. **Rooms:** 14 bedrooms 2 twins, 7 twins ensuite, 4 doubles ensuite, 1 family room ensuite. **Credit cards:** Visa, Access. **Other points:** open-air dining, Sunday lunch, children catered for – please check for age limits, coach/prior arr. **Directions:** on the B6341.
JAMES M CORRISH, tel (0669) 20305, fax (0669) 21500.

# ROTHERHAM, South Yorkshire Map 18

## BRECON HOTEL, Moorgate Road
*A small, family run-hotel where you will find true Yorkshire hospitality. The restaurant enjoys a good reputation locally for its quality, generous portions and friendliness of service. With its good food, comfortable accommodation, welcoming service and value for money, Brecon Hotel is highly recommended.*
*ACCOMMODATION £21–£30*
*FOOD up to £15*
**Hours:** breakfast 7:30am – 9:30am; lunch 12noon – 2pm; dinner 7pm – 9:15pm. **Cuisine:** English:- Dishes may include Beef Stroganoff, Roast Chicken Grandmere, Lamb Cutlets with Rosemary, Salmon Hollandaise. Bar meals. Traditional Sunday lunch. **Rooms:** 27 bedrooms 4 singles, 2 singles ensuite, 7 twins ensuite, 1 double, 13 doubles ensuite. **Credit cards:** Visa, Access, Diners, AmEx. **Other points:** licensed, children catered for – please check for age limits, pets allowed. **Directions:** off Junction 33, M1. Half mile past Rotherham General Hospital on A618.
DUNCAN CARR, tel (0709) 828811, fax (0709) 820213.

## BRENTWOOD HOTEL, Moorgate Road
*In a pleasant situation 1 mile from town centre in 2 acres of gardens. Gourmet wine list and restaurant with good value table d'hote menus.*
*ACCOMMODATION £31–£40*
*FOOD up to £15* ★
**Hours:** lunch 12:15pm – 2pm; dinner 7pm – 9:30pm. **Cuisine:** English:- Flambe dishes, char grills, fresh fish dishes, scampi George V, rack of lamb. **Rooms:** 43 bedrooms all with tea making facilities, telephone, TV: 17 singles ensuite, 6 twins ensuite, 20 doubles ensuite. **Credit cards:** Visa, Access, Diners, AmEx. **Other points:** licensed, Sunday lunch, children catered for – please check for age limits, coach/prior arr, pets/prior arr, disabled access, vegetarian meals, parking. **Directions:** leave M1, Junction 33, follow Bawtry signs to lights. Moorgate road on left.
JAMES LISTER, tel (0709) 382772, fax (0709) 820289.

## THE ELTON HOTEL, Main Street, Bramley
*Situated only 4 miles from Rotherham this is a popular spot for local business people at lunchtime and in the evening. The M18 is only half a mile away and the M1 and A1 are nearby making this an ideal stopover for travellers. Catering also available for private functions, conferences and receptions.*
*ACCOMMODATION £31–£40*
*FOOD £15–£20* ♀ ☺ CLUB ★
**Hours:** breakfast 7:15am – 9am; lunch – except Sunday 12noon – 2pm; lunch – Sunday 12noon – 3:30pm; dinner 7pm – 9:30pm. **Cuisine:** English / French. **Rooms:** 29 bedrooms all with tea making facilities, telephone, radio, TV: 9 singles ensuite, 4 twins ensuite, 16 doubles ensuite. **Credit cards:** Visa, Access, Diners, AmEx. **Other points:** licensed, Sunday lunch, children catered for – please check for age limits, baby-listening device, cots, 24hr reception. **Directions:** Junction 1, M18. From A631 in Bramley take Ravenfield turn B6093, first left.
PETER & WYNA KEARY, tel (0709) 545681, fax (0709) 549100.

## SALFORD, Greater Manchester Map 16

### BEAUCLIFFE HOTEL, 254 Eccles Old Road

*A large Victorian house in a convenient location, close to the motorway and all Manchester's amenities. The hotel has been in the family for 24 years, and the current resident proprietors pride themselves on their warm welcome, efficient service and good home-cooked food.*

ACCOMMODATION £21–£30

FOOD £15–£20

**Hours:** breakfast 7:30am – 9am; dinner 6:45pm – 8:45pm; bar meals 8pm – 10pm; closed Christmas 24/12 – 02/01. **Cuisine:** international:- Wide choice of dishes. **Rooms:** 21 bedrooms, 17 en suite. All bedrooms have colour TV and tea/coffee making facilities. **Credit cards:** Visa, Access, Diners, AmEx. **Other points:** licensed, Sunday lunch, children catered for – please check for age limits. **Directions:** quarter mile from Junction 2 of the M602, opposite the Hope Hospital.
ANTHONY & JACINTA WHITE, tel (061) 789 5092, fax (061) 787 7739.

## SCARBOROUGH, North Yorkshire Map 18

### AMBASSADOR HOTEL, Centre of the Esplanade, South Cliff

*The Ambassador is a gracious Victorian building commanding spectacular views of the south Bay. It is opposite the famous Italian Gardens & 150 yd from the Cliff. Lift to the Beach, Spa Entertainments & Conference Complex. All bedrooms have full facilities and direct-dial telephones. Excellent cuisine is served in the Bay View Restaurant. Tasteful entertainment in the Bay View Lounge. Bar, lift, ample unrestricted FREE parking. This family owned and managed Hotel ensures a pleasant and relaxing break.*

ACCOMMODATION £21–£30

FOOD up to £15

**Hours:** open New Year; breakfast 8am – 9:30am; bar lunches 12noon – 1:30pm; dinner 6pm – 7:45pm; closed November – February (inclusive). **Cuisine:** English:- Special dietary meals available on request. **Rooms:** 47 bedrooms 12 singles ensuite, 11 twins ensuite, 16 doubles ensuite, 8 family rooms ensuite. **Credit cards:** Access, Visa, Switch. **Other points:** no-smoking area, afternoon teas, morning coffee, garden, lounge bar. **Directions:** head down Avenue Victoria to the Cliff Top to locate the Ambassador.
RICHARD, KATHRYN & DAVID FRANK, tel (0723) 362841, fax (0723) 362841.

### ATTENBOROUGH HOTEL, 28–29 Albemarle Crescent

*A welcoming hotel set in a Victorian crescent, overlooking attractive gardens. Located in the centre of town, the train and bus station are only a short distance away.*

ACCOMMODATION under £20

FOOD up to £15

**Hours:** breakfast 8:30am – 9:15am; dinner 6pm.
**Cuisine:** English:- Traditional English cooking with continental influence. Daily fixed menu. **Rooms:** 4 single, 5 double, 8 twin and 8 family bedrooms and 5 with en suite. 2 bathrooms. 2 showers. Tea/coffee making facilities in all bedrooms. Colour TV in all bedrooms. **Other points:** central heating, children catered for – please check for age limits, residents' lounge, garden, vegetarian meals. **Directions:** A170, A171 or A165 to Scarborough. Located in centre of town.
MR & MRS J SNOW, tel (0723) 360857.

### AVONCROFT HOTEL, Crown Terrace

*A comfortable, family run private hotel in the centre of a Georgian Terrace overlooking Crown Gardens and within minutes walk of the beach, town centre, entertainments, Spa Complex, road and rail terminals. There is a quiet comfortable lounge with well stocked bar and Games Room, which provide ideal meeting points. Good British tradition, comfort and hospitality.*

ACCOMMODATION under £20

FOOD up to £15

**Hours:** breakfast 8:30am – 9:15am; bar meals 11am – 4pm; dinner 5:30pm – 6:15pm; bar meals 7pm – 11pm; closed part of December – part of January. **Cuisine:** English:- A daily changing menu, prepared with fresh ingredients. **Rooms:** 34 bedrooms, 20 ensuite. **Other points:** children catered for – please check for age limits, open bank holidays, afternoon tea, pets allowed, residents' lounge, vegetarian meals. **Directions:** from town centre take A165 Filey Road across Valley Bridge, at St Andrews Church turn left into Albion Road. First left into Crown Crescent, then first right into Crown Terrace.
CHRISTINE WILD, tel 0723 372737.

### BLACKSMITHS ARMS, High Street, Cloughton

*An old country pub, with oak beams and fires, set in a village near the north Yorkshire moors. The staff are very friendly and the food is not only excellently cooked, but also offers superb value for money. Ideal base for exploring the moors, Whitby, and for enjoying golf and pony trekking.*

ACCOMMODATION under £20

FOOD up to £15

**Hours:** breakfast 9am – 9:30am; lunch 12noon – 2pm; dinner 7pm – 10pm. **Cuisine:** modern English:- House specialities include fresh poached salmon in a white wine sauce, and trout grenobloise, fried with prawns, capers and lemon. Vegetarian dishes. **Rooms:** 6 double bedrooms all with tea making facilities, TV. **Credit cards:** Visa, Access. **Other points:** Sunday lunch, children catered for – please check for age limits, pets allowed, bank holidays. **Directions:** 5 miles north of Scarborough, on the A171 Whitby – Scarborough Road.
JEAN ANN ARNALL, tel (0723) 870244.

### THE CENTRAL HOTEL, 1–3 The Crescent

*Elegant yet comfortable, this newly refurbished hotel offers the discerning holiday maker or business person a chance to relax. Situated on Scarborough's elegant Georgian Crescent overlooking the gardens, yet only a short walk from all the major attractions of the town.*

*Ideal for exploring the nearby North Yorkshire Moors.*
*Jazz sessions Saturday and Sunday lunchtimes.*
ACCOMMODATION £21–£30
FOOD up to £15
**Hours:** breakfast 8am – 9:30am; bar snacks 12noon –
2pm; dinner 7pm – 10:30pm. **Cuisine:** English. **Rooms:**
33 bedrooms 1 single, 3 singles ensuite, 13 doubles
ensuite, 8 twins ensuite, 6 family rooms ensuite, 2 suites.
**Credit cards:** Visa, Access, Diners. **Other points:**
parking, children catered for – please check for age
limits, open all year, no-smoking area, afternoon tea,
disabled access, residents' lounge, vegetarian meals.
**Directions:** A64 from York, A171 from Whitby, A165
from Bridlington. 3 minutes from the railway station.
FRANK & YVONNE MILLARD, tel (0723) 365766,
fax (0723) 360448.

## THE COPPER HORSE, 15 Main Street, Seamer

*Traditional good homestyle cooking in a delightful pub*
*atmosphere, with efficient and helpful service in*
*comfortable surroundings. Ideally located for visiting*
*Scarborough and touring the North Yorkshire moors.*
FOOD up to £15 CLUB
**Hours:** open all year 7pm; lunch 12noon; dinner 6:30pm –
9:30pm. **Cuisine:** English:- Traditionally cooked food,
beautifully presented. Dishes may include, Crispy Boned
Half Duckling, Large Fillet of Haddock, plus Steaks, Grills
& Fish. **Credit cards:** Visa, Access. **Other points:**
licensed, Sunday lunch, no-smoking area, children catered
for – please check for age limits. **Directions:** situated off
the A64 in the main street of Seamer.
MR ST QUINTON, tel (0723) 862029.

## EAST AYTON LODGE COUNTRY HOTEL & RESTAURANT, Moor Lane, East Ayton

*An attractive country residence built in the early 19th*
*century and skilfully converted to a small but luxurious*
*hotel and restaurant. Situated 3 miles from Scarborough*
*in a beautiful 3 acre setting in the National Park, close*
*to the River Derwent.*
ACCOMMODATION £21–£30
FOOD £15–£20 CLUB ★
**Hours:** lunch 12noon – 2pm; dinner 6pm – 9pm.
**Cuisine:** English / French:- Home-grown produce in
season. A good selection of vegetarian meals. **Rooms:**
17 bedrooms all with tea making facilities, telephone,
radio, TV: 4 twins ensuite, 13 doubles ensuite. **Credit
cards:** Visa, Access. **Other points:** licensed, open-air
dining, Sunday lunch, children catered for – please
check for age limits, beer garden, baby-listening device,
cots, 24hr reception. **Directions:** turn left off A170 (to
Scarborough) in East Ayton. Close to Post Office.
BRIAN GARDNER, tel (0723) 864227, fax (0723)
862680.

## THE FALCON INN, Whitby Road, Cloughton

*A select Free House on the edge of the north Yorkshire*
*Moors, with open views of the sea. Good food served*

*by friendly, attentive staff. Three times winner of*
*"Scarborough in Bloom". Log fires in winter.*
ACCOMMODATION £21–£30
FOOD up to £15
**Hours:** open all year 6pm; lunch 12noon – 2pm; dinner
7pm – 9:30pm. **Cuisine:** English:- Bar meals, with
Carvery on Saturday evenings and Sunday lunchtimes in
the restaurant. **Rooms:** 8 bedrooms all with tea making
facilities, TV: 4 twins ensuite, 4 doubles ensuite.
**Directions:** 9 miles from Scarborough on A171 to
Whitby. Second Ravenscar turn off.
MESSRS STEWART & ROBERTS, tel (0723) 870717.

## LILMONT HOTEL, 44 Castle Road

*Ideally situated for both bays and town centre, this is a*
*family hotel with all modern amenities, and a reputation for*
*their excellent table and warm Yorkshire hospitality.*
*Nearby attractions include the harbour, castle, swimming*
*pool, water theme park, miniature railway, cricket ground,*
*indoor bowls centre, plus Scarborough's new multi-million*
*pound Brunswick Pavilion shopping centre.*
ACCOMMODATION under £20
FOOD up to £15
**Hours:** closed 2 weeks Oct or Nov; breakfast 8:30am –
9:15am; dinner 6pm; bar snacks 8:30pm – 11pm. **Cuisine:**
English:- Home cooked meals from a daily menu. Orders
taken at breakfast. **Rooms:** 8 bedrooms all with tea making
facilities, radio, TV: 1 single, 1 double, 1 single ensuite, 1
double ensuite, 2 twins ensuite, 2 family rooms ensuite.
**Credit cards:** Visa, Access. **Other points:** children catered
for – please check for age limits, open bank holidays, no-
smoking area, residents' lounge, vegetarian meals, parking,
special breaks. **Directions:** from A64 to town centre at
Railway station turn left, at traffic lights turn right, quarter
of a mile on left.
SHEILA AND WES SWIFT, tel (0723) 363687.

## MANOR HEATH HOTEL, 67 Northstead Manor Drive

*An attractive well appointed detached hotel overlooking*
*Peasholm Park and north Bay. Ideally situated close to*
*all the attractions of this English seaside resort – the*
*beach, swimming pools, Kinderland, miniature railway,*
*and Mr Marvels Fun Park, as well as golf links, bowling*
*and county cricket.*
ACCOMMODATION under £20
FOOD up to £15 ★
**Hours:** breakfast 9am; dinner 6pm; closed Christmas
day and New Year's day. **Cuisine:** English. **Rooms:** 16
bedrooms all with tea making facilities, TV: 2 singles, 1
single ensuite, 1 double, 6 doubles ensuite, 2 twins
ensuite, 4 family rooms ensuite. **Other points:** central
heating, children catered for – please check for age
limits, TV lounge. **Directions:** from Whitby, turn right
just before Peasholm Park traffic lights.
MRS JANET MOORE, tel (0723) 365720.

## RED LEA HOTEL, Prince of Wales Terrace

*One of Scarborough's most popular hotels having*
*undergone sympathetic conversion from six elegant*
*Victorian houses. Located on Scarborough's fashionable*

south Cliff, it provides an ideal base for summer
holidays, weekend breaks and conferences. Guests are
assured of a warm and sincere welcome. Superb heated
indoor swimming pool and fitness facilities.
ACCOMMODATION £31–£40
FOOD up to £15
**Hours:** breakfast 8:30am – 9:30am; bar meals 12noon –
2pm; lunch – Sunday 12:30pm – 1:30pm; dinner 6:30pm –
10pm. **Cuisine:** English. **Rooms:** 67 bedrooms all with tea
making facilities, telephone, radio, TV: 18 singles ensuite,
29 twins ensuite, 12 doubles ensuite, 7 triples ensuite, 1
quad ensuite. **Credit cards:** Visa, Access. **Other points:**
licensed, children catered for – please check for age limits,
Sunday lunch, open bank holidays, no-smoking area,
residents' lounge, vegetarian meals, 24 hr reception,
residents' bar, swimming pool, cots. **Directions:** Prince of
Wales Terrace runs between the Esplanade and Filey Road.
BRUCE & VALERIE LEE, tel (0723) 362431, fax
(0723) 371230.

### SOUTHLANDS HOTEL, 15 West Street, South Cliff
Southlands Hotel is ideally situated on Scarborough's
select south Cliff, enjoying close proximity to the Italian
Rose Gardens, Esplanade and South Bay. All bedrooms
in this centrally heated hotel are well appointed with
many facilities. The Windsor Restaurant offers a fine A
la Carte and Table d'Hote menu, and pre-luncheon
drinks can be enjoyed in the Windsor Bar. Evening
dances are held throughout the season, and in-house
conference facilities can cater for 20–100 delegates.
ACCOMMODATION £31–£40
FOOD up to £15
**Hours:** breakfast 8am – 9:30am; bar snacks 12noon –
1:45pm; dinner 6:30pm – 8:30pm. **Cuisine:** English.
**Rooms:** 58 bedrooms all with tea making facilities,
telephone, radio, TV: 8 singles ensuite, 21 twins ensuite,
20 doubles ensuite, 7 triples ensuite, 2 quads ensuite.
**Credit cards:** Visa, Access, Diners, AmEx. **Other
points:** parking, children catered for – please check for
age limits, open bank holidays, no-smoking area,
afternoon tea, pets allowed, residents' lounge, vegetarian
meals, residents' garden, licensed. **Directions:** A64, turn
right at Mere to Filey Road, turn left and second right.
MR & MRS DIXON, tel (0723) 361461, fax (0723)
376035.

## SCUNTHORPE, Humberside Map 18

### BRIGGATE LODGE INN, Ermine Street, Broughton, Brigg
An attractive hotel offering comfortable acommodation
and fine cuisine using only the freshest of produce.
Dishes may include Mustard Glazed Lamb Chops,
Supreme of Chicken Fromage, and Poached Salmon
Steak with a lime sauce.
ACCOMMODATION £31–£40
FOOD £21–£25
**Hours:** breakfast 7am – 10am; bar snacks 11am – 11pm;
lunch 12noon – 2pm; dinner 7pm – 10pm. **Cuisine:**

English /French. **Rooms:** 50 ensuite bedrooms.**Other
points:** parking, children catered for – please check for
age limits, Sunday lunch, open bank holidays, no-
smoking area, afternoon tea, Sunday dinner, disabled
access, residents' lounge, vegetarian meals, garden.
**Directions:** 200m from Junction 4 on M180. A18/A15.
MR M A MIDDLETON, tel (0652) 650770, fax (0652)
650495.

### TOWN HOUSE RESTAURANT, 62 Mary Street
Imaginative cooking and courteous service await you at the
Town House Restaurant. Well-cooked meals, a varied menu
and mouth-watering sweets are served in a congenial
atmosphere. Entrees cooked to your liking.
**Hours:** lunch 12noon – 3pm; dinner 7:30pm – 11pm;
closed Saturday lunch; closed Sunday. **Cuisine:** English /
French:- Exotic English and French cuisine. House
specialities are Beef Wellington, Chateaubriand, Steak
Tartare, Fondue. Flambes and sweets cooked at your table.
**Credit cards:** Visa, Access, AmEx. **Other points:** children
catered for – please check for age limits, vegetarian meals,
licensed. **Directions:** M180 Junction 3 for Scunthorpe.
STEPHEN WARD, tel (0724) 865111.

## SEAHOUSES, Northumberland Map 17

### BEACH HOUSE HOTEL, Seafront
A small, friendly family run hotel. Pleasantly situated
overlooking the Farne Islands. The Beach House Hotel
specialises in imaginative home cooking and baking.
Particularly suited to those looking for a quiet and
comfortable holiday.
ACCOMMODATION £31–£40
FOOD £15–£20
**Hours:** breakfast 8:30am – 9:30am; dinner 6:30pm –
7:30pm; closed November – March. **Cuisine:** English:-
Local produce. eg. game and fish including local
kippers. Clootie dumpling. **Rooms:** 14 bedrooms all en
suite. **Credit cards:** Visa, Access. **Other points:**
licensed, no-smoking area, children catered for – please
check for age limits. **Directions:** on the Seahouses to
Bamburgh road.
MR & MRS F R CRAIGS, tel (0665) 720337, fax (0665)
720921.

### THE LODGE, 146 Main Street
The falcon sign of this small hotel makes it easy to spot.
Styled along Scandinavian lines with pine panelling and
furniture throughout. Relaxing by the open fire in the
convivial bar is a perfect end to a day exploring this
historic and beautiful area.
ACCOMMODATION £21–£30
FOOD up to £15 ★
**Hours:** breakfast 8:30am – 9:30am; lunch 12noon –
2pm; dinner 6:30pm – 9:30pm. **Cuisine:** English /
seafood:- Local seafood. **Rooms:** 5 bedrooms all
with tea making facilities, TV: 4 doubles ensuite, 1 quad
ensuite. **Credit cards:** Visa, Access, AmEx.
**Other points:** Sunday lunch, children catered for –

please check for age limits, pets/prior arr, disabled access, vegetarian meals. **Directions:** on the main street in Seahouses (north Sunderland).
SELBY & JENIFER BROWN, tel (0665) 720158.

## THE ST AIDAN HOTEL AND RESTAURANT

*Built in 1919, the St Aidan Hotel boasts an unrivalled position on the seafront of the spectacular Northumbrian coastline, just a short distance from the bustling fishing village of Seahouses. The well appointed bedrooms have beautiful views – some towards the harbour, some towards the Farne Islands, Bamburgh Castle and Holy Island. A warm welcoming atmosphere prevails.*
*ACCOMMODATION £31–£40*
*FOOD up to £15*
**Hours:** breakfast 8am – 9.30am; dinner 6.30pm – 9pm. **Cuisine:** English/International. **Rooms:** 9 ensuite rooms all with TV, tea making facilities. **Credit cards:** Visa, Access, Diners, AmEx. **Other points:** parking, children catered for – please check for age limits, limited disabled access, pets allowed, residents' lounge, garden, vegetarian meals. **Directions:** 400m along seafront towards Bamburgh (next to filling station).
FREDDIE FORD-HUTCHINSON AND PETER AIREY, tel (0665) 720355, fax (0665) 830356.

# SEDBERGH, Cumbria Map 19

## THE DALESMAN COUNTRY INN, Main Street

*An olde worlde stone-built country inn, renovated by local craftsmen and situated in a village 'frozen-in-time'. Decorated in a country style throughout, with traditional log fires, this is a popular retreat for locals and tourists alike. Nice place to 'get away from it all'. Winter breaks very popular.*
*ACCOMMODATION £21–£30*
*FOOD up to £15*
**Hours:** breakfast 8:30am – 9:30am; lunch 12noon – 2pm; dinner 6pm – 9:30pm. **Cuisine:** English:- Grills and steaks, gammon, daily specials and roasts every Sunday. **Rooms:** 6 bedrooms all with tea making facilities, TV: 3 family rooms ensuite, 1 twin ensuite, 1 twin, 1 double. **Credit cards:** Visa, Access. **Other points:** licensed, Sunday lunch, children catered for – please check for age limits, afternoon tea, vegetarian meals. **Directions:** first pub on left entering Sedbergh, 5 miles from junction 37 of the M6.
BARRY & IRENE GARNETT, tel (05396) 21183.

## OAKDENE SEDBERGH COUNTRY HOUSE, Garsdale Road

*The hotel was built around 1880 for the Dover family who were leading mill owners in Sedburgh at the time. It retains many of its original Victorian fittings, such as gas lights, marble fireplaces and a splendid mahogany pannelled bath. Occupying an elevated position in the glorious Yorkshire Dales, it provides a perfect place to relax whilst enjoying simple, healthy, freshly prepared food in comfortable surroundings.*

*ACCOMMODATION £21–£30*
*FOOD up to £15*
**Hours:** closed January; breakfast 8am – 10am; dinner 7pm – 8:30pm. **Cuisine:** English:- Daily changing menu. **Rooms:** 6 bedrooms all with TV: 1 single ensuite, 1 twin ensuite, 3 doubles ensuite, 1 family room ensuite. **Credit cards:** Visa, Access. **Other points:** garden, children catered for – please check for age limits, no-smoking area, residents' lounge, vegetarian meals, garden. **Directions:** one mile east of Sedburgh on A684.
MRS H DIXON, tel (05396) 20280, fax (05396) 21501.

# SETTLE, North Yorkshire Map 18

## NEW INN HOTEL, Clapham

*The New Inn is over 200 years old and has provided a welcome stop for travellers to the Lake district and Scotland and visitors to the Yorkshire Dales since the 18th century. This coaching inn offers a relaxing and friendly atmosphere, comfortable accommodation and well cooked food in generous portions. Under the personal supervision of the resident proprietors.*
*ACCOMMODATION £21–£30*
*FOOD up to £15* ♉ ★
**Hours:** breakfast 8:30am – 9:30am; lunch 12noon – 2pm; dinner 7pm – 9:30pm. **Cuisine:** English:- Restaurant and bar meals. Dishes include Cheese and Leek Pie, Game Pie, and Sticky Toffee Pudding. **Rooms:** 13 bedrooms all with tea making facilities, telephone, TV: 3 twins ensuite, 10 doubles ensuite. **Credit cards:** Visa, Access, AmEx. **Other points:** licensed, Sunday lunch, children catered for – please check for age limits, garden, afternoon tea, pets allowed, games room, real ales, cots, residents' bar, residents' lounge, parking, vegetarian meals. **Directions:** situated on A65 to Lake District. Clapham is 5 miles north of Settle.
KEITH & BARBARA MANNION, tel (05242) 51203, fax (05242) 51496.

# SHEFFIELD, South Yorkshire Map 18

## HENRY'S CAFE BAR (SHEFFIELD), Cambridge Street

*A lively, popular cafe-bar serving an extensive range of international fast-food, American and non-alcoholic beers and speciality cocktails. The atmosphere is friendly and bustling.*
*FOOD up to £15*
**Hours:** closed Sunday; meals all day 8am – 7pm. **Cuisine:** international. **Credit cards:** Visa, Access. **Other points:** children catered for – please check for age limits, open bank holidays, no-smoking area, afternoon teas, disabled access, vegetarian meals.
ALASTAIR AMIV, tel (0742) 752342.

## THE OLD SIDINGS, 91 Chesterfield Road, Dronfield

*An attractive Victorian pub with railway memorabilia throughout waiting room lounge and buffet car dining room. Within the comfortable and welcoming*

surroundings there is a good choice of bar meals and snacks lunchtime and evening, in both lounge and dining room, with the emphasis on traditional, country style, home-made fayre.
*FOOD up to £15*
**Hours:** lunch 12noon – 2:30pm; dinner 6pm – 9:30pm.
**Cuisine:** Predominantly English. House speciality: Anne's Homemade Giant Yorkshire Pudding. Large Rump Steaks. A large selection of vegetarian meals. Family budget menus and children's menu. **Credit cards:** Visa, Access. **Other points:** licensed, Sunday lunch, no-smoking area, children catered for – please check for age limits, pets allowed, beer garden.
**Directions:** off main A61 on B6057. Next to only railway bridge in Dronfield.
WILLIAM & ANNE STANAWAY, tel (0246) 410023.

### ZING VAA RESTAURANT, 55 The Moor
*Genuine Cantonese dishes and atmosphere. Situated in the very heart of Sheffield's busy shopping area. Very popular with both locals, shoppers and business people.*
*FOOD up to £15*
**Hours:** meals all day 12noon – 12midnight; closed Christmas 25/12 – 26/12. **Cuisine:** Cantonese / Pekinese:- sliced fillet with king prawns marinated and cooked in a fruity sauce, duckling dishes. **Credit cards:** Visa, Access, Diners, AmEx. **Other points:** licensed, Sunday lunch, children catered for – please check for age limits, parking. **Directions:** in the heart of Sheffield's shopping centre opposite the bandstand.
ROGER CHEUNG, tel (0742) 722432, fax (0742) 729213.

## SHIPLEY, West Yorkshire Map 18

### THE CONNECTION, 41 Westgate
*A lively, family restaurant with eye-catching decor and a wide ranging menu. Much frequented by locals and tourists alike.*
*FOOD up to £15*
**Hours:** dinner – Sunday 4pm – 10pm; dinner – Saturday 5pm – 11pm; dinner – Mon-Fri 6pm – 11pm. **Cuisine:** international:- Hamburgers, pizzas, steaks, pancakes and chicken. **Credit cards:** Access, Visa, Switch. **Other points:** Sunday lunch. **Directions:** on the corner of the A657 and Westgate.
S R JENNINGS, tel (0274) 599461.

## SILLOTH ON SOLWAY, Cumbria Map 19

### THE GOLF HOTEL, Criffel Street
*Overlooking the Solway Firth within easy reach of the Lake District and the Scottish Borders. Excellent golf course 100 yd away. Golf-breaks a speciality.*
*FOOD £15–£20*
**Hours:** breakfast 7:30am – 9:30am; lunch 12noon – 2pm; dinner 7pm – 9:30pm; closed Christmas 25/12. **Cuisine:** English:- Solway special, medallion Golf Hotel, Sole van den Berg. **Rooms:** 23 bedrooms, all en suite. **Credit cards:** Visa, Access, Diners, AmEx. **Other**

**points:** Sunday lunch, children catered for – please check for age limits, coach/prior arr. **Directions:** B5300 or B5307, 20 miles from Carlisle.
FAUSTO & CHRISTINE PREVITALI, tel (06973) 31438.

## SKIPTON, North Yorkshire Map 18

### RANDELL'S HOTEL & LEISURE,
*Keighley Road, Snaygill*
*Randell's nestles in the Aire Valley next to the historic Leeds and Liverpool Canal with foothills to the Dales as a backdrop. Whether on business or pleasure, your every need is catered for. A health and beauty suite offers a tremendous range of treatments, whilst the ozone purified swimming pool ensures total relaxation. Extensive conference and banqueting facilities (350).*
*ACCOMMODATION £31–£40*
*FOOD £15–£20*
**Hours:** open all year; breakfast 7am – 10am; bar meals 11am – 7pm; dinner 7pm – 10pm. **Cuisine:** English:- Fixed price menu, offering fine dining in attractive and comfortable setting. Vegetarians catered for. A la carte menu. **Rooms:** 60 bedrooms all with tea making facilities, telephone, radio, TV: 25 doubles ensuite, 25 twins ensuite, 10 family rooms ensuite. **Credit cards:** Visa, Access, AmEx, Diners, Switch. **Other points:** licensed, Sunday lunch, children catered for – please check for age limits, playland, pets allowed, afternoon tea, leisure centre, squash, gym facilities, parking. **Directions:** 1 mile from the centre of Skipton, on the main A629 Keighley Road.
CHRISTOPHER HULL, tel (0756) 700100, fax (0756) 700107.

## SNAITH, Humberside Map 18

### BREWERS ARMS HOTEL, 10 Pontefract Road
*Theme Nights are a speciality at the Brewers Arms, from 'Gourmet Fish & Wine' evenings to Traditional Jazz, German Theme nights to Ye Old England. As well as the fine traditional cuisine, there is a good vegetarian menu, complemented by a wide range of beers and wines. Ideal for visiting the historic City of York.*
*ACCOMMODATION £21–£30*
**Hours:** breakfast 7am – 11:30am; bar snacks 11:30am – 2:30pm; lunch 12noon – 2:30pm; bar snacks 6pm – 9:30pm; dinner 6:30pm – 9:30pm/10pm. **Cuisine:** English/French. **Credit cards:** Visa, Access, AmEx. **Other points:** children catered for – please check for age limits, parking, no-smoking area, residents' lounge, garden, vegetarian meals, open-air dining. **Directions:** off A19 Selby / off M18/M62. Between York, Doncaster and Groote.
MR P P WAGSTAFF, tel (0405) 862404, fax (0405) 862397.

## SOUTH SHIELDS, Tyne & Wear Map 17

### SEA HOTEL, Sea Road
*This busy hotel is situated on the Sea Front in the heart of 'Catherine Cookson Country'. The hospitality,*

*for which the region is renowned, is reflected in the friendly service.*
ACCOMMODATION £31–£40
FOOD up to £15
**Hours:** breakfast 7am – 9:30am; lunch 12noon – 2:30pm; dinner 7pm – 9:30pm. **Cuisine:** English:- Traditional English menu using local produce, and a French based a la carte menu, both offering a wide choice of dishes. **Rooms:** 33 bedrooms 14 singles ensuite, 12 doubles ensuite, 5 twins ensuite, 2 triples ensuite. **Credit cards:** Visa, Access, Diners, AmEx. **Other points:** Sunday lunch, children catered for – please check for age limits. **Directions:** on the sea-front at A183 and A1018 junction.
MR JAMES, MR BASSETT & MR WATSON – MANAGERS, tel (091) 4270999, fax (091) 454 0500.

---

# SOUTHPORT, Merseyside Map 16

## THE AMBASSADOR PRIVATE HOTEL, 13 Bath Street
*Situated in an early Victorian terrace and family run since 1964. This small hotel offers a good standard of accomodation and is centrally situated for the main shopping areas and promenade, water sports and golf courses. The relaxed and comfortable surroundings are complemented by the friendly welcome provided by the proprietors Margaret and Harry Bennett.*
ACCOMMODATION £21–£30
FOOD up to £15
**Hours:** closed Xmas & New Year; breakfast 7:30am – 9:30am; bar snacks 12:30pm – 2pm; dinner 6pm – 7pm; bar snacks 9pm – 11pm. **Cuisine:** Predominantly English. **Rooms:** 8 bedrooms all with tea making facilities, radio, TV: 1 single ensuite, 2 twins ensuite, 2 doubles ensuite, 3 family rooms ensuite. **Credit cards:** Visa, Access. **Other points:** no-smoking area, pets allowed, residents' lounge, parking, children catered for – please check for age limits. **Directions:** from Lord Street, turn at traffic lights toward promenade, then second on the right.
MARGARET & HARRY BENNETT, tel (0704) 543998, (0704) 530459, fax (0704) 536269.

## THE CRIMOND HOTEL, Knowsley Road
*A small family-run hotel offering excellent facilities including indoor swimming pool, sauna and Jacuzzi. The good food, excellent service and comfortable accommodation combine to make this a pleasant and relaxing stay for tourists and businessmen alike. Conference facilities, including slide projector, TV and video.*
ACCOMMODATION £21–£30
FOOD up to £15
**Hours:** breakfast 7:30am – 9:30am; lunch 12noon – 2pm; dinner 7pm – 9pm. **Cuisine:** modern English:- Grey mullet, grilled, served with a savoury filling of apple onion/herbs with lemon. Crimond steak cooked with capsicums/mushrooms blended in cream sauce. **Rooms:** 15 bedrooms all with tea making facilities, telephone, radio, TV: 4 singles ensuite, 5 twins ensuite, 4 doubles ensuite, 2 family rooms ensuite. **Credit cards:** Visa, Access, Diners, AmEx. **Other points:** no-smoking

area, garden, pets allowed, conferences, functions. **Directions:** situated in Southport, off Park Road West. Near Municipal Golf Links.
PAT & GEOFF RANDLE, tel (0704) 536456, fax (0704) 548643.

## THE GILTON HOTEL, 7 Leicester Street
*A Victorian house with an attractive well-kept garden, situated in the centre of Southport. Gilton Hotel is traditionally decorated to provide a comfortable place to stay for tourists and business people alike. Mrs Cunliffe extends a warm welcome to all her guests and the hotel enjoys a friendly, homely atmosphere. Particularly attractive for golfers with 5 courses nearby.*
**Hours:** breakfast 7:30am – 9am; dinner 5:30pm – 8pm; bar meals 7pm – 10pm. **Cuisine:** English. **Rooms:** 13 bedrooms all with tea making facilities, radio, TV: 1 single ensuite, 7 twins ensuite, 5 doubles ensuite. **Credit cards:** Visa, Access. **Other points:** children catered for – please check for age limits, garden, TV lounge, residents' lounge, games room, table-tennis, golf nearby, baby sitting, baby-listening device, cots. **Directions:** M6; exit M62. Follow till M57: exit A565. Signposted Southport.
MR & MRS CUNLIFFE, tel (0704) 530646.

---

# STANDISH, Greater Manchester Map 16

## BEECHES HOTEL & RESTAURANT, School Lane, Wigan
*A privately-owned hotel set in picturesque grounds, providing a very personal and friendly service. A high standard of cuisine can be enjoyed in the new Brasserie with its informal atmosphere, or in the corniced Victorian dining room where guests can relax within the charm and elegance of a bygone era. Comfortable accommodation.*
ACCOMMODATION £21–£30
FOOD up to £15
**Hours:** coffee 8am – 11pm; Sunday lunch 12noon – 2:30pm; brasserie – 7 days 12noon – 2:30pm; dinner – Tue-Sat 5pm – 10pm; brasserie – 7 days 5pm – 10:30pm. **Cuisine:** seafood:- Extensive menus including upto 13 varieties of fish and seafood. Dishes may include Fillet of Scotch Beef, Roast Turbot, Sauteed Sea Scallops. **Rooms:** 11 bedrooms all with tea making facilities, telephone, TV: 1 single ensuite, 4 doubles ensuite, 6 twins ensuite. **Credit cards:** Visa, Access, AmEx. **Other points:** children catered for – please check for age limits, bank holidays, garden, guide dogs. **Directions:** 4 miles north of Wigan. 1.5 miles from Junction 27 of the M6 on the B5239.
MR F MOORE, tel (0257) 426432, fax (0257) 427503.

---

# STOKESLEY, North Yorkshire Map 18

## MILLERS RESTAURANT, 9 Bridge Road
*An attractive, family-run restaurant with an excellent reputation locally. Bookings are required for dinner. The lunchtime menu offers simpler meals at a very reasonable price. Lunch or dinner, all meals are well cooked and excellently served.*
FOOD up to £15 ☺

**Hours:** lunch 12noon – 2pm; dinner 7:30pm – 9:30pm; closed Sunday – Monday. **Cuisine:** English:- Steaks. Lighter meals served on the lunchtime menu. **Credit cards:** Visa, Access, Diners, AmEx. **Other points:** licensed, reservations, street parking. **Directions:** off Stokesley High Street (A172), by River Leven. KATHRYN ABBOTT, tel (0642) 710880.

## THE WAINSTONES HOTEL, 31 High Street, Great Broughton

*A most attractive village hotel with a real "local" bar. The restaurant has a homely atmosphere and serves both a la carte and table d'hote meals within its bright and airy setting. Great care and consideration is shown to all guests and the accommodation is of a high standard.*
ACCOMMODATION £21–£30
FOOD up to £15 ★
**Hours:** breakfast 7am – 9:30am; lunch 12noon – 2pm; bar meals 12noon – 2pm; bar meals 5pm – 10pm; dinner 7pm – 10pm. **Cuisine:** modern English:- Savoury cheese fritters, medallions of pork fillet, home-made beef burgers. **Rooms:** 23 bedrooms all with tea making facilities, telephone, radio, TV: 4 singles ensuite, 11 twins ensuite, 8 doubles ensuite. **Credit cards:** Visa, Access, AmEx. **Other points:** open-air dining, Sunday lunch, children catered for – please check for age limits, conferences, guide dogs. **Directions:** situated 2 miles south east of Stokesley on the B1257 Helmsley Road. JAMES KEITH PIGG, tel (0642) 712268, fax (0642) 711560.

## SULBY, Isle of Man Map 19

## PEPPER MILL RESTAURANT, Sulby Mill
*Situated in the heart of the beautiful countryside, this former woollen mill, now extensively refurbished, offers good food and friendly service in an informal setting. Excellent wine list and well stocked bar. Nearby visitor attractions include Sulby Claddagh and a Wildlife Park.*
FOOD up to £15
**Hours:** open all year 7pm; lunch 12noon – 2:30pm; dinner 6pm – 10pm. **Cuisine:** British:- Fixed price menus offering a wide choice of dishes, including Junior Gourmet's selection. Vegetarian dishes available. **Credit cards:** Visa, Access. **Other points:** licensed, open-air dining, Sunday lunch, children catered for – please check for age limits, parking, vegetarian meals. **Directions:** turn off Snaefell Mountain Road at bungalow. Centre of Sulby Glen. MITCHAEL HARVEY & KARL MEIER, tel (0624) 897436.

## SUNDERLAND, Tyne & Wear Map 17

## MOWBRAY PARK HOTEL, Borough Road
*A family-run private hotel, located within five minutes walk of the railway station, business and shopping areas and backing onto one of Sunderland's most impressive parks. The restaurant offers good food, well presented and at good value for money. Ideal for either a simple business lunch or for that special occasion.*

ACCOMMODATION £31–£40
FOOD £15–£20
**Hours:** breakfast 7am – 10am; bar meals 12noon – 2pm; dinner 7pm – 10pm. **Cuisine:** English / French:- English and French cuisine, including Chateaubriand au Mowbray and breast of Duck in a port sauce with green peppercorns. Imaginative vegetarian dishes. **Rooms:** 58 bedrooms, 40 en suite. **Credit cards:** Visa, Access, Diners, AmEx. **Other points:** licensed, Sunday lunch, children catered for – please check for age limits, afternoon tea, pets allowed, residents' lounge, functions, conferences. **Directions:** centre of Sunderland, next to Mowbray Park, town museum & library. EDWARD HUGHES, tel (091) 5678221.

## THE PULLMAN LODGE HOTEL, Whitburn Road, Seaburn

*A real dream for railway enthusiasts, this privately owned and personally run modern hotel is built in unique railway style offering the visitor every modern convenience. It is situated on one of the north east's most unspoilt beaches and close to some of Northumbria's finest heritage sites. Enjoy a drink in the Station Bar before retreating to the well appointed Carriage Restaurant overlooking the rugged coastline, where you can choose from an a la carte menu using only the freshest produce and cooked to perfection. The Pullman also offers a complete Wedding Package along with extensive conference and private function facilities.*
ACCOMMODATION £21–£30
FOOD up to £15
**Hours:** breakfast 7am – 10am; bar meals 12noon – 3pm; dinner 7pm – 10pm; bar meals 7pm – 10pm. **Cuisine:** English:- A range of choices on a la carte, table d'hote menu and bar menu. **Rooms:** 16 bedrooms all with tea making facilities, telephone, radio, TV: 8 twins ensuite, 8 family rooms ensuite. **Credit cards:** Visa, Access, Diners, AmEx. **Other points:** parking, children catered for – please check for age limits, Sunday lunch, open bank holidays, weekend breaks, disabled access, pets allowed, residents' lounge, vegetarian meals. DERRICK & PAULINE HARDY, tel (091) 5292020, fax (091) 5292077.

## THIRLMERE, Cumbria Map 19

## STYBECK FARM
*A working mixed farm with a friendly, non-smoking atmosphere. Situated at the foot of Helvellyn range of mountains, central for touring, walking, fishing and sailing on Lake Thirlmere.*
ACCOMMODATION under £20
**Hours:** breakfast 8:30am – 9am; dinner 7pm; closed Christmas 25/12. **Cuisine:** breakfast. **Rooms:** 4 bedrooms all with tea making facilities: 1 double ensuite, 1 double, 1 single, 1 family room. **Other points:** central heating, children catered for – please check for age limits, residents' lounge. **Directions:** A591 near the junction with the B5322. 5 miles Keswick. JOSEPH & JEAN HODGSON, tel (07687) 73232.

## THIRSK, North Yorkshire Map 18

### ANGEL INN, Long Street, Topcliffe

*Dating back to the 17th century, the Angle Inn is seeped in history being one of the main stopping points between the north and south in the days of stagecoach travel. In recent years it has been tastefully extended into a charming country inn which is renowned for its warm, friendly atmosphere, excellent food and traditional Yorkshire ales. A choice of suites provide the perfect setting for private functions and conferences. Car and coach park for 150 vehicles.*

ACCOMMODATION £21–£30

FOOD up to £15

**Hours:** breakfast 7am – 9:15am; lunch 12noon – 2:30pm; dinner 6:30pm – 9:30pm. **Cuisine:** English / international:- A wide choice including home-made steak and kidney pie, Chicken Switzerland, Leek and Gruyere Pithivier. **Rooms:** 15 bedrooms all with tea making facilities, telephone, mini bar, TV: 2 singles ensuite, 4 twins ensuite, 8 doubles ensuite, 1 family room ensuite. **Credit cards:** Access, Visa, Switch. **Other points:** parking, children catered for – please check for age limits, open bank holidays, afternoon tea, residents' lounge, vegetarian meals, garden, open-air dining, fishing, conferences, functions. **Directions:** on A167, just off A168. 3 miles from the A1 and A19. TONY & TRISH ARDRON, tel (0845) 577237, fax (0845) 578000.

### NAG'S HEAD HOTEL & RESTAURANT, Pickhill

*There has been an inn on this site for over 200 years, providing food and rest for travellers and horses using the A1 which was then the only road connecting London and Edinburgh. Today, the Nag's Head has been upgraded to an excellent standard, with comfortable rooms, superb cuisine and a wide selection of real ales and wines. Highly recommended.*

ACCOMMODATION £21–£30

FOOD £15–£20

**Hours:** breakfast 7am – 10:30am; lunch 12noon – 2pm; dinner – Sunday 6pm – 10pm; dinner – except Sunday 7pm – 9:30pm. **Cuisine:** English:- A la carte menu, dishes including grilled duck breast with blackcherry sauce, and supreme of chicken Americano. Desserts, eg. Highland Flummery. **Rooms:** 15 bedrooms all with tea making facilities, telephone, TV: 3 singles ensuite, 5 twins ensuite, 7 doubles ensuite. **Credit cards:** Visa, Access. **Other points:** Sunday lunch, children catered for – please check for age limits, pets allowed, garden, conferences. **Directions:** 1 mile off A1, near Thirsk. RAYMOND & EDWARD BOYNTON, tel (0845) 567391.

### SHEPPARD'S HOTEL, RESTAURANT & BISTRO, Front Street, Sowerby

*17th century brick buildings, ideally situated in Herriot Country. Sympathetically modernised, yet retaining a comfortable, country atmosphere which is a joy to relax and unwind in. Excellent cuisine and service amidst attractive surroundings.*

ACCOMMODATION £21–£30

FOOD £15–£20

**Hours:** open all year 7pm; breakfast 8:30am – 9am; lunch 12noon – 2pm; dinner 7pm – 9:30pm. **Cuisine:** English / international:- Fresh local produce used. Restaurant and Bistro. **Rooms:** 8 bedrooms all with tea making facilities, telephone, TV: 7 doubles ensuite, 1 triple ensuite. **Credit cards:** Visa, Access. **Other points:** licensed, Sunday lunch, children catered for – please check for age limits. **Directions:** off A19, into south west corner of Thirsk, half mile to Sowerby. ROY SHEPPARD, tel (0845) 523655, fax (0845) 524720.

## THORNABY, Cleveland Map 17

### GOLDEN EAGLE HOTEL, Trenchard Avenue

*Set in the heart of Teesside's commercial centre, the Golden Eagle is an excellent venue for conferences, yet provides prompt and easy access to the North Yorkshire Moors National Park. The hotel is situated only a few minutes from the A19 and is close to both main line rail and air communications. There is easy access to the A1 and M1 motorways.*

ACCOMMODATION £21–£30

FOOD up to £15

**Hours:** breakfast 7am – 10am; bar meals 11am – 9:30pm; dinner 7pm – 8:30pm. **Cuisine:** English. **Rooms:** 57 bedrooms 10 singles ensuite, 30 doubles ensuite, 17 twins ensuite. **Credit cards:** Visa, Access, Diners, AmEx. **Other points:** parking, children catered for – please check for age limits, disabled access, pets, vegetarian meals, reataurant, bar. **Directions:** leave A19 onto A174, turn left at traffic lights and hotel is half mile on the right. JOHN SNAITH & EDWARD HUGHES, tel (0642) 766511, fax (0642) 750336.

## THORNTON HOUGH, Merseyside Map 16

### THORNTON HALL HOTEL, Wirral

*Formerly the home of a major shipping family, Thornton Hall is a magnificent residence set in seven acres of gardens. Splendid wood carvings and panelling adorn the main staircase and many rooms. The Italian Room provides a perfect setting for the hotel restaurant, whilst The Pulford Suite is ideal for private functions. Suitably located in the lovely Wirral countryside.*

ACCOMMODATION £31–£40

FOOD £21–£25

**Hours:** breakfast 7am – 9:30am; dinner 7pm – 10pm. **Cuisine:** English:- An excellent choice of set and a la carte menus based on local produce and creative cooking. Comprehensive wine list complements our award winning chef recognised as one of the best on the Wirral. **Rooms:** 63 bedrooms all with tea making facilities, telephone, radio, TV: 32 twins ensuite, 31 doubles ensuite. **Credit cards:** Visa, Access, AmEx.

**Other points:** licensed, open-air dining, Sunday lunch, children catered for – please check for age limits, pets allowed, afternoon tea, parking, functions, special breaks, baby sitting, baby-listening device, cots, 24hr reception, foreign exchange, left luggage. **Directions:** exit Junction 4 of M53 and take B5151 – turn off right onto B5136. COLIN THOMPSON, tel (051) 336 3938, fax (051) 336 7864.

## ULVERSTON, Cumbria Map 19

### HILL FOOT HOTEL, Pennington Lane

*Within easy reach of the magnificence of the Lake District, this excellent family-run hotel is set in a charming cobbled market town and boasts meat suppliers appointed by Her Majesty the Queen. An ideal base for a relaxing vacation. The well-equipped bedrooms and facilities and friendly service ensure your personal comfort, while the superb cuisine offers maximum satisfaction.*

*ACCOMMODATION £21–£30*

*FOOD up to £15*

**Hours:** open all year 7pm; open bank holidays 7pm; breakfast 7:30am – 9am; lunch 11:30am – 2:30pm; dinner 6:30pm – 9:30pm. **Cuisine:** English:- Good quality English cooking. Charcoal grilled steaks a house speciality. Daily chef's specials. **Rooms:** 11 bedrooms all en suite. **Credit cards:** Visa, Access, AmEx. **Other points:** licensed, open-air dining, Sunday lunch, children catered for – please check for age limits, pets allowed. **Directions:** situated on the A590 past Ulverston by a garden centre. MARGARET NICOLSON, tel (0229) 580300.

## WALLASEY, Merseyside Map 16

### GROVE HOUSE HOTEL & RESTAURANT, Grove Road, Wirral

*A well-appointed Victorian hotel and restaurant, situated in its own attractive gardens in a quiet residential area of Wallasey. Offering fine cuisine using a comprehensive menu, including an extensive selection of vegetarian dishes. Excellent accommodation and warm, courteous service.*

*ACCOMMODATION £31–£40*

*FOOD £15–£20*

**Hours:** breakfast 7:30am – 9:30am; lunch 12noon – 2pm; dinner 7pm – 9:30pm. **Cuisine:** French / continental:- Comprehensive a la carte menu, featuring French and continental dishes. **Rooms:** 4 single, 2 twin and 8 double bedrooms, all en suite. **Credit cards:** Visa, Access. **Other points:** licensed, Sunday lunch, children catered for – please check for age limits, garden, functions, conferences. **Directions:** off the A554. MR N J BURN, tel (051) 639 3947.

### LEASOWE CASTLE, Leasowe, Moreton

*This 16th century castle has been converted to accommodate an excellent restaurant with varied table d'hote and a la carte menus. The Stables restaurant has recently opened and serves continental & English dishes in a very relaxed atmosphere. Sea views, outstanding accommodation, fine cuisine and excellent service, combine to make Leasowe Castle a delightful place to visit.*

*ACCOMMODATION £41–£50*

*FOOD up to £15*

**Hours:** breakfast 7am – 10am; lunch 12noon – 3pm; Stables Restaurant 4:30pm – 11pm; dinner 7pm – 10pm. **Cuisine:** English / continental:- A la carte and fixed 3 course menu, bar meals/snacks. A second restaurant has recently opened serving continental & English dishes. **Rooms:** 49 bedrooms all with tea making facilities, telephone, radio, TV: 23 twins ensuite, 23 doubles ensuite, 3 triples ensuite. **Credit cards:** Visa, Access, Diners, AmEx. **Other points:** licensed, Sunday lunch, no-smoking area, children catered for – please check for age limits, garden, afternoon tea, 24 hr reception, foreign exchange, residents' bar, residents' lounge, baby sitting, baby-listening device, cots. **Directions:** Wallasey is situated at the end of the M53, 3 miles from Liverpool. MR HARDING, tel (051) 606 9191.

### MONROES, 45 Wallasey Road

*A Bistro style restaurant with a 'Marilyn Monroe' theme, offering tasty and well presented food in a happy and relaxed atmosphere. Friendly, attentive service will assist you in your choice of over 24 steak dishes, vegetarian dishes and specials. 14 page menu and children's menu.*

*FOOD up to £15* CLUB

**Hours:** dinner – Sunday 5:30pm – 10pm; dinner – except Sunday 6pm – 11pm. **Cuisine:** English / international:- Specialities include over 24 steak dishes. Homemade profiteroles, cheesecake and apple pie, plus Vegetarian menu. Siumai, Cantonese beef balls, Texas rib starters, Buffalo pie, surf'n'turf chicken, pork marsala. **Credit cards:** Visa, Access, AmEx. **Other points:** children catered for – please check for age limits. **Directions:** situated in Liscard, 2 kilometres north west of Wallasey town centre. DAVID W CULLEN, tel (051) 638 3633.

## WARKWORTH, Northumberland Map 17

### THE JACKDAW RESTAURANT, 34 Castle Street

*Attractive cottage-restaurant with a friendly atmosphere and home-cooking with locally purchased produce. The a la carte menu features a wide selection of traditional dishes including mouthwatering sweets prepared daily. The menus change frequently. The fixed price Sunday lunch is deservedly very popular.*

*FOOD up to £15*

**Hours:** closed 01/01 – mid-February; lunch 12:30pm – 2pm; dinner 7pm – 9pm; closed Monday; closed Sunday evening; closed Thursday evening. **Cuisine:** English:- Menu changes for lunch and dinner. All dishes are home made. **Credit cards:** Visa, Access, Diners, AmEx. **Other points:** licensed, Sunday lunch, no-smoking area, children catered for – please check for age limits, bank holidays, morning tea, afternoon tea. **Directions:** 7 miles south of Alnwick on coast road A1068. RUPERT AND GILLIAN BELL, tel (0665) 711488.

## WATERMILLOCK, Cumbria Map 19

### WATERSIDE HOUSE, Near Penrith

*This is a lovely old house built in 1771, standing in its own 10 acre estate of gardens and meadows and facing Ullswater's shores. Built as two long arms around a cobbled courtyard, this setting gives the place that 'time gone by' atmosphere. A new brassserie-style restaurant is due to open in March 1994.*
**Hours:** breakfast 7am – 9:30am. **Other points:** parking, children catered for – please check for age limits, Sunday lunch, open bank holidays, no-smoking area, afternoon tea, Sunday dinner, disabled access, pets allowed, residents' lounge, vegetarian meals, open-air dining, garden. **Directions:** M6 (Exit 40) A66 for quarter mile. A592 for 6 miles.
MS S JENNER, tel (07684) 86038.

## WENSLEYDALE, North Yorkshire Map 18

### WENSLEYDALE HEIFER, West Witton, Leyburn

*A 17th century Dales inn situated in the heart of James Herriot country and in the Yorkshire Dales National Park. Restaurant and bistro style bar setting. With easy access to the A684, this typical beamed coaching inn is central for walking, fishing, shooting and touring.*
ACCOMMODATION £41–£50
FOOD £21–£25
**Hours:** open all year 7am; breakfast 8:30am – 9:30am; lunch 12noon – 2pm; dinner 7pm – 9:30pm. **Cuisine:** English:- Traditional Yorkshire cooking. All fresh and local produce. **Rooms:** 19 bedrooms all with tea making facilities, telephone, radio, TV: 6 twins ensuite, 12 doubles ensuite, 1 triple ensuite. **Credit cards:** Visa, Access, Diners, AmEx. **Other points:** Sunday lunch, children catered for – please check for age limits, baby sitting, baby-listening device, cots, left luggage. **Directions:** take A684 towards Hawes. West Witton is 4 miles from Leyburn.
MAJOR & MRS J B SHARP, tel (0969) 22322, fax (0969) 24183.

## WHITBY, North Yorkshire Map 18

### ANDERSONS, Silver Street

*Centrally located this bistro is popular for either a full meal or for a snack. Often gets very full in the evenings; booking recommended. Tables in the garden in summer.*
FOOD £15–£20
**Hours:** bar 10am – 11pm, lunch 11:30am – 2:15pm; dinner 6:30pm – 9:45pm. **Cuisine:** modern English:- Steaks with sauces, local fish dishes. Vegetarian menu available. **Credit cards:** Visa, Access, Diners, AmEx. **Other points:** open-air dining, Sunday lunch, children catered for – please check for age limits, pets allowed. **Directions:** Whitby is on A174 and A171, Bistro is located in town centre.
DAVID WHISSON, tel (0947) 605383.

### DUNSLEY HALL, Dunsley

*Dunsley Hall with its oak panelled hallways and rooms was built at the turn of the century, and offers a naturally warm*

*and welcoming atmosphere. There are 7 richly decorated bedrooms, including a 4 poster suite, which is perfect for honeymoon couples. For gentle recreation, the superb oak panelled billiard room is equipped with a full-size Matchplay table. Central for touring.*
ACCOMMODATION £31–£40
FOOD up to £15
**Hours:** breakfast 8:30am – 9:15am; dinner 7:30pm.
**Cuisine:** English. **Rooms:** 7 en suite bedrooms, airy and light, with private bath or shower, colour TV, radio, hair driers, telephones, tea/coffee facilities, full central heating. **Credit cards:** Visa, Access. **Other points:** bank holidays, residents' lounge, vegetarian meals, swimming pool, gym facilities, tennis, putting green. **Directions:** between A171 and coast road 3 miles north of Whitby at Dunsley.
IAN & ROASLIE BUCKLE, tel (0947) 83437, fax (0947) 83505.

### KIMBERLEY HOTEL, 7 Havelock Place

*Situated in the centre of Whitby the hotel acts as an ideal base for those exploring the town. Elegantly decorated to a high degree of comfort, the hotel is very popular with locals and holiday-makers. In the restaurant you can enjoy carefully presented meals, made from the freshest of ingredients in cosy surroundings. Highly recommended.*
ACCOMMODATION under £20
FOOD up to £15
**Hours:** breakfast 8:30am – 9:15am; dinner 7pm – 9:30pm. **Cuisine:** Italian / English:- Dishes may include Risotto with wild Mushrooms, Chicken breast stuffed with Mozzarella cheese & Parma ham, Tagliatelle with salmon. **Rooms:** 6 bedrooms all with telephone, TV: 6 doubles ensuite. **Credit cards:** Visa, Access. **Other points:** licensed, no-smoking area, street parking, vegetarian meals. **Directions:** situated on West Cliff close to sea-front.
MR & MRS CASTOLDI, tel (0947) 604125, fax (0947) 606147.

### THE MAGPIE CAFE, 14 Pier Road

*The McKenzie family have been serving superb fish in this historic building for nigh on 40 years. Window tables overlook the Abbey, 199 steps and picturesque harbour of Whitby. The restaurant is extremely popular with holiday-makers and locals alike. The food is always fresh and well cooked and the service friendly, quick and welcoming. Les Routiers Casserole Award 1991 & 1992.*
FOOD up to £15 ☜
**Hours:** meals all day 11:30am – 6:30pm; closed end November – early March. **Cuisine:** English:- Fresh, local fish and shellfish straight off the quayside including crab, lobster & salmon. Local ham, home-made steak pie and 30 home-made desserts. **Credit cards:** Visa, Access. **Other points:** Sunday lunch, children catered for – please check for age limits. **Directions:** Pier Road is main road from town centre to the beach and west Pier.
S & I MCKENZIE, A MCKENZIE-ROBSON & I RO, tel (0947) 602058.

### SEACLIFFE HOTEL, North Promenade, West Cliff

*A friendly, family-run hotel with a restaurant which is also open to non-residents. All food is of good quality and well presented, at very reasonable prices. Nicely decorated bedrooms, some with sea views, and situated close to local attractions such as Whitby Abbey, the museum and the local golf course.*

*ACCOMMODATION £21–£30*

*FOOD up to £15* ★

**Hours:** open all year; breakfast 8am – 9:30am; dinner 6pm – 9pm. **Cuisine:** English:- English cuisine, including fresh local seafood, steaks and vegetarian dishes. **Rooms:** 20 bedrooms all with tea making facilities, telephone, radio, TV: 1 single ensuite, 15 doubles ensuite, 3 triples ensuite, 1 quad ensuite. **Credit cards:** Visa, Access, Diners, AmEx. **Other points:** licensed, children catered for – please check for age limits, pets allowed, bank holidays, residents' lounge, residents' bar, vegetarian meals, parking. **Directions:** take A171 or A174 to Whitby. Follow signs to West Cliff.
J A PURCELL, tel (0947) 603139, fax (0947) 603139.

### STAKESBY MANOR, Manor Close, High Stakesby

*A lovely 17th century manor house, situated on the edge of Whitby, that has been owned and controlled by two generations of the Hodgson Family. Located in a quiet area approximately one mile from town centre, golf course and beach, 'Stakesby Manor' offers well cooked tasty food, friendly attentive service and comfortable accommodation in relaxed and attractive surroundings.*

*ACCOMMODATION £21–£30*

*FOOD £21–£25*

**Hours:** breakfast 8am – 9am; dinner 7pm – 9:30pm. **Cuisine:** modern English:- 3 course a la carte menu and table d'hote including salmon & lobster mousse, lobster cardinal, veal in leek & stilton sauce. **Rooms:** 8 bedrooms all with tea making facilities, TV: 2 twins ensuite, 6 doubles ensuite. **Credit cards:** Visa, Access, AmEx. **Other points:** vegetarian meals, special diets, children catered for – please check for age limits, garden, picnic lunches, functions, conferences, special breaks. **Directions:** off the A171.
MR & MRS HODGSON, tel (0947) 602773.

### TRENCHER'S RESTAURANT, New Quay Road

*A family-run seafood restaurant in the historic fishing town of Whitby. Fresh Whitby fish and seafoods are, needless to say, a speciality and are cooked to a high standard. Terry and his sisters Judy and Nicky have received thank you letters from as far away as Europe and the USA.*

*FOOD up to £15*

**Hours:** last orders 7pm; meals all day 11am – 12midnight; dinner 6pm – 9pm; closed January – February. **Cuisine:** seafood:- Fresh local fish, salad bar, freshly cut sandwiches, home-made desserts. **Other points:** licensed, Sunday lunch, children catered for – please check for age limits. **Directions:** opposite the Harbour offices and quayside car park, off main A174.
TERRY, JUDY & NICKY FOSTER, tel (0947) 603212.

### WHITE HOUSE HOTEL, Upgang Lane

*The Hotel is situated adjacent to Whitby Golf Course with panoramic views of Sandsend Bay. Whitby is a charming, picturesque fishing port with a history extending back 1000 years. An ideal location for discovering an intriguing part of Yorkshire.*

*ACCOMMODATION £21–£30*

*FOOD up to £15*

**Hours:** breakfast 8:30am – 10am; lunch 12noon – 2pm; dinner 7pm – 10pm. **Cuisine:** English:- Yorkshire pudding with stew. 'Galley' 5 course dinner. **Rooms:** 12 bedrooms, all en suite. **Credit cards:** Visa, Access. **Other points:** licensed, Sunday lunch, children catered for – please check for age limits. **Directions:** on the A174, beside Whitby golf course on the West Cliff.
THOMAS CAMPBELL, tel (0947) 600469, fax (0947) 821600.

## WHITLEY BAY, Tyne & Wear Map 17

### THE GRANGE RESTAURANT, East Holywell

*An 18th century farmhouse, which has been sympathetically extended to provide a relaxing, comfortable restaurant. Diners can choose from an extensive a la carte menu, created by one of the north's leading Chef's who uses only the freshest of local produce. Pre-dinner drinks can be enjoyed in the Cocktail Lounge. An excellent wine list is also available.*

*FOOD £21–£25*

**Hours:** closed Sunday evening 7pm; closed Monday 7pm; lunch 11am – 2pm; dinner 7pm – 11pm. **Cuisine:** English. **Credit cards:** Visa, Access, Diners, AmEx. **Other points:** parking, children catered for – please check for age limits, disabled access, residents' lounge, vegetarian meals, Sunday lunch, open bank holidays. **Directions:** near Earsdon village, Whitley Bay.
LYNN WAGNER, tel (091) 252 6980, fax (091) 252 0980.

### YORK HOUSE HOTEL, 30 Park Parade

*A family run hotel offering comfort, home cooking and good service in a friendly atmosphere. A mid terrace Victorian building in the town centre, the hotel is ideally situated for safe, sandy beaches, parks, indoor Leisure pool and the shopping centre. Much thought has been given to the comfort of their guests whether families on holiday or business people travelling in the area.*

*ACCOMMODATION under £20*

*FOOD up to £15* ★

**Hours:** breakfast 7am – 9:30am; dinner 6pm – 7pm. **Cuisine:** English. **Rooms:** 8 bedrooms all with tea making facilities, telephone, radio, TV: 1 single, 2 twins ensuite, 3 doubles ensuite, 2 family rooms ensuite. **Credit cards:** Visa, Access, AmEx. **Other points:** 24hr reception, lounge, central heating, children catered for –

please check for age limits, baby sitting, cots, disabled access. **Directions:** off A193 Park Avenue.
JUDY & MICHAEL RUDDY, tel (091) 252 8313, fax (091) 251 3953.

## WIGGLESWORTH, North Yorkshire Map 18

### THE PLOUGH INN, Nr Skipton
*This lovely country hotel is situated just two miles from the A65. Boasting early 18th century origins, the Plough Inn provides excellent food and service, comfortable furnishings and good service to meet all your needs. Good dining is offered in the bright conservatory restaurant.*
ACCOMMODATION £21–£30
FOOD up to £15
**Hours:** lunch 12noon – 2pm; dinner 7pm – 9:45pm.
**Cuisine:** English:- Beef and Cowheel Cobbler, seafood pancakes. **Rooms:** 12 bedrooms all with tea making facilities, telephone, radio, TV: 3 twins ensuite, 7 doubles ensuite, 2 family rooms ensuite. **Credit cards:** Visa, Access, Diners, AmEx. **Other points:** licensed, Sunday lunch, children catered for – please check for age limits. **Directions:** from the A65 at Long Preston, take the B6478 to Wigglesworth.
BRIAN GOODALL, tel (0729) 840243.

## WINDERMERE, Cumbria Map 19

### BECKMEAD HOUSE, 5 Park Avenue
*Delightful stone built Victorian house, with good reputation for high standards, comfort and friendliness. The breakfasts are famous. Convenient for lake, shops, restaurants and golf course.*
ACCOMMODATION under £20
**Hours:** breakfast 8:30am – 9am. **Cuisine:** breakfast.
**Rooms:** 5 bedrooms all with tea making facilities, TV: 1 double ensuite, 1 double – shower only, 1 twin – shower only, 1 family room ensuite, 1 single. **Other points:** central heating, children catered for – please check for age limits, residents' lounge, no evening meal, vegetarian meals. **Directions:** M6 Junction 36, westbound on A590 for 3 miles. A591 to Windermere.
MRS DOROTHY HEIGHTON, tel (05394) 42757.

### GILPIN LODGE HOTEL, Crook Road
*A small, family-run hotel and restaurant set in 20 very private acres of gardens, woodland and moors in the heart of the south Lakeland countryside. Fresh cut flowers, picture lined walls and antique furniture all add to the sophisticated atmosphere. Dinner is the highlight of the day and is served at prettily laid tables. Each bedroom is furnished to an exceptional standard and some rooms have four poster beds. This is the perfect location for a family holiday or a leisurely seasonal break.*
**Hours:** breakfast 7:30am – 9:30am; lunch 12noon – 2:30pm; bar snacks 12noon – 2:30pm; dinner 7pm – 8:45pm. **Cuisine:** English / French:- Very good food, and good range. **Other points:** children catered for – please check for age limits, parking, Sunday lunch, open bank holidays, no-smoking area, afternoon tea, Sunday

dinner, disabled access, residents' lounge, vegetarian meals, garden. **Directions:** M6 Junction 36, A590, A591, B5284 (Crook).
J AND C CUNLIFFE, tel (05394) 88818, fax (05394) 88058.

### GREEN GABLES GUEST HOUSE,
*37 Broad Street*
*A small, friendly guest house with very pretty bedrooms providing clean, comfortable accommodation, close to local amenities, bus and railway station. Guests are assured of a warm welcome, for the Green Gables' motto is 'Cleanliness, friendliness and a good hearty breakfast'.*
ACCOMMODATION under £20
**Hours:** breakfast 8.30am; dinner 7pm; closed Christmas; closed New Year's day. **Cuisine:** breakfast.
**Rooms:** 6 bedrooms all with tea making facilities, TV: 1 single ensuite, 2 doubles ensuite, 1 twin, 2 family rooms. **Other points:** central heating, children catered for – please check for age limits, residents' lounge, special breaks, no evening meal. **Directions:** leave M6, junction 36, A591 to Windermere.
MRS SHEILA LAWLESS, tel (05394) 43886.

### THE HIDEAWAY HOTEL, Phoenix Way
*A delightful Victorian stone building, The Hideaway has a reputation for good food, value and service. The easy access to the Lakes, a beautifully tended garden and well-appointed rooms keep people coming back.*
ACCOMMODATION £31–£40
FOOD up to £15
**Hours:** breakfast 8:30am – 9:30am; dinner 7:30pm – 8:30pm; open February – December. **Cuisine:** English / continental:- Modern English cuisine with continental influences. Menu changes daily. **Rooms:** 15 bedrooms all with tea making facilities, telephone, TV: 3 family rooms ensuite, 5 twins ensuite, 2 singles ensuite, 5 doubles ensuite. **Other points:** children catered for – please check for age limits, afternoon tea, residents' lounge, garden, pets allowed, leisure centre. **Directions:** situated on Phoenix Way off Ambleside Road (A591).
MRS GORNALL & MR SUMMERLEE, tel (05394) 43070.

### OLDFIELD HOUSE, Oldfield Road
*Bob and Maureen Theobald welcome you to Oldfield House, which has a friendly, informal atmosphere within a traditionally-built lakeland residence. Ideally situated close to Windermere village, yet away from the busy main road. Fully centrally heated, with a comfortable lounge and pleasant dining room. Guests are permitted to use the facilities at nearby Parklands Country Club.*
ACCOMMODATION £21–£30
**Hours:** open all year; breakfast 8:30am – 9am. **Cuisine:** breakfast. **Rooms:** 8 bedrooms all with tea making facilities, telephone, radio, TV: 1 single ensuite, 2 twins ensuite, 3 doubles ensuite, 1 double, 1 triple ensuite. **Credit cards:** Visa, Access. **Other points:** children catered for – please check for age limits, residents' lounge, parking, baby-listening device, cots. **Directions:**

Junction 36 of M6. A591 to Windermere, through village. Off Lake turn left into Ellerthaite Road, then second right and first left into Oldfield Road.
BOB & MAUREEN THEOBALD, tel (05394) 88445.

## ST JOHN'S LODGE, Lake Road

*A small, private hotel centrally situated for touring the Lake District, and only 10 minutes walk from the Lake Pier. Mini-breaks off-season. Facilities of local country sports club available to residents.*
ACCOMMODATION under £20
FOOD up to £15
**Hours:** breakfast 8:15am – 9am; dinner 7pm, order by 6pm; closed December – January. **Cuisine:** English:- All dishes made from fresh, local produce. Will cater for vegetarians. **Rooms:** 15 bedrooms all with tea making facilities, TV: 1 single ensuite, 1 single, 1 double, 3 family rooms ensuite, 1 twin ensuite, 8 doubles ensuite. **Credit cards:** Visa, Access. **Other points:** central heating, children catered for – please check for age limits, residents' lounge, residents' bar. **Directions:** midway between Windermere Village and Bowness on the A5074.
RAY & DOREEN GREGORY, tel (05394) 43078.

## THORNBANK HOTEL, Thornbarrow Road

*Thornbank is a family run hotel ideally situated in a pleasant residential area of Windermere in the beautiful Lake District, just a short distance from the lake shore. Bedrooms are fully equipped with many modern facilities, including Sky TV and there is a comfortable guest lounge with ample tourist information. Windermere is an excellent location for touring and exploring with endless amenities.*
ACCOMMODATION under £20
FOOD up to £15
**Hours:** breakfast 8:45am; dinner 6:45pm. **Cuisine:** English. **Credit cards:** Visa, Access, AmEx. **Other points:** parking, children catered for – please check for age limits, open bank holidays, no-smoking area, pets, residents' lounge, vegetarian meals. **Directions:** A591, turn left at Windermere Hotel towards Bowness, .75 mile along is Thornbarrow Road.
MR R & MRS P CHARNOCK, tel (05394) 43724.

# WITHERSLACK, Cumbria Map 19

## THE OLD VICARAGE COUNTRY HOUSE HOTEL, Church Road

*This outstanding establishment, a delightful Georgian period country vicarage, offers all the necessary qualities for a truly memorable evening. The ambiance, cuisine and service combine to make dining here a pleasure, totally in keeping with its setting in the peaceful and unspoiled countryside where it nestles under Yewbarrow Scar. Regional Newcomer 1991.*
ACCOMMODATION £41–£50
FOOD £21–£25 ♟ ♨
**Hours:** breakfast 8:30am – 9:30am; dinner 7:30pm – 8pm. **Cuisine:** English:- English regional cooking. **Rooms:** 15 bedrooms all with tea making facilities, telephone, radio, TV: 1 single ensuite, 4 twins ensuite,

10 doubles ensuite. **Credit cards:** Visa, Access, Diners, AmEx. **Other points:** licensed, afternoon tea, residents' lounge, garden, special breaks, children catered for – please check for age limits. **Directions:** off the A590 Barrow road, right turning to village, then first left in Witherslack village after the phonebox.
MR R BURRINGTON BROWN, tel (05395) 52381, fax (05395) 52373.

# YORK, North Yorkshire Map 18

## ABBOTS MEWS HOTEL, 6 Marygate Lane, Bootham

*Situated in the centre of York, only minutes away from the city's historic attractions. The hotel was an original coachman's cottage with coach-house and stables, but was converted in 1976. The restaurant is renowned for its high standard of cuisine and the service is very friendly and efficient.*
ACCOMMODATION £21–£30
FOOD up to £15 CLUB
**Hours:** breakfast – except Sunday 7:30am – 9:30am; breakfast – Sunday 8:30am – 10am; lunch 12noon – 2pm; dinner 7pm – 9:30pm. **Cuisine:** international:- Specialities include Sauted Medallions of Beef Hongroise, Chicken Madras, Stir Fried Beef on Oyster Sauce. Bar Lunches are also served weekdays. **Rooms:** 47 bedrooms all with tea making facilities, radio, TV: 16 twins ensuite, 20 doubles ensuite, 11 family rooms ensuite. **Credit cards:** Visa, Access, Diners, AmEx. **Other points:** licensed, Sunday lunch, children catered for – please check for age limits, garden, conferences. **Directions:** in centre of York. Close to Museum Gardens and Bootham Bar.
MR & MRS DEARNLEY, tel (0904) 622395, (0904) 634866.

## THE ALICE HAWTHORN, Nun Monkton

*An old cottage-style village pub, situated on the village green of the beautiful village of Nun Monkton, offering well cooked food in restaurant and bar. The welcoming and friendly atmosphere of the main bar attracts both locals and visitors to the area.*
FOOD up to £15
**Hours:** lunch 12noon – 2pm; dinner 7pm – 9:30pm. **Cuisine:** English:- Home cooked bar meals, using freshest produce available. Daily selection of vegetarian dishes. **Other points:** licensed, open-air dining, Sunday lunch, no-smoking area, children catered for – please check for age limits, garden, pets allowed. **Directions:** off the main A59 at Skipbridge filling station.
MR S WINSHIP, tel (0423) 330303.

## ARNOT HOUSE, 17 Grosvenor Terrace

*Overlooking Bootham Park and York Minster, Arnot House combines period elegance with modern amenities, from the original cornicing, fireplaces and fine old staircases to the large, warm, comfortable well-appointed rooms. The welcome is exemplary, and the Scotts take pride in their guest house.*
ACCOMMODATION under £20
FOOD up to £15

**Hours:** breakfast 8:15am – 9am; dinner 6:30pm – 7:30pm. **Cuisine:** English. **Rooms:** 6 bedrooms all with tea making facilities, TV: 1 single, 2 doubles, 1 twin, 2 family rooms. **Other points:** central heating, children catered for – please check for age limits. **Directions:** from the city wall at Bootham Bar, go along Bootham (A19). Grosvenor Terrace is the second on the right. SUE & RUPERT SCOTT, tel (0904) 641966.

## BYRON HOUSE HOTEL, 7 Driffield Terrace, The Mount

*Run by the proprietors, Byron House provides a high standard of accommodation, a friendly atmosphere and personal service in pleasant surroundings. Good food is served in the dining room and guests can relax in the lounge with its licensed bar and selection of wines. Within walking distance of the hotel are many attractions including the Minster.*

*ACCOMMODATION £21–£30*

*FOOD up to £15* ★

**Hours:** closed Christmas; breakfast 7:30am – 9:30am; dinner 7pm. **Cuisine:** English. **Rooms:** 10 bedrooms all with tea making facilities, telephone, radio, TV: 3 singles, 1 twin ensuite, 2 doubles ensuite, 4 family rooms ensuite. **Credit cards:** Visa, Access, Diners, AmEx. **Other points:** children catered for – please check for age limits, pets allowed, residents' lounge, vegetarian meals, baby-listening device, baby sitting, cots, left luggage, residents' bar, parking. **Directions:** A1036, signposted York west & Racecourse. Walking distance of centre. DICK & JEAN TYSON, tel (0904) 632525, fax (0904) 639424.

## CARLTON HOUSE HOTEL, 134 The Mount

*A cosy family run hotel conveniently located close to the racecourse and all city centre amenities. A popular choice for many visitors to York and the surrounding countryside.*

*ACCOMMODATION under £20*

**Hours:** closed Christmas; breakfast 7:45am – 9:15am. **Cuisine:** breakfast. **Rooms:** 15 bedrooms all with tea making facilities, radio, TV: 1 single, 3 doubles, 4 doubles ensuite, 2 twins, 1 family room, 4 family rooms ensuite. **Other points:** central heating, children catered for – please check for age limits, residents' lounge. **Directions:** on the A1036 close to York station. MALCOLM & LIZ GREAVES, tel (0904) 622265.

## DUKE OF CONNAUGHT HOTEL, Copmanthorpe Grange

*The hotel is set in a fascinating location, encircled by 14th century walls, ancient streets and buildings, and overlooked by the magnificent York Minster. With attractively 18th century style furnishings and equipped with many modern facilities, guests are assured of a warm welcome and comfortable stay. There is a bright, airy lounge bar and good access for disabled persons to all ground floor rooms. Self-catering cottage also available. Ideal base for touring the historic city of York.*

*ACCOMMODATION £31–£40* ★

**Hours:** closed Christmas; breakfast 8am – 9:30am; dinner 7pm – 10pm. **Cuisine:** English. **Rooms:** 15 bedrooms all with tea making facilities, telephone, TV: 5 family rooms ensuite, 6 doubles ensuite, 4 twins ensuite. **Credit cards:** Visa, Access. **Other points:** licensed, Sunday lunch, no-smoking area, children catered for – please check for age limits, disabled access, parking, vegetarian meals, afternoon tea, residents' lounge, garden, cots. **Directions:** off A64 York/Leeds road – between Appleton Roebuck and Bishopthorpe. JACK HUGHES, tel (0904) 744318.

## THE HAWNBY HOTEL, Hawnby, Near Helmsley

*Built in Yorkshire stone the Hawnby Hotel was originally a Drovers Inn in the 19th century. Decorated throughout to a high standard this hotel enjoys the peace of the unspoilt surrounding countryside. A high degree of personal attention is afforded to all guests. Fishing is free for residents, tennis and pony trekking can also be arranged locally.*

*ACCOMMODATION £31–£40*

*FOOD up to £15*

**Hours:** breakfast 8:30am – 9:30am; lunch 12noon – 2pm; dinner 7pm – 8:30pm; closed February. **Cuisine:** English:- Traditional English cooking using home-grown produce when possible. **Rooms:** 6 bedrooms, all en suite and with major facilities. **Credit cards:** Visa, Access. **Other points:** licensed, garden, special breaks. **Directions:** off the B127, 8 miles from Helmsley. LADY MEXBOROUGH, tel (04396) 202, fax (04396) 417.

## HEDLEY HOUSE, 3 Bootham Terrace

*A Victorian residence within walking distance of the city of York. Family run, the atmosphere is friendly and informal and complemented by good homecooking.*

*ACCOMMODATION £21–£30*

*FOOD up to £15*

**Hours:** breakfast 8am – 9am; dinner 6:30pm – 7pm. **Cuisine:** English. **Rooms:** 2 single, 5 double, 5 twin and 2 family bedrooms all en suite. Tea/coffee facilities, colour TVs, radio, and alarms in all bedrooms. Self catering apartments next door to hotel. **Credit cards:** Visa, Access, AmEx. **Other points:** children catered for – please check for age limits, pets allowed, residents' lounge, vegetarian meals. **Directions:** off the A19, third turning on left away from Bootham Bar. GRAHAM & SUSAN HARRAND, tel (0904) 637404.

## HUDSON'S HOTEL, 60 Bootham

*A Victorian hotel in the city centre only minutes from Bootham Bar, the Minster and the Roman Walls. The hotel was converted from 2 town houses and now provides elegant accommodation and high quality cuisine.*

*ACCOMMODATION £31–£40*

*FOOD up to £15*

**Hours:** breakfast 7:30am – 9:30am; lunch – prior arrangement 12noon – 2pm; dinner 6:30pm – 9:30pm. **Cuisine:** English / continental:- Extensive a la carte menu served in the 'Below Stairs' Restaurant. **Rooms:**

30 bedrooms all with tea making facilities, telephone, TV: 1 single ensuite, 15 doubles ensuite, 10 twins ensuite, 4 family rooms ensuite. **Credit cards:** Visa, Access, Diners, AmEx. **Other points:** Sunday lunch, children catered for – please check for age limits. **Directions:** very close to Bootham Bar and York Minster.

C R HUDSON, tel (0904) 621267, fax (0904) 654719.

## KITES RESTAURANT, 13 Grape Lane

*Tucked away in a small street very close to the Minster and Stonegate. Access to the restaurant is up a narrow staircase to the second floor. All herbs come from the proprietor's own herb garden. Local produce used where possible including a good selection of unusual cheeses from the Dales. Well chosen but affordable wine list.*

*FOOD £15–£20* `CLUB`

**Hours:** closed Sunday 6:30pm; lunch – Saturday 12noon – 1:45pm; dinner 6:30pm – 10:30pm. **Cuisine:** international:- Innovative international menu – Thai stuffed crab, Marinated duck breast with Chinese noodle and aubergine salad, Wood pigeon and Cumberland sauce. **Credit cards:** Visa, Access. **Other points:** licensed, children catered for – please check for age limits. **Directions:** from Bootham Bar, follow Petergate to Low Petergate to Grape Lane.

MS BOO ORMAN, tel (0904) 641750.

## MOUNT ROYALE, The Mount

*Gothic in appearance, but mainly William IV in style, the Mount Royale has been tastefully decorated and furnished to retain its character. The atmosphere is further enhanced by the presence of the old English garden, which can be seen from the restaurant. A very pleasant venue in which to enjoy good food and friendly, professional service.*

*ACCOMMODATION £31–£40*

*FOOD £21–£25* 🍲

**Hours:** breakfast 7:15am – 9:30am; dinner 7pm – 10:30pm. **Cuisine:** international:- including rack of lamb and duckling. **Rooms:** 23 bedrooms all with tea making facilities, telephone, radio, TV: 13 doubles ensuite, 10 twins ensuite. **Credit cards:** Visa, Access, Diners, AmEx. **Other points:** licensed, children catered for – please check for age limits, pets/prior arr, swimming pool, trimnasium, sauna, solarium. **Directions:** on A1036 past race course, up hill to traffic lights. On right side.

RICHARD & CHRISTINE OXTOBY, tel (0904) 628856.

## PLUNKETS RESTAURANT LTD, 9 High Petergate

*Plunkets is a cheerful restaurant set in a 17th century building near York Minster. It plays music of a gentle jazz/disco kind and is full of plants, prints and polished wooden tables.*

*FOOD £15–£20*

**Hours:** closed 01/01; meals all day 11am – 12noon; closed Christmas 25/12 – 26/12. **Cuisine:** international:- Dishes include fajitas, burritos, hamburgers, steaks, home-made pies, fresh salmon fishcakes, marinated chicken breasts, salads & various vegetarian dishes. **Other points:** licensed, Sunday lunch, children catered for – please check for age limits. **Directions:** located on one of York's principal streets, near Bootham Bar.

TREVOR BARRINGTON WARD, tel (0904) 637722.

## RED LION MOTEL & COUNTRY INN, Upper Poppleton

*A friendly, cheerful and welcoming country inn, offering fresh food amidst pleasant surroundings. Ideally located for those who wish to tour the famous Yorkshire Dales, the Moors, or for visiting York itself and nearby Harrogate.*

*ACCOMMODATION £21–£30*

*FOOD up to £15*

**Hours:** open all year; breakfast 7:30am – 9am; lunch 12noon – 2pm; dinner 6:30pm – 9:30pm. **Cuisine:** English:- A la carte menu. offering a choice of good homecooked dishes, including fresh Whitby fish. Vegetarian meals also available. **Rooms:** 18 bedrooms all with tea making facilities, telephone, TV: 2 twins ensuite, 8 doubles ensuite, 8 family rooms ensuite. **Credit cards:** Visa, Access. **Other points:** licensed, open-air dining, Sunday lunch, no-smoking area, children catered for – please check for age limits, parking, garden, bank holidays. **Directions:** situated half a mile from the outskirts of York on the A59.

DOUGLAS MALTBY, tel (0904) 781141, fax (0904) 785143.

## WHITE SWAN INN & RESTAURANT, Deighton, Escrick

*A family-run country inn, with an intimate restaurant and comfortable bar area. Offers well-prepared and presented dishes at excellent value for money – in a very pleasant, friendly atmosphere.*

*FOOD up to £15*

**Hours:** lunch – Sunday 12noon – 2pm; bar meals 12noon – 2pm; dinner 7pm – 9:30pm; bar meals 7pm – 9:30pm. **Cuisine:** British:- Salmon steak with prawn sauce, and half roast duckling in restaurant. Lasagne, and steak in the bar. Fillet of salmon in a piquant walnut sauce and half roast duckling available in restaurant. Steaks, salads, pies and special dishes of the day in the bar. Game available in season. **Credit cards:** Visa, Access. **Other points:** children catered for – please check for age limits, open bank holidays, Sunday lunch. **Directions:** on A19, 5 miles south of York.

MR & MRS WALKER, tel (0904) 728287.

# WALES

Wales is a small country with enormous appeal – it is a land of natural unspoilt beauty and endless scenic variety. But perhaps the best way to describe Wales is to say it is different. Although part of Britain, Wales is as different from England as France is from Spain. It has its own language, history and heritage, as well as its own culture and cuisine.

It is this difference, coupled with the traditional warm Welsh welcome, that makes a visit to Wales such a memorable and unique experience.

Wales is famed for its spectacular countryside and coastline – it has three National Parks, including Britain's only coastal park – as well as five areas designated as being of Outstanding Natural Beauty.

Each region and area of Wales has its own distinct character. In the north there are the magnificent moody mountain ranges of Snowdon whose rocky peaks rise to 3,560 ft, the highest point in England and Wales; there's the timeless beauty of the Llyn peninsula, the enchanting Isle of Anglesey and the green hills of the lush Clwydian Range. There are World Heritage Listed Sites like Beaumaris, Harlech, Caernarfon and Conwy Castles to discover, or the Victorian architectural elegance of Llandudno with its sweeping promenade, picturesque Betws-y-Coed and the famous Swallow Falls, or Llangollen which hosts the colourful annual International Musical Eisteddfod.

Mid Wales, an area of rural tranquillity, has mountain ranges, remote moorlands, ancient drovers' routes, an abundance of deep dark forests, lakes and waterfalls. This region is rich in scenic variety, ranging from the spectacular lakes and dams of the Elan Valley to the dramatic Abergwesyn Pass across the Roof of Wales. The elegant and historic spa towns of Wales can be found in Mid Wales as well as bustling market towns and a variety of coastal resorts.

South Wales is another area offering tremendous contrasts and encompassing the gentle rolling hills and peaks of the Brecon Beacons, the wooded glory of the Wye Valley and the bays and beaches of Pembrokeshire and the Gower peninsula. This region includes the cosmopolitan city of Cardiff, Britain's youngest capital and home of the acclaimed Welsh National Opera, the maritime city of Swansea, as well as the valleys, once the industrial heartland of Wales but now fascinating areas to explore.

Wales has a magnificent coastline stretching for more than 700 miles – there are vast sandy bays, towering cliffs, quiet little coves that can only be reached on foot, sleepy fishing villages, big bustling resorts and modern marinas.

The country also has a wealth of interesting and unusual attractions and fascinating places to visit, many of them unique like the Italianate village of Portmeirion, nestling on a secluded wooded hillside overlooking the Traeth Bach estuary, or the Centre of Alternative Technology – a green village of the future in Mid Wales where a host of environmentally friendly alternative technologies are demonstrated.

Wales has more castles per square mile than any country in Western Europe, splendid stately homes, world class gardens like Bodnant, miles of canals to cruise and off-shore islands to explore plus a host of visitor attractions.

If it is crafts you're looking for, then you will find them at Hay-on-Wye and Ruthin, where there are entire craft villages with workshops incorporating glassblowers, potters, stone masons and many more. At the Museum of the Welsh Woollen Industry near Llandysul, you can see regular hand carding, spinning and weaving demonstrations, alongside paper making and other craft workshops.

For good food look out for the distinctive red and blue Les Routiers sign, or the Taste of Wales/*Blas ar Gymru* symbol for creative Welsh cuisine where the very best of local produce is used.

For details of where to visit and what to see in Wales, contact the Wales Tourist Board, Brunel House, 2 Fitzalan Road, Cardiff CF2 1UY. Tel: (0222) 499909.

## ABERGAVENNY, Gwent Map 11

### THE SWAN HOTEL, Cross Street

*The hotel is situated adjacent to the bus station and within 10 minutes' walk from the railway station. It is centrally placed in the town thus affording easy access to the M4. Very popular because of its excellent menu and reasonable prices.*

ACCOMMODATION £21–£30

FOOD up to £15

**Hours:** bar meals 12noon – 2pm; dinner 7pm – 9:30pm. **Cuisine:** British:- Traditional home cooking, eg. Sunday lunch – roast beef with Yorkshire pud. Homemade pies, moussaka and fresh salads. **Rooms:** 11 bedrooms all with tea making facilities, telephone, radio, TV: 2 singles ensuite, 3 twins ensuite, 6 doubles ensuite. **Credit cards:** Visa, Access, AmEx. **Other points:** Sunday lunch. **Directions:** next to bus station in Abergavenny.
IAN S LITTLE, tel (0873) 852829, fax (0873) 852829.

## ABERGELE, Clwyd Map 12

### THE WHEATSHEAF INN, Betws-yn-Rhos

*Situated in the picturesque village of Betws-yn-Rhos, this inn was originally a 13th century ale house and later a 17th Century coaching inn which today boasts splendid brass strewn oak beams and original hay loft ladder. It provides a cosy and friendly olde-worlde charm where customers can enjoy its intimate atmosphere and extensive menus. Many tourist attractions nearby.*

ACCOMMODATION under £20

FOOD up to £15 ★

**Hours:** breakfast 8:30am – 9am; lunch 12noon – 2:30pm; bar meals 12noon – 2:30pm; dinner 6pm – 9:30pm; bar meals 6pm – 9:30pm. **Cuisine:** British:- A la carte, Table d'hote, Banqueting and Buffet menus. Chef's home-made specialities with seasonal vegetables. Special Festive Season Menus. **Rooms:** 4 bedrooms, all en suite with colour TV, radio and tea/coffee making facilities. **Credit cards:** Visa, Access. **Other points:** licensed, open-air dining, Sunday lunch, no-smoking area, children catered for – please check for age limits, parking, vegetarian meals. **Directions:** A55 to Abergele, A458 – 1 mile right turn, B5381 – 1 mile.
RAYMOND PERRY, tel (0492) 60218.

## ABERSOCH, Gwynedd Map 12

### TUDOR COURT HOTEL & RESTAURANT, Lon Sarn Bach

*Once the home of an old sea captain, but now extensively refurbished to provide a comfortable hotel with its own restaurant, offering fine cuisine using the best of local fresh produce. Sailing, Golfing, Fishing and many historical places of interest nearby. Open all Christmas and New Year. Mini breaks and inclusive golf breaks arranged.*

FOOD up to £15

**Hours:** breakfast 8am – 9am; lunch 12:30pm – 2pm; dinner 6:30pm – 9:30pm. **Cuisine:** French / English:-

Vegetarian meals also available. **Rooms:** 9 bedrooms 1 single ensuite, 4 doubles ensuite, 2 twins ensuite, 2 family rooms ensuite. **Credit cards:** Visa, Access, Diners. **Other points:** parking, children catered for – please check for age limits, afternoon teas, no-smoking area, pets – by arrangement, vegetarian meals. **Directions:** from Caernarfon or Porthmadog go to Pwllheli and drive along the coast to Abersoch. The hotel is on the right-hand side of the main road through the village.
MS J JONES, tel (0758) 713354, fax (0758) 713354.

### THE WHITE HOUSE HOTEL

*Overlooking the picturesque harbour of Abersoch, Cardigan Bay and St Tudwals Islands, this hotel is set back from the road in its own grounds. A warm welcome, comfortable accommodation and good food await you. The bedrooms have recently been modernised and the elegant dining room is comfortable and spacious. A 2 mile long sandy beach is within easy walking distance.*

ACCOMMODATION £21–£30

FOOD up to £15 ☜

**Hours:** bar meals 6:30pm – 9:30pm; dinner 7pm – 9pm. **Cuisine:** British:- Bar menu and a la carte restaurant menu (evenings). Fresh local produce used wherever possible. Local lobsters & crabs, Welsh lamb and beef. **Rooms:** 12 bedrooms all with tea making facilities, telephone, radio, TV: 1 single ensuite, 3 twins ensuite, 6 doubles ensuite, 1 triple ensuite, 1 quad ensuite. **Credit cards:** Access, Visa, Switch. **Other points:** licensed, children catered for – please check for age limits, garden, pets allowed, residents' lounge, baby sitting, cots. **Directions:** A499, 7 miles from Pwllheli.
JAYNE & DAVID SMITH, tel (0758) 713427, fax (0758) 713512.

## ABERYSTWYTH, Dyfed Map 10

### COURT ROYALE HOTEL, Eastgate

*A hotel dating back to the early 19th century, tastefully restored and fitted with 20th century comforts. The restaurant, in mahogany finish, has its own character and offers an extensive a la carte selection. Close to the beach and town centre.*

FOOD £15–£20

**Hours:** breakfast 8am – 9:30am; lunch 12noon – 2:30pm; bar meals 12noon – 2:30pm; dinner 7pm – 10pm; bar meals 7pm – 10pm. **Cuisine:** British:- Steaks. **Rooms:** 10 bedrooms, all en suite. **Credit cards:** Visa, Access, AmEx. **Other points:** Sunday lunch, children catered for – please check for age limits, pets allowed. **Directions:** A44 or A487 to Aberystwyth, close to beach and town centre.
MR & MRS JENKINS, tel (0970) 611722.

## BALA, Gwynedd Map 12

### PLAS COCH HOTEL, High Street

*This attractive stone building dating back to 1780, sits in the centre of Bala near Bala Lake, surrounded by Snowdonia National Park. The restaurant lends itself* to traditional Welsh cooking with an emphasis on local produce and a choice of good wines.

ACCOMMODATION £21–£30

FOOD up to £15

**Hours:** breakfast 8am – 9am; lunch 12noon – 2pm; dinner 7pm – 8:30pm; closed Christmas day – 25/12. **Cuisine:** Welsh:- A la carte menu, fixed 3 course menu, and Bar menu. **Rooms:** 10 bedrooms all with tea making facilities, telephone, radio, TV: 1 single ensuite, 1 twin ensuite, 4 doubles ensuite, 4 triples ensuite. **Credit cards:** Visa, Access, Diners, AmEx. **Other points:** licensed, Sunday lunch, no-smoking area, children catered for – please check for age limits, afternoon tea, baby-listening device, cots, left luggage, residents' bar, residents' lounge, vegetarian meals, parking. **Directions:** Bala is on the A494, 14 miles north of Dolgellau. MR & MRS EVANS, tel (0678) 520309, fax (0678) 521135.

---

# BARMOUTH, Gwynedd Map 12

## LLWYNDU FARMHOUSE HOTEL, Llanaber

*A delightful 17th century farmhouse dating from the early 17th century with wonderful views of the sea and mountains of Cardigan Bay. You can savour the imaginative cuisine in an atmosphere of oak beams, inglenooks, candlelight and a little music. Licensed. Llwyndu was praised for its hospitality even in the 17th century and a history of the house is available for guests. Occasional theme evenings for parties. All rooms have en suite bathrooms, TV, radio alarms, beverage facilities and great character. Four are in a converted barn next to the farmhouse.*

ACCOMMODATION £21–£30

FOOD up to £15

**Hours:** open all year Christmas day; breakfast 8:30am – 9:30am; dinner 6:30pm – 9pm. **Cuisine:** British:- Taste of Wales/Blas ar Gymru member. Local produce & seafood used in Welsh & international dishes: Welsh Black Beef & Black Olives with Cardamom Sauce, Ham Llwyndu, Old Welsh Rarebit. Selection of Welsh Cheeses. Good selection of vegetarian dishes also. **Rooms:** 7 bedrooms all with tea making facilities, TV: 1 single ensuite, 2 doubles ensuite, 4 family rooms ensuite. **Credit cards:** Visa. **Directions:** 2 miles north of Barmouth on the A496. PETER & PAULA THOMPSON, tel (0341) 280144.

## PANORAMA HOTEL, Panorama Road

*A warm welcome awaits you at this friendly, family-run hotel, set in 2 acres of wooded grounds, and overlooking the Mawddach estuary and Barmouth harbour. An excellent reputation for a la carte, table d'hote and home-made bar meals, and a comprehensive wine list.*

ACCOMMODATION £21–£30

FOOD up to £15 CLUB

**Hours:** breakfast 8:30am – 9:30am; lunch 12noon – 2pm; bar meals 12noon – 2pm; dinner 7pm – 9pm; bar meals 7pm – 9pm. **Cuisine:** British:- Homemade food. **Rooms:** 18 bedrooms 1 single ensuite, 4 doubles ensuite,

9 twins ensuite, 4 family rooms ensuite. **Credit cards:** Visa, Access. **Other points:** open-air dining, Sunday lunch, pets allowed, children catered for – please check for age limits, afternoon tea, vegetarian meals. **Directions:** Panorama Road is off the A496 ½ a mile east of Barmouth Harbour.
MR & MRS FLAVELL & MR & MRS MORGAN, tel (0341) 280550, fax (0341) 280346.

## WAVECREST, 8 Marine Parade

*Beachside Hotel with panoramic views over Cardigan Bay. Sensitively decorated and furnished to retain Victorian character. Highly commended by Wales Tourist Board. Meals of exceptional value, home-made soups and dessert a speciality.*

ACCOMMODATION under £20 ★

**Hours:** last orders 7pm – 5:30pm; breakfast 8:30am – 9:30am; dinner 6:30pm – 7pm. **Cuisine:** breakfast. **Rooms:** 11 bedrooms all with tea making facilities, TV: 3 singles, 1 double, 3 doubles ensuite, 4 family rooms ensuite. **Credit cards:** Visa, Access. **Other points:** children catered for – please check for age limits. **Directions:** on the seafront in Barmouth.
MRS SHELAGH JARMAN, tel (0341) 280330.

---

# BEDDGELERT, Gwynedd Map 12

## ROYAL GOAT HOTEL

*This Georgian building is situated in a charming little village in the heart of the Snowdonia National Park. The Royal Goat offers traditional Welsh hospitality in great comfort and style. The combination of excellent food, accommodation and service makes this hotel a pleasure to visit. Situated in town renowned for its 'Legend of Beddgelert'. Highly recommended.*

ACCOMMODATION £31–£40

FOOD up to £15

**Hours:** breakfast 7:45am – 10am; lunch 12noon – 2:30pm; dinner 7pm – 10pm. **Cuisine:** British:- A la carte and fixed 3 course menus. Serving fish, steak, duck and veal. **Rooms:** 34 bedrooms all with tea making facilities, telephone, radio, TV: 17 twins ensuite, 17 doubles ensuite. **Credit cards:** Visa, Access, Diners, AmEx. **Other points:** licensed, Sunday lunch, no-smoking area, children catered for – please check for age limits, garden, afternoon tea, pets allowed, car hire, pony trekking, baby-listening device, baby sitting, cots, 24hr reception, residents' lounge, residents' bar. **Directions:** located in the town centre.
IRENIE & EVAN ROBERTS, tel (076686) 224, (076686) 313, fax (076686) 422.

---

# BETWS Y COED, Gwynedd Map 12

## FAIRY GLEN HOTEL

*Built as a coaching inn 300 years ago, the Fairy Glen is now a small, family-owned and run hotel, situated in a quiet position overlooking the River Conwy. Situated only half a mile from the village centre, this is a popular hotel serving freshly prepared home cooked food in a friendly atmosphere.*

ACCOMMODATION £21–£30

FOOD up to £15

**Hours:** breakfast 8:30am – 9am; lunch 12noon – 2pm; dinner 7pm – 7:30pm; closed December & January. **Cuisine:** All dishes homecooked using fresh produce. Dishes may include Welsh Lamb, Conwy Salmon, grilled Trout, steaks, casseroles. Traditional breakfasts. Home made sweets. **Rooms:** 10 bedrooms 1 single ensuite, 1 double, 4 doubles ensuite, 1 twin, 1 twin ensuite, 2 family rooms ensuite. **Credit cards:** Visa, Access, Diners. **Other points:** Sunday lunch, children catered for – please check for age limits, pets allowed. **Directions:** half a mile south of the A5 by the Beaver Bridge on the A470.

JEAN & GRAHAM BALL, tel (0690) 710269.

## ROYAL OAK HOTEL, Holyhead Road

*Situated in a picturesque village in the heart of Snowdonia, the Royal Oak Hotel has been refurbished to provide excellent facilities and a high standard of comfort. All food is freshly made on the premises and can been enjoyed in the main dining room or in the more informal grill room.*

ACCOMMODATION £31–£40

FOOD up to £15

**Hours:** breakfast 7:45am – 9:30am; lunch 11:45am – 2pm; dinner 5:30pm – 9pm. **Cuisine:** British:- Fresh fish, home-made soups, grilled steaks. Traditional bar food served in the new bar. **Rooms:** 27 bedrooms all with telephone, TV: 5 family rooms ensuite, 13 twins ensuite, 5 doubles ensuite, 4 singles ensuite. **Credit cards:** Visa, Access, Diners, AmEx. **Other points:** licensed, Sunday lunch, children catered for – please check for age limits, coach/prior arr, functions. **Directions:** on the A5 in the centre of Betws y Coed. MR F KAVANAGH, tel (0690) 710219, fax (0690) 710603.

## TY GWYN HOTEL

*A delightful 16th century coaching inn which has captured the charm and character of the period with low beams, antique furnishings and tasteful decor. An idyllic setting overlooking the River Conwy in this beautiful Welsh village. Excellent home cooking ensures a strong local following. Routiers Newcomer of the Year 1987.*

ACCOMMODATION £21–£30

FOOD up to £15 ☜

**Hours:** breakfast 8:15am – 10am; lunch 12noon – 2pm; bar meals 12noon – 2pm; dinner 7pm – 9:30pm; bar meals 7pm – 9:30pm. **Cuisine:** Welsh / continental:- Pheasant braised in a Beaujolais and wild mushroom sauce, fresh local wild salmon served with a basil and vermouth sauce, breast of Chicken Rossini. **Rooms:** 13 bedrooms 1 single, 1 twin, 3 twins ensuite, 2 doubles, 5 doubles ensuite, 1 suite. **Credit cards:** Visa, Access. **Other points:** Sunday lunch, children catered for – please check for age limits, pets allowed. **Directions:** on the A5 south of Betws y Coed.

JAMES & SHELAGH RATCLIFFE, tel (0690) 710383, (0690) 710787.

# BRECON, Powys Map 10

## THE CASTLE INN, Llangorse

*A quiet, typical 200 year old road-side inn, with outside tables, two bars, traditional stone floors and fireplace. A good atmosphere abounds and the unflamboyant, wholesome cuisine is everything you would expect. An ideal point for visiting the Brecon Beacons, Llangorse Lake and the surrounding countryside.*

FOOD up to £15

**Hours:** lunch 12noon – 2pm; dinner – Sun-Thur 6pm – 9pm; dinner – Fri-Sat 6pm – 9:30pm. **Cuisine:** Welsh:- Traditional meals, local produce. **Credit cards:** Visa, Access. **Other points:** parking, children catered for – please check for age limits, open bank holidays, pets allowed, vegetarian meals. **Directions:** on B4560, turn off A40 Albwlch or A438 at Talgarth.

LITTLE, IAN, tel (0874) 84225.

## THE NANT DDU LODGE HOTEL, Cwm Taf, Nr Merthyr Tydfil

*The Nant Ddu Lodge Hotel is an imposing country house set in its own extensive grounds in the heart of the Brecon Beacons National Park. Formerly Lord Tredegar's shooting lodge, the lodge is now a family-run hotel which prides itself on its excellent home cooking and comfortable accommodation in peaceful and relaxed surroundings. All rooms offer spectacular views of the dramatic mountains.*

ACCOMMODATION £21–£30

FOOD up to £15

**Hours:** open all year 6pm; breakfast 7:30am – 9:30am; lunch 12noon – 2:30pm; dinner 6:30pm – 9:30pm. **Cuisine:** British:- Excellent home cooking, with a number of Welsh speciality dishes. **Rooms:** 15 bedrooms all with tea making facilities, telephone, radio, TV: 9 twins ensuite, 5 doubles ensuite, 1 family room ensuite. **Credit cards:** Visa, Access, AmEx. **Other points:** licensed, open-air dining, Sunday lunch, children catered for – please check for age limits, afternoon tea, residents' lounge, garden, pets allowed, baby sitting, baby-listening device, cots, parking, vegetarian meals, residents' bar, disabled access. **Directions:** on the A470, 6 miles north of Merthyr Tydfil.

DAVID AND PAULA RONSON, tel (0685) 379111, fax (0685) 377088.

## THE OLDE MASONS ARMS HOTEL, Hay Road, Talgarth

*A charming 16th century old hotel with pretty oak beams and country cottage ambiance, located in the little square of Talgarth, setting for the BBC TV series 'Morgan's Boy'. Enjoy a relaxing, special weekend or midweek break amidst outstanding beauty of the Brecon Beacons and Black Mountains. Ideal base for walking, pony trekking and fishing. Welsh Tourist Board '3 Crown' status.*

ACCOMMODATION £21–£30

FOOD up to £15 ★

**Hours:** open all year 6:30pm; breakfast 8am – 9am; lunch 12noon – 2pm; dinner 7pm – 9:30pm. **Cuisine:**

English:- Traditional English cuisine, complemented by vintage ports and clarets. **Rooms:** 7 bedrooms all with tea making facilities, radio, TV: 2 family rooms ensuite, 2 doubles ensuite, 1 twin ensuite, 2 singles ensuite. **Credit cards:** Visa, Access. **Other points:** licensed, Sunday lunch, children catered for – please check for age limits, pets allowed, parking, bank holidays, special breaks. **Directions:** situated in the centre of Talgarth – easy to locate.

PATRICIA BANFORD, tel (0874) 711688.

### PETERSTONE COURT, Llanhamlach Village

*A listed Georgian manor house, which has been carefully restored to an outstanding Country House Hotel, nestling amidst a breathtaking landscape in the Brecon Beacons National Park. Every effort has been made to ensure guests' comfort and relaxation – from the hotel's own high standard leisure facilities to many thoughtfully provided extras. The surrounding countryside of mountains and waterfalls is highly regarded for country sports and outdoor pursuits. For business guests, there is a fully equipped boardroom for up to 16 persons.*

*ACCOMMODATION £41–£50*

*FOOD £16–£20*

**Hours:** breakfast 7am; bar snacks 11am – 10pm; lunch 12noon – 2:30pm; dinner 7pm – 9:30pm. **Cuisine:** haute cuisine. **Credit cards:** Visa, Access, Diners, AmEx. **Other points:** parking, chidren welcome, afternoon teas, disabled access, residents' lounge, vegetarian meals, open-air dining. **Directions:** 2 miles east of Brecon towards Abergavenny.

MICHAEL TAYLOR, tel (0874) 86387, fax (0874) 86376.

### THE THREE COCKS HOTEL, Three Cocks

*The Three Cocks stands in grounds of one and a half acres in the parish of Aberllynfi on the edge of the Brecon Beacons. The Inn dates from the 15th century and has the unique distinction of being built around a tree, which can still be seen. It is complete with cobbled forecourt, mounting blocks, ivy-clad walls, great oak beams and log fires. Ideal location as a touring centre. Many of our clients come for famous second-hand bookshops in Hay-on-Wye, also activities such as walking and pony trekking.*

*ACCOMMODATION £21–£30*

*FOOD £21–£25*

**Hours:** breakfast 8am – 9:30am; lunch 12noon – 1:30pm; dinner 7pm – 9pm. **Cuisine:** continental:- continental cuisine with the accent on selected Belgian dishes, beautifully presented, using the finest fresh ingredients. The restaurant has been awarded 2 rosettes. **Rooms:** 7 bedrooms 4 doubles ensuite, 3 twins ensuite. **Credit cards:** Visa, Access. **Other points:** licensed, children catered for – please check for age limits, residents' lounge, bank holidays, afternoon tea, parking. **Directions:** situated on the A438 between Hereford and Brecon.

MR & MRS M WINSTONE, tel (0497) 847215.

## BRIDGEND, Mid Glamorgan Map 11

### ASHOKA TANDOORI, 68 Nolton Street

*Situated on the main road in Bridgend, the exterior suggests a Bengali connection. The interior is pleasantly decorated, with crisp, white tablecloths and unobtrusive background music. A popular restaurant.*

*FOOD up to £15*

**Hours:** lunch 12noon – 2:30pm; dinner 5:30pm – 12midnight. **Cuisine:** Indian:- Rogon chicken special, meat masala, sag ghosht. **Credit cards:** Visa, Access, Diners, AmEx. **Other points:** open-air dining, children catered for – please check for age limits. **Directions:** situated on the main road in Bridgend.

MR MISPAK MIAH, tel (0656) 650678.

## BROAD HAVEN, Dyfed Map 10

### BROAD HAVEN HOTEL, Nr Haverfordwest

*Situated on Broad Haven beach with magnificent views out over St Bride's Bay, this is an ideal holiday location for relaxing or to tour the whole of Pembrokeshire. This family-hotel has been extensively updated and modernised and now has its own large heated swimming pool, solarium, games room and sound-proofed dance hall. Nearby activities include boating, sailing, golf and tennis.*

*ACCOMMODATION £21–£30*

*FOOD up to £15*

**Hours:** breakfast 7:30am – 9:30am; bar meals 11am – 12midnight; dinner 6:30pm – 9:30pm. **Cuisine:** continental:- Dishes may include, Grilled Trout Almondine and Chicken Supreme with White Wine Cream and Lemon Sauce. Bistro Menu. Children and special diets catered for. **Rooms:** 39 bedrooms, 34 en suite with colour television and radio, direct-dial telephone and tea/coffee making facilities. **Credit cards:** Visa, Access, AmEx. **Other points:** licensed, open-air dining, Sunday lunch, no-smoking area, children catered for – please check for age limits, parking, residents' lounge, garden, pets allowed, afternoon tea. **Directions:** 6.5 miles past Haverfordwest on sea-front.

DAVID & SANDRA GLASGOW, tel (0437) 781366, fax (0437) 781070.

## CAERNARFON, Gwynedd Map 12

### THE BLACK BOY INN, North-gate Street

*A 15th century inn situated within the walls of Caernarfon Castle. Good sea and game fishing. Ideal for yachting on inland tidal waters. Traditional home cooking.*

*ACCOMMODATION under £20*

*FOOD up to £15*

**Hours:** lunch 12noon – 2:30pm; dinner 6:30pm – 9pm. **Cuisine:** English:- Traditional English cooking, eg. roast beef, roast lamb and the trimmings. **Rooms:** 12 bedrooms 1 single, 1 single ensuite, 1 double, 3 doubles ensuite, 1 twin, 3 twins ensuite, 1 family room, 1 family room ensuite. **Credit cards:** Visa, Access. **Other points:** Sunday lunch, children catered for – please check for age limits. **Directions:** located in the town centre.

MR ROBERT WILLIAMS, tel (0286) 673023.

## SEIONT MANOR HOTEL, *Llanrug*

*An outstanding rustic country mansion, remodelled to provide sport, leisure and conference facilities in 150 acres of parkland, overlooking a lake. The oak panelled bar, library and beautifully decorated rooms, with furnishings from around the world, make this a true country club.*

*ACCOMMODATION £41–£50*

*FOOD £15–£20*

**Hours:** open bank holidays 6:30pm; breakfast 7:30am – 10am; lunch 12:30pm – 2pm; dinner 7pm – 10pm. **Cuisine:** British / French:- Delicious food with a strong French influence and exceptionally well presented. Choose from the 4 course Table d'Hote or extensive Menu Gourmand. **Rooms:** 28 bedrooms all with tea making facilities, telephone, radio, TV: 16 twins ensuite, 8 doubles ensuite, 4 triples ensuite. **Credit cards:** Visa, Access, Diners, AmEx. **Other points:** licensed, open-air dining, Sunday lunch, no-smoking area, children catered for – please check for age limits, pets allowed, swimming pool, gym facilities, mountain bikes, sauna, golf, fishing, aromatherapy, conferences, video library, baby sitting, baby-listening device, cots, 24hr reception, left luggage. **Directions:** on A4086, 3 miles from Caernarfon heading towards Llanrug.

MR PHILIP WARREN, tel (0286) 673366.

## VICTORIA HOUSE, *13 Church Street*

*A Victorian terraced guest house offering comfortable accommodation in delightfully furnished surroundings. Snowdonia National Park and Caernarfon Castle are close by.*

*ACCOMMODATION under £20*

**Hours:** breakfast 8am. **Cuisine:** breakfast. **Rooms:** 7 bedrooms 2 doubles ensuite, 1 twin ensuite, 1 twin, 1 double, 2 singles. **Other points:** children catered for – please check for age limits, open bank holidays, pets – by arrangement, vegetarian meals. **Directions:** pass Castle entrance, turn right at end of street.

TERENCE & JANINE SMITH, tel (0286) 673133.

## CAPEL CURIG, Gwynedd Map 12

### COBDEN'S HOTEL

*A 200 year old country house hotel, set in the heart of Snowdonia. Comfortable, informal and fun; perfect for total rest and relaxation. Own 200 metre clear running water rock pool for swimming, canoeing and fishing.*

*ACCOMMODATION £21–£30*

*FOOD up to £15* ★

**Hours:** breakfast 8am – 10am; lunch 12noon – 2:30pm; bar meals 12noon – 2:30pm; dinner 7pm – 9pm; bar meals 7pm – 9:30pm. **Cuisine:** Earthy, international and healthy. **Rooms:** 16 bedrooms all with tea making facilities, TV: 4 singles ensuite, 5 twins ensuite, 5

doubles ensuite, 2 family rooms ensuite. **Credit cards:** Visa, Access, AmEx. **Other points:** licensed, Sunday lunch, children catered for – please check for age limits, pets allowed, bank holidays. **Directions:** on A5, between Betws-Y-Coed and Bangor.

CRAIG GOODALL & RUSSELL HONEYMAN, tel (06904) 243, (06904) 308, fax (06904) 354.

## CARDIFF, South Glamorgan Map 11

### HENRY'S CAFE BAR (CARDIFF), *Park Place*

*A trendy cafe-bar serving an extensive range of international fast-food, American and non-alcoholic beers and speciality cocktails. Bustling, happy, friendly atmosphere.*

*FOOD up to £15*

**Hours:** closed Sunday 7pm; meals all day 10:30am – 11pm. **Cuisine:** international. **Credit cards:** Visa, Access. **Other points:** children catered for – please check for age limits, open bank holidays, no-smoking area, afternoon teas, disabled access, vegetarian meals. **Directions:** adjacent to New Theatre.

RICHARD WESLEY, tel (0222) 224139.

## CARDIGAN, Dyfed Map 10

### SKIPPERS, *Tresaith Beach*

*Overlooking the unspoilt bay of Tresaith, this restaurant offers meals of 'outstanding quality' in a quiet, relaxed atmosphere. Efficient and friendly staff ensure an enjoyable meal. There is a definite nautical theme in the restaurant which also has a log fire. Comfortable accommodation. Highly recommended.*

*ACCOMMODATION under £20*

*FOOD up to £15* 🍽 ★

**Hours:** last orders 10:30am – 9pm; breakfast 7am – 12noon; lunch 12noon – 3pm; bar meals 12noon – 3pm; dinner 6pm – 11:30pm; bar meals 6pm – 9pm; closed January – Easter. **Cuisine:** seafood / international:- Extensive menu which may feature – Oysters, Fresh local Crab and Lobster, Rack of Lamb. **Rooms:** 3 bedrooms all with tea making facilities, telephone, radio, TV: 3 suites. **Credit cards:** Visa, Access, AmEx. **Other points:** licensed, open-air dining, Sunday lunch, children catered for – please check for age limits, afternoon tea, residents' lounge, residents' bar, vegetarian meals. **Directions:** B4333 to Aberporth, then unclassified road to Tresaith.

IAN & JANET DARROCH, tel (0239) 810113, fax (0239) 810176.

## CHEPSTOW, Gwent Map 11

### UPPER SEDBURY HOUSE, *Sedbury Lane, Sedbury*

*An atmosphere of homely comfort awaits guests at this delightful guest-house. Light, airy and spacious with comfortable accommodation, it is an ideal base for touring the beautiful Wye Valley.*

*ACCOMMODATION under £20*

*FOOD up to £15*

Hours: breakfast 8am – 9am; dinner 7pm. **Cuisine:**
English. **Rooms:** 4 bedrooms all with tea making facilities:
1 double ensuite, 1 family room, 1 double,
1 twin. **Other points:** parking, children catered for – please
check for age limits, open bank holidays, no-smoking area,
pets allowed, residents' lounge, vegetarian meals, garden,
swimming pool. **Directions:** through Sedbury until
reaching Sedbury Park, sharp left into Sedbury Lane,
quarter mile turn left, white painted house on left.
MS C F POTTS, tel (0291) 627173.

## COLWYN BAY, Clwyd Map 12

### CAFE NICOISE, 124 Abergele Road, Colwyn Bay
*Tastefully furnished restaurant, offering traditional and
modern provincial cookery. Close to beach and other
attractions, including Eirias Park, Conway Castle,
Great Orme, and Llandudno.*
*FOOD £15–£20* ★
**Hours:** lunch 12noon – 2pm; dinner 7pm – 10pm; closed
Sunday – Monday lunch. **Cuisine:** French:- Table d'hote
and a la carte menus. Dishes may include, Magret Duck
with a Blackcurrant Vinegar Sauce, and Smoked Salmon,
sauce gribiche. Vegetarian dishes available. **Credit cards:**
Visa, Access. **Other points:** licensed, children catered for –
please check for age limits, vegetarian meals, bank
holidays. **Directions:** Old Colwyn exit from A55. Situated
on main road through Colwyn Bay.
CARL SWIFT AND LYNNE SWIFT, tel (0492) 531555.

### EDELWEISS HOTEL, Lawson Road
*A 19th century country house set in its own wooded
gardens and tucked away in central Colwyn Bay. Large
car park, children's play area, games room and
solarium. Private pathway leading to the Promenade,
Eirias Park, and the Sports and Leisure Centre.*
*ACCOMMODATION under £20*
*FOOD up to £15* ☺
**Hours:** breakfast 7:45am – 9:30am; lunch 12noon – 2pm;
dinner 6:30pm – 9pm. **Cuisine:** Welsh / English:-
Vegetarian meals, fresh vegetables, home-cut meats.
**Rooms:** 26 en suite bedrooms, all with colour TV, video
films, radio, telephone and tea/coffee tray. **Credit cards:**
Visa, Access, Diners, AmEx. **Other points:** pets allowed.
**Directions:** situated off the A55 and then the B5104.
IAN BURT, tel (0492) 532314, fax (0492) 534707.

### NORTHWOOD HOTEL, 47 Rhos Road, Rhos On Sea
*Centrally situated in the heart of attractive Rhos-on-Sea.
Excellent tradition of fine cuisine with wide choice of
menu. Special diets catered for. Ground floor bedrooms.
Special "mini-break" rates. Easter and Christmas house
parties, golfing holidays arranged.*
*ACCOMMODATION under £20* ★
**Hours:** breakfast 8:15am – 9am; dinner 6:30pm – 7pm.
**Rooms:** 12 bedrooms all with tea making facilities,
radio, TV: 1 single, 1 single ensuite, 3 doubles ensuite,
4 twins ensuite, 3 family rooms ensuite. **Credit cards:**

Visa, Access. **Other points:** central heating, children
catered for – please check for age limits, pets allowed,
residents' lounge, patio, residents' bar. **Directions:** Rhos
Road, directly off the Promenade, turn opposite Tourist
Information Centre.
GORDON & AGNES PALLISER, tel (0492) 549931.

## CONWY, Gwynedd Map 12

### DEGANWY CASTLE HOTEL, Station Road, Deganwy
*Originally a cottage and over 250 years old, the
Degawny Castle Hotel offers a magnificent view of
Conwy Estuary and Castle. A main feature is the bar
which is built from beer barrels. Tourist Packages are
available. The many nearby places of interest, include
Conwy Castle, Bodnant Gardens, and the beautiful
Snowdonia National Park.*
*ACCOMMODATION £21–£30*
*FOOD £15–£20*
**Hours:** breakfast 7am – 9:30am; lunch 12noon – 2:30pm;
dinner 7pm – 9:30pm. **Cuisine:** British:- A la carte and
Table d'hote menus, offering an extensive choice of dishes.
Vegetarian dishes also available. **Rooms:** 31 bedrooms, all
en suite, with colour TV, radio, telephone & tea/coffee
making facilities. 2 four poster suites available. **Credit
cards:** Visa, Access, Diners, AmEx. **Other points:**
licensed, open-air dining, Sunday lunch, no-smoking area,
children catered for – please check for age limits, pets
allowed, residents' lounge, garden, parking, afternoon tea.
**Directions:** proceed along A55, and take signposted
turning to Deganwy.
DENNIS CHIN, tel (0492) 583555, fax (0492) 583555.

## CRICCIETH, Gwynedd Map 12

### BRON EIFION COUNTRY HOUSE HOTEL
*Built in the 1860's, Bron Eifion is set in the heart of the
tranquil Welsh countryside. The hotel is surrounded by
beautifully tended rose gardens and lawns with
stonewalled terraces. The decor is of tasteful pine
panelling adding to the hotel's character. Meals are well
prepared from fresh local produce.*
*ACCOMMODATION £31–£40*
*FOOD £15–£20* ☺
**Hours:** breakfast 8am – 9:30am; lunch 12noon – 2pm;
dinner – except Sunday 7pm – 9:15pm; dinner – Sunday
7pm – 9pm. **Cuisine:** British:- A la carte menu, bar
snacks, bar meals, fixed 3 course menu and vegetarian
meals. **Rooms:** 19 bedrooms all with tea making
facilities, telephone, radio, TV: 8 twins ensuite, 9
doubles ensuite, 2 family rooms ensuite. **Credit cards:**
Visa, Access, AmEx. **Other points:** licensed, Sunday
lunch, children catered for – please check for age limits,
garden, afternoon tea, conservatory, pets allowed, golf,
croquet, residents' lounge, residents' bar, vegetarian
meals, disabled access. **Directions:** from the east on
A497, through Criccieth. Hotel quarter mile on right.
MR R LILLEY, tel (0766) 522385, fax (0766) 522003.

## CAERWYLAN HOTEL, Beach Bank

*Caerwylan is an imposing hotel and the only one in Criccieth situated on the promenade. The lounge and several of the bedroom windows look out across the sandy beaches to the sea, or to the castle. The food is traditional Welsh. The warm welcome offered by the Davies' ensures many repeat bookings.*
*ACCOMMODATION under £20*

**Hours:** breakfast 8:45am – 9:30am; dinner 6:45pm – 7:30pm; closed November – Easter. **Cuisine:** Welsh. **Rooms:** 26 bedrooms all with tea making facilities, radio, TV: 6 singles ensuite, 4 doubles ensuite, 9 twins ensuite, 7 family rooms ensuite. **Other points:** pets allowed, children catered for – please check for age limits, residents' lounge, TV lounge. **Directions:** off the A497 onto B4411 to Criccieth. Hotel is on main promenade.
MR & MRS DAVIES, tel (0766) 522547.

## THE MOELWYN RESTAURANT WITH ROOMS, Mona Terrace

*A Victorian, creeper clad restaurant directly overlooking Cardigan Bay, with bar/lounge and well appointed bedrooms. The restaurant serves English and French cuisine including locally caught salmon. All food is carefully prepared and complemented by a comprehensive selection of wines. Public car park adjacent. Disabled access to restaurant only. Vegetarian menu.*
*ACCOMMODATION £21–£30*
*FOOD up to £15* 🍽

**Hours:** lunch – Sunday 12:30pm – 2pm; dinner 7pm – 9:30pm; closed January – March. **Cuisine:** English / French:- Seafood salmon and lamb, interesting sauces and fresh vegetables. Homemade sweets. Lobster when available. **Rooms:** 6 bedrooms, all en suite. all rooms have sea views. **Credit cards:** Visa, Access. **Other points:** licensed, Sunday lunch, children catered for – please check for age limits, pets/prior arr. **Directions:** on the seafront.
MR & MRS PETER BOOTH, tel (0766) 522500.

## CRICKHOWELL, Powys Map 10

## TY CROESO HOTEL, The Dardy, Llangattock

*Situated in the Brecon Beacons with magnificent views over the Usk Valley, this hotel was originally part of the Victorian Workhouse, now tastefully refurbished to provide comfort and every convenience for its guests. Log fires, stone walls, gardens and terrace all echo its traditional charm. Ideal for walking, visiting and touring. AA 2 Star & 3 Crown Highly Commended.*
*ACCOMMODATION £21–£30*
*FOOD £15–£20* ★

**Hours:** breakfast 7am – 9:30am; dinner 7pm – 9:30pm. **Cuisine:** Welsh / English:- Renowned for its excellent food with both locals and visitors. Interesting a la carte menu which includes traditional favourites and The Tastes of Wales Table d'Hote. **Rooms:** 8 bedrooms 4

doubles ensuite, 2 twins ensuite, 2 singles ensuite. **Credit cards:** Visa, Access, AmEx. **Other points:** licensed, open-air dining, Sunday lunch, garden, pets/prior arr, conferences. **Directions:** half mile from Crickhowell bridge – follow hotel sign.
KATE & PETER JONES, tel (0873) 810573, fax (0873) 810573.

## CWMBRAN, Gwent Map 11

## THE PARKWAY HOTEL & CONFERENCE CENTRE, Cwmbran Drive

*Outstanding in all aspects, The Parkway is ideal for holiday-makers and business visitors alike. Designed on a Mediterranean theme, the hotel offers accommodation of a very high standard, first-class restaurant meals, a leisure complex and excellent conference and banqueting facilities. Privately-owned and run, the service is excellent and a warm welcome guaranteed. Highly recommended.*
*ACCOMMODATION £31–£40*
*FOOD up to £15* 🍽

**Hours:** breakfast 7am – 9:30am; lunch 12noon – 2:30pm; dinner 7pm – 10pm. **Cuisine:** British / mediterranean:- Extensive choice of dishes such as River Wye Salmon, Lemon Sole Walewska, Grills, Tournedos Rossini. Carvery. **Rooms:** 70 bedrooms all with tea making facilities, telephone, radio, TV: 23 twins ensuite, 47 doubles ensuite. **Credit cards:** Visa, Access, Diners, AmEx. **Other points:** licensed, open-air dining, Sunday lunch, children catered for – please check for age limits, garden, residents' lounge, conferences, leisure centre, baby-listening device, cots, 24hr reception. **Directions:** off Junction 26 of the M4, onto A4042. Left into Cwmbran Drive.
JOHN WOODCOCK, tel (0633) 871199, fax (0633) 869160.

## DOLGELLAU, Gwynedd Map 12

## CLIFTON HOUSE HOTEL, Smithfield Square

*Dating from the 18th century when it was the County Gaol, the Clifton now offers a much warmer welcome as a hotel and restaurant. Mrs Dix, the chef, makes imaginative use of fresh, local produce and all the dishes are excellently cooked. The service is 'exemplary' and the warmth of the welcome is undoubtedly genuine. Highly recommended for food and accommodation.*
*ACCOMMODATION £21–£30*
*FOOD up to £15* 🍽

**Hours:** breakfast 8am – 9:30am; lunch 12:30pm – 2pm; dinner 7pm – 9:30pm; closed January. **Cuisine:** English:- Interesting and varied menu featuring traditional and vegetarian dishes and using fresh, local produce. **Rooms:** 7 bedrooms 3 doubles ensuite, 1 twin ensuite, 2 doubles, 1 twin. **Credit cards:** Visa, Access. **Other points:** licensed, garden, children catered for – please check for age limits. **Directions:** A470. Centre of Dolgellau.
ROB & PAULINE DIX, tel (0341) 422554.

## FISHGUARD, Dyfed Map 10

### GELLI FAWR COUNTRY HOUSE, Pontfaen

*An historic Welsh hill farm house, Gelli Fawr is now a comfortable, family-run hotel. Gelli Fawr is in the middle of the countryside and worth making a journey for its idyllic setting and excellent cuisine. A friendly yet relaxing hotel for all those who enjoy the peace of the country and good food.*

ACCOMMODATION £21–£30

FOOD £15–£20

**Hours:** breakfast 8:30am – 11am; bar meals 12:30pm - 2pm; bar meals 7pm – 10pm; dinner 7:30pm – 9:30pm. **Cuisine:** British:- Game pie, salmon en feuillette with fennel, caraway seed and cream sauce, Welsh lamb with apricots. Homemade bread. Tipsy bread and butter pudding. **Rooms:** 9 bedrooms 1 single, 1 twin ensuite, 2 twins, 4 doubles ensuite, 1 double. **Credit cards:** Visa, Access. **Other points:** licensed, open-air dining, Sunday lunch, children catered for – please check for age limits, pets allowed, afternoon tea, swimming pool, cookery school, baby-listening device, cots, residents' lounge, residents' bar. **Directions:** between B4329 & B4313, 5 miles from Newport Bay.
FRANCES ROUGHLEY & ANN CHURCHER, tel (0239) 820343, fax (0239) 820128.

### THE HOPE & ANCHOR INN, Goodwick

*This small family-run inn overlooks the harbour and is conveniently placed for both the station and the Irish ferries. There are miles of beaches nearby with a coastal path for walkers.*

ACCOMMODATION under £20

FOOD up to £15

**Hours:** lunch 12noon – 2:30pm; dinner 7pm – 10pm. **Cuisine:** English / Welsh. **Rooms:** 3 bedrooms 3 twins ensuite. **Other points:** open-air dining, Sunday lunch, children catered for – please check for age limits. **Directions:** end of A40.
MR T MCDONALD, tel (0348) 872314.

## GOWER, West Glamorgan Map 11

### OXWICH BAY HOTEL, Oxwich

*The hotel is situated in its own grounds just 10 yd from Oxwich Beach. Comfortable bedrooms, the majority of which have a sea view, provide an ideal base from which to explore the Gower peninsula.*

ACCOMMODATION £21–£30

FOOD up to £15 ★

**Hours:** breakfast 8am – 10:45am; bar meals 12noon – 2:30pm; dinner 7pm; closed Christmas 25/12. **Cuisine:** British:- Homemade sauces, eg. steak chasseur, steak with pepper sauce. **Rooms:** 14 bedrooms, 3 bathrooms. **Credit cards:** Visa, Access, Diners, AmEx. **Other points:** licensed, open-air dining, Sunday lunch, no-smoking area, children catered for – please check for age limits, coach/prior arr. **Directions:** from the A4118 take Oxwich turn then left at Oxwich crossroads.
MR IAN WILLIAMS, tel (0792) 390329.

## HARLECH, Gwynedd Map 12

### CASTLE COTTAGE HOTEL & RESTAURANT, Peh Llech

*An oak-beamed dining room and bar in one of the oldest houses in Harlech. Only 300 yd from the Castle. International cuisine plus modestly priced wine list. Ideally situated for the Royal St Davids Golf Course and surrounding area of natural beauty.*

ACCOMMODATION £21–£30

FOOD £15–£20 ♀

**Hours:** Sunday – lunch 12noon – 2pm; dinner – summer 7pm – 9:30pm; dinner – winter 7pm – 9pm. **Cuisine:** international:- Dishes include Local rack of lamb and honey & rosemary sauce. Brochette of scollops and smoked bacon, beurre blanc sauce. **Rooms:** 6 bedrooms all with tea making facilities, radio: 2 singles, 2 twins ensuite, 2 doubles ensuite. **Credit cards:** Visa, Access, AmEx. **Other points:** Sunday lunch, no-smoking area, children catered for – please check for age limits. **Directions:** on B4573 road to Porthmadog.
MR & MRS ROBERTS, tel (0766) 780479.

### THE CASTLE HOTEL, Castle Square

*A family-run hotel open all year offering a wide menu and warm, welcoming service. Local attractions include Harlech Castle, Cardigan Bay, a local golf club, Beddgelert copper mine and a dry ski slope. Nearby, Shell Island provides the opportunity for seal and bird spotting, and shell collecting.*

ACCOMMODATION £21–£30

FOOD £15–£20

**Hours:** last orders 7pm – 10pm; lunch 12noon – 3pm; meals all day – summer 12noon – 11pm; dinner 7pm – 11pm. **Cuisine:** English:- Pub menu, serving a range of dishes from dover sole and steak tartare to cow pie, lasagne and the Kiddies Corner selection. **Rooms:** 10 bedrooms all with tea making facilities, telephone, TV: 4 twins ensuite, 5 doubles ensuite, 1 single ensuite. **Credit cards:** Visa, Access. **Other points:** licensed, Sunday lunch, no-smoking area, children catered for – please check for age limits, pets allowed. **Directions:** opposite the castle in the centre of Harlech, which is on the A496.
R G & T M SWINSCOE, tel (0766) 780529.

## HAVERFORDWEST, Dyfed Map 10

### THE CASTLE HOTEL, Castle Square

*The Castle Hotel which has recently been refurbished, is ideally situated for touring the beautiful rugged mountains and coastline of Pembrokeshire. Comfortably and attractively furnished.*

ACCOMMODATION £21–£30

FOOD up to £15 ★

**Hours:** open all year 7pm; breakfast 7:30am – 9:30am; lunch 12noon – 2:45pm; bar meals 12noon – 2:45pm; dinner 7pm – 10pm; bar meals 7pm – 9pm. **Cuisine:** international:- Bistro style menu. Dishes may include, Honey Roasted Chicken, Pork & Apricot Stroganoff, Nutty Fettuccini, Rosemary Lamb Steak. Good selection

of steaks. Vegetarian dishes. **Rooms:** 8 bedrooms all with telephone, TV: 2 twins ensuite, 2 singles ensuite, 3 doubles ensuite, 1 family room ensuite. **Credit cards:** Visa, Access. **Other points:** licensed, Sunday lunch, children catered for – please check for age limits, afternoon tea, vegetarian meals, weekend breaks. **Directions:** turn off left at junction of A4076 and A40 over River Cleddau.
JULIET & PHILLIP LLEWELLYN, tel (0437) 769322, fax (0437) 769493.

## PEMBROKE HOUSE HOTEL, Spring Gardens

*A Virgina creeper clad, terraced Georgian house with a reputation for good food and friendly service.*
ACCOMMODATION £21–£30
FOOD up to £15
**Hours:** breakfast 7:30am – 9:30am; dinner 7pm – 9:30pm. **Cuisine:** English:- Steaks, grills and fresh fish. **Rooms:** 21 bedrooms 5 doubles ensuite, 1 double, 6 twins ensuite, 8 singles ensuite, 1 single. **Credit cards:** Visa, Access, Diners, AmEx. **Other points:** licensed, children catered for – please check for age limits, pets allowed, coach/prior arr. **Directions:** through the town centre, situated 2 blocks from Dew Street.
SIMON & SUZANNE DAVIES, tel (0437) 763652.

## ROCH GATE MOTEL, Roch

*A modern motel, providing excellent personal service to both long and short term visitors. Tasty meals with an emphasis on healthy eating and comfortable accommodation. With an indoor swimming pool, family sized Jacuzzi, solarium etc, there need never be a dull moment!*
ACCOMMODATION £31–£40
FOOD £15–£20
**Hours:** breakfast 7:45am – 9:30am; lunch 12noon – 3pm; dinner 6pm – 10pm. **Cuisine:** continental:- Menu may feature – tuna & prawn tagliatelle, cheese & walnut pasta bake, king prawns and apple pie. **Rooms:** 19 bedrooms, all en suite. **Credit cards:** Visa, Access, AmEx. **Other points:** licensed, Sunday lunch, children catered for – please check for age limits, bank holidays, pets allowed, sauna, gym facilities, Jacuzzi, solarium, swimming pool. **Directions:** 6 miles out of Haverfordwest towards St Davids.
JOHN SMITH, tel (0437) 710435.

## WOLFSCASTLE COUNTRY HOTEL, Wolf's Castle

*A country hotel where the traditional welcome of warmth, relaxation and friendliness has been maintained. Situated on a hillside amidst beautiful countryside, this hotel offers a high standard of accommodation. The restaurant enjoys an enviable reputation locally for its excellent food and imaginative bar meals are also available. A delightful hotel in which to stay or dine.*
ACCOMMODATION £31–£40
FOOD £15–£20
**Hours:** breakfast 7:30am – 9:30am; lunch – Sunday 12noon – 2pm; bar meals 12noon – 2pm; dinner 7pm – 9pm; bar meals 7pm – 9pm. **Cuisine:** British:- A blend of nouvelle cuisine and home cooking. Predominantly fresh, local produce used. Traditional Sunday lunch. Good wine list. **Rooms:** 20 bedrooms, all en suite. **Credit cards:** Visa, Access, AmEx. **Other points:** licensed, Sunday lunch, children catered for – please check for age limits, residents' lounge, log fire, functions, patio, squash. **Directions:** A40. 6 miles north of Haverfordwest in village of Wolf's Castle.
ANDREW STIRLING, tel (0437) 87225, (0437) 87688, fax (0437) 87383.

# HOLYHEAD, Gwynedd Map 12

## BULL HOTEL, London Road, Anglesey

*A pleasant, cream painted building on the main A5 road to Holyhead. There is a large, sheltered beer garden with children's play area outside, while inside the main, informal eating area is separate from the bar. For those wishing to linger a while the Bull offers comfortable accommodation.*
ACCOMMODATION under £20
FOOD up to £15
**Hours:** breakfast 7:30am – 9am; lunch 12noon – 2pm; bar meals 12noon – 9pm; dinner 7pm – 9:30pm. **Cuisine:** British:- Specials change daily. **Rooms:** 14 bedrooms 2 singles ensuite, 5 twins ensuite, 5 doubles ensuite, 2 family rooms ensuite. **Credit cards:** Visa, Access. **Other points:** open-air dining, Sunday lunch, pets allowed, children catered for – please check for age limits, afternoon tea. **Directions:** situated 200 yd from Holyhead side traffic lights at A5025 Junction.
DAVID HALL, tel (0407) 740351.

# LAMPETER, Dyfed Map 10

## PEPPERS RESTAURANT, 14 High Street

*Recently renovated and tastefully furnished, this bistro-style restaurant offers a cool, relaxed atmosphere in which to enjoy fine quality food in spotlessly clean surroundings.*
FOOD up to £15
**Hours:** snacks all day 10am – 9pm; lunch 12noon – 2:30pm; closed Christmas 23/12 – 03/01; closed Sunday. **Cuisine:** Daily changing menu, offering a good choice of typically bistro-style dishes, including vegetarian specialities and salads, all freshly prepared and cooked on the premises. **Other points:** licensed, no-smoking area, children catered for – please check for age limits, afternoon tea, morning tea. **Directions:** follow A482 from Aberaeron or Lllanwrda, A485 from Carmarthen or Aberystwyth, or A475 from Newcastle Emlyn.
STEPHANIE WARNES, tel (0570) 423796.

# LAMPHEY, Dyfed Map 10

## LAMPHEY HALL HOTEL, Pembroke

*This former Rectory stands in its own landscaped gardens within the Pembrokeshire Coast National Park. The resident proprietor offers you a warm and friendly welcome for your stay – whether a short break or annual holiday. Lamphey is an ideal base from which to explore*

*the miles of country lanes and explore the local scenery. At nearby Grassholm, you can see puffins and seals.*
ACCOMMODATION £21–£30
FOOD up to £15
**Hours:** open all year Sunday; breakfast 8am – 9am; bar meals 11:30am – 2pm; lunch 12noon – 1:30pm; bar meals 6pm – 10pm; dinner 7pm – 9pm. **Cuisine:** British:- A la carte and Table d'hote. All food is freshly prepared to order, including vegetarian dishes, complemented by a fine wine list. **Rooms:** 30 bedrooms all with tea making facilities, telephone, radio, TV: 3 singles ensuite, 2 twins ensuite, 3 doubles ensuite, 1 triple ensuite, 1 quad ensuite, 2 family rooms ensuite. **Credit cards:** Visa, Access, Diners, AmEx. **Other points:** licensed, open-air dining, Sunday lunch, pets allowed, parking, residents' lounge, garden, picnic lunches, children catered for – please check for age limits, baby-listening device, cots, residents' bar, vegetarian meals. **Directions:** situated in village centre on the A4139 Pembroke to Tenby Road.
CHRISTOPHER COCKER, tel (0646) 672394, fax (0646) 672369.

# LITTLE HAVEN, Dyfed Map 10

### THE NEST BISTRO, 12 Grove Place, Nr Haverfordwest
*A cosy bistro with a small cocktail bar, in an old rambling house in this unique seaside village. A wide choice of dishes such as Mexican Turkey & Breast of Duck. Fresh local fish includes Dover sole, monkfish, stuffed fillets of Lemon sole & lobster. 100 yd from the beach and coastal path. Little Haven provides a picturesque base for touring or enjoying the many water sports.*
ACCOMMODATION under £20
FOOD up to £15
**Hours:** lunch (high season only) 12noon – 2:30pm; dinner (booking advisable) 6:30pm – late; last orders 10pm; closed Monday. **Cuisine:** English / continental:- An imaginative menu with all dishes home-made, featuring fresh local fish, seafood & a selection of fine steaks. Extensive wine list. Welsh cheeseboard. **Rooms:** 2 bedrooms 2 doubles ensuite. **Credit cards:** Visa, Access. **Other points:** licensed, children catered for – please check for age limits, parking. **Directions:** off the B4341 in Broad Haven.
PAUL & MARGARET MERRICK, tel (0437) 781728.

# LLANBEDR, Gwynedd Map 12

### LLEW GLAS
*Originally 'Yr-Hen-Feudy' – Old Cow Sheds, today the Llew Glas Brasserie is a popular, tastefully furnished brasserie with character beams and Trevor in full view cooking in the kitchen. All food is home-made and purchased locally and fresh. All lamb is Welsh, and baked goods are from their own bakery. Vegetarians and those with special diets are catered for. Many places of interest nearby.*
FOOD up to £15
**Hours:** open all year; dinner 6pm – 10pm. **Cuisine:** British:- Traditional homecooked cuisine, using fresh local produce. **Credit cards:** Visa, Access, AmEx, Diners, Switch. **Other points:** licensed, open-air dining, no-smoking area, children catered for – please check for age limits. **Directions:** 3 miles south from Harlech. Turn left before bridge in centre of Llanbedr village on Cwm Bychan Road that leads to the Roman steps.
TREVOR & MARJ PHAROAH, tel (0341) 23555.

# LLANBERIS, Gwynedd Map 12

### LAKE VIEW HOTEL, Tan Y Pant
*The Lake View Hotel offers exceptional views of the surrounding terrain. Close to the narrow gauge railways and Snowdonia National Park. A friendly hotel with a homely atmosphere.*
ACCOMMODATION under £20
FOOD up to £15
**Hours:** open all day 6pm; breakfast 8:30am – 9:30am; lunch 12noon – 2pm; dinner 6:30pm – 9pm. **Cuisine:** English:- Veal our speciality, also fine steaks in home-made sauces. Local chef. **Rooms:** 10 bedrooms 1 double, 5 doubles ensuite, 4 family rooms ensuite. **Credit cards:** Visa, Access, Diners. **Other points:** licensed, Sunday lunch, children catered for – please check for age limits, coach/prior arr. **Directions:** on the A4086 on the Caernarfon side of Llanberis.
BRIAN TAYLOR & VAL TAYLOR, tel (0286) 870422.

# LLANDOVERY, Dyfed Map 10

### THE ROYAL OAK INN, Rhandirmwyn
*A 17th century village inn with restaurant, pool room, and en suite accommodation. Near Brecon Beacons, RSPB Bird Reserve, Llyn Brianne dam and reservoir, fishing, riding and fabulous scenery. 40 minutes from the coast and 7 miles north of Llandovery.*
ACCOMMODATION £21–£30
FOOD up to £15
**Hours:** breakfast 8am – 9:30am; lunch 11:30am – 3:30pm; bar meals 11:30am – 3:30pm; dinner 6pm – 10pm; bar meals 6pm – 10:30pm. **Cuisine:** English:- Good quality country food. Excellent value bar meals. **Rooms:** 5 bedrooms all with tea making facilities, TV: 1 double ensuite, 1 twin ensuite, 1 family room ensuite, 2 singles. **Credit cards:** Visa, Access. **Other points:** licensed, Sunday lunch, children catered for – please check for age limits, pets allowed, beer garden. **Directions:** from Llandovery, follow signs to Lyn Brianne & Rhandirmwyn.
MR & MRS L W ALEXANDER, tel (05506) 201, fax (05506) 332.

# LLANDRINDOD WELLS, Powys Map 10

### HOLLY FARM, Holly Farm
*Holly Farm is a lovely old house built in the early 18th century. It is tastefully decorated with full central heating and exposed beams. A comfortable lounge incorporates a large stone grate with log fire and colour TV. All around is the Welsh countryside, renowned for its*

beauty, peaceful walks, recreational facilities and places of historical interest.
ACCOMMODATION under £20
FOOD up to £15
**Hours:** breakfast 8:30am; dinner 7pm. **Cuisine:** breakfast. **Rooms:** 3 bedrooms all with tea making facilities: 1 twin – shower only, 1 double ensuite, 1 triple ensuite. **Other points:** children catered for – please check for age limits, residents' lounge, cots. **Directions:** 1.5 miles south of Llandrindod Wells near Howey, quarter mile off A483.
RUTH JONES, tel (0597) 822402.

## SEVERN ARMS HOTEL, Penybont
A former coaching inn ideally situated on a popular holiday route. The Inn has an olde worlde charm with a wealth of oak beams and a log fire which burns in the Lounge Bar during winter. The Severn Arms is one of the best known unaltered coaching houses in Mid Wales but has been modernised inside to a high standard. Reduced rates on 2 golf courses. 6 miles of fishing available.
ACCOMMODATION £21–£30
FOOD up to £15
**Hours:** closed Christmas 1 week; dinner 7pm – 9:30pm. **Cuisine:** English:- Grills, Roasts, home-made steak and kidney pie, cottage pie. Full A La Carte menu and Bar snacks are always available. **Rooms:** 10 bedrooms all with tea making facilities, telephone, radio, TV: 3 doubles ensuite, 1 twin ensuite, 6 family rooms ensuite. **Credit cards:** Visa, Access, Diners, AmEx. **Other points:** licensed, Sunday lunch, children catered for – please check for age limits, fishing, garden, caravan facilities.
**Directions:** on A44, Rhayader to Leominster road.
GEOFF & TESSA LLOYD, tel (0597) 851224, (0597) 851344, fax (0597) 851693.

# LLANDUDNO, Gwynedd Map 12

## AMBASSADOR HOTEL, Promenade
The Williams family have been in the hotel trade for 30 years, and in that time have built up a regular return business. The hotel is on the Promenade and gets the sun most of the day. The two sun lounges are relaxing places to sit whatever the weather.
ACCOMMODATION under £20
FOOD up to £15
**Hours:** closed 01/01 – 31/01; breakfast 8:30am – 9:15am; bar meals 12noon – 1:30pm; dinner 6:30pm – 7:30pm. **Cuisine:** British. **Rooms:** 66 bedrooms all with tea making facilities, TV: 9 singles, 4 singles ensuite, 2 doubles, 9 doubles ensuite, 5 twins, 28 twins ensuite, 6 family rooms ensuite, 3 family rooms. **Other points:** central heating, children catered for – please check for age limits, residents' lounge, lift, bar, cots, disabled access, vegetarian meals, parking, residents' bar. **Directions:** leave A55; take A470 to Llandudno. Follow to promenade then turn left.
DAVID T WILLIAMS, tel (0492) 876886, fax (0492) 876347.

## CASANOVA RESTAURANT, 18 Chapel Street
Situated in the heart of town. Gingham and red tablecloths, a cedar ceiling and lively music add to the bustling atmosphere. A very popular restaurant – advance booking recommended.
FOOD up to £15
**Hours:** dinner 6pm – 10:30pm. **Cuisine:** Italian:- Italian cuisine: eg. calimari fritti, insalata Casanova, filetto al funghi. **Credit cards:** Visa, Access. **Other points:** licensed, children catered for – please check for age limits, street parking. **Directions:** off Gloddaeth Street opposite the English Presbyterian Church.
MR K R BOONHAM, tel (0492) 878426.

## DUNOON HOTEL, Gloddaeth Street
Lavishly appointed with great attention to detail, the Dunoon exudes charm and comfort. The hotel has been in the same family for over 40 years which accounts for the care shown in the elegant accommodation and spacious restaurant. The Dunoon provides the ideal place to relax and enjoy the good food, civilised ambience and splendid facilities.
ACCOMMODATION £31–£40
FOOD up to £15
**Hours:** breakfast 9am – 10am; lunch 1pm – 2pm; dinner 6:30pm – 7:30pm. **Cuisine:** British:- Table d'hote, a la carte and bar meals. British cuisine specialising in fresh, local produce. **Rooms:** 56 bedrooms 12 singles ensuite, 12 family rooms ensuite, 14 doubles ensuite, 18 twins ensuite. **Credit cards:** Visa, Access. **Other points:** licensed, Sunday lunch, children catered for – please check for age limits, garden, afternoon tea, pets allowed, solarium. **Directions:** off Mostyn Street, close to Promenade.
MICHAEL C CHADDERTON, tel (0492) 860787.

## EMPIRE HOTEL, Church Walks
A family run hotel located near the centre of this popular holiday resort. The Empire has developed a reputation for good food served in two separate restaurants, friendly service and leisure facilities.
ACCOMMODATION £31–£40
FOOD up to £15
**Hours:** bar 11am – 11pm. **Cuisine:** British:- Watkins & Co serving traditional dishes and Grill Room/Coffee Shop fish and roasts. **Rooms:** 58 bedrooms, all en suite. **Credit cards:** Visa, Access, Diners, AmEx. **Other points:** licensed, Sunday lunch, no-smoking area, children catered for – please check for age limits, roof patio garden, swimming pool, sauna. **Directions:** Church Walks leads off the promenade.
MR & MRS MADDOCKS, tel (0492) 860555.

## EPPERSTONE HOTEL, 15 Abbey Road
Epperstone is a small detached hotel surrounded by gardens. Over 100 years old, the hotel has elegant, spacious rooms, original fireplaces, a superb mahogany staircase and a Victorian conservatory. The hotel caters for guests seeking peace and comfort with good home cooking, a high standard of accommodation and value for money prices.
ACCOMMODATION £21–£30
FOOD up to £15
**Hours:** breakfast 8:30am – 9am; dinner 6:30pm – 9pm. **Cuisine:** British. **Rooms:** 8 bedrooms all with tea making facilities, telephone, radio, TV: 4 doubles

ensuite, 2 twins ensuite, 2 family rooms ensuite. **Credit cards:** Visa, Access. **Other points:** children catered for – please check for age limits, vegetarian meals, afternoon tea, pets allowed, conservatory. **Directions:** from Promenade turn left at the Cenotaph, over the mini roundabout and proceed along Gloddaeth Avenue, turn third left into York Road. The hotel may then be seen fronting Abbey Road at the top of York Road. MR & MRS D J DREW, tel (0492) 878746, fax (0492) 871223.

### GRANBY GUEST HOUSE, *Deganwy Avenue*
*Situated in a popular avenue just a short distance between both shores, shops, cinemas and entertainments. Family guest house with resident proprietors. Children welcome at reduced rates if sharing room with parents. Vegetarian, diabetic, coeliac diets catered for.*
*ACCOMMODATION under £20*
**Hours:** last orders 6:30pm – 4:30pm; breakfast 9am – 9:30am; dinner 6pm. **Cuisine:** breakfast. **Rooms:** 2 double, 1 twin and 5 family bedrooms, all en suite. tea/coffee making facilities and colour TV in all bedrooms. **Credit cards:** Visa, Access. **Other points:** children catered for – please check for age limits, residents' lounge. **Directions:** located in the centre of town, 2 blocks from Mostyn St (main shops). JUNE ROBERTS, tel (0492) 76095.

### HEADLANDS HOTEL, *Hill Terrace*
*Situated above the town, but only a short walk to the beach and shops, Headlands Hotel offers superb views across the bay and Conwy estuary to the mountains of Snowdonia. Friendly service and home-cooked 5 course table d'hote dinner make this a popular choice with tourists.*
*ACCOMMODATION £21–£30*
*FOOD £15–£20* ★
**Hours:** breakfast 8:30am – 9:15am; bar meals 12noon – 1:30pm; dinner 6:45pm – 8pm; closed January – February. **Cuisine:** British:- A five-course table d'hote menu is offered. Wide choice of dishes, using local produce, both traditional and classical. Vegetarian meals by arrangement. **Rooms:** 17 bedrooms all with tea making facilities, telephone, radio, TV: 2 singles, 2 singles ensuite, 3 twins ensuite, 8 doubles ensuite, 2 triples ensuite. **Credit cards:** Visa, Access, Diners, AmEx. **Other points:** licensed, children catered for – please check for age limits, pets/prior arr, bar, lounge, central heating. **Directions:** at top of Hill Terrace, on the Great Orme in Llandudno. MR & MRS WOODS, tel (0492) 877485.

### HEATH HOUSE HOTEL, *Central Promenade*
*A comfortable family-run hotel on the sea-front, ideal for a short stop-over, a pleasant mini-break or a traditional holiday, with the same friendly welcome all year round. Children most welcome.*
*ACCOMMODATION £21–£30*
*FOOD up to £15*
**Hours:** breakfast 8:30am – 9:30am; dinner 6pm – 7:30pm. **Cuisine:** British:- Varied menus including traditional favourites. English breakfast. Comprehensive wine list. **Rooms:** 22 bedrooms all with tea making

facilities, telephone, radio, TV: 2 singles, 3 twins ensuite, 3 twins, 3 doubles ensuite, 3 doubles, 3 triples ensuite, 2 triples, 3 family rooms ensuite. **Credit cards:** Visa, Access, AmEx. **Other points:** residents' lounge, air-conditioned, baby-listening device, cots, no-smoking area, business facilities, entertainment, residents' bar, vegetarian meals, parking. **Directions:** on the A546 (Promenade), 250 yd west of the Conference Centre. JOHN & MARY HODGES, tel (0492) 876538, fax (0492) 860307.

### IMPERIAL HOTEL, *The Promenade*
*A large hotel with many facilities including the Speak easy Bar, based on 1920's American gangster style. Chantreys Restaurant plus Health & Fitness Centre.*
*ACCOMMODATION £41–£50*
*FOOD £15–£20*
**Hours:** bar meals 12noon – 2pm; lunch 12:30pm – 2pm; dinner 6:30pm – 9:30pm. **Cuisine:** international:- Daily table d'hote menu and monthly speciality menu. **Rooms:** 100 bedrooms 20 singles ensuite, 44 twins ensuite, 27 doubles ensuite, 4 family rooms ensuite, 5 suites. **Credit cards:** Visa, Access, Diners, AmEx. **Other points:** Sunday lunch, children catered for – please check for age limits, coach/prior arr. **Directions:** on promenade. GEOFFREY LOFTHOUSE, tel (0492) 877466, fax (0492) 878043.

### RAVENHURST HOTEL, *West Shore*
*The Ravenhurst is situated on the West Shore which runs alongside the Conwy Estuary. Wonderful views to Snowdonia and Anglesey. 50% of the bookings are from returning guests. No strangers only friends you haven't met.*
*ACCOMMODATION £21–£30*
*FOOD up to £15*
**Hours:** breakfast 8:15am – 10am; bar meals 12noon – 2pm; lunch 12:30pm – 2pm; bar meals 5:45pm – 11pm; dinner 6:15pm – 8pm; closed 30/11 – 01/02. **Cuisine:** British. **Rooms:** 19 bedrooms all with tea making facilities, TV: 6 singles ensuite, 10 twins ensuite, 3 family rooms ensuite. **Credit cards:** Visa, Access, Diners, AmEx. **Other points:** central heating, children catered for – please check for age limits, residents' lounge, garden, vegetarian meals, no-smoking area. **Directions:** on the seafront. Llandudno West. DAVID & KATHLEEN CARRINGTON & PETER CARR, tel (0492) 875525.

### ROSE TOR HOTEL, *124 Mostyn Street*
*Family run hotel with a very relaxed atmosphere. All the bedrooms have been individually styled and have colour TVs.*
*ACCOMMODATION under £20*
*FOOD up to £15*
**Hours:** breakfast 7:30am – 9:15am; dinner 6pm – 10:30pm. **Cuisine:** British. **Rooms:** 27 bedrooms all with TV: 1 single ensuite, 19 doubles ensuite, 4 twins ensuite, 3 family rooms ensuite. **Credit cards:** Visa, Access, Diners, AmEx. **Other points:** central heating, residents' lounge, bar. **Directions:** A546 or A470 to Llandudno. MRS B COTTON, tel (0492) 870433.

## SANDRINGHAM HOTEL, West Parade, West Shore

The bar has a definite naval flavour, with the cap bands of naval vessels and seascapes on the walls. Situated in the centre of the West Shore, it is a real suntrap all day long and has unimpeded views of Anglesey and the Conwy estuary. Happy, family atmosphere.

ACCOMMODATION £31–£40

FOOD up to £15

**Hours:** open all year 6pm; breakfast 8am – 9:15am; lunch 12noon – 2pm; dinner 6:30pm – 8:30pm. **Cuisine:** English:- Concentration on fresh wholesome food such as home made pies, lasagne, fish and roasts. **Rooms:** 18 bedrooms all with tea making facilities, telephone, TV: 3 family rooms ensuite, 5 twins ensuite, 3 singles ensuite, 7 doubles ensuite. **Credit cards:** Visa, Access. **Other points:** licensed, open-air dining, Sunday lunch, children catered for – please check for age limits, residents' lounge, residents' bar. **Directions:** on seafront of the quiet, sunny West Shore (not the main promenade). MR & MRS D KAVANAGH, tel (0492) 876513, (0492) 876447.

## TYNEDALE PRIVATE HOTEL, Central Promenade

Situated in a premier position opposite The Bandstand with excellent views of Llandudno Bay, a warm welcome is assured for all guests. Food is very important here and every effort is made to select the best. Guests can relax and enjoy the magnificent views from a luxurious 'no smoking' lounge, or retire to the Sun Lounge for peace and quiet. There are two bars and two dance floors, both air-conditioned, and comfortable accommodation with many facilities.

ACCOMMODATION £21–£30

FOOD up to £15

**Hours:** breakfast 8:15am – 9:15am; bar snacks 12noon – 2pm; dinner 6pm – 7pm. **Cuisine:** British. **Credit cards:** Visa, Access. **Other points:** parking, children catered for – please check for age limits, no-smoking area, disabled access, residents' lounge, vegetarian meals. **Directions:** on central promenade opposite the bandstand. GOODEY, MICHAEL, tel (0492) 877426, fax (0492) 871213.

## WHITE COURT HOTEL, 2 North Parade

An attractive hotel well-situated adjacent to the pier, beach and shopping area. All bedrooms and the charming sitting room offer a very high standard of comfort, allowing guests to relax and enjoy the ambiance of the hotel which is completely non-smoking. The dining room is renowned for its good food and comprehensive wine list.

ACCOMMODATION £21–£30

FOOD up to £15 ★

**Hours:** breakfast 8am – 9:30am; dinner 6:30pm – 8:30pm. **Cuisine:** British. **Rooms:** 14 bedrooms all with tea making facilities, telephone, radio, TV: 9 doubles ensuite, 1 family room ensuite, 3 twins ensuite, 1 suite.

**Credit cards:** Visa, Access. **Other points:** children catered for – please check for age limits, residents' lounge. **Directions:** near to Cenotaph, adjacent to pier, beach & shopping area. NATASHA & STEPHEN GARLINGE, tel (0492) 876719, fax (0492) 871583.

# LLANGOLLEN, Clwyd Map 12

## GALES, 18 Bridge Street

An 18th century establishment, opposite the River Dee, in the town famous for the international Eisteddfodd. Over 250 wines, on or off sales. Limited edition etchings and screen prints for sale. Overall winner of the Les Routiers/Mercier Wine List of the Year Award 1990.

ACCOMMODATION £21–£30

FOOD up to £15 ⚑

**Hours:** lunch 12noon – 2pm; dinner 6pm – 10pm; closed Sunday. **Cuisine:** international:- Specialises in home-made soups and ice creams and offers a variety of dishes of the day. **Rooms:** 14 bedrooms 1 triple ensuite, 2 suites, 11 doubles ensuite. **Credit cards:** Visa, Access. **Other points:** open-air dining, Sunday lunch, children catered for – please check for age limits, patio. **Directions:** located in the town centre. RICHARD & GILLIE GALE, tel (0978) 860089, fax (0978) 861313.

# LLANIDLOES, Powys Map 10

## GLYNGYNWYDD, Cwmbelan

Glyngynwydd is today a traditional farmhouse building which has been listed in local records as a "township" since very early times. Nestling on the Eastern slopes of an unspoilt valley, the house has been modernised to provide every comfort, but retaining its original exposed beams, oak and flagstone floors and inglenook fireplaces. Across the footbridge there are two-storey self-catering cottages with fully fitted kitchens and equipped with all modern facilities for four or six people. The area is superb for lovers of the countryside and its abundant wildlife.

ACCOMMODATION under £20

**Hours:** breakfast on request Sunday. **Cuisine:** breakfast. **Other points:** parking, children catered for – please check for age limits, no-smoking area, pets, residents' lounge, garden. **Directions:** 2 miles south of Llanidloes on A470 on the left-hand side. MS V DAVIES, tel (0686) 413854, fax (0686) 412012.

## UNICORN HOTEL, Long Bridge Street

Set in an attractive terrace, this is an extremely popular and sociable hotel, both with tourists and local townsfolk alike. The service is efficient and helpful complementing the welcoming atmosphere. This is an ideal base from which to tour the outstanding nearby countryside.

ACCOMMODATION under £20

FOOD up to £15

**Hours:** breakfast 7:30am – 9am; bar meals 12noon – 2pm; bar meals 7pm – 9pm. **Cuisine:** English:- Table d'hote menu offering traditional English fare. Vegetarian meals are also available. **Rooms:** 5 bedrooms, all en suite with colour TV, radio/alarm and tea/coffee making facilities, comfortable and attractively furnished. **Credit cards:** Visa, Access, AmEx. **Other points:** licensed, Sunday lunch, children catered for – please check for age limits. **Directions:** situated in Llanidloes town centre. CHRISTINE & DEREK HUMPHRIES, tel (0686) 413167.

# LLANTRISSENT, Gwent Map 11

## THE ROYAL OAK, Nr Usk
*A 15th century residential inn situated on the A449, only 10 minutes drive from junction 24 on the M4. An attractive white painted building standing in a well kept cottage garden in the valley of the River Usk. In the summer the beer garden and the children's play area are in great demand.*
*ACCOMMODATION £21–£30*
*FOOD £15–£20*
**Hours:** breakfast 7:30am – 9:30am; bar meals 12noon – 2pm; bar meals 7pm – 10pm; dinner 7:30pm – 10pm. **Cuisine:** international:- Paella, beef Wellington. **Rooms:** 23 bedrooms all with en suite bath or shower. **Credit cards:** Visa, Access, AmEx. **Other points:** open-air dining, pets allowed, children catered for – please check for age limits, coach/prior arr. **Directions:** near the A449. MR GASCOINE, tel (0291) 673317.

# LLANWDDYN, Powys Map 10

## LAKE VYRNWY HOTEL
*Lake Vyrnwy is everything you would expect from a unique first Class Country House and Sporting Hotel, set in the heart of beautiful mid-Wales. The comfort of the hotel echoes the peace of the surrounding countryside and its infinite views of outstanding natural beauty. A wide range of country pursuits are available on the Estate's 24,000 acres. Own Country Pub in grounds.*
*ACCOMMODATION £41–£50*
*FOOD £21–£25*
**Hours:** open all year 7:30pm; breakfast 8:30am – 9:30am; lunch 12:30pm – 2pm; bar meals 12:30pm – 2pm; bar meals 6pm – 9pm; dinner 7:30pm – 9:30pm. **Cuisine:** British:- Award winning traditional and innovative dishes. Hotel has daily changing menus, restaurant and the estate's fish and game. Own market garden. **Rooms:** 39 bedrooms all with tea making facilities, telephone, radio, TV: 2 singles ensuite, 16 twins ensuite, 21 doubles ensuite. **Credit cards:** Visa, Access, Diners, AmEx. **Other points:** licensed, Sunday lunch, no-smoking area, children catered for – please check for age limits, pets allowed, afternoon tea, vegetarian meals, garden, residents' lounge, residents' bar. **Directions:** from Shrewsbury A458 to Welshpool. Right onto B4393 to Lake Vyrnwy. JAMES TALBOT (GENERAL MANAGER), tel (0691) 73692, fax (0691) 73259.

# MACHYNLLETH, Powys Map 10

## THE WHITE LION COACHING INN, Heol Pentrerheydn
*The White Lion has been welcoming guests since the early 1800's. It was one of several coaching inns in town, and retains its original oak beams, inglenook fireplace and cobbled forecourt. Regular patrons appreciate the inn for its Dyffi salmon and traditional and innovative menus – well worth a visit.*
*ACCOMMODATION under £20*
*FOOD up to £15*
**Hours:** lunch 12noon – 2:30pm; bar meals 12noon – 2:30pm; dinner 6pm – 9pm; bar meals 6pm – 9pm. **Cuisine:** Welsh:- Traditional Welsh, including Sunday lunch. Bar meals. **Rooms:** 9 bedrooms all with tea making facilities, radio, TV: 2 singles ensuite, 1 single, 1 twin ensuite, 1 twin, 3 doubles ensuite, 1 double. **Credit cards:** Visa, Access, Diners, AmEx. **Other points:** licensed, Sunday lunch, children catered for – please check for age limits, pets allowed, bank holidays, cots, disabled access, residents' bar, vegetarian meals. **Directions:** hotel on junction A487/A489 by the Victorian Clock. M K & J F QUICK, tel (0654) 703455.

# MAENTWROG, Gwynedd Map 12

## GRAPES HOTEL
*Old, family owned coaching inn situated in the Vale of Ffestiniog – an area of outstanding beauty in the heart of Snowdonia National Park. Good fishing, walking and pony trekking country. Typical warm pub atmosphere.*
*ACCOMMODATION £21–£30*
*FOOD up to £15*
**Hours:** open all year 6pm; breakfast 8am – 9:30am; lunch 12noon – 2:15pm; dinner 6pm – 9:30pm. **Cuisine:** British / continental:- Homemade dishes, eg. lasagne, pizza, steak pie, curry, chilli, aubergine moussaka, wild mushroom stroganoff. **Rooms:** 6 bedrooms all with tea making facilities, TV: 3 doubles ensuite, 3 singles ensuite. **Credit cards:** Visa, Access. **Other points:** licensed, open-air dining, Sunday lunch, disabled access, children catered for – please check for age limits. **Directions:** 5 miles from Blaenau Ffestiniog on the main A470 from the north. BRIAN & GILLIAN TARBOX, tel (076685) 208, (076685) 365.

# MILFORD HAVEN, Dyfed Map 10

## BELHAVEN HOUSE HOTEL & RESTAURANT, 29 Hamilton Terrace
*A quiet hotel noted for its relaxed atmosphere. 6 of the bedrooms overlook the attractive waterway. The restaurant offers a large selection of scrumptious meals to cater for most tastes.*
*ACCOMMODATION £21–£30*
*FOOD up to £15* ★
**Hours:** breakfast 6am – 10:30am; lunch 12noon – 2pm; dinner 6:30pm – 10pm. **Cuisine:** British / continental:- Steaks, pavlovas, vegetarian dishes. Choice of over 40

main courses. **Rooms:** 11 bedrooms 3 singles, 1 single ensuite, 1 double ensuite, 2 twins, 4 family rooms. **Credit cards:** Visa, Access, AmEx, Diners, Switch. **Other points:** licensed, Sunday lunch, children catered for – please check for age limits, afternoon tea, coach/prior arr. **Directions:** on the front street, overlooking the haven, just past the monument. MR & MRS HENRICKSEN, tel (0646) 695983, fax (0646) 690787.

## THE TABERNA INN, *Herbrandston*

*Situated in the village of Herbrandston, the Taberna Inn offers a good range of bar and restaurant meals. Popular with locals, the Inn enjoys a bustling atmosphere and is well situated for both holiday-makers and commercial visitors to the area.*
ACCOMMODATION under £20
FOOD £15–£20
**Hours:** breakfast 8am – 10am; bar meals 12noon – 2pm; dinner 7pm – 10pm; bar meals 7pm – 10pm. **Cuisine:** international:- Dishes may include Shark Steaks, Lamb Shrewsbury, Italian Dish of the Day, Grilled Caribbean Gammon Steak. Local fish dishes. Bar meals lunch & evening. **Rooms:** 4 bedrooms. **Credit cards:** Visa, Access. **Other points:** licensed, open-air dining, Sunday lunch, children catered for – please check for age limits, pets allowed, beer garden. **Directions:** off main Milford Haven to Dale road. Signposted. NICK SKUDDER MHCIMA, tel (0646) 693498.

## MOLD, Clwyd Map 12

## CHEZ COLETTE, *56 High Street*

*An attractive French family-run restaurant, offering fine traditional cuisine. The panelled decor is adorned with French paintings and complemented by soft background music adding to the overall charm of this establishment, so popular with the locals. It is ideally situated for visits to the theatre and countryside walks, with the ancient parish church directly opposite.*
FOOD up to £15
**Hours:** lunch 11:30am – 2pm; dinner 6:30pm – 10pm; closed Monday; closed Sunday. **Cuisine:** French:- Quality French Provincial cuisine with table d'hote and a la carte menus. Dishes may include Mussels in Garlic Sauce, Escargot, Savoury Pancake, Navarin of Lamb, Poulet au Riesling, Steak au Poivre. **Credit cards:** Visa, Access, AmEx. **Other points:** licensed, children catered for – please check for age limits. **Directions:** A494, A541, top of Mold High Street, opposite the Parish Church. JACQUES & COLETTE DUVAUCHELLE, tel (0352) 759225.

## THEATR CLWYD, *Rakes Lane*

*Combine a meal with a visit to the Theatre at the only theatre-restaurant recommended by Les Routiers. The meals are well-cooked and provide very reasonable value for money, reason enough for visiting Theatr Clwyd at any time, lunch or dinner, whether you wish to enjoy a play or just relax over a meal.*
FOOD up to £15

**Hours:** closed Sunday. **Cuisine:** international:- Dishes May include, Tagliatelle Carbonara, Tarragon and Lemon Chicken, Vegetarian Chilli and Trout Cleopatra. Menu changed monthly. **Credit cards:** Visa, Access. **Other points:** no-smoking area, children catered for – please check for age limits, afternoon tea, conferences, functions. **Directions:** situated on A494, ½ mile outside Mold Town. Sign-posted. MR GORDON CARSON, tel (0352) 759304, fax (0352) 752302.

## MONMOUTH, Gwent Map 11

### Prix d'Elite
## THE CROWN AT WHITEBROOK, *Whitebrook*

*A small, intimate restaurant and hotel, remotely situated in beautiful scenery, 5 miles south of Monmouth, and one mile from the River Wye. Sandra Bates specialises in creating original dishes from fresh local ingredients and there is a good wine list. The cheerful hospitality of the proprietors and staff creates a relaxing, friendly atmosphere in which to dine or stay. Regional Newcomer of Year 1991.*
ACCOMMODATION £31–£40
FOOD £21–£25 ⦿ ⬡ ★
**Hours:** breakfast 8am – 9:30am; lunch 12noon – 2pm; dinner 7pm – 9pm; closed Christmas 25/12 – 26/12. **Cuisine:** French:- Specialities include Guinea Fowl poached in wine and herbs and Fresh Wye Salmon with cream and brandy sauce, local venison, salmon and Welsh lamb. All freshly cooked to order. **Rooms:** 11 bedrooms 3 twins ensuite, 8 doubles ensuite. **Credit cards:** Visa, Access, Diners, AmEx. **Other points:** licensed, Sunday lunch, children catered for – please check for age limits, garden, pets allowed. **Directions:** off A466, 2 miles from Bigsweir Bridge. In the Whitebrook Valley. ROGER & SANDRA BATES, tel (0600) 860254, fax (0600) 860607.

## MONMOUTH PUNCH HOUSE, *Agincourt Square*

*Situated in the centre of town and so enjoying both the local and the tourist trade.*
FOOD £15–£20
**Hours:** lunch 11:30am – 2pm; bar meals 11:30am – 2:30pm; bar meals 6:30pm – 9pm. **Cuisine:** British:- Traditional British dishes using finest, fresh local produce. **Credit cards:** Visa, Access. **Other points:** open-air dining, Sunday lunch, children catered for – please check for age limits, coach/prior arr. **Directions:** situated on the A466, in the town centre. W J L WILLS, tel (0600) 713855.

## NARBERTH, Dyfed Map 10

## ROBESTON HOUSE HOTEL & RESTAURANT, *Robeston Wathen*

*An elegant country house hotel with spacious views, set in six acre grounds high on a hill, giving spectacular*

views of the countryside. Robeston House provides an atmosphere of comfort and relaxation, where good food and wine and the personal attention of the resident owners combines to make your stay a happy and memorable one.
ACCOMMODATION £41–£50
FOOD £21–£25
**Hours:** breakfast 8am – 9:30am; dinner 7:30pm – 9:30pm. **Cuisine:** British:- Choice of a la carte, table d'hote or buttery meals. Fresh meat, fish and vegetables brought into kitchen daily. **Rooms:** 2 single, 1 twin, 5 double: all en suite. **Credit cards:** Visa, Access, Diners, AmEx. **Other points:** garden, afternoon tea, pets allowed, disabled access, vegetarian meals, parking, residents' bar, residents' lounge, children catered for – please check for age limits. **Directions:** Robeston Wathen is on the A40, 20 miles to the east of Carmarthen.
PETER, PAULINE & HELEN COPEMAN, tel (0834) 860392, fax (0834) 861195.

---

# NEW QUAY, Dyfed Map 10

## BLACK LION HOTEL, Glanmor Terrace
Built in 1830 of local stone, The Black Lion is essentially "off the beaten track" and an ideal stopping place between North and South Wales. There are comfortably appointed bedrooms, a Games and T.V. lounge, and an attractive dining room panelled with beams of Canadian pine. The well stocked Old Bar is where Dylan Thomas opened one of his stories, and offers a wide choice of snacks and meals for those wishing to eat informally.
ACCOMMODATION £21–£30
FOOD up to £15
**Hours:** breakfast 8:30am – 10am; bar snacks 12noon/12:30pm – 2:30pm/3pm; bar snacks 6pm – 10pm; dinner 7pm – 10pm. **Cuisine:** British. **Other points:** parking, children catered for – please check for age limits, no-smoking area, pets, residents' lounge, vegetarian meals, open-air dining. **Directions:** centre of town on approach to harbour and beach.
THOMAS JAMES HUNTER, tel (0545) 560209, fax (0545) 560585.

## CAMBRIAN HOTEL, New Road
On the outskirts of the old fishing port of New Quay, this small family-run hotel offers comfortable accommodation and well cooked meals. Frequented by holiday-makers it enjoys a relaxed, informal atmosphere. Within easy walking distance of several sandy beaches.
ACCOMMODATION under £20
FOOD up to £15 ★
**Hours:** breakfast 8:30am – 9:30am; lunch 12noon – 2pm; dinner 6:30pm – 9pm. **Cuisine:** British:- Dishes May include – poached Scotch salmon, home made chicken & mushroom pie, fillet steak, vegetarian lasagne and a selection of sweets. **Rooms:** 6 bedrooms all with tea making facilities, radio, TV: 1 twin, 1 twin ensuite, 2 doubles ensuite, 1 quad ensuite, 1 family room ensuite. **Credit cards:** Visa, Access. **Other points:** licensed,

open-air dining, Sunday lunch, no-smoking area, children catered for – please check for age limits, pets allowed, baby-listening device, cots, left luggage. **Directions:** turn off A487 at Llanarth, approx 2 miles further on.
MR BRIAN BLANCKENSEE, tel (0545) 560295, fax (0545) 560295.

## TY HEN FARM HOTEL & LEISURE CENTRE, Llwyndafydd, Nr New Quay
Situated in beautiful wooded countryside, near the spectacular Cardigan coast, this quiet stock farm offers a choice of self-catering cottages or guest accommodation. Facilities in the area include riding, fishing and water sports. On site Leisure Centre includes large indoor heated pool, fitness room, solarium, skittles etc. Restaurant & bar. Extra facilities planned for 1994.
ACCOMMODATION £21–£30 ★
**Hours:** breakfast 8:30am – 9:30am; dinner 6:30pm – 8pm. **Cuisine:** English. **Rooms:** 4 double, 2 bedsits suitable for wheelchair access, all ensuite. Colour TV and tea/coffee making facilities in all rooms. Central heating. Cottage suites (1–5 bedrooms). **Credit cards:** Visa, Access. **Other points:** central heating, children catered for – please check for age limits, residents' lounge, garden, self catering cottages, residents' bar, swimming pool, parking, disabled access. **Directions:** A487: follow signs to Llwyndafydd, with phone kiosk on left go up hill approx 1 mile, sharp right bend then into "No Through Road" on right. Entrance is 100 yd on right.
VERONICA KELLY, tel (0545) 560346.

---

# NEWPORT, Gwent Map 11

## VILLA DINO RESTAURANT, 103 Chepstow Road, Maindee
This attractive Italian restaurant serves excellent food in a very relaxing and welcoming atmosphere. All dishes are freshly cooked to order and well presented. A small family business in a delightful Victorian setting. The service is outstanding – professional, efficient and very warm and courteous. Highly recommended, a winner of many awards.
FOOD £15–£20
**Hours:** dinner 7pm – 11pm; closed Sunday. **Cuisine:** Italian:- A good choice of Italian dishes. Specialities include Chateaubriand Bouquetiere, Filletto al Stilton. Fish, veal, beef, chicken, pasta & vegetarian. Something for everyone. **Credit cards:** Visa, Access, Diners, AmEx. **Other points:** licensed, disabled access, functions. **Directions:** on main road from Newport to Chepstow. 5 minutes to station & motorway.
DINO GULOTTA, tel (0633) 251267.

---

# NEWTOWN, Powys Map 10

## YESTERDAYS, Severn Square
A delightful restaurant and take-away situated in Severn Square, offering a wide range of traditional fayre, including seafood, poultry, grills and light snacks. Easy

access to historic Powys Castle, Elan Valley and the beautiful mid-Welsh countryside.
*FOOD up to £15*
**Hours:** lunch 12noon – 2:30pm; dinner 6:30pm – 9:30pm. **Cuisine:** English. **Credit cards:** Visa, Access. **Other points:** children catered for – please check for age limits, Sunday lunch, open bank holidays, no-smoking area, disabled access, vegetarian meals. **Directions:** from Barclays Bank along Severn Street 80 yd to Severn Square.
MR J ASTON, tel (0686) 622644.

# PONTYPRIDD, Mid Glamorgan Map 11

## MARKET TAVERN HOTEL, *Market Street*
*A classic Victorian pub in town centre, the upper half of which has been sympathetically converted into a hotel with over 60 cover restaurant, offering traditional cuisine. Nearby attractions include Cardiff, museums and castle.*
*ACCOMMODATION under £20*
*FOOD up to £15*
**Hours:** breakfast 7:30am – 9:30am; lunch 12noon – 2:30pm; bar snacks 12noon – 2:30pm; Sunday 7pm – 11am; dinner 7:30pm – 9:30pm; bar snacks 7:30pm – 11pm; closed Christmas day. **Cuisine:** British:- Traditional a la carte and table d'hote menus. **Rooms:** 11 bedrooms 3 doubles ensuite, 6 twins ensuite, 2 singles ensuite. **Other points:** children catered for – please check for age limits, disabled access, residents' lounge, vegetarian meals, licensed. **Directions:** 2 minutes from Pontypridd intersection on A470.
PONTYPRIDD MARKET CO, tel (0443) 485331, fax (0443) 402806.

# PORTHMADOG, Gwynedd Map 12

## BLOSSOMS RESTAURANT, *Borth y Gest*
*Overlooking the bay at Borth y Gest with Snowdonia in the distance, Blossoms Restaurant is part of the 'Heartbeat Wales' programme to promote healthy eating. Log fires and classical jazz or blues music sets the atmosphere. It is a small restaurant so booking is advisable.*
*FOOD £15–£20*
**Hours:** lunch 12noon – 2pm; lunch 12noon – 2pm; dinner 7pm – 10:30pm; dinner 7pm – 10:30pm; closed Sunday. **Cuisine:** Mediterranean:-vegetarian dishes. **Credit cards:** Visa, Access. **Other points:** open-air dining, Sunday lunch, children catered for – please check for age limits. **Directions:** half a mile from A497 in the centre of Borth y Gest.
PAUL DENHAM & MEG BROOK, tel (0766) 513500.

## Y LLONG – THE SHIP, *Lombard Street*
*Built in 1824, this is the oldest Public House in Porthmadog and is mentioned in many maritime books of the area. Having undergone extensive refurbishment it still retains much of its original charm, with tiled floors, bench seats and a stone fireplace. Ideally situated for tourists and travellers. 'Heartbeat Wales Award', 'Vegetarian Good Food Guide', 'Good Beer Guide (CAMRA)'.*
*FOOD up to £15*
**Hours:** bar meals 12noon – 2:15pm; dinner 5:30pm –

11pm; bar meals 6:30pm – 9:30pm; closed Sunday. **Cuisine:** Cantonese / European:- A la carte, plus extensive choice of Cantonese and Peking dishes. Daily changing specials, excellent Vegetarian menu. Bar meals, snacks and traditional beers in both bars. **Credit cards:** Visa, Access. **Other points:** licensed, no-smoking area, children catered for – please check for age limits, parking, bank holidays. **Directions:** close to Porthmadog Harbour.
ROBERT JONES & NIA JONES, tel (0766) 512990, (0766) 514415.

# PRESTATYN, Clwyd Map 12

## SOPHIES, *17 Gronant Road*
*A black and white Georgian timbered building situated in a residential area close to the shops in Prestatyn High Street. The end of the Offa's Dyke footpath is only 100 yd away and the wealth of the Welsh countryside on the doorstep.*
*ACCOMMODATION under £20*
*FOOD up to £15*
**Hours:** breakfast 8am – 9am; lunch 12noon – 2pm; dinner 7pm – 9pm; closed Christmas 25/12 – 26/12. **Cuisine:** British:- Homemade soup, pate, pies, quiche and desserts. **Rooms:** 8 bedrooms, 8 en suite. **Credit cards:** Visa, Access. **Other points:** licensed, open-air dining, Sunday lunch. **Directions:** on A548 from Flint, left at 'Drivers' Garage, then half a mile.
SOPHIA DREW, tel (0745) 852442.

# PWLLHELI, Gwynedd Map 12

## TWNTI SEAFOOD RESTAURANT, *Rhydycladfy*
*Once the meeting place for the Monks Pilgrimage on their way to Bardsey Island, this family run restaurant, tastefully converted from a barn, now offers real fires in winter and a warm and friendly atmosphere. It is ideally situated for visiting nearby Caernarfon Castle, Portmerion Italianate Village, and the remote but beautiful wilderness of Snowdonia National Park.*
*FOOD £15–£20*
**Hours:** last orders 25/12 – 9pm; lunch – Sunday 12noon – 2pm; dinner 7pm – late; closed January and February. **Cuisine:** British:- A la carte menu, offering a wide choice of seafood dishes, all freshly prepared and cooked daily. Children's menu and vegetarian meals available if given 24 hours notice. **Credit cards:** Visa, Access. **Other points:** licensed, Sunday lunch, children catered for – please check for age limits, disabled access, bank holidays. **Directions:** from Pwllheli, left onto A497 for Nefyn. Turn left after Rugby Club.
KEITH JACKSON & STEPHEN WILLIAMS, tel (0758) 740929.

# RUTHIN, Clwyd Map 12

## SIOP NAIN (GRANNY'S SHOP), *6 Well Street*
*Small family cafe/restaurant built in 1490. Oak beams in the dining area and an olde worlde atmosphere throughout.*

*Situated just off the town centre square, Siop Nain offers hot meals all day and specialises in home cooking.*
FOOD up to £15
**Hours:** meals all day 9:30am – 5pm; closed bank holidays; closed Sunday. **Cuisine:** British:- Homemade steak pies and home-made cakes. **Credit cards:** Visa, Access. **Other points:** licensed, children catered for – please check for age limits, parking. **Directions:** on the town square in the centre, by the old courthouse.
MR & MRS C DAVIES, tel (0824) 703572.

## YE OLDE ANCHOR INN, *Rhos Street*

*Situated in the medieval town of Ruthin, Ye Olde Anchor Inn provides a perfect place to stay while touring beautiful North Wales. With its low oak-beamed ceilings, it offers the traveller a hearty welcome. The guestrooms are charming and characterful, each tastefully decorated in co-ordinating colours. Guests can also relax in the cosy bars where traditional cask beer is on tap. The a la carte restaurant is well known for its excellent cuisine, serving a wide range of imaginative dishes and home-made desserts.*
ACCOMMODATION £21–£30
FOOD up to £15
**Hours:** breakfast 7:30am – 9am; lunch 12noon – 2pm; bar snacks 12noon – 2pm; dinner 7pm – 9:30pm; bar snacks 7pm – 8pm. **Cuisine:** Welsh. **Credit cards:** Visa, Access. **Other points:** children catered for – please check for age limits, no-smoking area, disabled access, pets, vegetarian meals, parking. **Directions:** on the junction of A525 & A494. As you enter Ruthin from Wrexham on A525.
MR A R ENGLAND, tel (0824) 702813, fax (0824) 703050.

## SAUNDERSFOOT, Dyfed Map 10

### ST BRIDES HOTEL

*Excellent location overlooking Carmarthen Bay. A very high standard is maintained in all aspects of the hotel particularly with regard to the food and service.*
ACCOMMODATION £41–£50
FOOD £15–£20
**Hours:** breakfast 8am – 10am; lunch 12noon – 2pm; bar 12noon – 11pm; dinner 7pm – 9:15pm. **Cuisine:** British / continental:- Specialising in locally caught fish, lobster and crab. Flambe dishes. **Rooms:** 45 bedrooms all with tea making facilities, telephone, radio, mini bar, TV: 6 singles ensuite, 5 suites, 15 doubles ensuite, 19 twins ensuite. **Credit cards:** Visa, Access, Diners, AmEx. **Other points:** licensed, Sunday lunch, children catered for – please check for age limits, coach/prior arr, **Directions:** from the A40, A477 or A476, follow signposts to Saundersfoot.
IAN BELL, tel (0834) 812304, fax (0834) 813303.

## SHIRENEWTON, Gwent Map 11

### THE HUNTSMAN HOTEL, *Chepstow*

*A small country hotel serving well-presented food in generous portions, with polite unintrusive service. 3 miles to Chepstow racecourse and golfing facilities.*

ACCOMMODATION under £20
FOOD up to £15 ★
**Hours:** breakfast 7:30am – 10:30am; lunch 12noon – 2pm; dinner 7pm – 10pm. **Cuisine:** British / continental:- Chicken in leek and stilton sauce in the restaurant. Breaded plaice, chicken chasseur and lasagne in the bar. **Rooms:** 10 bedrooms all with tea making facilities, telephone, radio, TV: 3 singles ensuite, 3 doubles ensuite, 2 twins ensuite, 2 family rooms ensuite. **Credit cards:** Visa, Access, AmEx. **Other points:** licensed, Sunday lunch, playland, pets allowed, functions. **Directions:** approximately 4 miles out on the B4235 Chepstow to Usk road.
MR A C MOLES, tel (0291) 641521.

## ST ASAPH, Clwyd Map 12

### ORIEL HOUSE HOTEL, *Upper Denbigh Road*

*Set in own extensive grounds, this is a family-owned and run hotel. In quiet, relaxed surroundings you can enjoy well prepared and presented meals. Comfortable accommodation and attractive decor. Good venue for wedding receptions and conferences.*
ACCOMMODATION £31–£40
FOOD up to £15 ★
**Hours:** breakfast 7:15am – 9:30am; bar snacks 11am – 2:30pm; lunch 11:30am – 2pm; bar snacks 6:15pm – 10pm; dinner 7pm – 9:30pm. **Cuisine:** British:- Serving full a la carte menu, table d'hote and bar snacks. **Rooms:** 19 bedrooms all with tea making facilities, telephone, radio, TV: 5 singles ensuite, 7 doubles ensuite, 7 twins ensuite. **Credit cards:** Visa, Access, Diners, AmEx. **Other points:** licensed, Sunday lunch, children catered for – please check for age limits, afternoon tea, pets allowed, garden, conferences. **Directions:** A55 turn off for Denbigh, left at cathedral, 1 mile on right.
MR & MRS WIGGIN AND MR & MRS WOOD, tel (0745) 582716, fax (0745) 582716.

## ST DAVIDS, Dyfed Map 10

### HARBOUR HOUSE HOTEL & RESTAURANT, *The Harbour, Solva*

*Nestled in the heart of the Pembrokeshire Coast National Park, yet standing at the head of a fiord. Decorated in soothing colours and comfortably furnished. Serving tastefully presented excellent meals in a quiet atmosphere.*
ACCOMMODATION £21–£30
FOOD £15–£20 ⌣
**Hours:** breakfast 8:30am – 10am; lunch 12noon – 2:30pm; dinner 7pm – 9pm. **Cuisine:** British:- Dishes include trout pan-fried with capers & prawns & lemon, roast breast of duck with a blackberry and orange sauce. **Rooms:** 1 single, 2 twin and 2 double bedrooms, 3 en suite. **Credit cards:** Visa, Access. **Other points:** licensed, Sunday lunch, children catered for – please check for age limits, afternoon tea, pets allowed. **Directions:** A487, 3 miles east of St Davids.
PAUL HEMMING, tel (0437) 721267.

## OCEAN HAZE HOTEL & RESTAURANT,
### Haverfordwest Road

*A small family-run hotel on the outskirts of St Davids, within walking distance of the Cathedral. All rooms en suite, sea views, colour T.V, tea/coffee making facilities. Also disabled rooms, lounge, games room, childrens play area. A la carte menu, table d'hote, bar snacks, ample parking, car-hire available. Pleasant surroundings, attentive staff and good food available.*

ACCOMMODATION £21–£30

FOOD £15–£20

**Hours:** breakfast 7pm – 9:30am; lunch 12noon – 2:30pm; dinner 6pm – 10pm. **Cuisine:** British / continental:- 'Ocean Haze Special'(mixed grill). **Rooms:** 9 bedrooms, all en suite. **Credit cards:** Visa, Access. **Other points:** licensed, Sunday lunch, children catered for – please check for age limits, pets allowed, afternoon tea. **Directions:** off the A487, just outside St Davids. B & C MORRIS, tel (0437) 720826.

## RAMSEY HOUSE, Lower Moor

*Ramsey House offers you a unique combination of professional hotel standards of accommodation and food service, coupled with the friendly relaxing atmosphere of a pleasant country guest house. Situated just ½ mile from St Davids, with its 12th century Cathedral, this guest house enjoys a quiet location on the road to Porthclais and is an ideal base for touring the area.*

ACCOMMODATION £21–£30

FOOD up to £15 ♉ ★

**Hours:** breakfast 8am – 8:30am; dinner 7pm. **Cuisine:** Welsh:- Lamb steaks with laverbread and orange, "Dragons' Eggs", salmon with cucumber sauce. **Rooms:** 7 bedrooms all with tea making facilities: 3 twins ensuite, 4 doubles ensuite. **Other points:** garden, residents' lounge, pets allowed, Welsh Tourist Board – 3 crowns, parking, ground floor rooms, vegetarian meals, picnic lunches. **Directions:** off A487, centre of St Davids. Road from Cross Square, signposted Porthclais. MAC & SANDRA THOMPSON, tel (0437) 720321.

## Y GLENNYDD GUEST HOUSE, 51 Nun Street

*A cosy guest house in the charming village city of St Davids. Y Glennydd aims to make each guest's stay relaxed and comfortable. A full English breakfast dinner, picnic baskets etc. are available. Guests will also enjoy exploring this attractive area.*

ACCOMMODATION under £20

FOOD up to £15

**Hours:** breakfast 8am – 10am; dinner 7pm – 8:30pm; closed January. **Cuisine:** international:- Bistro Licensed Restaurant – a la carte and table d'hote. **Rooms:** 9 bedrooms all with tea making facilities, TV: 3 doubles, 1 double ensuite, 1 twin, 1 twin ensuite, 3 family rooms ensuite. **Credit cards:** Visa, Access, Diners. **Other points:** children catered for – please check for age limits, residents' lounge, picnic lunches, street parking, parking, residents' bar. **Directions:** A487. Nun Street is part of the one way system from Cross Square, next door to the Fire Station. TIMOTHY & TRACEY FOSTER, tel (0437) 720576, fax (0437) 720184.

---

## SWANSEA, West Glamorgan Map 11

## CEFN – BRYN, 6 Uplands Crescent, Uplands

*Built by a mariner a century ago, a calm, quiet atmosphere prevails throughout this vast semi-detached Victorian residence boasting some exceptional plaster work. The rooms are clean, comfortable and spacious with their own private bathrooms. Ideally situated for touring Mumbles and Gower.*

ACCOMMODATION £21–£30

**Hours:** closed Xmas & New Year and January; breakfast 7:30am – 9am. **Cuisine:** breakfast:- Full Welsh or continental breakfast. **Rooms:** 6 bedrooms 2 singles ensuite, 1 twin ensuite, 1 double ensuite, 2 family rooms ensuite. **Other points:** children catered for – please check for age limits, open bank holidays, no-smoking area, residents' lounge. **Directions:** on A4118, approx. 1 mile west of city centre. TELFER, ANN, tel (0792) 466687.

## LANGROVE LODGE AND COUNTRY CLUB, Parkmill, Gower

*Situated in 24 acres of grounds, 12 of which have been declared a nature reserve. Serving good food and providing comfortable accommodation, this establishment is ideal for anyone wanting to get away from the hustle and bustle of everyday life.*

ACCOMMODATION £21–£30

FOOD up to £15

**Hours:** breakfast 8am – 9:30am; dinner 7pm – 9pm; bar meals 7pm – 9pm. **Cuisine:** Extensive a la carte, set price menu and bar snacks available. **Rooms:** 24 bedrooms 12 twins ensuite, 12 doubles ensuite. **Credit cards:** Visa, Access, Diners. **Other points:** licensed, open-air dining, Sunday lunch, no-smoking area, afternoon tea. **Directions:** A4118 from Swansea. Located at the end of Fairwood Common. BRIAN STEWART, tel (0792) 232756, (0792) 232410.

## NORTON HOUSE HOTEL, Norton Road, Mumbles

*A grand neo-Gothic style mansion which has been tastefully converted to a fine hotel. Its quiet tranquillity and old fashioned ambiance makes it popular with the older age groups. Ideal for visiting Gower Peninsula and the Swansea Maritime Quarter.*

ACCOMMODATION £31–£40

FOOD £21–£25

**Hours:** breakfast 7am – 9:30am; dinner 7pm – 9:30pm. **Cuisine:** British. **Other points:** residents' lounge, garden, vegetarian meals, parking. **Directions:** 1 mile after "Welcome to Mumbles" road sign, turn right and the hotel is 50yds on the left. CHRISTOPHER, JOHN AND JANICE POWER, tel (0792) 404891, fax (0792) 403210.

## THE SCHOONER, *4 Prospect Place*

*Grade II listed building with wine bar, restaurant and function room. Situated in central Swansea on the fringe of the new Marina development and leisure centre.*
*FOOD up to £15*

**Hours:** lunch 12noon – 2pm; bar meals 12noon – 2pm; dinner 7pm – 9:30pm; bar meals 7pm – 7:30pm; closed Sunday evening. **Cuisine:** British:- Fresh local produce all home cooked. Traditional Sunday lunches (booking advisable). Evening special menu changes monthly. Carvery meals most evenings. **Other points:** Sunday lunch, no-smoking area, coach/prior arr, vegetarian meals. **Directions:** in the east of Swansea, close to Sainsburys.
RAYMOND & CHRISTINE PARKMAN, tel (0792) 649321.

## TAL-Y-BONT, Gwynedd Map 12

### THE LODGE SET, *Nr Conwy*

*An attractive and welcoming hotel and restaurant nestling in the Conwy Valley. The restaurant provides a relaxed and elegant setting in which to enjoy well prepared traditional cuisine. Fresh local produce is used whenever possible and most soft fruits and vegetables are grown in the hotel gardens.*
*ACCOMMODATION £21–£30*
*FOOD up to £15* ★

**Hours:** breakfast 8:15am – 9:30am; lunch 12noon – 2pm; dinner 7pm – 9:30pm. **Cuisine:** British:- Table d'hote and a la carte menus. Local fish specialities. Vegetarian meals are also available. **Rooms:** 10 bedrooms, all en suite. **Credit cards:** Visa, Access. **Other points:** licensed, open-air dining, Sunday lunch, children catered for – please check for age limits, pets/prior arr, residents' bar, parking, vegetarian meals, disabled access. **Directions:** follow A55 expressway to Conwy. At Castle turn left for the B5106.
MR & MRS BALDON, tel (0492) 660766, fax (0492) 660534.

## TENBY, Dyfed Map 10

### ATLANTIC HOTEL, *Esplanade*

*Fronted by magnificent gardens and with a spectacular view of the sea, this elegant Edwardian hotel fully deserves its loyal clientele. The rooms are richly furnished and fully fitted with an eye to comfort, the food is superbly prepared and presented with unobtrusive professionalism and your every need is catered for.*
*ACCOMMODATION £31–£40*
*FOOD £15–£20*

**Hours:** breakfast 8am – 9:30am; bar meals 12noon – 2pm; dinner 7pm – 8:30pm; closed Christmas 20/12 – 05/01. **Cuisine:** Welsh / international:- Welsh and international cuisine prepared using fresh local ingredients. **Rooms:** 40 bedrooms all with tea making facilities, telephone, radio, TV: 4 singles ensuite, 22 doubles ensuite, 9 family rooms ensuite, 5 twins ensuite. **Credit cards:** Visa, Access, AmEx. **Other points:**
licensed, Sunday lunch, children catered for – please check for age limits, residents' lounge, garden.
**Directions:** follow A477 to Tenby, continue through town past 5 Arches.
DORIS & WILLIAM JAMES, tel (0834) 842881, (0834) 844176, fax (0834) 842881 ext 256.

### FOURCROFT HOTEL, *North Beach*

*Over 150 years old, the Fourcroft is situated in the most peaceful and select part of the town. A seafront hotel set above Tenby's Blue Flag north Beach with magnificent views of Carmarthen Bay and Tenby Harbour.*
*ACCOMMODATION £31–£40*
*FOOD up to £15* ★

**Hours:** bar meals 8am – 12midnight; closed January – February. **Cuisine:** British:- Pembrokeshire turkey, honeyed Welsh lamb, local salmon, trout and plaice, interesting bar lunches. **Rooms:** 45 bedrooms all with tea making facilities, telephone, radio, TV: 6 singles ensuite, 19 twins ensuite, 13 doubles ensuite, 7 family rooms ensuite. **Credit cards:** Visa, Access. **Other points:** Sunday lunch, swimming pool, leisure centre, garden, parking. **Directions:** fork left after "Welcome to Tenby" sign, double back along seafront, past information office.
MR & MRS P L OSBORNE, tel (0834) 842886, fax (0834) 842888.

### THE IMPERIAL HOTEL, *The Paragon*

*Cliff-top location overlooking the south Beach towards St Catherine's and Caldy Islands. Private steps to the beach. The Imperial offers extensive menus and a good wine list, served by courteous staff in very pleasant surroundings. Three minutes level walk to the town centre.*
*ACCOMMODATION £21–£30*
*FOOD up to £15*

**Hours:** breakfast 8am – 9:30am; lunch 11:30am – 2:30pm; bar meals 11:30am – 9pm; dinner 7pm – 9pm. **Cuisine:** English:- Traditional English cuisine, with a la carte, table d'hote and bar meals. **Rooms:** 64 bedrooms all with tea making facilities, telephone, radio, TV: 7 singles ensuite, 10 twins – shower only, 10 doubles ensuite, 18 doubles ensuite, 18 triples ensuite, 1 quad ensuite. **Credit cards:** Visa, Access, Diners, AmEx. **Other points:** licensed, Sunday lunch, children catered for – please check for age limits, pets allowed, bank holidays, functions, baby-listening device, cots, 24hr reception, residents' lounge, residents' bar. **Directions:** M4, A40, A477 to Kilgetti – A478.
JAN-ROELOF EGGENS, tel (0834) 843737, fax (0834) 844342.

## TINTERN, Gwent Map 11

### THE FOUNTAIN INN, *Trellech Grange*

*A typical 17th century country Inn where the food is prepared to order. The bar provides the focal point and, on a chilly day, a log fire provides a warm welcome. Real ales and whisky a speciality.*
*ACCOMMODATION under £20*
*FOOD up to £15*

**Hours:** lunch – except Sunday 12noon – 3pm; lunch – Sunday 12noon – 2pm; dinner – except Sunday 7pm – 10:30pm; dinner – Sunday 7pm – 9:30pm; closed Christmas evening only. **Cuisine:** English:- Dishes include Jugged hare, Tudor roast, Venison, Rack of Lamb. **Rooms:** 5 bedrooms 2 family rooms, 1 single, 2 doubles. **Credit cards:** Visa, Access. **Other points:** licensed, Sunday lunch, children catered for – please check for age limits, caravan facilities. **Directions:** off B4283, 2 miles from Tintern Abbey. Turn by Royal George in Tintern and bear right around ponds.
CHRIS & JUDITH RABBITS, tel (0291) 689303.

---

# TRELLECH, Gwent Map 11

## THE LION INN, Nr Monmouth

*A 17th century Inn with original beams serving home made meals using fresh produce – most comes from the local farm. Situated in the ancient settlement of Trellech, known for its standing stones, Norman motte and 'virtuos' well. The Lion Inn is a friendly local set in beautiful surrounding countryside.*

ACCOMMODATION under £20

FOOD up to £15

**Hours:** last orders evening only – 9:30pm; lunch 12noon – 2pm; bar meals 12noon – 2pm; Sunday lunch 12noon – 2pm; dinner 7pm – 11pm. **Cuisine:** British:- Good quality home made meals made with local farm fresh produce. Fish a speciality. **Rooms:** 1 bedroom 1 twin. **Other points:** licensed, Sunday lunch, children catered for – please check for age limits, pets allowed. **Directions:** B4293 Monmouth to Chepstow road, opposite church in the village.
ALAN & CHRISTINE NIXON, tel (0600) 860322.

---

# WELSHPOOL, Powys Map 10

## THE LION HOTEL AND RESTAURANT, Berriew

*Situated in a quiet village on the Welsh borders surrounded by beautiful countryside, the Lion Hotel is a delightful 17th century Inn. The accommodation is of a high standard and good food is served in both the bars and restaurant.*

ACCOMMODATION £31–£40 ★

**Hours:** open bank holidays 7pm; breakfast 8am – 9:30am; lunch 12noon – 2pm; bar meals 12noon – 2pm; bar meals 7pm – 9pm; dinner 7:30pm – 9pm. **Cuisine:** Welsh / continental:- English, Welsh & continental cuisine. Dishes may include prawn and salmon cocktail, roast duck with vermouth and cranberry sauce. Fillet of Welsh lamb with a sauce of redcurrants, cranberries, mushrooms and port. **Rooms:** 7 bedrooms all with tea making facilities, TV: 1 single ensuite, 1 twin ensuite, 4 doubles ensuite, 1 family room ensuite. **Credit cards:** Visa, Access, Diners, AmEx. **Other points:** licensed, Sunday lunch, children catered for – please check for age limits. **Directions:** in village centre.
MR & MRS THOMAS, tel (0686) 640452, fax (0686) 640844.

## THE ROYAL OAK HOTEL

*Situated in the heart of Welshpool, an historic Georgian Border town nestling in the rolling green countryside of the old county of Montgomeryshire, the Royal Oak Hotel and Restaurant has been welcoming travellers for over 350 years. Once owned by the Earl of Powis, The Royal Oak has been in the same family for over 60 years and offers traditional cask ales, lunch/evening bar menus as well as table d'hote, a la carte menus and over 100 wines in the Acorn Restaurant. The Powis Suite provides comfortable rooms for seminars, banquets and wedding receptions for up to 200 guests. Welshpool is home to Powis Castle, the famous Llanfair light railway, Powysland Canal Museum. Situated close to Offas Dyke path it makes an ideal centre for walking and exploring wildlife.*

ACCOMMODATION £21–£30

FOOD up to £15

**Hours:** breakfast 7:30am – 9am; breakfast – Sunday 8:30am – 9:30am; lunch 12:30pm – 2:15pm; dinner 7pm – 9pm; dinner – Saturday 7:30pm – 9:30pm. **Cuisine:** Good traditional local and international cooking. Lamb and other roast meats and local popular dishes in bars and restaurant. **Rooms:** 24 bedrooms all with tea making facilities, telephone, TV: 7 singles ensuite, 7 doubles ensuite, 7 twins ensuite, 2 family rooms ensuite, 1 suite. **Credit cards:** Visa, Access, Diners, AmEx. **Other points:** parking, children catered for – please check for age limits, conferences, functions, afternoon tea, disabled access, pets – by prior arrangement, residents' lounge, vegetarian meals, morning coffee, bar meals, residents' bar. **Directions:** junction of A483 and A458 in the very centre of Welshpool, at only set of traffic lights.
MARGARET LANDGREBE, tel (0938) 552217, fax (0938) 552217.

---

# WREXHAM, Clwyd Map 12

## TREVOR ARMS HOTEL, Marford, Nr Wrexham

*An old Coaching Inn which maintains traditional pub hospitality, together with a wide range of modern facilities and tempting menus at affordable prices. Excellent staff team work ensures a relaxed, no fuss atmosphere in which to enjoy your meal. Comfortable accommodation, a safe childrens play area and an outdoor barbecue. Very highly recommended by the Les Routiers inspector.*

ACCOMMODATION under £20

FOOD up to £15 ★

**Hours:** breakfast 7:30am – 9am; lunch 12noon – 2:30pm; dinner – except Sunday 6pm – 10pm; dinner – Sunday 7pm – 10pm. **Cuisine:** British:- Extensive menu available in the Restaurant and Bar Areas. Dishes may include King Scampi, Sirloin Steak, Salmon with lemon & tarragon. Daily specials. **Rooms:** 17 bedrooms 3 twins ensuite, 2 singles ensuite, 12 doubles ensuite. **Credit cards:** Visa, Access. **Other points:** licensed, open-air dining, Sunday lunch, no-smoking area, playland, afternoon tea. **Directions:** midway between Chester and Wrexham. A short distance off A483.
MARTIN & DENISE BENNETT, tel (0244) 570436.

# SCOTLAND

Savour the wild beauty of the high heather-covered mountains, sparkling blue lochs and rivers, rich green glens – Scotland, land of legends and castles is a country made for the tourist.

Scotland's turbulent history has given it a great legacy of famous monarchs and romantic palaces and castles. Many of the country's historic buildings are open to the public from Edinburgh Castle to the stately residences of Royal Deeside. There are also many ruins to explore of ancient castles no longer intact.

Walk over hills and moors and follow in the footsteps of Bonnie Prince Charlie taking the road to the isles or experience the tingling thrill of the pipes at one of the many Highland gatherings. Stand in majestic Glencoe, scene of one of Scotland's most bloody massacres, or visit Dumfries and Ayrshire and see for yourself the Scotland which Robert Burns loved and knew so well. Make a pilgrimage to Dryburgh Abbey in the Borders to see the burial place of Sir Walter Scott and quietly admire the magnificence of Melrose Abbey which houses the heart of King Robert the Bruce.

Scotland is divided into nine regions and three island authorities – Orkney, Shetland and the Western Isles. Each has its own marked characteristics and has plenty to offer at all times of the year. Follow the famous whisky trail and sample the products of Scotland's greatest distilleries or visit Campbeltown Loch, reputed in song to consist entirely of whisky. Iona was the burying ground of Scottish Kings while on the misty Isle of Skye stands the mysterious Dunvegan Castle, ancestral home of the MacLeods. Tour the Trossachs and discover the Lake of Menteith, Scotland's only natural lake, or set sail on a steamer trip across Loch Lomond or in search of the Loch Ness monster from Inverness.

Experience the utter serenity, peace and tranquillity of life on a Scottish island, where wonderful folk make their living mostly from lobster fishing and crofting. The most famous of the islands is Skye, the largest of the Hebrides, with over one thousand miles of coastline. Visit Pictish brochs, castles and whitewashed croft homes which are the records in stone of Scotland's past. Don't miss the miles of white sands and beaches around the magnificent rugged coastline in the north and feel part of nature with a visit to the many wildlife parks and nature reserves. In the far west you will find Scotland's highest mountains, from Ben Nevis to the Cairngorms, which form a border between the Grampians and Highlands.

Scotland's northernmost areas are a group of sixty-seven islands forming the Orkneys and Shetlands; Orkney famed for its silverware and the Shetlands for its unique and unrivalled knitwear. Shetland has strong links with the Vikings who fished and farmed here.

Offering contrasting styles and rich in heritage, Scotland's two main cities, Glasgow and Edinburgh, are both important commercial centres. The famous Palace of Holyrood in Edinburgh is close to a host of museums, galleries, theatres and parks. Glasgow, however, is renowned for its splendid Victorian architecture. Its recent refurbishment gained it the distinguished title of Cultural Capital of Europe 1990. In contrast to these two giants Aberdeen, the 'Granite City,' is a thriving cosmopolitan town, also known as the oil capital of Europe.

If your taste runs to holidays on horseback, hill-walking, nature trailing, forest walks, climbing, canoeing, sailing, golfing, enjoying some of the finest fishing in the world, or simply quietly exploring the country's heritage, Scotland has it all. It also offers some of the finest cooking, hotels and guesthouses you will find, combined with an air of relaxed informality to make your visit to Scotland a truly memorable one.

For details of where to visit and what to see in Scotland, contact the Scottish Tourist Board, 23 Ravelston Terrace, Edinburgh, EH4 3EU. Tel: (031) 332 2433.

# ABERDEEN, Grampian Map 22

## BETTY BURKES, 45 Langstane Place

*Stylish and interesting bar, themed as a gentleman's club, with old portrait paintings, wood panelling and leather seats. The massive carved eagle dominating the entrance originated in America during the period of the Wars Of Independence. There are display cabinets full of old bar and glass curios. Bustling, local atmosphere.*
FOOD up to £15
**Hours:** breakfast 10am – 12noon; bar meals – Sun-Thur 12noon – 9:30pm; bar meals – Fri-Sat 12noon – 9pm. **Cuisine:** English / international:- Bar meals, including deep-fried mushrooms, potato skins, and home-made puddings. **Credit cards:** Visa, Access, AmEx. **Other points:** children catered for – please check for age limits, bank holidays. **Directions:** in city centre, close to Union Street, Aberdeen's main street.
MIKE COOK, tel (0224) 210359.

## OLD MILL INN & RESTAURANT, South Deeside Road, Mary Culter

*A historic 200 year old mill boasting original beams and timbers and set on the banks of the famous River Dee. It has been extensively refurbished to provide a high level of comfort and personal service in a friendly welcoming atmosphere. There are many nearby places of interest to visit, including Royal Deeside and several Whiskey trails.*
ACCOMMODATION £21–£30
FOOD up to £15
**Hours:** open all day 7:30am – 11:30pm; breakfast 7:30am – 10am; lunch 12noon – 2:30pm; dinner 5:30pm – 10pm. **Cuisine:** Titillate your taste-buds with our superb selection of traditional and innovative cuisine. Using only fresh, local produce, our house specialities are a must for the discerning diner. Our menus change with the seasons. **Rooms:** 7 bedrooms all with tea making facilities, TV: 1 family room ensuite, 3 doubles ensuite, 2 twins ensuite, 1 single ensuite. **Credit cards:** Visa, Access, Diners, AmEx. **Other points:** access to river fishing, golf, hill walking, pony trekking, parking, children catered for – please check for age limits, Sunday lunch, open bank holidays. **Directions:** from Aberdeen on south side of Dee Bridge, B9077 for 4 miles. The Inn is 300yds beyond Peterculter Bridge.
VICTOR SANG, tel (0224) 733212, fax (0224) 732884.

## THE PRINCE REGENT HOTEL, 20–22 Waverley Place, Off Albyn Place

*An attractive privately owned hotel in the heart of Aberdeen, Oil capital of Europe and gateway to Royal Deeside. It has undergone extensive refurbishment to provide a high level of comfort for guests whilst preserving the character of charm of this splendid Victorian building. The hotel is centrally situated in the heart of the west end business community and has a large customer car park. Nearby attractions include Aberdeen University founded in 1494, Marischal College with its extraordinary granite castellations and His Majestys Theatre.*
ACCOMMODATION £21–£30
FOOD £15–£20
**Hours:** open 24 hours. **Cuisine:** To suit all budgets from snacks to more formal meals. **Rooms:** 21 bedrooms all with tea making facilities, telephone, TV: 7 singles ensuite, 9 doubles ensuite, 3 twins ensuite, 2 family rooms ensuite. **Other points:** night porter, weekend breaks, sunbed, library, fax, parking.
PRINCE REGENT HOTEL (ABERDEEN) LTD., tel (0224) 645071, fax (0224) 648157.

## ST MAGNUS COURT HOTEL, 22 Guild Street

*The St Magnus Court Hotel is a family-run hotel catering principally for the commercial sector. The accommodation is very comfortable, whilst the food is well cooked and prepared. Pleasant, relaxed atmosphere.*
ACCOMMODATION £21–£30
FOOD up to £15
**Hours:** breakfast 5:30am – 9:30am; bar meals 12noon – 10:30am; dinner 6pm – 9pm. **Cuisine:** British:- Dishes include home-made soup of the day, rump steak garni, chicken fillet, omelettes, ice cream and fruit. **Rooms:** 19 bedrooms all with telephone, TV: 4 singles ensuite, 2 doubles ensuite, 4 twins, 8 twins ensuite, 1 family room ensuite. **Credit cards:** Visa, Access. **Other points:** licensed, residents' bar, residents' lounge. **Directions:** this commercial hotel is located in the centre of Aberdeen, directly opposite to Aberdeen Railway Station.
BOB PAGE, tel (0224) 589411, fax (0224) 584352.

# ABERFELDY, Tayside Map 22

## FORTINGALL HOTEL, Fortingall

*Fortingall, where the hotel is situated, has a yew tree reputed to be the oldest vegetation in Europe. The rooms have outstanding views of the hills with the River Tay and Lyon in the foreground. Widely known for its cuisine fully supported by an extensive wine list, this hotel provides a relaxing and enjoyable dinner.*
ACCOMMODATION £31–£40
FOOD £21–£25
**Hours:** breakfast 7:30am – 9:30am; lunch 12noon – 2pm; dinner 7pm – 9pm; closed November – February. **Cuisine:** Scottish:- Home-cooking, using local produce, the specialities being seafood and some Italian dishes. **Rooms:** 9 bedrooms – 3 family, 3 double and 3 twin. 8 en suite. **Credit cards:** Visa, Access, AmEx. **Other points:** licensed, central heating, children catered for – please check for age limits, residents' lounge, garden. **Directions:** off the A827 and B846, 8 miles from Aberfeldy.
MR ALAN SCHOFIELD, tel (0887) 830367.

# ABERLADY, Lothian Map 20

## GREEN CRAIGS

*A family-run country style house, recently refurbished to provide comfortable and welcoming accommodation with good food in homely surroundings. Ideal for golfers*

*with no less than 16 courses nearby, including Muirfield, Gullane, Dunbar and north Berwick. Edinburgh is 15 minutes away, and Aberlady Nature Reserve a short distance. A heavenly haven where everyone is welcome!*
ACCOMMODATION £41–£50
FOOD £15–£20 ♀

**Hours:** open all year; breakfast 7:30am – 11:30am; lunch 12noon – 2pm; dinner 6pm – 9:30pm. **Cuisine:** French / Scottish:- A la carte and Table d'hote, offering a mix of French and Scottish dishes. Lobster Thermidor, Baked Haddock, Escalope of Pork. Vegetarian dishes available. Breast of Chicken filled with Haggis. **Rooms:** 6 bedrooms all with tea making facilities, telephone, radio, TV: 3 twins ensuite, 1 double ensuite, 1 family room ensuite, 1 suite. **Credit cards:** Visa, Access, Diners, AmEx. **Other points:** licensed, open-air dining, Sunday lunch, children catered for – please check for age limits, pets allowed, afternoon tea, parking, residents' lounge, garden, parking. **Directions:** A198. Approximately 1 mile west of Aberlady. 'White House on Point'.
RAYMOND & OLLY CRAIG, tel (08757) 301/306, fax (08757) 440.

---

# ABERLOUR, Grampian Map 22

## ARCHIESTOWN HOTEL, Archiestown

*A family-run hotel in the small Moray village of Archiestown, a frequent winner of the 'Best Kept Village' competitions. Good, comfortable accommodation, excellent cuisine and knowledgeable service. The hotel appeals to anglers, holiday-makers and locals alike for its warm welcome and relaxing atmosphere.*
ACCOMMODATION £31–£40
FOOD £21–£25 ☜

**Hours:** breakfast 8am – 9:30am; bar meals 12noon – 2pm; lunch – Sunday 12:30pm – 2pm; bar meals 6pm – 8pm; dinner 7:30pm – 8:30pm; closed October – end February. **Cuisine:** English / seafood:- A la carte restaurant menu and bar meals, specialising in fish & seafood. Halibut with white butter sauce. Oxtail braised in port. **Rooms:** 8 bedrooms, 6 en suite. **Credit cards:** Visa, Access. **Other points:** licensed, open-air dining, Sunday lunch, children catered for – please check for age limits, afternoon tea, pets allowed, garden, residents' lounge, foreign exchange, residents' bar. **Directions:** B9102 in the village of Archiestown. 5 miles west of Craigellachie.
JUDITH & MICHAEL BULGER, tel (0340) 810218, fax (0340) 810239.

---

# ALFORD, Grampian Map 22

## FORBES ARMS HOTEL, Bridge Of Alford

*Owned by the same family since 1894, the Forbes Arms Hotel lies on the banks of the River Don, just over the picturesque Brig of Alford, one mile from the town. It has a deserved reputation for its friendly service and has been completely refurbished with a splendid conservatory and spacious dining room, offering traditional Scottish cuisine and fine wines. An ideal base for touring north-east Scotland.*

ACCOMMODATION £21–£30
FOOD up to £15

**Hours:** breakfast 8:30am – 9:30am; lunch 12noon – 1:30pm; bar snacks 12noon – 1:45pm; bar snacks 5pm – 8:30pm; dinner 7pm – 8:15pm. **Cuisine:** Scottish. **Credit cards:** Visa, Access, Diners, AmEx. **Other points:** children catered for – please check for age limits, no-smoking area, pets, disabled access, residents' lounge, garden, open-air dining, vegetarian meals, parking. **Directions:** from Alford take main A944 (signed Strathdon), and the hotel is located on the right after bridge over River Don.
CHARLES SPENCE, tel (097556) 2108, fax (097556) 3467.

---

# ALTNAHARRA, Highlands Map 24

## ALTNAHARRA HOTEL, By Lairg

*Privately owned and managed, 'Altnaharra' offers a warm welcome and friendly atmosphere together with good food and comfortable accommodation. With the choice of refurbished bedrooms and two annexe cottages, this hotel is ideal for families or a party of enthusiastic sports persons in the area to enjoy superb salmon and sea-trout fishing. Winter and spring breaks available.*
ACCOMMODATION over £50
FOOD £15–£20 ★

**Hours:** breakfast 7:45am – 9am; lunch 12noon – 2pm; closed 17/10 – 01/03; dinner 7:30pm – 8:30pm. **Cuisine:** Scottish:- Prime Scottish beef and lamb, game, fresh local fish and seafood. **Rooms:** 20 bedrooms all with tea making facilities: 3 singles ensuite, 14 twins ensuite, 3 doubles ensuite. **Credit cards:** Visa, Access. **Other points:** children catered for – please check for age limits, garden, fishing, drying facilities, residents' lounge, residents' bar. **Directions:** off the A836 Lairg road, follow sign for Tongue.
ALTNAHARRA HOTEL LTD, tel (054981) 222, fax (054981) 222.

---

# ANNAN, Dumfries & Galloway Map 23

## POWFOOT GOLF HOTEL, Links Avenue, Powfoot

*Standing beside an 18 hole Golf-Course with fishing nearby on the River Annan, the Golf Hotel is a tempting prospect for sport persons. With views over the unspoilt Powfoot Bay and with the countryside and history of south west Scotland on the doorstep, it is an excellent centre for touring. Excellent wildfowling from September till February.*
ACCOMMODATION £21–£30
FOOD up to £15

**Hours:** breakfast 8am – 9:30am; bar – weekdays 11am – 11pm; bar – weekends 11am – 12midnight; lunch 12noon – 2pm; dinner 7pm – 8:30pm. **Cuisine:** Scottish:- Traditional Scottish food prepared where possible using local produce eg. fresh Solway salmon, pheasant, venison, duck, prime Galloway beef. **Rooms:** 19 bedrooms all with tea making facilities, telephone, TV: 1 single, 2 doubles, 3 twins, 3 doubles ensuite, 8 twins ensuite, 2 family rooms ensuite. **Credit cards:** Visa, Access, AmEx. **Other points:** licensed, open-air

dining, Sunday lunch, children catered for – please check for age limits, beer garden, residents' lounge, residents' bar, foreign exchange. **Directions:** On the B724 in Powfoot next to the golf course.
ADAM T GRIBBON, tel (0461) 700254.

## ARBROATH, Tayside Map 22

### HOTEL SEAFORTH, *Dundee Road*
*A 19th century stone manor house with modern extension offering a warm, family welcome. Hotel Seaforth is a convenient base for visiting the nearby glens and castles, or you could spend a few days relaxing in the hotel's leisure centre. Surrounded by fine Golf Courses. Sea and river angling.*
ACCOMMODATION £41–£50
FOOD up to £15
**Hours:** breakfast 7:30am – 9:30am; lunch 12noon – 2pm; meals all day – Sunday 12:30pm – 8pm; dinner 7pm – 10pm. **Cuisine:** Traditional menus, featuring many Scottish dishes and local seafood. **Rooms:** 19 bedrooms all with tea making facilities, telephone, TV: 3 singles ensuite, 6 doubles ensuite, 8 twins ensuite, 2 family rooms ensuite. **Credit cards:** Visa, Access, Diners, AmEx. **Other points:** licensed, Sunday lunch, children catered for – please check for age limits, leisure centre, swimming pool, Jacuzzi, games room, ballroom, pets allowed, residents' bar. **Directions:** on the promenade.
ROBERT & CHRISTINE TINDALL, tel (0241) 72232, fax (0241) 77437.

## ARISAIG, Highlands Map 24

### THE OLD LIBRARY LODGE & RESTAURANT
*With magnificent views of the Hebrides, The Old Library Lodge and Restaurant is a lovely place to rest and relax. Offering tastefully furnished, spacious accommodation, this charming hotel is an ideal holiday place. Helpful staff will make you feel at home.*
ACCOMMODATION £21–£30
FOOD £15–£20
**Hours:** open bank holidays 7pm; breakfast 8:30am – 9:30am; lunch 11:30am – 2:30pm; dinner 6:30pm – 9:30pm; closed November – March. **Cuisine:** Scottish:- Traditional, well-prepared food using fresh local produce. Local fish and shellfish are house specialities and home-made bread adds a delicious touch. **Rooms:** 6 bedrooms 1 twin ensuite, 5 doubles ensuite. **Credit cards:** Access, Visa, Switch. **Other points:** licensed, Sunday lunch, children catered for – please check for age limits, residents' lounge. **Directions:** situated in the centre of village.
ALAN & ANGELA BROADHURST, tel (06875) 651.

## ARROCHAR, Strathclyde Map 21

### GREENBANK GUEST HOUSE & LICENSED RESTAURANT
*A small, family-run guest house and restaurant on the Loch side. There is a good choice of meals available*

throughout the day and the restaurant is licensed with a selection of wines, beers and spirits. An excellent base for fishing, climbing, boating and touring. A friendly, relaxed atmosphere prevails, with fine food and accommodation at good value.
ACCOMMODATION under £20
FOOD up to £15
**Hours:** meals all day 8am – 9:30pm. **Cuisine:** Scottish:- Meals available all day. Dishes may include Salmon steak, fresh baked Steak & Kidney Pie, Fried Loch Fyne Herring in Oatmeal, curries, vegetarian. **Rooms:** 4 bedrooms 1 single ensuite, 2 doubles ensuite, 1 family room ensuite. **Other points:** licensed, Sunday lunch, children catered for – please check for age limits, pets allowed, garden, disabled access. **Directions:** on the A83, opposite the famous Cobbler Mountain.
MR & MRS R CLUER, tel (03012) 305, (03012) 513.

## AUCHTERARDER, Tayside Map 22

### BLACKFORD HOTEL, *Moray Street, Blackford*
*A small, comfortable, family-run hotel, situated in the village of Blackford in the heart of Tayside – Scotland's Golfing County. The building is a 19th century Coaching Inn, attractively and comfortably furnished. Only 2 miles from Gleneagles, Blackford Hotel provides good food, comfortable accommodation, welcoming service and a friendly atmosphere.*
ACCOMMODATION £21–£30
FOOD up to £15
**Hours:** breakfast 8am – 9am; lunch 12noon – 2pm; dinner 6pm – 9pm. **Cuisine:** English:- 2 menus – one changes daily. Dishes may include Chicken Kiev, Herring in Oatmeal, Gammon steak, T-bone steak, salads. **Rooms:** 4 bedrooms, all en suite. **Credit cards:** Visa, Access, Diners, AmEx. **Other points:** licensed, Sunday lunch, children catered for – please check for age limits, garden, afternoon tea, pets allowed, central heating. **Directions:** just off the A9 in village of Blackford, 4 miles from Auchterarder.
MIKE & ROSEMARY TOMCZYNSKI, tel (0764) 682497.

## AUCHTERMUCHTY, Fife Map 22

### THE FOREST HILLS HOTEL, *The Square*
*A traditional 18th century Inn situated in the town square of the former Royal Burgh of Auchtermuchty, once a busy weaving centre. There is a comfortable oak-beamed cocktail bar with copper topped tables and ornate fireplace, which provides a cosy and intimate atmosphere. Nearby places of interest include Falkland with its Royal Palace and Freuchie. Function suite for up to 80 guests.*
ACCOMMODATION £21–£30
FOOD up to £15
**Hours:** breakfast 8am – 9am; breakfast – Sunday 9am – 10am; bar snacks 12noon – 2:15pm; lunch 12:30pm – 2pm; bar snacks 6pm – 10pm; dinner 7pm – 9:15pm. **Cuisine:** British / continental:- Table D'Hote and A la

Carte with some flambe dishes, complemented by an interesting wine list. **Rooms:** 9 bedrooms all with tea making facilities, telephone, TV: 1 single, 1 double, 2 family rooms ensuite, 2 twins ensuite, 1 single ensuite, 2 doubles ensuite. **Credit cards:** Visa, Access, Diners, AmEx. **Other points:** parking, children catered for – please check for age limits, Sunday lunch, open bank holidays, afternoon tea, pets allowed, residents' lounge, vegetarian meals, licensed, residents' bar. **Directions:** 7 miles from Cupar and 6 miles from exit 8 of M90.
VAN BEUSEKOM, ERNST, tel (0337) 828318, fax (0337) 828318.

## AVIEMORE, Highlands Map 24

### BALAVOULIN HOTEL, Main Road
*Located on the A9 well placed for skiing, climbing and Aviemore Centre complex. Luxury self-catering bungalows sleeping 4 are available for hire. Children's play area. A popular area for winter sports and summer touring.*
*ACCOMMODATION £21–£30*
*FOOD up to £15*
**Hours:** breakfast 8am – 9:30am; bar meals 12noon – 2:30pm; bar meals 5pm – 9pm; dinner 6pm – 8:45pm.
**Cuisine:** Scottish. **Rooms:** 8 bedrooms all with tea making facilities, telephone, TV: 3 twins ensuite, 5 doubles ensuite. **Credit cards:** Visa, Access, AmEx. **Other points:** central heating, children catered for – please check for age limits, pets/prior arr, foreign exchange. **Directions:** on the main village road, off the A9 to Aviemore.
MR & MRS MACKENZIE, tel (0479) 810672, fax (0479) 811575.

## AYR, Strathclyde Map 21

### FOUTERS BISTRO, 2a Academy Street
*Authentic cellar restaurant serving interesting French and British dishes using the best of local produce. Fouters Bistro is renowned for the high quality of its cuisine, steak and seafood specialities. Personally run by the proprietors. On-street parking opposite Town Hall.*
*FOOD £15–£20* � 🍽 🐦 CLUB ★
**Hours:** lunch 12noon – 2pm; dinner – except Sunday 6:30pm – 10:30pm; dinner – Sunday 7pm – 10pm; closed Christmas 4 days; closed 4 days over New Year.
**Cuisine:** Scottish / French:- Fine Scottish produce cooked in the French style. Vegetarians welcomed and special diets catered for. **Credit cards:** Visa, Access, Diners, AmEx. **Other points:** children catered for – please check for age limits. **Directions:** opposite Town hall, in a cobbled stone lane.
FRAN & LAURIE BLACK, tel (0292) 261391.

### THE KYLESTROME HOTEL, 11 Miller Road
*A large stone house in Ayr, which is in the heart of Burns Country. The seafront, railway station and town centre are a short walk away, and Prestwick Airport a few minutes' drive. The stylish restaurant provides a unique atmosphere in which to enjoy fine international cuisine.*
*ACCOMMODATION £41–£50*
*FOOD £15–£20*
**Hours:** breakfast 7:30am – 9:30am; lunch 12noon – 2pm; bar meals 12noon – 2pm; bar meals 5:30pm – 10pm; high tea 5:30pm – 7pm; dinner 7pm – 10pm.
**Cuisine:** Scottish / seafood:- Fresh seafood, local produce. In the bar: lamb cutlets with minted pear. In the restaurant: steak, seafood – a la carte. **Rooms:** 12 bedrooms 1 single ensuite, 7 doubles ensuite, 4 twins ensuite. **Credit cards:** Visa, Access, Diners, AmEx. **Other points:** licensed, Sunday lunch, no-smoking area, children catered for – please check for age limits, conferences. **Directions:** on a main street in Ayr, near the railway station.
Tel (0292) 262474, fax (0292) 260863.

### OLD RACECOURSE HOTEL, 2 Victoria Park
*An attractive stone building in pleasant garden surroundings 1 mile from the town centre and minutes from the beach. The beautiful scenery of Ayrshire is nearby, making this hotel a tempting base to return to. The hotel is justifiably proud of its fresh seafood and prime Scottish game.*
*ACCOMMODATION £21–£30*
*FOOD £15–£20*
**Hours:** breakfast 8am – 9am; lunch 12noon – 2pm; afternoon tea 3pm – 5pm; high tea 5pm – 7pm; bar meals 5pm – 9pm; dinner 7pm – 9pm. **Cuisine:** Scottish / seafood:- Specialising in fresh local seafood, game dishes and prime Scottish steaks. **Rooms:** 12 bedrooms all with tea making facilities, TV: 7 doubles ensuite, 4 twins ensuite, 1 single ensuite. **Credit cards:** Visa. **Other points:** open-air dining, children catered for – please check for age limits, pets allowed. **Directions:** A70 or A719 to Ayr, 1 mile from town centre, close to beach.
JOHN & MARGARET NICOL, tel (0292) 262873, fax (0292) 267598.

### TUDOR RESTAURANT, 6/8 Beresford Terrace
*Now in its 27th year of operation, the reasonably priced lunch and high tea menus and friendly staff make the Tudor a favourite with family parties. Children may choose from their own menus.*
*FOOD up to £15*
**Hours:** meals all day 9am – 8pm; closed Sunday except July/Aug. **Cuisine:** Scottish:- Traditional Scottish high teas served with cakes and scones from own bakery. **Other points:** no-smoking area, children catered for – please check for age limits. **Directions:** opposite the Burn's Statue Square off the A70 in the centre of Ayr.
KENNETH ANCELL, tel (0292) 261404.

## BALLATER, Grampian Map 22

### ALEXANDRA HOTEL, 12 Bridge Square
*An attractive, well-maintained exterior opens into a tastefully decorated hotel and restaurant. Table d'hote and a la carte meals are offered with a touch of French cuisine.*

Close to Balmoral, Crathie church and Scottish distilleries. For the anglers, there is fishing in the River Dee.
ACCOMMODATION £21–£30
FOOD £15–£20 ⊕ CLUB ★
**Hours:** breakfast 8am – 9:30am; bar 11am – 12midnight; lunch 12noon – 2:15pm; dinner 6pm – 9pm. **Cuisine:** Scottish / French:- Traditional Scottish and French – Entrecote au poivre, fillet steak Diane, trout with almonds, salmon, whole lemon sole, venison. Selection of cheese. **Rooms:** 7 bedrooms all with tea making facilities, telephone, radio, TV: 1 single ensuite, 2 twins ensuite, 3 doubles ensuite, 1 triple ensuite. **Credit cards:** Visa, Access, Diners, AmEx. **Other points:** licensed, central heating, children catered for – please check for age limits, pets allowed, baby-listening device, cots, foreign exchange, left luggage, disabled access, vegetarian meals, residents' lounge, residents' bar, parking. **Directions:** on the A93 Aberdeen to Braemar road, near the River Dee Bridge.
ALAIN TABUTEAU, tel (03397) 55376, fax (03397) 55466.

## AULD KIRK HOTEL, Braemar Road
Converted from a church to a hotel in 1990, the original structure including the front doors, bell tower, and many of the windows have been retained. The result is fascinating and well worth a visit. The resident proprietors provide a warm welcome, well-appointed accommodation, good food and good value.
ACCOMMODATION £21–£30
FOOD £15–£20
**Hours:** open all year 6pm; breakfast 8:30am – 9am; bar meals 11am – 4pm; lunch 12noon – 2pm; bar meals 4:30pm – 9pm; dinner 6:30pm – 9pm. **Cuisine:** Scottish:- Wide choice of meals from Royal Deeside Salmon with Hollandaise sauce to toasted sandwiches. **Rooms:** 6 bedrooms, all en suite. **Credit cards:** Visa, Access. **Other points:** licensed, open-air dining, Sunday lunch, children catered for – please check for age limits, afternoon tea, pets allowed, residents' lounge. **Directions:** on main Braemar/Aberdeen road at northern end of Ballater. A93.
MONICE CHIVAS, tel (03397) 55762.

## MONALTRIE HOTEL, Bridge Square
Monaltrie Hotel which was built in the reign of Queen Victoria, has been carefully and tastefully modernised to provide every comfort and convenience. Situated on the north banks of the River Dee, the head chef carefully selects fresh produce each day to guarantee the best quality. Royal Deeside is justly famed as an area of outstanding natural beauty with an extensive variety of scenery, flora and wildlife.
ACCOMMODATION £21–£30
FOOD up to £15
**Hours:** breakfast 8.30am – 9.30am; lunch 12 noon – 2.30pm; dinner 7pm – 10.30pm; bar snacks 12 noon – 2.30pm and 5.30pm – 9.30pm. **Cuisine:** International. **Rooms:** 25 bedrooms all with TV, telephone, tea making facilities. **Credit cards:** Visa, Access, diners. **Other points:** parking, children catered for – please check for

age limits, pets allowed, residents' lounge, vegetarian meals, garden. **Directions:** A93, on left on entering Ballater, overlooking the River Dee.
JAMES ANDERSON, tel (0339) 755417, fax (0339) 755180.

# BANCHORY, Grampian Map 22

## BANCHORY LODGE HOTEL
At the confluence of the Feugh with the Dee, the Banchory Lodge is in a striking and historic setting, with the river Dee, a celebrated salmon river, running through the grounds. As well as salmon fishing, there is also ample opportunity for golfing, nearby forest walks and nature trails. An abundance of National Trust properties to visit nearby.
ACCOMMODATION over £50
FOOD ⊖
**Hours:** lunch 6:30pm; dinner 6:30pm; bar 11am – 2pm; closed 12 December – 29 January; bar 5pm – 11pm. **Cuisine:** Scottish:- Prime Scottish beef, Dee salmon. **Rooms:** 22 bedrooms 5 twins ensuite, 8 doubles ensuite, 9 family rooms ensuite. **Credit cards:** Visa, Access, AmEx. **Other points:** children catered for – please check for age limits, fishing, sauna. **Directions:** off the A93, 18 miles west of Aberdeen in Banchory, off Dee Street.
DUGALD JAFFRAY, tel (03302) 2625, (03302) 4777, fax (03302) 5019.

# BEAULY, Highlands Map 24

## LOVAT ARMS HOTEL
This comfortable family-owned hotel is set in the very heart of Fraser Country, and offers excellent food and accommodation amidst warm and friendly surroundings. Just ten miles from the Highlands capital of Inverness, its intimate village setting has much to offer, including Campbell's Tweedhouse, a Winery, and Marr's Antiques. Fishing, Golf and Pony Trekking available nearby.
ACCOMMODATION £41–£50
FOOD £15–£20
**Hours:** open all year 5pm; breakfast 8am – 10am; lunch 12noon – 2pm; bar meals 12noon – 2pm; bar meals 5pm – 9pm; dinner 6pm – 9pm. **Cuisine:** Scottish:- A la carte and table d'hote menus offering traditional Scottish fare, including locally caught Salmon and Venison. Vegetarian dishes available. **Rooms:** 22 bedrooms 1 single ensuite, 5 doubles ensuite, 13 twins ensuite, 3 family rooms ensuite. **Credit cards:** Visa, Access. **Other points:** licensed, Sunday lunch, children catered for – please check for age limits, afternoon tea, residents' lounge, parking, vegetarian meals. **Directions:** A9 to Tore roundabout. Follow signs to Beauly. Hotel on edge of village.
WILLIAM & ANN FRASER, tel (0463) 782313, fax (0463) 782862.

# BIGGAR, Strathclyde Map 21

## TINTO HOTEL, Symington
Set in an area of great natural beauty near the romantic Borderland, yet only an hour from Glasgow and

*Edinburgh, this charming country house hotel is a perfect base for relaxation or business. Offering a very high standard of cuisine and accommodation, this hotel comes 'highly recommended'.*
*ACCOMMODATION £21–£30*
*FOOD up to £15* 🐕

**Hours:** breakfast 7am – 9:30am; lunch 12noon – 3pm; dinner 4:30pm – 10pm. **Cuisine:** British:- Dining room: A la carte menu, lunches and high teas. Bar and lounge: less formal meals and snacks. **Rooms:** 30 bedrooms 5 singles ensuite, 7 twins ensuite, 13 doubles ensuite, 3 family rooms ensuite, 2 suites. **Credit cards:** Visa, Access, Diners, AmEx. **Other points:** licensed, open-air dining, Sunday lunch, children catered for – please check for age limits, afternoon tea, pets allowed, garden, golf, fishing, bowls. **Directions:** 10 miles from M74, 9 miles south-east of Lanark.
BRIAN THOMPSON, tel (08993) 454.

---

## BLAIRGOWRIE, Tayside Map 22

### ANGUS HOTEL, 46 Wellmeadow
*Situated in the centre of the country town of Blairgowrie, the hotel is well located for touring the surrounding countryside. With golf and fishing nearby and a heated indoor swimming pool, sauna and squash court the hotel has something to interest most. Presenting tasty meals and offering accommodation of a high standard.*
*ACCOMMODATION £21–£30*
*FOOD up to £15* CLUB

**Hours:** breakfast 8am – 9:30am; bar meals 12noon – 1:45pm; dinner 7pm – 8:30pm; bar meals 7pm – 8:30pm. **Cuisine:** British:- Dishes may include Smoked Salmon with Capers and Lemon Wedges. Pan Fried Rainbow Trout in Almond Butter. Filo Tartlet with Broccoli and Mornay Sauce. **Rooms:** 86 bedrooms all with tea making facilities, telephone, TV: 18 singles ensuite, 21 doubles ensuite, 40 twins ensuite, 3 triples ensuite, 4 family rooms ensuite. **Credit cards:** Visa, Access, AmEx. **Other points:** licensed, open-air dining, Sunday lunch, no-smoking area, children catered for – please check for age limits, afternoon tea, pets allowed, conferences, swimming pool, sauna, squash. **Directions:** A93, Perth to Braemar road.
ARNOLD SCOTT, tel (0250) 872455, fax (0250) 875615.

---

## BO'NESS, Central Map 22

### HOLLYWOOD HOUSE, 25 Grahams Dyke Road
*House with outstanding character and superb views of Firth of Forth. With easy access of golf courses, stately homes, palaces. Only 30 minutes drive from Edinburgh city centre and 15 minutes from Airport.*
*ACCOMMODATION £21–£30*

**Hours:** breakfast 7am – 9am; dinner 6pm – 8pm. **Cuisine:** English. **Rooms:** 1 single, 3 double and 1 family bedroom, 2 bathrooms, 2 showers, colour TV in all rooms. **Other points:** central heating, children

catered for – please check for age limits, residents' lounge, garden. **Directions:** 5 mins from M9 motorway.
HARRY & CHRISTINA ROSS, tel (0506) 823260.

---

## BRAEMAR, Grampian Map 22

### CALLATER LODGE HOTEL, 9 Glenshee Road
*A typical Victorian villa built from local granite and standing in one acre of mature grounds on the southern edge of Braemar. Peter and Mary Nelson have built up an enviable reputation for the warmth of their welcome and the excellence of their hospitality towards guests. There are two separate self-catering units also available, Callater Cottage and Callater Chalet. Ideal location for tourists, sportsmen and walkers.*
*ACCOMMODATION under £20*
*FOOD up to £15*

**Hours:** breakfast 8:30am; dinner 7:30pm. **Cuisine:** British:- Fresh local produce is used extensively for the daily changing menu. **Rooms:** 9 bedrooms 3 twins ensuite, 2 doubles ensuite, 1 single ensuite, 1 twin, 1 double, 1 single. **Credit cards:** Visa, Access. **Other points:** parking, open bank holidays, no-smoking, pets allowed, residents' lounge, garden. **Directions:** on A93 (Perth to Aberdeen road), as it passes through Braemar.
PETER & MARY NELSON, tel (03397) 41275.

---

## BUCKIE, Grampian Map 22

### MILL HOUSE HOTEL, Tynet
*A converted, 18th-century water mill, offering all sporting and sightseeing activities. This hospitable, family-run establishment provides a relaxing atmosphere and is renowned for its excellent food and value. All 15 bedrooms are en-suite with full modern facilities. Open all year.*
*ACCOMMODATION £21–£30*
*FOOD up to £15* CLUB ★

**Hours:** breakfast 7:45am – 9:30am; lunch 12noon – 2pm; dinner 7pm – 9pm. **Cuisine:** Scottish:- A la carte – speciality Scottish cuisine from local produce. **Rooms:** 15 bedrooms all with tea making facilities, radio, TV: 3 doubles ensuite, 4 twins ensuite, 7 singles ensuite, 1 family room ensuite. **Credit cards:** Visa, Access, Diners, AmEx. **Other points:** licensed, Sunday lunch, functions, special breaks, golf packages, vegetarian meals, residents' bar, residents' lounge, disabled access, children catered for – please check for age limits. **Directions:** on the A98, east of Elgin. Hotel located between Buckie and Fochabers.
GILL & PHIL SILVER, tel (0542) 850233, fax (0542) 850331.

---

## BURNMOUTH, Borders Map 20

### THE FLEMINGTON INN
*An attractive, well run pub directly on the A1 in the pretty fishing village of Burnmouth. This is the 'first and last' pub in Scotland. Presenting home cooked meals made from fresh local produce at value for money*

prices, *The Flemington Inn is very popular, especially with locals.*
FOOD up to £15
**Hours:** lunch 12noon – 2:15pm; lunch – Sunday
12:30pm – 2:15pm; dinner 6:30pm – 9pm. **Cuisine:**
Scottish:- Traditional Scottish menu with good use of
local seafood. **Other points:** licensed, parking, children
catered for – please check for age limits, vegetarian
meals. **Directions:** 6 miles north of Berwick Upon
Tweed on A1.
MR & MRS SMILLIE, tel (08907) 81277.

## BURNTISLAND, Fife Map 22

### KINGSWOOD HOTEL, *Kinghorn Road*
*Set in 2 acres of grounds with outstanding views across
the River Forth towards Edinburgh. The hotel's
ambience, tasteful furnishings and first class cuisine all
combine to make every visit an enjoyable experience.*
ACCOMMODATION £21–£30
FOOD up to £15 🍵
**Hours:** breakfast 7:30am – 9am; lunch 12noon – 3pm;
bar meals 12noon – 10pm; dinner 7pm – 9:30pm.
**Cuisine:** Scottish:- Full a la carte and table d'hote
menus available. Choices include cullen skink and fresh
salmon. **Rooms:** 10 bedrooms 4 doubles ensuite, 5 twins
ensuite, 1 single. **Credit cards:** Visa, Access. **Other
points:** licensed, open-air dining, Sunday lunch, no-
smoking area, children catered for – please check for age
limits, pets/prior arr. **Directions:** on the A92 coast road
halfway between Kinghorn and Burntisland.
RANKIN & KATHRYN BELL, tel (0592) 872329, fax
(0592) 873123.

## CALLANDER, Central Map 22

### ABBOTSFORD LODGE HOTEL, *Stirling Road*
*A comfortable and friendly hotel which is surrounded by
places of interest, eg. Stirling Castle, Loch Lomond,
Glen Coe, Doune Castle and Doune Vintage Car
Museum. Private parking for all our guests.*
ACCOMMODATION £21–£30
FOOD up to £15
**Hours:** breakfast 8am – 9am; dinner 7pm – 8pm.
**Cuisine:** British:- Tea and home baking served in the
lounge at 10pm. **Rooms:** 18 bedrooms all with tea
making facilities: 1 single, 1 twin, 4 twins ensuite, 4
doubles ensuite, 3 family rooms, 5 family rooms ensuite.
**Other points:** central heating, children catered for –
please check for age limits, residents' lounge, garden.
**Directions:** east side of town, known by locals by its
monkey tree in front.
MR & MRS S SIBBALD, tel (0877) 330066.

## CARNOUSTIE, Tayside Map 22

### STATION HOTEL
*Originally an old Railway Hotel, now extensively
refurbished, providing comfortable accommodation and*

fine quality food. Very popular with golfers. Nearby places
of interest include Barry Mill and Broughton Ferry.
ACCOMMODATION £21–£30
**Hours:** breakfast 7:30am – 9:30am; lunch 12noon –
2pm; high tea 5pm – 7pm; dinner 7:30pm – 9pm.
**Cuisine:** English:- Traditional cuisine. Separate High
Tea menu. Bar Snacks. Children's menu. Vegetarian
dishes. **Rooms:** 9 bedrooms, 6 en suite with colour TV,
telephone, and room-service, all freshly and attractively
furnished. **Credit cards:** Visa, Access, AmEx. **Other
points:** Sunday lunch, children catered for – please
check for age limits, pets allowed, afternoon tea,
parking, bank holidays. **Directions:** off the A92, near
Carnoustie railway station.
ARTHUR CHRISTIESON, tel (0241) 52447.

## CONTIN BY STRATHPEFFER,
Highlands Map 24

### ACHILTY HOTEL, *Contin*
*Family run hotel, beautifully situated some 17 miles
from Inverness with spectacular views over the
surrounding mountains. Private fishing rights on River
Blackwater, marvellous walks and scenery. Good
comfortable accommodation. Popular restaurant and
good bar meals featuring the best local produce and
many French cordon bleu specialities. Warm welcome
and good value.*
ACCOMMODATION £21–£30
FOOD up to £15 CLUB
**Hours:** open all year 7:30pm; breakfast 7:30am –
9:30am; lunch 12noon – 2:30pm; bar meals 12noon –
2:30pm; dinner 5:30pm – 9:30pm; bar meals 5:30pm –
9:30pm. **Cuisine::-** A la carte and table d'hote menus
offering a good choice of traditional dishes. Vegetarians
also catered for. **Rooms:** 12 bedrooms all with tea
making facilities, TV: 5 twins ensuite, 3 doubles ensuite,
3 triples ensuite, 1 quad ensuite. **Credit cards:** Visa,
Access. **Other points:** licensed, open-air dining, Sunday
lunch, no-smoking area, children catered for – please
check for age limits, pets allowed, afternoon tea,
residents' lounge, parking, disabled access, bank
holidays, cots, foreign exchange, disabled access,
fishing, vegetarian meals, residents' bar. **Directions:**
from Inverness take A9 then A835 Ullapool Road.
CLAUDE & HELENA PONTY, tel (0997) 421355.

## CRAIL, Fife Map 22

### MARINE HOTEL, *54 Nethergate South*
*Small family-run hotel, with eight ensuite, well
appointed bedrooms, a residents' lounge and a
restaurant serving a la carte and table d'hote menus.
Beautiful views of the Firth of Forth and the Isle of May
can be enjoyed in the lounge bar which has a patio
leading into the garden.*
ACCOMMODATION £21–£30
FOOD up to £15
**Hours:** breakfast 8:30am – 9:30am; bar meals 12noon –
9pm; dinner 7pm – 9pm. **Cuisine:** seafood:- Local

seafood (in season). **Rooms:** 8 bedrooms all with tea making facilities, TV: 3 doubles ensuite, 4 twins ensuite, 1 family room ensuite. **Credit cards:** Visa, Access, Diners, AmEx. **Other points:** licensed, Sunday lunch, pets allowed, afternoon tea. **Directions:** on junction of B940 with A917, SE of St Andrews. Follow signs for Pottery.
IAIN & AILEEN GREENLEES, tel (0333) 50207.

## CRATHIE, Grampian Map 22

### INVER HOTEL, By Balmoral
*A fully licensed Country Inn, set amid the heather clad hills in the Upper Deeside Valley, on the A93. It is the nearest hostelry to Balmoral Castle. Sporting facilities include golfing, fishing, deer-stalking, pony trekking, skiing and more. Although 200 years old, the hotel has been renovated to provide personal attention and good food in quiet, comfortable surroundings.*
ACCOMMODATION £21–£30
FOOD up to £15
**Hours:** breakfast 8am – 9am; lunch 12noon – 2:15pm; bar snacks 12noon – 2:15pm; dinner 5:30pm – 8:30pm; bar snacks 5:30pm – 8:30pm. **Cuisine:** British. **Rooms:** 9 bedrooms all with tea making facilities, TV: 1 single ensuite, 2 doubles ensuite, 2 twins ensuite, 4 family rooms ensuite. **Credit cards:** Visa, Access, Eurocard. **Other points:** parking, children catered for – please check for age limits, Sunday lunch, Sunday dinner, open bank holidays, disabled access, pets allowed, residents' lounge, open-air dining, garden. **Directions:** 2 miles west of Balmoral Castle on main Braemar Road.
MR K & MRS J BOOTH, tel (0339) 742345.

## CRIANLARICH, Central Map 22

### THE ROD & REEL, Main Street
*A family-run bar and restaurant which offers a wide choice of good food at very reasonable prices. Personally run by Elspeth and Bill Paulin, you are assured a warm welcome and friendly service.*
FOOD up to £15
**Hours:** bar meals 12noon – 9pm; dinner 6pm – 9pm. **Cuisine:** British:- Bar meals and a la carte menu. Menus based on the use of fresh fish and local game. Good incorporation of Scottish meat for roasts and steaks, and an extensive selection of vegetarian dishes. **Credit cards:** Visa, Access. **Other points:** licensed, children catered for – please check for age limits. **Directions:** in the centre of Crianlarich.
ELSPETH & BILL PAULIN, tel (08383) 271, fax (08383) 261.

## CRIEFF, Tayside Map 22

### FOULFORD INN
*Originally a drovers' meeting place and coaching inn, this family-run hotel has much to explain its continuing success – comfortable, affordable accommodation, good home-style cooking, an unpretentious and lively family*

atmosphere and spectacular views of the southern Grampians. Good value for money.
ACCOMMODATION under £20
FOOD up to £15
**Hours:** open bank holidays 6pm; closed 01/02 – 28/02; breakfast 8am – 9am; lunch 12:15pm – 2pm; dinner 5pm – 9pm; bar meals 6:30pm – 9pm. **Cuisine:** Scottish:- Traditional Scottish fare, simple and sustaining. Well-cooked to a high standard. **Rooms:** 10 bedrooms, 3 en suite. **Credit cards:** Visa, Access. **Other points:** licensed, Sunday lunch, children catered for – please check for age limits, afternoon tea, vegetarian meals, residents' lounge, garden, disabled access, pets allowed, golf. **Directions:** situated off A85, turn right at . Gilmerton turn off on A822.
MESSRS BEAUMONT, tel (0764) 452407.

### MURRAYPARK HOTEL, Connaught Terrace
*Thoroughly spoil yourself at this delightful hotel – Anne & Noel ensure you receive a warm, friendly welcome, superb food and relaxed, quiet comfort in the heart of beautiful Perthshire.*
ACCOMMODATION £30–£40
FOOD £15–£20
**Hours:** lunch 12noon – 2pm; dinner 7:30pm – 9:30pm. **Cuisine:** Scottish:- Excellent, varied menu recommended by Taste of Scotland – local venison, pheasant, pigeon, beef and fish. Bar meals and packed lunches. **Rooms:** 15 bedrooms, 14 en suite. **Credit cards:** Visa, Diners. **Other points:** Sunday lunch, children catered for – please check for age limits, golf nearby. **Directions:** follow M90; exit onto A9. Take first left onto A85 for Crieff.
ANNE & NOEL SCOTT, tel (0764) 653731, (0764) 653732.

### SMUGGLERS RESTAURANT, The Hosh
*Previously an old warehouse, the restaurant forms part of the visitors' Heritage Centre at the Glenturret distillery. The site incorporates an audio-visual theatre and a 3-D exhibition. Visitors can also take the opportunity to taste the whiskies! For groups of up to 60 persons, try the Pagoda Room.*
FOOD up to £15
**Hours:** meals all day 10am – 4pm; lunch 12noon – 3pm. **Cuisine:** Scottish:- Glenturret pate, Tay salmon, venison in whisky sauce, gaugers – gateaux flavoured with malt liqueur. **Credit cards:** Visa, Access, AmEx. **Other points:** licensed, open-air dining, no-smoking area, children catered for – please check for age limits, coach/prior arr. Directions on the A85 in north west Crieff towards Comrie.
GLENTURRET DISTILLERY LTD, tel (0764) 656565, fax (0764) 654366.

## CROMARTY, Highlands Map 24

### ROYAL HOTEL, Marine Terrace
*A family-run hotel with attentive staff who guard their reputation for quality food and value for money with*

considerable pride – the best in Scottish hospitality. Cromarty is an unspoilt fishing village on the Black Isle where relaxation and peace are guaranteed.
ACCOMMODATION £21–£30
FOOD up to £15 CLUB ★
Hours: breakfast 8am – 9:30am; lunch 12noon – 2pm; bar meals 12noon – 2pm; bar meals 5:30pm – 9:30pm; dinner 7pm – 8:30pm. Cuisine: Scottish. Rooms: 10 bedrooms all with tea making facilities, TV: 3 singles ensuite, 2 twins ensuite, 5 doubles ensuite. Credit cards: Visa, AmEx. Other points: open-air dining, Sunday lunch, no-smoking area, children catered for – please check for age limits, coach/prior arr, residents' lounge, residents' bar. Directions: off the A832 in Cromarty overlooking the beach and harbour.
YVONNE & STEWART MORRISON, tel (0381) 600217.

## CULLEN, Grampian Map 22

### BAYVIEW HOTEL, 57 Seafield Street
A small, intimate hotel commanding spectacular views over the harbour, bay and Moray Firth, renowned for excellent food and personal service. The restaurant is open daily and meals are also served in the bar at lunchtime and in the evening. The inspector declared the food 'excellently prepared and presented' and the rooms 'attractive and very comfortable'. Daily changing menu.
ACCOMMODATION £21–£30
FOOD up to £15 🍽
Hours: breakfast 8am – 9:30am; lunch 12noon – 1:45pm; dinner 6:30pm – 9pm. Cuisine: Scottish:- Restaurant part of 'Taste of Scotland' scheme offering dishes such as Fillet of Salmon wrapped in Pastry with Lemon Thyme. Good range of bar meals. Rooms: 6 bedrooms all with tea making facilities, telephone, TV: 1 single ensuite, 2 twins ensuite, 2 doubles ensuite, 1 family room ensuite. Credit cards: Visa, Access. Other points: Sunday lunch. Directions: overlooking the Harbour.
DAVID EVANS, tel (0542) 841031.

## CUPAR, Fife Map 22

### EDEN HOUSE HOTEL, 2 Pitscottie Road
Built as a home for a Victorian merchant, this privately owned hotel reflects the architectural grandeur of the period. Immaculately furnished throughout, it offers impeccable standards of service and attention to details for all its guests. A large conservatory restaurant is a new addition to this lovely place. Ideal for both the businessman and holiday-maker.
ACCOMMODATION £21–£30
FOOD £26–£30
Hours: closed Sunday lunch; closed Christmas; breakfast 7:30am – 9:30am; bar snacks 12noon – 2pm; dinner 6:30pm – 9:30pm; bar snacks 6:30pm – 9:30pm. Cuisine: British. Rooms: 9 bedrooms all with tea making facilities, telephone, radio, TV: 2 singles ensuite, 4 twins ensuite, 1 double ensuite, 2 triples ensuite. Credit cards: Visa, Access. Other points: children catered for – please check for age limits, pets, disabled

access, residents' lounge, garden, parking, vegetarian meals, open-air dining, residents' bar, cots, baby-listening device. Directions: off A91, St Andrews Road, east of Cupar overlooking the park.
MR P A MEREDREW, tel (0334) 52510.

## DALKEITH, Lothian Map 20

### COUNTY HOTEL & RESTAURANT, 152 High Street
Family-run for over 40 years, this hotel has a well deserved reputation for friendly service, good food and value for money. Recently refurbished to provide additional bedrooms, a cocktail bar and bistro, two small meeting rooms and a well-designed function suite. Sporting and activity breaks such as golf, clay and game shooting and much more can be arranged. Ideal location for visiting Edinburgh and its many tourist attractions.
ACCOMMODATION £21–£30
FOOD up to £15
Hours: breakfast 7:30am – 11:30am; meals all day 11:30am – 10pm. Cuisine: international:- Attractively presented fresh food. Credit cards: Visa, Access. Other points: children catered for – please check for age limits, open bank holidays, no-smoking area, afternoon tea, disabled access, pets allowed, residents' lounge, vegetarian meals, functions, conferences. Directions: 1 mile from Edinburgh City bypass, 7 miles south of Edinburgh on A68 or A7.
MR P COPPOLA, tel (031) 663 3495, fax (031) 663 0208.

## DALMALLY, Strathclyde Map 21

### GLENORCHY LODGE HOTEL, Nr Oban
A small, family-run hotel in the village of Dalmally, offering warm, comfortable accommodation. Informal, lively bar and good bar meals served in generous portions. Ideal base for touring the area.
ACCOMMODATION £21–£30
FOOD up to £15
Hours: closed 01/01; breakfast 7am – 9am; lunch 11am – 2:30pm; dinner 5pm – 9pm; closed Christmas 25/12. Cuisine: Scottish:- Traditional cuisine using fresh, Scottish produce such as Highland Venison in a red wine sauce, Local Salmon, Awe Trout, Steaks. Rooms: 5 bedrooms all with tea making facilities, telephone, radio, TV: 1 double ensuite, 2 triples ensuite, 2 family rooms ensuite. Credit cards: Visa, Access, Diners, AmEx. Other points: licensed, children catered for – please check for age limits, afternoon tea, pets allowed, residents' lounge. Directions: A82 from Glasgow, A85 from Tyndrum. 16 miles Inveraray, 25 miles Oban.
HECTOR & PATRICIA WHYTE, tel (0838) 200312.

## DEESIDE, Highlands Map 22

### THE TOLBOOTH RESTAURANT, Kincardine
A building of historical interest, situated in the seaside holiday resort of Stonehaven, and offering good views

*across the working harbour. Excellent home-produced dishes using local produce with the emphasis on local fish dishes. A major nearby tourist attraction is Dunotter Castle, setting for Franco Zefferelli's portrayal of Hamlet in 1990.*

FOOD £15–£20

**Hours:** lunch 12noon – 2pm; dinner 7pm – 9pm; closed January; closed Monday. **Cuisine:** seafood:- A la carte menu. Blue Fin Tuna Steak, Red Snapper Ravioli, Monkfish Casserole, Loin of Venison, all home produced using only fresh produce. **Credit cards:** Visa. **Other points:** licensed, Sunday lunch, children catered for – please check for age limits, vegetarian meals. **Directions:** 15 miles south of Aberdeen. In Stonehaven, follow harbour signs.

MOYA BOTHWELL, tel (0569) 62287.

## DINGWALL, Highlands Map 24

### THE NATIONAL HOTEL, High Street

*This Victorian hotel offers spacious accommodation, warmly decorated with wood panelling and comfortable furnishings. With convenient access to the spectacular Highland countryside. Traditional home-cooking is welcome after an invigorating day spent exploring the nearby sights.*

ACCOMMODATION £31–£40

FOOD up to £15

**Hours:** breakfast 7am – 9:30am; lunch 12noon – 2:30pm; dinner 7pm – 9:30pm. **Cuisine:** Scottish:- Traditional homecooking. Vegetarians catered for. **Rooms:** 52 bedrooms all en suite, with colour TV, radio/alarm, trouser-press, telephone, baby-listening facilities, tea/coffee maker, room-service. **Credit cards:** Visa, Access, Diners, AmEx. **Other points:** licensed, Sunday lunch, children catered for – please check for age limits, afternoon tea, residents' lounge. **Directions:** 12 miles north of Inverness.

BERNARD & ROSEMARIE JUSTICE, tel (0349) 62166, fax (0349) 65178.

## DORNOCH, Highlands Map 24

### MALLIN HOUSE HOTEL, Church Street

*A family-run hotel situated close to the famous golf course in Dornoch. Good food and a friendly atmosphere complement the high standard of accommodation. Choose from the a la carte, table d'hote or bar meals menu. All dishes are freshly cooked to order and attractively presented. Good value for money. Especially popular with golfers and anglers.*

ACCOMMODATION £21–£30

FOOD £15–£20

**Hours:** breakfast 8:15am – 10am; lunch 12noon – 2:30pm; dinner 6:30pm – 9pm. **Cuisine:** English:- A la Carte and Table d'Hote menus. Dishes may include Rack of Spring Lamb, Lobster Thermidor. All dishes cooked to order. Good, imaginative bar meals. **Rooms:** 11 bedrooms, all en suite. **Credit cards:** Visa, Access, AmEx. **Other points:** licensed, Sunday lunch, children

catered for – please check for age limits, pets allowed, garden. **Directions:** in centre of Dornoch near to the famous golf course.

MALCOLM HOLDEN, tel (0862) 810335.

## DRUMNADROCHIT, Highlands Map 24

### LOCH NESS LODGE HOTEL

*A comfortable and friendly Highland lodge set in 8 acres of woodland near Loch Ness and Urquhart Castle. An ideal touring base for the Scottish Highlands. Regular Scottish entertainment. Loch Ness visitors centre, giftshop, and Loch Ness cruises.*

ACCOMMODATION £31–£40

FOOD up to £15

**Hours:** breakfast 8am – 10am; bar meals 11:30am – 6pm; bar meals 6:30pm – 9:30pm. **Cuisine:** Scottish:- Aberdeen Angus steaks and fresh seafood. Carte d'jour and full a la carte menus available. Bar snacks served in the bar/coffee shop. Children's menu. Homebaking. **Rooms:** 55 bedrooms all with tea making facilities, telephone, TV: 16 doubles ensuite, 36 twins ensuite, 2 triples ensuite, 1 quad ensuite. **Credit cards:** Visa, Access, Diners, AmEx. **Other points:** licensed, vegetarian meals, children catered for – please check for age limits, pets allowed, afternoon tea, coach/prior arr. **Directions:** on the A831 Cannich to Inverness Road.

D W SKINNER, tel (0456) 450342, fax (0456) 450429.

## DUMFRIES, Dumfries & Galloway Map 23

### CAIRNDALE HOTEL & LEISURE CLUB, English Street

*This privately-owned hotel offers all the comforts expected from one of the region's leading hotels. Executive room, suites, syndicate rooms and conference facilities are available. The Barracuda Leisure Club offers heated indoor swimming pool, sauna, steam room, hot spa-bath, air-conditioned gymnasium, sunbeds, toning table, health & beauty salon. Golf inclusive breaks, bargain breaks, leisure weekends available. (See colour advertisement in centre section.)*

ACCOMMODATION £31–£40

FOOD up to £15

**Hours:** breakfast 7:15am – 10am; lunch 12noon – 2pm; dinner 7pm – 9:30pm. **Cuisine:** Scottish:- Traditional Taste of Scotland fayre. Sawney Beans Bar & Grill: Carvery & Steaks. Forum Cafe Bar: Snacks & light meals in a continental cafe atmosphere. **Rooms:** 79 bedrooms 20 singles ensuite, 17 doubles ensuite, 37 twins ensuite, 2 family rooms ensuite, 3 suites. **Credit cards:** Visa, Access, Diners, AmEx. **Other points:** children catered for – please check for age limits, conferences, swimming pool, sauna, solarium, special breaks, parking, vegetarian meals, residents' bar, residents' lounge, disabled access. **Directions:** Close to town centre, just off A75 Dumfries to Carlisle route.

WALLACE FAMILY, tel (0387) 54111, fax (0387) 50555.

## HETLAND HALL HOTEL, *Carrutherstown*

*Originally built as a manor house, then converted into a boarding school, Hetland Hall is now a grand country house hotel and restaurant. Set in 45 acres of well tended parklands with fine views over the Solway Firth. The restaurant serves an international menu in relaxed, informal surroundings. Chalet Swimming Pool, Fitness Suite and Snooker are available.*

*ACCOMMODATION £41–£50*

*FOOD £15–£20*

**Hours:** breakfast 7:30am – 9:30am; lunch 12noon – 2pm; bar 12noon – 11pm; dinner 7pm – 9:30pm. **Cuisine:** international:- international menu. **Rooms:** 27 bedrooms all with tea making facilities, telephone, radio, TV: 5 singles ensuite, 11 twins ensuite, 11 doubles ensuite. **Credit cards:** Visa, Access, Diners, AmEx. **Other points:** open-air dining, Sunday lunch, no-smoking area, pets allowed, children catered for – please check for age limits, afternoon tea, swimming pool, gym facilities, games room, residents' lounge, residents' bar, foreign exchange, disabled access, parking. **Directions:** Hotel is located on the main A75 midway between Annan and Dumfries.
DAVID & MARY ALLEN, tel (0387) 84201, fax (0387) 84211.

## DUNBAR, Lothian Map 20

### REDHEUGH HOTEL, *Bayswell Park*

*A warm, friendly welcome awaits you at the Redheugh Hotel, situated on the cliff-top at Dunbar and with fine views over the Firth of Forth. Traditionally furnished, the hotel has a homely atmosphere and, with good food to match, you are sure of a relaxed stay. Golf and fishing packages can be arranged.*

*ACCOMMODATION £21–£30*

*FOOD up to £15*

**Hours:** breakfast 7:30am – 9am; dinner 7pm – 8:30pm; closed Christmas 24/12 – 03/01. **Cuisine:** British:- Predominantly British cuisine. Menu changes daily. Specialities include Sea Trout in a Cream sauce, home-made Casseroles and fresh Fruit Pies. **Rooms:** 10 bedrooms all with tea making facilities, telephone, radio, mini bar, TV: 2 family rooms ensuite, 2 singles ensuite, 3 twins ensuite, 3 doubles ensuite. **Credit cards:** Visa, Access, Diners, AmEx. **Other points:** licensed, pets allowed, golf, street parking. **Directions:** on the cliff-top at Dunbar.
MRS J YOUNG, tel (0368) 62793, fax (0368) 62793.

## DUNBEATH, Highlands Map 24

### DUNBEATH HOTEL

*Situated in a quiet Highland village with views to the sea, this old coaching inn dating from around 1830, offers true character with modern comfort. An ideal opportunity for the visitor to sample the best of Highland produce, complemented by a fine wine list. Caithness itself has much to offer the visitor with the Orkneys just off-shore, and a wealth of sporting activities available.*

*ACCOMMODATION £21–£30*

*FOOD up to £15* ★

**Hours:** closed 01/01 – 03/01; breakfast 8am – 9:30am; lunch 12noon – 2:30pm; bar snacks 12noon – 2:30pm; bar snacks 5pm – 9pm; dinner 7pm – 8pm; closed Christmas 25/12 – 26/12. **Cuisine:** Scottish:- Venison and Salmon from local estates and seafood from northern harbours. **Rooms:** 6 bedrooms all with tea making facilities, radio, TV: 2 twins ensuite, 4 doubles ensuite. **Credit cards:** Visa, Access, Diners, AmEx. **Other points:** licensed, Sunday lunch, no-smoking area, children catered for – please check for age limits, afternoon tea, pets allowed, garden, parking, cots, 24hr reception, residents' lounge, residents' bar. **Directions:** north on A9 from Inverness – signs to Wick/Thurso – left at roadbridge.
NEIL & PATRICIA BUCHANAN, tel (0593) 3208, fax (0593) 3242.

## DUNBLANE, Central Map 22

### SHERIFFMUIR INN, *Sheriffmuir*

*The Sherriffmuir is steeped in history, lying just east of where the famous battle of 1715 took place to stop the Jacobite advance to the south. This sense of history can be embraced whilst enjoying a bar meal or a drink in the grounds of this famous Scottish hostelry, where personal attention is of utmost importance. Nearby, endless recreational activities are also available.*

*ACCOMMODATION under £20*

*FOOD up to £15*

**Hours:** breakfast 9am – 9:30am; lunch – weekdays 12noon – 2pm; lunch – Saturday 12noon – 2:30pm; Sunday – food all day 12noon – 9pm; dinner 6pm – 9pm. **Cuisine:** English:- Fixed price menu. Excellent traditional country fare, including Steak & Guinness Pie, Deep Fried Haddock. Steaks. Vegetarians catered for. **Rooms:** 2 bedrooms all with tea making facilities, TV: 1 twin, 1 double. **Credit cards:** Visa, Access. **Other points:** licensed, open-air dining, Sunday lunch, children catered for – please check for age limits, parking, bank holidays, disabled access. **Directions:** follow local services – Dunblane from A9. Turn R at Fourways r'bout.
PETER & SUE COLLEY, tel (0786) 823285, fax (0786) 823969.

### STIRLING ARMS HOTEL, *Stirling Road*

*Originally a 17th century coaching inn by the bridge over the Allan Water, this family run hotel and restaurant has been extensively refurbished. The owners pride themselves in providing comfortable accommodation and excellent food in their Oak Room Restaurant. Good value for money. History records the patronage of Robert Burns and the Duke of Argyll to the inn.*

*ACCOMMODATION £21–£30*

*FOOD up to £15*

**Hours:** breakfast 8am – 9am; lunch 12noon – 2:30pm; dinner 6pm – 9pm. **Cuisine:** Scottish:- Modern Scottish/Continental cuisine. Specialities include Gaelic Steak. Bar meals. **Rooms:** 7 bedrooms, 4 en suite. **Credit cards:** Visa, Access, AmEx. **Other points:** licensed, open-air dining, Sunday lunch, no-smoking area, children catered for – please check for age limits,

pets allowed, garden. **Directions:** off B8033 Stirling – Perth road. Close to High Street.
JANE & RICHARD CASTELOW, MHCIMA, tel (0786) 822156, fax (0786) 825300.

## DUNDEE, Tayside Map 22

### LE BEAUBOURG, 188 Blackness Road
*A wide choice of delicious English and French dishes, served in a convivial atmosphere by efficient, courteous staff is the appeal of this elegant restaurant. The clientele are mainly professional people, looking for a place they can depend on for good food and service – and, in Le Beaubourg, this is obviously what they've found.*
*FOOD up to £15*
**Hours:** lunch 12noon – 2pm; dinner 6:30pm – 10pm; closed Saturday lunch; closed Sunday. **Cuisine:** English / French:- Dishes include, Breast of Duck with mixed berries, Rainbow Trout, Escalope of Veal with Apricots. Excellent Wine List. Vegetarian meals. **Credit cards:** Visa, Access. **Other points:** licensed, Sunday lunch, no-smoking area, children catered for – please check for age limits, vegetarian meals, bank holidays, street parking. **Directions:** from Dundee city centre, follow signs for Blackness.
MR ALLAN JAMES, tel (0382) 646752.

## DUNFERMLINE, Fife Map 22

### HALFWAY HOUSE HOTEL, Kingseat
*Scotland is renowned for its long tradition of warm hospitality and The Halfway House Hotel is no exception. Recently redecorated, the hotel is comfortable and welcoming and the food in the bar and restaurant well presented and served. Nearby Loch Fitty is famous for trout fishing, golf lovers can visit St Andrews and Gleneagles and Edinburgh is only 30 minutes away.*
*ACCOMMODATION £31–£40*
*FOOD up to £15*
**Hours:** breakfast 7:30am – 9:30am; lunch 12noon – 2:15pm; bar meals 12noon – 2:15pm; high tea – Sunday 4:30pm – 6pm; dinner 5:30pm – 9pm; bar meals 5:30pm – 9pm. **Cuisine:** Scottish:- Specialities include Salmon Gravadlax and a wide range of steaks. **Rooms:** 12 bedrooms all with tea making facilities, telephone, TV: 3 doubles ensuite, 9 twins ensuite. **Credit cards:** Visa, Access. **Other points:** licensed, Sunday lunch, children catered for – please check for age limits, residents' lounge, golf nearby, residents' bar, parking. **Directions:** take M90; exit 3 for Dunfermline. First right turn for Kingseat Rd.
ANN WITHEYMAN & VIC PEGG, tel (0383) 731661, fax (0383) 621274.

## DUNOON, Strathclyde Map 21

### ARGYLL HOTEL, Argyll Street
*A family run hotel centrally located overlooking Argyll Gardens and Dunoon Pier, also splendid views over the Firth of Clyde. The hotel offers comfortable*

accommodation where you can relax in a warm, friendly atmosphere and enjoy traditional fare.
*ACCOMMODATION £21–£30*
*FOOD up to £15*
**Hours:** meals all day 7.30am - 9.30pm. **Cuisine:** British. **Rooms:** 30 bedrooms all with telephone, TV, radio/alarm. **Credit cards:** Visa, Access, Diners. **Other points:** vegetarian meals, residents' lounge, children catered for – please check for age limts. **Directions:** prominently situated in Dunoon town centre.
MR & MRS FLETCHER, tel (0369) 2059.

### ROYAL MARINE HOTEL, Marine Parade, Hunter's Quay
*A family-run country style mansion with restaurant situated on the sea-front, offering well presented good food, making special use of Scottish produce especially local fresh seafood. Friendly, attentive service and comfortable accommodation. Easy access from Glasgow when using western ferries, as you will disembark immediately opposite the Royal Marine Hotel.*
*ACCOMMODATION £31–£40*
*FOOD up to £15*
**Hours:** breakfast 8am – 9:30am; bar meals 12noon – 9:30pm; dinner 7pm – 8:30pm. **Cuisine:** British / continental:- Escalope of pork cordon bleu, venison in red wine sauce, fillet steak in bernaise sauce. Baked Salmon Royale. **Rooms:** 35 bedrooms all with telephone, TV: 7 singles ensuite, 13 twins ensuite, 12 doubles ensuite, 3 triples ensuite. **Credit cards:** Visa, Access. **Other points:** Sunday lunch, garden, residents' lounge, games room, afternoon tea, children catered for – please check for age limits, baby-listening device, cots, foreign exchange, residents' bar. **Directions:** off A815 to Dunoon. On seafront. Opposite western Ferries terminal.
MESSRS ARNOLD & GREIG, tel (0369) 5810, fax (0369) 2329.

## DUNVEGAN, Highlands Map 24

### DUNORIN HOUSE HOTEL, Herebost, Isle Of Skye
*A new hotel offering luxury accommodation to suit modern requirements. It is situated in the beautiful north-west corner of Skye, enjoying a magnificent panorama across Loch Roag to the Cuillin Hills. The colour co-ordinated ground floor bedrooms and spacious corridors makes it an ideal hotel for disabled persons. Already it has acheived a reputation for attention to traditional island recipes, all home-made and complemented by a select wine list. Joan and Alasdair look forward to providing you with a true taste of island culture and hospitality.*
*ACCOMMODATION £21–£30*
*FOOD £15–£20*
**Hours:** breakfast 8am – 9am; dinner 6:45pm – 9pm. **Cuisine:** Scottish. **Rooms:** 10 bedrooms all with tea making facilities, TV: 6 doubles ensuite, 2 family rooms ensuite, 2 singles ensuite. **Credit cards:** Visa, Access, Eurocard. **Other points:** parking, children catered for –

please check for age limits, open bank holidays, no-smoking area, disabled access, residents' lounge, vegetarian meals, garden. **Directions:** from the ferry at Kyleakin follow A850 to Sligachan, then A860 to Dunvegan turn left at Roag / Orbost junction. The hotel is 200m along on the right.
ALASDAIR & JOAN MACLEAN, tel (047022) 488.

## DURNESS, Highlands Map 24

### CAPE WRATH HOTEL

*Originally built for the area tax official, this 200 year old hotel is furnished in country house style, providing an ambience of comfort and relaxation. Popular with locals and tourists alike, it is an ideal location for visiting Balnakeil Craft Village, Smoo Caves and exploring Cape Wrath.*
*ACCOMMODATION £31–£40*
*FOOD up to £15*
**Hours:** breakfast 8.30am; dinner 7.30pm; bar meals 12 noon – 2pm; closed November until Easter. **Cuisine:** International. **Rooms:** 14 ensuite rooms, 5 basic rooms in annexe. **Credit cards:** Visa, Access. **Other points:** vegetarian meals, residents' bar, residents' lounge, impressive wine cellar.
MR J WATSON, tel (0971) 511212.

### FAR NORTH HOTEL

*Situated near the Balnakeil Craft Village, offering interesting indoor opportunities to observe crafts people at work and buy their wares. With unspoilt views of hills and cape Wrath, as well as walks and outdoor activities,the peace and beauty of the area, and the excellent facilities of the hotel have kept people coming back year after year.*
*FOOD £15–£20* 🍴
**Hours:** closed Christmas 6:45pm; breakfast 7:30am – 11am; dinner 7:30pm. **Cuisine:** British. **Rooms:** 10 bedrooms. **Credit cards:** Visa, Access. **Other points:** children catered for – please check for age limits, pets allowed, afternoon tea, vegetarian meals. **Directions:** off the A838.
NICK & MARY WEATHERHEAD, tel (0971) 511221.

## EASDALE, Strathclyde Map 21

### INSHAIG PARK HOTEL (FORMERLY THE EASDALE), By Oban

*Fine Victorian House standing in its own grounds overlooking the sea and the islands with truly wonderful views. This is a small, family run, comfortable hotel in an idyllic location with good food served by friendly, helpful staff.*
*ACCOMMODATION £21–£30*
*FOOD up to £15*
**Hours:** breakfast 8:30am – 9:30am; dinner 7:30pm – 8:30pm. **Cuisine:** English. **Rooms:** 4 bedrooms all with tea making facilities, TV: 2 doubles ensuite, 1 twin ensuite, 1 twin. **Other points:** licensed, children catered for – please check for age limits, garden, pets allowed. **Directions:** 16 miles south of Oban.
B & S FLETCHER & G & C DALE, tel (08523) 256.

## EDINBURGH, Lothian Map 20

### ALBANY HOTEL, 39–43 Albany Street

*A small, friendly hotel in a quiet area yet only 5 minutes from Princes Street and the city centre. The fine Georgian exterior is matched by the elegantly refurbished interior. Under the personal supervision of the Swiss owner, all guests are assured a warm welcome. Comfortable bedrooms and excellent cuisine with a continental influence is served in the restaurant.*
*ACCOMMODATION £41–£50*
*FOOD £21–£25*
**Hours:** closed 25/12–26/12, 01/01 – 02/01; breakfast 7:30am – 9:30am; lunch 12noon – 2pm; bar meals 12noon – 2pm; dinner 6:30pm – 9:30pm; bar meals 6:30pm – 9pm; **Cuisine:** British:- Dishes may include Noisettes of lamb, Scottish Salmon Steak, Medallions of Beef on a whisky sauce, Garlic King Prawns, Albany Trio. **Rooms:** 20 bedrooms, all en suite. **Credit cards:** Visa, Access. **Other points:** licensed, open-air dining, Sunday lunch, children catered for – please check for age limits, conferences, pets allowed, residents' lounge. **Directions:** city centre, behind bus station and St James Centre.
PAULINE MARIDOR, tel (031) 556 0397, fax (031) 557663.

### ARD THOR, 10 Mentone Terrace

*A Victorian villa in unique 'terrace within a terrace' location. Modern amenities with 19th century character and elegance. Quiet residential area with good shopping facilities and Queen's Park and Commonwealth pool nearby. Easy access from main roads (A1, A68 and A7) and to city centre attractions.*
*ACCOMMODATION under £20*
**Hours:** breakfast 8am – 8:30am. **Cuisine:** breakfast. **Rooms:** 3 bedrooms all with tea making facilities, TV: 1 single, 1 double, 1 twin. **Other points:** central heating, children catered for – please check for age limits. **Directions:** west side of Minto St near Craigmillar Park Church via Mentone Gardens.
MRS A H TELFER, tel (031) 667 1647.

### BRUNSWICK HOTEL, Brunswick Street

*A centrally situated listed Georgian town house only a short walk from all transport facilities. Close to town centre. A friendly welcome from family owners.*
*ACCOMMODATION £21–£30*
**Hours:** open all year 8am; breakfast 8:30am – 9am. **Cuisine:** breakfast. **Rooms:** 10 bedrooms all with tea making facilities, TV: 4 doubles ensuite, 3 twins ensuite, 2 family rooms ensuite, 1 single ensuite. **Credit cards:** Visa, Access, AmEx. **Other points:** central heating, children catered for – please check for age limits, no evening meal, residents' lounge, street parking, vegetarian meals. **Directions:** in north east Edinburgh around the corner from the Playhouse Theatre.
MRS FREIDA MCGOVERN, tel (031) 556 1238, fax (031) 556 1238.

## CELLAR NO 1, 1a Chambers Street

*A characteristic bistro style wine bar with bare wooden floorboards and offering an interesting selection of dishes, including vegetarian, and an extensive choice of wines, spirits, liqueurs, beers and real ales.*

*FOOD up to £15*

**Hours:** bar meals 11:30am – 12midnight; lunch 12noon – 2:30pm; dinner 6pm – 10pm; closed Sunday. **Cuisine:** international:- A la carte menu. Jambalaya, Persian Style Lamb, Baked Salmon Fillet, Scampi Boscaiola. Vegetarian dishes. Extensive wine list. Booking advised. **Credit cards:** Visa, Access. **Other points:** licensed, vegetarian meals, bank holidays, parking. **Directions:** from east end of Princes St, go south along N & S Bridge, second on right. NIGEL MACLARDIE, tel (031) 220 4298.

## GLENERNE GUEST HOUSE, 4 Hampton Terrace, West Coates

*A friendly, family run guest house on the main Glasgow – Edinburgh Road yet with a quiet rear aspect. A detached Victorian villa, it is only 15 minutes walk from the centre of Edinburgh. Glenerne enjoys a friendly, welcoming atmosphere and is popular with holiday-makers, weekenders visiting Edinburgh and business travellers alike. Comfortable accommodation.*

*ACCOMMODATION £21–£30*

**Hours:** breakfast 8am – 9:30am. **Cuisine:** breakfast. **Rooms:** 5 bedrooms all with tea making facilities, TV: 1 twin, 2 doubles, 2 doubles ensuite. **Other points:** children catered for – please check for age limits, pets allowed, vegetarian meals. **Directions:** on main A8 Glasgow/Edinburgh road, about 1 mile west of city centre. M BALLENTYNE, tel (031) 337 1210.

## LANCERS BRASSERIE, 5 Hamilton Place

*Lancers Brasserie have a good selection of French and Indian dishes at reasonable prices. Their warm welcome and helpful, efficient staff, will make eating here a pleasureable experience.*

*FOOD £15–£20*

**Hours:** lunch 12noon – 2:30pm; dinner 5:30pm – 11:30pm. **Cuisine:** Indian:- Bengali and north Indian dishes, Kurji lamb (48 hours notice), Vegetarian Thali, Lancers assorted Tandoori, selection of French dishes. **Credit cards:** Visa, Access, Diners, AmEx. **Other points:** open-air dining, Sunday lunch, children catered for – please check for age limits. **Directions:** in Stockbridge area of the city. WALI UDDIN, tel (031) 332 3444, (031) 332 9559.

## THE OLD BORDEAUX, 47 Old Burdiehouse Road

*The principles of good food and friendly, efficient service in comfortable surroundings can be found at this pub on Edinburgh's southern boundary. Transformed from an original abode of exiled French silk weavers into today's warm, welcoming old world Inn, the Old Bordeaux is well worth a visit for its good food and service and very good value for money.*

*FOOD up to £15*

**Hours:** closed Christmas day 5:30pm; closed New Years day 5:30pm; bar meals 10am – 10pm. **Cuisine:** British:- An extensive choice of dishes such as Fresh mussels, Roast Beef, Steak Pie, Daily specials include game. Sea Bass, salmon, slads and vegetarian meals. **Credit cards:** Visa, Access, Diners, AmEx. **Other points:** licensed, Sunday lunch, children catered for – please check for age limits. **Directions:** A701. 5 miles south of city centre, adjacent to A720 city bypass. LINDA & ALAN THOMSON & ADRIAN DEMPSEY, tel (031) 664 1734.

## OSBOURNE HOTEL & SHELBOURNE LOUNGE, 53–59 York Place

*A city centre hotel, ideally located near the main coach and rail stations and only a short walk from the castle, Palace, Royal Mile, Princes Street shops and gardens. The dining room offers meals to residents and groups. Visitors receive a warm welcome and the service is polite and friendly.*

*ACCOMMODATION £31–£40*

*FOOD up to £15*

**Hours:** lunch 12noon – 2pm; dinner 5:30pm – 9pm. **Cuisine:** continental:- Traditional pub meals. continental cuisine. **Rooms:** 40 bedrooms all with tea making facilities, telephone, TV: 3 singles, 10 singles ensuite, 1 double, 13 doubles ensuite, 5 twins ensuite, 8 family rooms ensuite. **Credit cards:** Visa, Access, Diners, AmEx. **Other points:** licensed, children catered for – please check for age limits, pets/prior arr, residents' lounge, residents' bar. **Directions:** in Edinburgh city centre. Follow Queen Street east onto York Place. FEROZ WADIA, tel (031) 556 5577, (031) 556 2345, fax (031) 556 1012.

## ROYAL CIRCUS HOTEL, 19–21 Royal Circus

*This traditionally furnished listed building close to the city centre in a select area offers many modern facilities. At the rear is a garden which provides for alfresco dining and drinking. Other facilities include a Bistro Restaurant, comfortable lounge bar and small function room. Within easy walking distance are the Castle, Royal Mile, Holyrood Palace and Botanical Gardens.*

*ACCOMMODATION £21–£30*

*FOOD up to £15* ★

**Hours:** breakfast 7:30am – 9:30am; lunch 12noon – 2pm; bar meals 12noon – 2pm; dinner 5:30pm – 10pm; bar meals 5:30pm – 10pm. **Cuisine:** continental. **Rooms:** 29 bedrooms all with tea making facilities, telephone, TV: 6 twins, 2 doubles, 11 twins ensuite, 7 doubles ensuite, 1 triple, 2 triples ensuite. **Credit cards:** Visa, Access, Diners, AmEx. **Other points:** children catered for – please check for age limits, afternoon tea, pets allowed, vegetarian meals, garden, functions. **Directions:** from Princes Street head down Fredrick Street and Howe Street to Royal Circus. WADIA, FEROZ, tel (031) 220 5000, fax (031) 220 2020.

## THE TATTLER, 23 Commercial Street, Leith

*This 1992 winner of 'Les Routiers Pub of the Year' is a traditional pub and restaurant – originally four derelict shops in the heart of the historic port of Leith. Tastefully decorated in Victorian/Edwardian style, The Tattler recreates the glory of that era and offers a taste of Scotland to tourists, businessmen and locals alike.*

FOOD up to £15 ☺

**Hours:** closed Christmas day 5:30pm; closed New Years day 5:30pm; meals all day – Sat & Sun 5:30pm; lunch 12noon – 2pm; bar meals – Mon-Fri 12noon – 2pm; dinner 6pm – 10pm; bar meals – Mon-Fri 6pm – 10pm. **Cuisine:** Scottish:- Seafood, curries, casseroles & pies, vegetarian dishes. Border lamb, scampi, steaks, seafood, roast duckling. **Credit cards:** Visa, Access, Diners, AmEx. **Other points:** licensed, Sunday lunch, children catered for – please check for age limits. **Directions:** across from the Leith shore, opposite the historic Customs House.

LINDA & ALAN THOMSON & ADRIAN DEMPSEY, tel (031) 554 9999.

## TERRACE HOTEL, 37 Royal Terrace

*This listed Georgian hotel is beautifully decorated in the style of the era. The bedrooms are large and gracious, with high ceilings and cornices. Fireplaces adorn both the bedrooms and dining room. As this hotel is centrally situated with easy access to most of Edinburgh's attractions, it is well worth a visit, with its panoramic views of the Firth of Forth.*

ACCOMMODATION £21–£30

**Hours:** breakfast 8am – 9am. **Cuisine:** breakfast:- Scottish breakfast – choice of juices and cereals. Eggs cooked to your specifications. Oatcakes, toast, tea or coffee. **Rooms:** 14 bedrooms all with tea making facilities, TV: 1 single, 1 twin, 1 single ensuite, 2 twins ensuite, 3 doubles ensuite, 5 family rooms ensuite, 1 double. **Credit cards:** Visa, Access. **Other points:** bank holidays, residents' lounge, street parking, garden. **Directions:** half mile northeast of Princes Street. Near London Road.

ANNE & MICHAEL MANN, tel (031) 556 3423, fax (031) 556 2520.

## TEX MEX, 47 Hanover Street

*Authentic mix of "Cross Border" Mexican & Texan dishes, all prepared on the premises using only fresh ingredients of the highest quality. The restaurant and bar are decorated with bright colours and subtle lighting giving the feeling of being in sunnier climes! Situated just off Princes Street, there is a constant flow of people and the restaurant tends to get very full in the evenings. Booking is essential on Friday & Saturday nights, and advisable on other evenings.*

FOOD up to £15

**Hours:** meals all day 12noon – 12midnight; closed Christmas; closed New Years day. **Cuisine:** Mexican / American:- Mexican/American dishes: eg. nachos, flautas, carnitas, tortillas, burgers, home-made desserts and a wide selection of vegetarian meals. House Speciality – FLAMING FAJITAS. **Credit cards:** Visa, Access, AmEx,

Switch. **Other points:** Sunday lunch, children catered for – please check for age limits. **Directions:** situated just off Princes Street, opposite The Mound.

DONALD & SARAH MAVOR, tel (031) 225 1796, fax (031) 557 5585.

## THE TOWN HOUSE, 65 Gilmore Place

*A Victorian terraced town house on three floors. Built in 1876 as the manse for the church next door. Gilmore Place is situated opposite the King's Theatre and is within easy walking distance (15 minutes) of the city centre. It is also well placed on three city centre bus routes.*

ACCOMMODATION £21–£30

**Hours:** open all year New Years day; breakfast 8am – 9am. **Cuisine:** breakfast. **Rooms:** 5 bedrooms all with tea making facilities, TV: 1 single, 1 twin ensuite, 1 twin, 1 double ensuite, 1 triple ensuite. **Other points:** central heating, no evening meal, children catered for – please check for age limits, Scottish Tourist Board – 2 crown, baby sitting, left luggage, parking. **Directions:** take A702 towards city centre, turn left at the Kings Theatre.

MRS SUSAN VIRTUE, tel (031) 229 1985.

## VERANDAH TANDOORI RESTAURANT, 17 Dalry Road

*Winner of the Casserole Award 1988, 1989, 1990, 1991, 1992 and 1993. The Verandah Restaurant is one of Edinburgh's most popular eating establishments offering authentic Bangladeshi dishes. The light wicker chairs, and the matching timber blinds further enhance the Restaurant's already relaxed atmosphere.*

FOOD up to £15 ☺

**Hours:** lunch 12noon – 2:15pm; dinner 5pm – 11:45pm. **Cuisine:** Indian:- Lamb pasanda, chicken tikka massalla, tandoori mixed. **Credit cards:** Visa, Access, Diners, AmEx. **Other points:** Sunday lunch, children catered for – please check for age limits. **Directions:** close to Haymarket station in Edinburgh.

WALI TASAR UDDIN, tel (031) 337 5828, fax (031) 313 3853.

# EDZELL, Tayside Map 22

## PANMURE ARMS HOTEL, High Street

*Behind its imposing facade, the Panmure Arms Hotel offers good food and warm hospitality. The accommodation is comfortable and a lively atmosphere prevails.*

ACCOMMODATION £31–£40

FOOD up to £15

**Hours:** breakfast 7:30am – 9:30am; lunch 12noon – 2pm; Sunday roast 12:30pm – 7pm; bar meals 12:30pm – 9:30pm; supper 6:30pm – 9:30pm; dinner 7pm – 9pm. **Cuisine:** Scottish:- Traditional Scottish cooking. Adventurous menu and large portions. Good value for money. **Rooms:** 24 bedrooms 15 doubles ensuite, 2 family rooms ensuite, 5 twins ensuite, 2 singles ensuite. **Credit cards:** Visa, Access, Diners, AmEx. **Other points:** licensed, Sunday lunch, children catered for –

please check for age limits, pets allowed, residents' lounge, bank holidays. **Directions:** on main road through village.
MR CALE, tel (0356) 648420, fax (0356) 648588.

## FORFAR, Tayside Map 22

### ROYAL HOTEL, Castle Street
*Fine old coaching house in the centre of historic Forfar. All rooms are tastefully appointed with en suite facilities. The proprietors, both local, take special pride in making sure their guests enjoy excellent food in comfortable surroundings. The accommodation is being extended, with more rooms available from August 1994.*
ACCOMMODATION £31–£40
FOOD up to £15 ★
**Hours:** breakfast 7am – 10am; lunch 12noon – 2pm; dinner 7pm – 9pm. **Cuisine:** British:- Specialities include light fish mousse made from Arbroath Smokies, Prime Angus Sirloin Steak, Venison and Salmon from local rivers. **Rooms:** 5 single, 8 twin, 5 double, 1 family room, all en suite. 'royal suite' with four poster bed. **Credit cards:** Visa, Access, Diners, AmEx. **Other points:** licensed, Sunday lunch, children catered for – please check for age limits, garden, gym facilities, Jacuzzi, swimming pool, functions, conferences. **Directions:** off the A94, situated in the centre of Forfar.
ALISON & BRIAN BONNYMAN, tel (0307) 462691, fax (0307) 462691.

## FORT AUGUSTUS, Highlands Map 24

### THE BRAE HOTEL
*Originally a Church Manse, and standing in its own landscaped grounds, this hotel offers a quiet, relaxing atmosphere, with good food and drink. Some rooms offer a commanding view over the lochs nearby. The main nearby tourist attraction, is that of Loch Ness, famous with monster hunters.*
ACCOMMODATION £21–£30
FOOD £15–£20
**Hours:** breakfast 8:15am – 9:15am; dinner 7pm – 8:30pm. **Cuisine:** British / international:- Table d'hote menu, offering an imaginative selection of both national and international dishes of a very high standard, beautifully presented. **Rooms:** 8 bedrooms all with tea making facilities, TV: 2 twins ensuite, 3 doubles ensuite, 1 double, 2 singles. **Credit cards:** Visa, Access. **Other points:** licensed, no-smoking area, vegetarian meals, special diets, children catered for – please check for age limits, residents' lounge, pets allowed, parking. **Directions:** on A82, 200 yd off main road to the left of village.
ANDREW & MARI REIVE, tel (0320) 6289.

## FORT WILLIAM, Highlands Map 24

### ISLES OF GLENCOE HOTEL & LEISURE CENTRE, Ballachulish
*The hotel nestles on the side of a peninsula reaching into Loch Leven and affording stunning views of sky,*

*mountain and loch. The hotel offers spacious, well-appointed accommodation, good food and leisure facilities. Watersports, walking and climbing can all be enjoyed, and there is an informal Bistro Bar in which to relax during the evenings.*
ACCOMMODATION £31–£40
FOOD up to £15
**Hours:** breakfast 8am – 10am; bar meals 11am – 10pm; dinner 6pm – 10pm. **Cuisine:** Scottish / continental:- Exciting & varied Brasserie Menu, also featuring Traditional Scottish cuisine using fresh local produce, including Venison. Restaurant & bistro bar. **Rooms:** 39 bedrooms all with tea making facilities, telephone, TV: 17 twins ensuite, 9 doubles ensuite, 7 singles ensuite, 6 family rooms ensuite. **Credit cards:** Visa, Access. **Other points:** licensed, open-air dining, no-smoking area, children catered for – please check for age limits, afternoon tea, pets allowed, garden, leisure centre, swimming pool, residents' lounge, residents' bar, foreign exchange, disabled access, vegetarian meals, parking. **Directions:** A82 Glasgow – Fort William Road. On the Loch side at Ballachulish.
MR LAURENCE YOUNG, tel (08552) 602, fax (08552) 629.

### NEVISPORT RESTAURANT, High Street
*Situated in the Nevisport complex which also includes a large mountaineering/sports shop and a craft and books department featuring many local crafts. Cafeteria-style system and Climers Bar which is the newest addition to the complex. Pull up a chair in front of the open fire and relax. The bar serves snacks, meals and real ales.*
FOOD up to £15
**Hours:** meals all day – summer 9am – 7:30pm; meals all day – winter 9am – 5pm. **Cuisine:** Scottish:- Scottish influenced dishes, eg. pan-fried Lochy trout. **Credit cards:** Visa, Access, Diners, AmEx. **Other points:** licensed, children catered for – please check for age limits. **Directions:** on the A82 within the Nevisport complex on the high street.
IAIN SYKES & IAIN SUTHERLAND, tel (0397) 704921.

## FREUCHIE, Fife Map 22

### THE LOMOND HILLS HOTEL,
*Parliament Square*
*Set in the quiet, picturesque village in the Howe of Fife, at the foot of the Lomond hills, this is a comfortable hotel dating back to 1753 and now upgraded to a high standard. Intimate candlelit restaurant, comfortable lounges, 4 poster bedrooms, and a leisure centre which is free for guests use. An ideal centre for guests.*
ACCOMMODATION £31–£40
FOOD up to £15
**Hours:** breakfast 7:30am – 9am; breakfast 7:30am – 9am; bar snacks 12noon – 2:15pm; bar snacks 12noon – 2:15pm; lunch 12:30pm – 2pm; lunch 12:30pm – 2pm; bar snacks 6pm – 10pm; bar snacks 6pm – 10pm; dinner 7pm – 9:15pm; dinner 7pm – 9:15pm. **Cuisine:** British /

continental:- A la carte menu with special menu of flambed dishes. **Rooms:** 24 bedrooms all with tea making facilities, telephone, TV: 4 family rooms ensuite, 2 singles ensuite, 8 doubles ensuite, 10 twins ensuite. **Other points:** parking, children catered for – please check for age limits, Sunday lunch, open bank holidays, disabled access, pets allowed, residents' lounge, vegetarian meals, residents' garden, licensed, residents' bar, swimming pool. **Directions:** in centre of Fife, near Folkland, 14 miles from Kinross.
VAN BEUSEKOM, ERNST, tel (0337) 857329, fax (0337) 857498.

## GAIRLOCH, Highlands Map 24

### MILLCROFT HOTEL, Strath
*Small family-run hotel in centre of village, with magnificent views of the mountains, islands and sea. Comfortable rooms and quality cooking, with an Italian head chef. Places of interest nearby include Inverewe gardens, Gairloch Heritage museum and Peinn Eighe National Nature Reserve.*
*ACCOMMODATION £31–£40*
*FOOD £15–£20*
**Hours:** breakfast 8am – 9:30am; lunch 12noon – 2pm; bar meals 12noon – 10pm; dinner 6pm – 9pm. **Cuisine:** Scottish / Italian:- Good choice using local produce. ie. fresh local salmon, venison, Home baking and home-made jams when available. **Rooms:** 4 rooms, all en suite. **Credit cards:** Visa, Access. **Other points:** licensed, Sunday lunch, children catered for – please check for age limits, bank holidays. **Directions:** take B8021 off main road, signposted Melvaig. Hotel half mile along.
BERNARDI HOWES, tel (0445) 2376.

### MYRTLE BANK HOTEL, Low Road
*The Myrtle Bank is a small, family owned and personally run hotel, renowned for its friendly Highland welcome and personal service. Nestling amongst the unique and dramatic beauty of western Ross, it offers attractively furnished, fully equipped bedrooms, some of which overlook the sea. An elegantly furnished residents' lounge provides a quiet spot to relax with a drink or favourite book. An outstanding base for those who want to 'get away from it all'.*
*FOOD up to £15*
**Hours:** closed Christmas day 6pm; closed New Years day 6pm; breakfast 8am – 9am; lunch 12:30pm – 2pm; bar snacks 12:30pm – 2pm; bar snacks 6:30pm – 9pm; dinner 7pm – 9pm. **Cuisine:** Scottish. **Credit cards:** Visa, Access. **Other points:** children catered for – please check for age limits, no-smoking area, pets, residents' lounge, vegetarian meals, parking. **Directions:** in centre of Gairloch opposite school.
MR & MRS MACLEAN, tel (0445) 2004, fax (0445) 2214.

### STEADING RESTAURANT, Achtercairn
*A coffee house restaurant in a delightful converted 19th century farm building, which retains much of its olde worlde atmosphere. Adjoining the award winning Gairloch*

*Museum of west Highland Life, it offers good food using local fresh produce such as seafood and venison. Self-service by day and waitress service in evenings.*
*FOOD £21–£25*
**Hours:** breakfast 9am – all day; lunch 9am – 6pm; dinner 6pm – 9pm; closed Sunday October – March. **Cuisine:** Scottish:- Fresh local seafood and venison. Home baked cakes and scones. **Other points:** parking, children catered for – please check for age limits, open bank holidays, afternoon tea, disabled access, vegetarian meals. **Directions:** A832. From Inverness 80 miles. At junction of A832 and B8031 in centre of Gairloch.
MR W R MURDOCH, tel (0445) 2449.

### WHINDLEY GUEST HOUSE, Auchtercairn
*A comfortable modern guest house, with glorious views over Gairloch Bay, that offers their guests fresh home baked bread, warm comfortable bedrooms and a relaxing atmosphere. Ideal holiday guest house where you can relax with breakfast in bed before your day at the golf course or on the beach, both only a few minutes drive away. Special winter breaks featuring spinning & weaving courses.*
*ACCOMMODATION £21–£30*
**Hours:** breakfast 8:30am – 9:15am; lunch 12:30pm – 2pm; dinner 7pm – 8pm. **Cuisine:** Scottish. **Rooms:** 4 bedrooms, all en suite, colour TV, special winter breaks for the elderly who require care. **Other points:** children catered for – please check for age limits, residents' lounge, vegetarian meals, special diets, picnic lunches, garden, patio. **Directions:** up hill as you leave Gairloch on A832 towards Poolewe.
MICK & ELIZABETH PARK, tel (0445) 2340.

## GALASHIELS, Borders Map 20

### ABBOTSFORD ARMS HOTEL, 63 Stirling Street
*A beautifully modernised family hotel 32 miles south of Edinburgh. Completely refurbished to a high standard.*
*ACCOMMODATION £21–£30*
*FOOD up to £15*
**Hours:** breakfast 8am – 10am; meals all day 12noon – 9pm. **Cuisine:** Scottish:- Steak, chicken dishes. **Rooms:** 14 bedrooms all with tea making facilities, TV: 1 single, 2 singles ensuite, 3 twins, 2 twins ensuite, 3 doubles ensuite, 3 family rooms ensuite. **Credit cards:** Visa, Access. **Other points:** licensed, Sunday lunch, children catered for – please check for age limits, coach/prior arr. **Directions:** in Galashiels, opposite the bus station.
JAMES GORDON & CHRISTINA WILSON SCOTT, tel (0896) 2517, fax (0896) 50744.

### HERGES, 58 Island Street
*Karen and Sandy Craig offer imaginative, good value cuisine in a very friendly and relaxed atmosphere. A former yarn brokers store, Herges has been expertly converted to form this attractive continental-style wine bar. The service is most courteous and efficient, and all dishes freshly cooked to a high standard.*
*FOOD up to £15* CLUB

**Hours:** closed Monday all day 12noon; last orders 12noon – 9:30pm; open from 5.00pm Sunday 12noon; lunch 12noon – 2:30pm; dinner 6pm – 12midnight. **Cuisine:** continental:- Dishes may include Baked Rainbow Trout, Roast Gigot of Lamb, Supreme of Chicken Marango. Also lighter snacks such as filled baked potatoes & croissants. **Credit cards:** Visa, Access. **Other points:** licensed, Sunday lunch, no-smoking area, children catered for – please check for age limits. **Directions:** A72 to Peebles, near B & Q superstore.
KAREN & SANDY CRAIG, tel (0896) 50400.

## GATEHOUSE OF FLEET,
Dumfries & Galloway Map 23

### MURRAY ARMS HOTEL, *High Street*
*A warm, welcoming inn where Robert Burns wrote 'Scots Wha Hae'. Gatehouse-of-Fleet is one of Scotland's scenic heritage areas surrounded by unspoilt countryside. Residents enjoy free golf, tennis and fishing.*
*ACCOMMODATION £31–£40*
*FOOD up to £15*
**Hours:** meals all day 12noon – 9:45pm. **Cuisine:** Scottish:- Galloway beef, locally caught fish and smoked salmon, Scottish lamb, home-made soups and pate. Vegetarians catered for. **Rooms:** 13 bedrooms all with tea making facilities, telephone, TV: 1 single ensuite, 1 family room ensuite, 5 twins ensuite, 6 doubles ensuite. **Credit cards:** Visa, Access, Diners, AmEx. **Other points:** Sunday lunch, no-smoking area, children catered for – please check for age limits, disabled access, residents' lounge, residents' bar. **Directions:** Off A75, 60 miles west of Carlisle between Dumfries and Stranraer.
MURRAY ARMS HOTEL LTD, tel (0557) 814207, fax (0557) 814370.

## GLASGOW, Strathclyde Map 21

### AMRITSAR TANDOORI, *9 Kirk Road, Bearsdon*
*A popular and attractively furnished restaurant, situated just off the A808 and serving traditional tandoori dishes. An interesting computer displays dishes visually in colour. Good location from which to explore the nearby historic Roman baths.*
*FOOD up to £15*
**Hours:** dinner 5pm – 12midnight. **Cuisine:** Indian. **Credit cards:** Visa, Access, Diners, AmEx. **Other points:** children catered for – please check for age limits, open bank holidays, no-smoking area, vegetarian meals. **Directions:** just off A808. Kirk Road is just off Bearsden Cross.
M SINGH, tel (041) 942 7710.

### THE ARGYLL HOTEL, *973 Sauchiehall Street*
*This beautifully refurbished Georgian terrace hotel also disguises a particularly fine traditional and Italian restaurant, Scoffs. Whether staying for business or pleasure, the Argyll offers a warm, friendly atmosphere, newly refurbished and spacious rooms and efficient well trained staff. Close to the Scottish Exhibition Centre, Art Gallery, Museum and Kelvin Hall Sports Arena.*
*ACCOMMODATION £21–£30*
*FOOD up to £15*
**Hours:** breakfast 7am – 9:30am; lunch 12noon – 2pm; dinner 5:30pm – 9:30pm. **Cuisine:** British / Italian:- Scoffs Restaurant offers a wide choice of dining, from traditional to Italian style cuisine, including many gourmet specialities. Vegetarian dishes. **Rooms:** 34 bedrooms all with tea making facilities, TV: 7 singles, 6 twins ensuite, 14 doubles ensuite, 5 triples ensuite, 2 quads ensuite. **Credit cards:** Visa, Access, AmEx. **Other points:** licensed, children catered for – please check for age limits, residents' lounge, bank holidays, functions, street parking. **Directions:** exit Junction 18 of the M8 motorway. Turn right at end of Berkeley St.
IAN ALLISON, tel (041) 337 3313, fax (041) 337 3283.

### CATHAY CUISINE, *Rouken Glen Park, Giffnock*
*A fully-licensed traditional Peking and Cantonese restaurant, serving authentic food to delight any gourmet palate in the finest surroundings. The dining room is magnificently decorated in Charles Rennie Mackintosh design throughout, a style which creates the perfect ambience for any occasion.*
*FOOD £21–£25* ♀
**Hours:** lunch 12noon – 2:30pm; dinner 5pm – 11:30pm. **Cuisine:** Cantonese / Pekinese:- Traditional Peking and Cantonese of the highest standard. A la Carte and Table d'Hote. Vegetarian Menu also available. **Credit cards:** Visa, Access, Diners, AmEx. **Other points:** licensed, Sunday lunch, children catered for – please check for age limits, parking, bank holidays. **Directions:** off junction of A77 and A726 Roukenglen Road at Giffnock.
FRANCIS CHOW, tel (041) 620 0888, fax (041) 602 6988.

### EWINGTON HOTEL, *132 Queen's Drive*
*Ideally situated overlooking Queen's Park in u Victorian crescent, this historically listed terraced hotel offers accommodation of a high standard complemented by good food and an excellent wine list. For business people and tourists "the Ewington" is a friendly hotel to stay in. Golfing parties catered for. Convenient for Burrell Gallery.*
*ACCOMMODATION £31–£40*
*FOOD up to £15* ♀ 🍽 [CLUB]
**Hours:** breakfast 7am – 9:30am; lunch 12:30pm – last orders 2pm; dinner 6pm – last orders 9pm. **Cuisine:** international / Scottish:- All prepared on premises from fresh produce daily including vegetarian dishes. Excellent wine list. **Rooms:** 42 bedrooms all with tea making facilities, telephone, radio, TV: 12 singles ensuite, 21 twins ensuite, 8 doubles ensuite, 1 triple ensuite. **Credit cards:** Visa, Access, Diners, AmEx. **Other points:** licensed, children catered for – please check for age limits, pets allowed, afternoon tea, open

all year, conferences, room-service, baby-listening device, trouser-press, hair dryers, residents' lounge, residents' bar, parking, vegetarian meals. **Directions:** take Junction 20 from M8 on to A77, through 4 sets of lights, then second left is Queen's Drive. MARIE-CLARE WATSON (GENERAL MANAGER), tel (041) 423 1152, fax (041) 422 2030.

### LA FIORENTINA, *2 Paisley Road West*
*Situated in the west end of Glasgow, dining at La Fiorentina makes you feel you are in the Italian Riviera, surrounded by paintings and mirrors reflecting from one to the other, seaside and villages. You are dining in a friendly atmosphere, decorated and maintained to high class standard. The specialities of the house include, Fish-Veal Pasta, Seafood dishes and vegetarian, complemented by an extensive wine list.*
*FOOD up to £15* ☺
**Hours:** closed Monday 6pm; lunch 12noon – 2:15pm; dinner 5:30pm – 11pm. **Cuisine:** Italian. **Credit cards:** Visa, Access, Diners, AmEx. **Other points:** parking, disabled access, vegetarian meals, children catered for – please check for age limits.
MR PIEROTTI, tel (041) 420 1585, fax (041) 420 3090.

### LA RIVIERA RISTORANTE,
*147 Dumbarton Road*
*To experience a taste of the Italian Riviera while in Glasgow, La Riviera is a must. From the decor to the food and service the atmosphere is true Italian. An extensive wine list complements the impressive menu.*
*FOOD up to £15*
**Hours:** lunch 12noon – 2:15pm; dinner 5:30pm – 10:30pm. **Cuisine:** Italian / international:- Traditional Italian and international cuisine, seafood a speciality. **Credit cards:** Visa, Access, Diners, AmEx. **Directions:** situated in the west end of Glasgow.
MR PIEROTTI, tel (041) 334 8494.

### TURBAN TANDOORI RESTAURANT,
*2 Station Road, Giffnock*
*One of Scotland's finest tandoori restaurants in a residential suburb of Glasgow.*
*FOOD up to £15*
**Hours:** closed Christmas 5:30pm; dinner 5pm – 12midnight. **Cuisine:** Indian:- Tandoori dishes. **Credit cards:** Visa, Access, AmEx. **Other points:** Sunday lunch, children catered for – please check for age limits, coach/prior arr. **Directions:** close to the A726 and the A77.
KURBIR PUREWAL, tel (041) 638 0069.

# GLENBORRODALE, Highlands Map 24

### GLENBORRODALE CASTLE,
*Glenborrodale, By Acharacle*
*Everything you would expect from a first Class establishment can be found here at Glenborrodale, a wonderful place for relaxation. Enjoying a fine reputation for its good home cooking and well chosen wines, it is considered by many to be one of Scotland's*

*loveliest castles in an unrivalled setting. A truly perfect escape from the everyday pressures of modern life.*
*ACCOMMODATION over £50*
*FOOD £15–£20*
**Hours:** breakfast 8am – 10am; lunch 12:30pm – 2pm; dinner 7pm – 9pm; closed 31/10 – Easter. **Cuisine:** Scottish:- Table d'hote, using the very best of local produce: fruit and vegetables from the kitchen gardens, salmon, trout, shellfish, and game. **Rooms:** 16 bedrooms all with tea making facilities, telephone, radio, TV: 4 twins ensuite, 12 doubles ensuite. **Credit cards:** Visa, Access, AmEx. **Other points:** licensed, Sunday lunch, no-smoking area, children catered for – please check for age limits, fishing, shooting, beauty therapy, cots, left luggage. **Directions:** 41 miles west of Fort William on Ardnamurchan Peninsula.
CHARLES KINSLEY CARROLL, tel (09724) 266, fax (09724) 224.

# GLENFINNAN, Highlands Map 24

### THE STAGE HOUSE
*Originally an old staging post on the Road to the Isles, this stone built building has enormous character with a good homely atmosphere. The cuisine is mostly local using the freshest of produce, complemented by a fine Wine list. Ideal location for those seeking to get away from the pressures of modern day life.*
*ACCOMMODATION £21–£30*
*FOOD £15–£20*
**Hours:** breakfast 8am – 9am; bar meals 12:30pm – 2:30pm; bar meals 5pm – 9pm; diner 6:30pm – 8:30pm. **Cuisine:** Scottish:- Table d'hote and a la carte menus, offering salmon, venison, trout and fresh shellfish. **Rooms:** 9 bedrooms all with tea making facilities, telephone, mini bar, TV: 3 twins ensuite, 6 doubles ensuite. **Credit cards:** Visa, Access. **Other points:** licensed, no-smoking area, bank holidays, pets allowed, residents' lounge, afternoon tea, children catered for – please check for age limits, residents' bar, swimming pool, vegetarian meals, parking. **Directions:** on the main Fort William/Mallaig road in the centre of Glenfinnan.
ROBERT & CAROLE HAWKES, tel (0397) 722246, fax (0397) 722307.

# GLENLIVET, Grampian Map 22

### MINMORE HOUSE
*Formerly the residence of George Smith, the founder of Glenlivet Whisky, this is a family run hotel with a relaxed atmosphere, log fires, fresh flowers and an abundance of peace and quiet. Surrounded by 4 acres of secluded walled gardens, the comfortable bedrooms are named after local Speyside malts. Hearty breakfasts begin the day, followed by sumptuous afternoon teas and a 5-Course dinner as the finale, offering fresh salmon to fillet of venison. Glorious views over the glens.*
*ACCOMMODATION £31–£40*
*FOOD £15–£20*
**Hours:** breakfast 7:30am – 10am; bar snacks 12noon – 1:30pm; dinner 8pm – 8:30pm; closed November – April. **Cuisine:** Scottish. **Credit cards:** Visa, Access.

**Other points:** no-smoking area, parking, children catered for – please check for age limits, disabled access, pets, residents' lounge, garden, vegetarian meals. **Directions:** A95 from Grantown, 15 miles and turn right onto B9008 – follow signs to the Glenlivet Distillery. We are adjacent. BELINDA LUXMOORE, tel (0807) 590 378, fax (0807) 590 472.

# GLENMORISTON, Highlands Map 24

## CLUANIE INN

*A converted coaching house, this Inn offers good farmhouse cooking, comfortable accommodation and a warm welcome. With many beautiful walks through the mountains and glens, salmon and trout fishing, this is the ideal place to return to at the end of the day with its cosy, relaxing atmosphere, fitness centre including sauna, and the very best in comfort. Highly recommended.*
*ACCOMMODATION £31–£40*
*FOOD £15–£20*
**Hours:** breakfast 8am – 9:30am; lunch 12noon – 2:30pm; dinner 6pm – 9pm. **Cuisine:** Scottish:- Good farmhouse-style cooking. **Rooms:** 11 bedrooms, all ensuite. **Credit cards:** Visa, Access. **Other points:** licensed, Sunday lunch, children catered for – please check for age limits, bank holidays, pets allowed, garden, gym facilities, fishing. **Directions:** midway between Loch Ness and the ferry terminal to Isle of Skye.
MR JOHN DOUGLAS CLINTON, tel (0320) 40238.

# GLENROTHES, Fife Map 22

## TOWN HOUSE HOTEL, 1 High Street, Markinch

*A family-run hotel bringing together traditional values and quality. Centrally situated in the Kingdom of Fife, ideal for sporting breaks and for family holidays. The Town House Hotel provides a warm welcome and good value for money.*
*ACCOMMODATION £21–£30*
*FOOD up to £15*
**Hours:** breakfast 7am – 9am; lunch 12noon – 2pm; dinner 6:15pm – 8:30pm. **Cuisine:** international:- Dishes may include Chicken Stir-Fry, Tay Salmon Fillet, Chicken Tikka, Chinese Sweet & Sour Pork, grilled steaks. **Rooms:** 4 bedrooms all with tea making facilities, TV: 1 single, 1 single ensuite, 2 doubles ensuite. **Credit cards:** Visa, Access, Diners, AmEx. **Other points:** licensed, Sunday lunch, no-smoking area, children catered for – please check for age limits, pets allowed, special breaks, parking. **Directions:** B9130, opposite railway station in Markinch.
HARRY & LESLEY BAIN, tel (0592) 758459.

# GLENSHEE BY BLAIRGOWRIE, Tayside Map 22

## THE BLACKWATER INN

*Nestling at the base of a steep hill in a landscaped heather and waterfall garden, this quaint old inn gives the impression that you have stepped back in time into Brigadoon! Situated on the main road to Balmoral, there is skiing, golf, fishing, stalking and hang-gliding available nearby.*
*ACCOMMODATION under £20*
*FOOD up to £15* ⓒ
**Hours:** meals all day 6:15pm – 9pm. **Cuisine:** Scottish/Louisiana:- Homemade pies, pastas, curries, and Louisiana style dishes. Daily specials. **Rooms:** 8 bedrooms, 2 en suite. tea/coffee facilities in all rooms. **Credit cards:** Visa, Access. **Other points:** children catered for – please check for age limits, pets allowed. **Directions:** located in the west end of Aberdeen.
IVY BAILEY, tel (0250) 882234.

# GRANTOWN ON SPEY, Highlands Map 24

## THE BEN MHOR HOTEL, High Street

*Comfortable family run hotel in the heart of the Spey Valley. This is an ideal spot for the holiday-maker with an 18 hole golf course, salmon fishing, bowling green and woods nearby. Offering good food and comfortable accommodation.*
*ACCOMMODATION £21–£30*
*FOOD up to £15*
**Hours:** breakfast 8am – 9:30am; lunch 12:30pm – 2pm; bar meals 5:30pm – 9pm; dinner 7pm – 9pm. **Cuisine:** British / continental:- Meals made with an emphasis on local produce whenever possible. Dishes may include salmon en croute with dill sauce, Strathspey venison. **Rooms:** 24 bedrooms all with tea making facilities, radio, TV: 3 singles ensuite, 3 doubles ensuite, 16 twins ensuite, 2 family rooms ensuite. **Credit cards:** Visa, Access. **Other points:** licensed, open-air dining, Sunday lunch, children catered for – please check for age limits, bank holidays, afternoon tea, pets allowed, residents' bar, residents' lounge, foreign exchange, disabled access, vegetarian meals. **Directions:** on the main street in the town centre.
CLIVE & FIONA WILLIAMSON, tel (0479) 872056, fax (0479) 873537.

## CRAGGAN MILL RESTAURANT

*An old watermill, Craggan Mill has a rustic feel with candlelight, wooden tables and interesting relics from when the mill was still operational. All food is fresh and cooked to order by Mr Belleni, the owner. Well cooked food at good value prices and the very best in friendly yet efficient service.*
*FOOD £15–£20*
**Hours:** closed 01/10 – 14/10; dinner 6:30pm – 10pm. **Cuisine:** Italian / British:- House specialities include fillet of venison in a cream sauce. **Credit cards:** Visa, Access. **Other points:** licensed, children catered for – please check for age limits. **Directions:** on A95 Grantown to Aviemore road. 1 mile on south side of Grantown.
MR & MRS B BELLENI, tel (0479) 2288.

## GULLANE, Lothian Map 20

### QUEENS HOTEL, Main Street

*A family-run hotel situated in the picturesque village of Gullane. This is a welcoming and pleasant hotel with a good reputation, high standards, a relaxed atmosphere and friendly service. Golf and other packages are available.*
ACCOMMODATION £31–£40
FOOD up to £15
**Hours:** breakfast 7am – 9am; bar meals 12noon – 10pm; meals all day 7pm – 10pm. **Cuisine:** British:- Dinner menu May feature Beef Wellington, Baked Halibut Steak Caprice, Chicken and Mushroom Crepe au Gratin. Bar meals available all day. **Rooms:** 35 bedrooms all with tea making facilities, telephone, radio, TV: 16 twins ensuite, 3 family rooms, 6 twins – shower only, 10 twins. **Credit cards:** Visa, Access, Diners, AmEx. **Other points:** licensed, open-air dining, Sunday lunch, children catered for – please check for age limits, afternoon tea, residents' lounge, garden. **Directions:** off A1. A6137 Haddington to Aberlady, A198 to Gullane. ANN ROBERTSON, tel (0620) 842275, fax (0620) 842970.

## HALKIRK, Highlands Map 24

### THE ULBSTER ARMS HOTEL, Bridge Street

*Standing on the banks on the Thurso River at the centre of the village of Halkirk, this is a true sporting hotel. Both Shooting and Stalking can be arranged over a wide variety of moors, and also fly fishing on one of Scotland's finest 'Fly Only' salmon rivers. Other outdoor pursuits, include bird-watching, photography, rambling, painting, geology, and much more.*
ACCOMMODATION £31–£40
FOOD up to £15
**Hours:** open all year 7pm; breakfast 8am – 9:30am; lunch 12:30pm – 1:45pm; dinner 7pm – 8:45pm. **Cuisine:** British:- A Table D'Hote menu. Advance booking advisable for both lunch and dinner. **Rooms:** 25 bedrooms all with tea making facilities, telephone, TV: 9 singles ensuite, 3 doubles ensuite, 13 twins ensuite. **Credit cards:** Visa, Access. **Other points:** Sunday lunch, children catered for – please check for age limits, pets allowed, afternoon tea, parking, bank holidays. **Directions:** from Inverness via A9 Perth to Latheronwheel. Turn left onto A895. LOCHDHU HOTELS LTD, tel (084783) 206, (084783) 641, fax (084783) 206/641.

## HAWICK, Borders Map 20

### KIRKLANDS HOTEL, West Stewart Place

*A charming small hotel pleasantly situated in the beautiful Scottish borders. Ideal base for tourists and business people. Close to many attractions. Recommended by most leading hotel guides. Weekly terms and weekend breaks available. Colour brochure and tariff on request.*
ACCOMMODATION £31–£40
FOOD £15–£20
**Hours:** lunch 12noon – 2pm; dinner 7pm – 9:30pm. **Cuisine:** Scottish / continental:- Excellent choice of Scottish and a la carte dishes. Table d'hote and bar meals. Vegetarian dishes. **Rooms:** 12 bedrooms 7 doubles ensuite, 5 twins ensuite. **Credit cards:** Visa, Access, Diners, AmEx. **Other points:** open-air dining, no-smoking area, children catered for – please check for age limits, garden, games room, library. **Directions:** 200 yd off the main A7, a mile north of Hawick High Street. MR B NEWLAND, tel (0450) 72263, fax (0450) 370404.

## HELMSDALE, Highlands Map 24

### BUNILLIDH RESTAURANT, 2–4 Dunrobin Street

*A pleasant family-run restaurant offering good food and friendly service. Fresh lobster and crab from holding tanks complement the seafood specialities. There are spectacular views to be enjoyed all around.*
FOOD up to £15
**Hours:** meals all day 9am – 9pm. **Cuisine:** Scottish:- Good value home cooking. Langostines (local prawn) cooked from live. Drinks licence and full wine list. **Credit cards:** Visa. **Other points:** parking, children catered for – please check for age limits, open bank holidays, no-smoking area, afternoon tea, limited disabled access, vegetarian meals. **Directions:** off A9 just past Visitors Centre, opposite Time Span. EILEEN SHEWARD, tel (04312) 457, fax (04312) 205.

## HILLSWICK, Orkney & Shetland Islands Map 24

### ST MAGNUS BAY HOTEL

*A Norwegian Mansion set amidst the unspoiled coastal scenery of the northmavine region of Shetland and overlooking St Magnus Bay. The accommodation is comfortable and the restaurant provides good meals, with particular emphasis on local seafood. An ideal hotel for families.*
ACCOMMODATION £31–£40
FOOD £15–£20
**Hours:** breakfast 6am – 9am; bar meals 12:30pm – 2pm; bar meals 6:30pm – 9pm. **Cuisine:** Scottish:- Traditional Scottish cuisine with local seafood a speciality. **Rooms:** 27 bedrooms, all en suite. **Credit cards:** Visa, Access. **Other points:** licensed, Sunday lunch, children catered for – please check for age limits, afternoon tea, pets allowed, residents' lounge. **Directions:** A970 – end of road at Hillswick. 40 mins drive from Lerwick. PETER TITCOMB, tel (080623) 372, fax (080623) 373.

## INSCH, Grampian Map 22

### THE LODGE HOTEL, Old Rayne

*This large granite dwelling house is part of a small village with views of rolling hills and nearby fields. The*

*interior is stunning with a relaxed atmosphere finished off with vases of fresh flowers. The fixed price menu is excellent value and all food is freshly prepared.*
ACCOMMODATION £21–£30
*FOOD up to £15*
**Hours:** breakfast 8am – 9am; lunch 12noon – 2:30pm; dinner – weekdays 7pm – 8pm; dinner – weekends 7pm – 9pm. **Cuisine:** English / continental:- A la carte – Half Duckling in Cointreau and Orange, Prawn Marie Rose. **Rooms:** 6 bedrooms all with tea making facilities, telephone, mini bar, TV: 1 twin, 1 family room, 3 twins ensuite, 1 double ensuite. **Credit cards:** Visa, Access, AmEx. **Other points:** licensed, Sunday lunch, children catered for – please check for age limits, pets allowed, vegetarian meals, residents' lounge, residents' bar. **Directions:** off the A96, 9 miles north of Inverurie, 12 miles south of Huntly.
MR & MRS NEIL, tel (04645) 205, (04645) 636.

# INVERGARRY, Highlands Map 24

## INVERGARRY HOTEL
*A family-run, Highland hotel offering comfortable accommodation, good food and friendly service. The interior decor is in keeping with the distinctive and attractive Victorian building and provides comfortable and relaxed surroundings. Well placed to enjoy the beauty of the Scottish Highlands, fishing, golf, skiing or visits to the distilleries.*
ACCOMMODATION £31–£40
*FOOD up to £15* CLUB ★
**Hours:** breakfast 8:15am – 9:30am; meals all day 9am – 7pm; bar meals 12noon – 2pm; bar meals 6pm – 9pm; dinner 7pm – 8:30pm. **Cuisine:** Scottish / international:- Bar meals, self-service restaurant meals, and dinner featuring Scottish and international dishes and using fresh, predominantly local produce. **Rooms:** 10 bedrooms all with tea making facilities, telephone, TV: 1 single ensuite, 3 twins ensuite, 5 doubles ensuite, 1 triple ensuite. **Credit cards:** Visa, Access, AmEx. **Other points:** licensed, Sunday lunch, children catered for – please check for age limits, afternoon tea, pets allowed, residents' lounge, garden, baby-listening device, cots, foreign exchange, residents' bar, vegetarian meals. **Directions:** from A82, take the A87 Road for Kyle of Lochalsh. Hotel on the right.
MACCALLUM FAMILY, tel (08093) 206, fax (08093) 207.

# INVERGORDON, Highlands Map 24

## KINCRAIG HOUSE HOTEL
*Kincraig is a house of outstanding character, parts of which date back several centuries. Standing in its own grounds in an elevated position overlooking Cromarty Firth, it is ideal for both the business traveller and the holiday-maker. Spacious lounges, excellent food and friendly, personal service ensure any stay here is memorable.*
FOOD £15–£20
**Hours:** breakfast as required 7am; bar snacks as required 7pm; lunch 12noon – 2:30pm; dinner 6pm –

10pm. **Cuisine:** British. **Credit cards:** Visa, Access, Diners, AmEx. **Other points:** no-smoking area, children catered for – please check for age limits, parking, pets, disabled access, vegetarian meals, open-air dining, residents' lounge, garden. **Directions:** travel north on the A9 beyond both signs for Invergordon and Alness, and you will find our sign on the left approx. 1 mile beyond the Alness bypass, on the A9.
MR H DIXON, tel (0349) 852587, fax (0349) 852193.

# INVERNESS, Highlands Map 24

## ARDMUIR HOUSE HOTEL, 16 Ness Bank
*A small, family run hotel situated on the east bank of the river Ness a few minutes walk from both the town centre and Ness Islands. The Georgian residence has been improved to meet modern day requirements and all bedrooms have en suite facilities, tea/coffee making facilities, colour TVs and electric blankets. Traditional Scottish fare is served in the dining room.*
ACCOMMODATION £21 – £30
**Hours:** breakfast 8am – 9am; dinner 6:30pm – 7:30pm. **Cuisine:** Scottish. **Rooms:** 1 single, 2 twin, 6 double and 2 family bedrooms, all en suite. **Credit cards:** Visa. **Other points:** children catered for – please check for age limits, garden, pets allowed. **Directions:** off B862 to Loch Ness.
JEAN & TONY GATCOMBE, tel (0463) 231151.

## CULDUTHEL LODGE, 14 Culduthel Road
*A Georgian building set in its own grounds and enjoying views of the River Ness. The resident owners ensure that their guests enjoy a comfortable, relaxing stay. Tastefully decorated and furnished to a very high standard. Ideal touring base.*
ACCOMMODATION £31–£40
*FOOD up to £15*
**Hours:** breakfast 8am – 9am; dinner 7pm – 8pm. **Cuisine:** Scottish:- Table d'hote menu, changes each day offering delicious freshly prepared food. **Rooms:** 12 bedrooms all with tea making facilities, telephone, TV: 1 single ensuite, 1 twin ensuite, 9 doubles ensuite, 1 triple ensuite. **Credit cards:** Visa, Access. **Other points:** pets/prior arr, central heating, children catered for – please check for age limits, cots, left luggage. **Directions:** less than 1 mile from city centre. B861.
DAVID & MARION BONSOR, tel (0463) 240089, fax (0463) 240089.

## HEATHMOUNT HOTEL, Kingsmill Road
*A Victorian style building featuring ornate ceilings and decorative panels. Extremely popular local hostelry with busy restaurant and bars. The river Ness and Inverness Castle are within easy walking distance!*
ACCOMMODATION £21–£30
*FOOD up to £15*
**Hours:** breakfast 8am – 10am; bar meals 12:15pm – 2:15pm; bar meals 5:45pm – 9:15pm. **Cuisine:** Scottish / international:- A good selection from the menu, including the Scottish speciality, Haggis, also meals from the barbecue. Home made pies, pasta and

casseroles. **Rooms:** 4 bedrooms all with tea making facilities, TV: 2 family rooms ensuite, 1 twin ensuite, 1 double ensuite. **Credit cards:** Access, Visa, Switch. **Other points:** parking, children catered for – please check for age limits, Sunday lunch, open bank holidays, disabled access, residents' lounge, vegetarian meals, licensed. **Directions:** follow sign for Hilton Culcabock, left after flyover, right at roundabout, straight through traffic lights, bearing left at mini roundabout. Next set of lights, turn right into Kingsmills Road.
BUXTON, PATRICK & FIONA, tel (0463) 235877, fax (0463) 715749.

## LOCH NESS HOUSE HOTEL, Glen Urquhart Road

*Overlooking Caledonian Canal and the Torvean golf course, this family-owned and run hotel is ideal as a base for discovering the delights of Highland Scotland. A comfortable bar, dining room and residents' lounge await you after a day in the fresh air. Or join the locals in a ceilidh, held here most weekends. Loch Ness House is popular with locals and overseas visitors.*
ACCOMMODATION £31–£40
FOOD up to £15
**Hours:** open all year 5:45pm; breakfast 8am – 9:30am; bar meals 12noon – 2pm; bar meals 5:30pm – 9pm; dinner 7pm – 9pm. **Cuisine:** Scottish:- A la carte and Table d'hote menus, offering traditional and new Scottish recipes, using only the freshest of local produce. Vegetarian dishes available. **Rooms:** 22 bedrooms all with tea making facilities, telephone, radio, TV: 1 single ensuite, 8 twins ensuite, 5 doubles ensuite, 7 triples ensuite, 1 quad ensuite. **Credit cards:** Visa, Access, AmEx. **Other points:** licensed, open-air dining, Sunday lunch, children catered for – please check for age limits, pets allowed, residents' lounge, garden, parking, disabled access, baby-listening device, cots. **Directions:** 1.5 miles west of Inverness city centre on A82.
ALLISTER MILROY, tel (0463) 231248, fax (0463) 239327.

## WHINPARK HOTEL & RESTAURANT, 17 Ardross Street

*Our Inspector noted that this was 'a small, friendly restaurant with bedrooms'. The emphasis in this town house hotel is definitely on high quality food prepared from fresh seasonal ingredients. The hotel is close to central Inverness' shopping area and Eden Court Theatre.*
ACCOMMODATION £21–£30
FOOD up to £15
**Hours:** breakfast 7:30am – 9am; lunch 12noon – 2pm; dinner 6:30pm – 9:30pm. **Cuisine:** British:- A blend of modern and classical food. Smoked salmon mousse, fish soup, roast rack of lamb, steamed roulade of salmon and sole. **Rooms:** 9 bedrooms, 4 en suite. **Credit cards:** Visa, Access. **Other points:** licensed, no-smoking area, children catered for – please check for age limits, pets allowed, functions. **Directions:** city centre.
STEPHEN MACKENZIE, tel (0463) 232549.

## ISLE OF ARRAN, Strathclyde Map 21

### BURLINGTON HOTEL, Whiting Bay

*A small, family-run hotel on the beautiful Isle of Arran, offering comfortable accommodation, a friendly welcome and a wide choice of freshly cooked local produce. Both food and accommodation are excellent value for money. Bargain breaks available October to March. Ideal for walking, golf, sailing and fishing and there are splendid opportunities for both relaxing and adventure.*
ACCOMMODATION £21–£30
FOOD up to £15 CLUB
**Hours:** breakfast 8:30am – 9:30am; dinner 7pm – 9pm. **Cuisine:** British:- Dishes may include local seafood, beef, venison and other local specialities, such as Lamb gigot steak pan fried in cream, and a range of original vegetarian dishes. Traditional Arran cheeses. **Rooms:** 10 bedrooms all with tea making facilities: 1 single, 1 twin ensuite, 2 twins, 4 doubles ensuite, 1 double, 1 triple. **Credit cards:** Visa, Access. **Other points:** licensed, children catered for – please check for age limits, pets allowed, residents' lounge, garden, cots. **Directions:** opposite the beach on the A841 just north of Whiting Bay.
WILF & DIANE INGS, tel (0770) 700255.

### CATACOL BAY HOTEL, Catacol

*Small, comfortable family-run hotel. Seafront location over looking Kilbrannan Sound and Kintyre Peninsula. Ideally based for fishing, climbing, pony trekking, walking, golfing, bird-watching. Island breaks October to April.*
ACCOMMODATION under £20
FOOD £15–£20
**Hours:** bar meals 12noon – 10pm; dinner 6pm – 10pm. **Cuisine:** Scottish:- Steaks, seafood, salmon, duckling. **Rooms:** 6 bedrooms 2 singles, 1 double, 1 twin, 2 family rooms. **Credit cards:** Visa, Access, Diners, AmEx. **Other points:** licensed, open all day, Sunday buffet, children catered for – please check for age limits, pets allowed. **Directions:** on the A841, 1.25 miles south of Lochranza Pier.
DAVID C ASHCROFT, tel (0770) 830231, fax (0770) 830350.

## ISLE OF BARRA, Western Isles Map 24

### CASTLEBAY HOTEL, Castlebay

*A small family run hotel in the main village overlooking the harbour & the Isle of Vatersay. Comfortable accommodation and good food. While visiting here you can enjoy walking, fishing or sailing. If you would rather relax, there are plenty of beautiful, secluded sandy beaches to choose from.*
ACCOMMODATION £31–£40
FOOD £15–£20
**Hours:** breakfast 7:30am – 9:30am; bar meals 11am – 9pm; lunch 12:30pm – 2pm; dinner 6pm – 9pm. **Cuisine:** English:- Traditional cuisine, with an emphasis

on fresh fish. Dishes may include Mussels in White Wine Sauce, Lobster, Chicken Chasseur, Strawberry Gateau. **Rooms:** 12 bedrooms, 8 en suite. **Credit cards:** Visa, Access. **Other points:** licensed, open-air dining, Sunday lunch, children catered for – please check for age limits, afternoon tea, pets allowed, special breaks, foreign exchange, residents' lounge, residents' bar, parking. **Directions:** in the centre of Castlebay.
MR GEORGE MACLEOD, tel (08714) 223.

# ISLE OF BENBECULA, Western Isles Map 24

## DARK ISLAND HOTEL, Liniclate
*Privately owned hotel, offering comfortable, well-appointed accommodation, good food and service. Ideal holiday base, being well-situated for exploring adjacent islands: North Uist, Barra, Eriskay. Golf is available free of charge and there is trout fishing on over 70 lochs. This is also the perfect place to stay if you are a keen archaeologist or ornithologist.*
*ACCOMMODATION £31–£40*
*FOOD £15–£20*
**Hours:** bar meals 12noon; bar meals 6pm – 10pm. **Cuisine:** British:- Taste of Scotland cuisine, specialities sea food and shell fish. Also Laird's game casserole, Ben Mor Mountain Haggis, and Shepherd's Grill. **Rooms:** 44 bedrooms all with tea making facilities, radio, TV: 1 single, 7 singles ensuite, 1 double, 21 doubles ensuite, 13 twins ensuite, 1 family room ensuite. **Credit cards:** Visa, Access. **Other points:** children catered for – please check for age limits, pets allowed, bank holidays, residents' lounge. **Directions:** 4 miles from airport, 26 miles from ferry terminals: Loch Boisdale/Lochmaddy.
MR D J PETERANNA, tel (0870) 603030, fax (0870) 602347.

# ISLE OF COLONSAY, Highlands Map 21

## ISLE OF COLONSAY HOTEL
*There are few places in Britain which offer such a spectacular setting as can be found on Colonsay. A listed building, the hotel enjoys a fine reputation for its comfort, and its cuisine which uses the best of local fresh produce. On Colonsay there is an abundance of wildlife, including Golden Eagles and a major Atlantic seal colony. Important pre-Christian remains and portions of the ancient Caledonian Forest still survive here. A magical place for all ages.*
*ACCOMMODATION £31–£40*
*FOOD £15–£20*
**Hours:** breakfast 8:30am – 9:30am; bar snacks 12:30pm – 1:30pm; bar snacks 7pm – 8:30pm; dinner 7:30pm; closed 5 November – 28 February. **Cuisine:** Scottish / international. **Rooms:** 11 bedrooms all with tea making facilities, TV: 2 doubles ensuite, 4 twins ensuite, 2 family rooms ensuite, 3 singles. **Credit cards:** Visa, Access, Diners, AmEx. **Other points:** parking, children catered for – please check for age limits, open bank holidays, no-smoking area, afternoon tea, disabled access, pets allowed,

residents' lounge, vegetarian meals, garden, residents' bar, foreign exchange. **Directions:** ferry from Oban Mon/Wed/Fri. Hotel is 400yds west of the pier. A courtesy car meets all sailings.
BYRNE, KEVIN & CHRISTA, tel (09512) 316, fax (09512) 353.

# ISLE OF HARRIS, Western Isles Map 24

## THE HARRIS HOTEL
*An established family run hotel. J M Barrie once stayed here and etched his initials in the dining room window. The hotel is a perfect base for touring Harris and Lewis and people return year after year to soak up the history, peace and unspoilt beauty of these dramatic islands.*
*ACCOMMODATION £31–£40*
**Hours:** breakfast 8:30am – 9:15am; lunch 12noon – 2pm; dinner 7:30pm – 9pm. **Cuisine:** British. **Rooms:** 26 bedrooms 4 singles, 1 single ensuite, 1 double, 6 doubles ensuite, 2 twins, 7 twins ensuite, 2 family rooms ensuite. **Credit cards:** Visa, Access. **Other points:** central heating, children catered for – please check for age limits, residents' lounge, garden. **Directions:** on the A859 central to village of Tarbert.
HELEN & JOHN MORRISON, tel (0859) 2154, (0859) 2425.

# ISLE OF IONA, Strathclyde Map 21

## ARGYLL HOTEL
*A friendly hotel, right on the Iona seashore. Cars are not allowed on this tiny unspoilt Isle and must be left at Fionnphort or Oban. Iona, with its brilliant waters, clear light, and wealth of wildlife has inspired poets and painters for centuries. When staying at the Argyll Hotel, guests are also sure to be inspired by the superb home cooking and the comfort of the rooms.*
*ACCOMMODATION £31–£40*
*FOOD £15–£20*
**Hours:** breakfast 8:30am – 9am; closed 10/10 – Easter; lunch 12:30pm – 1:30pm; bar meals 12:30pm – 1:30pm; dinner 7pm. **Cuisine:** Scottish:- Scottish fayre, using fresh local produce, own vegetables in season, and also offering vegetarian dishes made with wholefoods. **Rooms:** 17 bedrooms all with tea making facilities: 6 singles, 4 singles ensuite, 1 double, 1 twin, 3 twins ensuite, 2 family rooms ensuite. **Credit cards:** Visa, Access. **Other points:** Sunday lunch, no-smoking area, children catered for – please check for age limits, pets allowed, bank holidays, residents' lounge, garden. **Directions:** ferry Oban-Craignure. Drive/bus to Fionnphort, then ferry to Iona.
MRS F MENZIES, tel (06817) 334, fax (06817) 334.

# ISLE OF MULL, Strathclyde Map 21

## GLENFORSA HOTEL, Salen, By Aros
*Delightfully situated in 6 acres of secluded woodland, this timber chalet style hotel offers tasty, well presented meals in a warm atmosphere. Accommodation is*

to a high standard. An ideal base for touring, walking, climbing or fishing.
ACCOMMODATION £31–£40
FOOD £15–£20
**Hours:** breakfast 8:30am – 9:30am; bar meals 12noon – 2pm; bar meals 6pm – 8:30pm; dinner 7pm – 8:30pm.
**Cuisine:** English:- Fixed price 3 course menu, bar snacks/meals and vegetarian meals. **Rooms:** 15 rooms. 7 twin, 7 double and 1 family bedroom. all en suite.
**Credit cards:** Visa, Access, AmEx. **Other points:** licensed, no-smoking area, children catered for – please check for age limits, garden, pets allowed. **Directions:** off the ferry turn right, 10 miles along the road.
JEAN & PAUL PRICE, tel (0680) 300377, fax (0680) 300535.

## PENNYGHAEL HOTEL, Pennyghael
An original 17th century farm, this family-run hotel provides a warm, welcoming atmosphere with personal, friendly service in a setting of unparalleled beauty on the shores of Loch Scridain. The restaurant offers spectacular views over the loch. The Island of Mull is a beautiful wilderness of coastline, moorland and mountain, which also boasts two 9 hole golf courses.
ACCOMMODATION £31–£40
FOOD £15–£20
**Hours:** breakfast 8:30am – 9:30am; lunch 11:30am – 6pm; dinner 6:30pm – 8:30pm; closed winter. **Cuisine:** British:- Dinner menu changes daily and offers the best of traditional cooking, including Wild Carsaig Salmon, Prawns, Scallops and Venison. Vegetarian dishes also available by arrangement. **Rooms:** 6 bedrooms all with tea making facilities, telephone, TV: 3 doubles ensuite, 3 twins ensuite. **Credit cards:** Visa, Access. **Other points:** licensed, open-air dining, Sunday lunch, children catered for – please check for age limits, pets allowed, parking, afternoon tea, pets allowed. **Directions:** turn left off ferry from Oban.
JAMES BOWMAN, tel (06814) 288.

## THE WESTERN ISLES HOTEL, Tobermory
A magnificent Gothic style building, personally run and commanding a spectacular position overlooking Tobermory Bay. The rooms also have marvellous views and are superbly furnished offering a high standard of comfort. Excellent menu using fresh local produce, including lobster and venison. Perfect location for those wishing to "get away from it all".
ACCOMMODATION £41–£50
FOOD £21–£25
**Hours:** breakfast 8am – 9.30am; dinner 7pm – 8.30pm; bar snacks 12 noon – 1.45pm; closed 3 January –1 March.
**Cuisine:** British. **Rooms:** 24 ensuite rooms with tea making facilities, telephone, TV. **Credit cards:** Visa, Access, Switch. **Other points:** children catered for – please check for age limits, residents' lounge, no-smoking area, pets, vegetarian meals, garden, parking.
**Directions:** above town of Tobermory.
SUE & MICHAEL FINK, tel (0688) 2012, fax (0688) 2297.

# ISLE OF SKYE, Highlands Map 24

## THE CASTLE MOIL RESTAURANT, Kyleakin
Comfortable restaurant serving reasonably priced snacks, lunches and evening meals. Just 300 yds from Skye ferry terminal, The Castle Moil is worthy of a visit to break your journey and to enjoy a good value meal or snack.
FOOD up to £15
**Hours:** open bank holidays; lunch 12noon – 5pm; dinner 5pm – 9:15pm; breakfast all day; closed November – February. **Cuisine:** British / seafood:- Self service during the day, table service in the evening. House speciality is sea food. Also salads, steaks, grills and all day breakfast. **Credit cards:** Visa, Access. **Other points:** licensed, Sunday lunch, children catered for – please check for age limits, meals all day, coach/prior arr. **Directions:** on the Skye side of the ferry.
ALEXANDER J C MACDIARMID, tel (0599) 4164.

## DUISDALE HOTEL, Isle Ornsay, Sleat
Built in a Scottish hunting lodge style, this family run hotel is set in 25 acres, overlooking the Sound of Sleat. Offering good food and comfortable accommodation, Duisdale is ideal for fishing, walking or observing the wildlife. Frequented by mixed ages, the atmosphere is quiet and peaceful.
ACCOMMODATION £31–£40
FOOD £15–£20 ★
**Hours:** breakfast 8:30am – 9:30am; lunch 12:30pm – 2pm; dinner 7:30pm – 8:30pm. **Cuisine:** Scottish:- Dishes include platter of oak smoked fish, casserole of venison and orange, Cloutie dumpling. **Rooms:** 19 bedrooms all with tea making facilities: 2 singles ensuite, 3 singles, 1 twin, 1 double, 2 triples ensuite, 2 family rooms ensuite, 1 double ensuite, 7 twins ensuite.
**Credit cards:** Visa, Access, AmEx. **Other points:** licensed, Sunday lunch, children catered for – please check for age limits, garden, afternoon tea, pets allowed, vegetarian meals, parking, residents' bar, residents' lounge. **Directions:** from Kyleakin Ferry take A850. At Skulamus turn left onto A851.
MARGARET COLPUS, tel (04713) 202, fax (04713) 363.

## FLODIGARRY COUNTRY HOUSE HOTEL, Staffin
Magnificently situated with panoramic views across the sea to the Torridon mountains. Family run, the hotel offers comfortable accommodation, Highland hospitality, and the best of traditional Scottish dishes and tempting specialities prepared from fresh local produce. The cottage next to the hotel was home to Flora MacDonald who helped in the escape of Bonnie Prince Charlie.
ACCOMMODATION £31–£40
FOOD £15–£20 ☁
**Hours:** breakfast 8:30am – 10:30am; bar meals 11am – 10:30pm; lunch – Sunday 12:30pm – 2:30pm; dinner

7pm – 10pm. **Cuisine:** Scottish:- Local salmon, lobster, langoustines and other fine fresh seafood. Highland venison and game along with the best of other fresh Scottish fayre. **Rooms:** 23 bedrooms all with tea making facilities: 2 twins, 3 doubles, 4 singles ensuite, 6 twins ensuite, 8 doubles ensuite. **Credit cards:** Visa, Access. **Other points:** licensed, open-air dining, Sunday lunch, no-smoking area, children catered for – please check for age limits, bank holidays, afternoon tea, pets allowed, residents' lounge, residents' bar, disabled access, vegetarian meals, parking. **Directions:** take the A855 from Portree north for Staffin (20 miles). Signposted. ANDREW & PAMELA BUTLER, tel (0470) 52203, fax (0470) 52301.

## HOTEL EILEAN IARMAIN, Sleat

*The hotel prides itself on continuing to provide a traditional welcome with blazing log fires, expert cooking using fresh local produce. Friendly Gaelic speaking management and staff. Each room has period furniture, offering special views of the sea and hills of Skye. All this in an idyllic and spectacular setting. Contact: Effie Kennedy (Manager). (See colour advertisement in centre section.)*
ACCOMMODATION £31–£40
FOOD £21–£25 ☐ CLUB

**Hours:** open all year 7pm; breakfast 8:30am – 9:30am; bar meals 12noon – 2:30pm; lunch 12:30pm – 2pm; bar meals 6:30pm – 9:30pm; dinner 7:30pm – 9pm. **Cuisine:** Scottish:- Lobsters, Scallops, Mussels used daily. Own Oyster beds. Best local game when in season. Exciting menus with fresh local produce. Extensive Wine List. **Rooms:** 12 bedrooms all with tea making facilities, telephone: 6 doubles ensuite, 5 twins ensuite, 1 family room ensuite. **Credit cards:** Visa, Access, Diners. **Other points:** Sunday lunch, no-smoking area, children catered for – please check for age limits, stalking, shooting, fishing, entertainment. **Directions:** situated between Broadford and Armadale, with its ferry to Mallaig. SIR IAIN NOBLE & LADY NOBLE, tel (04713) 332, fax (04713) 275.

## KINLOCH LODGE, Sleat

*Kinloch Lodge is the home of Lord & Lady MacDonald and family, who have turned their historic home into a small, comfortable hotel. The food is superb and Lady MacDonald's cooking and attention to detail has earned great praise from some of the best known gourmets and food writers. An ideal spot for a quiet, relaxing holiday and to enjoy the spectacular views.*
ACCOMMODATION £41–£50
FOOD £26–£30 ☺

**Hours:** breakfast 8:30am – 9:30am; dinner 8pm; closed December – February. **Cuisine:** modern English:- Excellent Table d'hote menu. Main courses may include Roast Loin of Pork with Mushroom & Vermouth Sauce, Smoked Haddock Roulade with Scallops. **Rooms:** 10 bedrooms, 8 en suite. the accommodation prices are just outside the Les Routiers price bracket during high season. **Credit cards:** Visa, Access. **Other points:**

licensed, afternoon tea, pets/prior arr, residents' lounge, garden. **Directions:** 1 mile from A851. 6 miles south of Broadford and 8 miles north of Armadale.
LORD & LADY MACDONALD, tel (04713) 214, (04713) 333, fax (04713) 277.

## ROSEDALE HOTEL, Portree

*A small hotel, created from a series of 19th century fishermen's dwellings, but with all modern comforts installed. An ideal base for exploring the surrounding area, with Dunnegan Castle and the Clan Donald Centre close by.*
ACCOMMODATION £31–£40
FOOD £15–£20

**Hours:** breakfast 8am – 9:30am; dinner 7pm – 8:30pm; closed October – April. **Cuisine:** Scottish. **Rooms:** 23 bedrooms all with tea making facilities, telephone, radio, TV: 5 singles ensuite, 5 doubles ensuite, 13 twins ensuite. **Credit cards:** Visa, Access. **Other points:** children catered for – please check for age limits, pets allowed, residents' lounge, garden. **Directions:** centre of village. On harbour side, facing water.
H M ANDREW, tel (0478) 613131, fax (0478) 612531.

## SKEABOST HOUSE HOTEL, Skeabost Bridge

*A former Victorian Shooting Lodge set in 12 acres of secluded woodland and gardens. It is a comfortable and relaxing, family run hotel with 3 lounges, cocktail bar and billiard room. The cuisine is excellent using fresh, local produce. The hotel has a 9 hole golf course and salmon and sea trout fishing on River Snizort – all free to guests who stay 3 days or more.*
ACCOMMODATION £31–£40
FOOD £15–£20

**Hours:** breakfast 8:30am – 9:30am; lunch 12noon – 1:30pm; dinner 7pm – 8:30pm; closed mid-October – April. **Cuisine:** Scottish:- Traditional Scottish cuisine using fresh, local ingredients. **Rooms:** 26 bedrooms 7 singles ensuite, 8 doubles ensuite, 11 twins ensuite. **Credit cards:** Visa, Access. **Other points:** licensed, open-air dining, Sunday lunch, no-smoking area, children catered for – please check for age limits, pets allowed, afternoon tea, fishing. **Directions:** Kyle of Lochalsh – Kyleakin Ferry. 38 miles to Skeabost Bridge.
THE STUART & MCNAB FAMILIES, tel (047032) 202, fax (047032) 454.

## UIG HOTEL, Uig, Portree

*An old Coaching Inn set on a hillside overlooking Loch Snizort. It is a family-run hotel offering excellent accommodation, good food and a warm welcome. The hotel has its own pony trekking and self catering apartments. Bargain breaks available.*
ACCOMMODATION £31–£40
FOOD £15–£20

**Hours:** breakfast 8am – 9am; lunch 12:30pm – 1:45pm; dinner 7:15pm – 8:15pm; closed mid-October – end March. **Cuisine:** British:- Traditional cuisine. House specialities are peat smoked salmon, venison casserole and bread & butter pudding. **Rooms:** 16 bedrooms 5

singles ensuite, 3 doubles ensuite, 8 twins ensuite.
**Credit cards:** Visa, Access, Diners, AmEx. **Other
points:** licensed, no-smoking area, children catered for –
please check for age limits, afternoon tea, pets/prior arr,
garden. **Directions:** A856. On right-hand side of road
approaching Uig from Portree.
GRACE GRAHAM & DAVID TAYLOR, tel (047042)
205, fax (047042) 308.

# ISLE OF WHITHORN,
Dumfries & Galloway Map 23

## STEAMPACKET HOTEL, *Harbour Row*
*A small family-run hotel with a distinct nautical atmosphere
where all the bedrooms overlook the harbour. Good food
served in friendly comfortable surroundings.*
*ACCOMMODATION £21–£30*
*FOOD up to £15*
**Hours:** breakfast 8am – 9:30am; lunch 12noon – 2pm;
dinner 7pm – 9:30pm. **Cuisine:** Scottish:- Lobster a
speciality. **Rooms:** 5 bedrooms all with tea making
facilities, telephone, TV: 1 twin ensuite, 3 doubles
ensuite, 1 family room ensuite. **Credit cards:** Visa,
Access. **Other points:** licensed, Sunday lunch, pets
allowed. **Directions:** on quayside.
MR SCOULAR, tel (0988) 500334.

# JEDBURGH, Borders Map 20

## THE GLENFRIARS HOTEL, *The Friars*
*Picturesquely situated on the high slopes overlooking
Jedburgh, yet only a short stroll from the town centre.
Only recently opened as a hotel, it offers a high degree
of comfort, a friendly atmosphere and the quality
expected by the more discerning guest. Ideally located
for touring the stunningly beautiful Border country, with
its soft green rolling hills and lush valleys.*
*ACCOMMODATION £21–£30*
*FOOD up to £15*
**Hours:** closed Christmas 6pm; breakfast 8am – 9am;
dinner 7pm – 8:30pm. **Cuisine:** Scottish:- A varied daily
menu, offering the best of Scottish food, with special
emphasis on local prime beef and lamb. Vegetarian meals
on request. **Rooms:** 6 bedrooms all with tea making
facilities, radio, TV: 2 singles ensuite, 2 twins ensuite, 2
doubles ensuite. **Credit cards:** Visa, Access, AmEx.
**Other points:** licensed, children catered for – please check
for age limits, pets allowed, residents' lounge, parking,
baby sitting, cots. **Directions:** A1 to north of Scots Corner
– then A68 to Jedburgh. Opposite school.
CLIVE & JENNY BYWATER, tel (0835) 862000.

# JOHNSTONE, Strathclyde Map 21

## LYNNHURST HOTEL, *Park Road*
*An original old Scottish stone-built house now
considerably modernised. Off the A737, 10 minutes from
Glasgow Airport. Golf courses nearby.*
*ACCOMMODATION £31–£40*
*FOOD up to £15*

**Hours:** lunch 12noon – 2pm; lunch – Sunday 12noon –
3pm; dinner 6:30pm – 9pm; dinner – Saturday 6:30pm –
10pm. **Cuisine:** British:- Home baked ham, home-made
soups, steaks. **Rooms:** 23 bedrooms all with tea making
facilities, telephone, radio, TV: 1 suite, 12 singles
ensuite, 2 family rooms ensuite, 3 doubles ensuite, 5
twins ensuite. **Credit cards:** Visa, Access. **Other
points:** licensed, Sunday lunch, children catered for –
please check for age limits. **Directions:** off the A737 in
Park Road.
MR N AND MISS J MACINTRYE, tel (0505) 324331,
fax (0505) 324219.

# KENMORE, Tayside Map 22

## CROFT-NA-CABER HOTEL, *Croft-na-caber*
*A unique leisure village, set in the beautiful hills of
Perthshire on the shores of Loch Tay. Comfortable
accommodation in the hotel and in luxury log chalets
and good food with the choice of good value bar menus
or dinner in the elegant Garden Restaurant. Relax and
absorb the beauty and peace of Loch Tay or enjoy the
extensive choice of activities available on both land and
loch. (See colour advertisement in centre section.)*
*ACCOMMODATION £21–£30*
*FOOD up to £15*
**Hours:** bar meals all day 6:30pm; breakfast 8:30am –
9:30am; lunch – restaurant 12:30pm – 2pm; dinner –
restaurant 7pm – 9pm. **Cuisine:** Scottish:- First class
reaturant menu with a selection of a la carte and table
d'hote available for lunch & dinner. Also a good
selection of bar meals. Taste of Scotland. **Rooms:** 5
bedrooms, 5 en suite and 17 chalets (2 chalets specially
designed for disabled guests). **Credit cards:** Visa,
Access. **Other points:** licensed, open-air dining, Sunday
lunch, no-smoking area, children catered for – please
check for age limits, afternoon tea, pets allowed, water
sports, special breaks, craft shop, coffee shop, parking,
vegetarian meals, residents' bar, residents' lounge,
disabled access. **Directions:** A827 to Kenmore, then
500yds along south side of Loch Tay.
AMBROSE CHARLES BARRATT, tel (0887) 830236,
fax (0887) 830649.

# KILFINAN, Highlands Map 21

## KILFINAN HOTEL, *Nr Tighnabruaich*
*An ancient coaching inn, tastefully modernised. Set
amidst thousands of acres of unspoilt countryside on
Loch Fyne. It is an ideal base for outdoor activities and
peaceful relaxation.*
*ACCOMMODATION £31–£40*
*FOOD £21–£25*
**Hours:** breakfast 7:30am – 9:30am; bar meals 12noon –
2:30pm; bar meals 6pm – 7:30pm; dinner 7pm –
9:30pm. **Cuisine:** international:- Chef/patron Rolf
Mueller, Member Master Chefs of Great Britain. His
cuisine gives an international flavour to Scottish
produce. **Rooms:** 11 bedrooms, all en suite. **Credit**

cards: Visa, Access, Diners, AmEx. **Other points:** no-smoking area, children catered for – please check for age limits. **Directions:** situated on B8000 between Strachur and Tighnabruaich.
MR N K S WILLS, tel (070 082) 201, fax (070) 082 205.

## KILLIN, Central Map 22

### CLACHAIG HOTEL, Gray Street, Falls Of Dochart
*A former 17th century coaching inn, overlooking the spectacular Falls of Dochart. The intimate and characterful restaurant offers a wide choice of quality food. Trout and salmon fishing is available on the hotel's private stretch of the River Dochart.*
ACCOMMODATION under £20
FOOD up to £15
**Hours:** breakfast 8:15am – 9:15am; lunch 12noon – 2:30pm; bar meals 12noon – 3:30pm; bar meals 5:30pm – 9:30pm; dinner 6:30pm – 9:30pm. **Cuisine:** Scottish:-Trout, salmon, Highland beef steaks, venison. **Rooms:** 9 bedrooms 1 single ensuite, 1 double, 4 doubles ensuite, 1 twin ensuite, 2 family rooms ensuite. **Credit cards:** Visa, Access. **Other points:** open-air dining, Sunday lunch, no-smoking area, disabled access, children catered for – please check for age limits, garden, afternoon tea, pets allowed. **Directions:** on A827 beside Falls of Dochart.
JOHN MALLINSON, tel (0567) 820270.

## KILMARNOCK, Strathclyde Map 21

### COFFEE CLUB, 30 Bank Street
*There is something for everyone here depending on your appetite, purse and time. There are three restaurants with separate menus, all housed under one roof. Each has the same lively atmosphere and friendly staff. You May bring your own wine.*
FOOD up to £15
**Hours:** meals all day 9am – 10pm; meals – Sunday 12noon – 5:30pm. **Cuisine:** international:- Fast food on ground floor, eg. American-style hamburgers. Downstairs, full service for special coffees, grills, omelettes, fish, pasta & vegetarian dishes. **Credit cards:** Visa, Access, AmEx. **Other points:** street parking, children catered for – please check for age limits, functions. **Directions:** Bank Street is off John Finnie Street close to BR and bus stations.
MESSRS S KAMMING & W MACDONALD, tel (0563) 22048.

## KILMELFORD, Strathclyde Map 21

### CUILFAIL HOTEL, By Oban
*A former coaching inn, attractively swathed in ivy on the outside, the interior is cosy and welcoming. The menu is imaginative and offers a healthy alternative. An ideal location for touring the beautiful west coast of Scotland.*
ACCOMMODATION £31–£40
FOOD £15–£20

**Hours:** open all year 12noon; breakfast 8:30am – 9:30am; bar meals 12noon – 2:30pm; dinner 6:30pm – 9:30pm; bar meals 6:30pm – 9:30pm. **Cuisine:** Scottish:- Traditional Scottish cuisine. **Rooms:** 12 bedrooms, all en suite. **Credit cards:** Visa, Access. **Other points:** licensed, open-air dining, Sunday lunch, no-smoking area, children catered for – please check for age limits, afternoon tea, pets allowed, residents' lounge, garden. **Directions:** on the A816 in Kilmelford, 14 miles south of Oban.
DAVID BIRRELL, tel (08522) 274, fax (08522) 264.

## KILWINNING, Strathclyde Map 21

### MONTGREENAN MANSION HOUSE HOTEL, Montgreenan Estate
*A magnificent 18th Century mansion with original brass and marble fireplaces and decorative plasterwork – its character carefully retained. Set in 45 acres of unspoilt parkland, there is tennis, croquet, golf, and billiards available. Award winning Scottish fare served in the restaurant. Scottish Tourist Board 4 Crown "Highly Commended".*
ACCOMMODATION £41–£50
FOOD £15–£20 🍲
**Hours:** breakfast 7am – 10:30am; lunch 12noon – 2:30pm; dinner 7pm – 9:30pm. **Cuisine:** Scottish:- Award winning fresh Scottish fayre. **Rooms:** 21 bedrooms 2 singles ensuite, 8 twins ensuite, 8 doubles ensuite, 3 suites. **Credit cards:** Visa, Access, Diners, AmEx. **Other points:** no-smoking area, children catered for – please check for age limits. **Directions:** 4 miles north of Irvine on the A736.
THE DOBSON FAMILY, tel (0294) 557733, fax (0294) 85397.

## KINCRAIG, Highlands Map 24

### THE BOATHOUSE RESTAURANT, Loch Insh
*Situated by Loch Insh, this restaurant is always a hub of activity because of the many sporting activities taking place, eg. mountain biking, fishing, dry slope skiing, sailing, skiing and canoeing. This restaurant offers a warm welcome, good well prepared food and value for money.*
ACCOMMODATION under £20
FOOD up to £15
**Hours:** last orders 7pm – 9pm; meals all day 10am – 10pm. **Cuisine:** British:- Home baking, fresh salads, Fondues, Bar meals served all day. A la carte evening menu. B.B.Q's every lunchtime (July/August). Children's menu. **Rooms:** 25 bedrooms 14 family rooms ensuite, 4 family rooms, 7 chalets. **Credit cards:** Visa, Access. **Other points:** licensed, open-air dining, Sunday lunch, no-smoking area, children catered for – please check for age limits, dry ski slope, water sports, fishing, mountain bikes. **Directions:** off A9 at Kingussie. Follow "Loch Insh Watersports" sign at Kincraig.
MR & MRS C FRESHWATER, tel (0540) 651272, fax (0540) 651208.

## KINGUSSIE, Highlands Map 24

### THE ROYAL HOTEL, High Street
*The Royal Hotel is in the centre of Kingussie in the beautiful Spey Valley. An ideal base for all types of outdoor activities, including skiing, and for touring the Highlands. The hotel is family owned and run offering good accommodation, food and a warm welcome.*
*ACCOMMODATION £21–£30*
*FOOD up to £15*
**Hours:** breakfast 8am – 9:30am; lunch 12noon – 2pm; dinner 7pm – 9:30pm. **Cuisine:** Scottish:- 3 course lunches, 4 course table d'hote dinner, a la carte. Traditional Scottish cuisine prepared from fresh local produce. **Rooms:** 52 bedrooms, all en suite. **Credit cards:** Visa, Access, Diners, AmEx. **Other points:** licensed, Sunday lunch, no-smoking area, children catered for – please check for age limits, garden, afternoon tea, pets allowed, foreign exchange, residents' lounge, residents' bar, vegetarian meals, parking, disabled access. **Directions:** Kingussie is just off the A9, 40 miles from Pitlochry and Inverness.
MRS JUSTICE, tel (0540) 661898, fax (0540) 661061.

## KINLOCHLEVEN, Highlands Map 24

### MACDONALD HOTEL, Wades Road
*This is a small, new, comfortable hotel, built in a traditional west Highland style, where the resident proprietors and staff pride themselves on a warm welcome and personal service. Good food and accommodation at value for money.*
*ACCOMMODATION £21–£30*
*FOOD £15–£20*
**Hours:** open bank holidays 7pm; breakfast 8am – 9am; bar meals 12noon – 9pm; dinner 7pm – 9pm. **Cuisine:** Scottish:- Menu may feature – Rack of Scottish Lamb glazed with Honey and Rosemary, Medallions of local Venison with a red wine sauce. **Rooms:** 10 bedrooms all with tea making facilities, TV: 4 twins ensuite, 1 twin, 3 doubles ensuite, 1 double, 1 triple ensuite. **Credit cards:** Visa, Access, AmEx. **Other points:** licensed, open-air dining, Sunday lunch, children catered for – please check for age limits, waterside location, cots, left luggage, fishing, foreign exchange, residents' bar. **Directions:** going north on A82 take turning at Glencoe Village.
PETER & SUSAN MACDONALD, tel (08554) 539, fax (08554) 539.

## KINROSS, Tayside Map 22

### BALGEDIE TOLL TAVERN, Wester Balgedie
*An original Toll House with open fires, wooden beams and brasses giving a pleasant olde world feel. The home-made food is excellent and all guests are made to feel immediately welcome by the friendly and efficient staff. A very popular rendezvous with many visitors travelling from far afield to enjoy the good food and convivial atmosphere.*
*FOOD up to £15*
**Hours:** bar 11am – 3pm; lunch 12noon – 2pm; bar 5pm – 11pm; dinner 5:30pm – 9pm. **Cuisine:** British:- Comprehensive & imaginative menu with specials board – traditional dishes may include, prime Scottish steaks with various garnishes, salmon, and venison. Assorted home-made vegetarian dishes available. **Credit cards:** Visa, Access. **Other points:** licensed, open-air dining, parking, children catered for – please check for age limits, beer garden, patio, real ales. **Directions:** 1 mile south east of Junction 8, M90, north shore of Loch Leven in fork of A911 & B919.
ALAN CHRISTIE, tel (0592) 84212.

### THE MUIRS INN KINROSS, 49 Muirs
*Situated on the "Moorland of Kinross", this Inn dates back to the 1800's when it was originally a small farmhouse where the blacksmith lodged. The food is appetising, well presented, generously portioned and of good quality, and the accommodation is also of a very high standard. A unique feature is the vast array of beers, lagers, ciders, wines and spirits that this little Inn stocks from all over the world, including its own branded brewery conditioned beers and connoisseurs choice of around 100 Malt Whiskies. A truly fascinating place for a weekend break or family holiday. Loch Leven Castle where 'Mary Queen of Scots' was imprisoned is nearby.*
*ACCOMMODATION £21–£30*
*FOOD up to £15*
**Hours:** closed Christmas day 5:30pm; breakfast 7am – 9am; breakfast – Sunday 8am – 10am; lunch 12noon – 2:30pm; bar snacks 12noon – 2:30pm; dinner 5pm – 9pm; bar snacks 5pm – 8:30pm; high tea 5pm – 6pm; country supper 5pm – 9pm. **Cuisine:** Scottish. **Rooms:** 5 bedrooms 3 doubles ensuite, 2 twins ensuite. **Credit cards:** Visa, Access. **Other points:** parking, children catered for – please check for age limits, high teas, disabled access, vegetarian meals, open-air dining. **Directions:** M90 exit junction 6, follow A922 (Milnathort) signs at T junction, The inn is diagonally opposite on right.
GORDON M WESTWOOD, tel (0577) 862270.

## KIRKCUDBRIGHT, Dumfries & Galloway Map 23

### SELKIRK ARMS HOTEL, Old High Street
*Family-run hotel set in a picturesque town. Guests can enjoy friendly hospitality, with good food and comfortable accommodation. Free squash for residents. Short breaks also available at special rates, an ideal base to tour Galloway.*
*ACCOMMODATION £31–£40*
*FOOD £15–£20* 🍷
**Hours:** breakfast 7:30am – 10am; lunch 12noon – 2pm; dinner 7pm – 9:30pm. **Cuisine:** British:- Dishes include local seafood, scallops, turbot, brill. Beef and lamb dishes. A la carte and daily changing table d'hote menus. **Rooms:** 15 bedrooms 5 singles ensuite, 3 twins ensuite, 5 doubles ensuite, 2 family rooms ensuite. **Credit cards:**

Visa, Access, Diners, AmEx. **Other points:** Sunday lunch, children catered for – please check for age limits. **Directions:** situated in the High Street.
MR E J MORRIS, tel (0557) 330402, fax (0557) 331639.

# KIRKMICHAEL, Tayside Map 22

## *THE LOG CABIN HOTEL*

*A large hotel built of whole Norwegian logs, set in the hills amidst a majestic pine forest. Family run, a definite apres ski atmosphere prevails in winter. A superb 4 course dinner can be enjoyed in the Edelweis restaurant, while the Viking Bar serves a comprehensive selection of bar meals. A unique base from which to explore the Perthshire area.*
ACCOMMODATION £21–£30
FOOD £15–£20
**Hours:** open all year 7pm; breakfast 8:45am – 9:30am; lunch 12noon – 1:45pm; dinner 7:30pm – 8:45pm.
**Cuisine:** British:- Daily specials in the bar. Table d'hote evening menu, using fresh local produce. **Rooms:** 13 bedrooms all with tea making facilities, radio: 4 twins ensuite, 5 doubles ensuite, 4 family rooms ensuite.
**Credit cards:** Visa, Access, Diners, AmEx. **Other points:** licensed, open-air dining, Sunday lunch, children catered for – please check for age limits, pets/prior arr, garden, disabled access. **Directions:** off the A924.
ALAN FINCH & DAPHNE KIRK, tel (0250) 881288, fax (0250) 881402.

# KIRKWALL, Orkney & Shetland Islands Map 24

## *ALBERT HOTEL, Mounthoolie Lane*

*A comfortable, family-run hotel in the centre of Kirkwall. Recently refurbished, the Albert Hotel is noted for its good food made from fresh, local produce. An ideal place to stay when exploring these unique islands.*
ACCOMMODATION £31–£40
FOOD £15–£20
**Hours:** closed 01/01; breakfast 7:30am – 9:30am; lunch 12noon – 2pm; bar meals 12noon – 2pm; bar meals 6pm – 10pm; dinner 7pm – 10pm; closed Christmas 25/12.
**Cuisine:** English / seafood:- A la carte restaurant meals and bar meals made from fresh, local produce. House speciality is the Seafood Platter, Stables Steak. **Rooms:** 19 bedrooms all with tea making facilities, telephone, TV: 9 singles ensuite, 5 doubles ensuite, 3 twins ensuite, 2 family rooms ensuite. **Credit cards:** Visa, Access.
**Other points:** licensed, Sunday lunch, children catered for – please check for age limits. **Directions:** in centre of Kirkwall, off Junction Road. Close to harbour.
ANJO CASEY, tel (0856) 876000, fax (0856) 875397.

## *KIRKWALL HOTEL*

*Orkney's largest hotel has, in its time, played host to a number of the crown heads of Europe. This fine historic hotel, overlooking the seafront and harbour, is justifiably popular with business and tourist clientele from around the world. The completely refurbished lounge and restaurant are ideal for relaxing or enjoying the exquisite Orkney cuisine. The Kirkwall Hotel is the*

*perfect location for those who want to 'get away from it all', to discover the delights that Orkney has to offer.*
ACCOMMODATION £31–£40
FOOD £16–£20
**Hours:** breakfast 7am – 9.30pm, lunch 12 noon – 2pm, dinner 6.30pm – 9pm. **Cuisine:** British:- Orkney cuisine including fresh local lobster, oysters, scallops and crab. Orkney steaks. **Rooms:** 44 bedrooms all with TV, telephone, tea making facilities. **Credit cards:** Access, Visa, AmEx. **Other points:** children catered for – please check for age limits, pets allowed, vegetarian meals, satellite TV, residents' lounge, residents' bar.
**Directions:** situated on the main town harbour.
GRAHAM WILKINS, tel (0856) 872232, fax (0856 872812.

# LARGS, Strathclyde Map 21

## *GLEN ELDON HOTEL, 2 Barr Crescent*

*Largs is a popular family seaside resort and the Glen Eldon Hotel caters for the needs of families on holiday. It is a family run establishment at the north end of Largs close to the sea-front, swimming pool, sports centre and golf course and not far from the town centre.*
ACCOMMODATION £21–£30
FOOD up to £15
**Hours:** breakfast 7am – 9am; dinner – Saturday 5pm – 9pm; dinner – Sunday 5pm – 7:45pm; dinner – weekdays 7pm – 7:45pm; closed mid-January – mid-March. **Cuisine:** Scottish:- Scottish dishes including haggis, venison, salmon and daily specials. **Rooms:** 6 bedrooms all with tea making facilities, telephone, TV: 1 single ensuite, 2 family rooms ensuite, 3 twins ensuite. **Credit cards:** Visa, Access, AmEx. **Other points:** children catered for – please check for age limits. **Directions:** on A78, midway between Glasgow & Prestwick airports.
MARY PATON, tel (0475) 673381, (0475) 674094, fax (00475) 673381.

## *THE MANOR PARK HOTEL*

*A well-kept, Grade B listed mansion house hotel with many architectural features, beautifully set in 15 acres of landscaped gardens on the coast overlooking the islands of the Firth of Clyde. Good food and accommodation make this an ideal base from which to tour, play golf or sail.*
ACCOMMODATION £41–£50
FOOD £15–£20 CLUB ★
**Hours:** breakfast 7:30am – 10am; lunch 12:30pm – 2:30pm; dinner 7pm – 10:30pm. **Cuisine:** Scottish:- All menus cooked to order using only fresh ingredients. Scottish dishes a speciality. Bar meals, table d'hote plus extensive a la carte menu. **Rooms:** 22 bedrooms 2 singles ensuite, 7 doubles ensuite, 10 twins ensuite, 3 family rooms ensuite. **Credit cards:** Visa, Access, Diners, AmEx. **Other points:** licensed, open-air dining, Sunday lunch, children catered for – please check for age limits, garden, afternoon tea. **Directions:** midway between Skelmorlie and Largs on the A78.
MR WILLIAMS (MANAGER), tel (0475) 520832, fax (0475) 520832.

## LEADBURN, Lothian Map 20

### THE LEADBURN INN, West Linton

*A country style hotel set in the beautiful Borders region. The Carriage Restaurant, aptly named, is a luxurious converted railway carriage which recreates the glory of the early trains. Only 25 minutes drive from the centre of Edinburgh, the hotel is popular with business people, tourists and locals alike, and was a Les Routiers 'Casserole' award winner in 1991.*

*ACCOMMODATION £21–£30*

*FOOD up to £15* ★

**Hours:** closed Christmas day 7pm; closed New Years day 7pm; breakfast 7am – 9am; bar meals 12noon – 10pm; dinner 6pm – 10pm. **Cuisine:** Scottish:- Local game and seafood are the specialities. Good value for money, extensive menu. **Rooms:** 6 bedrooms 1 twin ensuite, 1 double ensuite, 1 single, 1 twin, 2 family rooms. **Credit cards:** Visa, Access, Diners, AmEx. **Other points:** licensed, Sunday lunch, children catered for – please check for age limits, pets – prior arrangement, residents' lounge, residents' bar, vegetarian meals, disabled access. **Directions:** from Edinburgh, take the A701 to Penicuik. Continue to Leadburn.

LINDA & ALAN THOMSON & ADRIAN DEMPSEY, tel (0968) 672952.

## LETHAM, Fife Map 22

### FERNIE CASTLE HOTEL, Letham By Cupar

*An ancient Scottish royal hunting lodge, dating from the mid-14th century, Fernie Castle retains many original features and an air of olde-worlde comfort. All restoration work is personally supervised by its current owner. Situated in the geographic centre of Fife, the surrounding area is equally attractive, Falkland Palace, Scottish Deer Centre and Ladybank Golf Club nearby.*

*ACCOMMODATION £31–£40*

*FOOD up to £15* ★

**Hours:** breakfast 7:30am – 10am; bar meals & snacks 9:30am – 9:30pm; lunch 12noon – 2:30pm; dinner 6:30pm – 9:30pm. **Cuisine:** Scottish:- Predominantly Scottish fare. **Rooms:** 16 bedrooms all with tea making facilities, telephone, radio, TV: 4 singles ensuite, 5 twins ensuite, 6 doubles ensuite, 1 triple ensuite. **Credit cards:** Visa, Access, AmEx. **Other points:** licensed, open-air dining, Sunday lunch, children catered for – please check for age limits, residents' lounge, library, parking, bank holidays, baby sitting, baby-listening device, cots, foreign exchange. **Directions:** Half a mile north of Letham village on the A914.

NORMAN & ZOE SMITH, tel (033781) 381, fax (033781) 422.

## LOCHCARRON, Highlands Map 24

### ROCKVILLA HOTEL & RESTAURANT, Main Street

*Situated in Lochcarron village centre, overlooking the mountains and loch beyond, this hotel provides an excellent centre from which to explore some of the most beautiful and romantic scenery in Scotland. It offers comfortable accommodation and friendly, personal service within a warm, homely atmosphere. Nearby scenic beauty spots abound, including superb views of Skye.*

*ACCOMMODATION £21–£30*

*FOOD up to £15*

**Hours:** breakfast 8am – 9:15am; lunch 12noon – 2pm; bar meals 12noon – 2pm; bar meals 6pm – 9pm; dinner 6:30pm – 9pm. **Cuisine:** seafood / English:- Specialises in local fresh caught seafood, venison, and the finest steaks. Daily changing a la carte menu, complemented by a comprehensive wine list. **Rooms:** 4 bedrooms, 2 en suite, comfortably furnished with colour TV, heaters, razor points, and tea/coffee making facilities. All rooms bright and airy. **Credit cards:** Visa, Access. **Other points:** licensed, Sunday lunch, no-smoking area, children catered for – please check for age limits, parking. **Directions:** located in the centre of the village of Lochcarron.

KENNETH & LORNA WHEELAN, tel (05202) 379.

## LOCHEARNHEAD, Central Map 22

### LOCHEARNHEAD HOTEL, Lochside

*This small country house beside Loch Earn forms part of a lochside water sports development, offering such sports as sailing, waterskiing and windsurfing. Coupled with the friendly atmosphere of the hotel and the superb home-cooking, this is a perfect place for water sport enthusiasts of all ages. Ideal centre for golfers. Access to fifteen courses within the hour.*

*ACCOMMODATION £21–£30*

*FOOD up to £15*

**Hours:** breakfast 8:30am – 9:30am; lunch 11am – 2:30pm; dinner 7pm – 9:30pm. **Cuisine:** French:- A la carte and 3 course fixed menus. French. **Rooms:** 26 bedrooms all with tea making facilities, TV: 1 single, 5 twins, 4 doubles, 2 doubles ensuite, 2 twins ensuite, 4 doubles ensuite, 4 twins ensuite, 2 doubles, 2 twins. **Credit cards:** Visa, Access, Diners, AmEx. **Other points:** licensed, open-air dining, children catered for – please check for age limits, afternoon tea, pets allowed, garden. **Directions:** take the A84 from Oban; turn onto the A85 to Crieff.

ANGUS CAMERON, tel (0567) 830229, fax (0567) 830364.

## LOCHGILPHEAD, Strathclyde Map 21

### LOCHGAIR HOTEL, Lochgair

*A family run hotel offering a warm welcome to all discerning travellers who enjoy good food in friendly, comfortable surroundings. Situated in the village of Lochgair, only 200 yds from the Loch, the hotel enjoys wonderful views. Ideal base for exploring the west Highlands & islands. Activities include trout fishing, sea angling, pony trekking, golf and sailing.*

*ACCOMMODATION £21–£30*

*FOOD up to £15*

**Hours:** breakfast 8:30am – 9:30am; bar meals 12:15pm – 2:15pm; dinner 6:30pm – 9pm; bar meals 6:30pm – 9pm. **Cuisine:** international:- Local game dishes, spare ribs, home-made lasagne, chicken curry, beef stroganoff, haddock, trout, salmon and venison. **Rooms:** 14 bedrooms 3 twins ensuite, 4 doubles ensuite, 1 family room ensuite, 2 singles, 2 twins, 2 doubles. **Credit cards:** Visa, Access. **Other points:** licensed, open-air dining, Sunday lunch, no-smoking area, yacht anchorage, children catered for – please check for age limits, afternoon tea, residents' lounge. **Directions:** on A83 Glasgow – Campbeltown road. 7 miles north of Lochgilphead.
JOHN & ELSIE GALLOWAY, tel (0546) 86333.

### STAG HOTEL, Argyll Street
*A family-run, modern hotel, ideally situated in scenic Argyll for a touring, residential holiday or break. Good food and comfortable accommodation in a relaxed, informal atmosphere. Free golf available on local course.*
*ACCOMMODATION £21–£30*
*FOOD up to £15*
**Hours:** breakfast 7:30am – 9:30am; lunch 12noon – 2:30pm; bar meals 12noon – 2pm; bar meals 6pm – 8:30pm; dinner 7pm – 9pm. **Cuisine:** Scottish:- Traditional Scottish cuisine and bar meals. **Rooms:** 17 bedrooms all with tea making facilities, telephone, radio, TV: 4 singles ensuite, 9 twins ensuite, 4 doubles ensuite. **Credit cards:** Visa, Access. **Other points:** licensed, Sunday lunch, residents' lounge, pets allowed, sauna, solarium, disabled access, baby-listening device, cots. **Directions:** A83, A816. Loch Lomond to Inverary – 23 miles to Lochgilphead.
JOYCE & BILL ROSS, HEATHER & DREW MCGLYN, tel (0546) 602496, fax (0546) 603549.

---

## LOCKERBIE, Dumfries & Galloway Map 23

### LOCKERBIE MANOR COUNTRY HOTEL, Boreland Road
*Georgian mansion house retaining original Adam features about one half-mile north of Lockerbie provides well-appointed bedrooms and comfortable public rooms. The cuisine is truly international; Eastern flavours and cooking style blend easily with western recipes, to give a genuine East-meets-West experience that visitors will find truly unforgettable.*
*ACCOMMODATION £41–£50*
*FOOD up to £15* ★
**Hours:** breakfast 7:30am – 9:30am; dinner 6:30pm – 9·30pm. **Cuisine:** international. **Rooms:** 28 bedrooms all en suite. **Credit cards:** Visa, Access, AmEx. **Other points:** licensed, open-air dining, Sunday lunch, children catered for – please check for age limits, pets allowed, afternoon tea, bank holidays, residents' lounge, garden, parking, residents' bar, vegetarian meals. **Directions:** on the A74, 25 miles N of Carlisle. Follow B723 north – turn right.
JEFFREY YEH, tel (0576) 202610, fax (0576) 203046.

### SOMERTON HOUSE HOTEL, 35 Carlisle Road
*Victorian mansion built of local stone, standing in its own grounds 300 yds from main M6/A74. It is a family run hotel and restaurant, with a well-earned reputation for good food and accommodation. international a la carte menu and 'Taste of Scotland', real ales and interesting bar meals.*
*ACCOMMODATION £21–£30*
**Hours:** breakfast 8am – 9am; lunch 12noon – 2pm; dinner 7pm – 9pm. **Cuisine:** Scottish / international:- Dishes such as saute of beef stroganoff, lamb cooked with yoghurt and apricots, and Scottish salmon. **Rooms:** 7 bedrooms 1 single ensuite, 2 twins ensuite, 2 doubles ensuite, 2 family rooms ensuite. **Credit cards:** Visa, Access, AmEx. **Other points:** Sunday lunch, no-smoking area, children catered for – please check for age limits, pets allowed. **Directions:** on edge of Lockerbie, half mile from M74.
ALEX & JEAN ARTHUR, tel (0576) 202583, (0576) 202384, fax (0576) 204218.

---

## MALLAIG, Highlands Map 24

### MARINE HOTEL
*The Marine Hotel is a comfortable family owned hotel which overlooks Mallaig Harbour and is convenient for both rail and sea terminals. The west Highland line ends here, giving the train enthusiast an ideal opportunity to see steam trains at close quarters. All bedrooms have modern facilities and the restaurant provides excellent bar meals and dinners including fresh daily seafood and a good selection of malt whiskies. Arisaig and the beautiful Silver Sands of Morar, both ideal for bathing and picnics are nearby.*
*ACCOMMODATION £21–£30*
*FOOD £15–£20*
**Hours:** breakfast 8am – 9:30am; bar snacks 12noon – 2pm; bar meals 6pm – 9pm; bar snacks 6pm – 9:30pm; dinner 7pm – 9pm; lunch on request. **Cuisine:** Scottish:- Simple fresh food of local origin. **Credit cards:** Visa, Access. **Other points:** parking, children catered for – please check for age limits, Sunday lunch, open bank holidays, no-smoking area, Sunday dinner, disabled access, residents' lounge, vegetarian meals. **Directions:** hotel is adjacent to rail station and first on right coming off main road.
MR E AND MRS D IRONSIDE, tel (0687) 2217, fax (0687) 2821.

---

## MELROSE, Borders Map 20

### BURTS HOTEL, Market Square
*Built in 1722, Burts is a friendly family-run hotel, renowned for its excellent cuisine, fine Scottish hospitality and everything you would expect of a first-class establishment. Situated in the heart of Border country and convenient for visiting a wealth of stately homes, including Floors Castle. Nearby sporting activities include, fishing, golfing, game-shooting and*

hill walking. AA and RAC 3 star and Scottish Tourist Board 4 crown commended.
ACCOMMODATION £31–£40
FOOD £15–£20
**Hours:** breakfast 8am – 9:30am; bar meals 12noon – 2pm; lunch 12:30pm – 2pm; bar meals 6pm – 9:30pm; dinner 7pm – 9:30pm. **Cuisine:** Scottish:- Traditional Scottish fare. Dishes include, Medallions of Venison, Stuffed Brace of Boneless Quail, Steamed Fillet of Turbot, Supremes of Young Grouse. **Rooms:** 21 bedrooms all with tea making facilities, telephone, radio, TV: 8 singles ensuite, 10 twins ensuite, 3 doubles ensuite. **Credit cards:** Visa, Access, Diners, AmEx. **Other points:** licensed, open-air dining, Sunday lunch, parking, children catered for – please check for age limits, garden, residents' lounge, pets allowed, baby sitting, cots, left luggage, billiards. **Directions:** 3 miles from Galashiels off A7. 2 miles from A68, south of Earlston.
NICHOLAS HENDERSON (MANAGER), tel (089682) 2285, fax (089682) 2870.

## MILNATHORT, Tayside Map 22

### THE THISTLE HOTEL, 25–27 New Road
A small, residential country inn in a rural setting, only 1.5 miles from Kinross and M90 junction. Under the personal supervision of the managers, Mr & Mrs Quinn, the Thistle Hotel provides welcoming, friendly service and good food in the lounge bar and in the restaurant at weekends.
ACCOMMODATION under £20
FOOD up to £15
**Hours:** breakfast 8am – 9am; lunch 12noon – 2pm; bar meals 12noon – 2pm; high tea – weekends 5pm – 7:30pm; dinner 6pm – 9pm; bar meals 6pm – 9pm. **Cuisine:** English:- Specialities include steaks and home-made pate. A la carte and bar meals. Homemade sweets, own sticky toffee pudding and apple toffee pecan pie. **Rooms:** 5 bedrooms all with tea making facilities, TV: 2 twins, 1 family room, 1 single ensuite, 1 twin ensuite. **Credit cards:** Visa, Access. **Other points:** licensed, Sunday lunch, children catered for – please check for age limits, pets allowed. **Directions:** Junction 6 M90. A91 Perth – Stirling Road in Milnathort.
MR J. HARLEY, tel (0577) 863222.

## MOFFAT, Dumfries & Galloway Map 23

### BALMORAL HOTEL, High Street
Set in the picturesque Annan Valley, the Balmoral Hotel was once a Coaching Inn and frequented by Robert Burns. It is now a friendly, family owned hotel offering comfortable accommodation, fine cuisine and welcoming, friendly service. There is a wide choice of dishes and all offer very good value. Ideal place to relax in attractive surroundings and a warm, family atmosphere.
ACCOMMODATION £21–£30
FOOD up to £15 ★
**Hours:** breakfast 8am – 9:30am; bar meals 12noon – 2pm; dinner 6pm – 9pm; bar meals 6pm – 9pm. **Cuisine:** Scottish / French:- Traditional Scottish, English and French dishes. Specialities include venison, fresh

salmon, fillet steak. **Rooms:** 16 bedrooms all with tea making facilities: 3 singles, 4 twins, 3 twins ensuite, 2 doubles, 3 doubles ensuite, 1 family room. **Credit cards:** Visa, Access. **Other points:** licensed, Sunday lunch, children catered for – please check for age limits, pets allowed, residents' lounge. **Directions:** A701, main street in Moffat.
B STOKES & FAMILY, tel (0683) 20288, fax (0683) 20451.

### THE STAR HOTEL, 44 High Street
Although this hotel is listed in the Guinness Book of Records as the narrowest detached hotel, the interior and welcome is heartwarming and wholesome. If you enjoy good food at great value prices in splendidly comfortable surroundings then this is the place for you.
ACCOMMODATION £21–£30
FOOD up to £15
**Hours:** breakfast 8am – 9:30am; lunch 12noon – 2:30pm; dinner 5:30pm – 9pm. **Cuisine:** British / international:- Wide and varied menu, daily specials. **Rooms:** 8 bedrooms 2 twins ensuite, 4 doubles ensuite, 2 family rooms ensuite. **Credit cards:** Visa, Access. **Other points:** licensed, children catered for – please check for age limits, afternoon tea, pets allowed, coach/prior arr, functions, conferences. **Directions:** situated in the High Street.
MR HOUSE & MR LEIGHFIELD, tel (0683) 20156.

## MONTROSE, Tayside Map 22

### THE LINKS HOTEL, Mid Links
Recently refurbished to a high standard, the Links Hotel is located in a prime setting overlooking public gardens. The Hotel is ideally suited for touring the east coast of Scotland and the Grampian Mountains.
ACCOMMODATION £21–£30
FOOD up to £15
**Hours:** open all year 5:30pm; open bank holidays 5:30pm; breakfast 7:30am – 9:30am; breakfast – Sunday 8am – 10am; dinner & bar suppers 10:30am – 9:30pm. **Cuisine:** Scottish:- Traditional cuisine. **Rooms:** 21 bedrooms all with tea making facilities, telephone, radio, TV: 3 singles ensuite, 11 twins ensuite, 5 doubles ensuite, 2 doubles. **Credit cards:** Visa, Access, Diners, AmEx. **Other points:** licensed, Sunday lunch, children catered for – please check for age limits, afternoon tea, residents' lounge, baby-listening device, baby sitting, cots, 24hr reception, foreign exchange, left luggage. **Directions:** situated 2 minutes walk from the town centre.
MR NINTEMAN, tel (0674) 72288, fax (0674) 72698.

## MOTHERWELL, Strathclyde Map 21

### THE MOORINGS HOUSE HOTEL, 114 Hamilton Road
A family run hotel dating from the 1880's, offering a warm, relaxed atmosphere. The restaurant is in keeping with the original house and guests can choose from a wide selection of international dishes. All food is

*prepared under the supervision of the head chef who uses fresh Scottish produce whenever possible. The meals offer good value for money, particularly at lunchtime.*
ACCOMMODATION under £20
FOOD up to £15
**Hours:** breakfast 7am – 9am; lunch 12noon – 2pm; dinner 6:30pm – 9pm. **Cuisine:** French:- Table d'hote and a la carte meals. Classic French cooking with an accent on the unusual. **Rooms:** 14 bedrooms 6 singles ensuite, 4 twins ensuite, 4 doubles ensuite. **Credit cards:** Visa, Access, AmEx. **Other points:** licensed, Sunday lunch, children catered for – please check for age limits, afternoon tea, pets allowed, garden. **Directions:** Motherwell exit off M74. 500yds past Strathclyde Country Park.
DAVID KERR, tel (0698) 258131, fax (0698) 254973.

---

## NAIRN, Highlands Map 24

### THE ALBERT INN & LAMPLIGHTER RESTAURANT, 1 Albert Street

*An attractive Inn blending old with the new, and decorated to a high standard throughout. This inn offers excellent value for money which, together with the warm friendly atmosphere and good home cooking, makes it a popular choice for locals and tourists alike. Close to golf course.*
ACCOMMODATION under £20
FOOD up to £15
**Hours:** lunch 12noon – 2pm; dinner 5pm – 9pm. **Cuisine:** Scottish:- Traditional, a la carte and bar snack menus. **Rooms:** 8 bedrooms all with tea making facilities, TV: 4 twins ensuite, 3 doubles ensuite, 1 family room ensuite. **Credit cards:** Visa, Access. **Other points:** licensed, Sunday lunch, children catered for – please check for age limits, garden, disabled access. **Directions:** beside the bus station, on A96.
ROBERT MACKINTOSH, tel (0667) 54474.

### CLAYMORE HOUSE HOTEL, Seabank Road

*Set in a quiet residential area omly minutes from Nairn's miles of clean and sandy beaches and just 300 yd from the famous Championship Golf Course. Re-opened under new management, The Claymore House offers high standards and a warm, friendly welcome towards guests. All rooms have been tastefully furnished with many modern facilities. Golfing breaks are a speciality, with 25 courses within one hour. A golfer's paradise.*
ACCOMMODATION £21–£30
FOOD up to £15
**Hours:** breakfast 8am – 9:30am; bar snacks 12noon – 2pm; bar snacks 6pm – 9pm; dinner 7pm – 9pm. **Cuisine:** Scottish / international:- Traditional good food including Scottish and international. **Rooms:** 12 bedrooms 5 doubles ensuite, 3 twins ensuite, 3 singles ensuite, 1 family room ensuite. **Credit cards:** Visa, Access, AmEx. **Other points:** parking, children catered for – please check for age limits, afternoon teas, disabled access, pets, residents' lounge, garden, vegetarian meals, open-air dining. **Directions:** from A96, Inverness to Aberdeen, head toward the sea-front to approach Seabank Road. Take the A96 Inverness to Aberdeen road, to Nairn. In Nairn, turn left into Seabank Road from the A96.
ROSEMARY MACHEN-YOUNG, tel (0667) 53731, fax (0667) 55290.

### THE LINKS HOTEL, 1 Seafield Street

*A large stone villa with lovely views of the Moray Firth, decorated in warm colours and providing real country house comfort. Generous helpings of tasty meals made from fresh ingredients can be enjoyed in the relaxed atmosphere of the restaurant. Comfortable accommodation available at a reasonable price. Ideal base for touring or a golfing break.*
ACCOMMODATION £21–£30
FOOD up to £15
**Hours:** breakfast 8am – 9:30am; lunch 12:30pm – 2:30pm; bar meals 6:30pm – 9:30pm; dinner 7pm – 9pm. **Cuisine:** Scottish:- Menu may feature salmon en croute, local breast of wood pigeon Languedoc, fresh pink trout fillets with prawn and pernod sauce, sirloin steak. **Rooms:** 9 bedrooms all with tea making facilities, TV: 2 singles ensuite, 2 family rooms ensuite, 3 twins ensuite, 2 doubles ensuite. **Credit cards:** Visa, Access. **Other points:** licensed, open-air dining, children catered for – please check for age limits, bank holidays, afternoon tea, pets allowed. **Directions:** junction of Marine Road, turn down Marine Road or Albert St from A9.
IAN & CAROL COOPER, tel (0667) 53321, fax (0667) 53321.

### Restaurant of the Year
### RAMLEH HOTEL & FINGAL'S RESTAURANT, Ramleh House, 2 Academy Street

*This is a family-run hotel and restaurant offering good food and comfortable accommodation. The restaurant features a new conservatory for that relaxed, friendly atmosphere. Close to the High Street, beach, 2 golf courses, harbour, and all amenities.*
ACCOMMODATION £31–£40
FOOD up to £15 ★
**Hours:** breakfast 7:30am – 9am; lunch 12noon – 2pm; dinner 6:30pm – 9pm. **Cuisine:** British:- A wide variety of dishes served including fish and seafood, poultry and game, meat and also vegetarian meals. Desserts and a cheeseboard also on menu. **Rooms:** 20 bedrooms all with tea making facilities, TV: 2 singles, 1 single ensuite, 1 twin, 1 twin ensuite, 4 doubles ensuite, 1 family room ensuite. **Credit cards:** Visa, Access, AmEx. **Other points:** licensed, children catered for – please check for age limits, garden, afternoon tea, residents' lounge, residents' bar. **Directions:** Nairn is on the A96 Aberdeen to Inverness road, 15 miles/Inverness.
GEORGE & CAROL WOODHOUSE, tel (0667) 53551, fax (0667) 56577.

## NETHYBRIDGE, Highlands Map 24

### THE MOUNTVIEW HOTEL

*The hotel is situated in the beautiful Spey Valley, the centre for many attractions and central for touring the Highlands. Built in 1914 of granite and sandstone, this well-appointed hotel has an excellent bar and centrally-heated bedrooms. Aviemore Centre is a short drive away, providing cinema, theatre and other entertainment. Golf, fishing, pony trekking and more, nearby.*

*ACCOMMODATION £21–£30*

*FOOD up to £15*

**Hours:** breakfast 8am – 9am; lunch 12noon – 2pm; dinner 6:30pm – 9pm; closed Christmas 25/12. **Cuisine:** British:- A la carte menu, offering traditional homestyle cooking, with menu for children and vegetarians. **Rooms:** 9 bedrooms, 5 en suite, with tea/coffee making facilities. **Credit cards:** Visa, Access. **Other points:** licensed, open-air dining, Sunday lunch, children catered for – please check for age limits, pets allowed, residents' lounge. **Directions:** take Aviemore Road off A9. Next village after Boat of Garten. TRIXIE & STUART PARKINS, tel (0479) 821248.

## NEW GALLOWAY, Dumfries & Galloway Map 23

### THE SMITHY, The High Street

*As the name implies, this is a converted blacksmith's shop which houses a craft shop and B&B accommodation in an attached cottage. In the summer guests may dine outside beside the Mill Burn that flows through the property. This is the Official Tourist Information agency on behalf of the Dumfries & Galloway Tourist Board.*

*ACCOMMODATION under £20*

*FOOD up to £15*

**Hours:** meals – 1 March – Easter 10am – 6pm; meals – Easter – 31 May 10am – 8pm; meals – 1 June – 30 Sept 10am – 9pm; meals – 1 Oct – 31 Oct 10am – 7:30pm; closed 31/10 – 01/03. **Cuisine:** Scottish:- Home baking and cooking, trout in wine with almonds, home-made oatcakes & cheese, range of Scottish pates including wild garlic, smoked salmon, venison. **Rooms:** 2 bedrooms 1 double, 1 twin. **Other points:** open-air dining, Sunday lunch, no-smoking area, children catered for – please check for age limits, coach/prior arr. **Directions:** on the A762 to Kirkcudbright. MR & MRS MCPHEE, tel (06442) 269.

## NEWCASTLETON, Borders Map 20

### COPSHAW KITCHEN RESTAURANT, 4 North Hermitage Street

*A stone-built double-fronted antique shop, cafe and restaurant, offering a varied and interesting menu of well cooked tasty dishes, prepared by very well qualified and competent chef proprietor Jane Elliott. A friendly family run establishment that offers an exceptional range of facilities. Friendly attentive service in a pleasant relaxing atmosphere.*

*FOOD up to £15*

**Hours:** closed 01/01 – 28/02; meals all day 9:30am – 6pm; dinner 7:30pm – 9pm; closed Tuesday. **Cuisine:** British:- Varied and interesting menu, featuring Chef's Daily Choice, Scotch Gravadlax with cucumber & a mustard/dill dressing (Scandinavian sugar method). **Credit cards:** Visa, Access. **Other points:** Sunday lunch, children catered for – please check for age limits, afternoon tea. **Directions:** off B6357. JANE ELLIOTT, tel (03873) 75250, (03873) 75233.

## NEWTON STEWART, Dumfries & Galloway Map 23

### CROWN HOTEL, 101 Queen Street

*An attractive, cream, listed building carefully modernised in keeping with the character. The Crown Hotel has two private rods on the River Cree – a prime Salmon river – and several salmon dishes on the menu as a result!*

*ACCOMMODATION £21–£30*

*FOOD up to £15*

**Hours:** breakfast 8am – 9:30am; lunch 12noon – 2:30pm; bar meals 12noon – 2:30pm; bar meals 6pm – 9pm; dinner 6:30pm – 8:30pm. **Cuisine:** international:- A wide range of bar meals – chilli, curry, roast chicken, steaks. **Rooms:** 11 bedrooms all with tea making facilities, telephone, TV: 1 single ensuite, 1 single, 2 twins ensuite, 5 doubles ensuite, 1 double, 1 quad ensuite. **Credit cards:** Visa, Access. **Other points:** licensed, Sunday lunch, no-smoking area, children catered for – please check for age limits, baby-listening device, cots. **Directions:** on the southern outskirts of town. MR & MRS PRISE, tel (0671) 2727.

### INGLENOOK LICENSED RESTAURANT, 43 Main Street, Glenluce

*A small, intimate restaurant with a large inglenook fireplace. The menu offers an excellent choice of meals and snacks from 10.00am throughout the day until 9.00pm, all served within a friendly and relaxed atmosphere.*

*FOOD up to £15*

**Hours:** meals all day 10am – 9pm. **Cuisine:** British:- Wide range of dishes with Steak Pie and Inglenook mushrooms the house speciality. Full meals, snacks and drinks available. **Credit cards:** Visa, Access. **Other points:** Sunday lunch, children catered for – please check for age limits, afternoon tea. **Directions:** In Glenluce, 10 miles from Stranraer on the A75 to Dumfries. ROY & DIANA FLETCHER, tel (05813) 494.

## NEWTONMORE, Highlands Map 24

### BALAVIL SPORTS HOTEL, Main Street

*A family-run hotel situated in the centre of the village, offering a range of sporting amenities, including an indoor swimming pool. Recently renovated, the en suite bedrooms are spacious, airy and comfortable. Parties are welcomed. Good fresh Scottish food served all day. Golf, bowling, tennis, fishing.*

*ACCOMMODATION £21–£30*

*FOOD up to £15* ★

**Hours:** closed 01/01 – 14/01; breakfast 8am – 9:30am; lunch 12noon – 2:30pm; dinner 6:30pm – 8:30pm. **Cuisine:** Scottish:- Homestyle cooking. A la carte menu, includes Honeybaked Ham with an Orange & Cider sauce, Badenoch Venison Casserole, Haggis, Salmon and good home baking. **Rooms:** 50 bedrooms all with tea making facilities, telephone, TV: 5 singles ensuite, 10 doubles ensuite, 35 twins ensuite. **Credit cards:** Visa, Access. **Other points:** licensed, Sunday lunch, no-smoking area, children catered for – please check for age limits, pets allowed, parking, afternoon tea, residents' lounge, swimming pool, central heating, baby-listening device, cots, vegetarian meals, disabled access, residents' bar. **Directions:** A9, Situated on the main road running through the village.
JIM AND HELEN COYLE, tel (0540) 673220, fax (0540) 673773.

---

# NORTH UIST, Western Isles Map 24

## LOCHMADDY HOTEL, Lochmaddy

*Having undergone extensive restoration, this family-run sporting hotel offers good quality food and comfortable accommodation in tastefully furnished surroundings. The Lochmaddy is ideally situated for access to nearby beaches, fishing lochs, bird reserves, and archaeological sites.*
*ACCOMMODATION £31–£40*
*FOOD £15–£20* 🐮

**Hours:** open all year 6:30pm; breakfast 8am – 9:30am; bar meals 12noon – 2pm; bar meals 5:30pm – 9pm; dinner 6:30pm – 9pm. **Cuisine:** modern British:- Daily changing menus offering a wide selection of different dishes, including Honey Roast Duck with Apple and Cranberry Sauce, and Salmon Mornay. **Rooms:** 15 bedrooms all with tea making facilities, telephone, radio, TV: 5 singles ensuite, 5 twins ensuite, 5 doubles ensuite. **Credit cards:** Visa, Access. **Other points:** licensed, Sunday lunch, children catered for – please check for age limits, pets allowed, afternoon tea, garden, residents' lounge, parking, baby-listening device, cots, residents' bar. **Directions:** 100yds from Lochmaddy ferry terminal.
WILLIAM JOHN QUARM, tel (08763) 331, (08763) 332, fax (08763) 210.

---

# OBAN, Strathclyde Map 21

## ARDS HOUSE, Connel

*A family-owned guest house situated on the main Tyndrum to Oban road with magnificent views over the Firth of Lorn and Morvern Hills. An excellent touring base for the Highlands, all rooms are neatly furnished with most modern facilities, including central heating and colour television. There is an antique grand piano for the more artistic guests.*
*ACCOMMODATION £21– £30*
*FOOD up to £15*

**Hours:** breakfast 8:15am – 9am; dinner 7:15pm – later by arrangement. **Cuisine:** British. **Rooms:** 7 bedrooms, most ensuite. **Credit cards:** Visa, Access. **Other points:**

parking, open bank holidays, no-smoking, residents' lounge, vegetarian meals, garden. **Directions:** A85 Tyndrum to Oban, four miles north of Oban on the main A85.
JOHN & JEAN BOWMAN, tel (0631) 71 255.

## FALLS OF LORA HOTEL, Connel Ferry

*An imposing Victorian building in its own grounds set back from the A85. 100 yd from Connel railway station and overlooks Loch Etive. The cocktail bar has a roaring log fire and over 100 whiskies to tempt you. (See colour advertisement in centre section.)*
*ACCOMMODATION £21–£30*
*FOOD up to £15* ★

**Hours:** closed 01/01 – 01/02; breakfast 8am – 9:30am; lunch 12:30pm – 2pm; bar meals 12:30pm – 2pm; bar meals 5pm – 9:30pm; dinner 7pm – 8pm; closed Christmas day. **Cuisine:** Scottish / continental:- Sunday presentation buffet, Thursday 7 course Scottish dinner. **Rooms:** 30 bedrooms all with tea making facilities, telephone, radio, TV: 6 singles ensuite, 7 twins ensuite, 8 doubles ensuite, 3 triples ensuite, 3 quads ensuite, 3 luxury doubles. **Credit cards:** Visa, Access, Diners, AmEx. **Other points:** licensed, residents' lounge, no-smoking area, children catered for – please check for age limits, baby-listening device, cots, residents' bar. **Directions:** set back from A85, 5 miles before Oban, half mile from Connel Bridge.
MRS C M WEBSTER, tel (063171) 483, fax (063171) 694.

## FOXHOLES HOTEL, Cologin, Lerags

*Foxholes is peacefully situated in its own grounds in a quiet Glen just 3 miles south of Oban, with magnificent views of the surrounding countryside. An ideal spot for those who want to 'escape from it all', it offers tastefully furnished accommodation, a 6-Course Table d'Hote dinner menu and an A la Carte menu using the finest of fresh local Scottish produce. A marvellous place for any family holiday or romantic weekend break.*
*ACCOMMODATION £21–£30*

**Hours:** breakfast 8am – 9am; dinner 7pm – 8pm **Cuisine:** British:- Fresh local produce. **Other points:** parking, residents' lounge, vegetarian meals, garden. **Directions:** south from Oban, take A816 for approximately 2 miles, turn right, to Lerags, go for 0.75 miles, turn right and continue for 0.25 miles.
MR G AND MRS J WAUGH, tel (0631) 64982.

## LOCH ETIVE HOTEL, Connel Village

*A stone cottage style building, modernised to a high standard, and set in its own gardens bordered by a small river. The hotel derives its name from the nearby Loch Etive – and several of the rooms have views over the loch. Traditional Scottish hospitality is found here.*
*ACCOMMODATION under £20*
*FOOD up to £15*

**Hours:** breakfast 8:15am – 9am; dinner 7pm – 7:30pm; closed October – March. **Cuisine:** breakfast:- Dinner available May to mid July. **Rooms:** 2 double, 2 twin and 2 family bedrooms, 4 with en suite facilities. colour TV,

radio alarms and tea/coffee making facilities in all rooms. **Other points:** central heating, children catered for – please check for age limits, pets allowed, residents' lounge, parking. **Directions:** 100yds from the A85 in Connel village.
MISS FRANCOISE WEBER, tel (063117) 400.

# ORKNEY, Orkney & Shetland Islands Map 24

## QUOYBURRAY INN, Tankerness
*Dating back 100 years, the Quoyburray was once a grain store and is now undergoing extensive renovations by the proprietor, whose aim is to build it up into a reputable out-of-town restaurant. Nearby places of interest include the Covenanters Memorial.*
*FOOD up to £15*
**Hours:** bar snacks 12noon – 2pm; dinner 6pm – 9:30pm; closed Monday. **Cuisine:** English:- Traditional homestyle cooking. Vegetarians catered for. **Credit cards:** Visa, Access. **Other points:** Sunday lunch, children catered for – please check for age limits, bank holidays, parking. **Directions:** (A960) 5 miles east of Kirkwall.
JAMES & ISOBEL CURRIE, tel (0856) 86255.

# PAISLEY, Strathclyde Map 21

## BRABLOCH HOTEL, 62 Renfrew Road
*This pretty mansion house is set in 4 acres of land, conveniently situated within two miles of Glasgow airport, on the outskirts of Paisley. The restaurant serves a good selection of French and English cuisine, accompanied by a wide selection of wines.*
*ACCOMMODATION £41–£50*
*FOOD £15–£20*
**Hours:** breakfast 7am – 10am; lunch 12noon – 2pm; dinner 7:30pm – 10pm. **Cuisine:** French / English:- A la carte, Table d'hote and Bar menus. French/English – Duck a l'orange, Scampi Provincal. **Rooms:** 30 bedrooms, all en suite. **Credit cards:** Visa, Access, AmEx. **Other points:** licensed, Sunday lunch, no-smoking area, children catered for – please check for age limits, garden, afternoon tea, foreign exchange, residents' bar, residents' lounge, disabled access, vegetarian meals. **Directions:** on the A741. Less than 1 mile south of the M8, Junction 27.
LEWIS GRANT, tel (041) 889 5577.

## SHEZAN TANDOORI, 82 Glasgow Road
*A small comfortable restaurant serving Indian cuisine. A warm and courteous atmosphere prevails throughout. Close by for visiting Paisley Abbey.*
*FOOD up to £15*
**Hours:** Monday to Friday 12noon – 12midnight. **Cuisine:** Indian. **Credit cards:** Visa, Access, Diners, AmEx. **Other points:** open bank holidays, no-smoking area, vegetarian meals. **Directions:** A737 Glasgow Road towards Paisley Cross. On main Paisley Road from Glasgow.
MANJIT SINGH, tel (041) 887 2861.

## TRATTORIA LA TOSCANELLA, 16 Shuttle Street
*A traditionally furnished Italian-style restaurant, offering well prepared and presented Italian cuisine amidst a relaxed and friendly atmosphere. Popular with businessmen, locals and tourists alike.*
*FOOD up to £15*
**Hours:** closed New Years day 12noon; lunch 12noon – 2:15pm; dinner 5pm – 10:30pm. **Cuisine:** Italian. **Other points:** children catered for – please check for age limits, open bank holidays, no-smoking area, afternoon tea, disabled access, vegetarian meals. **Directions:** situated in Paisley town centre, off Cudsieside Street from High Street.
R J BRUCE, tel (041) 848 0898.

# PEEBLES, Borders Map 20

## CRINGLETIE HOUSE HOTEL
*Cringletie is a distinguished mansion house set well back in 28 acres of gardens and woodlands. Resident proprietors provide interesting and imaginative food, with fruit and vegetables in season from the hotel's extensive kitchen garden, which is featured in* The Gourmet Garden *by Geraldene Holt.*
*ACCOMMODATION £41–£50*
*FOOD £21–£25* 🍴
**Hours:** breakfast 8:15am – 9:15am; lunch 1pm – 1:45pm; dinner 7:30pm – 8:30pm. **Cuisine:** British:- Frequently changing menu – all home cooking. Afternoon tea including home baking. **Rooms:** 13 bedrooms 1 single ensuite, 8 twins ensuite, 4 doubles ensuite. **Credit cards:** Visa, Access. **Other points:** Sunday lunch, no-smoking area, children catered for – please check for age limits. **Directions:** on the Edinburgh/Peebles road (A703), 2.5 miles north of Peebles.
STANLEY & AILEEN MAGUIRE, tel (0721) 730233, fax (0721) 730244.

## KINGSMUIR HOTEL, Springhill Road
*A charming country house, built in the 1850s and set in leafy grounds in a quiet area, yet only 5 minutes walk through parkland to the High Street. The resident proprietors take great pride in their Taste of Scotland cuisine, to the delight of the many guests who have dined or stayed there. Winner of many local and regional awards.*
*ACCOMMODATION £31–£40*
*FOOD up to £15*
**Hours:** closed Christmas day 7:30pm; closed New Years day 7:30pm; breakfast 8:30am – 9:30am; lunch 12noon – 2pm; bar meals 12noon – 2pm; dinner 7pm – 9pm; bar meals 7pm – 9:30pm. **Cuisine:** Scottish:- Homemade soups, roasts, steak pie, sea and river fish, home-made desserts. **Rooms:** 10 bedrooms all with tea making facilities, telephone, radio, TV: 2 singles ensuite, 3 twins ensuite, 3 doubles ensuite, 1 triple ensuite, 1 family room ensuite. **Credit cards:** Visa, Access, AmEx. **Other points:** licensed, Sunday lunch, children catered for –

please check for age limits, pets allowed, conferences, baby-listening device, baby sitting, cots, foreign exchange, residents' lounge, residents' bar. **Directions:** High St; south over Tweed Bridge; Springhill Rd & half mile on right.
ELIZABETH & NORMAN KERR, tel (0721) 720151, fax (0721) 721795.

## PARK HOTEL, *Innerleithen Road*
*A friendly hotel on the outskirts of Peebles, overlooking the River Tweed. Guests can enjoy attractive gardens, well-appointed bedrooms and the popular hotel restaurant. When available, guests can also benefit from the facilities at the Peebles Hydro Hotel (only 700 yd away) – leisure centre with pool, saunas and Jacuzzi; squash courts; tennis courts and riding.*
*ACCOMMODATION £31–£40*
*FOOD up to £15*
**Hours:** breakfast 8am – 10am; lunch 12noon – 2pm; bar snacks 12noon – 2pm; dinner 7pm – 9:30pm; bar snacks 7pm – 9pm. **Cuisine:** Scottish:- Traditional cuisine featuring local produce such as smoked Scottish salmon and fresh local trout. **Rooms:** 24 bedrooms, all en suite. **Credit cards:** Visa, Access, Diners, AmEx. **Other points:** licensed, open-air dining, Sunday lunch, pets allowed, afternoon tea, garden, residents' lounge, leisure centre. **Directions:** on the A72 south of Edinburgh.
PEEBLES HOTEL HYDRO PATHIC LTD, tel (0721) 720451.

## PEEBLES HOTEL HYDRO, *Innerleithen Road*
*Few hotels offer facilities comparable to the Peebles Hydro. A 'resort' hotel with a full range of indoor and outdoor recreation facilities. There is a superb range of top value holiday packages all year round. Friendly staff and a warm welcome await you and the quality of the food is excellent. Magnificent grounds of 30 acres. Sister to the Park Hotel, also in Peebles.*
*ACCOMMODATION £41–£50*
*FOOD £21–£25* ☕
**Hours:** breakfast 8am – 9:30am; bar meals 12noon – 3:30pm; lunch 12:45pm – 2pm; dinner 7:30pm – 9pm. **Cuisine:** modern English:- Table d'hote dinner menu using local produce eg. Roast leg of Border lamb with a coriander sauce. Separate vegetarian menu. **Rooms:** 137 bedrooms, all en suite. **Credit cards:** Visa, Access, Diners, AmEx. **Other points:** licensed, Sunday lunch, no-smoking area, children catered for – please check for age limits, garden, leisure centre, residents' bar, residents' lounge, swimming pool, parking. **Directions:** on the A72, Peebles to Galashiels road.
MR P J VAN DIJK (MGR), tel (0721) 720602, fax (0721) 722999.

## VENLAW CASTLE HOTEL, *Tweedale*
*Venlaw Castle, on the slopes of the Moorfoot Hills yet within five minutes from the centre of Peebles, is a family owned hotel run in the country manner with the accent on personal attention. Reputed for their good quality home*

cooked dishes, using only the freshest produce, and for providing excellent accommodation, you will find the hospitality of the Cumming family outstanding.
*ACCOMMODATION £21–£30*
*FOOD £16–£20*
**Hours:** breakfast 8.30am – 9.30pm; dinner 7pm – 8pm; closed November until March. **Cuisine:** British. Dishes include baked salmon served with Hollandaise sauce, aubergine bake served with green salad. **Rooms:** 1 single, 4 twin, 4 double and 3 family bedrooms, 9 ensuite. **Credit cards:** Visa, Access, AmEx, Diners. **Other points:** children catered for – please check for age limits, garden, no smoking area, dogs allowed, residents' bar, residents' lounge. **Directions:** A72 to Peebles, 5 minutes from town centre.
MR & MRS CUMMING, tel (0721) 720384.

## PERTH, Tayside Map 22

## ALMONDBANK INN, *Almondbank*
*Olde worlde inn overlooking the River Almond in an attractive country village. Good food at very reasonable prices, friendly staff and a fun local atmosphere.*
*FOOD up to £15*
**Hours:** lunch 12noon – 2:15pm; lunch – Sunday 12:30pm – 2:15pm; dinner – Monday 5pm – 8:30pm; dinner – Tuesday 5pm – 8:30pm; dinner – Wednesday 5pm – 8:30pm; dinner – Thursday 5pm – 8:30pm; dinner – Sunday 5pm – 8:30pm; dinner – Friday 6:30pm – 10pm; dinner – Saturday 6:30pm – 10pm. **Cuisine:** English:- All fresh ingredients used: fresh melon, prawn & cheese salad, steaks, fresh salmon and prawn salad, plus a wide variety of special dishes. **Credit cards:** Visa, Access. **Other points:** licensed, Sunday lunch, children catered for – please check for age limits, beer garden. **Directions:** middle of main street of Almondbank village, about 3 miles from Perth.
MR & MRS C LINDSAY, tel (0738) 83242.

## PETERHEAD, Grampian Map 22

## BAYVIEW HOTEL, *3 St Peter Street*
*Pleasant family-run hotel situated on the coastline of Scotland. Peterhead is the home of the largest fishing fleet in Europe, and during your visit, you may have the opportunity to see the fish being landed. There is also a golf course nearby and Aviemore and Inverness are just a short drive away.*
*ACCOMMODATION £21–£30*
*FOOD up to £15*
**Hours:** breakfast 7am – 9:30am; lunch 12noon – 2pm; dinner 5pm – 8:30pm. **Cuisine:** Scottish:- Traditional Scottish cuisine using fresh fish and seafood, chicken, beef, pork and duck. **Rooms:** 17 bedrooms 4 twins ensuite, 11 doubles ensuite, 2 singles. **Credit cards:** Visa, Access. **Other points:** licensed, Sunday lunch, children catered for – please check for age limits, pets allowed. **Directions:** off the A952 between Aberdeen and Fraserburgh.
MR JAMES ELDER, tel (0779) 72523, fax (0779) 79495.

## PITLOCHRY, Tayside Map 22

### CRAIGOWER HOTEL, 134 Atholl Road

*A delightful family-run hotel occupying a prime position in the centre of Pitlochry, offering every comfort. Ideally situated within reach of all amenities, Pitlochry itself has much to offer, including golf, tennis, bowling, fishing, a cinema and more. Nearby attractions, include Blair Castle, The Historical Pass of Killiecrankie, and many breathtaking countryside walks.*

ACCOMMODATION £21–£30

FOOD up to £15

**Hours:** breakfast 8am – 10am; morning coffee 10am – 12noon; dinner 6:30pm – 9:30pm; bar meals 9pm – 11pm. **Cuisine:** British:- Grilled Rainbow Trout, Roast Gigot of Lamb, Baked Madeira, Choice of Salads. Extensive Wine List. Restaurant open all day for meals or snacks. **Rooms:** 26 bedrooms all with tea making facilities, telephone, TV: 2 singles ensuite, 10 twins ensuite, 10 doubles ensuite, 4 triples. **Credit cards:** Visa, Access. **Other points:** open-air dining, Sunday lunch, no-smoking area, children catered for – please check for age limits, pets allowed, afternoon tea, vegetarian meals, residents' lounge, garden, parking, baby-listening device, cots, left luggage. **Directions:** Pitlochry, situated in the town centre.
ROBERT & JEAN WILSON, tel (0796) 472590, fax (0796) 472590.

### GREEN PARK HOTEL, Clunie Bridge Road

*This is a country house hotel situated on the banks of the lovely Loch Faskally and although secluded it is only five minutes walk from the centre of the town. Popular with golfers because of the nearby golf course. Other facilities include fishing, sailing, golf and walking. Casserole Award winner 1990 and 1991.*

ACCOMMODATION £31–£40

FOOD up to £15 🍽

**Hours:** bar meals 12noon – 2:30pm; bar meals 6:30pm – 8:30pm; dinner 6:30pm – 8:30pm; closed November – mid-March. **Cuisine:** Scottish:- Scottish cuisine, eg. salmon, venison, Highland bonnets. **Rooms:** 37 bedrooms 23 twins ensuite, 12 doubles ensuite, 2 singles ensuite. **Credit cards:** Access, Visa, Switch. **Other points:** children catered for – please check for age limits, no-smoking area, fishing. **Directions:** on the A924 in north-west Pitlochry, on the left as you leave town.
MR & MRS GRAHAM BROWN, tel (0796) 473248, fax (0796) 473520.

### SCOTLAND'S HOTEL, Bonnethill Road

*Centrally, yet quietly located in picturesque Pitlochry, this friendly family owned and operated hotel enjoys a good reputation for comfortable bedrooms, fine food and attentive service. A new indoor leisure club features a 12m swimming pool, spa-bath, solarium, sauna, mini-gym and beauty salon. Complimentary mini-bus to/from the Festival Theatre, railway station and golf course.*

ACCOMMODATION £31–£40

FOOD £15–£20

**Hours:** breakfast 7:30am – 9:30am; lunch 12noon – 2pm; dinner 6:30pm – 8:30pm. **Cuisine:** Scottish:- Table d'hote with ample choice. A la carte also available. Speciality – Salmon. **Rooms:** 60 bedrooms all with tea making facilities, telephone, radio, TV: 13 singles ensuite, 11 doubles ensuite, 23 twins ensuite, 13 family rooms ensuite. **Credit cards:** Access, Visa, Switch. **Other points:** licensed, parking, children catered for – please check for age limits, garden, pets allowed, launderette, cots, bar. **Directions:** follow slip road from A9 or A924 into the centre of town. Turn off opposite Co-op, to find hotel on the right.
ERHARD J PENKER & FAMILY, tel (0796) 472292, fax (0769) 473284.

## POOLEWE, Highlands Map 24

### POOL HOUSE HOTEL, Nr Gairloch

*Situated at the heart of Wester Ross, at the head of Loch Ewe, Pool House Hotel offers an exciting alternative to those seeking a hotel base from which to explore the natural beauty of the Scottish Highlands. From the pleasant candlelit restaurant, guests can watch otters, seals and cormorants feeding by day and night. The hotel has a unique, comfortable and friendly atmosphere in astonishingly beautiful surroundings. Renowned for its exceptional local fare.*

ACCOMMODATION over £50

FOOD up to £15

**Hours:** breakfast 7:45am – 9:30am; bar snacks 12noon – 9pm; dinner 7pm – 9pm. **Cuisine:** British. **Credit cards:** Visa, Access. **Other points:** children catered for – please check for age limits, parking, no smoking area, residents' lounge, vegetarian meals, open-air dining. **Directions:** on main A832, on edge of River Ewe and Loch Ewe.
MR P L HARRISON, tel (0445) 86 272, fax (0445) 86 403.

## PORTPATRICK, Dumfries & Galloway Map 23

### FERNHILL HOTEL, Heugh Road

*Fernhill Hotel is situated in its own quiet, secluded grounds in the picturesque village of Portpatrick, which brings visitors back time after time. They have a proud reputation for their high standards, where every need is catered for. The hotel also caters for small golfing groups which can enjoy the freedom of their own house.*

ACCOMMODATION £31–£40

FOOD up to £15

**Hours:** breakfast 7:30am – 9:30am; lunch 12noon – 2pm; bar snacks 12noon – 2pm; bar snacks 6pm – 10pm; dinner 6:30pm – 10pm. **Cuisine:** English. **Rooms:** 20 bedrooms all with tea making facilities, radio, TV: 2 singles ensuite, 6 doubles ensuite, 12 twins ensuite. **Credit cards:** Visa, Access, Diners, AmEx. **Other points:** parking, children catered for – please check for age limits, Sunday lunch, open bank holidays, no-smoking area, afternoon tea, Sunday dinner, disabled

access, pets allowed, residents' lounge, vegetarian meals, open-air dining, garden, residents' bar, foreign exchange. **Directions:** at the end of A77. On approach to village take right fork at the War Memorial.
MR & MRS HARVIE, tel (0776)81220, (0776) 810220, fax (0776) 81596/810596.

## PORTREE, Highlands Map 24

### ROYAL HOTEL, Bank Street
*From Portree's Royal Hotel, the whole of Skye is on the doorstep. With a coastline of over 900 miles, the Isle of Skye enjoys a bountiful harvest from the sea – prawns, lobsters, oysters and salmon. From the hill there is lamb and venison and from the rich pastures sizzling prime steaks. Most comfortably furnished bedrooms face the sea and have stunning views, making this a popular holiday retreat for families.*
*ACCOMMODATION £21–£30*
**Hours:** breakfast 7:30am – 10am; lunch 12noon – 2pm; bar snacks 12noon – 2pm; bar snacks 5pm – 7:30pm; dinner 7pm – 9:30pm. **Cuisine:** Scottish. **Credit cards:** Visa, Access. **Other points:** parking, children catered for – please check for age limits, no-smoking area, disabled access, pets, residents' lounge, vegetarian meals. **Directions:** off A850 to A855, quarter mile on left-hand side overlooking Harbour.
MACLEOD HOTELS LTD, tel (0478) 612525, fax (0478) 613198.

## RENFREW, Strathclyde Map 21

### PICCOLO MONDO & LA TOSCANELLA, 63 Hairst Street
*This bustling Italian Restaurant has gained an excellent reputation for its imaginative menus which offer outstanding value for money. From Monday to Saturday the owner has introduced a marvellous "Grande Buffet Italiano" which allows you to help yourself to starters, Main courses and desserts. Of course there are also Table D'Hote menus and full international a la carte menu available at all times, all of this makes Piccolo Mondo one of the most popular Italian Restaurants in the west of Scotland. Highly recommended. Adjoining Piccolo Mondo is Trattoria La Toscanella, which is a lovely little restaurant specialising in Pizza and Pasta, and is open 7 days for lunch and dinner and all day every Sunday. The menu includes a vast selection of Authentic Tuscan Cuisine dishes all freshly cooked.*
*FOOD up to £15* 🍽
**Hours:** lunch 12noon – 2:15pm; dinner 5pm – 11pm, closed bank holidays; closed Sunday. **Cuisine:** Italian / seafood:- Italian/French cuisine – veal, steak, chicken, pasta and shellfish dishes. **Credit cards:** Visa, Access, Diners, AmEx. **Other points:** licensed, children catered for – please check for age limits. **Directions:** 5 miles from Glasgow centre. Centre of Renfrew, near Glasgow airport.
MR R J BRUCE, tel (041) 886 3055, fax (041) 885 2688.

## ROSEHALL, Highlands Map 24

### ACHNESS HOTEL, Sutherland
*Formerly a turn-of-the-century farmhouse, the main building of the Achness Hotel is a highly successful conversion into a quadrangle, which allows parking outside the door of your room. Specially popular with holiday-makers and fishermen the emphasis is on home-made meals and no doubt the reason for its popularity at lunchtimes.*
*ACCOMMODATION £31–£40*
*FOOD £15–£20*
**Hours:** breakfast 8:30am; bar meals 12:30pm – 2pm; bar meals 6pm – 9pm; dinner 8pm. **Cuisine:** English:- Fixed price menu, with an emphasis on home-made soups and sweets. **Rooms:** 12 bedrooms all with tea making facilities: 2 doubles ensuite, 2 twins, 5 twins ensuite, 3 singles. **Credit cards:** Visa, Access. **Other points:** licensed, Sunday lunch, children catered for – please check for age limits, pets allowed, afternoon tea, residents' lounge, parking, disabled access. **Directions:** situated off the A837 in Rosehall village. Well signposted.
NEIL GRAESSER & PARTNERS, tel (054984) 239, fax (054984) 324.

## ROSLIN, Lothian Map 20

### OLD ORIGINAL INN
*This historic inn was first opened in 1827 and has remained open for business ever since. The village is in a rural area and the inn's old fashioned decor gives it a charming atmosphere.*
*FOOD £15–£20*
**Hours:** breakfast 7:30am – 9:30am; lunch 12noon – 2pm; dinner – weekends 5pm – 10pm; dinner – weekdays 6pm – 10pm. **Cuisine:** British:- Grills, daily specials such as Salmon Vol au vents, Grilled Spring Lamb, Walnut Sundae. **Rooms:** 6 bedrooms all en suite. **Credit cards:** Visa, Access, AmEx. **Other points:** open-air dining, Sunday lunch, children catered for – please check for age limits, coach/prior arr. **Directions:** just off A701, just outside Edinburgh.
MR G A HARRIS, tel (031) 440 2384.

## ROSYTH, Fife Map 22

### GLADYER INN, Heath Road, Ridley Drive
*A modern, purpose built hotel with up to date facilities to match. The best of Scottish hospitality is extended to all guests whether they are staying overnight, dining or having a drink. Good value for money.*
*ACCOMMODATION £21–£30*
*FOOD up to £15*
**Hours:** breakfast 7am – 9:30am; lunch 12noon – 2pm; bar meals 12noon – 2pm; dinner 7pm – 9:30pm; bar meals 7pm – 9:30pm. **Cuisine:** Scottish:- Table d'hote menu including traditional dishes. **Rooms:** 21 bedrooms all with tea making facilities, telephone, TV: 4 doubles ensuite, 1 family room ensuite, 16 twins ensuite. **Credit cards:** Visa, Access, AmEx. **Other points:** licensed, Sunday lunch, no-smoking area, children catered for –

please check for age limits, functions, pets allowed.
**Directions:** from M90 junction 1 towards Kincardine Bridge, Ridley Drive on left.
JANET & JIM INNES, tel (0383) 419977, fax (0383) 411728.

## SCOURIE, Highlands Map 24

### EDDRACHILLES HOTEL, Badcall Bay
*Eddrachilles Hotel stands in its own 320 acre estate in a magnificent situation at the head of the island-studded Badcall Bay. This is a family run, comfortable hotel offering good food in friendly relaxing surroundings. If you are looking for a peaceful, tranquil holiday this hotel is well worth a visit.*
ACCOMMODATION £31–£40
FOOD up to £15
**Hours:** breakfast 8am – 9am; dinner 6:30pm – 8:30pm.
**Cuisine:** English:- Dishes include salmon pate, pepper steak, lemon sole meuniere, and desserts such as blackberry & apple pie, rhum baba and pear belle helen. **Rooms:** 11 rooms. 7 twinbeds, 3 double and 1 family room, all en suite. TV, radio, telephone, trouser-press, iron & tea making facilities in all rooms. **Credit cards:** Visa, Access. **Other points:** licensed. **Directions:** on A894 it is approximately 6 miles north of Kylesku Bridge.
MR & MRS A C M WOOD, tel (0971) 502080, (0971) 502211, fax (0971) 502477.

## SELKIRK, Borders Map 20

### PHILIPBURN HOUSE HOTEL & RESTAURANT
*A charming 18th century house, carefully converted into a warm hostelry with very interesting gourmet cooking. Set in very beautiful gardens amidst superb historical buildings, abbeys and houses, this is the Borders premier hotel for guided and unguided hill walking.*
ACCOMMODATION £21–£30
FOOD up to £15 ☜
**Hours:** breakfast 8am – 9:30am; lunch 12:15pm – 2:15pm; bar meals 12:25pm – 2:15pm; bar meals 7pm – 10pm; dinner 7:30pm – 9:30pm. **Cuisine:** Scottish / French:- Innovative French and Scottish cooking, including local Saddle of Roe Deer Cassis, and Rosace of Langoustines, Sachertorte. Unusual Scottish bar menu. **Rooms:** 16 bedrooms, all en suite, with colour TV, radio, alarm, telephone, and tea/coffee making facilities. **Credit cards:** Visa, Access. **Other points:** licensed, Sunday lunch, no-smoking area, children catered for – please check for age limits, pets/prior arr, afternoon tea, bank holidays, residents' lounge, garden.
**Directions:** near Selkirk rugby ground.
JIM & ANNE HILL, tel (0750) 720747, fax (0750) 721690.

## SHETLAND, Orkney & Shetland Islands Map 24

### SHETLAND HOTEL, Holmsgarth Road
*Warm hospitality is offered at this efficient, modern hotel, overlooking Lerwick Harbour, just 3 minutes from the ferry terminal. All rooms have the most up-to-date facilities for maximum comfort. Special Package Holidays are available, and conferences and private functions can be catered for.*
ACCOMMODATION £31–£40
FOOD £15–£20
**Hours:** 7:30pm. **Cuisine:** British. **Other points:** children catered for – please check for age limits, no-smoking area, disabled access, pets, vegetarian meals, parking, garden. **Directions:** situated north end of Lerwick directly opposite ferry terminal.
LERWICK HARBOUR TRUST, tel (0595) 5515, fax (0595) 5828.

## SOUTH UIST, Western Isles Map 24

### BORRODALE HOTEL, Daliburgh, Lochboisdale
*The Borrodale Hotel is a small family run hotel famous for its shellfish dishes and friendly atmosphere. Offering comfortable accommodation. The helpful staff will arrange golfing, fishing or tell you of the best beaches or where to spot rare and splendid birds.*
ACCOMMODATION £21–£30
FOOD up to £15
**Hours:** breakfast 7:30am – 9:30am; lunch 12:30pm – 2pm; bar meals 6:30pm – 9pm; dinner 7pm – 9pm. **Cuisine:** British:- Dishes may include Scotch Cockles in Whisky & Oatmeal, Venison with Red Wine and Mushroom Sauce, Strawberry Cheesecake. Speciality dishes – Seafood. **Rooms:** 14 bedrooms all with tea making facilities, TV: 3 singles ensuite, 4 twins ensuite, 6 doubles ensuite, 1 triple ensuite. **Credit cards:** Visa, Access. **Other points:** licensed, Sunday lunch, children catered for – please check for age limits, afternoon tea, pets allowed, caravan facilities, residents' lounge, residents' bar. **Directions:** 2.5 miles from Lochboisdale ferry, on Junction of the A865 and B888.
MR DONALD PETERANNA, tel (08784) 444, fax (08784) 611.

## ST ANDREWS, Fife Map 22

### THE PANCAKE PLACE, 177/9 South Street
*A cheerful family restaurant serving satisfying meals at good value for money. Spacious surroundings and relaxed atmosphere. Famous golf course, university, and sea-life centre nearby. Also, beaches and cathedral ruins.*
FOOD up to £15
**Hours:** closed 01/01; meals all day 9:30am – 5:30pm; closed Christmas 25/12. **Cuisine:** Scottish:- Pancakes traditional Scottish style, savoury and sweet. Also, baked potatoes, rice and monthly specials. **Other points:** licensed, Sunday lunch, no-smoking area, children catered for – please check for age limits.
**Directions:** towards the west port along South Street, near Madras College.
C D BURHOUSE, tel (0334) 75671.

## STIRLING, Central Map 22

### STIRLING MANAGEMENT CENTRE,
*University Of Stirling*
*Conveniently located in a splendid rural setting, Stirling Management Centre is an ideal venue for business conferences and training courses. Purpose built meeting rooms, executive accommodation, sports and leisure facilities combined with educational resources of a progressive, modern University ensure the success of your visit here.*
*ACCOMMODATION £31–£40*
*FOOD £15–£20*
**Hours:** breakfast 7:30am – 9am; lunch 12:30pm – 2:30pm; dinner 6:30pm – 8:30pm. **Cuisine:** British. **Credit cards:** Visa, Access. **Other points:** parking, children catered for – please check for age limits, no-smoking area, disabled access, vegetarian meals, garden. **Directions:** from the north follow A9 from south, follow A74, leading to the A80/M80.
MS G MACINTYRE, tel (0786) 451666, fax (0786) 450472.

## STRACHUR, Strathclyde Map 21

### THE CREGGANS INN
*Stupendous views over Loch Fyne. Genuine country lodge atmosphere of log fires and own house Malt Whisky 'McPhunns'. Private walks, deerstalking and fishing by arrangement. All the food is based on Lady MacLean's famous cookbook recipes. Only 1 hour from Glasgow. Also, via Gournock, ferry across Clyde and A815 to Strachur.*
*ACCOMMODATION £31–£40*
*FOOD £15–£20* 🍷 🥄 CLUB
**Hours:** open all day 8am – 12midnight. **Cuisine:** British:- Homemade soups, rainbow trout, Aberdeen Angus steaks, poached salmon, local seafood table inc. oysters, smoked salmon and langoustines, wild game. **Rooms:** 21 bedrooms all with tea making facilities, telephone, TV: 1 single ensuite, 3 singles, 8 doubles ensuite, 9 twins ensuite. **Credit cards:** Visa, Access, Diners, AmEx. **Other points:** children catered for – please check for age limits, residents' lounge, residents' bar. **Directions:** from Glasgow & M8 over Erskine Bridge, left Lom', A815 to Strachur.
SIR FITZROY MACLEAN, tel (036986) 279, fax (036986) 637.

## STROMNESS, Orkney & Shetland Islands Map 24

### STANDING STONES HOTEL, Stenness
*One of Orkney's finest fishing hotels situated on the tranquil shores of the Stenness Loch, providing an ideal base for touring Orkney's many other attractions. There are two comfortable lounges in which to relax, with a welcoming and popular Lounge Bar serving bar meals. Surrounded by many historical monuments, fishing, golf and bird-watching are also very popular.*
*ACCOMMODATION £31–£40*
*FOOD up to £15*
**Hours:** open all year 8am; breakfast 8am – 9am; bar snacks 12noon – 2:30pm; bar snacks 6:30pm – 9:30pm; dinner 7:30pm – 9:30pm. **Cuisine:** modern British:- A la carte and table d'hote first Class cuisine prepared with fresh local produce, including Deepdale Duck, Germiston Grouse, St Magnus Salmon Steak. **Rooms:** 17 bedrooms all with tea making facilities, telephone, radio, TV: 3 singles ensuite, 2 doubles ensuite, 3 family rooms ensuite, 9 twins ensuite. **Credit cards:** Visa, Access. **Other points:** licensed, Sunday lunch, children catered for – please check for age limits, parking, residents' lounge, garden, vegetarian meals, afternoon tea, disabled access, residents' bar. **Directions:** 3 miles from Stromness ferry terminal on main Kirkwall road.
COLIN INNES, tel (0856) 850449, fax (0856) 851262.

### STROMNESS HOTEL, Victoria Street
*A comfortable hotel situated in the heart of the unique fishing port of Stromness which is also the main ferry terminal between the mainland and Orkney. The hotel overlooks the harbour and Scapa Flow which served as the British naval base for both World Wars. All bedrooms have modern facilities and bar lunches are served daily in the lounge bar, which enjoys panoramic views.*
*ACCOMMODATION £21–£30*
*FOOD £15–£20*
**Hours:** breakfast 7:15am – 9:30am; bar snacks 12noon – 2pm; bar snacks 6:30pm – 9:30pm; dinner 7pm – 9pm. **Cuisine:** international. **Rooms:** 40 bedrooms 34 doubles ensuite, 6 singles ensuite. **Credit cards:** Visa, Access. **Other points:** parking, children catered for – please check for age limits, open bank holidays, pets allowed, vegetarian meals, garden. **Directions:** the Stromness is situated at the main pier in Stromness, on the harbour.
LEONA KIRKNESS, tel (0856) 850298, fax (0856) 850610.

## TAIN, Highlands Map 24

### MORANGIE HOUSE HOTEL, Morangie Road
*A fine old Victorian mansion with luxurious rooms and stained glass windows. Professionally managed yet friendly and welcoming and offering an extensive range of menus to suit all tastes, with food of excellent quality. Reduced price golf to residents. Tain museum and 14th century church nearby.*
*ACCOMMODATION £31–£40*
*FOOD up to £15* ★
**Hours:** breakfast 7am – 10am; lunch 12noon – 2:30pm; bar meals 12noon – 2:30pm; bar meals 5pm – 10pm; dinner 7pm – 10pm. **Cuisine:** Scottish / continental:- Scottish and continental cuisine, fresh seafood being the speciality. A la carte, table d'hote and bar menus. **Rooms:** 13 bedrooms all with tea making facilities, telephone, TV: 7 doubles ensuite, 2 twins ensuite, 4 singles ensuite. **Credit cards:** Visa, Access, Diners,

AmEx. **Other points:** licensed, Sunday lunch, children catered for – please check for age limits. **Directions:** north on A9, take last turn off into Tain on right-hand side.
AVRIL & JOHN WYNNE, tel (0862) 892281, fax (0862) 892872.

# TAYVALLICH, Strathclyde Map 21

## TAYVALLICH INN, By Lochgilphead
*Tayvallich Inn is situated in one of the most beautiful and picturesque locations in Scotland. Mr Grafton and his staff offer a warm welcome and serve really good food. Steaks and locally caught mussels, prawns and lobsters are the house specialities.*
*FOOD £15–£20*
**Hours:** lunch 12noon – 2pm; dinner 6pm – 9pm; closed Monday – November – March. **Cuisine:** British:- Traditional meals. House speciality – seafood. **Credit cards:** Visa, Access. **Other points:** licensed, open-air dining, Sunday lunch, children catered for – please check for age limits, bank holidays, pets allowed.
**Directions:** off A816 Lochgilphead to Crinan road.
JOHN & PAT GRAFTON, tel (05467) 282.

# THORNHILL, Central Map 23

## BUCCLEUGH AND QUEENSBERRY HOTEL, 112 Drumcanrigg Street
*A family run comfortable hotel in the centre of Thornhill surrounded by scenic Nithsdale. Built in 1855 by the Duke of Buccleuch, it provides a friendly, welcoming atmosphere and freshly prepared food in pleasant surroundings.*
*ACCOMMODATION under £20*
*FOOD up to £15*
**Hours:** meals all day 7:30am – 10:30pm. **Cuisine:** English / continental. **Credit cards:** Visa, Access, Diners. **Other points:** parking, children catered for – please check for age limits, afternoon teas, pets, residents' lounge, vegetarian meals, open-air dining.
**Directions:** situated in the centre of Thornhill.
MR & MRS STACK, tel (0848) 330215.

# THURSO, Highlands Map 24

## THE CASTLE ARMS HOTEL, Mey
*A former 19th century coaching inn, situated on the John O' Groats peninsula in the north coast village of Mey, and only a short distance from the Queen Mother's Highland home, the Castle of Mey. In the evenings, relax in front of the Caithness flagstone fireplace and enjoy a wee dram from a choice of fine malt whiskies. A seal colony is just one of the main nearby attractions.*
*ACCOMMODATION £21–£30*
*FOOD £15–£20*
**Hours:** open all year 7:30am; breakfast 8:30am – 9:30am; lunch 12:30pm – 2pm; bar meals 5:30pm – 9pm; high tea 5:30pm – 7:30pm; dinner 7pm – 9pm. **Cuisine:** Scottish:- For dinner, a comprehensive table

d'hote menu is available, which includes locally caught fresh salmon, crab and succulent steaks. Extremely fine wine list. **Rooms:** 8 bedrooms all with tea making facilities, telephone, TV: 3 twins ensuite, 4 doubles ensuite, 1 triple ensuite. **Credit cards:** Visa, Access. **Other points:** open-air dining, Sunday lunch, children catered for – please check for age limits, pets allowed, parking, afternoon tea, cots, left luggage, residents' lounge, residents' bar.
**Directions:** 7 miles west of John O' Groats.
MRS MORRISON, tel (084 785) 244, fax (084 785) 244.

# TONGUE, Highlands Map 24

## BEN LOYAL HOTEL, Main Street
*Situated between Durness & Thurso, this small crofting village enjoys some of Scotland's most spectacular coastal and mountain scenery and wonderful clean beaches. The warmth of welcome and the genuine friendliness of the staff and proprietors, add to its reputation as a mecca for fishermen and hillwalkers and a holiday/touring centre. A true sanctuary from the stress of urban living.*
*ACCOMMODATION £21–£30*
*FOOD £15–£20* 🍽
**Hours:** breakfast 8am – 9:15am; bar meals 12noon – 2pm; bar meals 6pm – 8:30pm; dinner 7pm – 8pm. **Cuisine:** Scottish:- Traditional and modern Scottish cooking using fresh local produce. **Rooms:** 17 bedrooms all with tea making facilities, TV: 1 single ensuite, 2 singles, 1 twin, 8 doubles ensuite, 5 twins ensuite. **Credit cards:** Visa, Access. **Other points:** licensed, no-smoking area, coach/prior arr, vegetarian meals, cots, 24hr reception.
**Directions:** at the junction of the A836 and A838.
MEL & PAULINE COOK, tel (084 755) 216.

# TWEEDSMUIR, Borders Map 20

## THE CROOK INN, By Biggar
*The Crook is Scotland's oldest licensed Inn, which has been sympathetically updated over many years. This family run establishment, offers good food, comfortable accommodation and a very warm welcome. Ideally located for touring the beautiful Border country and a centre for country pursuits. New for 1993 is a Craft Centre demonstrating a wide range of local crafts.*
*ACCOMMODATION £21–£30*
*FOOD up to £15*
**Hours:** meals all day 8am – 9:30pm. **Cuisine:** British:- Dishes may include Beef Stroganoff, Roast Duck, Poached Salmon Steak. Bar meals include fish dishes and the very popular home-made steak pies. **Rooms:** 3 twin, 4 double, and 1 family room, 6 of them en suite. **Credit cards:** Visa, Access, Diners, AmEx. **Other points:** Sunday lunch, no-smoking area, children catered for – please check for age limits, garden, afternoon tea, pets allowed, residents' lounge, residents' bar, parking.
**Directions:** 17 miles north of Moffat on the A7O1, between Moffat and Edinburgh.
STUART & ANGELA REID, tel (08997) 272, fax (08997) 294.

## TYNDRUM, Central Map 22

### CLIFTON COFFEE HOUSE

*Spacious self-service restaurant with adjoining shops, specialising in the best Scottish dishes, whisky and confectionery. Outstanding Scottish crafts. Extensive car park and filling station facilities.*
*FOOD up to £15*
**Hours:** meals all day 8:30am – 5:30pm; closed January – end March. **Cuisine:** Scottish:- Homemade soups, good country cooking including game pies, hot pots and casseroles, fresh and smoked salmon and extensive salad table. **Credit cards:** Visa, Access, AmEx, Diners, Switch. **Other points:** Sunday lunch, no-smoking area, children catered for – please check for age limits. **Directions:** Tyndrum is located on the A82. The Coffee House is in the middle of the village on the road side.
GOSDEN OF TYNDRUM, tel (08384) 271, fax (08384) 330.

### INVERVEY HOTEL

*Standing on the Road to the Isles in some of Scotland's most stunning scenery, the hotel is ideal for either an overnight stop or for staying a while to explore the area.*
*ACCOMMODATION £21–£30*
**Hours:** breakfast 8am – 10am; lunch 12 noon – 2pm; dinner 5pm – 8.30pm. **Rooms:** 3 single, 7 double, 7 twin and 4 family bedrooms, 9 ensuite. **Credit cards:** Visa, Access, AmEx. **Other points:** children catered for – please check for age limits, licensed, residents' lounge. s**Directions:** on the A82/A85.
MR RILEY, tel (08384) 219, (08384) 289.

## ULLAPOOL, Highlands Map 24

### CEILIDH PLACE, West Argyle Street

*Originally two cottages, the buildings have been carefully renovated with quality fabrics and wood panelling to provide a relaxing, comfortable hotel with a friendly atmosphere. As the Gaelic name suggests it is a "place to meet, eat, talk or sing". There are regular concerts throughout the year, traditional music with some folk, classical and jazz. Ullapool is a convenient centre from which to explore some of the finest mountain scenery in Scotland. Special winter rates 27th October 94 until 27th March 95.*
*ACCOMMODATION £41–£50*
*FOOD £21–£25*
**Hours:** breakfast 8am – 10am; bar snacks 12noon – 6pm; bar snacks 6:30pm – 9:30pm; dinner 7pm – 9pm; closed 9 January – 23 January. **Cuisine:** Scottish, **Rooms:** 13 bedrooms 2 singles, 1 double, 4 twins ensuite, 6 doubles ensuite. **Credit cards:** Visa, Access, Diners, AmEx. **Other points:** parking, children catered

for – please check for age limits, no-smoking area, pets, residents' lounge, vegetarian meals. **Directions:** A835, first right after the pier.
JEAN AND ROBERT URQUHART, tel (0854) 612103, fax (0854) 612886.

### THE HARBOUR LIGHTS HOTEL, Garve Road

*A family-run hotel and restaurant offering excellent food, a warm welcome and comfortable accommodation. The spacious lounge has a panoramic view of the harbour, Loch Broom and the surrounding hills and the hotel is only a short walk from the centre of the old fishing port of Ullapool.*
*ACCOMMODATION £21–£30*
*FOOD £15–£20*
**Hours:** breakfast 8am – 9am; bar meals 12noon – 2pm; lunch – Sunday 12:30pm – 2pm; dinner 7pm – 9:30pm. **Cuisine:** British:- Specialities include local salmon, seafood, Scotch beef and venison, Turf and Surf – Fillet steak, with fresh scallops, prawn tails & shellfish sauce. **Rooms:** 22 bedrooms all with tea making facilities, telephone, TV: 8 twins ensuite, 8 doubles ensuite, 2 family rooms ensuite, 1 single ensuite, 3 singles. **Credit cards:** Visa, Access. **Other points:** licensed, Sunday lunch, children catered for – please check for age limits, garden, afternoon tea, pets allowed, residents' lounge, residents' bar. **Directions:** on the outskirts of Ullapool.
MARILYN & DANNY GORDON, tel (0854) 612222.

## WEST WEMYSS, Fife Map 22

### THE BELVEDERE, Coxstool, Nr Kirkcaldy

*A waterside hotel, beautifully situated on the Firth Of Forth, in the picturesque Fife village of West Wemyss. Only 10 minutes drive from Kirkcaldy, with plenty of places to visit, including golf courses, nearby fishing and activities centre and the historic East Neuk of Fife. Edinburgh only 40 minutes by road or rail.*
*ACCOMMODATION £21–£30*
*FOOD £15–£20* ★
**Hours:** breakfast 7am – 10am; lunch 12noon – 2:30pm; bar meals 12noon – 2:30pm; dinner 6pm – 9:30pm; bar meals 6pm – 9:30pm; bar and snacks all day. **Cuisine:** European cuisine with good local seafood. **Rooms:** 21 bedrooms all with tea making facilities, TV: 12 doubles ensuite, 5 twins ensuite, 1 single ensuite, 1 suite, 2 family rooms ensuite. **Credit cards:** Visa, Access, AmEx, Switch. **Other points:** licensed, children catered for – please check for age limits, bank holidays, sauna, solarium, high tea. **Directions:** take A955 from Kirkcaldy to Leven. 3 miles from Kirkcaldy.
WEMYSS HOTELS LTD, tel (0592) 654167, fax (0592) 655279.

# THE NORTH OF IRELAND

Ireland is excellent touring country – a world where time stands still – a wild and enchanting land of emerald green windswept moors, remote lakes, ever changing scenery and dramatic skies.

History has generated a wealth of castles, churches and abbeys, many of which remain intact. In Ulster, the craggy North Antrim coast – shaped over thousands of years by the sea – is home to some spectacular wildlife. It was also here in 7000 BC that Ireland's first inhabitants came ashore, nomadic boatmen from Scotland, later followed by early Christians and Vikings. It was not until the arrival of the Normans, however, that the building of many of Ireland's finest castles commenced.

In the north the Sperrin Mountains, with their network of tiny streams and roads, are frequented by a wide range of wildlife, where walkers and naturalists are often rewarded with sightings of golden plover and red grouse. The famous glens of Antrim and their lush green valleys are steeped in folklore and legend. Take the road from Larne to Ballycastle and stop off to visit the Giant's Causeway. As the largest lake in the British Isles, Lough Neagh is a favourite with sailing enthusiasts, while Lough Erne at 50 miles long offers unrestricted cruising and watersports, and is also a paradise for birdwatchers and anglers. Belfast is an exciting city with a wealth of Edwardian and Victorian architecture. Dominating the main shopping centre is The City Hall, built in the early 1900s. Not far away is Queen's University, a large imposing building of mellow brick with original Tudor cloisters and mullioned windows. South of Belfast is Carrickfergus Castle, built in 1180 by Henry II to guard Belfast Lough.

County Down is known as St Patrick's country where the saint is buried in Downe Cathedral churchyard. Along the shores of Strangford Lough in the twelfth century, many monasteries were built including Inch Abbey near Downpatrick. A windswept coast road takes you from the popular seaside resort of Bangor past Ballycopeland windmill and down to Portavogie harbour where you can see seals bobbing among the fishing boats. Travel south-east to view the splendour of Ireland's most famous mountains – the Mountains of Mourne, idolized in song and covering an area of 15 miles long and 8 miles wide, with twelve magnificent rounded summits including Slieve Donard which dominates the surrounding landscape. Fermanagh boasts many National Trust properties including Castle Coole, a fine Palladian house designed by James Wyatt for the Earl of Belmore at Enniskillen, and in the grounds of Florence Court, seat of the Earls of Enniskillen, is the original Florence Court Yew from which the yew tree originated.

Wherever you are planning to travel throughout Ireland, you will always find a good choice of comfortable places to stay offering good food and accommodation.

For details of where to visit and what to see in the North of Ireland, contact the Northern Ireland Tourist Board, St Anne's Court, 59 North Street, Belfast BT1 1NB. Tel: (0232) 231221/246609.

---

## BANGOR, County Down Map 25

### GILLESPIES' PLACE / GRYPHON RESTAURANT, 12 Ballyholme Esplanade

*Situated on Ballyholme Esplanade and enjoying full panoramic views over Belfast Lough, this Bar/Restaurant has undergone extensive refurbishment throughout. A bright, spacious 54 seater restaurant, attractively furnished lounge bars, excellent food, and highly efficient service are all part of the warm friendly, relaxed atmosphere at this highly popular meeting place.*
FOOD up to £15 ♈ 🍲
**Hours:** bar meals – Mon-Sat 12noon – 2:30pm; Sunday lunch 12:30pm – 2pm; high tea 5:50pm – 7pm; bar meals – Tue-Sat 6pm – 9:15pm; dinner – except Sun & Mon 7pm – 9:15pm. **Cuisine:** modern:- Set price menu changes each week. Two courses – £10.00, Three courses – £13.00. May include: Salmon escalope with saffron and ginger sauce; steamed chicken fillet stuffed with prawn mousse in lemon and pink peppercorn sauce. **Credit cards:** Visa, Access. **Other points:** licensed, Sunday lunch, parking, disabled access, vegetarian meals, bank holidays. **Directions:** one mile from Bangor Town Centre, overlooking Ballyholme Bay.
RAYMOND MCELROY (DIRECTOR), tel (0247) 473294, (0247) 270954, fax (0247) 463883.

## BELFAST, County Antrim Map 25

### SAINTS & SCHOLARS LTD, 3 University Street, University & Malone

*Highly popular and attractively furnished bistro style restaurant on two floors with a bar on each. The atmosphere is warm, welcoming and lively. Nearby places of interest include the Ulster Museum and Queens University.*

*FOOD up to £15*

**Hours:** meals all day 12noon – 11am; lunch – Sunday 12noon – 2:30pm; dinner – Sunday 5:30pm – 9:30pm. **Cuisine:** British:- A La Carte menu, combining traditional and modern dishes, complemented by a fine wine list. Vegetarian dishes available. Express menu for luncheon. **Credit cards:** Visa, Access, Diners, AmEx. **Other points:** licensed, Sunday lunch, children catered for – please check for age limits, vegetarian meals, bank holidays, parking. **Directions:** situated on the left, off University Road, before Queens University.
DIRK LAKEMAN, tel (0232) 325137, fax (0232) 323240.

## BUSHMILLS, County Antrim Map 25

### Restaurant of the Year
### HILLCREST COUNTRY HOUSE & RESTAURANT, 306 Whitepark Road

*An internationally renowned award winning guesthouse, offering comfortable and well appointed accommodation in spacious en suite rooms, all with marvellous coastal or rural views. The restaurant offers traditional menus using the finest fresh ingredients, specialising in local seafood and game. Beautifully furnished throughout – highly recommended.*

*ACCOMMODATION £21–£30*

*FOOD up to £15* 🕭

**Hours:** breakfast 8:30am – 9:30am; closed Monday to Thursday 1 September – 31 March; lunch 12:30pm – 2:30pm; dinner 5pm – 9pm. **Cuisine:** British:- Food and service of the highest standard. **Credit cards:** Visa, Access. **Other points:** parking, children catered for – please check for age limits, Sunday lunch, no-smoking area, disabled access, residents' lounge, vegetarian meals, garden. **Directions:** half mile out of Bushmills Village. On the main road to Giants Causeway.
MR M MCKEEVER, tel (02657) 31577, fax (02657) 31577.

## COLERAINE, Londonderry Map 25

### BROOKS WINE BAR, 21 Park Street

*A delightful wine bar, situated in the business centre of Coleraine, on the edge of the town centre car park. 'Olde Worlde' atmosphere, on ground floor level with car park, affording easy access for the disabled. All tastes catered for by choosing from light meals to more imaginative dishes on the a la carte menu, all served with politeness and care. Good wine list also available.*

*FOOD up to £15*

**Hours:** closed Sunday 5pm; bar snacks 12noon – 3pm; bar snacks 5:30pm – 9pm. **Other points:** parking, children catered for – please check for age limits, open bank holidays, no-smoking area, disabled access, vegetarian meals. **Directions:** 100m from Town Hall, town centre. Situated at the Mall car park.
CAMERON, FRANCES & ALWYN, tel (0265) 42552.

## COOKSTOWN, County Tyrone Map 25

### GLENAVON HOUSE HOTEL, 52 Drum Road

*An attractively furnished, modern purpose built hotel, where the emphasis is on healthy eating. The large hotel has managed to retain the intimate, friendly atmosphere which is only expected of much smaller hotels. The staff are also polite and efficient. An ideal location for a family holiday, with golf, fishing, riding and many historical places of interest nearby.*

*ACCOMMODATION £21–£30*

*FOOD up to £15*

**Hours:** breakfast 7am – 10am; bar snacks 10am – 9:30pm; lunch 12noon – 5pm; dinner 5pm – 10pm. **Cuisine:** British / continental. **Rooms:** 53 bedrooms 26 twins, 16 doubles, 11 family rooms. **Credit cards:** Visa, Access, AmEx. **Other points:** children catered for – please check for age limits, parking, afternoon teas, disabled access, residents' lounge, vegetarian meals. **Directions:** on the A29 off M1 or M2.
MR AND MRS MORRIS, tel (06487) 64949, fax (06487) 64396.

## DUNGANNON, County Tyrone Map 25

### INN ON THE PARK, Moy Rd

*Set in 10 acres of mature landscaped gardens, this was once the home of the Finneys, one of Ireland's dynastic linen families. Now extensively refurbished by the present owner, it prides itself on its standards of cuisine and service. A comprehensive Wedding Package is available, also attractively furnished Function Rooms catering for 6 – 250 persons. Own Outdoor Tennis Court.*

*ACCOMMODATION £31–£40*

*FOOD up to £15*

**Hours:** breakfast 7:30am – 10:30am; lunch 12:30pm – 2:30pm; bar meals 12:30pm – 2:30pm; bar meals 2:30pm – 10pm; dinner 6pm – 9:30pm; closed Christmas 25/12 – 26/12. **Cuisine:** Irish:- Award Winning restaurant specialising in fresh local produce. **Rooms:** 14 en suite bedrooms, with television, telephone, radio, alarm and room-service. **Credit cards:** Visa, Access, Diners, AmEx. **Other points:** licensed, Sunday lunch, no-smoking area, children catered for – please check for age limits, pets allowed, parking, afternoon tea, special breaks. **Directions:** junction 15 of M1 Motorway – half a mile from Dungannon Town.
ROBERT WATERSON, tel (08687) 25151, fax (08687) 24953.

## ENNISKILLEN, County Fermanagh Map 25

### FRANCOS, Queen Elizabeth Road
*A popular restaurant with a distinctly warm and friendly continental atmosphere, where you can choose imaginative fresh food from an extensive menu. Ideal location for visiting and exploring the Lakeland Arena.*
**FOOD up to £15**
**Hours:** meals all day 12noon – 12midnight; closed Christmas 25/12; closed Sunday lunch. **Cuisine:** cosmopolitan:- Dishes may include, Roast Monkfish, Local Wild Salmon, Guinea Fowl, Game Terrine, Duck Breasts, Swordfish Steak. Fresh Pizzas & Pastas. **Credit cards:** AmEx. **Other points:** licensed, no-smoking area, children catered for – please check for age limits, pets allowed, vegetarian meals, disabled access. **Directions:** on the A4 in the town centre, behind the Town Hall, on the river.
RUAIRI & FRANK SWEENEY & FAMILY, tel (0365) 324424, fax (0365) 323584.

### OSCARS RESTAURANT, 29 Belmore Street
*A lovely little Town House restaurant situated in the centre of Enniskillen. Attractively decorated in pine, it has a friendly, fun atmosphere. Diners can choose from an extensive range of mouthwatering dishes. Nearby attractions include the Lakes of Fermanagh, Marble Arch Caves and Castle Coole.*
**FOOD up to £15**
**Hours:** closed Christmas day Sunday lunch; dinner 5pm – 10:30pm. **Cuisine:** international. **Credit cards:** Visa, Access. **Other points:** parking, children catered for – please check for age limits, open bank holidays, disabled access, vegetarian meals. **Directions:** Enniskillen town centre.
MR D MAGEE, tel (0365) 327037, (0365) 326886.

## KILKEEL, County Down Map 25

### KILMOREY ARMS HOTEL, 41–43 Greencastle Street
*Situated in County Down exactly where "The Mountains of Mourne sweep down to the sea", this is the ideal location from which to experience an incredibly beautiful part of Ireland. This family-run hotel with many modern facilities, offering an unobtrusive, relaxed and friendly atmosphere, with attention to detail at all times. Surrounded by breathtaking beauty, there are miles of pathways for walkers, sports, historic houses and nearby seaside resorts to visit.*
**ACCOMMODATION £21–£30**
**FOOD up to £15**
**Hours:** breakfast 7:30am – 9:30am; bar snacks 12noon – 3pm; lunch 12:30pm – 2:30pm; bar snacks 5pm – 8pm; dinner 5:30pm – 9pm. **Cuisine:** international. **Rooms:** 27 bedrooms 5 singles ensuite, 6 doubles ensuite, 11 twins ensuite, 2 triples ensuite, 3 family rooms ensuite. **Credit cards:** Visa, Access. **Other points:** parking, children catered for – please check for age limits, open bank holidays, no-smoking area, afternoon tea, disabled access, pets allowed, vegetarian meals, garden.
**Directions:** on A2.
LINDSAY MCMURRAY, HUGH & ROBERT GIFFEN, tel (06937) 62220, fax (06937) 65399.

## KILLYLEAGH, County Down Map 25

### DUFFERIN ARMS, 35 High Street
*The Dufferin Arms offers a warm, welcome friendly atmosphere for travellers and businessmen. Very popular and highly recommended. Ideal for visiting the many nearby attractions, including Killyleagh Castle, Strangford Lough and Delamont Country Park. Dufferin Arms also offers comfortable accommodation, self-catering apartments and studios with large lounge, country style kitchen and access to barbeque and picnic table.*
**ACCOMMODATION under £20**
**FOOD £15–£20** ★
**Hours:** lunch 12:30pm – 2:30pm; Sunday brunch 12:30pm – 2:30pm; supper – Mon-Wed 5pm – 9pm; supper – Thur-Sat 7pm – 11pm; dinner – Thur-Sat 7pm – 2:30pm; closed Sunday evening. **Cuisine:** international:- A la carte menu, offering Baked Killyleagh Trout, Char Grilled Steak, and Lamb Kebabs, all with fresh seasonal vegetables. Excellent wine list. **Rooms:** 3 bedrooms 3 self-catering rooms. **Credit cards:** Visa, Access. **Other points:** licensed, open-air dining, Sunday brunch, children catered for – please check for age limits, afternoon tea, bank holidays, vegetarian meals.
**Directions:** located in front of Killyleagh Castle.
MORRIS CRAWFORD & KITTY STEWART, tel (0396) 828229, fax (0396) 828755.

## OMAGH, County Tyrone Map 25

### GREENMOUNT LODGE, 58 Greenmount Road, Gortaclare
*An early 18th century estate which nestles peacefully in the heart of County Tyrone. Completely re-built in 1970 – only the courtyard remains intact – this new country house is approached by a tree-lined avenue set amidst mature woodland where the peace is disturbed only by birdsong or the bark of a fox. Luxurious accommodation with many modern facilities and a long-established reputation for its fine cuisine makes any stay here a memorable one. Excellent game shooting can be arranged.*
**ACCOMMODATION under £20**
**FOOD up to £15**
**Hours:** breakfast 7:30am – 9:30am; dinner 6:30pm – 8pm. **Cuisine:** British:- Home style country cooking. **Rooms:** 8 bedrooms all with tea making facilities, TV: 1 single ensuite, 1 double ensuite, 3 twins ensuite, 3 family rooms ensuite. **Other points:** parking, children catered for – please check for age limits, vegetarian meals, disabled access, residents' lounge, garden.
**Directions:** 8 miles south on A5 from Omagh, right 1 mile after Travellers Rest.
LOUIE REID, tel (0662) 841325.

## THE MELLON COUNTRY INN,
### 134 Beltany Road

*The extensive a la carte menu has been developed to suit both the cosmopolitan and regular clientele, offering dishes with recipes from all over Europe and complemented by more than 100 fine wines. One special feature of the dinner menu is a Flambe dish. The restaurant also caters for "late risers", offering traditional Ulster and continental breakfasts, coffee and scones from 10.30, meals from noon and early evening high-tea until 7.30pm. Special childrens menu is also available.*

*FOOD £15–£20* ♀

**Hours:** breakfast 10:30am – 12noon; lunch 12noon – 2:30pm; bar meals 12noon – 5:30pm; dinner 5:30pm – 9:30pm; high tea & bistro 5:30pm – 7:30pm; a la carte 6:30pm – 9:30pm. **Cuisine:** British / continental:- A la Carte & Table D'Hote menus. Dishes may include, Lobster & Fillet Steak with Onions, Lemon & Garlic, Fresh Duckling in a puddle of Peach sauce. **Credit cards:** Visa, Access, Diners, AmEx. **Other points:** licensed, open-air dining, Sunday lunch, no-smoking area, children catered for – please check for age limits, pets allowed, vegetarian meals, garden, afternoon tea, parking. **Directions:** halfway between Omagh and Newtonstewart. 1 mile from the Ulster American Folk Park.

KEN RUSSELL, tel (06626) 61946, fax (06626) 62245.

## THE WOODLANDER, 28 Gorton Road

*The Woodlander stands in an area that was historically part of Mountjoy Forest. Surrounded by great swathes of trees, this is where woodlanders once lived enjoying the abundant provisions of the forest. Today's visitors no longer have to hunt for their food and can choose from a wide range of wholesome dishes, served by courteous waitresses. Function rooms available for Weddings, Parties and Conferences.*

*FOOD up to £15* 🍲

**Hours:** closed Christmas day 6:30pm; bar meals 12noon – 8:30pm; dinner 6pm – 10pm. **Cuisine:** British. **Credit cards:** Visa, Access, Diners. **Other points:** parking, children catered for – please check for age limits, Sunday lunch, open bank holidays, no-smoking area, afternoon teas, disabled access, vegetarian meals. **Directions:** take Gorton Road from Omagh town to reach the restaurant.

MR J J MCQUINN, tel (0662) 251038, fax (0662) 246287.

## PORTRUSH, County Antrim Map 25

## CAUSEWAY COAST HOTEL & CONFERENCE CENTRE, 36 Ballyreagh Road

*Overlooking the Atlantic Ocean and hills of Donegal, this is a new building which has been well furnished to provide a popular venue with lovers of Nouvelle Cuisine. The atmosphere is busy and efficient, warm and friendly, with live music on Sunday lunchtimes. Comfortable accommodation and conference facilities are provided.*

*ACCOMMODATION £31–£40*

*FOOD up to £15*

**Hours:** breakfast 7:30am – 10am; bar snacks 12noon – 2:30pm; bar snacks 5pm – 9:30pm; dinner 7:30pm – 9:30pm. **Cuisine:** British. **Credit cards:** Visa, Access, AmEx. **Other points:** parking, children catered for – please check for age limits, Sunday lunch, no-smoking area, afternoon teas, disabled access, residents' lounge, vegetarian meals. **Directions:** located on A2 Coastal Road between resorts of Portrush and Portstewart.

MR W O'NEILL, tel (0265) 822435, fax (0265) 824495.

## THE ABBEY BAR AND COURTYARD CAFE

*Winchester, Hampshire*

**LES ROUTIERS**

*Special Offer*

**10% off food**

## ALEXANDRA HOTEL

*Ballater, Grampian*

**LES ROUTIERS**

*Special Offer*

**10% off accommodation**
**10% off food**

## ALLHAYS COUNTRY HOUSE

*Looe, Cornwall*

**LES ROUTIERS**

*Special Offer*

**10% off accommodation**

## ALTNAHARRA HOTEL

*Altnaharra, Highlands*

**LES ROUTIERS**

*Special Offer*

**10% off food**

## ALVERBANK HOUSE HOTEL

*Gosport, Hampshire*

**LES ROUTIERS**

*Special Offer*

**10% off accommodation**
**10% off food**

## ARCHES HOTEL

*Bristol, Avon*

**LES ROUTIERS**

*Special Offer*

**10% off accommodation**

## ASHLING TARA HOTEL

*Sutton, Surrey*

**LES ROUTIERS**

*Special Offer*

**10% off accommodation**

## BALAVIL SPORTS HOTEL

*Newtonmore, Highlands*

**LES ROUTIERS**

*Special Offer*

**10% off food**

## BALMORAL HOTEL

*Moffat, Dumfries & Galloway*

**LES ROUTIERS**

*Special Offer*

**10% off accommodation**

## BAYLEY ARMS

*Whalley, Lancashire*

**LES ROUTIERS**

*Special Offer*

**10% off accommodation**
**10% off food**

# Terms and Conditions

Only one voucher accepted per person per visit

Only one offer per Voucher, e.g. FOOD or
ACCOMMODATION or WINE

Establishments must be informed when booking that a
voucher will be used as part-payment for
ACCOMMODATION

Vouchers for FOOD or WINE must be handed
in on arrival

All offers are subject to the establishment's regulations

# Terms and Conditions

Only one voucher accepted per person per visit

Only one offer per Voucher, e.g. FOOD or
ACCOMMODATION or WINE

Establishments must be informed when booking that a
voucher will be used as part-payment for
ACCOMMODATION

Vouchers for FOOD or WINE must be handed
in on arrival

All offers are subject to the establishment's regulations

# Terms and Conditions

Only one voucher accepted per person per visit

Only one offer per Voucher, e.g. FOOD or
ACCOMMODATION or WINE

Establishments must be informed when booking that a
voucher will be used as part-payment for
ACCOMMODATION

Vouchers for FOOD or WINE must be handed
in on arrival

All offers are subject to the establishment's regulations

# Terms and Conditions

Only one voucher accepted per person per visit

Only one offer per Voucher, e.g. FOOD or
ACCOMMODATION or WINE

Establishments must be informed when booking that a
voucher will be used as part-payment for
ACCOMMODATION

Vouchers for FOOD or WINE must be handed
in on arrival

All offers are subject to the establishment's regulations

# Terms and Conditions

Only one voucher accepted per person per visit

Only one offer per Voucher, e.g. FOOD or
ACCOMMODATION or WINE

Establishments must be informed when booking that a
voucher will be used as part-payment for
ACCOMMODATION

Vouchers for FOOD or WINE must be handed
in on arrival

All offers are subject to the establishment's regulations

# Terms and Conditions

Only one voucher accepted per person per visit

Only one offer per Voucher, e.g. FOOD or
ACCOMMODATION or WINE

Establishments must be informed when booking that a
voucher will be used as part-payment for
ACCOMMODATION

Vouchers for FOOD or WINE must be handed
in on arrival

All offers are subject to the establishment's regulations

# Terms and Conditions

Only one voucher accepted per person per visit

Only one offer per Voucher, e.g. FOOD or
ACCOMMODATION or WINE

Establishments must be informed when booking that a
voucher will be used as part-payment for
ACCOMMODATION

Vouchers for FOOD or WINE must be handed
in on arrival

All offers are subject to the establishment's regulations

# Terms and Conditions

Only one voucher accepted per person per visit

Only one offer per Voucher, e.g. FOOD or
ACCOMMODATION or WINE

Establishments must be informed when booking that a
voucher will be used as part-payment for
ACCOMMODATION

Vouchers for FOOD or WINE must be handed
in on arrival

All offers are subject to the establishment's regulations

# Terms and Conditions

Only one voucher accepted per person per visit

Only one offer per Voucher, e.g. FOOD or
ACCOMMODATION or WINE

Establishments must be informed when booking that a
voucher will be used as part-payment for
ACCOMMODATION

Vouchers for FOOD or WINE must be handed
in on arrival

All offers are subject to the establishment's regulations

# Terms and Conditions

Only one voucher accepted per person per visit

Only one offer per Voucher, e.g. FOOD or
ACCOMMODATION or WINE

Establishments must be informed when booking that a
voucher will be used as part-payment for
ACCOMMODATION

Vouchers for FOOD or WINE must be handed
in on arrival

All offers are subject to the establishment's regulations

## BEACH DUNES HOTEL

*Perranporth, Cornwall*

**Special Offer**

**10% off accommodation**

## BELHAVEN HOUSE HOTEL AND RESTAURANT

*Milford Haven, Dyfed*

**Special Offer**

**10% off food**

## BELOW STAIRS RESTAURANT

*Cheltenham, Gloucestershire*

**Special Offer**

**Free bottle of house wine**

## THE BELVEDERE

*West Wemyss, Fife*

**Special Offer**

**10% off accommodation**
**10% off food**

## THE BENETT ARMS

*Shaftesbury, Dorset*

**Special Offer**

**10% off accommodation**

## BENT ARMS

*Lindfield, West Sussex*

**Special Offer**

**10% off accommodation**
**10% off food**
**Free bottle of house wine**

## BESWICKS RESTAURANT

*Broughton in Furness, Cumbria*

**Special Offer**

**10% off food**

## THE BOARS HEAD

*Bishops Castle, Shropshire*

**Special Offer**

**10% off accommodation**
**10% off food**
**Free bottle of house wine**

## BOSSINEY HOUSE HOTEL & RESTAURANT

*Tintagel, Cornwall*

**Special Offer**

**10% off accommodation**
**10% off food**

## BRENTWOOD HOTEL

*Rotherham, South Yorkshire*

**Special Offer**

**10% off accommodation**

# Terms and Conditions

Only one voucher accepted per person per visit

Only one offer per Voucher, e.g. FOOD or
ACCOMMODATION or WINE

Establishments must be informed when booking that a
voucher will be used as part-payment for
ACCOMMODATION

Vouchers for FOOD or WINE must be handed
in on arrival

All offers are subject to the establishment's regulations

# Terms and Conditions

Only one voucher accepted per person per visit

Only one offer per Voucher, e.g. FOOD or
ACCOMMODATION or WINE

Establishments must be informed when booking that a
voucher will be used as part-payment for
ACCOMMODATION

Vouchers for FOOD or WINE must be handed
in on arrival

All offers are subject to the establishment's regulations

# Terms and Conditions

Only one voucher accepted per person per visit

Only one offer per Voucher, e.g. FOOD or
ACCOMMODATION or WINE

Establishments must be informed when booking that a
voucher will be used as part-payment for
ACCOMMODATION

Vouchers for FOOD or WINE must be handed
in on arrival

All offers are subject to the establishment's regulations

# Terms and Conditions

Only one voucher accepted per person per visit

Only one offer per Voucher, e.g. FOOD or
ACCOMMODATION or WINE

Establishments must be informed when booking that a
voucher will be used as part-payment for
ACCOMMODATION

Vouchers for FOOD or WINE must be handed
in on arrival

All offers are subject to the establishment's regulations

# Terms and Conditions

Only one voucher accepted per person per visit

Only one offer per Voucher, e.g. FOOD or
ACCOMMODATION or WINE

Establishments must be informed when booking that a
voucher will be used as part-payment for
ACCOMMODATION

Vouchers for FOOD or WINE must be handed
in on arrival

All offers are subject to the establishment's regulations

# Terms and Conditions

Only one voucher accepted per person per visit

Only one offer per Voucher, e.g. FOOD or
ACCOMMODATION or WINE

Establishments must be informed when booking that a
voucher will be used as part-payment for
ACCOMMODATION

Vouchers for FOOD or WINE must be handed
in on arrival

All offers are subject to the establishment's regulations

# Terms and Conditions

Only one voucher accepted per person per visit

Only one offer per Voucher, e.g. FOOD or
ACCOMMODATION or WINE

Establishments must be informed when booking that a
voucher will be used as part-payment for
ACCOMMODATION

Vouchers for FOOD or WINE must be handed
in on arrival

All offers are subject to the establishment's regulations

# Terms and Conditions

Only one voucher accepted per person per visit

Only one offer per Voucher, e.g. FOOD or
ACCOMMODATION or WINE

Establishments must be informed when booking that a
voucher will be used as part-payment for
ACCOMMODATION

Vouchers for FOOD or WINE must be handed
in on arrival

All offers are subject to the establishment's regulations

# Terms and Conditions

Only one voucher accepted per person per visit

Only one offer per Voucher, e.g. FOOD or
ACCOMMODATION or WINE

Establishments must be informed when booking that a
voucher will be used as part-payment for
ACCOMMODATION

Vouchers for FOOD or WINE must be handed
in on arrival

All offers are subject to the establishment's regulations

# Terms and Conditions

Only one voucher accepted per person per visit

Only one offer per Voucher, e.g. FOOD or
ACCOMMODATION or WINE

Establishments must be informed when booking that a
voucher will be used as part-payment for
ACCOMMODATION

Vouchers for FOOD or WINE must be handed
in on arrival

All offers are subject to the establishment's regulations

## BRITANNIA LODGE HOTEL

*Harrogate, North Yorkshire*

**LES ROUTIERS**

*Special Offer*

**10% off accommodation**

## BRYN-Y-MOR

*St Aubin's Bay, Jersey*

**LES ROUTIERS**

*Special Offer*

**10% off accommodation**
**10% off food**

## THE BULL TERRIER

*Wells, Somerset*

**LES ROUTIERS**

*Special Offer*

**10% off accommodation**
**10% off food**

## BURLEY COURT HOTEL

*Bournemouth, Dorset*

**LES ROUTIERS**

*Special Offer*

**10% off accommodation**

## THE BUTLERS HOTEL

*Leeds, West Yorkshire*

**LES ROUTIERS**

*Special Offer*

**10% off accommodation**
**10% off food**

## BYES LINKS HOTEL

*Sidmouth, Devon*

**LES ROUTIERS**

*Special Offer*

**Free bottle of house wine**

## BYRON HOUSE HOTEL

*York, North Yorkshire*

**LES ROUTIERS**

*Special Offer*

**10% off accommodation**

## CAFE NICOISE

*Colwyn Bay, Clwyd*

**LES ROUTIERS**

*Special Offer*

**Free bottle of house wine**

## CAMBRIAN HOTEL

*New Quay, Dyfed*

**LES ROUTIERS**

*Special Offer*

**10% off accommodation**

## CAPS

*Kensington, London*

**LES ROUTIERS**

*Special Offer*

**10% off food**

# Terms and Conditions

Only one voucher accepted per person per visit

Only one offer per Voucher, e.g. FOOD or ACCOMMODATION or WINE

Establishments must be informed when booking that a voucher will be used as part-payment for ACCOMMODATION

Vouchers for FOOD or WINE must be handed in on arrival

All offers are subject to the establishment's regulations

# Terms and Conditions

Only one voucher accepted per person per visit

Only one offer per Voucher, e.g. FOOD or ACCOMMODATION or WINE

Establishments must be informed when booking that a voucher will be used as part-payment for ACCOMMODATION

Vouchers for FOOD or WINE must be handed in on arrival

All offers are subject to the establishment's regulations

# Terms and Conditions

Only one voucher accepted per person per visit

Only one offer per Voucher, e.g. FOOD or ACCOMMODATION or WINE

Establishments must be informed when booking that a voucher will be used as part-payment for ACCOMMODATION

Vouchers for FOOD or WINE must be handed in on arrival

All offers are subject to the establishment's regulations

# Terms and Conditions

Only one voucher accepted per person per visit

Only one offer per Voucher, e.g. FOOD or ACCOMMODATION or WINE

Establishments must be informed when booking that a voucher will be used as part-payment for ACCOMMODATION

Vouchers for FOOD or WINE must be handed in on arrival

All offers are subject to the establishment's regulations

# Terms and Conditions

Only one voucher accepted per person per visit

Only one offer per Voucher, e.g. FOOD or ACCOMMODATION or WINE

Establishments must be informed when booking that a voucher will be used as part-payment for ACCOMMODATION

Vouchers for FOOD or WINE must be handed in on arrival

All offers are subject to the establishment's regulations

# Terms and Conditions

Only one voucher accepted per person per visit

Only one offer per Voucher, e.g. FOOD or ACCOMMODATION or WINE

Establishments must be informed when booking that a voucher will be used as part-payment for ACCOMMODATION

Vouchers for FOOD or WINE must be handed in on arrival

All offers are subject to the establishment's regulations

# Terms and Conditions

Only one voucher accepted per person per visit

Only one offer per Voucher, e.g. FOOD or ACCOMMODATION or WINE

Establishments must be informed when booking that a voucher will be used as part-payment for ACCOMMODATION

Vouchers for FOOD or WINE must be handed in on arrival

All offers are subject to the establishment's regulations

# Terms and Conditions

Only one voucher accepted per person per visit

Only one offer per Voucher, e.g. FOOD or ACCOMMODATION or WINE

Establishments must be informed when booking that a voucher will be used as part-payment for ACCOMMODATION

Vouchers for FOOD or WINE must be handed in on arrival

All offers are subject to the establishment's regulations

# Terms and Conditions

Only one voucher accepted per person per visit

Only one offer per Voucher, e.g. FOOD or ACCOMMODATION or WINE

Establishments must be informed when booking that a voucher will be used as part-payment for ACCOMMODATION

Vouchers for FOOD or WINE must be handed in on arrival

All offers are subject to the establishment's regulations

# Terms and Conditions

Only one voucher accepted per person per visit

Only one offer per Voucher, e.g. FOOD or ACCOMMODATION or WINE

Establishments must be informed when booking that a voucher will be used as part-payment for ACCOMMODATION

Vouchers for FOOD or WINE must be handed in on arrival

All offers are subject to the establishment's regulations

## THE CASTLE HOTEL
*Haverfordwest, Dyfed*

**LES ROUTIERS**

*Special Offer*

**10% off accommodation**

## CHASE LODGE HOTEL
*Kingston upon Thames, Surrey*

**LES ROUTIERS**

*Special Offer*

**Free bottle of house wine**

## THE CHASER INN
*Tonbridge, Kent*

**LES ROUTIERS**

*Special Offer*

**10% off accommodation**

## CHY-AN-DOUR HOTEL
*St Ives, Cornwall*

**LES ROUTIERS**

*Special Offer*

**10% off accommodation**

## CLARENDON HOTEL AND WIGHT MOUSE INN
*Chale, Isle of Wight*

**LES ROUTIERS**

*Special Offer*

**10% off accommodation**

## CLIFF HOTEL
*Harwich, Essex*

**LES ROUTIERS**

*Special Offer*

**Free bottle of house wine**

## COBDEN'S HOTEL
*Capel Curig, Gwynedd*

**LES ROUTIERS**

*Special Offer*

**10% off food**

## THE COPPER SKILLET
*Christchurch, Dorset*

**LES ROUTIERS**

*Special Offer*

**10% off food**

## COSMOPOLITAN HOTEL
*Brighton & Hove, East Sussex*

**LES ROUTIERS**

*Special Offer*

**10% off accommodation**

## COURT BARN COUNTRY HOUSE HOTEL
*Clawton-Holesworthy, Devon*

**LES ROUTIERS**

*Special Offer*

**Free bottle of house wine**

## Terms and Conditions

Only one voucher accepted per person per visit

Only one offer per Voucher, e.g. FOOD or
ACCOMMODATION or WINE

Establishments must be informed when booking that a
voucher will be used as part-payment for
ACCOMMODATION

Vouchers for FOOD or WINE must be handed
in on arrival

All offers are subject to the establishment's regulations

## Terms and Conditions

Only one voucher accepted per person per visit

Only one offer per Voucher, e.g. FOOD or
ACCOMMODATION or WINE

Establishments must be informed when booking that a
voucher will be used as part-payment for
ACCOMMODATION

Vouchers for FOOD or WINE must be handed
in on arrival

All offers are subject to the establishment's regulations

## Terms and Conditions

Only one voucher accepted per person per visit

Only one offer per Voucher, e.g. FOOD or
ACCOMMODATION or WINE

Establishments must be informed when booking that a
voucher will be used as part-payment for
ACCOMMODATION

Vouchers for FOOD or WINE must be handed
in on arrival

All offers are subject to the establishment's regulations

## Terms and Conditions

Only one voucher accepted per person per visit

Only one offer per Voucher, e.g. FOOD or
ACCOMMODATION or WINE

Establishments must be informed when booking that a
voucher will be used as part-payment for
ACCOMMODATION

Vouchers for FOOD or WINE must be handed
in on arrival

All offers are subject to the establishment's regulations

## Terms and Conditions

Only one voucher accepted per person per visit

Only one offer per Voucher, e.g. FOOD or
ACCOMMODATION or WINE

Establishments must be informed when booking that a
voucher will be used as part-payment for
ACCOMMODATION

Vouchers for FOOD or WINE must be handed
in on arrival

All offers are subject to the establishment's regulations

## Terms and Conditions

Only one voucher accepted per person per visit

Only one offer per Voucher, e.g. FOOD or
ACCOMMODATION or WINE

Establishments must be informed when booking that a
voucher will be used as part-payment for
ACCOMMODATION

Vouchers for FOOD or WINE must be handed
in on arrival

All offers are subject to the establishment's regulations

## Terms and Conditions

Only one voucher accepted per person per visit

Only one offer per Voucher, e.g. FOOD or
ACCOMMODATION or WINE

Establishments must be informed when booking that a
voucher will be used as part-payment for
ACCOMMODATION

Vouchers for FOOD or WINE must be handed
in on arrival

All offers are subject to the establishment's regulations

## Terms and Conditions

Only one voucher accepted per person per visit

Only one offer per Voucher, e.g. FOOD or
ACCOMMODATION or WINE

Establishments must be informed when booking that a
voucher will be used as part-payment for
ACCOMMODATION

Vouchers for FOOD or WINE must be handed
in on arrival

All offers are subject to the establishment's regulations

## Terms and Conditions

Only one voucher accepted per person per visit

Only one offer per Voucher, e.g. FOOD or
ACCOMMODATION or WINE

Establishments must be informed when booking that a
voucher will be used as part-payment for
ACCOMMODATION

Vouchers for FOOD or WINE must be handed
in on arrival

All offers are subject to the establishment's regulations

## Terms and Conditions

Only one voucher accepted per person per visit

Only one offer per Voucher, e.g. FOOD or
ACCOMMODATION or WINE

Establishments must be informed when booking that a
voucher will be used as part-payment for
ACCOMMODATION

Vouchers for FOOD or WINE must be handed
in on arrival

All offers are subject to the establishment's regulations

## COW & CALF HOTEL

*Ilkley, West Yorkshire*

**LES ROUTIERS**

*Special Offer*

**10% off accommodation**

## CRESCENT LODGE HOTEL

*Harrow, Middlesex*

**LES ROUTIERS**

*Special Offer*

**10% off accommodation**

## THE CROWN AT WHITEBROOK

*Monmouth, Gwent*

**LES ROUTIERS**

*Special Offer*

**10% off accommodation**

## THE CROWN OF CRUCIS HOTEL & RESTAURANT

*Cirencester, Gloucestershire*

**LES ROUTIERS**

*Special Offer*

**10% off accommodation**
**10% off food**

## CULVER LODGE HOTEL & RESTAURANT

*Sandown, Isle of Wight*

**LES ROUTIERS**

*Special Offer*

**Free bottle of house wine**

## DUFFERIN ARMS

*Killyleagh, Co. Down*

**LES ROUTIERS**

*Special Offer*

**10% off food**

## DUISDALE HOTEL

*Isle of Skye, Highlands*

**LES ROUTIERS**

*Special Offer*

**10% off accommodation**
**10% off food**

## DUKE OF CONNAUGHT HOTEL

*York, North Yorkshire*

**LES ROUTIERS**

*Special Offer*

**Free bottle of house wine**

## DUNBEATH HOTEL

*Dunbeath, Highlands*

**LES ROUTIERS**

*Special Offer*

**10% off food**

## EAST AYTON LODGE

*Scarborough, North Yorkshire*

**LES ROUTIERS**

*Special Offer*

**10% off accommodation**

## Terms and Conditions

Only one voucher accepted per person per visit

Only one offer per Voucher, e.g. FOOD or
ACCOMMODATION or WINE

Establishments must be informed when booking that a
voucher will be used as part-payment for
ACCOMMODATION

Vouchers for FOOD or WINE must be handed
in on arrival

All offers are subject to the establishment's regulations

## Terms and Conditions

Only one voucher accepted per person per visit

Only one offer per Voucher, e.g. FOOD or
ACCOMMODATION or WINE

Establishments must be informed when booking that a
voucher will be used as part-payment for
ACCOMMODATION

Vouchers for FOOD or WINE must be handed
in on arrival

All offers are subject to the establishment's regulations

## Terms and Conditions

Only one voucher accepted per person per visit

Only one offer per Voucher, e.g. FOOD or
ACCOMMODATION or WINE

Establishments must be informed when booking that a
voucher will be used as part-payment for
ACCOMMODATION

Vouchers for FOOD or WINE must be handed
in on arrival

All offers are subject to the establishment's regulations

## Terms and Conditions

Only one voucher accepted per person per visit

Only one offer per Voucher, e.g. FOOD or
ACCOMMODATION or WINE

Establishments must be informed when booking that a
voucher will be used as part-payment for
ACCOMMODATION

Vouchers for FOOD or WINE must be handed
in on arrival

All offers are subject to the establishment's regulations

## Terms and Conditions

Only one voucher accepted per person per visit

Only one offer per Voucher, e.g. FOOD or
ACCOMMODATION or WINE

Establishments must be informed when booking that a
voucher will be used as part-payment for
ACCOMMODATION

Vouchers for FOOD or WINE must be handed
in on arrival

All offers are subject to the establishment's regulations

## Terms and Conditions

Only one voucher accepted per person per visit

Only one offer per Voucher, e.g. FOOD or
ACCOMMODATION or WINE

Establishments must be informed when booking that a
voucher will be used as part-payment for
ACCOMMODATION

Vouchers for FOOD or WINE must be handed
in on arrival

All offers are subject to the establishment's regulations

## Terms and Conditions

Only one voucher accepted per person per visit

Only one offer per Voucher, e.g. FOOD or
ACCOMMODATION or WINE

Establishments must be informed when booking that a
voucher will be used as part-payment for
ACCOMMODATION

Vouchers for FOOD or WINE must be handed
in on arrival

All offers are subject to the establishment's regulations

## Terms and Conditions

Only one voucher accepted per person per visit

Only one offer per Voucher, e.g. FOOD or
ACCOMMODATION or WINE

Establishments must be informed when booking that a
voucher will be used as part-payment for
ACCOMMODATION

Vouchers for FOOD or WINE must be handed
in on arrival

All offers are subject to the establishment's regulations

## Terms and Conditions

Only one voucher accepted per person per visit

Only one offer per Voucher, e.g. FOOD or
ACCOMMODATION or WINE

Establishments must be informed when booking that a
voucher will be used as part-payment for
ACCOMMODATION

Vouchers for FOOD or WINE must be handed
in on arrival

All offers are subject to the establishment's regulations

## Terms and Conditions

Only one voucher accepted per person per visit

Only one offer per Voucher, e.g. FOOD or
ACCOMMODATION or WINE

Establishments must be informed when booking that a
voucher will be used as part-payment for
ACCOMMODATION

Vouchers for FOOD or WINE must be handed
in on arrival

All offers are subject to the establishment's regulations

## ELM CREST GUEST HOUSE

*Huddersfield, West Yorkshire*

**LES ROUTIERS**

*Special Offer*

**10% off accommodation**

## THE ELTON HOTEL

*Rotherham, South Yorkshire*

**LES ROUTIERS**

*Special Offer*

**10% off accommodation**

## THE FALCON HOTEL

*Uppingham, Leicestershire*

**LES ROUTIERS**

*Special Offer*

**10% off accommodation**
**10% off food**

## FALLS OF LORA HOTEL

*Oban, Strathclyde*

**LES ROUTIERS**

*Special Offer*

**10% off accommodation**

## FERNIE CASTLE HOTEL

*Letham, Fife*

**LES ROUTIERS**

*Special Offer*

**10% off accommodation**

## FOOD FOR THOUGHT

*Covent Garden, London*

**LES ROUTIERS**

*Special Offer*

**10% off food**

## FORTFIELD HOTEL

*Sidmouth, Devon*

**LES ROUTIERS**

*Special Offer*

**Free bottle of house wine**

## FOURCROFT HOTEL

*Tenby, Dyfed*

**LES ROUTIERS**

*Special Offer*

**Free bottle of house wine**

## FOUTERS BISTRO

*Ayr, Strathclyde*

**LES ROUTIERS**

*Special Offer*

**10% off food**

## FRANCS RESTAURANT

*Chester, Cheshire*

**LES ROUTIERS**

*Special Offer*

**10% off food**

# Terms and Conditions

Only one voucher accepted per person per visit

Only one offer per Voucher, e.g. FOOD or ACCOMMODATION or WINE

Establishments must be informed when booking that a voucher will be used as part-payment for ACCOMMODATION

Vouchers for FOOD or WINE must be handed in on arrival

All offers are subject to the establishment's regulations

# Terms and Conditions

Only one voucher accepted per person per visit

Only one offer per Voucher, e.g. FOOD or ACCOMMODATION or WINE

Establishments must be informed when booking that a voucher will be used as part-payment for ACCOMMODATION

Vouchers for FOOD or WINE must be handed in on arrival

All offers are subject to the establishment's regulations

# Terms and Conditions

Only one voucher accepted per person per visit

Only one offer per Voucher, e.g. FOOD or ACCOMMODATION or WINE

Establishments must be informed when booking that a voucher will be used as part-payment for ACCOMMODATION

Vouchers for FOOD or WINE must be handed in on arrival

All offers are subject to the establishment's regulations

# Terms and Conditions

Only one voucher accepted per person per visit

Only one offer per Voucher, e.g. FOOD or ACCOMMODATION or WINE

Establishments must be informed when booking that a voucher will be used as part-payment for ACCOMMODATION

Vouchers for FOOD or WINE must be handed in on arrival

All offers are subject to the establishment's regulations

# Terms and Conditions

Only one voucher accepted per person per visit

Only one offer per Voucher, e.g. FOOD or ACCOMMODATION or WINE

Establishments must be informed when booking that a voucher will be used as part-payment for ACCOMMODATION

Vouchers for FOOD or WINE must be handed in on arrival

All offers are subject to the establishment's regulations

# Terms and Conditions

Only one voucher accepted per person per visit

Only one offer per Voucher, e.g. FOOD or ACCOMMODATION or WINE

Establishments must be informed when booking that a voucher will be used as part-payment for ACCOMMODATION

Vouchers for FOOD or WINE must be handed in on arrival

All offers are subject to the establishment's regulations

# Terms and Conditions

Only one voucher accepted per person per visit

Only one offer per Voucher, e.g. FOOD or ACCOMMODATION or WINE

Establishments must be informed when booking that a voucher will be used as part-payment for ACCOMMODATION

Vouchers for FOOD or WINE must be handed in on arrival

All offers are subject to the establishment's regulations

# Terms and Conditions

Only one voucher accepted per person per visit

Only one offer per Voucher, e.g. FOOD or ACCOMMODATION or WINE

Establishments must be informed when booking that a voucher will be used as part-payment for ACCOMMODATION

Vouchers for FOOD or WINE must be handed in on arrival

All offers are subject to the establishment's regulations

# Terms and Conditions

Only one voucher accepted per person per visit

Only one offer per Voucher, e.g. FOOD or ACCOMMODATION or WINE

Establishments must be informed when booking that a voucher will be used as part-payment for ACCOMMODATION

Vouchers for FOOD or WINE must be handed in on arrival

All offers are subject to the establishment's regulations

# Terms and Conditions

Only one voucher accepted per person per visit

Only one offer per Voucher, e.g. FOOD or ACCOMMODATION or WINE

Establishments must be informed when booking that a voucher will be used as part-payment for ACCOMMODATION

Vouchers for FOOD or WINE must be handed in on arrival

All offers are subject to the establishment's regulations

## GAMMAGE'S RESTAURANT
### Newdigate, Surrey

**LES ROUTIERS**

*Special Offer*

**10% off food**

## GARLANDS
### Beer, Devon

**LES ROUTIERS**

*Special Offer*

**10% off accommodation**

## THE GEORGE
### Great Missenden, Buckinghamshire

**LES ROUTIERS**

*Special Offer*

**10% off accommodation**

## GEORGE HOTEL
### Darlington, North Yorkshire

**LES ROUTIERS**

*Special Offer*

**10% off accommodation**

## GLENTHORNE
### St Helier, Jersey

**LES ROUTIERS**

*Special Offer*

**Free bottle of house wine**

## GRANGE HOTEL
### Norwich, Norfolk

**LES ROUTIERS**

*Special Offer*

**Free bottle of house wine**

## GRAPEVINE HOTEL
### Stow on the Wold, Gloucestershire

**LES ROUTIERS**

*Special Offer*

**10% off accommodation**
**10% off food**
**Free bottle of house wine**

## THE GREAT WESTERN HOTEL
### Newquay, Cornwall

**LES ROUTIERS**

*Special Offer*

**10% off accommodation**
**10% off food**

## GREEN LAWNS HOTEL
### Falmouth, Cornwall

**LES ROUTIERS**

*Special Offer*

**10% off accommodation**

## THE GROVE HOTEL
### Falmouth, Cornwall

**LES ROUTIERS**

*Special Offer*

**10% off accommodation**

# Terms and Conditions

Only one voucher accepted per person per visit

Only one offer per Voucher, e.g. FOOD or ACCOMMODATION or WINE

Establishments must be informed when booking that a voucher will be used as part-payment for ACCOMMODATION

Vouchers for FOOD or WINE must be handed in on arrival

All offers are subject to the establishment's regulations

# Terms and Conditions

Only one voucher accepted per person per visit

Only one offer per Voucher, e.g. FOOD or ACCOMMODATION or WINE

Establishments must be informed when booking that a voucher will be used as part-payment for ACCOMMODATION

Vouchers for FOOD or WINE must be handed in on arrival

All offers are subject to the establishment's regulations

# Terms and Conditions

Only one voucher accepted per person per visit

Only one offer per Voucher, e.g. FOOD or ACCOMMODATION or WINE

Establishments must be informed when booking that a voucher will be used as part-payment for ACCOMMODATION

Vouchers for FOOD or WINE must be handed in on arrival

All offers are subject to the establishment's regulations

# Terms and Conditions

Only one voucher accepted per person per visit

Only one offer per Voucher, e.g. FOOD or ACCOMMODATION or WINE

Establishments must be informed when booking that a voucher will be used as part-payment for ACCOMMODATION

Vouchers for FOOD or WINE must be handed in on arrival

All offers are subject to the establishment's regulations

# Terms and Conditions

Only one voucher accepted per person per visit

Only one offer per Voucher, e.g. FOOD or ACCOMMODATION or WINE

Establishments must be informed when booking that a voucher will be used as part-payment for ACCOMMODATION

Vouchers for FOOD or WINE must be handed in on arrival

All offers are subject to the establishment's regulations

# Terms and Conditions

Only one voucher accepted per person per visit

Only one offer per Voucher, e.g. FOOD or ACCOMMODATION or WINE

Establishments must be informed when booking that a voucher will be used as part-payment for ACCOMMODATION

Vouchers for FOOD or WINE must be handed in on arrival

All offers are subject to the establishment's regulations

# Terms and Conditions

Only one voucher accepted per person per visit

Only one offer per Voucher, e.g. FOOD or ACCOMMODATION or WINE

Establishments must be informed when booking that a voucher will be used as part-payment for ACCOMMODATION

Vouchers for FOOD or WINE must be handed in on arrival

All offers are subject to the establishment's regulations

# Terms and Conditions

Only one voucher accepted per person per visit

Only one offer per Voucher, e.g. FOOD or ACCOMMODATION or WINE

Establishments must be informed when booking that a voucher will be used as part-payment for ACCOMMODATION

Vouchers for FOOD or WINE must be handed in on arrival

All offers are subject to the establishment's regulations

# Terms and Conditions

Only one voucher accepted per person per visit

Only one offer per Voucher, e.g. FOOD or ACCOMMODATION or WINE

Establishments must be informed when booking that a voucher will be used as part-payment for ACCOMMODATION

Vouchers for FOOD or WINE must be handed in on arrival

All offers are subject to the establishment's regulations

# Terms and Conditions

Only one voucher accepted per person per visit

Only one offer per Voucher, e.g. FOOD or ACCOMMODATION or WINE

Establishments must be informed when booking that a voucher will be used as part-payment for ACCOMMODATION

Vouchers for FOOD or WINE must be handed in on arrival

All offers are subject to the establishment's regulations

## HAGLEY COURT HOTEL
*Birmingham, West Midlands*

**LES ROUTIERS**

*Special Offer*

**10% off accommodation
Free bottle of house wine**

## HARDWICK GUEST HOUSE
*Stratford upon Avon, Warwickshire*

**LES ROUTIERS**

*Special Offer*

**10% off accommodation**

## HAVEN HOTEL
*Poole, Dorset*

**LES ROUTIERS**

*Special Offer*

**10% off accommodation**

## HEADLANDS HOTEL
*Llandudno, Gwynedd*

**LES ROUTIERS**

*Special Offer*

**10% off accommodation
10% off food**

## HILLCREST HOTEL
*Lincoln, Lincolnshire*

**LES ROUTIERS**

*Special Offer*

**10% off accommodation**

## HINGSTON HOUSE COUNTRY HOTEL
*Gunnislake, Cornwall*

**LES ROUTIERS**

*Special Offer*

**Free bottle of house wine**

## HOTEL SYDORE
*Torquay, Devon*

**LES ROUTIERS**

*Special Offer*

**10% off accommodation
10% off food
Free bottle of house wine**

## THE HUNDRED HOUSE HOTEL
*Norton, Shropshire*

**LES ROUTIERS**

*Special Offer*

**10% off accommodation**

## THE HUNTSMAN HOTEL
*Shirenewton, Gwent*

**LES ROUTIERS**

*Special Offer*

**10% off accommodation
10% off food**

## THE ILFRACOMBE CARLTON
*Ilfracombe, Devon*

**LES ROUTIERS**

*Special Offer*

**10% off accommodation**

# Terms and Conditions

Only one voucher accepted per person per visit

Only one offer per Voucher, e.g. FOOD or ACCOMMODATION or WINE

Establishments must be informed when booking that a voucher will be used as part-payment for ACCOMMODATION

Vouchers for FOOD or WINE must be handed in on arrival

All offers are subject to the establishment's regulations

# Terms and Conditions

Only one voucher accepted per person per visit

Only one offer per Voucher, e.g. FOOD or ACCOMMODATION or WINE

Establishments must be informed when booking that a voucher will be used as part-payment for ACCOMMODATION

Vouchers for FOOD or WINE must be handed in on arrival

All offers are subject to the establishment's regulations

# Terms and Conditions

Only one voucher accepted per person per visit

Only one offer per Voucher, e.g. FOOD or ACCOMMODATION or WINE

Establishments must be informed when booking that a voucher will be used as part-payment for ACCOMMODATION

Vouchers for FOOD or WINE must be handed in on arrival

All offers are subject to the establishment's regulations

# Terms and Conditions

Only one voucher accepted per person per visit

Only one offer per Voucher, e.g. FOOD or ACCOMMODATION or WINE

Establishments must be informed when booking that a voucher will be used as part-payment for ACCOMMODATION

Vouchers for FOOD or WINE must be handed in on arrival

All offers are subject to the establishment's regulations

# Terms and Conditions

Only one voucher accepted per person per visit

Only one offer per Voucher, e.g. FOOD or ACCOMMODATION or WINE

Establishments must be informed when booking that a voucher will be used as part-payment for ACCOMMODATION

Vouchers for FOOD or WINE must be handed in on arrival

All offers are subject to the establishment's regulations

# Terms and Conditions

Only one voucher accepted per person per visit

Only one offer per Voucher, e.g. FOOD or ACCOMMODATION or WINE

Establishments must be informed when booking that a voucher will be used as part-payment for ACCOMMODATION

Vouchers for FOOD or WINE must be handed in on arrival

All offers are subject to the establishment's regulations

# Terms and Conditions

Only one voucher accepted per person per visit

Only one offer per Voucher, e.g. FOOD or ACCOMMODATION or WINE

Establishments must be informed when booking that a voucher will be used as part-payment for ACCOMMODATION

Vouchers for FOOD or WINE must be handed in on arrival

All offers are subject to the establishment's regulations

# Terms and Conditions

Only one voucher accepted per person per visit

Only one offer per Voucher, e.g. FOOD or ACCOMMODATION or WINE

Establishments must be informed when booking that a voucher will be used as part-payment for ACCOMMODATION

Vouchers for FOOD or WINE must be handed in on arrival

All offers are subject to the establishment's regulations

# Terms and Conditions

Only one voucher accepted per person per visit

Only one offer per Voucher, e.g. FOOD or ACCOMMODATION or WINE

Establishments must be informed when booking that a voucher will be used as part-payment for ACCOMMODATION

Vouchers for FOOD or WINE must be handed in on arrival

All offers are subject to the establishment's regulations

# Terms and Conditions

Only one voucher accepted per person per visit

Only one offer per Voucher, e.g. FOOD or ACCOMMODATION or WINE

Establishments must be informed when booking that a voucher will be used as part-payment for ACCOMMODATION

Vouchers for FOOD or WINE must be handed in on arrival

All offers are subject to the establishment's regulations

## INVERGARRY HOTEL

*Invergarry, Highlands*

**LES ROUTIERS** *Special Offer*

**10% off accommodation**

## THE JOLLY SAILORS

*Brancaster Staithe, Norfolk*

**LES ROUTIERS** *Special Offer*

**10% off food**

## KEMPTON HOUSE HOTEL

*Brighton, East Sussex*

**LES ROUTIERS** *Special Offer*

**10% off accommodation**

## KINGS HEAD HOTEL

*Cirencester, Gloucestershire*

**LES ROUTIERS** *Special Offer*

**10% off accommodation**

## KING'S HEAD HOTEL

*Malton, North Yorkshire*

**LES ROUTIERS** *Special Offer*

**10% off food**

## THE KINGS HEAD HOTEL

*Great Bircham, Norfolk*

**LES ROUTIERS** *Special Offer*

**10% off accommodation**

## KINGSDOWN HOTEL

*Margate, Kent*

**LES ROUTIERS** *Special Offer*

**10% off accommodation**

## KINGSTOWN HOTEL

*Hull, Humberside*

**LES ROUTIERS** *Special Offer*

**10% off accommodation**

## KINGSWAY HOTEL

*Worthing, West Sussex*

**LES ROUTIERS** *Special Offer*

**10% off food**

## THE KNIFE & CLEAVER

*Bedford, Bedfordshire*

**LES ROUTIERS** *Special Offer*

**10% off accommodation**

# Terms and Conditions

Only one voucher accepted per person per visit

Only one offer per Voucher, e.g. FOOD or ACCOMMODATION or WINE

Establishments must be informed when booking that a voucher will be used as part-payment for ACCOMMODATION

Vouchers for FOOD or WINE must be handed in on arrival

All offers are subject to the establishment's regulations

---

# Terms and Conditions

Only one voucher accepted per person per visit

Only one offer per Voucher, e.g. FOOD or ACCOMMODATION or WINE

Establishments must be informed when booking that a voucher will be used as part-payment for ACCOMMODATION

Vouchers for FOOD or WINE must be handed in on arrival

All offers are subject to the establishment's regulations

---

# Terms and Conditions

Only one voucher accepted per person per visit

Only one offer per Voucher, e.g. FOOD or ACCOMMODATION or WINE

Establishments must be informed when booking that a voucher will be used as part-payment for ACCOMMODATION

Vouchers for FOOD or WINE must be handed in on arrival

All offers are subject to the establishment's regulations

---

# Terms and Conditions

Only one voucher accepted per person per visit

Only one offer per Voucher, e.g. FOOD or ACCOMMODATION or WINE

Establishments must be informed when booking that a voucher will be used as part-payment for ACCOMMODATION

Vouchers for FOOD or WINE must be handed in on arrival

All offers are subject to the establishment's regulations

---

# Terms and Conditions

Only one voucher accepted per person per visit

Only one offer per Voucher, e.g. FOOD or ACCOMMODATION or WINE

Establishments must be informed when booking that a voucher will be used as part-payment for ACCOMMODATION

Vouchers for FOOD or WINE must be handed in on arrival

All offers are subject to the establishment's regulations

---

# Terms and Conditions

Only one voucher accepted per person per visit

Only one offer per Voucher, e.g. FOOD or ACCOMMODATION or WINE

Establishments must be informed when booking that a voucher will be used as part-payment for ACCOMMODATION

Vouchers for FOOD or WINE must be handed in on arrival

All offers are subject to the establishment's regulations

---

# Terms and Conditions

Only one voucher accepted per person per visit

Only one offer per Voucher, e.g. FOOD or ACCOMMODATION or WINE

Establishments must be informed when booking that a voucher will be used as part-payment for ACCOMMODATION

Vouchers for FOOD or WINE must be handed in on arrival

All offers are subject to the establishment's regulations

---

# Terms and Conditions

Only one voucher accepted per person per visit

Only one offer per Voucher, e.g. FOOD or ACCOMMODATION or WINE

Establishments must be informed when booking that a voucher will be used as part-payment for ACCOMMODATION

Vouchers for FOOD or WINE must be handed in on arrival

All offers are subject to the establishment's regulations

---

# Terms and Conditions

Only one voucher accepted per person per visit

Only one offer per Voucher, e.g. FOOD or ACCOMMODATION or WINE

Establishments must be informed when booking that a voucher will be used as part-payment for ACCOMMODATION

Vouchers for FOOD or WINE must be handed in on arrival

All offers are subject to the establishment's regulations

---

# Terms and Conditions

Only one voucher accepted per person per visit

Only one offer per Voucher, e.g. FOOD or ACCOMMODATION or WINE

Establishments must be informed when booking that a voucher will be used as part-payment for ACCOMMODATION

Vouchers for FOOD or WINE must be handed in on arrival

All offers are subject to the establishment's regulations

## LA CACHETTE

*Biggleswade, Bedfordshire*

**LES ROUTIERS**

## Special Offer

**10% off food**

## LANGLEY CASTLE HOTEL

*Hexham, Northumberland*

**LES ROUTIERS**

## Special Offer

**10% off accommodation**

## THE LEADBURN INN

*Leadburn, Lothian*

**LES ROUTIERS**

## Special Offer

**10% off accommodation
10% off food**

## LEIGHTON HOUSE

*Bath, Avon*

**LES ROUTIERS**

## Special Offer

**10% off accommodation**

## THE LINDUM HOTEL

*Lytham St Annes, Lancashire*

**LES ROUTIERS**

## Special Offer

**10% off accommodation**

## THE LION HOTEL AND RESTAURANT

*Welshpool, Powys*

**LES ROUTIERS**

## Special Offer

**10% off accommodation**

## LOCKERBIE MANOR COUNTRY HOTEL

*Lockerbie, Dumfries & Galloway*

**LES ROUTIERS**

## Special Offer

**Free bottle of house wine**

## THE LODGE

*Seahouses, Northumberland*

**LES ROUTIERS**

## Special Offer

**10% off food**

## THE LODGE SET

*Tal-y-Bont, Gwynedd*

**LES ROUTIERS**

## Special Offer

**10% off food**

## LYNDHURST HOTEL

*Birmingham, West Midlands*

**LES ROUTIERS**

## Special Offer

**Free bottle of house wine**

## Terms and Conditions

Only one voucher accepted per person per visit

Only one offer per Voucher, e.g. FOOD or
ACCOMMODATION or WINE

Establishments must be informed when booking that a
voucher will be used as part-payment for
ACCOMMODATION

Vouchers for FOOD or WINE must be handed
in on arrival

All offers are subject to the establishment's regulations

## Terms and Conditions

Only one voucher accepted per person per visit

Only one offer per Voucher, e.g. FOOD or
ACCOMMODATION or WINE

Establishments must be informed when booking that a
voucher will be used as part-payment for
ACCOMMODATION

Vouchers for FOOD or WINE must be handed
in on arrival

All offers are subject to the establishment's regulations

## Terms and Conditions

Only one voucher accepted per person per visit

Only one offer per Voucher, e.g. FOOD or
ACCOMMODATION or WINE

Establishments must be informed when booking that a
voucher will be used as part-payment for
ACCOMMODATION

Vouchers for FOOD or WINE must be handed
in on arrival

All offers are subject to the establishment's regulations

## Terms and Conditions

Only one voucher accepted per person per visit

Only one offer per Voucher, e.g. FOOD or
ACCOMMODATION or WINE

Establishments must be informed when booking that a
voucher will be used as part-payment for
ACCOMMODATION

Vouchers for FOOD or WINE must be handed
in on arrival

All offers are subject to the establishment's regulations

## Terms and Conditions

Only one voucher accepted per person per visit

Only one offer per Voucher, e.g. FOOD or
ACCOMMODATION or WINE

Establishments must be informed when booking that a
voucher will be used as part-payment for
ACCOMMODATION

Vouchers for FOOD or WINE must be handed
in on arrival

All offers are subject to the establishment's regulations

## Terms and Conditions

Only one voucher accepted per person per visit

Only one offer per Voucher, e.g. FOOD or
ACCOMMODATION or WINE

Establishments must be informed when booking that a
voucher will be used as part-payment for
ACCOMMODATION

Vouchers for FOOD or WINE must be handed
in on arrival

All offers are subject to the establishment's regulations

## Terms and Conditions

Only one voucher accepted per person per visit

Only one offer per Voucher, e.g. FOOD or
ACCOMMODATION or WINE

Establishments must be informed when booking that a
voucher will be used as part-payment for
ACCOMMODATION

Vouchers for FOOD or WINE must be handed
in on arrival

All offers are subject to the establishment's regulations

## Terms and Conditions

Only one voucher accepted per person per visit

Only one offer per Voucher, e.g. FOOD or
ACCOMMODATION or WINE

Establishments must be informed when booking that a
voucher will be used as part-payment for
ACCOMMODATION

Vouchers for FOOD or WINE must be handed
in on arrival

All offers are subject to the establishment's regulations

## Terms and Conditions

Only one voucher accepted per person per visit

Only one offer per Voucher, e.g. FOOD or
ACCOMMODATION or WINE

Establishments must be informed when booking that a
voucher will be used as part-payment for
ACCOMMODATION

Vouchers for FOOD or WINE must be handed
in on arrival

All offers are subject to the establishment's regulations

## Terms and Conditions

Only one voucher accepted per person per visit

Only one offer per Voucher, e.g. FOOD or
ACCOMMODATION or WINE

Establishments must be informed when booking that a
voucher will be used as part-payment for
ACCOMMODATION

Vouchers for FOOD or WINE must be handed
in on arrival

All offers are subject to the establishment's regulations

## MAER LODGE HOTEL

*Bude, Cornwall*

**LES ROUTIERS**

*Special Offer*

**10% off accommodation
Free bottle of house wine**

## MANOR HEATH HOTEL

*Scarborough, North Yorkshire*

**LES ROUTIERS**

*Special Offer*

**10% off accommodation**

## THE MANOR HOTEL

*Dorchester, Dorset*

**LES ROUTIERS**

*Special Offer*

**10% off accommodation
10% off food**

## THE MANOR HOUSE

*Studland, Dorset*

**LES ROUTIERS**

*Special Offer*

**10% off accommodation**

## THE MANOR PARK HOTEL

*Largs, Strathclyde*

**LES ROUTIERS**

*Special Offer*

**Free bottle of house wine**

## MARKINGTON HOTEL

*South Croydon, Surrey*

**LES ROUTIERS**

*Special Offer*

**10% off accommodation**

## MELFORD HALL HOTEL

*Brighton & Hove, East Sussex*

**LES ROUTIERS**

*Special Offer*

**10% off accommodation**

## THE MILBURN ARMS HOTEL

*Rosedale Abbey, North Yorkshire*

**LES ROUTIERS**

*Special Offer*

**10% off food**

## MILL AT OUNDLE

*Oundle, Northamptonshire*

**LES ROUTIERS**

*Special Offer*

**10% off food**

## MILL HOUSE HOTEL

*Buckie, Grampian*

**LES ROUTIERS**

*Special Offer*

**10% off accommodation**

## Terms and Conditions

Only one voucher accepted per person per visit

Only one offer per Voucher, e.g. FOOD or
ACCOMMODATION or WINE

Establishments must be informed when booking that a
voucher will be used as part-payment for
ACCOMMODATION

Vouchers for FOOD or WINE must be handed
in on arrival

All offers are subject to the establishment's regulations

## Terms and Conditions

Only one voucher accepted per person per visit

Only one offer per Voucher, e.g. FOOD or
ACCOMMODATION or WINE

Establishments must be informed when booking that a
voucher will be used as part-payment for
ACCOMMODATION

Vouchers for FOOD or WINE must be handed
in on arrival

All offers are subject to the establishment's regulations

## Terms and Conditions

Only one voucher accepted per person per visit

Only one offer per Voucher, e.g. FOOD or
ACCOMMODATION or WINE

Establishments must be informed when booking that a
voucher will be used as part-payment for
ACCOMMODATION

Vouchers for FOOD or WINE must be handed
in on arrival

All offers are subject to the establishment's regulations

## Terms and Conditions

Only one voucher accepted per person per visit

Only one offer per Voucher, e.g. FOOD or
ACCOMMODATION or WINE

Establishments must be informed when booking that a
voucher will be used as part-payment for
ACCOMMODATION

Vouchers for FOOD or WINE must be handed
in on arrival

All offers are subject to the establishment's regulations

## Terms and Conditions

Only one voucher accepted per person per visit

Only one offer per Voucher, e.g. FOOD or
ACCOMMODATION or WINE

Establishments must be informed when booking that a
voucher will be used as part-payment for
ACCOMMODATION

Vouchers for FOOD or WINE must be handed
in on arrival

All offers are subject to the establishment's regulations

## Terms and Conditions

Only one voucher accepted per person per visit

Only one offer per Voucher, e.g. FOOD or
ACCOMMODATION or WINE

Establishments must be informed when booking that a
voucher will be used as part-payment for
ACCOMMODATION

Vouchers for FOOD or WINE must be handed
in on arrival

All offers are subject to the establishment's regulations

## Terms and Conditions

Only one voucher accepted per person per visit

Only one offer per Voucher, e.g. FOOD or
ACCOMMODATION or WINE

Establishments must be informed when booking that a
voucher will be used as part-payment for
ACCOMMODATION

Vouchers for FOOD or WINE must be handed
in on arrival

All offers are subject to the establishment's regulations

## Terms and Conditions

Only one voucher accepted per person per visit

Only one offer per Voucher, e.g. FOOD or
ACCOMMODATION or WINE

Establishments must be informed when booking that a
voucher will be used as part-payment for
ACCOMMODATION

Vouchers for FOOD or WINE must be handed
in on arrival

All offers are subject to the establishment's regulations

## Terms and Conditions

Only one voucher accepted per person per visit

Only one offer per Voucher, e.g. FOOD or
ACCOMMODATION or WINE

Establishments must be informed when booking that a
voucher will be used as part-payment for
ACCOMMODATION

Vouchers for FOOD or WINE must be handed
in on arrival

All offers are subject to the establishment's regulations

## Terms and Conditions

Only one voucher accepted per person per visit

Only one offer per Voucher, e.g. FOOD or
ACCOMMODATION or WINE

Establishments must be informed when booking that a
voucher will be used as part-payment for
ACCOMMODATION

Vouchers for FOOD or WINE must be handed
in on arrival

All offers are subject to the establishment's regulations

## THE MILLER OF MANSFIELD HOTEL

*Goring on Thames, Oxfordshire*

**LES ROUTIERS**

*Special Offer*

**10% off accommodation
10% off food**

## THE MOAT HOUSE RESTAURANT

*Stafford, Staffordshire*

**LES ROUTIERS**

*Special Offer*

**Free bottle of house wine**

## MORANGIE HOUSE HOTEL

*Tain, Highlands*

**LES ROUTIERS**

*Special Offer*

**10% off accommodation**

## MORTON'S FORK

*Ramsgate, Kent*

**LES ROUTIERS**

*Special Offer*

**10% off accommodation**

## MOTEL LEEMING

*Leeming Bar, North Yorkshire*

**LES ROUTIERS**

*Special Offer*

**10% off accommodation**

## MYRA RESTAURANT

*Putney, London*

**LES ROUTIERS**

*Special Offer*

**10% off food**

## NEEDHAMS FARM

*Hyde, Cheshire*

**LES ROUTIERS**

*Special Offer*

**10% off accommodation**

## THE NESS HOUSE HOTEL

*Shaldon, Devon*

**LES ROUTIERS**

*Special Offer*

**10% off accommodation
Free bottle of house wine**

## NEW INN HOTEL

*Settle, North Yorkshire*

**LES ROUTIERS**

*Special Offer*

**10% off accommodation
10% off food**

## NEWPARK HOUSE HOTEL

*St Albans, Hertfordshire*

**LES ROUTIERS**

*Special Offer*

**10% off food**

# Terms and Conditions

Only one voucher accepted per person per visit

Only one offer per Voucher, e.g. FOOD or
ACCOMMODATION or WINE

Establishments must be informed when booking that a
voucher will be used as part-payment for
ACCOMMODATION

Vouchers for FOOD or WINE must be handed
in on arrival

All offers are subject to the establishment's regulations

# Terms and Conditions

Only one voucher accepted per person per visit

Only one offer per Voucher, e.g. FOOD or
ACCOMMODATION or WINE

Establishments must be informed when booking that a
voucher will be used as part-payment for
ACCOMMODATION

Vouchers for FOOD or WINE must be handed
in on arrival

All offers are subject to the establishment's regulations

# Terms and Conditions

Only one voucher accepted per person per visit

Only one offer per Voucher, e.g. FOOD or
ACCOMMODATION or WINE

Establishments must be informed when booking that a
voucher will be used as part-payment for
ACCOMMODATION

Vouchers for FOOD or WINE must be handed
in on arrival

All offers are subject to the establishment's regulations

# Terms and Conditions

Only one voucher accepted per person per visit

Only one offer per Voucher, e.g. FOOD or
ACCOMMODATION or WINE

Establishments must be informed when booking that a
voucher will be used as part-payment for
ACCOMMODATION

Vouchers for FOOD or WINE must be handed
in on arrival

All offers are subject to the establishment's regulations

# Terms and Conditions

Only one voucher accepted per person per visit

Only one offer per Voucher, e.g. FOOD or
ACCOMMODATION or WINE

Establishments must be informed when booking that a
voucher will be used as part-payment for
ACCOMMODATION

Vouchers for FOOD or WINE must be handed
in on arrival

All offers are subject to the establishment's regulations

# Terms and Conditions

Only one voucher accepted per person per visit

Only one offer per Voucher, e.g. FOOD or
ACCOMMODATION or WINE

Establishments must be informed when booking that a
voucher will be used as part-payment for
ACCOMMODATION

Vouchers for FOOD or WINE must be handed
in on arrival

All offers are subject to the establishment's regulations

# Terms and Conditions

Only one voucher accepted per person per visit

Only one offer per Voucher, e.g. FOOD or
ACCOMMODATION or WINE

Establishments must be informed when booking that a
voucher will be used as part-payment for
ACCOMMODATION

Vouchers for FOOD or WINE must be handed
in on arrival

All offers are subject to the establishment's regulations

# Terms and Conditions

Only one voucher accepted per person per visit

Only one offer per Voucher, e.g. FOOD or
ACCOMMODATION or WINE

Establishments must be informed when booking that a
voucher will be used as part-payment for
ACCOMMODATION

Vouchers for FOOD or WINE must be handed
in on arrival

All offers are subject to the establishment's regulations

# Terms and Conditions

Only one voucher accepted per person per visit

Only one offer per Voucher, e.g. FOOD or
ACCOMMODATION or WINE

Establishments must be informed when booking that a
voucher will be used as part-payment for
ACCOMMODATION

Vouchers for FOOD or WINE must be handed
in on arrival

All offers are subject to the establishment's regulations

# Terms and Conditions

Only one voucher accepted per person per visit

Only one offer per Voucher, e.g. FOOD or
ACCOMMODATION or WINE

Establishments must be informed when booking that a
voucher will be used as part-payment for
ACCOMMODATION

Vouchers for FOOD or WINE must be handed
in on arrival

All offers are subject to the establishment's regulations

## NORTHWOOD HOTEL
*Colwyn Bay, Clwyd*

**LES ROUTIERS**

*Special Offer*

**Free bottle of house wine**

## OAKLANDS HOTEL
*Sandown, Isle of Wight*

**LES ROUTIERS**

*Special Offer*

**10% off accommodation**

## OAKWOOD HALL HOTEL
*Bingley, West Yorkshire*

**LES ROUTIERS**

*Special Offer*

**10% off accommodation**
**Free bottle of house wine**

## THE OLD COURT HOTEL & RESTAURANT
*Ross on Wye, Hereford & Worcester*

**LES ROUTIERS**

*Special Offer*

**10% off accommodation**

## THE OLD MALT HOUSE HOTEL
*Bath, Avon*

**LES ROUTIERS**

*Special Offer*

**Free bottle of house wine**

## THE OLDE MASONS ARMS HOTEL
*Brecon, Powys*

**LES ROUTIERS**

*Special Offer*

**Free bottle of house wine**

## ORIEL HOUSE HOTEL
*St Asaph, Clwyd*

**LES ROUTIERS**

*Special Offer*

**Free bottle of house wine**

## THE ORIGINAL FARMERS ARMS
*Eccleston, Lancashire*

**LES ROUTIERS**

*Special Offer*

**10% off accommodation**

## OXWICH BAY HOTEL
*Gower, West Glamorgan*

**LES ROUTIERS**

*Special Offer*

**10% off accommodation**

## PARKEND HOUSE HOTEL
*Parkend, Gloucestershire*

**LES ROUTIERS**

*Special Offer*

**Free bottle of house wine**

# Terms and Conditions

Only one voucher accepted per person per visit

Only one offer per Voucher, e.g. FOOD or
ACCOMMODATION or WINE

Establishments must be informed when booking that a
voucher will be used as part-payment for
ACCOMMODATION

Vouchers for FOOD or WINE must be handed
in on arrival

All offers are subject to the establishment's regulations

# Terms and Conditions

Only one voucher accepted per person per visit

Only one offer per Voucher, e.g. FOOD or
ACCOMMODATION or WINE

Establishments must be informed when booking that a
voucher will be used as part-payment for
ACCOMMODATION

Vouchers for FOOD or WINE must be handed
in on arrival .

All offers are subject to the establishment's regulations

# Terms and Conditions

Only one voucher accepted per person per visit

Only one offer per Voucher, e.g. FOOD or
ACCOMMODATION or WINE

Establishments must be informed when booking that a
voucher will be used as part-payment for
ACCOMMODATION

Vouchers for FOOD or WINE must be handed
in on arrival

All offers are subject to the establishment's regulations

# Terms and Conditions

Only one voucher accepted per person per visit

Only one offer per Voucher, e.g. FOOD or
ACCOMMODATION or WINE

Establishments must be informed when booking that a
voucher will be used as part-payment for
ACCOMMODATION

Vouchers for FOOD or WINE must be handed
in on arrival

All offers are subject to the establishment's regulations

# Terms and Conditions

Only one voucher accepted per person per visit

Only one offer per Voucher, e.g. FOOD or
ACCOMMODATION or WINE

Establishments must be informed when booking that a
voucher will be used as part-payment for
ACCOMMODATION

Vouchers for FOOD or WINE must be handed
in on arrival

All offers are subject to the establishment's regulations

# Terms and Conditions

Only one voucher accepted per person per visit

Only one offer per Voucher, e.g. FOOD or
ACCOMMODATION or WINE

Establishments must be informed when booking that a
voucher will be used as part-payment for
ACCOMMODATION

Vouchers for FOOD or WINE must be handed
in on arrival

All offers are subject to the establishment's regulations

# Terms and Conditions

Only one voucher accepted per person per visit

Only one offer per Voucher, e.g. FOOD or
ACCOMMODATION or WINE

Establishments must be informed when booking that a
voucher will be used as part-payment for
ACCOMMODATION

Vouchers for FOOD or WINE must be handed
in on arrival

All offers are subject to the establishment's regulations

# Terms and Conditions

Only one voucher accepted per person per visit

Only one offer per Voucher, e.g. FOOD or
ACCOMMODATION or WINE

Establishments must be informed when booking that a
voucher will be used as part-payment for
ACCOMMODATION

Vouchers for FOOD or WINE must be handed
in on arrival

All offers are subject to the establishment's regulations

# Terms and Conditions

Only one voucher accepted per person per visit

Only one offer per Voucher, e.g. FOOD or
ACCOMMODATION or WINE

Establishments must be informed when booking that a
voucher will be used as part-payment for
ACCOMMODATION

Vouchers for FOOD or WINE must be handed
in on arrival

All offers are subject to the establishment's regulations

# Terms and Conditions

Only one voucher accepted per person per visit

Only one offer per Voucher, e.g. FOOD or
ACCOMMODATION or WINE

Establishments must be informed when booking that a
voucher will be used as part-payment for
ACCOMMODATION

Vouchers for FOOD or WINE must be handed
in on arrival

All offers are subject to the establishment's regulations

## PASKINS HOTEL
*Brighton, East Sussex*

**Special Offer**

**10% off accommodation**

## PINEWOOD PRIVATE HOTEL
*Leeds, West Yorkshire*

**Special Offer**

**10% off accommodation**
**Free bottle of house wine**

## PLATTERS RESTAURANT
*Chichester, West Sussex*

**Special Offer**

**10% off food**

## THE POLASH RESTAURANT
*Shoeburyness, Essex*

**Special Offer**

**10% off food**

## PORTLAND HOTEL
*Lincoln, Lincolnshire*

**Special Offer**

**10% off accommodation**

## POWDERMILLS HOTEL
*Battle, East Sussex*

**Special Offer**

**Free bottle of house wine**

## THE QUEENS HOTEL
*Bournemouth, Dorset*

**Special Offer**

**10% off accommodation**
**10% off food**

## QUIGGINS RESTAURANT
*Beccles, Suffolk*

**Special Offer**

**Free bottle of house wine**

## RAMLEH HOTEL & FINGAL'S RESTAURANT
*Nairn, Highlands*

**Special Offer**

**10% off accommodation**

## RAMSEY HOUSE
*St Davids, Dyfed*

**Special Offer**

**10% off food**

403

# Terms and Conditions

Only one voucher accepted per person per visit

Only one offer per Voucher, e.g. FOOD or
ACCOMMODATION or WINE

Establishments must be informed when booking that a
voucher will be used as part-payment for
ACCOMMODATION

Vouchers for FOOD or WINE must be handed
in on arrival

All offers are subject to the establishment's regulations

# Terms and Conditions

Only one voucher accepted per person per visit

Only one offer per Voucher, e.g. FOOD or
ACCOMMODATION or WINE

Establishments must be informed when booking that a
voucher will be used as part-payment for
ACCOMMODATION

Vouchers for FOOD or WINE must be handed
in on arrival

All offers are subject to the establishment's regulations

# Terms and Conditions

Only one voucher accepted per person per visit

Only one offer per Voucher, e.g. FOOD or
ACCOMMODATION or WINE

Establishments must be informed when booking that a
voucher will be used as part-payment for
ACCOMMODATION

Vouchers for FOOD or WINE must be handed
in on arrival

All offers are subject to the establishment's regulations

# Terms and Conditions

Only one voucher accepted per person per visit

Only one offer per Voucher, e.g. FOOD or
ACCOMMODATION or WINE

Establishments must be informed when booking that a
voucher will be used as part-payment for
ACCOMMODATION

Vouchers for FOOD or WINE must be handed
in on arrival

All offers are subject to the establishment's regulations

# Terms and Conditions

Only one voucher accepted per person per visit

Only one offer per Voucher, e.g. FOOD or
ACCOMMODATION or WINE

Establishments must be informed when booking that a
voucher will be used as part-payment for
ACCOMMODATION

Vouchers for FOOD or WINE must be handed
in on arrival

All offers are subject to the establishment's regulations

# Terms and Conditions

Only one voucher accepted per person per visit

Only one offer per Voucher, e.g. FOOD or
ACCOMMODATION or WINE

Establishments must be informed when booking that a
voucher will be used as part-payment for
ACCOMMODATION

Vouchers for FOOD or WINE must be handed
in on arrival

All offers are subject to the establishment's regulations

# Terms and Conditions

Only one voucher accepted per person per visit

Only one offer per Voucher, e.g. FOOD or
ACCOMMODATION or WINE

Establishments must be informed when booking that a
voucher will be used as part-payment for
ACCOMMODATION

Vouchers for FOOD or WINE must be handed
in on arrival

All offers are subject to the establishment's regulations

# Terms and Conditions

Only one voucher accepted per person per visit

Only one offer per Voucher, e.g. FOOD or
ACCOMMODATION or WINE

Establishments must be informed when booking that a
voucher will be used as part-payment for
ACCOMMODATION

Vouchers for FOOD or WINE must be handed
in on arrival

All offers are subject to the establishment's regulations

# Terms and Conditions

Only one voucher accepted per person per visit

Only one offer per Voucher, e.g. FOOD or
ACCOMMODATION or WINE

Establishments must be informed when booking that a
voucher will be used as part-payment for
ACCOMMODATION

Vouchers for FOOD or WINE must be handed
in on arrival

All offers are subject to the establishment's regulations

# Terms and Conditions

Only one voucher accepted per person per visit

Only one offer per Voucher, e.g. FOOD or
ACCOMMODATION or WINE

Establishments must be informed when booking that a
voucher will be used as part-payment for
ACCOMMODATION

Vouchers for FOOD or WINE must be handed
in on arrival

All offers are subject to the establishment's regulations

## RAPHAELS RESTAURANT

*Telford, Shropshire*

**LES ROUTIERS**

*Special Offer*

**10% off food**

## THE RED LION HOTEL

*Spalding, Lincolnshire*

**LES ROUTIERS**

*Special Offer*

**10% off accommodation**

## THE REDFERN HOTEL

*Cleobury Mortimer, Shropshire*

**LES ROUTIERS**

*Special Offer*

**10% off accommodation**
**10% off food**

## RIVERSFORD HOTEL

*Bideford, Devon*

**LES ROUTIERS**

*Special Offer*

**10% off accommodation**

## THE ROSE & CROWN FREEHOUSE

*Snettisham, Norfolk*

**LES ROUTIERS**

*Special Offer*

**Free bottle of house wine**

## ROSE & CROWN HOTEL

*Colchester, Essex*

**LES ROUTIERS**

*Special Offer*

**10% off accommodation**

## ROSLIN HOTEL

*Southend, Essex*

**LES ROUTIERS**

*Special Offer*

**10% off accommodation**

## ROYAL CASTLE HOTEL

*Dartmouth, Devon*

**LES ROUTIERS**

*Special Offer*

**Free bottle of house wine**

## ROYAL CIRCUS HOTEL

*Edinburgh, Lothian*

**LES ROUTIERS**

*Special Offer*

**10% off food**

## ROYAL HOTEL

*Cromarty, Highlands*

**LES ROUTIERS**

*Special Offer*

**Free bottle of house wine**

# Terms and Conditions

Only one voucher accepted per person per visit

Only one offer per Voucher, e.g. FOOD or
ACCOMMODATION or WINE

Establishments must be informed when booking that a
voucher will be used as part-payment for
ACCOMMODATION

Vouchers for FOOD or WINE must be handed
in on arrival

All offers are subject to the establishment's regulations

# Terms and Conditions

Only one voucher accepted per person per visit

Only one offer per Voucher, e.g. FOOD or
ACCOMMODATION or WINE

Establishments must be informed when booking that a
voucher will be used as part-payment for
ACCOMMODATION

Vouchers for FOOD or WINE must be handed
in on arrival

All offers are subject to the establishment's regulations

# Terms and Conditions

Only one voucher accepted per person per visit

Only one offer per Voucher, e.g. FOOD or
ACCOMMODATION or WINE

Establishments must be informed when booking that a
voucher will be used as part-payment for
ACCOMMODATION

Vouchers for FOOD or WINE must be handed
in on arrival

All offers are subject to the establishment's regulations

# Terms and Conditions

Only one voucher accepted per person per visit

Only one offer per Voucher, e.g. FOOD or
ACCOMMODATION or WINE

Establishments must be informed when booking that a
voucher will be used as part-payment for
ACCOMMODATION

Vouchers for FOOD or WINE must be handed
in on arrival

All offers are subject to the establishment's regulations

# Terms and Conditions

Only one voucher accepted per person per visit

Only one offer per Voucher, e.g. FOOD or
ACCOMMODATION or WINE

Establishments must be informed when booking that a
voucher will be used as part-payment for
ACCOMMODATION

Vouchers for FOOD or WINE must be handed
in on arrival

All offers are subject to the establishment's regulations

# Terms and Conditions

Only one voucher accepted per person per visit

Only one offer per Voucher, e.g. FOOD or
ACCOMMODATION or WINE

Establishments must be informed when booking that a
voucher will be used as part-payment for
ACCOMMODATION

Vouchers for FOOD or WINE must be handed
in on arrival

All offers are subject to the establishment's regulations

# Terms and Conditions

Only one voucher accepted per person per visit

Only one offer per Voucher, e.g. FOOD or
ACCOMMODATION or WINE

Establishments must be informed when booking that a
voucher will be used as part-payment for
ACCOMMODATION

Vouchers for FOOD or WINE must be handed
in on arrival

All offers are subject to the establishment's regulations

# Terms and Conditions

Only one voucher accepted per person per visit

Only one offer per Voucher, e.g. FOOD or
ACCOMMODATION or WINE

Establishments must be informed when booking that a
voucher will be used as part-payment for
ACCOMMODATION

Vouchers for FOOD or WINE must be handed
in on arrival

All offers are subject to the establishment's regulations

# Terms and Conditions

Only one voucher accepted per person per visit

Only one offer per Voucher, e.g. FOOD or
ACCOMMODATION or WINE

Establishments must be informed when booking that a
voucher will be used as part-payment for
ACCOMMODATION

Vouchers for FOOD or WINE must be handed
in on arrival

All offers are subject to the establishment's regulations

# Terms and Conditions

Only one voucher accepted per person per visit

Only one offer per Voucher, e.g. FOOD or
ACCOMMODATION or WINE

Establishments must be informed when booking that a
voucher will be used as part-payment for
ACCOMMODATION

Vouchers for FOOD or WINE must be handed
in on arrival

All offers are subject to the establishment's regulations

# Terms and Conditions

Only one voucher accepted per person per visit

Only one offer per Voucher, e.g. FOOD or
ACCOMMODATION or WINE

Establishments must be informed when booking that a
voucher will be used as part-payment for
ACCOMMODATION

Vouchers for FOOD or WINE must be handed
in on arrival

All offers are subject to the establishment's regulations

# Terms and Conditions

Only one voucher accepted per person per visit

Only one offer per Voucher, e.g. FOOD or
ACCOMMODATION or WINE

Establishments must be informed when booking that a
voucher will be used as part-payment for
ACCOMMODATION

Vouchers for FOOD or WINE must be handed
in on arrival

All offers are subject to the establishment's regulations

## ROYAL HOTEL
*Forfar, Tayside*

**LES ROUTIERS**

## Special Offer

**10% off food**

---

## THE ROYAL HOTEL
*Winchester, Hampshire*

**LES ROUTIERS**

## Special Offer

**10% off accommodation**

---

## RUDLOE PARK HOTEL & RESTAURANT
*Corsham, Wiltshire*

**LES ROUTIERS**

## Special Offer

**10% off accommodation**

---

## SANDY COVE HOTEL
*Combe Martin, Devon*

**LES ROUTIERS**

## Special Offer

**10% off accommodation**

---

## SEACLIFFE HOTEL
*Whitby, North Yorkshire*

**LES ROUTIERS**

## Special Offer

**10% off accommodation**

---

## SKIPPERS
*Cardigan, Dyfed*

**LES ROUTIERS**

## Special Offer

**Free bottle of house wine**

---

## THE SMOKE HOUSE
*Mildenhall, Suffolk*

**LES ROUTIERS**

## Special Offer

**10% off accommodation**

---

## SOLE MIO ITALIAN RESTAURANT
*Chelmsford, Essex*

**LES ROUTIERS**

## Special Offer

**10% off food**

---

## SPREAD EAGLE HOTEL
*Clitheroe, Lancashire*

**LES ROUTIERS**

## Special Offer

**10% off accommodation**

---

## ST CATHERINES LODGE HOTEL
*Brighton & Hove, East Sussex*

**LES ROUTIERS**

## Special Offer

**10% off accommodation
10% off food
Free bottle of house wine**

# Terms and Conditions

Only one voucher accepted per person per visit

Only one offer per Voucher, e.g. FOOD or ACCOMMODATION or WINE

Establishments must be informed when booking that a voucher will be used as part-payment for ACCOMMODATION

Vouchers for FOOD or WINE must be handed in on arrival

All offers are subject to the establishment's regulations

# Terms and Conditions

Only one voucher accepted per person per visit

Only one offer per Voucher, e.g. FOOD or ACCOMMODATION or WINE

Establishments must be informed when booking that a voucher will be used as part-payment for ACCOMMODATION

Vouchers for FOOD or WINE must be handed in on arrival

All offers are subject to the establishment's regulations

# Terms and Conditions

Only one voucher accepted per person per visit

Only one offer per Voucher, e.g. FOOD or ACCOMMODATION or WINE

Establishments must be informed when booking that a voucher will be used as part-payment for ACCOMMODATION

Vouchers for FOOD or WINE must be handed in on arrival

All offers are subject to the establishment's regulations

# Terms and Conditions

Only one voucher accepted per person per visit

Only one offer per Voucher, e.g. FOOD or ACCOMMODATION or WINE

Establishments must be informed when booking that a voucher will be used as part-payment for ACCOMMODATION

Vouchers for FOOD or WINE must be handed in on arrival

All offers are subject to the establishment's regulations

# Terms and Conditions

Only one voucher accepted per person per visit

Only one offer per Voucher, e.g. FOOD or ACCOMMODATION or WINE

Establishments must be informed when booking that a voucher will be used as part-payment for ACCOMMODATION

Vouchers for FOOD or WINE must be handed in on arrival

All offers are subject to the establishment's regulations

# Terms and Conditions

Only one voucher accepted per person per visit

Only one offer per Voucher, e.g. FOOD or ACCOMMODATION or WINE

Establishments must be informed when booking that a voucher will be used as part-payment for ACCOMMODATION

Vouchers for FOOD or WINE must be handed in on arrival

All offers are subject to the establishment's regulations

# Terms and Conditions

Only one voucher accepted per person per visit

Only one offer per Voucher, e.g. FOOD or ACCOMMODATION or WINE

Establishments must be informed when booking that a voucher will be used as part-payment for ACCOMMODATION

Vouchers for FOOD or WINE must be handed in on arrival

All offers are subject to the establishment's regulations

# Terms and Conditions

Only one voucher accepted per person per visit

Only one offer per Voucher, e.g. FOOD or ACCOMMODATION or WINE

Establishments must be informed when booking that a voucher will be used as part-payment for ACCOMMODATION

Vouchers for FOOD or WINE must be handed in on arrival

All offers are subject to the establishment's regulations

# Terms and Conditions

Only one voucher accepted per person per visit

Only one offer per Voucher, e.g. FOOD or ACCOMMODATION or WINE

Establishments must be informed when booking that a voucher will be used as part-payment for ACCOMMODATION

Vouchers for FOOD or WINE must be handed in on arrival

All offers are subject to the establishment's regulations

# Terms and Conditions

Only one voucher accepted per person per visit

Only one offer per Voucher, e.g. FOOD or ACCOMMODATION or WINE

Establishments must be informed when booking that a voucher will be used as part-payment for ACCOMMODATION

Vouchers for FOOD or WINE must be handed in on arrival

All offers are subject to the establishment's regulations

## STANSHOPE HALL
*Ashbourne, Derbyshire*

**LES ROUTIERS**

*Special Offer*

**10% off accommodation**

## SUNRAY
*Blackpool, Lancashire*

**LES ROUTIERS**

*Special Offer*

**10% off accommodation**

## THE SWAN HOTEL
*Bampton, Devon*

**LES ROUTIERS**

*Special Offer*

**Free bottle of house wine**

## SYDNEY HOUSE HOTEL
*Shrewsbury, Shropshire*

**LES ROUTIERS**

*Special Offer*

**10% off accommodation**

## TERRACE RESTAURANT
*Brownhills, West Midlands*

**LES ROUTIERS**

*Special Offer*

**Free bottle of house wine**

## THREE HORSESHOES INN & RESTAURANT
*Leek, Staffordshire*

**LES ROUTIERS**

*Special Offer*

**10% off accommodation**
**10% off food**

## TREVOR ARMS HOTEL
*Wrexham, Clwyd*

**LES ROUTIERS**

*Special Offer*

**Free bottle of house wine**

## TROUVILLE HOTEL
*Brighton, East Sussex*

**LES ROUTIERS**

*Special Offer*

**10% off accommodation**
**10% off food**
**Free bottle of house wine**

## TY CROESO HOTEL
*Crickhowell, Powys*

**LES ROUTIERS**

*Special Offer*

**10% off accommodation**
**Free bottle of house wine**

## TY HEN FARM HOTEL & LEISURE CENTRE
*New Quay, Dyfed*

**LES ROUTIERS**

*Special Offer*

**10% off accommodation**

# Terms and Conditions

Only one voucher accepted per person per visit

Only one offer per Voucher, e.g. FOOD or ACCOMMODATION or WINE

Establishments must be informed when booking that a voucher will be used as part-payment for ACCOMMODATION

Vouchers for FOOD or WINE must be handed in on arrival

All offers are subject to the establishment's regulations

# Terms and Conditions

Only one voucher accepted per person per visit

Only one offer per Voucher, e.g. FOOD or ACCOMMODATION or WINE

Establishments must be informed when booking that a voucher will be used as part-payment for ACCOMMODATION

Vouchers for FOOD or WINE must be handed in on arrival

All offers are subject to the establishment's regulations

# Terms and Conditions

Only one voucher accepted per person per visit

Only one offer per Voucher, e.g. FOOD or ACCOMMODATION or WINE

Establishments must be informed when booking that a voucher will be used as part-payment for ACCOMMODATION

Vouchers for FOOD or WINE must be handed in on arrival

All offers are subject to the establishment's regulations

# Terms and Conditions

Only one voucher accepted per person per visit

Only one offer per Voucher, e.g. FOOD or ACCOMMODATION or WINE

Establishments must be informed when booking that a voucher will be used as part-payment for ACCOMMODATION

Vouchers for FOOD or WINE must be handed in on arrival

All offers are subject to the establishment's regulations

# Terms and Conditions

Only one voucher accepted per person per visit

Only one offer per Voucher, e.g. FOOD or ACCOMMODATION or WINE

Establishments must be informed when booking that a voucher will be used as part-payment for ACCOMMODATION

Vouchers for FOOD or WINE must be handed in on arrival

All offers are subject to the establishment's regulations

# Terms and Conditions

Only one voucher accepted per person per visit

Only one offer per Voucher, e.g. FOOD or ACCOMMODATION or WINE

Establishments must be informed when booking that a voucher will be used as part-payment for ACCOMMODATION

Vouchers for FOOD or WINE must be handed in on arrival

All offers are subject to the establishment's regulations

# Terms and Conditions

Only one voucher accepted per person per visit

Only one offer per Voucher, e.g. FOOD or ACCOMMODATION or WINE

Establishments must be informed when booking that a voucher will be used as part-payment for ACCOMMODATION

Vouchers for FOOD or WINE must be handed in on arrival

All offers are subject to the establishment's regulations

# Terms and Conditions

Only one voucher accepted per person per visit

Only one offer per Voucher, e.g. FOOD or ACCOMMODATION or WINE

Establishments must be informed when booking that a voucher will be used as part-payment for ACCOMMODATION

Vouchers for FOOD or WINE must be handed in on arrival

All offers are subject to the establishment's regulations

# Terms and Conditions

Only one voucher accepted per person per visit

Only one offer per Voucher, e.g. FOOD or ACCOMMODATION or WINE

Establishments must be informed when booking that a voucher will be used as part-payment for ACCOMMODATION

Vouchers for FOOD or WINE must be handed in on arrival

All offers are subject to the establishment's regulations

# Terms and Conditions

Only one voucher accepted per person per visit

Only one offer per Voucher, e.g. FOOD or ACCOMMODATION or WINE

Establishments must be informed when booking that a voucher will be used as part-payment for ACCOMMODATION

Vouchers for FOOD or WINE must be handed in on arrival

All offers are subject to the establishment's regulations

## THE WAINSTONES HOTEL
*Stokesley, North Yorkshire*

**LES ROUTIERS**

*Special Offer*

**10% off accommodation**
**10% off food**
**Free bottle of house wine**

## WALNUT TREE INN
*Bridgwater, Somerset*

**LES ROUTIERS**

*Special Offer*

**10% off accommodation**

## WAVECREST
*Barmouth, Gwynedd*

**LES ROUTIERS**

*Special Offer*

**Free bottle of house wine**

## THE WAVERLEY HOTEL
*Felixstowe, Suffolk*

**LES ROUTIERS**

*Special Offer*

**10% off accommodation**

## WELL FARM
*Throwleigh, Devon*

**LES ROUTIERS**

*Special Offer*

**10% off accommodation**

## WELLINGTON HOTEL
*St Just in Penwith, Cornwall*

**LES ROUTIERS**

*Special Offer*

**10% off accommodation**
**10% off food**

## WESTCLIFF HOTEL
*Sidmouth, Devon*

**LES ROUTIERS**

*Special Offer*

**10% off accommodation**
**10% off food**
**Free bottle of house wine**

## THE WHEATSHEAF INN
*Abergele, Clwyd*

**LES ROUTIERS**

*Special Offer*

**10% off food**

## WHITE COURT HOTEL
*Llandudno, Gwynedd*

**LES ROUTIERS**

*Special Offer*

**Free bottle of house wine**

## WHITE LODGE HOTEL
*Newquay, Cornwall*

**LES ROUTIERS**

*Special Offer*

**Free bottle of house wine**

411

# Terms and Conditions

Only one voucher accepted per person per visit

Only one offer per Voucher, e.g. FOOD or ACCOMMODATION or WINE

Establishments must be informed when booking that a voucher will be used as part-payment for ACCOMMODATION

Vouchers for FOOD or WINE must be handed in on arrival

All offers are subject to the establishment's regulations

# Terms and Conditions

Only one voucher accepted per person per visit

Only one offer per Voucher, e.g. FOOD or ACCOMMODATION or WINE

Establishments must be informed when booking that a voucher will be used as part-payment for ACCOMMODATION

Vouchers for FOOD or WINE must be handed in on arrival

All offers are subject to the establishment's regulations

# Terms and Conditions

Only one voucher accepted per person per visit

Only one offer per Voucher, e.g. FOOD or ACCOMMODATION or WINE

Establishments must be informed when booking that a voucher will be used as part-payment for ACCOMMODATION

Vouchers for FOOD or WINE must be handed in on arrival

All offers are subject to the establishment's regulations

# Terms and Conditions

Only one voucher accepted per person per visit

Only one offer per Voucher, e.g. FOOD or ACCOMMODATION or WINE

Establishments must be informed when booking that a voucher will be used as part-payment for ACCOMMODATION

Vouchers for FOOD or WINE must be handed in on arrival

All offers are subject to the establishment's regulations

# Terms and Conditions

Only one voucher accepted per person per visit

Only one offer per Voucher, e.g. FOOD or ACCOMMODATION or WINE

Establishments must be informed when booking that a voucher will be used as part-payment for ACCOMMODATION

Vouchers for FOOD or WINE must be handed in on arrival

All offers are subject to the establishment's regulations

# Terms and Conditions

Only one voucher accepted per person per visit

Only one offer per Voucher, e.g. FOOD or ACCOMMODATION or WINE

Establishments must be informed when booking that a voucher will be used as part-payment for ACCOMMODATION

Vouchers for FOOD or WINE must be handed in on arrival

All offers are subject to the establishment's regulations

# Terms and Conditions

Only one voucher accepted per person per visit

Only one offer per Voucher, e.g. FOOD or ACCOMMODATION or WINE

Establishments must be informed when booking that a voucher will be used as part-payment for ACCOMMODATION

Vouchers for FOOD or WINE must be handed in on arrival

All offers are subject to the establishment's regulations

# Terms and Conditions

Only one voucher accepted per person per visit

Only one offer per Voucher, e.g. FOOD or ACCOMMODATION or WINE

Establishments must be informed when booking that a voucher will be used as part-payment for ACCOMMODATION

Vouchers for FOOD or WINE must be handed in on arrival

All offers are subject to the establishment's regulations

# Terms and Conditions

Only one voucher accepted per person per visit

Only one offer per Voucher, e.g. FOOD or ACCOMMODATION or WINE

Establishments must be informed when booking that a voucher will be used as part-payment for ACCOMMODATION

Vouchers for FOOD or WINE must be handed in on arrival

All offers are subject to the establishment's regulations

# Terms and Conditions

Only one voucher accepted per person per visit

Only one offer per Voucher, e.g. FOOD or ACCOMMODATION or WINE

Establishments must be informed when booking that a voucher will be used as part-payment for ACCOMMODATION

Vouchers for FOOD or WINE must be handed in on arrival

All offers are subject to the establishment's regulations

## WIDBROOK GRANGE

*Bradford-on-Avon, Wiltshire*

**LES ROUTIERS**

*Special Offer*

**Free bottle of house wine**

## THE WILLOW TREE INN

*Newark, Nottinghamshire*

**LES ROUTIERS**

*Special Offer*

**10% off accommodation
10% off food
Free bottle of house wine**

## WINDSOR HOUSE HOTEL

*Worthing, West Sussex*

**LES ROUTIERS**

*Special Offer*

**10% off food**

## WINSTON MANOR HOTEL

*Tunbridge Wells, East Sussex*

**LES ROUTIERS**

*Special Offer*

**10% off accommodation
Free bottle of house wine**

## WOODBRIDGE INN

*Pewsey, Wiltshire*

**LES ROUTIERS**

*Special Offer*

**10% off accommodation**

## YARN MARKET HOTEL

*Dunster, Somerset*

**LES ROUTIERS**

*Special Offer*

**10% off accommodation
10% off food**

## YE OLDE SALUTATION INN

*Weobley, Hereford & Worcester*

**LES ROUTIERS**

*Special Offer*

**Free bottle of house wine**

## THE YEW TREE HOTEL

*Birkenhead, Merseyside*

**LES ROUTIERS**

*Special Offer*

**Free bottle of house wine**

## YORK HOUSE HOTEL

*Whitley Bay, Tyne & Wear*

**LES ROUTIERS**

*Special Offer*

**10% off accommodation**

# Terms and Conditions

Only one voucher accepted per person per visit

Only one offer per Voucher, e.g. FOOD or ACCOMMODATION or WINE

Establishments must be informed when booking that a voucher will be used as part-payment for ACCOMMODATION

Vouchers for FOOD or WINE must be handed in on arrival

All offers are subject to the establishment's regulations

# Terms and Conditions

Only one voucher accepted per person per visit

Only one offer per Voucher, e.g. FOOD or ACCOMMODATION or WINE

Establishments must be informed when booking that a voucher will be used as part-payment for ACCOMMODATION

Vouchers for FOOD or WINE must be handed in on arrival

All offers are subject to the establishment's regulations

# Terms and Conditions

Only one voucher accepted per person per visit

Only one offer per Voucher, e.g. FOOD or ACCOMMODATION or WINE

Establishments must be informed when booking that a voucher will be used as part-payment for ACCOMMODATION

Vouchers for FOOD or WINE must be handed in on arrival

All offers are subject to the establishment's regulations

# Terms and Conditions

Only one voucher accepted per person per visit

Only one offer per Voucher, e.g. FOOD or ACCOMMODATION or WINE

Establishments must be informed when booking that a voucher will be used as part-payment for ACCOMMODATION

Vouchers for FOOD or WINE must be handed in on arrival

All offers are subject to the establishment's regulations

# Terms and Conditions

Only one voucher accepted per person per visit

Only one offer per Voucher, e.g. FOOD or ACCOMMODATION or WINE

Establishments must be informed when booking that a voucher will be used as part-payment for ACCOMMODATION

Vouchers for FOOD or WINE must be handed in on arrival

All offers are subject to the establishment's regulations

# Terms and Conditions

Only one voucher accepted per person per visit

Only one offer per Voucher, e.g. FOOD or ACCOMMODATION or WINE

Establishments must be informed when booking that a voucher will be used as part-payment for ACCOMMODATION

Vouchers for FOOD or WINE must be handed in on arrival

All offers are subject to the establishment's regulations

# Terms and Conditions

Only one voucher accepted per person per visit

Only one offer per Voucher, e.g. FOOD or ACCOMMODATION or WINE

Establishments must be informed when booking that a voucher will be used as part-payment for ACCOMMODATION

Vouchers for FOOD or WINE must be handed in on arrival

All offers are subject to the establishment's regulations

# Terms and Conditions

Only one voucher accepted per person per visit

Only one offer per Voucher, e.g. FOOD or ACCOMMODATION or WINE

Establishments must be informed when booking that a voucher will be used as part-payment for ACCOMMODATION

Vouchers for FOOD or WINE must be handed in on arrival

All offers are subject to the establishment's regulations

# Terms and Conditions

Only one voucher accepted per person per visit

Only one offer per Voucher, e.g. FOOD or ACCOMMODATION or WINE

Establishments must be informed when booking that a voucher will be used as part-payment for ACCOMMODATION

Vouchers for FOOD or WINE must be handed in on arrival

All offers are subject to the establishment's regulations

# Terms and Conditions

Only one voucher accepted per person per visit

Only one offer per Voucher, e.g. FOOD or ACCOMMODATION or WINE

Establishments must be informed when booking that a voucher will be used as part-payment for ACCOMMODATION

Vouchers for FOOD or WINE must be handed in on arrival

All offers are subject to the establishment's regulations

# Club B●N Viveur!

## THE ULTIMATE DINING SCHEME!

CLUB BON VIVEUR is an exciting National Dining Scheme operated by Les Routiers, which invites you to rediscover the *Joie de Vivre* in hundreds of restaurants throughout the country, offering more than 23 types of international cuisine!

As a Club Bon Viveur cardholder, you are entitled to a range of substantial discounts and benefits, including reductions of up to 50% on food bills (subject to individual restaurant's restrictions), when dining with one or more guests. You can use your card as often as you wish, in any of the establishments listed in the *Joie de Vivre* Directory. The directory will be sent to you with your Members Pack, when you join.

Membership to Club Bon Viveur costs just £30 per annum, which can very quickly be recouped through discounts.

MEMBERSHIP BENEFITS INCLUDE:

* Discounted food prices when dining out.
* The *Joie de Vivre* Handbook for easy reference.
* Discounts on purchases of Les Routiers guidebooks and publications.
* Other Promotional offers.

To apply for your Club Bon Viveur membership, simply complete the application form (overleaf) and return it with your payment of £30 to:

**The Club Secretary**
**CLUB BON VIVEUR**
**25 Vanston Place**
**London SW6 1AZ**

## Your personal invitation . . .

To Club Bon Viveur
25 Vanston Place, London SW6 1AZ
Telephone: 071 385 6644 Fax: 071 385 7136

Please enrol me in the Club Bon Viveur
National Dining Scheme, at an annual
subscription of £30.00 inc. VAT.
PLEASE COMPLETE IN BLOCK CAPITALS

Mr/Mrs/Ms/Miss

Forename

Surname

Address

Postcode

Telephone

Profession

THE ABOVE INFORMATION WILL BE KEPT IN THE
STRICTEST CONFIDENCE AND USED FOR
INTERNAL PURPOSES ONLY.

I enclose my cheque for £30.00 inc. Vat, made
payable to Club Bon Viveur
Or
Charge my Access/Visa/Mastercard/Amex No.

Expiry Date

IF YOU ARE INTRODUCING A NEW MEMBER,
PLEASE COMPLETE YOUR DETAILS BELOW

Restaurant Name
Postcode
OR
Cardmember Name:
Membership No:
Postcode:

**Membership Application Form**
**Britannia Rescue**
**FREEPOST**
**Huddersfield**
**HD1 1WP**

BRITANNIA RESCUE

BLOCK LETTERS PLEASE

SURNAME ➤ _____ INITIALS ➤ _____ TITLE (Mr/Mrs/Miss/Ms) ➤ _____

ADDRESS ➤ _____

_____

_____ POSTCODE ➤ _____ TEL NO ➤ _____

Cover commences from midnight of date of our receipt of this application form or later if you specify here ➤

**COMPLETE SECTIONS A OR B, AND C TOGETHER WITH METHOD OF PAYMENT DETAILS.**

| A  ANNUAL RATES applicable to 31.12.94 or later review date. | Single Vehicle | ✓ Tick | Two Vehicles | ✓ Tick |
|---|---|---|---|---|
| SUPERSTART | £26.50 | | £53.00 | |
| RESCUE PLUS | £40.00 | | £60.00 | |
| STANDARD | £64.50 | | £81.75 | |
| COMPREHENSIVE | £72.00 | | £108.00 | |
| DELUXE | £88.00 | | £132.00 | |
| Optional extra PERSONAL COVER (with Free Card for Spouse  Please tick [  ] ) | | | £18.00 | |
| JOINING FEE (waived if payment made by Direct Debit or Continuous Credit Card Authority) | | | £10.00 | |
| ENTER TOTAL COST OF TICKED OPTIONS | | ➤ £ | | |

Note: ANNUAL RATE is a single payment, providing 12 months cover.

| B  MONTHLY PREMIUMS (Direct Debit Only) | Single Vehicle | ✓ Tick | Two Vehicles | ✓ Tick |
|---|---|---|---|---|
| STANDARD | £5.50 | | £8.25 | |
| COMPREHENSIVE | £7.25 | | £10.75 | |
| DELUXE | £8.75 | | £13.25 | |
| Optional extra PERSONAL COVER (with Free Card for Spouse  Please tick [  ] ) | | | £1.80 | |
| ENTER TOTAL COST OF TICKED OPTIONS | | ➤ £ | | |

**Note: MONTHLY PREMIUMS are continuous payments available only by DIRECT DEBIT until cancelled by either party and are subject to amendments from time to time. Members are given prior notice of any change of payment.**
CAR GRILLE BADGE (inc. VAT and P&P) £4.35 payment by cheque only [  ] Additional vehicles – details on request

| C  1st CAR DETAILS | Reg No ▼ | Year New ▼ | Make ▼ | Model ▼ |
|---|---|---|---|---|
| | | | | |
| 2nd CAR DETAILS  Reg No ▼ | | Year New ▼ | Make ▼ | Model ▼ |
| | | | | |

The above rates are applicable only to vehicles under 2.5 tonnes/2,540 kilos gross vehicle weight.

I wish to apply for membership of Britannia Rescue and I certify that the vehicle(s) to be covered is/are fully roadworthy and in normal use and is/are insured and kept at my home address here given. I agree to abide by the Terms and Conditions of Britannia Rescue. **ALL MEMBERS MUST SIGN.**

SIGNATURE ➤ _____ DATE ➤ _____

**METHODS OF PAYMENT**

1. TRANSCASH ➤ Complete Transcash forms from the Post Office, make payable to Britannia Recovery Ltd., Girobank Account No 3006980. Please enclose receipt with application form. Standard Transcash fee will be payable.

2. CHEQUE/P.O. ➤ Make payable to Britannia Recovery Ltd.   Cheque/P.O [_____]

3. CREDIT CARD ➤ Please debit my  ACCESS [  ]  VISA [  ]  (please tick)

Card No [  ][  ][  ][  ][  ][  ][  ][  ][  ][  ][  ][  ][  ][  ][  ][  ]   Card Expiry Date [_____]

4. CONTINUOUS CREDIT CARD AUTHORITY ➤ Sign here only if you wish to authorise automatic renewal by credit card:
I authorise Britannia Recovery Ltd. until further written notice, to charge my Access/Visa card account with unspecified amounts in respect of my annual Britannia Rescue membership.

SIGNATURE ➤ _____ DATE ➤ _____

5. DIRECT DEBIT ➤ Please complete the direct debit mandate overleaf.

As part of our service, Britannia Rescue will send you information about valuable offers especially negotiated members. If you prefer not to receive this information, please tick here. [  ]

# DIRECT DEBITING MANDATE

1. NAME OF ACCOUNT HOLDER

2. BANK SORTING CODE

3. BANK ACCOUNT NUMBER

NAME AND FULL POSTAL ADDRESS OF YOUR BANK

4. THE MANAGER

BANK LTD

After signature please return this form to: Britannia Recovery Limited, FREEPOST (No stamp required) Huddersfield HD1 1WP. Instructions cannot be accepted to charge Direct Debits to a Deposit or Savings Account.

WE REGRET THAT NO ALTERATIONS MAY BE MADE TO THE WORDING OF THIS MANDATE.

Complete the Direct Debiting Mandate by entering:
(1) The name of the Account to be debited; (2) Your bank's Sorting Code; (3)Your Bank Account Number; (4) The name and address of your Bank; and (5) Sign and date the Mandate.

Your Direct Debit Mandate will only be used to collect your Britannia Rescue subscription. Should you wish to cancel your mandate you can do this by notifying your Bank and Britannia Rescue in writing.

Should any error be made by us you may claim reimbursement through your bankers under an indemnity effected by the Company in their favour and lodged with the committee of London Clearing Banks.

OFFICE USE ONLY

I/we authorise you until further notice in writing to charge to my/our account with you unspecified amounts which Britannia Rescue may debit thereto by Direct Debit.

5. SIGNATURE

DATE

419

# LES ROUTIERS

# Your Opinion

Do you have a favourite pub, restaurant or hotel which you would like to recommend to us, which is not recommended by Les Routiers.

If so, please let us know on the page below so that we can arrange for one of our inspectors to call on them. Alternatively, if you have visited a Les Routiers establishment and are in any way dissatisfied, again we would like to receive your comments.

Your cooperation is invaluable in helping Les Routiers to maintain the high standards for which it is widely renown. All correspondence will be treated in the strictest of confidence.

Name of Establishment: _____

Address/Location: _____

_____

Establishment type (please circle):

| Restaurant | Public House | Hotel |
| Wine Bar/Bistro | B&B | Other |

Please Circle:   NOMINATION   or   COMPLAINT

Your comments (you may prefer to write separately to us): _____

_____

_____

_____

_____

# Participating Voucher Establishments

The Queens Hotel, Bournemouth, Dorset [A][F]

Quiggins Restaurant, Beccles, Suffolk [W]

Ramleh Hotel & Fingal's Restaurant, Nairn, Highlands [A]

Ramsey House, St Davids, Dyfed [F]

Raphaels Restaurant, Telford, Shropshire [F]

The Red Lion Hotel, Spalding, Lincolnshire [A]

The Redfern Hotel, Cleobury Mortimer, Shropshire [A][F]

Riversford Hotel, Bideford, Devon [A]

The Rose & Crown Freehouse, Snettisham, Norfolk [W]

Rose & Crown Hotel, Colchester, Essex [A]

Roslin Hotel, Thorpe Bay, Essex [A]

Royal Castle Hotel, Dartmouth, Devon [W]

Royal Circus Hotel, Edinburgh, Lothian [F]

Royal Hotel, Cromarty, Highlands [W]

Royal Hotel, Forfar, Tayside [F]

The Royal Hotel, Winchester, Hampshire [A]

The Rudloe Park Hotel & Restaurant, Corsham, Wiltshire [A]

Sandy Cove Hotel, Combe Martin, Devon [A]

Seacliffe Hotel, Whitby, North Yorkshire [A]

Skippers, Cardigan, Dyfed [W]

The Smoke House, Mildenhall, Suffolk [A]

Sole Mio Italian Restaurant, Chelmsford, Essex [F]

Spread Eagle Hotel, Clitheroe, Lancashire [A]

St Catherines Lodge Hotel, Brighton & Hove, East Sussex [W][A][F]

Stanshope Hall, Ashbourne, Derbyshire [A]

Sunray, Blackpool, Lancashire [A]

The Swan Hotel, Bampton, Devon [W]

Sydney House Hotel, Shrewsbury, Shropshire [A]

Terrace Restaurant, Brownhills, West Midlands [W]

The Three Horseshoes Inn & Restaurant, Leek, Staffordshire [A][F]

Trevor Arms Hotel, Wrexham, Clwyd [W]

Trouville Hotel, Brighton, East Sussex [W][A][F]

Ty Croeso Hotel, Crickhowell, Powys [W][A]

Ty Hen Farm Hotel & Leisure Centre, New Quay, Dyfed [A]

The Wainstones Hotel, Stokesley, North Yorkshire [A][F][W]

Walnut Tree Inn, Bridgwater, Somerset [A]

Wavecrest, Barmouth, Gwynedd [W]

The Waverley Hotel, Felixstowe, Suffolk [A]

Well Farm, Throwleigh, Devon [A]

Wellington Hotel, St Just in Penwith, Cornwall [A][F]

Westcliff Hotel, Sidmouth, Devon [A][W][F]

The Wheatsheaf Inn, Abergele, Clwyd [F]

White Court Hotel, Llandudno, Gwynedd [W]

White Lodge Hotel, Newquay, Cornwall [W]

Widbrook Grange, Bradford-on-Avon, Wiltshire [W]

The Willow Tree Inn, Newark, Nottinghamshire [A][F][W]

Windsor House Hotel, Worthing, West Sussex [F]

Winston Manor Hotel, Tunbridge Wells, East Sussex [A][W]

Woodbridge Inn, Pewsey, Wiltshire [A]

Yarn Market Hotel, Dunster, Somerset [A][F]

Yc Olde Salutation Inn, Weobley, Hereford & Worcester [W]

The Yew Tree Hotel, Birkenhead, Merseyside [W]

York House Hotel, Whitley Bay, Tyne & Wear [A]

Index

# Index of Towns

Index

427

430

# Index

432